Literature
A Portable Anthology

Literature
A Portable Anthology
Fourth Edition

Edited by

JANET E. GARDNER

BEVERLY LAWN

Emerita, Adelphi University

JACK RIDL

Hope College

PETER SCHAKEL

Hope College

with the assistance of

JOANNE DIAZ

Illinois Wesleyan University

bedford/st.martin's
Macmillan Learning
Boston | New York

For Bedford/St. Martin's

Vice President, Editorial, Macmillan Learning Humanities: Edwin Hill
Editorial Director, English: Karen S. Henry
Executive Editor: Vivian Garcia
Executive Development Manager: Maura Shea
Editorial Assistant: Julia Domenicucci
Production Editor: Lidia MacDonald-Carr
Senior Media Producer: Allison Hart
Production Supervisor: Carolyn Quimby
Marketing Manager: Sophia LaTorre-Zengierski
Project Management: Jouve
Permissions Manager: Kalina Ingham
Senior Art Director: Anna Palchik
Cover Design: John Callahan
Cover Art/Cover Photo: Dennis Hallinan/Getty Images
Composition: Jouve
Printing and Binding: Edwards Brothers Malloy

Manufactured in the United States of America.

1 0 9 8 7 6
f e d c b a

For information, write: Bedford/St. Martin's, 75 Arlington Street, Boston, MA 02116
  (617-399-4000)

ISBN: 978-1-319-03534-1

Acknowledgments

Text acknowledgments and copyrights appear at the back of the book on pages 1439–1448, which constitute an extension of the copyright page.

Preface for Instructors

The fourth edition of *Literature: A Portable Anthology* presents, in a compact and highly affordable format, an ample and flexible choice of contemporary and classic fiction, poetry, and drama for introductory literature courses. Arranged chronologically by genre, the stories, poems, and plays are complemented by editorial matter that offers enough help for students learning to think, read, and write about literature, without interfering with their enjoyment of the literary works.

In these pages students will discover a full array of literary works:

- Forty engaging and significant short stories, from classic authors such as Kate Chopin, Ernest Hemingway, and Flannery O'Connor to contemporary writers such as Jhumpa Lahiri, Junot Díaz, and Sherman Alexie.
- A judicious and varied collection of 200 poems—not only an abundant selection of many classic and frequently assigned works by canonical writers such as John Keats, Emily Dickinson, and Langston Hughes, but also the most diverse selection of contemporary American poetry in an anthology of this scope, including poems by Patricia Lockwood, Naomi Shihab Nye, and Solmaz Sharif, among many others.
- A teaching canon of nine plays — from Sophocles's classical tragedy *Oedipus the King* to modern masterpieces such as Tennessee Williams's *Cat on a Hot Tin Roof* to deeply admired contemporary works such as August Wilson's *Fences*. The selection represents not only important works in the Western dramatic tradition but also a core of the most frequently assigned and popular plays in today's classroom.

At the back of the book, in addition to biographical notes on every author and a glossary of literary terms, students will find Part Four, a section devoted to helping them read literature closely and write about it effectively. Also available to students as a separate volume (*Reading and Writing about Literature: A Portable Guide*), this section explains how to think critically, read analytically, and write a variety of commonly assigned papers about literature, from summaries to research papers, with several sample student papers included as models.

New to the Fourth Edition

The fourth edition has been significantly revised and updated with a wide choice of literary selections that includes the following:

- A more contemporary and diverse selection of fiction. Of the sixteen new stories, several are by classic authors such as Willa Cather and Richard Wright, but most are contemporary, including recent gems by T. Coraghessan Boyle, Dagoberto Gilb, and Jhumpa Lahiri.
- Several canonical poets represented in greater depth, and an exciting selection of fresh, contemporary poems. The eighty-nine new poems include more classic selections from the works of Ezra Pound and Langston Hughes as well as recent pieces by current poets such as Patricia Smith, Claudia Rankine, Martín Espada, and Amit Majmudar.
- Four new plays: a classic comedy, Oscar Wilde's *The Importance of Being Earnest*; a modern classic, Tennessee Williams's *Cat on a Hot Tin Roof*; and two award-winning contemporary plays, Lynn Nottage's *Ruined* and Ayad Akhtar's *Disgraced*.

We have also expanded our coverage of close reading with the addition of Active Reading questions that precede the selections in each genre and can be easily applied to a specific work. We have fully updated the writing about literature instruction in Part Four of the book with current guidelines on finding, integrating, and citing sources in academic writing. We have expanded the glossary of literary terms to include more coverage of the literary elements.

While the table of contents is arranged chronologically within each genre, we recognize that there are multiple ways to organize a literature course, and have therefore added Selections by Form and Theme, an alternate table of contents for those who prefer to teach thematically. For our readers' convenience, we continue to offer the alphabetical list of authors at the front of the book.

ACKNOWLEDGMENTS

For their helpful responses to a questionnaire about their experiences using previous editions of the book, the editors are grateful to Jay Adler, Los Angeles Southwest College; Nathan Austin, York College CUNY; Ethel Bonds, Virginia Western Community College; Nissa Cannon, University of California at Santa Barbara; Nikola Champlin, University of Iowa; John Chandler, Merrimack College; Margaret Clark, Florida State

College at Jacksonville; Genvieve Des Georges, New Mexico State University; John Domini; Marcia Douglas, University of Colorado at Boulder; Matt Evertson, Chadron State College; Lori Franklin, Northern New Mexico College; Angela Fulk, Canisius College; Mara Grayson, LaGuardia Community College; Grace Haddox, El Paso Community College; Michael Herman, St. John's University; Peter Herman, San Diego State University; Carolina Hospital, Miami Dade College; Lutfi Hussein, Mesa Community College; Miriam Janechek, University of Iowa; Trevor Kearns, Greenfield Community College; Nancy Kennedy, Edmonds Community College; Tracey Lander-Garrett, Borough of Manhattan Community College; Vince Locke, Delta College; John McDermott, Stephen F. Austin State University; James Merrill, Oxnard College; Duygu Minton, Georgia Regents University; Sherry Moore, Eastern Oklahoma State College; Cecilia Muhlstein, Borough of Manhattan Community College; Lonnie Pidel, Mount Wachusett Community College; Sheila Raeschild, Northern New Mexico College; Joseph Sabado, College of New Rochelle; Melissa Sande, Union County College; David Shimkin, Queensborough Community College; Michael Stubbs, Idaho State University; Gregory Sydoriw, Morrisville State College; Diane Thompson, Harrisburg Area Community College; David Vilandre, Quinsigamond Community College; Karen Weyant, Jamestown Community College.

The editors would like to thank several individuals at Macmillan Learning including Edwin Hill, Karen Henry, Vivian Garcia, and Steve Scipione whose vision was instrumental in shaping the fourth edition. Thank you to our editor, Maura Shea, whose wisdom, foresight, and rigorous attention to detail made the work such a pleasure, and to our editorial assistant, Julia Domenicucci, for her tremendous work on preparing the manuscript. We appreciate Virginia Creeden's work in clearing permissions and Sophia LaTorre-Zengierski's marketing expertise. We especially appreciate those in production who turned the manuscript into a book: Elise Kaiser, and Lidia MacDonald-Carr at Macmillan Learning, and Kevin Bradley at Jouve North America.

Joanne Diaz prepared all sections of this revised fourth edition. She thanks Brandi Reissenweber, Gayle Rogers, Grace Talusan, Michael Theune, and Abram Van Engen for their advice on the new table of contents. In past editions, the fiction section was prepared by Beverly Lawn, the poetry section was prepared by Jack Ridl and Peter Schakel, and the drama section and reading and writing about literature section were prepared by Janet Gardner.

GET THE MOST OUT OF YOUR COURSE WITH ADDITIONAL RESOURCES FOR TEACHING AND LEARNING WITH *LITERATURE: A PORTABLE ANTHOLOGY.*

Join Our Community. The Macmillan English Community is home to Bedford/St. Martin's professional resources, featuring content to support the teaching of literature—including our popular blog, *LitBits*, as well as articles, research studies, and testimonials on the importance of literature in our classrooms and in our lives. Community members may also review projects and ideas in the pipeline. Join at **community.macmillan .com.**

Package One of Our Best-selling Brief Handbooks at a Discount. Do you need a pocket-sized handbook for your course? Package *Easy Writer* by Andrea Lunsford or *A Pocket Style Manual* by Diana Hacker and Nancy Sommers with this text at a 20 percent discount. For more information, go to **macmillanlearning.com/easywriter/catalog** or **macmillanlearning .com/pocket/catalog.**

Teach Longer Works at a Nice Price. Volumes from our Literary Reprint series—the Case Studies in Contemporary Criticism series, The Bedford Cultural Edition series, the Bedford Shakespeare series, and the Bedford College Editions—can be shrinkwrapped with Approaching Literature at a discount. For a complete list of available titles, visit **macmillanlearning.com/literaryreprints/catalog.**

Trade Up and Save 50 Percent. Add more value and choice to your students' learning experiences by packaging their Macmillan textbook with one of a thousand titles from our sister publishers, including Farrar, Straus & Giroux and St. Martin's Press—at a discount of 50 percent off the regular prices. Visit **macmillanlearning.com/tradeup** for details.

LaunchPad Solo
macmillan learning

Pairing *Literature: A Portable Anthology* with *LaunchPad Solo for Literature* helps students succeed.

Available for free when packaged with *Literature: A Portable Anthology*, *LaunchPad Solo for Literature* gets to the heart of close reading. It offers a set of online materials that helps beginning literature students learn and practice close reading and critical thinking skills in an interactive environment.

To package *LaunchPad Solo for Literature*, use ISBN 978-1-319-08497-4.

How can *LaunchPad Solo for Literature* enhance your course?

It helps students come prepared to class. Assign one of almost 500 reading comprehension quizzes on commonly taught stories, poems, plays, and essays to ensure that your students complete and understand their reading. For homework assignments, have students work through close reading modules that will prepare them for lively, informed classroom discussions.

It gives students hands-on practice in close reading. Easy-to-use and easy-to-assign modules based on widely taught literary selections guide students through three common assignment types:

- **Respond to a Reading**
  Marginal questions that refer to specific passages in a publisher-provided literary work prompt students to read carefully and think critically about key issues raised by the text.

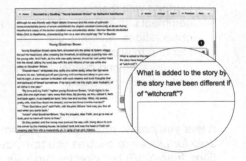

- **Draw Connections**
  Students read and compare
  two or more publisher-provided
  texts that illuminate each other.
     Students can download
  these texts, which have
  been annotated to highlight
  key moments and contextual
  information, and respond in
  writing to a series of questions
  that highlight important
  similarities and differences
  between and among
  the texts.

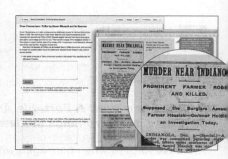

- **Collaborate on a Reading**
  Instructors can upload their
  favorite text or choose from over
  200 publisher-provided texts to
  create a customized lesson on
  close reading. Using the
  highlighting tools and notes
  feature in LaunchPad, the
  instructor can post notes
  or questions about specific
  passages or issues in a text,
  prompting students to
  respond with their own
  comments, questions, or
  observations. Students can also
  respond to each other, further
  collaborating and deepening their
  understanding of a text.

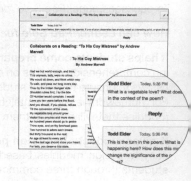

It lets you create multimedia assignments about literature. *LaunchPad Solo for Literature* enables you to embed videos, including favorite selections from YouTube, directly into your digital course. Whether you want students to analyze a Shakespearean scene, listen to W. B. Yeats reading his poems, or compare *The Great Gatsby* in print and on film, the tools are at your fingertips. You can annotate these videos for your students, or ask them to leave their own comments directly on the video content itself. Consider some of these assignment suggestions:

- **Create a Dialogue Around an Assignment**
  Some projects are complicated because they involve many choices
  and stages. Record yourself explaining the project, and upload the
  video to the Video Assignment tool. Require students to comment by
  asking a question or by proposing a topic.

- **Critique a Video as a Group**
  Embed a video from YouTube or from another source. In your
  assignment instructions, provide discussion questions. Require
  students to add two or three comments on the video that respond
  to the prompt. You may grade this assignment with a rubric.

- **Collaborate on Acting out a Scene from a Play**
  Although students most often study plays as written texts, it can be
  fun and informative to have them act out scenes for their classmates.
  Assign small groups of students to record themselves acting out their
  favorite scene from a play and upload the video for the class to watch.
  You can add your feedback and comments directly on the video.

- **Compare and Share Poems Your Students Read Aloud**
  Sound is essential in poetry, and how a poem is read can be as
  important to understanding as the words themselves. Invite students
  to record themselves — either using video, or audio only — and share
  the results with the class. Consider giving each student a "mood"
  for their reading, so that the class can hear how different tones and
  interpretations affect their response to the poem.

Brief Contents

Contents

Selections by Form and Theme

(Arranged Alphabetically by Author's Name)

AGING

ALCOHOLISM

ALLUSIONS TO MYTHOLOGY, LEGENDS,
AND FAIRY TALES

DEATH AND ELEGY

DISAPPOINTMENT AND DESPAIR

DRAMATIC MONOLOGUE

EDUCATION

EKPHRASIS

EPIGRAMS

FATE

FEMINISM

FOUND POEMS

GHAZAL

GOD, FAITH, PRAYER, RELIGIOUS DOUBT

GOTHIC

HEROISM

HISTORY

HUMOR AND SATIRE

ILLNESS

IMMIGRANT EXPERIENCE

MAGICAL REALISM

MINIMALISM

MOON, STARS, PLANETS

MONEY

PHILOSOPHY OF MIND

THE POETRY OF PLACE

SONNETS

SOUTHERN LIFE

THE WRITING PROCESS

YOUTH

PART ONE

40 Stories

QUESTIONS FOR ACTIVE READING:
FICTION

- *The plot is, simply put, the series of events that transpire in a story. How would you summarize the plot of each story? What, if anything, makes it difficult to do so?*

- *Who, in your opinion, are the most sympathetic characters? Who are the most antagonistic? What kinds of information do we learn about the emotional lives of these characters? How do they grow, develop, or change their minds?*

- *What is the point of view of the story? If the author has chosen first-person or omniscient narration, what are the advantages and disadvantages of those choices?*

- *How would you describe the setting of each story? What details of setting contribute to the tone or atmosphere of the story?*

- *How would you describe the style of writing in each story? Is the prose formal? Casual? Archaic? Conversational? Melodramatic? Be as specific as possible, and note examples that bolster your claims.*

- *What kinds of symbols recur in each story? Are they fanciful? Ordinary? Conventional? Surprising? How do they move the narrative forward?*

- *All good short stories use vivid physical details and images to bring the story to life. What details are most memorable to you? How do they affect your interpretation of the characters and events?*

- *What insights do you gather from this story? Do you learn something? Does the author challenge your value system? Do the characters undergo a transformation that is surprising, troubling, or inspiring, and what does that reveal about the story itself?*

Theme

NATHANIEL HAWTHORNE [1804–1864]

Young Goodman Brown

Young Goodman Brown came forth at sunset into the street at Salem village; but put his head back, after crossing the threshold, to exchange a parting kiss with his young wife. And Faith, as the wife was aptly named, thrust her own pretty head into the street, letting the wind play with the pink ribbons of her cap while she called to Goodman Brown.

"Dearest heart," whispered she, softly and rather sadly, when her lips were close to his ear, "prithee put off your journey until sunrise and sleep in your own bed to-night. A lone woman is troubled with such dreams and such thoughts that she's afeared of herself sometimes. Pray tarry with me this night, dear husband, of all nights in the year."

"My love and my Faith," replied young Goodman Brown, "of all nights in the year, this one night must I tarry away from thee. My journey, as thou callest it, forth and back again, must needs be done 'twixt now and sunrise. What, my sweet, pretty wife, dost thou doubt me already, and we but three months married?"

"Then God bless you!" said Faith, with the pink ribbons, "and may you find all well when you come back."

"Amen!" cried Goodman Brown. "Say thy prayers, dear Faith, and go to bed at dusk, and no harm will come to thee."

So they parted; and the young man pursued his way until, being about to turn the corner by the meeting-house, he looked back and saw the head of Faith still peeping after him with a melancholy air, in spite of her pink ribbons.

"Poor little Faith!" thought he, for his heart smote him. "What a wretch am I to leave her on such an errand! She talks of dreams, too. Methought as she spoke there was trouble in her face, as if a dream had warned her what work is to be done to-night. But no, no; 't would kill her to think it. Well, she's a blessed angel on earth, and after this one night I'll cling to her skirts and follow her to heaven."

With this excellent resolve for the future, Goodman Brown felt himself justified in making more haste on his present evil purpose. He had taken a dreary road, darkened by all the gloomiest trees of the forest, which barely stood aside to let the narrow path creep through, and closed immediately behind. It was all as lonely as could be; and there is this

3

peculiarity in such a solitude, that the traveller knows not who may be concealed by the innumerable trunks and the thick boughs overhead; so that with lonely footsteps he may yet be passing through an unseen multitude.

"There may be a devilish Indian behind every tree," said Goodman Brown to himself; and he glanced fearfully behind him as he added, "What if the devil himself should be at my very elbow!"

His head being turned back, he passed a crook of the road, and, looking forward again, beheld the figure of a man, in grave and decent attire, seated at the foot of an old tree. He arose at Goodman Brown's approach and walked onward side by side with him.

"You are late, Goodman Brown," said he. "The clock of the Old South was striking as I came through Boston, and that is full fifteen minutes agone."

"Faith kept me back a while," replied the young man, with a tremor in his voice, caused by the sudden appearance of his companion, though not wholly unexpected.

It was now deep dusk in the forest, and deepest in that part of it where these two were journeying. As nearly as could be discerned, the second traveller was about fifty years old, apparently in the same rank of life as Goodman Brown, and bearing a considerable resemblance to him, though perhaps more in expression than features. Still they might have been taken for father and son. And yet, though the elder person was as simply clad as the younger, and as simple in manner too, he had an indescribable air of one who knew the world, and who would not have felt abashed at the governor's dinner table or in King William's court, were it possible that his affairs should call him thither. But the only thing about him that could be fixed upon as remarkable was his staff, which bore the likeness of a great black snake, so curiously wrought that it might almost be seen to twist and wriggle itself like a living serpent. This, of course, must have been an ocular deception, assisted by the uncertain light.

"Come, Goodman Brown," cried his fellow-traveller, "this is a dull pace for the beginning of a journey. Take my staff, if you are so soon weary."

"Friend," said the other, exchanging his slow pace for a full stop, "having kept covenant by meeting thee here, it is my purpose now to return whence I came. I have scruples touching the matter thou wot'st of."

"Sayest thou so?" replied he of the serpent, smiling apart. "Let us walk on, nevertheless, reasoning as we go; and if I convince thee not thou shalt turn back. We are but a little way in the forest yet."

"Too far! too far!" exclaimed the goodman, unconsciously resuming his walk. "My father never went into the woods on such an errand, nor his father before him. We have been a race of honest men and good Christians since the days of the martyrs; and shall I be the first of the name of Brown that ever took this path and kept"—

"Such company, thou wouldst say," observed the elder person, interpreting his pause. "Well said Goodman Brown! I have been as well acquainted with your family as with ever a one among the Puritans; and that's no trifle to say. I helped your grandfather, the constable, when he lashed the Quaker woman so smartly through the streets of Salem; and it was I that brought your father a pitch-pine knot, kindled at my own hearth, to set fire to an Indian village, in King Philip's war.° They were my good friends, both; and many a pleasant walk have we had along this path, and returned merrily after midnight. I would fain be friends with you for their sake."

"If it be as thou sayest," replied Goodman Brown, "I marvel they never spoke of these matters; or, verily, I marvel not, seeing that the least rumor of the sort would have driven them from New England. We are a people of prayer, and good works to boot, and abide no such wickedness."

"Wickedness or not," said the traveller with the twisted staff, "I have a very general acquaintance here in New England. The deacons of many a church have drunk the communion wine with me; the selectmen of divers towns make me their chairman; and a majority of the Great and General Court are firm supporters of my interest. The governor and I, too—But these are state secrets."

"Can this be so?" cried Goodman Brown, with a stare of amazement at his undisturbed companion. "Howbeit, I have nothing to do with the governor and council; they have their own ways, and are no rule for a simple husbandman like me. But, were I to go on with thee, how should I meet the eye of that good old man, our minister, at Salem village? Oh, his voice would make me tremble both Sabbath day and lecture day."

Thus far the elder traveller had listened with due gravity; but now burst into a fit of irrepressible mirth, shaking himself so violently that his snake-like staff actually seemed to wriggle in sympathy.

"Ha! ha! ha!" shouted he again and again; then composing himself, "Well, go on, Goodman Brown, go on; but, prithee, don't kill me with laughing."

"Well, then, to end the matter at once," said Goodman Brown, considerably nettled, "there is my wife, Faith. It would break her dear little heart; and I'd rather break my own."

"Nay, if that be the case," answered the other, "e'en go thy ways, Goodman Brown. I would not for twenty old women like the one hobbling before us that Faith should come to any harm."

As he spoke he pointed his staff at a female figure on the path, in whom Goodman Brown recognized a very pious and exemplary dame, who had taught him his catechism in youth, and was still his moral and spiritual adviser, jointly with the minister and Deacon Gookin.

King Philip: Wampanoag chief, waged war against the New England colonists (1675–1676).

arranged diction

"A marvel, truly that Goody Cloyse should be so far in the wilderness at nightfall," said he. "But with your leave, friend, I shall take a cut through the woods until we have left this Christian woman behind. Being a stranger to you, she might ask whom I was consorting with and whither I was going."

"Be it so," said his fellow-traveller. "Betake you to the woods, and let me keep the path."

Accordingly the young man turned aside, but took care to watch his companion, who advanced softly along the road until he had come within a staff's length of the old dame. She, meanwhile, was making the best of her way, with singular speed for so aged a woman, and mumbling some indistinct words—a prayer, doubtless—as she went. The traveller put forth his staff and touched her withered neck with what seemed the serpent's tail.

"The devil!" screamed the pious old lady.

"Then Goody Cloyse knows her old friend?" observed the traveller, confronting her and leaning on his writhing stick.

"Ah, forsooth, and is it your worship indeed?" cried the good dame. "Yea, truly is it, and in the very image of my old gossip, Goodman Brown, the grandfather of the silly fellow that now is. But—would your worship believe it?—my broomstick hath strangely disappeared, stolen, as I suspect, by that unhanged witch, Goody Cory, and that, too, when I was all anointed with the juice of smallage, and cinquefoil, and wolf's bane"°—

"Mingled with fine wheat and the fat of a new-born babe," said the shape of old Goodman Brown.

"Ah, your worship knows the recipe," cried the old lady, cackling aloud. "So, as I was saying, being all ready for the meeting, and no horse to ride on, I made up my mind to foot it; for they tell me there is a nice young man to be taken into communion to-night. But now your good worship will lend me your arm, and we shall be there in a twinkling."

"That can hardly be," answered her friend. "I may not spare you my arm, Goody Cloyse; but here is my staff, if you will."

So saying, he threw it down at her feet, where, perhaps, it assumed life, being one of the rods which its owner had formerly lent to the Egyptian magi. Of this fact, however, Goodman Brown could not take cognizance. He had cast up his eyes in astonishment, and, looking down again, beheld neither Goody Cloyse nor the serpentine staff, but his fellow-traveller alone, who waited for him as calmly as if nothing had happened.

Smallage, cinquefoil, and wolf's bane: Three plants sometimes associated with witchcraft. Smallage refers to varieties of parsley and celery; cinquefoil to plants with compound leaves, each having five leaflets; wolf's bane to plants with dull green leaves and yellow foliage, sometimes called winter wheat or aconite.

"That old woman taught me my catechism," said the young man; and there was a world of meaning in this simple comment.

They continued to walk onward, while the elder traveller exhorted his companion to make good speed and persevere in the path, discoursing so aptly that his arguments seemed rather to spring up in the bosom of his auditor than to be suggested by himself. As they went, he plucked a branch of maple to serve for a walking stick, and began to strip it of the twigs and little boughs, which were wet with evening dew. The moment his fingers touched them they became strangely withered and dried up as with a week's sunshine. Thus the pair proceeded, at a good free pace, until suddenly, in a gloomy hollow of the road, Goodman Brown sat himself down on the stump of a tree and refused to go any farther.

"Friend," he said, stubbornly, "my mind is made up. Not another step will I budge on this errand. What if a wretched old woman do choose to go to the devil when I thought she was going to heaven: is that any reason why I should quit my dear Faith and go after her?"

"You will think better of this by and by," said his acquaintance, composedly. "Sit here and rest yourself a while; and when you feel like moving again, there is my staff to help you along."

Without more words, he threw his companion the maple stick, and was as speedily out of sight as if he had vanished into the deepening gloom. The young man sat a few moments by the roadside, applauding himself greatly, and thinking with how clear a conscience he should meet the minister in his morning walk, nor shrink from the eye of good old Deacon Gookin. And what calm sleep would be his that very night, which was to have been spent so wickedly, but so purely and sweetly now, in the arms of Faith! Amidst these pleasant and praiseworthy meditations, Goodman Brown heard the tramp of horses along the road, and deemed it advisable to conceal himself within the verge of the forest, conscious of the guilty purpose that had brought him thither, though now so happily turned from it.

On came the hoof tramps and the voices of the riders, two grave old voices, conversing soberly as they drew near. These mingled sounds appeared to pass along the road, within a few yards of the young man's hiding-place; but, owing doubtless to the depth of the gloom at that particular spot, neither the travellers nor their steeds were visible. Though their figures brushed the small boughs by the wayside, it could not be seen that they intercepted, even for a moment, the faint gleam from the strip of bright sky athwart which they must have passed. Goodman Brown alternately crouched and stood on tiptoe, pulling aside the branches and thrusting forth his head as far as he durst without discerning so much as a shadow. It vexed him the more, because he could have sworn, were such a thing possible, that he recognized the voices of the minister and

Deacon Gookin, jogging along quietly, as they were wont to do, when bound to some ordination or ecclesiastical council. While yet within hearing, one of the riders stopped to pluck a switch.

"Of the two, reverend sir," said the voice like the deacon's, "I had rather miss an ordination dinner than to-night's meeting. They tell me that some of our community are to be here from Falmouth and beyond, and others from Connecticut and Rhode Island, besides several of the Indian powwows, who, after their fashion, know almost as much deviltry as the best of us. Moreover, there is a goodly young woman to be taken into communion."

"Mighty well, Deacon Gookin!" replied the solemn old tones of the minister. "Spur up, or we shall be late. Nothing can be done, you know, until I get on the ground."

The hoofs clattered again; and the voices, talking so strangely in the empty air, passed on through the forest, where no church had ever been gathered or solitary Christian prayed. Whither, then, could these holy men be journeying so deep into the heathen wilderness? Young Goodman Brown caught hold of a tree for support, being ready to sink down on the ground, faint and overburdened with the heavy sickness of his heart. He looked up to the sky, doubting whether there really was a heaven above him. Yet there was the blue arch, and the stars brightening in it.

"With heaven above and Faith below, I will yet stand firm against the devil!" cried Goodman Brown.

While he still gazed upward into the deep arch of the firmament and had lifted his hands to pray, a cloud, though no wind was stirring, hurried across the zenith and hid the brightening stars. The blue sky was still visible, except directly overhead, where this black mass of cloud was sweeping swiftly northward. Aloft in the air, as if from the depths of the cloud, came a confused and doubtful sound of voices. Once the listener fancied that he could distinguish the accents of towns-people of his own, men and women, both pious and ungodly, many of whom he had met at the communion table, and had seen others rioting at the tavern. The next moment, so indistinct were the sounds, he doubted whether he had heard aught but the murmur of the old forest, whispering without a wind. Then came a stronger swell of those familiar tones, heard daily in the sunshine at Salem village, but never until now from a cloud of night. There was one voice, of a young woman, uttering lamentations, yet with an uncertain sorrow, and entreating for some favor, which, perhaps, it would grieve her to obtain; and all the unseen multitude, both saints and sinners, seemed to encourage her onward.

"Faith!" shouted Goodman Brown, in a voice of agony and desperation; and the echoes of the forest mocked him, crying, "Faith! Faith!" as if bewildered wretches were seeking her all through the wilderness.

The cry of grief, rage, and terror was yet piercing the night, when the unhappy husband held his breath for a response. There was a scream, drowned immediately in a louder murmur of voices, fading into far-off laughter, as the dark cloud swept away, leaving the clear and silent sky above Goodman Brown. But something fluttered lightly down through the air and caught on the branch of a tree. The young man seized it, and beheld a pink ribbon.

"My Faith is gone!" cried he after one stupefied moment. "There is no good on earth; and sin is but a name. Come, devil; for to thee is this world given."

And, maddened with despair, so that he laughed loud and long, did Goodman Brown grasp his staff and set forth again, at such a rate that he seemed to fly along the forest path rather than to walk or run. The road grew wilder and drearier and more faintly traced, and vanished at length, leaving him in the heart of the dark wilderness, still rushing onward with the instinct that guides mortal man to evil. The whole forest was peopled with frightful sounds—the creaking of the trees, the howling of wild beasts, and the yell of Indians; while sometimes the wind tolled like a distant church bell, and sometimes gave a broad roar around the traveller, as if all Nature were laughing him to scorn. But he was himself the chief horror of the scene, and shrank not from its other horrors.

"Ha! ha! ha!" roared Goodman Brown when the wind laughed at him. "Let us hear which will laugh loudest. Think not to frighten me with your deviltry. Come witch, come wizard, come Indian powwow, come devil himself, and here comes Goodman Brown. You may as well fear him as he fear you."

In truth, all through the haunted forest there could be nothing more frightful than the figure of Goodman Brown. On he flew among the black pines, brandishing his staff with frenzied gestures, now giving vent to an inspiration of horrid blasphemy, and now shouting forth such laughter as set all the echoes of the forest laughing like demons around him. The fiend in his own shape is less hideous than when he rages in the breast of man. Thus sped the demoniac on his course, until, quivering among the trees, he saw a red light before him, as when the felled trunks and branches of a clearing have been set on fire, and throw up their lurid blaze against the sky, at the hour of midnight. He paused, in a lull of the tempest that had driven him onward, and heard the swell of what seemed a hymn, rolling solemnly from a distance with the weight of many voices. He knew the tune; it was a familiar one in the choir of the village meeting-house. The verse died heavily away, and was lengthened by a chorus, not of human voices, but of all the sounds of the benighted wilderness pealing in awful harmony together. Goodman Brown cried out, and his cry was lost to his own ear by its unison with the cry of the desert.

In the interval of silence he stole forward until the light glared full upon his eyes. At one extremity of an open space, hemmed in by the dark wall of the forest, arose a rock, bearing some rude, natural resemblance either to an altar or a pulpit, and surrounded by four blazing pines, their tops aflame, their stems untouched, like candles at an evening meeting. The mass of foliage that had overgrown the summit of the rock was all on fire, blazing high into the night and fitfully illuminating the whole field. Each pendent twig and leafy festoon was in a blaze. As the red light arose and fell, a numerous congregation alternately shone forth, then disappeared in shadow, and again grew, as it were, out of the darkness, peopling the heart of the solitary woods at once.

"A grave and dark-clad company," quoth Goodman Brown.

In truth they were such. Among them, quivering to and fro between gloom and splendor, appeared faces that would be seen next day at the council board of the province, and others which, Sabbath after Sabbath, looked devoutly heavenward, and benignantly over the crowded pews, from the holiest pulpits in the land. Some affirm that the lady of the governor was there. At least there were high dames well known to her, and wives of honored husbands, and widows, a great multitude, and ancient maidens, all of excellent repute, and fair young girls, who trembled lest their mothers should espy them. Either the sudden gleams of light flashing over the obscure field bedazzled Goodman Brown, or he recognized a score of the church members of Salem village famous for their especial sanctity. Good old Deacon Gookin had arrived, and waited at the skirts of that venerable saint, his revered pastor. But, irreverently consorting with these grave, reputable, and pious people, these elders of the church, these chaste dames and dewy virgins, there were men of dissolute lives and women of spotted fame, wretches given over to all mean and filthy vice, and suspected even of horrid crimes. It was strange to see that the good shrank not from the wicked, nor were the sinners abashed by the saints. Scattered also among their pale-faced enemies were the Indian priests, or powwows, who had often scared their native forest with more hideous incantations than any known to English witchcraft.

"But where is Faith?" thought Goodman Brown; and, as hope came into his heart, he trembled.

Another verse of the hymn arose, a slow and mournful strain, such as the pious love, but joined to words which expressed all that our nature can conceive of sin, and darkly hinted at far more. Unfathomable to mere mortals is the lore of fiends. Verse after verse was sung; and still the chorus of the desert swelled between like the deepest tone of a mighty organ; and with the final peal of that dreadful anthem there came a sound, as if the roaring wind, the rushing streams, the howling beasts, and every other voice of the unconcerted wilderness were mingling and according with the voice of guilty man in homage to the prince of all. The four blazing pines threw up a loftier flame, and obscurely discovered shapes and visages of horror on the smoke wreaths above the impious assembly. At the same moment the fire on the rock shot redly forth and formed a flowing arch above its base, where now appeared a figure. With reverence be it spoken, the figure bore no slight similitude, both in garb and manner, to some grave divine of the New England churches.

"Bring forth the converts!" cried a voice that echoed through the field and rolled into the forest.

At the word, Goodman Brown stepped forth from the shadow of the trees and approached the congregation, with whom he felt a loathful brotherhood by the sympathy of all that was wicked in his heart. He could have well-nigh sworn that the shape of his own dead father beckoned him to advance, looking downward from a smoke wreath, while a woman, with dim features of despair, threw out her hand to warn him back. Was it his mother? But he had no power to retreat one step, nor to resist, even in thought, when the minister and good old Deacon Gookin seized his arms and led him to the blazing rock. Thither came also the slender form of a veiled female, led between Goody Cloyse, that pious teacher of the catechism, and Martha Carrier, who had received the devil's promise to be queen of hell. A rampant hag was she. And there stood the proselytes beneath the canopy of fire.

"Welcome, my children," said the dark figure, "to the communion of your race. Ye have found thus young your nature and your destiny. My children, look behind you!"

They turned; and flashing forth, as it were, in a sheet of flame, the fiend worshippers were seen; the smile of welcome gleamed darkly on every visage.

"There," resumed the sable form, "are all whom ye have reverenced from youth. Ye deemed them holier than yourselves and shrank from your own sin, contrasting it with their lives of righteousness and prayerful aspirations heavenward. Yet here are they all in my worshipping assembly. This night it shall be granted you to know their secret deeds: how hoary-bearded elders of the church have whispered wanton words to the young maids of their households; how many a woman, eager for widows' weeds, has given her husband a drink at bedtime and let him sleep his last sleep in her bosom; how beardless youths have made haste to inherit their fathers' wealth; and how fair damsels—blush not, sweet ones—have dug little graves in the garden, and bidden me, the sole guest, to an infant's funeral. By the sympathy of your human hearts for sin ye shall scent out all the places—whether in church, bedchamber, street, field, or forest—where crime has been committed, and shall exult to behold the whole earth one stain of guilt, one mighty blood spot. Far more than this. It shall be yours to penetrate, in every bosom, the deep mystery of sin, the fountain of all wicked arts, and which inexhaustibly supplies more evil impulses than human power—than my power at its utmost—can make manifest in deeds. And now, my children, look upon each other."

They did so; and, by the blaze of the hell-kindled torches, the wretched man beheld his Faith, and the wife her husband, trembling before that unhallowed altar.

"Lo, there ye stand, my children," said the figure, in a deep and solemn tone, almost sad with its despairing awfulness, as if his once angelic nature could yet mourn for our miserable race. "Depending upon one another's hearts, ye had still hoped that virtue were not all a dream. Now are ye undeceived. Evil is the nature of mankind. Evil must be your only happiness. Welcome again, my children, to the communion of your race."

"Welcome," repeated the fiend worshippers, in one cry of despair and triumph.

And there they stood, the only pair, as it seemed, who were yet hesitating on the verge of wickedness in this dark world. A basin was hallowed, naturally, in the rock. Did it contain water, reddened by the lurid light? or was it blood? or, perchance, a liquid flame? Herein did the shape of evil dip his hand and prepare to lay the mark of baptism upon their foreheads, that they might be partakers of the mystery of sin, more conscious of the secret guilt of others, both in deed and thought, than they could now be of their own. The husband cast one look at his pale wife, and Faith at him. What polluted wretches would the next glance show them to each other, shuddering alike at what they disclosed and what they saw!

"Faith! Faith!" cried the husband, "look up to heaven, and resist the wicked one."

Whether Faith obeyed he knew not. Hardly had he spoken when he found himself amid calm night and solitude, listening to a roar of the wind which died heavily away through the forest. He staggered against the rock, and felt it chill and damp; while a hanging twig, that had been all on fire, besprinkled his cheek with the coldest dew.

The next morning young Goodman Brown came slowly into the street of Salem village, staring around him like a bewildered man. The good old minister was taking a walk along the graveyard to get an appetite for breakfast and meditate his sermon, and bestowed a blessing, as he passed, on Goodman Brown. He shrank from the venerable saint as if to avoid an anathema. Old Deacon Gookin was at domestic worship, and the holy words of his prayer were heard through the open window. "What God doth the wizard pray to?" quoth Goodman Brown. Goody Cloyse, that excellent old Christian, stood in the early sunshine at her own lattice, catechizing a little girl who had brought her a pint of morning's milk. Goodman Brown snatched away the child as from the grasp of the fiend himself. Turning the corner by the meeting-house, he spied the head of Faith, with the pink ribbons, gazing anxiously forth, and bursting into such joy at sight of him that she skipped along the street and almost kissed her husband before the whole village. But Goodman Brown looked sternly and sadly into her face, and passed on without a greeting.

Had Goodman Brown fallen asleep in the forest and only dreamed a wild dream of a witch-meeting?

Be it so if you will; but, alas! it was a dream of evil omen for young Goodman Brown. A stern, a sad, a darkly meditative, a distrustful, if not a desperate man did he become from the night of that fearful dream. On the Sabbath day, when the congregation were singing a holy psalm, he could not listen because an anthem of sin rushed loudly upon his ear and drowned all the blessed strain. When the minister spoke from the pulpit with power and fervid eloquence, and, with his hand on the open Bible, of the sacred truths of our religion, and of saint-like lives and triumphant deaths, and of future bliss or misery unutterable, then did Goodman Brown turn pale, dreading lest the roof should thunder down upon the gray blasphemer and his hearers. Often, awaking suddenly at midnight, he shrank from the bosom of Faith; and at morning or eventide, when the family knelt down at prayer, he scowled and muttered to himself, and gazed sternly at his wife, and turned away. And when he had lived long, and was borne to his grave a hoary corpse, followed by Faith, an aged woman, and children and grandchildren, a goodly procession, besides neighbors not a few, they carved no hopeful verse upon his tombstone, for his dying hour was gloom.

[1835]

EDGAR ALLAN POE   [1809–1849]

The Cask of Amontillado

The thousand injuries of Fortunato I had borne as I best could; but when he ventured upon insult, I vowed revenge. You, who so well know the nature of my soul, will not suppose, however, that I gave utterance to a threat. *At length* I would be avenged; this was a point definitely settled — but the very definitiveness with which it was resolved precluded the idea of risk. I must not only punish, but punish with impunity. A wrong is unredressed when retribution overtakes its redresser. It is equally unredressed when the avenger fails to make himself felt as such to him who has done the wrong.

It must be understood, that neither by word nor deed had I given Fortunato cause to doubt my good-will. I continued, as was my wont, to smile in his face, and he did not perceive that my smile *now* was at the thought of his immolation.

He had a weak point—this Fortunato—although in other regards he was a man to be respected and even feared. He prided himself on his connoisseurship in wine. Few Italians have the true virtuoso spirit. For the most part their enthusiasm is adopted to suit the time and opportunity — to practise imposture upon the British and Austrian *millionaires*. In painting and gemmary Fortunato, like his countrymen, was a quack—but in the matter of old wines he was sincere. In this respect I did not differ from him materially: I was skilful in the Italian vintages myself, and bought largely whenever I could.

It was about dusk, one evening during the supreme madness of the carnival season, that I encountered my friend. He accosted me with excessive warmth, for he had been drinking much. The man wore motley. He had on a tight-fitting parti-striped dress, and his head was surmounted by the conical cap and bells. I was so pleased to see him, that I thought I should never have done wringing his hand.

I said to him: "My dear Fortunato, you are luckily met. How remarkably well you are looking to-day! But I have received a pipe° of what passes for Amontillado, and I have my doubts."

"How?" said he. "Amontillado? A pipe? Impossible! And in the middle of the carnival!"

Pipe: A large cask.

"I have my doubts," I replied; "and I was silly enough to pay the full Amontillado price without consulting you in the matter. You were not to be found, and I was fearful of losing a bargain."

"Amontillado!"

"I have my doubts."

"Amontillado!"

"And I must satisfy them."

"Amontillado!"

"As you are engaged, I am on my way to Luchesi. If any one has a critical turn, it is he. He will tell me——"

"Luchesi cannot tell Amontillado from Sherry."

"And yet some fools will have it that his taste is a match for your own."

"Come, let us go."

"Whither?"

"To your vaults."

"My friend, no; I will not impose upon your good nature. I perceive you have an engagement. Luchesi——"

"I have no engagement;—come."

"My friend, no. It is not the engagement, but the severe cold with which I perceive you are afflicted. The vaults are insufferably damp. They are encrusted with nitre."°

"Let us go, nevertheless. The cold is merely nothing. Amontillado! You have been imposed upon. And as for Luchesi, he cannot distinguish Sherry from Amontillado."

Thus speaking, Fortunato possessed himself of my arm. Putting on a mask of black silk, and drawing a *roquelaire*° closely about my person, I suffered him to hurry me to my palazzo.

There were no attendants at home; they had absconded to make merry in honor of the time. I had told them that I should not return until the morning, and had given them explicit orders not to stir from the house. These orders were sufficient, I well knew, to insure their immediate disappearance, one and all, as soon as my back was turned.

I took from their sconces two flambeaux, and giving one to Fortunato, bowed him through several suites of rooms to the archway that led into the vaults. I passed down a long and winding staircase, requesting him to be cautious as he followed. We came at length to the foot of the descent, and stood together on the damp ground of the catacombs of the Montresors.

The gait of my friend was unsteady, and the bells upon his cap jingled as he strode.

Nitre: Potassium nitrate, or saltpeter; believed at the end of the eighteenth century to be an element in air and plants.
Roquelaire: A cloak.

"The pipe?" said he.

"It is farther on," said I; "but observe the white web-work which gleams from these cavern walls."

He turned toward me, and looked into my eyes with two filmy orbs that distilled the rheum of intoxication.

"Nitre?" he asked, at length.

"Nitre," I replied. "How long have you had that cough?"

"Ugh! ugh! ugh!—ugh! ugh! ugh!—ugh! ugh! ugh!—ugh! ugh! ugh!—ugh! ugh! ugh!"

My poor friend found it impossible to reply for many minutes.

"It is nothing," he said, at last.

"Come," I said, with decision, "we will go back; your health is precious. You are rich, respected, admired, beloved; you are happy, as once I was. You are a man to be missed. For me it is no matter. We will go back; you will be ill, and I cannot be responsible. Besides, there is Luchesi—"

"Enough," he said; "the cough is a mere nothing; it will not kill me. I shall not die of a cough."

"True—true," I replied; "and, indeed, I had no intention of alarming you unnecessarily; but you should use all proper caution. A draught of this Medoc will defend us from the damps."

Here I knocked off the neck of a bottle which I drew from a long row of its fellows that lay upon the mould.

"Drink," I said, presenting him the wine.

He raised it to his lips with a leer. He paused and nodded to me familiarly, while his bells jingled.

"I drink," he said, "to the buried that repose around us."

"And I to your long life."

He again took my arm, and we proceeded.

"These vaults," he said, "are extensive."

"The Montresors," I replied, "were a great and numerous family."

"I forget your arms."

"A huge human foot d'or,° in a field azure; the foot crushes a serpent rampant whose fangs are imbedded in the heel."

"And the motto?"

"*Nemo me impune lacessit.*"°

"Good!" he said.

The wine sparkled in his eyes and the bells jingled. My own fancy grew warm with the Medoc. We had passed through walls of piled bones, with casks and puncheons intermingling into the inmost recesses of the

---

D'or: Of gold.
Nemo me impune lacessit: No one wounds me with impunity (Latin); the motto of the Scottish royal arms.

catacombs. I paused again, and this time I made bold to seize Fortunato by an arm above the elbow.

"The nitre!" I said; "see, it increases. It hangs like moss upon the vaults. We are below the river's bed. The drops of moisture trickle among the bones. Come, we will go back ere it is too late. Your cough——"

"It is nothing," he said; "let us go on. But first, another draught of the Medoc."

I broke and reached him a flagon of De Grâve. He emptied it at a breath. His eyes flashed with a fierce light. He laughed and threw the bottle upward with a gesticulation I did not understand.

I looked at him in surprise. He repeated the movement—a grotesque one.

"You do not comprehend?" he said.

"Not I," I replied.

"Then you are not of the brotherhood."

"How?"

"You are not of the masons."

"Yes, yes," I said; "yes, yes."

"You? Impossible! A mason?"

"A mason," I replied.

"A sign," he said.

"It is this," I answered, producing a trowel from beneath the folds of my *roquelaire*.

"You jest," he exclaimed, recoiling a few paces. "But let us proceed to the Amontillado."

"Be it so," I said, replacing the tool beneath the cloak, and again offering him my arm. He leaned upon it heavily. We continued our route in search of the Amontillado. We passed through a range of low arches, descended, passed on, and descending again, arrived at a deep crypt, in which the foulness of the air caused our flambeaux rather to glow than flame.

At the most remote end of the crypt there appeared another less spacious. Its walls had been lined with human remains, piled to the vault overhead, in the fashion of the great catacombs of Paris. Three sides of this interior crypt were still ornamented in this manner. From the fourth the bones had been thrown down, and lay promiscuously upon the earth, forming at one point a mound of some size. Within the wall thus exposed by the displacing of the bones, we perceived a still interior recess, in depth about four feet, in width three, in height six or seven. It seemed to have been constructed for no especial use within itself, but formed merely the interval between two of the colossal supports of the roof of the catacombs, and was backed by one of their circumscribing walls of solid granite.

It was in vain that Fortunato, uplifting his dull torch, endeavored to pry into the depth of the recess. Its termination the feeble light did not enable us to see.

"Proceed," I said; "herein is the Amontillado. As for Luchesi——"

"He is an ignoramus," interrupted my friend, as he stepped unsteadily forward, while I followed immediately at his heels. In an instant he had reached the extremity of the niche, and finding his progress arrested by the rock, stood stupidly bewildered. A moment more and I had fettered him to the granite. In its surface were two iron staples, distant from each other about two feet, horizontally. From one of these depended a short chain, from the other a padlock. Throwing the links about his waist, it was but the work of a few seconds to secure it. He was too much astounded to resist. Withdrawing the key I stepped back from the recess.

"Pass your hand," I said, "over the wall; you cannot help feeling the nitre. Indeed it is *very* damp. Once more let me *implore* you to return. No? Then I must positively leave you. But I must first render you all the little attentions in my power."

"The Amontillado!" ejaculated my friend, not yet recovered from his astonishment.

"True," I replied; "the Amontillado."

As I said these words I busied myself among the pile of bones of which I have before spoken. Throwing them aside, I soon uncovered a quantity of building stone and mortar. With these materials and with the aid of my trowel, I began vigorously to wall up the entrance of the niche.

I had scarcely laid the first tier of the masonry when I discovered that the intoxication of Fortunato had in a great measure worn off. The earliest indication I had of this was a low moaning cry from the depth of the recess. It was *not* the cry of a drunken man. There was then a long and obstinate silence. I laid the second tier, and the third, and the fourth; and then I heard the furious vibrations of the chain. The noise lasted for several minutes, during which, that I might hearken to it with the more satisfaction, I ceased my labors and sat down upon the bones. When at last the clanking subsided, I resumed the trowel, and finished without interruption the fifth, the sixth, and the seventh tier. The wall was now nearly upon a level with my breast. I again paused, and holding the flambeaux over the masonwork, threw a few feeble rays upon the figure within.

A succession of loud and shrill screams, bursting suddenly from the throat of the chained form, seemed to thrust me violently back. For a brief moment I hesitated—I trembled. Unsheathing my rapier, I began to grope with it about the recess; but the thought of an instant reassured me. I placed my hand upon the solid fabric of the catacombs, and felt satisfied. I reapproached the wall. I replied to the yells of him who clamored. I reechoed—I aided—I surpassed them in volume and in strength. I did this, and the clamorer grew still.

It was now midnight, and my task was drawing to a close. I had completed the eighth, the ninth, and the tenth tier. I had finished a portion of the last and the eleventh; there remained but a single stone to be fitted and plastered in. I struggled with its weight; I placed it partially in its destined position. But now there came from out the niche a low laugh that erected the hairs upon my head. It was succeeded by a sad voice, which I had difficulty in recognizing as that of the noble Fortunato. The voice said—

"Ha! ha! ha!—he! he!—a very good joke indeed—an excellent jest. We will have many a rich laugh about it at the palazzo—he! he! he!—over our wine—he! he! he!"

"The Amontillado!" I said.

"He! he! he!—he! he! he!—yes, the Amontillado. But is it not getting late? Will not they be awaiting us at the palazzo, the Lady Fortunato and the rest? Let us be gone."

"Yes," I said, "let us be gone "

"For the love of God, Montresor!"

"Yes," I said, "for the love of God!"

But to these words I hearkened in vain for a reply. I grew impatient. I called aloud:

"Fortunato!"

No answer. I called again:

"Fortunato!"

No answer still, I thrust a torch through the remaining aperture and let it fall within. There came forth in return only a jingling of the bells. My heart grew sick—on account of the dampness of the catacombs. I hastened to make an end of my labor. I forced the last stone into its position; I plastered it up. Against the new masonry I reerected the old rampart of bones. For the half of a century no mortal has disturbed them. *In pace requiescat!°*

[1846]

In pace requiescat: May he rest in peace (Latin).

SUI SIN FAR (EDITH MAUD EATON)

[1865–1914]

In the Land of the Free

I

"See, Little One—the hills in the morning sun. There is thy home for years to come. It is very beautiful and thou wilt be very happy there."

The Little One looked up into his mother's face in perfect faith. He was engaged in the pleasant occupation of sucking a sweetmeat;° but that did not prevent him from gurgling responsively.

"Yes, my olive bud; there is where thy father is making a fortune for thee. Thy father! Oh, wilt thou not be glad to behold his dear face. 'Twas for thee I left him."

The Little One ducked his chin sympathetically against his mother's knee. She lifted him on to her lap. He was two years old, a round, dimple-cheeked boy with bright brown eyes and a sturdy little frame.

"Ah! Ah! Ah! Ooh! Ooh! Ooh!" puffed he, mocking a tugboat steaming by.

San Francisco's waterfront was lined with ships and steamers, while other craft, large and small, including a couple of white transports from the Philippines, lay at anchor here and there off shore. It was some time before the *Eastern Queen* could get docked, and even after that was accomplished, a lone Chinaman who had been waiting on the wharf for an hour was detained that much longer by men with the initials U.S.C. on their caps, before he could board the steamer and welcome his wife and child.

"This is thy son," announced the happy Lae Choo.

Hom Hing lifted the child, felt of his little body and limbs, gazed into his face with proud and joyous eyes; then turned inquiringly to a customs officer at his elbow.

"That's a fine boy you have there," said the man. "Where was he born?"

"In China," answered Hom Hing, swinging the Little One on his right shoulder, preparatory to leading his wife off the steamer.

Sweetmeat: A piece of candy.

20

"Ever been to America before?"

"No, not he," answered the father with a happy laugh.

The customs officer beckoned to another.

"This little fellow," said he, "is visiting America for the first time."

The other customs officer stroked his chin reflectively.

"Good day," said Hom Hing.

"Wait!" commanded one of the officers. "You cannot go just yet."

"What more now?" asked Hom Hing.

"I'm afraid," said the customs officer, "that we cannot allow the boy to go ashore. There is nothing in the papers that you have shown us—your wife's papers and your own—having any bearing upon the child."

"There was no child when the papers were made out," returned Hom Hing. He spoke calmly; but there was apprehension in his eyes and in his tightening grip on his son.

"What is it? What is it?" quavered Lae Choo, who understood a little English.

The second customs officer regarded her pityingly.

"I don't like this part of the business," he muttered.

The first officer turned to Hom Hing and in an official tone of voice, said:

"Seeing that the boy has no certificate entitling him to admission to this country you will have to leave him with us."

"Leave my boy!" exclaimed Hom Hing.

"Yes; he will be well taken care of, and just as soon as we can hear from Washington he will be handed over to you."

"But," protested Hom Hing, "he is my son."

"We have no proof," answered the man with a shrug of his shoulders; "and even if so we cannot let him pass without orders from the Government."

"He is my son," reiterated Hom Hing, slowly and solemnly. "I am a Chinese merchant and have been in business in San Francisco for many years. When my wife told to me one morning that she dreamed of a green tree with spreading branches and one beautiful red flower growing thereon, I answered her that I wished my son to be born in our country, and for her to prepare to go to China. My wife complied with my wish. After my son was born my mother fell sick and my wife nursed and cared for her; then my father, too, fell sick, and my wife also nursed and cared for him. For twenty moons my wife care for and nurse the old people, and when they die they bless her and my son, and I send for her to return to me. I had no fear of trouble. I was a Chinese merchant and my son was my son."

"Very good, Hom Hing," replied the first officer. "Nevertheless, we take your son."

"No, you not take him; he my son too."

It was Lae Choo. Snatching the child from his father's arms she held and covered him with her own.

The officers conferred together for a few moments; then one drew Hom Hing aside and spoke in his ear.

Resignedly Hom Hing bowed his head, then approached his wife. "'Tis the law," said he, speaking in Chinese, "and 'twill be but for a little while—until tomorrow's sun arises."

"You, too," reproached Lae Choo in a voice eloquent with pain. But accustomed to obedience she yielded the boy to her husband, who in turn delivered him to the first officer. The Little One protested lustily against the transfer; but his mother covered her face with her sleeve and his father silently led her away. Thus was the law of the land complied with.

II

Day was breaking. Lae Choo, who had been awake all night, dressed herself, then awoke her husband.

"'Tis the morn," she cried. "Go, bring our son."

The man rubbed his eyes and arose upon his elbow so that he could see out of the window. A pale star was visible in the sky. The petals of a lily in a bowl on the windowsill were unfurled.

"'Tis not yet time," said he, laying his head down again.

"Not yet time. Ah, all the time that I lived before yesterday is not so much as the time that has been since my Little One was taken from me."

The mother threw herself down beside the bed and covered her face.

Hom Hing turned on the light, and touching his wife's bowed head with a sympathetic hand inquired if she had slept.

"Slept!" she echoed, weepingly. "Ah, how could I close my eyes with my arms empty of the little body that has filled them every night for more than twenty moons! You do not know—man—what it is to miss the feel of the little fingers and the little toes and the soft round limbs of your little one. Even in the darkness his darling eyes used to shine up to mine, and often have I fallen into slumber with his pretty babble at my ear. And now, I see him not; I touch him not; I hear him not. My baby, my little fat one!"

"Now! Now! Now!" consoled Hom Hing, patting his wife's shoulder reassuringly; "there is no need to grieve so; he will soon gladden you again. There cannot be any law that would keep a child from its mother!"

Lae Choo dried her tears.

"You are right, my husband," she meekly murmured. She arose and stepped about the apartment, setting things to rights. The box of presents she had brought for her California friends had been opened the evening before; and silks, embroideries, carved ivories, ornamental laccquerware, brasses, camphorwood boxes, fans, and chinaware were scattered around in confused heaps. In the midst of unpacking the thought of her child in the hands of strangers had overpowered her, and she had left everything to crawl into bed and weep.

Having arranged her gifts in order she stepped out on to the deep balcony.

The star had faded from view and there were bright streaks in the western sky. Lae Choo looked down the street and around. Beneath the flat occupied by her and her husband were quarters for a number of bachelor Chinamen, and she could hear them from where she stood, taking their early morning breakfast. Below their dining-room was her husband's grocery store. Across the way was a large restaurant. Last night it had been resplendent with gay colored lanterns and the sound of music. The rejoicings over "the completion of the moon," by Quong Sum's firstborn, had been long and loud, and had caused her to tie a handkerchief over her ears. She, a bereaved mother, had it not in her heart to rejoice with other parents. This morning the place was more in accord with her mood. It was still and quiet. The revellers had dispersed or were asleep.

A roly-poly woman in black sateen, with long pendant earrings in her ears, looked up from the street below and waved her a smiling greeting. It was her old neighbor, Kuie Hoe, the wife of the gold embosser, Mark Sing. With her was a little boy in yellow jacket and lavender pantaloons. Lae Choo remembered him as a baby. She used to like to play with him in those days when she had no child of her own. What a long time ago that seemed! She caught her breath in a sigh, and laughed instead.

"Why are you so merry?" called her husband from within.

"Because my Little One is coming home," answered Lae Choo. "I am a happy mother—a happy mother."

She pattered into the room with a smile on her face.

The noon hour had arrived. The rice was steaming in the bowls and a fragrant dish of chicken and bamboo shoots was awaiting Hom Hing. Not for one moment had Lae Choo paused to rest during the morning hours; her activity had been ceaseless. Every now and again, however, she had raised her eyes to the gilded clock on the curiously carved mantelpiece. Once, she had exclaimed:

"Why so long, oh! why so long?" Then, apostrophizing herself: "Lae Choo, be happy. The Little One is coming! The Little One is coming!" Several times she burst into tears, and several times she laughed aloud.

Hom Hing entered the room; his arms hung down by his side.

"The Little One!" shrieked Lae Choo.

"They bid me call tomorrow."

With a moan the mother sank to the floor.

The noon hour passed. The dinner remained on the table.

III

The winter rains were over: the spring had come to California, flushing the hills with green and causing an ever-changing pageant of flowers to pass over them. But there was no spring in Lae Choo's heart, for the Little One remained away from her arms. He was being kept in a mission. White women were caring for him, and though for one full moon he had pined for his mother and refused to be comforted he was now apparently happy and contented. Five moons or five months had gone by since the day he had passed with Lae Choo through the Golden Gate; but the great Government at Washington still delayed sending the answer which would return him to his parents.

Hom Hing was disconsolately rolling up and down the balls in his abacus box when a keen-faced young man stepped into his store.

"What news?" asked the Chinese merchant.

"This!" The young man brought forth a typewritten letter. Hom Hing read the words:

"Re Chinese child, alleged to be the son of Hom Hing, Chinese merchant, doing business at 425 Clay Street, San Francisco.

"Same will have attention as soon as possible."

Hom Hing returned the letter, and without a word continued his manipulation of the counting machine.

"Have you anything to say?" asked the young man.

"Nothing. They have sent the same letter fifteen times before. Have you not yourself showed it to me?"

"True!" The young man eyed the Chinese merchant furtively. He had a proposition to make and was pondering whether or not the time was opportune.

"How is your wife?" he inquired solicitously—and diplomatically.

Hom Hing shook his head mournfully.

"She seems less every day," he replied. "Her food she takes only when I bid her and her tears fall continually. She finds no pleasure in dress or flowers and cares not to see her friends. Her eyes stare all night. I think before another moon she will pass into the land of spirits."

"No!" exclaimed the young man, genuinely startled.

"If the boy not come home I lose my wife sure," continued Hom Hing with bitter sadness.

"It's not right," cried the young man indignantly. Then he made his proposition.

The Chinese father's eyes brightened exceedingly.

"Will I like you to go to Washington and make them give you the paper to restore my son?" cried he. "How can you ask when you know my heart's desire?"

"Then," said the young fellow, "I will start next week. I am anxious to see this thing through if only for the sake of your wife's peace of mind."

"I will call her. To hear what you think to do will make her glad," said Hom Hing.

He called a message to Lae Choo upstairs through a tube in the wall.

In a few moments she appeared, listless, wan, and hollow-eyed; but when her husband told her the young lawyer's suggestion she became electrified; her form straightened, her eyes glistened; the color flushed to her cheeks.

"Oh," she cried, turning to James Clancy. "You are a hundred man good!"

The young man felt somewhat embarrassed; his eyes shifted a little under the intense gaze of the Chinese mother.

"Well, we must get your boy for you," he responded. "Of course" —turning to Hom Hing— "it will cost a little money. You can't get fellows to hurry the Government for you without gold in your pocket."

Hom Hing stared blankly for a moment. Then: "How much do you want, Mr. Clancy?" he asked quietly.

"Well, I will need at least five hundred to start with."

Hom Hing cleared his throat.

"I think I told to you the time I last paid you for writing letters for me and seeing the Custom boss here that nearly all I had was gone!"

"Oh, well then we won't talk about it, old fellow. It won't harm the boy to stay where he is, and your wife may get over it all right."

"What that you say?" quavered Lae Choo.

James Clancy looked out of the window.

"He says," explained Hom Hing in English, "that to get our boy we have to have much money."

"Money! Oh, yes."

Lae Choo nodded her head.

"I have not got the money to give him."

For a moment Lae Choo gazed wonderingly from one face to the other; then, comprehension dawning upon her, with swift anger, pointing to the lawyer, she cried: "You not one hundred man good; you just common white man."

"Yes, ma'am," returned James Clancy, bowing and smiling ironically.

Hom Hing pushed his wife behind him and addressed the lawyer again: "I might try," said he, "to raise something; but five hundred—it is not possible."

"What about four?"

"I tell you I have next to nothing left and my friends are not rich."

"Very well!"

The lawyer moved leisurely toward the door, pausing on its threshold to light a cigarette.

"Stop, white man; white man, stop!"

Lae Choo, panting and terrified, had started forward and now stood beside him, clutching his sleeve excitedly.

"You say you can go to get paper to bring my Little One to me if Hom Hing give you five hundred dollars?"

The lawyer nodded carelessly; his eyes were intent upon the cigarette which would not take the fire from the match.

"Then you go get paper. If Hom Hing not can give you five hundred dollars—I give you perhaps what more that much."

She slipped a heavy gold bracelet from her wrist and held it out to the man. Mechanically he took it.

"I go get more!"

She scurried away, disappearing behind the door through which she had come.

"Oh, look here, I can't accept this," said James Clancy, walking back to Hom Hing and laying down the bracelet before him.

"It's all right," said Hom Hing, seriously, "pure China gold. My wife's parent give it to her when we married."

"But I can't take it anyway," protested the young man.

"It is all same as money. And you want money to go to Washington," replied Hom Hing in a matter-of-fact manner.

"See, my jade earrings—my gold buttons—my hairpins—my comb of pearl and my rings—one, two, three, four, five rings; very good—very good—all same much money. I give them all to you. You take and bring me paper for my Little One."

Lae Choo piled up her jewels before the lawyer.

Hom Hing laid a restraining hand upon her shoulder. "Not all, my wife," he said in Chinese. He selected a ring—his gift to Lae Choo when she dreamed of the tree with the red flower. The rest of the jewels he pushed toward the white man.

"Take them and sell them," said he. "They will pay your fare to Washington and bring you back with the paper."

For one moment James Clancy hesitated. He was not a sentimental man; but something within him arose against accepting such payment for his services.

"They are good, good." pleadingly asserted Lae Choo, seeing his hesitation.

Whereupon he seized the jewels, thrust them into his coat pocket, and walked rapidly away from the store.

IV

Lae Choo followed after the missionary woman through the mission nursery school. Her heart was beating so high with happiness that she could scarcely breathe. The paper had come at last—the precious paper which gave Hom Hing and his wife the right to the possession of their own child. It was ten months now since he had been taken from them—ten months since the sun had ceased to shine for Lae Choo.

The room was filled with children—most of them wee tots, but none so wee as her own. The mission woman talked as she walked. She told Lae Choo that little Kim, as he had been named by the school, was the pet of the place, and that his little tricks and ways amused and delighted every one. He had been rather difficult to manage at first and had cried much for his mother; "but children so soon forget, and after a month he seemed quite at home and played around as bright and happy as a bird."

"Yes," responded Lae Choo. "Oh, yes, yes!"

But she did not hear what was said to her. She was walking in a maze of anticipatory joy.

"Wait here, please," said the mission woman, placing Lae Choo in a chair. "The very youngest ones are having their breakfast."

She withdrew for a moment—it seemed like an hour to the mother—then she reappeared leading by the hand a little boy dressed in blue cotton overalls and white-soled shoes. The little boy's face was round and dimpled and his eyes were very bright.

"Little One, ah, my Little One!" cried Lae Choo.

She fell on her knees and stretched her hungry arms toward her son.

But the Little One shrank from her and tried to hide himself in the folds of the white woman's skirt.

"Go 'way, go 'way!" he bade his mother.

[c. 1900]

STEPHEN CRANE [1871–1900]

The Open Boat

A Tale Intended to Be after the Fact,
Being the Experience of Four Men from
the Sunk Steamer *Commodore*

I

None of them knew the color of the sky. Their eyes glanced level, and were fastened upon the waves that swept toward them. These waves were of the hue of slate, save for the tops, which were of foaming white, and all of the men knew the colors of the sea. The horizon narrowed and widened, and dipped and rose, and at all times its edge was jagged with waves that seemed thrust up in points like rocks.

Many a man ought to have a bath-tub larger than the boat which here rode upon the sea. These waves were most wrongfully and barbarously abrupt and tall, and each froth-top was a problem in small boat navigation.

The cook squatted in the bottom and looked with both eyes at the six inches of gunwale which separated him from the ocean. His sleeves were rolled over his fat forearms, and the two flaps of his unbuttoned vest dangled as he bent to bail out the boat. Often he said: "Gawd! That was a narrow clip." As he remarked it he invariably gazed eastward over the broken sea.

The oiler, steering with one of the two oars in the boat, sometimes raised himself suddenly to keep clear of water that swirled in over the stern. It was a thin little oar and it seemed often ready to snap.

The correspondent, pulling at the other oar, watched the waves and wondered why he was there.

The injured captain, lying in the bow, was at this time buried in that profound dejection and indifference which comes, temporarily at least, to even the bravest and most enduring when, willy nilly, the firm fails, the army loses, the ship goes down. The mind of the master of a vessel is rooted deep in the timbers of her, though he command for a day or a decade, and this captain had on him the stern impression of a scene in the grays of dawn of seven turned faces, and later a stump of a top-mast with a white ball on it that slashed to and fro at the waves, went low and lower, and down. Thereafter there was something strange in his voice.

28

Although steady, it was deep with mourning, and of a quality beyond oration or tears.

"Keep 'er a little more south, Billie," said he.

"'A little more south,' sir," said the oiler in the stern.

A seat in this boat was not unlike a seat upon a bucking broncho, and, by the same token, a broncho is not much smaller. The craft pranced and reared, and plunged like an animal. As each wave came, and she rose for it, she seemed like a horse making at a fence outrageously high. The manner of her scramble over these walls of water is a mystic thing, and, moreover, at the top of them were ordinarily these problems in white water, the foam racing down from the summit of each wave, requiring a new leap, and a leap from the air. Then, after scornfully bumping a crest, she would slide, and race, and splash down a long incline and arrive bobbing and nodding in front of the next menace.

A singular disadvantage of the sea lies in the fact that after successfully surmounting one wave you discover that there is another behind it just as important and just as nervously anxious to do something effective in the way of swamping boats. In a ten-foot dingey one can get an idea of the resources of the sea in the line of waves that is not probable to the average experience, which is never at sea in a dingey. As each slaty wall of water approached, it shut all else from the view of the men in the boat, and it was not difficult to imagine that this particular wave was the final outburst of the ocean, the last effort of the grim water. There was a terrible grace in the move of the waves, and they came in silence, save for the snarling of the crests.

In the wan light, the faces of the men must have been gray. Their eyes must have glinted in strange ways as they gazed steadily astern. Viewed from a balcony, the whole thing would doubtlessly have been weirdly picturesque. But the men in the boat had no time to see it, and if they had had leisure there were other things to occupy their minds. The sun swung steadily up the sky, and they knew it was broad day because the color of the sea changed from slate to emerald-green, streaked with amber lights, and the foam was like tumbling snow. The process of the breaking day was unknown to them. They were aware only of this effect upon the color of the waves that rolled toward them.

In disjointed sentences the cook and the correspondent argued as to the difference between a life-saving station and a house of refuge. The cook had said: "There's a house of refuge just north of the Mosquito Inlet Light, and as soon as they see us, they'll come off in their boat and pick us up."

"As soon as who see us?" said the correspondent.

"The crew," said the cook.

"Houses of refuge don't have crews," said the correspondent. "As I understand them, they are only places where clothes and grub are stored for the benefit of shipwrecked people. They don't carry crews."

"Oh, yes, they do," said the cook.

"No, they don't," said the correspondent.

"Well, we're not there yet, anyhow," said the oiler, in the stern.

"Well," said the cook, "perhaps it's not a house of refuge that I'm thinking of as being near Mosquito Inlet Light. Perhaps it's a life-saving station."

"We're not there yet," said the oiler, in the stern.

II

As the boat bounced from the top of each wave, the wind tore through the hair of the hatless men, and as the craft plopped her stern down again the spray slashed past them. The crest of each of these waves was a hill, from the top of which the men surveyed, for a moment, a broad tumultuous expanse, shining and wind-riven. It was probably splendid. It was probably glorious, this play of the free sea, wild with lights of emerald and white and amber.

"Bully good thing it's an on-shore wind," said the cook. "If not where would we be? Wouldn't have a show."

"That's right," said the correspondent.

The busy oiler nodded his assent.

Then the captain, in the bow, chuckled in a way that expressed humor, contempt, tragedy, all in one. "Do you think we've got a show, now, boys?" said he.

Whereupon the three went silent, save for a trifle of hemming and hawing. To express any particular optimism at this time they felt to be childish and stupid, but they all doubtless possessed this sense of the situation in their mind. A young man thinks doggedly at such times. On the other hand, the ethics of their condition was decidedly against any open suggestion of hopelessness. So they were silent.

"Oh, well," said the captain, soothing his children, "we'll get ashore all right."

But there was that in his tone which made them think, so the oiler quoth: "Yes! If this wind holds!"

The cook was bailing. "Yes! If we don't catch hell in the surf."

Canton flannel gulls flew near and far. Sometimes they sat down on the sea, near patches of brown sea-weed that rolled over the waves with a movement like carpets on a line in a gale. The birds sat comfortably in groups, and they were envied by some in the dingey, for the wrath of the sea was no more to them than it was to a covey of prairie chickens a thousand miles inland. Often they came very close and stared at the men with black bead-like eyes. At these times they were uncanny and sinister in their unblinking scrutiny, and the men hooted angrily at them, telling them to be gone. One came, and evidently decided to alight on the top of the captain's head. The bird flew parallel to the boat and did not circle, but made short sidelong jumps in the air in chicken-fashion. His black eyes were wistfully fixed upon the captain's head. "Ugly brute," said the oiler to the bird. "You look as if you were made with a jack-knife." The cook and the correspondent swore darkly at the creature. The captain naturally wished to knock it away with the end of the heavy painter, but he did not dare do it, because anything resembling an emphatic gesture would have capsized this freighted boat, and so with his open hand, the captain gently and carefully waved the gull away. After it had been discouraged from the pursuit the captain breathed easier on account of his hair, and others breathed easier because the bird struck their minds at this time as being somehow gruesome and ominous.

In the meantime the oiler and the correspondent rowed. And also they rowed.

They sat together in the same seat, and each rowed an oar. Then the oiler took both oars; then the correspondent took both oars; then the oiler; then the correspondent. They rowed and they rowed. The very ticklish part of the business was when the time came for the reclining one in the stern to take his turn at the oars. By the very last star of truth, it is easier to steal eggs from under a hen than it was to change seats in the dingey. First the man in the stern slid his hand along the thwart and moved with care, as if he were of Sèvres. Then the man in the rowing seat slid his hand along the other thwart. It was all done with the most extraordinary care. As the two sidled past each other, the whole party kept watchful eyes on the coming wave, and the captain cried: "Look out now! Steady there!"

The brown mats of sea-weed that appeared from time to time were like islands, bits of earth. They were travelling, apparently, neither one way nor the other. They were, to all intents, stationary. They informed the men in the boat that it was making progress slowly toward the land.

The captain, rearing cautiously in the bow, after the dingey soared on a great swell, said that he had seen the light-house at Mosquito Inlet. Presently the cook remarked that he had seen it. The correspondent was at the oars, then, and for some reason he too wished to look at the light-house, but his back was toward the far shore and the waves were important, and for some time he could not seize an opportunity to turn his head. But at last there came a wave more gentle than the others, and when at the crest of it he swiftly scoured the western horizon.

"See it?" said the captain.

"No," said the correspondent, slowly, "I didn't see anything."

"Look again," said the captain. He pointed. "It's exactly in that direction."

At the top of another wave, the correspondent did as he was bid, and this time his eyes chanced on a small still thing on the edge of the swaying horizon. It was precisely like the point of a pin. It took an anxious eye to find a light-house so tiny.

"Think we'll make it, Captain?"

"If this wind holds and the boat don't swamp, we can't do much else," said the captain.

The little boat, lifted by each towering sea, and splashed viciously by the crests, made progress that in the absence of sea-weed was not apparent to those in her. She seemed just a wee thing wallowing, miraculously, top-up, at the mercy of five oceans. Occasionally, a great spread of water, like white flames, swarmed into her.

"Bail her, cook," said the captain, serenely.

"All right, Captain," said the cheerful cook.

III

It would be difficult to describe the subtle brotherhood of men that was here established on the seas. No one said that it was so. No one mentioned it. But it dwelt in the boat, and each man felt it warm him. They were a captain, an oiler, a cook, and a correspondent, and they were friends, friends in a more curiously iron-bound degree than may be common. The hurt captain, lying against the water-jar in the bow, spoke always in a low voice and calmly, but he could never command a more ready and swiftly obedient crew than the motley three of the dingey. It was more than a mere recognition of what was best for the common safety. There was surely in it a quality that was personal and heartfelt. And after this devotion to the commander of the boat there was this comradeship that the correspondent, for instance, who had been taught to be cynical of men, knew even at the time was the best experience of his life. But no one said that it was so. No one mentioned it.

"I wish we had a sail," remarked the captain. "We might try my overcoat on the end of an oar and give you two boys a chance to rest." So the cook and the correspondent held the mast and spread wide the overcoat. The oiler steered, and the little boat made good way with her new rig. Sometimes the oiler had to scull sharply to keep a sea from breaking into the boat, but otherwise sailing was a success.

Meanwhile the light-house had been growing slowly larger. It had now almost assumed color, and appeared like a little gray shadow on the sky.

The man at the oars could not be prevented from turning his head rather often to try for a glimpse of this little gray shadow.

At last, from the top of each wave the men in the tossing boat could see land. Even as the light-house was an upright shadow on the sky, this land seemed but a long black shadow on the sea. It certainly was thinner than paper. "We must be about opposite New Smyrna," said the cook, who had coasted this shore often in schooners. "Captain, by the way, I believe they abandoned that life-saving station there about a year ago."

"Did they?" said the captain.

The wind slowly died away. The cook and the correspondent were not now obliged to slave in order to hold high the oar. But the waves continued their old impetuous swooping at the dingey, and the little craft, no longer under way, struggled woundily over them. The oiler or the correspondent took the oars again.

Shipwrecks are *apropos* of nothing. If men could only train for them and have them occur when the men had reached pink condition, there would be less drowning at sea. Of the four in the dingey none had slept any time worth mentioning for two days and two nights previous to embarking in the dingey, and in the excitement of clambering about the deck of a foundering ship they had also forgotten to eat heartily.

For these reasons, and for others, neither the oiler nor the correspondent was fond of rowing at this time. The correspondent wondered ingenuously how in the name of all that was sane could there be people who thought it amusing to row a boat. It was not an amusement; it was a diabolical punishment, and even a genius of mental aberrations could never conclude that it was anything but a horror to the muscles and a crime against the back. He mentioned to the boat in general how the amusement of rowing struck him, and the weary-faced oiler smiled in full sympathy. Previously to the foundering, by the way, the oiler had worked double-watch in the engine-room of the ship.

"Take her easy, now, boys," said the captain. "Don't spend yourselves. If we have to run a surf you'll need all your strength, because we'll sure have to swim for it. Take your time."

Slowly the land arose from the sea. From a black line it became a line of black and a line of white—trees and sand. Finally, the captain said that he could make out a house on the shore. "That's the house of refuge, sure," said the cook. "They'll see us before long, and come out after us."

The distant light-house reared high. "The keeper ought to be able to make us out now, if he's looking through a glass," said the captain. "He'll notify the life-saving people."

"None of those other boats could have got ashore to give word of the wreck," said the oiler, in a low voice. "Else the life-boat would be out hunting us."

Slowly and beautifully the land loomed out of the sea. The wind came again. It had veered from the northeast to the southeast. Finally, a new sound struck the ears of the men in the boat. It was the low thunder of the surf on the shore. "We'll never be able to make the light-house now," said the captain. "Swing her head a little more north, Billie."

"'A little more north,' sir," said the oiler.

Whereupon the little boat turned her nose once more down the wind, and all but the oarsman watched the shore grow. Under the influence of this expansion doubt and direful apprehension were leaving the minds of the men. The management of the boat was still most absorbing, but it could not prevent a quiet cheerfulness. In an hour, perhaps, they would be ashore.

Their back-bones had become thoroughly used to balancing in the boat and they now rode this wild colt of a dingey like circus men. The correspondent thought that he had been drenched to the skin, but happening to feel in the top pocket of his coat, he found therein eight cigars. Four of them were soaked with sea-water; four were perfectly scatheless. After a search, somebody produced three dry matches, and thereupon the four waifs rode impudently in their little boat, and with an assurance of an impending rescue shining in their eyes, puffed at the big cigars and judged well and ill of all men. Everybody took a drink of water.

IV

"Cook," remarked the captain, "there don't seem to be any signs of life about your house of refuge."

"No," replied the cook. "Funny they don't see us!"

A broad stretch of lowly coast lay before the eyes of the men. It was of dunes topped with dark vegetation. The roar of the surf was plain, and sometimes they could see the white lip of a wave as it spun up the beach. A tiny house was blocked out black upon the sky. Southward, the slim light-house lifted its little gray length.

Tide, wind, and waves were swinging the dingey northward. "Funny they don't see us," said the men.

The surf's roar was here dulled, but its tone was, nevertheless, thunderous and mighty. As the boat swam over the great rollers, the men sat listening to this roar. "We'll swamp sure," said everybody.

It is fair to say here that there was not a life-saving station within twenty miles in either direction, but the men did not know this fact and in consequence they made dark and opprobrious remarks concerning the eyesight of the nation's life-savers. Four scowling men sat in the dingey and surpassed records in the invention of epithets.

"Funny they don't see us."

The light-heartedness of a former time had completely faded. To their sharpened minds it was easy to conjure pictures of all kinds of incompetency and blindness and, indeed, cowardice. There was the shore of the populous land, and it was bitter and bitter to them that from it came no sign.

"Well," said the captain, ultimately, "I suppose we'll have to make a try for ourselves. If we stay out here too long, we'll none of us have strength left to swim after the boat swamps."

And so the oiler, who was at the oars, turned the boat straight for the shore. There was a sudden tightening of muscles. There was some thinking.

"If we don't all get ashore—" said the captain. "If we don't all get ashore, I suppose you fellows know where to send news of my finish?"

They then briefly exchanged some addresses and admonitions. As for the reflections of the men, there was a great deal of rage in them. Perchance they might be formulated thus: "If I am going to be drowned—if I am going to be drowned—if I am going to be drowned, why, in the name of the seven mad gods who rule the sea, was I allowed to come thus far and contemplate sand and trees? Was I brought here merely to have my nose dragged away as I was about to nibble the sacred cheese of life? It is preposterous. If this old ninny-woman, Fate, cannot do better than this, she should be deprived of the management of men's fortunes. She is an old hen who knows not her intention. If she has decided to drown me, why did she not do it in the beginning and save me all this trouble. The whole affair is absurd. . . . But, no, she cannot mean to drown me. She dare not drown me. She cannot drown me. Not after all this work." Afterward the man might have had an impulse to shake his fist at the clouds. "Just you drown me, now and then hear what I call you!"

The billows that came at this time were more formidable. They seemed always just about to break and roll over the little boat in a turmoil of foam. There was a preparatory and long growl in the speech of them. No mind unused to the sea would have concluded that the dingey could ascend these sheer heights in time. The shore was still afar. The oiler was a wily surfman. "Boys," he said, swiftly, "she won't live three minutes more and we're too far out to swim. Shall I take her to sea again, Captain?"

"Yes! Go ahead!" said the captain.

This oiler, by a series of quick miracles, and fast and steady oarsmanship, turned the boat in the middle of the surf and took her safely to sea again.

There was a considerable silence as the boat bumped over the furrowed sea to deeper water. Then somebody in gloom spoke. "Well, anyhow, they must have seen us from the shore by now."

The gulls went in slanting flight up the wind toward the gray desolate east. A squall, marked by dingy clouds, and clouds brick-red, like smoke from a burning building, appeared from the southeast.

"What do you think of those life-saving people? Ain't they peaches?"

"Funny they haven't seen us."

"Maybe they think we're out here for sport! Maybe they think we're fishin'. Maybe they think we're damned fools."

It was a long afternoon. A changed tide tried to force them southward, but wind and wave said northward. Far ahead, where coast-line, sea, and sky formed their mighty angle, there were little dots which seemed to indicate a city on the shore.

"St. Augustine?"

The captain shook his head. "Too near Mosquito Inlet."

And the oiler rowed, and then the correspondent rowed. Then the oiler rowed. It was a weary business. The human back can become the seat of more aches and pains than are registered in books for the composite anatomy of a regiment. It is a limited area, but it can become the theatre of innumerable muscular conflicts, tangles, wrenches, knots, and other comforts.

"Did you ever like to row, Billie?" asked the correspondent.

"No," said the oiler, "Hang it."

When one exchanged the rowing-seat for a place in the bottom of the boat, he suffered a bodily depression that caused him to be careless of everything save an obligation to wiggle one finger. There was cold sea-water swashing to and fro in the boat, and he lay in it. His head, pillowed on a thwart, was within an inch of the swirl of a wave crest, and some-times a particularly obstreperous sea came in-board and drenched him once more. But these matters did not annoy him. It is almost certain that if the boat had capsized he would have tumbled comfortably out upon the ocean as if he felt sure that it was a great soft mattress.

"Look! There's a man on the shore!"

"Where?"

"There! See 'im? See 'im?"

"Yes, sure! He's walking along."

"Now he's stopped. Look! He's facing us!"

"He's waving at us!"

"So he is! By thunder!"

"Ah, now, we're all right! There'll be a boat out here for us in half an hour."

"He's going on. He's running. He's going up to that house there."

The remote beach seemed lower than the sea, and it required a search-ing glance to discern the little black figure. The captain saw a floating stick and they rowed to it. A bath-towel was by some weird chance in the boat, and, tying this on the stick, the captain waved it. The oarsman did not dare turn his head, so he was obliged to ask questions.

"What's he doing now?"

"He's standing still again. He's looking, I think. . . . There he goes again. Toward the house. . . . Now he's stopped again."

"Is he waving at us?"

"No, not now! He was, though."

"Look! There comes another man!"

"He's running."

"Look at him go, would you."

"Why, he's on a bicycle. Now he's met the other man. They're both waving at us. Look!"

"There comes something up the beach."

"What the devil is that thing?"

"Why, it looks like a boat."

"Why, certainly it's a boat."

"No, it's on wheels."

"Yes, so it is. Well, that must be the life-boat. They drag them along shore on a wagon."

"That's the life-boat, sure."

"No, by, it's—it's an omnibus."

"I tell you it's a life-boat."

"It is not! It's an omnibus. I can see it plain. See? One of those big hotel omnibuses."

"By thunder, you're right. It's an omnibus, sure as fate. What do you suppose they are doing with an omnibus? Maybe they are going around collecting the life-crew, hey?"

"That's it, likely. Look! There's a fellow waving a little black flag. He's standing on the steps of the omnibus. There come those other two fellows. Now they're all talking together. Look at the fellow with the flag. Maybe he ain't waving it!"

"That ain't a flag, is it? That's his coat. Why, certainly, that's his coat."

"So it is. It's his coat. He's taken it off and is waving it around his head. But would you look at him swing it!"

"Oh, say, there isn't any life-saving station there. That's just a winter resort hotel omnibus that has brought over some of the boarders to see us drown."

"What's that idiot with the coat mean? What's he signaling, anyhow?"

"It looks as if he were trying to tell us to go north. There must be a life-saving station up there."

"No! He thinks we're fishing. Just giving us a merry hand. See? Ah, there, Willie."

"Well, I wish I could make something out of those signals. What do you suppose he means?"

"He don't mean anything. He's just playing."

"Well, if he'd just signal us to try the surf again, or to go to sea and wait, or go north, or go south, or go to hell—there would be some reason in it. But look at him. He just stands there and keeps his coat revolving like a wheel. The ass!"

"There come more people."

"Now there's quite a mob. Look! Isn't that a boat?"

"Where? Oh, I see where you mean. No, that's no boat."

"That fellow is still waving his coat."

"He must think we like to see him do that. Why don't he quit it. It don't mean anything."

"I don't know. I think he is trying to make us go north. It must be that there's a life-saving station there somewhere."

"Say, he ain't tired yet. Look at 'im wave."

"Wonder how long he can keep that up. He's been revolving his coat ever since he caught sight of us. He's an idiot. Why aren't they getting men to bring a boat out. A fishing boat—one of those big yawls—could come out here all right. Why don't he do something?"

"Oh, it's all right, now."

"They'll have a boat out here for us in less than no time, now that they've seen us."

A faint yellow tone came into the sky over the low land. The shadows on the sea slowly deepened. The wind bore coldness with it, and the men began to shiver.

"Holy smoke!" said one, allowing his voice to express his impious mood, "if we keep on monkeying out here! If we've got to flounder out here all night!"

"Oh, we'll never have to stay here all night! Don't you worry. They've seen us now, and it won't be long before they'll come chasing out after us."

The shore grew dusky. The man waving a coat blended gradually into this gloom, and it swallowed in the same manner the omnibus and the group of people. The spray, when it dashed uproariously over the side, made the voyagers shrink and swear like men who were being branded.

"I'd like to catch the chump who waved the coat. I feel like soaking him one, just for luck."

"Why? What did he do?"

"Oh, nothing, but then he seemed so damned cheerful."

In the meantime the oiler rowed, and then the correspondent rowed, and then the oiler rowed. Gray-faced and bowed forward, they mechanically, turn by turn, plied the leaden oars. The form of the light-house had vanished from the southern horizon, but finally a pale star appeared, just lifting from the sea. The streaked saffron in the west passed before the all-merging darkness, and the sea to the east was black. The land had vanished, and was expressed only by the low and drear thunder of the surf.

"If I am going to be drowned—if I am going to be drowned—if I am going to be drowned, why, in the name of the seven mad gods who rule the sea, was I allowed to come thus far and contemplate sand and trees? Was I brought here merely to have my nose dragged away as I was about to nibble the sacred cheese of life?"

The patient captain, drooped over the water-jar, was sometimes obliged to speak to the oarsman.

"Keep her head up! Keep her head up!"

"'Keep her head up,' sir." The voices were weary and low.

This was surely a quiet evening. All save the oarsman lay heavily and listlessly in the boat's bottom. As for him, his eyes were just capable of noting the tall black waves that swept forward in a most sinister silence, save for an occasional subdued growl of a crest.

The cook's head was on a thwart, and he looked without interest at the water under his nose. He was deep in other scenes. Finally he spoke. "Billie," he murmured, dreamfully, "what kind of pie do you like best?"

V

"Pie," said the oiler and the correspondent, agitatedly. "Don't talk about those things, blast you!"

"Well," said the cook, "I was just thinking about ham sandwiches, and —"

A night on the sea in an open boat is a long night. As darkness settled finally, the shine of the light, lifting from the sea in the south, changed to full gold. On the northern horizon a new light appeared, a small bluish gleam on the edge of the waters. These two lights were the furniture of the world. Otherwise there was nothing but waves.

Two men huddled in the stern, and distances were so magnificent in the dingey that the rower was enabled to keep his feet partly warmed by thrusting them under his companions. Their legs indeed extended far under the rowing-seat until they touched the feet of the captain forward. Sometimes, despite the efforts of the tired oarsman, a wave came piling into the boat, an icy wave of the night, and the chilling water soaked them anew. They would twist their bodies for a moment and groan, and sleep the dead sleep once more, while the water in the boat gurgled about them as the craft rocked.

The plan of the oiler and the correspondent was for one to row until he lost the ability, and then arouse the other from his sea-water couch in the bottom of the boat.

The oiler plied the oars until his head drooped forward, and the overpowering sleep blinded him. And he rowed yet afterward. Then he touched a man in the bottom of the boat, and called his name. "Will you spell me for a little while?" he said, meekly.

"Sure, Billie," said the correspondent, awakening and dragging himself to a sitting position. They exchanged places carefully, and the oiler, cuddling down in the sea-water at the cook's side, seemed to go to sleep instantly.

The particular violence of the sea had ceased. The waves came without snarling. The obligation of the man at the oars was to keep the boat headed so that the tilt of the rollers would not capsize her, and to preserve her from filling when the crests rushed past. The black waves were silent and hard to be seen in the darkness. Often one was almost upon the boat before the oarsman was aware.

In a low voice the correspondent addressed the captain. He was not sure that the captain was awake, although this iron man seemed to be always awake. "Captain, shall I keep her making for that light north, sir?"

The same steady voice answered him. "Yes. Keep it about two points off the port bow."

The cook had tied a life-belt around himself in order to get even the warmth which this clumsy cork contrivance could donate, and he seemed almost stove-like when a rower, whose teeth invariably chattered wildly as soon as he ceased his labor, dropped down to sleep.

The correspondent, as he rowed, looked down at the two men sleeping under foot. The cook's arm was around the oiler's shoulders, and, with their fragmentary clothing and haggard faces, they were the babes of the sea, a grotesque rendering of the old babes in the wood.

Later he must have grown stupid at his work, for suddenly there was a growling of water, and a crest came with a roar and a swash into the boat, and it was a wonder that it did not set the cook afloat in his lifebelt. The cook continued to sleep, but the oiler sat up, blinking his eyes and shaking with the new cold.

"Oh, I'm awful sorry, Billie," said the correspondent, contritely.

"That's all right, old boy," said the oiler, and lay down again and was asleep.

Presently it seemed that even the captain dozed, and the correspondent thought that he was the one man afloat on all the oceans. The wind had a voice as it came over the waves, and it was sadder than the end.

There was a long, loud swishing astern of the boat, and a gleaming trail of phosphorescence, like blue flame, was furrowed on the black waters. It might have been made by a monstrous knife.

Then there came a stillness, while the correspondent breathed with the open mouth and looked at the sea.

Suddenly there was another swish and another long flash of bluish light, and this time it was alongside the boat, and might almost have been reached with an oar. The correspondent saw an enormous fin speed like a shadow through the water, hurling the crystalline spray and leaving the long glowing trail.

The correspondent looked over his shoulder at the captain. His face was hidden, and he seemed to be asleep. He looked at the babes of the sea. They certainly were asleep. So, being bereft of sympathy, he leaned a little way to one side and swore softly into the sea.

But the thing did not then leave the vicinity of the boat. Ahead or astern, on one side or the other, at intervals long or short, fled the long sparkling streak, and there was to be heard the whirroo of the dark fin. The speed and power of the thing were greatly to be admired. It cut the water like a gigantic and keen projectile.

The presence of this biding thing did not affect the man with the same horror that it would if he had been a picnicker. He simply looked at the sea dully and swore in an undertone.

Nevertheless, it is true that he did not wish to be alone with the thing. He wished one of his companions to awaken by chance and keep him company with it. But the captain hung motionless over the water-jar and the oiler and the cook in the bottom of the boat were plunged in slumber.

VI

"If I am going to be drowned—if I am going to be drowned—if I am going to be drowned, why, in the name of the seven mad gods who rule the sea, was I allowed to come thus far and contemplate sand and trees?"

During this dismal night, it may be remarked that a man would conclude that it was really the intention of the seven mad gods to drown him, despite the abominable injustice of it. For it was certainly an abominable injustice to drown a man who had worked so hard, so hard. The man felt it would be a crime most unnatural. Other people had drowned at sea since galleys swarmed with painted sails, but still—

When it occurs to a man that nature does not regard him as important, and that she feels she would not maim the universe by disposing of him, he at first wishes to throw bricks at the temple, and he hates deeply the fact that there are no bricks and no temples. Any visible expression of nature would surely be pelleted with his jeers.

Then, if there be no tangible thing to hoot he feels, perhaps, the desire to confront a personification and indulge in pleas, bowed to one knee, and with hands supplicant, saying: "Yes, but I love myself."

A high cold star on a winter's night is the word he feels that she says to him. Thereafter he knows the pathos of his situation.

The men in the dingey had not discussed these matters, but each had, no doubt, reflected upon them in silence and according to his mind. There was seldom any expression upon their faces save the general one of complete weariness. Speech was devoted to the business of the boat.

To chime the notes of his emotion, a verse mysteriously entered the correspondent's head. He had even forgotten that he had forgotten this verse, but it suddenly was in his mind.

A soldier of the Legion lay dying in Algiers,
There was lack of woman's nursing, there was dearth of woman's tears;
But a comrade stood beside him, and he took that comrade's hand,
And he said: "I never more shall see my own, my native land."

In his childhood, the correspondent had been made acquainted with the fact that a soldier of the Legion lay dying in Algiers, but he had never regarded it as important. Myriads of his school-fellows had informed him of the soldier's plight, but the dinning had naturally ended by making him perfectly indifferent. He had never considered it his affair that a soldier of the Legion lay dying in Algiers, nor had it appeared to him as a matter for sorrow. It was less to him than the breaking of a pencil's point.

Now, however, it quaintly came to him as a human, living thing. It was no longer merely a picture of a few throes in the breast of a poet, meanwhile drinking tea and warming his feet at the grate; it was an actuality— stern, mournful, and fine.

The correspondent plainly saw the soldier. He lay on the sand with his feet out straight and still. While his pale left hand was upon his chest in an attempt to thwart the going of his life, the blood came between his fingers. In the far Algerian distance, a city of low square forms was set against a sky that was faint with the last sunset hues. The correspondent, plying the oars and dreaming of the slow and slower movements of the lips of the soldier, was moved by a profound and perfectly impersonal comprehension. He was sorry for the soldier of the Legion who lay dying in Algiers.

The thing which had followed the boat and waited had evidently grown bored at the delay. There was no longer to be heard the slash of the cutwater, and there was no longer the flame of the long trail. The light in the north still glimmered, but it was apparently no nearer to the boat. Sometimes the boom of the surf rang in the correspondent's ears, and he turned the craft seaward then and rowed harder. Southward, some one had evidently built a watch-fire on the beach. It was too low and too far to be seen, but it made a shimmering, roseate reflection upon the bluff back of it, and this could be discerned from the boat. The wind came stronger, and sometimes a wave suddenly raged out like a mountain-cat and there was to be seen the sheen and sparkle of a broken crest.

The captain, in the bow, moved on his water-jar and sat erect. "Pretty long night," he observed to the correspondent. He looked at the shore. "Those life-saving people take their time."

"Did you see that shark playing around?"

"Yes, I saw him. He was a big fellow, all right."

"Wish I had known you were awake."

Later the correspondent spoke into the bottom of the boat.

"Billie!" There was a slow and gradual disentanglement. "Billie, will you spell me?"

"Sure," said the oiler.

As soon as the correspondent touched the cold comfortable sea-water in the bottom of the boat, and had huddled close to the cook's life-belt he was deep in sleep, despite the fact that his teeth played all the popular airs. This sleep was so good to him that it was but a moment before he heard a voice call his name in a tone that demonstrated the last stages of exhaustion. "Will you spell me?"

"Sure, Billie."

The light in the north had mysteriously vanished, but the correspondent took his course from the wide-awake captain.

Later in the night they took the boat farther out to sea, and the captain directed the cook to take one oar at the stern and keep the boat facing the seas. He was to call out if he should hear the thunder of the surf. This plan enabled the oiler and the correspondent to get respite together. "We'll give those boys a chance to get into shape again," said the captain. They curled down and, after a few preliminary chatterings and trembles, slept once more the dead sleep. Neither knew they had bequeathed to the cook the company of another shark, or perhaps the same shark.

As the boat caroused on the waves, spray occasionally bumped over the side and gave them a fresh soaking, but this had no power to break their repose. The ominous slash of the wind and the water affected them as it would have affected mummies.

"Boys," said the cook, with the notes of every reluctance in his voice, "she's drifted in pretty close. I guess one of you had better take her to sea again." The correspondent, aroused, heard the crash of the toppled crests.

As he was rowing, the captain gave him some whiskey and water, and this steadied the chills out of him. "If I ever get ashore and anybody shows me even a photograph of an oar —"

At last there was a short conversation.

"Billie. . . . Billie, will you spell me?"
"Sure," said the oiler.

VII

When the correspondent again opened his eyes, the sea and the sky were each of the gray hue of the dawning. Later, carmine and gold was painted upon the waters. The morning appeared finally, in its splendor, with a sky of pure blue, and the sunlight flamed on the tips of the waves.

On the distant dunes were set many little black cottages, and a tall white wind-mill reared above them. No man, nor dog, nor bicycle appeared on the beach. The cottages might have formed a deserted village.

The voyagers scanned the shore. A conference was held in the boat. "Well," said the captain, "if no help is coming, we might better try a run through the surf right away. If we stay out here much longer we will be too weak to do anything for ourselves at all." The others silently acquiesced in this reasoning. The boat was headed for the beach. The correspondent wondered if none ever ascended the tall wind-tower, and if then they never looked seaward. This tower was a giant, standing with its back to the plight of the ants. It represented in a degree, to the correspondent, the serenity of nature amid the struggles of the individual— nature in the wind, and nature in the vision of men. She did not seem cruel to him then, nor beneficent, nor treacherous, nor wise. But she was indifferent, flatly indifferent. It is, perhaps, plausible that a man in this situation, impressed with the unconcern of the universe, should see the innumerable flaws of his life and have them taste wickedly in his mind and wish for another chance. A distinction between right and wrong seems absurdly clear to him, then, in this new ignorance of the grave-edge, and he understands that if he were given another opportunity he would mend his conduct and his words, and be better and brighter during an introduction, or at a tea.

"Now, boys," said the captain, "she is going to swamp sure. All we can do is to work her in as far as possible, and then when she swamps, pile out and scramble for the beach. Keep cool now, and don't jump until she swamps sure."

The oiler took the oars. Over his shoulders he scanned the surf. "Captain," he said, "I think I'd better bring her about, and keep her head-on to the seas and back her in."

"All right, Billie," said the captain. "Back her in." The oiler swung the boat then and, seated in the stern, the cook and the correspondent were obliged to look over their shoulders to contemplate the lonely and indifferent shore.

The monstrous inshore rollers heaved the boat high until the men were again enabled to see the white sheets of water scudding up the slanted beach. "We won't get in very close," said the captain. Each time a man could wrest his attention from the rollers, he turned his glance toward the shore, and in the expression of the eyes during this contemplation there was a singular quality. The correspondent, observing the others, knew that they were not afraid, but the full meaning of their glances was shrouded.

As for himself, he was too tired to grapple fundamentally with the fact. He tried to coerce his mind into thinking of it, but the mind was dominated at this time by the muscles, and the muscles said they did not care. It merely occurred to him that if he should drown it would be a shame.

There were no hurried words, no pallor, no plain agitation. The men simply looked at the shore. "Now, remember to get well clear of the boat when you jump," said the captain.

Seaward the crest of a roller suddenly fell with a thunderous crash, and the long white comber came roaring down upon the boat.

"Steady now," said the captain. The men were silent. They turned their eyes from the shore to the comber and waited. The boat slid up the incline, leaped at the furious top, bounced over it, and swung down the long back of the wave. Some water had been shipped and the cook bailed it out.

But the next crest crashed also. The tumbling boiling flood of white water caught the boat and whirled it almost perpendicular. Water swarmed in from all sides. The correspondent had his hands on the gunwale at this time, and when the water entered at that place he swiftly withdrew his fingers, as if he objected to wetting them.

The little boat, drunken with this weight of water, reeled and snuggled deeper into the sea.

"Bail her out, cook! Bail her out," said the captain.

"All right, Captain," said the cook.

"Now boys, the next one will do for us, sure," said the oiler. "Mind to jump clear of the boat."

The third wave moved forward, huge, furious, implacable. It fairly swallowed the dingey, and almost simultaneously the men tumbled into the sea. A piece of life-belt had lain in the bottom of the boat, and as the correspondent went overboard he held this to his chest with his left hand.

The January water was icy, and he reflected immediately that it was colder than he had expected to find it off the coast of Florida. This appeared to his dazed mind as a fact important enough to be noted at the time. The coldness of the water was sad; it was tragic. This fact was somehow so mixed and confused with his opinion of his own situation that it seemed almost a proper reason for tears. The water was cold.

When he came to the surface he was conscious of little but the noisy water. Afterward he saw his companions in the sea. The oiler was ahead in the race. He was swimming strongly and rapidly. Off to the correspondent's left, the cook's great white and corked back bulged out of the water, and in the rear the captain was hanging with his one good hand to the keel of the overturned dingey.

There is a certain immovable quality to a shore, and the correspondent wondered at it amid the confusion of the sea.

It seemed also very attractive, but the correspondent knew that it was a long journey, and he paddled leisurely. The piece of life-preserver lay under him, and sometimes he whirled down the incline of a wave as if he were on a hand-sled.

But finally he arrived at a place in the sea where travel was beset with difficulty. He did not pause swimming to inquire what manner of current had caught him, but there his progress ceased. The shore was set before him like a bit of scenery on a stage, and he looked at it and understood with his eyes each detail of it.

As the cook passed, much farther to the left, the captain was calling to him, "Turn over on your back, cook! Turn over on your back and use the oar."

"All right, sir." The cook turned on his back, and, paddling with an oar, went ahead as if he were a canoe.

Presently the boat also passed to the left of the correspondent with the captain clinging with one hand to the keel. He would have appeared like a man raising himself to look over a board fence, if it were not for the extraordinary gymnastics of the boat. The correspondent marvelled that the captain could still hold to it.

They passed on, nearer to shore—the oiler, the cook, the captain—and following them went the water-jar, bouncing gayly over the seas.

The correspondent remained in the grip of this strange new enemy—a current. The shore, with its white slope of sand and its green bluff, topped with little silent cottages, was spread like a picture before him. It was very near to him then, but he was impressed as one who in a gallery looks at a scene from Brittany or Holland.

He thought: "I am going to drown? Can it be possible? Can it be possible? Can it be possible?" Perhaps an individual must consider his own death to be the final phenomenon of nature.

But later a wave perhaps whirled him out of his small deadly current, for he found suddenly that he could again make progress toward the shore. Later still, he was aware that the captain, clinging with one hand to the keel of the dingey, had his face turned away from the shore and toward him, and was calling his name. "Come to the boat! Come to the boat!"

In his struggle to reach the captain and the boat, he reflected that when one gets properly wearied, drowning must really be a comfortable arrangement, a cessation of hostilities accompanied by a large degree of relief, and he was glad of it, for the main thing in his mind for some moments had been the horror of the temporary agony. He did not wish to be hurt.

Presently he saw a man running along the shore. He was undressing with most remarkable speed. Coat, trousers, shirt, everything flew magically off him.

"Come to the boat," called the captain.

"All right, Captain." As the correspondent paddled, he saw the captain let himself down to bottom and leave the boat. Then the correspondent performed his one little marvel of the voyage. A large wave caught him and flung him with ease and supreme speed completely over the boat and far beyond it. It struck him even then as an event in gymnastics, and a true miracle of the sea. An overturned boat in the surf is not a plaything to a swimming man.

The correspondent arrived in water that reached only to his waist, but his condition did not enable him to stand for more than a moment. Each wave knocked him into a heap, and the under-tow pulled at him.

Then he saw the man who had been running and undressing, and undressing and running, come bounding into the water. He dragged ashore the cook, and then waded toward the captain, but the captain waved him away, and sent him to the correspondent. He was naked, naked as a tree in winter, but a halo was about his head, and he shone like a saint. He gave a strong pull, and a long drag, and a bully heave at the correspondent's hand. The correspondent, schooled in the minor formulae, said: "Thanks, old man." But suddenly the man cried: "What's that?" He pointed a swift finger. The correspondent said: "Go."

In the shallows, face downward, lay the oiler. His forehead touched sand that was periodically, between each wave, clear of the sea.

The correspondent did not know all that transpired afterward. When he achieved safe ground he fell, striking the sand with each particular part of his body. It was as if he had dropped from a roof, but the thud was grateful to him.

It seems that instantly the beach was populated with men with blankets, clothes, and flasks, and women with coffee-pots and all the remedies sacred to their minds. The welcome of the land to the men from the sea was warm and generous, but a still and dripping shape was carried slowly up the beach, and the land's welcome for it could only be the different and sinister hospitality of the grave.

When it came night, the white waves paced to and fro in the moonlight, and the wind brought the sound of the great sea's voice to the men on shore, and they felt that they could then be interpreters.

[1897]

KATE CHOPIN [1851–1904]

The Story of an Hour

Knowing that Mrs. Mallard was afflicted with a heart trouble, great care was taken to break to her as gently as possible the news of her husband's death.

It was her sister Josephine who told her, in broken sentences; veiled hints that revealed in half concealing. Her husband's friend Richards was there, too, near her. It was he who had been in the newspaper office when intelligence of the railroad disaster was received, with Brently Mallard's name leading the list of "killed." He had only taken the time to assure himself of its truth by a second telegram, and had hastened to forestall any less careful, less tender friend in bearing the sad message.

She did not hear the story as many women have heard the same, with a paralyzed inability to accept its significance. She wept at once, with sudden, wild abandonment, in her sister's arms. When the storm of grief had spent itself she went away to her room alone. She would have no one follow her.

There stood, facing the open window, a comfortable, roomy armchair. Into this she sank, pressed down by a physical exhaustion that haunted her body and seemed to reach into her soul.

She could see in the open square before her house the tops of trees that were all aquiver with the new spring life. The delicious breath of rain was in the air. In the street below a peddler was crying his wares. The notes of a distant song which some one was singing reached her faintly, and countless sparrows were twittering in the eaves.

There were patches of blue sky showing here and there through the clouds that had met and piled one above the other in the west facing her window.

She sat with her head thrown back upon the cushion of the chair, quite motionless, except when a sob came up into her throat and shook her, as a child who had cried itself to sleep continues to sob in its dreams.

She was young, with a fair, calm face, whose lines bespoke repression and even a certain strength. But now there was a dull stare in her eyes, whose gaze was fixed away off yonder on one of those patches of blue sky. It was not a glance of reflection, but rather indicated a suspension of intelligent thought.

There was something coming to her and she was waiting for it, fearfully. What was it? She did not know; it was too subtle and elusive to name. But she felt it, creeping out of the sky, reaching toward her through the sounds, the scents, the color that filled the air.

Now her bosom rose and fell tumultuously. She was beginning to recognize this thing that was approaching to possess her, and she was striving to beat it back with her will—as powerless as her two white slender hands would have been.

When she abandoned herself a little whispered word escaped her slightly parted lips. She said it over and over under her breath: "free, free, free!" The vacant stare and the look of terror that had followed it went from her eyes. They stayed keen and bright. Her pulses beat fast, and the coursing blood warmed and relaxed every inch of her body.

She did not stop to ask if it were or were not a monstrous joy that held her. A clear and exalted perception enabled her to dismiss the suggestion as trivial.

She knew that she would weep again when she saw the kind, tender hands folded in death; the face that had never looked save with love upon her, fixed and gray and dead. But she saw beyond that bitter moment a long procession of years to come that would belong to her absolutely. And she opened and spread her arms out to them in welcome.

There would be no one to live for her during those coming years: she would live for herself. There would be no powerful will bending hers in that blind persistence with which men and women believe they have a right to impose a private will upon a fellow-creature. A kind intention or a cruel intention made the act seem no less a crime as she looked upon it in that brief moment of illumination.

And yet she had loved him—sometimes. Often she had not. What did it matter! What could love, the unsolved mystery, count for in face of this possession of self-assertion which she suddenly recognized as the strongest impulse of her being!

"Free! Body and soul free!" she kept whispering.

Josephine was kneeling before the closed door with her lips to the keyhole, imploring for admission. "Louise, open the door! I beg; open the door—you will make yourself ill. What are you doing, Louise? For heaven's sake open the door."

"Go away. I am not making myself ill." No; she was drinking in a very elixir of life through that open window.

Her fancy was running riot along those days ahead of her. Spring days, and summer days, and all sorts of days that would be her own. She breathed a quick prayer that life might be long. It was only yesterday she had thought with a shudder that life might be long.

She arose at length and opened the door to her sister's importunities. There was a feverish triumph in her eyes, and she carried herself unwittingly like a goddess of Victory. She clasped her sister's waist, and together they descended the stairs. Richards stood waiting for them at the bottom.

Some one was opening the front door with a latchkey. It was Brently Mallard who entered, a little travel-stained, composedly carrying his gripsack and umbrella. He had been far from the scene of accident, and did not even know there had been one. He stood amazed at Josephine's piercing cry; at Richards' quick motion to screen him from the view of his wife.

But Richards was too late.

When the doctors came they said she had died of heart disease—of joy that kills.

[1894]

ANTON CHEKHOV   [1860–1904]

The Lady with the Dog

TRANSLATED BY CONSTANCE GARNETT, 1899

I

It was said that a new person had appeared on the sea-front: a lady with a little dog. Dmitri Dmitritch Gurov, who had by then been a fortnight at Yalta, and so was fairly at home there, had begun to take an interest in new arrivals. Sitting in Verney's pavilion, he saw, walking on the sea-front, a fair-haired young lady of medium height, wearing a *béret*; a white Pomeranian dog was running behind her.

And afterwards he met her in the public gardens and in the square several times a day. She was walking alone, always wearing the same *béret*, and always with the same white dog; no one knew who she was, and every one called her simply "the lady with the dog."

"If she is here alone without a husband or friends, it wouldn't be amiss to make her acquaintance," Gurov reflected.

He was under forty, but he had a daughter already twelve years old, and two sons at school. He had been married young, when he was a student in his second year, and by now his wife seemed half as old again as he. She was a tall, erect woman with dark eyebrows, staid and dignified, and, as she said of herself, intellectual. She read a great deal, used phonetic spelling, called her husband, not Dmitri, but Dimitri, and he secretly considered her unintelligent, narrow, inelegant, was afraid of her, and did not like to be at home. He had begun being unfaithful to her long ago—had been unfaithful to her often, and, probably on that account, almost always spoke ill of women, and when they were talked about in his presence, used to call them "the lower race."

It seemed to him that he had been so schooled by bitter experience that he might call them what he liked, and yet he could not get on for two days together without "the lower race." In the society of men he was bored and not himself, with them he was cold and uncommunicative; but when he was in the company of women he felt free, and knew what to say to them and how to behave; and he was at ease with them even when he was silent. In his appearance, in his character, in his whole nature, there was something attractive and elusive which allured women and disposed them in his favour; he knew that, and some force seemed to draw him, too, to them.

Experience often repeated, truly bitter experience, had taught him long ago that with decent people, especially Moscow people—always slow to move and irresolute—every intimacy, which at first so agreeably diversifies life and appears a light and charming adventure, inevitably grows into a regular problem of extreme intricacy, and in the long run the situation becomes unbearable. But at every fresh meeting with an interesting woman this experience seemed to slip out of his memory, and he was eager for life, and everything seemed simple and amusing.

One evening he was dining in the gardens, and the lady in the *béret* came up slowly to take the next table. Her expression, her gait, her dress, and the way she did her hair told him that she was a lady, that she was married, that she was in Yalta for the first time and alone, and that she was dull there. . . . The stories told of the immorality in such places as Yalta are to a great extent untrue; he despised them, and knew that such stories were for the most part made up by persons who would themselves have been glad to sin if they had been able; but when the lady sat down at the next table three paces from him, he remembered these tales of easy conquests, of trips to the mountains, and the tempting thought of a swift, fleeting love affair, a romance with an unknown woman, whose name he did not know, suddenly took possession of him.

He beckoned coaxingly to the Pomeranian, and when the dog came up to him he shook his finger at it. The Pomeranian growled: Gurov shook his finger at it again.

The lady looked at him and at once dropped her eyes.

"He doesn't bite," she said, and blushed.

"May I give him a bone?" he asked; and when she nodded he asked courteously, "Have you been long in Yalta?"

"Five days."

"And I have already dragged out a fortnight here."

There was a brief silence.

"Time goes fast, and yet it is so dull here!" she said, not looking at him.

"That's only the fashion to say it is dull here. A provincial will live in Belyov or Zhidra and not be dull, and when he comes here it's 'Oh, the dullness! Oh, the dust!' One would think he came from Grenada."

She laughed. Then both continued eating in silence, like strangers, but after dinner they walked side by side; and there sprang up between them the light jesting conversation of people who are free and satisfied, to whom it does not matter where they go or what they talk about. They walked and talked of the strange light on the sea: the water was of a soft warm lilac hue, and there was a golden streak from the moon upon it. They talked of how sultry it was after a hot day. Gurov told her that he came from Moscow, that he had taken his degree in Arts, but had a post in a bank; that he had trained as an opera-singer, but had given it up, that he owned two houses in Moscow. . . . And from her he learnt that she had grown up in Petersburg, but had lived in S—— since her marriage two years before, that she was staying another month in Yalta, and that her husband, who needed a holiday too, might perhaps come and fetch her. She was not sure whether her husband had a post in a Crown Department or under the Provincial Council—and was amused by her own ignorance. And Gurov learnt, too, that she was called Anna Sergeyevna.

Afterwards he thought about her in his room at the hotel—thought she would certainly meet him next day; it would be sure to happen. As he got into bed he thought how lately she had been a girl at school, doing lessons like his own daughter; he recalled the diffidence, the angularity, that was still manifest in her laugh and her manner of talking with a stranger. This must have been the first time in her life she had been alone in surroundings in which she was followed, looked at, and spoken to merely from a secret motive which she could hardly fail to guess. He recalled her slender, delicate neck, her lovely grey eyes.

"There's something pathetic about her, anyway," he thought, and fell asleep.

II

A week had passed since they had made acquaintance. It was a holiday. It was sultry indoors, while in the street the wind whirled the dust round and round, and blew people's hats off. It was a thirsty day, and Gurov often went into the pavilion, and pressed Anna Sergeyevna to have syrup and water or an ice. One did not know what to do with oneself.

In the evening when the wind had dropped a little, they went out on the groyne° to see the steamer come in. There were a great many people walking about the harbor; they had gathered to welcome some one, bringing bouquets. And two peculiarities of a well-dressed Yalta crowd were very conspicuous: the elderly ladies were dressed like young ones, and there were great numbers of generals.

Owing to the roughness of the sea, the steamer arrived late, after the sun had set, and it was a long time turning about before it reached the groyne. Anna Sergeyevna looked through her lorgnette at the steamer and the passengers as though looking for acquaintances, and when she turned to Gurov her eyes were shining. She talked a great deal and asked disconnected questions, forgetting next moment what she had asked; then she dropped her lorgnette in the crush.

The festive crowd began to disperse; it was too dark to see people's faces. The wind had completely dropped, but Gurov and Anna Sergeyevna still stood as though waiting to see some one else come from the steamer. Anna Sergeyevna was silent now, and sniffed the flowers without looking at Gurov.

"The weather is better this evening," he said. "Where shall we go now? Shall we drive somewhere?"

She made no answer.

Then he looked at her intently, and all at once put his arm round her and kissed her on the lips, and breathed in the moisture and the fragrance of the flowers; and he immediately looked round him, anxiously wondering whether any one had seen them.

"Let us go to your hotel," he said softly. And both walked quickly.

The room was close and smelt of the scent she had bought at the Japanese shop. Gurov looked at her and thought: "What different people one meets in the world!" From the past he preserved memories of careless, good-natured women, who loved cheerfully and were grateful to him for the happiness he gave them, however brief it might be; and of women like his wife who loved without any genuine feeling, with superfluous phrases, affectedly, hysterically, with an expression that suggested that it was not love nor passion, but something more significant; and of two or three others, very beautiful, cold women, on whose faces he had caught a glimpse of a rapacious expression—an obstinate desire to snatch from life more than it could give, and these were capricious, unreflecting, domineering, unintelligent women not in their first youth, and when Gurov grew cold to them their beauty excited his hatred, and the lace on their linen seemed to him like scales.

Groyne: A wall or jetty built out from a shore to control erosion.

But in this case there was still the diffidence, the angularity of inexperienced youth, an awkward feeling; and there was a sense of consternation as though some one had suddenly knocked at the door. The attitude of Anna Sergeyevna—"the lady with the dog"—to what had happened was somehow peculiar, very grave, as though it were her fall—so it seemed, and it was strange and inappropriate. Her face dropped and faded, and on both sides of it her long hair hung down mournfully; she mused in a dejected attitude like "the woman who was a sinner" in an old-fashioned picture.

"It's wrong," she said. "You will be the first to despise me now."

There was a water-melon on the table. Gurov cut himself a slice and began eating it without haste. There followed at least half an hour of silence.

Anna Sergeyevna was touching; there was about her the purity of a good, simple woman who had seen little of life. The solitary candle burning on the table threw a faint light on her face, yet it was clear that she was very unhappy.

"How could I despise you?" asked Gurov. "You don't know what you are saying."

"God forgive me," she said, and her eyes filled with tears. "It's awful."

"You seem to feel you need to be forgiven."

"Forgiven? No. I am a bad, low woman; I despise myself and don't attempt to justify myself. It's not my husband but myself I have deceived. And not just now; I have been deceiving myself for a long time. My husband may be a good, honest man, but he is a flunkey! I don't know what he does there, what his work is, but I know he is a flunkey! I was twenty when I was married to him. I have been tormented by curiosity; I wanted something better. 'There must be a different sort of life,' I said to myself. I wanted to live! To live, to live! . . . I was fired by curiosity . . . you don't understand it, but, I swear to God, I could not control myself; something happened to me: I could not be restrained. I told my husband I was ill, and came here. . . . And here I have been walking about as though I were dazed, like a mad creature; . . . and now I have become a vulgar, contemptible woman whom any one may despise."

Gurov felt bored already, listening to her. He was irritated by the naïve tone, by this remose, so unexpected and inopportune; but for the tears in her eyes, he might have thought she was jesting or playing a part.

"I don't understand," he said softly. "What is it you want?"

She hid her face on his breast and pressed close to him.

"Believe me, believe me, I beseech you . . ." she said. "I love a pure, honest life, and sin is loathsome to me. I don't know what I am doing. Simple people say: 'The Evil One has beguiled me.' And I may say of myself now that the Evil One has beguiled me."

"Hush, hush! . . ." he muttered.

He looked at her fixed, scared eyes, kissed her, talked softly and affectionately, and by degrees she was comforted, and her gaiety returned; they both began laughing.

Afterwards when they went out there was not a soul on the sea-front. The town with its cypresses had quite a deathlike air, but the sea still broke noisily on the shore; a single barge was rocking on the waves, and a lantern was blinking sleepily on it.

They found a cab and drove to Oreanda.

"I found out your surname in the hall just now: it was written on the board—Von Diderits," said Gurov. "Is your husband a German?"

"No; I believe his grandfather was a German, but he is an Orthodox Russian himself."

At Oreanda they sat on a seat not far from the church, looked down at the sea, and were silent. Yalta was hardly visible through the morning mist; white clouds stood motionless on the mountain-tops. The leaves did not stir on the trees, grasshoppers chirruped, and the monotonous hollow sound of the sea rising up from below, spoke of the peace, of the eternal sleep awaiting us. So it must have sounded when there was no Yalta, no Oreanda here; so it sounds now, and it will sound as indifferently and monotonously when we are all no more. And in this constancy, in this complete indifference to the life and death of each of us, there lies hid, perhaps, a pledge of our eternal salvation, of the unceasing movement of life upon earth, of unceasing progress towards perfection. Sitting beside a young woman who in the dawn seemed so lovely, soothed and spellbound in these magical surroundings—the sea, mountains, clouds, the open sky—Gurov thought how in reality everything is beautiful in this world when one reflects: everything except what we think or do ourselves when we forget our human dignity and the higher aims of our existence.

A man walked up to them—probably a keeper—looked at them and walked away. And this detail seemed mysterious and beautiful, too. They saw a steamer come from Theodosia, with its lights out in the glow of dawn.

"There is dew on the grass," said Anna Sergeyevna, after a silence.

"Yes. It's time to go home."

They went back to the town.

Then they met every day at twelve o'clock on the sea-front, lunched and dined together, went for walks, admired the sea. She complained that she slept badly, that her heart throbbed violently; asked the same questions, troubled now by jealousy and now by the fear that he did not respect her sufficiently. And often in the square or gardens, when there was no one near them, he suddenly drew her to him and kissed her passionately. Complete idleness, these kisses in broad daylight while he looked round in dread of some one's seeing them, the heat, the smell of the sea, and the continual passing to and fro before him of idle, well-dressed, well-fed people, made a new man of him; he told Anna Sergeyevna how beautiful she was, how fascinating. He was impatiently passionate, he would not move a step away from her, while she was often pensive and continually urged him to confess that he did not respect her, did not love her in the least, and thought of her as nothing but a common woman. Rather late almost every evening they drove somewhere out of town, to Oreanda or to the waterfall; and the expedition was always a success, the scenery invariably impressed them as grand and beautiful.

They were expecting her husband to come, but a letter came from him, saying that there was something wrong with his eyes, and he entreated his wife to come home as quickly as possible. Anna Sergeyevna made haste to go.

"It's a good thing I am going away," she said to Gurov. "It's the finger of destiny!"

She went by coach and he went with her. They were driving the whole day. When she had got into a compartment of the express, and when the second bell had rung, she said:

"Let me look at you once more . . . look at you once again. That's right."

She did not shed tears, but was so sad that she seemed ill, and her face was quivering.

"I shall remember you . . . think of you," she said. "God be with you; be happy. Don't remember evil against me. We are parting forever—it must be so, for we ought never to have met. Well, God be with you."

The train moved off rapidly, its lights soon vanished from sight, and a minute later there was no sound of it, as though everything had conspired together to end as quickly as possible that sweet delirium, that madness. Left alone on the platform, and gazing into the dark distance, Gurov listened to the chirrup of the grasshoppers and the hum of the telegraph wires, feeling as though he had only just waked up. And he thought, musing, that there had been another episode or adventure in his life, and it, too, was at an end, and nothing was left of it but a memory. . . . He was moved, sad, and conscious of a slight remorse. This young woman whom he would never meet again had not been happy with him; he was genuinely warm and affectionate with her, but yet in his manner, his tone, and his caresses there had been a shade of light irony, the coarse condescension of a happy man who was, besides, almost twice her age. All the time she had called him kind, exceptional, lofty; obviously he had seemed to her different from what he really was, so he had unintentionally deceived her. . . .

Here at the station was already a scent of autumn; it was a cold evening.

"It's time for me to go north," thought Gurov as he left the platform. "High time!"

III

At home in Moscow everything was in its winter routine; the stoves were heated, and in the morning it was still dark when the children were having breakfast and getting ready for school, and the nurse would light the lamp for a short time. The frosts had begun already. When the first snow has fallen, on the first day of sledge-driving it is pleasant to see the white earth, the white roofs, to draw soft, delicious breath, and the season brings back the days of one's youth. The old limes and birches, white with hoar-frost, have a good-natured expression; they are nearer to one's heart than cypresses and palms, and near them one doesn't want to be thinking of the sea and the mountains.

Gurov was Moscow born; he arrived in Moscow on a fine frosty day, and when he put on his fur coat and warm gloves, and walked along Petrovka, and when on Saturday evening he heard the ringing of the bells, his recent trip and the places he had seen lost all charm for him. Little by little he became absorbed in Moscow life, greedily read three newspapers a day, and declared he did not read the Moscow papers on principle! He already felt a longing to go to restaurants, clubs, dinner-parties, anniversary celebrations, and he felt flattered at entertaining distinguished lawyers and artists, and at playing cards with a professor at the doctors' club. He could already eat a whole plateful of salt fish and cabbage. . . .

In another month, he fancied, the image of Anna Sergeyevna would be shrouded in a mist in his memory, and only from time to time would visit him in his dreams with a touching smile as others did. But more than a month passed, real winter had come, and everything was still clear in his memory as though he had parted with Anna Sergeyevna only the day before. And his memories glowed more and more vividly. When in the evening stillness he heard from his study the voices of his children, preparing their lessons, or when he listened to a song or the organ at the restaurant, or the storm howled in the chimney, suddenly everything would rise up in his memory: what had happened on the groyne, and the early morning with the mist on the mountains, and the steamer coming from Theodosia, and the kisses. He would pace a long time about his room, remembering it all and smiling; then his memories passed into dreams, and in his fancy the past was mingled with what was to come.

Anna Sergeyevna did not visit him in dreams, but followed him about everywhere like a shadow and haunted him. When he shut his eyes he saw her as though she were living before him, and she seemed to him lovelier, younger, tenderer than she was; and he imagined himself finer than he had been in Yalta. In the evenings she peeped out at him from the bookcase, from the fireplace, from the corner—he heard her breathing, the caressing rustle of her dress. In the street he watched the women, looking for some one like her.

He was tormented by an intense desire to confide his memories to some one. But in his home it was impossible to talk of his love, and he had no one outside; he could not talk to his tenants nor to any one at the bank. And what had he to talk of? Had he been in love, then? Had there been anything beautiful, poetical, or edifying or simply interesting in his relations with Anna Sergeyevna? And there was nothing for him but to talk vaguely of love, of woman, and no one guessed what it meant; only his wife twitched her black eyebrows, and said: "The part of a lady-killer does not suit you at all, Dimitri."

One evening, coming out of the doctors' club with an official with whom he had been playing cards, he could not resist saying:

"If only you knew what a fascinating woman I made the acquaintance of in Yalta!"

The official got into his sledge and was driving away, but turned suddenly and shouted:

"Dmitri Dmitritch!"

"What?"

"You were right this evening: the sturgeon was a bit too strong!"

These words, so ordinary, for some reason moved Gurov to indignation, and struck him as degrading and unclean. What savage manners, what people! What senseless nights, what uninteresting, uneventful days! The rage for card-playing, the gluttony, the drunkenness, the continual talk always about the same thing. Useless pursuits and conversations always about the same things absorb the better part of one's time, the better part of one's strength, and in the end there is left a life grovelling and curtailed, worthless and trivial, and there is no escaping or getting away from it—just as though one were in a madhouse or a prison.

Gurov did not sleep all night, and was filled with indignation. And he had a headache all next day. And the next night he slept badly; he sat up in bed, thinking, or paced up and down his room. He was sick of his children, sick of the bank; he had no desire to go anywhere or to talk of anything.

In the holidays in December he prepared for a journey, and told his wife he was going to Petersburg to do something in the interests of a young friend—and he set off for S——. What for? He did not very well know himself. He wanted to see Anna Sergeyevna and to talk with her—to arrange a meeting, if possible.

He reached S—— in the morning, and took the best room at the hotel, in which the floor was covered with grey army cloth, and on the table was an inkstand, grey with dust and adorned with a figure on horseback, with its hat in its hand and its head broken off. The hotel porter gave him the necessary information; Von Diderits lived in a house of his own in Old Gontcharny Street—it was not far from the hotel: he was rich and lived in good style, and had his own horses; every one in the town knew him. The porter pronounced the name "Dridirits."

Gurov went without haste to Old Gontcharny Street and found the house. Just opposite the house stretched a long grey fence adorned with nails.

"One would run away from a fence like that," thought Gurov, looking from the fence to the windows of the house and back again.

He considered: to-day was a holiday, and the husband would probably be at home. And in any case it would be tactless to go into the house and upset her. If he were to send her a note it might fall into her husband's hands, and then it might ruin everything. The best thing was to trust to chance. And he kept walking up and down the street by the fence, waiting for the chance. He saw a beggar go in at the gate and dogs fly at him; then an hour later he heard a piano, and the sounds were faint and indistinct. Probably it was Anna Sergeyevna playing. The front door suddenly opened, and an old woman came out, followed by the familiar white Pomeranian. Gurov was on the point of calling to the dog, but his heart began beating violently, and in his excitement he could not remember the dog's name.

He walked up and down, and loathed the grey fence more and more, and by now he thought irritably that Anna Sergeyevna had forgotten him, and was perhaps already amusing herself with some one else, and that that was very natural in a young woman who had nothing to look at from morning till night but that confounded fence. He went back to his hotel room and sat for a long while on the sofa, not knowing what to do, then he had dinner and a long nap.

"How stupid and worrying it is!" he thought when he woke and looked at the dark windows: it was already evening. "Here I've had a good sleep for some reason. What shall I do in the night?"

He sat on the bed, which was covered by a cheap grey blanket, such as one sees in hospitals, and he taunted himself in his vexation:

"So much for the lady with the dog . . . so much for the adventure. . . . You're in a nice fix. . . ."

That morning at the station a poster in large letters had caught his eye. *The Geisha* was to be performed for the first time. He thought of this and went to the theatre.

"It's quite possible she may go to the first performance," he thought.

The theatre was full. As in all provincial theatres, there was a fog above the chandelier, the gallery was noisy and restless; in the front row the local dandies were standing up before the beginning of the performance, with their hands behind them; in the Governor's box the Governor's daughter, wearing a boa, was sitting in the front seat, while the Governor himself lurked modestly behind the curtain with only his hands visible; the orchestra was a long time tuning up; the stage curtain swayed. All the time the audience were coming in and taking their seats Gurov looked at them eagerly.

Anna Sergeyevna, too, came in. She sat down in the third row, and when Gurov looked at her his heart contracted, and he understood clearly that for him there was in the whole world no creature so near, so precious, and so important to him; she, this little woman, in no way remarkable, lost in a provincial crowd, with a vulgar lorgnette in her hand, filled his whole life now, was his sorrow and his joy, the one happiness that he now desired for himself, and to the sounds of the inferior orchestra, of the wretched provincial violins, he thought how lovely she was. He thought and dreamed.

A young man with small side-whiskers, tall and stooping, came in with Anna Sergeyevna and sat down beside her; he bent his head at every step and seemed to be continually bowing. Most likely this was the husband whom at Yalta, in a rush of bitter feeling, she had called a flunkey. And there really was in his long figure, his side-whiskers, and the small bald patch on his head, something of the flunkey's obsequiousness; his smile was sugary, and in his buttonhole there was some badge of distinction like the number on a waiter.

During the first interval the husband went away to smoke; she remained alone in her stall. Gurov, who was sitting in the stalls, too, went up to her and said in a trembling voice, with a forced smile:

"Good-evening."

She glanced at him and turned pale, then glanced again with horror, unable to believe her eyes, and tightly gripped the fan and the lorgnette in her hands, evidently struggling with herself not to faint. Both were silent. She was sitting, he was standing, frightened by her confusion and not venturing to sit down beside her. The violins and the flute began tuning up. He felt suddenly frightened; it seemed as though all the people in the boxes were looking at them. She got up and went quickly to the door; he followed her, and both walked senselessly along passages, and up and down stairs, and figures in legal, scholastic, and civil service uniforms, all wearing badges, flitted before their eyes. They caught glimpses of ladies, of fur coats hanging on pegs; the draughts blew on them, bringing a smell of stale tobacco. And Gurov, whose heart was beating violently, thought:

"Oh, heavens! Why are these people here and this orchestra! . . ."

And at that instant he recalled how when he had seen Anna Sergeyevna off at the station he had thought that everything was over and they would never meet again. But how far they were still from the end!

On the narrow, gloomy staircase over which was written "To the Amphitheatre," she stopped.

"How you have frightened me!" she said, breathing hard, still pale and overwhelmed. "Oh, how you have frightened me! I am half dead. Why have you come? Why?"

"But do understand, Anna, do understand . . ." he said hastily in a low voice. "I entreat you to understand. . . ."

She looked at him with dread, with entreaty, with love; she looked at him intently, to keep his features more distinctly in her memory.

"I am so unhappy," she went on, not heeding him. "I have thought of nothing but you all the time; I live only in the thought of you. And I wanted to forget, to forget you; but why, oh, why, have you come?"

On the landing above them two schoolboys were smoking and looking down, but that was nothing to Gurov; he drew Anna Sergeyevna to him, and began kissing her face, her cheeks, and her hands.

"What are you doing, what are you doing!" she cried in horror, pushing him away. "We are mad. Go away to-day; go away at once. . . . I beseech you by all that is sacred, I implore you. . . . There are people coming this way!"

Some one was coming up the stairs.

"You must go away," Anna Sergeyevna went on in a whisper. "Do you hear, Dmitri Dmitritch? I will come and see you in Moscow. I have never been happy; I am miserable now, and I never, never shall be happy, never! Don't make me suffer still more! I swear I'll come to Moscow. But now let us part. My precious, good, dear one, we must part!"

She pressed his hand and began rapidly going downstairs, looking round at him, and from her eyes he could see that she really was unhappy. Gurov stood for a little while, listened, then, when all sound had died away, he found his coat and left the theatre.

IV

And Anna Sergeyevna began coming to see him in Moscow. Once in two or three months she left S——, telling her husband that she was going to consult a doctor about an internal complaint—and her husband believed her, and did not believe her. In Moscow she stayed at the Slaviansky Bazaar hotel, and at once sent a man in a red cap to Gurov. Gurov went to see her, and no one in Moscow knew of it.

Once he was going to see her in this way on a winter morning (the messenger had come the evening before when he was out). With him walked his daughter, whom he wanted to take to school: it was on the way. Snow was falling in big wet flakes.

"It's three degrees above freezing-point, and yet it is snowing," said Gurov to his daughter. "The thaw is only on the surface of the earth; there is quite a different temperature at a greater height in the atmosphere."

"And why are there no thunderstorms in the winter, father?"

He explained that, too. He talked, thinking all the while that he was going to see *her*, and no living soul knew of it, and probably never would know. He had two lives: one, open, seen and known by all who cared to know, full of relative truth and of relative falsehood, exactly like the lives of his friends and acquaintances; and another life running its course in secret. And through some strange, perhaps accidental, conjunction of circumstances, everything that was essential, of interest and of value to him, everything in which he was sincere and did not deceive himself, everything that made the kernel of his life, was hidden from other people; and all that was false in him, the sheath in which he hid himself to conceal the truth—such, for instance, as his work in the bank, his discussions at the club, his "lower race," his presence with his wife at anniversary festivities—all that was open. And he judged others by himself, not believing in what he saw, and always believing that every man had his real, most interesting life under the cover of secrecy and under the cover of night. All personal life rested on secrecy, and possibly it was partly on that account that civilised man was so nervously anxious that personal privacy should be respected.

After leaving his daughter at school, Gurov went on to the Slaviansky Bazaar. He took off his fur coat below, went upstairs, and softly knocked at the door. Anna Sergeyevna, wearing his favourite grey dress, exhausted by the journey and the suspense, had been expecting him since the evening before. She was pale; she looked at him, and did not smile, and he had hardly come in when she fell on his breast. Their kiss was slow and prolonged, as though they had not met for two years.

"Well, how are you getting on there?" he asked. "What news?"

"Wait; I'll tell you directly. . . . I can't talk."

She could not speak; she was crying. She turned away from him, and pressed her handkerchief to her eyes.

"Let her have her cry out. I'll sit down and wait," he thought, and he sat down in an arm-chair.

Then he rang and asked for tea to be brought him, and while he drank his tea she remained standing at the window with her back to him. She was crying from emotion, from the miserable consciousness that their

explorers who have left their ears and fingers north of Franz-Josef-Land,° or their health somewhere along the Upper Congo. My Aunt Georgiana had been a music teacher at the Boston Conservatory, somewhere back in the latter sixties. One summer, while visiting in the little village among the Green Mountains where her ancestors had dwelt for generations, she had kindled the callow fancy of the most idle and shiftless of all the village lads, and had conceived for this Howard Carpenter one of those extravagant passions which a handsome country boy of twenty-one sometimes inspires in an angular, spectacled woman of thirty. When she returned to her duties in Boston, Howard followed her, and the upshot of this inexplicable infatuation was that she eloped with him, eluding the reproaches of her family and the criticisms of her friends by going with him to the Nebraska frontier. Carpenter, who, of course, had no money, had taken a homestead in Red Willow County, fifty miles from the railroad. There they had measured off their quarter section themselves by driving across the prairie in a wagon, to the wheel of which they had tied a red cotton handkerchief, and counting off its revolutions. They built a dugout in the red hillside, one of those cave dwellings whose inmates so often reverted to primitive conditions. Their water they got from the lagoons where the buffalo drank, and their slender stock of provisions was always at the mercy of bands of roving Indians. For thirty years my aunt had not been further than fifty miles from the homestead.

But Mrs. Springer knew nothing of all this, and must have been considerably shocked at what was left of my kinswoman. Beneath the soiled linen duster which, on her arrival, was the most conspicuous feature of her costume, she wore a black stuff dress, whose ornamentation showed that she had surrendered herself unquestioningly into the hands of a country dressmaker. My poor aunt's figure, however, would have presented astonishing difficulties to any dressmaker. Originally stooped, her shoulders were now almost bent together over her sunken chest. She wore no stays, and her gown, which trailed unevenly behind, rose in a sort of peak over her abdomen. She wore ill-fitting false teeth, and her skin was as yellow as a Mongolian's from constant exposure to a pitiless wind and to the alkaline water which hardens the most transparent cuticle into a sort of flexible leather.

I owed to this woman most of the good that ever came my way in my boyhood, and had a reverential affection for her. During the years when I was riding herd for my uncle, my aunt, after cooking the three meals — the first of which was ready at six o'clock in the morning — and putting the six children to bed, would often stand until midnight at her ironingboard, with me at the kitchen table beside her, hearing me recite Latin

Franz-Josef-Land: An archipelago of islands just north of Russia.

declensions and conjugations, gently shaking me when my drowsy head sank down over a page of irregular verbs. It was to her, at her ironing or mending, that I read my first Shakespere, and her old text-book on mythology was the first that ever came into my empty hands. She taught me my scales and exercises, too—on the little parlour organ, which her husband had bought her after fifteen years, during which she had not so much as seen any instrument, but an accordion that belonged to one of the Norwegian farmhands. She would sit beside me by the hour, darning and counting while I struggled with the "Joyous Farmer," but she seldom talked to me about music, and I understood why. She was a pious woman; she had the consolations of religion and, to her at least, her martyrdom was not wholly sordid. Once when I had been doggedly beating out some easy passages from an old score of *Euryanthe* I had found among her music books, she came up to me and, putting her hands over my eyes, gently drew my head back upon her shoulder, saying tremulously, "Don't love it so well, Clark, or it may be taken from you. Oh! dear boy, pray that whatever your sacrifice may be, it be not that."

When my aunt appeared on the morning after her arrival, she was still in a semi-somnambulant state. She seemed not to realize that she was in the city where she had spent her youth, the place longed for hungrily half a lifetime. She had been so wretchedly train-sick throughout the journey that she had no recollection of anything but her discomfort, and, to all intents and purposes, there were but a few hours of nightmare between the farm in Red Willow County and my study on Newbury Street. I had planned a little pleasure for her that afternoon, to repay her for some of the glorious moments she had given me when we used to milk together in the straw-thatched cowshed and she, because I was more than usually tired, or because her husband had spoken sharply to me, would tell me of the splendid performance of the *Huguenots* she had seen in Paris, in her youth. At two o'clock the Symphony Orchestra was to give a Wagner programme, and I intended to take my aunt; though, as I conversed with her, I grew doubtful about her enjoyment of it. Indeed, for her own sake, I could only wish her taste for such things quite dead, and the long struggle mercifully ended at last. I suggested our visiting the Conservatory and the Common before lunch, but she seemed altogether too timid to wish to venture out. She questioned me absently about various changes in the city, but she was chiefly concerned that she had forgotten to leave instructions about feeding half-skimmed milk to a certain weakling calf, "old Maggie's calf, you know, Clark," she explained, evidently having forgotten how long I had been away. She was further troubled because she had neglected to tell her daughter about the freshly-opened kit of mackerel in the cellar, which would spoil if it were not used directly.

I asked her whether she had ever heard any of the Wagnerian operas, and found that she had not, though she was perfectly familiar with their respective situations, and had once possessed the piano score of *The Flying Dutchman*. I began to think it would have been best to get her back to Red Willow County without waking her, and regretted having suggested the concert.

From the time we entered the concert hall, however, she was a trifle less passive and inert, and for the first time seemed to perceive her surroundings. I had felt some trepidation lest she might become aware of the absurdities of her attire, or might experience some painful embarrassment at stepping suddenly into the world to which she had been dead for a quarter of a century. But, again, I found how superficially I had judged her. She sat looking about her with eyes as impersonal, almost as stony, as those with which the granite Rameses° in a museum watches the froth and fret that ebbs and flows about his pedestal — separated from it by the lonely stretch of centuries. I have seen this same aloofness in old miners who drift into the Brown hotel at Denver, their pockets full of bullion,° their linen soiled, their haggard faces unshaven; standing in the thronged corridors as solitary as though they were still in a frozen camp on the Yukon, conscious that certain experiences have isolated them from their fellows by a gulf no haberdasher could bridge.

We sat at the extreme left of the first balcony, facing the arc of our own and the balcony above us, veritable hanging gardens, brilliant as tulip beds. The matinée audience was made up chiefly of women. One lost the contour of faces and figures, indeed any effect of line whatever, and there was only the colour of bodices past counting, the shimmer of fabrics soft and firm, silky and sheer; red, mauve, pink, blue, lilac, purple, ecru, rose, yellow, cream, and white, all the colours that an impressionist finds in a sunlit landscape, with here and there the dead shadow of a frock coat. My Aunt Georgiana regarded them as though they had been so many daubs of tube-paint on a palette.

When the musicians came out and took their places, she gave a little stir of anticipation and looked with quickening interest down over the rail at that invariable grouping, perhaps the first wholly familiar thing that had greeted her eye since she had left old Maggie and her weakling calf. I could feel how all those details sank into her soul, for I had not forgotten how they had sunk into mine when I came fresh from ploughing forever and forever between green aisles of corn, where, as in a treadmill, one might walk from daybreak to dusk without perceiving a shadow of change. The clean profiles of the musicians, the gloss of their linen,

Rameses: (Ramses) The name of eleven different Egyptian pharaohs.
Bullion: A bar of gold.

the dull black of their coats, the beloved shapes of the instruments, the patches of yellow light thrown by the green shaded lamps on the smooth, varnished bellies of the 'cellos and the bass viols in the rear, the restless, wind-tossed forest of fiddle necks and bows—I recalled how, in the first orchestra I had ever heard, those long bow strokes seemed to draw the heart out of me, as a conjurer's stick reels out yards of paper ribbon from a hat.

The first number was the *Tannhauser* overture. When the horns drew out the first strain of the Pilgrim's chorus, my Aunt Georgiana clutched my coat sleeve. Then it was I first realized that for her this broke a silence of thirty years; the inconceivable silence of the plains. With the battle between the two motives, with the frenzy of the Venusberg theme and its ripping of strings, there came to me an overwhelming sense of the waste and wear we are so powerless to combat; and I saw again the tall, naked house on the prairie, black and grim as a wooden fortress; the black pond where I had learned to swim, its margin pitted with sun-dried cattle tracks; the rain gullied clay banks about the naked house, the four dwarf ash seedlings where the dish-cloths were always hung to dry before the kitchen door. The world there was the flat world of the ancients; to the east, a cornfield that stretched to daybreak; to the west, a corral that reached to sunset; between, the conquests of peace, dearer bought than those of war.

The overture closed, my aunt released my coat sleeve, but she said nothing. She sat staring at the orchestra through a dullness of thirty years, through the films made little by little by each of the three hundred and sixty-five days in every one of them. What, I wondered, did she get from it? She had been a good pianist in her day I knew, and her musical education had been broader than that of most music teachers of a quarter of a century ago. She had often told me of Mozart's operas and Meyerbeer's, and I could remember hearing her sing, years ago, certain melodies of Verdi's. When I had fallen ill with a fever in her house she used to sit by my cot in the evening—when the cool, night wind blew in through the faded mosquito netting tacked over the window and I lay watching a certain bright star that burned red above the cornfield—and sing "Home to our mountains, O, let us return!" in a way fit to break the heart of a Vermont boy near dead of homesickness already.

I watched her closely through the prelude to *Tristan and Isolde*, trying vainly to conjecture what that seething turmoil of strings and winds might mean to her, but she sat mutely staring at the violin bows that drove obliquely downward, like the pelting streaks of rain in a summer shower. Had this music any message for her? Had she enough left to at all comprehend this power which had kindled the world since she had left it? I was in a fever of curiosity, but Aunt Georgiana sat silent upon her peak in Darien.° She preserved this utter immobility throughout the number from *The Flying Dutchman*, though her fingers worked mechanically upon her black dress, as though, of themselves, they were recalling the piano score they had once played. Poor old hands! They had been stretched and twisted into mere tentacles to hold and lift and knead with; the palms unduly swollen, the fingers bent and knotted—on one of them a thin, worn band that had once been a wedding ring. As I pressed and gently quieted one of those groping hands, I remembered with quivering eyelids their services for me in other days.

Soon after the tenor began the "Prize Song," I heard a quick drawn breath and turned to my aunt. Her eyes were closed, but the tears were glistening on her cheeks, and I think, in a moment more, they were in my eyes as well. It never really died, then—the soul that can suffer so excruciatingly and so interminably; it withers to the outward eye only; like that strange moss which can lie on a dusty shelf half a century and yet, if placed in water, grows green again. She wept so throughout the development and elaboration of the melody.

During the intermission before the second half of the concert, I questioned my aunt and found that the "Prize Song" was not new to her. Some years before there had drifted to the farm in Red Willow County a young German, a tramp cow puncher, who had sung the chorus at Bayreuth, when he was a boy, along with the other peasant boys and girls. Of a Sunday morning he used to sit on his gingham-sheeted bed in the hands' bedroom which opened off the kitchen, cleaning the leather of his boots and saddle, singing the "Prize Song," while my aunt went about her work in the kitchen. She had hovered about him until she had prevailed upon him to join the country church, though his sole fitness for this step, in so far as I could gather, lay in his boyish face and his possession of this divine melody. Shortly afterward he had gone to town on the Fourth of July, been drunk for several days, lost his money at a faro° table, ridden a saddled Texan steer on a bet, and disappeared with a fractured collar-bone. All this my aunt told me huskily, wanderingly, as though she were talking in the weak lapses of illness.

"Well, we have come to better things than the old *Trovatore* at any rate, Aunt Georgie?" I queried, with a well meant effort at jocularity.

Her lip quivered and she hastily put her handkerchief up to her mouth. From behind it she murmured, "And you have been hearing this ever since you left me, Clark?" Her question was the gentlest and saddest of reproaches.

peak in Darien: A reference to John Keats's sonnet "On First Looking into Chapman's Homer." Keats alludes to the peak that Hernan Cortez would have climbed when he first discovered and stared at the Pacific Ocean in the 1530s.
Faro: A card game.

The second half of the programme consisted of four numbers from the *Ring*, and closed with Siegfried's funeral march. My aunt wept quietly, but almost continuously, as a shallow vessel overflows in a rainstorm. From time to time her dim eyes looked up at the lights which studded the ceiling, burning softly under their dull glass globes; doubtless they were stars in truth to her. I was still perplexed as to what measure of musical comprehension was left to her, she who had heard nothing but the singing of Gospel Hymns at Methodist services in the square frame schoolhouse on Section Thirteen for so many years. I was wholly unable to gauge how much of it had been dissolved in soapsuds, or worked into bread, or milked into the bottom of a pail.

The deluge of sound poured on and on; I never knew what she found in the shining current of it; I never knew how far it bore her, or past what happy islands. From the trembling of her face I could well believe that before the last numbers she had been carried out where the myriad graves are, into the grey, nameless burying grounds of the sea; or into some world of death vaster yet, where, from the beginning of the world, hope has lain down with hope and dream with dream and, renouncing, slept.

The concert was over; the people filed out of the hall chattering and laughing, glad to relax and find the living level again, but my kinswoman made no effort to rise. The harpist slipped its green felt cover over his instrument; the flute-players shook the water from their mouthpieces; the men of the orchestra went out one by one, leaving the stage to the chairs and music stands, empty as a winter cornfield.

I spoke to my aunt. She burst into tears and sobbed pleadingly. "I don't want to go, Clark, I don't want to go!"

I understood. For her, just outside the door of the concert hall, lay the black pond with the cattle-tracked bluffs; the tall, unpainted house, with weather-curled boards; naked as a tower, the crook-backed ash seedlings where the dish-cloths hung to dry; the gaunt, moulting turkeys picking up refuse about the kitchen door.

[1904]

JAMES JOYCE [1882–1941]

Araby

North Richmond Street, being blind, was a quiet street except at the hour when the Christian Brothers' School set the boys free. An uninhabited house of two storeys stood at the blind end, detached from its neighbours in a square ground. The other houses of the street, conscious of decent lives within them, gazed at one another with brown imperturbable faces.

The former tenant of our house, a priest, had died in the back drawing-room. Air, musty from having been long enclosed, hung in all the rooms, and the waste room behind the kitchen was littered with old useless papers. Among these I found a few paper-covered books, the pages of which were curled and damp: *The Abbot*, by Walter Scott, *The Devout Communicant*, and *The Memoirs of Vidocq*. I liked the last best because its leaves were yellow. The wild garden behind the house contained a central apple-tree and a few straggling bushes under one of which I found the late tenant's rusty bicycle-pump. He had been a very charitable priest; in his will he had left all his money to institutions and the furniture of his house to his sister.

When the short days of winter came dusk fell before we had well eaten our dinners. When we met in the street the houses had grown sombre. The space of sky above us was the colour of ever-changing violet and towards it the lamps of the street lifted their feeble lanterns. The cold air stung us and we played till our bodies glowed. Our shouts echoed in the silent street. The career of our play brought us through the dark muddy lanes behind the houses where we ran the gauntlet of the rough tribes from the cottages, to the back doors of the dark dripping gardens where odours arose from the ashpits, to the dark odorous stables where a coachman smoothed and combed the horse or shook music from the buckled harness. When we returned to the street light from the kitchen windows had filled the areas. If my uncle was seen turning the corner we hid in the shadow until we had seen him safely housed. Or if Mangan's sister came out on the doorstep to call her brother in to his tea we watched her from our shadow peer up and down the street. We waited to see whether she would remain or go in and, if she remained, we left our shadow and walked up to Mangan's steps resignedly. She was waiting for us, her figure defined by the light from the half-opened door. Her brother always teased her before he obeyed and I stood by the railings looking at her. Her dress swung as she moved her body and the soft rope of her hair tossed from side to side.

Every morning I lay on the floor in the front parlour watching her door. The blind was pulled down to within an inch of the sash so that I could not be seen. When she came out on the doorstep my heart leaped. I ran to the hall, seized my books, and followed her. I kept her brown figure always in my eye and, when we came near the point at which our ways diverged, I quickened my pace and passed her. This happened morning after morning. I had never spoken to her, except for a few casual words, and yet her name was like a summons to all my foolish blood.

Her image accompanied me even in places the most hostile to romance. On Saturday evenings when my aunt went marketing I had to go to carry some of the parcels. We walked through the flaring streets, jostled by drunken men and bargaining women, amid the curses of labourers, the shrill litanies of shop-boys who stood on guard by the barrel of pigs' cheeks, the nasal chanting of street-singers, who sang a *come-all-you* about O'Donovan Rossa,° or a ballad about the troubles in our native land. These noises converged in a single sensation of life for me: I imagined that I bore my chalice safely through a throng of foes. Her name sprang to my lips at moments in strange prayers and praises which I myself did not understand. My eyes were often full of tears (I could not tell why) and at times a flood from my heart seemed to pour itself out into my bosom. I thought little of the future. I did not know whether I would ever speak to her or not or, if I spoke to her, how I could tell her of my confused adoration. But my body was like a harp and her words and gestures were like fingers running upon the wires.

One evening I went into the back drawing-room in which the priest had died. It was a dark rainy evening and there was no sound in the house. Through one of the broken panes I heard the rain impinge upon the earth, the fine incessant needles of water playing in the sodden beds. Some distant lamp or lighted window gleamed below me. I was thankful that I could see so little. All my senses seemed to desire to veil themselves and, feeling that I was about to slip from them, I pressed the palms of my hands together until they trembled, murmuring: *"O love! O love!"* many times.

At last she spoke to me. When she addressed the first words to me I was so confused that I did not know what to answer. She asked me was I

O'Donovan Rossa: Jeremiah O'Donovan (1831–1915) was nicknamed "Dynamite Rossa" for his militant pursuit of Irish independence.

going to *Araby*. I forgot whether I answered yes or no. It would be a splendid bazaar, she said she would love to go.

"And why can't you?" I asked.

While she spoke she turned a silver bracelet round and round her wrist. She could not go, she said, because there would be a retreat that week in her convent. Her brother and two other boys were fighting for their caps and I was alone at the railings. She held one of the spikes, bowing her head towards me. The light from the lamp opposite our door caught the white curve of her neck, lit up her hair that rested there and, falling, lit up the hand upon the railing. It fell over one side of her dress and caught the white border of a petticoat, just visible as she stood at ease.

"It's well for you," she said.

"If I go," I said, "I will bring you something."

What innumerable follies laid waste my waking and sleeping thoughts after that evening! I wished to annihilate the tedious intervening days. I chafed against the work of school. At night in my bedroom and by day in the classroom her image came between me and the page I strove to read. The syllables of the word *Araby* were called to me through the silence in which my soul luxuriated and cast an Eastern enchantment over me. I asked for leave to go to the bazaar on Saturday night. My aunt was surprised and hoped it was not some Freemason affair. I answered few questions in class. I watched my master's face pass from amiability to sternness; he hoped I was not beginning to idle. I could not call my wandering thoughts together. I had hardly any patience with the serious work of life which, now that it stood between me and my desire, seemed to me child's play, ugly monotonous child's play.

On Saturday morning I reminded my uncle that I wished to go to the bazaar in the evening. He was fussing at the hallstand, looking for the hat-brush, and answered me curtly:

"Yes, boy, I know."

As he was in the hall I could not go into the front parlour and lie at the window. I left the house in bad humour and walked slowly towards the school. The air was pitilessly raw and already my heart misgave me.

When I came home to dinner my uncle had not yet been home. Still it was early. I sat staring at the clock for some time and, when its ticking began to irritate me, I left the room. I mounted the staircase and gained the upper part of the house. The high cold empty gloomy rooms liberated me and I went from room to room singing. From the front window I saw my companions playing below in the street. Their cries reached me weakened and indistinct and, leaning my forehead against the cool glass, I looked over at the dark house where she lived. I may have stood there for an hour, seeing nothing but the brown-clad figure cast by my imagination, touched discreetly by the lamplight at the curved neck, at the hand upon the railings and at the border below the dress.

When I came downstairs again I found Mrs. Mercer sitting at the fire. She was an old garrulous woman, a pawnbroker's widow, who collected used stamps for some pious purpose. I had to endure the gossip of the tea-table. The meal was prolonged beyond an hour and still my uncle did not come. Mrs. Mercer stood up to go: she was sorry she couldn't wait any longer, but it was after eight o'clock and she did not like to be out late, as the night air was bad for her. When she had gone I began to walk up and down the room, clenching my fists. My aunt said:

"I'm afraid you may put off your bazaar for this night of Our Lord."

At nine o'clock I heard my uncle's latchkey in the halldoor. I heard him talking to himself and heard the hallstand rocking when it had received the weight of his overcoat. I could interpret these signs. When he was midway through his dinner I asked him to give me the money to go to the bazaar. He had forgotten.

"The people are in bed and after their first sleep now," he said.

I did not smile. My aunt said to him energetically:

"Can't you give him the money and let him go? You've kept him late enough as it is."

My uncle said he was very sorry he had forgotten. He said he believed in the old saying: "All work and no play makes Jack a dull boy." He asked me where I was going and, when I had told him a second time he asked me did I know *The Arab's Farewell to his Steed*.° When I left the kitchen he was about to recite the opening lines of the piece to my aunt.

I held a florin° tightly in my hand as I strode down Buckingham Street towards the station. The sight of the streets thronged with buyers and glaring with gas recalled to me the purpose of my journey. I took my seat in a third-class carriage of a deserted train. After an intolerable delay the train moved out of the station slowly. It crept onward among ruinous houses and over the twinkling river. At Westland Row Station a crowd of people pressed to the carriage doors; but the porters moved them back, saying that it was a special train for the bazaar. I remained alone in the bare carriage. In a few minutes the train drew up beside an improvised wooden platform. I passed out on to the road and saw by the lighted dial of a clock that it was ten minutes to ten. In front of me was a large building which displayed the magical name.

I could not find any sixpenny entrance and, fearing that the bazaar would be closed, I passed in quickly through a turnstile, handing a shilling

The Arab's Farewell to his Steed: A nostalgic poem by Caroline Norton (1808–1877).
Florin: A silver coin worth two shillings.

to a weary-looking man. I found myself in a big hall girdled at half its height by a gallery. Nearly all the stalls were closed and the greater part of the hall was in darkness. I recognised a silence like that which pervades a church after a service. I walked into the centre of the bazaar timidly. A few people were gathered about the stalls which were still open. Before a curtain, over which the words *Café Chantant* were written in coloured lamps, two men were counting money on a salver. I listened to the fall of the coins.

Remembering with difficulty why I had come I went over to one of the stalls and examined porcelain vases and flowered tea-sets. At the door of the stall a young lady was talking and laughing with two young gentlemen. I remarked their English accents and listened vaguely to their conversation.

"O, I never said such a thing!"

"O, but you did!"

"O, but I didn't!"

"Didn't she say that?"

"Yes. I heard her."

"O, there's a . . . fib!"

Observing me the young lady came over and asked me did I wish to buy anything. The tone of her voice was not encouraging; she seemed to have spoken to me out of a sense of duty. I looked humbly at the great jars that stood like eastern guards at either side of the dark entrance to the stall and murmured:

"No, thank you."

The young lady changed the position of one of the vases and went back to the two young men. They began to talk of the same subject. Once or twice the young lady glanced at me over her shoulder.

I lingered before her stall, though I knew my stay was useless, to make my interest in her wares seem the more real. Then I turned away slowly and walked down the middle of the bazaar. I allowed the two pennies to fall against the sixpence in my pocket. I heard a voice call from one end of the gallery that the light was out. The upper part of the hall was now completely dark.

Gazing up into the darkness I saw myself as a creature driven and derided by vanity; and my eyes burned with anguish and anger.

[1914]

FRANZ KAFKA [1883–1924]

The Metamorphosis

TRANSLATED BY ANN CHARTERS

I

As Gregor Samsa awoke one morning from troubled dreams, he found himself transformed in his bed into a monstrous insect. He was lying on his hard, armor-plated back, and when he lifted his head a little he could see his dome-like brown belly divided into bow-shaped ridges, on top of which the precariously perched bed quilt was about to slide off completely. His numerous legs, pitiably thin compared to the rest of him, fluttered helplessly before his eyes.

"What has happened to me?" he thought. It was no dream. His room—a normal, though rather small, human bedroom—lay quiet within its four familiar walls. Above the table, where a collection of cloth samples was unpacked and laid out—Samsa was a traveling salesman—hung the picture that he had recently cut from an illustrated magazine and put in a pretty gilt frame. It showed a lady wearing a small fur hat and a fur stole, sitting upright, holding out to the viewer a heavy fur muff into which her entire forearm had vanished.

Then Gregor looked toward the window, and the dreary weather—he heard the rain falling on the metal ledge of the window—made him feel quite melancholy. "What if I went back to sleep again for awhile and forgot about all this nonsense?" he thought, but it was absolutely impossible, since he was used to sleeping on his right side, and he was unable to get into that position in his present state. No matter how hard he tried to heave himself over onto his right side, he always rocked onto his back again. He tried a hundred times, closing his eyes so he wouldn't have to look at his wriggly legs, and he didn't give up until he began to feel a faint, dull ache in his side that he had never felt before.

"Oh God," he thought, "what a hard job I picked for myself! Traveling day in and day out. Much more stressful than working in the home office; on top of that, the strain of traveling, the worry about making connections, the bad meals at all hours, meeting new people, no real human contact, no one who ever becomes a friend. The devil take it all!" He felt a slight itch on top of his belly; slowly he pushed himself on his back closer to the bedpost, so he could lift his head better; he found the itchy place, which was covered with little white spots he couldn't identify; he tried to touch the place with one of his legs, but he immediately drew it back, for the contact sent icy shudders through his entire body.

He slid back to his former position. "Getting up so early like this," he thought, "makes you quite stupid. A man has to have his sleep. Other traveling salesmen live like women in a harem. For instance, when I return to the hotel during the morning to write up my orders, I find these gentlemen just sitting down to breakfast. I should try that with my boss; I would be fired on the spot. Anyway, who knows if that wouldn't be a good thing for me after all. If it weren't for my parents, I would have quit long ago, I would have gone to the boss and told him off. That would knock him off his desk! It's a strange thing, too, the way he sits on top of his desk and talks down to his employees from this height, especially since he's hard of hearing and we have to come so close to him. Now, I haven't totally given up hope; as soon as I've saved the money to pay back what my parents owe him—that should take another five or six years—I'll certainly do it. Then I'll take the big step. Right now, though, I have to get up, because my train leaves at five."

He looked over at the alarm clock, which was ticking on the chest of drawers. "Heavenly Father," he thought. It was half past six, and the hands of the clock were quietly moving forward; in fact, it was after half past, it was nearly quarter to seven. Was it possible the alarm hadn't rung? He saw from the bed that it was correctly set at four o'clock; surely it had rung. Yes, but was it possible to sleep peacefully right through that furniture-rattling noise? Well, he hadn't exactly slept peacefully, but probably all the more soundly. What should he do now? The next train left at seven o'clock; to catch it, he would have to rush like mad, and his samples weren't even packed yet, and he definitely didn't feel particularly fresh and rested. And even if he did catch the train, he wouldn't escape a scene with his boss, since the firm's office boy would have been waiting at the five o'clock train and would have reported back to the office long ago that he hadn't turned up. The office boy was the boss's own creature, without backbone or brains. Now, what if he called in sick? But that would be embarrassing, and it would look suspicious, because in the five years he'd been with the company, he'd never been sick before. His boss would be sure to show up with the doctor from the Health Insurance; he'd reproach his parents for their son's laziness, and he'd cut short any excuses by repeating the doctor's argument that people don't get sick, they're just lazy. And in this case, would he be so wrong? The fact was that except for being drowsy, which was certainly unnecessary after his long sleep, Gregor felt quite well, and he was even hungrier than usual.

As he was hurriedly turning all these thoughts over in his mind, still not able to decide to get out of bed—the alarm clock was just striking a quarter to seven—he heard a cautious tap on the door, close by the head of his bed. "Gregor"—someone called—it was his mother—"it's a quarter to seven. Didn't you want to leave?" That gentle voice! Gregor was shocked when he heard his own voice reply; it was unmistakably his old familiar voice, but mixed with it could be heard an irrepressible undertone of painful squeaking, which left the words clear for only a moment, immediately distorting their sound so that you didn't know if you had really heard them right. Gregor would have liked to answer fully and explain everything, but under the circumstances, he contented himself by saying, "Yes, yes, thank you, mother. I'm just getting up." No doubt the wooden door between them must have kept her from noticing the change in Gregor's voice, for his mother was reassured with his announcement and shuffled off. But because of this brief conversation, the other family members had become aware that Gregor unexpectedly was still at home, and soon his father began knocking on a side door softly, but with his fist. "Gregor, Gregor," he called, "what's the matter with you?" And after a little while, in a deeper, warning tone, "Gregor! Gregor!" At the other side door, his sister was asking plaintively, "Gregor, aren't you feeling well? Do you need anything?" To both sides of the room, Gregor answered, "I'm getting ready," and he forced himself to pronounce each syllable carefully and to separate his words by inserting long pauses, so his voice sounded normal. His father went back to his breakfast, but his sister whispered, "Gregor, open the door, please do." But Gregor had no intention of opening the door, and he congratulated himself on having developed the prudent habit during his travels of always locking all doors during the night, even at home.

As a start, he would get up quietly and undisturbed, get dressed, and—what was most important—eat breakfast, and then he would consider what to do next, since he realized that he would never come to a sensible conclusion about the situation if he stayed in bed. He remembered how many times before, perhaps when he was lying in bed in an unusual position, he had felt slight pains that turned out to be imaginary when he got up, and he was looking forward to finding out how this morning's fantasy would fade away. As for the change in his voice, he didn't doubt at all that it was nothing more than the first warning of a serious cold, a traveling salesman's occupational hazard.

It was easy to push off the quilt; all he had to do was to take a deep breath and it fell off by itself. But things got difficult with the next step, especially since he was now much broader. He could have used hands and arms to prop himself up, but all he had were his numerous little legs that never stopped moving in all directions and that he couldn't control at all. Whenever he tried to bend one of his legs, that was the first one to straighten itself out; and when it was finally doing what he wanted it to do, then all the other legs waved uncontrollably, in very painful agitation. "There's simply no use staying idle in bed," said Gregor to himself.

The first thing he meant to do was get the lower part of his body out of bed, but this lower part, which he still hadn't seen, and couldn't imagine either, proved to be too difficult to move, it shifted so slowly; and when finally, growing almost frantic, he gathered his strength and lurched forward, he miscalculated the direction, and banged himself violently into the bottom bedpost, and from the burning pain he felt, he realized that for the moment, it was the lower part of his body that was the most sensitive.

Next he tried to get the upper part of his body out first, and cautiously brought his head to the edge of the bed. This he managed easily, and eventually the rest of his body, despite its width and weight, slowly followed the direction of his head. But when he finally had moved his head off the bed into open space, he became afraid of continuing any further, because if he were to fall in this position, it would be a miracle if he didn't injure his head. And no matter what happened, he must not lose consciousness just now; he would be better off staying in bed.

But when he repeated his efforts and, sighing, found himself stretched out just as before, and again he saw his little legs struggling if possible even more wildly than ever, despairing of finding a way to bring discipline and order to this random movement, he once again realized that it was impossible to stay in bed, and that the wisest course was to make every sacrifice, if there was even the slightest hope of freeing himself from the bed. But at the same time, he continued to remind himself that it was always better to think calmly and coolly than make desperate decisions. In such stressful moments he usually turned his eyes toward the window, but unfortunately the view of the morning fog didn't inspire confidence or comfort; it was so thick that it obscured the other side of the narrow street. "Already seven o'clock," he said as the alarm clock rang again, "already seven o'clock and still such a heavy fog." And for a little while longer he lay quietly, breathing very gently as if expecting perhaps that the silence would restore real and normal circumstances.

But then he told himself, "Before it reaches quarter past seven, I must absolutely be out of bed without fail. Besides, by then someone from the office will be sent here to ask about me, since it opens at seven." And he began to rock the entire length of his body in a steady rhythm to swing it out of bed. If he maneuvered out of bed in this way, then his head, which he intended to lift up as he fell, would presumably escape injury. His back seemed to be hard; it wouldn't be harmed if he fell on the carpet. His biggest worry was the loud crash he was bound to make, which would certainly cause anxiety, perhaps even alarm, behind all the doors. Still, he had to take the risk.

When Gregor was already jutting halfway out of bed—his new approach was more a game than an exertion, for all he needed was to see-saw himself on his back—it occurred to him how easy his task would become if only he had help. Two strong people—he thought of his father and the maid—would have been enough; all they had to do was to slide their arms under his round back, lift him out of bed, bend down with their burden, and then wait patiently while he swung himself onto the ground, where he hoped that his little legs would find some purpose. Well, quite aside from the fact that the doors were locked, should he really have called for help? Despite his misery, he couldn't help smiling at the very thought of it.

By now he had pushed himself so far off the bed with his steady rocking that he could feel himself losing his balance, and he would finally have to decide what he was going to do, because in five minutes it would be quarter after seven—when the front doorbell rang. "That's somebody from the office," he said to himself, and his body became rigid, while his little legs danced in the air even faster. For a moment everything was quiet. "They won't open the door," Gregor told himself, with a surge of irrational hope. But then, as usual, the maid walked to the door with her firm step and opened it. Gregor needed only to hear the first words of greeting from the visitor to know who it was—the office manager himself. Why on earth was Gregor condemned to work for a company where the slightest sign of negligence was seized upon with the gravest suspicion? Were the employees, without exception, all scoundrels? Was no one among them a loyal and dedicated man, who, if he did happen to miss a few hours of work one morning, might drive himself so crazy with remorse that he couldn't get out of bed? Wouldn't it have been enough to send an apprentice to inquire—if inquiries were really necessary—did the manager himself have to come, and make it clear to the whole innocent family that any investigation into this suspicious matter could only be entrusted to a manager? And responding to these irritating thoughts more than to any conscious decision, Gregor swung himself out of bed with all his strength. There was a loud thud, but not really a crash. The carpet softened his fall, and his back was more resilient than Gregor had thought, so the resulting thud wasn't so noticeable. Only he hadn't held his head carefully enough and had banged it; he twisted it and rubbed it against the carpet in pain and annoyance.

"Something fell in there," said the manager in the adjoining room on the left. Gregor tried to imagine whether something similar to what had happened to him today might happen one day to the office manager; one really had to admit this possibility. But, as if in brusque reply, the manager took a few decisive steps in the next room, which made his patent leather boots creak. And in the adjoining room to the right, Gregor's sister whispered, as if warning him, "Gregor, the office manager is here." "I know," said Gregor to himself; but he didn't dare to raise his voice high enough so that his sister could hear.

"Gregor," said his father from the room to his left, "the office manager has come and wants to know why you didn't catch the early train. We don't know what to tell him. Besides, he wants to talk to you in person. So, please, open the door. Surely he will be kind enough to excuse the disorder in your room.' "Good morning, Mr. Samsa," the manager was calling in a friendly tone. "He's not well," said his mother to the manager, while his father continued talking through the door. "He's not well, believe me, sir. Why else would Gregor miss a train! That boy doesn't have anything in his head but business. I'm almost upset, as it is, that he never goes out at night; he's been in town for the past week, but he's stayed home every evening. He just sits here with us at the table, quietly reading the newspaper or studying the railroad timetables. His only recreation is when he occupies himself with his fretsaw. For instance, during the past two or three evenings, he's made a small picture frame; you'd be surprised how pretty it is; it's hanging in his room; you'll see it as soon as Gregor opens up. I'm really glad you've come, sir, we haven't been able to persuade Gregor to open the door; he's so obstinate; and he must definitely be feeling unwell, although he denied it earlier this morning." "I'll be right there," said Gregor slowly and deliberately, but he didn't move, so as not to miss a word of the conversation. "Dear madam, I can think of no other explanation, either," said the office manager. "Let us only hope it's nothing serious. Though, on the other hand, I must say, that we business people—fortunately or unfortunately—often very simply must overlook a slight indisposition in order to get on with business." "Well, can the office manager come in now?" asked his father impatiently and knocked again on the door. "No," said Gregor. In the room to the left, there was an embarrassed silence; in the room to the right, his sister began sobbing.

Why hadn't she joined the others? Probably she had just gotten out of bed and hadn't yet begun dressing. And why was she crying? Because he hadn't gotten up and let the office manager in, because he was in danger of losing his job, and because his boss would pester his parents again about their old debts? But surely for the moment these were unnecessary worries. Gregor was still here and would never consider abandoning the family. True, at this very moment he was lying on the carpet, and no one who could have seen his condition, could seriously expect him to open his door for the office manager. But Gregor could hardly be fired for this small discourtesy, for which he could easily find a plausible excuse later on. And it seemed to Gregor, that it would be much more sensible, just to leave him in peace for now, instead of pestering him with tears and speeches. But it was just this uncertainty about him that upset the others and excused their behavior.

"Mr. Samsa," the office manager now called out, raising his voice, "what is the matter with you? You are barricading yourself in your room, answering with only Yes and No, causing your parents serious and needless worries, and—I mention this only in passing—now suddenly you neglect your duties to the firm in an absolutely shocking manner. I'm speaking here in the name of your parents and your employer, and I must ask you to give an immediate and satisfactory explanation. I'm amazed, amazed! I took you for a quiet, sensible person, and now suddenly you seem intent on behaving in an absolutely strange manner. Early this morning, the head of the firm did suggest to me a possible explanation for your absence—it concerned the cash payment for sales that you received recently—but I practically gave him my word of honor that this couldn't be true. But now that I'm witness to your unbelievable obstinacy here, I haven't the slightest desire to defend you in any way whatsoever. And your job is by no means secure. I'd originally intended to confide this to you privately, but since you force me to waste my time here needlessly, I see no reason why your parents shouldn't hear it as well. For some time your sales have been quite unsatisfactory; to be sure, it's not the best season for business, we recognize that, but a season for doing no business at all just doesn't exist, Mr. Samsa, it *must* not exist."

"But, sir," Gregor called out, beside himself and forgetting everything in his agitation, "I'll open the door immediately, this very minute. A slight indisposition, a dizzy spell, kept me from getting up. I'm still lying in bed. But I feel completely well again. I'm just climbing out of bed. Please be patient for a moment. It's not going quite so well as I thought. But I'm really all right. How suddenly a thing like this can happen to a person! Just last night I felt fine, my parents know that, or rather last night I already had a slight foreboding. It must have been noticeable. Why didn't I let them know at the office! But you always think that you can recover from an illness without having to stay at home. Please, sir, please spare my parents! Because there are no grounds for all the accusations you just made; no one has ever said a word to me about them. Perhaps you haven't seen the last orders that I sent in. Anyway, I can still catch the eight o'clock train; the last couple hours of rest have made me feel much stronger. Don't delay here any longer, sir; I'll soon be back at work, and please be kind enough to report that to the office, and put in a good word for me with the head of the firm."

And while Gregor was hastily blurting all this out, hardly aware of what he was saying, he had easily reached the chest of drawers, perhaps as a result of his practice in bed, and he was trying to raise himself up against it. He actually wanted to open his door, he actually looked forward to showing himself and speaking with the manager; he was eager to find out what the others, who so wanted to see him, would say when they caught sight of him. If they were frightened, then Gregor was no longer responsible and he could rest in peace. But if they took everything calmly, then he, too, had no grounds for alarm, and could still get to the station in time for the eight o'clock train—if he hurried. At first he kept sliding a few times down the side of the polished chest, but finally, giving one last heave, he stood upright; he no longer paid attention to the pain in his lower abdomen, though it hurt a lot. Then he let himself fall against the back of a nearby chair, clinging to its edges with his little legs. By doing this, he gained control over himself, and he stayed very quiet so he could listen to the office manager.

"Did you understand even a single word?" the manager asked the parents. "Surely he can't be trying to make fools of us?" "For Heaven's sake," cried his mother, already in tears, "perhaps he's seriously ill, and we're torturing him. Grete! Grete!" she then called. "Mother?" answered his sister from the other side—they were communicating across Gregor's room. "You must get the doctor immediately. Gregor is sick. Hurry, run for the doctor. Didn't you hear Gregor talking just now?" "That was an animal voice," said the office manager, in a tone much lower than the mother's shouting. "Anna! Anna!" yelled the father through the hallway into the kitchen, clapping his hands. "Get the locksmith at once!" And already the two young girls were running through the hallway with a rustling of skirts—how had his sister gotten dressed so quickly?—and tearing open the front door to the apartment. There was no sound of the door closing; they must have just left it open, as you sometimes do in homes where a great misfortune had occurred.

But Gregor had grown calmer. Apparently no one understood his words any longer, though they were sufficiently clear to himself, even clearer than before; perhaps his ears were getting adjusted to the sound. But at least people knew now that something was wrong with him and were ready to help him. His parents' first orders had been given with such confidence and dispatch that he already felt comforted. Once more he'd been drawn back into the circle of humanity, and he expected miraculous results from both the doctor and the locksmith, without distinguishing precisely between them. In order to make his voice as clear as possible for the conversations he anticipated in the future, he coughed a little, but as quietly as he could, because it might not sound like a human cough, and he could no longer trust his judgment. Meanwhile, it had become completely quiet in the next room. Perhaps his parents sat at the table whispering with the office manager; perhaps they were all leaning against his door and listening.

Gregor pushed himself along slowly to the door holding onto the chair, then he let go of it and fell against the door, holding himself upright—the balls of his little feet secreted a sticky substance—and rested there a moment from his efforts. Then he attempted to use his mouth to turn the key in the lock. It seemed, unfortunately, that he had no real teeth—then how was he to hold onto the key?—but to compensate for that, his jaws were certainly very powerful; with their help, he succeeded in getting the key to turn, ignoring the fact that he was undoubtedly somehow injuring himself, since a brown fluid was streaming out of his mouth, oozing over the lock and dripping onto the floor. "Listen to that," said the office manager in the next room, "he's turning the key." Gregor felt greatly encouraged; but he felt that all of them, mother and father too, should have been cheering him on. "Keep it up, Gregor," they should have shouted, "Keep going, keep working on that lock!" And imagining that everyone was eagerly following his efforts, he bit down on the key with all the strength he had in his jaws. As the key began to turn, he danced around the lock; hanging on with only his mouth, he used the full weight of his body to either push up on the key or press down on it. The clear click of the lock as it finally snapped open, broke Gregor's concentration. With a sigh of relief, he said to himself, "I didn't need the locksmith after all," and he laid his head down on the handle so the door could open wide.

Since he had to open the door in this manner, it could open out fairly widely while he himself wasn't yet visible. Next he had to turn his body slowly around one half of the double door, moving very carefully so he wouldn't fall flat on his back while crossing over the threshold. He was concentrating on this difficult maneuver, not thinking of anything else, when he heard the manager exclaim a loud "Oh"—it sounded like the wind howling—and then he could see him too, standing closest to the door, pressing his hand against his open mouth and slowly staggering back, as if driven by some invisible and intensely powerful force. His mother—despite the presence of the manager, she was standing in the room with untidy hair sticking out in all directions from the night before—first looked toward his father with her hands clasped; then she took two steps toward Gregor and collapsed on the floor, her skirts billowing out around her and her face hidden on her breast. His father clenched his fist with a menacing air, as if he wanted to knock Gregor back into his room; then he looked uncertainly around the living room, covered his eyes with his hands, and sobbed so hard that his powerful chest heaved.

Now Gregor decided not to enter the room after all; instead he leaned against his side of the firmly bolted wing of the double door, so that only half of his body was visible, his head tilting above it while he peered at the others. Meanwhile, it had become much brighter; across the street a section of an endlessly long, dark gray building was clearly visible—it was a hospital—with its facade starkly broken by regularly placed windows; it was still raining, but now large individual drops were falling, striking the ground one at a time. On the table, the breakfast dishes were set out in a lavish display, since his father considered breakfast the most important meal of the day; he lingered over it for hours, reading various newspapers. Directly on the opposite wall hung a photograph of Gregor, taken during his military service, wearing a lieutenant's uniform, his hand on his sword, with a carefree smile, demanding respect for his bearing and his rank. The door to the entrance hall was open, and since the apartment door also stood open, you could see out to the landing and the top of the descending stairs.

"Well, now," said Gregor, and he was quite aware that he was the only one who had remained calm. "I'll get dressed at once, pack my samples, and be on my way. Will you, will you all let me go catch my train? Now you see, sir, I'm not obstinate, and I'm glad to work; traveling is a hard job, but I couldn't live without it. Where are you going, sir? Back to the office? Yes? Will you give a true account of everything? A man may temporarily seem incapable of working, but that is precisely the moment to remember his past accomplishments and to consider that later on, after overcoming his obstacles, he's sure to work all the harder and more diligently. As you know very well, I'm deeply obligated to the head of the firm. And then I have to take care of my parents and my sister. I'm in a tight spot, but I'll work myself out of it again. Please don't make it harder for me than it already is. I beg you to put in a good word for me at the office. Traveling salesmen aren't regarded highly there, I know. They think we make lots of money and lead easy lives. They have no particular reason to think differently. But you, sir, you have a better idea of what's really going on than the rest of the office, why—speaking just between ourselves—you have an even better idea than the head of the firm himself, who, in his role as our employer, lets his judgment be swayed against his employees. You know very well that a traveling salesman, who's out of the office most of the year, can easily become a victim of gossip, coincidences, and unfounded complaints, against which he can't possibly defend himself, since he almost never hears about them, except perhaps after he returns exhausted from a trip, and then he himself personally suffers the grim consequences without understanding the reasons for them. Sir, please don't leave without having told me that you think I'm at least partly right!"

But at Gregor's very first words the office manager had already turned away, and now with open mouth, he simply stared back at him over a twitching shoulder. And during Gregor's speech, he never stood still for a moment, but—without taking his eyes off Gregor—he kept moving very gradually toward the door, as if there were a secret ban on leaving the room. He was already in the front hall, and from the abrupt way that he pulled his leg out of the living room, you might have thought that he had just scorched the sole of his foot. In the hall, however, he stretched out his right hand as far as he could toward the stairs, as if some supernatural deliverance were awaiting him there.

Gregor realized that he must not let the office manager leave in this frame of mind, or his position in the firm would be seriously compromised. His parents didn't quite understand the situation; over the years they'd convinced themselves that Gregor was set up for life in this firm, and besides, they were now so preoccupied by their immediate worries that they'd lost any sense of the future. But Gregor had more foresight. The office manager must be stopped, calmed down, persuaded, and finally won over; Gregor's future and that of his family depended on it! If only his sister had been here! She had understood, she had even started to cry when Gregor was still lying quietly on his back. And the office manager, a ladies' man, would certainly have listened to her; she would have shut the front door and talked him out of his fright in the hall. But she wasn't there; Gregor would have to handle the situation by himself. And forgetting that he was still completely unfamiliar with his present powers of movement, and also that very possibly, indeed probably once again his words hadn't been understood, he let go of the wing of the door, shoved himself through the opening, and tried to move toward the office manager, who was already on the landing, foolishly clutching the banister with both hands; but instead, groping for support, Gregor fell down with a small cry upon his many little legs. The instant that happened he felt a sense of physical well-being for the first time that morning; his little legs had solid ground under them; he was delighted to discover that they obeyed him perfectly; they even seemed eager to carry him off in whatever direction he chose; and now he felt sure that the end to all his suffering was at hand. But at that same moment, as he lay on the floor rocking with suppressed motion, not far away from his mother, directly opposite her, she—who had seemed so completely self-absorbed—suddenly jumped up, stretched out her arms, spread her fingers out wide, crying "Help, for Heaven's sake, help!" She craned her head forward, as if she wanted to get a better look at Gregor, but then inconsistently, she backed away instead; forgetting that the table laden with breakfast dishes was right behind her, she sat down on it hastily, as if distracted, and then failed to notice that next to her, the coffee was pouring out of the big, overturned pot in a steady stream onto the carpet.

"Mother, mother," Gregor said softly and looked up at her. For a moment, the office manager had completely slipped from his mind; on the other hand, at the sight of the flowing coffee, he couldn't help snapping his jaws a few times. That made his mother scream again; she fled from the table and collapsed into his father's arms as he was rushing towards her. But Gregor had no time now for his parents; the office manager was already on the stairs; his chin on the banister, he was taking a final look back. Gregor leaped forward, moving as fast as he could to catch him; the office manager must have anticipated this, for he jumped down several steps and vanished; but he was still yelling "Aaah!" and the sound echoed through the entire staircase. Unfortunately, the manager's flight seemed to confuse Gregor's father, who had remained relatively calm until now; for instead of running after the office manager himself, or at least not preventing Gregor from going after him, his father seized with his right hand the manager's cane—it had been left behind on a chair along with his hat and overcoat—and with his left hand, he picked up a large newspaper from the table, and stamping his feet, he began to brandish the cane and the newspaper to drive Gregor back to his room. No plea of Gregor's helped; indeed, no plea was understood; no matter how humbly he bent his head, his father only stamped his feet harder. Across the room, his mother had flung open a window despite the cold weather, and she was leaning far out of it with her face buried in her hands. A strong draft was created between the street and the staircase, so that the window curtains billowed up, the newspapers rustled on the table, and a few pages flew across the floor. Relentlessly, his father charged, making hissing noises like a savage. Since Gregor had as yet no practice in moving backwards, it was really slow going. If Gregor had only been able to turn around, he would have returned to his room right away, but he was afraid of making his father impatient by his slow rotation, while at any moment now the cane in his father's hand threatened a deadly blow to his back or his head. Finally, however, Gregor had no other choice when he realized with dismay that while moving backwards he had no control over his direction; and so with constant, fearful glances at his father, he began to turn himself around as quickly as he could, which was in reality very slowly. Perhaps his father sensed Gregor's good intentions, since he didn't interfere—occasionally he even steered the movement from a distance with the tip of the cane. If only his father would stop that unbearable hissing! It made Gregor lose his head completely. He had almost turned totally around, when distracted by the hissing, he made a mistake and briefly shifted the wrong way back again. But when at last he successfully brought his head around to the doorway, he discovered that his body was too wide to squeeze through. Naturally, in his father's present mood it didn't occur to him to open the other wing of the double door and create a passage wide enough for Gregor. He was simply obsessed with the idea that Gregor must return to his room as fast as possible. And he would never have allowed the intricate maneuvers that Gregor needed, in order to pull himself upright and try to fit through the door this way. Instead, as if there were no obstacles, he drove Gregor forward, making a lot of noise; the noise behind Gregor didn't sound any longer like the voice of a single father; now this was really getting serious, and Gregor—regardless of what would happen—jammed into the doorway. One side of his body lifted up, he lay lopsided in the opening, one of his sides was scraped raw, ugly blotches appeared on the white door, soon he was wedged in tightly and unable to move any further by himself; on one side his little legs were trembling in midair, while on the other side they were painfully crushed against the floor—when his father gave him a strong shove from behind that was truly his deliverance, so that he flew far into his room, bleeding profusely. The door was slammed shut with the cane, and at last there was silence.

II

Not until dusk did Gregor awaken from his heavy, torpid sleep. He would certainly have awakened by himself before long, even without being disturbed, for he felt that he had rested and slept long enough, but it seemed to him that a furtive step and a cautious closing of the hall door had aroused him. The light of the electric street lamps were reflected in pale patches here and there on the ceiling and on the upper parts of the furniture, but down below where Gregor lay, it was dark. Slowly, still groping awkwardly with his antennae, which he was just beginning to appreciate, he dragged himself toward the door to see what had been going on there. His left side felt like a single long, unpleasantly tightening scab, and he actually had to limp on his two rows of legs. One little leg, moreover, had been badly hurt during the morning's events—it seemed almost a miracle that only one had been injured—and it dragged along lifelessly.

Only when he reached the door did he discover what had really attracted him: it was the smell of something edible. For there stood a bowl filled with fresh milk in which floated small slices of white bread. He practically laughed with joy, since he was even hungrier now than in the morning, and he immediately plunged his head into the milk almost over his eyes. But he soon pulled it out again in disappointment; not only did he find eating difficult on account of his tender left side—and he could only eat if his whole heaving body joined in—but he also didn't care at all for the milk, which used to be his favorite drink, and that was surely why his sister had placed it there for him; in fact, he turned away from the bowl almost with disgust and crawled back into the middle of the room.

Through the crack in the double door, Gregor could look into the living room where the gas was lit, but while during this time his father was usually in the habit of reading the afternoon newspaper in a loud voice to his mother and sometimes to his sister as well, there wasn't a sound at present. Well, perhaps this practice of reading aloud that his sister was always telling him about and often mentioned in her letters, had recently been dropped altogether. But it was silent in all the other rooms too, though the apartment was certainly not empty. "What a quiet life the family's been leading," Gregor said to himself, and while he sat there staring into the darkness, he felt a great sense of pride that he had been able to provide such a life in so beautiful an apartment for his parents and sister. But what if all the peace, all the comfort, all the contentment were now to come to a terrible end? Rather than lose himself in such thoughts, Gregor decided to start moving and crawled up and down the room.

Once during the long evening, first one of the side doors and then the other was opened a tiny crack and quickly closed again; probably someone had felt the need to come in and then decided against it. Gregor now settled himself directly in front of the living room door, determined to persuade the hesitating visitor to come in or else at least to discover who it might be; but the door wasn't opened again, and Gregor waited in vain. That morning, when the doors had been locked, they all had wanted to come in to see him; now after he had opened one of the doors himself and the others had obviously been unlocked during the day, no one came in, and the keys were even put into the locks on the other side of the doors.

It wasn't until late at night that the light in the living room was turned off, and Gregor could easily tell that his parents and sister had stayed awake until then, because as he could clearly hear, all three of them were tiptoeing away. Certainly now no one would come into Gregor's room until morning; so he had ample time to reflect in peace and quiet about how he should restructure his life. But the high-ceilinged, spacious room in which he had to lie flat on the floor filled him with an anxiety he couldn't explain, since it was his own room and he had lived in it for the past five years; and with a half-unconscious movement—and not without a slight feeling of shame—he scurried under the sofa, where even though his back was slightly squeezed and he couldn't raise his head, he immediately felt quite comfortable, regretting only that his body was too wide to fit completely under the sofa.

There he stayed the entire night, which he spent either dozing and waking up from hunger with a start, or else fretting with vague hopes, but it all led him to the same conclusion, that for now he would have to stay calm and, by exercising patience and trying to be as considerate as possible, help the family to endure the inconveniences he was bound to cause them in his present condition.

Very early in the morning—it was still almost night—Gregor had the opportunity to test the strength of his new resolutions, because his sister, nearly fully dressed, opened the door from the hall and peered in uncertainly. She couldn't locate him immediately, but when she caught sight of him under the sofa—God, he had to be somewhere, he couldn't have flown away, could he?—she was so startled that, unable to control herself, she slammed the door shut again from the outside. But, apparently regretting her behavior, she immediately opened the door again and came in on tiptoe as if she were visiting someone seriously ill or even a complete stranger. Gregor had pushed his head forward just to the edge of the sofa and was watching her. Would she notice that he had left the milk standing, certainly not because he wasn't hungry, and would she bring in some other kind of food he liked better? If she didn't do it on her own, he would rather starve than bring it to her attention, though he felt a tremendous urge to dart out from under the sofa, throw himself at her feet and beg for something good to eat. But, to Gregor's surprise, his sister noticed at once that his bowl was still full, except for a little milk that had spilled around the edges; she immediately picked it up, to be sure not with her bare hands but with an old rag, and carried it out. Gregor was wildly curious to know what she would bring in its place, and he made various guesses about it. But he could never have guessed what his sister, in the goodness of her heart, actually did. To find out what he liked, she brought him a wide selection that she spread out on an old newspaper. There were old, half-rotten vegetables, bones left over from the evening meal covered with a congealed white sauce, a few raisins and almonds, some cheese that Gregor had considered inedible two days ago, a slice of dry bread, a slice of bread and butter, and a slice of bread and butter with some salt. In addition, she set down the bowl, now presumably reserved for Gregor's exclusive use, into which she had poured some water. And from a sense of delicacy, since she understood that Gregor was unlikely to eat in her presence, she quickly left the room and even turned the key in the lock outside so that Gregor would understand that he could indulge himself as freely as he liked. Gregor's little legs whirled as he hurried toward the food. His injuries must have fully healed already; he no longer felt any handicap, which amazed him, and made him think that over a month ago he had nicked his finger with a knife, and that this injury had still been hurting him the day before yesterday. "Could I have become less sensitive?" he wondered, sucking greedily at the cheese, which he was drawn to immediately, more than the other foods. Quickly, one after another, with tears of contentment streaming from his eyes, he devoured the cheese, the vegetables, and the white sauce; on the other hand, the fresh food didn't appeal to him; he couldn't stand the smell, and he even dragged the things he wanted to eat a little distance away. He had finished with everything long ago and was just resting lazily in the same spot, when his sister slowly turned the key in the lock as a signal that he should withdraw. That startled him at once, even though he was almost dozing off, and he scuttled back under the sofa again. But it took a lot of self-control to stay there, even for the brief time that his sister was in the room, because his body was bloated after his heavy meal, and he could hardly breathe in that cramped space. In between brief bouts of near suffocation, he watched with somewhat bulging eyes as his unsuspecting sister swept up with a broom not only the scraps he hadn't eaten, but also the foods that he hadn't touched, as if they were also no longer fit to eat, and then she hastily dumped everything into a bucket which she covered with a wooden lid, and carried it out. She had scarcely turned her back when Gregor came out from under the sofa to stretch himself and let his belly expand.

In this way Gregor was fed each day, once in the morning while his parents and the maid were still sleeping, and the second time in the afternoon after the family's meal, while his parents took a short nap and his sister sent the maid on some errand or other. Certainly they didn't want Gregor to starve either, but perhaps they couldn't stand to know about his feeding arrangements except by hearsay; or perhaps his sister also wished to spare them anything even mildly distressing, since they were already suffering enough as it was.

Gregor couldn't discover what excuses had been made that first morning to get rid of the doctor and the locksmith, for since the others couldn't understand him, no one thought that he could understand them—including his sister—and so whenever she was in his room, he had to content himself with hearing her occasional sighs and appeals to the saints. Not until later on, when she had become a little more used to it all—of course her complete adjustment was out of the question—Gregor sometimes caught a remark that was meant to be friendly or could be interpreted that way. "Today he really liked it," she said, when Gregor had gobbled up his food, or when he hadn't eaten much, as was gradually happening more and more frequently, she would say almost sadly, "Now he hasn't touched anything again."

But while Gregor couldn't get any news directly, he overheard many things from the adjoining rooms, and as soon as he heard the sound of voices, he would immediately run to the corresponding door and press his entire body against it. Especially in the early days, there was no conversation that didn't refer to him somehow, if only indirectly. For two whole days, there were family discussions at every meal about what they should do now; but they also talked about the same subject between meals, because now there were always at least two family members at home, since probably no one wanted to stay alone in the apartment. And yet, on no account could they leave it empty. Besides, on the very first day, the cook—it wasn't entirely clear what or how much she knew of the situation—had begged his mother on bended knees to let her leave at once, and when she departed fifteen minutes later, she thanked them tearfully for her dismissal as if it were the greatest favor they had ever bestowed on her in this house, and without being asked, she swore a solemn oath, promising not to say a word about what had happened to anyone.

So now his sister, together with his mother, had to do the cooking as well; this wasn't much trouble, of course, since they ate almost nothing. Again and again Gregor would hear how one encouraged another to eat, always getting the answer, "Thanks, I've had enough" or something similar. They didn't seem to drink anything either. Often his sister asked his father if he wanted some beer, and she kindly offered to get it herself; and then when his father didn't answer, she suggested that if he didn't want her to bother, she could send the janitor's wife for it, but in the end his father answered with a firm "No," and there wasn't any further discussion.

In the course of the very first day his father explained the family's financial situation and prospects to both the mother and sister. Every now and then he stood up from the table to get some receipt or account book from the small safe that he'd managed to salvage from the collapse of his business five years earlier. He could be heard opening the complicated lock, taking out what he was looking for, and closing it again. The father's explanations, to some extent, were the first encouraging news that Gregor had heard since his captivity. He had always supposed that his father had nothing at all left from his old business, at least his father had never told him anything to the contrary, though Gregor had never actually asked him about it. In those days Gregor's only concern had been to do all that he could to help the family forget as quickly as possible the business catastrophe that had plunged them all into complete despair. And so he had begun to work with exceptional zeal and was promoted almost overnight from a junior clerk to a traveling salesman, who naturally had a much greater earning potential, and his successes were immediately converted by way of commissions into cash that he could bring home and lay on the table for the astonished and delighted family. Those had been happy times, and they had never been repeated, at least not with such splendor, even though Gregor was eventually earning so much money that he was capable of meeting the expenses of the entire family, and in fact did so. They had simply grown used to it, the family as well as Gregor; they accepted the money gratefully and he gave it gladly, but it didn't arouse any especially warm feelings any longer.

Only Gregor's sister had stayed close to him, and it was his secret plan that she, who—unlike Gregor—loved music and could play the violin very movingly, should be sent to the conservatory next year despite the considerable expense involved, and which he would certainly have to meet somehow. During Gregor's brief visits home, the conservatory was often mentioned in his conversations with his sister, but it was always only as a beautiful dream that could never come true, and his parents even disliked hearing those innocent allusions; but Gregor had definitely set his mind on it and had intended to announce his plan solemnly on Christmas Eve.

Such were the thoughts, quite futile in his present condition, that passed through his mind as he stood upright, glued to the door, eavesdropping. Sometimes he grew so weary that he could no longer listen and let his head bump carelessly against the door, but then he held it up again immediately, because even the slightest noise that he inadvertently made was enough to be heard next door and to reduce everyone to silence. "Just what's he up to now?" his father would say after a pause, obviously turning toward the door, and only then would the interrupted conversation gradually resume.

Gregor now had ample opportunity to discover—since his father would often repeat his explanations, partly because he hadn't concerned himself with these matters for a long time, and also partly because his mother couldn't always grasp everything the first time—that despite all their misfortune, a sum of money, to be sure a very small one, still remained from the old days and had even increased slightly in the meantime since the interest had never been touched. And besides that, the money Gregor had been bringing home every month—he'd only kept a little for himself—had not been entirely spent and had accumulated into a modest capital. Behind his door, Gregor nodded his head eagerly, delighted at this unexpected foresight and thrift. In fact, he could have used this surplus money to pay off more of his father's debt to the head of the firm, so the day when he could have quit his job would have been a lot closer, but now things were doubtless better the way his father had arranged them.

However, this money was by no means sufficient to allow the family to live off the interest; it might be enough to support them for a year, or for two at the most, but no more than that. It was really just a sum that shouldn't be touched, but instead saved for an emergency; money to live on would have to be earned. Now his father was still certainly healthy, but he was an old man who hadn't done any work for the past five years and couldn't be expected to take on very much; in those five years, which was his first vacation in his hardworking if unsuccessful life, he had put on weight and as a result, had become very sluggish. And as for his old mother, should she really start trying to earn money, when she suffered from asthma and found it a strain just to walk through the apartment, and spent every second day gasping for breath on the couch by the open window? And should his sister go out to work, she who was still a child at seventeen and whose life it would be a pity to disturb, since it consisted of wearing nice clothes, sleeping late, helping out with the housework, enjoying a few modest amusements, and most of all, playing the violin? At first, whenever the conversation turned to the necessity of earning money, Gregor would always let go of the door immediately and then throw himself down on the cool leather sofa beside it, because he felt so flushed with shame and grief.

Often he lay there throughout the long nights, not sleeping a wink and just scrabbling on the leather for hours. Or else, undaunted by the great effort of shoving an armchair to the window, he would crawl to the sill and, propping himself up on the chair, lean against the panes, evidently inspired by some memory of the sense of freedom that he used to experience looking out the window. Because, in fact, from day to day he saw objects only a short distance away becoming more indistinct; the hospital across the street, which he used to curse because he saw it all too often, he now couldn't see at all, and if he weren't certain that he lived on the quiet but decidedly urban Charlotte Street, he might have believed that he was gazing out of his window into a barren wasteland where the gray sky and the gray earth merged indistinguishably. Only twice had his attentive sister needed to see the armchair standing by the window; from then on whenever she cleaned the room, she carefully pushed the chair back to the window, and now she even left the inside windowpane open.

If Gregor had only been able to speak to his sister and thank her for all she had to do for him, he could have endured her services more easily, but as it was, they oppressed him. To be sure, she tried to ease the embarrassment of the situation as much as possible, and the longer time went on, the better she became at it, but in time Gregor too became more keenly aware of everything. Even the way she came in was terrible for him. Hardly had she entered the room when—not even taking time to close the door, though she was usually so careful to spare everyone the sight of Gregor's room—she'd run straight to the window and tear it open with impatient fingers, almost as if she were suffocating, and then she stayed there for a while, taking deep breaths no matter how cold it was. With this hustle and bustle, she scared Gregor twice a day; he lay quaking under the sofa the entire time, and yet he knew perfectly well that she would surely have spared him if she had only found it possible to stand being in a room with him with the windows closed.

One time—it must have been a month since Gregor's transformation, so there was no particular reason for his sister to be surprised by his appearance any more—she came a little earlier than usual and caught Gregor as he was looking out the window, motionless and terrifyingly upright. It wouldn't have surprised Gregor if she hadn't come in, since his position prevented her from opening the window immediately, but not only did she not enter, she also actually jumped back and shut the door; a stranger might easily have thought that Gregor had been lying in wait for her and meant to bite her. Gregor naturally hid at once under the sofa, but he had to wait until noon before she came back, and she seemed much more uneasy than usual. From this he concluded that the sight of him was still unbearable to her and was bound to remain unbearable in the future, and that she probably was exercising great self-control not to run away at the sight of even the small portion of his body that protruded from under the sofa. To spare her even this sight, he draped the sheet on his back and dragged it over to the sofa one day—he needed four hours for this task—and placed it in such a way so as to conceal himself completely, so that she couldn't see him even if she stooped down. If she considered this sheet unnecessary, then of course she could remove it, because it was clear enough that Gregor was hardly shutting himself off so completely for his own sake; but she left the sheet the way it was, and Gregor believed he caught a grateful look when he once cautiously raised the sheet a little with his head to see how she was reacting to the new arrangement.

During the first two weeks his parents couldn't bring themselves to come in to him, and often he heard them say how much they appreciated his sister's work, whereas previously they'd been annoyed with her because she'd appeared to be a little useless. But often now, both his father and mother waited outside of Gregor's room while his sister was cleaning up inside, and as soon as she emerged, she had to give a detailed report about how the room looked, what Gregor had eaten, how he had behaved this time, and whether perhaps some slight improvement was noticeable. Gregor's mother, incidentally, wanted to visit him relatively soon, but at first his father and sister put her off with sensible arguments, which Gregor listened to most attentively and fully endorsed. But later his mother had to be held back by force, and when she cried out, "Let me go to Gregor; after all, he's my unfortunate son! Don't you understand that I must go to him?" then Gregor thought that perhaps it would be a good idea after all if she did come in; not every day, of course, but perhaps once a week; she surely understood everything much better than his sister, who for all her courage, was still only a child, and had perhaps, in the final analysis, merely taken on this demanding task out of childish recklessness.

Gregor's wish to see his mother was soon fulfilled. During the daytime Gregor didn't want to show himself at the window, if only out of consideration for his parents, but he couldn't crawl very far on his few square yards of floor space, either, nor could he bear to lie still during the night; eating had soon ceased to give him the slightest pleasure, and so as a distraction he got into the habit of crawling crisscross over the walls and ceiling. He especially enjoyed hanging from the ceiling; it was quite different from lying on the floor; he could breathe more freely, and a mild tingle ran through his body; and in the almost blissful oblivion in which Gregor found himself up there, it could happen that, to his surprise, he let himself go and crashed onto the floor. But now of course he had much greater control over his body than before, and he never hurt himself by even this great fall. Gregor's sister immediately noticed the new pastime that he had found for himself—after all, he left some traces of the sticky tracks of his crawling here and there—and she then took it into her head to enable Gregor to crawl around to the greatest possible extent, so she decided to remove the furniture that stood in his way, first of all, the chest of drawers and the desk. But she couldn't do this alone; she didn't dare ask her father for help; and the maid would most certainly not help her, because this girl (about sixteen years old) was bravely staying on since the previous cook had quit, but she'd asked permission to keep the kitchen locked at all times and to open it only when expressly called; so his sister had no other choice than to get her mother one day when her father was out. And indeed, with cries of eager delight, Gregor's mother approached his room, but she fell silent at the door. Of course his sister first looked in to check that everything in the room was in order; only then did she let her mother enter. Gregor had hastily pulled the sheet even lower down in tighter folds; the whole thing really looked like a sheet casually tossed over the sofa. This time Gregor also refrained from peering out from under the sheet; he denied himself the sight of his mother, and was only pleased to know that she had finally come. "Come on in, you can't see him," said his sister, and evidently she was leading her mother by the hand. Now Gregor heard the two weak women shifting the really heavy old chest of drawers from its place, and how his sister obstinately took on the hardest part of the work for herself, ignoring the warnings of her mother, who was afraid she'd strain herself. It took a very long time. After about a quarter of an hour's work, Gregor's mother said that it would be better to leave the chest where it was, because for one thing, it was just too heavy, they would not be finished before the father arrived, and with the chest in the middle of the room, Gregor's path would be blocked; and for the second, it wasn't at all certain that they were doing Gregor a favor to move the furniture. It seemed to her that the opposite was true; the sight of the bare walls made her heart ache; and why shouldn't Gregor also feel the same way, since after all he'd been accustomed to the furniture for so long and might feel abandoned in an empty room. "And doesn't it really look," concluded his mother very softly, in fact she'd been almost whispering the whole time, as if she were anxious that Gregor, whose exact whereabouts she didn't know, couldn't hear even the sound of her voice, for of course she was convinced that he couldn't understand her words, "and doesn't it look as if by moving the furniture we were showing that we'd given up all hope for improvement and were callously abandoning him to his own resources? I think it would be best if we tried to keep the room just as it was, so that when Gregor comes back to us again, everything will be unchanged and it can be easier to forget what happened in the meantime."

Hearing his mother's words, Gregor realized that the lack of all direct human exchange, together with his monotonous life in the midst of the family, must have confused his mind during these past two months, because otherwise he couldn't explain to himself how he could seriously have wanted his room cleared out. Had he really wanted his warm room, with its comfortable old family furniture, to be transformed into a cave in which he could crawl freely around in all directions, no doubt, but only at the cost of swiftly and totally losing his human past? Indeed, he was already on the verge of forgetting it, and only his mother's voice, which he hadn't heard for so long, had brought him to his senses. Nothing should be removed; everything must stay; he couldn't do without the beneficial effects of the furniture on his state of mind; and if the furniture interfered with his mindless crawling about, then it was not a loss but a great gain.

But unfortunately his sister thought differently; she had grown accustomed, to be sure not entirely without reason, to being the great expert on Gregor in any discussion with her parents, and so now her mother's proposal was cause enough for the sister to insist on removing not only the chest of drawers and the desk, as she had originally planned, but also the rest of the furniture in the room except for the indispensable sofa. It was, of course, not only her childish defiance and the self-confidence she had recently and so unexpectedly gained at such cost that led to this determination; but she had also in fact observed that Gregor needed more space to crawl around in, while on the other hand, as far as she could see, he never used the furniture. But, perhaps, what also played some part was the romantic spirit of girls of her age, which seeks satisfaction at every opportunity and tempted Grete to make Gregor's predicament even more frightening so that she might then be able to do even more for him than before. For most likely no one but Grete would ever dare to enter into a room where Gregor ruled the bare walls all by himself.

And so she refused to be dissuaded from her resolve by her mother, who in any case seemed unsure of herself in that room and who soon fell silent out of sheer nervousness, and helped the sister as best she could to move the chest of drawers out of the room. Well, Gregor could do without the chest, if necessary, but the desk had to stay. And no sooner had the two women, groaning and shoving the chest, left the room, when Gregor poked his head out from under the sofa to see how he could intervene as cautiously and tactfully as possible. Unfortunately, it was his mother who returned first, while Grete kept her arms around the chest in the next room, rocking it back and forth, and naturally unable to move it by herself from its spot. Gregor's mother, however, was not used to the sight of him; it might make her sick, and so Gregor scurried backwards in alarm to the other end of the sofa, though not in time to prevent the front of the sheet from stirring a little. That was enough to catch his mother's attention. She stopped short, stood still a moment, and then went back to Grete.

Although Gregor kept telling himself that nothing out of the ordinary was happening, that just a couple of pieces of furniture were being moved around, all the same he soon had to admit to himself that this walking back and forth by the women, their little cries to each other, the scraping of the furniture along the floor, were affecting him on all sides like a tremendous uproar, and no matter how tightly he tucked in his head and legs and pressed his body against the floor, he was forced to admit that he couldn't endure the fuss much longer. They were emptying out his room, stripping him of everything he loved; they had already removed the chest, which contained his fretsaw and other tools; and now they were prying loose the desk, which was almost embedded in the floor, and at which he'd done his homework when he was in business school, high school, and even as far back as elementary school—at this point he really had no more time to consider the good intentions of the two women, whose existence he had indeed almost forgotten, because by now they were working away in silence from sheer exhaustion, and he heard only the heavy shuffling of their feet.

And so he broke out—just at the moment the women were in the next room, leaning against the desk to catch their breath—and he changed direction four times, not really knowing what he should rescue first, and then he spotted the picture of the lady dressed in nothing but furs, hanging conspicuously on what was otherwise a bare wall opposite him; he crawled rapidly up to it and pressed himself against the glass, which held him fast and soothed his hot belly. At least this picture, which Gregor now completely covered, was definitely not going to be removed by anyone. He twisted his head around toward the door of the living room to observe the women on their return.

They had not given themselves much of a rest and were already coming back; Grete had put her arm around her mother and was almost carrying her. "Well, what should we take now?" said Grete and looked around. Then her eyes met Gregor's on the wall. No doubt it was only due to the presence of her mother that she kept her composure, lowered her head to keep her mother from looking about, and said, although rather shakily and without thinking, "Come on, why don't we go back to the living room for a moment?" Grete's intention was clear to Gregor; she wanted to get her mother to safety and then chase him down from the wall. Well, just let her try! He clung to his picture and wouldn't give it up. He would rather fly in Grete's face.

But Grete's words had made her mother even more anxious; she stepped to one side, caught sight of the huge brown splotch on the flowered wallpaper, and before realizing that what she saw was Gregor, she cried out in a hoarse, shrieking voice, "Oh God, oh God," and collapsed across the sofa with outstretched arms, as if giving up completely, and didn't move. "You, Gregor," cried the sister, raising her fist and glaring at him. These were the first words that she had addressed directly to him since his transformation. She ran into the next room to get some sort of medicine to revive her mother from her fainting fit; Gregor also wanted to help—there was time enough to save his picture later on—but he was stuck fast to the glass and had to wrench himself free; then he also ran into the next room, as if he could give some advice to his sister as in the old days; but once there he had to stand uselessly behind her while she was rummaging among various little bottles; she got frightened when she turned around; one of the bottles fell to the floor and shattered; a splinter of glass sliced Gregor's face, and some kind of burning medicine splashed around him; then without further delay, Grete grabbed as many bottles as she could hold and ran back to her mother with them; she slammed the door closed with her foot. Gregor was now cut off from his mother, who was perhaps nearly dying because of him; he dared not open the door for fear of frightening away his sister, who had to stay with his mother; now he had nothing to do but wait; and so, in an agony of self-reproach and anxiety, he began to crawl, to crawl over everything, walls, furniture, and ceiling; until finally when the entire room was spinning, he dropped in despair onto the middle of the big table.

A little while passed. Gregor lay worn out, all was quiet, perhaps that was a good sign. Then the doorbell rang. The maid, of course, was locked in the kitchen, and Grete had to open the door. Father was back. "What's happened?" were his first words; Grete's face must have told him everything. Grete replied in a muffled voice, evidently with her face pressing against her father's chest. "Mother fainted. But she's better now. Gregor's broken loose." "Just what I expected," said his father. "Just what I've always told you, but you women wouldn't listen." It was clear to Gregor that his father had misinterpreted Grete's all too brief statement and assumed that Gregor was guilty of some act of violence. That meant that he must now try to pacify his father, for he had neither the time nor the means to explain things to him. And so Gregor fled to the door of his room and pressed himself against it, so that as soon as his father came in from the hall, he should see that Gregor had the best intention of return- ing to his room immediately, and that it was unnecessary to drive him back; but that someone only had to open the door, and he would imme- diately disappear.

But his father was in no mood to observe such subtlety; "Ah ha!" he cried as soon as he entered, in a tone both furious and elated. Gregor drew his head back from the door and raised it toward his father. He hadn't really pictured his father at all, standing that way; admittedly he had been too preoccupied by the new sensation of crawling around to concern himself with what was going on in the rest of the household as before, and he really ought to have been prepared for some changes. And yet, and yet, was this really his father? The same man who used to lie wearily in bed when Gregor left early on one of his business trips; who always greeted him on his return in the evening wearing a robe and sit- ting in an armchair; who was actually hardly capable of standing up, but had merely raised his arms to show his pleasure; and who, during the rare family walks on a few Sundays a year and on the high holidays, would always shuffle laboriously along between Gregor and his mother, who walked slowly anyway, walking even a little slower than they walked, bundled in his old overcoat, planting his cane before him for each step he took, and when he wanted to say something, nearly always standing still and gathering his escorts around him? Now, however, he held him- self erect, dressed in a tight blue uniform with gold buttons, like that worn by bank messengers; his heavy double chin bulged over the high stiff collar of his jacket; from under his bushy eyebrows, his black eyes flashed alert and observant glances; his previously tousled white hair was combed flat, meticulously parted and gleaming. He tossed his cap, on which was a gold monogram, probably that of some bank, right across the room in a wide arc onto the couch, and started toward Gregor with a grimly set face, the ends of his long uniform jacket thrown back, and his hands in his pockets. Probably he didn't know himself what he intended; nevertheless, he lifted his feet unusually high, and Gregor was astonished at the gigantic size of his boot soles. But Gregor didn't dwell on his reflections; he had known from the very first day of his new life that his father considered only the strictest measures appropriate for dealing with him. And so he fled from his father, pausing only when his father stood still, and immediately hurrying on again when he made any kind of a move. In that way they circled the room several times, without anything decisive happening; in fact, they proceeded in such a slow tempo that it didn't have the appearance of a chase. For this reason, Gregor stayed on the floor for the time being, especially since he feared his father might regard any escape onto the walls or ceiling as a particularly wicked act. At the same time, Gregor had to admit that he couldn't keep up with this kind of running for long; for while his father took a single step, he had to carry out a countless number of movements. Shortness of breath was beginning to appear, and even in his earlier days his lungs had never been entirely reliable. As he went staggering along, saving all his energy for running, hardly keeping his eyes open, in his stupor not even thinking of any other refuge than running, and having almost forgotten that the walls were available, though admittedly here these walls were blocked by elaborately carved furniture full of sharp points and corners—suddenly something came sailing past him, lightly tossed; it landed next to him and rolled away in front of him. It was an apple; immediately a second one came flying after it; Gregor stopped dead in fright; any further running was useless, because his father was determined to bombard him. He had filled his pockets from the fruit bowl on the sideboard and now, without taking careful aim, he was throwing one apple after another. These small red apples rolled around on the floor as if electrified, colliding with one another. One weakly thrown apple grazed Gregor's back and glanced off harmlessly. But another one thrown directly afterwards actually penetrated into Gregor's back; Gregor wanted to drag himself further, as if the surprising and unbelievable pain might pass if he changed his position; but he felt as if nailed to the spot and stretched himself flat out, all his senses in complete confusion. Now with his last conscious sight he saw how the door of his room was flung open, and his mother rushed out in her chemise, ahead of his screaming sister, for his sister had undressed her when she had fainted to make it easier for her to breathe; he saw his mother running to his father, shedding her loosened petticoats one by one on the floor behind her, and stumbling over her petticoats to fling herself upon his father, and embracing him, in complete union with him—but now Gregor's vision failed him— begging him, with her hands clasped around his father's neck, to spare Gregor's life.

III

Gregor suffered from his serious injury for over a month—the apple remained embedded in his flesh as a visible reminder since no one dared to remove it—and it even seemed to bring home to his father that despite Gregor's present deplorable and repulsive shape, he was still a member of the family who ought not to be treated as an enemy, but that on the contrary, family duty required them to swallow their disgust and put up with him, simply put up with him.

And now, although Gregor had probably suffered some permanent loss of mobility as a result of his injury and for the present needed long, long minutes to cross his room like an old invalid—crawling up the walls was out of the question—yet he thought he was granted entirely satisfactory compensation for this deterioration of his condition, since every day toward evening the living room door, which he used to watch intently for an hour or two beforehand, would be opened, so that lying in the darkness of his room and not visible from the living room, he could see the entire family at the lamp-lit table and could listen to the conversation as if by general consent, not at all as he had been obliged earlier to eavesdrop.

Of course, there were no longer the lively discussions of earlier days that Gregor used to recall wistfully in small hotel rooms whenever he had to sink down wearily into the damp bedding. Now it was mostly very quiet. The father fell asleep in his armchair shortly after supper; the mother and sister would caution each other to keep quiet; the mother, hunched forward under the light, stitched away at fine lingerie for a fashion boutique; the sister, who had taken a job as a salesgirl, studied shorthand and French every evening, in the hope of getting a better job some day. Occasionally the father woke up, and as if he didn't know he'd been sleeping, he said to the mother, "How long you've been sewing again today!" and instantly he'd doze off again, while the mother and sister smiled wearily at each other.

With a kind of perverse obstinacy, the father refused to take off his messenger's uniform even in the house, and while his robe hung uselessly on the clothes hook, he slept fully dressed in his chair, as if he were ever ready for duty and waiting for his superior's call even here. As a result, his uniform—not new to begin with—started to look less clean despite all the efforts of the mother and sister, and Gregor would often spend whole evenings staring at the soiled and spotted uniform, with its gleaming, constantly polished gold buttons, in which the old man slept in great discomfort and yet very peacefully.

As soon as the clock struck ten, the mother tried to wake up the father with a few gentle words, trying to persuade him to go to bed, because here he couldn't get any proper rest, which the father sorely needed, since he had to go on duty at six. But with the obstinacy that had possessed him since he'd become a bank messenger, he always insisted on staying at the table a little longer, though he regularly fell asleep, and it was then only with the greatest effort that he could be coaxed into exchanging his armchair for his bed. No matter how much the mother and sister cajoled and admonished him, he would go on shaking his head slowly for a quarter of an hour, keeping his eyes shut and refusing to get up. The mother plucked at his sleeve, whispering sweet words into his ear; the sister would leave her homework to help her mother, but none of this had any effect on the father. He merely sank deeper into his chair. He would open his eyes only when the two women took hold of him under his arms, look back and forth at the mother and sister, and usually say, "What a life. Such is the peace of my old age." And supported by both women, he rose to his feet laboriously, as if he himself were his greatest burden, and allowed the women to lead him to the door, where he waved them away and went on by himself, while the mother hastily dropped her sewing and the sister her pen, to run after the father and provide further assistance.

Who in this overworked and exhausted family had time to worry about Gregor any more than was absolutely necessary? The household was neglected even more; the maid was dismissed after all; a gigantic, bony cleaning woman with white hair fluttering around her head now came every morning and evening to do the heaviest chores; everything else was taken care of by the mother, along with all her sewing. It even came to pass that various pieces of family jewelry, which the mother and sister used to wear with great pleasure at parties and on great occasions, had to be sold, as Gregor learned in the evenings from the family's discussion of the prices they had fetched. But always their greatest complaint was that they couldn't leave this apartment, which was much too large for their present circumstances, since no one could imagine how to move Gregor. But Gregor fully understood that it was not only concern for him that prevented a move, for he could easily have been shipped in a suitable crate with a few air holes; what mostly stopped them was the complete hopelessness of their situation and their sense that they had been struck by a misfortune unlike anyone else in their entire circle of friends and relations. They were suffering to the limit what the world requires of poor people: the father brought in breakfast for junior bank clerks; the mother sacrificed herself sewing underwear for strangers; the sister ran to and fro behind a counter at the bidding of customers, but the family had no more strength beyond that. And the wound in Gregor's back began to hurt again whenever the mother and sister returned after putting the father to bed, dropped their work, drew close together, and sat cheek to cheek; then the mother, pointing to Gregor's room, said "Close the door, Grete," so that Gregor was again left in darkness while in the next room, the women mingled their tears or stared dry eyed at the table.

Gregor spent his nights and days almost entirely without sleep. Sometimes he fancied that the next time the door opened, he would once again take charge of the family affairs just as he had done in the past; in his thoughts there reappeared, as after a long absence, the director and the office manager, the clerks and the trainees, the slow-witted office boy, two or three friends from other firms, a maid in a country hotel (a charming, fleeting memory), a cashier in a hat shop whom he'd courted earnestly but too slowly—they all appeared mixed up with strangers or people he'd forgotten, but instead of helping him and his family, they were all inaccessible, and he was glad when they disappeared. But at other times he was in no mood to worry about his family; he was filled with rage over how badly he was looked after; and even though he couldn't imagine having an appetite for anything, he still invented plans for getting into the pantry so he could help himself to the food that was coming to him, even if he wasn't hungry. No longer considering what might give Gregor some special pleasure, the sister now quickly pushed any old food into Gregor's room with her foot before she rushed off to work both in the morning and at noon; then in the evening, not caring whether the food had only been nibbled at or—most frequently—left completely untouched, she swept it out with a swing of her broom. The cleaning of his room, which she now always took care of in the evening, couldn't have been more perfunctory. Grimy dirt streaked the walls, and balls of dust and filth lay here and there. At first Gregor would stand in particularly offensive corners when the sister came in, as if intending to reproach her. But he could have waited there for weeks without the sister making any improvement; she could see the dirt just as well as he could, of course, but she had simply made up her mind to leave it there. At the same time, with a touchiness that was new to her, and that indeed was felt in the entire family, she made certain that the cleaning of Gregor's room remained her exclusive responsibility. Once Gregor's mother subjected his room to a thorough cleaning, which she managed only by using several buckets of water—the resulting dampness made Gregor sick, of course, and he lay stretched out on the sofa, embittered and immobile—but the mother didn't escape her punishment. Because that evening, the moment Gregor's sister noticed the change in his room, she ran into the living room, deeply insulted, and although the mother raised her hands imploringly, the sister broke out in a fit of weeping, while the parents—the father had of course been frightened out of his armchair—gaped in helpless astonishment, until they too started in; the father reproached the mother on his right for not leaving the cleaning of Gregor's room to the sister, and he shouted at the sister on his left, warning her that she would never again be allowed to clean Gregor's room; meanwhile the mother tried to drag the father, who was beside himself with rage, into the bedroom; the sister, shaking with sobs, beat the table with her small fists; and Gregor hissed loudly in his fury because no one thought of closing the door and sparing him this spectacle and commotion.

But even if Gregor's sister, exhausted by her work at the shop, was fed up with taking care of him as before, it was by no means necessary for the mother to take her place to make sure that Gregor wouldn't be neglected. For now the cleaning woman was there. This old widow, who in her long life must have weathered the worst thanks to her sturdy constitution, wasn't really repelled by Gregor. Without being in the least nosy, she happened one day to open the door to Gregor's room, and at the sight of Gregor, who was completely taken by surprise and began scrambling back and forth though no one was chasing him, she had merely stood still in amazement, her hands folded on her stomach. Since then, she never failed to open his door a crack every morning and night to peep in at Gregor. Initially she would even call him over with words she probably considered friendly, such as "Come on over here, you old dung beetle," or "Just look at that old dung beetle!" Gregor never responded to such calls, but remained motionless where he stood, as if the door had never been opened. If only they had ordered this woman to clean out his room every day, instead of letting her disturb him whenever she pleased! Once, early in the morning—a heavy rain, perhaps a sign of the coming spring, was pelting the windowpanes—Gregor was so annoyed when the cleaning woman again launched into her phrases that he charged toward her as if to attack, but slowly and feebly. Instead of being frightened, the cleaning woman simply raised a chair placed near the door and stood there with her mouth wide open, obviously not intending to close it again until the chair in her hand came crashing down on Gregor's back. "So you're not coming any closer?" she asked, when Gregor turned around again, and she calmly put the chair back in the corner.

By this time Gregor was eating next to nothing. Only when he happened by chance to pass by the food spread out for him, would he take a bite in his mouth just for pleasure, hold it there for hours, and then mostly spit it back out again. At first he thought it was distress at the condition of his room that kept him from eating, but he soon became adjusted to these very changes. The family had gotten into the habit of putting things that had no other place into his room, and now there were plenty of such things, because they had rented a bedroom in the apartment to three boarders. These serious gentlemen—all three had full beards, as Gregor once observed through a crack in the door—were obsessed with order, not only in their room, but also, since they were paying rent there, throughout the apartment, particularly the kitchen. They couldn't stand any kind of useless odds and ends, let alone dirty ones. Furthermore, they had for the most part brought along their own furnishings. For this reason, many things had become superfluous that couldn't be sold but also couldn't be thrown away. All these things ended up in Gregor's room. As did the ash bucket and the garbage pail from the kitchen. Whatever was not being used at the moment was simply flung into Gregor's room by the cleaning woman, who was always in a hurry; Gregor was usually fortunate enough to see only the object in question and the hand that held it. Perhaps the cleaning woman intended to retrieve these objects when she had time and opportunity to do so, or else to throw out everything at once, but in fact they lay wherever they happened to land, unless Gregor waded through the junk pile and set it in motion, at first out of necessity because there was no free space to crawl; but later on with growing pleasure, though after such excursions he would lie still for hours, dead tired and miserable.

Since the boarders also sometimes took their evening meal at home in the common living room, Gregor's door stayed shut on many evenings, but he found it very easy to give up the open door, for when it was left open on many earlier evenings he had already not taken advantage of it, but without the family's notice, he had lain in the darkest corner of his room. Once, however, the cleaning woman had left the door to the living room open a small crack; and it stayed open, even when the boarders entered in the evening and the lamp was lit. They sat at the head of the table where the father, mother, and Gregor had sat in the old days, unfolded their napkins and picked up their knives and forks. Immediately the mother appeared in the doorway with a platter of meat, and right behind her was the sister with a platter piled high with potatoes. The food gave off thick clouds of steam. The boarders bent over the platters placed in front of them as if to examine them before eating, and in fact the man sitting in the middle (whom the other two seemed to regard as an authority) cut up a piece of meat on the platter, obviously in order to determine whether it was tender enough or should perhaps need to be sent back to the kitchen. He was satisfied, and so the mother and sister, who had been watching anxiously, breathed freely again and began to smile.

The family itself ate in the kitchen. Nevertheless, before the father headed for the kitchen, he came into the living room, bowed once, his cap in hand, and walked around the table. The boarders all rose simultaneously and muttered something into their beards. When they were alone again, they ate in almost complete silence. It seemed strange to Gregor that out of the various noises of eating, he could always distinguish the sound of their chomping teeth, as if to demonstrate to Gregor that teeth were necessary for eating, and that even the most wonderful toothless jaws could accomplish nothing. "I do have an appetite," said Gregor mournfully to himself, "but not for these things. How those boarders gorge themselves, and I'm starving to death."

On that very evening—Gregor couldn't remember having once heard the violin during all this time—it was heard from the kitchen. The boarders had already finished their supper, the middle one had taken out a newspaper, handing over a sheet apiece to the two others, and they were now leaning back, reading and smoking. When the violin began to play, they noticed it, stood up, and tiptoed to the hall, where they paused, huddled together. They must have been heard from the kitchen, because the father called, "Are the gentlemen disturbed by the music, perhaps? It can be stopped at once." "On the contrary," said the middle boarder, "wouldn't the young lady like to come in here with us and play in the living room, which is more spacious and comfortable?" "Oh, with pleasure," cried the father, as if he were the violinist. The boarders went back into the living room and waited. Soon the father came with the music stand, the mother with the sheet music, and the sister with the violin. The sister calmly got everything ready to play; the parents, who'd never rented rooms before and therefore were excessively polite to the boarders, didn't dare to sit on their own chairs; the father leaned against the door, his right hand thrust between two buttons of his closed uniform jacket; the mother, however, was offered a chair by one of the boarders and sat down on it just where he happened to put it, off to the side in a corner.

The sister began to play; the father and mother on either side of her followed the movements of her hands attentively. Gregor, attracted by her playing, had ventured out a little further, and his head was already in the living room. He was hardly surprised that he had recently begun to show so little concern for others; previously such thoughtfulness had been his pride. And yet right now he would have had even more reason than ever to stay hidden, because he was completely covered with dust as a result of the particles that lay everywhere in his room and flew about with his slightest movement; bits of fluff, hair, and food remnants also stuck to his back and trailed from his sides; his indifference to everything was much too great for him to lie on his back and rub himself against the carpet, as he had once done several times a day. And in spite of his condition, he felt no shame in edging forward a little onto the immaculate floor of the living room.

To be sure, no one paid any attention to him. The family was completely absorbed by the violin playing; on the other hand, the boarders, with their hands in their pockets, stood at first much too closely behind the sister's music stand so that they all would have been able to read the music, which surely must have distracted the sister, but they soon retreated to the window and stayed there with lowered heads, softly talking with each other, while the father watched them anxiously. Indeed it now appeared all too clearly that they seemed disappointed in their hopes of hearing beautiful or entertaining violin playing, as if they had had enough of the recital and were merely suffering this disturbance of their peace out of politeness. In particular, the way in which they all blew their cigar smoke through their nose and mouth into the air suggested their high degree of irritability. And yet the sister was playing so beautifully. Her face was inclined to one side, her eyes followed the notes of the music with a searching and sorrowful look. Gregor crawled a little bit further forward and kept his head close to the floor so that it might be possible for their eyes to meet. Was he an animal, that music could move him so? It seemed as if he were being shown the way to the unknown nourishment he longed for. He was determined to push his way up to his sister and tug at her skirt, and thus suggest that she should come into his room with her violin, for nobody here was worthy of her playing as he would be worthy of it. He would never let her out of his room again, at least not so long as he lived; his terrible shape would be useful to him for the first time; he would stand guard at all the doors of his room simultaneously, hissing at the intruders; his sister, however, wouldn't be forced to stay with him but should remain of her own free will; she should sit next to him on the sofa, bending her ear down to him, and then he would confide to her that he had made a firm resolve to send her to the Conservatory, and that if misfortune hadn't intervened, he would have announced this to everyone at Christmas—had Christmas passed already?—without listening to any objections. After this declaration his sister would burst into tears of emotion, and Gregor would raise himself up to her shoulder and kiss her on the neck, which—now that she went out to work—she kept free of ribbon or collar.

"Mr. Samsa!" cried the middle boarder to the father, and without wasting another word, he pointed with his forefinger at Gregor, who was slowly crawling forward. The violin fell silent, the middle boarder first smiled at his friends with a shake of his head and then looked at Gregor again. The father seemed to think that it was more urgent to pacify the boarders than to drive Gregor out, though they weren't at all upset, and Gregor seemed to entertain them more than the violin playing. With outstretched arms, the father rushed to them and tried to herd them back to their room, while simultaneously blocking their view of Gregor with his body. Now they really became a bit angry; it wasn't clear whether the father's behavior was to blame or whether the realization was dawning on them that they had unknowingly had a next door neighbor like Gregor. They demanded explanations from the father, waving their arms at him, nervously plucking their beards, and then they backed toward their room very reluctantly. In the meantime, the sister had recovered from the bewildered state she had fallen into with the sudden interruption of her music; after having dangled her violin and bow listlessly for awhile in her slack hands, continuing to gaze at the music as if she were still playing, she had suddenly pulled herself together, placed her instrument in her mother's lap (her mother was still sitting in her chair, gasping for breath with heaving lungs) and run into the next room, which the boarders were approaching more rapidly now under pressure from the father. One could see the blankets and pillows on the beds obeying the sister's skillful hands and arranging themselves neatly. Before the boarders had even reached their room, she finished making the beds and slipped out. Once again the father seemed so overcome by his obstinacy that he was forgetting any respect he still owed his boarders. He kept crowding them and crowding them until, just at the doorway to their room, the middle boarder thunderously stamped his foot and brought the father to a halt. "I hereby declare," he said, raising his hand and looking around for the mother and sister too, "that in view of the disgusting conditions prevailing in this household and family"—here he promptly spit on the floor—"I give immediate notice. I will of course not pay a cent for the days that I have been living here, either; on the contrary, I will think seriously about taking some sort of legal action against you, with claims—believe me—that would be very easy to substantiate." He was silent and looked straight ahead of him, as if he were expecting something. And in fact his two friends immediately chimed in with the words, "We're also leaving tomorrow." Thereupon he seized the door handle and banged the door shut.

Gregor's father staggered with groping hands to his armchair and let himself fall into it; he looked as if he were stretching out for his usual evening nap, but the rapid nodding of his head, as if it were out of control, showed that he was anything but asleep. All this time Gregor had been lying still in the same place where the boarders had caught sight of him. His disappointment over the failure of his plan, and perhaps also the weakness caused by his great hunger, made it impossible for him to move. With a fair degree of certainty, he feared that in the very next moment everything would collapse over him, and he was waiting. He was not even startled when the violin slipped through the mother's trembling fingers, fell off her lap, and gave off a reverberating clang.

"My dear parents," the sister said, striking the table with her hand by way of introduction, "things can't go on like this. Perhaps you don't realize that, but I do. I refuse to utter my brother's name in the presence of this monster, and so I say: we have to try to get rid of it. We've done everything humanly possible to take care of it and put up with it; I think no one could reproach us in the slightest."

"She's right a thousand times over," the father said to himself. Still struggling to catch her breath, a wild look in her eyes, the mother began to cough hollowly into her hand.

The sister rushed to the mother and held her forehead. The father's thoughts seemed to have become clearer as a result of the sister's words;

he had sat up straight and was playing with his uniform cap among the dishes that still lay on the table from the boarder's supper, and from time to time he glanced over at Gregor, who remained motionless.

"We must try to get rid of it," said the sister, now only addressing the father, since the mother couldn't hear anything over her coughing. "It'll kill both of you, I can see that coming. When we all have to work as hard as we do, how can we stand this constant torment at home? At least I can't stand it anymore." And she burst out into such violent weeping that her tears flowed down onto her mother's face, where she mechanically wiped them away.

"My child," said the father compassionately and with remarkable comprehension, "but what are we supposed to do?"

The sister just shrugged her shoulders to show the helplessness that had now come over her during her crying fit, in contrast to her former self-confidence.

"If he understood us," said the father, half-questioningly; the sister, still sobbing, waved her hand vehemently to show how unthinkable it was.

"If he understood us," repeated the father, closing his eyes to absorb the sister's conviction that this was impossible, "then perhaps we might be able to come to some sort of agreement with him. But as it is —"

"He's got to go," cried the sister, "that's the only answer, father. You must just try to stop thinking that this is Gregor. The fact that we've believed it for so long is actually our true misfortune. But how can it be Gregor? If it were Gregor, he would long since have understood that it's impossible for people to live together with such a creature, and he would have gone away of his own free will. Then we wouldn't have a brother, but we could go on living and honor his memory. But instead this creature persecutes us, drives away the boarders, obviously wants to take over the entire apartment and let us sleep out in the street. Just look, father," she suddenly shrieked, "he's at it again!" And—in a state of panic that was totally incomprehensible to Gregor—the sister even abandoned her mother, literally bolting away from her chair as if she would rather sacrifice her mother than stay near Gregor, and she rushed behind her father, who got to his feet as well, alarmed at her behavior, and half raised his arms as if to protect her.

But Gregor hadn't the slightest intention of frightening anyone, least of all his sister. He had merely begun to turn himself around so as to return to his room, and that admittedly did attract attention, since in his feeble condition he had to use his head to achieve these difficult turns, raising it and bumping it against the floor several times. He paused and looked around. His good intentions seemed to have been recognized; it had only been a momentary alarm. Now they all watched him, silent and sad. His mother lay back in her chair, her legs stretched out and pressed together, her eyes almost shut from exhaustion; his father and sister were sitting side by side, his sister had placed her hand around her father's neck.

"Perhaps I'm allowed to turn around now," Gregor thought, and he resumed his work. He couldn't suppress his panting from the exertion and also had to stop and rest every once in awhile. Otherwise no one hurried him, it was all left entirely to him. When he had completed the turn, he started to crawl back in a straight line. He was astonished at the great distance separating him from his room and couldn't comprehend how in his weak condition he could have covered the same ground a short time ago almost without noticing it. So intent was he on crawling rapidly, he scarcely noticed that no word or outcry from the family was disturbing his progress. Only when he was already in the doorway did he turn his head, not completely, for he felt his neck stiffening, but enough to see that nothing had changed behind him, except that his sister had stood up. His final gaze fell on his mother, who was now sound asleep.

No sooner was he inside his room than the door was hurriedly slammed shut, firmly bolted, and locked. The sudden noise behind him frightened Gregor so much that his little legs buckled. It was his sister who had been in such a hurry. She had been standing there ready and waiting, then she had swiftly leaped forward, Gregor hadn't even heard her coming, and she had cried "At last!" to her parents as she turned the key in the lock.

"And now?" Gregor asked himself, and peered around in the darkness. He soon made the discovery that he couldn't move at all. It didn't surprise him; rather it seemed unnatural to him that until now he had actually been able to get around on those thin little legs. Otherwise he felt relatively comfortable. He had pains throughout his body, of course, but it seemed to him that they were gradually getting weaker and weaker and would eventually disappear completely. The rotten apple in his back and the inflamed area around it, completely covered over by soft dust, scarcely bothered him. His thoughts went back to his family with tenderness and love. His conviction that he must disappear was, if possible, even stronger than his sister's. He remained in this state of empty, peaceful meditation until the tower clock struck three in the morning. He was just conscious of the beginning of the dawn outside his window. Then his head sank down completely, involuntarily, and his last breath issued faintly from his nostrils.

Early in the morning when the cleaning woman arrived—from sheer energy and impatience she would slam all the doors so loudly, no matter how many times she'd been asked not to do so, that it was impossible to sleep peacefully anywhere in the apartment—she found nothing unusual at first during her customary brief visit to Gregor. She thought that he was deliberately lying motionless like that, acting insulted; she credited him with unlimited intelligence. Since she happened to be holding the long broom in her hand, she tried to tickle Gregor with it from the doorway. When this produced no response, she became annoyed and jabbed Gregor a little, and it was only when she had moved him from his place without his resistance that she began to take notice. When she quickly grasped the fact of the matter, she opened her eyes wide and gave a low whistle, but she didn't stay there long; instead she tore open the bedroom door and shouted at the top of her voice into the darkness, "Come and take a look; it's croaked; it's lying there, completely and totally croaked!"

The Samsa parents sat up in their marriage bed and had to overcome the shock that the cleaning woman had given them before they could finally grasp her message. Then Mr. and Mrs. Samsa quickly climbed out of bed, one from each side; Mr. Samsa wrapped the blanket around his shoulders, Mrs. Samsa came out only in her nightgown; in this way they entered Gregor's room. Meanwhile the living room door had also opened; Grete had been sleeping there since the boarders had moved in; she was fully dressed, as if she'd not slept at all, and her pale face seemed to confirm this. "Dead?" asked Mrs. Samsa, and looked up inquiringly at the cleaning woman, though she could have examined everything herself, and the situation was plain enough without her doing so. "I'll say!" replied the cleaning woman, and to prove it she pushed Gregor's corpse with her broom off to one side. Mrs. Samsa made a movement as if she wanted to hold back the broom, but she didn't do it. "Well," said Mr. Samsa, "now we can thank God." He crossed himself, and the three women followed his example. Grete, who never took her eyes off the corpse, said, "Just look how thin he was. After all, he hadn't been eating anything for so long. The food came out of his room again just the way it went in." As a matter of fact, Gregor's body was completely flat and dry; this was really evident now for the first time when he was no longer lifted up by his little legs and also when nothing else diverted their gaze.

"Come in with us, Grete, for a little while," said Mrs. Samsa with a melancholy smile, and Grete followed her parents into their bedroom, not without looking back at the corpse. The cleaning woman shut Gregor's door and opened his window wide. Although it was early in the morning, the fresh air held a touch of mildness. By now it was nearly the end of March.

The three boarders emerged from their room and looked around in astonishment for their breakfast; they had been forgotten. "Where is breakfast?" the middle one gruffly asked the cleaning woman. But she put her finger to her lips and hastily and silently beckoned them to come into Gregor's room. In they went and stood with their hands in the pockets of their somewhat shabby jackets in a circle around Gregor's corpse in the room that by now was filled with light.

Just then the bedroom door opened, and Mr. Samsa appeared in his uniform with his wife on one arm and his daughter on the other. They all looked as if they had been crying; from time to time Grete pressed her face against her father's sleeve.

"Leave my apartment at once!" said Mr. Samsa and pointed to the door without letting go of the women. "What do you mean?" asked the middle boarder, somewhat dismayed and with a sugary smile. The two others held their hands behind their backs and rubbed them together incessantly, as if in gleeful anticipation of a major quarrel that could only turn out in their favor. "I mean exactly what I say," answered Mr. Samsa, and he marched in a line with his two women companions toward the boarder. At first the boarder quietly stood still and looked at the floor, as if he were rearranging matters in his head. "Well, then, we'll go," he said, and suddenly overcome with humility he looked up at Mr. Samsa as if he were seeking new approval for this decision. Mr. Samsa merely nodded several times, staring at him hard. At that the boarder immediately took long strides into the hall; his two friends, who had been listening for awhile, their hands entirely still, now practically went hopping right after him, as if afraid that Mr. Samsa would reach the hall ahead of them and cut them off from their leader. In the hall, all three took their hats from the coat rack, drew their canes out of the umbrella stand, bowed silently and left the apartment. Impelled by a mistrust that proved to be entirely unfounded, Mr. Samsa and the two women stepped out onto the landing and, leaning over the banister, they watched the three boarders slowly but surely descend the long staircase, disappearing on each floor at a certain turn and then reappearing a few moments later; the lower they got, the more the Samsa family's interest in them dwindled, and when a butcher's boy proudly carrying a tray on his head swung past them on up the stairs, Mr. Samsa and the women left the banister and, as if relieved, all went back to the apartment.

They decided to spend this day resting and going for a walk; they not only deserved a break from their work, they also desperately needed it. And so they sat down at the table to write their letters of excuse, Mr. Samsa to the bank manager, Mrs. Samsa to her employer, and Grete to the store owner. While they were writing, the cleaning woman came in to announce that she was going because her morning work was finished. The three letter writers merely nodded at first without looking up, but as the cleaning woman still kept lingering, they all looked up irritably. "Well?" asked Mr. Samsa. The cleaning woman stood smiling in the doorway as if she had some great news for the family but would only tell it if they questioned her properly. The little ostrich feather sticking up almost straight on her hat, which had annoyed Mr. Samsa during all the time she had been working for them, was fluttering in all directions. "Well, what is it you really want?" asked Mrs. Samsa, for whom the cleaning woman still had the most respect. "Well," answered the cleaning woman, and she couldn't go on immediately for her own good natured chuckling, "well, you don't have to worry about getting rid of the thing next door. It's already been taken care of." Mrs. Samsa and Grete bent their heads down over their letters, as if they intended to resume writing; Mr. Samsa, who realized that the cleaning woman was now eager to start describing everything in detail, cut her short with an outstretched hand. But since she couldn't tell her story, she remembered that she was in a great hurry and cried out, obviously offended, "Goodbye, everyone," then whirled around wildly and left the apartment with a thunderous slamming of the door.

"She'll be fired tonight," said Mr. Samsa, but he received no reply from either his wife or his daughter, because the cleaning woman seemed to have disturbed the peace of mind they had just recently acquired. They got up, went over to the window, and stayed there, their arms around each other. Mr. Samsa turned toward them in his chair and watched them quietly for awhile. Then he called, "Oh, come on over here. Stop brooding over the past. And have a little consideration for me, too." The women obeyed him at once, rushed over to him, caressed him, and hurriedly finished their letters.

Then they all three left the apartment together, which they hadn't done in months, and took the trolley out to the open country on the outskirts of the city. The car, in which they were the only passengers, was flooded with warm sunshine. Leaning back comfortably in their seats, they discussed their prospects for the future and it turned out that, on closer inspection, these weren't bad at all, because all three had positions which—though they hadn't ever really asked one another about them in any detail—were thoroughly advantageous and especially promising for the future. The greatest immediate improvement in their situation would easily result, of course, from a change in apartments; now they would move to a smaller and cheaper apartment, but one better located and in general more practical than their present one, which Gregor had chosen. While they were talking in this way, it occurred almost simultaneously to both Mr. and Mrs. Samsa, as they watched their daughter's increasing liveliness, that despite all the recent cares that had made her cheeks pale, she had blossomed into a good looking and well-developed girl. Growing quieter and almost unconsciously communicating through glances, they thought it would soon be time, too, to find a good husband for her. And it was like a confirmation of their new dreams and good intentions when at the end of their ride, their daughter stood up first and stretched her young body.

[1915]

SHERWOOD ANDERSON   [1876–1941]

Death in the Woods

She was an old woman and lived on a farm near the town in which I lived. All country and small-town people have seen such old women, but no one knows much about them. Such an old woman comes into town driving an old worn-out horse or she comes afoot carrying a basket. She may own a few hens and have eggs to sell. She brings them in a basket and takes them to a grocer. There she trades them in. She gets some salt pork and some beans. Then she gets a pound or two of sugar and some flour.

Afterwards she goes to the butcher's and asks for some dog-meat. She may spend ten or fifteen cents, but when she does she asks for something. Formerly the butchers gave liver to anyone who wanted to carry it away. In our family we were always having it. Once one of my brothers got a whole cow's liver at the slaughterhouse near the fair grounds in our town. We had it until we were sick of it. It never cost a cent. I have hated the thought of it ever since.

The old farm woman got some liver and a soup-bone. She never visited with anyone, and as soon as she got what she wanted she lit out for home. It made quite a load for such an old body. No one gave her a lift. People drive right down a road and never notice an old woman like that.

There was such an old woman who used to come into town past our house one summer and fall when I was a young boy and was sick with what was called inflammatory rheumatism. She went home later carrying a heavy pack on her back. Two or three large gaunt-looking dogs followed at her heels.

The old woman was nothing special. She was one of the nameless ones that hardly anyone knows, but she got into my thoughts. I have just suddenly now, after all these years, remembered her and what happened. It is a story. Her name was Grimes, and she lived with her husband and son in a small unpainted house on the bank of a small creek four miles from town.

The husband and son were a tough lot. Although the son was but twenty-one, he had already served a term in jail. It was whispered about that the woman's husband stole horses and ran them off to some other county. Now and then, when a horse turned up missing, the man had

129

also disappeared. No one ever caught him. Once, when I was loafing at Tom Whitehead's livery-barn, the man came there and sat on the bench in front. Two or three other men were there, but no one spoke to him. He sat for a few minutes and then got up and went away. When he was leaving he turned around and stared at the men. There was a look of defiance in his eyes. "Well, I have tried to be friendly. You don't want to talk to me. It has been so wherever I have gone in this town. If, some day, one of your fine horses turns up missing, well, then what?" He did not say anything actually. "I'd like to bust one of you on the jaw," was about what his eyes said. I remember how the look in his eyes made me shiver.

The old man belonged to a family that had had money once. His name was Jake Grimes. It all comes back clearly now. His father, John Grimes, had owned a sawmill when the country was new, and had made money. Then he got to drinking and running after women. When he died there wasn't much left.

Jake blew in the rest. Pretty soon there wasn't any more lumber to cut and his land was nearly all gone.

He got his wife off a German farmer, for whom he went to work one June day in the wheat harvest. She was a young thing then and scared to death. You see, the farmer was up to something with the girl—she was, I think, a bound girl and his wife had her suspicions. She took it out on the girl when the man wasn't around. Then, when the wife had to go off to town for supplies, the farmer got after her. She told young Jake that nothing really ever happened, but he didn't know whether to believe it or not.

He got her pretty easy himself, the first time he was out with her. He wouldn't have married her if the German farmer hadn't tried to tell him where to get off. He got her to go riding with him in his buggy one night when he was threshing on the place, and then he came for her the next Sunday night.

She managed to get out of the house without her employer's seeing, but when she was getting into the buggy he showed up. It was almost dark, and he just popped up suddenly at the horse's head. He grabbed the horse by the bridle and Jake got out his buggy-whip.

They had it out all right! The German was a tough one. Maybe he didn't care whether his wife knew or not. Jake hit him over the face and shoulders with the buggy-whip, but the horse got to acting up and he had to get out.

Then the two men went for it. The girl didn't see it. The horse started to run away and went nearly a mile down the road before the girl got him stopped. Then she managed to tie him to a tree beside the road. (I wonder how I know all this. It must have stuck in my mind from small-town tales when I was a boy.) Jake found her there after he got through with the German. She was huddled up in the buggy seat, crying, scared to death. She told Jake a lot of stuff, how the German had tried to get her, how he chased her once into the barn, how another time, when they happened to be alone in the house together, he tore her dress open clear down the front. The German, she said, might have got her that time if he hadn't heard his old woman drive in at the gate. She had been off to town for supplies. Well, she would be putting the horse in the barn. The German managed to sneak off to the fields without his wife seeing. He told the girl he would kill her if she told. What could she do? She told a lie about ripping her dress in the barn when she was feeding the stock. I remember now that she was a bound girl and did not know where her father and mother were. Maybe she did not have any father. You know what I mean.

Such bound children were often enough cruelly treated. They were children who had no parents, slaves really. There were very few orphan homes then. They were legally bound into some home. It was a matter of pure luck how it came out.

II

She married Jake and had a son and daughter, but the daughter died.

Then she settled down to feed stock. That was her job. At the German's place she had cooked the food for the German and his wife. The wife was a strong woman with big hips and worked most of the time in the fields with her husband. She fed them and fed the cows in the barn, fed the pigs, the horses and the chickens. Every moment of every day, as a young girl, was spent feeding something.

Then she married Jake Grimes and he had to be fed. She was a slight thing, and when she had been married for three or four years, and after the two children were born, her slender shoulders became stooped.

Jake always had a lot of big dogs around the house, that stood near the unused sawmill near the creek. He was always trading horses when he wasn't stealing something and had a lot of poor bony ones about. Also he kept three or four pigs and a cow. They were all pastured in the few acres left of the Grimes place and Jake did little enough work.

He went into debt for a threshing outfit and ran it for several years, but it did not pay. People did not trust him. They were afraid he would steal the grain at night. He had to go a long way off to get work and it cost too much to get there. In the winter he hunted and cut a little firewood, to be sold in some nearby town. When the son grew up he was just like the father. They got drunk together. If there wasn't anything to eat in the house when they came home the old man gave his old woman a cut over the head. She had a few chickens of her own and had to kill one of them in a hurry. When they were all killed she wouldn't have any eggs to sell when she went to town, and then what would she do?

She had to scheme all her life about getting things fed, getting the pigs fed so they would grow fat and could be butchered in the fall. When they were butchered her husband took most of the meat off to town and sold it. If he did not do it first the boy did. They fought sometimes and when they fought the old woman stood aside trembling.

She had got the habit of silence anyway—that was fixed. Sometimes, when she began to look old—she wasn't forty yet—and when the husband and son were both off, trading horses or drinking or hunting or stealing, she went around the house and the barnyard muttering to herself.

How was she going to get everything fed?—that was her problem. The dogs had to be fed. There wasn't enough hay in the barn for the horses and the cow. If she didn't feed the chickens how could they lay eggs? Without eggs to sell how could she get things in town, things she had to have to keep the life of the farm going? Thank heaven, she did not have to feed her husband—in a certain way. That hadn't lasted long after their marriage and after the babies came. Where he went on his long trips she did not know. Sometimes he was gone from home for weeks, and after the boy grew up they went off together.

They left everything at home for her to manage and she had no money. She knew no one. No one ever talked to her in town. When it was winter she had to gather sticks of wood for her fire, had to try to keep the stock fed with very little grain.

The stock in the barn cried to her hungrily, the dogs followed her about. In the winter the hens laid few enough eggs. They huddled in the corners of the barn and she kept watching them. If a hen lays an egg in the barn in the winter and you do not find it, it freezes and breaks.

One day in winter the old woman went off to town with a few eggs and the dogs followed her. She did not get started until nearly three o'clock and the snow was heavy. She hadn't been feeling very well for several days and so she went muttering along, scantily clad, her shoulders stooped. She had an old grain bag in which she carried her eggs, tucked away down in the bottom. There weren't many of them, but in winter the price of eggs is up. She would get a little meat in exchange for the eggs, some salt pork, a little sugar, and some coffee perhaps. It might be the butcher would give her a piece of liver.

When she had got to town and was trading in her eggs the dogs lay by the door outside. She did pretty well, got the things she needed, more than she had hoped. Then she went to the butcher and he gave her some liver and some dog-meat.

It was the first time anyone had spoken to her in a friendly way for a long time. The butcher was alone in his shop when she came in and was annoyed by the thought of such a sick-looking old woman out on such a day. It was bitter cold and the snow, that had let up during the afternoon, was falling again. The butcher said something about her husband and her son, swore at them, and the old woman stared at him, a look of mild surprise in her eyes as he talked. He said that if either the husband or the son were going to get any of the liver or the heavy bones with scraps of meat hanging to them that he had put into the grain bag, he'd see him starve first.

Starve, eh? Well, things had to be fed. Men had to be fed, and the horses that weren't any good but maybe could be traded off, and the poor thin cow that hadn't given any milk for three months.

Horses, cows, pigs, dogs, men.

III

The old woman had to get back before darkness came if she could. The dogs followed at her heels, sniffing at the heavy grain bag she had fastened on her back. When she got to the edge of town she stopped by a fence and tied the bag on her back with a piece of rope she had carried in her dress-pocket for just that purpose. That was an easier way to carry it. Her arms ached. It was hard when she had to crawl over fences and once she fell over and landed in the snow. The dogs went frisking about. She had to struggle to get to her feet again, but she made it. The point of climbing over the fences was that there was a short cut over a hill and through a woods. She might have gone around by the road, but it was a mile farther that way. She was afraid she couldn't make it. And then, besides, the stock had to be fed. There was a little hay left and a little corn. Perhaps her husband and son would bring some home when they came. They had driven off in the only buggy the Grimes family had, a rickety thing, a rickety horse hitched to the buggy, two other rickety horses led by halters. They were going to trade horses, get a little money if they could. They might come home drunk. It would be well to have something in the house when they came back.

The son had an affair on with a woman at the county seat, fifteen miles away. She was a rough enough woman, a tough one. Once, in the summer, the son had brought her to the house. Both she and the son had been drinking. Jake Grimes was away and the son and his woman ordered the old woman about like a servant. She didn't mind much; she was used to it. Whatever happened she never said anything. That was her way of getting along. She had managed that way when she was a young girl at the German's and ever since she had married Jake. That time her son brought his woman to the house they stayed all night, sleeping together just as though they were married. It hadn't shocked the old woman, not much. She had got past being shocked early in life.

With the pack on her back she went painfully along across an open field, wading in the deep snow, and got into the woods.

There was a path, but it was hard to follow. Just beyond the top of the hill, where the woods was thickest, there was a small clearing. Had someone once thought of building a house there? The clearing was as large as a building lot in town, large enough for a house and a garden. The path ran along the side of the clearing, and when she got there the old woman sat down to rest at the foot of a tree.

It was a foolish thing to do. When she got herself placed, the pack against the tree's trunk, it was nice, but what about getting up again? She worried about that for a moment and then quietly closed her eyes.

She must have slept for a time. When you are about so cold you can't get any colder. The afternoon grew a little warmer and the snow came thicker than ever. Then after a time the weather cleared. The moon even came out.

There were four Grimes dogs that had followed Mrs. Grimes into town, all tall gaunt fellows. Such men as Jake Grimes and his son always keep just such dogs. They kick and abuse them, but they stay. The Grimes dogs, in order to keep from starving, had to do a lot of foraging for themselves, and they had been at it while the old woman slept with her back to the tree at the side of the clearing. They had been chasing rabbits in the woods and in adjoining fields and in their ranging had picked up three other farm dogs.

After a time all the dogs came back to the clearing. They were excited about something. Such nights, cold and clear and with a moon, do things to dogs. It may be that some old instinct, come down from the time when they were wolves and ranged the woods in packs on winter nights, comes back into them.

The dogs in the clearing, before the old woman, had caught two or three rabbits and their immediate hunger had been satisfied. They began to play, running in circles in the clearing. Round and round they ran, each dog's nose at the tail of the next dog. In the clearing, under the snow-laden trees and under the wintry moon they made a strange picture, running thus silently, in a circle their running had beaten in the soft snow. The dogs made no sound. They ran around and around in the circle.

It may have been that the old woman saw them doing that before she died. She may have awakened once or twice and looked at the strange sight with dim old eyes.

She wouldn't be very cold now, just drowsy. Life hangs on a long time. Perhaps the old woman was out of her head. She may have dreamed of her girlhood, at the German's, and before that, when she was a child and before her mother lit out and left her.

Her dreams couldn't have been very pleasant. Not many pleasant things had happened to her. Now and then one of the Grimes dogs left the running circle and came to stand before her. The dog thrust his face close to her face. His red tongue was hanging out.

The running of the dogs may have been a kind of death ceremony. It may have been that the primitive instinct of the wolf, having been aroused in the dogs by the night and the running, made them somehow afraid.

"Now we are no longer wolves. We are dogs, the servants of men. Keep alive, man! When man dies we become wolves again."

When one of the dogs came to where the old woman sat with her back against the tree and thrust his nose close to her face he seemed satisfied and went back to run with the pack. All the Grimes dogs did it at some time during the evening, before she died. I knew all about it afterward, when I grew to be a man, because once in a woods in Illinois, on another winter night, I saw a pack of dogs act just like that. The dogs were waiting for me to die as they had waited for the old woman that night when I was a child, but when it happened to me I was a young man and had no intention whatever of dying.

The old woman died softly and quietly. When she was dead and when one of the Grimes dogs had come to her and had found her dead all the dogs stopped running.

They gathered about her.

Well, she was dead now. She had fed the Grimes dogs when she was alive, what about now?

There was the pack on her back, the grain bag containing the piece of salt pork, the liver the butcher had given her, the dog-meat, the soup bones. The butcher in town, having been suddenly overcome with a feeling of pity, had loaded her grain bag heavily. It had been a big haul for the old woman.

It was a big haul for the dogs now.

IV

One of the Grimes dogs sprang suddenly out from among the others and began worrying the pack on the old woman's back. Had the dogs really been wolves that one would have been the leader of the pack. What he did, all the others did.

All of them sank their teeth into the grain bag the old woman had fastened with ropes to her back.

They dragged the old woman's body out into the open clearing. The worn-out dress was quickly torn from her shoulders. When she was found, a day or two later, the dress had been torn from her body clear to the hips, but the dogs had not touched her body. They had got the meat out of the grain bag, that was all. Her body was frozen stiff when it was found, and the shoulders were so narrow and the body so slight that in death it looked like the body of some charming young girl.

Such things happened in towns of the Middle West, on farms near town, when I was a boy. A hunter out after rabbits found the old woman's body and did not touch it. Something, the beaten round path in the little snow-covered clearing, the silence of the place, the place where the dogs had worried the body trying to pull the grain bag away or tear it open — something startled the man and he hurried off to town.

I was in Main Street with one of my brothers who was town newsboy and who was taking the afternoon papers to the stores. It was almost night.

The hunter came into a grocery and told his story. Then he went to a hardware shop and into a drugstore. Men began to gather on the sidewalks. Then they started out along the road to the place in the woods.

My brother should have gone on about his business of distributing papers but he didn't. Everyone was going to the woods. The undertaker went and the town marshal. Several men got on a dray and rode out to where the path left the road and went into the woods, but the horses weren't very sharply shod and slid about on the slippery roads. They made no better time than those of us who walked.

The town marshal was a large man whose leg had been injured in the Civil War. He carried a heavy cane and limped rapidly along the road. My brother and I followed at his heels, and as we went other men and boys joined the crowd.

It had grown dark by the time we got to where the old woman had left the road but the moon had come out. The marshal was thinking there might have been a murder. He kept asking the hunter questions. The hunter went along with his gun across his shoulders, a dog following at his heels. It isn't often a rabbit hunter has a chance to be so conspicuous. He was taking full advantage of it, leading the procession with the town marshal. "I didn't see any wounds. She was a beautiful young girl. Her face was buried in the snow. No, I didn't know her." As a matter of fact, the hunter had not looked closely at the body. He had been frightened. She might have been murdered and someone might spring out from behind a tree and murder him. In a woods, in the late afternoon, when the trees are all bare and there is white snow on the ground, when all is silent, something creepy steals over the mind and body. If something strange or uncanny has happened in the neighborhood all you think about is getting away from there as fast as you can.

The crowd of men and boys had got to where the old woman had crossed the field and went, following the marshal and the hunter, up the slight incline and into the woods.

My brother and I were silent. He had his bundle of papers in a bag slung across his shoulder. When he got back to town he would have to go on distributing his papers before he went home to supper. If I went along, as he had no doubt already determined I should, we would both be late. Either mother or our older sister would have to warm our supper.

Well, we would have something to tell. A boy did not get such a chance very often. It was lucky we just happened to go into the grocery when the hunter came in. The hunter was a country fellow. Neither of us had ever seen him before.

Now the crowd of men and boys had got to the clearing. Darkness comes quickly on such winter nights, but the full moon made everything clear. My brother and I stood near the tree, beneath which the old woman had died.

She did not look old, lying there in that light, frozen and still. One of the men turned her over in the snow and I saw everything. My body trembled with some strange mystical feeling and so did my brother's. It might have been the cold.

Neither of us had ever seen a woman's body before. It may have been the snow, clinging to the frozen flesh, that made it look so white and lovely, so like marble. No woman had come with the party from town; but one of the men, he was the town blacksmith, took off his overcoat and spread it over her. Then he gathered her into his arms and started off to town, all the others following silently. At that time no one knew who she was.

V

I had seen everything, had seen the oval in the snow, like a miniature race track, where the dogs had run, had seen how the men were mystified, had seen the white bare young-looking shoulders, had heard the whispered comments of the men.

The men were simply mystified. They took the body to the undertaker's, and when the blacksmith, the hunter, the marshal and several others had got inside they closed the door. If father had been there perhaps he could have got in, but we boys couldn't.

I went with my brother to distribute the rest of his papers and when we got home it was my brother who told the story.

I kept silent and went to bed early. It may have been I was not satisfied with the way he told it.

Later, in the town, I must have heard other fragments of the old woman's story. She was recognized the next day and there was an investigation.

The husband and son were found somewhere and brought to town and there was an attempt to connect them with the woman's death, but it did not work. They had perfect enough alibis.

However, the town was against them. They had to get out. Where they went I never heard.

I remember only the picture there in the forest, the men standing about, the naked girlish-looking figure, face down in the snow, the tracks made by the running dogs and the clear cold winter sky above. White fragments of clouds were drifting across the sky. They went racing across the little open space among the trees.

The scene in the forest had become for me, without my knowing it, the foundation for the real story I am now trying to tell. The fragments, you see, had to be picked up slowly, long afterwards.

Things happened. When I was a young man I worked on the farm of a German. The hired-girl was afraid of her employer. The farmer's wife hated her.

I saw things at the place. Once later, I had a half-uncanny, mystical adventure with dogs in an Illinois forest on a clear, moonlit winter night. When I was a schoolboy, and on a summer day, I went with a boy friend out along a creek some miles from town and came to the house where the old woman had lived. No one had lived in the house since her death. The doors were broken from the hinges; the window lights were all broken. As the boy and I stood in the road outside, two dogs, just roving farm dogs no doubt, came running around the corner of the house. The dogs were tall, gaunt fellows and came down to the fence and glared through at us, standing in the road.

The whole thing, the story of the old woman's death, was to me as I grew older like music heard from far off. The notes had to be picked up slowly one at a time. Something had to be understood.

The woman who died was one destined to feed animal life. Anyway, that is all she ever did. She was feeding animal life before she was born, as a child, as a young woman working on the farm of the German, after she married, when she grew old and when she died. She fed animal life in cows, in chickens, in pigs, in horses, in dogs, in men. Her daughter had died in childhood and with her one son she had no articulate relations. On the night when she died she was hurrying homeward, bearing on her body food for animal life.

She died in the clearing in the woods and even after her death continued feeding animal life.

You see it is likely that, when my brother told the story, that night when we got home and my mother and sister sat listening, I did not think he got the point. He was too young and so was I. A thing so complete has its own beauty.

I shall not try to emphasize the point. I am only explaining why I was dissatisfied then and have been ever since. I speak of that only that you may understand why I have been impelled to try to tell the simple story over again.

[1933]

ZORA NEALE HURSTON   [1891–1960]

Sweat

It was eleven o'clock of a Spring night in Florida. It was Sunday. Any other night, Delia Jones would have been in bed for two hours by this time. But she was a washwoman, and Monday morning meant a great deal to her. So she collected the soiled clothes on Saturday when she returned the clean things. Sunday night after church, she sorted them and put the white things to soak. It saved her almost a half day's start. A great hamper in the bedroom held the clothes that she brought home. It was so much neater than a number of bundles lying around.

She squatted in the kitchen floor beside the great pile of clothes, sorting them into small heaps according to color, and humming a song in a mournful key, but wondering through it all where Sykes, her husband, had gone with her horse and buckboard.

Just then something long, round, limp, and black fell upon her shoulders and slithered to the floor beside her. A great terror took hold of her. It softened her knees and dried her mouth so that it was a full minute before she could cry out or move. Then she saw that it was the big bull whip her husband liked to carry when he drove.

She lifted her eyes to the door and saw him standing there bent over with laughter at her fright. She screamed at him.

"Sykes, what you throw dat whip on me like dat? You know it would skeer me—looks just like a snake, an' you knows how skeered Ah is of snakes."

"Course Ah knowed it! That's how come Ah done it." He slapped his leg with his hand and almost rolled on the ground in his mirth. "If you such a big fool dat you got to have a fit over a earth worm or a string, Ah don't keer how bad Ah skeer you."

"You aint got no business doing it. Gawd knows it's a sin. Some day Ah'm gointuh drop dead from some of yo' foolishness. 'Nother thing, where you been wid mah rig? Ah feeds dat pony. He aint fuh you to be drivin' wid no bull whip."

"You sho is one aggravatin' nigger woman!" he declared and stepped into the room. She resumed her work and did not answer him at once. "Ah done tole you time and again to keep them white folks' clothes outa dis house."

He picked up the whip and glared down at her. Delia went on with her work. She went out into the yard and returned with a galvanized tub and sat it on the washbench. She saw that Sykes had kicked all of the clothes together again, and now stood in her way truculently, his whole manner hoping, *praying*, for an argument. But she walked calmly around him and commenced to re-sort the things.

"Next time, Ah'm gointer kick 'em outdoors," he threatened as he struck a match along the leg of his corduroy breeches.

Delia never looked up from her work, and her thin, stooped shoulders sagged further.

"Ah aint for no fuss t'night, Sykes. Ah just come from taking sacrament at the church house."

He snorted scornfully. "Yeah, you just come from de church house on a Sunday night, but heah you is gone to work on them clothes. You ain't nothing but a hypocrite. One of them amen-corner Christians—sing, whoop, and shout, then come home and wash white folks clothes on the Sabbath."

He stepped roughly upon the whitest pile of things, kicking them helter-skelter as he crossed the room. His wife gave a little scream of dismay, and quickly gathered them together again.

"Sykes, you quit grindin' dirt into these clothes! How can Ah git through by Sat'day if Ah don't start on Sunday?"

"Ah don't keer if you never git through. Anyhow, Ah done promised Gawd and a couple of other men, Ah aint gointer have it in mah house. Don't gimme no lip neither, else Ah'll throw 'em out and put mah fist up side yo' head to boot."

Delia's habitual meekness seemed to slip from her shoulders like a blown scarf. She was on her feet; her poor little body, her bare knuckly hands bravely defying the strapping hulk before her.

"Looka heah, Sykes, you done gone too fur. Ah been married to you fur fifteen years, and Ah been takin' in washin' fur fifteen years. Sweat, sweat, sweat! Work and sweat, cry and sweat, pray and sweat!"

"What's that got to do with me?" he asked brutally.

"What's it got to do with you, Sykes? Mah tub of suds is filled yo' belly with vittles more times than yo' hands is filled it. Mah sweat is done paid for this house and Ah reckon Ah kin keep on sweatin' in it."

She seized the iron skillet from the stove and struck a defensive pose, which act surprised him greatly, coming from her. It cowed him and he did not strike her as he usually did.

"Naw you won't," she panted, "that ole snaggle-toothed black woman you runnin' with aint comin' heah to pile up on *mah* sweat and blood. You aint paid for nothin' on this place, and Ah'm gointer stay right heah till Ah'm toted out foot foremost."

"Well, you better quit gittin' me riled up, else they'll be totin' you out sooner than you expect. Ah'm so tired of you Ah don't know whut to do. Gawd! how Ah hates skinny wimmen!"

A little awed by this new Delia, he sidled out of the door and slammed the back gate after him. He did not say where he had gone, but she knew too well. She knew very well that he would not return until nearly daybreak also. Her work over, she went on to bed but not to sleep at once. Things had come to a pretty pass!

She lay awake, gazing upon the debris that cluttered their matrimonial trail. Not an image left standing along the way. Anything like flowers had long ago been drowned in the salty stream that had been pressed from her heart. Her tears, her sweat, her blood. She had brought love to the union and he had brought a longing after the flesh. Two months after the wedding, he had given her the first brutal beating. She had the memory of his numerous trips to Orlando with all of his wages when he had returned to her penniless, even before the first year had passed. She was young and soft then, but now she thought of her knotty, muscled limbs, her harsh knuckly hands, and drew herself up into an unhappy little ball in the middle of the big feather bed. Too late now to hope for love, even if it were not Bertha it would be someone else. This case differed from the others only in that she was bolder than the others. Too late for everything except her little home. She had built it for her old days, and planted one by one the trees and flowers there. It was lovely to her, lovely.

Somehow, before sleep came, she found herself saying aloud: "Oh well, whatever goes over the Devil's back, is got to come under his belly. Sometime or ruther, Sykes, like everybody else, is gointer reap his sowing." After that she was able to build a spiritual earthworks against her husband. His shells could no longer reach her. *Amen.* She went to sleep and slept until he announced his presence in bed by kicking her feet and rudely snatching the cover away.

"Gimme some kivah heah, an' git yo' damn foots over on yo' own side! Ah oughter mash you in yo' mouf fuh drawing dat skillet on me."

Delia went clear to the rail without answering him. A triumphant indifference to all that he was or did.

The week was as full of work for Delia as all other weeks, and Saturday found her behind her little pony, collecting and delivering clothes.

It was a hot, hot day near the end of July. The village men on Joe Clarke's porch even chewed cane listlessly. They did not hurl the cane-knots as usual. They let them dribble over the edge of the porch. Even conversation had collapsed under the heat.

"Heah come Delia Jones," Jim Merchant said, as the shaggy pony came 'round the bend of the road toward them. The rusty buckboard was heaped with baskets of crisp, clean laundry.

"Yep," Joe Lindsay agreed. "Hot or col', rain or shine, jes ez reg'lar ez de weeks roll roun' Delia carries 'em an' fetches 'em on Sat'day."

"She better if she wanter eat," said Moss. "Sykes Jones aint wuth de shot an' powder hit would tek tuh kill 'em. Not to *huh* he aint."

"He sho' aint," Walter Thomas chimed in. "It's too bad, too, cause she wuz a right pritty li'l trick when he got huh. Ah'd uh mah'ied huh mah-seff if he hadnter beat me to it."

Delia nodded briefly at the men as she drove past.

"Too much knockin' will ruin *any* 'oman. He done beat huh 'nough tuh kill three women, let 'lone change they looks," said Elijah Moseley. "How Sykes kin stommuck dat big black greasy Mogul he's layin' roun' wid, gits me. Ah swear dat eight-rock couldn't kiss a sardine can Ah done thowed out de back do' 'way las' yeah."

"Aw, she's fat, thass how come. He's allus been crazy 'bout fat women," put in Merchant. "He'd a' been tied up wid one long time ago if he could a' found one tuh have him. Did Ah tell yuh 'bout im come sidlin' roun' *mah* wife—bringin' her a basket uh pee-cans outa his yard fuh a present? Yessir, mah wife! She tol' him tuh take 'em right straight back home, cause Delia works so hard ovah dat washtub she reckon eveything on de place taste lak sweat an' soapsuds. Ah jus' wisht Ah'd a' caught 'im 'roun' dere! Ah'd a' made his hips ketch on fiah down dat shell road."

"Ah know he done it, too. Ah sees 'im grinnin' at every 'oman dat passes," Walter Thomas said. "But even so, he useter eat some mighty big hunks uh humble pie tuh git dat lil' 'oman he got. She wuz ez pritty ez a speckled pup! Dat wuz fifteen yeahs ago. He useter be so skeered uh losin' huh, she could make him do some parts of a husband's duty. Dey never wuz de same in de mind."

"There oughter be a law about him," said Lindsay. "He aint fit tuh carry guts tuh a bear."

Clarke spoke for the first time. "Taint no law on earth dat kin make a man be decent if it aint in 'im. There's plenty men dat takes a wife lak dey do a joint uh sugar-cane. It's round, juicy an' sweet when dey gits it. But dey squeeze an' grind, squeeze an' grind an' wring tell dey wring every drop uh pleasure dat's in 'em out. When dey's satisfied dat dey is wrung dry, dey treats 'em jes lak dey do a cane-chew. Dey throws 'em away. Dey knows whut dey is doin' while dey is at it, an' hates theirselves fuh it but

they keeps on hangin' after huh tell she's empty. Den dey hates huh fuh
bein' a cane-chew an' in de way."

"We oughter take Sykes an' dat stray 'oman uh his'n down in Lake
Howell swamp an' lay on de rawhide till they cain't say 'Lawd a' mussy.'
He allus wuz uh ovahbearin' niggah, but since dat white 'oman from up
north done teached 'im how to run a automobile, he done got too biggety
to live—an' we oughter kill 'im," Old Man Anderson advised.

A grunt of approval went around the porch. But the heat was melting
their civic virtue and Elijah Moseley began to bait Joe Clarke.

"Come on, Joe, git a melon outa dere an' slice it up for yo' customers.
We'se all sufferin' wid de heat. De bear's done got *me*!"

"Thass right, Joe, a watermelon is jes' whut Ah needs tuh cure de
eppizudicks." Walter Thomas joined forces with Moseley. "Come on dere,
Joe. We all is steady customers an' you aint set us up in a long time. Ah
chooses dat long, bowlegged Floridy favorite."

"A god, an' be dough. You all gimme twenty cents and slice away,"
Clarke retorted. "Ah needs a col' slice m'self. Heah, everybody chip in.
Ah'll lend y'all mah meat knife."

The money was quickly subscribed and the huge melon brought forth.
At that moment, Sykes and Bertha arrived. A determined silence fell on
the porch and the melon was put away again.

Merchant snapped down the blade of his jack-knife and moved toward
the store door.

"Come on in, Joe, an' gimme a slab uh sow belly an' uh pound uh
coffee—almost fuhgot 'twas Sat'day. Got to git on home." Most of the
men left also.

Just then Delia drove past on her way home, as Sykes was ordering
magnificently for Bertha. It pleased him for Delia to see.

"Git whutsoever yo' heart desires, Honey. Wait a minute, Joe. Give huh
two botles uh strawberry soda-water, uh quart uh parched ground-peas,
an a block uh chewin' gum."

With all this they left the store, with Sykes reminding Bertha that this
was his town and she could have it if she wanted it.

The men returned soon after they left, and held their watermelon feast.

"Where did Sykes Jones git dat 'oman from nohow?" Lindsay asked.

"Ovah Apopka. Guess dey musta been cleanin' out de town when she
lef'. She don't look lak a thing but a hunk uh liver wid hair on it."

"Well, she sho' kin squall," Dave Carter contributed. "When she gits
ready tuh laff, she jes' opens huh mouf an' latches it back tuh de las' notch.
No ole grandpa alligator down in Lake Bell aint got nothin' on huh."

Bertha had been in town three months now. Sykes was still paying her
room rent at Della Lewis'—the only house in town that would have

taken her in. Sykes took her frequently to Winter Park to "stomps." He still assured her that he was the swellest man in the state.

"Sho' you kin have dat lil' ole house soon's Ah kin git dat 'oman outa dere. Everything b'longs tuh me an' you sho' kin have it. Ah sho' 'bominates uh skinny 'oman. Lawdy, you sho' is got one portly shape on you! You kin git *anything* you wants. Dis is *mah* town an' you sho' kin have it."

Delia's work-worn knees crawled over the earth in Gethsemane and up the rocks of Calvary many, many times during these months. She avoided the villagers and meeting places in her efforts to be blind and deaf. But Bertha nullified this to a degree, by coming to Delia's house to call Sykes out to her at the gate.

Delia and Sykes fought all the time now with no peaceful interludes. They slept and ate in silence. Two or three times Delia had attempted a timid friendliness, but she was repulsed each time. It was plain that the breaches must remain agape.

The sun had burned July to August. The heat streamed down like a million hot arrows, smiting all things living upon the earth. Grass withered, leaves browned, snakes went blind in shedding, and men and dogs went mad. Dog days!

Delia came home one day and found Sykes there before her. She wondered, but started to go on into the house without speaking, even though he was standing in the kitchen door and she must either stoop under his arm or ask him to move. He made no room for her. She noticed a soap box beside the steps, but paid no particular attention to it, knowing that he must have brought it there. As she was stooping to pass under his outstretched arm, he suddenly pushed her backward, laughingly.

"Look in de box dere Delia, Ah done brung yuh somethin'!"

She nearly fell upon the box in her stumbling, and when she saw what it held, she all but fainted outright.

"Sykes! Sykes, mah Gawd! You take dat rattlesnake 'way from heah! You *gottuh*. Oh, Jesus, have mussy!"

"Ah aint gut tuh do nothin' uh de kin'—fact is Ah aint got tuh do nothin' but die. Taint no use uh you puttin' on airs makin' out lak you skeered uh dat snake—he's gointer stay right heah tell he die. He wouldn't bite me cause Ah knows how tuh handle 'im. Nohow he wouldn't risk breakin' out his fangs 'gin yo' skinny laigs."

"Naw, now Sykes, don't keep dat thing 'roun' heah tuh skeer me tuh death. You knows Ah'm even feared uh earth worms. Thass de biggest snake Ah evah did see. Kill 'im Sykes, please."

"Doan ast me tuh do nothin' fuh yuh. Goin' 'roun' tryin' tuh be so damn astorperious. Naw, Ah aint gonna kill it. Ah think uh damn sight mo' uh him dan you! Dat's a nice snake an' anybody doan lak 'im kin jes' hit de grit."

The village soon heard that Sykes had the snake, and came to see and ask questions.

"How de hen-fire did you ketch dat six-foot rattler, Sykes?" Thomas asked.

"He's full uh frogs so he caint hardly move, thass how Ah eased up on 'm. But Ah'm a snake charmer an' knows how tuh handle 'em. Shux, dat aint nothin'. Ah could ketch one eve'y day if Ah so wanted tuh."

"Whut he needs is a heavy hick'ry club leaned real heavy on his head. Dat's de bes 'way tuh charm a rattlesnake."

"Naw, Walt, y'all jes' don't understand dese diamon' backs lak Ah do," said Sykes in a superior tone of voice.

The village agreed with Walter, but the snake stayed on. His box remained by the kitchen door with its screen wire covering. Two or three days later it had digested its meal of frogs and literally came to life. It rattled at every movement in the kitchen or the yard. One day as Delia came down the kitchen steps she saw his chalky-white fangs curved like scimitars hung in the wire meshes. This time she did not run away with averted eyes as usual. She stood for a long time in the doorway in a red fury that grew bloodier for every second that she regarded the creature that was her torment.

That night she broached the subject as soon as Sykes sat down to the table.

"Sykes, Ah wants you tuh take dat snake 'way fum heah. You done starved me an' Ah put up widcher, you done beat me an Ah took dat, but you done kilt all mah insides bringin' dat varmint heah."

Sykes poured out a saucer full of coffee and drank it deliberately before he answered her.

"A whole lot Ah keer 'bout how you feels inside uh out. Dat snake aint goin' no damn wheah till Ah gits ready fuh 'im tuh go. So fur as beatin' is concerned, yuh aint took near all dat you gointer take ef yuh stay 'roun' me."

Delia pushed back her plate and got up from the table. "Ah hates you, Sykes," she said calmly. "Ah hates you tuh de same degree dat Ah useter love yuh. Ah done took an' took till mah belly is full up tuh mah neck. Dat's de reason Ah got mah letter fum de church an' moved mah membership tuh Woodbridge—so Ah don't haftuh take no sacrament wid yuh. Ah don't wantuh see yuh 'roun' me a-tall. Lay 'roun' wid dat 'oman all yuh wants tuh, but gwan 'way fum me an' mah house. Ah hates yuh lak uh suck-egg dog."

Sykes almost let the huge wad of corn bread and collard greens he was chewing fall out of his mouth in amazement. He had a hard time whipping himself up to the proper fury to try to answer Delia.

"Well, Ah'm glad you does hate me. Ah'm sho' tiahed uh you hangin' ontuh me. Ah don't want yuh. Look at yuh stringey ole neck! Yo' rawbony laigs an' arms is enough tuh cut uh man tuh death. You looks jes' lak de devvul's doll-baby tuh *me*. You cain't hate me no worse dan Ah hates you. Ah been hatin' *you* fuh years."

"Yo' ole black hide don't look lak nothin' tuh me, but uh passed uh wrinkled up rubber, wid yo' big ole yeahs flappin' on each side lak uh paih uh buzzard wings. Don't think Ah'm gointuh be run 'way fum mah house neither. Ah'm goin' tuh de white folks bout *you*, mah young man, de very nex' time you lay yo' han's on me. Mah cup is done run ovah."
Delia said this with no signs of fear and Sykes departed from the house, threatening her, but made not the slightest move to carry out any of them.

That night he did not return at all, and the next day being Sunday, Delia was glad that she did not have to quarrel before she hitched up her pony and drove the four miles to Woodbridge.

She stayed to the night service—"love feast"—which was very warm and full of spirit. In the emotional winds her domestic trials were borne far and wide so that she sang as she drove homeward,

> Jurden water, black an' col'
> Chills de body, not de soul
> An' Ah wantah cross Jurden in uh calm time.

She came from the barn to the kitchen door and stopped.

"Whut's de mattah, ol' satan, you aint kickin' up yo' racket?" She addressed the snake's box. Complete silence. She went on into the house with a new hope in its birth struggles. Perhaps her threat to go to the white folks had frightened Sykes! Perhaps he was sorry! Fifteen years of misery and suppression had brought Delia to the place where she would hope *anything* that looked towards a way over or through her wall of inhibitions.

She felt in the match safe behind the stove at once for a match. There was only one there.

"Dat niggah wouldn't fetch nothin' heah tuh save his rotten neck, but he kin run thew whut Ah brings quick enough. Now he done toted off nigh on tuh haff uh box uh matches. He done had dat 'oman heah in mah house, too."

Nobody but a woman could tell how she knew this even before she struck the match. But she did and it put her into a new fury.

Presently she brought in the tubs to put the white things to soak. This time she decided she need not bring the hamper out of the bedroom; she would go in there and do the sorting. She picked up the pot-bellied lamp and went in. The room was small and the hamper stood hard by the foot

of the white iron bed. She could sit and reach through the bedposts—
resting as she worked.

"Ah wantah cross Jurden in uh calm time." She was singing again. The
mood of the "love feast" had returned. She threw back the lid of the basket almost gaily. Then, moved by both horror and terror, she sprung back
toward the door. *There lay the snake in the basket!* He moved sluggishly at
first, but even as she turned round and round, jumped up and down in an
insanity of fear, he began to stir vigorously. She saw him pouring his awful beauty from the basket upon the bed, then she seized the lamp and
ran as fast as she could to the kitchen. The wind from the open door blew
out the light and the darkness added to her terror. She sped to the darkness of the yard, slamming the door after her before she thought to set
down the lamp. She did not feel safe even on the ground, so she climbed
up in the hay barn.

There for an hour or more she lay sprawled upon the hay a gibbering
wreck.

Finally she grew quiet, and after that, coherent thought. With this,
stalked through her a cold, bloody rage. Hours of this. A period of introspection, a space of retrospection, then a mixture of both. Out of this an
awful calm.

"Well, Ah done de bes' Ah could. If things aint right, Gawd knows taint
mah fault."

She went to sleep—a twitchy sleep—and woke up to a faint gray sky.
There was a loud hollow sound below. She peered out. Sykes was at the
wood-pile, demolishing a wire-covered box.

He hurried to the kitchen door, but hung outside there some minutes
before he entered, and stood some minutes more inside before he closed
it after him.

The gray in the sky was spreading. Delia descended without fear now,
and crouched beneath the low bedroom window. The drawn shade shut
out the dawn, shut in the night. But the thin walls held back no sound.

"Dat ol' scratch is woke up now!" She mused at the tremendous whirr
inside, which every woodsman knows, is one of the sound illusions. The
rattler is a ventriloquist. His whirr sounds to the right, to the left, straight
ahead, behind, close under foot—everywhere but where it is. Woe to him
who guesses wrong unless he is prepared to hold up his end of the argument! Sometimes he strikes without rattling at all.

Inside, Sykes heard nothing until he knocked a pot lid off the stove
while trying to reach the match safe in the dark. He had emptied his
pockets at Bertha's.

The snake seemed to wake up under the stove and Sykes made a quick
leap into the bedroom. In spite of the gin he had had, his head was clearing now.

"Mah Gawd!" he chattered, "ef Ah could on'y strack uh light!"

The rattling ceased for a moment as he stood paralyzed. He waited. It seemed that the snake waited also.

"Oh fuh de light! Ah thought he'd be too sick"—Sykes was muttering to himself when the whirr began again, closer, right underfoot this time. Long before this, Sykes' ability to think had been flattened down to primitive instinct and he leaped—onto the bed.

Outside Delia hears a cry that might have come from a maddened chimpanzee, a stricken gorilla. All the terror, all the horror, all the rage that man possibly could express, without a recognizable human sound.

A tremendous stir inside there, another series of animal screams, the intermittent whirr of the reptile. The shade torn violently down from the window, letting in the red dawn, a huge brown hand seizing the window stick, great dull blows upon the wooden floor punctuating the gibberish of sound long after the rattle of the snake had abruptly subsided. All this Delia could see and hear from her place beneath the window, and it made her ill. She crept over to the four-o'clocks and stretched herself on the cool earth to recover.

She lay there. "Delia, Delia!" She could hear Sykes calling in a most despairing tone as one who expected no answer. The sun crept on up, and he called. Delia could not move—her legs were gone flabby. She never moved, he called, and the sun kept rising.

"Mah Gawd!" she heard him moan. "Mah Gawd fum Heben!" She heard him stumbling about and got up from her flower-bed. The sun was growing warm. As she approached the door she heard him call out hopefully, "Delia, is dat you Ah heah?"

She saw him on his hands and knees as soon as she reached the door. He crept an inch or two toward her—all that he was able, and she saw his horribly swollen neck and his one open eye shining with hope. A surge of pity too strong to support bore her away from that eye that must, could not, fail to see the tubs. He would see the lamp. Orlando with its doctors was too far. She could scarcely reach the Chinaberry tree, where she waited in the growing heat while inside she knew the cold river was creeping up and up to extinguish that eye which must know by now that she knew.

[1926]

F. SCOTT FITZGERALD [1896–1940]

Winter Dreams

I

Some of the caddies were poor as sin and lived in one-room houses with a neurasthenic cow in the front yard, but Dexter Green's father owned the second best grocery-store in Black Bear—the best one was "The Hub," patronized by the wealthy people from Sherry Island—and Dexter caddied only for pocket-money.

In the fall when the days became crisp and gray, and the long Minnesota winter shut down like the white lid of a box, Dexter's skis moved over the snow that hid the fairways of the golf course. At these times the country gave him a feeling of profound melancholy—it offended him that the links should lie in enforced fallowness, haunted by ragged sparrows for the long season. It was dreary, too, that on the tees where the gay colors fluttered in summer there were now only the desolate sandboxes knee-deep in crusted ice. When he crossed the hills the wind blew cold as misery, and if the sun was out he tramped with his eyes squinted up against the hard dimensionless glare.

In April the winter ceased abruptly. The snow ran down into Black Bear Lake scarcely tarrying for the early golfers to brave the season with red and black balls. Without elation, without an interval of moist glory, the cold was gone.

Dexter knew that there was something dismal about this Northern spring, just as he knew there was something gorgeous about the fall. Fall made him clinch his hands and tremble and repeat idiotic sentences to himself, and make brisk abrupt gestures of command to imaginary audiences and armies. October filled him with hope which November raised to a sort of ecstatic triumph, and in this mood the fleeting brilliant impressions of the summer at Sherry Island were ready grist to his mill. He became a golf champion and defeated Mr. T. A. Hedrick in a marvellous match played a hundred times over the fairways of his imagination, a match each detail of which he changed about untiringly—sometimes he won with almost laughable ease, sometimes he came up magnificently from behind. Again, stepping from a Pierce-Arrow automobile, like Mr. Mortimer Jones, he strolled frigidly into the lounge of the Sherry

Island Golf Club—or perhaps, surrounded by an admiring crowd, he gave an exhibition of fancy diving from the spring-board of the club raft. . . . Among those who watched him in open-mouthed wonder was Mr. Mortimer Jones.

And one day it came to pass that Mr. Jones—himself and not his ghost—came up to Dexter with tears in his eyes and said that Dexter was the——best caddy in the club, and wouldn't he decide not to quit if Mr. Jones made it worth his while, because every other——caddy in the club lost one ball a hole for him—regularly——

"No, sir," said Dexter decisively, "I don't want to caddy any more." Then, after a pause: "I'm too old."

"You're not more than fourteen. Why the devil did you decide just this morning that you wanted to quit? You promised that next week you'd go over to the State tournament with me."

"I decided I was too old."

Dexter handed in his "A Class" badge, collected what money was due him from the caddy master, and walked home to Black Bear Village.

"The best——caddy I ever saw," shouted Mr. Mortimer Jones over a drink that afternoon. "Never lost a ball! Willing! Intelligent! Quiet! Honest! Grateful!"

The little girl who had done this was eleven—beautifully ugly as little girls are apt to be who are destined after a few years to be inexpressibly lovely and bring no end of misery to a great number of men. The spark, however, was perceptible. There was a general ungodliness in the way her lips twisted down at the corners when she smiled, and in the—Heaven help us!—in the almost passionate quality of her eyes. Vitality is born early in such women. It was utterly in evidence now, shining through her thin frame in a sort of glow.

She had come eagerly out on to the course at nine o'clock with a white linen nurse and five small new golf-clubs in a white canvas bag which the nurse was carrying. When Dexter first saw her she was standing by the caddy house, rather ill at ease and trying to conceal the fact by engaging her nurse in an obviously unnatural conversation graced by startling and irrelevant grimaces from herself.

"Well, it's certainly a nice day, Hilda," Dexter heard her say. She drew down the corners of her mouth, smiled, and glanced furtively around, her eyes in transit falling for an instant on Dexter.

Then to the nurse:

"Well, I guess there aren't very many people out here this morning, are there?"

The smile again—radiant, blatantly artificial—convincing.

"I don't know what we're supposed to do now," said the nurse, looking nowhere in particular.

"Oh, that's all right. I'll fix it up."

Dexter stood perfectly still, his mouth slightly ajar. He knew that if he moved forward a step his stare would be in her line of vision—if he moved backward he would lose his full view of her face. For a moment he had not realized how young she was. Now he remembered having seen her several times the year before—in bloomers.

Suddenly, involuntarily, he laughed, a short abrupt laugh—then, startled by himself, he turned and began to walk quickly away.

"Boy!"

Dexter stopped.

"Boy——"

Beyond question he was addressed. Not only that, but he was treated to that absurd smile, that preposterous smile—the memory of which at least a dozen men were to carry into middle age.

"Boy, do you know where the golf teacher is?"

"He's giving a lesson."

"Well, do you know where the caddy-master is?"

"He isn't here yet this morning."

"Oh." For a moment this baffled her. She stood alternately on her right and left foot.

"We'd like to get a caddy," said the nurse. "Mrs. Mortimer Jones sent us out to play golf, and we don't know how without we get a caddy."

Here she was stopped by an ominous glance from Miss Jones, followed immediately by the smile.

"There aren't any caddies here except me," said Dexter to the nurse, "and I got to stay here in charge until the caddy-master gets here."

"Oh."

Miss Jones and her retinue now withdrew, and at a proper distance from Dexter became involved in a heated conversation, which was concluded by Miss Jones taking one of the clubs and hitting it on the ground with violence. For further emphasis she raised it again and was about to bring it down smartly upon the nurse's bosom, when the nurse seized the club and twisted it from her hands.

"You damn little mean old *thing*!" cried Miss Jones wildly.

Another argument ensued. Realizing that the elements of the comedy were implied in the scene, Dexter several times began to laugh, but each time restrained the laugh before it reached audibility. He could not resist the monstrous conviction that the little girl was justified in beating the nurse.

The situation was resolved by the fortuitous appearance of the caddy-master, who was appealed to immediately by the nurse.

"Miss Jones is to have a little caddy, and this one says he can't go."

"Mr. McKenna said I was to wait here till you came," said Dexter quickly.

"Well, he's here now." Miss Jones smiled cheerfully at the caddy-master. Then she dropped her bag and set off at a haughty mince toward the first tee.

"Well?" The caddy-master turned to Dexter. "What you standing there like a dummy for? Go pick up the young lady's clubs."

"I don't think I'll go out to-day," said Dexter.

"You don't ——"

"I think I'll quit."

The enormity of his decision frightened him. He was a favorite caddy, and the thirty dollars a month he earned through the summer were not to be made elsewhere around the lake. But he had received a strong emotional shock, and his perturbation required a violent and immediate outlet.

It is not so simple as that, either. As so frequently would be the case in the future, Dexter was unconsciously dictated to by his winter dreams.

II

Now, of course, the quality and the seasonability of these winter dreams varied, but the stuff of them remained. They persuaded Dexter several years later to pass up a business course at the State university—his father, prospering now, would have paid his way—for the precarious advantage of attending an older and more famous university in the East, where he was bothered by his scanty funds. But do not get the impression, because his winter dreams happened to be concerned at first with musings on the rich, that there was anything merely snobbish in the boy. He wanted not association with glittering things and glittering people— he wanted the glittering things themselves. Often he reached out for the best without knowing why he wanted it—and sometimes he ran up against the mysterious denials and prohibitions in which life indulges. It is with one of those denials and not with his career as a whole that this story deals.

He made money. It was rather amazing. After college he went to the city from which Black Bear Lake draws its wealthy patrons. When he was only twenty-three and had been there not quite two years, there were already people who liked to say: "Now *there's* a boy—" All about him rich men's sons were peddling bonds precariously, or investing patrimonies precariously, or plodding through the two dozen volumes of the "George Washington Commercial Course," but Dexter borrowed a thousand dollars on his college degree and his confident mouth, and bought a partnership in a laundry.

It was a small laundry when he went into it but Dexter made a specialty of learning how the English washed fine woollen golf-stockings without shrinking them, and within a year he was catering to the trade that wore knickerbockers. Men were insisting that their Shetland hose and sweaters go to his laundry just as they had insisted on a caddy who could find golf-balls. A little later he was doing their wives' lingerie as well—and running five branches in different parts of the city. Before he was twenty-seven he owned the largest string of laundries in his section of the country. It was then that he sold out and went to New York. But the part of his story that concerns us goes back to the days when he was making his first big success.

When he was twenty-three Mr. Hart—one of the gray-haired men who like to say "Now there's a boy"—gave him a guest card to the Sherry Island Golf Club for a week-end. So he signed his name one day on the register, and that afternoon played golf in a foursome with Mr. Hart and Mr. Sandwood and Mr. T. A. Hedrick. He did not consider it necessary to remark that he had once carried Mr. Hart's bag over this same links, and that he knew every trap and gully with his eyes shut—but he found himself glancing at the four caddies who trailed them, trying to catch a gleam or gesture that would remind him of himself, that would lessen the gap which lay between his present and his past.

It was a curious day, slashed abruptly with fleeting, familiar impressions. One minute he had the sense of being a trespasser—in the next he was impressed by the tremendous superiority he felt toward Mr. T. A. Hedrick, who was a bore and not even a good golfer any more.

Then, because of a ball Mr. Hart lost near the fifteenth green, an enormous thing happened. While they were searching the stiff grasses of the rough there was a clear call of "Fore!" from behind a hill in their rear. And as they all turned abruptly from their search a bright new ball sliced abruptly over the hill and caught Mr. T. A. Hedrick in the abdomen.

"By Gad!" cried Mr. T. A. Hedrick, "they ought to put some of these crazy women off the course. It's getting to be outrageous."

A head and a voice came up together over the hill:

"Do you mind if we go through?"

"You hit me in the stomach!" declared Mr. Hedrick wildly.

"Did I?" The girl approached the group of men. "I'm sorry. I yelled 'Fore!'"

Her glance fell casually on each of the men—then scanned the fairway for her ball.

"Did I bounce into the rough?"

It was impossible to determine whether this question was ingenuous or malicious. In a moment, however, she left no doubt, for as her partner came up over the hill she called cheerfully:

"Here I am! I'd have gone on the green except that I hit something."

As she took her stance for a short mashie shot, Dexter looked at her closely. She wore a blue gingham dress, rimmed at throat and shoulders with a white edging that accentuated her tan. The quality of exaggeration, of thinness, which had made her passionate eyes and down-turning mouth absurd at eleven, was gone now. She was arrestingly beautiful. The color in her cheeks was centered like the color in a picture—it was not a "high" color, but a sort of fluctuating and feverish warmth, so shaded that it seemed at any moment it would recede and disappear. This color and the mobility of her mouth gave a continual impression of flux, of intense life, of passionate vitality—balanced only partially by the sad luxury of her eyes.

She swung her mashie impatiently and without interest, pitching the ball into a sand-pit on the other side of the green. With a quick, insincere smile and a careless "Thank you!" she went on after it.

"That Judy Jones!" remarked Mr. Hedrick on the next tee, as they waited—some moments—for her to play on ahead. "All she needs is to be turned up and spanked for six months and then to be married off to an old-fashioned cavalry captain."

"My God, she's good-looking!" said Mr. Sandwood, who was just over thirty.

"Good-looking!" cried Mr. Hedrick contemptuously, "she always looks as if she wanted to be kissed! Turning those big cow-eyes on every calf in town!"

It was doubtful if Mr. Hedrick intended a reference to the maternal instinct.

"She'd play pretty good golf if she'd try," said Mr. Sandwood.

"She has no form," said Mr. Hedrick solemnly.

"She has a nice figure," said Mr. Sandwood.

"Better thank the Lord she doesn't drive a swifter ball," said Mr. Hart, winking at Dexter.

Later in the afternoon the sun went down with a riotous swirl of gold and varying blues and scarlets, and left the dry, rustling night of Western summer. Dexter watched from the veranda of the Golf Club, watched the even overlap of the waters in the little wind, silver molasses under the harvest-moon. Then the moon held a finger to her lips and the lake became a clear pool, pale and quiet. Dexter put on his bathing-suit and swam out to the farthest raft, where he stretched dripping on the wet canvas of the spring-board.

There was a fish jumping and a star shining and the lights around the lake were gleaming. Over on a dark peninsula a piano was playing the songs of last summer and of summers before that—songs from "Chin-Chin" and "The Count of Luxemburg" and "The Chocolate Soldier"—and because the sound of a piano over a stretch of water had always seemed beautiful to Dexter he lay perfectly quiet and listened.

The tune the piano was playing at that moment had been gay and new five years before when Dexter was a sophomore at college. They had played it at a prom once when he could not afford the luxury of proms, and he had stood outside the gymnasium and listened. The sound of the tune precipitated in him a sort of ecstasy and it was with that ecstasy he viewed what happened to him now. It was a mood of intense appreciation, a sense that, for once, he was magnificently attuned to life and that everything about him was radiating a brightness and a glamour he might never know again.

A low, pale oblong detached itself suddenly from the darkness of the Island, spitting forth the reverberate sound of a racing motor-boat. Two white streamers of cleft water rolled themselves out behind it and almost immediately the boat was beside him, drowning out the hot tinkle of the piano in the drone of its spray. Dexter raising himself on his arms was aware of a figure standing at the wheel, of two dark eyes regarding him over the lengthening space of water—then the boat had gone by and was sweeping in an immense and purposeless circle of spray round and round in the middle of the lake. With equal eccentricity one of the circles flattened out and headed back toward the raft.

"Who's that?" she called, shutting off her motor. She was so near now that Dexter could see her bathing-suit, which consisted apparently of pink rompers.

The nose of the boat bumped the raft, and as the latter tilted rakishly he was precipitated toward her. With different degrees of interest they recognized each other.

"Aren't you one of those men we played through this afternoon?" she demanded.

He was.

"Well, do you know how to drive a motor-boat? Because if you do I wish you'd drive this one so I can ride on the surf-board behind. My name is Judy Jones"—she favored him with an absurd smirk—rather, what tried to be a smirk, for, twist her mouth as she might, it was not grotesque, it was merely beautiful—"and I live in a house over there on the Island, and in that house there is a man waiting for me. When he drove up at the door I drove out of the dock because he says I'm his ideal."

There was a fish jumping and a star shining and the lights around the lake were gleaming. Dexter sat beside Judy Jones and she explained how her boat was driven. Then she was in the water, swimming to the floating surf-board with a sinuous crawl. Watching her was without effort to the eye, watching a branch waving or a sea-gull flying. Her arms, burned to butternut, moved sinuously among the dull platinum ripples, elbow appearing first, casting the forearm back with a cadence of falling water, then reaching out and down, stabbing a path ahead.

They moved out into the lake; turning, Dexter saw that she was kneeling on the low rear of the now uptilted surf-board.

"Go faster," she called, "fast as it'll go."

Obediently he jammed the lever forward and the white spray mounted at the bow. When he looked around again the girl was standing up on the rushing board, her arms spread wide, her eyes lifted toward the moon.

"It's awful cold," she shouted. "What's your name?"

He told her.

"Well, why don't you come to dinner to-morrow night?"

His heart turned over like the fly-wheel of the boat, and, for the second time, her casual whim gave a new direction to his life.

III

Next evening while he waited for her to come down-stairs, Dexter peopled the soft deep summer room and the sun-porch that opened from it with the men who had already loved Judy Jones. He knew the sort of men they were—the men who when he first went to college had entered from the great prep schools with graceful clothes and the deep tan of healthy summers. He had seen that, in one sense, he was better than these men. He was newer and stronger. Yet in acknowledging to himself that he wished his children to be like them he was admitting that he was but the rough, strong stuff from which they eternally sprang.

When the time had come for him to wear good clothes, he had known who were the best tailors in America, and the best tailors in America had made him the suit he wore this evening. He had acquired that particular reserve peculiar to his university, that set it off from other universities. He recognized the value to him of such a mannerism and he had adopted it; he knew that to be careless in dress and manner required more confidence than to be careful. But carelessness was for his children. His mother's name had been Krimslich. She was a Bohemian of the peasant class and she had talked broken English to the end of her days. Her son must keep to the set patterns.

At a little after seven Judy Jones came down-stairs. She wore a blue silk afternoon dress, and he was disappointed at first that she had not put on something more elaborate. This feeling was accentuated when, after a brief greeting, she went to the door of a butler's pantry and pushing it open called: "You can serve dinner, Martha." He had rather expected that a butler would announce dinner, that there would be a cocktail. Then he put these thoughts behind him as they sat down side by side on a lounge and looked at each other.

"Father and mother won't be here," she said thoughtfully.

He remembered the last time he had seen her father, and he was glad the parents were not to be here to-night—they might wonder who he was. He had been born in Keeble, a Minnesota village fifty miles farther north, and he always gave Keeble as his home instead of Black Bear Village. Country towns were well enough to come from if they weren't inconveniently in sight and used as footstools by fashionable lakes.

They talked of his university, which she had visited frequently during the past two years, and of the near-by city which supplied Sherry Island with its patrons, and whither Dexter would return next day to his prospering laundries.

During dinner she slipped into a moody depression which gave Dexter a feeling of uneasiness. Whatever petulance she uttered in her throaty voice worried him. Whatever she smiled at—at him, at a chicken liver, at nothing—it disturbed him that her smile could have no root in mirth, or even in amusement. When the scarlet corners of her lips curved down, it was less a smile than an invitation to a kiss.

Then, after dinner, she led him out on the dark sun-porch and deliberately changed the atmosphere.

"Do you mind if I weep a little?" she said.

"I'm afraid I'm boring you," he responded quickly.

"You're not. I like you. But I've just had a terrible afternoon. There was a man I cared about, and this afternoon he told me out of a clear sky that he was poor as a church-mouse. He'd never even hinted it before. Does this sound horribly mundane?"

"Perhaps he was afraid to tell you."

"Suppose he was," she answered. "He didn't start right. You see, if I'd thought of him as poor—well, I've been mad about loads of poor men, and fully intended to marry them all. But in this case, I hadn't thought of him that way, and my interest in him wasn't strong enough to survive the shock. As if a girl calmly informed her fiancé that she was a widow. He might not object to widows, but——

"Let's start right," she interrupted herself suddenly. "Who are you, anyhow?"

For a moment Dexter hesitated. Then:

"I'm nobody," he announced. "My career is largely a matter of futures."

"Are you poor?"

"No," he said frankly, "I'm probably making more money than any man my age in the Northwest. I know that's an obnoxious remark, but you advised me to start right."

There was a pause. Then she smiled and the corners of her mouth drooped and an almost imperceptible sway brought her closer to him, looking up into his eyes. A lump rose in Dexter's throat, and he waited breathless for the experiment, facing the unpredictable compound that would form mysteriously from the elements of their lips. Then he saw—she communicated her excitement to him, lavishly, deeply, with kisses that were not a promise but a fulfillment. They aroused in him not hunger demanding renewal but surfeit that would demand more surfeit . . . kisses that were like charity, creating want by holding back nothing at all.

It did not take him many hours to decide that he had wanted Judy Jones ever since he was a proud, desirous little boy.

IV

It began like that—and continued, with varying shades of intensity, on such a note right up to the dénouement. Dexter surrendered a part of himself to the most direct and unprincipled personality with which he had ever come in contact. Whatever Judy wanted, she went after with the full pressure of her charm. There was no divergence of method, no jockeying for position or premeditation of effects—there was a very little mental side to any of her affairs. She simply made men conscious to the highest degree of her physical loveliness. Dexter had no desire to change her. Her deficiencies were knit up with a passionate energy that transcended and justified them.

When, as Judy's head lay against his shoulder that first night, she whispered, "I don't know what's the matter with me. Last night I thought I was in love with a man and to-night I think I'm in love with you——"—it seemed to him a beautiful and romantic thing to say. It was the exquisite excitability that for the moment he controlled and owned. But a week later he was compelled to view this same quality in a different light. She took him in her roadster to a picnic supper, and after supper she disappeared, likewise in her roadster, with another man. Dexter became enormously upset and was scarcely able to be decently civil to the other people present. When she assured him that she had not kissed the other man, he knew she was lying—yet he was glad that she had taken the trouble to lie to him.

He was, as he found before the summer ended, one of a varying dozen who circulated about her. Each of them had at one time been favored above all others—about half of them still basked in the solace of occasional sentimental revivals. Whenever one showed signs of dropping out through long neglect, she granted him a brief honeyed hour, which encouraged him to tag along for a year or so longer. Judy made these forays upon the helpless and defeated without malice, indeed half unconscious that there was anything mischievous in what she did.

When a new man came to town every one dropped out—dates were automatically cancelled.

The helpless part of trying to do anything about it was that she did it all herself. She was not a girl who could be "won" in the kinetic sense—she was proof against cleverness, she was proof against charm; if any of these assailed her too strongly she would immediately resolve the affair to a physical basis, and under the magic of her physical splendor the strong as well as the brilliant played her game and not their own. She was entertained only by the gratification of her desires and by the direct exercise of her own charm. Perhaps from so much youthful love, so many youthful lovers, she had come, in self-defense, to nourish herself wholly from within.

Succeeding Dexter's first exhilaration came restlessness and dissatisfaction. The helpless ecstasy of losing himself in her was opiate rather than tonic. It was fortunate for his work during the winter that those moments of ecstasy came infrequently. Early in their acquaintance it had seemed for a while that there was a deep and spontaneous mutual attraction—that first August. for example—three days of long evenings on her dusky veranda, of strange wan kisses through the late afternoon, in shadowy alcoves or behind the protecting trellises of the garden arbors, of mornings when she was fresh as a dream and almost shy at meeting him in the clarity of the rising day. There was all the ecstasy of an engagement about it, sharpened by his realization that there was no engagement. It was during those three days that, for the first time, he had asked her to marry him. She said "maybe some day," she said "kiss me," she said "I'd like to marry you," she said "I love you"—she said—nothing.

The three days were interrupted by the arrival of a New York man who visited at her house for half September. To Dexter's agony, rumor engaged them. The man was the son of the president of a great trust company. But at the end of a month it was reported that Judy was yawning. At a dance one night she sat all evening in a motor-boat with a local beau, while the New Yorker searched the club for her frantically. She told the local beau that she was bored with her visitor, and two days later he left. She was seen with him at the station, and it was reported that he looked very mournful indeed.

On this note the summer ended. Dexter was twenty-four, and he found himself increasingly in a position to do as he wished. He joined two clubs in the city and lived at one of them. Though he was by no means an integral part of the stag-lines at these clubs, he managed to be on hand at dances where Judy Jones was likely to appear. He could have gone out socially as much as he liked—he was an eligible young man, now, and popular with down-town fathers. His confessed devotion to Judy Jones had rather solidified his position. But he had no social aspirations and rather despised the dancing men who were always on tap for the Thursday or Saturday parties and who filled in at dinners with the younger married set. Already he was playing with the idea of going East to New York. He wanted to take Judy Jones with him. No disillusion as to the world in which she had grown up could cure his illusion as to her desirability.

Remember that—for only in the light of it can what he did for her be understood.

Eighteen months after he first met Judy Jones he became engaged to another girl. Her name was Irene Scheerer, and her father was one of the men who had always believed in Dexter. Irene was light-haired and sweet and honorable, and a little stout, and she had two suitors whom she pleasantly relinquished when Dexter formally asked her to marry him.

Summer, fall, winter, spring, another summer, another fall—so much he had given of his active life to the incorrigible lips of Judy Jones. She had treated him with interest, with encouragement, with malice, with indifference, with contempt. She had inflicted on him the innumerable little slights and indignities possible in such a case—as if in revenge for having ever cared for him at all. She had beckoned him and yawned at him and beckoned him again and he had responded often with bitterness and narrowed eyes. She had brought him ecstatic happiness and intolerable agony of spirit. She had caused him untold inconvenience and not a little trouble. She had insulted him, and she had ridden over him, and she had played his interest in her against his interest in his work—for fun. She had done everything to him except to criticise him—this she had not done—it seemed to him only because it might have sullied the utter indifference she manifested and sincerely felt toward him.

When autumn had come and gone again it occurred to him that he could not have Judy Jones. He had to beat this into his mind but he convinced himself at last. He lay awake at night for a while and argued it over. He told himself the trouble and the pain she had caused him, he enumerated her glaring deficiencies as a wife. Then he said to himself that he loved her, and after a while he fell asleep. For a week, lest he imagined her husky voice over the telephone or her eyes opposite him at lunch, he worked hard and late, and at night he went to his office and plotted out his years.

At the end of a week he went to a dance and cut in on her once. For almost the first time since they had met he did not ask her to sit out with him or tell her that she was lovely. It hurt him that she did not miss these things—that was all. He was not jealous when he saw that there was a new man to-night. He had been hardened against jealousy long before.

He stayed late at the dance. He sat for an hour with Irene Scheerer and talked about books and about music. He knew very little about either. But he was beginning to be master of his own time now, and he had a rather priggish notion that he—the young and already fabulously successful Dexter Green—should know more about such things.

That was in October, when he was twenty-five. In January, Dexter and Irene became engaged. It was to be announced in June, and they were to be married three months later.

The Minnesota winter prolonged itself interminably, and it was almost May when the winds came soft and the snow ran down into Black Bear Lake at last. For the first time in over a year Dexter was enjoying a certain tranquility of spirit. Judy Jones had been in Florida, and afterward in Hot Springs, and somewhere she had been engaged, and somewhere she had broken it off. At first, when Dexter had definitely given her up, it had made him sad that people still linked them together and asked for news of her, but when he began to be placed at dinner next to Irene Scheerer people didn't ask him about her any more—they told him about her. He ceased to be an authority on her.

May at last. Dexter walked the streets at night when the darkness was damp as rain, wondering that so soon, with so little done, so much of ecstasy had gone from him. May one year back had been marked by Judy's poignant, unforgivable, yet forgiven turbulence—it had been one of those rare times when he fancied she had grown to care for him. That old penny's worth of happiness he had spent for this bushel of content. He knew that Irene would be no more than a curtain spread behind him, a hand moving among gleaming teacups, a voice calling to children . . . fire and loveliness were gone, the magic of nights and the wonder of the varying hours and seasons . . . slender lips, down-turning, dropping to his lips and bearing him up into a heaven of eyes. . . . The thing was deep in him. He was too strong and alive for it to die lightly.

In the middle of May when the weather balanced for a few days on the thin bridge that led to deep summer he turned in one night at Irene's house. Their engagement was to be announced in a week now—no one would be surprised at it. And to-night they would sit together on the lounge at the University Club and look on for an hour at the dancers. It gave him a sense of solidity to go with her—she was so sturdily popular, so intensely "great."

He mounted the steps of the brownstone house and stepped inside.

"Irene," he called.

Mrs. Scheerer came out of the living-room to meet him.

"Dexter," she said, "Irene's gone up-stairs with a splitting headache. She wanted to go with you but I made her go to bed."

"Nothing serious, I——"

"Oh, no. She's going to play golf with you in the morning. You can spare her for just one night, can't you, Dexter?"

Her smile was kind. She and Dexter liked each other. In the living-room he talked for a moment before he said good-night.

Returning to the University Club, where he had rooms, he stood in the doorway for a moment and watched the dancers. He leaned against the door-post, nodded at a man or two—yawned.

"Hello, darling."

The familiar voice at his elbow startled him. Judy Jones had left a man and crossed the room to him—Judy Jones, a slender enamelled doll in cloth of gold: gold in a band at her head, gold in two slipper points at her dress's hem. The fragile glow of her face seemed to blossom as she smiled at him. A breeze of warmth and light blew through the room. His hands in the pockets of his dinner-jacket tightened spasmodically. He was filled with a sudden excitement.

"When did you get back?" he asked casually.

"Come here and I'll tell you about it."

She turned and he followed her. She had been away—he could have wept at the wonder of her return. She had passed through enchanted streets, doing things that were like provocative music. All mysterious happenings, all fresh and quickening hopes, had gone away with her, come back with her now.

She turned in the doorway.

"Have you a car here? If you haven't, I have."

"I have a coupé."

In then, with a rustle of golden cloth. He slammed the door. Into so many cars she had stepped—like this—like that—her back against the leather, so—her elbow resting on the door—waiting. She would have been soiled long since had there been anything to soil her—except herself—but this was her own self outpouring.

With an effort he forced himself to start the car and back into the street. This was nothing, he must remember. She had done this before, and he had put her behind him, as he would have crossed a bad account from his books.

He drove slowly down-town and, affecting abstraction, traversed the deserted streets of the business section, peopled here and there where a movie was giving out its crowd or where consumptive or pugilistic youth lounged in front of pool halls. The clink of glasses and the slap of hands on the bars issued from saloons, cloisters of glazed glass and dirty yellow light.

She was watching him closely and the silence was embarrassing, yet in this crisis he could find no casual word with which to profane the hour. At a convenient turning he began to zigzag back toward the University Club.

"Have you missed me?" she asked suddenly.

"Everybody missed you."

He wondered if she knew of Irene Scheerer. She had been back only a day—her absence had been almost contemporaneous with his engagement.

"What a remark!" Judy laughed sadly—without sadness. She looked at him searchingly. He became absorbed in the dashboard.

"You're handsomer than you used to be," she said thoughtfully. "Dexter, you have the most rememberable eyes."

He could have laughed at this, but he did not laugh. It was the sort of thing that was said to sophomores. Yet it stabbed at him.

"I'm awfully tired of everything, darling." She called every one darling, endowing the endearment with careless, individual comraderie. "I wish you'd marry me."

The directness of this confused him. He should have told her now that he was going to marry another girl, but he could not tell her. He could as easily have sworn that he had never loved her.

"I think we'd get along," she continued, on the same note, "unless probably you've forgotten me and fallen in love with another girl."

Her confidence was obviously enormous. She had said, in effect, that she found such a thing impossible to believe, that if it were true he had merely committed a childish indiscretion—and probably to show off. She would forgive him, because it was not a matter of any moment but rather something to be brushed aside lightly.

"Of course you could never love anybody but me," she continued. "I like the way you love me. Oh, Dexter, have you forgotten last year?"

"No, I haven't forgotten."

"Neither have I!"

Was she sincerely moved—or was she carried along by the wave of her own acting?

"I wish we could be like that again," she said, and he forced himself to answer:

"I don't think we can."

"I suppose not. . . . I hear you're giving Irene Scheerer a violent rush."

There was not the faintest emphasis on the name, yet Dexter was suddenly ashamed.

"Oh, take me home," cried Judy suddenly; "I don't want to go back to that idiotic dance—with those children."

Then, as he turned up the street that led to the residence district, Judy began to cry quietly to herself. He had never seen her cry before.

The dark street lightened, the dwellings of the rich loomed up around them, he stopped his coupé in front of the great white bulk of the Mortimer Joneses house, somnolent, gorgeous, drenched with the splendor of the damp moonlight. Its solidity startled him. The strong walls, the steel of the girders, the breadth and beam and pomp of it were there only to bring out the contrast with the young beauty beside him. It was sturdy to accentuate her slightness—as if to show what a breeze could be generated by a butterfly's wing.

He sat perfectly quiet, his nerves in wild clamor, afraid that if he moved he would find her irresistibly in his arms. Two tears had rolled down her wet face and trembled on her upper lip.

"I'm more beautiful than anybody else," she said brokenly, "why can't I be happy?" Her moist eyes tore at his stability—her mouth turned slowly downward with an exquisite sadness: "I'd like to marry you if you'll have me, Dexter. I suppose you think I'm not worth having, but I'll be so beautiful for you, Dexter."

A million phrases of anger, pride, passion, hatred, tenderness fought on his lips. Then a perfect wave of emotion washed over him, carrying off with it a sediment of wisdom, of convention, of doubt, of honor. This was his girl who was speaking, his own, his beautiful, his pride.

"Won't you come in?" He heard her draw in her breath sharply.

Waiting.

"All right," his voice was trembling, "I'll come in."

V

It was strange that neither when it was over nor a long time afterward did he regret that night. Looking at it from the perspective of ten years, the fact that Judy's flare for him endured just one month seemed of little importance. Nor did it matter that by his yielding he subjected himself to a deeper agony in the end and gave serious hurt to Irene Scheerer and to Irene's parents, who had befriended him. There was nothing sufficiently pictorial about Irene's grief to stamp itself on his mind.

Dexter was at bottom hard-minded. The attitude of the city on his action was of no importance to him, not because he was going to leave the city, but because any outside attitude on the situation seemed superficial. He was completely indifferent to popular opinion. Nor, when he had seen that it was no use, that he did not possess in himself the power to move fundamentally or to hold Judy Jones, did he bear any malice toward her. He loved her, and he would love her until the day he was too old for loving—but he could not have her. So he tasted the deep pain that is reserved only for the strong, just as he had tasted for a little while the deep happiness.

Even the ultimate falsity of the grounds upon which Judy terminated the engagement that she did not want to "take him away" from Irene—Judy, who had wanted nothing else—did not revolt him. He was beyond any revulsion or any amusement.

He went East in February with the intention of selling out his laundries and settling in New York—but the war came to America in March and changed his plans. He returned to the West, handed over the management of the business to his partner, and went into the first officers' training-camp in late April. He was one of those young thousands who greeted the war with a certain amount of relief, welcoming the liberation from webs of tangled emotion.

VI

This story is not his biography, remember, although things creep into it which have nothing to do with those dreams he had when he was young. We are almost done with them and with him now. There is only one more incident to be related here, and it happens seven years farther on.

It took place in New York, where he had done well—so well that there were no barriers too high for him. He was thirty-two years old, and, except for one flying trip immediately after the war, he had not been West in seven years. A man named Devlin from Detroit came into his office to see him in a business way, and then and there this incident occurred, and closed out, so to speak, this particular side of his life.

"So you're from the Middle West," said the man Devlin with careless curiosity. "That's funny—I thought men like you were probably born and raised on Wall Street. You know—wife of one of my best friends in Detroit came from your city. I was usher at the wedding."

Dexter waited with no apprehension of what was coming.

"Judy Simms," said Devlin with no particular interest; "Judy Jones she was once."

"Yes, I knew her." A dull impatience spread over him. He had heard, of course, that she was married—perhaps deliberately he had heard no more.

"Awfully nice girl," brooded Devlin meaninglessly, "I'm sort of sorry for her."

"Why?" Something in Dexter was alert, receptive, at once.

"Oh, Lud Simms has gone to pieces in a way. I don't mean he ill-uses her, but he drinks and runs around——"

"Doesn't she run around?"

"No. Stays at home with her kids."

"Oh."

"She's a little too old for him," said Devlin.

"Too old!" cried Dexter. "Why, man, she's only twenty-seven."

He was possessed with a wild notion of rushing out into the streets and taking a train to Detroit. He rose to his feet spasmodically.

"I guess you're busy," Devlin apologized quickly. "I didn't realize——"

"No, I'm not busy," said Dexter, steadying his voice. "I'm not busy at all. Not busy at all. Did you say she was—twenty-seven? No, I said she was twenty-seven."

"Yes, you did," agreed Devlin dryly.

"Go on, then. Go on."

"What do you mean?"

"About Judy Jones."

Devlin looked at him helplessly.

"Well, that's—I told you all there is to it. He treats her like the devil. Oh, they're not going to get divorced or anything. When he's particularly outrageous she forgives him. In fact, I'm inclined to think she loves him. She was a pretty girl when she first came to Detroit."

A pretty girl! The phrase struck Dexter as ludicrous.

"Isn't she—a pretty girl, any more?"

"Oh, she's all right."

"Look here," said Dexter, sitting down suddenly, "I don't understand. You say she was a 'pretty girl' and now you say she's 'all right.' I don't understand what you mean—Judy Jones wasn't a pretty girl, at all. She was a great beauty. Why, I knew her, I knew her. She was——"

Devlin laughed pleasantly.

"I'm not trying to start a row," he said. "I think Judy's a nice girl and I like her. I can't understand how a man like Lud Simms could fall madly in love with her, but he did." Then he added: "Most of the women like her."

Dexter looked closely at Devlin, thinking wildly that there must be a reason for this, some insensitivity in the man or some private malice.

"Lots of women fade just like *that*," Devlin snapped his fingers. "You must have seen it happen. Perhaps I've forgotten how pretty she was at her wedding. I've seen her so much since then, you see. She has nice eyes."

A sort of dullness settled down upon Dexter. For the first time in his life he felt like getting very drunk. He knew that he was laughing loudly at something Devlin had said, but he did not know what it was or why it was funny. When, in a few minutes, Devlin went he lay down on his lounge and looked out the window at the New York sky-line into which the sun was sinking in dull lovely shades of pink and gold.

He had thought that having nothing else to lose he was invulnerable at last—but he knew that he had just lost something more, as surely as if he had married Judy Jones and seen her fade away before his eyes.

The dream was gone. Something had been taken from him. In a sort of panic he pushed the palms of his hands into his eyes and tried to bring up a picture of the waters lapping on Sherry Island and the moonlit veranda, and gingham on the golf-links and the dry sun and the gold color of her neck's soft down. And her mouth damp to his kisses and her eyes plaintive with melancholy and her freshness like new fine linen in the morning. Why, these things were no longer in the world! They had existed and they existed no longer.

For the first time in years the tears were streaming down his face. But they were for himself now. He did not care about mouth and eyes and moving hands. He wanted to care, and he could not care. For he had gone away and he could never go back any more. The gates were closed, the sun was gone down, and there was no beauty but the gray beauty of steel that withstands all time. Even the grief he could have borne was left behind in the country of illusion, of youth, of the richness of life, where his winter dreams had flourished.

"Long ago," he said, "long ago, there was something in me, but now that thing is gone. Now that thing is gone, that thing is gone. I cannot cry. I cannot care. That thing will come back no more."

[1922]

WILLIAM FAULKNER [1897–1962]

A Rose for Emily

I

When Miss Emily Grierson died, our whole town went to her funeral: the men through a sort of respectful affection for a fallen monument, the women mostly out of curiosity to see the inside of her house, which no one save an old manservant—a combined gardener and cook—had seen in at least ten years.

It was a big, squarish frame house that had once been white, decorated with cupolas and spires and scrolled balconies in the heavily lightsome style of the seventies, set on what had once been our most select street. But garages and cotton gins had encroached and obliterated even the august names of that neighborhood; only Miss Emily's house was left, lifting its stubborn and coquettish decay above the cotton wagons and the gasoline pumps—an eyesore among eyesores. And now Miss Emily had gone to join the representatives of those august names where they lay in the cedar-bemused cemetery among the ranked and anonymous graves of Union and Confederate soldiers who fell at the battle of Jefferson.

Alive, Miss Emily had been a tradition, a duty, and a care; a sort of hereditary obligation upon the town, dating from that day in 1894 when Colonel Sartoris, the mayor—he who fathered the edict that no Negro woman should appear on the streets without an apron—remitted her taxes, the dispensation dating from the death of her father on into perpetuity. Not that Miss Emily would have accepted charity. Colonel Sartoris invented an involved tale to the effect that Miss Emily's father had loaned money to the town, which the town, as a matter of business, preferred this way of repaying. Only a man of Colonel Sartoris's generation and thought could have invented it, and only a woman could have believed it.

When the next generation, with its more modern ideas, became mayors and aldermen, this arrangement created some little dissatisfaction. On the first of the year they mailed her a tax notice. February came, and there was no reply. They wrote her a formal letter, asked her to call at the sheriff's office at her convenience. A week later the mayor wrote her himself, offering to call or to send his car for her, and received in reply a note on paper of an archaic shape, in a thin, flowing calligraphy in faded ink, to the effect that she no longer went out at all. The tax notice was also enclosed, without comment.

They called a special meeting of the Board of Aldermen. A deputation waited upon her, knocked at the door through which no visitor had passed since she ceased giving china-painting lessons eight or ten years earlier. They were admitted by the old Negro into a dim hall from which a stairway mounted into still more shadow. It smelled of dust and disuse—a close, dank smell. The Negro led them into the parlor. It was furnished in heavy, leather-covered furniture. When the Negro opened the blinds of one window, they could see that the leather was cracked; and when they sat down, a faint dust rose sluggishly about their thighs, spinning with slow motes in the single sun-ray. On a tarnished gilt easel before the fireplace stood a crayon portrait of Miss Emily's father.

They rose when she entered—a small, fat woman in black, with a thin gold chain descending to her waist and vanishing into her belt, leaning on an ebony cane with a tarnished gold head. Her skeleton was small and spare; perhaps that was why what would have been merely plumpness in another was obesity in her. She looked bloated, like a body long submerged in motionless water, and of that pallid hue. Her eyes, lost in the fatty ridges of her face, looked like two small pieces of coal pressed into a lump of dough as they moved from one face to another while the visitors stated their errand.

She did not ask them to sit. She just stood in the door and listened quietly until the spokesman came to a stumbling halt. Then they could hear the invisible watch ticking at the end of the gold chain.

Her voice was dry and cold. "I have no taxes in Jefferson. Colonel Sartoris explained it to me. Perhaps one of you can gain access to the city records and satisfy yourselves."

"But we have. We are the city authorities, Miss Emily. Didn't you get a notice from the sheriff, signed by him?"

"I received a paper, yes," Miss Emily said. "Perhaps he considers himself the sheriff. . . . I have no taxes in Jefferson."

"But there is nothing on the books to show that, you see. We must go by the—"

"See Colonel Sartoris. I have no taxes in Jefferson."

"But, Miss Emily—"

"See Colonel Sartoris." (Colonel Sartoris had been dead almost ten years.) "I have no taxes in Jefferson. Tobe!" The Negro appeared. "Show these gentlemen out."

II

So she vanquished them, horse and foot, just as she had vanquished their fathers thirty years before about the smell. That was two years after her father's death and a short time after her sweetheart—the one we believed would marry her—had deserted her. After her father's death she went out very little; after her sweetheart went away, people hardly saw her at all. A few of the ladies had the temerity to call, but were not received, and the only sign of life about the place was the Negro man—a young man then—going in and out with a market basket.

"Just as if a man—any man—could keep a kitchen properly," the ladies said; so they were not surprised when the smell developed. It was another link between the gross, teeming world and the high and mighty Griersons.

A neighbor, a woman, complained to the mayor, Judge Stevens, eighty years old.

"But what will you have me do about it, madam?" he said.

"Why, send her word to stop it," the woman said. "Isn't there a law?"

"I'm sure that won't be necessary," Judge Stevens said. "It's probably just a snake or a rat that nigger of hers killed in the yard. I'll speak to him about it."

The next day he received two more complaints, one from a man who came in diffident deprecation. "We really must do something about it, Judge. I'd be the last one in the world to bother Miss Emily, but we've got to do something." That night the Board of Aldermen met—three gray-beards and one younger man, a member of the rising generation.

"It's simple enough," he said. "Send her word to have her place cleaned up. Give her a certain time to do it in, and if she don't. . . ."

"Dammit, sir," Judge Stevens said, "will you accuse a lady to her face of smelling bad?"

So the next night, after midnight, four men crossed Miss Emily's lawn and slunk about the house like burglars, sniffing along the base of the brickwork and at the cellar openings while one of them performed a regular sowing motion with his hand out of a sack slung from his shoulder. They broke open the cellar door and sprinkled lime there, and in all the outbuildings. As they recrossed the lawn, a window that had been dark was lighted and Miss Emily sat in it, the light behind her, and her upright torso motionless as that of an idol. They crept quietly across the lawn and into the shadow of the locusts that lined the street. After a week or two the smell went away.

That was when people had begun to feel really sorry for her. People in our town, remembering how old lady Wyatt, her great-aunt, had gone completely crazy at last, believed that the Griersons held themselves a little too high for what they really were. None of the young men were quite good enough for Miss Emily and such. We had long thought of them as a tableau. Miss Emily a slender figure in white in the background, her father a spraddled silhouette in the foreground, his back to her and clutching a horsewhip, the two of them framed by the backflung front door. So when she got to be thirty and was still single, we were not pleased exactly, but vindicated; even with insanity in the family she wouldn't have turned down all of her chances if they had really materialized.

When her father died, it got about that the house was all that was left to her; and in a way, people were glad. At last they could pity Miss Emily. Being left alone, and a pauper, she had become humanized. Now she too would know the old thrill and the old despair of a penny more or less.

The day after his death all the ladies prepared to call at the house and offer condolence and aid, as is our custom. Miss Emily met them at the door, dressed as usual and with no trace of grief on her face. She told them that her father was not dead. She did that for three days, with the ministers calling on her, and the doctors, trying to persuade her to let them dispose of the body. Just as they were about to resort to law and force, she broke down, and they buried her father quickly.

We did not say she was crazy then. We believed she had to do that. We remembered all the young men her father had driven away, and we knew that with nothing left, she would have to cling to that which had robbed her, as people will.

III

She was sick for a long time. When we saw her again, her hair was cut short, making her look like a girl, with a vague resemblance to those angels in colored church windows—sort of tragic and serene.

The town had just let the contracts for paving the sidewalks, and in the summer after her father's death they began the work. The construction company came with niggers and mules and machinery, and a foreman named Homer Barron, a Yankee—a big, dark, ready man, with a big voice and eyes lighter than his face. The little boys would follow in groups to hear him cuss the niggers, and the niggers singing in time to the rise and fall of picks. Pretty soon he knew everybody in town. Whenever you heard a lot of laughing anywhere about the square, Homer Barron would be in the center of the group. Presently, we began to see him and Miss Emily on Sunday afternoons driving in the yellow-wheeled buggy and the matched team of bays from the livery stable.

At first we were glad that Miss Emily would have an interest, because the ladies all said, "Of course a Grierson would not think seriously of a Northerner, a day laborer." But there were still others, older people, who said that even grief could not cause a real lady to forget *noblesse oblige* — without calling it *noblesse oblige*. They just said, "Poor Emily. Her kinsfolk should come to her." She had some kin in Alabama; but years ago her father had fallen out with them over the estate of old lady Wyatt, the crazy woman, and there was no communication between the two families. They had not even been represented at the funeral.

And as soon as the old people said, "Poor Emily," the whispering began. "Do you suppose it's really so?" they said to one another. "Of course it is. What else could. . . ." This behind their hands; rustling of craned silk and satin behind jalousies closed upon the sun of Sunday afternoon as the thin, swift clop-clop-clop of the matched team passed: "Poor Emily."

She carried her head high enough — even when we believed that she was fallen. It was as if she demanded more than ever the recognition of her dignity as the last Grierson; as if it had wanted that touch of earthiness to reaffirm her imperviousness. Like when she bought the rat poison, the arsenic. That was over a year after they had begun to say "Poor Emily," and while the two female cousins were visiting her.

"I want some poison," she said to the druggist. She was over thirty then, still a slight woman, though thinner than usual, with cold, haughty black eyes in a face the flesh of which was strained across the temples and about the eye-sockets as you imagine a lighthouse-keeper's face ought to look. "I want some poison," she said.

"Yes, Miss Emily. What kind? For rats and such? I'd recom——"

"I want the best you have. I don't care what kind."

The druggist named several. "They'll kill anything up to an elephant. But what you want is——"

"Arsenic," Miss Emily said. "Is that a good one?"

"Is . . . arsenic? Yes, ma'am. But what you want——"

"I want arsenic."

The druggist looked down at her. She looked back at him, erect, her face like a strained flag. "Why, of course," the druggist said. "If that's what you want. But the law requires you to tell what you are going to use it for."

Miss Emily just stared at him, her head tilted back in order to look him eye for eye, until he looked away and went and got the arsenic and wrapped it up. The Negro delivery boy brought her the package: the druggist didn't come back. When she opened the package at home there was written on the box, under the skull and bones: "For rats."

IV

So the next day we all said, "She will kill herself"; and we said it would be the best thing. When she had first begun to be seen with Homer Barron, we had said, "She will marry him." Then we said, "She will persuade him yet," because Homer himself had remarked—he liked men, and it was known that he drank with the younger men in the Elks' Club—that he was not a marrying man. Later we said, "Poor Emily" behind the jalousies as they passed on Sunday afternoon in the glittering buggy, Miss Emily with her head high and Homer Barron with his hat cocked and a cigar in his teeth, reins and whip in a yellow glove.

Then some of the ladies began to say it was a disgrace to the town and a bad example to the young people. The men did not want to interfere; but at last the ladies forced the Baptist minister—Miss Emily's people were Episcopal—to call upon her. He would never divulge what happened during that interview, but he refused to go back again. The next Sunday they again drove about the streets, and the following day the minister's wife wrote to Miss Emily's relations in Alabama.

So she had blood-kin under her roof again and we sat back to watch developments. At first nothing happened. Then we were sure that they were to be married. We learned that Miss Emily had been to the jeweler's and ordered a man's toilet set in silver, with the letters H.B. on each piece. Two days later we learned that she had bought a complete outfit of men's clothing, including a nightshirt, and we said, "They are married." We were really glad. We were glad because the two female cousins were even more Grierson than Miss Emily had ever been.

So we were not surprised when Homer Barron—the streets had been finished some time since—was gone. We were a little disappointed that there was not a public blowing-off, but we believed that he had gone on to prepare for Miss Emily's coming, or to give her a chance to get rid of the cousins. (By that time it was a cabal, and we were all Miss Emily's allies to help circumvent the cousins.) Sure enough, after another week they departed. And, as we had expected all along, within three days Homer Barron was back in town. A neighbor saw the Negro man admit him at the kitchen door at dusk one evening.

And that was the last we saw of Homer Barron. And of Miss Emily for some time. The Negro man went in and out with the market basket, but the front door remained closed. Now and then we would see her at the window for a moment, as the men did that night when they sprinkled the lime, but for almost six months she did not appear on the streets. Then we knew that this was to be expected too; as if that quality of her father which had thwarted her woman's life so many times had been too virulent and too furious to die.

When we next saw Miss Emily, she had grown fat and her hair was turning gray. During the next few years it grew grayer and grayer until it attained an even pepper-and-salt iron-gray, when it ceased turning. Up to the day of her death at seventy-four it was still that vigorous iron-gray, like the hair of an active man.

From that time on her front door remained closed, save during a period of six or seven years, when she was about forty, during which she gave lessons in china-painting. She fitted up a studio in one of the downstairs rooms, where the daughters and granddaughters of Colonel Sartoris's contemporaries were sent to her with the same regularity and in the same spirit that they were sent to church on Sundays with a twenty-five-cent piece for the collection plate. Meanwhile her taxes had been remitted.

Then the newer generation became the backbone and the spirit of the town, and the painting pupils grew up and fell away and did not send their children to her with boxes of color and tedious brushes and pictures cut from the ladies' magazines. The front door closed upon the last one and remained closed for good. When the town got free postal delivery, Miss Emily alone refused to let them fasten the metal numbers above her door and attach a mailbox to it. She would not listen to them.

Daily, monthly, yearly we watched the Negro grow grayer and more stooped, going in and out with the market basket. Each December we sent her a tax notice, which would be returned by the post office a week later, unclaimed. Now and then we would see her in one of the downstairs windows—she had evidently shut up the top floor of the house—like the carven torso of an idol in a niche, looking or not looking at us, we could never tell which. Thus she passed from generation to generation—dear, inescapable, impervious, tranquil, and perverse.

And so she died. Fell ill in the house filled with dust and shadows, with only a doddering Negro man to wait on her. We did not even know she was sick; we had long since given up trying to get any information from the Negro. He talked to no one, probably not even to her, for his voice had grown harsh and rusty, as if from disuse.

She died in one of the downstairs rooms, in a heavy walnut bed with a curtain, her gray head propped on a pillow yellow and moldy with age and lack of sunlight.

V

The Negro met the first of the ladies at the front door and let them in, with their hushed, sibilant voices and their quick, curious glances, and then he disappeared. He walked right through the house and out the back and was not seen again.

The two female cousins came at once. They held the funeral on the second day, with the town coming to look at Miss Emily beneath a mass of bought flowers, with the crayon face of her father musing profoundly above the bier and the ladies sibilant and macabre; and the very old men—some in their brushed Confederate uniforms—on the porch and the lawn, talking of Miss Emily as if she had been a contemporary of theirs, believing that they had danced with her and courted her perhaps, confusing time with its mathematical progression, as the old do, to whom all the past is not a diminishing road but, instead, a huge meadow which no winter ever quite touches, divided from them now by the narrow bottleneck of the most recent decade of years.

Already we knew that there was one room in that region above stairs which no one had seen in forty years, and which would have to be forced. They waited until Miss Emily was decently in the ground before they opened it.

The violence of breaking down the door seemed to fill this room with pervading dust. A thin, acrid pall as of the tomb seemed to lie everywhere upon this room decked and furnished as for a bridal: upon the valance curtains of faded rose color, upon the rose-shaded lights, upon the dressing table, upon the delicate array of crystal and the man's toilet things backed with tarnished silver, silver so tarnished that the monogram was obscured. Among them lay a collar and tie, as if they had just been removed, which, lifted, left upon the surface a pale crescent in the dust. Upon a chair hung the suit, carefully folded; beneath it the two mute shoes and the discarded socks.

The man himself lay in the bed.

For a long while we just stood there, looking down at the profound and fleshless grin. The body had apparently once lain in the attitude of an embrace, but now the long sleep that outlasts love, that conquers even the grimace of love, had cuckolded him. What was left of him, rotted beneath what was left of the nightshirt, had become inextricable from the bed in which he lay; and upon him and upon the pillow beside him lay that even coating of the patient and biding dust.

Then we noticed that in the second pillow was the indentation of a head. One of us lifted something from it, and leaning forward, that faint and invisible dust dry and acrid in the nostrils, we saw a long strand of iron-gray hair.

[1931]

ERNEST HEMINGWAY   [1899–1961]

Hills Like White Elephants

The hills across the valley of the Ebro were long and white. On this side there was no shade and no trees and the station was between two lines of rails in the sun. Close against the side of the station there was the warm shadow of the building and a curtain, made of strings of bamboo beads, hung across the open door into the bar, to keep out flies. The American and the girl with him sat at a table in the shade, outside the building. It was very hot and the express from Barcelona would come in forty minutes. It stopped at this junction for two minutes and went on to Madrid.

"What should we drink?" the girl asked. She had taken off her hat and put it on the table.

"It's pretty hot," the man said.

"Let's drink beer."

"*Dos cervezas,*" the man said into the curtain.

"Big ones?" a woman asked from the doorway.

"Yes. Two big ones."

The woman brought two glasses of beer and two felt pads. She put the felt pads and the beer glasses on the table and looked at the man and the girl. The girl was looking off at the line of hills. They were white in the sun and the country was brown and dry.

"They look like white elephants," she said.

"I've never seen one," the man drank his beer.

"No, you wouldn't have."

"I might have," the man said. "Just because you say I wouldn't have doesn't prove anything."

The girl looked at the bead curtain. "They've painted something on it," she said. "What does it say?"

"Anis del Toro. It's a drink."

"Could we try it?"

The man called "Listen" through the curtain. The woman came out from the bar.

"Four reales."°

"We want two Anis del Toro."

Reales: Spanish silver coins.

176

"With water?"

"Do you want it with water?"

"I don't know," the girl said. "Is it good with water?"

"It's all right."

"You want them with water?" asked the woman.

"Yes, with water."

"It tastes like licorice," the girl said and put the glass down.

"That's the way with everything."

"Yes," said the girl. "Everything tastes of licorice. Especially all the things you've waited so long for, like absinthe."

"Oh, cut it out."

"You started it," the girl said. "I was being amused. I was having a fine time."

"Well, let's try and have a fine time."

"All right. I was trying. I said the mountains looked like white elephants. Wasn't that bright?"

"That was bright."

"I wanted to try this new drink. That's all we do, isn't it—look at things and try new drinks?"

"I guess so."

The girl looked across at the hills.

"They're lovely hills," she said. "They don't really look like white elephants. I just meant the coloring of their skin through the trees."

"Should we have another drink?"

"All right."

The warm wind blew the bead curtain against the table.

"The beer's nice and cool," the man said.

"It's lovely," the girl said.

"It's really an awfully simple operation, Jig," the man said. "It's not really an operation at all."

The girl looked at the ground the table legs rested on.

"I know you wouldn't mind it, Jig. It's really not anything. It's just to let the air in."

The girl did not say anything.

"I'll go with you and I'll stay with you all the time. They just let the air in and then it's all perfectly natural."

"Then what will we do afterward?"

"We'll be fine afterward. Just like we were before."

"What makes you think so?"

"That's the only thing that bothers us. It's the only thing that's made us unhappy."

The girl looked at the bead curtain, put her hand out, and took hold of two of the strings of beads.

"And you think then we'll be all right and be happy."

"I know we will. You don't have to be afraid. I've known lots of people that have done it."

"So have I," said the girl. "And afterward they were all so happy."

"Well," the man said, "if you don't want to you don't have to. I wouldn't have you do it if you didn't want to. But I know it's perfectly simple."

"And you really want to?"

"I think it's the best thing to do. But I don't want you to do it if you don't really want to."

"And if I do it you'll be happy and things will be like they were and you'll love me?"

"I love you now. You know I love you."

"I know. But if I do it, then it will be nice again if I say things are like white elephants, and you'll like it?"

"I'll love it. I love it now but I just can't think about it. You know how I get when I worry."

"If I do it you won't ever worry?"

"I won't worry about that because it's perfectly simple."

"Then I'll do it. Because I don't care about me."

"What do you mean?"

"I don't care about me."

"Well, I care about you."

"Oh, yes. But I don't care about me. And I'll do it and then everything will be fine."

"I don't want you to do it if you feel that way."

The girl stood up and walked to the end of the station. Across, on the other side, were fields of grain and trees along the banks of the Ebro. Far away, beyond the river, were mountains. The shadow of a cloud moved across the field of grain and she saw the river through the trees.

"And we could have all this," she said. "And we could have everything and every day we make it more impossible."

"What did you say?"

"I said we could have everything."

"We can have everything."

"No, we can't."

"We can have the whole world."

"No, we can't."

"We can go everywhere."

"No, we can't. It isn't ours any more."

"It's ours."

"No, it isn't. And once they take it away, you never get it back."

"But they haven't taken it away."

"We'll wait and see."

"Come on back in the shade," he said. "You mustn't feel that way."

"I don't feel any way," the girl said. "I just know things."

"I don't want you to do anything that you don't want to do——"

"Nor that isn't good for me," she said. "I know. Could we have another beer?"

"All right. But you've got to realize——"

"I realize," the girl said. "Can't we maybe stop talking?"

They sat down at the table and the girl looked across at the hills on the dry side of the valley and the man looked at her and at the table.

"You've got to realize," he said, "that I don't want you to do it if you don't want to. I'm perfectly willing to go through with it if it means anything to you."

"Doesn't it mean anything to you? We could get along."

"Of course it does. But I don't want anybody but you. I don't want any one else. And I know it's perfectly simple."

"Yes, you know it's perfectly simple."

"It's all right for you to say that, but I do know it."

"Would you do something for me now?"

"I'd do anything for you."

"Would you please please please please please please please stop talking?"

He did not say anything but looked at the bags against the wall of the station. There were labels on them from all the hotels where they had spent nights.

"But I don't want you to," he said, "I don't care anything about it."

"I'll scream," the girl said.

The woman came out through the curtains with two glasses of beer and put them down on the damp felt pads. "The train comes in five minutes," she said.

"What did she say?" asked the girl.

"That the train is coming in five minutes."

The girl smiled brightly at the woman, to thank her.

"I'd better take the bags over to the other side of the station," the man said. She smiled at him.

"All right. Then come back and we'll finish the beer."

He picked up the two heavy bags and carried them around the station to the other tracks. He looked up the tracks but could not see the train. Coming back, he walked through the barroom, where people waiting for the train were drinking. He drank an Anis at the bar and looked at the people. They were all waiting reasonably for the train. He went out through the bead curtain. She was sitting at the table and smiled at him.

"Do you feel better?" he asked.

"I feel fine," she said. "There's nothing wrong with me. I feel fine."

[1927]

RICHARD WRIGHT   [1908–1960]

The Man Who Was
Almost a Man

Dave struck out across the fields, looking homeward through paling light. Whut's the use talkin wid em niggers in the field? Anyhow, his mother was putting supper on the table. Them niggers can't understan nothing. One of these days he was going to get a gun and practice shooting, then they couldn't talk to him as though he were a little boy. He slowed, looking at the ground. Shucks, Ah ain scareda them even ef they are biggern me! Aw, Ah know whut Ahma do. Ahm going by ol Joe's sto n git that Sears Roebuck catlog n look at them guns. Mebbe Ma will lemme buy one when she gits mah pay from ol man Hawkins. Ahma beg her t gimme some money. Ahm ol ernough to hava gun. Ahm seventeen. Almost a man. He strode, feeling his long loose-jointed limbs. Shucks, a man oughta hava little gun aftah he done worked hard all day.

He came in sight of Joe's store. A yellow lantern glowed on the front porch. He mounted steps and went through the screen door, hearing it bang behind him. There was a strong smell of coal oil and mackerel fish. He felt very confident until he saw fat Joe walk in through the rear door, then his courage began to ooze.

"Howdy, Dave! Whutcha want?"

"How yuh, Mistah Joe? Aw, Ah don wanna buy nothing. Ah jus wanted t see ef yuhd lemme look at tha catlog erwhile."

"Sure! You wanna see it here?"

"Nawsuh. Ah wans t take it home wid me. Ah'll bring it back termorrow when Ah come in from the fiels."

"You plannin on buying something?"

"Yessuh."

"Your ma lettin you have your own money now?"

"Shucks. Mistah Joe, Ahm gittin t be a man like anybody else!"

Joe laughed and wiped his greasy white face with a red bandanna.

"Whut you plannin on buyin?"

Dave looked at the floor, scratched his head, scratched his thigh, and smiled. Then he looked up shyly.

"Ah'll tell yuh, Mistah Joe, ef yuh promise yuh won't tell."

180

"I promise."

"Waal, Ahma buy a gun."

"A gun? Whut you want with a gun?"

"Ah wanna keep it."

"You ain't nothing but a boy. You don't need a gun."

"Aw, lemme have the catlog, Mistah Joe. Ah'll bring it back."

Joe walked through the rear door. Dave was elated. He looked around at barrels of sugar and flour. He heard Joe coming back. He craned his neck to see if he were bringing the book. Yeah, he's got it. Gawddog, he's got it!

"Here, but be sure you bring it back. It's the only one I got."

"Sho, Mistah Joe."

"Say, if you wanna buy a gun, why don't you buy one from me? I gotta gun to sell."

"Will it shoot?"

"Sure it'll shoot."

"Whut kind is it?"

"Oh, it's kinda old . . . a left-hand Wheeler. A pistol. A big one."

"Is it got bullets in it?"

"It's loaded."

"Kin Ah see it?"

"Where's your money?"

"Whut yuh wan fer it?"

"I'll let you have it for two dollars."

"Just two dollahs? Shucks, Ah could buy tha when Ah git mah pay."

"I'll have it here when you want it."

"Awright, suh. Ah be in fer it."

He went through the door, hearing it slam again behind him. Ahma git some money from Ma n buy me a gun! Only two dollahs! He tucked the thick catalogue under his arm and hurried.

"Where yuh been, boy?" His mother held a steaming dish of black-eyed peas.

"Aw, Ma, Ah jus stopped down the road t talk wid the boys."

"Yuh know bettah t keep suppah waitin."

He sat down, resting the catalogue on the edge of the table.

"Yuh git up from there and git to the well n wash yosef! Ah ain feedin no hogs in mah house!"

She grabbed his shoulder and pushed him. He stumbled out of the room, then came back to get the catalogue.

"Whut this?"

"Aw, Ma, it's jusa catlog."

"Who yuh git it from?"

"From Joe, down at the sto."

"Waal, thas good. We kin use it in the outhouse."

"Naw, Ma." He grabbed for it. "Gimme ma catlog, Ma."

She held onto it and glared at him.

"Quit hollerin at me! Whut's wrong wid yuh? Yuh crazy?"

"But Ma, please. It ain mine! It's Joe's! He tol me t bring it back t im termorrow."

She gave up the book. He stumbled down the back steps, hugging the thick book under his arm. When he had splashed water on his face and hands, he groped back to the kitchen and fumbled in a corner for the towel. He bumped into a chair; it clattered to the floor. The catalogue sprawled at his feet. When he had dried his eyes he snatched up the book and held it again under his arm. His mother stood watching him.

"Now, ef yuh gonna act a fool over that ol book, Ah'll take it n burn it up."

"Naw, Ma, please."

"Waal, set down n be still!"

He sat down and drew the oil lamp close. He thumbed page after page, unaware of the food his mother set on the table. His father came in. Then his small brother.

"Whutcha got there, Dave?" his father asked.

"Jusa catlog," he answered, not looking up.

"Yeah, here they is!" His eyes glowed at blue-and-black revolvers. He glanced up, feeling sudden guilt. His father was watching him. He eased the book under the table and rested it on his knees. After the blessing was asked, he ate. He scooped up peas and swallowed fat meat without chewing. Buttermilk helped to wash it down. He did not want to mention money before his father. He would do much better by cornering his mother when she was alone. He looked at his father uneasily out of the edge of his eye.

"Boy, how come yuh don quit foolin wid tha book n eat yo suppah?"

"Yessuh."

"How you n ol man Hawkins gitten erlong?"

"Suh?"

"Can't yuh hear? Why don yuh lissen? Ah ast yu how wuz yuh n ol man Hawkins gittin erlong?"

"Oh, swell, Pa. Ah plows mo lan than anybody over there."

"Waal, yuh oughta keep yo mind on whut yuh doin."

"Yessuh."

He poured his plate full of molasses and sopped it up slowly with a chunk of cornbread. When his father and brother had left the kitchen, he still sat and looked again at the guns in the catalogue, longing to muster courage enough to present his case to his mother. Lawd, ef Ah only had tha pretty one! He could almost feel the slickness of the weapon with his fingers. If he had a gun like that he would polish it and keep it shining so it would never rust. N Ah'd keep it loaded, by Gawd!

"Ma?" His voice was hesitant.

"Hunh?"

"Ol man Hawkins give yuh mah money yit?"

"Yeah, but ain no usa yuh thinking bout throwin nona it erway. Ahm keepin tha money sos yuh kin have cloes t go to school this winter."

He rose and went to her side with the open catalogue in his palms. She was washing dishes, her head bent low over a pan. Shyly he raised the book. When he spoke, his voice was husky, faint.

"Ma, Gawd knows Ah wans one of these."

"One of whut?" she asked, not raising her eyes.

"One of these," he said again, not daring even to point. She glanced up at the page, then at him with wide eyes.

"Nigger, is yuh gone plumb crazy?"

"Aw, Ma—"

"Git outta here! Don yuh talk t me bout no gun! Yuh a fool!"

"Ma, Ah kin buy one fer two dollahs."

"Not ef Ah knows it, yuh ain!"

"But yuh promised me one—"

"Ah don care whut Ah promised! Yuh ain nothing but a boy yit!"

"Ma, ef yuh lemme buy one Ah'll *never* ast yuh fer nothing no mo."

"Ah tol yuh t git outta here! Yuh ain gonna toucha penny of tha money fer no gun! Thas how come Ah has Mistah Hawkins t pay yo wages t me, cause Ah knows yuh ain got no sense."

"But, Ma, we needa gun. Pa ain got no gun. We needa gun in the house. Yuh kin never tell whut might happen."

"Now don yuh try to maka fool outta me, boy! Ef we did hava gun, yuh wouldn't have it!"

He laid the catalogue down and slipped his arm around her waist.

"Aw, Ma, Ah done worked hard alla summer n ain ast yuh fer nothin, is Ah, now?"

"Thas whut yuh spose t do!"

"But Ma, Ah wans a gun. Yuh kin lemme have two dollahs outta mah money. Please, Ma. I kin give it to Pa . . . Please, Ma! Ah loves yuh, Ma."

When she spoke her voice came soft and low.

"Whut yu wan wida gun, Dave? Yuh don need no gun. Yuh'll git in trouble. N ef yo pa jus thought Ah let yuh have money t buy a gun he'd hava fit."

"Ah'll hide it, Ma. It ain but two dollahs."

"Lawd, chil, whut's wrong wid yuh?"

"Ain nothin wrong, Ma. Ahm almos a man now. Ah wans a gun."

"Who gonna sell yuh a gun?"

"Ol Joe at the sto."

"N it don cos but two dollahs?"

"Thas all, Ma. Jus two dollahs. Please, Ma."

She was stacking the plates away; her hands moved slowly, reflectively. Dave kept an anxious silence. Finally, she turned to him.

"Ah'll let yuh git tha gun ef yuh promise me one thing."

"Whut's tha, Ma?"

"Yuh bring it straight back t me, yuh hear? It be fer Pa."

"Yessum! Lemme go now, Ma."

She stooped, turned slightly to one side, raised the hem of her dress, rolled down the top of her stocking, and came up with a slender wad of bills.

"Here," she said. "Lawd knows yuh don need no gun. But yer pa does. Yuh bring it right back t me, yuh hear? Ahma put it up. Now ef yuh don, Ahma have yuh pa lick yuh so hard yuh won fergit it."

"Yessum."

He took the money, ran down the steps, and across the yard.

"Dave! Yuuuuuh Daaaaave!"

He heard, but he was not going to stop now. "Naw, Lawd!"

The first movement he made the following morning was to reach under his pillow for the gun. In the gray light of dawn he held it loosely, feeling a sense of power. Could kill a man with a gun like this. Kill anybody, black or white. And if he were holding his gun in his hand, nobody could run over him; they would have to respect him. It was a big gun, with a long barrel and a heavy handle. He raised and lowered it in his hand, marveling at its weight.

He had not come straight home with it as his mother had asked; instead he had stayed out in the fields, holding the weapon in his hand, aiming it now and then at some imaginary foe. But he had not fired it; he had been afraid that his father might hear. Also he was not sure he knew how to fire it.

To avoid surrendering the pistol he had not come into the house until he knew that they were all asleep. When his mother had tiptoed to his bedside late that night and demanded the gun, he had first played possum;° then he had told her that the gun was hidden outdoors, that he would bring it to her in the morning. Now he lay turning it slowly in his hands. He broke it, took out the cartridges, felt them, and then put them back.

played possum: Made believe that he was sleeping.

He slid out of bed, got a long strip of old flannel from a trunk, wrapped the gun in it, and tied it to his naked thigh while it was still loaded. He did not go in to breakfast. Even though it was not yet daylight, he started for Jim Hawkins' plantation. Just as the sun was rising he reached the barns where the mules and plows were kept.

"Hey! That you, Dave?"

He turned. Jim Hawkins stood eying him suspiciously.

"What're yuh doing here so early?"

"Ah didn't know Ah wuz gittin up so early, Mistah Hawkins. Ah wuz fixin t hitch up ol Jenny n take her t the fiels."

"Good. Since you're so early, how about plowing that stretch down by the woods?"

"Suits me, Mistah Hawkins."

"O.K. Go to it!"

He hitched Jenny to a plow and started across the fields. Hot dog! This was just what he wanted. If he could get down by the woods, he could shoot his gun and nobody would hear. He walked behind the plow, hearing the traces creaking, feeling the gun tied tight to his thigh.

When he reached the woods, he plowed two whole rows before he decided to take out the gun. Finally, he stopped, looked in all directions, then untied the gun and held it in his hand. He turned to the mule and smiled.

"Know whut this is, Jenny? Naw, yuh wouldn know! Yuhs jusa ol mule! Anyhow, this is a gun, n it kin shoot, by Gawd!"

He held the gun at arm's length. Whut t hell, Ahma shoot this thing! He looked at Jenny again.

"Lissen here, Jenny! When Ah pull this ol trigger, Ah don wan yuh t run n acka fool now!"

Jenny stood with head down, her short ears pricked straight. Dave walked off about twenty feet, held the gun far out from him at arm's length, and turned his head. Hell, he told himself, Ah ain afraid. The gun felt loose in his fingers; he waved it wildly for a moment. Then he shut his eyes and tightened his forefinger. Bloom! A report half deafened him and he thought his right hand was torn from his arm. He heard Jenny whinnying and galloping over the field, and he found himself on his knees, squeezing his fingers hard between his legs. His hand was numb; he jammed it into his mouth, trying to warm it, trying to stop the pain. The gun lay at his feet. He did not quite know what had happened. He stood up and stared at the gun as though it were a living thing. He gritted his teeth and kicked the gun. Yuh almos broke mah arm! He turned to look for Jenny; she was far over the fields, tossing her head and kicking wildly.

"Hol on there, ol mule!"

When he caught up with her she stood trembling, walling her big white eyes at him. The plow was far away; the traces had broken. Then Dave stopped short, looking, not believing. Jenny was bleeding. Her left side was red and wet with blood. He went closer. Lawd, have mercy! Wondah did Ah shoot this mule? He grabbed for Jenny's mane. She flinched, snorted, whirled, tossing her head.

"Hol on now! Hol on."

Then he saw the hole in Jenny's side, right between the ribs. It was round, wet, red. A crimson stream streaked down the front leg, flowing fast. Good Gawd! Ah wuzn't shootin at tha mule. He felt panic. He knew he had to stop that blood, or Jenny would bleed to death. He had never seen so much blood in all his life. He chased the mule for half a mile, trying to catch her. Finally she stopped, breathing hard, stumpy tail half arched. He caught her mane and led her back to where the plow and gun lay. Then he stooped and grabbed handfuls of damp black earth and tried to plug the bullet hole. Jenny shuddered, whinnied, and broke from him.

"Hol on! Hol on now!"

He tried to plug it again, but blood came anyhow. His fingers were hot and sticky. He rubbed dirt into his palms, trying to dry them. Then again he attempted to plug the bullet hole, but Jenny shied away, kicking her heels high. He stood helpless. He had to do something. He ran at Jenny; she dodged him. He watched a red stream of blood flow down Jenny's leg and form a bright pool at her feet.

"Jenny . . . Jenny," he called weakly.

His lips trembled. She's bleeding t death! He looked in the direction of home, wanting to go back, wanting to get help. But he saw the pistol lying in the damp black clay. He had a queer feeling that if he only did something, this would not be; Jenny would not be there bleeding to death.

When he went to her this time, she did not move. She stood with sleepy, dreamy eyes; and when he touched her she gave a low-pitched whinny and knelt to the ground, her front knees slopping in blood.

"Jenny . . . Jenny . . ." he whispered.

For a long time she held her neck erect; then her head sank, slowly. Her ribs swelled with a mighty heave and she went over.

Dave's stomach felt empty, very empty. He picked up the gun and held it gingerly between his thumb and forefinger. He buried it at the foot of a tree. He took a stick and tried to cover the pool of blood with dirt—but what was the use? There was Jenny lying with her mouth open and her eyes walled and glassy. He could not tell Jim Hawkins he had shot his mule. But he had to tell something. Yeah, Ah'll tell em Jenny started gittin wil n fell on the joint of the plow. . . . But that would hardly happen to a mule. He walked across the field slowly, head down.

It was sunset. Two of Jim Hawkins' men were over near the edge of the woods digging a hole in which to bury Jenny. Dave was surrounded by a knot of people, all of whom were looking down at the dead mule.

"I don't see how in the world it happened," said Jim Hawkins for the tenth time.

The crowd parted and Dave's mother, father, and small brother pushed into the center.

"Where Dave?" his mother called.

"There he is," said Jim Hawkins.

His mother grabbed him.

"Whut happened, Dave? Whut yuh done?"

"Nothin."

"C mon, boy, talk," his father said.

Dave took a deep breath and told the story he knew nobody believed.

"Waal," he drawled. "Ah brung ol Jenny down here sos Ah could do mah plowin. Ah plowed bout two rows, just like yuh see." He stopped and pointed at the long rows of upturned earth. "Then somethin musta been wrong wid ol Jenny. She wouldn ack right a-tall. She started snortin n kickin her heels. Ah tried t hol her, but she pulled erway, rearin n goin in. Then when the point of the plow was stickin up in the air, she swung erroun n twisted herself back on it . . . She stuck herself n started t bleed. N fo Ah could do anything, she wuz dead."

"Did you ever hear of anything like that in all your life?" asked Jim Hawkins.

There were white and black standing in the crowd. They murmured. Dave's mother came close to him and looked hard into his face. "Tell the truth, Dave," she said.

"Looks like a bullet hole to me," said one man.

"Dave, whut yuh do wid the gun?" his mother asked.

The crowd surged in, looking at him. He jammed his hands into his pockets, shook his head slowly from left to right, and backed away. His eyes were wide and painful.

"Did he hava gun?" asked Jim Hawkins.

"By Gawd, Ah tol yuh tha wuz a gun wound," said a man, slapping his thigh.

His father caught his shoulders and shook him till his teeth rattled.

"Tell whut happened, yuh rascal! Tell whut . . ."

Dave looked at Jenny's stiff legs and began to cry.

"Whut yuh do wid tha gun?" his mother asked.

"Whut wuz he doin wida gun?" his father asked.

"Come on and tell the truth," said Hawkins. "Ain't nobody going to hurt you . . ."

His mother crowded close to him.

"Did yuh shoot tha mule, Dave?"

Dave cried, seeing blurred white and black faces.

"Ahh ddinn gggo tt sshooot hher . . . Ah ssswear ffo Gawd Ahh ddin. . . . Ah wuz a-tryin t sssee ef the old gggun would sshoot—"

"Where yuh git the gun from?" his father asked.

"Ah got it from Joe, at the sto."

"Where yuh git the money?"

"Ma give it t me."

"He kept worryin me, Bob. Ah had t. Ah tol im t bring the gun right back t me . . . It was fer yuh, the gun."

"But how yuh happen to shoot that mule?" asked Jim Hawkins.

"Ah wuzn shootin at the mule, Mistah Hawkins. The gun jumped when Ah pulled the trigger . . . N fo Ah knowed anythin Jenny was there a-bleedin."

Somebody in the crowd laughed. Jim Hawkins walked close to Dave and looked into his face.

"Well, looks like you have bought you a mule, Dave."

"Ah swear fo Gawd, Ah didn go t kill the mule, Mistah Hawkins!"

"But you killed her!"

All the crowd was laughing now. They stood on tiptoe and poked heads over one another's shoulders.

"Well, boy, looks like yuh done bought a dead mule! Hahaha!"

"Ain tha ershame."

"Hohohohoho."

Dave stood, head down, twisting his feet in the dirt.

"Well, you needn't worry about it, Bob," said Jim Hawkins to Dave's father. "Just let the boy keep on working and pay me two dollars a month."

"Whut yuh wan fer yo mule, Mistah Hawkins?"

Jim Hawkins screwed up his eyes.

"Fifty dollars."

"Whut yuh do wid tha gun?" Dave's father demanded.

Dave said nothing.

"Yuh wan me t take a tree n beat yuh till yuh talk!"

"Nawsuh!"

"Whut yuh do wid it?"

"Ah throwed it erway."

"Where?"

"Ah . . . Ah throwed it in the creek."

"Waal, c mon home. N firs thing in the mawnin git to tha creek n fin tha gun."

"Yessuh."

"Whut yuh pay fer it?"

"Two dollahs."

"Take tha gun n git yo money back n carry it t Mistah Hawkins, yuh hear? N don fergit Ahma lan you black bottom good fer this! Now march yosef on home, suh!"

Dave turned and walked slowly. He heard people laughing. Dave glared, his eyes welling with tears. Hot anger bubbled in him. Then he swallowed and stumbled on.

That night Dave did not sleep. He was glad that he had gotten out of killing the mule so easily, but he was hurt. Something hot seemed to turn over inside him each time he remembered how they had laughed. He tossed on his bed, feeling his hard pillow. N Pa says he's gonna beat me . . . He remembered other beatings, and his back quivered. Naw, naw, Ah sho don wan im t beat me tha way no mo. Dam em all! Nobody ever gave him anything. All he did was work. They treat me like a mule, n then they beat me. He gritted his teeth. N Ma had t tell on me.

Well, if he had to, he would take old man Hawkins that two dollars. But that meant selling the gun. And he wanted to keep that gun. Fifty dollars for a dead mule.

He turned over, thinking how he had fired the gun. He had an itch to fire it again. Ef other men kin shoota gun, by Gawd, Ah kin! He was still, listening. Mebbe they all sleepin now. The house was still. He heard the soft breathing of his brother. Yes, now! He would go down and get that gun and see if he could fire it! He eased out of bed and slipped into overalls.

The moon was bright. He ran almost all the way to the edge of the woods. He stumbled over the ground, looking for the spot where he had buried the gun. Yeah, here it is. Like a hungry dog scratching for a bone, he pawed it up. He puffed his black cheeks and blew dirt from the trigger and barrel. He broke it and found four cartridges unshot. He looked around; the fields were filled with silence and moonlight. He clutched the gun stiff and hard in his fingers. But, as soon as he wanted to pull the trigger, he shut his eyes and turned his head. Naw, Ah can't shoot wid mah eyes closed n mah head turned. With effort he held his eyes open; then he squeezed. *Blooooom!* He was stiff, not breathing. The gun was still in his hands. Dammit, he'd done it! He fired again. *Blooooom!* He smiled. *Blooooom! Blooooom! Click, click*. There! It was empty. If anybody could shoot a gun, he could. He put the gun into his hip pocket and started across the fields.

When he reached the top of a ridge he stood straight and proud in the moonlight, looking at Jim Hawkins' big white house, feeling the gun sagging in his pocket. Lawd, ef Ah had just one mo bullet Ah'd taka shot at tha house. Ah'd like t scare ol man Hawkins jusa little . . . Jusa enough t let im know Dave Saunders is a man.

To his left the road curved, running to the tracks of the Illinois Central. He jerked his head, listening. From far off came a faint *hoooof-hoooof; hoooof-hoooof; hoooof-hoooof*. . . . He stood rigid. Two dollahs a mont. Les see now . . . Tha means it'll take bout two years. Shucks! Ah'll be dam!

He started down the road, toward the tracks. Yeah, here she comes! He stood beside the track and held himself stiffly. Here she comes, erroun the ben . . . C mon, yuh slow poke! C mon! He had his hand on his gun; something quivered in his stomach. Then the train thundered past, the gray and brown box cars rumbling and clinking. He gripped the gun tightly; then he jerked his hand out of his pocket. Ah betcha Bill wouldn't do it! Ah betcha . . . The cars slid past, steel grinding upon steel. Ahm ridin yuh ternight, so hep me Gawd! He was hot all over. He hesitated just a moment; then he grabbed, pulled atop of a car, and lay flat. He felt his pocket; the gun was still there. Ahead the long rails were glinting in the moonlight, stretching away, away to somewhere, somewhere where he could be a man . . .

[1961]

EUDORA WELTY   [1909-2001]

Why I Live at the P.O.

I was getting along fine with Mama, Papa-Daddy, and Uncle Rondo until my sister Stella-Rondo just separated from her husband and came back home again. Mr. Whitaker! Of course I went with Mr. Whitaker first, when he first appeared here in China Grove, taking "Pose Yourself" photos, and Stella-Rondo broke us up. Told him I was one-sided. Bigger on one side than the other, which is a deliberate, calculated falsehood: I'm the same. Stella-Rondo is exactly twelve months to the day younger than I am and for that reason she's spoiled.

She's always had anything in the world she wanted and then she'd throw it away. Papa-Daddy gave her this gorgeous Add-a-Pearl necklace when she was eight years old and she threw it away playing baseball when she was nine, with only two pearls.

So as soon as she got married and moved away from home the first thing she did was separate! From Mr. Whitaker! This photographer with the popeyes she said she trusted. Came home from one of those towns up in Illinois and to our complete surprise brought this child of two.

Mama said she like to make her drop dead for a second. "Here you had this marvelous blonde child and never so much as wrote your mother a word about it," says Mama. "I'm thoroughly ashamed of you." But of course she wasn't.

Stella-Rondo just calmly takes off this *hat*, I wish you could see it. She says, "Why, Mama, Shirley-T.'s adopted, I can prove it."

"How?" says Mama, but all I says was, "H'm!" There I was over the hot stove, trying to stretch two chickens over five people and a completely unexpected child into the bargain, without one moment's notice.

"What do you mean — 'H'm!'?" says Stella-Rondo, and Mama says, "I heard that, Sister."

I said that oh, I didn't mean a thing, only that whoever Shirley-T. was, she was the spit-image of Papa-Daddy if he'd cut off his beard, which of course he'd never do in the world. Papa-Daddy's Mama's papa and sulks.

Stella-Rondo got furious! She said, "Sister, I don't need to tell you you got a lot of nerve and always did have and I'll thank you to make no future reference to my adopted child whatsoever."

"Very well," I said. "Very well, very well. Of course I noticed at once she looks like Mr. Whitaker's side too. That frown. She looks like a cross between Mr. Whitaker and Papa-Daddy."

"Well, all I can say is she isn't."

"She looks exactly like Shirley Temple to me," says Mama, but Shirley-T. just ran away from her.

So the first thing Stella-Rondo did at the table was turn Papa-Daddy against me.

"Papa-Daddy," she says. He was trying to cut up his meat. "Papa-Daddy!" I was taken completely by surprise. Papa-Daddy is about a million years old and's got this long-long beard. "Papa-Daddy, Sister says she fails to understand why you don't cut off your beard."

So Papa-Daddy l-a-y-s down his knife and fork! He's real rich. Mama says he is, he says he isn't. So he says, "Have I heard correctly? You don't understand why I don't cut off my beard?"

"Why," I says, "Papa-Daddy, of course I understand, I did not say any such of a thing, the idea!"

He says, "Hussy!"

I says, "Papa-Daddy, you know I wouldn't any more want you to cut off your beard than the man in the moon. It was the farthest thing from my mind! Stella-Rondo sat there and made that up while she was eating breast of chicken."

But he says, "So the postmistress fails to understand why I don't cut off my beard. Which job I got you through my influence with the government. 'Bird's nest' — is that what you call it?"

Not that it isn't the next to smallest P.O. in the entire state of Mississippi.

I says, "Oh, Papa-Daddy," I says, "I didn't say any such of a thing, I never dreamed it was a bird's nest, I have always been grateful though this is the next to smallest P.O. in the state of Mississippi, and I do not enjoy being referred to as a hussy by my own grandfather."

But Stella-Rondo says, "Yes, you did say it too. Anybody in the world could of heard you, that had ears."

"Stop right there," says Mama, looking at *me*.

So I pulled my napkin straight back through the napkin ring and left the table.

As soon as I was out of the room Mama says, "Call her back, or she'll starve to death," but Papa-Daddy says, "This is the beard I started growing on the Coast when I was fifteen years old." He would of gone on till nightfall if Shirley-T. hadn't lost the Milky Way she ate in Cairo.°

So Papa-Daddy says, "I am going out and lie in the hammock, and you can all sit here and remember my words: I'll never cut off my beard as long as I live, even one inch, and I don't appreciate it in you at all." Passed right by me in the hall and went straight out and got in the hammock.

It would be a holiday. It wasn't five minutes before Uncle Rondo suddenly appeared in the hall in one of Stella-Rondo's flesh-colored kimonos, all cut on the bias, like something Mr. Whitaker probably thought was gorgeous.

"Uncle Rondo!" I says. "I didn't know who that was! Where are you going?"

"Sister," he says, "get out of my way, I'm poisoned."

"If you're poisoned stay away from Papa-Daddy," I says. "Keep out of the hammock. Papa-Daddy will certainly beat you on the head if you come within forty miles of him. He thinks I deliberately said he ought to cut off his beard after he got me the P.O., and I've told him and told him and told him, and he acts like he just don't hear me. Papa-Daddy must of gone stone deaf."

"He picked a fine day to do it then," says Uncle Rondo, and before you could say "Jack Robinson" flew out in the yard.

What he'd really done, he'd drunk another bottle of that prescription. He does it every single Fourth of July as sure as shooting, and it's horribly expensive. Then he falls over in the hammock and snores. So he insisted on zigzagging right on out to the hammock, looking like a half-wit.

Papa-Daddy woke up with this horrible yell and right there without moving an inch he tried to turn Uncle Rondo against me. I heard every word he said. Oh, he told Uncle Rondo I didn't learn to read till I was eight years old and he didn't see how in the world I ever got the mail put

Cairo: Cairo, Illinois.

up at the P.O., much less read it all, and he said if Uncle Rondo could only fathom the lengths he had gone to get me that job! And he said on the other hand he thought Stella-Rondo had a brilliant mind and deserved credit for getting out of town. All the time he was just lying there swinging as pretty as you please and looping out his beard, and poor Uncle Rondo was *pleading* with him to slow down the hammock, it was making him as dizzy as a witch to watch it. But that's what Papa-Daddy likes about a hammock. So Uncle Rondo was too dizzy to get turned against me for the time being. He's Mama's only brother and is a good case of a one-track mind. Ask anybody. A certified pharmacist.

Just then I heard Stella-Rondo raising the upstairs window. While she was married she got this peculiar idea that it's cooler with the windows shut and locked. So she has to raise the window before she can make a soul hear her outdoors.

So she raises the window and says, "*Oh!*" You would have thought she was mortally wounded.

Uncle Rondo and Papa-Daddy didn't even look up, but kept right on with what they were doing. I had to laugh.

I flew up the stairs and threw the door open! I says, "What in the wide world's the matter, Stella-Rondo? You mortally wounded?"

"No," she says, "I am not mortally wounded but I wish you would do me the favor of looking out that window there and telling me what you see."

So I shade my eyes and look out the window.

"I see the front yard," I says.

"Don't you see any human beings?" she says.

"I see Uncle Rondo trying to run Papa-Daddy out of the hammock," I says. "Nothing more. Naturally, it's so suffocating-hot in the house, with all the windows shut and locked, everybody who cares to stay in their right mind will have to go out and get in the hammock before the Fourth of July is over."

"Don't you notice anything different about Uncle Rondo?" asks Stella-Rondo.

"Why, no, except he's got on some terrible-looking flesh-colored contraption I wouldn't be found dead in, is all I can see," I says.

"Never mind, you won't be found dead in it, because it happens to be part of my trousseau, and Mr. Whitaker took several dozen photographs of me in it," says Stella-Rondo. "What on earth could Uncle Rondo *mean* by wearing part of my trousseau out in the broad open daylight without saying so much as 'Kiss my foot,' *knowing* I only got home this morning after my separation and hung my negligee up on the bathroom door, just as nervous as I could be?"

"I'm sure I don't know, and what do you expect me to do about it?" I says. "Jump out the window?"

"No, I expect nothing of the kind. I simply declare that Uncle Rondo looks like a fool in it, that's all," she says. "It makes me sick to my stomach."

"Well, he looks as good as he can," I says. "As good as anybody in reason could." I stood up for Uncle Rondo, please remember. And I said to Stella-Rondo, "I think I would do well not to criticize so freely if I were you and came home with a two-year-old child I had never said a word about, and no explanation whatever about my separation."

"I asked you the instant I entered this house not to refer one more time to my adopted child, and you gave me your word of honor you would not," was all Stella-Rondo would say, and started pulling out every one of her eyebrows with some cheap Kress tweezers.

So I merely slammed the door behind me and went down and made some green-tomato pickle. Somebody had to do it. Of course Mama had turned both the niggers loose; she always said no earthly power could hold one anyway on the Fourth of July, so she wouldn't even try. It turned out that Jaypan fell in the lake and came within a very narrow limit of drowning.

So Mama trots in. Lifts up the lid and says, "H'm! Not very good for your Uncle Rondo in his precarious condition, I must say. Or poor little adopted Shirley-T. Shame on you!"

That made me tired. I says, "Well, Stella-Rondo had better thank her lucky stars it was her instead of me came trotting in with that very peculiar-looking child. Now if it had been me that trotted in from Illinois and brought a peculiar-looking child of two, I shudder to think of the reception I'd of got, much less controlled the diet of an entire family."

"But you must remember, Sister, that you were never married to Mr. Whitaker in the first place and didn't go up to Illinois to live," says Mama, shaking a spoon in my face. "If you had I would of been just as overjoyed to see you and your little adopted girl as I was to see Stella-Rondo, when you wound up with your separation and came on back home."

"You would not," I says.

"Don't contradict me, I would," says Mama.

But I said she couldn't convince me though she talked till she was blue in the face. Then I said, "Besides, you know as well as I do that that child is not adopted."

"She most certainly is adopted," says Mama, stiff as a poker.

I says, "Why, Mama, Stella-Rondo had her just as sure as anything in this world, and just too stuck up to admit it."

"Why, Sister," said Mama. "Here I thought we were going to have a pleasant Fourth of July, and you start right out not believing a word your own baby sister tells you!"

"Just like Cousin Annie Flo. Went to her grave denying the facts of life," I remind Mama.

"I told you if you ever mentioned Annie Flo's name I'd slap your face," says Mama, and slaps my face.

"All right, you wait and see," I says.

"I," says Mama, "*I* prefer to take my children's word for anything when it's humanly possible." You ought to see Mama, she weighs two hundred pounds and has real tiny feet.

Just then something perfectly horrible occurred to me.

"Mama," I says, "can that child talk?" I simply had to whisper! "Mama, I wonder if that child can be — you know — in any way? Do you realize," I says, "that she hasn't spoken one single, solitary word to a human being up to this minute? This is the way she looks," I says, and I looked like this.

Well, Mama and I just stood there and stared at each other. It was horrible!

"I remember well that Joe Whitaker frequently drank like a fish," says Mama. "I believed to my soul he drank *chemicals*." And without another word she marches to the foot of the stairs and calls Stella-Rondo.

"Stella-Rondo? O-o-o-o-o! Stella-Rondo!"

"What?" says Stella-Rondo from upstairs. Not even the grace to get up off the bed.

"Can that child of yours talk?" asks Mama.

Stella-Rondo says, "Can she what?"

"Talk! Talk!" says Mama. "Burdyburdyburdyburdy!"

So Stella-Rondo yells back, "Who says she can't talk?"

"Sister says so," says Mama.

"You didn't have to tell me, I know whose word of honor don't mean a thing in this house," says Stella-Rondo.

And in a minute the loudest Yankee voice I ever heard in my life yells out, "OE'm Pop-OE the Sailor-r-r-r Ma-a-an!" and then somebody jumps up and down in the upstairs hall. In another second the house would of fallen down.

"Not only talks, she can tap-dance!" calls Stella-Rondo. "Which is more than some people I won't name can do."

"Why, the little precious darling thing!" Mama says, so surprised. "Just as smart as she can be!" Starts talking baby talk right there. Then she turns on me. "Sister, you ought to be thoroughly ashamed! Run upstairs this instant and apologize to Stella-Rondo and Shirley-T."

"Apologize for what?" I says. "I merely wondered if the child was normal, that's all. Now that she's proved she is, why, I have nothing further to say."

But Mama just turned on her heel and flew out, furious. She ran right upstairs and hugged the baby. She believed it was adopted. Stella-Rondo hadn't done a thing but turn her against me from upstairs while I stood there helpless over the hot stove. So that made Mama, Papa-Daddy, and the baby all on Stella-Rondo's side.

Next, Uncle Rondo.

I must say that Uncle Rondo has been marvelous to me at various times in the past and I was completely unprepared to be made to jump out of my skin, the way it turned out. Once Stella-Rondo did something perfectly horrible to him — broke a chain letter from Flanders Field° — and he took the radio back he had given her and gave it to me. Stella-Rondo was furious! For six months we all had to call her Stella instead of Stella-Rondo, or she wouldn't answer. I always thought Uncle Rondo had all the brains of the entire family. Another time he sent me to Mammoth Cave,° with all expenses paid.

But this would be the day he was drinking that prescription, the Fourth of July.

So at supper Stella-Rondo speaks up and says she thinks Uncle Rondo ought to try to eat a little something. So finally Uncle Rondo said he would try a little cold biscuits and ketchup, but that was all. So *she* brought it to him.

"Do you think it wise to disport with ketchup in Stella-Rondo's flesh-colored kimono?" I says. Trying to be considerate! If Stella-Rondo couldn't watch out for her trousseau, somebody had to.

"Any objections?" asks Uncle Rondo, just about to pour out all the ketchup.

"Don't mind what she says, Uncle Rondo," says Stella-Rondo. "Sister has been devoting this solid afternoon to sneering out my bedroom window at the way you look."

"What's that?" says Uncle Rondo. Uncle Rondo has got the most terrible temper in the world. Anything is liable to make him tear the house down if it comes at the wrong time.

So Stella-Rondo says, "Sister says, 'Uncle Rondo certainly does look like a fool in that pink kimono!'"

Do you remember who it was really said that?

Uncle Rondo spills out all the ketchup and jumps out of his chair and tears off the kimono and throws it down on the dirty floor and puts his foot on it. It had to be sent all the way to Jackson to the cleaners and repleated.

Flanders Field: American military cemetery in Belgium dating from World War I.
Mammoth Cave: Mammoth Cave, Kentucky, a network of natural underground caverns.

"So that's your opinion of your Uncle Rondo, is it?" he says. "I look like a fool, do I? Well, that's the last straw. A whole day in this house with nothing to do, and then to hear you come out with a remark like that behind my back!"

"I didn't say any such of a thing, Uncle Rondo," I says, "and I'm not saying who did, either. Why, I think you look all right. Just try to take care of yourself and not talk and eat at the same time," I says. "I think you better go lie down."

"Lie down my foot," says Uncle Rondo. I ought to of known by that he was fixing to do something perfectly horrible.

So he didn't do anything that night in the precarious state he was in — just played Casino with Mama and Stella-Rondo and Shirley-T. and gave Shirley-T. a nickel with a head on both sides. It tickled her nearly to death, and she called him "Papa." But at 6:30 A.M. the next morning, he threw a whole five-cent package of some unsold one-inch firecrackers from the store as hard as he could into my bedroom and they every one went off. Not one bad one in the string. Anybody else, there'd be one that wouldn't go off.

Well, I'm just terribly susceptible to noise of any kind, the doctor has always told me I was the most sensitive person he had ever seen in his whole life, and I was simply prostrated. I couldn't eat! People tell me they heard it as far as the cemetery, and old Aunt Jep Patterson, that had been holding her own so good, thought it was Judgment Day and she was going to meet her whole family. It's usually so quiet here.

And I'll tell you it didn't take me any longer than a minute to make up my mind what to do. There I was with the whole entire house on Stella-Rondo's side and turned against me. If I have anything at all I have pride.

So I just decided I'd go straight down to the P.O. There's plenty of room there in the back, I says to myself.

Well! I made no bones about letting the family catch on to what I was up to. I didn't try to conceal it.

The first thing they knew, I marched in where they were all playing Old Maid and pulled the electric oscillating fan out by the plug, and everything got real hot. Next I snatched the pillow I'd done the needlepoint on right off the davenport from behind Papa-Daddy. He went "Ugh!" I beat Stella-Rondo up the stairs and finally found my charm bracelet in her bureau drawer under a picture of Nelson Eddy.°

"So that's the way the land lies," says Uncle Rondo. There he was, piecing on the ham. "Well, Sister, I'll be glad to donate my army cot if you got

Nelson Eddy: A singer in many Hollywood musical films of the 1930s.

any place to set it up, providing you'll leave right this minute and let me get some peace." Uncle Rondo was in France.

"Thank you kindly for the cot and 'peace' is hardly the word I would select if I had to resort to firecrackers at 6:30 A.M. in a young girl's bedroom," I says back to him. "And as to where I intend to go, you seem to forget my position as postmistress of China Grove, Mississippi," I says. "I've always got the P.O."

Well, that made them all sit up and take notice.

I went out front and started digging up some four-o'clocks to plant around the P.O.

"Ah-ah-ah!" says Mama, raising the window. "Those happen to be my four-o'clocks. Everything planted in that star is mine. I've never known you to make anything grow in your life."

"Very well," I says. "But I take the fern. Even you, Mama, can't stand there and deny that I'm the one watered that fern. And I happen to know where I can send in a box top and get a packet of one thousand mixed seeds, no two the same kind, free."

"Oh, where?" Mama wants to know.

But I says, "Too late. You 'tend to your house, and I'll 'tend to mine. You hear things like that all the time if you know how to listen to the radio. Perfectly marvelous offers. Get anything you want free."

So I hope to tell you I marched in and got that radio, and they could of all bit a nail in two, especially Stella-Rondo, that it used to belong to, and she well knew she couldn't get it back, I'd sue for it like a shot. And I very politely took the sewing-machine motor I helped pay the most on to give Mama for Christmas back in 1929, and a good big calendar, with the first-aid remedies on it. The thermometer and the Hawaiian ukulele certainly were rightfully mine, and I stood on the step-ladder and got all my watermelon-rind preserves and every fruit and vegetable I'd put up, every jar. Then I began to pull the tacks out of the bluebird wall vases on the archway to the dining room.

"Who told you you could have those, Miss Priss?" says Mama, fanning as hard as she could.

"I bought 'em and I'll keep track of 'em," I says. "I'll tack 'em up one on each side the post-office window, and you can see 'em when you come to ask me for your mail, if you're so dead to see 'em."

"Not I! I'll never darken the door to that post office again if I live to be a hundred," Mama says. "Ungrateful child! After all the money we spent on you at the Normal."°

Normal: A two-year school for teacher training.

"Me either," says Stella-Rondo. "You can just let my mail lie there and *rot*, for all I care. I'll never come and relieve you of a single, solitary piece."

"I should worry," I says. "And who you think's going to sit down and write you all those big fat letters and postcards, by the way? Mr. Whitaker? Just because he was the only man ever dropped down in China Grove and you got him—unfairly—is he going to sit down and write you a lengthy correspondence after you come home giving no rhyme nor reason whatsoever for your separation and no explanation for the presence of that child? I may not have your brilliant mind, but I fail to see it."

So Mama says, "Sister, I've told you a thousand times that Stella-Rondo simply got homesick, and this child is far too big to be hers," and she says, "Now, why don't you just sit down and play Casino?"

Then Shirley-T. sticks out her tongue at me in this perfectly horrible way. She has no more manners than the man in the moon. I told her she was going to cross her eyes like that some day and they'd stick.

"It's too late to stop me now," I says. "You should have tried that yesterday. I'm going to the P.O. and the only way you can possibly see me is to visit me there."

So Papa-Daddy says, "You'll never catch me setting foot in that post office, even if I should take a notion into my head to write a letter some place." He says, "I won't have you reachin' out of that little old window with a pair of shears and cuttin' off any beard of mine. I'm too smart for you!"

"We all are," says Stella-Rondo.

But I said, "If you're so smart, where's Mr. Whitaker?"

So then Uncle Rondo says, "I'll thank you from now on to stop reading all the orders I get on postcards and telling everybody in China Grove what you think is the matter with them," but I says, "I draw my own conclusions and will continue in the future to draw them." I says, "If people want to write their inmost secrets on penny postcards, there's nothing in the wide world you can do about it, Uncle Rondo."

"And if you think we'll ever *write* another postcard you're sadly mistaken," says Mama.

"Cutting off your nose to spite your face then," I says. "But if you're all determined to have no more to do with the U.S. mail, think of this: What will Stella-Rondo do now, if she wants to tell Mr. Whitaker to come after her?"

"Wah!" says Stella-Rondo. I knew she'd cry. She had a conniption fit right there in the kitchen.

"It will be interesting to see how long she holds out," I says. "And now—I am leaving."

"Good-bye," says Uncle Rondo.

"Oh, I declare," says Mama, "to think that a family of mine should quarrel on the Fourth of July, or the day after, over Stella-Rondo leaving old Mr. Whitaker and having the sweetest little adopted child! It looks like we'd all be glad!"

"Wah!" says Stella-Rondo, and has a fresh conniption fit.

"*He* left *her* — you mark my words," I says. "That's Mr. Whitaker. I know Mr. Whitaker. After all, I knew him first. I said from the beginning he'd up and leave her. I foretold every single thing that's happened."

"Where did he go?" asks Mama.

"Probably to the North Pole, if he knows what's good for him," I says.

But Stella-Rondo just bawled and wouldn't say another word. She flew to her room and slammed the door.

"Now look what you've gone and done, Sister," says Mama. "You go apologize."

"I haven't got time, I'm leaving," I says.

"Well, what are you waiting around for?" asks Uncle Rondo.

So I just picked up the kitchen clock and marched off, without saying "Kiss my foot," or anything, and never did tell Stella-Rondo good-bye.

There was a nigger girl going along on a little wagon right in front.

"Nigger girl," I says, "come help me haul these things down the hill, I'm going to live in the post office."

Took her nine trips in her express wagon. Uncle Rondo came out on the porch and threw her a nickel.

And that's the last I've laid eyes on any of my family or my family laid eyes on me for five solid days and nights. Stella-Rondo may be telling the most horrible tales in the world about Mr. Whitaker, but I haven't heard them. As I tell everybody, I draw my own conclusions.

But oh, I like it here. It's ideal, as I've been saying. You see, I've got everything cater-cornered, the way I like it. Hear the radio? All the war news. Radio, sewing machine, book ends, ironing board and that great big piano lamp — peace, that's what I like. Butter-bean vines planted all along the front where the strings are.

Of course, there's not much mail. My family are naturally the main people in China Grove, and if they prefer to vanish from the face of the earth, for all the mail they get or the mail they write, why, I'm not going to open my mouth. Some of the folks here in town are taking up for me and some turned against me. I know which is which. There are always people who will quit buying stamps just to get on the right side of Papa-Daddy.

But here I am, and here I'll stay. I want the world to know I'm happy.

And if Stella-Rondo should come to me this minute, on bended knees, and *attempt* to explain the incidents of her life with Mr. Whitaker, I'd simply put my fingers in both my ears and refuse to listen.

[1941]

JOHN CHEEVER [1912–1982]

Reunion

The last time I saw my father was in Grand Central Station. I was going from my grandmother's in the Adirondacks to a cottage on the Cape that my mother had rented, and I wrote my father that I would be in New York between trains for an hour and a half, and asked if we could have lunch together. His secretary wrote to say that he would meet me at the information booth at noon, and at twelve o'clock sharp I saw him coming through the crowd. He was a stranger to me—my mother divorced him three years ago and I hadn't been with him since—but as soon as I saw him I felt that he was my father, my flesh and blood, my future and my doom. I knew that when I was grown I would be something like him; I would have to plan my campaigns within his limitations. He was a big, good-looking man, and I was terribly happy to see him again. He struck me on the back and shook my hand. "Hi, Charlie," he said. "Hi, boy. I'd like to take you up to my club, but it's in the Sixties, and if you have to catch an early train I guess we'd better get something to eat around here." He put his arm around me, and I smelled my father the way my mother sniffs a rose. It was a rich compound of whiskey, after-shave lotion, shoe polish, woolens, and the rankness of a mature male. I hoped that someone would see us together. I wished that we could be photographed. I wanted some record of our having been together.

We went out of the station and up a side street to a restaurant. It was still early, and the place was empty. The bartender was quarreling with a delivery boy, and there was one very old waiter in a red coat down by the kitchen door. We sat down, and my father hailed the waiter in a loud voice. "*Kellner!*" he shouted. "*Garçon! Cameriere! You!*" His boisterousness in the empty restaurant seemed out of place. "Could we have a little service here!" he shouted. "Chop-chop." Then he clapped his hands. This caught the waiter's attention, and he shuffled over to our table.

"Were you clapping your hands at me?" he asked.

"Calm down, calm down, *sommelier*," my father said. "If it isn't too much to ask of you—if it wouldn't be too much above and beyond the call of duty, we would like a couple of Beefeater Gibsons."

"I don't like to be clapped at," the waiter said.

201

"I should have brought my whistle," my father said. "I have a whistle that is audible only to the ears of old waiters. Now, take out your little pad and your little pencil and see if you can get this straight: two Beefeater Gibsons. Repeat after me: two Beefeater Gibsons."

"I think you'd better go somewhere else," the waiter said quietly.

"That," said my father, "is one of the most brilliant suggestions I have ever heard. Come on, Charlie, let's get the hell out of here."

I followed my father out of that restaurant into another. He was not so boisterous this time. Our drinks came, and he cross-questioned me about the baseball season. He then struck the edge of his empty glass with his knife and began shouting again. "*Garçon! Kellner! Cameriere! You!* Could we trouble you to bring us two more of the same."

"How old is the boy?" the waiter asked.

"That," my father said, "is none of your God-damned business."

"I'm sorry, sir," the waiter said, "but I won't serve the boy another drink."

"Well, I have some news for you," my father said. "I have some very interesting news for you. This doesn't happen to be the only restaurant in New York. They've opened another on the corner. Come on, Charlie."

He paid the bill, and I followed him out of that restaurant into another. Here the waiters wore pink jackets like hunting coats, and there was a lot of horse tack on the walls. We sat down, and my father began to shout again. "Master of the hounds! Tallyhoo and all that sort of thing. We'd like a little something in the way of a stirrup cup. Namely, two Bibson Geefeaters."

"Two Bibson Geefeaters?" the waiter asked, smiling.

"You know damned well what I want," my father said angrily. "I want two Beefeater Gibsons, and make it snappy. Things have changed in jolly old England. So my friend the duke tells me. Let's see what England can produce in the way of a cocktail."

"This isn't England," the waiter said.

"Don't argue with me," my father said. "Just do as you're told."

"I just thought you might like to know where you are," the waiter said.

"If there is one thing I cannot tolerate," my father said, "it is an impudent domestic. Come on, Charlie."

The fourth place we went to was Italian. "*Buon giorno,*" my father said. "*Per favore, possiamo avere due cocktail americani, forti, forti. Molto gin, poco vermut.*"

"I don't understand Italian," the waiter said.

"Oh, come off it," my father said. "You understand Italian, and you know damned well you do. *Vogliamo due cocktail americani. Subito.*"

The waiter left us and spoke with the captain, who came over to our table and said, "I'm sorry, sir, but this table is reserved."

"All right," my father said. "Get us another table."

"All the tables are reserved," the captain said.

"I get it," my father said. "You don't desire our patronage. Is that it? Well, the hell with you. *Vada all' inferno*. Let's go, Charlie."

"I have to get my train," I said.

"I'm sorry, sonny," my father said. "I'm terribly sorry." He put his arm around me and pressed me against him. "I'll walk you back to the station. If there had only been time to go up to my club."

"That's all right, Daddy," I said.

"I'll get you a paper," he said. "I'll get you a paper to read on the train."

Then he went up to a newsstand and said, "Kind sir, will you be good enough to favor me with one of your God-damned, no-good, ten-cent afternoon papers?" The clerk turned away from him and stared at a magazine cover. "Is it asking too much, kind sir," my father said, "is it asking too much for you to sell me one of your disgusting specimens of yellow journalism?"

"I have to go, Daddy," I said. "It's late."

"Now, just wait a second, sonny," he said. "Just wait a second. I want to get a rise out of this chap."

"Goodbye, Daddy," I said, and I went down the stairs and got my train, and that was the last time I saw my father.

[1962]

RALPH ELLISON   [1914–1994]

Battle Royal

It goes a long way back, some twenty years. All my life I had been looking for something, and everywhere I turned someone tried to tell me what it was. I accepted their answers too, though they were often in contradiction and even self-contradictory. I was naïve. I was looking for myself and asking everyone except myself questions which I, and only I, could answer. It took me a long time and much painful boomeranging of my expectations to achieve a realization everyone else appears to have been born with: That I am nobody but myself. But first I had to discover that I am an invisible man!

And yet I am no freak of nature, nor of history. I was in the cards, other things having been equal (or unequal) eighty-five years ago. I am not ashamed of my grandparents for having been slaves. I am only ashamed of myself for having at one time been ashamed. About eighty-five years ago they were told that they were free, united with others of our country in everything pertaining to the common good, and, in everything social, separate like the fingers of the hand. And they believed it. They exulted in it. They stayed in their place, worked hard, and brought up my father to do the same. But my grandfather is the one. He was an odd old guy, my grandfather, and I am told I take after him. It was he who caused the trouble. On his deathbed he called my father to him and said, "Son, after I'm gone I want you to keep up the good fight. I never told you, but our life is a war and I have been a traitor all my born days, a spy in the enemy's country ever since I give up my gun back in the Reconstruction. Live with your head in the lion's mouth. I want you to overcome 'em with yeses, undermine 'em with grins, agree 'em to death and destruction, let 'em swoller you till they vomit or bust wide open." They thought the old man had gone out of his mind. He had been the meekest of men. The younger children were rushed from the room, the shades drawn, and the flame of the lamp turned so low that it sputtered on the wick like the old man's breathing. "Learn it to the younguns," he whispered fiercely; then he died.

But my folks were more alarmed over his last words than over his dying. It was as though he had not died at all, his words caused so much anxiety. I was warned emphatically to forget what he had said and, indeed, this is the first time it has been mentioned outside the family circle. It had a tremendous effect upon me, however. I could never be sure of what he meant. Grandfather had been a quiet old man who never made any trouble, yet on his deathbed he had called himself a traitor and a spy, and he had spoken of his meekness as a dangerous activity. It became a constant puzzle which lay unanswered in the back of my mind. And whenever things went well for me I remembered my grandfather and felt guilty and uncomfortable. It was as though I was carrying out his advice in spite of myself. And to make it worse, everyone loved me for it. I was praised by the most lily-white men of the town. I was considered an example of desirable conduct—just as my grandfather had been. And what puzzled me was that the old man had defined it as *treachery*. When I was praised for my conduct I felt a guilt that in some way I was doing something that was really against the wishes of the white folks, that if they had understood they would have desired me to act just the opposite, that I should have been sulky and mean, and that that really would have been what they wanted, even though they were fooled and thought they wanted me to act as I did. It made me afraid that some day they would look upon me as a traitor and I would be lost. Still I was more afraid to act any other way because they didn't like that at all. The old man's words were like a curse. On my graduation day I delivered an oration in which I showed that humility was the secret, indeed, the very essence of progress. (Not that I believed this—how could I, remembering my grandfather?—I only believed that it worked.) It was a great success. Everyone praised me and I was invited to give the speech at a gathering of the town's leading white citizens. It was a triumph for our whole community.

It was in the main ballroom of the leading hotel. When I got there I discovered that it was on the occasion of a smoker, and I was told that since I was to be there anyway I might as well take part in the battle royal to be fought by some of my schoolmates as part of the entertainment. The battle royal came first.

All of the town's big shots were there in their tuxedoes, wolfing down the buffet foods, drinking beer and whiskey and smoking black cigars. It was a large room with a high ceiling. Chairs were arranged in neat rows around three sides of a portable boxing ring. The fourth side was clear, revealing a gleaming space of polished floor. I had some misgivings over the battle royal, by the way. Not from a distaste for fighting, but because I didn't care too much for the other fellows who were to take part. They were tough guys who seemed to have no grandfather's curse worrying their minds. No one could mistake their toughness. And besides, I suspected that fighting a battle royal might detract from the dignity of my speech. In those pre-invisible days I visualized myself as a potential Booker T. Washington.° But the other fellows didn't care too much for me either, and there were nine of them. I felt superior to them in my way, and I didn't like the manner in which we were all crowded together into the servants' elevator. Nor did they like my being there. In fact, as the warmly lighted floors flashed past the elevator we had words over the fact that I, by taking part in the fight, had knocked one of their friends out of a night's work.

We were led out of the elevator through a rococo hall into an anteroom and told to get into our fighting togs. Each of us was issued a pair of boxing gloves and ushered out into the big mirrored hall, which we entered looking cautiously about us and whispering, lest we might accidentally be heard above the noise of the room. It was foggy with cigar smoke. And already the whiskey was taking effect. I was shocked to see some of the most important men of the town quite tipsy. They were all there— bankers, lawyers, judges, doctors, fire chiefs, teachers, merchants. Even one of the more fashionable pastors. Something we could not see was

---

Booker T. Washington: (1856–1915) African American educator, reformer, and political leader. He advocated education in industry and economic security for post-Reconstruction African Americans.

going on up front. A clarinet was vibrating sensuously and the men were standing up and moving eagerly forward. We were a small tight group, clustered together, our bare upper bodies touching and shining with anticipatory sweat; while up front the big shots were becoming increasingly excited over something we still could not see. Suddenly I heard the school superintendent, who had told me to come, yell, "Bring up the shines, gentlemen! Bring up the little shines!"

We were rushed up to the front of the ballroom, where it smelled even more strongly of tobacco and whiskey. Then we were pushed into place. I almost wet my pants. A sea of faces, some hostile, some amused, ringed around us, and in the center, facing us, stood a magnificent blonde—stark naked. There was dead silence. I felt a blast of cold air chill me. I tried to back away, but they were behind me and around me. Some of the boys stood with lowered heads, trembling. I felt a wave of irrational guilt and fear. My teeth chattered, my skin turned to goose flesh, my knees knocked. Yet I was strongly attracted and looked in spite of myself. Had the price of looking been blindness, I would have looked. The hair was yellow like that of a circus kewpie doll, the face heavily powdered and rouged, as though to form an abstract mask, the eyes hollow and smeared a cool blue, the color of a baboon's butt. I felt a desire to spit upon her as my eyes brushed slowly over her body. Her breasts were firm and round as the domes of East Indian temples, and I stood so close as to see the fine skin texture and beads of pearly perspiration glistening like dew around the pink and erected buds of her nipples. I wanted at one and the same time to run from the room, to sink through the floor, or go to her and cover her from my eyes and the eyes of the others with my body; to feel the soft thighs, to caress her and destroy her, to love her and murder her, to hide from her, and yet to stroke where below the small American flag tattooed upon her belly her thighs formed a capital V. I had a notion that of all in the room she saw only me with her impersonal eyes.

And then she began to dance, a slow sensuous movement; the smoke of a hundred cigars clinging to her like the thinnest of veils. She seemed like a fair bird-girl girdled in veils calling to me from the angry surface of some gray and threatening sea. I was transported. Then I became aware of the clarinet playing and the big shots yelling at us. Some threatened us if we looked and others if we did not. On my right I saw one boy faint. And now a man grabbed a silver pitcher from a table and stepped close as he dashed ice water upon him and stood him up and forced two of us to support him as his head hung and moans issued from his thick bluish lips. Another boy began to plead to go home. He was the largest of the group, wearing dark red fighting trunks much too small to conceal the erection which projected from him as though in answer to the insinuating low-registered moaning of the clarinet. He tried to hide himself with his boxing gloves.

And all the while the blonde continued dancing, smiling faintly at the big shots who watched her with fascination, and faintly smiling at our fear. I noticed a certain merchant who followed her hungrily, his lips loose and drooling. He was a large man who wore diamond studs in a shirtfront which swelled with the ample paunch underneath, and each time the blonde swayed her undulating hips he ran his hand through the thin hair of his bald head and, with his arms upheld, his posture clumsy like that of an intoxicated panda, wound his belly in a slow and obscene grind. This creature was completely hypnotized. The music had quickened. As the dancer flung herself about with a detached expression on her face, the men began reaching out to touch her. I could see their beefy fingers sink into her soft flesh. Some of the others tried to stop them and she began to move around the floor in graceful circles, as they gave chase, slipping and sliding over the polished floor. It was mad. Chairs went crashing, drinks were spilt, as they ran laughing and howling after her. They caught her just as she reached a door, raised her from the floor, and tossed her as college boys are tossed at a hazing, and above her red fixed-smiling lips I saw the terror and disgust in her eyes, almost like my own terror and that which I saw in some of the other boys. As I watched, they tossed her twice and her soft breasts seemed to flatten against the air and her legs flung wildly as she spun. Some of the more sober ones helped her to escape. And I started off the floor, heading for the anteroom with the rest of the boys.

Some were still crying and in hysteria. But as we tried to leave we were stopped and ordered to get into the ring. There was nothing to do but what we were told. All ten of us climbed under the ropes and allowed ourselves to be blindfolded with broad bands of white cloth. One of the men seemed to feel a bit sympathetic and tried to cheer us up as we stood with our backs against the ropes. Some of us tried to grin. "See that boy over there?" one of the men said. "I want you to run across at the bell and give it to him right in the belly. If you don't get him, I'm going to get you. I don't like his looks." Each of us was told the same. The blindfolds were put on. Yet even then I had been going over my speech. In my mind each word was as bright as flame. I felt the cloth pressed into place, and frowned so that it would be loosened when I relaxed.

But now I felt a sudden fit of blind terror. I was unused to darkness. It was as though I had suddenly found myself in a dark room filled with poisonous cottonmouths. I could hear the bleary voices yelling insistently for the battle royal to begin.

"Get going in there!"

"Let me at that big nigger!"

I strained to pick up the school superintendent's voice, as though to squeeze some security out of that slightly more familiar sound.

"Let me at those black sonsabitches!" someone yelled.

"No, Jackson, no!" another voice yelled. "Here, somebody, help me hold Jack."

"I want to get at that ginger-colored nigger. Tear him limb from limb," the first voice yelled.

I stood against the ropes trembling. For in those days I was what they called ginger-colored, and he sounded as though he might crunch me between his teeth like a crisp ginger cookie.

Quite a struggle was going on. Chairs were being kicked about and I could hear voices grunting as with a terrific effort. I wanted to see, to see more desperately than ever before. But the blindfold was as tight as a thick skin-puckering scab and when I raised my gloved hands to push the layers of white aside a voice yelled, "Oh, no you don't, black bastard! Leave that alone!"

"Ring the bell before Jackson kills him a coon!" someone boomed in the sudden silence. And I heard the bell clang and the sound of the feet scuffling forward.

A glove smacked against my head. I pivoted, striking out stiffly as someone went past, and felt the jar ripple along the length of my arm to my shoulder. Then it seemed as though all nine of the boys had turned upon me at once. Blows pounded me from all sides while I struck out as best I could. So many blows landed upon me that I wondered if I were not the only blindfolded fighter in the ring, or if the man called Jackson hadn't succeeded in getting me after all.

Blindfolded, I could no longer control my motions. I had no dignity. I stumbled about like a baby or a drunken man. The smoke had become thicker and with each new blow it seemed to sear and further restrict my lungs. My saliva became like hot bitter glue. A glove connected with my head, filling my mouth with warm blood. It was everywhere. I could not tell if the moisture I felt upon my body was sweat or blood. A blow landed hard against the nape of my neck. I felt myself going over, my head hitting the floor. Streaks of blue light filled the black world behind the blindfold. I lay prone, pretending that I was knocked out, but felt myself seized by hands and yanked to my feet. "Get going, black boy! Mix it up!" My arms were like lead, my head smarting from blows. I managed to feel my way to the ropes and held on, trying to catch my breath. A glove landed in my midsection and I went over again, feeling as though the smoke had become a knife jabbed into my guts. Pushed this way and that by the legs milling around me, I finally pulled erect and discovered that I could see the black, sweat-washed forms weaving in the smoky-blue atmosphere like drunken dancers weaving to the rapid drum-like thuds of blows.

Everyone fought hysterically. It was complete anarchy. Everybody fought everybody else. No group fought together for long. Two, three, four, fought one, then turned to fight each other, were themselves attacked. Blows landed below the belt and in the kidney, with the gloves open as well as closed, and with my eye partly opened now there was not so much terror. I moved carefully, avoiding blows, although not too many to attract attention, fighting from group to group. The boys groped about like blind, cautious crabs crouching to protect their mid-sections, their heads pulled in short against their shoulders, their arms stretched nervously before them, with their fists testing the smoke-filled air like the knobbed feelers of hypersensitive snails. In one corner I glimpsed a boy violently punching the air and heard him scream in pain as he smashed his hand against a ring post. For a second I saw him bent over holding his hand, then going down as a blow caught his unprotected head. I played one group against the other, slipping in and throwing a punch then stepping out of range while pushing the others into the melee to take the blows blindly aimed at me. The smoke was agonizing and there were no rounds, no bells at three minute intervals to relieve our exhaustion. The room spun round me, a swirl of lights, smoke, sweating bodies surrounded by tense white faces. I bled from both nose and mouth, the blood spattering upon my chest.

The men kept yelling, "Slug him, black boy! Knock his guts out!"

"Uppercut him! Kill him! Kill that big boy!"

Taking a fake fall, I saw a boy going down heavily beside me as though we were felled by a single blow, saw a sneaker-clad foot shoot into his groin as the two who had knocked him down stumbled upon him. I rolled out of range, feeling a twinge of nausea.

The harder we fought the more threatening the men became. And yet, I had begun to worry about my speech again. How would it go? Would they recognize my ability? What would they give me?

I was fighting automatically and suddenly I noticed that one after another of the boys was leaving the ring. I was surprised, filled with panic, as though I had been left alone with an unknown danger. Then I understood. The boys had arranged it among themselves. It was the custom for the two men left in the ring to slug it out for the winner's prize. I discovered this too late. When the bell sounded two men in tuxedoes leaped into the ring and removed the blindfold. I found myself facing Tatlock, the biggest of the gang. I felt sick at my stomach. Hardly had the bell stopped ringing in my ears than it clanged again and I saw him moving swiftly toward me. Thinking of nothing else to do I hit him smash on the nose. He kept coming, bringing the rank sharp violence of stale sweat. His face was a black blank of a face, only his eyes alive — with hate of me and aglow with a feverish terror from what had happened to us all. I became anxious. I wanted to deliver my speech and he came at me as though he meant to beat it out of me. I smashed him again and again, taking his blows as they came. Then on a sudden impulse I struck him lightly and as we clinched, I whispered, "Fake like I knocked you out, you can have the prize."

"I'll break your behind," he whispered hoarsely.

"For *them*?"

"For *me*, sonofabitch!"

They were yelling for us to break it up and Tatlock spun me half around with a blow, and as a joggled camera sweeps in a reeling scene, I saw the howling red faces crouching tense beneath the cloud of blue-gray smoke. For a moment the world wavered, unraveled, flowed, then my head cleared and Tatlock bounced before me. That fluttering shadow before my eyes was his jabbing left hand. Then falling forward, my head against his damp shoulder, I whispered,

"I'll make it five dollars more."

"Go to hell!"

But his muscles relaxed a trifle beneath my pressure and I breathed, "Seven!"

"Give it to your ma," he said, ripping me beneath the heart.

And while I still held him I butted him and moved away. I felt myself bombarded with punches. I fought back with hopeless desperation. I wanted to deliver my speech more than anything else in the world, because I felt that only these men could judge truly my ability, and now this stupid clown was ruining my chances. I began fighting carefully now, moving in to punch him and out again with my greater speed. A lucky blow to his chin and I had him going too—until I heard a loud voice yell, "I got my money on the big boy."

Hearing this, I almost dropped my guard. I was confused: Should I try to win against the voice out there? Would not this go against my speech, and was not this a moment for humility, for nonresistance? A blow to my head as I danced about sent my right eye popping like a jack-in-the-box and settled my dilemma. The room went red as I fell. It was a dream fall, my body languid and fastidious as to where to land, until the floor became impatient and smashed up to meet me. A moment later I came to. An hypnotic voice said FIVE emphatically. And I lay there, hazily watching a dark red spot of my own blood shaping itself into a butterfly, glistening and soaking into the soiled gray world of the canvas.

When the voice drawled TEN I was lifted up and dragged to a chair. I sat dazed. My eye pained and swelled with each throb of my pounding heart and I wondered if now I would be allowed to speak. I was wringing wet, my mouth still bleeding. We were grouped along the wall now. The other boys ignored me as they congratulated Tatlock and speculated as to how much they would be paid. One boy whimpered over his smashed hand. Looking up front, I saw attendants in white jackets rolling the portable ring away and placing a small square rug in the vacant space surrounded by chairs. Perhaps, I thought, I will stand on the rug to deliver my speech.

Then the M.C. called to us. "Come on up here boys and get your money."

We ran forward to where the men laughed and talked in their chairs, waiting. Everyone seemed friendly now.

"There it is on the rug," the man said. I saw the rug covered with coins of all dimensions and a few crumpled bills. But what excited me, scattered here and there, were the gold pieces.

"Boys, it's all yours," the man said. "You get all you grab."

"That's right, Sambo," a blond man said, winking at me confidentially.

I trembled with excitement, forgetting my pain. I would get the gold and the bills, I thought. I would use both hands. I would throw my body against the boys nearest me to block them from the gold.

"Get down around the rug now," the man commanded, "and don't anyone touch it until I give the signal."

"This ought to be good," I heard.

As told, we got around the square rug on our knees. Slowly the man raised his freckled hand as we followed it upward with our eyes.

I heard, "These niggers look like they're about to pray!"

Then, "Ready," the man said. "Go!"

I lunged for a yellow coin lying on the blue design of the carpet, touching it and sending a surprised shriek to join those rising around me. I tried frantically to remove my hand but could not let go. A hot, violent force tore through my body, shaking me like a wet rat. The rug was electrified. The hair bristled up on my head as I shook myself free. My muscles jumped, my nerves jangled, writhed. But I saw that this was not stopping the other boys. Laughing in fear and embarrassment, some were holding back and scooping up the coins knocked off by the painful contortions of the others. The men roared above us as we struggled.

"Pick it up, goddamnit, pick it up!" someone called like a bass-voiced parrot. "Go on, get it!"

I crawled rapidly around the floor, picking up the coins, trying to avoid the coppers and to get greenbacks and the gold. Ignoring the shock by laughing, as I brushed the coins off quickly, I discovered that I could contain the electricity—a contradiction, but it works. Then the men began to push us onto the rug. Laughing embarrassedly, we struggled out of their hands and kept after the coins. We were all wet and slippery and hard to hold. Suddenly I saw a boy lifted into the air, glistening with sweat like a circus seal, and dropped, his wet back landing flush upon the charged rug, heard him yell and saw him literally dance upon his back, his elbows beating a frenzied tattoo upon the floor, his muscles twitching like the flesh of a horse stung by many flies. When he finally rolled off, his face was gray and no one stopped him when he ran from the floor amid booming laughter.

"Get the money," the M.C. called. "That's good hard American cash!"

And we snatched and grabbed, snatched and grabbed. I was careful not to come too close to the rug now, and when I felt the hot whiskey breath descend upon me like a cloud of foul air I reached out and grabbed the leg of a chair. It was occupied and I held on desperately.

"Leggo, nigger! Leggo!"

The huge face wavered down to mine as he tried to push me free. But my body was slippery and he was too drunk. It was Mr. Colcord, who owned a chain of movie houses and "entertainment palaces." Each time he grabbed me I slipped out of his hands. It became a real struggle. I feared the rug more than I did the drunk, so I held on, surprising myself for a moment by trying to topple *him* upon the rug. It was such an enormous idea that I found myself actually carrying it out. I tried not to be obvious, yet when I grabbed his leg, trying to tumble him out of the chair, he raised up roaring with laughter, and, looking at me with soberness dead in the eye, kicked me viciously in the chest. The chair leg flew out of my hand. I felt myself going and rolled. It was as though I had rolled through a bed of hot coals. It seemed a whole century would pass before I would roll free, a century in which I was seared through the deepest levels of my body to the fearful breath within me and the breath seared and heated to the point of explosion. It'll all be over in a flash, I thought as I rolled clear. It'll all be over in a flash.

But not yet, the men on the other side were waiting, red faces swollen as though from apoplexy as they bent forward in their chairs. Seeing their fingers coming toward me I rolled away as a fumbled football rolls off the receiver's fingertips, back into the coals. That time I luckily sent the rug sliding out of place and heard the coins ringing against the floor and the boys scuffling to pick them up and the M.C. calling, "All right, boys, that's all. Go get dressed and get your money."

I was limp as a dish rag. My back felt as though it had been beaten with wires.

When we had dressed the M.C. came in and gave us each five dollars, except Tatlock, who got ten for being last in the ring. Then he told us to leave. I was not to get a chance to deliver my speech, I thought. I was going out into the dim alley in despair when I was stopped and told to go back. I returned to the ballroom, where the men were pushing back their chairs and gathering in groups to talk.

The M.C. knocked on a table for quiet. "Gentlemen," he said, "we almost forgot an important part of the program. A most serious part, gentlemen. This boy was brought here to deliver a speech which he made at his graduation yesterday. . . ."

"Bravo!"

"I'm told that he is the smartest boy we've got out there in Greenwood. I'm told that he knows more big words than a pocket-sized dictionary."

Much applause and laughter.

"So now, gentlemen, I want you to give him your attention."

There was still laughter as I faced them, my mouth dry, my eye throbbing. I began slowly, but evidently my throat was tense, because they began shouting, "Louder! Louder!"

"We of the younger generation extol the wisdom of that great leader and educator," I shouted, "who first spoke these flaming words of wisdom: 'A ship lost at sea for many days suddenly sighted a friendly vessel. From the mast of the unfortunate vessel was seen a signal: "Water, water; we die of thirst!" The answer from the friendly vessel came back: "Cast down your bucket where you are." The captain of the distressed vessel, at last heeding the injunction, cast down his bucket, and it came up full of fresh sparkling water from the mouth of the Amazon River.' And like him I say, and in his words, 'To those of my race who depend upon bettering their condition in a foreign land, or who underestimate the importance of cultivating friendly relations with the Southern white man, who is his next-door neighbor, I would say: "Cast down your bucket where you are"—cast it down in making friends in every manly way of the people of all races by whom we are surrounded. . . .'"

I spoke automatically and with such fervor that I did not realize that the men were still talking and laughing until my dry mouth, filling up with blood from the cut, almost strangled me. I coughed, wanting to stop and go to one of the tall brass, sand-filled spittoons to relieve myself, but a few of the men, especially the superintendent, were listening and I was afraid. So I gulped it down, blood, saliva, and all, and continued. (What powers of endurance I had during those days! What enthusiasm! What a belief in the rightness of things!) I spoke even louder in spite of the pain. But still they talked and still they laughed, as though deaf with cotton in dirty ears. So I spoke with greater emotional emphasis. I closed my ears and swallowed blood until I was nauseated. The speech seemed a hundred times as long as before, but I could not leave out a single word. All had to be said, each memorized nuance considered, rendered. Nor was that all. Whenever I uttered a word of three or more syllables a group of voices would yell for me to repeat it. I used the phrase "social responsibility" and they yelled:

"What's the word you say, boy?"

"Social responsibility," I said.

"What?"

"Social . . ."

"Louder."

"... responsibility."

"More!"

"Respon—"

"Repeat!"

"—sibility."

The room filled with the uproar of laughter until, no doubt, distracted by having to gulp down my blood, I made a mistake and yelled a phrase I had often seen denounced in newspaper editorials, heard debated in private.

"Social ..."

"What?" they yelled.

"... equality—"

The laughter hung smokelike in the sudden stillness. I opened my eyes, puzzled. Sounds of displeasure filled the room. The M.C. rushed forward. They shouted hostile phrases at me. But I did not understand.

A small dry mustached man in the front row blared out, "Say that slowly, son!"

"What sir?"

"What you just said!"

"Social responsibility, sir," I said.

"You weren't being smart, were you, boy?" he said, not unkindly.

"No, sir!"

"You sure that about 'equality' was a mistake?"

"Oh, yes, sir," I said. "I was swallowing blood."

"Well, you had better speak more slowly so we can understand. We mean to do right by you, but you've got to know your place at all times. All right, now, go on with your speech."

I was afraid. I wanted to leave but I wanted also to speak and I was afraid they'd snatch me down.

"Thank you, sir," I said, beginning where I had left off, and having them ignore me as before.

Yet when I finished there was a thunderous applause. I was surprised to see the superintendent come forth with a package wrapped in white tissue paper, and, gesturing for quiet, address the men.

"Gentlemen, you see that I did not overpraise this boy. He makes a good speech and some day he'll lead his people in the proper paths. And I don't have to tell you that that is important in these days and times. This is a good, smart boy, and so to encourage him in the right direction, in the name of the Board of Education I wish to present him a prize in the form of this ..."

He paused, removing the tissue paper and revealing a gleaming calf-skin brief case.

"... in the form of this first-class article from Shad Whitmore's shop."

"Boy," he said, addressing me, "take this prize and keep it well. Consider it a badge of office. Prize it. Keep developing as you are and some day it will be filled with important papers that will help shape the destiny of your people."

I was so moved that I could hardly express my thanks. A rope of bloody saliva forming a shape like an undiscovered continent drooled upon the leather and I wiped it quickly away. I felt an importance that I had never dreamed.

"Open it and see what's inside," I was told.

My fingers a-tremble, I complied, smelling the fresh leather and finding an official-looking document inside. It was a scholarship to the state college for Negroes. My eyes filled with tears and I ran awkwardly off the floor.

I was overjoyed; I did not even mind when I discovered that the gold pieces I had scrambled for were brass pocket tokens advertising a certain make of automobile.

When I reached home everyone was excited. Next day the neighbors came to congratulate me. I even felt safe from grandfather, whose deathbed curse usually spoiled my triumphs. I stood beneath his photograph with my brief case in hand and smiled triumphantly into his stolid black peasant's face. It was a face that fascinated me. The eyes seemed to follow everywhere I went.

That night I dreamed I was at a circus with him and that he refused to laugh at the clowns no matter what they did. Then later he told me to open my brief case and read what was inside and I did, finding an official envelope stamped with the state seal; and inside the envelope I found another and another, endlessly, and I thought I would fall of weariness. "Them's years," he said. "Now open that one." And I did and in it I found an engraved document containing a short message in letters of gold. "Read it," my grandfather said. "Out loud."

"To Whom It May Concern," I intoned. "Keep This Nigger-Boy Running."

I awoke with the old man's laughter ringing in my ears.

(It was a dream I was to remember and dream again for many years after. But at the time I had no insight into its meaning. First I had to attend college.)

[1952]

SHIRLEY JACKSON   [1919–1965]

The Lottery

The morning of June 27th was clear and sunny, with the fresh warmth of a full-summer day; the flowers were blossoming profusely and the grass was richly green. The people of the village began to gather in the square, between the post office and the bank, around ten o'clock; in some towns there were so many people that the lottery took two days and had to be started on June 26th, but in this village, where there were only about three hundred people, the whole lottery took less than two hours, so it could begin at ten o'clock in the morning and still be through in time to allow the villagers to get home for noon dinner.

The children assembled first, of course. School was recently over for the summer, and the feeling of liberty sat uneasily on most of them; they tended to gather together quietly for a while before they broke into bois-terous play, and their talk was still of the classroom and teacher, of books and reprimands. Bobby Martin had already stuffed his pockets full of stones, and the other boys soon followed his example, selecting the smoothest and roundest stones; Bobby and Harry Jones and Dickie Delacroix—the villagers pronounced this name "Dellacroy"—eventually made a great pile of stones in one corner of the square and guarded it against the raids of the other boys. The girls stood aside, talking among themselves, looking over their shoulders at the boys, and the very small children rolled in the dust or clung to the hands of their older brothers or sisters.

Soon the men began to gather, surveying their own children, speaking of planting and rain, tractors and taxes. They stood together, away from the pile of stones in the corner, and their jokes were quiet and they smiled rather than laughed. The women, wearing faded house dresses and sweaters, came shortly after their menfolk. They greeted one an-other and exchanged bits of gossip as they went to join their husbands. Soon the women, standing by their husbands, began to call to their chil-dren, and the children came reluctantly, having to be called four or five times. Bobby Martin ducked under his mother's grasping hand and ran, laughing, back to the pile of stones. His father spoke up sharply, and Bobby came quickly and took his place between his father and his oldest brother.

216

The lottery was conducted—as were the square dances, the teen-age club, the Halloween program—by Mr. Summers, who had time and energy to devote to civic activities. He was a round-faced, jovial man and he ran the coal business, and people were sorry for him, because he had no children and his wife was a scold. When he arrived in the square, carrying the black wooden box, there was a murmur of conversation among the villagers, and he waved and called, "Little late today, folks." The postmaster, Mr. Graves, followed him, carrying a three-legged stool, and the stool was put in the center of the square and Mr. Summers set the black box down on it. The villagers kept their distance, leaving a space between themselves and the stool, and when Mr. Summers said, "Some of you fellows want to give me a hand?" there was a hesitation before two men, Mr. Martin and his oldest son, Baxter, came forward to hold the box steady on the stool while Mr. Summers stirred up the papers inside it.

The original paraphernalia for the lottery had been lost long ago, and the black box now resting on the stool had been put into use even before Old Man Warner, the oldest man in town, was born. Mr. Summers spoke frequently to the villagers about making a new box, but no one liked to upset even as much tradition as was represented by the black box. There was a story that the present box had been made with some pieces of the box that had preceded it, the one that had been constructed when the first people settled down to make a village here. Every year, after the lottery, Mr. Summers began talking again about a new box, but every year the subject was allowed to fade off without anything's being done. The black box grew shabbier each year; by now it was no longer completely black but splintered badly along one side to show the original wood color, and in some places faded or stained.

Mr. Martin and his oldest son, Baxter, held the black box securely on the stool until Mr. Summers had stirred the papers thoroughly with his hand. Because so much of the ritual had been forgotten or discarded, Mr. Summers had been successful in having slips of paper substituted for the chips of wood that had been used for generations. Chips of wood, Mr. Summers had argued, had been all very well when the village was tiny, but now that the population was more than three hundred and likely to keep on growing, it was necessary to use something that would fit more easily into the black box. The night before the lottery, Mr. Summers and Mr. Graves made up the slips of paper and put them in the box, and it was then taken to the safe of Mr. Summers's coal company and locked up until Mr. Summers was ready to take it to the square next morning. The rest of the year, the box was put away, sometimes one place, sometimes another; it had spent one year in Mr. Graves's barn and another year underfoot in the post office, and sometimes it was set on a shelf in the Martin grocery and left there.

There was a great deal of fussing to be done before Mr. Summers declared the lottery open. There were the lists to make up—of heads of families, heads of households in each family, members of each household in each family. There was the proper swearing-in of Mr. Summers by the postmaster, as the official of the lottery; at one time, some people remembered, there had been a recital of some sort, performed by the official of the lottery, a perfunctory, tuneless chant that had been rattled off duly each year; some people believed that the official of the lottery used to stand just so when he said or sang it, others believed that he was supposed to walk among the people, but years and years ago this part of the ritual had been allowed to lapse. There had been, also, a ritual salute, which the official of the lottery had had to use in addressing each person who came up to draw from the box, but this also had changed with time, until now it was felt necessary only for the official to speak to each person approaching. Mr. Summers was very good at all this; in his clean white shirt and blue jeans, with one hand resting carelessly on the black box, he seemed very proper and important as he talked interminably to Mr. Graves and the Martins.

Just as Mr. Summers finally left off talking and turned to the assembled villagers, Mrs. Hutchinson came hurriedly along the path to the square, her sweater thrown over her shoulders, and slid into place in the back of the crowd. "Clean forgot what day it was," she said to Mrs. Delacroix, who stood next to her, and they both laughed softly. "Thought my old man was out back stacking wood," Mrs. Hutchinson went on, "and then I looked out the window and the kids was gone, and then I remembered it was the twenty-seventh and came a-running." She dried her hands on her apron, and Mrs. Delacroix said, "You're in time, though. They're still talking away up there."

Mrs. Hutchinson craned her neck to see through the crowd and found her husband and children standing near the front. She tapped Mrs. Delacroix on the arm as a farewell and began to make her way through the crowd. The people separated good-humoredly to let her through; two or three people said, in voices just loud enough to be heard across the crowd, "Here comes your Missus, Hutchinson," and "Bill, she made it after all." Mrs. Hutchinson reached her husband, and Mr. Summers, who had been waiting, said cheerfully, "Thought we were going to have to get on without you, Tessie." Mrs. Hutchinson said, grinning, "Wouldn't have me leave m'dishes in the sink, now, would you, Joe?" and soft laughter ran through the crowd as the people stirred back into position after Mrs. Hutchinson's arrival.

"Well, now," Mr. Summers said soberly, "guess we better get started, get this over with, so's we can go back to work. Anybody ain't here?"

"Dunbar," several people said. "Dunbar, Dunbar."

Mr. Summers consulted his list. "Clyde Dunbar," he said. "That's right. He's broke his leg, hasn't he? Who's drawing for him?"

"Me, I guess," a woman said, and Mr. Summers turned to look at her. "Wife draws for her husband," Mr. Summers said. "Don't you have a grown boy to do it for you, Janey?" Although Mr. Summers and everyone else in the village knew the answer perfectly well, it was the business of the official of the lottery to ask such questions formally. Mr. Summers waited with an expression of polite interest while Mrs. Dunbar answered.

"Horace's not but sixteen yet," Mrs. Dunbar said regretfully. "Guess I gotta fill in for the old man this year."

"Right," Mr. Summers said. He made a note on the list he was holding. Then he asked, "Watson boy drawing this year?"

A tall boy in the crowd raised his hand. "Here," he said. "I'm drawing for m'mother and me." He blinked his eyes nervously and ducked his head as several voices in the crowd said things like "Good fellow, Jack," and "Glad to see your mother's got a man to do it."

"Well," Mr. Summers said, "guess that's everyone. Old Man Warner make it?"

"Here," a voice said, and Mr. Summers nodded.

A sudden hush fell on the crowd as Mr. Summers cleared his throat and looked at the list. "All ready?" he called. "Now, I'll read the names—heads of families first—and the men come up and take a paper out of the box. Keep the paper folded in your hand without looking at it until everyone has had a turn. Everything clear?"

The people had done it so many times that they only half listened to the directions; most of them were quiet, wetting their lips, not looking around. Then Mr. Summers raised one hand high and said, "Adams." A man disengaged himself from the crowd and came forward. "Hi, Steve," Mr. Summers said, and Mr. Adams said, "Hi, Joe." They grinned at one another humorlessly and nervously. Then Mr. Adams reached into the black box and took out a folded paper. He held it firmly by one corner as he turned and went hastily back to his place in the crowd, where he stood a little apart from his family, not looking down at his hand.

"Allen," Mr. Summers said, "Anderson. . . . Bentham."

"Seems like there's no time at all between lotteries any more," Mrs. Delacroix said to Mrs. Graves in the back row. "Seems like we got through with the last one only last week."

"Time sure goes fast," Mrs. Graves said.

"Clark. . . . Delacroix."

"There goes my old man," Mrs. Delacroix said. She held her breath while her husband went forward.

"Dunbar," Mr. Summers said, and Mrs. Dunbar went steadily to the box while one of the women said, "Go on, Janey," and another said, "There she goes."

"We're next," Mrs. Graves said. She watched while Mr. Graves came around from the side of the box, greeted Mr. Summers gravely, and selected a slip of paper from the box. By now, all through the crowd there were men holding the small folded papers in their large hands, turning them over and over nervously. Mrs. Dunbar and her two sons stood together, Mrs. Dunbar holding the slip of paper.

"Harburt. . . . Hutchinson."

"Get up there, Bill," Mrs. Hutchinson said, and the people near her laughed.

"Jones."

"They do say," Mr. Adams said to Old Man Warner, who stood next to him, "that over in the north village they're talking of giving up the lottery."

Old Man Warner snorted. "Pack of crazy fools," he said. "Listening to the young folks, nothing's good enough for *them*. Next thing you know, they'll be wanting to go back to living in caves, nobody work any more, live *that* way for a while. Used to be a saying about 'Lottery in June, corn be heavy soon.' First thing you know, we'd all be eating stewed chickweed and acorns. There's *always* been a lottery," he added petulantly. "Bad enough to see young Joe Summers up there joking with everybody."

"Some places have already quit lotteries," Mrs. Adams said.

"Nothing but trouble in *that*," Old Man Warner said stoutly. "Pack of young fools."

"Martin." And Bobby Martin watched his father go forward. "Overdyke. . . . Percy."

"I wish they'd hurry," Mrs. Dunbar said to her older son. "I wish they'd hurry."

"They're almost through," her son said.

"You get ready to run tell Dad," Mrs. Dunbar said.

Mr. Summers called his own name and then stepped forward precisely and selected a slip from the box. Then he called, "Warner."

"Seventy-seventh year I been in the lottery," Old Man Warner said as he went through the crowd. "Seventy-seventh time."

"Watson." The tall boy came awkwardly through the crowd. Someone said, "Don't be nervous, Jack," and Mr. Summers said, "Take your time, son."

"Zanini."

After that, there was a long pause, a breathless pause, until Mr. Summers, holding his slip of paper in the air, said, "All right, fellows." For a minute, no one moved, and then all the slips of paper were opened. Suddenly, all the women began to speak at once, saying, "Who is it?" "Who's got it?" "Is it the Dunbars?" "Is it the Watsons?" Then the voices began to say, "It's Hutchinson. It's Bill," "Bill Hutchinson's got it."

"Go tell your father," Mrs. Dunbar said to her older son.

People began to look around to see the Hutchinsons. Bill Hutchinson was standing quiet, staring down at the paper in his hand. Suddenly, Tessie Hutchinson shouted to Mr. Summers, "You didn't give him time enough to take any paper he wanted. I saw you. It wasn't fair!"

"Be a good sport, Tessie," Mrs. Delacroix called, and Mrs. Graves said, "All of us took the same chance."

"Shut up, Tessie," Bill Hutchinson said.

"Well, everyone," Mr. Summers said, "that was done pretty fast, and now we've got to be hurrying a little more to get done in time." He consulted his next list. "Bill," he said, "you draw for the Hutchinson family. You got any other households in the Hutchinsons?"

"There's Don and Eva," Mrs. Hutchinson yelled. "Make *them* take their chance!"

"Daughters drew with their husbands' families, Tessie," Mr. Summers said gently. "You know that as well as anyone else."

"It wasn't *fair*," Tessie said.

"I guess not, Joe," Bill Hutchinson said regretfully. "My daughter draws with her husband's family, that's only fair. And I've got no other family except the kids."

"Then, as far as drawing for families is concerned, it's you," Mr. Summers said in explanation, "and as far as drawing for households is concerned, that's you, too. Right?"

"Right," Bill Hutchinson said.

"How many kids, Bill?" Mr. Summers asked formally.

"Three," Bill Hutchinson said. "There's Bill, Jr., and Nancy, and little Dave. And Tessie and me."

"All right, then," Mr. Summers said. "Harry, you got their tickets back?"

Mr. Graves nodded and held up the slips of paper. "Put them in the box, then," Mr. Summers directed. "Take Bill's and put it in."

"I think we ought to start over," Mrs. Hutchinson said, as quietly as she could. "I tell you it wasn't *fair*. You didn't give him time enough to choose. *Every*body saw that."

Mr. Graves had selected the five slips and put them in the box, and he dropped all the papers but those onto the ground, where the breeze caught them and lifted them off.

"Listen, everybody," Mrs. Hutchinson was saying to the people around her.

"Ready, Bill?" Mr. Summers asked, and Bill Hutchinson, with one quick glance around at his wife and children, nodded.

"Remember," Mr. Summers said, "take the slips and keep them folded until each person has taken one. Harry, you help little Dave." Mr. Graves took the hand of the little boy, who came willingly with him up to the box. "Take a paper out of the box, Davy," Mr. Summers said. Davy put his hand into the box and laughed. "Take just *one* paper," Mr. Summers said. "Harry, you hold it for him." Mr. Graves took the child's hand and removed the folded paper from the tight fist and held it while little Dave stood next to him and looked up at him wonderingly.

"Nancy next," Mr. Summers said. Nancy was twelve, and her school friends breathed heavily as she went forward, switching her skirt, and took a slip daintily from the box. "Bill, Jr.," Mr. Summers said, and Billy, his face red and his feet overlarge, nearly knocked the box over as he got a paper out. "Tessie," Mr. Summers said. She hesitated for a minute, looking around defiantly, and then set her lips and went up to the box. She snatched a paper out and held it behind her.

"Bill," Mr. Summers said, and Bill Hutchinson reached into the box and felt around, bringing his hand out at last with the slip of paper in it.

The crowd was quiet. A girl whispered, "I hope it's not Nancy," and the sound of the whisper reached the edges of the crowd.

"It's not the way it used to be," Old Man Warner said clearly. "People ain't the way they used to be."

"All right," Mr. Summers said. "Open the papers. Harry, you open little Dave's."

Mr. Graves opened the slip of paper and there was a general sigh through the crowd as he held it up and everyone could see that it was blank. Nancy and Bill, Jr., opened theirs at the same time, and both beamed and laughed, turning around to the crowd and holding their slips of paper above their heads.

"Tessie," Mr. Summers said. There was a pause, and then Mr. Summers looked at Bill Hutchinson, and Bill unfolded his paper and showed it. It was blank.

"It's Tessie," Mr. Summers said, and his voice was hushed. "Show us her paper, Bill."

Bill Hutchinson went over to his wife and forced the slip of paper out of her hand. It had a black spot on it, the black spot Mr. Summers had made the night before with the heavy pencil in the coal-company office. Bill Hutchinson held it up and there was a stir in the crowd.

"All right, folks," Mr. Summers said. "Let's finish quickly."

Although the villagers had forgotten the ritual and lost the original black box, they still remembered to use stones. The pile of stones the boys had made earlier was ready; there were stones on the ground with the blowing scraps of paper that had come out of the box. Mrs. Delacroix selected a stone so large she had to pick it up with both hands and turned to Mrs. Dunbar. "Come on," she said. "Hurry up."

Mrs. Dunbar had small stones in both hands, and she said, gasping for breath, "I can't run at all. You'll have to go ahead and I'll catch up with you."

The children had stones already, and someone gave little Davy Hutchinson a few pebbles.

Tessie Hutchinson was in the center of a cleared space by now, and she held her hands out desperately as the villagers moved in on her. "It isn't fair," she said. A stone hit her on the side of the head.

Old Man Warner was saying, "Come on, come on, everyone." Steve Adams was in the front of the crowd of villagers, with Mrs. Graves beside him.

"It isn't fair, it isn't right," Mrs. Hutchinson screamed and then they were upon her.

[1948]

JAMES BALDWIN   [1924–1987]

Sonny's Blues

I read about it in the paper, in the subway, on my way to work. I read it, and I couldn't believe it, and I read it again. Then perhaps I just stared at it, at the newsprint spelling out his name, spelling out the story. I stared at it in the swinging lights of the subway car, and in the faces and bodies of the people, and in my own face, trapped in the darkness which roared outside.

It was not to be believed and I kept telling myself that, as I walked from the subway station to the high school. And at the same time I couldn't doubt it. I was scared, scared for Sonny. He became real to me again. A great block of ice got settled in my belly and kept melting there slowly all day long, while I taught my classes algebra. It was a special kind of ice. It kept melting, sending trickles of ice water all up and down my veins, but it never got less. Sometimes it hardened and seemed to expand until I felt my guts were going to come spilling out or that I was going to choke or scream. This would always be at a moment when I was remembering some specific thing Sonny had once said or done.

When he was about as old as the boys in my classes his face had been bright and open, there was a lot of copper in it; and he'd had wonderfully direct brown eyes, and great gentleness and privacy. I wondered what he looked like now. He had been picked up, the evening before, in a raid on an apartment downtown, for peddling and using heroin.

I couldn't believe it: but what I mean by that is that I couldn't find any room for it anywhere inside me. I had kept it outside me for a long time.

I hadn't wanted to know. I had had suspicions, but I didn't name them, I kept putting them away. I told myself that Sonny was wild, but he wasn't crazy. And he'd always been a good boy, he hadn't ever turned hard or evil or disrespectful, the way kids can, so quick, so quick, especially in Harlem. I didn't want to believe that I'd ever see my brother going down, coming to nothing, all that light in his face gone out, in the condition I'd already seen so many others. Yet it had happened and here I was, talking about algebra to a lot of boys who might, every one of them for all I knew, be popping off needles every time they went to the head. Maybe it did more for them than algebra could.

I was sure that the first time Sonny had ever had horse, he couldn't have been much older than these boys were now. These boys, now, were living as we'd been living then, they were growing up with a rush and their heads bumped abruptly against the low ceiling of their actual possibilities. They were filled with rage. All they really knew were two darknesses, the darkness of their lives, which was now closing in on them, and the darkness of the movies, which had blinded them to that other darkness, and in which they now, vindictively, dreamed, at once more together than they were at any other time, and more alone.

When the last bell rang, the last class ended, I let out my breath. It seemed I'd been holding it for all that time. My clothes were wet—I may have looked as though I'd been sitting in a steam bath, all dressed up, all afternoon. I sat alone in the classroom a long time. I listened to the boys outside, downstairs, shouting and cursing and laughing. Their laughter struck me for perhaps the first time. It was not the joyous laughter which—God knows why—one associates with children. It was mocking and insular, its intent to denigrate. It was disenchanted, and in this, also, lay the authority of their curses. Perhaps I was listening to them because I was thinking about my brother and in them I heard my brother. And myself.

One boy was whistling a tune, at once very complicated and very simple, it seemed to be pouring out of him as though he were a bird, and it sounded very cool and moving through all that harsh, bright air, only just holding its own through all those other sounds.

I stood up and walked over to the window and looked down into the courtyard. It was the beginning of the spring and the sap was rising in the boys. A teacher passed through them every now and again, quickly, as though he or she couldn't wait to get out of that courtyard, to get those boys out of their sight and off their minds. I started collecting my stuff. I thought I'd better get home and talk to Isabel.

The courtyard was almost deserted by the time I got downstairs. I saw this boy standing in the shadow of a doorway, looking just like Sonny. I almost called his name. Then I saw that it wasn't Sonny, but somebody we used to know, a boy from around our block. He'd been Sonny's friend. He'd never been mine, having been too young for me, and, anyway, I'd never liked him. And now, even though he was a grown-up man, he still hung around that block, still spent hours on the street corners, was always high and raggy. I used to run into him from time to time and he'd often work around to asking me for a quarter or fifty cents. He always had some real good excuse, too, and I always gave it to him, I don't know why.

But now, abruptly, I hated him. I couldn't stand the way he looked at me, partly like a dog, partly like a cunning child. I wanted to ask him what the hell he was doing in the school courtyard.

He sort of shuffled over to me, and he said, "I see you got the papers. So you already know about it."

"You mean about Sonny? Yes, I already know about it. How come they didn't get you?"

He grinned. It made him repulsive and it also brought to mind what he'd looked like as a kid. "I wasn't there. I stay away from them people."

"Good for you." I offered him a cigarette and I watched him through the smoke. "You come all the way down here just to tell me about Sonny?"

"That's right." He was sort of shaking his head and his eyes looked strange, as though they were about to cross. The bright sun deadened his damp dark brown skin and it made his eyes look yellow and showed up the dirt in his kinked hair. He smelled funky. I moved a little away from him and I said, "Well, thanks. But I already know about it and I got to get home."

"I'll walk you a little ways," he said. We started walking. There were a couple of kids still loitering in the courtyard and one of them said goodnight to me and looked strangely at the boy beside me.

"What're you going to do?" he asked me. "I mean, about Sonny?"

"Look. I haven't seen Sonny for over a year. I'm not sure I'm going to do anything. Anyway, what the hell *can* I do?"

"That's right," he said quickly, "ain't nothing you can do. Can't much help old Sonny no more, I guess."

It was what I was thinking and so it seemed to me he had no right to say it.

"I'm surprised at Sonny, though," he went on—he had a funny way of talking, he looked straight ahead as though he were talking to himself—"I thought Sonny was a smart boy, I thought he was too smart to get hung."

"I guess he thought so too," I said sharply, "and that's how he got hung. And how about you? You're pretty goddamn smart, I bet."

Then he looked directly at me, just for a minute. "I ain't smart," he said. "If I was smart, I'd have reached for a pistol a long time ago."

"Look. Don't tell *me* your sad story, if it was up to me, I'd give you one."
Then I felt guilty—guilty, probably, for never having supposed that the
poor bastard *had* a story of his own, much less a sad one, and I asked,
quickly, "What's going to happen to him now?"

He didn't answer this. He was off by himself some place. "Funny
thing," he said, and from his tone we might have been discussing the
quickest way to get to Brooklyn, "when I saw the papers this morning,
the first thing I asked myself was if I had anything to do with it. I felt sort
of responsible."

I began to listen more carefully. The subway station was on the corner,
just before us, and I stopped. He stopped, too. We were in front of a bar
and he ducked slightly, peering in, but whoever he was looking for didn't
seem to be there. The juke box was blasting away with something black
and bouncy and I half watched the barmaid as she danced her way from
the juke box to her place behind the bar. And I watched her face as she
laughingly responded to something someone said to her, still keeping
time to the music. When she smiled one saw the little girl, one sensed the
doomed, still-struggling woman beneath the battered face of the semi-
whore.

"I never *give* Sonny nothing," the boy said finally, "but a long time ago
I come to school high and Sonny asked me how it felt." He paused, I
couldn't bear to watch him, I watched the barmaid, and I listened to the
music which seemed to be causing the pavement to shake. "I told him it
felt great." The music stopped, the barmaid paused and watched the juke
box until the music began again. "It did."

All this was carrying me some place I didn't want to go. I certainly
didn't want to know how it felt. It filled everything, the people, the houses,
the music, the dark, quicksilver barmaid, with menace; and this menace
was their reality.

"What's going to happen to him now?" I asked again.

"They'll send him away some place and they'll try to cure him." He
shook his head. "Maybe he'll even think he's kicked the habit. Then they'll
let him loose"—he gestured, throwing his cigarette into the gutter.
"That's all."

"What do you mean, that's *all*?"

But I knew what he meant.

"I *mean*, that's *all*." He turned his head and looked at me, pulling down
the corners of his mouth. "Don't you know what I mean?" he asked,
softly.

"How the hell *would* I know what you mean?" I almost whispered it, I
don't know why.

"That's right," he said to the air, "how would *he* know what I mean?" He
turned toward me again, patient and calm, and yet I somehow felt him

shaking, shaking as though he were going to fall apart. I felt that ice in my guts again, the dread I'd felt all afternoon; and again I watched the barmaid, moving about the bar, washing glasses, and singing. "Listen. They'll let him out and then it'll just start all over again. That's what I mean."

"You mean—they'll let him out. And then he'll just start working his way back in again. You mean he'll never kick the habit. Is that what you mean?"

"That's right," he said, cheerfully. "*You* see what I mean."

"Tell me," I said at last, "why does he want to die? He must want to die, he's killing himself, why does he want to die?"

He looked at me in surprise. He licked his lips. "He don't want to die. He wants to live. Don't nobody want to die, ever."

Then I wanted to ask him—too many things. He could not have answered, or if he had, I could not have borne the answers. I started walking. "Well, I guess it's none of my business."

"It's going to be rough on old Sonny," he said. We reached the subway station. "This is your station?" he asked. I nodded. I took one step down. "Damn!" he said, suddenly. I looked up at him. He grinned again. "Damn it if I didn't leave all my money home. You ain't got a dollar on you, have you? Just for a couple of days, is all."

All at once something inside gave and threatened to come pouring out of me. I didn't hate him any more. I felt that in another moment I'd start crying like a child.

"Sure," I said. "Don't sweat." I looked in my wallet and didn't have a dollar, I only had a five. "Here," I said. "That hold you?"

He didn't look at it—he didn't want to look at it. A terrible closed look came over his face, as though he were keeping the number on the bill a secret from him and me. "Thanks," he said, and now he was dying to see me go. "Don't worry about Sonny. Maybe I'll write him or something."

"Sure," I said. "You do that. So long."

"Be seeing you," he said. I went on down the steps.

And I didn't write Sonny or send him anything for a long time. When I finally did, it was just after my little girl died, he wrote me back a letter which made me feel like a bastard.

Here's what he said:

Dear brother,

You don't know how much I needed to hear from you. I wanted to write you many a time but I dug how much I must have hurt you and so I didn't write. But now I feel like a man who's been trying to climb up out of some deep, real deep and funky hole and just saw the sun up there, outside. I got to get outside.

I can't tell you much about how I got here. I mean I don't know how to tell you. I guess I was afraid of something or I was trying to escape from something and you know I have never been very strong in the head (smile). I'm glad Mama and Daddy are dead and can't see what's happened to their son and I swear if I'd known what I was doing I would never have hurt you so, you and a lot of other fine people who were nice to me and who believed in me.

I don't want you to think it had anything to do with me being a musician. It's more than that. Or maybe less than that. I can't get anything straight in my head down here and I try not to think about what's going to happen to me when I get outside again. Sometime I think I'm going to flip and never get outside and sometime I think I'll come straight back. I tell you one thing, though, I'd rather blow my brains out than go through this again. But that's what they all say, so they tell me. If I tell you when I'm coming to New York and if you could meet me, I sure would appreciate it. Give my love to Isabel and the kids and I was sure sorry to hear about little Gracie. I wish I could be like Mama and say the Lord's will be done, but I don't know it seems to me that trouble is the one thing that never does get stopped and I don't know what good it does to blame it on the Lord. But maybe it does some good if you believe it.

Your brother,
Sonny

Then I kept in constant touch with him and I sent him whatever I could and I went to meet him when he came back to New York. When I saw him many things I thought I had forgotten came flooding back to me. This was because I had begun, finally, to wonder about Sonny, about the life that Sonny lived inside. This life, whatever it was, had made him older and thinner and it had deepened the distant stillness in which he had always moved. He looked very unlike my baby brother. Yet, when he smiled, when we shook hands, the baby brother I'd never known looked out from the depths of his private life, like an animal waiting to be coaxed into the light.

"How you been keeping?" he asked me.

"All right. And you?"

"Just fine." He was smiling all over his face. "It's good to see you again."

"It's good to see you."

The seven years' difference in our ages lay between us like a chasm: I wondered if these years would ever operate between us as a bridge. I was remembering, and it made it hard to catch my breath, that I had been there when he was born; and I had heard the first words he had ever spoken. When he started to walk, he walked from our mother straight to me. I caught him just before he fell when he took the first steps he ever took in this world.

"How's Isabel?"

"Just fine. She's dying to see you."

"And the boys?"

"They're fine, too. They're anxious to see their uncle."

"Oh, come on. You know they don't remember me."

"Are you kidding? Of course they remember you."

He grinned again. We got into a taxi. We had a lot to say to each other, far too much to know how to begin.

As the taxi began to move, I asked, "You still want to go to India?"

He laughed. "You still remember that. Hell, no. This place is Indian enough for me."

"It used to belong to them," I said.

And he laughed again. "They damn sure knew what they were doing when they got rid of it."

Years ago, when he was around fourteen, he'd been all hipped on the idea of going to India. He read books about people sitting on rocks, naked, in all kinds of weather, but mostly bad, naturally, and walking barefoot through hot coals and arriving at wisdom. I used to say that it sounded to me as though they were getting away from wisdom as fast as they could. I think he sort of looked down on me for that.

"Do you mind," he asked, "if we have the driver drive alongside the park? On the west side—I haven't seen the city in so long."

"Of course not," I said. I was afraid that I might sound as though I were humoring him, but I hoped he wouldn't take it that way.

So we drove along, between the green of the park and the stony, lifeless elegance of hotels and apartment buildings, toward the vivid, killing streets of our childhood. These streets hadn't changed, though housing projects jutted up out of them now like rocks in the middle of a boiling sea. Most of the houses in which we had grown up had vanished, as had the stores from which we had stolen, the basements in which we had first tried sex, the rooftops from which we had hurled tin cans and bricks. But houses exactly like the houses of our past yet dominated the landscape, boys exactly like the boys we once had been found themselves smothering in these houses, came down into the streets for light and air and found themselves encircled by disaster. Some escaped the trap, most didn't. Those who got out always left something of themselves behind, as some animals amputate a leg and leave it in the trap. It might be said, perhaps, that I had escaped, after all, I was a school teacher; or that Sonny had, he hadn't lived in Harlem for years. Yet, as the cab moved uptown through streets which seemed, with a rush, to darken with dark people, and as I covertly studied Sonny's face, it came to me that what we both were seeking through our separate cab windows was that part of ourselves which had been left behind. It's always at the hour of trouble and confrontation that the missing member aches.

We hit 110th Street and started rolling up Lenox Avenue. And I'd known this avenue all my life, but it seemed to me again, as it had seemed on the day I'd first heard about Sonny's trouble, filled with a hidden menace which was its very breath of life.

"We almost there," said Sonny.

"Almost." We were both too nervous to say anything more.

We live in a housing project. It hasn't been up long. A few days after it was up it seemed uninhabitably new, now, of course, it's already run-down. It looks like a parody of the good, clean, faceless life—God knows the people who live in it do their best to make it a parody. The beat-looking grass lying around isn't enough to make their lives green, the hedges will never hold out the streets, and they know it. The big windows fool no one, they aren't big enough to make space out of no space. They don't bother with the windows, they watch the TV screen instead. The playground is most popular with the children who don't play at jacks, or skip rope, or roller skate, or swing, and they can be found in it after dark. We moved in partly because it's not too far from where I teach, and partly for the kids; but it's really just like the houses in which Sonny and I grew up. The same things happen, they'll have the same things to remember. The moment Sonny and I started into the house I had the feeling that I was simply bringing him back into the danger he had almost died trying to escape.

Sonny has never been talkative. So I don't know why I was sure he'd be dying to talk to me when supper was over the first night. Everything went fine, the oldest boy remembered him, and the youngest boy liked him, and Sonny had remembered to bring something for each of them; and Isabel, who is really much nicer than I am, more open and giving, had gone to a lot of trouble about dinner and was genuinely glad to see him. And she's always been able to tease Sonny in a way that I haven't. It was nice to see her face so vivid again and to hear her laugh and watch her make Sonny laugh. She wasn't, or, anyway, she didn't seem to be, at all uneasy or embarrassed. She chatted as though there were no subject which had to be avoided and she got Sonny past his first, faint stiffness. And thank God she was there, for I was filled with that icy dread again. Everything I did seemed awkward to me, and everything I said sounded freighted with hidden meaning. I was trying to remember everything I'd heard about dope addiction and I couldn't help watching Sonny for signs. I wasn't doing it out of malice. I was trying to find out something about my brother. I was dying to hear him tell me he was safe.

"Safe!" my father grunted, whenever Mama suggested trying to move to a neighborhood which might be safer for children. "Safe, hell! Ain't no place safe for kids, nor nobody."

He always went on like this, but he wasn't, ever, really as bad as he sounded, not even on weekends, when he got drunk. As a matter of fact, he was always on the lookout for "something a little better," but he died before he found it. He died suddenly, during a drunken weekend in the middle of the war, when Sonny was fifteen. He and Sonny hadn't ever got on too well. And this was partly because Sonny was the apple of his father's eye. It was because he loved Sonny so much and was frightened for him, that he was always fighting with him. It doesn't do any good to fight with Sonny. Sonny just moves back, inside himself, where he can't be reached. But the principal reason that they never hit it off is that they were so much alike. Daddy was big and rough and loud-talking, just the opposite of Sonny, but they both had—that same privacy.

Mama tried to tell me something about this, just after Daddy died. I was home on leave from the army.

This was the last time I ever saw my mother alive. Just the same, this picture gets all mixed up in my mind with pictures I had of her when she was younger. The way I always see her is the way she used to be on a Sunday afternoon, say, when the old folks were talking after the big Sunday dinner. I always see her wearing pale blue. She'd be sitting on the sofa. And my father would be sitting in the easy chair, not far from her. And the living room would be full of church folks and relatives. There they sit, in chairs all around the living room, and the night is creeping up outside, but nobody knows it yet. You can see the darkness growing against the windowpanes and you hear the street noises every now and again, or maybe the jangling beat of a tambourine from one of the churches close by, but it's real quiet in the room. For a moment nobody's talking, but every face looks darkening, like the sky outside. And my mother rocks a little from the waist, and my father's eyes are closed. Everyone is looking at something a child can't see. For a minute they've forgotten the children. Maybe a kid is lying on the rug, half asleep. Maybe somebody's got a kid in his lap and is absent-mindedly stroking the kid's head. Maybe there's a kid, quiet and big-eyed, curled up in a big chair in the corner. The silence, the darkness coming, and the darkness in the faces frightens the child obscurely. He hopes that the hand which strokes his forehead will never stop—will never die. He hopes that there will never come a time when the old folks won't be sitting around the living room, talking about where they've come from, and what they've seen, and what's happened to them and their kinfolk.

But something deep and watchful in the child knows that this is bound to end, is already ending. In a moment someone will get up and turn on the light. Then the old folks will remember the children and they won't talk any more that day. And when light fills the room, the child is filled with darkness. He knows that every time this happens he's moved just a little closer to that darkness outside. The darkness outside is what the old folks have been talking about. It's what they've come from. It's what they endure. The child knows that they won't talk any more because if he knows too much about what's happened to *them*, he'll know too much too soon, about what's going to happen to *him*.

The last time I talked to my mother, I remember I was restless. I wanted to get out and see Isabel. We weren't married then and we had a lot to straighten out between us.

There Mama sat, in black, by the window. She was humming an old church song, *Lord, you brought me from a long ways off.* Sonny was out somewhere. Mama kept watching the streets.

"I don't know," she said, "if I'll ever see you again, after you go off from here. But I hope you'll remember the things I tried to teach you."

"Don't talk like that," I said, and smiled. "You'll be here a long time yet."

She smiled, too, but she said nothing. She was quiet for a long time. And I said, "Mama, don't you worry about nothing. I'll be writing all the time, and you be getting the checks. . . ."

"I want to talk to you about your brother," she said, suddenly. "If anything happens to me he ain't going to have nobody to look out for him."

"Mama," I said, "ain't nothing going to happen to you or Sonny. Sonny's all right. He's a good boy and he's got good sense."

"It ain't a question of his being a good boy," Mama said, "nor of his having good sense. It ain't only the bad ones, nor yet the dumb ones that gets sucked under." She stopped, looking at me. "Your Daddy once had a brother," she said, and she smiled in a way that made me feel she was in pain. "You didn't never know that, did you?"

"No," I said, "I never knew that," and I watched her face.

"Oh, yes," she said, "your Daddy had a brother." She looked out of the window again. "I know you never saw your Daddy cry. But *I* did—many a time, through all these years."

I asked her, "What happened to his brother? How come nobody's ever talked about him?"

This was the first time I ever saw my mother look old.

"His brother got killed," she said, "when he was just a little younger than you are now. I knew him. He was a fine boy. He was maybe a little full of the devil, but he didn't mean nobody no harm."

Then she stopped and the room was silent, exactly as it had sometimes been on those Sunday afternoons. Mama kept looking out into the streets.

"He used to have a job in the mill," she said, "and, like all young folks, he just liked to perform on Saturday nights. Saturday nights, him and your father would drift around to different places, go to dances and things like that, or just sit around with people they knew, and your father's brother would sing, he had a fine voice, and play along with himself on his guitar. Well, this particular Saturday night, him and your father was coming home from some place, and they were both a little drunk and there was a moon that night, it was bright like day. Your father's brother was feeling kind of good, and he was whistling to himself, and he had his guitar slung over his shoulder. They was coming down a hill and beneath them was a road that turned off from the highway. Well, your father's brother, being always kind of frisky, decided to run down this hill, and he did, with that guitar banging and clanging behind him, and he ran across the road, and he was making water behind a tree. And your father was sort of amused at him and he was still coming down the hill, kind of slow. Then he heard a car motor and that same minute his brother stepped from behind the tree, into the road, in the moonlight. And he started to cross the road. And your father started to run down the hill, he says he don't know why. This car was full of white men. They was all drunk, and when they seen your father's brother they let out a great whoop and holler and they aimed the car straight at him. They was having fun, they just wanted to scare him, the way they do sometimes, you know. But they was drunk. And I guess the boy, being drunk, too, and scared, kind of lost his head. By the time he jumped it was too late. Your father says he heard his brother scream when the car rolled over him, and he heard the wood of that guitar when it give, and he heard them strings go flying, and he heard them white men shouting, and the car kept on a-going and it ain't stopped till this day. And, time your father got down the hill, his brother weren't nothing but blood and pulp."

Tears were gleaming on my mother's face. There wasn't anything I could say.

"He never mentioned it," she said, "because I never let him mention it before you children. Your Daddy was like a crazy man that night and for many a night thereafter. He says he never in his life seen anything as dark as that road after the lights of that car had gone away. Weren't nothing, weren't nobody on that road, just your Daddy and his brother and that busted guitar. Oh, yes. Your Daddy never did really get right again. Till the day he died he weren't sure but that every white man he saw was the man that killed his brother."

She stopped and took out her handkerchief and dried her eyes and looked at me.

"I ain't telling you all this," she said, "to make you scared or bitter or to make you hate nobody. I'm telling you this because you got a brother. And the world ain't changed."

I guess I didn't want to believe this. I guess she saw this in my face. She turned away from me, toward the window again, searching those streets.

"But I praise my Redeemer," she said at last, "that He called your Daddy home before me. I ain't saying it to throw no flowers at myself, but, I declare, it keeps me from feeling too cast down to know I helped your father get safely through this world. Your father always acted like he was the roughest, strongest man on earth. And everybody took him to be like that. But if he hadn't had *me* there—to see his tears!"

She was crying again. Still, I couldn't move. I said, "Lord, Lord, Mama, I didn't know it was like that."

"Oh, honey," she said, "there's a lot that you don't know. But you are going to find it out." She stood up from the window and came over to me. "You got to hold on to your brother," she said, "and don't let him fall, no matter what it looks like is happening to him and no matter how evil you gets with him. You going to be evil with him many a time. But don't you forget what I told you, you hear?"

"I won't forget," I said. "Don't you worry, I won't forget. I won't let nothing happen to Sonny."

My mother smiled as though she were amused at something she saw in my face. Then, "You may not be able to stop nothing from happening. But you got to let him know you's *there*."

Two days later I was married, and then I was gone. And I had a lot of things on my mind and I pretty well forgot my promise to Mama until I got shipped home on a special furlough for her funeral.

And, after the funeral, with just Sonny and me alone in the empty kitchen, I tried to find out something about him.

"What do you want to do?" I asked him.

"I'm going to be a musician," he said.

For he had graduated, in the time I had been away, from dancing to the juke box to finding out who was playing what, and what they were doing with it, and he had bought himself a set of drums.

"You mean, you want to be a drummer?" I somehow had the feeling that being a drummer might be all right for other people but not for my brother Sonny.

"I don't think," he said, looking at me very gravely, "that I'll ever be a good drummer. But I think I can play a piano."

I frowned. I'd never played the role of the older brother quite so seriously before, had scarcely ever, in fact, *asked* Sonny a damn thing. I sensed myself in the presence of something I didn't really know how to handle, didn't understand. So I made my frown a little deeper as I asked: "What kind of musician do you want to be?"

He grinned. "How many kinds do you think there are?"

"Be *serious*," I said.

He laughed, throwing his head back, and then looked at me. "I *am* serious."

"Well, then, for Christ's sake, stop kidding around and answer a serious question. I mean, do you want to be a concert pianist, you want to play classical music and all that, or—or what?" Long before I finished he was laughing again. "For Christ *sake*, Sonny!"

He sobered, but with difficulty. "I'm sorry. But you sound so—*scared!*" and he was off again.

"Well, you may think it's funny now, baby, but it's not going to be so funny when you have to make your living at it, let me tell you *that*." I was furious because I knew he was laughing at me and I didn't know why.

"No," he said, very sober now, and afraid, perhaps, that he'd hurt me, "I don't want to be a classical pianist. That isn't what interests me. I mean"—he paused, looking hard at me, as though his eyes would help me to understand, and then gestured helplessly, as though perhaps his hand would help—"I mean, I'll have a lot of studying to do, and I'll have to study *everything*, but, I mean, I want to play *with*—jazz musicians." He stopped. "I want to play jazz," he said.

Well, the word had never before sounded as heavy, as real, as it sounded that afternoon in Sonny's mouth. I just looked at him and I was probably frowning a real frown by this time. I simply couldn't see why on earth he'd want to spend his time hanging around nightclubs, clowning around on bandstands, while people pushed each other around a dance floor. It seemed—beneath him, somehow. I had never thought about it before, had never been forced to, but I suppose I had always put jazz musicians in a class with what Daddy called "good-time people."

"Are you *serious*?"

"Hell, *yes*, I'm serious."

He looked more helpless than ever, and annoyed, and deeply hurt.

I suggested, helpfully: "You mean—like Louis Armstrong?"

His face closed as though I'd struck him. "No. I'm not talking about none of that old-time, down home crap."

"Well, look, Sonny, I'm sorry, don't get mad. I just don't altogether get it, that's all. Name somebody—you know, a jazz musician you admire."

"Bird."

"Who?"

"Bird! Charlie Parker! Don't they teach you nothing in the goddamn army?"

I lit a cigarette. I was surprised and then a little amused to discover that I was trembling. "I've been out of touch," I said. "You'll have to be patient with me. Now. Who's this Parker character?"

"He's just one of the greatest jazz musicians alive," said Sonny, sullenly, his hands in his pockets, his back to me. "Maybe *the* greatest," he added, bitterly, "that's probably why *you* never heard of him."

"All right," I said, "I'm ignorant. I'm sorry. I'll go out and buy all the cat's records right away, all right?"

"It don't," said Sonny, with dignity, "make any difference to me. I don't care what you listen to. Don't do me no favors."

I was beginning to realize that I'd never seen him so upset before. With another part of my mind I was thinking that this would probably turn out to be one of those things kids go through and that I shouldn't make it seem important by pushing it too hard. Still, I didn't think it would do any harm to ask: "Doesn't all this take a lot of time? Can you make a living at it?"

He turned back to me and half leaned, half sat, on the kitchen table. "Everything takes time," he said, "and—well, yes, sure, I can make a living at it. But what I don't seem to be able to make you understand is that it's the only thing I want to do."

"Well, Sonny," I said, gently, "you know people can't always do exactly what they *want* to do—"

"*No*, I don't know that," said Sonny, surprising me. "I think people *ought* to do what they want to do, what else are they alive for?"

"You getting to be a big boy," I said desperately, "it's time you started thinking about your future."

"I'm thinking about my future," said Sonny, grimly. "I think about it all the time."

I gave up. I decided, if he didn't change his mind, that we could always talk about it later. "In the meantime," I said, "you got to finish school." We had already decided that he'd have to move in with Isabel and her folks. I knew this wasn't the ideal arrangement because Isabel's folks are inclined to be dicty° and they hadn't especially wanted Isabel to marry me. But I didn't know what else to do. "And we have to get you fixed up at Isabel's."

There was a long silence. He moved from the kitchen table to the window. "That's a terrible idea. You know it yourself."

"Do you have a *better* idea?"

He just walked up and down the kitchen for a minute. He was as tall as I was. He had started to shave. I suddenly had the feeling that I didn't know him at all.

He stopped at the kitchen table and picked up my cigarettes. Looking at me with a kind of mocking, amused defiance, he put one between his lips. "You mind?"

"You smoking already?"

He lit the cigarette and nodded, watching me through the smoke. "I just wanted to see if I'd have the courage to smoke in front of you." He grinned

Dicty: High-class, snobbish.

and blew a great cloud of smoke to the ceiling. "It was easy." He looked at my face. "Come on, now. I bet you was smoking at my age, tell the truth."

I didn't say anything but the truth was on my face, and he laughed. But now there was something very strained in his laugh. "Sure. And I bet that ain't all you was doing."

He was frightening me a little. "Cut the crap," I said. "We already decided that you was going to go and live at Isabel's. Now what's got into you all of a sudden?"

"*You* decided it," he pointed out. "*I* didn't decide nothing." He stopped in front of me, leaning against the stove, arms loosely folded. "Look, brother. I don't want to stay in Harlem no more, I really don't." He was very earnest. He looked at me, then over toward the kitchen window. There was something in his eyes I'd never seen before, some thoughtfulness, some worry all his own. He rubbed the muscle of one arm. "It's time I was getting out of here."

"Where do you want to go, Sonny?"

"I want to join the army. Or the navy, I don't care. If I say I'm old enough, they'll believe me."

Then I got mad. It was because I was so scared. "You must be crazy. You goddamn fool, what the hell do you want to go and join the *army* for?"

"I just told you. To get out of Harlem."

"Sonny, you haven't even finished *school.* And if you really want to be a musician, how do you expect to study if you're in the *army?*"

He looked at me, trapped, and in anguish. "There's ways. I might be able to work out some kind of deal. Anyway, I'll have the G.I. Bill when I come out."

"*If* you come out." We stared at each other. "Sonny, please. Be reasonable. I know the setup is far from perfect. But we got to do the best we can."

"I ain't learning nothing in school," he said. "Even when I go." He turned away from me and opened the window and threw his cigarette out into the narrow alley. I watched his back. "At least, I ain't learning nothing you'd want me to learn." He slammed the window so hard I thought the glass would fly out, and turned back to me. "And I'm sick of the stink of these garbage cans!"

"Sonny," I said, "I know how you feel. But if you don't finish school now, you're going to be sorry later that you didn't." I grabbed him by the shoulders. "And you only got another year. It ain't so bad. And I'll come back and I swear I'll help you do *whatever* you want to do. Just try to put up with it till I come back. Will you please do that? For me?"

He didn't answer and he wouldn't look at me.

"Sonny. You hear me?"

He pulled away. "I hear you. But you never hear anything *I* say."

I didn't know what to say to that. He looked out of the window and then back at me. "OK," he said, and sighed. "I'll try."

Then I said, trying to cheer him up a little, "They got a piano at Isabel's. You can practice on it."

And as a matter of fact, it did cheer him up for a minute. "That's right," he said to himself. "I forgot that." His face relaxed a little. But the worry, the thoughtfulness, played on it still, the way shadows play on a face which is staring into the fire.

But I thought I'd never hear the end of that piano. At first, Isabel would write me, saying how nice it was that Sonny was so serious about his music and how, as soon as he came in from school, or wherever he had been when he was supposed to be at school, he went straight to that piano and stayed there until suppertime. And, after supper, he went back to that piano and stayed there until everybody went to bed. He was at the piano all day Saturday and all day Sunday. Then he bought a record player and started playing records. He'd play one record over and over again, all day long sometimes, and he'd improvise along with it on the piano. Or he'd play one section of the record, one chord, one change, one progression, then he'd do it on the piano. Then back to the record. Then back to the piano.

Well, I really don't know how they stood it. Isabel finally confessed that it wasn't like living with a person at all, it was like living with sound. And the sound didn't make any sense to her, didn't make any sense to any of them—naturally. They began, in a way, to be afflicted by this presence that was living in their home. It was as though Sonny were some sort of god, or monster. He moved in an atmosphere which wasn't like theirs at all. They fed him and he ate, he washed himself, he walked in and out of their door; he certainly wasn't nasty or unpleasant or rude, Sonny isn't any of those things; but it was as though he were all wrapped up in some cloud, some fire, some vision all his own; and there wasn't any way to reach him.

At the same time, he wasn't really a man yet, he was still a child, and they had to watch out for him in all kinds of ways. They certainly couldn't throw him out. Neither did they dare to make a great scene about that piano because even they dimly sensed, as I sensed, from so many thousands of miles away, that Sonny was at that piano playing for his life.

But he hadn't been going to school. One day a letter came from the school board and Isabel's mother got it—there had, apparently, been other letters but Sonny had torn them up. This day, when Sonny came in, Isabel's mother showed him the letter and asked where he'd been spending his time. And she finally got it out of him that he'd been down in

Greenwich Village, with musicians and other characters, in a white girl's apartment. And this scared her and she started to scream at him and what came up, once she began—though she denies it to this day—was what sacrifices they were making to give Sonny a decent home and how little he appreciated it.

Sonny didn't play the piano that day. By evening, Isabel's mother had calmed down but then there was the old man to deal with, and Isabel herself. Isabel says she did her best to be calm but she broke down and started crying. She says she just watched Sonny's face. She could tell, by watching him, what was happening with him. And what was happening was that they penetrated his cloud, they had reached him. Even if their fingers had been a thousand times more gentle than human fingers ever are, he could hardly help feeling that they had stripped him naked and were spitting on that nakedness. For he also had to see that his presence, that music, which was life or death to him, had been torture for them and that they had endured it, not at all for his sake, but only for mine. And Sonny couldn't take that. He can take it a little better today than he could then but he's still not very good at it and, frankly, I don't know anybody who is.

The silence of the next few days must have been louder than the sound of all the music ever played since time began. One morning, before she went to work, Isabel was in his room for something and she suddenly realized that all of his records were gone. And she knew for certain that he was gone. And he was. He went as far as the navy would carry him. He finally sent me a postcard from some place in Greece and that was the first I knew that Sonny was still alive. I didn't see him any more until we were both back in New York and the war had long been over.

He was a man by then, of course, but I wasn't willing to see it. He came by the house from time to time, but we fought almost every time we met. I didn't like the way he carried himself, loose and dreamlike all the time, and I didn't like his friends, and his music seemed to be merely an excuse for the life he led. It sounded just that weird and disordered.

Then we had a fight, a pretty awful fight, and I didn't see him for months. By and by I looked him up, where he was living, in a furnished room in the Village, and I tried to make it up. But there were lots of people in the room and Sonny just lay on his bed, and he wouldn't come downstairs with me, and he treated these other people as though they were his family and I weren't. So I got mad and then he got mad, and then I told him that he might just as well be dead as live the way he was living. Then he stood up and he told me not to worry about him any more in life, that he was dead as far as I was concerned. Then he pushed me to the door and the other people looked on as though nothing were happening, and he slammed the door behind me. I stood in the hallway, staring at the door. I heard somebody laugh in the room and then the tears came to my eyes. I started down the steps, whistling to keep from crying, I kept whistling to myself, *You going to need me, baby, one of these cold, rainy days.*

I read about Sonny's trouble in the spring. Little Grace died in the fall. She was a beautiful little girl. But she only lived a little over two years. She died of polio and she suffered. She had a slight fever for a couple of days, but it didn't seem like anything and we just kept her in bed. And we would certainly have called the doctor, but the fever dropped, she seemed to be all right. So we thought it had just been a cold. Then, one day, she was up, playing, Isabel was in the kitchen fixing lunch for the two boys when they'd come in from school, and she heard Grace fall down in the living room. When you have a lot of children you don't always start running when one of them falls, unless they start screaming or something. And, this time, Grace was quiet. Yet, Isabel says that when she heard that *thump* and then that silence, something happened in her to make her afraid. And she ran to the living room and there was little Grace on the floor, all twisted up, and the reason she hadn't screamed was that she couldn't get her breath. And when she did scream, it was the worst sound, Isabel says, that she'd ever heard in all her life, and she still hears it sometimes in her dreams. Isabel will sometimes wake me up with a low, moaning, strangled sound and I have to be quick to awaken her and hold her to me and where Isabel is weeping against me seems a mortal wound.

I think I may have written Sonny the very day that little Grace was buried. I was sitting in the living room in the dark, by myself, and I suddenly thought of Sonny. My trouble made his real.

One Saturday afternoon, when Sonny had been living with us, or, anyway, been in our house, for nearly two weeks, I found myself wandering aimlessly about the living room, drinking from a can of beer, and trying to work up the courage to search Sonny's room. He was out, he was usually out whenever I was home, and Isabel had taken the children to see their grandparents. Suddenly I was standing still in front of the living room window, watching Seventh Avenue. The idea of searching Sonny's room made me still. I scarcely dared to admit to myself what I'd be searching for. I didn't know what I'd do if I found it. Or if I didn't.

On the sidewalk across from me, near the entrance to a barbecue joint, some people were holding an old-fashioned revival meeting. The barbecue cook, wearing a dirty white apron, his conked hair reddish and metallic in the pale sun, and a cigarette between his lips, stood in the doorway, watching them. Kids and older people paused in their errands and stood there, along with some older men and a couple of very tough-looking women who watched everything that happened on the avenue, as though they owned it, or were maybe owned by it. Well, they were watching this, too. The revival was being carried on by three sisters in black, and a brother. All they had were their voices and their Bibles and a tambourine. The brother was testifying and while he testified two of the sisters stood together, seeming to say, amen, and the third sister walked around with the tambourine outstretched and a couple of people dropped coins into it. Then the brother's testimony ended and the sister who had been taking up the collection dumped the coins into her palm and transferred them to the pocket of her long black robe. Then she raised both hands, striking the tambourine against the air, and then against one hand, and she started to sing. And the two other sisters and the brother joined in.

It was strange, suddenly, to watch, though I had been seeing these street meetings all my life. So of course, had everybody else down there. Yet, they paused and watched and listened and I stood still at the window. *"Tis the old ship of Zion,"* they sang, and the sister with the tambourine kept a steady, jangling beat, *"it has rescued many a thousand!"* Not a soul under the sound of their voices was hearing this song for the first time, not one of them had been rescued. Nor had they seen much in the way of rescue work being done around them. Neither did they especially believe in the holiness of the three sisters and the brother, they knew too much about them, knew where they lived, and how. The woman with the tambourine, whose voice dominated the air, whose face was bright with joy, was divided by very little from the woman who stood watching her, a cigarette between her heavy, chapped lips, her hair a cuckoo's nest, her face scarred and swollen from many beatings, and her black eyes glittering like coal. Perhaps they both knew this, which was why, when, as rarely, they addressed each other they addressed each other as Sister. As the singing filled the air the watching, listening faces underwent a change, the eyes focusing on something within; the music seemed to soothe a poison out of them; and time seemed, nearly, to fall away from the sullen, belligerent, battered faces, as though they were fleeing back to their first condition, while dreaming of their last. The barbecue cook half shook his head and smiled, and dropped his cigarette and disappeared into his joint. A man fumbled in his pockets for change and stood holding it in his hand impatiently, as though he had just remembered a pressing appointment further up the avenue. He looked furious. Then I saw Sonny, standing on the edge of the crowd. He was carrying a wide, flat notebook with a green cover, and it made him look, from where I was standing, almost like a schoolboy. The coppery sun brought out the copper in his skin, he was very faintly smiling, standing very still. Then the singing stopped, the tambourine turned into a collection plate again. The furious man dropped in his coins and vanished, so did a couple of the women, and Sonny dropped some change in the plate, looking directly at the woman with a little smile. He started across the avenue, toward the house. He has a slow, loping walk, something like the way Harlem hipsters walk, only he's imposed on this his own half-beat. I had never really noticed it before.

I stayed at the window, both relieved and apprehensive. As Sonny disappeared from my sight, they began singing again. And they were still singing when his key turned in the lock.

"Hey," he said.

"Hey, yourself. You want some beer?"

"No. Well, maybe." But he came up to the window and stood beside me, looking out. "What a warm voice," he said.

They were singing *If I could only hear my mother pray again!*

"Yes," I said, "and she can sure beat that tambourine."

"But what a terrible song," he said, and laughed. He dropped his notebook on the sofa and disappeared into the kitchen. "Where's Isabel and the kids?"

"I think they went to see their grandparents. You hungry?"

"No." He came back into the living room with his can of beer. "You want to come some place with me tonight?"

I sensed, I don't know how, that I couldn't possibly say no. "Sure. Where?"

He sat down on the sofa and picked up his notebook and started leafing through it. "I'm going to sit in with some fellows in a joint in the Village."

"You mean, you're going to play, tonight?"

"That's right." He took a swallow of his beer and moved back to the window. He gave me a sidelong look. "If you can stand it."

"I'll try," I said.

He smiled to himself and we both watched as the meeting across the way broke up. The three sisters and the brother, heads bowed, were singing *God be with you till we meet again*. The faces around them were very quiet. Then the song ended. The small crowd dispersed. We watched the three women and the lone man walk slowly up the avenue.

"When she was singing before," said Sonny, abruptly, "her voice reminded me for a minute of what heroin feels like sometimes—when it's in your veins. It makes you feel sort of warm and cool at the same time. And distant. And—and sure." He sipped his beer, very deliberately not looking at me. I watched his face. "It makes you feel—in control. Sometimes you've got to have that feeling."

"Do you?" I sat down slowly in the easy chair.

"Sometimes." He went to the sofa and picked up his notebook again. "Some people do."

"In order," I asked, "to play?" And my voice was very ugly, full of contempt and anger.

"Well"—he looked at me with great, troubled eyes, as though, in fact, he hoped his eyes would tell me things he could never otherwise say—"they *think* so. And *if* they think so—!"

"And what do *you* think?" I asked.

He sat on the sofa and put his can of beer on the floor. "I don't know," he said, and I couldn't be sure if he were answering my question or pursuing his thoughts. His face didn't tell me. "It's not so much to *play*. It's to *stand* it, to be able to make it at all. On any level." He frowned and smiled: "In order to keep from shaking to pieces."

"But these friends of yours," I said, "they seem to shake themselves to pieces pretty goddamn fast."

"Maybe." He played with the notebook. And something told me that I should curb my tongue, that Sonny was doing his best to talk, that I should listen. "But of course you only know the ones that've gone to pieces. Some don't—or at least they haven't *yet* and that's just about all *any* of us can say." He paused. "And then there are some who just live, really, in hell, and they know it and they see what's happening and they go right on. I don't know." He sighed, dropped the notebook, folded his arms. "Some guys, you can tell from the way they play, they on something *all* the time. And you can see that, well, it makes something real for them. But of course," he picked up his beer from the floor and sipped it and put the can down again, "they *want* to, too, you've got to see that. Even some of them that say they don't—*some*, not all."

"And what about you?" I asked—I couldn't help it. "What about you? Do *you* want to?"

He stood up and walked to the window and remained silent for a long time. Then he sighed. "Me," he said. Then: "While I was downstairs before, on my way here, listening to that woman sing, it struck me all of a sudden how much suffering she must have had to go through—to sing like that. It's *repulsive* to think you have to suffer that much."

I said: "But there's no way not to suffer—is there, Sonny?"

"I believe not," he said and smiled, "but that's never stopped anyone from trying." He looked at me. "Has it?" I realized, with this mocking look, that there stood between us, forever, beyond the power of time or forgiveness, the fact that I had held silence—so long!—when he had needed human speech to help him. He turned back to the window. "No, there's no way not to suffer. But you try all kinds of ways to keep from drowning in it, to keep on top of it, and to make it seem—well, like *you*. Like you did something, all right, and now you're suffering for it. You know?" I said nothing. "Well you know," he said, impatiently, "why *do* people suffer? Maybe it's better to do something to give it a reason, *any* reason."

"But we just agreed," I said, "that there's no way not to suffer. Isn't it better, then, just to—take it?"

"But nobody just takes it," Sonny cried, "that's what I'm telling you! *Everybody* tries not to. You're just hung up on the *way* some people try—it's not *your* way!"

The hair on my face began to itch, my face felt wet. "That's not true," I said, "that's not true. I don't give a damn what other people do, I don't even care how they suffer. I just care how *you* suffer." And he looked at me. "Please believe me," I said, "I don't want to see you—die—trying not to suffer."

"I won't," he said, flatly, "die trying not to suffer. At least, not any faster than anybody else."

"But there's no need," I said, trying to laugh, "is there? in killing yourself."

I wanted to say more, but I couldn't. I wanted to talk about will power and how life could be—well, beautiful. I wanted to say that it was all within; but was it? or, rather, wasn't that exactly the trouble? And I wanted to promise that I would never fail him again. But it would all have sounded—empty words and lies.

So I made the promise to myself and prayed that I would keep it.

"It's terrible sometimes, inside," he said, "that's what's the trouble. You walk these streets, black and funky and cold, and there's not really a living ass to talk to, and there's nothing shaking, and there's no way of getting it out—that storm inside. You can't talk it and you can't make love with it, and when you finally try to get with it and play it, you realize *nobody's* listening. So *you've* got to listen. You got to find a way to listen."

And then he walked away from the window and sat on the sofa again, as though all the wind had suddenly been knocked out of him. "Sometimes you'll do *anything* to play, even cut your mother's throat." He laughed and looked at me. "Or your brother's." Then he sobered. "Or your own." Then: "Don't worry. I'm all right now and I think I'll *be* all right. But I can't forget—where I've been. I don't mean just the physical place I've been, I mean where I've *been*. And *what* I've been."

"What have you been, Sonny?" I asked.

He smiled—but sat sideways on the sofa, his elbow resting on the back, his fingers playing with his mouth and chin, not looking at me. "I've been something I didn't recognize, didn't know I could be. Didn't know anybody could be." He stopped, looking inward, looking helplessly young, looking old. "I'm not talking about it now because I feel *guilty* or anything like that—maybe it would be better if I did, I don't know. Anyway, I can't really talk about it. Not to you, not to anybody," and now he turned and faced me. "Sometimes, you know, and it was actually when I was most *out* of the world, I felt that I was in it, that I was *with* it, really, and I could play or I didn't really have to *play*, it just came out of me, it was there. And I don't know how I played, thinking about it now, but I know I did awful things, those times, sometimes, to people. Or it wasn't that I *did* anything to them—it was that they weren't real." He picked up the beer can; it was empty; he rolled it between his palms: "And other times—well, I needed a fix, I needed to find a place to lean, I needed to clear a space to *listen*—and I couldn't find it, and I—went crazy, I did terrible things to *me*, I was terrible *for* me." He began pressing the beer can between his hands, I watched the metal begin to give. It glittered, as he played with it, like a knife, and I was afraid he would cut himself, but I said nothing. "Oh well. I can never tell you. I was all by myself at the bottom of something, stinking and sweating and crying and shaking, and I smelled it, you know? *my* stink, and I thought I'd die if I couldn't get away from it and yet, all the same, I knew that everything I was doing was just locking me in with it. And I didn't know," he paused, still flattening the beer can, "I didn't know, I still *don't* know, something kept telling me that maybe it was good to smell your own stink, but I didn't think that *that* was what I'd been trying to do—and—who can stand it?" and he abruptly dropped the ruined beer can, looking at me with a small, still smile, and then rose, walking to the window as though it were the lodestone rock. I watched his face, he watched the avenue. "I couldn't tell you when Mama died—but the reason I wanted to leave Harlem so bad was to get away from drugs. And then, when I ran away, that's what I was running from—really. When I came back, nothing had changed, *I* hadn't changed, I was just—older." And he stopped, drumming with his fingers on the windowpane. The sun had vanished, soon darkness would fall. I watched his face. "It can come again," he said, almost as though speaking to himself. Then he turned to me. "It can come again," he repeated. "I just want you to know that."

"All right," I said, at last. "So it can come again. All right."

He smiled, but the smile was sorrowful. "I had to try to tell you," he said.

"Yes," I said. "I understand that."

"You're my brother," he said, looking straight at me, and not smiling at all.

"Yes," I repeated, "yes. I understand that."

He turned back to the window, looking out. "All that hatred down there," he said, "all that hatred and misery and love. It's a wonder it doesn't blow the avenue apart."

We went to the only nightclub on a short, dark street, downtown. We squeezed through the narrow, chattering, jam-packed bar to the entrance of the big room, where the bandstand was. And we stood there for a moment, for the lights were very dim in this room and we couldn't see. Then, "Hello, boy," said a voice and an enormous black man, much older than Sonny or myself, erupted out of all that atmospheric lighting and put an arm around Sonny's shoulder. "I been sitting right here," he said, "waiting for you."

He had a big voice, too, and heads in the darkness turned toward us.

Sonny grinned and pulled a little away, and said, "Creole, this is my brother. I told you about him."

Creole shook my hand. "I'm glad to meet you, son," he said, and it was clear that he was glad to meet me *there*, for Sonny's sake. And he smiled, "You got a real musician in *your* family," and he took his arm from Sonny's shoulder and slapped him, lightly, affectionately, with the back of his hand.

"Well. Now I've heard it all," said a voice behind us. This was another musician, and a friend of Sonny's, a coal-black, cheerful-looking man, built close to the ground. He immediately began confiding to me, at the top of his lungs, the most terrible things about Sonny, his teeth gleaming like a lighthouse and his laugh coming up out of him like the beginning of an earthquake. And it turned out that everyone at the bar knew Sonny, or almost everyone; some were musicians, working there, or nearby, or not working, some were simply hangers-on, and some were there to hear Sonny play. I was introduced to all of them and they were all very polite to me. Yet, it was clear that, for them, I was only Sonny's brother. Here, I was in Sonny's world. Or, rather: his kingdom. Here, it was not even a question that his veins bore royal blood.

They were going to play soon and Creole installed me, by myself, at a table in a dark corner. Then I watched them, Creole, and the little black man, and Sonny, and the others, while they horsed around, standing just below the bandstand. The light from the bandstand spilled just a little short of them and, watching them laughing and gesturing and moving about, I had the feeling that they, nevertheless, were being most careful not to step into that circle of light too suddenly: that if they moved into the light too suddenly, without thinking, they would perish in flame. Then, while I watched, one of them, the small, black man, moved into the light and crossed the bandstand and started fooling around with his drums. Then—being funny and being, also, extremely ceremonious—Creole took Sonny by the arm and led him to the piano. A woman's voice called Sonny's name and a few hands started clapping. And Sonny, also being funny and being ceremonious, and so touched, I think, that he could have cried, but neither hiding it nor showing it, riding it like a man, grinned, and put both hands to his heart and bowed from the waist.

Creole then went to the bass fiddle and a lean, very bright-skinned brown man jumped up on the bandstand and picked up his horn. So there they were, and the atmosphere on the bandstand and in the room began to change and tighten. Someone stepped up to the microphone and announced them. Then there were all kinds of murmurs. Some people at the bar shushed others. The waitress ran around, frantically getting in the last orders, guys and chicks got closer to each other, and the lights on the bandstand, on the quartet, turned to a kind of indigo. Then they all looked different there. Creole looked about him for the last time, as though he were making certain that all his chickens were in the coop, and then he—jumped and struck the fiddle. And there they were.

All I know about music is that not many people ever really hear it. And even then, on the rare occasions when something opens within, and the music enters, what we mainly hear, or hear corroborated, are personal, private, vanishing evocations. But the man who creates the music is hearing something else, is dealing with the roar rising from the void and imposing order on it as it hits the air. What is evoked in him, then, is of another order, more terrible because it has no words, and triumphant, too, for that same reason. And his triumph, when he triumphs, is ours. I just watched Sonny's face. His face was troubled, he was working hard, but he wasn't with it. And I had the feeling that, in a way, everyone on the bandstand was waiting for him, both waiting for him and pushing him along. But as I began to watch Creole, I realized that it was Creole who held them all back. He had them on a short rein. Up there, keeping the beat with his whole body, wailing on the fiddle, with his eyes half closed, he was listening to everything, but he was listening to Sonny. He was having a dialogue with Sonny. He wanted Sonny to leave the shoreline and strike out for the deep water. He was Sonny's witness that deep water and drowning were not the same thing—he had been there, and he knew. And he wanted Sonny to know. He was waiting for Sonny to do the things on the keys which would let Creole know that Sonny was in the water.

And, while Creole listened, Sonny moved, deep within, exactly like someone in torment. I had never before thought of how awful the relationship must be between the musician and his instrument. He has to fill it, this instrument, with the breath of life, his own. He has to make it do what he wants it to do. And a piano is just a piano. It's made out of so much wood and wires and little hammers and big ones, and ivory. While there's only so much you can do with it, the only way to find this out is to try; to try and make it do everything.

And Sonny hadn't been near a piano for over a year. And he wasn't on much better terms with his life, not the life that stretched before him now. He and the piano stammered, started one way, got scared, stopped;

started another way, panicked, marked time, started again; then seemed to have found a direction, panicked again, got stuck. And the face I saw on Sonny I'd never seen before. Everything had been burned out of it, and, at the same time, things usually hidden were being burned in, by the fire and fury of the battle which was occurring in him up there.

Yet, watching Creole's face as they neared the end of the first set, I had the feeling that something had happened, something I hadn't heard. Then they finished, there was scattered applause, and then, without an instant's warning, Creole started into something else, it was almost sardonic, it was *Am I Blue*. And, as though he commanded, Sonny began to play. Something began to happen. And Creole let out the reins. The dry, low, black man said something awful on the drums, Creole answered, and the drums talked back. Then the horn insisted, sweet and high, slightly detached perhaps, and Creole listened, commenting now and then, dry, and driving, beautiful and calm and old. Then they all came together again, and Sonny was part of the family again. I could tell this from his face. He seemed to have found, right there beneath his fingers, a damn brand-new piano. It seemed that he couldn't get over it. Then, for awhile, just being happy with Sonny, they seemed to be agreeing with him that brand-new pianos certainly were a gas.

Then Creole stepped forward to remind them that what they were playing was the blues. He hit something in all of them, he hit something in me, myself, and the music tightened and deepened, apprehension began to beat the air. Creole began to tell us what the blues were all about. They were not about anything very new. He and his boys up there were keeping it new, at the risk of ruin, destruction, madness, and death, in order to find new ways to make us listen. For, while the tale of how we suffer, and how we are delighted, and how we may triumph is never new, it always must be heard. There isn't any other tale to tell, it's the only light we've got in all this darkness.

And this tale, according to that face, that body, those strong hands on those strings, has another aspect in every country, and a new depth in every generation. Listen, Creole seemed to be saying, listen. Now these are Sonny's blues. He made the little black man on the drums know it, and the bright, brown man on the horn. Creole wasn't trying any longer to get Sonny in the water. He was wishing him Godspeed. Then he stepped back, very slowly, filling the air with the immense suggestion that Sonny speak for himself.

Then they all gathered around Sonny and Sonny played. Every now and again one of them seemed to say, amen. Sonny's fingers filled the air with life, his life. But that life contained so many others. And Sonny went all the way back, he really began with the spare, flat statement of the opening phrase of the song. Then he began to make it his. It was very beautiful because it wasn't hurried and it was no longer a lament. I seemed to hear with what burning he had made it his, with what burning we had yet to make it ours, how we could cease lamenting. Freedom lurked around us and I understood, at last, that he could help us to be free if we would listen, that he would never be free until we did. Yet, there was no battle in his face now. I heard what he had gone through, and would continue to go through until he came to rest in earth. He had made it his: that long line, of which we knew only Mama and Daddy. And he was giving it back, as everything must be given back, so that, passing through death, it can live forever. I saw my mother's face again, and felt, for the first time, how the stories of the road she had walked on must have bruised her feet. I saw the moonlit road where my father's brother died. And it brought something else back to me, and carried me past it. I saw my little girl again and felt Isabel's tears again, and I felt my own tears begin to rise. And I was yet aware that this was only a moment, that the world waited outside, as hungry as a tiger, and that trouble stretched above us, longer than the sky.

Then it was over. Creole and Sonny let out their breath, both soaking wet, and grinning. There was a lot of applause and some of it was real. In the dark, the girl came by and I asked her to take drinks to the bandstand. There was a long pause, while they talked up there in the indigo light and after awhile I saw the girl put a Scotch and milk on top of the piano for Sonny. He didn't seem to notice it, but just before they started playing again, he sipped from it and looked toward me, and nodded. Then he put it back on top of the piano. For me, then, as they began to play again, it glowed and shook above my brother's head like the very cup of trembling.

[1957]

FLANNERY O'CONNOR [1925–1964]

A Good Man Is Hard to Find

The dragon is by the side of the road, watching those who pass.
Beware lest he devour you. We go to the Father of Souls, but it is
necessary to pass by the dragon. —ST. CYRIL OF JERUSALEM

The grandmother didn't want to go to Florida. She wanted to visit some of her connections in east Tennessee and she was seizing at every chance to change Bailey's mind. Bailey was the son she lived with, her only boy. He was sitting on the edge of his chair at the table, bent over the orange sports section of the *Journal.* "Now look here, Bailey," she said, "see here, read this," and she stood with one hand on her thin hip and the other rattling the newspaper at his bald head. "Here this fellow that calls himself The Misfit is aloose from the Federal Pen and headed toward Florida and you read here what it says he did to these people. Just you read it. I wouldn't take my children in any direction with a criminal like that aloose in it. I couldn't answer to my conscience if I did."

Bailey didn't look up from his reading so she wheeled around then and faced the children's mother, a young woman in slacks, whose face was as broad and innocent as a cabbage and was tied around with a green headkerchief that had two points on the top like rabbit's ears. She was sitting on the sofa, feeding the baby his apricots out of a jar. "The children have been to Florida before," the old lady said. "You all ought to take them somewhere else for a change so they would see different parts of the world and be broad. They never have been to east Tennessee."

The children's mother didn't seem to hear her but the eight-year-old boy, John Wesley, a stocky child with glasses, said, "If you don't want to go to Florida, why dontcha stay at home?" He and the little girl, June Star, were reading the funny papers on the floor.

"She wouldn't stay at home to be queen for a day," June Star said without raising her yellow head.

"Yes and what would you do if this fellow, The Misfit, caught you?" the grandmother asked.

"I'd smack his face," John Wesley said.

"She wouldn't stay at home for a million bucks," June Star said. "Afraid she'd miss something. She has to go everywhere we go."

"All right, Miss," the grandmother said. "Just remember that the next time you want me to curl your hair."

June Star said her hair was naturally curly.

The next morning the grandmother was the first one in the car, ready to go. She had her big black valise that looked like the head of a hippopotamus in one corner, and underneath it she was hiding a basket with Pitty Sing, the cat, in it. She didn't intend for the cat to be left alone in the house for three days because he would miss her too much and she was afraid he might brush against one of the gas burners and accidentally asphyxiate himself. Her son, Bailey, didn't like to arrive at a motel with a cat.

She sat in the middle of the back seat with John Wesley and June Star on either side of her. Bailey and the children's mother and the baby sat in front and they left Atlanta at eight forty-five with the mileage on the car at 55890. The grandmother wrote this down because she thought it would be interesting to say how many miles they had been when they got back. It took them twenty minutes to reach the outskirts of the city.

The old lady settled herself comfortably, removing her white cotton gloves and putting them up with her purse on the shelf in front of the back window. The children's mother still had on slacks and still had her head tied up in a green kerchief, but the grandmother had on a navy blue straw sailor hat with a bunch of white violets on the brim and a navy blue dress with a small white dot in the print. Her collars and cuffs were white organdy trimmed with lace and at her neckline she had pinned a purple spray of cloth violets containing a sachet. In case of an accident, anyone seeing her dead on the highway would know at once that she was a lady.

She said she thought it was going to be a good day for driving, neither too hot nor too cold, and she cautioned Bailey that the speed limit was fifty-five miles an hour and that the patrolmen hid themselves behind billboards and small clumps of trees and sped out after you before you had a chance to slow down. She pointed out interesting details of the scenery: Stone Mountain; the blue granite that in some places came up to both sides of the highway; the brilliant red clay banks slightly streaked with purple; and the various crops that made rows of green lace-work on the ground. The trees were full of silver-white sunlight and the meanest of them sparkled. The children were reading comic magazines and their mother had gone back to sleep.

"Let's go through Georgia fast so we won't have to look at it much," John Wesley said.

"If I were a little boy," said the grandmother, "I wouldn't talk about my native state that way. Tennessee has the mountains and Georgia has the hills."

"Tennessee is just a hillbilly dumping ground," John Wesley said, "and Georgia is a lousy state too."

"You said it," June Star said.

"In my time," said the grandmother, folding her thin veined fingers, "children were more respectful of their native states and their parents and everything else. People did right then. Oh look at the cute little pickaninny!" she said and pointed to a Negro child standing in the door of a shack. "Wouldn't that make a picture, now?" she asked and they all turned and looked at the little Negro out of the back window. He waved.

"He didn't have any britches on," June Star said.

"He probably didn't have any," the grandmother explained. "Little niggers in the country don't have things like we do. If I could paint, I'd paint that picture," she said.

The children exchanged comic books.

The grandmother offered to hold the baby and the children's mother passed him over the front seat to her. She set him on her knee and bounced him and told him about the things they were passing. She rolled her eyes and screwed up her mouth and stuck her leathery thin face into his smooth bland one. Occasionally he gave her a faraway smile. They passed a large cotton field with five or six graves fenced in the middle of it, like a small island. "Look at the graveyard!" the grandmother said, pointing it out. "That was the old family burying ground. That belonged to the plantation."

"Where's the plantation?" John Wesley asked.

"Gone with the Wind," said the grandmother. "Ha. Ha."

When the children finished all the comic books they had brought, they opened the lunch and ate it. The grandmother ate a peanut butter sandwich and an olive and would not let the children throw the box and the paper napkins out the window. When there was nothing else to do they played a game by choosing a cloud and making the other two guess what shape it suggested. John Wesley took one the shape of a cow and June Star guessed a cow and John Wesley said, no, an automobile, and June Star said he didn't play fair, and they began to slap each other over the grandmother.

The grandmother said she would tell them a story if they would keep quiet. When she told a story, she rolled her eyes and waved her head and was very dramatic. She said once when she was a maiden lady she had been courted by a Mr. Edgar Atkins Teagarden from Jasper, Georgia. She said he was a very good-looking man and a gentleman and that he brought her a watermelon every Saturday afternoon with his initials cut in it, E. A. T. Well, one Saturday, she said, Mr. Teagarden brought the watermelon and there was nobody at home and he left it on the front porch and returned in his buggy to Jasper, but she never got the watermelon, she said, because a nigger boy ate it when he saw the initials,

E. A. T.! This story tickled John Wesley's funny bone and he giggled and giggled but June Star didn't think it was any good. She said she wouldn't marry a man that just brought her a watermelon on Saturday. The grandmother said she would have done well to marry Mr. Teagarden because he was a gentleman and had bought Coca-Cola stock when it first came out and that he had died only a few years ago, a very wealthy man.

They stopped at The Tower for barbecued sandwiches. The Tower was a part stucco and part wood filling station and dance hall set in a clearing outside of Timothy. A fat man named Red Sammy Butts ran it and there were signs stuck here and there on the building and for miles up and down the highway saying, TRY RED SAMMY'S FAMOUS BARBECUE. NONE LIKE FAMOUS RED SAMMY'S! RED SAM! THE FAT BOY WITH THE HAPPY LAUGH. A VETERAN! RED SAMMY'S YOUR MAN!

Red Sammy was lying on the bare ground outside The Tower with his head under a truck while a gray monkey about a foot high, chained to a small chinaberry tree, chattered nearby. The monkey sprang back into the tree and got on the highest limb as soon as he saw the children jump out of the car and run toward him.

Inside, The Tower was a long dark room with a counter at one end and tables at the other and dancing space in the middle. They all sat down at a board table next to the nickelodeon and Red Sam's wife, a tall burnt-brown woman with hair and eyes lighter than her skin, came and took their order. The children's mother put a dime in the machine and played "The Tennessee Waltz," and the grandmother said that tune always made her want to dance. She asked Bailey if he would like to dance but he only glared at her. He didn't have a naturally sunny disposition like she did and trips made him nervous. The grandmother's brown eyes were very bright. She swayed her head from side to side and pretended she was dancing in her chair. June Star said play something she could tap to so the children's mother put in another dime and played a fast number and June Star stepped out onto the dance floor and did her tap routine.

"Ain't she cute?" Red Sam's wife said, leaning over the counter. "Would you like to come be my little girl?"

"No I certainly wouldn't," June Star said. "I wouldn't live in a broken-down place like this for a million bucks!" and she ran back to the table.

"Ain't she cute?" the woman repeated, stretching her mouth politely.

"Aren't you ashamed?" hissed the grandmother.

Red Sam came in and told his wife to quit lounging on the counter and hurry up with these people's order. His khaki trousers reached just to his hip bones and his stomach hung over them like a sack of meal swaying under his shirt. He came over and sat down at a table nearby and let out a combination sigh and yodel. "You can't win," he said. "You can't win," and he wiped his sweating red face off with a gray handkerchief. "These days you don't know who to trust," he said. "Ain't that the truth?"

"People are certainly not nice like they used to be," said the grandmother.

"Two fellers come in here last week," Red Sammy said, "driving a Chrysler. It was a old beat-up car but it was a good one and these boys looked all right to me. Said they worked at the mill and you know I let them fellers charge the gas they bought? Now why did I do that?"

"Because you're a good man!" the grandmother said at once.

"Yes'm, I suppose so," Red Sam said as if he were struck with this answer.

His wife brought the orders, carrying the five plates all at once without a tray, two in each hand and one balanced on her arm. "It isn't a soul in this green world of God's that you can trust," she said. "And I don't count nobody out of that, not nobody," she repeated, looking at Red Sammy.

"Did you read about that criminal, The Misfit, that's escaped?" asked the grandmother.

"I wouldn't be a bit surprised if he didn't attack this place right here," said the woman. "If he hears about it being here, I wouldn't be none surprised to see him. If he hears it's two cent in the cash register, I wouldn't be a tall surprised if he . . ."

"That'll do," Red Sam said. "Go bring these people their Co'-Colas," and the woman went off to get the rest of the order.

"A good man is hard to find," Red Sammy said. "Everything is getting terrible. I remember the day you could go off and leave your screen door unlatched. Not no more."

He and the grandmother discussed better times. The old lady said that in her opinion Europe was entirely to blame for the way things were now. She said the way Europe acted you would think we were made of money and Red Sam said it was no use talking about it, she was exactly right. The children ran outside into the white sunlight and looked at the monkey in the lacy chinaberry tree. He was busy catching fleas on himself and biting each one carefully between his teeth as if it were a delicacy.

They drove off again into the hot afternoon. The grandmother took cat naps and woke up every few minutes with her own snoring. Outside of Toombsboro she woke up and recalled an old plantation that she had visited in this neighborhood once when she was a young lady. She said the house had six white columns across the front and that there was an avenue of oaks leading up to it and two little wooden trellis arbors on either side in front where you sat down with your suitor after a stroll in the garden. She recalled exactly which road to turn off to get to it. She knew that Bailey would not be willing to lose any time looking at an old house, but the more she talked about it, the more she wanted to see it once again and find out if the little twin arbors were still standing. "There was a secret panel in this house," she said craftily, not telling the truth but wishing that she were, "and the story went that all the family silver was hidden in it when Sherman came through but it was never found . . ."

"Hey!" John Wesley said. "Let's go see it! We'll find it! We'll poke all the woodwork and find it! Who lives there? Where do you turn off at? Hey Pop, can't we turn off there?"

"We never have seen a house with a secret panel!" June Star shrieked. "Let's go to the house with the secret panel! Hey Pop, can't we go see the house with the secret panel!"

"It's not far from here, I know." the grandmother said. "It wouldn't take over twenty minutes."

Bailey was looking straight ahead. His jaw was as rigid as a horseshoe. "No," he said.

The children began to yell and scream that they wanted to see the house with the secret panel. John Wesley kicked the back of the front seat and June Star hung over her mother's shoulder and whined desperately into her ear that they never had any fun even on their vacation, that they could never do what THEY wanted to do. The baby began to scream and John Wesley kicked the back of the seat so hard that his father could feel the blows in his kidney.

"All right!" he shouted and drew the car to a stop at the side of the road. "Will you all shut up? Will you all just shut up for one second? If you don't shut up, we won't go anywhere."

"It would be very educational for them," the grandmother murmured.

"All right," Bailey said, "but get this: this is the only time we're going to stop for anything like this. This is the one and only time."

"The dirt road that you have to turn down is about a mile back," the grandmother directed. "I marked it when we passed."

"A dirt road," Bailey groaned.

After they had turned around and were headed toward the dirt road, the grandmother recalled other points about the house, the beautiful glass over the front doorway and the candle-lamp in the hall. John Wesley said that the secret panel was probably in the fireplace.

"You can't go inside this house," Bailey said. "You don't know who lives there."

"While you all talk to the people in front, I'll run around behind and get in a window," John Wesley suggested.

"We'll all stay in the car," his mother said.

They turned onto the dirt road and the car raced roughly along in a swirl of pink dust. The grandmother recalled the times when there were no paved roads and thirty miles was a day's journey. The dirt road was hilly and there were sudden washes in it and sharp curves on dangerous embankments. All at once they would be on a hill, looking down over the blue tops of trees for miles around, then the next minute, they would be in a red depression with the dust-coated trees looking down on them.

"This place had better turn up in a minute," Bailey said, "or I'm going to turn around."

The road looked as if no one had traveled on it in months.

"It's not much farther," the grandmother said and just as she said it, a horrible thought came to her. The thought was so embarrassing that she turned red in the face and her eyes dilated and her feet jumped up, upsetting her valise in the corner. The instant the valise moved, the newspaper top she had over the basket under it rose with a snarl and Pitty Sing, the cat, sprang onto Bailey's shoulder.

The children were thrown to the floor and their mother, clutching the baby, was thrown out the door onto the ground; the old lady was thrown into the front seat. The car turned over once and landed right-side-up in a gulch off the side of the road. Bailey remained in the driver's seat with the cat—gray-striped with a broad white face and an orange nose—clinging to his neck like a caterpillar.

As soon as the children saw they could move their arms and legs, they scrambled out of the car, shouting, "We've had an ACCIDENT!" The grandmother was curled up under the dashboard, hoping she was injured so that Bailey's wrath would not come down on her all at once. The horrible thought she had had before the accident was that the house she had remembered so vividly was not in Georgia but in Tennessee.

Bailey removed the cat from his neck with both hands and flung it out the window against the side of a pine tree. Then he got out of the car and started looking for the children's mother. She was sitting against the side of the red gutted ditch, holding the screaming baby, but she only had a cut down her face and a broken shoulder. "We've had an ACCIDENT!" the children screamed in a frenzy of delight.

"But nobody's killed," June Star said with disappointment as the grandmother limped out of the car, her hat still pinned to her head but the broken front brim standing up at a jaunty angle and the violet spray hanging off the side. They all sat down in the ditch, except the children, to recover from the shock. They were all shaking.

"Maybe a car will come along," said the children's mother hoarsely.

"I believe I have injured an organ," said the grandmother, pressing her side, but no one answered her. Bailey's teeth were clattering. He had on a yellow sport shirt with bright blue parrots designed in it and his face was as yellow as the shirt. The grandmother decided that she would not mention that the house was in Tennessee.

The road was about ten feet above and they could only see the tops of the trees on the other side of it. Behind the ditch they were sitting in there were more woods, tall and dark and deep. In a few minutes they saw a car some distance away on top of a hill, coming slowly as if the occupants were watching them. The grandmother stood up and waved both arms dramatically to attract their attention. The car continued to come on slowly, disappeared around a bend and appeared again, moving even slower, on top of the hill they had gone over. It was a big black battered hearse-like automobile. There were three men in it.

It came to a stop just over them and for some minutes, the driver looked down with a steady expressionless gaze to where they were sitting, and didn't speak. Then he turned his head and muttered something to the other two and they got out. One was a fat boy in black trousers and a red sweat shirt with a silver stallion embossed on the front of it. He moved around on the right side of them and stood staring, his mouth partly open in a kind of loose grin. The other had on khaki pants and a blue striped coat and a gray hat pulled very low, hiding most of his face. He came around slowly on the left side. Neither spoke.

The driver got out of the car and stood by the side of it, looking down at them. He was an older man than the other two. His hair was just beginning to gray and he wore silver-rimmed spectacles that gave him a scholarly look. He had a long creased face and didn't have on any shirt or undershirt. He had on blue jeans that were too tight for him and was holding a black hat and a gun. The two boys also had guns.

"We've had an ACCIDENT!" the children screamed.

The grandmother had the peculiar feeling that the bespectacled man was someone she knew. His face was as familiar to her as if she had known him all her life but she could not recall who he was. He moved away from the car and began to come down the embankment, placing his feet carefully so that he wouldn't slip. He had on tan and white shoes and no socks, and his ankles were red and thin. "Good afternoon," he said. "I see you all had you a little spill."

"We turned over twice!" said the grandmother.

"Oncet," he corrected. "We seen it happen. Try their car and see will it run, Hiram," he said quietly to the boy with the gray hat.

"What you got that gun for?" John Wesley asked. "Whatcha gonna do with that gun?"

"Lady," the man said to the children's mother, "would you mind calling them children to sit down by you? Children make me nervous. I want all you all to sit down right together there where you're at."

"What are you telling US what to do for?" June Star asked.

Behind them the line of woods gaped like a dark open mouth. "Come here," said the mother.

"Look here now," Bailey began suddenly, "we're in a predicament! We're in . . ."

The grandmother shrieked. She scrambled to her feet and stood staring. "You're The Misfit!" she said. "I recognized you at once!"

"Yes'm," the man said, smiling slightly as if he were pleased in spite of himself to be known, "but it would have been better for all of you, lady, if you hadn't of reckernized me."

Bailey turned his head sharply and said something to his mother that shocked even the children. The old lady began to cry and The Misfit reddened.

"Lady," he said, "don't you get upset. Sometimes a man says things he don't mean. I don't reckon he meant to talk to you thataway."

"You wouldn't shoot a lady, would you?" the grandmother said and removed a clean handkerchief from her cuff and began to slap at her eyes with it.

The Misfit pointed the toe of his shoe into the ground and made a little hole and then covered it up again. "I would hate to have to," he said.

"Listen," the grandmother almost screamed, "I know you're a good man. You don't look a bit like you have common blood. I know you must come from nice people!"

"Yes mam," he said, "finest people in the world." When he smiled he showed a row of strong white teeth. "God never made a finer woman than my mother and my daddy's heart was pure gold," he said. The boy with the red sweat shirt had come around behind them and was standing with his gun at his hip. The Misfit squatted down on the ground. "Watch them children, Bobby Lee," he said. "You know they make me nervous." He looked at the six of them huddled together in front of him and he seemed to be embarrassed as if he couldn't think of anything to say. "Ain't a cloud in the sky," he remarked, looking up at it. "Don't see no sun but don't see no cloud neither."

"Yes, it's a beautiful day," said the grandmother. "Listen," she said, "you shouldn't call yourself The Misfit because I know you're a good man at heart. I can just look at you and tell."

"Hush!" Bailey yelled. "Hush! Everybody shut up and let me handle this!" He was squatting in the position of a runner about to sprint forward but he didn't move.

"I pre-chate that, lady," The Misfit said and drew a little circle in the ground with the butt of his gun.

"It'll take a half a hour to fix this here car," Hiram called, looking over the raised hood of it.

"Well, first you and Bobby Lee get him and that little boy to step over yonder with you," The Misfit said, pointing to Bailey and John Wesley. "The boys want to ast you something," he said to Bailey. "Would you mind stepping back in them woods there with them?"

"Listen," Bailey began, "we're in a terrible predicament! Nobody realizes what this is," and his voice cracked. His eyes were as blue and intense as the parrots in his shirt and he remained perfectly still.

The grandmother reached up to adjust her hat brim as if she were going to the woods with him but it came off in her hand. She stood staring at it and after a second she let it fall on the ground. Hiram pulled Bailey up by the arm as if he were assisting an old man. John Wesley caught hold of his father's hand and Bobby Lee followed. They went off toward the woods and just as they reached the dark edge, Bailey turned and supporting himself against a gray naked pine trunk, he shouted, "I'll be back in a minute, Mamma, wait on me!"

"Come back this instant!" his mother shrilled but they all disappeared into the woods.

"Bailey Boy!" the grandmother called in a tragic voice but she found she was looking at The Misfit squatting on the ground in front of her. "I just know you're a good man," she said desperately. "You're not a bit common!"

"Nome, I ain't a good man," The Misfit said after a second as if he had considered her statement carefully, "but I ain't the worst in the world neither. My daddy said I was a different breed of dog from my brothers and sisters. 'You know,' Daddy said, 'it's some that can live their whole life out without asking about it and it's others has to know why it is, and this boy is one of the latters. He's going to be into everything!'" He put on his black hat and looked up suddenly and then away deep into the woods as if he were embarrassed again. "I'm sorry I don't have on a shirt before you ladies," he said, hunching his shoulders slightly. "We buried our clothes that we had on when we escaped and we're just making do until we can get better. We borrowed these from some folks we met," he explained.

"That's perfectly all right," the grandmother said. "Maybe Bailey has an extra shirt in his suitcase."

"I'll look and see terrectly," The Misfit said.

"Where are they taking him?" the children's mother screamed.

"Daddy was a card himself," The Misfit said. "You couldn't put anything over on him. He never got in trouble with the Authorities though. Just had the knack of handling them."

"You could be honest too if you'd only try," said the grandmother. "Think how wonderful it would be to settle down and live a comfortable life and not have to think about somebody chasing you all the time."

The Misfit kept scratching in the ground with the butt of his gun as if he were thinking about it. "Yes'm, somebody is always after you," he murmured.

The grandmother noticed how thin his shoulder blades were just be-hind his hat because she was standing up looking down at him. "Do you ever pray?" she asked.

He shook his head. All she saw was the black hat wiggle between his shoulder blades. "Nome," he said.

There was a pistol shot from the woods, followed closely by another. Then silence. The old lady's head jerked around. She could hear the wind move through the tree tops like a long satisfied insuck of breath. "Bailey Boy!" she called.

"I was a gospel singer for a while," The Misfit said. "I been most every-thing. Been in the arm service, both land and sea, at home and abroad, been twict married, been an undertaker, been with the railroads, plowed Mother Earth, been in a tornado, seen a man burnt alive oncet," and he looked up at the children's mother and the little girl who were sitting close together, their faces white and their eyes glassy; "I even seen a woman flogged," he said.

"Pray, pray," the grandmother began, "pray, pray . . ."

"I never was a bad boy that I remember of," The Misfit said in an al-most dreamy voice, "but somewheres along the line I done something wrong and got sent to the penitentiary. I was buried alive," and he looked up and held her attention to him by a steady stare.

"That's when you should have started to pray," she said. "What did you do to get sent to the penitentiary, that first time?"

"Turn to the right, it was a wall," The Misfit said, looking up again at the cloudless sky. "Turn to the left, it was a wall. Look up it was a ceiling, look down it was a floor. I forgot what I done, lady. I set there and set there, trying to remember what it was I done and I ain't recalled it to this day. Oncet in a while, I would think it was coming to me, but it never come."

"Maybe they put you in by mistake," the old lady said vaguely.

"Nome," he said. "It wasn't no mistake. They had the papers on me."

"You must have stolen something," she said.

The Misfit sneered slightly. "Nobody had nothing I wanted," he said. "It was a head-doctor at the penitentiary said what I had done was kill my daddy but I known that for a lie. My daddy died in nineteen ought nineteen of the epidemic flu and I never had a thing to do with it. He was buried in the Mount Hopewell Baptist churchyard and you can go there and see for yourself."

"If you would pray," the old lady said, "Jesus would help you."

"That's right," The Misfit said.

"Well then, why don't you pray?" she asked trembling with delight suddenly.

"I don't want no hep," he said. "I'm doing all right by myself."

Bobby Lee and Hiram came ambling back from the woods. Bobby Lee was dragging a yellow shirt with bright blue parrots in it.

"Thow me that shirt, Bobby Lee," The Misfit said. The shirt came flying at him and landed on his shoulder and he put it on. The grandmother couldn't name what the shirt reminded her of. "No, lady," The Misfit said while he was buttoning it up. "I found out the crime don't matter. You can do one thing or you can do another, kill a man or take a tire off his car, because sooner or later you're going to forget what it was you done and just be punished for it."

The children's mother had begun to make heaving noises as if she couldn't get her breath. "Lady," he asked, "would you and that little girl like to step off yonder with Bobby Lee and Hiram and join your husband?"

"Yes, thank you," the mother said faintly. Her left arm dangled helplessly and she was holding the baby, who had gone to sleep, in the other. "Hep that lady up, Hiram," The Misfit said as she struggled to climb out of the ditch, "and Bobby Lee, you hold onto that little girl's hand."

"I don't want to hold hands with him," June Star said. "He reminds me of a pig."

The fat boy blushed and laughed and caught her by the arm and pulled her off into the woods after Hiram and her mother.

Alone with The Misfit, the grandmother found that she had lost her voice. There was not a cloud in the sky nor any sun. There was nothing around her but woods. She wanted to tell him that he must pray. She opened and closed her mouth several times before anything came out. Finally she found herself saying, "Jesus. Jesus," meaning, Jesus will help you, but the way she was saying it, it sounded as if she might be cursing.

"Yes'm," The Misfit said as if he agreed. "Jesus thown everything off balance. It was the same case with Him as with me except He hadn't committed any crime and they could prove I had committed one because they had the papers on me. Of course," he said, "they never shown me my papers. That's why I sign myself now. I said long ago, you get you a signature and sign everything you do and keep a copy of it. Then you'll know what you done and you can hold up the crime to the punishment and see do they match and in the end you'll have something to prove you ain't been treated right. I call myself The Misfit," he said, "because I can't make what all I done wrong fit what all I gone through in punishment."

There was a piercing scream from the woods, followed closely by a pistol report. "Does it seem right to you, lady, that one is punished a heap and another ain't punished at all?"

"Jesus!" the old lady cried. "You've got good blood! I know you wouldn't shoot a lady! I know you come from nice people! Pray! Jesus, you ought not to shoot a lady. I'll give you all the money I've got!"

"Lady," The Misfit said, looking beyond her far into the woods, "there never was a body that give the undertaker a tip."

There were two more pistol reports and the grandmother raised her head like a parched old turkey hen crying for water and called, "Bailey Boy, Bailey Boy!" as if her heart would break.

"Jesus was the only One that ever raised the dead," The Misfit continued, "and He shouldn't have done it. He thown everything off balance. If He did what He said, then it's nothing for you to do but thow away everything and follow Him, and if He didn't, then it's nothing for you to do but enjoy the few minutes you got left the best you can — by killing somebody or burning down his house or doing some other meanness to him. No pleasure but meanness," he said and his voice had become almost a snarl.

"Maybe He didn't raise the dead," the old lady mumbled, not knowing what she was saying and feeling so dizzy that she sank down in the ditch with her legs twisted under her.

"I wasn't there so I can't say He didn't," The Misfit said. "I wisht I had of been there," he said, hitting the ground with his fist. "It ain't right I wasn't there because if I had of been there I would of known. Listen lady," he said in a high voice, "if I had of been there I would of known and I wouldn't be like I am now." His voice seemed about to crack and the grandmother's head cleared for an instant. She saw the man's face twisted close to her own as if he were going to cry and she murmured, "Why you're one of my babies. You're one of my own children!" She reached out and touched him on the shoulder. The Misfit sprang back as if a snake had bitten him and shot her three times through the chest. Then he put his gun down on the ground and took off his glasses and began to clean them.

Hiram and Bobby Lee returned from the woods and stood over the ditch, looking down at the grandmother who half sat and half lay in a puddle of blood with her legs crossed under her like a child's and her face smiling up at the cloudless sky.

Without his glasses, The Misfit's eyes were red-rimmed and pale and defenseless-looking. "Take her off and thow her where you thown the others," he said, picking up the cat that was rubbing itself against his leg.

"She was a talker, wasn't she?" Bobby Lee said, sliding down the ditch with a yodel.

"She would of been a good woman," The Misfit said, "if it had been somebody there to shoot her every minute of her life."

"Some fun!" Bobby Lee said.

"Shut up, Bobby Lee," The Misfit said. "It's no real pleasure in life."

[1955]

GABRIEL GARCÍA MÁRQUEZ   [1927-2014]

A Very Old Man with Enormous Wings

TRANSLATED BY GREGORY RABASSA, 1955

On the third day of rain they had killed so many crabs inside the house that Pelayo had to cross his drenched courtyard and throw them into the sea, because the newborn child had a temperature all night and they thought it was due to the stench. The world had been sad since Tuesday. Sea and sky were a single ash-gray thing and the sands of the beach, which on March nights glimmered like powdered light, had become a stew of mud and rotten shellfish. The light was so weak at noon that when Pelayo was coming back to the house after throwing away the crabs, it was hard for him to see what it was that was moving and groaning in the rear of the courtyard. He had to go very close to see that it was an old man, a very old man, lying face down in the mud, who, in spite of his tremendous efforts, couldn't get up, impeded by his enormous wings.

Frightened by that nightmare, Pelayo ran to get Elisenda, his wife, who was putting compresses on the sick child, and he took her to the rear of the courtyard. They both looked at the fallen body with mute stupor. He was dressed like a ragpicker. There were only a few faded hairs left on his bald skull and very few teeth in his mouth, and his pitiful condition of a drenched great-grandfather had taken away any sense of grandeur he might have had. His huge buzzard wings, dirty and half-plucked, were forever entangled in the mud. They looked at him so long and so closely that Pelayo and Elisenda very soon overcame their surprise and in the end found him familiar. Then they dared speak to him, and he answered in an incomprehensible dialect with a strong sailor's voice. That was how they skipped over the inconvenience of the wings and quite intelligently concluded that he was a lonely castaway from some foreign ship wrecked by the storm. And yet, they called in a neighbor woman who knew everything about life and death to see him, and all she needed was one look to show them their mistake.

"He's an angel," she told them. "He must have been coming for the child, but the poor fellow is so old that the rain knocked him down."

On the following day everyone knew that a flesh-and-blood angel was held captive in Pelayo's house. Against the judgment of the wise neighbor

263

woman, for whom angels in those times were the fugitive survivors of a celestial conspiracy, they did not have the heart to club him to death. Pelayo watched over him all afternoon from the kitchen, armed with his bailiff's club, and before going to bed he dragged him out of the mud and locked him up with the hens in the wire chicken coop. In the middle of the night, when the rain stopped, Pelayo and Elisenda were still killing crabs. A short time afterward the child woke up without a fever and with a desire to eat. Then they felt magnanimous and decided to put the angel on a raft with fresh water and provisions for three days and leave him to his fate on the high seas. But when they went out into the courtyard with the first light of dawn, they found the whole neighborhood in front of the chicken coop having fun with the angel, without the slightest reverence, tossing him things to eat through the openings in the wire as if he weren't a supernatural creature but a circus animal.

Father Gonzaga arrived before seven o'clock, alarmed at the strange news. By that time onlookers less frivolous than those at dawn had already arrived and they were making all kinds of conjectures concerning the captive's future. The simplest among them thought that he should be named mayor of the world. Others of sterner mind felt that he should be promoted to the rank of five-star general in order to win all wars. Some visionaries hoped that he could be put to stud in order to implant on earth a race of winged wise men who could take charge of the universe. But Father Gonzaga, before becoming a priest, had been a robust wood-cutter. Standing by the wire, he reviewed his catechism in an instant and asked them to open the door so that he could take a close look at that pitiful man who looked more like a huge decrepit hen among the fasci-nated chickens. He was lying in a corner drying his open wings in the sunlight among the fruit peels and breakfast leftovers that the early ris-ers had thrown him. Alien to the impertinences of the world, he only lifted his antiquarian eyes and murmured something in his dialect when Father Gonzaga went into the chicken coop and said good morning to him in Latin. The parish priest had his first suspicion of an impostor when he saw that he did not understand the language of God or know how to greet His ministers. Then he noticed that seen close up he was much too human: he had an unbearable smell of the outdoors, the back side of his wings was strewn with parasites and his main feathers had been mistreated by terrestrial winds, and nothing about him measured up to the proud dignity of angels. Then he came out of the chicken coop and in a brief sermon warned the curious against the risks of being in-genuous. He reminded them that the devil had the bad habit of making use of carnival tricks in order to confuse the unwary. He argued that if wings were not the essential element in determining the difference be-tween a hawk and an airplane, they were even less so in the recognition of angels. Nevertheless, he promised to write a letter to his bishop so that the latter would write to his primate so that the latter would write to the Supreme Pontiff in order to get the final verdict from the highest courts.

His prudence fell on sterile hearts. The news of the captive angel spread with such rapidity that after a few hours the courtyard had the bustle of a marketplace and they had to call in troops with fixed bayonets to disperse the mob that was about to knock the house down. Elisenda, her spine all twisted from sweeping up so much marketplace trash, then got the idea of fencing in the yard and charging five cents admission to see the angel.

The curious came from far away. A traveling carnival arrived with a flying acrobat who buzzed over the crowd several times, but no one paid any attention to him because his wings were not those of an angel but, rather, those of a sidereal° bat. The most unfortunate invalids on earth came in search of health: a poor woman who since childhood had been counting her heartbeats and had run out of numbers; a Portuguese man who couldn't sleep because the noise of the stars disturbed him; a sleep-walker who got up at night to undo the things he had done while awake; and many others with less serious ailments. In the midst of that ship-wreck disorder that made the earth tremble, Pelayo and Elisenda were happy with fatigue, for in less than a week they had crammed their rooms with money and the line of pilgrims waiting their turn to enter still reached beyond the horizon.

The angel was the only one who took no part in his own act. He spent his time trying to get comfortable in his borrowed nest, befuddled by the hellish heat of the oil lamps and sacramental candles that had been placed along the wire. At first they tried to make him eat some mothballs, which, according to the wisdom of the wise neighbor woman, were the food prescribed for angels. But he turned them down, just as he turned down the papal lunches that the penitents brought him, and they never found out whether it was because he was an angel or because he was an old man that in the end he ate nothing but eggplant mush. His only su-pernatural virtue seemed to be patience. Especially during the first days, when the hens pecked at him, searching for the stellar parasites that proliferated in his wings, and the cripples pulled out feathers to touch their defective parts with, and even the most merciful threw stones at him, trying to get him to rise so they could see him standing. The only time they succeeded in arousing him was when they burned his side with an iron for branding steers, for he had been motionless for so many hours that they thought he was dead. He awoke with a start, ranting in his hermetic language and with tears in his eyes, and he flapped his wings a couple of times, which brought on a whirlwind of chicken dung

Sidereal: Coming from the stars.

and lunar dust and a gale of panic that did not seem to be of this world. Although many thought that his reaction had been one not of rage but of pain, from then on they were careful not to annoy him, because the majority understood that his passivity was not that of a hero taking his ease but that of a cataclysm in repose.

Father Gonzaga held back the crowd's frivolity with formulas of maidservant inspiration while awaiting the arrival of a final judgment on the nature of the captive. But the mail from Rome showed no sense of urgency. They spent their time finding out if the prisoner had a navel, if his dialect had any connection with Aramaic, how many times he could fit on the head of a pin, or whether he wasn't just a Norwegian with wings. Those meager letters might have come and gone until the end of time if a providential event had not put an end to the priest's tribulations.

It so happened that during those days, among so many other carnival attractions, there arrived in town the traveling show of the woman who had been changed into a spider for having disobeyed her parents. The admission to see her was not only less than the admission to see the angel, but people were permitted to ask her all manner of questions about her absurd state and to examine her up and down so that no one would ever doubt the truth of her horror. She was a frightful tarantula the size of a ram and with the head of a sad maiden. What was most heart-rending, however, was not her outlandish shape but the sincere affliction with which she recounted the details of her misfortune. While still practically a child she had sneaked out of her parents' house to go to a dance, and while she was coming back through the woods after having danced all night without permission, a fearful thunderclap rent the sky in two and through the crack came the lightning bolt of brimstone that changed her into a spider. Her only nourishment came from the meatballs that charitable souls chose to toss into her mouth. A spectacle like that, full of so much human truth and with such a fearful lesson, was bound to defeat without even trying that of a haughty angel who scarcely deigned to look at mortals. Besides, the few miracles attributed to the angel showed a certain mental disorder, like the blind man who didn't recover his sight but grew three new teeth, or the paralytic who didn't get to walk but almost won the lottery, and the leper whose sores sprouted sunflowers. Those consolation miracles, which were more like mocking fun, had already ruined the angel's reputation when the woman who had been changed into a spider finally crushed him completely. That was how Father Gonzaga was cured forever of his insomnia and Pelayo's courtyard went back to being as empty as during the time it had rained for three days and crabs walked through the bedrooms.

The owners of the house had no reason to lament. With the money they saved they built a two-story mansion with balconies and gardens and high netting so that crabs wouldn't get in during the winter, and with iron bars on the windows so that angels wouldn't get in. Pelayo also set up a rabbit warren close to town and gave up his job as bailiff for good, and Elisenda bought some satin pumps with high heels and many dresses of iridescent silk, the kind worn on Sunday by the most desirable women in those times. The chicken coop was the only thing that didn't receive any attention. If they washed it down with creolin and burned tears of myrrh inside it every so often, it was not in homage to the angel but to drive away the dungheap stench that still hung everywhere like a ghost and was turning the new house into an old one. At first, when the child learned to walk, they were careful that he not get too close to the chicken coop. But then they began to lose their fears and got used to the smell, and before the child got his second teeth he'd gone inside the chicken coop to play, where the wires were falling apart. The angel was no less standoffish with him than with other mortals, but he tolerated the most ingenious infamies with the patience of a dog who had no illusions. They both came down with chicken pox at the same time. The doctor who took care of the child couldn't resist the temptation to listen to the angel's heart, and he found so much whistling in the heart and so many sounds in his kidneys that it seemed impossible for him to be alive. What surprised him most, however, was the logic of his wings. They seemed so natural on that completely human organism that he couldn't understand why other men didn't have them too.

When the child began school it had been some time since the sun and rain had caused the collapse of the chicken coop. The angel went dragging himself about here and there like a stray dying man. They would drive him out of the bedroom with a broom and a moment later find him in the kitchen. He seemed to be in so many places at the same time that they grew to think that he'd been duplicated, that he was reproducing himself all through the house, and the exasperated and unhinged Elisenda shouted that it was awful living in that hell full of angels. He could scarcely eat and his antiquarian eyes had also become so foggy that he went about bumping into posts. All he had left were the bare cannulae° of his last feathers. Pelayo threw a blanket over him and extended him the charity of letting him sleep in the shed, and only then did they notice that he had a temperature at night, and was delirious with the tongue twisters of an old Norwegian. That was one of the few times they became alarmed, for they thought he was going to die and not even the wise neighbor woman had been able to tell them what to do with dead angels.

And yet he not only survived his worst winter, but seemed improved with the first sunny days. He remained motionless for several days in the farthest corner of the courtyard, where no one would see him, and at the beginning of December some large, stiff feathers began to grow on his

Cannulae: The tubular pieces by which feathers are attached to a body.

wings, the feathers of a scarecrow, which looked more like another misfortune of decrepitude. But he must have known the reason for those changes, for he was quite careful that no one should notice them, that no one should hear the sea chanteys that he sometimes sang under the stars. One morning Elisenda was cutting some bunches of onions for lunch when a wind that seemed to come from the high seas blew into the kitchen. Then she went to the window and caught the angel in his first attempts at flight. They were so clumsy that his fingernails opened a furrow in the vegetable patch and he was on the point of knocking the shed down with the ungainly flapping that slipped on the light and couldn't get a grip on the air. But he did manage to gain altitude. Elisenda let out a sigh of relief, for herself and for him, when she saw him pass over the last houses, holding himself up in some way with the risky flapping of a senile vulture. She kept watching him even when she was through cutting the onions and she kept on watching until it was no longer possible for her to see him, because then he was no longer an annoyance in her life but an imaginary dot on the horizon of the sea.

[1955]

JOHN UPDIKE   [1932–2009]

A & P

In walks these three girls in nothing but bathing suits. I'm in the third checkout slot, with my back to the door, so I don't see them until they're over by the bread. The one that caught my eye first was the one in the plaid green two-piece. She was a chunky kid, with a good tan and a sweet broad soft-looking can with those two crescents of white just under it, where the sun never seems to hit, at the top of the backs of her legs. I stood there with my hand on a box of HiHo crackers trying to remember if I rang it up or not. I ring it up again and the customer starts giving me hell. She's one of these cash-register-watchers, a witch about fifty with rouge on her cheekbones and no eyebrows, and I know it made her day to trip me up. She'd been watching cash registers for fifty years and probably never seen a mistake before.

By the time I got her feathers smoothed and her goodies into a bag—she gives me a little snort in passing, if she'd been born at the right time they would have burned her over in Salem—by the time I get her on her way the girls had circled around the bread and were coming back, without a pushcart, back my way along the counters, in the aisle between the checkouts and the Special bins. They didn't even have shoes on. There was this chunky one, with the two-piece—it was bright green and the seams on the bra were still sharp and her belly was still pretty pale so I guessed she just got it (the suit)—there was this one, with one of those chubby berry-faces, the lips all bunched together under her nose, this one, and a tall one, with black hair that hadn't quite frizzed right, and one of these sunburns right across under the eyes, and a chin that was too long—you know, the kind of girl other girls think is very "striking" and "attractive" but never quite makes it, as they very well know, which is why they like her so much—and then the third one, that wasn't quite so tall. She was the queen. She kind of led them, the other two peeking around and making their shoulders round. She didn't look around, not this queen, she just walked straight on slowly, on these long white prima-donna legs. She came down a little hard on her heels, as if she didn't walk in her bare feet that much, putting down her heels and then letting the weight move along to her toes as if she was testing the floor with every step, putting a little deliberate extra action into it. You never know for sure how girls' minds work (do you really think it's a mind in there or just a little buzz like a bee in a glass jar?) but you got the idea she had talked the other two into coming in here with her, and now she was showing them how to do it, walk slow and hold yourself straight.

She had on a kind of dirty-pink—beige maybe, I don't know—bathing suit with a little nubble all over it, and what got me, the straps were down. They were off her shoulders looped loose around the cool tops of her arms, and I guess as a result the suit had slipped a little on her, so all around the top of the cloth there was this shining rim. If it hadn't been there you wouldn't have known there could have been anything whiter than those shoulders. With the straps pushed off, there was nothing be-tween the top of the suit and the top of her head except just *her*, this clean bare plane of the top of her chest down from the shoulder bones like a dented sheet of metal tilted in the light. I mean, it was more than pretty.

She had sort of oaky hair that the sun and salt had bleached, done up in a bun that was unravelling, and a kind of prim face. Walking into the A & P with your straps down, I suppose it's the only kind of face you *can* have. She held her head so high her neck, coming up out of those white shoulders, looked kind of stretched, but I didn't mind. The longer her neck was, the more of her there was.

She must have felt in the corner of her eye me and over my shoulder Stokesie in the second slot watching, but she didn't tip. Not this queen. She kept her eyes moving across the racks, and stopped, and turned so slow it made my stomach rub the inside of my apron, and buzzed to the other two, who kind of huddled against her for relief, and then they all three of them went up the cat-and-dog-food-breakfast-cereal-macaroni-rice-raisins-seasonings-spreads-spaghetti-soft-drinks-crackers-and-cookies aisle. From the third slot I look straight up this aisle to the meat counter, and I watched them all the way. The fat one with the tan sort of fumbled with the cookies, but on second thought she put the package back. The sheep pushing their carts down the aisle—the girls were walking against the usual traffic (not that we have one-way signs or anything)—were pretty hilarious. You could see them, when Queenie's white shoulders dawned on them, kind of jerk, or hop, or hiccup, but their eyes snapped back to their own baskets and on they pushed. I bet you could set off dynamite in an A & P and the people would by and large keep reaching and checking oatmeal off their lists and muttering "Let me see, there was a third thing, began with A, asparagus, no, ah, yes, apple-sauce!" or whatever it is they do mutter. But there was no doubt, this jiggled them. A few houseslaves in pin curlers even looked around after pushing their carts past to make sure what they had seen was correct.

You know, it's one thing to have a girl in a bathing suit down on the beach, where what with the glare nobody can look at each other much anyway, and another thing in the cool of the A & P, under the fluorescent lights, against all those stacked packages, with her feet paddling along naked over our checkboard green-and-cream rubber-tile floor.

"Oh Daddy," Stokesie said beside me. "I feel so faint."

"Darling," I said. "Hold me tight." Stokesie's married, with two babies chalked up on his fuselage already, but as far as I can tell that's the only difference. He's twenty-two, and I was nineteen this April.

"Is it done?" he asks, the responsible married man finding his voice. I forgot to say he thinks he's going to be manager some sunny day, maybe in 1990 when it's called the Great Alexandrov and Petrooshki Tea Company or something.

What he meant was, our town is five miles from a beach, with a big summer colony out on the Point, but we're right in the middle of town, and the women generally put on a shirt or shorts or something before they get out of the car into the street. And anyway these are usually women with six children and varicose veins mapping their legs and no-body, including them, could care less. As I say, we're right in the middle of town, and if you stand at our front doors you can see two banks and the Congregational church and the newspaper store and three real-estate offices and about twenty-seven old freeloaders tearing up Central Street because the sewer broke again. It's not as if we're on the Cape; we're north of Boston and there's people in this town haven't seen the ocean for twenty years.

The girls had reached the meat counter and were asking McMahon something. He pointed, they pointed, and they shuffled out of sight behind a pyramid of Diet Delight peaches. All that was left for us to see was old McMahon patting his mouth and looking after them sizing up their joints. Poor kids, I began to feel sorry for them, they couldn't help it.

Now here comes the sad part of the story, at least my family says it's sad, but I don't think it's so sad myself. The store's pretty empty, it being Thursday afternoon, so there was nothing much to do except lean on the register and wait for the girls to show up again. The whole store was like a pinball machine and I didn't know which tunnel they'd come out of. After a while they come around out of the far aisle, around the light bulbs, records at discount of the Caribbean Six or Tony Martin Sings or some such gunk you wonder they waste the wax on, sixpacks of candy bars, and plastic toys done up in cellophane that fall apart when a kid looks at them anyway. Around they come, Queenie still leading the way, and holding a little gray jar in her hand. Slots Three through Seven are unmanned and I could see her wondering between Stokes and me, but Stokesie with his usual luck draws an old party in baggy gray pants who stumbles up with four giant cans of pineapple juice (what do these bums *do* with all that pineapple juice? I've often asked myself) so the girls come to me. Queenie puts down the jar and I take it into my fingers icy cold. Kingfish Fancy Herring Snacks in Pure Sour Cream: 49¢. Now her hands are empty, not a ring or a bracelet, bare as God made them, and I wonder where the money's coming from. Still with that prim look she lifts a folded dollar bill out of the hollow at the center of her nubbled pink top. The jar went heavy in my hand. Really, I thought that was so cute.

Then everybody's luck begins to run out. Lengel comes in from haggling with a truck full of cabbages on the lot and is about to scuttle into that door marked MANAGER behind which he hides all day when the girls touch his eye. Lengel's pretty dreary, teaches Sunday school and the rest, but he doesn't miss that much. He comes over and says, "Girls, this isn't the beach."

Queenie blushes, though maybe it's just a brush of sunburn I was noticing for the first time, now that she was so close. "My mother asked me to pick up a jar of herring snacks." Her voice kind of startled me, the way voices do when you see the people first, coming out so flat and dumb yet kind of tony, too, the way it ticked over "pick up" and "snacks." All of a sudden I slid right down her voice into her living room. Her father and the other men were standing around in ice-cream coats and bow ties and the women were in sandals picking up herring snacks on toothpicks off a big glass plate and they were all holding drinks the color of water with olives and sprigs of mint in them. When my parents have somebody over they get lemonade and if it's a real racy affair Schlitz in tall glasses with "They'll Do It Every Time" cartoons stencilled on.

"That's all right," Lengel said. "But this isn't the beach." His repeating this struck me as funny, as if it had just occurred to him, and he had been thinking all these years the A & P was a great big sand dune and he was the head lifeguard. He didn't like my smiling—as I say he doesn't miss much—but he concentrates on giving the girls that sad Sunday-school–superintendent stare.

Queenie's blush is no sunburn now, and the plump one in plaid, that I liked better from the back—a really sweet can—pipes up, "We weren't doing any shopping. We just came in for the one thing."

"That makes no difference," Lengel tells her, and I could see from the way his eyes went that he hadn't noticed she was wearing a two-piece before. "We want you decently dressed when you come in here."

"We *are* decent," Queenie says suddenly, her lower lip pushing, getting sore now that she remembers her place, a place from which the crowd that runs the A & P must look pretty crummy. Fancy Herring Snacks flashed in her very blue eyes.

"Girls, I don't want to argue with you. After this come in here with your shoulders covered. It's our policy." He turns his back. That's policy for you. Policy is what the kingpins want. What the others want is juvenile delinquency.

All this while, the customers had been showing up with their carts but, you know, sheep, seeing a scene, they had all bunched up on Stokesie, who shook open a paper bag as gently as peeling a peach, not wanting to miss a word. I could feel in the silence everybody getting nervous, most of all Lengel, who asks me, "Sammy, have you rung up their purchase?"

I thought and said "No" but it wasn't about that I was thinking. I go through the punches, 4, 9, GROC, TOT—it's more complicated than you think, and after you do it often enough, it begins to make a little song, that you hear words to, in my case "Hello (*bing*) there, you (*gung*) hap-py pee-pul (*splat*)!"—the *splat* being the drawer flying out. I uncrease the bill, tenderly as you may imagine, it just having come from between the two smoothest scoops of vanilla I had ever known were there, and pass a half and a penny into her narrow pink palm, and nestle the herrings in a bag and twist its neck and hand it over, all the time thinking.

The girls, and who'd blame them, are in a hurry to get out, so I say "I quit" to Lengel quick enough for them to hear, hoping they'll stop and watch me, their unsuspected hero. They keep right on going, into the electric eye; the door flies open and they flicker across the lot to their car, Queenie and Plaid and Big Tall Goony-Goony (not that as raw material she was so bad), leaving me with Lengel and a kink in his eyebrow.

"Did you say something, Sammy?"

"I said I quit."

"I thought you did."

"You didn't have to embarrass them."

"It was they who were embarrassing us."

I started to say something that came out "Fiddle-de-doo." It's a saying of my grandmother's, and I know she would have been pleased.

"I don't think you know what you're saying," Lengel said.

"I know you don't," I said. "But I do." I pull the bow at the back of my apron and start shrugging it off my shoulders. A couple customers that had been heading for my slot begin to knock against each other, like scared pigs in a chute.

Lengel sighs and begins to look very patient and old and gray. He's been a friend of my parents for years. "Sammy, you don't want to do this to your Mom and Dad," he tells me. It's true, I don't. But it seems to me that once you begin a gesture it's fatal not to go through with it. I fold the apron, "Sammy" stitched in red on the pocket, and put it on the counter, and drop the bow tie on top of it. The bow tie is theirs, if you've ever wondered. "You'll feel this for the rest of your life," Lengel says, and I know that's true, too, but remembering how he made that pretty girl blush makes me so scrunchy inside I punch the No Sale tab and the machine whirs "pee-pul" and the drawer splats out. One advantage to this scene taking place in summer, I can follow this up with a clean exit, there's no fumbling around getting your coat and galoshes, I just saunter into the electric eye in my white shirt that my mother ironed the night before, and the door heaves itself open, and outside the sunshine is skating around on the asphalt.

I look around for my girls, but they're gone, of course. There wasn't anybody but some young married screaming with her children about some candy they didn't get by the door of a powder-blue Falcon station wagon. Looking back in the big windows, over the bags of peat moss and aluminum lawn furniture stacked on the pavement, I could see Lengel in my place in the slot, checking the sheep through. His face was dark gray and his back stiff, as if he'd just had an injection of iron, and my stomach kind of fell as I felt how hard the world was going to be to me hereafter.

[1961]

RAYMOND CARVER [1938–1988]

Cathedral

This blind man, an old friend of my wife's, he was on his way to spend the night. His wife had died. So he was visiting the dead wife's relatives in Connecticut. He called my wife from his in-laws'. Arrangements were made. He would come by train, a five-hour trip, and my wife would meet him at the station. She hadn't seen him since she worked for him one summer in Seattle ten years ago. But she and the blind man had kept in touch. They made tapes and mailed them back and forth. I wasn't enthusiastic about his visit. He was no one I knew. And his being blind bothered me. My idea of blindness came from the movies. In the movies, the blind moved slowly and never laughed. Sometimes they were led by seeing-eye dogs. A blind man in my house was not something I looked forward to.

That summer in Seattle she had needed a job. She didn't have any money. The man she was going to marry at the end of the summer was in officers' training school. He didn't have any money, either. But she was in love with the guy, and he was in love with her, etc. She'd seen something in the paper: HELP WANTED—*Reading to Blind Man*, and a telephone number. She phoned and went over, was hired on the spot. She'd worked with this blind man all summer. She read stuff to him, case studies, reports, that sort of thing. She helped him organize his little office in the county social-service department. They'd become good friends, my wife and the blind man. How do I know these things? She told me. And she told me something else. On her last day in the office, the blind man asked if he could touch her face. She agreed to this. She told me he touched his fingers to every part of her face, her nose—even her neck! She never forgot it. She even tried to write a poem about it. She was always trying to write a poem. She wrote a poem or two every year, usually after something really important had happened to her.

When we first started going out together, she showed me the poem. In the poem, she recalled his fingers and the way they had moved around over her face. In the poem, she talked about what she had felt at the time, about what went through her mind when the blind man touched her nose and lips. I can remember I didn't think much of the poem. Of course, I didn't tell her that. Maybe I just don't understand poetry. I admit it's not the first thing I reach for when I pick up something to read.

Anyway, this man who'd first enjoyed her favors, the officer-to-be, he'd been her childhood sweetheart. So okay. I'm saying that at the end of the summer she let the blind man run his hands over her face, said good-bye to him, married her childhood etc., who was now a commissioned officer, and she moved away from Seattle. But they'd kept in touch, she and the blind man. She made the first contact after a year or so. She called him up one night from an Air Force base in Alabama. She wanted to talk. They talked. He asked her to send him a tape and tell him about her life. She did this. She sent the tape. On the tape, she told the blind man about her husband and about their life together in the military. She told the blind man she loved her husband but she didn't like it where they lived and she didn't like it that he was part of the military-industrial thing. She told the blind man she'd written a poem and he was in it. She told him that she was writing a poem about what it was like to be an Air Force officer's wife. The poem wasn't finished yet. She was still writing it. The blind man made a tape. He sent her the tape. She made a tape. This went on for years. My wife's officer was posted to one base and then another. She sent tapes from Moody AFB, McGuire, McConnell, and finally Travis, near Sacramento, where one night she got to feeling lonely and cut off from the people she kept losing in that moving-around life. She got to feeling she couldn't go it another step. She went in and swallowed all the pills and capsules in the medicine chest and washed them down with a bottle of gin. Then she got into a hot bath and passed out.

But instead of dying, she got sick. She threw up. Her officer—why should he have a name? he was the childhood sweetheart, and what more does he want?—came home from somewhere, found her, and called the ambulance. In time, she put it all on a tape and sent the tape to the blind man. Over the years, she put all kinds of stuff on tapes and sent the tapes off lickety-split. Next to writing a poem every year, I think it was her chief means of recreation. On one tape, she told the blind man she'd decided to live away from her officer for a time. On another tape, she told him about her divorce. She and I began going out, and of course she told her blind man about it. She told him everything, or so it seemed to me. Once she asked me if I'd like to hear the latest tape from the blind man. This was a year ago. I was on the tape, she said. So I said okay, I'd listen to it. I got us drinks and we settled down in the living room. We made ready to listen. First she inserted the tape into the player and adjusted a couple of dials. Then she pushed a lever. The tape squeaked and someone began to talk in this loud voice. She lowered the volume. After a few minutes of harmless chitchat, I heard my own name in the mouth of this stranger, this blind man I didn't even know! And then this: "From all you've said about him, I can only conclude—" But we were interrupted, a knock at the door, something, and we didn't ever get back to the tape. Maybe it was just as well. I'd heard all I wanted to.

Now this same blind man was coming to sleep in my house.

"Maybe I could take him bowling," I said to my wife. She was at the draining board doing scalloped potatoes. She put down the knife she was using and turned around.

"If you love me," she said, "you can do this for me. If you don't love me, okay. But if you had a friend, any friend, and the friend came to visit, I'd make him feel comfortable." She wiped her hands with the dish towel.

"I don't have any blind friends," I said.

"You don't have *any* friends," she said. "Period. Besides," she said, "goddamn it, his wife's just died! Don't you understand that? The man's lost his wife!"

I didn't answer. She'd told me a little about the blind man's wife. Her name was Beulah. Beulah! That's a name for a colored woman.

"Was his wife a Negro?" I asked.

"Are you crazy?" my wife said. "Have you just flipped or something?" She picked up a potato. I saw it hit the floor, then roll under the stove. "What's wrong with you?" she said. "Are you drunk?"

"I'm just asking," I said.

Right then my wife filled me in with more detail than I cared to know. I made a drink and sat at the kitchen table to listen. Pieces of the story began to fall into place.

Beulah had gone to work for the blind man the summer after my wife had stopped working for him. Pretty soon Beulah and the blind man had themselves a church wedding. It was a little wedding—who'd want to go to such a wedding in the first place?—just the two of them, plus the minister and the minister's wife. But it was a church wedding just the same. It was what Beulah had wanted, he'd said. But even then Beulah must have been carrying the cancer in her glands. After they had been inseparable for eight years—my wife's word, *inseparable*—Beulah's health went into a rapid decline. She died in a Seattle hospital room, the blind man sitting beside the bed and holding on to her hand. They'd married, lived and worked together, slept together—had sex, sure—and then the blind man had to bury her. All this without his having ever seen what the goddamned woman looked like. It was beyond my understanding. Hearing this, I felt sorry for the blind man for a little bit. And then I found myself thinking what a pitiful life this woman must have led. Imagine a woman who could never see herself as she was seen in the eyes of her loved one. A woman who could go on day after day and never receive the smallest compliment from her beloved. A woman whose husband could never read the expression on her face, be it misery or something better. Someone who could wear makeup or not—what difference to him? She could, if she wanted, wear green eye-shadow around one eye, a straight pin in her nostril, yellow slacks and purple shoes, no matter. And then to slip off into death, the blind man's hand on her hand, his blind eyes streaming tears—I'm imagining now—her last thought maybe this: that he never even knew what she looked like, and she on an express to the grave. Robert was left with a small insurance policy and half of a twenty-peso Mexican coin. The other half of the coin went into the box with her. Pathetic.

So when the time rolled around, my wife went to the depot to pick him up. With nothing to do but wait—sure, I blamed him for that—I was having a drink and watching the TV when I heard the car pull into the drive. I got up from the sofa with my drink and went to the window to have a look.

I saw my wife laughing as she parked the car. I saw her get out of the car and shut the door. She was still wearing a smile. Just amazing. She went around to the other side of the car to where the blind man was already starting to get out. This blind man, feature this, he was wearing a full beard! A beard on a blind man! Too much, I say. The blind man reached into the back seat and dragged out a suitcase. My wife took his arm, shut the car door, and, talking all the way, moved him down the drive and then up the steps to the front porch. I turned off the TV. I finished my drink, rinsed the glass, dried my hands. Then I went to the door.

My wife said, "I want you to meet Robert. Robert, this is my husband. I've told you all about him." She was beaming. She had this blind man by his coat sleeve.

The blind man let go of his suitcase and up came his hand.

I took it. He squeezed hard, held my hand, and then he let it go.

"I feel like we've already met," he boomed.

"Likewise," I said. I didn't know what else to say. Then I said, "Welcome. I've heard a lot about you." We began to move then, a little group, from the porch into the living room, my wife guiding him by the arm. The blind man was carrying his suitcase in his other hand. My wife said things like, "To your left here, Robert. That's right. Now watch it, there's a chair. That's it. Sit down right here. This is the sofa. We just bought this sofa two weeks ago."

I started to say something about the old sofa. I'd liked that old sofa. But I didn't say anything. Then I wanted to say something else, small-talk, about the scenic ride along the Hudson. How going *to* New York, you should sit on the right-hand side of the train, and coming *from* New York, the left-hand side.

"Did you have a good train ride?" I said. "Which side of the train did you sit on, by the way?"

"What a question, which side!" my wife said. "What's it matter which side?" she said.

"I just asked," I said.

"Right side," the blind man said. "I hadn't been on a train in nearly forty years. Not since I was a kid. With my folks. That's been a long time. I'd nearly forgotten the sensation. I have winter in my beard now," he said. "So I've been told, anyway. Do I look distinguished, my dear?" the blind man said to my wife.

"You look distinguished, Robert," she said. "Robert," she said. "Robert, it's just so good to see you."

My wife finally took her eyes off the blind man and looked at me. I had the feeling she didn't like what she saw. I shrugged.

I've never met, or personally known, anyone who was blind. This blind man was late forties, a heavy-set, balding man with stooped shoulders, as if he carried a great weight there. He wore brown slacks, brown shoes, a light-brown shirt, a tie, a sports coat. Spiffy. He also had this full beard. But he didn't use a cane and he didn't wear dark glasses. I'd always thought dark glasses were a must for the blind. Fact was, I wished he had a pair. At first glance, his eyes looked like anyone else's eyes. But if you looked close, there was something different about them. Too much white in the iris, for one thing, and the pupils seemed to move around in the sockets without his knowing it or being able to stop it. Creepy. As I stared at his face, I saw the left pupil turn in toward his nose while the other made an effort to keep in one place. But it was only an effort, for that eye was on the roam without his knowing it or wanting it to be.

I said, "Let me get you a drink. What's your pleasure? We have a little of everything. It's one of our pastimes."

"Bub, I'm a Scotch man myself," he said fast enough in this big voice.

"Right," I said. Bub! "Sure you are. I knew it."

He let his fingers touch his suitcase, which was sitting alongside the sofa. He was taking his bearings. I didn't blame him for that.

"I'll move that up to your room," my wife said.

"No, that's fine," the blind man said loudly. "It can go up when I go up."

"A little water with the Scotch?" I said.

"Very little," he said.

"I knew it," I said.

He said, "Just a tad. The Irish actor, Barry Fitzgerald? I'm like that fellow. When I drink water, Fitzgerald said, I drink water. When I drink whiskey, I drink whiskey." My wife laughed. The blind man brought his hand up under his beard. He lifted his beard slowly and let it drop.

I did the drinks, three big glasses of Scotch with a splash of water in each. Then we made ourselves comfortable and talked about Robert's travels. First the long flight from the West Coast to Connecticut, we covered that. Then from Connecticut up here by train. We had another drink concerning that leg of the trip.

I remembered having read somewhere that the blind didn't smoke because, as speculation had it, they couldn't see the smoke they exhaled. I thought I knew that much and that much only about blind people. But this blind man smoked his cigarette down to the nubbin and then lit another one. This blind man filled his ashtray and my wife emptied it.

When we sat down at the table for dinner, we had another drink. My wife heaped Robert's plate with cube steak, scalloped potatoes, green beans. I buttered him up two slices of bread. I said, "Here's bread and butter for you." I swallowed some of my drink. "Now let us pray," I said, and the blind man lowered his head. My wife looked at me, her mouth agape. "Pray the phone won't ring and the food doesn't get cold," I said.

We dug in. We ate everything there was to eat on the table. We ate like there was no tomorrow. We didn't talk. We ate. We scarfed. We grazed that table. We were into serious eating. The blind man had right away located his foods, he knew just where everything was on his plate. I watched with admiration as he used his knife and fork on the meat. He'd cut two pieces of meat, fork the meat into his mouth, and then go all out for the scalloped potatoes, the beans next, and then he'd tear off a hunk of buttered bread and eat that. He'd follow this up with a big drink of milk. It didn't seem to bother him to use his fingers once in a while, either.

We finished everything, including half a strawberry pie. For a few moments, we sat as if stunned. Sweat beaded on our faces. Finally, we got up from the table and left the dirty plates. We didn't look back. We took ourselves into the living room and sank into our places again. Robert and my wife sat on the sofa. I took the big chair. We had us two or three more drinks while they talked about the major things that had come to pass for them in the past ten years. For the most part, I just listened. Now and then I joined in. I didn't want him to think I'd left the room, and I didn't want her to think I was feeling left out. They talked of things that had happened to them—to them!—these past ten years. I waited in vain to hear my name on my wife's sweet lips: "And then my dear husband came into my life"—something like that. But I heard nothing of the sort. More talk of Robert. Robert had done a little of everything, it seemed, a regular blind jack-of-all-trades. But most recently he and his wife had had an Amway distributorship, from which, I gathered, they'd earned their living, such as it was. The blind man was also a ham radio operator. He talked in his loud voice about conversations he'd had with fellow operators in Guam, in the Philippines, in Alaska, and even in Tahiti. He said he'd have a lot of friends there if he ever wanted to go visit those places. From time to time, he'd turn his blind face toward me, put his hand under his beard, ask me something. How long had I been in my present position? (Three years.) Did I like my work? (I didn't.) Was I going to stay with it? (What were the options?) Finally, when I thought he was beginning to run down, I got up and turned on the TV.

My wife looked at me with irritation. She was heading toward a boil. Then she looked at the blind man and said, "Robert, do you have a TV?"

The blind man said, "My dear, I have two TVs. I have a color set and a black-and-white thing, an old relic. It's funny, but if I turn the TV on, and I'm always turning it on, I turn on the color set. It's funny, don't you think?"

I didn't know what to say to that. I had absolutely nothing to say to that. No opinion. So I watched the news program and tried to listen to what the announcer was saying.

"This is a color TV," the blind man said. "Don't ask me how, but I can tell."

"We traded up a while ago," I said.

The blind man had another taste of his drink. He lifted his beard, sniffed it, and let it fall. He leaned forward on the sofa. He positioned his ashtray on the coffee table, then put the lighter to his cigarette. He leaned back on the sofa and crossed his legs at the ankles.

My wife covered her mouth, and then she yawned. She stretched. She said, "I think I'll go upstairs and put on my robe. I think I'll change into something else. Robert, you make yourself comfortable," she said.

"I'm comfortable," the blind man said.

"I want you to feel comfortable in this house," she said.

"I am comfortable," the blind man said.

After she'd left the room, he and I listened to the weather report and then to the sports roundup. By that time, she'd been gone so long I didn't know if she was going to come back. I thought she might have gone to bed. I wished she'd come back downstairs. I didn't want to be left alone with a blind man. I asked him if he wanted another drink, and he said sure. Then I asked if he wanted to smoke some dope with me. I said I'd just rolled a number. I hadn't, but I planned to do so in about two shakes.

"I'll try some with you," he said.

"Damn right," I said. "That's the stuff."

I got our drinks and sat down on the sofa with him. Then I rolled us two fat numbers. I lit one and passed it. I brought it to his fingers. He took it and inhaled.

"Hold it as long as you can," I said. I could tell he didn't know the first thing.

My wife came back downstairs wearing her pink robe and her pink slippers.

"What do I smell?" she said.

"We thought we'd have us some cannabis," I said.

My wife gave me a savage look. Then she looked at the blind man and said, "Robert, I didn't know you smoked."

He said, "I do now, my dear. There's a first time for everything. But I don't feel anything yet."

"This stuff is pretty mellow," I said. "This stuff is mild. It's dope you can reason with," I said. "It doesn't mess you up."

"Not much it doesn't, bub," he said, and laughed.

My wife sat on the sofa between the blind man and me. I passed her the number. She took it and toked and then passed it back to me. "Which way is this going?" she said. Then she said, "I shouldn't be smoking this. I can hardly keep my eyes open as it is. That dinner did me in. I shouldn't have eaten so much."

"It was the strawberry pie," the blind man said. "That's what did it," he said, and he laughed his big laugh. Then he shook his head.

"There's more strawberry pie," I said.

"Do you want some more, Robert?" my wife said.

"Maybe in a little while," he said.

We gave our attention to the TV. My wife yawned again. She said, "Your bed is made up when you feel like going to bed, Robert. I know you must have had a long day. When you're ready to go to bed, say so." She pulled his arm. "Robert?"

He came to and said, "I've had a real nice time. This beats tapes, doesn't it?"

I said, "Coming at you," and I put the number between his fingers. He inhaled, held the smoke, and then let it go. It was like he'd been doing it since he was nine years old.

"Thanks, bub," he said. "But I think this is all for me. I think I'm beginning to feel it," he said. He held the burning roach out for my wife.

"Same here," she said. "Ditto. Me, too." She took the roach and passed it to me. "I may just sit here for a while between you two guys with my eyes closed. But don't let me bother you, okay? Either one of you. If it bothers you, say so. Otherwise, I may just sit here with my eyes closed until you're ready to go to bed," she said. "Your bed's made up, Robert, when you're ready. It's right next to our room at the top of the stairs. We'll show you up when you're ready. You wake me up now, you guys, if I fall asleep." She said that and then she closed her eyes and went to sleep.

The news program ended. I got up and changed the channel. I sat back down on the sofa. I wished my wife hadn't pooped out. Her head lay across the back of the sofa, her mouth open. She'd turned so that her robe slipped away from her legs, exposing a juicy thigh. I reached to draw her robe back over her, and it was then that I glanced at the blind man. What the hell! I flipped the robe open again.

"You say when you want some strawberry pie," I said.

"I will," he said.

I said, "Are you tired? Do you want me to take you up to your bed? Are you ready to hit the hay?"

"Not yet," he said. "No, I'll stay up with you, bub. If that's all right. I'll stay up until you're ready to turn in. We haven't had a chance to talk. Know what I mean? I feel like me and her monopolized the evening." He lifted his beard and he let it fall. He picked up his cigarettes and his lighter.

"That's all right," I said. Then I said, "I'm glad for the company."

And I guess I was. Every night I smoked dope and stayed up as long as I could before I fell asleep. My wife and I hardly ever went to bed at the same time. When I did go to sleep, I had these dreams. Sometimes I'd wake up from one of them, my heart going crazy.

Something about the church and the Middle Ages was on the TV. Not your run-of-the-mill TV fare. I wanted to watch something else. I turned to the other channels. But there was nothing on them, either. So I turned back to the first channel and apologized.

"Bub, it's all right," the blind man said. "It's fine with me. Whatever you want to watch is okay. I'm always learning something. Learning never ends. It won't hurt me to learn something tonight. I got ears," he said.

We didn't say anything for a time. He was leaning forward with his head turned at me, his right ear aimed in the direction of the set. Very disconcerting. Now and then his eyelids drooped and then they snapped open again. Now and then he put his fingers into his beard and tugged, like he was thinking about something he was hearing on the television.

On the screen, a group of men wearing cowls was being set upon and tormented by men dressed in skeleton costumes and men dressed as devils. The men dressed as devils wore devil masks, horns, and long tails. This pageant was part of a procession. The Englishman who was narrating the thing said it took place in Spain once a year. I tried to explain to the blind man what was happening.

"Skeletons," he said. "I know about skeletons," he said, and he nodded.

The TV showed this one cathedral. Then there was a long, slow look at another one. Finally, the picture switched to the famous one in Paris, with its flying buttresses and its spires reaching up to the clouds. The camera pulled away to show the whole of the cathedral rising above the skyline.

There were times when the Englishman who was telling the thing would shut up, would simply let the camera move around over the cathedrals. Or else the camera would tour the countryside, men in fields walking behind oxen. I waited as long as I could. Then I felt I had to say something. I said, "They're showing the outside of this cathedral now. Gargoyles. Little statues carved to look like monsters. Now I guess they're in Italy. Yeah, they're in Italy. There's paintings on the walls of this one church."

"Are those fresco paintings, bub?" he asked, and he sipped from his drink.

I reached for my glass. But it was empty. I tried to remember what I could remember. "You're asking me are those frescoes?" I said. "That's a good question. I don't know."

The camera moved to a cathedral outside Lisbon. The differences in the Portuguese cathedral compared with the French and Italian were not that great. But they were there. Mostly the interior stuff. Then something occurred to me, and I said, "Something has occurred to me. Do you have any idea what a cathedral is? What they look like, that is? Do you follow me? If somebody says cathedral to you, do you have any notion what they're talking about? Do you know the difference between that and a Baptist church, say?"

He let the smoke dribble from his mouth. "I know they took hundreds of workers fifty or a hundred years to build," he said. "I just heard the man say that, of course. I know generations of the same families worked on a cathedral. I heard him say that, too. The men who began their life's work on them, they never lived to see the completion of their work. In that wise, bub, they're no different from the rest of us, right?" He laughed. Then his eyelids drooped again. His head nodded. He seemed to be snoozing. Maybe he was imagining himself in Portugal. The TV was showing another cathedral now. This one was in Germany. The Englishman's voice droned on. "Cathedrals," the blind man said. He sat up and rolled his head back and forth "If you want the truth, bub, that's about all I know. What I just said. What I heard him say. But maybe you could describe one to me? I wish you'd do it. I'd like that. If you want to know, I really don't have a good idea."

I stared hard at the shot of the cathedral on the TV. How could I even begin to describe it? But say my life depended on it. Say my life was being threatened by an insane guy who said I had to do it or else.

I stared some more at the cathedral before the picture flipped off into the countryside. There was no use. I turned to the blind man and said, "To begin with, they're very tall." I was looking around the room for clues. "They reach way up. Up and up. Toward the sky. They're so big, some of them, they have to have these supports. To help hold them up, so to speak. These supports are called buttresses. They remind me of viaducts, for some reason. But maybe you don't know viaducts, either? Sometimes the cathedrals have devils and such carved into the front. Sometimes lords and ladies. Don't ask me why this is," I said.

He was nodding. The whole upper part of his body seemed to be moving back and forth.

"I'm not doing so good, am I?" I said.

He stopped nodding and leaned forward on the edge of the sofa. As he listened to me, he was running his fingers through his beard. I wasn't getting through to him, I could see that. But he waited for me to go on just the same. He nodded, like he was trying to encourage me. I tried to think what else to say. "They're really big," I said. "They're massive. They're built of stone. Marble, too, sometimes. In those olden days, when they built cathedrals, men wanted to be close to God. In those olden days, God was an important part of everyone's life. You could tell this from their cathedral-building. I'm sorry," I said, "but it looks like that's the best I can do for you. I'm just no good at it."

"That's all right, bub," the blind man said. "Hey, listen. I hope you don't mind my asking you. Can I ask you something? Let me ask you a simple question, yes or no. I'm just curious and there's no offense. You're my host. But let me ask if you are in any way religious? You don't mind my asking?"

I shook my head. He couldn't see that, though. A wink is the same as a nod to a blind man. "I guess I don't believe in it. In anything. Sometimes it's hard. You know what I'm saying?"

"Sure, I do," he said.

"Right," I said.

The Englishman was still holding forth. My wife sighed in her sleep. She drew a long breath and went on with her sleeping.

"You'll have to forgive me," I said. "But I can't tell you what a cathedral looks like. It just isn't in me to do it. I can't do any more than I've done."

The blind man sat very still, his head down, as he listened to me.

I said, "The truth is, cathedrals don't mean anything special to me. Nothing. Cathedrals. They're something to look at on late-night TV. That's all they are."

It was then that the blind man cleared his throat. He brought something up. He took a handkerchief from his back pocket. Then he said, "I get it, bub. It's okay. It happens. Don't worry about it," he said. "Hey, listen to me. Will you do me a favor? I got an idea. Why don't you find us some heavy paper? And a pen. We'll do something. We'll draw one together. Get us a pen and some heavy paper. Go on, bub, get the stuff," he said.

So I went upstairs. My legs felt like they didn't have any strength in them. They felt like they did after I'd done some running. In my wife's room, I looked around. I found some ballpoints in a little basket on her table. And then I tried to think where to look for the kind of paper he was talking about.

Downstairs, in the kitchen, I found a shopping bag with onion skins in the bottom of the bag. I emptied the bag and shook it. I brought it into the living room and sat down with it near his legs. I moved some things, smoothed the wrinkles from the bag, spread it out on the coffee table.

The blind man got down from the sofa and sat next to me on the carpet.

He ran his fingers over the paper. He went up and down the sides of the paper. The edges, even the edges. He fingered the corners.

"All right," he said. "All right, let's do her."

He found my hand, the hand with the pen. He closed his hand over my hand. "Go ahead, bub, draw," he said. "Draw. You'll see. I'll follow along with you. It'll be okay. Just begin now like I'm telling you. You'll see. Draw," the blind man said.

So I began. First I drew a box that looked like a house. It could have been the house I lived in. Then I put a roof on it. At either end of the roof, I drew spires. Crazy.

"Swell," he said. "Terrific. You're doing fine," he said. "Never thought anything like this could happen in your lifetime, did you, bub? Well, it's a strange life, we all know that. Go on now. Keep it up."

I put in windows with arches. I drew flying buttresses. I hung great doors. I couldn't stop. The TV station went off the air. I put down the pen and closed and opened my fingers. The blind man felt around over the paper. He moved the tips of his fingers over the paper, all over what I had drawn, and he nodded.

"Doing fine," the blind man said.

I took up the pen again, and he found my hand. I kept at it. I'm no artist. But I kept drawing just the same.

My wife opened up her eyes and gazed at us. She sat up on the sofa, her robe hanging open. She said, "What are you doing? Tell me, I want to know."

I didn't answer her.

The blind man said, "We're drawing a cathedral. Me and him are working on it. Press hard," he said to me. "That's right. That's good," he said. "Sure. You got it, bub. I can tell. You didn't think you could. But you can, can't you? You're cooking with gas now. You know what I'm saying? We're going to really have us something here in a minute. How's the old arm?" he said. "Put some people in there now. What's a cathedral without people?"

My wife said, "What's going on? Robert, what are you doing? What's going on?"

"It's all right," he said to her. "Close your eyes now," the blind man said to me.

I did it. I closed them just like he said.

"Are they closed?" he said. "Don't fudge."

"They're closed," I said.

"Keep them that way," he said. He said, "Don't stop now. Draw."

So we kept on with it. His fingers rode my fingers as my hand went over the paper. It was like nothing else in my life up to now.

Then he said, "I think that's it. I think you got it," he said. "Take a look. What do you think?"

But I had my eyes closed. I thought I'd keep them that way for a little longer. I thought it was something I ought to do.

"Well?" he said. "Are you looking?"

My eyes were still closed. I was in my house. I knew that. But I didn't feel like I was inside anything.

"It's really something," I said.

[1981]

JOYCE CAROL OATES   [b. 1938]

Where Are You Going, Where Have You Been?

For Bob Dylan

Her name was Connie. She was fifteen and she had a quick nervous giggling habit of craning her neck to glance into mirrors, or checking other people's faces to make sure her own was all right. Her mother, who noticed everything and knew everything and who hadn't much reason any longer to look at her own face, always scolded Connie about it. "Stop gawking at yourself, who are you? You think you're so pretty?" she would say. Connie would raise her eyebrows at these familiar complaints and look right through her mother, into a shadowy vision of herself as she was right at that moment: she knew she was pretty and that was everything. Her mother had been pretty once too, if you could believe those old snapshots in the album, but now her looks were gone and that was why she was always after Connie.

"Why don't you keep your room clean like your sister? How've you got your hair fixed—what the hell stinks? Hair spray? You don't see your sister using that junk."

Her sister June was twenty-four and still lived at home. She was a secretary in the high school Connie attended, and if that wasn't bad enough—with her in the same building—she was so plain and chunky and steady that Connie had to hear her praised all the time by her mother and her mother's sisters. June did this, June did that, she saved money and helped clean the house and cooked and Connie couldn't do a thing, her mind was all filled with trashy daydreams. Their father was away at work most of the time and when he came home he wanted supper and he read the newspaper at supper and after supper he went to bed. He didn't bother talking much to them, but around his bent head Connie's mother kept picking at her until Connie wished her mother was dead and she herself was dead and it was all over. "She makes me want to throw up sometimes," she complained to her friends. She had a high, breathless, amused voice which made everything she said a little forced, whether it was sincere or not.

There was one good thing: June went places with girl friends of hers, girls who were just as plain and steady as she, and so when Connie wanted to do that her mother had no objections. The father of Connie's best girl friend drove the girls the three miles to town and left them off at a shopping plaza, so that they could walk through the stores or go to a movie, and when he came to pick them up again at eleven he never bothered to ask what they had done.

They must have been familiar sights, walking around that shopping plaza in their shorts and flat ballerina slippers that always scuffed the sidewalk, with charm bracelets jingling on their thin wrists; they would lean together to whisper and laugh secretly if someone passed by who amused or interested them. Connie had long dark blond hair that drew anyone's eye to it, and she wore part of it pulled up on her head and puffed out and the rest of it she let fall down her back. She wore a pullover jersey blouse that looked one way when she was at home and another way when she was away from home. Everything about her had two sides to it, one for home and one for anywhere that was not home: her walk that could be childlike and bobbing, or languid enough to make anyone think she was hearing music in her head, her mouth which was pale and smirking most of the time, but bright and pink on these evenings out, her laugh which was cynical and drawling at home—"Ha, ha, very funny"—but high-pitched and nervous anywhere else, like the jingling of the charms on her bracelet.

Sometimes they did go shopping or to a movie, but sometimes they went across the highway, ducking fast across the busy road, to a drive-in restaurant where older kids hung out. The restaurant was shaped like a big bottle, though squatter than a real bottle, and on its cap was a revolving figure of a grinning boy who held a hamburger aloft. One night in midsummer they ran across, breathless with daring, and right away someone leaned out a car window and invited them over, but it was just a boy from high school they didn't like. It made them feel good to be able to ignore him. They went up through the maze of parked and cruising cars to the bright-lit, fly-infested restaurant, their faces pleased and expectant as if they were entering a sacred building that loomed out of the night to give them what haven and what blessing they yearned for. They sat at the counter and crossed their legs at the ankles, their thin shoulders rigid with excitement and listened to the music that made everything so good: the music was always in the background like music at a church service, it was something to depend upon.

A boy named Eddie came in to talk with them. He sat backwards on his stool, turning himself jerkily around in semi-circles and then stopping and turning again, and after a while he asked Connie if she would like something to eat. She said she did and so she tapped her friend's arm on her way out—her friend pulled her face up into a brave droll look—and Connie said she would meet her at eleven, across the way. "I just hate to leave her like that," Connie said earnestly, but the boy said that she wouldn't be alone for long. So they went out to his car and on the way Connie couldn't help but let her eyes wander over the windshields and faces all around her, her face gleaming with the joy that had nothing to do with Eddie or even this place; it might have been the music. She drew her shoulders up and sucked in her breath with the pure pleasure of being alive, and just at that moment she happened to glance at a face just a few feet from hers. It was a boy with shaggy black hair, in a convertible jalopy painted gold. He stared at her and then his lips widened into a grin. Connie slit her eyes at him and turned away, but she couldn't help glancing back and there he was still watching her. He wagged a finger and laughed and said, "Gonna get you, baby," and Connie turned away again without Eddie noticing anything.

She spent three hours with him, at the restaurant where they ate hamburgers and drank Cokes in wax cups that were always sweating, and then down an alley a mile or so away, and when he left her off at five to eleven only the movie house was still open at the plaza. Her girl friend was there, talking with a boy. When Connie came up the two girls smiled at each other and Connie said, "How was the movie?" and the girl said, "*You* should know." They rode off with the girl's father, sleepy and pleased, and Connie couldn't help but look at the darkened shopping plaza with its big empty parking lot and its signs that were faded and ghostly now, and over at the drive-in restaurant where cars were still circling tirelessly. She couldn't hear the music at this distance.

Next morning June asked her how the movie was and Connie said, "So-so."

She and that girl and occasionally another girl went out several times a week that way, and the rest of the time Connie spent around the house—it was summer vacation—getting in her mother's way and thinking, dreaming, about the boys she met. But all the boys fell back and dissolved into a single face that was not even a face, but an idea, a feeling, mixed up with the urgent insistent pounding of the music and the humid night air of July. Connie's mother kept dragging her back to the daylight by finding things for her to do or saying suddenly, "What's this about the Pettinger girl?"

And Connie would say nervously, "Oh, her. That dope." She always drew thick clear lines between herself and such girls, and her mother was simple and kindly enough to believe her. Her mother was so simple, Connie thought, that it was maybe cruel to fool her so much. Her mother went scuffling around the house in old bedroom slippers and complained over the telephone to one sister about the other, then the other called up and the two of them complained about the third one. If June's name was mentioned her mother's tone was approving, and if Connie's name was mentioned it was disapproving. This did not really mean she disliked Connie and actually Connie thought that her mother preferred her to June because she was prettier, but the two of them kept up a pretense of exasperation, a sense that they were tugging and struggling over something of little value to either of them. Sometimes, over coffee, they were almost friends, but something would come up—some vexation that was like a fly buzzing suddenly around their heads—and their faces went hard with contempt.

One Sunday Connie got up at eleven—none of them bothered with church—and washed her hair so that it could dry all day long, in the sun. Her parents and sister were going to a barbecue at an aunt's house and Connie said no, she wasn't interested, rolling her eyes, to let mother know just what she thought of it. "Stay home alone then," her mother said sharply. Connie sat out back in a lawn chair and watched them drive away, her father quiet and bald, hunched around so that he could back the car out, her mother with a look that was still angry and not at all softened through the windshield, and in the back seat poor old June all dressed up as if she didn't know what a barbecue was, with all the running yelling kids and the flies. Connie sat with her eyes closed in the sun, dreaming and dazed with the warmth about her as if this were a kind of love, the caresses of love, and her mind slipped over onto thoughts of the boy she had been with the night before and how nice he had been, how sweet it always was, not the way someone like June would suppose but sweet, gentle, the way it was in movies and promised in songs; and when she opened her eyes she hardly knew where she was, the back yard ran off into weeds and a fenceline of trees and behind it the sky was perfectly blue and still. The asbestos "ranch house" that was now three years old startled her—it looked small. She shook her head as if to get awake.

It was too hot. She went inside the house and turned on the radio to drown out the quiet. She sat on the edge of her bed, barefoot, and listened for an hour and a half to a program called XYZ Sunday Jamboree, record after record of hard, fast, shrieking songs she sang along with, interspersed by exclamations from "Bobby King": "An' look here you girls at Napoleon's—Son and Charley want you to pay real close attention to this song coming up!"

And Connie paid close attention herself, bathed in a glow of slow-pulsed joy that seemed to rise mysteriously out of the music itself and lay languidly about the airless little room, breathed in and breathed out with each gentle rise and fall of her chest.

After a while she heard a car coming up the drive. She sat up at once, startled, because it couldn't be her father so soon. The gravel kept crunching all the way in from the road—the driveway was long—and Connie ran to the window. It was a car she didn't know. It was an open jalopy, painted a bright gold that caught the sun opaquely. Her heart began to pound and her fingers snatched at her hair, checking it, and she whispered "Christ. Christ," wondering how bad she looked. The car came to a stop at the side door and the horn sounded four short taps as if this were a signal Connie knew.

She went into the kitchen and approached the door slowly, then hung out the screen door, her bare toes curling down off the step. There were two boys in the car and now she recognized the driver: he had shaggy, shabby black hair that looked crazy as a wig and he was grinning at her.

"I ain't late, am I?" he said.

"Who the hell do you think you are?" Connie said.

"Toldja I'd be out, didn't I?"

"I don't even know who you are."

She spoke sullenly, careful to show no interest or pleasure, and he spoke in a fast bright monotone. Connie looked past him to the other boy, taking her time. He had fair brown hair, with a lock that fell onto his forehead. His sideburns gave him a fierce, embarrassed look, but so far he hadn't even bothered to glance at her. Both boys wore sunglasses. The driver's glasses were metallic and mirrored everything in miniature.

"You wanta come for a ride?" he said.

Connie smirked and let her hair fall loose over one shoulder.

"Don'tcha like my car? New paint job," he said. "Hey."

"What?"

"You're cute."

She pretended to fidget, chasing flies away from the door.

"Don'tcha believe me, or what?" he said.

"Look, I don't even know who you are," Connie said in disgust.

"Hey, Ellie's got a radio, see. Mine's broke down." He lifted his friend's arm and showed her the little transistor the boy was holding, and now Connie began to hear the music. It was the same program that was playing inside the house.

"Bobby King?" she said.

"I listen to him all the time. I think he's great."

"He's kind of great," Connie said reluctantly.

"Listen, that guy's *great*. He knows where the action is."

Connie blushed a little, because the glasses made it impossible for her to see just what this boy was looking at. She couldn't decide if she liked him or if he was just a jerk, and so she dawdled in the doorway and wouldn't come down or go back inside. She said, "What's all that stuff painted on your car?"

"Can'tcha read it?" He opened the door very carefully, as if he was afraid it might fall off. He slid out just as carefully, planting his feet firmly on the ground, the tiny metallic world in his glasses slowing down like gelatine hardening and in the midst of it Connie's bright green blouse. "This here is my name, to begin with," he said. ARNOLD FRIEND was written in tar-like black letters on the side, with a drawing of a round grinning face that reminded Connie of a pumpkin, except it wore sunglasses. "I wanta introduce myself, I'm Arnold Friend and that's my real name and I'm gonna be your friend, honey, and inside the car's Ellie Oscar, he's kinda shy." Ellie brought his transistor up to his shoulder and balanced it there. "Now these numbers are a secret code, honey," Arnold Friend explained. He read off the numbers 33, 19, 17 and raised his eyebrows at her to see what she thought of that, but she didn't think much of it. The left rear fender had been smashed and around it was written, on the gleaming gold background: DONE BY CRAZY WOMAN DRIVER. Connie had to laugh at that. Arnold Friend was pleased at her laughter and looked up at her. "Around the other side's a lot more—you wanta come and see them?"

"No."

"Why not?"

"Why should I?"

"Don'tcha wanta see what's on the car? Don'tcha wanta go for a ride?"

"I don't know."

"Why not?"

"I got things to do."

"Like what?"

"Things."

He laughed as if she had said something funny. He slapped his thighs. He was standing in a strange way, leaning back against the car as if he were balancing himself. He wasn't tall, only an inch or so taller than she would be if she came down to him. Connie liked the way he was dressed, which was the way all of them dressed: tight faded jeans stuffed into black, scuffed boots, a belt that pulled his waist in and showed how lean he was, and a white pull-over shirt that was a little soiled and showed the hard small muscles of his arms and shoulders. He looked as if he probably did hard work, lifting and carrying things. Even his neck looked muscular. And his face was a familiar face, somehow: the jaw and chin and cheeks slightly darkened, because he hadn't shaved for a day or two, and the nose long and hawk-like, sniffing as if she were a treat he was going to gobble up and it was all a joke.

"Connie, you ain't telling the truth. This is your day set aside for a ride with me and you know it," he said, still laughing. The way he straightened and recovered from his fit of laughing showed that it had been all fake.

"How do you know what my name is?" she said suspiciously.

"It's Connie."

"Maybe and maybe not."

"I know my Connie," he said, wagging his finger. Now she remembered him even better, back at the restaurant, and her cheeks warmed at the thought of how she sucked in her breath just at the moment she passed him—how she must have looked to him. And he had remembered her. "Ellie and I come out here especially for you," he said. "Ellie can sit in back. How about it?"

"Where?"

"Where what?"

"Where're we going?"

He looked at her. He took off the sunglasses and she saw how pale the skin around his eyes was, like holes that were not in shadow but instead in light. His eyes were like chips of broken glass that catch the light in an amiable way. He smiled. It was as if the idea of going for a ride somewhere, to some place, was a new idea to him.

"Just for a ride, Connie sweetheart."

"I never said my name was Connie," she said.

"But I know what it is. I know your name and all about you, lots of things," Arnold Friend said. He had not moved yet but stood still leaning back against the side of his jalopy. "I took a special interest in you, such a pretty girl, and found out all about you like I know your parents and sister are gone somewheres and I know where and how long they're going to be gone, and I know who you were with last night, and your best friend's name is Betty. Right?"

He spoke in a simple lilting voice, exactly as if he were reciting the words to a song. His smile assured her that everything was fine. In the car Ellie turned up the volume on his radio and did not bother to look around at them.

"Ellie can sit in the back seat," Arnold Friend said. He indicated his friend with a casual jerk of his chin, as if Ellie did not count and she could not bother with him.

"How'd you find out all that stuff?" Connie said.

"Listen: Betty Schultz and Tony Fitch and Jimmy Pettinger and Nancy Pettinger," he said, in a chant. "Raymond Stanley and Bob Hutter—"

"Do you know all those kids?"

"I know everybody."

"Look, you're kidding. You're not from around here."

"Sure."

"But—how come we never saw you before?"

"Sure you saw me before," he said. He looked down at his boots, as if he were a little offended. "You just don't remember."

"I guess I'd remember you," Connie said.

"Yeah?" He looked up at this, beaming. He was pleased. He began to mark time with the music from Ellie's radio, tapping his fists lightly together. Connie looked away from his smile to the car, which was painted so bright it almost hurt her eyes to look at it. She looked at that name, ARNOLD FRIEND. And up at the front fender was an expression that was familiar—MAN THE FLYING SAUCERS. It was an expression kids had used the year before, but didn't use this year. She looked at it for a while as if the words meant something to her that she did not yet know.

"What're you thinking about? Huh?" Arnold Friend demanded. "Not worried about your hair blowing around in the car, are you?"

"No."

"Think I maybe can't drive good?"

"How do I know?"

"You're a hard girl to handle. How come?" he said. "Don't you know I'm your friend? Didn't you see me put my sign in the air when you walked by?"

"What sign?"

"My sign." And he drew an X in the air, leaning out toward her. They were maybe ten feet apart. After his hand fell back to his side the X was still in the air, almost visible. Connie let the screen door close and stood perfectly still inside it, listening to the music from her radio and the boy's blend together. She stared at Arnold Friend. He stood there so stiffly relaxed, pretending to be relaxed, with one hand idly on the door handle as if he were keeping himself up that way and had no intention of ever moving again. She recognized most things about him, the tight jeans that showed his thighs and buttocks and the greasy leather boots and the tight shirt, and even that slippery friendly smile of his, that sleepy dreamy smile that all the boys used to get across ideas they didn't want to put into words. She recognized all this and also the singsong way he talked, slightly mocking, kidding, but serious and a little melancholy, and she recognized the way he tapped one fist against the other in homage to the perpetual music behind him. But all these things did not come together.

She said suddenly, "Hey, how old are you?"

His smile faded. She could see then that he wasn't a kid, he was much older—thirty, maybe more. At this knowledge her heart began to pound faster.

"That's a crazy thing to ask. Can'tcha see I'm your own age?"

"Like hell you are."

"Or maybe a coupla years older, I'm eighteen."

"Eighteen?" she said doubtfully.

He grinned to reassure her and lines appeared at the corners of his mouth. His teeth were big and white. He grinned so broadly his eyes became slits and she saw how thick the lashes were, thick and black as if painted with a black tar-like material. Then he seemed to become embarrassed, abruptly, and looked over his shoulder at Ellie. "*Him*, he's crazy," he said. "Ain't he a riot, he's a nut, a real character." Ellie was still listening to the music. His sunglasses told nothing about what he was thinking. He wore a bright orange shirt unbuttoned halfway to show his chest, which was a pale, bluish chest and not muscular like Arnold Friend's. His shirt collar was turned up all around and the very tips of the collar pointed out past his chin as if they were protecting him. He was pressing the transistor radio up against his ear and sat there in a kind of daze, right in the sun.

"He's kinda strange," Connie said.

"Hey, she says you're kinda strange! Kinda strange!" Arnold Friend cried. He pounded on the car to get Ellie's attention. Ellie turned for the first time and Connie saw with shock that he wasn't a kid either—he had a fair, hairless face, cheeks reddened slightly as if the veins grew too close to the surface of his skin, the face of a forty-year-old baby. Connie felt a wave of dizziness rise in her at this sight and she stared at him as if waiting for something to change the shock of the moment, make it all right again. Ellie's lips kept shaping words, mumbling along with the words blasting his ear.

"Maybe you two better go away," Connie said faintly.

"What? How come?" Arnold Friend cried. "We come out here to take you for a ride. It's Sunday." He had the voice of the man on the radio now. It was the same voice, Connie thought. "Don'tcha know it's Sunday all day and honey, no matter who you were with last night today you're with Arnold Friend and don't you forget it!—Maybe you better step out here," he said, and this last was in a different voice. It was a little flatter, as if the heat was finally getting to him.

"No. I got things to do."

"Hey."

"You two better leave."

"We ain't leaving until you come with us."

"Like hell I am—"

"Connie, don't fool around with me. I mean—I mean, don't fool *around*," he said, shaking his head. He laughed incredulously. He placed his sunglasses on top of his head, carefully, as if he were indeed wearing a wig, and brought the stems down behind his ears. Connie stared at him, another wave of dizziness and fear rising in her so that for a moment he wasn't even in focus but was just a blur, standing there against his gold car, and she had the idea that he had driven up the driveway all right but had come from nowhere before that and belonged nowhere and that everything about him and even the music that was so familiar to her was only half real.

"If my father comes and sees you—"

"He ain't coming. He's at a barbecue."

"How do you know that?"

"Aunt Tillie's. Right now they're—uh—they're drinking. Sitting around," he said vaguely, squinting as if he were staring all the way to town and over to Aunt Tillie's back yard. Then the vision seemed to clear and he nodded energetically. "Yeah. Sitting around. There's your sister in a blue dress, huh? And high heels, the poor sad bitch—nothing like you, sweetheart! And your mother's helping some fat woman with the corn, they're cleaning the corn—husking the corn—"

"What fat woman?" Connie cried.

"How do I know what fat woman. I don't know every goddamn fat woman in the world!" Arnold Friend laughed.

"Oh, that's Mrs. Hornby. . . . Who invited her?" Connie said. She felt a little light-headed. Her breath was coming quickly.

"She's too fat. I don't like them fat. I like them the way you are, honey," he said, smiling sleepily at her. They stared at each other for a while, through the screen door. He said softly, "Now what you're going to do is this: you're going to come out that door. You're going to sit up front with me and Ellie's going to sit in the back, the hell with Ellie, right? This isn't Ellie's date. You're my date. I'm your lover, honey."

"What? You're crazy—"

"Yes, I'm your lover. You don't know what that is but you will," he said. "I know that too. I know all about you. But look: it's real nice and you couldn't ask for nobody better than me, or more polite. I always keep my word. I'll tell you how it is, I'm always nice at first, the first time. I'll hold you so tight you won't think you have to try to get away or pretend anything because you'll know you can't. And I'll come inside you where it's all secret and you'll give in to me and you'll love me—"

"Shut up! You're crazy!" Connie said. She backed away from the door. She put her hands against her ears as if she'd heard something terrible, something not meant for her. "People don't talk like that, you're crazy," she muttered. Her heart was almost too big now for her chest and its pumping made sweat break out all over her. She looked out to see Arnold Friend pause and then take a step toward the porch lurching. He almost fell. But, like a clever drunken man, he managed to catch his balance. He wobbled in his high boots and grabbed hold of one of the porch posts.

"Honey?" he said. "You still listening?"

"Get the hell out of here!"

"Be nice, honey. Listen."

"I'm going to call the police—"

He wobbled again and out of the side of his mouth came a fast spat curse, an aside not meant for her to hear. But even this "Christ!" sounded forced. Then he began to smile again. She watched this smile come, awkward as if he were smiling from inside a mask. His whole face was a mask, she thought wildly, tanned down onto his throat but then running out as if he had plastered make-up on his face but had forgotten about his throat.

"Honey—? Listen, here's how it is. I always tell the truth and I promise you this: I ain't coming in that house after you."

"You better not! I'm going to call the police if you—if you don't—"

"Honey," he said, talking right through her voice, "honey, I'm not coming in there but you are coming out here. You know why?"

She was panting. The kitchen looked like a place she had never seen before, some room she had run inside but which wasn't good enough, wasn't going to help her. The kitchen window had never had a curtain, after three years, and there were dishes in the sink for her to do—probably—and if you ran your hand across the table you'd probably feel something sticky there.

"You listening, honey? Hey?"

"—going to call the police—"

"Soon as you touch the phone I don't need to keep my promise and can come inside. You won't want that."

She rushed forward and tried to lock the door. Her fingers were shaking. "But why lock it," Arnold Friend said gently, talking right into her face. "It's just a screen door. It's just nothing." One of his boots was at a strange angle, as if his foot wasn't in it. It pointed out to the left, bent at the ankle. "I mean, anybody can break through a screen door and glass and wood and iron or anything else if he needs to, anybody at all and specially Arnold Friend. If the place got lit up with a fire, honey, you'd come runnin' out into my arms, right into my arms an' safe at home—like you knew I was your lover and'd stopped fooling around, I don't mind a nice shy girl but I don't like no fooling around." Part of those words were spoken with a slight rhythmic lilt, and Connie somehow recognized them—the echo of a song from last year, about a girl rushing into her boy friend's arms and coming home again—

Connie stood barefoot on the linoleum floor, staring at him. "What do you want?" she whispered.

"I want you," he said.

"What?"

"Seen you that night and thought, that's the one, yes sir. I never needed to look any more."

"But my father's coming back. He's coming to get me. I had to wash my hair first—" She spoke in a dry, rapid voice, hardly raising it for him to hear.

"No, your daddy is not coming and yes, you had to wash your hair and you washed it for me. It's nice and shining and all for me. I thank you, sweetheart," he said, with a mock bow, but again he almost lost his balance. He had to bend and adjust his boots. Evidently his feet did not go all the way down; the boots must have been stuffed with something so that he would seem taller. Connie stared out at him and behind him at Ellie in the car, who seemed to be looking off toward Connie's right, into nothing. Then Ellie said, pulling the words out of the air one after another as if he were just discovering them, "You want me to pull out the phone?"

"Shut your mouth and keep it shut," Arnold Friend said, his face red from bending over or maybe from embarrassment because Connie had seen his boots. "This ain't none of your business."

"What—what are you doing? What do you want?" Connie said. "If I call the police they'll get you, they'll arrest you—"

"Promise was not to come in unless you touch that phone, and I'll keep that promise," he said. He resumed his erect position and tried to force his shoulders back. He sounded like a hero in a movie, declaring something important. He spoke too loudly and it was as if he were speaking to someone behind Connie. "I ain't made plans for coming in that house where I don't belong but just for you to come out to me, the way you should. Don't you know who I am?"

"You're crazy," she whispered. She backed away from the door but did not want to go into another part of the house, as if this would give him permission to come through the door. "What do you . . . You're crazy, you. . . ."

"Huh? What're you saying, honey?"

Her eyes darted everywhere in the kitchen. She could not remember what it was, this room.

"This is how it is, honey: you come out and we'll drive away, have a nice ride. But if you don't come out we're gonna wait till your people come home and then they're all going to get it."

"You want that telephone pulled out?" Ellie said. He held the radio away from his ear and grimaced, as if without the radio the air was too much for him.

"I toldja shut up, Ellie," Arnold Friend said, "you're deaf, get a hearing aid, right? Fix yourself up. This little girl's no trouble and's gonna be nice to me, so Ellie keep to yourself, this ain't your date—right? Don't hem in on me, don't hog, don't crush, don't bird dog, don't trail me," he said in a rapid, meaningless voice, as if he were running through all the expressions he'd learned but was no longer sure which one of them was in style, then rushing on to new ones, making them up with his eyes closed. "Don't crawl under my fence, don't squeeze in my chipmunk hole, don't sniff my glue, suck my popsicle, keep your own greasy fingers on yourself!" He shaded his eyes and peered in at Connie, who was backed against the kitchen table. "Don't mind him, honey, he's just a creep. He's a dope. Right? I'm the boy for you and like I said, you come out here nice like a lady and give me your hand, and nobody else gets hurt, I mean, your nice old bald-headed daddy and your mummy and your sister in her high heels. Because listen: why bring them in this?"

"Leave me alone," Connie whispered.

"Hey, you know that old woman down the road, the one with the chickens and stuff—you know her?"

"She's dead!"

"Dead? What? You know her?" Arnold Friend said.

"She's dead—"

"Don't you like her?"

"She's dead—she's—she isn't here any more—"

"But don't you like her, I mean, you got something against her? Some grudge or something?" Then his voice dipped as if he were conscious of rudeness. He touched the sunglasses on top of his head as if to make sure they were still there. "Now you be a good girl."

"What are you going to do?"

"Just two things, or maybe three," Arnold Friend said. "But I promise it won't last long and you'll like me that way you get to like people you're close to. You will. It's all over for you here, so come on out. You don't want your people in any trouble, do you?"

She turned and bumped against a chair or something, hurting her leg, but she ran into the back room and picked up the telephone. Something roared in her ear, a tiny roaring, and she was so sick with fear that she could do nothing but listen to it—the telephone was clammy and very heavy and her fingers groped down to the dial but were too weak to touch it. She began to scream into the phone, into the roaring. She cried out, she cried for her mother, she felt her breath start jerking back and forth in her lungs as if it were something Arnold Friend was stabbing her with again and again with no tenderness. A noisy sorrowful wailing rose all about her and she was locked inside it the way she was locked inside this house.

After a while she could hear again. She was sitting on the floor, with her wet back against the wall.

Arnold Friend was saying from the door, "That's a good girl. Put the phone back."

She kicked the phone away from her.

"No, honey. Pick it up. Put it back right."

She picked it up and put it back. The dial tone stopped.

"That's a good girl. Now you come outside."

She was hollow with what had been fear but what was now just an emptiness. All that screaming had blasted it out of her. She sat, one leg cramped under her, and deep inside her brain was something like a pinpoint of light that kept going and would not let her relax. She thought, I'm not going to see my mother again. She thought, I'm not going to sleep in my bed again. Her bright green blouse was all wet.

Arnold Friend said, in a gentle-loud voice that was like a stage voice, "The place where you came from ain't there any more, and where you had in mind to go is cancelled out. This place you are now—inside your daddy's house—is nothing but a cardboard box I can knock down any time. You know that and always did know it. You hear me?"

She thought, I have got to think. I have got to know what to do.

"We'll go out to a nice field, out in the country here where it smells so nice and it's sunny," Arnold Friend said. "I'll have my arms tight around you so you won't need to try to get away and I'll show you what love is like, what it does. The hell with this house! It looks solid all right," he said. He ran a fingernail down the screen and the noise did not make Connie shiver, as it would have the day before. "Now put your hand on your heart, honey. Feel that? That feels solid too but we know better. Be nice to me, be sweet like you can because what else is there for a girl like you but to be sweet and pretty and give in?—and get away before her people get back?"

She felt her pounding heart. Her hand seemed to enclose it. She thought for the first time in her life that it was nothing that was hers, that belonged to her, but just a pounding, living thing inside this body that wasn't really hers either.

"You don't want them to get hurt," Arnold Friend went on. "Now get up, honey. Get up all by yourself."

She stood.

"Now turn this way. That's right. Come over to me—Ellie, put that away, didn't I tell you? You dope. You miserable creepy dope," Arnold Friend said. His words were not angry but only part of an incantation. The incantation was kindly. "Now come out through the kitchen to me honey and let's see a smile, try it, you're a brave sweet little girl and now they're eating corn and hotdogs cooked to bursting over an outdoor fire, and they don't know one thing about you and never did and honey you're better than them because not a one of them would have done this for you."

Connie felt the linoleum under her feet; it was cool. She brushed her hair back out of her eyes. Arnold Friend let go of the post tentatively and opened his arms for her, his elbows pointing in toward each other and his wrists limp, to show that this was an embarrassed embrace and a little mocking, he didn't want to make her self-conscious.

She put out her hand against the screen. She watched herself push the door slowly open as if she were back safe somewhere in the other doorway, watching this body and this head of long hair moving out into the sunlight where Arnold Friend waited.

"My sweet little blue-eyed girl," he said in a half-sung sigh that had nothing to do with her brown eyes but was taken up just the same by the vast sunlit reaches of the land behind him and on all sides of him—so much land that Connie had never seen before and did not recognize except to know that she was going to it.

[1966]

MARGARET ATWOOD   [b. 1939]

Happy Endings

John and Mary meet.
   What happens next?
   If you want a happy ending, try A.

A

John and Mary fall in love and get married. They both have worthwhile and remunerative jobs which they find stimulating and challenging. They buy a charming house. Real estate values go up. Eventually, when they can afford live-in help, they have two children, to whom they are devoted. The children turn out well. John and Mary have a stimulating and challenging sex life and worthwhile friends. They go on fun vacations together. They retire. They both have hobbies which they find stimulating and challenging. Eventually they die. This is the end of the story.

B

Mary falls in love with John but John doesn't fall in love with Mary. He merely uses her body for selfish pleasure and ego gratification of a tepid kind. He comes to her apartment twice a week and she cooks him dinner, you'll notice that he doesn't even consider her worth the price of a dinner out, and after he's eaten the dinner he fucks her and after that he falls asleep, while she does the dishes so he won't think she's untidy, having all those dirty dishes lying around, and puts on fresh lipstick so she'll look good when he wakes up, but when he wakes up he doesn't even notice, he puts on his socks and his shorts and his pants and his shirt and his tie and his shoes, the reverse order from the one in which he took them off. He doesn't take off Mary's clothes, she takes them off herself, she acts as if she's dying for it every time, not because she likes sex exactly, she doesn't, but she wants John to think she does because if they do it often enough surely he'll get used to her, he'll come to depend on her and they will get married, but John goes out the door with hardly so much as a goodnight and three days later he turns up at six o'clock and they do the whole thing over again.

Mary gets run down. Crying is bad for your face, everyone knows that and so does Mary but she can't stop. People at work notice. Her friends tell her John is a rat, a pig, a dog, he isn't good enough for her, but she can't believe it. Inside John, she thinks, is another John, who is much nicer. This other John will emerge like a butterfly from a cocoon, a Jack from a box, a pit from a prune, if the first John is only squeezed enough.

One evening John complains about the food. He has never complained about the food before. Mary is hurt.

Her friends tell her they've seen him in a restaurant with another woman, whose name is Madge. It's not even Madge that finally gets to Mary: it's the restaurant. John has never taken Mary to a restaurant. Mary collects all the sleeping pills and aspirins she can find, and takes them and half a bottle of sherry. You can see what kind of a woman she is by the fact that it's not even whiskey. She leaves a note for John. She hopes he'll discover her and get her to the hospital in time and repent and then they can get married, but this fails to happen and she dies.

John marries Madge and everything continues as in A.

C

John, who is an older man, falls in love with Mary, and Mary, who is only twenty-two, feels sorry for him because he's worried about his hair falling out. She sleeps with him even though she's not in love with him. She met him at work. She's in love with someone called James, who is twenty-two also and not yet ready to settle down.

John on the contrary settled down long ago: this is what is bothering him. John has a steady respectable job and is getting ahead in his field, but Mary isn't impressed by him, she's impressed by James, who has a motorcycle and a fabulous record collection. But James is often away on his motorcycle, being free. Freedom isn't the same for girls, so in the meantime Mary spends Thursday evenings with John. Thursdays are the only days John can get away.

John is married to a woman called Madge and they have two children, a charming house which they bought just before the real estate values went up, and hobbies which they find stimulating and challenging, when they have the time. John tells Mary how important she is to him, but of course he can't leave his wife because a commitment is a commitment. He goes on about this more than is necessary and Mary finds it boring, but older men can keep it up longer so on the whole she has a fairly good time.

One day James breezes in on his motorcycle with some top-grade California hybrid and James and Mary get higher than you'd believe possible and they climb into bed. Everything becomes very underwater, but along comes John, who has a key to Mary's apartment. He finds them stoned and entwined. He's hardly in any position to be jealous, considering Madge, but nevertheless he's overcome with despair. Finally he's middle-aged, in two years he'll be bald as an egg, and he can't stand it. He purchases a handgun, saying he needs it for target practice—this is the thin part of the plot, but it can be dealt with later—and shoots the two of them and himself.

Madge, after a suitable period of mourning, marries an understanding man called Fred and everything continues as in A, but under different names.

D

Fred and Madge have no problems. They get along exceptionally well and are good at working out any little difficulties that may arise. But their charming house is by the seashore and one day a giant tidal wave approaches. Real estate values go down. The rest of the story is about what caused the tidal wave and how they escape from it. They do, though thousands drown. Some of the story is about how the thousands drown, but Fred and Madge are virtuous and lucky. Finally on high ground they clasp each other, wet and dripping and grateful, and continue as in A.

E

Yes, but Fred has a bad heart. The rest of the story is about how kind and understanding they both are until Fred dies. Then Madge devotes herself to charity work until the end of A. If you like, it can be "Madge," "cancer," "guilty and confused," and "bird watching."

F

If you think this is all too bourgeois, make John a revolutionary and Mary a counterespionage agent and see how far that gets you. Remember, this is Canada. You'll still end up with A, though in between you may get a lustful brawling saga of passionate involvement, a chronicle of our times, sort of.

You'll have to face it, the endings are the same however you slice it. Don't be deluded by any other endings, they're all fake, either deliberately fake, with malicious intent to deceive, or just motivated by excessive optimism if not by downright sentimentality.

The only authentic ending is the one provided here:

John and Mary die. John and Mary die. John and Mary die.

So much for endings. Beginnings are always more fun. True connoisseurs, however, are known to favor the stretch in between, since it's the hardest to do anything with.

That's about all that can be said for plots, which anyway are just one thing after another, a what and a what and a what.

Now try How and Why.

[1994]

TONI CADE BAMBARA   [1939–1995]

The Lesson

Back in the days when everyone was old and stupid or young and foolish and me and Sugar were the only ones just right, this lady moved on our block with nappy hair and proper speech and no makeup. And quite naturally we laughed at her, laughed the way we did at the junk man who went about his business like he was some big-time president and his sorry-ass horse his secretary. And we kinda hated her too, hated the way we did the winos who cluttered up our parks and pissed on our handball walls and stank up our hallways and stairs so you couldn't halfway play hide-and-seek without a goddamn gas mask. Miss Moore was her name. The only woman on the block with no first name. And she was black as hell, cept for her feet, which were fish-white and spooky. And she was always planning these boring-ass things for us to do, us being my cousin, mostly, who lived on the block cause we all moved North the same time and to the same apartment then spread out gradual to breathe. And our parents would yank our heads into some kinda shape and crisp up our clothes so we'd be presentable for travel with Miss Moore, who always looked like she was going to church, though she never did. Which is just one of the things the grownups talked about when they talked behind her back like a dog. But when she came calling with some sachet she'd sewed up or some gingerbread she'd made or some book, why then they'd all be too embarrassed to turn her down and we'd get handed over all spruced up. She'd been to college and said it was only right that she should take responsibility for the young ones' education, and she not even related by marriage or blood. So they'd go for it. Specially Aunt Gretchen. She was the main gofer in the family. You got some ole dumb shit foolishness you want somebody to go for, you send for Aunt Gretchen. She been screwed into the go-along for so long, it's a blood-deep natural thing with her. Which is how she got saddled with me and Sugar and Junior in the first place while our mothers were in a la-de-da apartment up the block having a good ole time.

So this one day, Miss Moore rounds us all up at the mailbox and it's puredee hot and she's knockin herself out about arithmetic. And school suppose to let up in summer I heard, but she don't never let up. And the starch in my pinafore scratching the shit outta me and I'm really hating this nappy-head bitch and her goddamn college degree. I'd much rather go to the pool or to the show where it's cool. So me and Sugar leaning on the mailbox being surly, which is a Miss Moore word. And Flyboy checking out what everybody brought for lunch. And Fat Butt already wasting his peanut-butter-and-jelly sandwich like the pig he is. And Junebug punchin on Q.T.'s arm for potato chips. And Rosie Giraffe shifting from one hip to the other waiting for somebody to step on her foot or ask her if she from Georgia so she can kick ass, preferably Mercedes'. And Miss Moore asking us do we know what money is, like we a bunch of retards. I mean real money, she say, like it's only poker chips or monopoly papers we lay on the grocer. So right away I'm tired of this and say so. And would much rather snatch Sugar and go to the Sunset and terrorize the West Indian kids and take their hair ribbons and their money too. And Miss Moore files that remark away for next week's lesson on brotherhood, I can tell. And finally I say we oughta get to the subway cause it's cooler and besides we might meet some cute boys. Sugar done swiped her mama's lipstick, so we ready.

So we heading down the street and she's boring us silly about what things cost and what our parents make and how much goes for rent and how money ain't divided up right in this country. And then she gets to the part about we all poor and live in the slums, which I don't feature. And I'm ready to speak on that, but she steps out in the street and hails two cabs just like that. Then she hustles half the crew in with her and hands me a five-dollar bill and tells me to calculate 10 percent tip for the driver. And we're off. Me and Sugar and Junebug and Flyboy hangin out the window and hollering to everybody, putting lipstick on each other cause Flyboy a faggot anyway, and making farts with our sweaty armpits. But I'm mostly trying to figure how to spend this money. But they all fascinated with the meter ticking and Junebug starts laying bets as to how much it'll read when Flyboy can't hold his breath no more. Then Sugar lays bets as to how much it'll be when we get there. So I'm stuck. Don't nobody want to go for my plan, which is to jump out at the next light and run off to the first bar-b-que we can find. Then the driver tells us to get the hell out cause we there already. And the meter reads eighty-five cents. And I'm stalling to figure out the tip and Sugar say give him a dime. And I decide he don't need it bad as I do, so later for him. But then he tries to take off with Junebug foot still in the door so we talk about his mama something ferocious. Then we check out that we on Fifth Avenue and everybody dressed up in stockings. One lady in a fur coat, hot as it is. White folks crazy.

"This is the place," Miss Moore say, presenting it to us in the voice she uses at the museum. "Let's look in the windows before we go in."

"Can we steal?" Sugar asks very serious like she's getting the ground rules squared away before she plays. "I beg your pardon," say Miss

Moore, and we fall out. So she leads us around the windows of the toy store and me and Sugar screamin, "This is mine, that's mine, I gotta have that, that was made for me, I was born for that," till Big Butt drowns us out.

"Hey, I'm going to buy that there."

"That there? You don't even know what it is, stupid."

"I do so," he say punchin on Rosie Giraffe. "It's a microscope."

"Whatcha gonna do with a microscope, fool?"

"Look at things."

"Like what, Ronald?" ask Miss Moore. And Big Butt ain't got the first notion. So here go Miss Moore gabbing about the thousands of bacteria in a drop of water and the somethinorother in a speck of blood and the million and one living things in the air around us is invisible to the naked eye. And what she say that for? Junebug go to town on that "naked" and we rolling. Then Miss Moore ask what it cost. So we all jam into the window smudgin it up and the price tag say $300. So then she ask how long'd take for Big Butt and Junebug to save up their allowances. "Too long," I say. "Yeh," adds Sugar, "outgrown it by that time." And Miss Moore say no, you never outgrow learning instruments. "Why, even medical students and interns and," blah, blah, blah. And we ready to choke Big Butt for bringing it up in the first damn place.

"This here costs four hundred eighty dollars," say Rosie Giraffe. So we pile up all over her to see what she pointin out. My eyes tell me it's a chunk of glass cracked with something heavy, and different-color inks dripped into the splits, then the whole thing put into a oven or something. But for $480 it don't make sense.

"That's a paperweight made of semi-precious stones fused together under tremendous pressure," she explains slowly, with her hands doing the mining and all the factory work.

"So what's a paperweight?" ask Rosie Giraffe.

"To weigh paper with, dumbbell," say Flyboy, the wise man from the East.

"Not exactly," say Miss Moore, which is what she say when you warm or way off too. "It's to weigh paper down so it won't scatter and make your desk untidy." So right away me and Sugar curtsy to each other and then to Mercedes who is more the tidy type.

"We don't keep paper on top of the desk in my class," say Junebug, figuring Miss Moore crazy or lyin one.

"At home, then," she say. "Don't you have a calendar and a pencil case and a blotter and a letter-opener on your desk at home where you do your homework?" And she know damn well what our homes look like cause she nosys around in them every chance she gets.

"I don't even have a desk," say Junebug. "Do we?"

"No. And I don't get no homework neither," say Big Butt.

"And I don't even have a home," say Flyboy like he do at school to keep the white folks off his back and sorry for him. Send this poor kid to camp posters, is his specialty.

"I do," says Mercedes. "I have a box of stationery on my desk and a picture of my cat. My godmother bought the stationery and the desk. There's a big rose on each sheet and the envelopes smell like roses."

"Who wants to know about your smelly-ass stationery," say Rosie Giraffe fore I can get my two cents in.

"It's important to have a work area all your own so that . . ."

"Will you look at this sailboat, please," say Flyboy, cutting her off and pointin to the thing like it was his. So once again we tumble all over each other to gaze at this magnificent thing in the toy store which is just big enough to maybe sail two kittens across the pond if you strap them to the posts tight. We all start reciting the price tag like we in assembly. "Handcrafted sailboat of fiberglass at one thousand one hundred ninety-five dollars."

"Unbelievable," I hear myself say and am really stunned. I read it again for myself just in case the group recitation put me in a trance. Same thing. For some reason this pisses me off. We look at Miss Moore and she lookin at us, waiting for I dunno what.

"Who'd pay all that when you can buy a sailboat set for a quarter at Pop's, a tube of glue for a dime, and a ball of string for eight cents? It must have a motor and a whole lot else besides," I say. "My sailboat cost me about fifty cents."

"But will it take water?" say Mercedes with her smart ass.

"Took mine to Alley Pond Park once," say Flyboy. "String broke. Lost it. Pity."

"Sailed mine in Central Park and it keeled over and sank. Had to ask my father for another dollar."

"And you got the strap," laugh Big Butt. "The jerk didn't even have a string on it. My old man wailed on his behind."

Little Q.T. was staring hard at the sailboat and you could see he wanted it bad. But he too little and somebody'd just take it from him. So what the hell. "This boat for kids, Miss Moore?"

"Parents silly to buy something like that just to get all broke up," say Rosie Giraffe.

"That much money it should last forever," I figure.

"My father'd buy it for me if I wanted it."

"Your father, my ass," say Rosie Giraffe getting a chance to finally push Mercedes.

"Must be rich people shop here," say Q.T.

"You are a very bright boy," say Flyboy. "What was your first clue?" And he rap him on the head with the back of his knuckles, since Q.T. the only one he could get away with. Though Q.T. liable to come up behind you years later and get his licks in when you half expect it.

"What I want to know is," I says to Miss Moore though I never talk to her, I wouldn't give the bitch that satisfaction, "is how much a real boat costs? I figure a thousand'd get you a yacht any day."

"Why don't you check that out," she says, "and report back to the group?" Which really pains my ass. If you gonna mess up a perfectly good swim day least you could do is have some answers. "Let's go in," she say like she got something up her sleeve. Only she don't lead the way. So me and Sugar turn the corner to where the entrance is, but when we get there I kinda hang back. Not that I'm scared, what's there to be afraid of, just a toy store. But I feel funny, shame. But what I got to be shamed about? Got as much right to go in as anybody. But somehow I can't seem to get hold of the door, so I step away from Sugar to lead. But she hangs back too. And I look at her and she looks at me and this is ridiculous. I mean, damn, I have never been shy about doing nothing or going nowhere. But then Mercedes steps up and then Rosie Giraffe and Big Butt crowd in behind and shove, and next thing we all stuffed into the doorway with only Mercedes squeezing past us, smoothing out her jumper and walking right down the aisle. Then the rest of us tumble in like a glued-together jigsaw done all wrong. And people lookin at us. And it's like the time me and Sugar crashed into the Catholic church on a dare. But once we got in there and everything so hushed and holy and the candles and the bowin and the handkerchiefs on all the drooping heads, I just couldn't go through with the plan. Which was for me to run up to the altar and do a tap dance while Sugar played the nose flute and messed around in the holy water. And Sugar kept given me the elbow. Then later teased me so bad I tied her up in the shower and turned it on and locked her in. And she'd be there till this day if Aunt Gretchen hadn't finally figured I was lying about the boarder takin a shower.

Same thing in the store. We all walkin on tiptoe and hardly touchin the games and puzzles and things. And I watched Miss Moore who is steady watchin us like she waitin for a sign. Like Mama Drewery watches the sky and sniffs the air and takes note of just how much slant is in the bird formation. Then me and Sugar bump smack into each other, so busy gazing at the toys, 'specially the sailboat. But we don't laugh and go into our fat-lady bump-stomach routine. We just stare at that price tag. Then Sugar run a finger over the whole boat. And I'm jealous and want to hit her. Maybe not her, but I sure want to punch somebody in the mouth.

"Watcha bring us here for, Miss Moore?"

"You sound angry, Sylvia. Are you mad about something?" Givin me one of them grins like she tellin a grown-up joke that never turns out to be funny. And she's lookin very closely at me like maybe she plannin to do my portrait from memory. I'm mad, but I won't give her that satisfaction. So I slouch around the store being very bored and say, "Let's go."

Me and Sugar at the back of the train watchin the tracks whizzin by large then small then getting gobbled up in the dark. I'm thinkin about this tricky toy I saw in the store. A clown that somersaults on a bar then does chin-ups just cause you yank lightly at his leg. Cost $35. I could see me askin my mother for a $35 birthday clown. "You wanna who that costs what?" she'd say, cocking her head to the side to get a better view of the hole in my head. Thirty-five dollars could buy new bunk beds for Junior and Gretchen's boy. Thirty-five dollars and the whole household could go visit Grand-daddy Nelson in the country. Thirty-five dollars would pay for the rent and the piano bill too. Who are these people that spend that much for performing clowns and $1000 for toy sailboats? What kinda work they do and how they live and how come we ain't in on it? Where we are is who we are, Miss Moore always pointin out. But it don't necessarily have to be that way, she always adds then waits for somebody to say that poor people have to wake up and demand their share of the pie and don't none of us know what kind of pie she talking about in the first damn place. But she ain't so smart cause I still got her four dollars from the taxi and she sure ain't gettin it. Messin up my day with this shit. Sugar nudges me in my pocket and winks.

Miss Moore lines us up in front of the mailbox where we started from, seem like years ago, and I got a headache for thinkin so hard. And we lean all over each other so we can hold up under the draggy-ass lecture she always finishes us off with at the end before we thank her for borin us to tears. But she just looks at us like she readin tea leaves. Finally she say, "Well, what did you think of F.A.O. Schwarz?"

Rosie Giraffe mumbles, "White folks crazy."

"I'd like to go there again when I get my birthday money," says Mercedes, and we shove her out the pack so she has to lean on the mailbox by herself.

"I'd like a shower. Tiring day," say Flyboy.

Then Sugar surprises me by sayin, "You know, Miss Moore, I don't think all of us here put together eat in a year what that sailboat costs." And Miss Moore lights up like somebody goosed her. "And?" she say, urging Sugar on. Only I'm standin on her foot so she don't continue.

"Imagine for a minute what kind of society it is in which some people can spend on a toy what it would cost to feed a family of six or seven. What do you think?"

"I think," say Sugar pushing me off her feet like she never done before, cause I whip her ass in a minute, "that this is not much of a democracy if you ask me. Equal chance to pursue happiness means an equal crack at the dough, don't it?" Miss Moore is besides herself and I am disgusted with Sugar's treachery. So I stand on her foot one more time to see if she'll shove me. She shuts up, and Miss Moore looks at me, sorrowfully I'm thinkin. And somethin weird is goin on, I can feel it in my chest.

"Anybody else learn anything today?" lookin dead at me. I walk away and Sugar has to run to catch up and don't even seem to notice when I shrug her arm off my shoulder.

"Well, we got four dollars anyway," she says.

"Uh, hunh."

"We could go to Hascombs and get half a chocolate layer and then go to the Sunset and still have plenty money for potato chips and ice cream sodas."

"Uh, hunh."

"Race you to Hascombs," she say.

We start down the block and she gets ahead which is O.K. by me cause I'm going to the West End and then over to the Drive to think this day through. She can run if she want to and even run faster. But ain't nobody gonna beat me at nuthin.

[1972]

ALICE WALKER   [b. 1944]

Everyday Use

For Your Grandmama

I will wait for her in the yard that Maggie and I made so clean and wavy yesterday afternoon. A yard like this is more comfortable than most people know. It is not just a yard. It is like an extended living room. When the hard clay is swept clean as a floor and the fine sand around the edges lined with tiny, irregular grooves, anyone can come and sit and look up into the elm tree and wait for the breezes that never come inside the house.

Maggie will be nervous until after her sister goes: she will stand hopelessly in corners, homely and ashamed of the burn scars down her arms and legs, eying her sister with a mixture of envy and awe. She thinks her sister has held life always in the palm of one hand, that "no" is a word the world never learned to say to her.

You've no doubt seen those TV shows where the child who has "made it" is confronted, as a surprise, by her own mother and father, tottering in weakly from backstage. (A pleasant surprise, of course: What would they do if parent and child came on the show only to curse out and insult each other?) On TV mother and child embrace and smile into each other's faces. Sometimes the mother and father weep, the child wraps them in her arms and leans across the table to tell how she would not have made it without their help. I have seen these programs.

Sometimes I dream a dream in which Dee and I are suddenly brought together on a TV program of this sort. Out of a dark and soft-seated limousine I am ushered into a bright room filled with many people. There I meet a smiling, gray, sporty man like Johnny Carson° who shakes my hand and tells me what a fine girl I have. Then we are on the stage and Dee is embracing me with tears in her eyes. She pins on my dress a large orchid, even though she has told me once that she thinks orchids are tacky flowers.

In real life I am a large, big-boned woman with rough, man-working hands. In the winter I wear flannel nightgowns to bed and overalls during the day. I can kill and clean a hog as mercilessly as a man. My fat keeps me hot in zero weather. I can work outside all day, breaking ice to get water for washing; I can eat pork liver cooked over the open fire minutes after it comes steaming from the hog. One winter I knocked a bull calf straight in the brain between the eyes with a sledge hammer and had the meat hung up to chill before nightfall. But of course all this does not show on television. I am the way my daughter would want me to be: a hundred pounds lighter, my skin like an uncooked barley pancake. My hair glistens in the hot bright lights. Johnny Carson has much to do to keep up with my quick and witty tongue.

But that is a mistake. I know even before I wake up. Who ever knew a Johnson with a quick tongue? Who can even imagine me looking a strange white man in the eye? It seems to me I have talked to them always with one foot raised in flight, with my head turned in whichever way is farthest from them. Dee, though. She would always look anyone in the eye. Hesitation was no part of her nature.

"How do I look, Mama?" Maggie says, showing just enough of her thin body enveloped in pink skirt and red blouse for me to know she's there, almost hidden by the door.

"Come out into the yard," I say.

Have you ever seen a lame animal, perhaps a dog run over by some careless person rich enough to own a car, sidle up to someone who is ignorant enough to be kind to him? That is the way my Maggie walks.

Johnny Carson (1925–2005): Late-night talk-show host and comedian. *The Tonight Show* starring Johnny Carson was on the air from 1962 to 1992.

She has been like this, chin on chest, eyes on ground, feet in shuffle, ever since the fire that burned the other house to the ground.

Dee is lighter than Maggie, with nicer hair and a fuller figure. She's a woman now, though sometimes I forget. How long ago was it that the other house burned? Ten, twelve years? Sometimes I can still hear the flames and feel Maggie's arms sticking to me, her hair smoking and her dress falling off her in little black papery flakes. Her eyes seemed stretched open, blazed open by the flames reflected in them. And Dee. I see her standing off under the sweet gum tree she used to dig gum out of; a look of concentration on her face as she watched the last dingy gray board of the house fall in toward the red-hot brick chimney. Why don't you do a dance around the ashes? I'd want to ask her. She had hated the house that much.

I used to think she hated Maggie, too. But that was before we raised the money, the church and me, to send her to Augusta to school. She used to read to us without pity; forcing words, lies, other folks' habits, whole lives upon us two, sitting trapped and ignorant underneath her voice. She washed us in a river of make-believe, burned us with a lot of knowledge we didn't necessarily need to know. Pressed us to her with the serious way she read, to shove us away at just the moment, like dimwits, we seemed about to understand.

Dee wanted nice things. A yellow organdy dress to wear to her graduation from high school; black pumps to match a green suit she'd made from an old suit somebody gave me. She was determined to stare down any disaster in her efforts. Her eyelids would not flicker for minutes at a time. Often I fought off the temptation to shake her. At sixteen she had a style of her own: and knew what style was.

I never had an education myself. After second grade the school was closed down. Don't ask me why: in 1927 colored asked fewer questions than they do now. Sometimes Maggie reads to me. She stumbles along good-naturedly but can't see well. She knows she is not bright. Like good looks and money, quickness passed her by. She will marry John Thomas (who has mossy teeth in an earnest face) and then I'll be free to sit here and I guess just sing church songs to myself. Although I never was a good singer. Never could carry a tune. I was always better at a man's job. I used to love to milk till I was hooked in the side in '49. Cows are soothing and slow and don't bother you, unless you try to milk them the wrong way.

I have deliberately turned my back on the house. It is three rooms, just like the one that burned, except the roof is tin; they don't make shingle roofs any more. There are no real windows, just some holes cut in the sides, like the portholes in a ship, but not round and not square, with rawhide holding the shutters up on the outside. This house is in a pasture, too, like the other one. No doubt when Dee sees it she will want to tear it down. She wrote me once that no matter where we "choose" to live, she will manage to come see us. But she will never bring her friends. Maggie and I thought about this and Maggie asked me, "Mama, when did Dee ever *have* any friends?"

She had a few. Furtive boys in pink shirts hanging about on wash-day after school. Nervous girls who never laughed. Impressed with her they worshipped the well-turned phrase, the cute shape, the scalding humor that erupted like bubbles in lye. She read to them.

When she was courting Jimmy T she didn't have much time to pay to us, but turned all her faultfinding power on him. He *flew* to marry a cheap city girl from a family of ignorant flashy people. She hardly had time to recompose herself.

When she comes I will meet—but there they are!

Maggie attempts to make a dash for the house, in her shuffling way, but I stay her with my hand. "Come back here," I say. And she stops and tries to dig a well in the sand with her toe.

It is hard to see them clearly through the strong sun. But even the first glimpse of leg out of the car tells me it is Dee. Her feet were always neat-looking, as if God himself had shaped them with a certain style. From the other side of the car comes a short, stocky man. Hair is all over his head a foot long and hanging from his chin like a kinky mule tail. I hear Maggie suck in her breath. "Uhnnnh," is what it sounds like. Like when you see the wriggling end of a snake just in front of your foot on the road. "Uhnnnh."

Dee next. A dress down to the ground, in this hot weather. A dress so loud it hurts my eyes. There are yellows and oranges enough to throw back the light of the sun. I feel my whole face warming from the heat waves it throws out. Earrings gold, too, and hanging down to her shoulders. Bracelets dangling and making noises when she moves her arm up to shake the folds of the dress out of her armpits. The dress is loose and flows, and as she walks closer, I like it. I hear Maggie go "Uhnnnh" again. It is her sister's hair. It stands straight up like the wool on a sheep. It is black as night and around the edges are two long pigtails that rope about like small lizards disappearing behind her ears.

"Wa-su-zo-Tean-o!" she says, coming on in that gliding way the dress makes her move. The short stocky fellow with the hair to his navel is all grinning and he follows up with "Asalamalakim, my mother and sister!" He moves to hug Maggie but she falls back, right up against the back of my chair. I feel her trembling there and when I look up I see the perspiration falling off her chin.

"Don't get up," says Dee. Since I am stout it takes something of a push. You can see me trying to move a second or two before I make it. She turns, showing white heels through her sandals, and goes back to the car. Out she peeks next with a Polaroid. She stoops down quickly and lines up picture after picture of me sitting there in front of the house with Maggie cowering behind me. She never takes a shot without making sure the house is included. When a cow comes nibbling around the edge of the yard she snaps it and me and Maggie *and* the house. Then she puts the Polaroid in the back seat of the car, and comes up and kisses me on the forehead.

Meanwhile Asalamalakim is going through motions with Maggie's hand. Maggie's hand is as limp as a fish, and probably as cold, despite the sweat, and she keeps trying to pull it back. It looks like Asalamalakim wants to shake hands but wants to do it fancy. Or maybe he don't know how people shake hands. Anyhow, he soon gives up on Maggie.

"Well," I say. "Dee."

"No, Mama," she says. "Not 'Dee,' Wangero Leewanika Kemanjo!"

"What happened to 'Dee'?" I wanted to know.

"She's dead," Wangero said. "I couldn't bear it any longer, being named after the people who oppress me."

"You know as well as me you was named after your aunt Dicie," I said. Dicie is my sister. She named Dee. We called her "Big Dee" after Dee was born.

"But who was *she* named after?" asked Wangero.

"I guess after Grandma Dee," I said.

"And who was she named after?" asked Wangero.

"Her mother," I said, and saw Wangero was getting tired. "That's about as far back as I can trace it," I said. Though, in fact, I probably could have carried it back beyond the Civil War through the branches.

"Well," said Asalamalakim, "there you are."

"Uhnnnh," I heard Maggie say.

"There I was not," I said, "before 'Dicie' cropped up in our family, so why should I try to trace it that far back?"

He just stood there grinning, looking down on me like somebody inspecting a Model A car. Every once in a while he and Wangero sent eye signals over my head.

"How do you pronounce this name?" I asked.

"You don't have to call me by it if you don't want to," said Wangero.

"Why shouldn't I?" I asked. "If that's what you want us to call you, we'll call you."

"I know it might sound awkward at first," said Wangero.

"I'll get used to it," I said. "Ream it out again."

Well, soon we got the name out of the way. Asalamalakim had a name twice as long and three times as hard. After I tripped over it two or three times he told me to just call him Hakim-a-barber. I wanted to ask him was he a barber, but I didn't really think he was, so I didn't ask.

"You must belong to those beef-cattle peoples down the road," I said. They said "Asalamalakim" when they met you, too, but they didn't shake hands. Always too busy: feeding the cattle, fixing the fences, putting up salt-lick shelters, throwing down hay. When the white folks poisoned some of the herd the men stayed up all night with rifles in their hands. I walked a mile and a half just to see the sight.

Hakim-a-barber said, "I accept some of their doctrines, but farming and raising cattle is not my style." (They didn't tell me, and I didn't ask, whether Wangero (Dee) had really gone and married him.)

We sat down to eat and right away he said he didn't eat collards and pork was unclean. Wangero, though, went on through the chitlins and corn bread, the greens and everything else. She talked a blue streak over the sweet potatoes. Everything delighted her. Even the fact that we still used the benches her daddy made for the table when we couldn't afford to buy chairs.

"Oh, Mama!" she cried. Then turned to Hakim-a-barber. "I never knew how lovely these benches are. You can feel the rump prints," she said, running her hands underneath her and long the bench. Then she gave a sigh and her hand closed over Grandma Dee's butter dish. "That's it!" she said. "I knew there was something I wanted to ask you if I could have." She jumped up from the table and went over in the corner where the churn stood, the milk in it clabber by now. She looked at the churn and looked at it.

"This churn top is what I need," she said. "Didn't Uncle Buddy whittle it out of a tree you all used to have?"

"Yes," I said.

"Uh huh," she said happily. "And I want the dasher, too."

"Uncle Buddy whittle that, too?" asked the barber.

Dee (Wangero) looked up at me.

"Aunt Dee's first husband whittled the dash," said Maggie so low you almost couldn't hear her. "His name was Henry, but they called him Stash."

"Maggie's brain is like an elephant's," Wangero said, laughing. "I can use the churn top as a centerpiece for the alcove table," she said, sliding a plate over the churn, "and I'll think of something artistic to do with the dasher."

When she finished wrapping the dasher the handle stuck out. I took it for a moment in my hands. You didn't even have to look close to see where hands pushing the dasher up and down to make butter had left a kind of sink in the wood. In fact, there were a lot of small sinks; you could see where thumbs and fingers had sunk into the wood. It was beautiful light yellow wood, from a tree that grew in the yard where Big Dee and Stash had lived.

After dinner Dee (Wangero) went to the trunk at the foot of my bed and started rifling through it. Maggie hung back in the kitchen over the dishpan. Out came Wangero with two quilts. They had been pieced by Grandma Dee and then Big Dee and me had hung them on the quilt frames on the front porch and quilted them. One was in the Lone Star pattern. The other was Walk Around the Mountain. In both of them were scraps of dresses Grandma Dee had worn fifty and more years ago. Bits and pieces of Grandpa Jarrell's Paisley shirts. And one teeny faded blue piece, about the size of a penny matchbox, that was from Great Grandpa Ezra's uniform that he wore in the Civil War.

"Mama," Wangero said sweet as a bird. "Can I have these old quilts?"

I heard something fall in the kitchen, and a minute later the kitchen door slammed.

"Why don't you take one or two of the others?" I asked. "These old things was just done by me and Big Dee from some tops your grandma pieced before she died."

"No," said Wangero. "I don't want those. They are stitched around the borders by machine."

"That'll make them last better," I said.

"That's not the point," said Wangero. "These are all pieces of dresses Grandma used to wear. She did all this stitching by hand. Imagine!" She held the quilts securely in her arms, stroking them.

"Some of the pieces, like those lavender ones, come from old clothes her mother handed down to her," I said, moving up to touch the quilts. Dee (Wangero) moved back just enough so that I couldn't reach the quilts. They already belonged to her.

"Imagine!" she breathed again, clutching them closely to her bosom.

"The truth is," I said, "I promised to give them quilts to Maggie, for when she marries John Thomas."

She gasped like a bee had stung her.

"Maggie can't appreciate these quilts!" she said. "She'd probably be backward enough to put them to everyday use."

"I reckon she would," I said. "God knows I been saving 'em for long enough with nobody using 'em. I hope she will!" I didn't want to bring up how I had offered Dee (Wangero) a quilt when she went away to college. Then she had told me they were old-fashioned, out of style.

"But they're *priceless*!" she was saying now, furiously; for she has a temper. "Maggie would put them on the bed and in five years they'd be in rags. Less than that!"

"She can always make some more," I said. "Maggie knows how to quilt."

Dee (Wangero) looked at me with hatred. "You just will not understand. The point is these quilts, *these* quilts!"

"Well," I said, stumped. "What would *you* do with them?"

"Hang them," she said. As if that was the only thing you *could* do with quilts.

Maggie by now was standing in the door. I could almost hear the sound her feet made as they scraped over each other.

"She can have them, Mama," she said, like somebody used to never winning anything, or having anything reserved for her. "I can 'member Grandma Dee without the quilts."

I looked at her hard. She had filled her bottom lip with checkerberry snuff and it gave her face a kind of dopey, hangdog look. It was Grandma Dee and Big Dee who taught her how to quilt herself. She stood there with her scarred hands hidden in the folds of her skirt. She looked at her sister with something like fear but she wasn't mad at her. This was Maggie's portion. This was the way she knew God to work.

When I looked at her like that something hit me in the top of my head and ran down to the soles of my feet. Just like when I'm in church and the spirit of God touches me and I get happy and shout. I did something I never had done before: hugged Maggie to me, then dragged her on into the room, snatched the quilts out of Miss Wangero's hands and dumped them into Maggie's lap. Maggie just sat there on my bed with her mouth open.

"Take one or two of the others," I said to Dee.

But she turned without a word and went out to Hakim-a-barber.

"You just don't understand," she said, as Maggie and I came out to the car.

"What don't I understand?" I wanted to know.

"Your heritage," she said. And then she turned to Maggie, kissed her, and said, "You ought to try to make something of yourself, too, Maggie. It's really a new day for us. But from the way you and Mama still live you'd never know it."

She put on some sunglasses that hid everything above the tip of her nose and her chin.

Maggie smiled; maybe at the sunglasses. But a real smile, not scared. After we watched the car dust settle I asked Maggie to bring me a dip of snuff. And then the two of us sat there just enjoying, until it was time to go in the house and go to bed.

[1973]

TOBIAS WOLFF   [b. 1945]

Bullet in the Brain

Anders couldn't get to the bank until just before it closed, so of course the line was endless and he got stuck behind two women whose loud, stupid conversation put him in a murderous temper. He was never in the best of tempers anyway, Anders — a book critic known for the weary, elegant savagery with which he dispatched almost everything he reviewed.

With the line still doubled around the rope, one of the tellers stuck a "POSITION CLOSED" sign in her window and walked to the back of the bank, where she leaned against a desk and began to pass the time with a man shuffling papers. The women in front of Anders broke off their conversation and watched the teller with hatred. "Oh, that's nice," one of them said. She turned to Anders and added, confident of his accord, "One of those little human touches that keep us coming back for more."

Anders had conceived his own towering hatred of the teller, but he immediately turned it on the presumptuous crybaby in front of him. "Damned unfair," he said. "Tragic, really. If they're not chopping off the wrong leg, or bombing your ancestral village, they're closing their positions."

She stood her ground. "I didn't say it was tragic," she said. "I just think it's a pretty lousy way to treat your customers."

"Unforgivable," Anders said. "Heaven will take note."

She sucked in her cheeks but stared past him and said nothing. Anders saw that the other woman, her friend, was looking in the same direction. And then the tellers stopped what they were doing, and the customers slowly turned, and silence came over the bank. Two men wearing black ski masks and blue business suits were standing to the side of the door. One of them had a pistol pressed against the guard's neck. The guard's eyes were closed, and his lips were moving. The other man had a sawed-off shotgun. "Keep your big mouth shut!" the man with the pistol said, though no one had spoken a word. "One of you tellers hits the alarm, you're all dead meat. Got it?"

The tellers nodded.

"Oh, bravo," Anders said. "*Dead meat.*" He turned to the woman in front of him. "Great script, eh? The stern, brass-knuckled poetry of the dangerous classes."

318

She looked at him with drowning eyes.

The man with the shotgun pushed the guard to his knees. He handed the shotgun to his partner and yanked the guard's wrists up behind his back and locked them together with a pair of handcuffs. He toppled him onto the floor with a kick between the shoulder blades. Then he took his shotgun back and went over to the security gate at the end of the counter. He was short and heavy and moved with peculiar slowness, even torpor. "Buzz him in," his partner said. The man with the shotgun opened the gate and sauntered along the line of tellers, handing each of them a Hefty bag. When he came to the empty position he looked over at the man with the pistol, who said, "Whose slot is that?"

Anders watched the teller. She put her hand to her throat and turned to the man she'd been talking to. He nodded. "Mine," she said.

"Then get your ugly ass in gear and fill that bag."

"There you go," Anders said to the woman in front of him. "Justice is done."

"Hey! Bright boy! Did I tell you to talk?"

"No," Anders said.

"Then shut your trap."

"Did you hear that?" Anders said. " 'Bright boy.' Right out of 'The Killers.' "°

"Please be quiet," the woman said.

"Hey, you deaf or what?" The man with the pistol walked over to Anders. He poked the weapon into Anders' gut. "You think I'm playing games?"

"No," Anders said, but the barrel tickled like a stiff finger and he had to fight back the titters. He did this by making himself stare into the man's eyes, which were clearly visible behind the holes in the mask: pale blue and rawly red-rimmed. The man's left eyelid kept twitching. He breathed out a piercing, ammoniac smell that shocked Anders more than anything that had happened, and he was beginning to develop a sense of unease when the man prodded him again with the pistol.

"You like me, bright boy?" he said. "You want to suck my dick?"

"No," Anders said.

"Then stop looking at me."

Anders fixed his gaze on the man's shiny wing-tip shoes.

"Not down there. Up there." He stuck the pistol under Anders' chin and pushed it upward until Anders was looking at the ceiling.

Anders had never paid much attention to that part of the bank, a pompous old building with marble floors and counters and pillars, and gilt scrollwork over the tellers' cages. The domed ceiling had been decorated

'The Killers': A short story about two gangsters written by Ernest Hemingway.

with mythological figures whose fleshy, toga-draped ugliness Anders had taken in at a glance many years earlier and afterward declined to notice. Now he had no choice but to scrutinize the painter's work. It was even worse than he remembered, and all of it executed with the utmost gravity. The artist had a few tricks up his sleeve and used them again and again — a certain rosy blush on the underside of the clouds, a coy backward glance on the faces of the cupids and fauns. The ceiling was crowded with various dramas, but the one that caught Anders' eye was Zeus and Europa — portrayed, in this rendition, as a bull ogling a cow from behind a haystack. To make the cow sexy, the painter had canted her hips suggestively and given her long, droopy eyelashes through which she gazed back at the bull with sultry welcome. The bull wore a smirk and his eyebrows were arched. If there'd been a bubble coming out of his mouth, it would have said, "Hubba hubba."

"What's so funny, bright boy?"

"Nothing."

"You think I'm comical? You think I'm some kind of clown?"

"No."

"You think you can fuck with me?"

"No."

"Fuck with me again, you're history. *Capiche?*"

Anders burst out laughing. He covered his mouth with both hands and said, "I'm sorry, I'm sorry," then snorted helplessly through his fingers and said, "*Capiche* — oh, God, *capiche*," and at that the man with the pistol raised the pistol and shot Anders right in the head.

The bullet smashed Anders' skull and ploughed through his brain and exited behind his right ear, scattering shards of bone into the cerebral cortex, the corpus callosum, back toward the basal ganglia, and down into the thalamus. But before all this occurred, the first appearance of the bullet in the cerebrum set off a crackling chain of ion transports and neuro-transmissions. Because of their peculiar origin these traced a peculiar pattern, flukishly calling to life a summer afternoon some forty years past, and long since lost to memory. After striking the cranium the bullet was moving at 900 feet per second, a pathetically sluggish, glacial pace compared to the synaptic lightning that flashed around it. Once in the brain, that is, the bullet came under the mediation of brain time, which gave Anders plenty of leisure to contemplate the scene that, in a phrase he would have abhorred, "passed before his eyes."

It is worth noting what Anders did not remember, given what he did remember. He did not remember his first lover, Sherry, or what he had most madly loved about her, before it came to irritate him — her unembarrassed carnality, and especially the cordial way she had with his unit, which she called Mr. Mole as in, "Uh-oh, looks like Mr. Mole wants to play," and, "Let's hide Mr. Mole!" Anders did not remember his wife, whom he had also loved before she exhausted him with her predictability, or his daughter, now a sullen professor of economics at Dartmouth. He did not remember standing just outside his daughter's door as she lectured her bear about his naughtiness and described the truly appalling punishments Paws would receive unless he changed his ways. He did not remember a single line of the hundreds of poems he had committed to memory in his youth so that he could give himself the shivers at will — not "Silent, upon a peak in Darien," or "My God, I heard this day," or "All my pretty ones? Did you say all? O hell-kite! All?" None of these did he remember; not one. Anders did not remember his dying mother saying of his father, "I should have stabbed him in his sleep."

He did not remember Professor Josephs telling his class how Athenian prisoners in Sicily had been released if they could recite Aeschylus, and then reciting Aeschylus himself, right there, in the Greek. Anders did not remember how his eyes had burned at those sounds. He did not remember the surprise of seeing a college classmate's name on the jacket of a novel not long after they graduated, or the respect he had felt after reading the book. He did not remember the pleasure of giving respect.

Nor did Anders remember seeing a woman leap to her death from the building opposite his own just days after his daughter was born. He did not remember shouting, "Lord have mercy!" He did not remember deliberately crashing his father's car into a tree, or having his ribs kicked in by three policemen at an anti-war rally, or waking himself up with laughter. He did not remember when he began to regard the heap of books on his desk with boredom and dread, or when he grew angry at writers for writing them. He did not remember when everything began to remind him of something else.

This is what he remembered. Heat. A baseball field. Yellow grass, the whirr of insects, himself leaning against a tree as the boys of the neighborhood gather for a pickup game. He looks on as the others argue the relative genius of Mantle and Mays. They have been worrying this subject all summer, and it has become tedious to Anders: an oppression, like the heat.

Then the last two boys arrive, Coyle and a cousin of his from Mississippi. Anders has never met Coyle's cousin before and will never see him again. He says hi with the rest but takes no further notice of him until they've chosen sides and someone asks the cousin what position he wants to play. "Shortstop," the boy says. "Short's the best position they is." Anders turns and looks at him. He wants to hear Coyle's cousin repeat what he's just said, but he knows better than to ask. The others will think he's being a jerk, ragging the kid for his grammar. But that isn't it, not at all—it's that Anders is strangely roused, elated, by those final two words, their pure unexpectedness and their music. He takes the field in a trance, repeating them to himself.

The bullet is already in the brain; it won't be outrun forever, or charmed to a halt. In the end it will do its work and leave the troubled skull behind, dragging its comet's tail of memory and hope and talent and love into the marble hall of commerce. That can't be helped. But for now Anders can still make time. Time for the shadows to lengthen on the grass, time for the tethered dog to bark at the flying ball, time for the boy in right field to smack his sweat-blackened mitt and softly chant, *They is, they is, they is*.

[1995]

TIM O'BRIEN [b. 1946]

The Things They Carried

First Lieutenant Jimmy Cross carried letters from a girl named Martha, a junior at Mount Sebastian College in New Jersey. They were not love letters, but Lieutenant Cross was hoping, so he kept them folded in plastic at the bottom of his rucksack. In the late afternoon, after a day's march, he would dig his foxhole, wash his hands under a canteen, unwrap the letters, hold them with the tips of his fingers, and spend the last hour of light pretending. He would imagine romantic camping trips into the White Mountains in New Hampshire. He would sometimes taste the envelope flaps, knowing her tongue had been there. More than anything, he wanted Martha to love him as he loved her, but the letters were mostly chatty, elusive on the matter of love. She was a virgin, he was almost sure. She was an English major at Mount Sebastian, and she wrote beautifully about her professors and roommates and midterm exams, about her respect for Chaucer and her great affection for Virginia Woolf. She often quoted lines of poetry; she never mentioned the war, except to say, Jimmy, take care of yourself. The letters weighed ten ounces. They were signed "Love, Martha," but Lieutenant Cross understood that "Love" was only a way of signing and did not mean what he sometimes pretended it meant. At dusk, he would carefully return the letters to his rucksack. Slowly, a bit distracted, he would get up and move among his men, checking the perimeter, then at full dark he would return to his hole and watch the night and wonder if Martha was a virgin.

The things they carried were largely determined by necessity. Among the necessities or near necessities were P-38 can openers, pocket knives, heat tabs, wrist watches, dog tags, mosquito repellant, chewing gum, candy, cigarettes, salt tablets, packets of Kool-Aid, lighters, matches, sewing kits, Military Payment Certificates, C rations,° and two or three canteens of water. Together, these items weighed between fifteen and twenty pounds, depending upon a man's habits or rate of metabolism. Henry Dobbins, who was a big man, carried extra rations; he was especially fond of canned peaches in heavy syrup over pound cake. Dave Jensen, who practiced field hygiene, carried a toothbrush, dental floss, and several hotel-size bars of soap he'd stolen on R&R in Sydney, Australia. Ted Lavender, who was scared, carried tranquilizers until he was shot in the head outside the village of Than Khe in mid-April. By necessity, and because it was SOP,° they all carried steel helmets that weighed five pounds including the liner and camouflage cover. They carried the standard fatigue jackets and trousers. Very few carried underwear. On their feet they carried jungle boots — 2.1 pounds — and Dave Jensen carried three pairs of socks and a can of Dr. Scholl's foot powder as a precaution against trench foot. Until he was shot, Ted Lavender carried six or seven ounces of premium dope, which for him was a necessity. Mitchell Sanders, the RTO,° carried condoms. Norman Bowker carried a diary. Rat Kiley carried comic books. Kiowa, a devout Baptist, carried an illustrated New Testament that had been presented to him by his father, who taught Sunday school in Oklahoma City, Oklahoma. As a hedge against bad times, however, Kiowa also carried his grandmother's distrust of the white man, his grandfather's old hunting hatchet. Necessity dictated. Because the land was mined and booby-trapped, it was SOP for each man to carry a steel-centered, nylon-covered flak jacket, which weighed 6.7 pounds, but which on hot days seemed much heavier. Because you could die so quickly, each man carried at least one large compress bandage, usually in the helmet band for easy access. Because the nights were cold, and because the monsoons were wet, each carried a green plastic poncho that could be used as a raincoat or ground sheet or makeshift tent. With its quilted liner, the poncho weighed almost two pounds, but it was worth every ounce. In April, for instance, when Ted Lavender

C rations: Combat rations.
SOP: Standard operating procedure.
RTO: Radiotelephone operator.

was shot, they used his poncho to wrap him up, then to carry him across the paddy, then to lift him into the chopper that took him away.

They were called legs or grunts.

To carry something was to "hump" it, as when Lieutenant Jimmy Cross humped his love for Martha up the hills and through the swamps. In its intransitive form, "to hump" meant "to walk," or "to march," but it implied burdens far beyond the intransitive.

Almost everyone humped photographs. In his wallet, Lieutenant Cross carried two photographs of Martha. The first was a Kodachrome snapshot signed "Love," though he knew better. She stood against a brick wall. Her eyes were gray and neutral, her lips slightly open as she stared straight-on at the camera. At night, sometimes, Lieutenant Cross wondered who had taken the picture, because he knew she had boyfriends, because he loved her so much, and because he could see the shadow of the picture taker spreading out against the brick wall. The second photograph had been clipped from the 1968 Mount Sebastian yearbook. It was an action shot—women's volleyball—and Martha was bent horizontal to the floor, reaching, the palms of her hands in sharp focus, the tongue taut, the expression frank and competitive. There was no visible sweat. She wore white gym shorts. Her legs, he thought, were almost certainly the legs of a virgin, dry and without hair, the left knee cocked and carrying her entire weight, which was just over one hundred pounds. Lieutenant Cross remembered touching that left knee. A dark theater, he remembered, and the movie was *Bonnie and Clyde*, and Martha wore a tweed skirt, and during the final scene, when he touched her knee, she turned and looked at him in a sad, sober way that made him pull his hand back, but he would always remember the feel of the tweed skirt and the knee beneath it and the sound of the gunfire that killed Bonnie and Clyde, how embarrassing it was, how slow and oppressive. He remembered kissing her good night at the dorm door. Right then, he thought, he should've done something brave. He should've carried her up the stairs to her room and tied her to the bed and touched that left knee all night long. He should've risked it. Whenever he looked at the photographs, he thought of new things he should've done.

What they carried was partly a function of rank, partly of field specialty.

As a first lieutenant and platoon leader, Jimmy Cross carried a compass, maps, code books, binoculars, and a .45-caliber pistol that weighed 2.9 pounds fully loaded. He carried a strobe light and the responsibility for the lives of his men.

As an RTO, Mitchell Sanders carried the PRC-25 radio, a killer, twenty-six pounds with its battery.

As a medic, Rat Kiley carried a canvas satchel filled with morphine and plasma and malaria tablets and surgical tape and comic books and all the things a medic must carry, including M&M's for especially bad wounds, for a total weight of nearly twenty pounds.

As a big man, therefore a machine gunner, Henry Dobbins carried the M-60, which weighed twenty-three pounds unloaded, but which was almost always loaded. In addition, Dobbins carried between ten and fifteen pounds of ammunition draped in belts across his chest and shoulders.

As PFCs° or Spec 4s,° most of them were common grunts and carried the standard M-16 gas-operated assault rifle. The weapon weighed 7.5 pounds unloaded, 8.2 pounds with its full twenty-round magazine. Depending on numerous factors, such as topography and psychology, the riflemen carried anywhere from twelve to twenty magazines, usually in cloth bandoliers, adding on another 8.4 pounds at minimum, fourteen pounds at maximum. When it was available, they also carried M-16 maintenance gear—rods and steel brushes and swabs and tubes of LSA oil°—all of which weighed about a pound. Among the grunts, some carried the M-79 grenade launcher, 5.9 pounds unloaded, a reasonably light weapon except for the ammunition, which was heavy. A single round weighed ten ounces. The typical load was twenty-five rounds. But Ted Lavender, who was scared, carried thirty-four rounds when he was shot and killed outside Than Khe, and he went down under an exceptional burden, more than twenty pounds of ammunition, plus the flak jacket and helmet and rations and water and toilet paper and tranquilizers and all the rest, plus the unweighed fear. He was dead weight. There was no twitching or flopping. Kiowa, who saw it happen, said it was like watching a rock fall, or a big sandbag or something—just boom, then down—not like the movies where the dead guy rolls around and does fancy spins and goes ass over teakettle—not like that, Kiowa said, the poor bastard just flat-fuck fell. Boom. Down. Nothing else. It was a bright morning in mid-April. Lieutenant Cross felt the pain. He blamed himself. They stripped off Lavender's canteens and ammo, all the heavy things, and Rat Kiley said the obvious, the guy's dead, and Mitchell Sanders used his radio to report one U.S. KIA° and to request a chopper. Then they wrapped Lavender in his poncho. They carried him out to a dry paddy, established security, and sat smoking the dead man's dope until the chopper came. Lieutenant Cross kept to himself. He pictured Martha's smooth young face, thinking he loved her more than anything, more

PFCs: Privates first class.
Spec 4s: Specialists fourth class, rank equivalent to that of corporal.
LSA oil: Lube-small-arms oil.
KIA: Killed in action.

than his men, and now Ted Lavender was dead because he loved her so much and could not stop thinking about her. When the dust-off arrived, they carried Lavender aboard. Afterward they burned Than Khe. They marched until dusk, then dug their holes, and that night Kiowa kept explaining how you had to be there, how fast it was, how the poor guy just dropped like so much concrete. Boom-down, he said. Like cement.

In addition to the three standard weapons—the M-60, M-16, and M-79—they carried whatever presented itself, or whatever seemed appropriate as a means of killing or staying alive. They carried catch-as-catch-can. At various times, in various situations, they carried M-14s and CAR-15s and Swedish Ks and grease guns and captured AK-47s and Chi-Coms and RPGs and Simonov carbines and black-market Uzis and .38-caliber Smith & Wesson handguns and 66 mm LAWs and shotguns and silencers and blackjacks and bayonets and C-4 plastic explosives. Lee Strunk carried a slingshot; a weapon of last resort, he called it. Mitchell Sanders carried brass knuckles. Kiowa carried his grandfather's feathered hatchet. Every third or fourth man carried a Claymore antipersonnel mine—3.5 pounds with its firing device. They all carried fragmentation grenades—fourteen ounces each. They all carried at least one M-18 colored smoke grenade—twenty-four ounces. Some carried CS or tear-gas grenades. Some carried white-phosphorus grenades. They carried all they could bear, and then some, including a silent awe for the terrible power of the things they carried.

In the first week of April, before Lavender died, Lieutenant Jimmy Cross received a good-luck charm from Martha. It was a simple pebble, an ounce at most. Smooth to the touch, it was a milky-white color with flecks of orange and violet, oval-shaped, like a miniature egg. In the accompanying letter, Martha wrote that she had found the pebble on the Jersey shoreline, precisely where the land touched water at high tide, where things came together but also separated. It was this separate-but-together quality, she wrote, that had inspired her to pick up the pebble and to carry it in her breast pocket for several days, where it seemed weightless, and then to send it through the mail, by air, as a token of her truest feelings for him. Lieutenant Cross found this romantic. But he wondered what her truest feelings were, exactly, and what she meant by separate-but-together. He wondered how the tides and waves had come into play on that afternoon along the Jersey shoreline when Martha saw the pebble and bent down to rescue it from geology. He imagined bare feet. Martha was a poet, with the poet's sensibilities, and her feet would be brown and bare, the toenails unpainted, the eyes chilly and somber like the ocean in March, and though it was painful, he wondered who had been with her that afternoon. He imagined a pair of shadows moving along the strip of sand where things came together but also separated. It was phantom jealousy, he knew, but he couldn't help himself. He loved her so much. On the march, through the hot days of early April, he carried the pebble in his mouth, turning it with his tongue, tasting sea salts and moisture. His mind wandered. He had difficulty keeping his attention on the war. On occasion he would yell at his men to spread out the column, to keep their eyes open, but then he would slip away into daydreams, just pretending, walking barefoot along the Jersey shore, with Martha, carrying nothing. He would feel himself rising. Sun and waves and gentle winds, all love and lightness.

What they carried varied by mission.

When a mission took them to the mountains, they carried mosquito netting, machetes, canvas tarps, and extra bug juice.

If a mission seemed especially hazardous, or if it involved a place they knew to be bad, they carried everything they could. In certain heavily mined AOs,° where the land was dense with Toe Poppers° and Bouncing Betties,° they took turns humping a twenty-eight-pound mine detector. With its headphones and big sensing plate, the equipment was a stress on the lower back and shoulders, awkward to handle, often useless because of the shrapnel in the earth, but they carried it anyway, partly for safety, partly for the illusion of safety.

On ambush, or other night missions, they carried peculiar little odds and ends. Kiowa always took along his New Testament and a pair of moccasins for silence. Dave Jensen carried night-sight vitamins high in carotin. Lee Strunk carried his slingshot; ammo, he claimed, would never be a problem. Rat Kiley carried brandy and M&M's. Until he was shot, Ted Lavender carried the starlight scope, which weighed 6.3 pounds with its aluminum carrying case. Henry Dobbins carried his girlfriend's pantyhose wrapped around his neck as a comforter. They all carried ghosts. When dark came, they would move out single file across the meadows and paddies to their ambush coordinates, where they would quietly set up the Claymores and lie down and spend the night waiting.

Other missions were more complicated and required special equipment. In mid-April, it was their mission to search out and destroy the elaborate tunnel complexes in the Than Khe area south of Chu Lai. To blow the tunnels, they carried one-pound blocks of pentrite high explosives, four blocks to a man, sixty-eight pounds in all. They carried wiring,

---

AOs: Areas of operations.
Toe Poppers: Viet Cong antipersonnel land mines with small firing pins.
Bouncing Betties: Bounding fragmentation land mines, the deadliest of all land mines.

detonators, and battery-powered clackers. Dave Jensen carried earplugs. Most often, before blowing the tunnels, they were ordered by higher command to search them, which was considered bad news, but by and large they just shrugged and carried out orders. Because he was a big man, Henry Dobbins was excused from tunnel duty. The others would draw numbers. Before Lavender died there were seventeen men in the platoon, and whoever drew the number seventeen would strip off his gear and crawl in head first with a flashlight and Lieutenant Cross's .45-caliber pistol. The rest of them would fan out as security. They would sit down or kneel, not facing the hole, listening to the ground beneath them, imagining cobwebs and ghosts, whatever was down there—the tunnel walls squeezing in—how the flashlight seemed impossibly heavy in the hand and how it was tunnel vision in the very strictest sense, compression in all ways, even time, and how you had to wiggle in—ass and elbows—a swallowed-up feeling—and how you found yourself worrying about odd things—will your flashlight go dead? Do rats carry rabies? If you screamed, how far would the sound carry? Would your buddies hear it? Would they have the courage to drag you out? In some respects, though not many, the waiting was worse than the tunnel itself. Imagination was a killer.

On April 16, when Lee Strunk drew the number seventeen, he laughed and muttered something and went down quickly. The morning was hot and very still. Not good, Kiowa said. He looked at the tunnel opening, then out across a dry paddy toward the village of Than Khe. Nothing moved. No clouds or birds or people. As they waited, the men smoked and drank Kool-Aid, not talking much, feeling sympathy for Lee Strunk but also feeling the luck of the draw. You win some, you lose some, said Mitchell Sanders, and sometimes you settle for a rain check. It was a tired line and no one laughed.

Henry Dobbins ate a tropical chocolate bar. Ted Lavender popped a tranquilizer and went off to pee.

After five minutes, Lieutenant Jimmy Cross moved to the tunnel, leaned down, and examined the darkness. Trouble, he thought—a cave-in maybe. And then suddenly, without willing it, he was thinking about Martha. The stresses and fractures, the quick collapse, the two of them buried alive under all that weight. Dense, crushing love. Kneeling, watching the hole, he tried to concentrate on Lee Strunk and the war, all the dangers, but his love was too much for him, he felt paralyzed, he wanted to sleep inside her lungs and breathe her blood and be smothered. He wanted her to be a virgin and not a virgin, all at once. He wanted to know her. Intimate secrets—why poetry? Why so sad? Why the grayness in her eyes? Why so alone? Not lonely, just alone—riding her bike across campus or sitting off by herself in the cafeteria. Even dancing, she danced alone—and it was the aloneness that filled him with love. He remembered telling her that one evening. How she nodded and looked away. And how, later, when he kissed her, she received the kiss without returning it, her eyes wide open, not afraid, not a virgin's eyes, just flat and uninvolved.

Lieutenant Cross gazed at the tunnel. But he was not there. He was buried with Martha under the white sand at the Jersey shore. They were pressed together, and the pebble in his mouth was her tongue. He was smiling. Vaguely, he was aware of how quiet the day was, the sullen paddies, yet he could not bring himself to worry about matters of security. He was beyond that. He was just a kid at war, in love. He was twenty-two years old. He couldn't help it.

A few moments later Lee Strunk crawled out of the tunnel. He came up grinning, filthy but alive. Lieutenant Cross nodded and closed his eyes while the others clapped Strunk on the back and made jokes about rising from the dead.

Worms, Rat Kiley said. Right out of the grave. Fuckin' zombie.

The men laughed. They all felt great relief.

Spook City, said Mitchell Sanders.

Lee Strunk made a funny ghost sound, a kind of moaning, yet very happy, and right then, when Strunk made that high happy moaning sound, when he went *Ahhooooo*, right then Ted Lavender was shot in the head on his way back from peeing. He lay with his mouth open. The teeth were broken. There was a swollen black bruise under his left eye. The cheekbone was gone. Oh shit, Rat Kiley said, the guy's dead. The guy's dead, he kept saying, which seemed profound—the guy's dead. I mean really.

The things they carried were determined to some extent by superstition. Lieutenant Cross carried his good-luck pebble. Dave Jensen carried a rabbit's foot. Norman Bowker, otherwise a very gentle person, carried a thumb that had been presented to him as a gift by Mitchell Sanders. The thumb was dark brown, rubbery to the touch, and weighed four ounces at most. It had been cut from a VC° corpse, a boy of fifteen or sixteen. They'd found him at the bottom of an irrigation ditch, badly burned, flies in his mouth and eyes. The boy wore black shorts and sandals. At the time of his death he had been carrying a pouch of rice, a rifle, and three magazines of ammunition.

You want my opinion, Mitchell Sanders said, there's a definite moral here.

VC: Vietcong, a guerrilla fighter of the Vietnamese Communist movement.

He put his hand on the dead boy's wrist. He was quiet for a time, as if counting a pulse, then he patted the stomach, almost affectionately, and used Kiowa's hunting hatchet to remove the thumb.

Henry Dobbins asked what the moral was.

Moral?

You know. *Moral.*

Sanders wrapped the thumb in toilet paper and handed it across to Norman Bowker. There was no blood. Smiling, he kicked the boy's head, watched the flies scatter, and said, It's like with that old TV show— Paladin. Have gun, will travel.

Henry Dobbins thought about it.

Yeah, well, he finally said. I don't see no moral.

There it *is*, man.

Fuck off.

They carried USO stationery and pencils and pens. They carried Sterno, safety pins, trip flares, signal flares, spools of wire, razor blades, chewing tobacco, liberated joss sticks° and statuettes of the smiling Buddha, candles, grease pencils, *The Stars and Stripes*, fingernail clippers, Psy Ops° leaflets, bush hats, bolos, and much more. Twice a week, when the resupply choppers came in, they carried hot chow in green Mermite cans and large canvas bags filled with iced beer and soda pop. They carried plastic water containers, each with a two-gallon capacity. Mitchell Sanders carried a set of starched tiger fatigues for special occasions. Henry Dobbins carried Black Flag insecticide. Dave Jensen carried empty sandbags that could be filled at night for added protection. Lee Strunk carried tanning lotion. Some things they carried in common. Taking turns, they carried the big PRC-77 scrambler radio, which weighed thirty pounds with its battery. They shared the weight of memory. They took up what others could no longer bear. Often, they carried each other, the wounded or weak. They carried infections. They carried chess sets, basketballs, Vietnamese-English dictionaries, insignia of rank, Bronze Stars and Purple Hearts, plastic cards imprinted with the Code of Conduct. They carried diseases, among them malaria and dysentery. They carried lice and ringworm and leeches and paddy algae and various rots and molds. They carried the land itself—Vietnam, the place, the soil—a powdery orange-red dust that covered their boots and fatigues and faces. They carried the sky. The whole atmosphere, they carried it, the humidity, the monsoons, the stink of fungus and decay, all of it, they carried gravity. They moved like mules. By daylight they took

Joss sticks: Slender sticks of incense.
Psy Ops: Psychological operations.

sniper fire, at night they were mortared, but it was not battle, it was just the endless march, village to village, without purpose, nothing won or lost. They marched for the sake of the march. They plodded along slowly, dumbly, leaning forward against the heat, unthinking, all blood and bone, simple grunts, soldiering with their legs, toiling up the hills and down into the paddies and across the rivers and up again and down, just humping, one step and then the next and then another, but no volition, no will, because it was automatic, it was anatomy, and the war was entirely a matter of posture and carriage, the hump was everything, a kind of inertia, a kind of emptiness, a dullness of desire and intellect and conscience and hope and human sensibility. Their principles were in their feet. Their calculations were biological. They had no sense of strategy or mission. They searched the villages without knowing what to look for, not caring, kicking over jars of rice, frisking children and old men, blowing tunnels, sometimes setting fires and sometimes not, then forming up and moving on to the next village, then other villages, where it would always be the same. They carried their own lives. The pressures were enormous. In the heat of early afternoon, they would remove their helmets and flak jackets, walking bare, which was dangerous but which helped ease the strain. They would often discard things along the route of march. Purely for comfort, they would throw away rations, blow their Claymores and grenades, no matter, because by nightfall the resupply choppers would arrive with more of the same, then a day or two later still more, fresh watermelons and crates of ammunition and sunglasses and woolen sweaters — the resources were stunning — sparklers for the Fourth of July, colored eggs for Easter. It was the great American war chest — the fruits of science, the smokestacks, the canneries, the arsenals at Hartford, the Minnesota forests, the machine shops, the vast fields of corn and wheat — they carried like freight trains; they carried it on their backs and shoulders — and for all the ambiguities of Vietnam, all the mysteries and unknowns, there was at least the single abiding certainty that they would never be at a loss for things to carry.

After the chopper took Lavender away, Lieutenant Jimmy Cross led his men into the village of Than Khe. They burned everything. They shot chickens and dogs, they trashed the village well, they called in artillery and watched the wreckage, then they marched for several hours through the hot afternoon, and then at dusk, while Kiowa explained how Lavender died, Lieutenant Cross found himself trembling.

He tried not to cry. With his entrenching tool, which weighed five pounds, he began digging a hole in the earth.

He felt shame. He hated himself. He had loved Martha more than his men, and as a consequence Lavender was now dead, and this was something he would have to carry like a stone in his stomach for the rest of the war.

All he could do was dig. He used his entrenching tool like an ax, slashing, feeling both love and hate, and then later, when it was full dark, he sat at the bottom of his foxhole and wept. It went on for a long while. In part, he was grieving for Ted Lavender, but mostly it was for Martha, and for himself, because she belonged to another world, which was not quite real, and because she was a junior at Mount Sebastian College in New Jersey, a poet and a virgin and uninvolved, and because he realized she did not love him and never would.

Like cement, Kiowa whispered in the dark. I swear to God—boom-down. Not a word.

I've heard this, said Norman Bowker.

A pisser, you know? Still zipping himself up. Zapped while zipping.

All right, fine. That's enough.

Yeah, but you had to see it, the guy just—

I *heard*, man. Cement. So why not shut the fuck *up*?

Kiowa shook his head sadly and glanced over at the hole where Lieutenant Jimmy Cross sat watching the night. The air was thick and wet. A warm, dense fog had settled over the paddies and there was the stillness that precedes rain.

After a time Kiowa sighed.

One thing for sure, he said. The Lieutenant's in some deep hurt. I mean that crying jag—the way he was carrying on—it wasn't fake or anything, it was real heavy-duty hurt. The man cares.

Sure, Norman Bowker said.

Say what you want, the man does care.

We all got problems.

Not Lavender.

No, I guess not, Bowker said. Do me a favor, though.

Shut up?

That's a smart Indian. Shut up.

Shrugging, Kiowa pulled off his boots. He wanted to say more, just to lighten up his sleep, but instead he opened his New Testament and arranged it beneath his head as a pillow. The fog made things seem hollow and unattached. He tried not to think about Ted Lavender, but then he was thinking how fast it was, no drama, down and dead, and how it was hard to feel anything except surprise. It seemed un-Christian. He wished he could find some great sadness, or even anger, but the emotion wasn't there and he couldn't make it happen. Mostly he felt pleased to be alive. He liked the smell of the New Testament under his cheek, the leather and ink and paper and glue, whatever the chemicals were. He liked hearing the sounds of night. Even his fatigue, it felt fine, the stiff muscles and the prickly awareness of his own body, a floating feeling. He enjoyed not being dead. Lying there, Kiowa admired Lieutenant Jimmy Cross's capacity for grief. He wanted to share the man's pain, he wanted to care as Jimmy Cross cared. And yet when he closed his eyes, all he could think was Boom-down, and all he could feel was the pleasure of having his boots off and the fog curling in around him and the damp soil and the Bible smells and the plush comfort of night.

After a moment Norman Bowker sat up in the dark.

What the hell, he said. You want to talk, *talk*. Tell it to me.

Forget it.

No, man, go on. One thing I hate, it's a silent Indian.

For the most part they carried themselves with poise, a kind of dignity. Now and then, however, there were times of panic, when they squealed or wanted to squeal but couldn't, when they twitched and made moaning sounds and covered their heads and said Dear Jesus and flopped around on the earth and fired their weapons blindly and cringed and sobbed and begged for the noise to stop and went wild and made stupid promises to themselves and to God and to their mothers and fathers, hoping not to die. In different ways, it happened to all of them. Afterward, when the firing ended, they would blink and peek up. They would touch their bodies, feeling shame, then quickly hiding it. They would force themselves to stand. As if in slow motion, frame by frame, the world would take on the old logic—absolute silence, then the wind, then sunlight, then voices. It was the burden of being alive. Awkwardly, the men would reassemble themselves, first in private, then in groups, becoming soldiers again. They would repair the leaks in their eyes. They would check for casualties, call in dust-offs, light cigarettes, try to smile, clear their throats and spit and begin cleaning their weapons. After a time someone would shake his head and say, No lie, I almost shit my pants, and someone else would laugh, which meant it was bad, yes, but the guy had obviously not shit his pants, it wasn't that bad, and in any case nobody would ever do such a thing and then go ahead and talk about it. They would squint into the dense, oppressive sunlight. For a few moments, perhaps, they would fall silent, lighting a joint and tracking its passage from man to man, inhaling, holding in the humiliation. Scary stuff, one of them might say. But then someone else would grin or flick his eyebrows and say, Roger-dodger, almost cut me a new asshole, *almost*.

There were numerous such poses. Some carried themselves with a sort of wistful resignation, others with pride or stiff soldierly discipline or good humor or macho zeal. They were afraid of dying but they were even more afraid to show it.

They found jokes to tell.

They used a hard vocabulary to contain the terrible softness. *Greased,* they'd say. *Offed, lit up, zapped while zipping.* It wasn't cruelty, just stage presence. They were actors and the war came at them in 3-D. When someone died, it wasn't quite dying, because in a curious way it seemed scripted, and because they had their lines mostly memorized, irony mixed with tragedy, and because they called it by other names, as if to encyst and destroy the reality of death itself. They kicked corpses. They cut off thumbs. They talked grunt lingo. They told stories about Ted Lavender's supply of tranquilizers, how the poor guy didn't feel a thing, how incredibly tranquil he was.

There's a moral here, said Mitchell Sanders.

They were waiting for Lavender's chopper, smoking the dead man's dope.

The moral's pretty obvious, Sanders said, and winked. Stay away from drugs. No joke, they'll ruin your day every time.

Cute, said Henry Dobbins.

Mind-blower, get it? Talk about wiggy—nothing left, just blood and brains.

They made themselves laugh.

There it is, they'd say, over and over, as if the repetition itself were an act of poise, a balance between crazy and almost crazy, knowing without going. There it is, which meant be cool, let it ride, because oh yeah, man, you can't change what can't be changed, there it is, there it absolutely and positively and fucking well *is.*

They were tough.

They carried all the emotional baggage of men who might die. Grief, terror, love, longing—these were intangibles, but the intangibles had their own mass and specific gravity, they had tangible weight. They carried shameful memories. They carried the common secret of cowardice barely restrained, the instinct to run or freeze or hide, and in many respects this was the heaviest burden of all, for it could never be put down, it required perfect balance and perfect posture. They carried their reputations. They carried the soldier's greatest fear, which was the fear of blushing. Men killed, and died, because they were embarrassed not to. It was what had brought them to the war in the first place, nothing positive, no dreams of glory or honor, just to avoid the blush of dishonor. They died so as not to die of embarrassment. They crawled into tunnels and walked point and advanced under fire. Each morning, despite the unknowns, they made their legs move. They endured. They kept humping. They did not submit to the obvious alternative, which was simply to close the eyes and fall. So easy, really. Go limp and tumble to the ground and let the muscles unwind and not speak and not budge until your buddies picked you up and lifted you into the chopper that would roar and dip its nose and carry you off to the world. A mere matter of falling, yet no one ever fell. It was not courage, exactly; the object was not valor. Rather, they were too frightened to be cowards.

By and large they carried these things inside, maintaining the masks of composure. They sneered at sick call. They spoke bitterly about guys who had found release by shooting off their own toes or fingers. Pussies, they'd say. Candyasses. It was fierce, mocking talk, with only a trace of envy or awe, but even so, the image played itself out behind their eyes.

They imagined the muzzle against flesh. They imagined the quick, sweet pain, then the evacuation to Japan, then a hospital with warm beds and cute geisha nurses.

They dreamed of freedom birds.

At night, on guard, staring into the dark, they were carried away by jumbo jets. They felt the rush of takeoff. *Gone!* they yelled. And then velocity, wings and engines, a smiling stewardess—but it was more than a plane, it was a real bird, a big sleek silver bird with feathers and talons and high screeching. They were flying. The weights fell off, there was nothing to bear. They laughed and held on tight, feeling the cold slap of wind and altitude, soaring, thinking *It's over, I'm gone!*—they were naked, they were light and free—it was all lightness, bright and fast and buoyant, light as light, a helium buzz in the brain, a giddy bubbling in the lungs as they were taken up over the clouds and the war, beyond duty, beyond gravity and mortification and global entanglements—*Sin loi!*° they yelled, *I'm sorry, motherfuckers, but I'm out of it, I'm goofed, I'm on a space cruise, I'm gone!*—and it was a restful, disencumbered sensation, just riding the light waves, sailing that big silver freedom bird over the mountains and oceans, over America, over the farms and great sleeping cities and cemeteries and highways and the golden arches of McDonald's. It was flight, a kind of fleeing, a kind of falling, falling higher and higher, spinning off the edge of the earth and beyond the sun and through the vast, silent vacuum where there were no burdens and where everything weighed exactly nothing. *Gone!* they screamed, *I'm sorry but I'm gone!* And so at night, not quite dreaming, they gave themselves over to lightness, they were carried, they were purely borne.

On the morning after Ted Lavender died, First Lieutenant Jimmy Cross crouched at the bottom of his foxhole and burned Martha's letters. Then he burned the two photographs. There was a steady rain falling, which made it difficult, but he used heat tabs and Sterno to build a small fire, screening it with his body, holding the photographs over the tight blue flame with the tips of his fingers.

Sin loi!: "Sorry about that!"

He realized it was only a gesture. Stupid, he thought. Sentimental, too, but mostly just stupid.

Lavender was dead. You couldn't burn the blame.

Besides, the letters were in his head. And even now, without photographs, Lieutenant Cross could see Martha playing volleyball in her white gym shorts and yellow T-shirt. He could see her moving in the rain.

When the fire died out, Lieutenant Cross pulled his poncho over his shoulders and ate breakfast from a can.

There was no great mystery, he decided.

In those burned letters Martha had never mentioned the war, except to say, Jimmy, take care of yourself. She wasn't involved. She signed the letters "Love," but it wasn't love, and all the fine lines and technicalities did not matter.

The morning came up wet and blurry. Everything seemed part of everything else, the fog and Martha and the deepening rain.

It was a war, after all.

Half smiling, Lieutenant Jimmy Cross took out his maps. He shook his head hard, as if to clear it, then bent forward and began planning the day's march. In ten minutes, or maybe twenty, he would rouse the men and they would pack up and head west, where the maps showed the country to be green and inviting. They would do what they had always done. The rain might add some weight, but otherwise it would be one more day layered upon all the other days.

He was realistic about it. There was that new hardness in his stomach.

No more fantasies, he told himself.

Henceforth, when he thought about Martha, it would be only to think that she belonged elsewhere. He would shut down the daydreams. This was not Mount Sebastian, it was another world, where there were no pretty poems or midterm exams, a place where men died because of carelessness and gross stupidity. Kiowa was right. Boom-down, and you were dead, never partly dead.

Briefly, in the rain, Lieutenant Cross saw Martha's gray eyes gazing back at him.

He understood.

It was very sad, he thought. The things men carried inside. The things men did or felt they had to do.

He almost nodded at her, but didn't.

Instead he went back to his maps. He was now determined to perform his duties firmly and without negligence. It wouldn't help Lavender, he knew that, but from this point on he would comport himself as a soldier. He would dispose of his good-luck pebble. Swallow it, maybe, or use Lee Strunk's slingshot, or just drop it along the trail. On the march he would impose strict field discipline. He would be careful to send out flank security, to prevent straggling or bunching up, to keep his troops moving at the proper pace and at the proper interval. He would insist on clean weapons. He would confiscate the remainder of Lavender's dope. Later in the day, perhaps, he would call the men together and speak to them plainly. He would accept the blame for what had happened to Ted Lavender. He would be a man about it. He would look them in the eyes, keeping his chin level, and he would issue the new SOPs in a calm, impersonal tone of voice, an officer's voice, leaving no room for argument or discussion. Commencing immediately, he'd tell them, they would no longer abandon equipment along the route of march. They would police up their acts. They would get their shit together, and keep it together, and maintain it neatly and in good working order.

He would not tolerate laxity. He would show strength, distancing himself.

Among the men there would be grumbling, of course, and maybe worse, because their days would seem longer and their loads heavier, but Lieutenant Cross reminded himself that his obligation was not to be loved but to lead. He would dispense with love; it was not now a factor. And if anyone quarreled or complained, he would simply tighten his lips and arrange his shoulders in the correct command posture. He might give a curt little nod. Or he might not. He might just shrug and say Carry on, then they would saddle up and form into a column and move out toward the villages west of Than Khe.

[1986]

T. CORAGHESSAN BOYLE   [b. 1948]

After the Plague

After the plague—it was some sort of Ebola mutation passed from hand
to hand and nose to nose like the common cold—life was different. More
relaxed and expansive, more natural. The rat race was over, the freeways
were clear all the way to Sacramento, and the poor dwindling ravaged
planet was suddenly big and mysterious again. It was a kind of miracle
really, what the environmentalists had been hoping for all along, though
of course even the most strident of them wouldn't have wished for his
own personal extinction, but there it was. I don't mean to sound callous—
my parents are long dead and I'm unmarried and siblingless, but I lost
friends, colleagues and neighbors, the same as any other survivor. What
few of us there are, that is. We're guessing it's maybe one in ten thousand, here in the States anyway. I'm sure there are whole tribes that escaped it somewhere in the Amazon or the interior valleys of Indonesia,
meteorologists in isolated weather stations, fire lookouts, goatherds and
the like. But the president's gone, the vice president, the cabinet, Congress, the joint chiefs of staff, the chairmen of the boards and CEOs of
the Fortune 500 companies, along with all their stockholders, employees
and retainers. There's no TV. No electricity or running water. And there
won't be any dining out anytime soon.

Actually, I'm lucky to be here to tell you about it—it was sheer serendipity, really. You see, I wasn't among my fellow human beings when it
hit—no festering airline cabins or snaking supermarket lines for me, no
concerts, sporting events or crowded restaurants—and the closest I
came to intimate contact was a telephone call to my on-and-off girlfriend, Danielle, from a gas station in the Sierra foothills. I think I may
have made a kissing noise over the wire, my lips very possibly coming
into contact with the molded plastic mouthpiece into which hordes of
strangers had breathed before me, but this was a good two weeks before
the first victim carried the great dripping bag of infection that was himself back from a camcorder safari to the Ngorongoro Crater or a conference on economic development in Malawi. Danielle, whose voice was a
drug I was trying to kick, at least temporarily, promised to come join me
for a weekend in the cabin after my six weeks of self-imposed isolation
were over, but sadly, she never made it. Neither did anyone else.

I *was* isolated up there in the mountains—that was the whole point—
and the first I heard of anything amiss was over the radio. It was a warm,
full-bodied day in early fall, the sun caught like a child's ball in the crown
of the Jeffrey pine outside the window, and I was washing up after lunch
when a smooth melodious voice interrupted *Afternoon Classics* to say
that people were bleeding from the eyeballs and vomiting up bile in the
New York subways and collapsing en masse in the streets of the capital.
The authorities were fully prepared to deal with what they were calling a
minor outbreak of swine flu, the voice said, and people were cautioned
not to panic, but all at once the announcer seemed to chuckle deep in his
throat, and then, right in the middle of the next phrase, he sneezed—a
controlled explosion hurtling out over the airwaves to detonate ominously in ten million trembling speakers—and the radio fell silent.
Somebody put on a CD of Richard Strauss' *Death and Transfiguration*,
and it played over and over through the rest of the afternoon.

I didn't have access to a telephone—not unless I hiked two and a half
miles out to the road where I'd parked my car and then drove another six
to Fish Fry Flats, pop. 28, and used the public phone at the bar/restau-
rant/gift shop/one-stop grocery/gas station there—so I ran the dial up
and down the radio to see if I could get some news. Reception is pretty
spotty up in the mountains—you never knew whether you'd get Bakersfield, Fresno, San Luis Obispo or even Tijuana—and I couldn't pull in
anything but white noise on that particular afternoon, except for the
aforementioned tone poem, that is. I was powerless. What would happen
would happen, and I'd find out all the sordid details a week later, just as
I found out about all the other crises, scandals, scoops, coups, typhoons,
wars and cease-fires that held the world spellbound while I communed
with the ground squirrels and woodpeckers. It was funny. The big events
didn't seem to mean much up here in the mountains, where life was so
much more elemental and immediate and the telling concerns of the day
revolved around priming the water pump and lighting the balky old gas
stove without blowing the place up. I picked up a worn copy of John
Cheever's stories somebody had left in the cabin during one of its previous incarnations and forgot all about the news out of New York and
Washington.

Later, when it finally came to me that I couldn't live through another
measure of Strauss without risk of permanent impairment, I flicked off
the radio, put on a light jacket and went out to glory in the way the season had touched the aspens along the path out to the road. The sun was
leaning way over to the west now, the shrubs and ground litter gathering
up the night, the tall trees trailing deep blue shadows. There was the
faintest breath of a chill in the air, a premonition of winter, and I thought

of the simple pleasures of building a fire, preparing a homely meal and sitting through the evening with a book in one hand and a scotch and Drambuie in the other. It wasn't until nine or ten at night that I remembered the bleeding eyeballs and the fateful sneeze, and though I was half-convinced it was a hoax or maybe one of those fugitive terrorist attacks with a colorless, odorless gas—sarin or the like—I turned on the radio, eager for news.

There was nothing, no Strauss, no crisp and efficient NPR correspondent delivering news of riots in Cincinnati and the imminent collapse of the infrastructure, no right-wing talk, no hip-hop, no jazz, no rock. I switched to AM, and after a painstaking search I hit on a weak signal that sounded as if it were coming from the bottom of Santa Monica Bay. *This is only a test*, a mechanical voice pronounced in what was now just the faintest whispering squeak, *in the event of an actual emergency please stay tuned to* . . . and then it faded out. While I was fumbling to bring it back in, I happened upon a voice shouting something in Spanish. It was just a single voice, very agitated, rolling on tirelessly, and I listened in wonder and dread until the signal went dead just after midnight.

I didn't sleep that night. I'd begun to divine the magnitude of what was going on in the world below me—this was no hoax, no casual atrocity or ordinary attrition; this was the beginning of the end, the Apocalypse, the utter failure and ultimate demise of all things human. I felt sick at heart. Lying there in the fastness of the cabin in the absolute and abiding dark of the wilderness, I was consumed with fear. I lay on my stomach and listened to the steady thunder of my heart pounding through the mattress, attuned to the slightest variation, waiting like a condemned man for the first harrowing sneeze.

Over the course of the next several days, the radio would sporadically come to life (I left it switched on at all times, day and night, as if I were going down in a sinking ship and could shout "Mayday!" into the receiver at the first stirring of a human voice). I'd be pacing the floor or spooning sugar into my tea or staring at a freshly inserted and eternally blank page in my ancient manual typewriter when the static would momentarily clear and a harried newscaster spoke out of the void to provide me with the odd and horrific detail: an oceanliner had run aground off Cape Hatteras and nothing left aboard except three sleek and frisky cats and various puddles of flesh swathed in plaid shorts, polo shirts and sunglasses; no sound or signal had come out of South Florida in over thirty-six hours; a group of survivalists had seized Bill Gates' private jet in an attempt to escape to Antarctica, where it was thought the infection hadn't yet reached, but everyone aboard vomited black bile and died before the plane could leave the ground. Another announcer broke down in the middle of an unconfirmed report that every man, woman and child in

Minneapolis was dead, and yet another came over the air early one morning shouting, "It kills! It kills! It kills in three days!" At that point, I jerked the plug out of the wall.

My first impulse, of course, was to help. To save Danielle, the frail and the weak, the young and the old, the chairman of the social studies department at the school where I teach (or taught), a student teacher with cropped red hair about whom I'd had several minutely detailed sexual fantasies. I even went so far as to hike out to the road and take the car into Fish Fry Flats, but the bar/restaurant/gift shop/one-stop grocery/gas station was closed and locked and the parking lot deserted. I drove round the lot three times, debating whether I should continue on down the road or not, but then a lean furtive figure darted out of a shed at the corner of the lot and threw itself—himself—into the shadows beneath the deck of the main building. I recognized the figure immediately as the splay-footed and pony-tailed proprietor of the place, a man who would pump your gas with an inviting smile and then lure you into the gift shop to pay in the hope that the hand-carved Tule Indian figurines and Pen-Lite batteries would prove irresistible. I saw his feet protruding from beneath the deck, and they seemed to be jittering or trembling as if he were doing some sort of energetic new contra-dance that began in the prone position. For a long moment I sat there and watched those dancing feet, then I hit the lock button, rolled up the windows and drove back to the cabin.

What did I do? Ultimately? Nothing. Call it enlightened self-interest. Call it solipsism, self-preservation, cowardice, I don't care. I was terrified—who wouldn't be?—and I decided to stay put. I had plenty of food and firewood, fuel for the generator and propane for the stove, three reams of twenty-five percent cotton fiber bond, correction fluid, books, board games—Parcheesi and Monopoly—and a complete set of *National Geographic*, 1947–1962. (By way of explanation, I should mention that I am—or was—a social studies teacher at the Montecito School, a preparatory academy in a pricey suburb of Santa Barbara, and that the serendipity that spared me the fate of nearly all my fellow men and women was as simple and fortuitous a thing as a sabbatical leave. After fourteen years of unstinting service, I applied for and was granted a one-semester leave at half-salary for the purpose of writing a memoir of my deprived and miserable Irish-Catholic upbringing. The previous year a high school teacher from New York—the name escapes me now—had enjoyed a spectacular *succès d'estime*, not to mention *d'argent*, with a memoir about his own miserable and deprived Irish-Catholic boyhood, and I felt I could profitably mine the same territory. And I got a good start on it too, until the plague hit. Now I ask myself what's the use—the publishers are all dead. Ditto the editors, agents, reviewers, book-sellers and the great congenial book-buying public itself. What's the sense of writing? What's the sense of anything?)

At any rate, I stuck close to the cabin, writing at the kitchen table through the mornings, staring out the window into the ankles of the pines and redwoods as I summoned degrading memories of my alcoholic mother, father, aunts, uncles, cousins and grandparents, and in the afternoons I hiked up to the highest peak and looked down on the deceptive tranquillity of the San Joaquin Valley spread out like a continent below me. There were no planes in the sky overhead, no sign of traffic or movement anywhere, no sounds but the calling of the birds and the soughing of the trees as the breeze sifted through them. I stayed up there past dark one night and felt as serene and terrible as a god when I looked down at the velvet expanse of the world and saw no ray or glimmer of light. I plugged the radio back in that night, just to hear the fading comfort of man-made noise, of the static that emanates from nowhere and nothing. Because there was nothing out there, not anymore.

It was four weeks later—just about the time I was to have ended my hermitage and enjoyed the promised visit from Danielle—that I had my first human contact of the new age. I was at the kitchen window, beating powdered eggs into a froth for dinner, one ear half-attuned to the perfect and unbroken static hum of the radio, when there was a heavy thump on the deteriorating planks of the front deck. My first thought was that a branch had dropped out of the Jeffrey pine—or worse, that a bear had got wind of the corned beef hash I'd opened to complement the powdered eggs—but I was mistaken on both counts. The thump was still reverberating through the floorboards when I was surprised to hear a moan and then a curse—a distinctly human curse. "Oh, shit-fuck!" a woman's voice cried. "Open the goddamned door! Help, for shit's sake, help!"

I've always been a cautious animal. This may be one of my great failings, as my mother and later my fraternity brothers were always quick to point out, but on the other hand, it may be my greatest virtue. It's kept me alive when the rest of humanity has gone on to a quick and brutal extinction, and it didn't fail me in that moment. The door was locked. Once I'd got wind of what was going on in the world, though I was devastated and the thought of the radical transformation of everything I'd ever known gnawed at me day and night, I took to locking it against just such an eventuality as this. "Shit!" the voice raged. "I can hear you in there, you son of a bitch—I can *smell* you!"

I stood perfectly still and held my breath. The static breathed dismally through the speakers and I wished I'd had the sense to disconnect the radio long ago. I stared down at the half-beaten eggs.

"I'm dying out here!" the voice cried. "I'm starving to death—hey, are you deaf in there or what? I said, I'm *starving!*"

And now of course I was faced with a moral dilemma. Here was a fellow human being in need of help, a member of a species whose value had just vaulted into the rarefied atmosphere occupied by the gnatcatcher, the condor and the beluga whale by virtue of its rarity. Help her? Of course I would help her. But at the same time, I knew if I opened that door I would invite the pestilence in and that three days hence both she and I would be reduced to our mortal remains.

"Open up!" she demanded, and the tattoo of her fists was the thunder of doom on the thin planks of the door.

It occurred to me suddenly that she couldn't be infected—she'd have been dead and wasted by now if she were. Maybe she was like me, maybe she'd been out brooding in her own cabin or hiking the mountain trails, utterly oblivious and immune to the general calamity. Maybe she was beautiful, nubile, a new Eve for a new age, maybe she would fill my nights with passion and my days with joy. As if in a trance, I crossed the room and stood at the door, my fingers on the long brass stem of the bolt. "Are you alone?" I said, and the rasp of my own voice, so long in disuse, sounded strange in my ears.

I heard her draw in a breath of astonishment and outrage from the far side of the thin panel that separated us. "What the hell do you think, you son of a bitch? I've been lost out here in these stinking woods for I don't know how long and I haven't had a scrap for days, not a goddamn scrap, not even bark or grass or a handful of soggy trail mix. *Now will you fucking open this door?!*"

Still, I hesitated.

A rending sound came to me then, a sound that tore me open as surely as a surgical knife, from my groin to my throat: she was sobbing. Gagging for breath, and sobbing. "A frog," she sobbed, "I ate a goddamn slimy little putrid *frog!*"

God help me. God save and preserve me. I opened the door.

Sarai was thirty-eight years old—that is, three years older than I—and she was no beauty. Not on the surface, anyway. Even if you discounted the twenty-odd pounds she'd lost and her hair that was like some crushed rodent's pelt and the cuts and bites and suppurating sores that made her skin look like a leper's, and tried, by a powerful leap of the imagination, to see her as she once might have been, safely ensconced in her condo in Tarzana and surrounded by all the accoutrements of feminine hygiene and beauty, she still wasn't much.

This was her story: she and her live-in boyfriend, Howard, were nature enthusiasts—at least Howard was, anyway—and just before the plague hit they'd set out to hike an interlocking series of trails in the Golden Trout Wilderness. They were well provisioned, with the best of everything—Howard managed a sporting goods store—and for the first three weeks everything went according to plan. They ate delicious freeze-dried fettuccine Alfredo and shrimp couscous, drank cognac from a bota bag and made love wrapped in propylene, Gore-Tex and nylon. Mosquitoes and horseflies sampled her legs, but she felt good, born again, liberated from the traffic and the smog and her miserable desk in a miserable corner of the electronics company her father had founded. Then one morning, when they were camped by a stream, Howard went off with his day pack and a fly rod and never came back. She waited. She searched. She screamed herself hoarse. A week went by. Every day she searched in a new direction, following the stream both ways and combing every tiny rill and tributary, until finally she got herself lost. All streams were one stream, all hills and ridges alike. She had three Kudos bars with her and a six-ounce bag of peanuts, but no shelter and no freeze-dried entrées— all that was back at the camp she and Howard had made in happier times. A cold rain fell. There were no stars that night, and when something moved in the brush beside her she panicked and ran blindly through the dark, hammering her shins and destroying her face, her hair and her clothes. She'd been wandering ever since.

I made her a package of Top Ramen, gave her a towel and a bar of soap and showed her the primitive shower I'd rigged up above the ancient slab of the tub. I was afraid to touch her or even come too close to her. Sure I was skittish. Who wouldn't be when ninety-nine percent of the human race had just died off on the tailwind of a simple sneeze? Besides, I'd begun to adopt all the habits of the hermit—talking to myself, performing elaborate rituals over my felicitous stock of foodstuffs, dredging bursts of elementary school songs and beer jingles out of the depths of my impacted brain—and I resented having my space invaded. *Still.* Still, though, I felt that Sarai had been delivered to me by some higher power and that she'd been blessed in the way that I was—we'd escaped the infection. We'd survived. And we weren't just errant members of a selfish, suspicious and fragmented society, but the very foundation of a new one. She was a woman. I was a man.

At first, she wouldn't believe me when I waved a dismissive hand at the ridge behind the cabin and all that lay beyond it and informed her that the world was depeopled, that the Apocalypse had come and that she and I were among the solitary survivors—and who could blame her? As she sipped my soup and ate my flapjacks and treated her cuts and abrasions with my Neosporin and her hair with my shampoo, she must have thought she'd found a lunatic as her savior. "If you don't believe me," I said, and I was gloating, I was, sick as it may seem, "try the radio."

She looked up at me out of the leery brooding eyes of the one sane woman in a madhouse of impostors, plugged the cord in the socket and calibrated the dial as meticulously as a safecracker. She was rewarded by static—no dynamics even, just a single dull continuum—but she glared up at me as if I'd rigged the thing to disappoint her. "So," she spat, skinny as a refugee, her hair kinked and puffed up with my shampoo till it devoured her parsimonious and disbelieving little sliver of a face, "that doesn't prove a thing. It's broken, that's all."

When she got her strength back, we hiked out to the car and drove into Fish Fry Flats so she could see for herself. I was half-crazy with the terrible weight of the knowledge I'd been forced to hold inside me, and I can't describe the irritation I felt at her utter lack of interest—she treated me like a street gibberer, a psychotic, Cassandra in long pants. She condescended to me. She was *humoring* me, for God's sake, and the whole world lay in ruins around us. But she would have a rude awakening, she would, and the thought of it was what kept me from saying something I'd regret—I didn't want to lose my temper and scare her off, but I hate stupidity and willfulness. It's the one thing I won't tolerate in my students. Or wouldn't. Or didn't.

Fish Fry Flats, which in the best of times could hardly be mistaken for a metropolis, looked now as if it had been deserted for a decade. Weeds had begun to sprout up through invisible cracks in the pavement, dust had settled over the idle gas pumps and the windows of the main building were etched with grime. And the animals—the animals were everywhere, marmots waddling across the lot as if they owned it, a pair of coyotes asleep in the shade of an abandoned pickup, ravens cawing and squirrels chittering. I cut the engine just as a bear the color of cinnamon toast tumbled stupendously through an already shattered window and lay on his back, waving his bloodied paws in the air as if he were drunk, which he was. As we discovered a few minutes later—once he'd lurched to his feet and staggered off into the bushes—a whole host of creatures had raided the grocery, stripping the candy display right down to the twisted wire rack, scattering Triscuits and Doritos, shattering jars of jam and jugs of port wine and grinding the hand-carved Tule Indian figurines underfoot. There was no sign of the formerly sunny proprietor or of his dancing feet—I could only imagine that the ravens, coyotes and ants had done their work.

But Sarai—she was still an unbeliever, even after she dropped a quarter into the public telephone and put the dead black plastic receiver to her ear. For all the good it did her, she might as well have tried coaxing a dial tone out of a stone or a block of wood, and I told her so. She gave me a sour look, the sticks of her bones briefly animated beneath a sweater and jacket I'd loaned her—it was the end of October and getting cold at seventy-two hundred feet—and then she tried another quarter, and then another, before she slammed the receiver down in a rage and turned her seething face on me. "The lines are down, that's all," she sneered. And then her mantra: "It doesn't prove a thing."

While she'd been frustrating herself, I'd been loading the car with canned goods, after entering the main building through the broken window and unlatching the door from the inside. "And what about all this?" I said, irritated, hot with it, sick to death of her and her thick-headedness. I gestured at the bloated and lazy coyotes, the hump in the bushes that was the drunken bear, the waddling marmots and the proprietary ravens.

"I don't know," she said, clenching her jaws. "And I don't care." Her eyes had a dull sheen to them. They were insipid and bovine, exactly the color of the dirt at her feet. And her lips—thin and stingy, collapsed in a riot of vertical lines like a dried-up mud puddle. I hated her in that moment, godsend or no. Oh, how I hated her.

"What are you *doing?*" she demanded as I loaded the last of the groceries into the car, settled into the driver's seat and turned the engine over. She was ten feet from me, caught midway between the moribund phone booth and the living car. One of the coyotes lifted its head at the vehemence of her tone and gave her a sleepy, yellow-eyed look.

"Going back to the cabin," I said.

"You're *what?*" Her face was pained. She'd been through agonies. I was a devil and a madman.

"Listen, Sarai, it's all over. I've told you time and again. You don't have a job anymore. You don't have to pay rent, utility bills, don't have to make car payments or remember your mother's birthday. It's over. Don't you get it?"

"You're insane! You're a shithead! I hate you!"

The engine was purring beneath my feet, fuel awasting, but there was infinite fuel now, and though I realized the gas pumps would no longer work, there were millions upon millions of cars and trucks out there in the world with full tanks to siphon, and no one around to protest. I could drive a Ferrari if I wanted, a Rolls, a Jag, anything. I could sleep on a bed of jewels, stuff the mattress with hundred-dollar bills, prance through the streets in a new pair of Italian loafers and throw them into the gutter each night and get a new pair in the morning. But I was afraid. Afraid of the infection, the silence, the bones rattling in the wind. "I know it," I said. "I'm insane. I'm a shithead. I admit it. But I'm going back to the cabin and you can do anything you want—it's a free country. Or at least it used to be."

I wanted to add that it was a free world now, a free universe, and that God was in the details, the biblical God, the God of famine, flood and pestilence, but I never got the chance. Before I could open my mouth she bent for a stone and heaved it into the windshield, splintering me with flecks and shards of safety glass. "Die!" she shrieked. "*You* die, you shit!"

That night we slept together for the first time. In the morning, we packed up a few things and drove down the snaking mountain road to the charnel house of the world.

I have to confess that I've never been much of a fan of the apocalyptic potboiler, the doomsday film shot through with special effects and asinine dialogue or the cyberpunk version of a grim and relentless future. What these entertainments had led us to expect—the roving gangs, the inhumanity, the ascendancy of machines and the redoubled pollution and ravaging of the earth—wasn't at all what it was like. There were no roving gangs—they were all dead, to a man, woman and tattooed punk— and the only machines still functioning were the automobiles and weed whippers and such that we the survivors chose to put into prosaic action. And a further irony was that the survivors were the least likely and least qualified to organize anything, either for better or worse. We were the fugitive, the misfit, the recluse, and we were so widely scattered we'd never come into contact with one another, anyway—and that was just the way we liked it. There wasn't even any looting of the supermarkets— there was no need. There was more than enough for everybody who ever was or would be.

Sarai and I drove down the mountain road, through the deserted small town of Springville and the deserted larger town of Porterville, and then we turned south for Bakersfield, the Grapevine and Southern California. She wanted to go back to her apartment, to Los Angeles, and see if her parents and her sisters were alive still—she became increasingly vociferous on that score as the reality of what had happened began to seep through to her—but I was driving and I wanted to avoid Los Angeles at all costs. To my mind, the place had been a pit before the scourge hit, and now it was a pit heaped with seven million moldering corpses. She carped and moaned and whined and threatened, but she was in shock too and couldn't quite work herself up to her usual pitch, and so we turned west and north on Route 126 and headed toward Montecito, where for the past ten years I'd lived in a cottage on one of the big estates there—the DuPompier place. *Mírame*.

By the way, when I mentioned earlier that the freeways were clear, I was speaking metaphorically—they were free of traffic, but cluttered with abandoned vehicles of all sorts, take your pick, from gleaming choppers with thousand-dollar gold-fleck paint jobs to sensible family cars, Corvettes, Winnebagos, eighteen-wheelers and even fire engines and police cruisers. Twice, when Sarai became especially insistent, I pulled alongside one or another of these abandoned cars, swung open her door and said, "Go ahead. Take this Cadillac"—or BMW or whatever—"and drive yourself any damn place you please. Go on. What are you waiting for?" But her face shrank till it was as small as a doll's and her eyes went stony with fear: those cars were catacombs, each and every one of them, and the horror of that was more than anybody could bear.

So we drove on, through a preternatural silence and a world that already seemed primeval, up the Coast Highway and along the frothing bright boatless sea and into Montecito. It was evening when we arrived, and there wasn't a soul in sight. If it weren't for that—and a certain creeping untended look to the lawns, shrubs and trees—you wouldn't have noticed anything out of the ordinary. My cottage, built in the twenties of local sandstone and draped in wisteria till it was all but invisible, was exactly as I'd left it. We pulled into the silent drive with the great house looming in the near distance, a field of dark reflective glass that held the blood of the declining sun in it, and Sarai barely glanced up. Her thin shoulders were hunched and she was staring at a worn place on the mat between her feet.

"We're here," I announced, and I got out of the car.

She turned her eyes to me, stricken, suffering, a waif. "Where?"

"Home."

It took her a moment, but when she responded she spoke slowly and carefully, as if she were just learning the language. "I have no home," she said. "Not anymore."

So. What to tell you? We didn't last long, Sarai and I, though we were pioneers, though we were the last hope of the race, drawn together by the tenacious glue of fear and loneliness. I knew there wouldn't be much opportunity for dating in the near future, but we just weren't suited to each other. In fact, we were as unsuited as any two people could ever be, and our sex was tedious and obligatory, a ballet of mutual need and loathing, but to my mind at least, there was a bright side—here was the chance to go forth and be fruitful and do what we could to repopulate the vast and aching sphere of the planet. Within the month, however, Sarai had disabused me of that notion.

It was a silky, fog-hung morning, the day deepening around us, and we'd just gone through the mechanics of sex and were lying exhausted and unsatisfied in the rumple of my gritty sheets (water was a problem and we did what laundry we could with what we were able to haul down from the estate's swimming pool). Sarai was breathing through her mouth, an irritating snort and burble that got on my nerves, but before I could say anything, she spoke in a hard shriveled little nugget of a voice. "You're no Howard," she said.

"Howard's dead," I said. "He deserted you."

She was staring at the ceiling. "Howard was gold," she mused in a languid, reflective voice, "and you're shit."

It was childish, I know, but the dig at my sexual performance really stung—not to mention the ingratitude of the woman—and I came back at her. "You came to me," I said. "I didn't ask for it—I was doing fine out there on the mountain without you. And where do you think you'd be now if it wasn't for me? Huh?"

She didn't answer right away, but I could feel her consolidating in the bed beside me, magma becoming rock. "I'm not going to have sex with you again," she said, and still she was staring at the ceiling. "Ever. I'd rather use my finger."

"You're no Danielle," I said

She sat up then, furious, all her ribs showing and her shrunken breasts clinging to the remains of them like an afterthought. "Fuck Danielle," she spat. "And fuck you."

I watched her dress in silence, but as she was lacing up her hiking boots I couldn't resist saying, "It's no joy for me either, Sarai, but there's a higher principle involved here than our likes and dislikes or any kind of animal gratification, and I think you know what I'm talking about—"

She was perched on the edge of a leather armchair I'd picked up at a yard sale years ago, when money and things had their own reality. She'd laced up the right boot and was working on the left, laces the color of rust, blunt white fingers with the nails bitten to the quick. Her mouth hung open slightly and I could see the pink tip of her tongue caught between her teeth as she worked mindlessly at her task, reverting like a child to her earliest training and her earliest habits. She gave me a blank look.

"Procreation, I mean. If you look at it in a certain way, it's—well, it's our duty."

Her laugh stung me. It was sharp and quick, like the thrust of a knife. "You idiot," she said, and she laughed again, showing the gold in her back teeth. "I hate children, always have—they're little monsters that grow up to be uptight fussy pricks like you." She paused, smiled, and released an audible breath. "I had my tubes tied fifteen years ago."

That night she moved into the big house, a replica of a Moorish castle in Seville, replete with turrets and battlements. The paintings and furnishings were exquisite, and there were some twelve thousand square feet of living space, graced with carved wooden ceilings, colored tiles, rectangular arches, a loggia and formal gardens. Nor had the DuPompiers spoiled the place by being so thoughtless as to succumb inside— they'd died, Julius, Eleanor and their daughter, Kelly, under the arbor in back, the white bones of their hands eternally clasped. I wished Sarai good use of the place. I did. Because by that point I didn't care if she moved into the White House so long as I didn't have to deal with her anymore.

Weeks slipped by. Months. Occasionally I would see the light of Sarai's Coleman lantern lingering in one of the high windows of *Mírame* as night fell over the coast, but essentially I was as solitary—and as lonely—as I'd been in the cabin in the mountains. The rains came and went. It was spring. Everywhere the untended gardens ran wild, the lawns became fields, the orchards forests, and I took to walking round the neighborhood with a baseball bat to ward off the packs of feral dogs for which Alpo would never again materialize in a neat bowl in the corner of a dry and warm kitchen. And then one afternoon, while I was at Von's, browsing the aisles for pasta, bottled marinara and Green Giant asparagus spears amid a scattering of rats and the lingering stench of the perished perishables, I detected movement at the far end of the next aisle over. My first thought was that it must be a dog or a coyote that had somehow managed to get in to feed on the rats or the big twenty-five-pound bags of Purina Dog Chow, but then, with a shock, I realized I wasn't alone in the store.

In all the time I'd been coming here for groceries, I'd never seen a soul, not even Sarai or one of the six or seven other survivors who were out there occupying the mansions in the hills. Every once in a while I'd see lights shining in the wall of the night—someone had even managed to fire up a generator at Las Tejas, a big Italianate villa half a mile away—and every so often a car would go helling up the distant freeway, but basically we survivors were shy of one another and kept to ourselves. It was fear, of course, the little spark of panic that told you the contagion was abroad again and that the best way to avoid it was to avoid all human contact. So we did. Strenuously.

But I couldn't ignore the squeak and rattle of a shopping cart wheeling up the bottled water aisle, and when I turned the corner, there she was, Felicia, with her flowing hair and her scared and sorry eyes. I didn't know her name then, not at first, but I recognized her—she was one of the tellers at the Bank of America branch where I cashed my checks. Formerly cashed them, that is. My first impulse was to back wordlessly away, but I mastered it—how could I be afraid of what was human, so palpably human, and appealing? "Hello," I said, to break the tension, and then I was going to say something stupid like "I see you made it too" or "Tough times, huh?" but instead I settled for "Remember me?"

She looked stricken. Looked as if she were about to bolt—or die on the spot. But her lips were brave and they came together and uttered my name. "Mr. Halloran?" she said, and it was so ordinary, so plebeian, so real.

I smiled and nodded. My name is—was—Francis Xavier Halloran III, a name I've hated since Tyrone Johnson (now presumably dead) tormented me with it in kindergarten, chanting "Francis, Francis, Francis" till I wanted to sink through the floor. But it was a new world now, a world burgeoning and bursting at the seams to discover the lineaments of its new forms and rituals. "Call me Jed," I said.

Nothing happens overnight, especially not in plague times. We were wary of each other, and every banal phrase and stultifying cliché of the small talk we made as I helped her load her groceries into the back of her Range Rover reverberated hugely with the absence of all the multitudes who'd used those phrases before us. Still, I got her address that afternoon — she'd moved into Villa Ruscello, a mammoth place set against the mountains, with a creek, pond and Jacuzzi for fresh water — and I picked her up two nights later in a Rolls Silver Cloud and took her to my favorite French restaurant. The place was untouched and pristine, with a sweeping view of the sea, and I lit some candles and poured us each a glass of twenty-year-old Bordeaux, after which we feasted on canned crab, truffles, cashews and marinated artichoke hearts.

I'd like to tell you that she was beautiful, because that's the way it should be, the way of the fable and the fairy tale, but she wasn't — or not conventionally, anyway. She was a little heavier than she might have been ideally, but that was a relief after stringy Sarai, and her eyes were ever so slightly crossed. Yet she was decent and kind, sweet even, and more important, she was available.

We took walks together, raided overgrown gardens for lettuce, tomatoes and zucchini, planted strawberries and snow peas in the middle of the waist-high lawn at Villa Ruscello. One day we drove to the mountains and brought back the generator so we could have lights and refrigeration in the cottage — ice cubes, now there was a luxury — and begin to work our way through the eight thousand titles at the local video store. It was nearly a month before anything happened between us — anything sexual, that is. And when it did, she first felt obligated, out of a sense of survivor's guilt, I suppose, to explain to me how she came to be alive and breathing still when everyone she'd ever known had vanished off the face of the earth. We were in the beamed living room of my cottage, sharing a bottle of Dom Pérignon 1970, with the three-hundred-ten-dollar price tag still on it, and I'd started a fire against the gathering night and the wet raw smell of rain on the air. "You're going to think I'm an idiot," she said.

I made a noise of demurral and put my arm round her.

"Did you ever hear of a sensory deprivation tank?" She was peering up at me through the scrim of her hair, gold and red highlights, health in a bottle.

"Yeah, sure," I said. "But you don't mean — ?"

"It was an older one, a model that's not on the market anymore — one of the originals. My roommate's sister — Julie Angier? — she had it out in her garage on Padaro, and she was really into it. You could get in touch with your inner self, relax, maybe even have an out-of-body experience, that's what she said, and I figured why not?" She gave me a look, shy and passionate at once, to let me know that she was the kind of girl who took experience seriously. "They put salt water in it, three hundred gallons, heated to your body temperature, and then they shut the lid on you and there's nothing, absolutely nothing there—it's like going to outer space. Or inner space. Inside yourself."

"And you were in there when—?"

She nodded. There was something in her eyes I couldn't read—pride, triumph, embarrassment, a spark of sheer lunacy. I gave her an encouraging smile.

"For days, I guess," she said. "I just sort of lost track of everything, who I was, where I was—you know? And I didn't wake up till the water started getting cold"—she looked at her feet—"which I guess is when the electricity went out because there was nobody left to run the power plants. And then I pushed open the lid and the sunlight through the window was like an atom bomb, and then, then I called out Julie's name, and she . . . well, she never answered."

Her voice died in her throat and she turned those sorrowful eyes on me. I put my other arm around her and held her. "Hush," I whispered, "it's all right now, everything's all right." It was a conventional thing to say, and it was a lie, but I said it, and I held her and felt her relax in my arms.

It was then, almost to the precise moment, that Sarai's naked sliver of a face appeared at the window, framed by her two uplifted hands and a rock the size of my Webster's unabridged. "What about *me*, you son of a bitch!" she shouted, and there it was again, everlasting stone and frangible glass, and not a glazier left alive on the planet.

I wanted to kill her. It was amazing—three people I knew of had survived the end of everything, and it was one too many. I felt vengeful. Biblical. I felt like storming Sarai's ostentatious castle and wringing her chicken neck for her, and I think I might have if it weren't for Felicia. "Don't let her spoil it for us," she murmured, the gentle pressure of her fingers on the back of my neck suddenly holding my full attention, and we went into the bedroom and closed the door on all that mess of emotion and glass.

In the morning, I stepped into the living room and was outraged all over again. I cursed and stomped and made a fool of myself over heaving the rock back through the window and attacking the shattered glass as if it were alive—I admit I was upset out of all proportion to the crime. This was a new world, a new beginning, and Sarai's nastiness and negativity had no place in it. Christ, there were only three of us—couldn't we get along?

Felicia had repaired dozens of windows in her time. Her little brothers (dead now) and her fiancé (dead too) were forever throwing balls around the house, and she assured me that a shattered window was nothing to get upset over (though she bit her lip and let her eyes fill at the mention of her fiancé, and who could blame her?). So we consulted the Yellow Pages, drove to the nearest window glass shop and broke in as gently as possible. Within the hour, the new pane had been installed and the putty was drying in the sun, and watching Felicia at work had so elevated my spirits I suggested a little shopping spree to celebrate.

"Celebrate what?" She was wearing a No Fear T-shirt and an Anaheim Angels cap and there was a smudge of off-white putty on her chin.

"You," I said. "The simple miracle of you."

And that was fine. We parked on the deserted streets of down-town Santa Barbara and had the stores to ourselves—clothes, the latest (and last) bestsellers, CDs, a new disc player to go with our newly electrified house. Others had visited some of the stores before us, of course, but they'd been polite and neat about it, almost as if they were afraid to betray their presence, and they always closed the door behind them. We saw deer feeding in the courtyards and one magnificent tawny mountain lion stalking the wrong way up a one-way street. By the time we got home, I was elated. Everything was going to work out, I was sure of it.

The mood didn't last long. As I swung into the drive, the first thing I saw was the yawning gap where the new window had been, and beyond it, the undifferentiated heap of rubble that used to be my living room. Sarai had been back. And this time she'd done a thorough job, smashing lamps and pottery, poking holes in our cans of beef stew and chili con carne, scattering coffee, flour and sugar all over everything and dumping sand in the generator's fuel tank. Worst of all, she'd taken half a dozen pairs of Felicia's panties and nailed them to the living room wall, a crude X slashed across the crotch of each pair. It was hateful and savage—human, that's what it was, human—and it killed all the joy we'd taken in the afternoon and the animals and the infinite and various riches of the mall. Sarai had turned it all to shit.

"We'll move to my place," Felicia said. "Or any place you want. How about an oceanfront house—didn't you say you'd always wanted to live right on the ocean?"

I had. But I didn't want to admit it. I stood in the middle of the desecrated kitchen and clenched my fists. "I don't want any other place. This is my home. I've lived here for ten years and I'll be damned if I'm going to let *her* drive me out."

It was an irrational attitude—again, childish—and Felicia convinced me to pack up a few personal items (my high school yearbook, my reggae albums, a signed first edition of *For Whom the Bell Tolls*, a pair of deer antlers I'd found in the woods when I was eight) and move into a place on the ocean for a few days. We drove along the coast road at a slow, stately pace, looking over this house or that, until we finally settled on a grand modern place that was all angles and glass and broad sprawling decks. I got lucky and caught a few perch in the surf, and we barbecued them on the beach and watched the sun sink into the western bluffs.

The next few days were idyllic, and we thought about little beyond love and food and the way the water felt on our skin at one hour of the day or another, but still, the question of Sarai nagged at me. I was reminded of her every time I wanted a cold drink, for instance, or when the sun set and we had to make do with candles and kerosene lanterns—we'd have to go out and dig up another generator, we knew that, but they weren't exactly in demand in a place like Santa Barbara (in the old days, that is) and we didn't know where to look. And so yes, I couldn't shake the image of Sarai and the look on her face and the things she'd said and done. And I missed my house, because I'm a creature of habit, like anybody else. Or more so. Definitely more so.

Anyway, the solution came to us a week later, and it came in human form—at least it appeared in human form, but it was a miracle and no doubt about it. Felicia and I were both on the beach—naked, of course, as naked and without shame or knowledge of it as Eve and Adam—when we saw a figure marching resolutely up the long curving finger of sand that stretched away into the haze of infinity. As the figure drew closer, we saw that it was a man, a man with a scraggly salt-and-pepper beard and hair the same color trailing away from a bald spot worn into his crown. He was dressed in hiking clothes, big-grid boots, a bright blue pack riding his back like a second set of shoulders. We stood there, naked, and greeted him.

"Hello," he said, stopping a few feet from us and staring first at my face, then at Felicia's breasts, and finally, with an effort, bending to check the laces of his boots. "Glad to see you two made it," he said, speaking to the sand.

"Likewise," I returned.

Over lunch on the deck—shrimp salad sandwiches on Felicia-baked bread—we traded stories. It seems he was hiking in the mountains when the pestilence descended—"The mountains?" I interrupted. "Whereabouts?"

"Oh," he said, waving a dismissive hand, "up in the Sierras, just above this little town—you've probably never heard of it—Fish Fry Flats?"

I let him go on a while, explaining how he'd lost his girlfriend and wandered for days before he finally came out on a mountain road and appropriated a car to go on down to Los Angeles—"One big cemetery"—and how he'd come up the coast and had been wandering ever since. I don't think I've ever felt such exhilaration, such a rush of excitement, such perfect and inimitable a sense of closure.

I couldn't keep from interrupting him again. "I'm clairvoyant," I said, raising my glass to the man sitting opposite me, to Felicia and her breasts, to the happy fishes in the teeming seas and the birds flocking without number in the unencumbered skies. "Your name's Howard, right?"

Howard was stunned. He set down his sandwich and wiped a fleck of mayonnaise from his lips. "How did you guess?" he said, gaping up at me out of eyes that were innocent and pure, the newest eyes in the world.

I just smiled and shrugged, as if it were my secret. "After lunch," I said, "I've got somebody I want you to meet."

[2001]

JAMAICA KINCAID   [b. 1949]

Girl

Wash the white clothes on Monday and put them on the stone heap; wash the color clothes on Tuesday and put them on the clothesline to dry; don't walk barehead in the hot sun; cook pumpkin fritters in very hot sweet oil; soak your little cloths right after you take them off; when buying cotton to make yourself a nice blouse, be sure that it doesn't have gum on it, because that way it won't hold up well after a wash; soak salt fish overnight before you cook it; is it true that you sing benna° in Sunday school?; always eat your food in such a way that it won't turn someone else's stomach; on Sundays try to walk like a lady and not like the slut you are so bent on becoming; don't sing benna in Sunday school; you mustn't speak to wharf-rat boys, not even to give directions; don't eat fruits on the street—flies will follow you; *but I don't sing benna on Sundays at all and never in Sunday school*; this is how to sew on a button; this is how to make a button-hole for the button you have just sewed on; this is how to hem a dress when you see the hem coming down and so to prevent yourself from looking like the slut I know you are so bent on becoming; this is how you iron your father's khaki shirt so that it doesn't

Benna: Calypso music.

have a crease; this is how you iron your father's khaki pants so that they don't have a crease; this is how you grow okra—far from the house, because okra tree harbors red ants; when you are growing dasheen,° make sure it gets plenty of water or else it makes your throat itch when you are eating it; this is how you sweep a corner; this is how you sweep a whole house; this is how you sweep a yard; this is how you smile to someone you don't like too much; this is how you smile to someone you don't like at all; this is how you smile to someone you like completely; this is how you set a table for tea; this is how you set a table for dinner; this is how you set a table for dinner with an important guest; this is how you set a table for lunch; this is how you set a table for breakfast; this is how to behave in the presence of men who don't know you very well, and this way they won't recognize immediately the slut I have warned you against becoming; be sure to wash every day, even if it is with your own spit; don't squat down to play marbles—you are not a boy, you know; don't pick people's flowers—you might catch something; don't throw stones at blackbirds, because it might not be a blackbird at all; this is how to make a bread pudding; this is how to make doukona;° this is how to make pepper pot; this is how to make a good medicine for a cold; this is how to make a good medicine to throw away a child before it even becomes a child; this is how to catch a fish; this is how to throw back a fish you don't like, and that way something bad won't fall on you; this is how to bully a man; this is how a man bullies you; this is how to love a man, and if this doesn't work there are other ways, and if they don't work don't feel too bad about giving up; this is how to spit up in the air if you feel like it, and this is how to move quick so that it doesn't fall on you; this is how to make ends meet; always squeeze bread to make sure it's fresh; *but what if the baker won't let me feel the bread?*; you mean to say that after all you are really going to be the kind of woman who the baker won't let near the bread?

[1978]

Dasheen: Taro, an edible starchy plant.
Doukona: A spicy plantain pudding.

DAGOBERTO GILB   [b. 1950]

Shout

He beat on the screen door. "Will somebody open this?!" Unlike most men, he didn't leave his hard hat in his truck, took it inside his home; and he had it in his hand. His body was dry now, at least it wasn't like it was two hours ago at work, when he wrung his T-shirt of sweat, made it drool between the fingers of his fist, he and his partner making as much of a joke out of it as they could. That's how hot it was, how humid, and it'd been like this, in the nineties and hundreds, for two weeks, and it'd been hot enough before that. All he could think about was unlacing his dirty boots, then peeling off those stinky socks, then the rest. He'd take a cold one into the shower. The second one. He'd down the first one right at the refrigerator. "Come on!" Three and four were to be appreciated, five was mellow, and six let him nap before bed.

"I didn't hear you," his wife said.

"Didn't *hear* me? How *couldn't* you hear me? And why's it locked anyways? When I get here I don't feel like waiting to come in. Why can't you leave the thing unlocked?"

"Why do you think?"

"Well don't let the baby open it. I want this door open when I get home." He carried on in Spanish, *hijos de* and *putas* and *madres* and *chingadas*. This was the only Spanish he used at home. He tossed the hard hat near the door, relieved to be inside, even though it was probably hotter than outside, even though she was acting mad. He took it that she'd been that way all day already.

Their children, three boys, were seven, four, and almost two, and they were, as should be expected, battling over something.

"Everybody shut up and be quiet!" he yelled. Of course that worsened the situation, because when he got mad he scared the baby, who immediately started crying.

"I'm so tired," he muttered.

She glared at him, the baby in her arms.

"You know sometimes I wish you were a man cuz I wouldn't let you get away with looks like that. I wouldn't take half the shit I take from you." He fell back into the wooden chair nobody sat in except him when he laced the high-top boots on, or off, as he already had. "You know how hot

357

it was today? A hundred and five. It's unbelievable." He looked at her closely, deeply, which he didn't often do, especially this month. She was trying to settle down the baby and turned the TV on to distract the other two.

"It's too hard to breathe," he said to her. He walked barefooted for the beer and took out two. They were in the door tray of the freezer and almost frozen.

"So nothing happened today?" she asked. Already she wasn't mad at him. It was how she was, why they could get along.

"Nothing else was said. Maybe nothing's gonna happen. God knows this heat's making everybody act unnatural. But tomorrow's check day. If he's gonna get me most likely it'll be tomorrow." He finished a beer leaning against the tile near the kitchen sink, enjoying a peace that had settled into the apartment. The baby was content, the TV was on, the Armenians living an arm's reach away were chattering steadily, there was a radio on from an apartment in a building across from them, Mexican TV upstairs, pigeons, a dog, traffic noise, the huge city out there groaning its sound—all this silence in the apartment.

"There's other jobs," he said. "All of 'em end no matter what anyways."

It was a job neither of them wanted to end too soon. This year he'd been laid up for months after he fell and messed up his shoulder and back. He'd been drunk—a happy one that started after work—but he did it right there at his own front door, playing around. At the same time the duplex apartment they'd been living in for years had been sold and they had to move here. It was all they could get, all they were offered, since so few landlords wanted three children, boys no less, at a monthly rent they could afford. They were lucky to find it and it wasn't bad as places went, but they didn't like it much. They felt like they were starting out again, and that did not seem right. They'd talked this over since they'd moved in until it degenerated into talk about separation. And otherwise, in other details, it also wasn't the best year of their lives.

He showered in warm water, gradually turning the hot water down until it came out as cold as the summer allowed, letting the iced beer do the rest.

She was struggling getting dinner together, the boys were loud and complaining about being hungry, and well into the fifth beer, as he sat near the bright color and ever-happy tingle of the TV set, his back stiffening up, he snapped.

"Everybody has to shut up! I can't stand this today! I gotta relax some!"

She came back at him screaming too. "I can't stand *you!*"

He leaped. "You don't talk to me like that!"

She came right up to him. "You gonna hit me?!" she dared him.

The seven-year-old ran to his bed but the other two froze up, waiting for the tension to ease enough before their tears squeezed out.

"Get away from me," he said trying to contain himself. "You better get away from me right now. You know, just go home, go to your mother's, just go."

"*You* go! *You* get out! We're gonna stay!"

He looked through her, then slapped a wall, rocking what seemed like the whole building. "You don't know how close you are."

He wouldn't leave. He walked into the bedroom, then walked out, sweating. He went into the empty kitchen—they were all in the children's room, where there was much crying—and he took a plate and filled it with what she'd made and went in front of the tube and he clicked on a ball game, told himself to calm himself and let it all pass at least tonight, at least while the weather was like it was and while these other things were still bothering both of them, and then he popped the sixth beer. He wasn't going to fall asleep on the couch tonight.

Eventually his family came out, one by one peeking around a corner to see what he looked like. Then they ate in a whisper, even cutting loose here and there with a little giggle or gripe. Eventually the sun did set, though that did nothing to wash off the glue of heat.

And eventually the older boys felt comfortable enough to complain about bedtime. Only the baby cried—he was tired and wanted to sleep but couldn't because a cold had clogged his nose. Still, they were all trying to maintain the truce when from outside, a new voice came in: SHUT THAT FUCKING KID UP YOU FUCKING PEOPLE! HEY! SHUT THAT FUCKING KID UP OVER THERE!

It was like an explosion except that he flew toward it. He shook the window screen with his voice. "You fuck yourself, asshole! You stupid asshole, you shut your mouth!" He ran out the other way, out the screen door and around and under the heated stars. "Come on out here, mouth! Come out and say that to my face!" He squinted at all the windows around him, no idea where it came from. "So come on! Say it right now!" There was no taker, and he turned away, his blood still bright red.

When he came back inside, the children had gone to bed and she was lying down with the baby, who'd fallen asleep. He went back to the chair. The game ended, she came out, half-closing the door behind her, and went straight to their bed. He followed.

"I dunno," he said after some time. He'd been wearing shorts and nothing else since his shower, and it shouldn't have taken him so long, yet he just sat there on the bed. Finally he turned on the fan and it whirred, ticking as it pivoted left and right. "It doesn't do any good, but it's worse without it." He looked at her like he did earlier. "I'm kinda glad nobody came out. Afterwards I imagined some nut just shooting me, or a few guys coming. I'm getting too old for that shit."

She wasn't talking.

"So what did they say?" he asked her. "At the clinic?"

"Yes."

"Yes what?"

"That I am."

They both listened to the fan and to the mix of music from the Armenians and that TV upstairs.

"I would've never thought it could happen," he said. "That one time, and it wasn't even good."

"Maybe for you. I knew it then."

"You did?"

She rolled on her side.

"I'm sorry about all the yelling," he said.

"I was happy you went after that man. I always wanna do stuff like that."

He rolled to her.

"I'm too sticky. It's too hot."

"I have to. We do. It's been too long, and now it doesn't matter."

"It does matter," she said. "I love you."

"I'm sorry," he said, reaching over to touch her breast. "You know I'm sorry."

He took another shower afterward. A cold shower. His breath sputtered and noises hopped from his throat. He crawled into the bed naked, onto the sheet that seemed as hot as ever, and listened to outside, to that mournful Armenian music mixing with Spanish, and to the fan, and it had stilled him. It was joy, and it was so strange. She'd fallen asleep and so he resisted kissing her, telling her. He thought he should hold on to this as long as he could, until he heard the pitch of the freeway climb, telling him that dawn was near and it was almost time to go back to work.

[2002]

LOUISE ERDRICH [b.1954]

The Red Convertible

Lyman Lamartine

I was the first one to drive a convertible on my reservation. And of course it was red, a red Olds. I owned that car along with my brother Henry Junior. We owned it together until his boots filled with water on a windy night and he bought out my share. Now Henry owns the whole car, and his younger brother Lyman (that's myself), Lyman walks everywhere he goes.

How did I earn enough money to buy my share in the first place? My own talent was I could always make money. I had a touch for it, unusual in a Chippewa. From the first I was different that way, and everyone recognized it. I was the only kid they let in the American Legion Hall to shine shoes, for example, and one Christmas I sold spiritual bouquets for the mission door to door. The nuns let me keep a percentage. Once I started, it seemed the more money I made the easier the money came. Everyone encouraged it. When I was fifteen I got a job washing dishes at the Joliet Café, and that was where my first big break happened.

It wasn't long before I was promoted to busing tables, and then the short-order cook quit and I was hired to take her place. No sooner than you know it I was managing the Joliet. The rest is history. I went on managing. I soon became part owner, and of course there was no stopping me then. It wasn't long before the whole thing was mine.

After I'd owned the Joliet for one year, it blew over in the worst tornado ever seen around here. The whole operation was smashed to bits. A total loss. The fryalator was up in a tree, the grill torn in half like it was paper. I was only sixteen. I had it all in my mother's name, and I lost it quick, but before I lost it I had every one of my relatives, and their relatives, to dinner, and I also bought that red Olds I mentioned, along with Henry.

The first time we saw it! I'll tell you when we first saw it. We had gotten a ride up to Winnipeg, and both of us had money. Don't ask me why, because we never mentioned a car or anything, we just had all our money. Mine was cash, a big bankroll from the Joliet's insurance. Henry had two checks—a week's extra pay for being laid off, and his regular check from the Jewel Bearing Plant.

361

We were walking down Portage anyway, seeing the sights, when we saw it. There it was, parked, large as life. Really as if it was alive. I thought of the word *repose*, because the car wasn't simply stopped, parked, or whatever. That car reposed, calm and gleaming, a for sale sign in its left front window. Then, before we had thought it over at all, the car belonged to us and our pockets were empty. We had just enough money for gas back home.

We went places in that car, me and Henry. We took off driving all one whole summer. We started off toward the Little Knife River and Mandaree in Fort Berthold and then we found ourselves down in Wakpala somehow, and then suddenly we were over in Montana on the Rocky Boy, and yet the summer was not even half over. Some people hang on to details when they travel, but we didn't let them bother us and just lived our everyday lives here to there.

I do remember this one place with willows. I remember I laid under those trees and it was comfortable. So comfortable. The branches bent down all around me like a tent or a stable. And quiet, it was quiet, even though there was a powwow close enough so I could see it going on. The air was not too still, not too windy either. When the dust rises up and hangs in the air around the dancers like that, I feel good. Henry was asleep with his arms thrown wide. Later on, he woke up and we started driving again. We were somewhere in Montana, or maybe on the Blood Reserve— it could have been anywhere. Anyway it was where we met the girl.

All her hair was in buns around her ears, that's the first thing I noticed about her. She was posed alongside the road with her arm out, so we stopped. That girl was short, so short her lumber shirt looked comical on her, like a nightgown. She had jeans on and fancy moccasins and she carried a little suitcase.

"Hop on in," says Henry. So she climbs in between us.

"We'll take you home," I says. "Where do you live?"

"Chicken," she says.

"Where the hell's that?" I ask her.

"Alaska."

"Okay," says Henry, and we drive.

We got up there and never wanted to leave. The sun doesn't truly set there in summer, and the night is more a soft dusk. You might doze off, sometimes, but before you know it you're up again, like an animal in nature. You never feel like you have to sleep hard or put away the world. And things would grow up there. One day just dirt or moss, the next day flowers and long grass. The girl's name was Susy. Her family really took to us. They fed us and put us up. We had our own tent to live in by their house, and the kids would be in and out of there all day and night. They couldn't get over me and Henry being brothers, we looked so different. We told them we knew we had the same mother, anyway.

One night Susy came in to visit us. We sat around in the tent talking of this and that. The season was changing. It was getting darker by that time, and the cold was even getting just a little mean. I told her it was time for us to go. She stood up on a chair.

"You never seen my hair," Susy said.

That was true. She was standing on a chair, but still, when she unclipped her buns the hair reached all the way to the ground. Our eyes opened. You couldn't tell how much hair she had when it was rolled up so neatly. Then my brother Henry did something funny. He went up to the chair and said, "Jump on my shoulders." So she did that, and her hair reached down past his waist, and he started twirling, this way and that, so her hair was flung out from side to side.

"I always wondered what it was like to have long pretty hair," Henry says. Well we laughed. It was a funny sight, the way he did it. The next morning we got up and took leave of those people.

On to greener pastures, as they say. It was down through Spokane and across Idaho then Montana and very soon we were racing the weather right along under the Canadian border through Columbus, Des Lacs, and then we were in Bottineau County and soon home. We'd made most of the trip, that summer, without putting up the car hood at all. We got home just in time, it turned out, for the army to remember Henry had signed up to join it.

I don't wonder that the army was so glad to get my brother that they turned him into a Marine. He was built like a brick outhouse anyway. We liked to tease him that they really wanted him for his Indian nose. He had a nose big and sharp as a hatchet, like the nose on Red Tomahawk, the Indian who killed Sitting Bull, whose profile is on signs all along the North Dakota highways. Henry went off to training camp, came home once during Christmas, then the next thing you know we got an overseas letter from him. It was 1970, and he said he was stationed up in the northern hill country. Whereabouts I did not know. He wasn't such a hot letter writer, and only got off two before the enemy caught him. I could never keep it straight, which direction those good Vietnam soldiers were from.

I wrote him back several times, even though I didn't know if those letters would get through. I kept him informed all about the car. Most of the time I had it up on blocks in the yard or half taken apart, because that long trip did a hard job on it under the hood.

I always had good luck with numbers, and never worried about the draft myself. I never even had to think about what my number was. But Henry was never lucky in the same way as me. It was at least three years before Henry came home. By then I guess the whole war was solved in the government's mind, but for him it would keep on going. In those years I'd put his car into almost perfect shape. I always thought of it as his car while he was gone, even though when he left he said, "Now it's yours," and threw me his key.

"Thanks for the extra key," I'd said. "I'll put it up in your drawer just in case I need it." He laughed.

When he came home, though, Henry was very different, and I'll say this: the change was no good. You could hardly expect him to change for the better, I know. But he was quiet, so quiet, and never comfortable sitting still anywhere but always up and moving around. I thought back to times we'd sat still for whole afternoons, never moving a muscle, just shifting our weight along the ground, talking to whoever sat with us, watching things. He'd always had a joke, then, too, and now you couldn't get him to laugh, or when he did it was more the sound of a man choking, a sound that stopped up the throats of other people around him. They got to leaving him alone most of the time, and I didn't blame them. It was a fact: Henry was jumpy and mean.

I'd bought a color TV set for my mom and the rest of us while Henry was away. Money still came very easy. I was sorry I'd ever bought it though, because of Henry. I was also sorry I'd bought color, because with black-and-white the pictures seem older and farther away. But what are you going to do? He sat in front of it, watching it, and that was the only time he was completely still. But it was the kind of stillness that you see in a rabbit when it freezes and before it will bolt. He was not easy. He sat in his chair gripping the armrests with all his might, as if the chair itself was moving at a high speed and if he let go at all he would rocket forward and maybe crash right through the set.

Once I was in the room watching TV with Henry and I heard his teeth click at something. I looked over, and he'd bitten through his lip. Blood was going down his chin. I tell you right then I wanted to smash that tube to pieces. I went over to it but Henry must have known what I was up to. He rushed from his chair and shoved me out of the way, against the wall. I told myself he didn't know what he was doing.

My mom came in, turned the set off real quiet, and told us she had made something for supper. So we went and sat down. There was still blood going down Henry's chin, but he didn't notice it and no one said anything, even though every time he took a bite of his bread his blood fell onto it until he was eating his own blood mixed in with the food.

While Henry was not around we talked about what was going to happen to him. There were no Indian doctors on the reservation, and my mom was afraid of trusting the old man, Moses Pillager, because he courted her long ago and was jealous of her husband. He might take revenge through her son. We were afraid that if we brought Henry to a regular hospital they would keep him.

"They don't fix them in those places," Mom said; "they just give them drugs."

"We wouldn't get him there in the first place," I agreed, "so let's just forget about it."

Then I thought about the car.

Henry had not even looked at the car since he'd gotten home, though like I said, it was in tip-top condition and ready to drive. I thought the car might bring the old Henry back somehow. So I bided my time and waited for my chance to interest him in the vehicle.

One night Henry was off somewhere. I took myself a hammer. I went out to that car and I did a number on its underside. Whacked it up. Bent the tail pipe double. Ripped the muffler loose. By the time I was done with the car it looked worse than any typical Indian car that has been driven all its life on reservation roads, which they always say are like government promises—full of holes. It just about hurt me, I'll tell you that! I threw dirt in the carburetor and I ripped all the electric tape off the seats. I made it look just as beat up as I could. Then I sat back and waited for Henry to find it.

Still, it took him over a month. That was all right, because it was just getting warm enough, not melting, but warm enough to work outside.

"Lyman," he says, walking in one day, "that red car looks like shit."

"Well it's old," I says. "You got to expect that."

"No way!" says Henry. "That car's a classic! But you went and ran the piss right out of it, Lyman, and you know it don't deserve that. I kept that car in A-one shape. You don't remember. You're too young. But when I left, that car was running like a watch. Now I don't even know if I can get it to start again, let alone get it anywhere near its old condition."

"Well you try," I said, like I was getting mad, "but I say it's a piece of junk."

Then I walked out before he could realize I knew he'd strung together more than six words at once.

After that I thought he'd freeze himself to death working on that car. He was out there all day, and at night he rigged up a little lamp, ran a cord out the window, and had himself some light to see by while he worked. He was better than he had been before, but that's still not saying much. It was easier for him to do the things the rest of us did. He ate more slowly and didn't jump up and down during the meal to get this or that or look out the window. I put my hand in the back of the TV set, I admit, and fiddled around with it good, so that it was almost impossible now to get a clear picture. He didn't look at it very often anyway. He was always out with that car or going off to get parts for it. By the time it was really melting outside, he had it fixed.

I had been feeling down in the dumps about Henry around this time. We had always been together before. Henry and Lyman. But he was such a loner now that I didn't know how to take it. So I jumped at the chance one day when Henry seemed friendly. It's not that he smiled or anything. He just said, "Let's take that old shitbox for a spin." Just the way he said it made me think he could be coming around.

We went out to the car. It was spring. The sun was shining very bright. My only sister, Bonita, who was just eleven years old, came out and made us stand together for a picture. Henry leaned his elbow on the red car's windshield, and he took his other arm and put it over my shoulder, very carefully, as though it was heavy for him to lift and he didn't want to bring the weight down all at once.

"Smile," Bonita said, and he did.

That picture, I never look at it anymore. A few months ago, I don't know why, I got his picture out and tacked it on the wall. I felt good about Henry at the time, close to him. I felt good having his picture on the wall, until one night when I was looking at television. I was a little drunk and stoned. I looked up at the wall and Henry was staring at me. I don't know what it was, but his smile had changed, or maybe it was gone. All I know is I couldn't stay in the same room with that picture. I was shaking. I got up, closed the door, and went into the kitchen. A little later my friend Ray came over and we both went back into that room. We put the picture in a brown bag, folded the bag over and over tightly, then put it way back in a closet.

I still see that picture now, as if it tugs at me, whenever I pass that closet door. The picture is very clear in my mind. It was so sunny that day Henry had to squint against the glare. Or maybe the camera Bonita held flashed like a mirror, blinding him, before she snapped the picture. My face is right out in the sun, big and round. But he might have drawn back, because the shadows on his face are deep as holes. There are two shadows curved like little hooks around the ends of his smile, as if to frame it and try to keep it there—that one, first smile that looked like it might have hurt his face. He has his field jacket on and the worn-in clothes he'd come back in and kept wearing ever since. After Bonita took the picture, she went into the house and we got into the car. There was a full cooler in the trunk. We started off, east, toward Pembina and the Red River because Henry said he wanted to see the high water.

The trip over there was beautiful. When everything starts changing, drying up, clearing off, you feel like your whole life is starting. Henry felt it, too. The top was down and the car hummed like a top. He'd really put it back in shape, even the tape on the seats was very carefully put down and glued back in layers. It's not that he smiled again or even joked, but his face looked to me as if it was clear, more peaceful. It looked as though he wasn't thinking of anything in particular except the bare fields and windbreaks and houses we were passing.

The river was high and full of winter trash when we got there. The sun was still out, but it was colder by the river. There were still little clumps of dirty snow here and there on the banks. The water hadn't gone over the banks yet, but it would, you could tell. It was just at its limit, hard swollen glossy like an old gray scar. We made ourselves a fire, and we sat down and watched the current go. As I watched it I felt something squeezing inside me and tightening and trying to let go all at the same time. I knew I was not just feeling it myself; I knew I was feeling what Henry was going through at that moment. Except that I couldn't stand it, the closing and opening. I jumped to my feet. I took Henry by the shoulders and I started shaking him. "Wake up," I says, "wake up, wake up, wake up!" I didn't know what had come over me. I sat down beside him again.

His face was totally white and hard. Then it broke, like stones break all of a sudden when water boils up inside them.

"I know it," he says. "I know it. I can't help it. It's no use."

We start talking. He said he knew what I'd done with the car. It was obvious it had been whacked out of shape and not just neglected. He said he wanted to give the car to me for good now, it was no use. He said he'd fixed it just to give it back and I should take it.

"No way," I says, "I don't want it."

"That's okay," he says, "you take it."

"I don't want it, though," I says back to him, and then to emphasize, just to emphasize, you understand, I touch his shoulder. He slaps my hand off.

"Take that car," he says.

"No," I say. "Make me," I say, and then he grabs my jacket and rips the arm loose. That jacket is a class act, suede with tags and zippers. I push Henry backwards, off the log. He jumps up and bowls me over. We go down in a clinch and come up swinging hard, for all we're worth, with our fists. He socks my jaw so hard I feel like it swings loose. Then I'm at his rib cage and land a good one under his chin so his head snaps back. He's dazzled. He looks at me and I look at him and then his eyes are full of tears and blood and at first I think he's crying. But no, he's laughing. "Ha! Ha!" he says. "Ha! Ha! Take good care of it."

"Okay," I says, "okay, no problem. Ha! Ha!"

I can't help it, and I start laughing, too. My face feels fat and strange, and after a while I get a beer from the cooler in the trunk, and when I hand it to Henry he takes his shirt and wipes my germs off. "Hoof-and-mouth disease," he says. For some reason this cracks me up, and so we're really laughing for a while, and then we drink all the rest of the beers one by one and throw them in the river and see how far, how fast, the current takes them before they fill up and sink.

"You want to go on back?" I ask after a while. "Maybe we could snag a couple nice Kashpaw girls."

He says nothing. But I can tell his mood is turning again.

"They're all crazy, the girls up here, every damn one of them."

"You're crazy too," I say, to jolly him up. "Crazy Lamartine boys!"

He looks as though he will take this wrong at first. His face twists, then clears, and he jumps up on his feet. "That's right!" he says. "Crazier 'n hell. Crazy Indians!"

I think it's the old Henry again. He throws off his jacket and starts swinging his legs out from the knees like a fancy dancer. He's down doing something between a grass dance and a bunny hop, no kind of dance I ever saw before, but neither has anyone else on all this green growing earth. He's wild. He wants to pitch whoopee! He's up and at me and all over. All this time I'm laughing so hard, so hard my belly is getting tied up in a knot.

"Got to cool me off!" he shouts all of a sudden. Then he runs over to the river and jumps in.

There's boards and other things in the current. It's so high. No sound comes from the river after the splash he makes, so I run right over. I look around. It's getting dark. I see he's halfway across the water already, and I know he didn't swim there but the current took him. It's far. I hear his voice, though, very clearly across it.

"My boots are filling," he says.

He says this in a normal voice, like he just noticed and he doesn't know what to think of it. Then he's gone. A branch comes by. Another branch. And I go in.

By the time I get out of the river, off the snag I pulled myself onto, the sun is down. I walk back to the car, turn on the high beams, and drive it up the bank. I put it in first gear and then I take my foot off the clutch. I get out, close the door, and watch it plow softly into the water. The head-lights reach in as they go down, searching, still lighted even after the water swirls over the back end. I wait. The wires short out. It is all finally dark. And then there is only the water, the sound of it going and running and going and running and running.

[1984]

LEILA ABOULELA [b. 1964]

The Museum

At first Shadia was afraid to ask him for his notes. The earring made her afraid; the straight long hair that he tied up with a rubber band. She had never seen a man with an earring and such long hair. But then she had never known such cold, so much rain. His silver earring was the strangeness of the West, another culture shock. She stared at it during classes, her eyes straying from the white scribbles on the board. Most times she could hardly understand anything. Only the notation was familiar. But how did it all fit together? How did *this* formula lead to *this*? Her ignorance and the impending exams were horrors she wanted to escape. His long hair was a dull colour between yellow and brown. It reminded her of a doll she had when she was young. She had spent hours combing that doll's hair, stroking it. She had longed for such straight hair. When she went to Paradise she would have hair like that. When she ran it would fly behind her; if she bent her head down it would fall over her like silk and sweep the flowers on the grass. She watched his ponytail move as he wrote and then looked up at the board. She pictured her doll, vivid suddenly, after years, and felt sick that she was daydreaming in class, not learning a thing.

The first days of term, when the classes started for the M.Sc. in Statistics, she was like someone tossed around by monstrous waves — battered, as she lost her way to the different lecture rooms, fumbled with the photocopying machine, could not find anything in the library. She could scarcely hear or eat or see. Her eyes bulged with fright, watered from the cold. The course required a certain background, a background she didn't have. So she floundered, she and the other African students, the two Turkish girls, and the men from Brunei. Asafa, the short, round-faced Ethiopian, said, in his grave voice — as this collection from the Third World whispered their anxieties in grim Scottish corridors, the girls in nervous giggles — "Last year, last year a Nigerian on this very same course committed suicide. *Cut his wrists.*"

Us and them, she thought. The ones who would do well, the ones who would crawl and sweat and barely pass. Two predetermined groups. Asafa, generous and wise (he was the oldest), leaned over and whispered to Shadia: "The Spanish girl is good. Very good." His eyes bulged redder

369

than Shadia's. He cushioned his fears every night in the university pub; she only cried. Their countries were nextdoor neighbours but he had never been to Sudan, and Shadia had never been to Ethiopia. "But we meet in Aberdeen!" she had shrieked when this information was exchanged, giggling furiously. Collective fear had its euphoria.

"That boy Bryan," said Asafa, "is excellent."

"The one with the earring?"

Asafa laughed and touched his own unadorned ear. "The earring doesn't mean anything. He'll get the Distinction. He was an undergraduate here; got First Class Honours. That gives him an advantage. He knows all the lecturers, he knows the system."

So the idea occurred to her of asking Bryan for the notes of his graduate year. If she strengthened her background in stochastic processes and time series, she would be better able to cope with the new material they were bombarded with every day. She watched him to judge if he was approachable. Next to the courteous Malaysian students, he was devoid of manners. He mumbled and slouched and did not speak with respect to the lecturers. He spoke to them as if they were his equals. And he did silly things. When he wanted to throw a piece of paper in the bin, he squashed it into a ball and aimed it at the bin. If he missed, he muttered under his breath. She thought that he was immature. But he was the only one who was sailing through the course.

The glossy handbook for overseas students had explained about the "famous British reserve" and hinted that they should be grateful, things were worse further south, less "hospitable." In the cafeteria, drinking coffee with Asafa and the others, the picture of "hospitable Scotland" was something different. Badr, the Malaysian, blinked and whispered, "Yesterday our windows got smashed; my wife today is afraid to go out."

"Thieves?" asked Shadia, her eyes wider than anyone else's.

"Racists," said the Turkish girl, her lipstick chic, the word tripping out like silver, like ice.

Wisdom from Asafa, muted, before the collective silence: "These people think they own the world . . ." and around them the aura of the dead Nigerian student. They were ashamed of that brother they had never seen. He had weakened, caved in. In the cafeteria, Bryan never sat with them. They never sat with him. He sat alone, sometimes reading the local paper. When Shadia walked in front of him he didn't smile. "These people are strange . . . One day they greet you, the next day they don't . . ."

On Friday afternoon, as everyone was ready to leave the room after Linear Models, she gathered her courage and spoke to Bryan. He had spots on his chin and forehead, was taller than her, restless, as if he was in a hurry to go somewhere else. He put his calculator back in its case, his pen in his pocket. She asked him for his notes, and his blue eyes behind his glasses took on the blankest look she had ever seen in her life. What was all the surprise for? Did he think she was an insect? Was he surprised that she could speak?

A mumble for a reply, words strung together. So taken aback, he was. He pushed his chair back under the table with his foot.

"Pardon?"

He slowed down, separated each word. "Ah'll have them for ye on Monday."

"Thank you." She spoke English better than he did! How pathetic. The whole of him was pathetic. He wore the same shirt every blessed day. Grey and white stripe.

On the weekends, Shadia never went out of the halls and, unless someone telephoned long-distance from home, she spoke to no one. There was time to remember Thursday nights in Khartoum: a wedding to go to with Fareed, driving in his red Mercedes. Or the club with her sisters. Sitting by the pool drinking lemonade with ice, the waiters all dressed in white. Sometimes people swam at night, dived in the water—dark like the sky above. Here, in this country's weekend of Saturday and Sunday, Shadia washed her clothes and her hair. Her hair depressed her. The damp weather made it frizz up after she straightened it with hot tongs. So she had given up and now wore it in a bun all the time, tightly pulled back away from her face, the curls held down by pins and Vaseline Tonic. She didn't like this style, her corrugated hair, and in the mirror her eyes looked too large. The mirror in the public bathroom, at the end of the corridor to her room, had printed on it: "This is the face of someone with HIV." She had written about this mirror to her sister, something foreign and sensational like hail, and cars driving on the left. But she hadn't written that the mirror made her feel as if she had left her looks behind in Khartoum.

On the weekends, she made a list of the money she had spent: the sterling enough to keep a family alive back home. Yet she might fail her exams after all that expense, go back home empty-handed without a degree. Guilt was cold like the fog of this city. It came from everywhere. One day she forgot to pray in the morning. She reached the bus stop and then realized that she hadn't prayed. That morning folded out like the nightmare she sometimes had, of discovering that she had gone out into the street without any clothes.

In the evening, when she was staring at multidimensional scaling, the telephone in the hall rang. She ran to answer it. Fareed's cheerful greeting: "Here, Shadia, Mama and the girls want to speak to you." His mother's endearments: "They say it's so cold where you are . . ."

Shadia was engaged to Fareed. Fareed was a package that came with the 7UP franchise, the paper factory, the big house he was building, his sisters and widowed mother. Shadia was going to marry them all. She was going to be happy and make her mother happy. Her mother deserved happiness after the misfortunes of her life. A husband who left her for another woman. Six girls to bring up. People felt sorry for her mother. Six girls to educate and marry off. But your Lord is generous: each of the girls, it was often said, was lovelier than the other. They were clever too: dentist, pharmacist, architect, and all with the best of manners.

"We are just back from looking at the house." Fareed's turn again to talk. "It's coming along fine, they're putting the tiles down . . ."

"That's good, that's good," her voice strange from not talking to anyone all day.

"The bathroom suites. If I get them all the same colour for us and the girls and Mama, I could get them on a discount. Blue, the girls are in favour of blue," his voice echoed from one continent to another. Miles and miles.

"Blue is nice. Yes, better get them all the same colour."

He was building a block of flats, not a house. The ground floor flat for his mother and the girls until they married, the first floor for him and Shadia. When Shadia had first got engaged to Fareed, he was the son of a rich man. A man with the franchise for 7UP and the paper factory which had a monopoly in ladies' sanitary towels. Fareed's sisters never had to buy sanitary towels; their house was abundant with boxes of *Pinky*, fresh from the production line. But Fareed's father died of an unexpected heart attack soon after the engagement party (five hundred guests at the Hilton). Now Shadia was going to marry the rich man himself. "You are a lucky, lucky girl," her mother had said, and Shadia had rubbed soap in her eyes so that Fareed would think she was weeping about his father's death.

There was no time to talk about her course on the telephone, no space for her anxieties. Fareed was not interested in her studies. He had said, "I am very broad-minded to allow you to study abroad. Other men would not have put up with this . . ." It was her mother who was keen for her to study, to get a postgraduate degree from Britain and then have a career after she got married. "This way," her mother had said, "you will have your in-laws' respect. They have money but you will have a degree. Don't end up like me. I left my education to marry your father and now . . ." Many conversations ended with her mother bitter; with her mother saying, "No one suffers like I suffer," and making Shadia droop. At night her mother sobbed in her sleep, noises that woke Shadia and her sisters.

No, on the long-distance line, there was no space for her worries. Talk about the Scottish weather. Picture Fareed, generously perspiring, his stomach straining the buttons of his shirt. Often she had nagged him to lose weight, without success. His mother's food was too good; his sisters were both overweight. On the long-distance line, listen to the Khartoum gossip as if listening to a radio play.

On Monday, without saying anything, Bryan slid two folders across the table towards her as if he did not want to come near her, did not want to talk to her. She wanted to say, "I won't take them till you hand them to me politely." But smarting, she said, "Thank you very much." *She* had manners. *She* was well brought up.

Back in her room, at her desk, the clearest handwriting she had ever seen. Sparse on the pages, clean. Clear and rounded like a child's, the tidiest notes. She cried over them, wept for no reason. She cried until she wetted one of the pages, smudged the ink, blurred one of the formulas. She dabbed at it with a tissue but the paper flaked and became transparent. Should she apologize about the stain, say that she was drinking water, say that it was rain? Or should she just keep quiet, hope he wouldn't notice? She chided herself for all that concern. *He* wasn't concerned about wearing the same shirt every day. She was giving him too much attention thinking about him. He was just an immature and closed-in sort of character. He probably came from a small town, his parents were probably poor, low-class. In Khartoum, she never mixed with people like that. Her mother liked her to be friends with people who were higher up. How else were she and her sisters going to marry well? She must study the notes and stop crying over this boy's handwriting. His handwriting had nothing to do with her, nothing to do with her at all.

Understanding after not understanding is fog lifting, pictures swinging into focus, missing pieces slotting into place. It is fragments gelling, a sound vivid whole, a basis to build on. His notes were the knowledge she needed, the gap filled. She struggled through them, not skimming them with the carelessness of incomprehension, but taking them in, making them a part of her, until in the depth of concentration, in the late hours of the nights, she lost awareness of time and place, and at last, when she slept she became epsilon and gamma, and she became a variable, making her way through discrete space from state "i" to state "j."

It felt natural to talk to him. As if now that she had spent hours and days with his handwriting, she knew him in some way. She forgot the offence she had taken when he had slid his folders across the table to her, all the times he didn't say hello.

In the computer room, at the end of the Statistical Packages class, she went to him and said: "Thanks for the notes. They are really good. I think I might not fail, after all. I might have a chance to pass." Her eyes were dry from all the nights she had stayed up. She was tired and grateful.

He nodded and they spoke a little about the Poisson distribution, queuing theory. Everything was clear in his mind; his brain was a clear pane of glass where all the concepts were written out boldly and neatly. Today, he seemed more at ease talking to her, though he still shifted about from foot to foot, avoiding her eyes.

He said, "Do ye want to go for a coffee?"

She looked up at him. He was tall and she was not used to speaking to people with blue eyes. Then she made a mistake. Perhaps because she had been up late last night, she made that mistake. Perhaps there were other reasons for that mistake. The mistake of shifting from one level to another.

She said, "I don't like your earring."

The expression in his eyes, a focusing, no longer shifting away. He lifted his hand to his ear and tugged the earring off. His earlobe without the silver looked red and scarred.

She giggled because she was afraid, because he wasn't smiling, wasn't saying anything. She covered her mouth with her hand, then wiped her forehead and eyes. A mistake had been made and it was too late to go back. She plunged ahead, careless now, reckless. "I don't like your long hair."

He turned and walked away.

The next morning, Multivariate Analysis, and she came in late, dishevelled from running and the rain. The professor, whose name she wasn't sure of (there were three who were Mc-something), smiled, unperturbed. All the lecturers were relaxed and urbane, in tweed jackets and polished shoes. Sometimes she wondered how the incoherent Bryan, if he did pursue an academic career, was going to transform himself into a professor like that. But it was none of her business.

Like most of the other students, she sat in the same seat in every class. Bryan sat a row ahead which was why she could always look at his hair. But he had cut it, there was no ponytail today! Just his neck and the collar of the grey and white striped shirt.

Notes to take down. *In discriminant analysis, a linear combination of variables serves as the basis for assigning cases to groups.*

She was made up of layers. Somewhere inside, deep inside, under the crust of vanity, in the untampered-with essence, she would glow and be in awe, and be humble and think, this is just for me, he cut his hair for me. But there were other layers, bolder, more to the surface. Giggling. Wanting to catch hold of a friend. Guess what? You wouldn't *believe* what this idiot did!

Find a weighted average of variables . . . The weights are estimated so that they result in the best separation between the groups.

After the class he came over and said very seriously, without a smile, "Ah've cut my hair."

A part of her hollered with laughter, sang: "You stupid boy, you stupid boy, I can see that, can't I?"

She said, "It looks nice." She said the wrong thing and her face felt hot and she made herself look away so that she would not know his reaction. It was true though, he did look nice; he looked decent now.

She should have said to Bryan, when they first held their coffee mugs in their hands and were searching for an empty table. "Let's sit with Asafa and the others." Mistakes follow mistakes. Across the cafeteria, the Turkish girl saw them together and raised her perfect eyebrows. Badr met Shadia's eyes and quickly looked away. Shadia looked at Bryan and he was different, different without the earring and the ponytail, transformed in some way. If he would put lemon juice on his spots . . . but it was none of her business. Maybe the boys who smashed Badr's windows looked like Bryan, but with fiercer eyes, no glasses. She must push him away from her. She must make him dislike her.

He asked her where she came from and when she replied, he said, "Where's that?"

"Africa," with sarcasm. "Do you know where *that* is?"

His nose and cheeks under the rims of his glasses went red. Good, she thought, good. He will leave me now in peace.

He said, "Ah know Sudan is in Africa, I meant where exactly in Africa."

"Northeast, south of Egypt. Where are *you* from?"

"Peterhead. It's north of here. By the sea."

It was hard to believe that there was anything north of Aberdeen. It seemed to her that they were on the northernmost corner of the world. She knew better now than to imagine suntanning and sandy beaches for his "by the sea." More likely dismal skies, pale, bad-tempered people shivering on the rocky shore.

"Your father works in Peterhead?"

"Aye, he does."

She had grown up listening to the proper English of the BBC World Service only to come to Britain and find people saying "yes" like it was said back home in Arabic: "aye."

"What does he do, your father?"

He looked surprised, his blue eyes surprised. "Ma dad's a joiner."

Fareed hired people like that to work on the house. Ordered them about.

"And your mother?" she asked.

He paused a little, stirred sugar in his coffee with a plastic spoon. "She's a lollipop lady."

Shadia smirked into her coffee, took a sip.

"My father," she said proudly, "is a doctor, a specialist." Her father was a gynaecologist. The woman who was now his wife had been one of his patients. Before that, Shadia's friends had teased her about her father's job, crude jokes that made her laugh. It was all so sordid now.

"And my mother," she blew the truth up out of proportion, "comes from a very big family. A ruling family. If you British hadn't colonized us, my mother would have been a princess now."

"Ye walk like a princess," he said.

What a gullible, silly boy! She wiped her forehead with her hand and said, "You mean I am conceited and proud?"

"No, Ah didnae mean that, no . . ." The packet of sugar he was tearing open tipped from his hand, its contents scattered over the table. "Ah shit . . . sorry . . ." He tried to scoop up the sugar and knocked against his coffee mug, spilling a little on the table.

She took out a tissue from her bag, reached over and mopped up the stain. It was easy to pick up all the bits of sugar with the damp tissue.

"Thanks," he mumbled and they were silent. The cafeteria was busy: full of the humming, buzzing sound of people talking to each other, trays and dishes. In Khartoum, she avoided being alone with Fareed. She preferred it when they were with others: their families, their many mutual friends. If they were ever alone, she imagined that her mother or her sister was with them, could hear them, and she spoke to Fareed with that audience in mind.

Bryan was speaking to her, saying something about rowing on the River Dee. He went rowing on the weekends, he belonged to a rowing club.

To make herself pleasing to people was a skill Shadia was trained in. It was not difficult to please people. Agree with them, never dominate the conversation, be economical with the truth. Now, here was someone to whom all these rules needn't apply.

She said to him, "The Nile is superior to the Dee. I saw your Dee, it is nothing, it is like a stream. There are two Niles, the Blue and the White, named after their colours. They come from the south, from two different places. They travel for miles over countries with different names, never knowing they will meet. I think they get tired of running alone, it is such a long way to the sea. They want to reach the sea so that they can rest, stop running. There is a bridge in Khartoum, and under this bridge the two Niles meet. If you stand on the bridge and look down you can see the two waters mixing together."

"Do ye get homesick?" he asked. She felt tired now, all this talk of the river running to rest in the sea. She had never talked like this before. Luxury words, and this question he asked.

"Things I should miss I don't miss. Instead I miss things I didn't think I would miss. The *azan*, the Muslim call to prayer from the mosque. I don't know if you know about it. I miss that. At dawn it used to wake me up. I would hear 'prayer is better than sleep' and just go back to sleep.

I never got up to pray." She looked down at her hands on the table. There was no relief in confessions, only his smile, young, and something like wonder in his eyes.

"We did Islam in school," he said. "Ah went on a trip to Mecca." He opened out his palms on the table.

"What!"

"In a book."

"Oh."

The coffee was finished. They should go now. She should go to the library before the next lecture and photocopy previous exam papers. Asafa, full of helpful advice, had shown her where to find them.

"What is your religion?" she asked.

"Dunno, nothing I suppose."

"That's terrible! That's really terrible!" Her voice was too loud, concerned.

His face went red again and he tapped his spoon against the empty mug.

Waive all politeness, make him dislike her. Badr had said, even before his windows got smashed, that here in the West they hate Islam. Standing up to go, she said flippantly, "Why don't you become a Muslim then?"

He shrugged. "Ah wouldnae mind travelling to Mecca, I was keen on that book."

Her eyes filled with tears. They blurred his face when he stood up. In the West they hate Islam and he . . . She said, "Thanks for the coffee," and walked away, but he followed her.

"Shadiya, Shadiya," he pronounced her name wrongly, three syllables instead of two, "there's this museum about Africa. I've never been before. If you'd care to go, tomorrow . . ."

No sleep for the guilty, no rest she should have said no, I can't go, no I have too much catching up to do. No sleep for the guilty, the memories come from another continent. Her father's new wife, happier than her mother, fewer worries. When Shadia visits she offers fruit in a glass bowl, icy oranges and guavas, soothing in the heat. Shadia's father hadn't wanted a divorce, hadn't wanted to leave them; he wanted two wives, not a divorce. But her mother had too much pride, she came from fading money, a family with a "name." Of the new wife her mother says, bitch, whore, the dregs of the earth, a nobody.

Tomorrow she need not show up at the museum, even though she said that she would. She should have told Bryan she was engaged to be married, mentioned it casually. What did he expect from her? Europeans had different rules, reduced, abrupt customs. If Fareed knew about this . . .

her secret thoughts like snakes . . . Perhaps she was like her father, a traitor. Her mother said that her father was devious. Sometimes Shadia was devious. With Fareed in the car, she would deliberately say, "I need to stop at the grocer, we need things at home." At the grocer he would pay for all her shopping and she would say, "No, you shouldn't do that, no, you are too generous, you are embarrassing me." With the money she saved, she would buy a blouse for her mother, nail varnish for her mother, a magazine, imported apples.

It was strange to leave her desk, lock her room and go out on a Saturday. In the hall the telephone rang. It was Fareed. If he knew where she was going now . . . Guilt was like a hard-boiled egg stuck in her chest. A large cold egg.

"Shadia, I want you to buy some of the fixtures for the bathrooms. Taps and towel hangers. I'm going to send you a list of what I want exactly and the money . . ."

"I can't, I can't."

"What do you mean you can't? If you go into any large department store . . ."

"I can't, I wouldn't know where to put these things, how to send them."

There was a rustle on the line and she could hear someone whispering, Fareed distracted a little. He would be at work this time in the day, glass bottles filling up with clear effervescent, the words 7UP written in English and Arabic, white against the dark green.

"You can get good things, things that aren't available here. Gold would be good. It would match . . ."

Gold. Gold toilet seats!

"People are going to burn in hell for eating out of gold dishes, you want to sit on gold!"

He laughed. He was used to getting his own way, not easily threatened. "Are you joking with me?"

"No."

In a quieter voice, "This call is costing . . ."

She knew, she knew. He shouldn't have let her go away. She was not coping with the whole thing, she was not handling the stress. Like the Nigerian student.

"Shadia, gold-coloured, not gold. It's smart."

"Allah is going to punish us for this, it's not right . . ."

"Since when have you become so religious!"

Bryan was waiting for her on the steps of the museum, familiar-looking against the strange grey of the city streets where cars had their headlamps on in the middle of the afternoon. He wore a different shirt, a navy-blue jacket. He said, not looking at her, "Ah was beginning to think you wouldnae turn up."

There was no entry fee to the museum, no attendant handing out tickets. Bryan and Shadia walked on soft carpets; thick blue carpets that made Shadia want to take off her shoes. The first thing they saw was a Scottish man from Victorian times. He sat on a chair surrounded by possessions from Africa: overflowing trunks, an ancient map strewn on the floor of the glass cabinet. All the light in the room came from this and other glass cabinets and gleamed on the waxed floors. Shadia turned away; there was an ugliness in the lifelike wispiness of his hair, his determined expression, the way he sat. A hero who had gone away and come back, laden, ready to report.

Bryan began to conscientiously study every display cabinet, to read the posters on the wall. She followed him around and thought that he was studious, careful; that was why he did so well in his degree. She watched the intent expression on his face as he looked at everything. For her the posters were an effort to read, the information difficult to take in. It had been so long since she had read anything outside the requirements of the course. But she persevered saying the words to herself, moving her lips . . . *"During the 18th and 19th centuries, northeast Scotland made a disproportionate impact on the world at large by contributing so many skilled and committed individuals. In serving an empire they gave and received, changed others and were themselves changed and often returned home with tangible reminders of their experiences."*

The tangible reminders were there to see, preserved in spite of the years. Her eyes skimmed over the disconnected objects out of place and time. Iron and copper, little statues. Nothing was of her, nothing belonged to her life at home, what she missed. Here was Europe's vision, the clichés about Africa: cold and old.

She had not expected the dim light and the hushed silence. Apart from Shadia and Bryan, there was only a man with a briefcase, a lady who took down notes, unless there were others out of sight on the second floor. Something electrical, the heating or the lights, gave out a humming sound like that of an air conditioner. It made Shadia feel as if they were in an aeroplane without windows, detached from the world outside.

"He looks like you, don't you think?" she said to Bryan. They stood in front of a portrait of a soldier who died in the first year of the twentieth century. It was the colour of his eyes and his hair. But Bryan did not answer her, did not agree with her. He was preoccupied with reading the caption. When she looked at the portrait again, she saw that she was mistaken. That strength in the eyes, the purpose, was something Bryan didn't have. They had strong faith in those days long ago.

Biographies of explorers who were educated in Edinburgh; they knew what to take to Africa: doctors, courage, Christianity, commerce, civilization. They knew what they wanted to bring back: cotton—watered by the Blue Nile, the Zambezi River. She walked after Bryan, felt his concentration, his interest in what was before him and thought. "In a photograph we would not look nice together."

She touched the glass of a cabinet showing papyrus rolls, copper pots. She pressed her forehead and nose against the cool glass. If she could enter the cabinet, she would not make a good exhibit. She wasn't right, she was too modern, too full of mathematics.

Only the carpet, its petroleum blue, pleased her. She had come to this museum expecting sunlight and photographs of the Nile, something to relieve her homesickness: a comfort, a message. But the messages were not for her, not for anyone like her. A letter from West Africa, 1762, an employee to his employer in Scotland. An employee trading European goods for African curiosities. *It was difficult to make the natives understand my meaning, even by an interpreter, it being a thing so seldom asked of them, but they have all undertaken to bring something and laughed heartily at me and said, I was a good man to love their country so much . . .*

Love my country so much. She should not be here, there was nothing for her here. She wanted to see minarets, boats fragile on the Nile, people. People like her father. The times she had sat in the waiting room of his clinic, among pregnant women, a pain in her heart because she was going to see him in a few minutes. His room, the air conditioner and the smell of his pipe, his white coat. When she hugged him, he smelled of Listerine mouthwash. He could never remember how old she was, what she was studying; six daughters, how could he keep track. In his confusion, there was freedom for her, games to play, a lot of teasing. She visited his clinic in secret, telling lies to her mother. She loved him more than she loved her mother. Her mother who did everything for her, tidied her room, sewed her clothes from *Burda* magazine. Shadia was twenty-five and her mother washed everything for her by hand, even her pants and bras.

"I know why they went away," said Bryan. "I understand why they travelled." At last he was talking. She had not seen him intense before. He spoke in a low voice. "They had to get away, to leave here . . ."

"To escape from the horrible weather . . ." She was making fun of him. She wanted to put him down. The imperialists who had humiliated her history were heroes in his eyes.

He looked at her. "To escape . . ." he repeated.

"They went to benefit themselves," she said, "people go away because they benefit in some way."

"I want to get away," he said.

She remembered when he had opened his palms on the table and said, "I went on a trip to Mecca." There had been pride in his voice.

"I should have gone somewhere else for the course," he went on. "A new place, somewhere down south."

He was on a plateau, not like her. She was fighting and struggling for a piece of paper that would say she was awarded an M.Sc. from a British university. For him, the course was a continuation.

"Come and see," he said, and he held her arm. No one had touched her before, not since she had hugged her mother goodbye. Months now in this country and no one had touched her.

She pulled her arm away. She walked away, quickly up the stairs. Metal steps rattled under her feet. She ran up the stairs to the next floor. Guns, a row of guns aiming at her. They had been waiting to blow her away. Scottish arms of centuries ago, gunfire in service of the empire.

Silver muzzles, a dirty grey now. They must have shone prettily once, under a sun far away. If they blew her away now, where would she fly and fall? A window that looked out at the hostile sky. She shivered in spite of the wool she was wearing, layers of clothes. Hell is not only blazing fire, a part of it is freezing cold, torturous ice and snow. In Scotland's winter you have a glimpse of this unseen world, feel the breath of it in your bones.

There was a bench and she sat down. There was no one here on this floor. She was alone with sketches of jungle animals, words on the wall. A diplomat away from home, in Ethiopia in 1903: Asafa's country long before Asafa was born. *It is difficult to imagine anything more satisfactory or better worth taking part in than a lion drive. We rode back to camp feeling very well indeed. Archie was quite right when he said that this was the first time since we have started that we have really been in Africa—the real Africa of jungle inhabited only by game, and plains where herds of antelope meet your eye in every direction.*

"Shadiya, don't cry." He still pronounced her name wrongly because she had not told him how to say it properly.

He sat next to her on the bench, the blur of his navy jacket blocking the guns, the wall-length pattern of antelope herds. She should explain that she cried easily, there was no need for the alarm on his face. His awkward voice: "Why are ye crying?"

He didn't know, he didn't understand. He was all wrong, not a substitute . . .

"They are telling lies in this museum," she said. "Don't believe them. It's all wrong. It's not jungles and antelopes, it's people. We have things like computers and cars. We have 7UP in Africa, and some people, a few people, have bathrooms with golden taps . . . I shouldn't be here with you. You shouldn't talk to me . . ."

He said, "Museums change, I can change . . ."

He didn't know it was a steep path she had no strength for. He didn't understand. Many things, years and landscapes, gulfs. If she had been strong she would have explained, and not tired of explaining. She would have patiently taught him another language, letters curved like the epsilon and gamma he knew from mathematics. She would have shown him that words could be read from right to left. If she had not been small in the museum, if she had been really strong, she would have made his trip to Mecca real, not only in a book.

[1997]

SHERMAN ALEXIE   [b. 1966]

The Lone Ranger and Tonto Fistfight in Heaven

Too hot to sleep so I walked down to the Third Avenue 7-11 for a Creamsicle and the company of a graveyard-shift cashier. I know that game. I worked graveyard for a Seattle 7-11 and got robbed once too often. The last time the bastard locked me in the cooler. He even took my money and basketball shoes.

The graveyard-shift worker in the Third Avenue 7-11 looked like they all do. Acne scars and a bad haircut, work pants that showed off his white socks, and those cheap black shoes that have no support. My arches still ache from my year at the Seattle 7-11.

"Hello," he asked when I walked into his store. "How you doing?"

I gave him a half-wave as I headed back to the freezer. He looked me over so he could describe me to the police later. I knew the look. One of my old girlfriends said I started to look at her that way, too. She left me not long after that. No, I left her and don't blame her for anything. That's how it happened. When one person starts to look at another like a criminal, then the love is over. It's logical.

"I don't trust you," she said to me. "You get too angry."

She was white and I lived with her in Seattle. Some nights we fought so bad that I would just get in my car and drive all night, only stop to fill up on gas. In fact, I worked the graveyard shift to spend as much time away from her as possible. But I learned all about Seattle that way, driving its back ways and dirty alleys.

Sometimes, though, I would forget where I was and get lost. I'd drive for hours, searching for something familiar. Seems like I'd spent my whole life that way, looking for anything I recognized. Once, I ended up in a nice residential neighborhood and somebody must have been worried because the police showed up and pulled me over.

"What are you doing out here?" the police officer asked me as he looked over my license and registration.

"I'm lost."

"Well, where are you supposed to be?" he asked me, and I knew there were plenty of places I wanted to be, but none where I was supposed to be.

"I got in a fight with my girlfriend," I said. "I was just driving around, blowing off steam, you know?"

"Well, you should be more careful where you drive," the officer said. "You're making people nervous. You don't fit the profile of the neighborhood."

I wanted to tell him that I didn't really fit the profile of the country but I knew it would just get me into trouble.

"Can I help you?" the 7-11 clerk asked me loudly, searching for some response that would reassure him that I wasn't an armed robber. He knew this dark skin and long, black hair of mine was dangerous. I had potential.

"Just getting a Creamsicle," I said after a long interval. It was a sick twist to pull on the guy, but it was late and I was bored. I grabbed my Creamsicle and walked back to the counter slowly, scanned the aisles for effect. I wanted to whistle low and menacingly but I never learned to whistle.

"Pretty hot out tonight?" he asked, that old rhetorical weather bullshit question designed to put us both at ease.

"Hot enough to make you go crazy," I said and smiled. He swallowed hard like a white man does in those situations. I looked him over. Same old green, red, and white 7-11 jacket and thick glasses. But he wasn't ugly, just misplaced and marked by loneliness. If he wasn't working there that night, he'd be at home alone flipping through channels and wishing he could afford HBO or Showtime.

"Will this be all?" he asked me, in that company effort to make me do some impulse shopping. Like adding a clause onto a treaty. *We'll take Washington and Oregon, and you get six pine trees and a brand-new Chrysler Cordoba.* I knew how to make and break promises.

"No," I said and paused. "Give me a Cherry Slushie, too."

"What size?" he asked, relieved.

"Large," I said, and he turned his back to me to make the drink. He realized his mistake but it was too late. He stiffened, ready for the gunshot or the blow behind the ear. When it didn't come, he turned back to me.

"I'm sorry," he said. "What size did you say?"

"Small," I said and changed the story.

"But I thought you said large."

"If you knew I wanted a large, then why did you ask me again?" I asked him and laughed. He looked at me, couldn't decide if I was giving him serious shit or just goofing. There was something about him I liked, even if it was three in the morning and he was white.

"Hey," I said. "Forget the Slushie. What I want to know is if you know all the words to the theme from *The Brady Bunch?*"

He looked at me, confused at first, then laughed.

"Shit," he said. "I was hoping you weren't crazy. You were scaring me."

"Well, I'm going to get crazy if you don't know the words."

He laughed loudly then, told me to take the Creamsicle for free. He was the graveyard-shift manager and those little demonstrations of power tickled him. All seventy-five cents of it. I knew how much everything cost.

"Thanks," I said to him and walked out the door. I took my time walking home, let the heat of the night melt the Creamsicle all over my hand. At three in the morning I could act just as young as I wanted to act. There was no one around to ask me to grow up.

In Seattle, I broke lamps. She and I would argue and I'd break a lamp, just pick it up and throw it down. At first she'd buy replacement lamps, expensive and beautiful. But after a while she'd buy lamps from Goodwill or garage sales. Then she just gave up the idea entirely and we'd argue in the dark.

"You're just like your brother," she'd yell. "Drunk all the time and stupid."

"My brother don't drink that much."

She and I never tried to hurt each other physically. I did love her, after all, and she loved me. But those arguments were just as damaging as a fist. Words can be like that, you know? Whenever I get into arguments now, I remember her and I also remember Muhammad Ali. He knew the power of his fists but, more importantly, he knew the power of his words, too. Even though he only had an IQ of 80 or so, Ali was a genius. And she was a genius, too. She knew exactly what to say to cause me the most pain.

But don't get me wrong. I walked through that relationship with an executioner's hood. Or more appropriately, with war paint and sharp arrows. She was a kindergarten teacher and I continually insulted her for that.

"Hey, schoolmarm," I asked. "Did your kids teach you anything new today?"

And I always had crazy dreams. I always have had them, but it seemed they became nightmares more often in Seattle.

In one dream, she was a missionary's wife and I was a minor war chief. We fell in love and tried to keep it secret. But the missionary caught us fucking in the barn and shot me. As I lay dying, my tribe learned of the shooting and attacked the whites all across the reservation. I died and my soul drifted above the reservation.

Disembodied, I could see everything that was happening. Whites killing Indians and Indians killing whites. At first it was small, just my tribe and the few whites who lived there. But my dream grew, intensified. Other tribes arrived on horseback to continue the slaughter of whites, and the United States Cavalry rode into battle.

The most vivid image of that dream stays with me. Three mounted soldiers played polo with a dead Indian woman's head. When I first dreamed it, I thought it was just a product of my anger and imagination. But since then, I've read similar accounts of that kind of evil in the old West. Even more terrifying, though, is the fact that those kinds of brutal things are happening today in places like El Salvador.

All I know for sure, though, is that I woke from that dream in terror, packed up all my possessions, and left Seattle in the middle of the night.

"I love you," she said as I left her. "And don't ever come back."

I drove through the night, over the Cascades, down into the plains of central Washington, and back home to the Spokane Indian Reservation.

When I finished the Creamsicle that the 7-11 clerk gave me, I held the wooden stick up into the air and shouted out very loudly. A couple lights flashed on in windows and a police car cruised by me a few minutes later. I waved to the men in blue and they waved back accidentally. When I got home it was still too hot to sleep so I picked up a week-old newspaper from the floor and read.

There was another civil war, another terrorist bomb exploded, and one more plane crashed and all aboard were presumed dead. The crime rate was rising in every city with populations larger than 100,000, and a farmer in Iowa shot his banker after foreclosure on his 1,000 acres.

A kid from Spokane won the local spelling bee by spelling the word *rhinoceros*.

When I got back to the reservation, my family wasn't surprised to see me. They'd been expecting me back since the day I left for Seattle. There's an old Indian poet who said that Indians can reside in the city, but they can never live there. That's as close to truth as any of us can get.

Mostly I watched television. For weeks I flipped through channels, searched for answers in the game shows and soap operas. My mother would circle the want ads in red and hand the paper to me.

"What are you going to do with the rest of your life?" she asked.

"Don't know," I said, and normally, for almost any other Indian in the country, that would have been a perfectly fine answer. But I was special, a former college student, a smart kid. I was one of those Indians who was supposed to make it, to rise above the rest of the reservation like a fucking eagle or something. I was the new kind of warrior.

For a few months I didn't even look at the want ads my mother circled, just left the newspaper where she had set it down. After a while, though, I got tired of television and started to play basketball again. I'd been a good player in high school, nearly great, and almost played at the college I attended for a couple years. But I'd been too out of shape from drinking and sadness to ever be good again. Still, I liked the way the ball felt in my hands and the way my feet felt inside my shoes.

At first I just shot baskets by myself. It was selfish, and I also wanted to learn the game again before I played against anybody else. Since I had been good before and embarrassed fellow tribal members, I knew they would want to take revenge on me. Forget about the cowboys versus Indians business. The most intense competition on any reservation is Indians versus Indians.

But on the night I was ready to play for real, there was this white guy at the gym, playing with all the Indians.

"Who is that?" I asked Jimmy Seyler.

"He's the new BIA° chief's kid."

"Can he play?"

"Oh, yeah."

And he could play. He played Indian ball, fast and loose, better than all the Indians there.

"How long's he been playing here?" I asked.

"Long enough."

I stretched my muscles, and everybody watched me. All these Indians watched one of their old and dusty heroes. Even though I had played most of my ball at the white high school I went to, I was still all Indian, you know? I was Indian when it counted, and this BIA kid needed to be beaten by an Indian, any Indian.

I jumped into the game and played well for a little while. It felt good. I hit a few shots, grabbed a rebound or two, played enough defense to keep the other team honest. Then that white kid took over the game. He was too good. Later, he'd play college ball back East and would nearly

---

BIA: Bureau of Indian Affairs.

make the Knicks team a couple years on. But we didn't know any of that would happen. We just knew he was better that day and every other day.

The next morning I woke up tired and hungry, so I grabbed the want ads, found a job I wanted, and drove to Spokane to get it. I've been working at the high school exchange program ever since, typing and answering phones. Sometimes I wonder if the people on the other end of the line know that I'm Indian and if their voices would change if they did know.

One day I picked up the phone and it was her, calling from Seattle.

"I got your number from your mom," she said. "I'm glad you're working."

"Yeah, nothing like a regular paycheck."

"Are you drinking?"

"No, I've been on the wagon for almost a year."

"Good. "

The connection was good. I could hear her breathing in the spaces between our words. How do you talk to the real person whose ghost has haunted you? How do you tell the difference between the two?

"Listen," I said. "I'm sorry for everything."

"Me, too."

"What's going to happen to us?" I asked her and wished I had the answer for myself.

"I don't know," she said. "I want to change the world."

These days, living alone in Spokane, I wish I lived closer to the river, to the falls where ghosts of salmon jump. I wish I could sleep. I put down my paper or book and turn off all the lights, lie quietly in the dark. It may take hours, even years, for me to sleep again. There's nothing surprising or disappointing in that.

I know how all my dreams end anyway.

[1993]

JHUMPA LAHIRI   [b. 1967]

A Temporary Matter

The notice informed them that it was a temporary matter: for five days their electricity would be cut off for one hour, beginning at eight P.M. A line had gone down in the last snowstorm, and the repairmen were going to take advantage of the milder evenings to set it right. The work would affect only the houses on the quiet tree-lined street, within walking distance of a row of brick-faced stores and a trolley stop, where Shoba and Shukumar had lived for three years.

"It's good of them to warn us," Shoba conceded after reading the notice aloud, more for her own benefit than Shukumar's. She let the strap of her leather satchel, plump with files, slip from her shoulders, and left it in the hallway as she walked into the kitchen. She wore a navy blue poplin raincoat over gray sweatpants and white sneakers, looking, at thirty-three, like the type of woman she'd once claimed she would never resemble.

She'd come from the gym. Her cranberry lipstick was visible only on the outer reaches of her mouth, and her eyeliner had left charcoal patches beneath her lower lashes. She used to look this way sometimes, Shukumar thought, on mornings after a party or a night at a bar, when she'd been too lazy to wash her face, too eager to collapse into his arms. She dropped a sheaf of mail on the table without a glance. Her eyes were still fixed on the notice in her other hand. "But they should do this sort of thing during the day."

"When I'm here, you mean," Shukumar said. He put a glass lid on a pot of lamb, adjusting it so only the slightest bit of steam could escape. Since January he'd been working at home, trying to complete the final chapters of his dissertation on agrarian revolts in India. "When do the repairs start?"

"It says March nineteenth. Is today the nineteenth?" Shoba walked over to the framed corkboard that hung on the wall by the fridge, bare except for a calendar of William Morris wallpaper patterns. She looked at it as if for the first time, studying the wallpaper pattern carefully on the top half before allowing her eyes to fall to the numbered grid on the bottom. A friend had sent the calendar in the mail as a Christmas gift, even though Shoba and Shukumar hadn't celebrated Christmas that year.

"Today then," Shoba announced. "You have a dentist appointment next Friday, by the way."

He ran his tongue over the tops of his teeth; he'd forgotten to brush them that morning. It wasn't the first time. He hadn't left the house at all that day, or the day before. The more Shoba stayed out, the more she began putting in extra hours at work and taking on additional projects, the more he wanted to stay in, not even leaving to get the mail, or to buy fruit or wine at the stores by the trolley stop.

Six months ago, in September, Shukumar was at an academic conference in Baltimore when Shoba went into labor, three weeks before her due date. He hadn't wanted to go to the conference, but she had insisted; it was important to make contacts, and he would be entering the job market next year. She told him that she had his number at the hotel, and a copy of his schedule and flight numbers, and she had arranged with her friend Gillian for a ride to the hospital in the event of an emergency. When the cab pulled away that morning for the airport, Shoba stood waving good-bye in her robe, with one arm resting on the mound of her belly as if it were a perfectly natural part of her body.

Each time he thought of that moment, the last moment he saw Shoba pregnant, it was the cab he remembered most, a station wagon, painted red with blue lettering. It was cavernous compared to their own car. Although Shukumar was six feet tall, with hands too big ever to rest comfortably in the pockets of his jeans, he felt dwarfed in the back seat. As the cab sped down Beacon Street, he imagined a day when he and Shoba might need to buy a station wagon of their own, to cart their children back and forth from music lessons and dentist appointments. He imagined himself gripping the wheel, as Shoba turned around to hand the children juice boxes. Once, these images of parenthood had troubled Shukumar, adding to his anxiety that he was still a student at thirty-five. But that early autumn morning, the trees still heavy with bronze leaves, he welcomed the image for the first time.

A member of the staff had found him somehow among the identical convention rooms and handed him a stiff square of stationery. It was only a telephone number, but Shukumar knew it was the hospital. When he returned to Boston it was over. The baby had been born dead. Shoba was lying on a bed, asleep, in a private room so small there was barely enough space to stand beside her, in a wing of the hospital they hadn't been to on the tour for expectant parents. Her placenta had weakened and she'd had a cesarean, though not quickly enough. The doctor explained that these things happen. He smiled in the kindest way it was possible to smile at people known only professionally. Shoba would be back on her feet in a few weeks. There was nothing to indicate that she would not be able to have children in the future.

These days Shoba was always gone by the time Shukumar woke up. He would open his eyes and see the long black hairs she shed on her pillow and think of her, dressed, sipping her third cup of coffee already, in her office downtown, where she searched for typographical errors in textbooks and marked them, in a code she had once explained to him, with an assortment of colored pencils. She would do the same for his dissertation, she promised, when it was ready. He envied her the specificity of her task, so unlike the elusive nature of his. He was a mediocre student who had a facility for absorbing details without curiosity. Until September he had been diligent if not dedicated, summarizing chapters, outlining arguments on pads of yellow lined paper. But now he would lie in their bed until he grew bored, gazing at his side of the closet which Shoba always left partly open, at the row of the tweed jackets and corduroy trousers he would not have to choose from to teach his classes that semester. After the baby died it was too late to withdraw from his teaching duties. But his adviser had arranged things so that he had the spring semester to himself. Shukumar was in his sixth year of graduate school. "That and the summer should give you a good push," his adviser had said. "You should be able to wrap things up by next September."

But nothing was pushing Shukumar. Instead he thought of how he and Shoba had become experts at avoiding each other in their three-bedroom house, spending as much time on separate floors as possible. He thought of how he no longer looked forward to weekends, when she sat for hours on the sofa with her colored pencils and her files, so that he feared that putting on a record in his own house might be rude. He thought of how long it had been since she looked into his eyes and smiled, or whispered his name on those rare occasions they still reached for each other's bodies before sleeping.

In the beginning he had believed that it would pass, that he and Shoba would get through it all somehow. She was only thirty-three. She was strong, on her feet again. But it wasn't a consolation. It was often nearly lunchtime when Shukumar would finally pull himself out of bed and head downstairs to the coffeepot, pouring out the extra bit Shoba left for him, along with an empty mug, on the countertop.

Shukumar gathered onion skins in his hands and let them drop into the garbage pail, on top of the ribbons of fat he'd trimmed from the lamb. He ran the water in the sink, soaking the knife and the cutting board, and rubbed a lemon half along his fingertips to get rid of the garlic smell, a trick he'd learned from Shoba. It was seven-thirty. Through the window he saw the sky, like soft black pitch. Uneven banks of snow still lined the sidewalks, though it was warm enough for people to walk about without hats or gloves. Nearly three feet had fallen in the last storm, so that for a week people had to walk single file, in narrow trenches. For a week that was Shukumar's excuse for not leaving the house. But now the trenches were widening, and water drained steadily into grates in the pavement.

"The lamb won't be done by eight," Shukumar said. "We may have to eat in the dark."

"We can light candles," Shoba suggested. She unclipped her hair, coiled neatly at her nape during the days, and pried the sneakers from her feet without untying them. "I'm going to shower before the lights go," she said, heading for the staircase. "I'll be down."

Shukumar moved her satchel and her sneakers to the side of the fridge. She wasn't this way before. She used to put her coat on a hanger, her sneakers in the closet, and she paid bills as soon as they came. But now she treated the house as if it were a hotel. The fact that the yellow chintz armchair in the living room clashed with the blue-and-maroon Turkish carpet no longer bothered her. On the enclosed porch at the back of the house, a crisp white bag still sat on the wicker chaise, filled with lace she had once planned to turn into curtains.

While Shoba showered, Shukumar went into the downstairs bathroom and found a new toothbrush in its box beneath the sink. The cheap, stiff bristles hurt his gums, and he spit some blood into the basin. The spare brush was one of many stored in a metal basket. Shoba had bought them once when they were on sale, in the event that a visitor decided, at the last minute, to spend the night.

It was typical of her. She was the type to prepare for surprises, good and bad. If she found a skirt or a purse she liked she bought two. She kept the bonuses from her job in a separate bank account in her name. It hadn't bothered him. His own mother had fallen to pieces when his father died, abandoning the house he grew up in and moving back to Calcutta, leaving Shukumar to settle it all. He liked that Shoba was different. It astonished him, her capacity to think ahead. When she used to do the shopping, the pantry was always stocked with extra bottles of olive and corn oil, depending on whether they were cooking Italian or Indian. There were endless boxes of pasta in all shapes and colors, zippered sacks of basmati rice, whole sides of lambs and goats from the Muslim butchers at Haymarket, chopped up and frozen in endless plastic bags. Every other Saturday they wound through the maze of stalls Shukumar eventually knew by heart. He watched in disbelief as she bought more food, trailing behind her with canvas bags as she pushed through the crowd, arguing under the morning sun with boys too young to shave but already missing teeth, who twisted up brown paper bags of artichokes, plums, gingerroot, and yams, and dropped them on their scales, and tossed them to Shoba one by one. She didn't mind being jostled, even when she was pregnant. She was tall, and broad-shouldered, with hips that her obstetrician assured her were made for childbearing. During the drive back home, as the car curved along the Charles, they invariably marveled at how much food they'd bought.

It never went to waste. When friends dropped by, Shoba would throw together meals that appeared to have taken half a day to prepare, from things she had frozen and bottled, not cheap things in tins but peppers she had marinated herself with rosemary, and chutneys that she cooked on Sundays, stirring boiling pots of tomatoes and prunes. Her labeled mason jars lined the shelves of the kitchen, in endless sealed pyramids, enough, they'd agreed, to last for their grandchildren to taste. They'd eaten it all by now. Shukumar had been going through their supplies steadily, preparing meals for the two of them, measuring out cupfuls of rice, defrosting bags of meat day after day. He combed through her cookbooks every afternoon, following her penciled instructions to use two teaspoons of ground coriander seeds instead of one, or red lentils instead of yellow. Each of the recipes was dated, telling the first time they had eaten the dish together. April 2, cauliflower with fennel. January 14, chicken with almonds and sultanas. He had no memory of eating those meals, and yet there they were, recorded in her neat proofreader's hand. Shukumar enjoyed cooking now. It was the one thing that made him feel productive. If it weren't for him, he knew, Shoba would eat a bowl of cereal for her dinner.

Tonight, with no lights, they would have to eat together. For months now they'd served themselves from the stove, and he'd taken his plate into his study, letting the meal grow cold on his desk before shoving it into his mouth without pause, while Shoba took her plate to the living room and watched game shows, or proofread files with her arsenal of colored pencils at hand.

At some point in the evening she visited him. When he heard her approach he would put away his novel and begin typing sentences. She would rest her hands on his shoulders and stare with him into the blue glow of the computer screen. "Don't work too hard," she would say after a minute or two, and head off to bed. It was the one time in the day she sought him out, and yet he'd come to dread it. He knew it was something she forced herself to do. She would look around the walls of the room, which they had decorated together last summer with a border of marching ducks and rabbits playing trumpets and drums. By the end of August there was a cherry crib under the window, a white changing table with mint-green knobs, and a rocking chair with checkered cushions. Shukumar had disassembled it all before bringing Shoba back from the hospital, scraping off the rabbits and ducks with a spatula. For some reason the room did not haunt him the way it haunted Shoba. In January, when he stopped working at his carrel in the library, he set up his desk there deliberately, partly because the room soothed him, and partly because it was a place Shoba avoided.

Shukumar returned to the kitchen and began to open drawers. He tried to locate a candle among the scissors, the eggbeaters and whisks, the mortar and pestle she'd bought in a bazaar in Calcutta, and used to pound garlic cloves and cardamom pods, back when she used to cook. He found a flashlight, but no batteries, and a half-empty box of birthday candles. Shoba had thrown him a surprise birthday party last May. One hundred and twenty people had crammed into the house—all the friends and the friends of friends they now systematically avoided. Bottles of vinho verde had nested in a bed of ice in the bathtub. Shoba was in her fifth month, drinking ginger ale from a martini glass. She had made a vanilla cream cake with custard and spun sugar. All night she kept Shukumar's long fingers linked with hers as they walked among the guests at the party.

Since September their only guest had been Shoba's mother. She came from Arizona and stayed with them for two months after Shoba returned from the hospital. She cooked dinner every night, drove herself to the supermarket, washed their clothes, put them away. She was a religious woman. She set up a small shrine, a framed picture of a lavender-faced goddess and a plate of marigold petals, on the bedside table in the guest room, and prayed twice a day for healthy grandchildren in the future. She was polite to Shukumar without being friendly. She folded his sweaters with an expertise she had learned from her job in a department store. She replaced a missing button on his winter coat and knit him a beige and brown scarf, presenting it to him without the least bit of ceremony, as if he had only dropped it and hadn't noticed. She never talked to him about Shoba; once, when he mentioned the baby's death, she looked up from her knitting, and said, "But you weren't even there."

It struck him as odd that there were no real candles in the house. That Shoba hadn't prepared for such an ordinary emergency. He looked now for something to put the birthday candles in and settled on the soil of a potted ivy that normally sat on the windowsill over the sink. Even though the plant was inches from the tap, the soil was so dry that he had to water it first before the candles would stand straight. He pushed aside the things on the kitchen table, the piles of mail, the unread library books. He remembered their first meals there, when they were so thrilled to be married, to be living together in the same house at last, that they would just reach for each other foolishly, more eager to make love than to eat. He put down two embroidered place mats, a wedding gift from an uncle in Lucknow, and set out the plates and wineglasses they usually saved for guests. He put the ivy in the middle, the white-edged, star-shaped leaves girded by ten little candles. He switched on the digital clock radio and tuned it to a jazz station.

"What's all this?" Shoba said when she came downstairs. Her hair was wrapped in a thick white towel. She undid the towel and draped it over a chair, allowing her hair, damp and dark, to fall across her back. As she walked absently toward the stove she took out a few tangles with her fingers. She wore a clean pair of sweatpants, a T-shirt, an old flannel robe. Her stomach was flat again, her waist narrow before the flare of her hips, the belt of the robe tied in a floppy knot.

It was nearly eight. Shukumar put the rice on the table and the lentils from the night before into the microwave oven, punching the numbers on the timer.

"You made *rogan josh*," Shoba observed, looking through the glass lid at the bright paprika stew.

Shukumar took out a piece of lamb, pinching it quickly between his fingers so as not to scald himself. He prodded a larger piece with a serving spoon to make sure the meat slipped easily from the bone. "It's ready," he announced.

The microwave had just beeped when the lights went out, and the music disappeared.

"Perfect timing," Shoba said.

"All I could find were birthday candles." He lit up the ivy, keeping the rest of the candles and a book of matches by his plate.

"It doesn't matter," she said, running a finger along the stem of her wineglass. "It looks lovely."

In the dimness, he knew how she sat, a bit forward in her chair, ankles crossed against the lowest rung, left elbow on the table. During his search for the candles, Shukumar had found a bottle of wine in a crate he had thought was empty. He clamped the bottle between his knees while he turned in the corkscrew. He worried about spilling, and so he picked up the glasses and held them close to his lap while he filled them. They served themselves, stirring the rice with their forks, squinting as they extracted bay leaves and cloves from the stew. Every few minutes Shukumar lit a few more birthday candles and drove them into the soil of the pot.

"It's like India," Shoba said, watching him tend his makeshift candelabra. "Sometimes the current disappears for hours at a stretch. I once had to attend an entire rice ceremony in the dark. The baby just cried and cried. It must have been so hot."

Their baby had never cried, Shukumar considered. Their baby would never have a rice ceremony, even though Shoba had already made the guest list, and decided on which of her three brothers she was going to ask to feed the child its first taste of solid food, at six months if it was a boy, seven if it was a girl.

"Are you hot?" he asked her. He pushed the blazing ivy pot to the other end of the table, closer to the piles of books and mail, making it even more difficult for them to see each other. He was suddenly irritated that he couldn't go upstairs and sit in front of the computer.

"No. It's delicious," she said, tapping her plate with her fork. "It really is."
He refilled the wine in her glass. She thanked him.

They weren't like this before. Now he had to struggle to say something
that interested her, something that made her look up from her plate, or
from her proofreading files. Eventually he gave up trying to amuse her.
He learned not to mind the silences.

"I remember during power failures at my grandmother's house, we all
had to say something," Shoba continued. He could barely see her face,
but from her tone he knew her eyes were narrowed, as if trying to focus
on a distant object. It was a habit of hers.

"Like what?"

"I don't know. A little poem. A joke. A fact about the world. For some
reason my relatives always wanted me to tell them the names of my
friends in America. I don't know why the information was so interesting
to them. The last time I saw my aunt she asked after four girls I went to
elementary school with in Tucson. I barely remember them now."

Shukumar hadn't spent as much time in India as Shoba had. His
parents, who settled in New Hampshire, used to go back without him.
The first time he'd gone as an infant he'd nearly died of amoebic dysentery. His father, a nervous type, was afraid to take him again, in case
something were to happen, and left him with his aunt and uncle in
Concord. As a teenager he preferred sailing camp or scooping ice
cream during the summers to going to Calcutta. It wasn't until after
his father died, in his last year of college, that the country began to
interest him, and he studied its history from course books as if it were
any other subject. He wished now that he had his own childhood story
of India.

"Let's do that," she said suddenly.

"Do what?"

"Say something to each other in the dark."

"Like what? I don't know any jokes."

"No, no jokes." She thought for a minute. "How about telling each
other something we've never told before."

"I used to play this game in high school," Shukumar recalled. "When I
got drunk."

"You're thinking of truth or dare. This is different. Okay, I'll start." She
took a sip of wine. "The first time I was alone in your apartment, I looked
in your address book to see if you'd written me in. I think we'd known
each other two weeks."

"Where was I?"

"You went to answer the telephone in the other room. It was your
mother, and I figured it would be a long call. I wanted to know if you'd
promoted me from the margins of your newspaper."

"Had I?"

"No. But I didn't give up on you. Now it's your turn."

He couldn't think of anything, but Shoba was waiting for him to speak. She hadn't appeared so determined in months. What was there left to say to her? He thought back to their first meeting, four years earlier at a lecture hall in Cambridge, where a group of Bengali poets were giving a recital. They'd ended up side by side, on folding wooden chairs. Shukumar was soon bored; he was unable to decipher the literary diction, and couldn't join the rest of the audience as they sighed and nodded solemnly after certain phrases. Peering at the newspaper folded in his lap, he studied the temperatures of cities around the world. Ninety-one degrees in Singapore yesterday, fifty-one in Stockholm. When he turned his head to the left, he saw a woman next to him making a grocery list on the back of a folder, and was startled to find that she was beautiful.

"Okay," he said, remembering. "The first time we went out to dinner, to the Portuguese place, I forgot to tip the waiter. I went back the next morning, found out his name, left money with the manager."

"You went all the way back to Somerville just to tip a waiter?"

"I took a cab."

"Why did you forget to tip the waiter?"

The birthday candles had burned out, but he pictured her face clearly in the dark, the wide tilting eyes, the full grape-toned lips, the fall at age two from her high chair still visible as a comma on her chin. Each day, Shukumar noticed, her beauty, which had once overwhelmed him, seemed to fade. The cosmetics that had seemed superfluous were necessary now, not to improve her but to define her somehow.

"By the end of the meal I had a funny feeling that I might marry you," he said, admitting it to himself as well as to her for the first time. "It must have distracted me."

The next night Shoba came home earlier than usual. There was lamb left over from the evening before, and Shukumar heated it up so that they were able to eat by seven. He'd gone out that day, through the melting snow, and bought a packet of taper candles from the corner store, and batteries to fit the flashlight. He had the candles ready on the countertop, standing in brass holders shaped like lotuses, but they ate under the glow of the copper-shaded ceiling lamp that hung over the table.

When they had finished eating, Shukumar was surprised to see that Shoba was stacking her plate on top of his, and then carrying them over to the sink. He had assumed she would retreat to the living room, behind her barricade of files.

"Don't worry about the dishes," he said, taking them from her hands.

"It seems silly not to," she replied, pouring a drop of detergent onto a sponge. "It's nearly eight o'clock."

His heart quickened. All day Shukumar had looked forward to the lights going out. He thought about what Shoba had said the night before, about looking in his address book. It felt good to remember her as she was then, how bold yet nervous she'd been when they first met, how hopeful. They stood side by side at the sink, their reflections fitting together in the frame of the window. It made him shy, the way he felt the first time they stood together in a mirror. He couldn't recall the last time they'd been photographed. They had stopped attending parties, went nowhere together. The film in his camera still contained pictures of Shoba, in the yard, when she was pregnant.

After finishing the dishes, they leaned against the counter, drying their hands on either end of a towel. At eight o'clock the house went black. Shukumar lit the wicks of the candles, impressed by their long, steady flames.

"Let's sit outside," Shoba said. "I think it's warm still."

They each took a candle and sat down on the steps. It seemed strange to be sitting outside with patches of snow still on the ground. But everyone was out of their houses tonight, the air fresh enough to make people restless. Screen doors opened and closed. A small parade of neighbors passed by with flashlights.

"We're going to the bookstore to browse," a silver-haired man called out. He was walking with his wife, a thin woman in a windbreaker, and holding a dog on a leash. They were the Bradfords, and they had tucked a sympathy card into Shoba and Shukumar's mailbox back in September. "I hear they've got their power."

"They'd better," Shukumar said. "Or you'll be browsing in the dark."

The woman laughed, slipping her arm through the crook of her husband's elbow. "Want to join us?"

"No thanks," Shoba and Shukumar called out together. It surprised Shukumar that his words matched hers.

He wondered what Shoba would tell him in the dark. The worst possibilities had already run through his head. That she'd had an affair. That she didn't respect him for being thirty-five and still a student. That she blamed him for being in Baltimore the way her mother did. But he knew those things weren't true. She'd been faithful, as had he. She believed in him. It was she who had insisted he go to Baltimore. What didn't they know about each other? He knew she curled her fingers tightly when she slept, that her body twitched during bad dreams. He knew it was honeydew she favored over cantaloupe. He knew that when they returned from the hospital the first thing she did when she walked into the house was pick out objects of theirs and toss them into a pile in the hallway: books from the shelves, plants from the windowsills, paintings from walls, photos from tables, pots and pans that hung from the hooks over the stove. Shukumar had stepped out of her way, watching as she moved methodically from room to room. When she was satisfied, she stood there staring at the pile she'd made, her lips drawn back in such distaste that Shukumar had thought she would spit. Then she'd started to cry.

He began to feel cold as he sat there on the steps. He felt that he needed her to talk first, in order to reciprocate.

"That time when your mother came to visit us," she said finally. "When I said one night that I had to stay late at work, I went out with Gillian and had a martini."

He looked at her profile, the slender nose, the slightly masculine set of her jaw. He remembered that night well; eating with his mother, tired from teaching two classes back to back, wishing Shoba were there to say more of the right things because he came up with only the wrong ones. It had been twelve years since his father had died, and his mother had come to spend two weeks with him and Shoba, so they could honor his father's memory together. Each night his mother cooked something his father had liked, but she was too upset to eat the dishes herself, and her eyes would well up as Shoba stroked her hand. "It's so touching," Shoba had said to him at the time. Now he pictured Shoba with Gillian, in a bar with striped velvet sofas, the one they used to go to after the movies, making sure she got her extra olive, asking Gillian for a cigarette. He imagined her complaining, and Gillian sympathizing about visits from in-laws. It was Gillian who had driven Shoba to the hospital.

"Your turn," she said, stopping his thoughts.

At the end of their street Shukumar heard sounds of a drill and the electricians shouting over it. He looked at the darkened facades of the houses lining the street. Candles glowed in the windows of one. In spite of the warmth, smoke rose from the chimney.

"I cheated on my Oriental Civilization exam in college," he said. "It was my last semester, my last set of exams. My father had died a few months before. I could see the blue book of the guy next to me. He was an American guy, a maniac. He knew Urdu and Sanskrit. I couldn't remember if the verse we had to identify was an example of a *ghazal* or not. I looked at his answer and copied it down."

It had happened over fifteen years ago. He felt relief now, having told her.

She turned to him, looking not at his face, but at his shoes—old moccasins he wore as if they were slippers, the leather at the back permanently flattened. He wondered if it bothered her, what he'd said. She took his hand and pressed it. "You didn't have to tell me why you did it," she said, moving closer to him.

They sat together until nine o'clock, when the lights came on. They heard some people across the street clapping from their porch, and televisions being turned on. The Bradfords walked back down the street, eating ice-cream cones and waving. Shoba and Shukumar waved back. Then they stood up, his hand still in hers, and went inside.

Somehow, without saying anything, it had turned into this. Into an exchange of confessions—the little ways they'd hurt or disappointed each other, and themselves. The following day Shukumar thought for hours about what to say to her. He was torn between admitting that he once ripped out a photo of a woman in one of the fashion magazines she used to subscribe to and carried it in his books for a week, or saying that he really hadn't lost the sweater-vest she bought him for their third wedding anniversary but had exchanged it for cash at Filene's, and that he had gotten drunk alone in the middle of the day at a hotel bar. For their first anniversary, Shoba had cooked a ten-course dinner just for him. The vest depressed him. "My wife gave me a sweater-vest for our anniversary," he complained to the bartender, his head heavy with cognac. "What do you expect?" the bartender had replied. "You're married."

As for the picture of the woman, he didn't know why he'd ripped it out. She wasn't as pretty as Shoba. She wore a white sequined dress, and had a sullen face and lean, mannish legs. Her bare arms were raised, her fists around her head, as if she were about to punch herself in the ears. It was an advertisement for stockings. Shoba had been pregnant at the time, her stomach suddenly immense, to the point where Shukumar no longer wanted to touch her. The first time he saw the picture he was lying in bed next to her, watching her as she read. When he noticed the magazine in the recycling pile he found the woman and tore out the page as carefully as he could. For about a week he allowed himself a glimpse each day. He felt an intense desire for the woman, but it was a desire that turned to disgust after a minute or two. It was the closest he'd come to infidelity.

He told Shoba about the sweater on the third night, the picture on the fourth. She said nothing as he spoke, expressed no protest or reproach. She simply listened, and then she took his hand, pressing it as she had before. On the third night, she told him that once after a lecture they'd attended, she let him speak to the chairman of his department without telling him that he had a dab of pâté on his chin. She'd been irritated with him for some reason, and so she'd let him go on and on, about securing his fellowship for the following semester, without putting a finger to her own chin as a signal. The fourth night, she said that she never liked the one poem he'd ever published in his life, in a literary magazine in Utah. He'd written the poem after meeting Shoba. She added that she found the poem sentimental.

Something happened when the house was dark. They were able to talk to each other again. The third night after supper they'd sat together on the sofa, and once it was dark he began kissing her awkwardly on her forehead and her face, and though it was dark he closed his eyes, and knew that she did, too. The fourth night they walked carefully upstairs, to bed, feeling together for the final step with their feet before the landing, and making love with a desperation they had forgotten. She wept without sound, and whispered his name, and traced his eyebrows with her finger in the dark. As he made love to her he wondered what he would say to her the next night, and what she would say, the thought of it exciting him. "Hold me," he said, "hold me in your arms." By the time the lights came back on downstairs, they'd fallen asleep.

The morning of the fifth night Shukumar found another notice from the electric company in the mailbox. The line had been repaired ahead of schedule, it said. He was disappointed. He had planned on making shrimp *malai* for Shoba, but when he arrived at the store he didn't feel like cooking anymore. It wasn't the same, he thought, knowing that the lights wouldn't go out. In the store the shrimp looked gray and thin. The coconut milk tin was dusty and overpriced. Still, he bought them, along with a beeswax candle and two bottles of wine.

She came home at seven-thirty. "I suppose this is the end of our game," he said when he saw her reading the notice.

She looked at him. "You can still light candles if you want." She hadn't been to the gym tonight. She wore a suit beneath the raincoat. Her makeup had been retouched recently.

When she went upstairs to change, Shukumar poured himself some wine and put on a record, a Thelonius Monk album he knew she liked.

When she came downstairs they ate together. She didn't thank him or compliment him. They simply ate in a darkened room, in the glow of a beeswax candle. They had survived a difficult time. They finished off the shrimp. They finished off the first bottle of wine and moved on to the second. They sat together until the candle had nearly burned away. She shifted in her chair, and Shukumar thought that she was about to say something. But instead she blew out the candle, stood up, turned on the light switch, and sat down again.

"Shouldn't we keep the lights off?" Shukumar asked.

She set her plate aside and clasped her hands on the table. "I want you to see my face when I tell you this," she said gently.

His heart began to pound. The day she told him she was pregnant, she had used the very same words, saying them in the same gentle way, turning off the basketball game he'd been watching on television. He hadn't been prepared then. Now he was.

Only he didn't want her to be pregnant again. He didn't want to have to pretend to be happy.

"I've been looking for an apartment and I've found one," she said, narrowing her eyes on something, it seemed, behind his left shoulder. It was nobody's fault, she continued. They'd been through enough. She needed some time alone. She had money saved up for a security deposit. The apartment was on Beacon Hill, so she could walk to work. She had signed the lease that night before coming home.

She wouldn't look at him, but he stared at her. It was obvious that she'd rehearsed the lines. All this time she'd been looking for an apartment, testing the water pressure, asking a Realtor if heat and hot water were included in the rent. It sickened Shukumar, knowing that she had spent these past evenings preparing for a life without him. He was relieved and yet he was sickened. This was what she'd been trying to tell him for the past four evenings. This was the point of her game.

Now it was his turn to speak. There was something he'd sworn he would never tell her, and for six months he had done his best to block it from his mind. Before the ultrasound she had asked the doctor not to tell her the sex of their child, and Shukumar had agreed. She had wanted it to be a surprise.

Later, those few times they talked about what had happened, she said at least they'd been spared that knowledge. In a way she almost took pride in her decision, for it enabled her to seek refuge in a mystery. He knew that she assumed it was a mystery for him, too. He'd arrived too late from Baltimore—when it was all over and she was lying on the hospital bed. But he hadn't. He'd arrived early enough to see their baby, and to hold him before they cremated him. At first he had recoiled at the suggestion, but the doctor said holding the baby might help him with the process of grieving. Shoba was asleep. The baby had been cleaned off, his bulbous lids shut tight to the world.

"Our baby was a boy," he said. "His skin was more red than brown. He had black hair on his head. He weighed almost five pounds. His fingers were curled shut, just like yours in the night."

Shoba looked at him now, her face contorted with sorrow. He had cheated on a college exam, ripped a picture of a woman out of a magazine. He had returned a sweater and got drunk in the middle of the day instead. These were the things he had told her. He had held his son, who had known life only within her, against his chest in a darkened room in an unknown wing of the hospital. He had held him until a nurse knocked and took him away, and he promised himself that day that he would never tell Shoba, because he still loved her then, and it was the one thing in her life that she had wanted to be a surprise.

Shukumar stood up and stacked his plate on top of hers. He carried the plates to the sink, but instead of running the tap he looked out the window. Outside the evening was still warm, and the Bradfords were walking arm in arm. As he watched the couple the room went dark, and he spun around. Shoba had turned the lights off. She came back to the table and sat down, and after a moment Shukumar joined her. They wept together, for the things they now knew.

[1998]

JUNOT DÍAZ   [b. 1968]

How to Date a Browngirl, Blackgirl, Whitegirl, or Halfie

Wait for your brother and your mother to leave the apartment. You've already told them that you're feeling too sick to go to Union City to visit that tía° who likes to squeeze your nuts. (He's gotten big, she'll say.) And even though your moms knows you ain't sick you stuck to your story until finally she said, Go ahead and stay, malcriado.°

Clear the government cheese from the refrigerator. If the girl's from the Terrace stack the boxes behind the milk. If she's from the Park or Society Hill hide the cheese in the cabinet above the oven, way up where she'll never see. Leave yourself a reminder to get it out before morning or your moms will kick your ass. Take down any embarrassing photos of your family in the campo,° especially the one with the half-naked kids dragging a goat on a rope leash. The kids are your cousins and by now they're old enough to understand why you're doing what you're doing. Hide the pictures of yourself with an Afro. Make sure the bathroom is presentable. Put the basket with all the crapped-on toilet paper under the sink. Spray the bucket with Lysol, then close the cabinet.

Shower, comb, dress. Sit on the couch and watch TV. If she's an outsider her father will be bringing her, maybe her mother. Neither of them want her seeing any boys from the Terrace—people get stabbed in the Terrace—but she's strong-headed and this time will get her way. If she's a whitegirl you know you'll at least get a hand job.

tía: Aunt.
malcriado: A spoiled or ill-mannered child.
campo: countryside

The directions were in your best handwriting, so her parents won't think you're an idiot. Get up from the couch and check the parking lot. Nothing. If the girl's local, don't sweat it. She'll flow over when she's good and ready. Sometimes she'll run into her other friends and a whole crowd will show up at your apartment and even though that means you ain't getting shit it will be fun anyway and you'll wish these people would come over more often. Sometimes the girl won't flow over at all and the next day in school she'll say sorry, smile and you'll be stupid enough to believe her and ask her out again.

Wait and after an hour go out to your corner. The neighborhood is full of traffic. Give one of your boys a shout and when he says, Are you still waiting on that bitch? say, Hell yeah.

Get back inside. Call her house and when her father picks up ask if she's there. He'll ask, Who is this? Hang up. He sounds like a principal or a police chief, the sort of dude with a big neck, who never has to watch his back. Sit and wait. By the time your stomach's ready to give out on you, a Honda or maybe a Jeep pulls in and out she comes.

Hey, you'll say.

Look, she'll say. My mom wants to meet you. She's got herself all worried about nothing.

Don't panic. Say, Hey, no problem. Run a hand through your hair like the whiteboys do even though the only thing that runs easily through your hair is Africa. She will look good. The white ones are the ones you want the most, aren't they, but usually the out-of-towners are black, blackgirls who grew up with ballet and Girl Scouts, who have three cars in their driveways. If she's a halfie don't be surprised that her mother is white. Say, Hi. Her moms will say hi and you'll see that you don't scare her, not really. She will say that she needs easier directions to get out and even though she has the best directions in her lap give her new ones. Make her happy.

You have choices. If the girl's from around the way, take her to El Cibao for dinner. Order everything in your busted-up Spanish. Let her correct you if she's Latina and amaze her if she's black. If she's not from around the way, Wendy's will do. As you walk to the restaurant talk about school. A local girl won't need stories about the neighborhood but the other ones might. Supply the story about the loco who'd been storing canisters of tear gas in his basement for years, how one day the canisters cracked and the whole neighborhood got a dose of the military strength stuff. Don't tell her that your moms knew right away what it was, that she recognized its smell from the year the United States invaded your island.

Hope that you don't run into your nemesis, Howie, the Puerto Rican kid with the two killer mutts. He walks them all over the neighborhood and every now and then the mutts corner themselves a cat and tear it to shreds, Howie laughing as the cat flips up in the air, its neck twisted around like an owl, red meat showing through the soft fur. If his dogs haven't cornered a cat, he will walk behind you and ask, Hey, Yunior, is that your new fuckbuddy?

Let him talk. Howie weighs about two hundred pounds and could eat you if he wanted. At the field he will turn away. He has new sneakers, and doesn't want them muddy. If the girl's an outsider she will hiss now and say, What a fucking asshole. A homegirl would have been yelling back at him the whole time, unless she was shy. Either way don't feel bad that you didn't do anything. Never lose a fight on a first date or that will be the end of it.

Dinner will be tense. You are not good at talking to people you don't know. A halfie will tell you that her parents met in the Movement, will say, Back then people thought it a radical thing to do. It will sound like something her parents made her memorize. Your brother once heard that one and said, Man, that sounds like a whole lot of Uncle Tomming to me. Don't repeat this.

Put down your hamburger and say, It must have been hard.

She will appreciate your interest. She will tell you more. Black people, she will say, treat me real bad. That's why I don't like them. You'll wonder how she feels about Dominicans. Don't ask. Let her speak on it and when you're both finished eating walk back into the neighborhood. The skies will be magnificent. Pollutants have made Jersey sunsets one of the wonders of the world. Point it out. Touch her shoulder and say, That's nice, right?

Get serious. Watch TV but stay alert. Sip some of the Bermúdez your father left in the cabinet, which nobody touches. A local girl may have hips and a thick ass but she won't be quick about letting you touch. She has to live in the same neighborhood you do, has to deal with you being all up in her business. She might just chill with you and then go home. She might kiss you and then go, or she might, if she's reckless, give it up, but that's rare. Kissing will suffice. A whitegirl might just give it up right then. Don't stop her. She'll take her gum out of her mouth, stick it to the plastic sofa covers and then will move close to you. You have nice eyes, she might say.

Tell her that you love her hair, that you love her skin, her lips, because, in truth, you love them more than you love your own.

She'll say, I like Spanish guys, and even though you've never been to Spain, say, I like you. You'll sound smooth.

You'll be with her until about eight-thirty and then she will want to wash up. In the bathroom she will hum a song from the radio and her waist will keep the beat against the lip of the sink. Imagine her old lady coming to get her, what she would say if she knew her daughter had just lain under you and blown your name, pronounced with her eighth-grade Spanish, into your ear. While she's in the bathroom call one of your boys and say, Lo hice, loco.° Or just sit back on the couch and smile.

Lo hice, loco: A boast about his sexual interactions with the girl, whether real or fabricated.

But usually it won't work this way. Be prepared. She will not want to kiss you. Just cool it, she'll say. The halfie might lean back, breaking away from you. She will cross her arms, say, I hate my tits. Stroke her hair but she will pull away. I don't like anybody touching my hair, she will say. She will act like somebody you don't know. In school she is known for her attention-grabbing laugh, as high and far-ranging as a gull, but here she will worry you. You will not know what to say.

You're the only kind of guy who asks me out, she will say. Your neighbors will start their hyena calls, now that the alcohol is in them. You and the blackboys.

Say nothing. Let her button her shirt, let her comb her hair, the sound of it stretching like a sheet of fire between you. When her father pulls in and beeps, let her go without too much of a good-bye. She won't want it. During the next hour the phone will ring. You will be tempted to pick it up. Don't. Watch the shows you want to watch, without a family around to debate you. Don't go downstairs. Don't fall asleep. It won't help. Put the government cheese back in its place before your moms kills you.

[1996]

YIYUN LI   [b. 1972]

A Thousand Years of Good Prayers

A rocket scientist, Mr. Shi tells people when they ask about his profession in China. Retired, he then adds, out of modesty, when people marvel. Mr. Shi learned the phrase from a woman during a layover at Detroit, when he tried to explain to her his work, drawing pictures when his English failed to help. "A rocket scientist!" the woman exclaimed, laughing out loud.

People he meets in America, already friendly, seem more so when they learn his profession, so he likes to repeat the words whenever possible. Five days into his visit at his daughter's place, in this Midwest town, Mr. Shi has made quite a few acquaintances. Mothers with babies in strollers wave at him. An old couple, the husband in suit and the wife in skirt, show up in the park every morning at nine o'clock, her hand on his arm; they stop and greet him, the husband always the one speaking, the wife smiling. A woman living in the retirement home a block away comes to talk to him. She is seventy-seven, two years his senior, and was originally from Iran. Despite the fact they both speak little English, they have no problem understanding each other, and in no time they become friends.

"America good country," she says often. "Sons make rich money."

America is indeed a good country. Mr. Shi's daughter works as a librarian in the East Asian department in the college library and earns more in a year than he made in twenty.

"My daughter, she make lots of money, too."

"I love America. Good country for everybody."

"Yes, yes. A rocket scientist I am in China. But very poor. Rocket scientist, you know?" Mr. Shi says, his hands making a peak.

"I love China. China a good country, very old," the woman says.

"America is young country, like young people."

"America a happy country."

"Young people are more happy than old people," Mr. Shi says, and then realizes that it is too abrupt a conclusion. He himself feels happier at this moment than he remembers he ever did in his life. The woman in front of him, who loves everything with or without a good reason, seems happy, too.

Sometimes they run out of English. She switches to Persian, mixed with a few English words. Mr. Shi finds it hard to speak Chinese to her. It is she who carries the conversation alone then, for ten or twenty minutes. He nods and smiles effusively. He does not understand much of what she is saying, but he feels her joy in talking to him, the same joy he feels listening to her.

Mr. Shi starts to look forward to the mornings when he sits in the park and waits for her. "Madam" is what he uses to address her, as he has never asked her name. Madam wears colors that he does not imagine a woman of her age, or where she came from, would wear, red and orange and purple and yellow. She has a pair of metal barrettes, a white elephant and blue-and-green peacock. They clasp on her thin hair in a wobbly way that reminds him of his daughter when she was a small child—before her hair was fully grown, with a plastic butterfly hanging loose on her forehead. Mr. Shi, for a brief moment, wants to tell Madam how much he misses the days when his daughter was small and life was hopeful. But he is sure, even before he starts, that his English would fail him. Besides, it is never his habit to talk about the past.

In the evenings, when his daughter comes home, Mr. Shi has the supper ready. He took a cooking class after his wife died, a few years ago, and ever since has studied the culinary art with the same fervor with which he studied mathematics and physics when he was a college student. "Every man is born with more talents than he knows how to use," he says at dinner. "I would've never imagined taking up cooking, but here I am, better than I imagined."

"Yes, very impressive," his daughter says.

"And likewise"—Mr. Shi takes a quick glance at his daughter—"life provides more happiness than we ever know. We have to train ourselves to look for it."

His daughter does not reply. Despite the pride he takes in his cooking and her praises for it, she eats little and eats out of duty. It worries him that she is not putting enough enthusiasm into life as she should be. Of course, she has her reasons, newly divorced after seven years of marriage. His ex-son-in-law went back to Beijing permanently after the divorce. Mr. Shi does not know what led the boat of their marriage to run into a hidden rock, but whatever the reason is, it must not be her fault. She is made for a good wife, soft-voiced and kindhearted, dutiful and beautiful, a younger version of her mother. When his daughter called to inform him of the divorce, Mr. Shi imagined her in inconsolable pain, and asked to come to America, to help her recover. She refused, and he started calling daily and pleading, spending a good solid month of his pension on the long-distance bill. She finally agreed when he announced that his wish for his seventy-fifth birthday was to take a look at America. A lie it was, but the lie turned out to be a good reason. America is worth taking a look at; more than that, America makes him a new person, a rocket scientist, a good conversationalist, a loving father, a happy man.

After dinner, Mr. Shi's daughter either retreats to her bedroom to read or drives away and comes home at late hours. Mr. Shi asks to go out with her, to accompany her to the movies he imagines that she watches alone, but she refuses in a polite but firm manner. It is certainly not healthy for a woman, especially a contemplative woman like his daughter, to spend too much time alone. He starts to talk more to tackle her solitude, asking questions about the part of her life he is not witnessing. How was her work of the day? he asks. Fine, she says tiredly. Not discouraged, he asks about her colleagues, whether there are more females than males, how old they are, and, if they are married, whether they have children. He asks what she eats for lunch and whether she eats alone, what kind of computer she uses, and what books she reads. He asks about her old school friends, people he believes she is out of contact with because of the shame of the divorce. He asks about her plan for the future, hoping she understands the urgency of her situation. Women in their marriage-able twenties and early thirties are like lychees that have been picked from the tree; each passing day makes them less fresh and less desirable, and only too soon will they lose their value, and have to be gotten rid of at a sale price.

Mr. Shi knows enough not to mention the sale price. Still, he cannot help but lecture on the fruitfulness of life. The more he talks, the more he is moved by his own patience. His daughter, however, does not improve. She eats less and becomes quieter each day. When he finally points out that she is not enjoying her life as she should, she says, "How do you get this conclusion? I'm enjoying my life all right."

"But that's a lie. A happy person will never be so quiet!"

She looks up from the bowl of rice. "Baba, you used to be very quiet, remember? Were you unhappy then?"

Mr. Shi, not prepared for such directness from his daughter, is unable to reply. He waits for her to apologize and change the topic, as people with good manners do when they realize they are embarrassing others with their questions, but she does not let him go. Her eyes behind her glasses, wide open and unrelenting, remind him of her in her younger years. When she was four or five, she went after him every possible moment, asking questions and demanding answers. The eyes remind him of her mother too; at one time in their marriage, she gazed at him with this questioning look, waiting for an answer he did not have for her.

He sighs. "Of course I've always been happy."

"There you go, Baba. We can be quiet *and* happy, can't we?"

"Why not talk about your happiness with me?" Mr. Shi says. "Tell me more about your work."

"You didn't talk much about your work either, remember? Even when I asked."

"A rocket scientist, you know how it was. My work was confidential."

"You didn't talk much about anything," his daughter says.

Mr. Shi opens his mouth but finds no words coming. After a long moment, he says, "I talk more now. I'm improving, no?"

"Sure," his daughter says.

"That's what you need to do. Talk more," Mr. Shi says. "And start now."

His daughter, however, is less enthusiastic. She finishes her meal quickly in her usual silence and leaves the apartment before he finishes his.

The next morning, Mr. Shi confesses to Madam, "The daughter, she's not happy."

"Daughter a happy thing to have," Madam says.

"She's divorced."

Madam nods, and starts to talk in Persian. Mr. Shi is not sure if Madam knows what divorce means. A woman so boldly in love with the world like her must have been shielded from life's unpleasantness, by her husband, or her sons maybe. Mr. Shi looks at Madam, her face brightened by her talking and laughing, and almost envies her for the energy that his daughter, forty years younger, does not possess. For the day Madam wears a bright orange blouse with prints of purple monkeys, all tumbling and grinning; on her head she wears a scarf with the same pattern. A displaced woman she is, but no doubt happily displaced. Mr. Shi tries to recall what he knows about Iran and the country's recent history; with his limited knowledge, all he can conclude is that Madam must be a lucky woman. A lucky man he is, too, despite all the big and small imperfections. How extraordinary, Mr. Shi thinks, that Madam and he, from different worlds and with different languages, have this opportunity to sit and talk in the autumn sunshine.

"In China we say, *Xiu bai shi ke tong zhou,*" Mr. Shi says when Madam stops. It takes three hundred years of prayers to have the chance to cross a river with someone in the same boat, he thinks of explaining to Madam in English, but then, what's the difference between the languages? Madam would understand him, with or without the translation. "*That we get to meet and talk to each other—it must have taken a long time of good prayers to get us here,*" he says in Chinese to Madam.

Madam smiles in agreement.

"*There's a reason for every relationship, that's what the saying means. Husband and wife, parents and children, friends and enemies, strangers you bump into in the street. It takes three thousand years of prayers to place your head side by side with your loved one's on the pillow. For father and daughter? A thousand years, maybe. People don't end up randomly as father and daughter, that's for sure. But the daughter, she doesn't understand this. She must be thinking I'm a nuisance. She prefers I shut up because that's how she's known me always. She doesn't understand that I didn't talk much with her mother and her because I was a rocket scientist back then. Everything was confidential. We worked all day and when evening came, the security guards came to collect all our notebooks and scratch papers. We signed our names on the archive folders, and that was a day's work. Never allowed to tell our family what we were doing. We were trained not to talk.*"

Madam listens, both hands folding on her heart. Mr. Shi hasn't been sitting so close to a woman his age since his wife died; even when she was alive, he had never talked this much to her. His eyes feel heavy. Imagine he's traveled half a world to his daughter, to make up for all the talks he denied her when she was younger, but only to find her uninterested in his words. Imagine Madam, a stranger who does not even know his language, listens to him with more understanding. Mr. Shi massages his eyes with his two thumbs. A man his age shouldn't indulge himself in unhealthy emotions; he takes long breaths, and laughs slightly. "*Of course, there's a reason for a bad relationship, too—I must be praying half-heartedly for a thousand years for the daughter."*

Madam nods solemnly. She understands him, he knows, but he does not want to burden her with his petty unhappiness. He rubs his hands as if to get rid of the dust of memory. "Old stories," he says in his best English. "Old stories are not exciting."

"I love stories," Madam says, and starts to talk. Mr. Shi listens, and she smiles all the time. He looks at the grinning monkeys on her head, bobbing up and down when she breaks out laughing.

"Lucky people we are," he says after she finishes talking. "In America, we can talk anything."

"America good country." Madam nods. "I love America."

That evening, Mr. Shi says to his daughter, "I met this Iranian lady in the park. Have you met her?"

"No."

"You should meet her sometime. She's so very optimistic. You may find her illuminating for your situation."

"What's my situation?" his daughter asks without looking up from her food.

"You tell me," Mr. Shi says. When his daughter makes no move to help the conversation, he says, "You're experiencing a dark time."

"How do you know she would shed light on my life?"

Mr. Shi opens his mouth, but cannot find an answer. He is afraid that if he explains he and Madam talk in different languages, his daughter will think of him as a crazy old man. Things that make sense at one time suddenly seem absurd in a different light. He feels disappointed in his daughter, someone he shares a language with but with whom he can no longer share a dear moment. After a long pause, he says, "You know, a woman shouldn't ask such direct questions. A good woman is deferential and knows how to make people talk."

"I'm divorced, so certainly I'm not a good woman according to your standard."

Mr. Shi, thinking his daughter is unfairly sarcastic, ignores her. "Your mother was an example of a good woman."

"Did she succeed in making you talk?" his daughter asks, and her eyes, looking directly into his, are fiercer than he knows.

"Your mother wouldn't be so confrontational."

"Baba, first you accused me of being too quiet. I start to talk, and you are saying I'm talking in a wrong way."

"Talking is not only asking questions. Talking is you telling people how you feel about them, and inviting them to tell you how they feel about you."

"Baba, since when did you become a therapist?"

"I'm here to help you, and I'm trying my best," Mr. Shi says. "I need to know why you ended up in a divorce. I need to know what went wrong and help you to find the right person the next time. You're my daughter and I want you to be happy. I don't want you to fall twice."

"Baba, I didn't ask you before, but how long do you plan to stay in America?" his daughter says.

"Until you recover."

His daughter stands up, the legs of the chair scraping the floor.

"We're the only family for each other now," Mr. Shi says, almost pleading, but his daughter closes her bedroom door before he says more. Mr. Shi looks at the dishes that are barely touched by his daughter, the fried tofu cubes stuffed with chopped mushrooms, shrimps, and ginger, the collage of bamboo shoots, red peppers, and snow peas. Even though his daughter admires his cooking every evening, he senses the halfheartedness in her praise; she does not know the cooking has become his praying, and she leaves the prayers unanswered.

"The wife would've done a better job of cheering the daughter up," Mr. Shi says to Madam the next morning. He feels more at ease speaking to her in Chinese now. *"They were closer to each other. Wasn't that I was not close to them. I loved them dearly. It's what happened when you were a rocket scientist. I worked hard during the day, and at night I couldn't stop thinking about my work. Everything was confidential so I couldn't talk to my family about what I was thinking about. But the wife, she was the most understanding woman in the world. She knew I was so occupied with my work, and she wouldn't interrupt my thoughts, and wouldn't let the daughter, either. I know now that it was not healthy for the daughter. I should've left my working self in the office. I was too young to understand that. Now the daughter, she doesn't have anything to say to me."*

Truly it was his mistake, never establishing a habit of talking to his daughter. But then, he argues for himself—in his time, a man like him, among the few chosen to work for a grand cause, he had to bear more duties toward his work than his family. Honorable and sad, but honorable more than sad.

At the dinner table that evening, Mr. Shi's daughter informs him that she's found a Chinese-speaking travel agency that runs tours both on the East Coast and the West. "You're here to take a look at America. I think it's best you take a couple of tours before winter comes."

"Are they expensive?"

"I'll pay, Baba. It's what you wanted for your birthday, no?"

She is his daughter after all; she remembers his wish and she honors it. But what she does not understand is that the America he wants to see is the country where she is happily married. He scoops vegetables and fish into her bowl. "You should eat more," he says in a gentle voice.

"So, I'm going to call them tomorrow and book the tours," his daughter says.

"You know, staying here probably does more good for me. I'm an old man now, not very good for traveling."

"But there's not much to see here."

"Why not? This is the America I wanted to see. Don't worry. I have my friends here. I won't be too much of an annoyance to you."

The phone rings before his daughter replies. She picks up the phone and automatically goes into her bedroom. He waits for the bang of the door. She never takes a call in front of him, even with strangers trying to sell her something on the phone. A few evenings when she talked longer and talked in a hushed voice, he had to struggle not to put his ear on the door and listen. This evening, however, she seems to have a second thought, and leaves the bedroom door open.

He listens to her speak English on the phone, her voice shriller than he has ever known it to be. She speaks fast and laughs often. He does not understand her words, but even more, he does not understand her manner. Her voice, too sharp, too loud, too immodest, is so unpleasant to his ears that for a moment he feels as if he had accidentally caught a glimpse of her naked body, a total stranger, not the daughter he knows.

He stares at her when she comes out of the room. She puts the receiver back, and sits down at the table without saying anything. He watches her face for a moment, and asks, "Who was it on the phone?"

"A friend."

"A male friend, or a female?"

"A male."

He waits for her to give further explanation, but she seems to have no such intention. After a while, he says, "Is this man—is he a special friend?"

"Special? Sure."

"How special is he?"

"Baba, maybe this'll make you worry less about me—yes, he is a very special one. More than a friend," his daughter says. "A lover. Do you feel better now that you know my life isn't as miserable as you thought?"

"Is he American?"

"An American now, yes, but he came from Romania."

At least the man grew up in a communist country, Mr. Shi thinks, trying to be positive. "Do you know him well? Does he understand you—where you were from, and your culture—well? Remember, you can't make the same mistakes twice. You have to be really careful."

"We've known each other for a long time."

"A long time? A month is not a long time!"

"Longer than that, Baba."

"One and half months at most, right? Listen, I know you are in pain, but a woman shouldn't rush, especially in your situation. Abandoned women—they make mistakes in loneliness!"

His daughter looks up. "Baba, my marriage wasn't what you thought. I wasn't abandoned."

Mr. Shi looks at his daughter, her eyes candid with resolve and relief. For a moment he almost wants her to spare him any further detail, but like all people, once she starts talking, he cannot stop her. "Baba, we were divorced because of this man. I was the abandoner, if you want to use the term."

"But why?"

"Things go wrong in a marriage, Baba."

"*One night of being husband and wife in bed makes them in love for a hundred days.* You were married for seven years! How could you do this to your husband? What was the problem, anyway, besides your little extramarital affair?" Mr. Shi says. A disloyal woman is the last thing he raised his daughter to be.

"There's no point talking about it now."

"I'm your father. I have a right to know," Mr. Shi says, banging on the table with a hand.

"Our problem was I never talked enough for my husband. He always suspected that I was hiding something from him because I was quiet."

"You were hiding a lover from him."

Mr. Shi's daughter ignores his words. "The more he asked me to talk, the more I wanted to be quiet and alone. I'm not good at talking, as you've pointed out."

"But that's a lie. You just talked over the phone with such immodesty! You talked, you laughed, like a prostitute!"

Mr. Shi's daughter, startled by the vehemence of his words, looks at him for a long moment before she replies in a softer voice. "It's different, Baba. We talk in English, and it's easier. I don't talk well in Chinese."

"That's a ridiculous excuse!"

"Baba, if you grew up in a language that you never used to express your feelings, it would be easier to take up another language and talk more in the new language. It makes you a new person."

"Are you blaming your mother and me for your adultery?"

"That's not what I'm saying, Baba!"

"But isn't it what you meant? We didn't do a good job bringing you up in Chinese so you decided to find a new language and a new lover when you couldn't talk to your husband honestly about your marriage."

"You never talked, and Mama never talked, when you both knew there was a problem in your marriage. I learned not to talk."

"Your mother and I never had a problem. We were just quiet people."

"But it's a lie!"

"No, it's not. I know I made the mistake of being too preoccupied with my work, but you have to understand I was quiet because of my profession."

"Baba," Mr. Shi's daughter said, pity in her eyes. "You know it's a lie, too. You were never a rocket scientist. Mama knew. I knew. Everybody knew."

Mr. Shi stares at his daughter for a long time. "I don't understand what you mean."

"But you know, Baba. You never talked about what you did at work, true, but other people—they talked about you."

Mr. Shi tries to find some words to defend himself, but his lips quiver without making a sound.

His daughter says, "I'm sorry, Baba. I didn't mean to hurt you."

Mr. Shi takes long breaths and tries to maintain his dignity. It is not hard to do so, after all, as he has, for all his life, remained calm about disasters. "You didn't hurt me. Like you said, you were only talking about truth," he says, and stands up. Before he retreats to the guest bedroom, she says quietly behind him, "Baba, I'll book the tours for you tomorrow."

Mr. Shi sits in the park and waits to say his farewell to Madam. He has asked his daughter to arrange for him to leave from San Francisco after his tour of America. There'll still be a week before he leaves, but he has only the courage to talk to Madam one last time, to clarify all the lies he has told about himself. He was not a rocket scientist. He had had the training, and had been one for three years out of the thirty-eight years he worked for the Institute. *Hard for a young man to remain quiet about his work*, Mr. Shi rehearses in his mind. *A young rocket scientist, such pride and glory. You just wanted to share the excitement with someone.*

That someone—twenty-five years old, forty-two years ago—was the girl working on the card-punching machine for Mr. Shi. Punchers they were called back then, a profession that has long been replaced by more advanced computers, but of all the things that have disappeared from his life, a card puncher is what he misses most. *His* card puncher. *"Name is Yilan,"* Mr. Shi says aloud to the air, and someone greets the name with a happy hello. Madam is walking toward him with basket of autumn leaves. She picks up one and hands it to Mr. Shi. "Beautiful," she says.

Mr. Shi studies the leaf, its veins to the tiniest branches, the different shades of yellow and orange. Never before has he seen the world in such detail. He tries to remember the softened edges and dulled colors he was more used to, but like a patient with his cataracts taken away, he finds everything sharp and bright, appalling yet attractive. "I want to tell something to you," Mr. Shi says, and Madam flashes an eager smile.

Mr. Shi shifts on the bench and says in English, "I was not a rocket scientist."

Madam nods hard. Mr. Shi looks at her, and then looks away. *"I was not a rocket scientist because of a woman. The only thing we did was talk. Nothing wrong with talking, you would imagine, but no, talking between a married man and an unmarried girl was not accepted. That's how sad our time was back then."* Yes, sad is the word, not crazy as young people use to talk about that period. *"One would always want to talk, even when not talking was part of our training."* And talking, such a commonplace thing, but how people got addicted to it! Their talking started from five minutes of break in the office, and later they sat in the cafeteria and talked the whole lunch break. They talked about their hope and excitement in the grand history they were taking part in, of building the first rocket for their young communist mother.

"Once you started talking, you talked more, and more. It was different than going home and talking to your wife because you didn't have to hide anything. We talked about our own lives, of course. Talking is like riding with an unreined horse, you don't know where you end up and you don't have to think about it. That's what our talking was like, but we weren't having an affair as they said. We were never in love," Mr. Shi says, and then, for a short moment, is confused by his own words. What kind of love is he talking about? Surely they were in love, not the love they were suspected of having—he always kept a respectful distance, their hands never touched. But a love in which they talked freely, a love in which their minds touched—wasn't it love, too? Wasn't it how his daughter ended her marriage, because of all the talking with another man? Mr. Shi shifts on the bench, and starts to sweat despite the cool breeze of October. He insisted they were innocent when they were accused of having an affair; he appealed for her when she was sent down to a provincial town. She was a good puncher, but a puncher was always easier to train. He was, however, promised to remain in the position on the condition that he publicly admitted his love affair and gave a self-criticism. He refused because he believed he was wronged. *"I stopped being a rocket scientist at thirty-two. Never was I involved in any research after that, but everything at work was confidential so the wife didn't know."* At least that was what he thought until the previous night. He was assigned to the lowest position that could happen to someone with his training—he decorated offices for the birthdays of Chairman Mao and the Party; he wheeled the notebooks and paperwork from one research group to the other; in the evening he collected his colleagues' notebooks and paperwork, logged them in, and locked them in the file cabinet in the presence of two security guards. He maintained his dignity at work, and went home to his wife as a preoccupied and silent rocket scientist. He looked away from

the questions in his wife's eyes until the questions disappeared one day; he watched his daughter grow up, quiet and understanding as his wife was, a good girl, a good woman. Thirty-two guards he worked with during his career, young men in uniforms and carrying empty holsters on their belts, but the bayonets on their rifles were real.

But then, there was no other choice for him. The decision he made — wasn't it out of loyalty to the wife, and to the other woman? How could he have admitted the love affair, hurt his good wife, and remained a selfish rocket scientist — or, even more impossible, given up a career, a wife, and a two-year-old daughter for the not so glorious desire to spend a lifetime with another woman? *"It is what we sacrifice that makes life meaningful"* — Mr. Shi says the line that was often repeated in their training. He shakes his head hard. A foreign country gives one foreign thoughts, he thinks. For an old man like him, it is not healthy to ponder too much over memory. A good man should live in the present moment, with Madam, a dear friend sitting next to him, holding up a perfect golden ginkgo leaf to the sunshine for him to see.

[2006]

PART TWO

200 Poems

QUESTIONS FOR ACTIVE READING: POETRY

- *Wallace Stevens once said that "the poem is the cry of its occasion." What occasion forced this poem into utterance? Why did the poet have to write it? For example, Marilyn Nelson felt compelled to commemorate the death of Emmett Till in her sonnet sequence* A Wreath for Emmett Till *(p. 603). What other occasions do you see throughout this poem?*

- *Who is the main speaker of the poem? How would this poem sound if it were spoken from another perspective? For example, how would Robert Browing's dramatic monologue "My Last Duchess" (p. 468) sound if it were spoken by the Duke's guest?*

- *For whom is the speaker writing the poem? What evidence do you see for this reading? For example, in Bernadette Mayer's "Sonnet (You jerk you didn't call me up)" (p. 598) it is clear that the speaker is furious with her boyfriend.*

- *Imagery creates a sensory experience on the page. How does the poetry use imagery to make you feel the experience in the poem? For example, how does Yusef Komunyakaa's "Facing It" (p. 604) create an image of the Vietnam Veterans Memorial that makes you feel like you are really there?*

- *How is the poem arranged on the page? How would you describe the shape of the stanzas? The shape of the lines? How long or short are the lines? Why does this matter to the content of the poem? You might consider the more experimental techniques of Emmett Williams, whose arrangement of three words in his poem "like attracts like" (p. 549) creates a unique experience just by virtue of its layout on the page.*

- *Where do you see patterns of repetition? In shape, in language, in image? What effect does this achieve? For example, Joy Harjo's "She Had Some Horses" (p. 621) takes on an incantatory, songlike quality just by virtue of its use of repetition.*

- *What has the speaker realized (or not realized) by the end of the poem? Where does the poem take you, and how do you get there? Most poems include a turn, or an "aha" moment, when the poet makes a shift toward discovery. For example, Seamus Heaney's "Digging" (p. 578) offers insights into labor, family, and the writing process.*

- *How would you describe the language of the poem? What kind of diction does the speaker use? What verb tense? What references? For example, consider Naomi Shihab Nye's use of Arabic in "Gate A-4" (p. 629).*

ANONYMOUS

Barbara Allen

In Scarlet town, where I was born,
   There was a fair maid dwellin',
Made every youth cry *Well-a-way*!
   Her name was Barbara Allen.

All in the merry month of May,   5
   When green buds they were swellin',
Young Jemmy Grove on his death-bed lay,
   For love of Barbara Allen.

He sent his man in to her then,
   To the town where she was dwellin';   10
"O haste and come to my master dear,
   If your name be Barbara Allen."

So slowly, slowly rase she up,
   And slowly she came nigh him,
And when she drew the curtain by–   15
   "Young man, I think you're dyin'."

"O it's I am sick and very very sick,
   And it's all for Barbara Allen."–
O the better for me ye'se never be,
   Tho' your heart's blood were a-spillin'!   20

"O dinna ye mind, young man," says she,
   "When the red wine ye were fillin',
That ye made the healths go round and round,
   And slighted Barbara Allen?"

He turned his face unto the wall,   25
   And death was with him dealin':
"Adieu, adieu, my dear friends all,
   And be kind to Barbara Allen!"

As she was walking o'er the fields,
   She heard the dead-bell knellin';   30

And every jow the dead-bell gave
 Cried "Woe to Barbara Allen."

"O mother, mother, make my bed,
 O make it saft and narrow:
My love has died for me today,   35
 I'll die for him tomorrow."

"Farewell," she said, "ye virgins all,
 And shun the fault I fell in:
Henceforth take warning by the fall
 Of cruel Barbara Allen."   40

SIR THOMAS WYATT [1503–1542]

Whoso list to hunt°

Whoso list° to hunt, I know where is an hind,°   *cares / female deer*
But as for me, alas, I may no more.
The vain travail hath wearied me so sore,
I am of them that farthest cometh behind.
Yet may I, by no means, my wearied mind   5
Draw from the deer, but as she fleeth afore,
Fainting I follow. I leave off, therefore,
Since in a net I seek to hold the wind.
Who list her hunt, I put him out of doubt,
As well as I, may spend his time in vain.   10
And graven with diamonds in letters plain
There is written, her fair neck round about,
"*Noli me tangere*, for Caesar's I am,°
And wild for to hold, though I seem tame."

                    [1557]

Whoso list to hunt: Wyatt's sonnet is a loose translation of Petrarch's *Rima 190*.
13. Noli me tangere, for Caesar's I am: Touch me not, for I belong to Caesar.
"Caesar" in this case may have referred to Henry VIII, King of England, whose
wife, Anne Boleyn, may have been Wyatt's object of desire.

HENRY HOWARD, EARL
OF SURREY   [c. 1517–1547]

The Soote Season°

The soote° season, that bud and bloom forth brings,	*sweet*
With green hath clad the hill and eke° the vale;	*also*
The nightingale with feathers new she sings;	
The turtle° to her make° hath told her tale.	*turtledove/mate*
Summer is come, for every spray now springs;	5
The hart hath hung his old head on the pale;°	
The buck in brake° his winter coat he flings,	*the bushes*
The fishes float with new repairèd scale;	
The adder all her slough away she slings,	
The swift swallow pursueth the flies small;	10
The busy bee her honey now she mings.°	*discharges*
Winter is worn, that was the flowers' bale.°	*harm*
And thus I see among these pleasant things,	
Each care decays, and yet my sorrow springs.	

[1557]

The Soote Season: Surrey's sonnet is a loose translation of Petrarch's *Rima 310*.
6. The hart hath hung his old head on the pale: The male deer has hung his
antlers, or "old head," on the fence.

QUEEN ELIZABETH I [1533–1603]

On Monsieur's Departure°

I grieve and dare not show my discontent,
I love and yet am forced to seem to hate,
I do, yet dare not say I ever meant,
I seem stark mute but inwardly do prate.°   *chatter*
 I am and not, I freeze and yet am burned,   5
 Since from myself another self I turned.

My care is like my shadow in the sun,
Follows me flying, flies when I pursue it,
Stands and lies by me, doth what I have done.
His too familiar care doth make me rue° it.   *regret*   10
 No means I find to rid him from my breast,
 Till by the end of things it be suppressed.

Some gentler passion slide into my mind,
For I am soft and made of melting snow;
Or be more cruel, love, and so be kind.   15
Let me or° float or sink, be high or low.   *either*
 Or let me live with some more sweet content,
 Or die and so forget what love ere meant.

                [c. 1582]

On Monsieur's Departure: The "monsieur" of the title might refer to French
Duke of Anjou, who courted Queen Elizabeth. After several years of court visits
and intimate communication, Elizabeth ended the relationship in 1581.

EDMUND SPENSER [1552–1599]

Sonnet 64°

Comming to kisse her lyps (such grace I found)
  Me seemd I smelt a gardin of sweet flowers
  That dainty odours from them threw around,
  For damzels fit to decke their lovers bowres.
Her lips did smell lyke unto Gillyflowers,°   *carnations* 5
  Her ruddy cheeks lyke unto Roses red;
  Her snowy browes lyke budded Bellamoures,°
  Her lovely eyes like Pincks but newly spred,
Her goodly bosome lyke a Strawberry bed,
  Her neck lyke to a bounch of Cullambynes;   10
  Her brest lyke lillyes, ere theyr leaves be shed,°
  Her nipples lyke yong blossomd Jessemynes.°   *jasmines*
Such fragrant flowres doe give most odorous smell,
  But her sweet odour did them all excell.

[1594]

Sonnet 64: Adapted from the Song of Solomon 4.10–16.
7. Bellamoures: An unidentified white flower.
11. leaves: Pages.

PHILIP SIDNEY [1554–1586]

Sonnet 1°

From Astrophil and Stella

Loving in truth, and fain° in verse my love to show,   *desirous*
That the dear She might take some pleasure of my pain,
Pleasure might cause her read, reading might make her know,

Sonnet 1: The first of six sonnets in a sequence written in hexameters.

Knowledge might pity win, and pity grace obtain,
  I sought fit words to paint the blackest face of woe,
Studying inventions fine, her wits to entertain,
Oft turning others' leaves, to see if thence would flow
Some fresh and fruitful showers upon my sunburned brain.
    But words came halting forth, wanting Invention's stay;°   *prop*
Invention, Nature's child, fled step-dame Study's blows,   1(
And others' feet still seemed but strangers in my way.
Thus great with child to speak, and helpless in my throes,
    Biting my trewand° pen, beating myself for spite,   *truant*
    "Fool," said my Muse to me, "look in thy heart and write."

CHRISTOPHER MARLOWE [1564–1593]

The Passionate Shepherd to His Love

Come live with me and be my love,
And we will all the pleasures prove
That valleys, groves, hills, and fields,
Woods, or steepy mountain yields.

And we will sit upon the rocks,
Seeing the shepherds feed their flocks,
By shallow rivers, to whose falls
Melodious birds sing madrigals.

And I will make thee beds of roses
And a thousand fragrant posies,
A cap of flowers, and a kirtle°   *a long gown*   1
Embroidered all with leaves of myrtle.

A gown made of the finest wool
Which from our pretty lambs we pull,
Fair lined slippers for the cold,   1
With buckles of the purest gold.

A belt of straw and ivy buds,
With coral clasps and amber studs,
And if these pleasures may thee move,
Come live with me, and be my love.   2

The shepherd swains shall dance and sing
For thy delight each May morning.
If these delights thy mind may move,
Then live with me and be my love.

[1599]

WALTER RALEGH [1554–1618]

The Nymph's Reply to the Shepherd

If all the world and love were young,
And truth in every shepherd's tongue,
These pretty pleasures might me move
To live with thee and be thy love.

Time drives the flocks from field to fold   5
When rivers rage and rocks grow cold,
And Philomel° becometh dumb;   *the nightingale*
The rest complains of cares to come.

The flowers do fade, and wanton fields
To wayward winter reckoning yields;   10
A honey tongue, a heart of gall,
Is fancy's spring, but sorrow's fall.

Thy gowns, thy shoes, thy beds of roses,
Thy cap, thy kirtle,° and thy posies   *skirt, outer petticoat*
Soon break, soon wither, soon forgotten—   15
In folly ripe, in reason rotten.

Thy belt of straw and ivy buds,
Thy coral clasps and amber studs,
All these in me no means can move
To come to thee and be thy love.   20

But could youth last and love still breed,
Had joys no date° nor age no need,   *ending*
Then these delights my mind might move
To live with thee and be thy love.

[1600]

WILLIAM SHAKESPEARE [1564–1616]

Sonnet 18

Shall I compare thee to a summer's day?
Thou art more lovely and more temperate:
Rough winds do shake the darling buds of May,
And summer's lease° hath all too short a date;°   *allotted time / duration*
Sometimes too hot the eye of heaven shines,
And often is his gold complexion dimmed;
And every fair° from fair° sometimes declines,   *beautiful thing / beauty*
By chance or nature's changing course untrimmed;°   *stripped of its beauty*
But thy eternal summer shall not fade,
Nor lose possession of that fair thou ow'st;°   *beauty you own*   1
Nor shall death brag thou wand'rest in his shade,
When in eternal lines° to time thou grow'st:°
    So long as men can breathe, or eyes can see,
    So long lives this,° and this gives life to thee.   *this sonnet*

[1609]

12. lines: (Of poetry); **to . . . grow'st:** You are grafted to time.

WILLIAM SHAKESPEARE [1564–1616]

Sonnet 73

That time of year thou mayst in me behold
When yellow leaves, or none, or few, do hang
Upon those boughs which shake against the cold,
Bare ruined choirs,° where late° the sweet birds sang.   *choir stalls / lately*
In me thou seest the twilight of such day
As after sunset fadeth in the west,
Which by and by black night doth take away,

Death's second self, that seals up all in rest.
In me thou seest the glowing of such fire
That on the ashes of his youth doth lie,   10
As the deathbed whereon it must expire,
Consumed with that which it was nourished by.
  This thou perceiv'st, which makes thy love more strong,
  To love that well which thou must leave ere long.

[1609]

WILLIAM SHAKESPEARE   [1564–1616]

Sonnet 116

Let me not to the marriage of true minds
Admit impediments. Love is not love
Which alters when it alteration finds,
Or bends with the remover to remove:
Oh, no! it is an ever-fixed mark,   5
That looks on tempests and is never shaken;
It is the star to every wandering bark,°   *a small sailing ship*
Whose worth's unknown, although his height be taken.
Love's not Time's fool, though rosy lips and cheeks
Within his bending sickle's compass come;   10
Love alters not with his brief hours and weeks,
But bears it out even to the edge of doom.
  If this be error, and upon me prov'd,
  I never writ, nor no man ever lov'd.

[1609]

AEMILIA LANYER   [1569–1645]

Eve's Apology in Defense of Women

Now Pontius Pilate° is to judge the cause°   *case*
Of faultless Jesus, who before him stands,
Who neither hath offended prince, nor laws,
Although he now be brought in woeful bands.
O noble governor, make thou yet a pause,   5
Do not in innocent blood inbrue° thy hands;   *stain*
   But hear the words of thy most worthy wife,
   Who sends to thee, to beg her Savior's life.°

Let barb'rous cruelty far depart from thee,
And in true justice take affliction's part;   10
Open thine eyes, that thou the truth may'st see.
Do not the thing that goes against thy heart,
Condemn not him that must thy Savior be;
But view his holy life, his good desert.
   Let not us women glory in men's fall,   15
   Who had power given to overrule us all.

Till now your indiscretion sets us free.
And makes our former fault much less appear;
Our mother Eve, who tasted of the tree,
Giving to Adam what she held most dear,   20
Was simply good, and had no power to see;°
The after-coming harm did not appear:
   The subtle serpent that our sex betrayed
   Before our fall so sure a plot had laid.

1. **Pontius Pilate:** The Roman prefect who, bowing to popular pressure, authorized
the crucifixion of Jesus. In Lanyer's poem, Pilate and Adam represent all
of mankind, and Eve and Pilate's wife represent all of womankind.
8. **her Savior's life:** In Matthew 27.19, Pilate's wife is mentioned as having sent
her husband an urgent message pleading him to spare Jesus' life.
21. **had no power to see:** In Genesis, Eve is persuaded by the serpent to eat the
forbidden fruit first before Adam.

428

That undiscerning ignorance perceived   25
No guile or craft that was by him intended;
For had she known of what we were bereaved,°   *deprived*
To his request she had not condescended.°   *consented*
But she, poor soul, by cunning was deceived;
No hurt therein her harmless heart intended: 30
   For she alleged° God's word, which he° denies,   *asserted/serpent*
   That they should die, but even as gods be wise.

But surely Adam cannot be excused;
Her fault though great, yet he was most to blame;
What weakness offered, strength might have refused,   35
Being lord of all, the greater was his shame.
Although the serpent's craft had her abused,
God's holy word ought all his actions frame,°   *determine*
   For he was lord and king of all the earth,
   Before poor Eve had either life or breath,   40

Who being framed° by God's eternal hand   *fashioned*
The perfectest man that ever breathed on earth;
And from God's mouth received that strait° command,   *strict*
The breach whereof he knew was present death;
Yea, having power to rule both sea and land,   45
Yet with one apple won to lose that breath
   Which God had breathed in his beauteous face,
   Bringing us all in danger and disgrace.

And then to lay the fault on Patience' back,
That we (poor women) must endure it all.   50
We know right well he did discretion lack,
Being not persuaded thereunto at all.
If Eve did err, it was for knowledge sake;
The fruit being fair persuaded him to fall:
   No subtle serpent's falsehood did betray him;   55
   If he would eat it, who had power to stay° him?   *prevent*

Not Eve, whose fault was only too much love,
Which made her give this present to her dear,
That what she tasted he likewise might prove,°   *experience*
Whereby his knowledge might become more clear;   60
He never sought her weakness to reprove
With those sharp words which he of God did hear;
   Yet men will boast of knowledge, which he took
   From Eve's fair hand, as from a learned book.

If any evil did in her remain,   65
Being made of him,° he was the ground of all.
If one of many worlds could lay a stain
Upon our sex, and work so great a fall
To wretched man by Satan's subtle train,°
What will so foul a fault amongst you all?   70
   Her weakness did the serpent's words obey,
   But you in malice God's dear Son betray,

Whom, if unjustly you condemn to die,
Her sin was small to what you do commit;
All mortal sins that do for vengeance cry   75
Are not to be compared unto it.
If many worlds would altogether try
By all their sins the wrath of God to get,
   This sin of yours surmounts them all as far
   As doth the sun another little star.   80

Then let us have our liberty again,
And challenge° to yourselves no sovereignty.   *claim*
You came not in the world without our pain,
Make that a bar against your cruelty;
Your fault being greater, why should you disdain   85
Our being your equals, free from tyranny?
   If one weak woman simply did offend,
   This sin of yours hath no excuse nor end,

To which, poor souls, we never gave consent.
Witness, thy wife, O Pilate, speaks for all,   90
Who did but dream, and yet a message sent
That thou shouldest have nothing to do at all
With that just man° which, if thy heart relent,   *Christ*
Why wilt thou be a reprobate° with Saul°   *damned*
   To seek the death of him that is so good,   95
   For thy soul's health to shed his dearest blood?

[1611]

---

66. **Being made of him:** In Genesis 2.21–22, God creates Eve from Adam's rib.
69. **Satan's subtle train:** Common interpretation of Genesis identifies the
serpent as Satan.
94. **Saul:** The King of Israel (11th century BCE.) who sought the death of David,
the prophet-king.

JOHN DONNE   [1572–1631]

A Valediction:
Forbidding Mourning

As virtuous men pass mildly away,
    And whisper to their souls to go,
Whilst some of their sad friends do say
    The breath goes now, and some say, No;

So let us melt, and make no noise,   5
    No tear-floods, nor sigh-tempests move;
'Twere profanation of our joys
    To tell the laity our love.

Moving of th' earth brings harms and fears,
    Men reckon what it did and meant;   10
But trepidation of the spheres,
    Though greater far, is innocent.°

Dull sublunary° lovers' love   *under the moon; hence, inconstant*
    (Whose soul is sense) cannot admit
Absence, because it doth remove   15
    Those things which elemented° it.   *composed*

But we, by a love so much refined
    That our selves know not what it is,
Inter-assurèd of the mind,
    Care less, eyes, lips, and hands to miss.   20

Our two souls therefore, which are one,
    Though I must go, endure not yet
A breach, but an expansion,
    Like gold to airy thinness beat.

9–12. Moving . . . innocent: Earthquakes cause damage and were taken as por-
tending further changes or dangers. Trepidation (an oscillating motion of the
eighth or ninth sphere, in the Ptolemaic cosmological system) is greater than an
earthquake, but not harmful or ominous.

431

If they be two, they are two so   2
   As stiff twin compasses° are two;   *drawing compasses*
Thy soul, the fixed foot, makes no show
   To move, but doth, if th' other do.

And though it in the center sit,
   Yet when the other far doth roam,   3
It leans and hearkens after it,
   And grows erect, as that comes home.

Such wilt thou be to me, who must,
   Like th' other foot, obliquely run;
Thy firmness makes my circle just,   3
   And makes me end where I begun.

[1633]

JOHN DONNE   [1572–1631]

Death, be not proud

Death, be not proud, though some have callèd thee
Mighty and dreadful, for thou art not so;
For those whom thou think'st thou dost overthrow
Die not, poor Death, nor yet canst thou kill me.
From rest and sleep, which but thy pictures be,
Much pleasure; then from thee much more must flow,
And soonest our best men with thee do go,
Rest of their bones, and soul's delivery.
Thou art slave to fate, chance, kings, and desperate men,
And dost with poison, war, and sickness dwell,
And poppy° or charms can make us sleep as well   *opium*   1
And better than thy stroke; why swell'st° thou then?   *(with pride)*
One short sleep past, we wake eternally
And death shall be no more; Death, thou shalt die.

[1633]

BEN JONSON [1572–1637]

On My First Son

Farewell, thou child of my right hand,° and joy;
My sin was too much hope of thee, loved boy:
Seven years thou'wert lent to me, and I thee pay,
Exacted by thy fate, on the just day.
O could I lose all father now! for why   5
Will man lament the state he should envy,
To have so soon 'scaped world's and flesh's rage,
And, if no other misery, yet age?
Rest in soft peace, and asked. say, "Here doth lie
Ben Jonson his best piece of poetry."   10
For whose sake henceforth all his° vows be such   (the father's)
As what he loves may never like° too much.

[1616]

1. **child . . . hand:** A literal translation of the Hebrew name "Benjamin." The boy, named for his father, was born in 1596 and died on his birthday ("the [exact] day"—that on which the loan came due) in 1603.
12. **like:** Archaic meaning "please."

LADY MARY WROTH [1587–1653]

Am I Thus Conquer'd?

Am I thus conquer'd? have I lost the powers,
    That to withstand which joyes to ruine me?
    Must I bee still, while it my strength devoures,
    And captive leads me prisoner bound, unfree?

Love first shall leane mens fant'sies to them free,   5
    Desire shall quench loves flames, Spring, hate sweet showers,

Love shall loose all his Darts, have sight, and see
His shame and wishings, hinder happy houres.

Why should we not Loves purblinde charmes resist?
    Must we be servile, doing what he list?
    No, seeke some host to harbour thee: I flye

Thy Babish° tricks, and freedome doe professe;
    But O, my hurt makes my lost heart confesse:
    I love, and must; so farewell liberty.

[1621]

12. **Babish:** Like a babe, childish, babyish.

ROBERT HERRICK   [1591–1674]

To the Virgins, to Make Much of Time

Gather ye rosebuds while ye may,
    Old time is still a-flying;
And this same flower that smiles today
    Tomorrow will be dying.

The glorious lamp of heaven, the sun,
    The higher he's a-getting,
The sooner will his race be run,
    And nearer he's to setting.

That age is best which is the first,
    When youth and blood are warmer;
But being spent, the worse, and worst
    Times still succeed the former.

Then be not coy, but use your time,
    And while ye may, go marry;
For having lost but once your prime,
    You may forever tarry.

[1648]

GEORGE HERBERT [1593–1633]

Easter-wings°

Lord, who createdst man in wealth and store,°
   Though foolishly he lost the same,°
      Decaying   more   and   more
         Till   he   became
           Most   poor: 5
           With   thee
         O   let   me   rise
      As   larks,   harmoniously,
   And   sing   this   day   thy   victories:
Then   shall   the   fall   further   the   flight   in   me.   10

My   tender   age   in   sorrow   did   begin:
   And still with sicknesses and shame
      Thou   didst   so   punish   sin,
         That   I   became
           Most   thin.   15
           With   thee
        Let   me   combine,
      And   feel   thy   victory;
   For,   if   I   imp°   my   wing   on   thine,
Affliction   shall   advance   the   flight   in   me.   20

[1633]

Easter-wings: Originally the stanzas were printed on facing pages, lines 1–10
on the right page, to be read first, then lines 11–20 on the left page.
1. store: Abundance.
2. lost the same: Through the Fall in the Garden of Eden. Early editions include
the words "this day" in line 18 (perhaps repeated by mistake from line 9); they
do not appear in the only surviving manuscript and are not required for the
meter.
19. imp: A term from falconry—to graft additional feathers onto the wings of a
hawk to improve its flight.

JOHN MILTON [1608–1674]

When I consider
how my light is spent

When I consider how my light is spent°
  Ere half my days, in this dark world and wide,
  And that one talent which is death to hide
  Lodged with me useless, though my soul more bent
To serve therewith my Maker, and present
  My true account, lest he returning chide.
  "Doth God exact day-labor, light denied?"
  I fondly ask; but patience to prevent
That murmur, soon replies, "God doth not need
  Either man's work or his own gifts; who best
  Bear his mild yoke, they serve him best. His state
Is kingly. Thousands at his bidding speed
  And post o'er land and ocean without rest:
  They also serve who only stand and wait."

1

[c. 1652; 1673]°

1. **When . . . spent:** Milton went blind in 1652. Lines 1–2 allude to Matthew 25:1–13; line 3, to Matthew 25:14–30; and line 11, to Matthew 11:30.
[*c. 1652;* 1673]: When two dates appear, the first date (in italics) is an approximate time of composition and the second date is the year of earliest publication. Both dates are included when the two dates are so far apart that publication doesn't reflect the time the poem was written.

ANNE BRADSTREET   [c. 1612–1672]

Here Follows Some Verses upon the Burning of Our House July 10th, 1666. Copied Out of a Loose Paper

In silent night when rest I took
For sorrow near I did not look
I wakened was with thund'ring noise
And piteous shrieks of dreadful voice.
That fearful sound of "Fire!" and "Fire!" 5
Let no man know is my desire.
I, starting up, the light did spy,
And to my God my heart did cry
To strengthen me in my distress
And not to leave me succorless. 10
Then, coming out, beheld a space
The flame consume my dwelling place.
And when I could no longer look,
I blest His name that gave and took,
That laid my goods now in the dust. 15
Yea, so it was, and so 'twas just.
It was His own, it was not mine,
Far be it that I should repine;
He might of all justly bereft
But yet sufficient for us left. 20
When by the ruins oft I past
My sorrowing eyes aside did cast,
And here and there the places spy
Where oft I sat and long did lie:
Here stood that trunk, and there that chest, 25
There lay that store I counted best.
My pleasant things in ashes lie,
And them behold no more shall I.
Under thy roof no guest shall sit,

Nor at thy table eat a bit.   30
No pleasant tale shall e'er be told,
Nor things recounted done of old.
No candle e'er shall shine in thee,
Nor bridegroom's voice e'er heard shall be.
In silence ever shall thou lie,   35
Adieu, Adieu, all's vanity.
Then straight I 'gin my heart to chide,
And did thy wealth on earth abide?°
Didst fix thy hope on mold'ring° dust?
The arm of flesh didst make thy trust?   40
Raise up thy thoughts above the sky
That dunghill mists away may fly.
Thou hast an house on high erect,
Framed by that mighty Architect,
With glory richly furnished,   45
Stands permanent though this be fled.
It's purchased and paid for too
By Him who hath enough to do.
A price so vast as is unknown
Yet by His gift is made thine own;   50
There's wealth enough, I need no more,
Farewell, my pelf,° farewell my store.
The world no longer let me love,
My hope and treasure lies above.

                                                          [1666]

38. abide: Wait for, expect.
39. mold'ring: Crumbling, decaying.
52. pelf: Material possessions.

ANDREW MARVELL   [1621–1678]

To His Coy Mistress°

Had we but world enough, and time,
This coyness, lady, were no crime.
We would sit down, and think which way
To walk, and pass our long love's day.
Thou by the Indian Ganges' side   5
Shouldst rubies find; I by the tide
Of Humber° would complain. I would
Love you ten years before the Flood,
And you should, if you please, refuse
Till the conversion of the Jews.°   10
My vegetable° love should grow   *living and growing*
Vaster than empires, and more slow;
An hundred years should go to praise
Thine eyes, and on thy forehead gaze;
Two hundred to adore each breast,   15
But thirty thousand to the rest;
An age at least to every part,
And the last age should show your heart.
For, lady, you deserve this state,°   *dignity*
Nor would I love at lower rate.   20
    But at my back I always hear
Time's wingèd chariot hurrying near;
And yonder all before us lie
Deserts of vast eternity.
Thy beauty shall no more be found,   25
Nor, in thy marble vault, shall sound

Coy Mistress: In the seventeenth century, "coy" could carry its older meaning,
"shy," or the modern sense of "coquettish." "Mistress" then could mean "a
woman loved and courted by a man; a female sweetheart."
5–7. Indian Ganges', Humber: The Ganges River in India, with its distant,
romantic associations, contrasts with the Humber River, running through Hull
in northeast England, Marvell's hometown.
10. conversion . . . Jews: An occurrence foretold, in some traditions, as one of
the concluding events of human history.

439

My echoing song; then worms shall try
That long-preserved virginity,
And your quaint honor turn to dust,
And into ashes all my lust:
The grave's a fine and private place,
But none, I think, do there embrace.
   Now therefore, while the youthful hue
Sits on thy skin like morning dew,
And while thy willing soul transpires°   *breathes forth*
At every pore with instant fires,°   *urgent passion*
Now let us sport us while we may,
And now, like amorous birds of prey,
Rather at once our time devour
Than languish in his slow-chapped° power.
Let us roll all our strength and all
Our sweetness up into one ball,
And tear our pleasures with rough strife
Thorough° the iron gates of life;   *through*
Thus, though we cannot make our sun
Stand still,° yet we will make him run.

                                                [*c. 1650;* 1681]

40. **slow-chapped:** Slow-jawed, devouring slowly.
45–46. **make our sun stand still:** An allusion to Joshua 10:12. In answer to Joshua's prayer, God made the sun stand still, to prolong the day and give the Israelites more time to defeat the Amorites.

KATHERINE PHILIPS   [1631–1664]

Friendship's Mystery, To My Dearest *Lucasia*°

1

Come, my Lucasia, since we see
   That miracles men's faith do move,
By wonder and by prodigy
   To the dull angry world let's prove
   There's a religion in our love.

Lucasia: Refers to Philips's friend, Anne Owen.

2

For though we were designed t' agree,
  That fate no liberty destroys,
But our election is as free
  As angels, who with greedy choice
  Are yet determined to their joys.°   10

3

Our hearts are doubled by the loss,
  Here mixture is addition grown;
We both diffuse,° and both engross:°   *spread out/collect*
  And we whose minds are so much one,
  Never, yet ever are alone.   15

4

We court our own captivity
  Than thrones more great and innocent:
'Twere banishment to be set free,
  Since we wear fetters whose intent
  Not bondage is, but ornament.   20

5

Divided joys are tedious found,
  And griefs united easier grow:
We are selves but by rebound,
  And all our titles shuffled so,
  Both princes, and both subjects too.   25

6

Our hearts are mutual victims laid,
  While they (such power in friendship lies)
Are altars, priests, and off'rings made:
  And each heart which thus kindly° dies,   *benevolently, naturally*
  Grows deathless by the sacrifice.   30

[*1655*, 1664]

9–10. As angels . . . to their joys: Just as angels are chosen by God and revel in
that appointment, so too have the poetic speaker and Lucasia been "elected" into
their friendship.

THOMAS GRAY [1716–1771]

Elegy Written in a Country Churchyard

The curfew° tolls the knell of parting day,   *evening bell*
  The lowing herd wind slowly o'er the lea,
The plowman homeward plods his weary way,
  And leaves the world to darkness and to me.

Now fades the glimmering landscape on the sight,
  And all the air a solemn stillness holds,
Save where the beetle wheels his droning flight,
  And drowsy tinklings lull the distant folds;

Save that from yonder ivy-mantled tower
  The moping owl does to the moon complain   1
Of such, as wandering near her secret bower,
  Molest her ancient solitary reign.

Beneath those rugged elms, that yew tree's shade,
  Where heaves the turf in many a moldering heap,
Each in his narrow cell forever laid,   1
  The rude forefathers° of the hamlet sleep.   *humble ancestors*

The breezy call of incense-breathing morn,
  The swallow twittering from the straw-built shed,
The cock's shrill clarion, or the echoing horn,°   *(of a hunter)*
  No more shall rouse them from their lowly bed.   2

For them no more the blazing hearth shall burn,
  Or busy housewife ply her evening care;
No children run to lisp their sire's return,
  Or climb his knees the envied kiss to share.

Oft did the harvest to their sickle yield,   2
  Their furrow oft the stubborn glebe° has broke;   *soil*
How jocund did they drive their team afield!
  How bowed the woods beneath their sturdy stroke!

Let not Ambition mock their useful toil,
    Their homely joys, and destiny obscure;   30
Nor Grandeur hear with a disdainful smile
    The short and simple annals of the poor.

The boast of heraldry,° the pomp of power,   *noble ancestry*
    And all that beauty, all that wealth e'er gave,
Awaits alike the inevitable hour.   35
    The paths of glory lead but to the grave.

Nor you, ye proud, impute to these the fault,
    If memory o'er their tomb no trophies° raise,   *memorials*
Where through the long-drawn aisle and fretted° vault   *ornamented*
    The pealing anthem swells the note of praise.   40

Can storied° urn or animated° bust   *decorated/lifelike*
    Back to its mansion call the fleeting breath?
Can Honor's voice provoke° the silent dust,   *call forth*
    Or Flattery soothe the dull cold ear of Death?

Perhaps in this neglected spot is laid   45
    Some heart once pregnant with celestial fire;
Hands that the rod of empire might have swayed,
    Or waked to ecstasy the living lyre.

But Knowledge to their eyes her ample page
    Rich with the spoils of time did ne'er unroll;   50
Chill Penury repressed their noble rage,
    And froze the genial current of the soul.

Full many a gem of purest ray serene,
    The dark unfathomed caves of ocean bear:
Full many a flower is born to blush unseen,   55
    And waste its sweetness on the desert air.

Some village Hampden,that with dauntless breast
    The little tyrant of his fields withstood;
Some mute inglorious Milton here may rest,
    Some Cromwell° guiltless of his country's blood.   60

The applause of listening senates to command,
    The threats of pain and ruin to despise,

57–60. Hampden, Cromwell: John Hampden (1594–1643) refused to pay a
special tax imposed in 1636 and led a defense of the people's rights in Parliament. Oliver Cromwell (1599–1658) was a rebel leader in the English Civil War.

To scatter plenty o'er a smiling land,
   And read their history in a nation's eyes,

Their lot forbade: nor° circumscribed alone   *not*   6
   Their growing virtues, but their crimes confined;
Forbade to wade through slaughter to a throne,
   And shut the gates of mercy on mankind,

The struggling pangs of conscious truth to hide,
   To quench the blushes of ingenuous shame,
Or heap the shrine of Luxury and Pride   7
   With incense kindled at the Muse's flame.

Far from the madding crowd's ignoble strife,
   Their sober wishes never learned to stray;
Along the cool sequestered vale of life   7
   They kept the noiseless tenor of their way.

Yet even these bones from insult to protect
   Some frail memorial° still erected nigh,   *(simple tombstone)*
With uncouth rhymes and shapeless sculpture decked,
   Implores the passing tribute of a sigh.   8

Their name, their years, spelt by the unlettered Muse,
   The place of fame and elegy supply:
And many a holy text around she strews,
   That teach the rustic moralist to die.

For who to dumb Forgetfulness a prey,   8
   This pleasing anxious being e'er resigned,
Left the warm precincts of the cheerful day,
   Nor cast one longing lingering look behind?

On some fond breast the parting soul relies,
   Some pious drops° the closing eye requires;   *tears* 9
Even from the tomb the voice of Nature cries,
   Even in our ashes live their wonted fires.

For thee,° who mindful of the unhonored dead   *(the poet himself)*
   Dost in these lines their artless tale relate;
If chance, by lonely contemplation led,   9
   Some kindred spirit shall inquire thy fate,

Haply° some hoary-headed swain° may say,   *perhaps/elderly shepherd*
   "Oft have we seen him° at the peep of dawn   *the poet*
Brushing with hasty steps the dews away
   To meet the sun upon the upland lawn.   10

"There at the foot of yonder nodding beech
    That wreathes its old fantastic roots so high,
His listless length at noontide would he stretch,
    And pore upon the brook that babbles by.

"Hard by yon wood, now smiling as in scorn,   105
    Muttering his wayward fancies he would rove,
Now drooping, woeful wan, like one forlorn,
    Or crazed with care, or crossed in hopeless love.

"One morn I missed him on the customed hill,
    Along the heath and near his favorite tree;   110
Another° came; nor yet beside the rill,°   (another day)/small brook
    Nor up the lawn, nor at the wood was he;

"The next with dirges due in sad array
    Slow through the churchway path we saw him borne.
Approach and read (for thou canst read) the lay,   115
    Graved on the stone beneath yon aged thorn."

THE EPITAPH

Here rests his head upon the lap of Earth
    A youth to fortune and to Fame unknown.
Fair Science° frowned not on his humble birth,   *learning*
    And Melancholy marked him for her own.   120

Large was his bounty, and his soul sincere,
    Heaven did a recompense as largely send:
He gave to Misery all he had, a tear,
    He gained from Heaven ('twas all he wished) a friend.

No farther seek his merits to disclose,   125
    Or draw his frailties from their dread abode
(There they alike in trembling hope repose),
    The bosom of his Father and his God.

[1751]

PHILLIS WHEATLEY   [1753–1784]

On Being Brought from Africa to America

'Twas mercy brought me from my *Pagan* land,
Taught my benighted soul to understand
That there's a God, that there's a *Saviour* too:
Once I redemption neither sought nor knew.
Some view our sable race with scornful eye,
"Their colour is a diabolic die."
Remember, *Christians*, *Negros*, black as *Cain*,°
May be refin'd, and join th' angelic train.

[1773]

7. **black as Cain:** According to Genesis (4:15), Cain was the eldest son of Adam and Eve. He murdered his brother Abel and was consequently cursed by God, who put a mark on him—a mark that was commonly associated with blackness by readers of the Bible.

WILLIAM BLAKE   [1757–1827]

The Lamb

Little Lamb, who made thee?
Dost thou know who made thee?
Gave thee life & bid thee feed,
By the stream & o'er the mead;
Gave thee clothing of delight,
Softest clothing wooly bright;
Gave thee such a tender voice,

Making all the vales rejoice!
  Little Lamb who made thee?
  Dost thou know who made thee?   10

  Little Lamb I'll tell thee,
  Little Lamb I'll tell thee!
He is callèd by thy name,
For he calls himself a Lamb:
He is meek & he is mild,   15
He became a little child:
I a child & thou a lamb,
We are callèd by his name.
  Little Lamb God bless thee.
  Little Lamb God bless thee.   20

[1789]

WILLIAM BLAKE   [1757–1827]

The Tyger

Tyger, Tyger, burning bright
In the forests of the night,
What immortal hand or eye
Could frame thy fearful symmetry?

In what distant deeps or skies   5
Burnt the fire of thine eyes?
On what wings dare he aspire?
What the hand, dare seize the fire?

And what shoulder, & what art,
Could twist the sinews of thy heart?   10
And when thy heart began to beat,
What dread hand? & what dread feet?

What the hammer? what the chain?
In what furnace was thy brain?
What the anvil? what dread grasp   15
Dare its deadly terrors clasp?

When the stars threw down their spears
And water'd heaven with their tears,
Did he smile his work to see?
Did he who made the Lamb make thee?

Tyger, Tyger, burning bright
In the forests of the night,
What immortal hand or eye
Dare frame thy fearful symmetry?

[1794]

WILLIAM WORDSWORTH   [1770–1850]

Lines Composed a Few Miles Above Tintern Abbey°

*On Revisiting the Banks
of the Wye during a Tour, July 13, 1798*

Five years have past; five summers, with the length
Of five long winters! and again I hear
These waters, rolling from their mountain-springs
With a soft inland murmur.—Once again
Do I behold these steep and lofty cliffs,   5
That on a wild secluded scene impress
Thoughts of more deep seclusion; and connect
The landscape with the quiet of the sky.
The day is come when I again repose
Here, under this dark sycamore, and view   10
These plots of cottage-ground, these orchard-tufts,
Which at this season, with their unripe fruits,
Are clad in one green hue, and lose themselves

Lines . . . Tintern Abbey: No poem of mine was composed under circumstances more pleasant for me to remember than this. I began it upon leaving Tintern, after crossing the Wye, and concluded it just as I was entering Bristol in the evening, after a ramble of 4 or 5 days, with my sister. Not a line of it was altered, and not any part of it written down till I reached Bristol [Wordsworth's note]. The poem was printed as the last item in *Lyrical Ballads*.

'Mid groves and copses. Once again I see
These hedge-rows, hardly hedge-rows, little lines   15
Of sportive wood run wild: these pastoral farms,
Green to the very door; and wreaths of smoke
Sent up, in silence, from among the trees!
With some uncertain notice, as might seem
Of vagrant dwellers in the houseless woods,   20
Or of some Hermit's cave, where by his fire
The Hermit sits alone.

        These beauteous forms,
Through a long absence, have not been to me
As is a landscape to a blind man's eye:
But oft, in lonely rooms, and 'mid the din   25
Of towns and cities, I have owed to them
In hours of weariness, sensations sweet,
Felt in the blood, and felt along the heart;
And passing even into my purer mind,
With tranquil restoration:—feelings too   30
Of unremembered pleasure: such, perhaps,
As have no slight or trivial influence
On that best portion of a good man's life,
His little, nameless, unremembered, acts
Of kindness and of love. Nor less, I trust,   35
To them I may have owed another gift,
Of aspect more sublime; that blessed mood,
In which the burthen of the mystery,
In which the heavy and the weary weight
Of all this unintelligible world,   40
Is lightened:—that serene and blessed mood,
In which the affections gently lead us on,—
Until, the breath of this corporeal frame
And even the motion of our human blood
Almost suspended, we are laid asleep   45
In body, and become a living soul:
While with an eye made quiet by the power
Of harmony, and the deep power of joy,
We see into the life of things.

        If this
Be but a vain belief, yet, oh! how oft—   50
In darkness and amid the many shapes
Of joyless daylight; when the fretful stir
Unprofitable, and the fever of the world,
Have hung upon the beatings of my heart—

How oft, in spirit, have I turned to thee,   5
O sylvan Wye! thou wanderer thro' the woods,
How often has my spirit turned to thee!

   And now, with gleams of half-extinguished thought,
With many recognitions dim and faint,
And somewhat of a sad perplexity,   6
The picture of the mind revives again:
While here I stand, not only with the sense
Of present pleasure, but with pleasing thoughts
That in this moment there is life and food
For future years. And so I dare to hope,   6
Though changed, no doubt, from what I was when first
I came among these hills; when like a roe
I bounded o'er the mountains, by the sides
Of the deep rivers, and the lonely streams,
Wherever nature led: more like a man   7
Flying from something that he dreads, than one
Who sought the thing he loved. For nature then
 (The coarser pleasures of my boyish days,
And their glad animal movements all gone by)
To me was all in all.—I cannot paint   7
What then I was. The sounding cataract
Haunted me like a passion: the tall rock,
The mountain, and the deep and gloomy wood,
Their colours and their forms, were then to me
An appetite; a feeling and a love,   8
That had no need of a remoter charm,
By thought supplied, nor any interest
Unborrowed from the eye.—That time is past,
And all its aching joys are now no more,
And all its dizzy raptures. Not for this   8
Faint I, nor mourn nor murmur; other gifts
Have followed; for such loss, I would believe,
Abundant recompense. For I have learned
To look on nature, not as in the hour
Of thoughtless youth; but hearing oftentimes   9
The still, sad music of humanity,
Nor harsh nor grating, though of ample power
To chasten and subdue. And I have felt
A presence that disturbs me with the joy
Of elevated thoughts; a sense sublime   9
Of something far more deeply interfused,
Whose dwelling is the light of setting suns,

And the round ocean and the living air,
And the blue sky, and in the mind of man:
A motion and a spirit, that impels   100
All thinking things, all objects of all thought,
And rolls through all things. Therefore am I still
A lover of the meadows and the woods,
And mountains; and of all that we behold
From this green earth; of all the mighty world   105
Of eye, and ear,—both what they half create,
And what perceive; well pleased to recognise
In nature and the language of the sense,
The anchor of my purest thoughts, the nurse,
The guide, the guardian of my heart, and soul   110
Of all my moral being.

           Nor perchance,
If I were not thus taught, should I the more
Suffer my genial° spirits genius to decay: *genius*
For thou art with me here upon the banks
Of this fair river; thou my dearest Friend,°   115
My dear, dear Friend; and in thy voice I catch
The language of my former heart, and read
My former pleasures in the shooting lights
Of thy wild eyes. Oh! yet a little while
May I behold in thee what I was once,   120
My dear, dear Sister! and this prayer I make,
Knowing that Nature never did betray
The heart that loved her; 'tis her privilege,
Through all the years of this our life, to lead
From joy to joy: for she can so inform   125
The mind that is within us, so impress
With quietness and beauty, and so feed
With lofty thoughts, that neither evil tongues,
Rash judgments, nor the sneers of selfish men,
Nor greetings where no kindness is, nor all   130
The dreary intercourse of daily life,
Shall e'er prevail against us, or disturb
Our cheerful faith, that all which we behold
Is full of blessings. Therefore let the moon
Shine on thee in thy solitary walk;   135
And let the misty mountain-winds be free
To blow against thee: and, in after years,

115. dearest Friend: Refers to his sister, Dorothy.

When these wild ecstasies shall be matured
Into a sober pleasure; when thy mind
Shall be a mansion for all lovely forms,   14
Thy memory be as a dwelling-place
For all sweet sounds and harmonies; oh! then,
If solitude, or fear, or pain, or grief,
Should be thy portion, with what healing thoughts
Of tender joy wilt thou remember me,   14
And these my exhortations! Nor, perchance —
If I should be where I no more can hear
Thy voice, nor catch from thy wild eyes these gleams
Of past existence — wilt thou then forget
That on the banks of this delightful stream   15
We stood together; and that I, so long
A worshipper of Nature, hither came
Unwearied in that service; rather say
With warmer love — oh! with far deeper zeal
Of holier love. Nor wilt thou then forget,   15
That after many wanderings, many years
Of absence, these steep woods and lofty cliffs,
And this green pastoral landscape, were to me
More dear, both for themselves and for thy sake!

[1798]

SAMUEL TAYLOR COLERIDGE   [1772–1834]

This Lime-Tree Bower My Prison

In the June of 1797, some long-expected Friends paid a visit to the author's cottage; and on the morning of their arrival, he met with an accident, which disabled him from walking during the whole time of their stay. One evening, when they had left him for a few hours, he composed the following lines in the garden-bower.°

the garden-bower: The original version of this poem was relayed in a letter from the poet to Robert Southey. The author's note refers to a visit from his friends, William and Dorothy Wordsworth and Charles Lamb in the summer of 1797, during which his wife Sara accidentally spilled scalding hot milk on his foot. The "lime-tree bower" in the title of his poem refers to the linden trees in the neighboring garden.

Well, they are gone, and here must I remain,
This lime-tree bower my prison! I have lost
Beauties and feelings, such as would have been
Most sweet to my remembrance even when age
Had dimmed mine eyes to blindness! They, meanwhile,   5
Friends, whom I never more may meet again,
On springy° heath, along the hill-top edge,
Wander in gladness, and wind down, perchance,
To that still roaring dell, of which I told;
The roaring dell, o'erwooded, narrow, deep,   10
And only speckled by the mid-day sun;
Where its slim trunk the ash from rock to rock
Flings arching like a bridge;—that branchless ash,
Unsunned and damp, whose few poor yellow leaves
Ne'er tremble in the gale, yet tremble still,   15
Fanned by the water-fall! and there my friends
Behold the dark green file of long lank weeds,
That all at once (a most fantastic sight!)
Still nod and drip beneath the dripping edge
Of the blue clay-stone.

                Now, my friends emerge   20
Beneath the wide wide Heaven—and view again
The many-steepled tract magnificent
Of hilly fields and meadows, and the sea,
With some fair bark, perhaps, whose sails light up
The slip of smooth clear blue betwixt two Isles   25
Of purple shadow! Yes! they wander on
In gladness all; but thou, methinks, most glad,
My gentle-hearted Charles! for thou hast pined
And hungered after Nature, many a year,
In the great City pent, winning thy way   30
With sad yet patient soul, through evil and pain
And strange calamity!° Ah! slowly sink
Behind the western ridge, thou glorious sun!
Shine in the slant beams of the sinking orb,
Ye purple heath-flowers! richlier burn, ye clouds!   35
Live in the yellow light, ye distant groves!
And kindle, thou blue ocean! So my Friend
Struck with deep joy may stand, as I have stood,

7. **springy:** *Elastic*, I mean [Coleridge's note].
32. **strange calamity:** Coleridge refers to a tragedy in Charles Lamb's life when several months prior, his mother was stabbed to death by his sister, who was mentally ill.

Silent with swimming sense; yea, gazing round
On the wide landscape, gaze till all doth seem
Less gross than bodily; and of such hues
As veil the Almighty Spirit, when yet he makes
Spirits perceive his presence.
                              A delight
Comes sudden on my heart, and I am glad
As I myself were there! Nor in this bower,
This little lime-tree bower, have I not marked
Much that has soothed me. Pale beneath the blaze
Hung the transparent foliage; and I watched
Some broad and sunny leaf, and loved to see
The shadow of the leaf and stem above
Dappling its sunshine! And that walnut-tree
Was richly tinged, and a deep radiance lay
Full on the ancient ivy, which usurps
Those fronting elms, and now, with blackest mass
Makes their dark branches gleam a lighter hue
Through the late twilight: and though now the bat
Wheels silent by, and not a swallow twitters,
Yet still the solitary humble bee
Sings in the bean-flower! Henceforth I shall know
That Nature ne'er deserts the wise and pure;
No plot so narrow, be but Nature there,
No waste so vacant, but may well employ
Each faculty of sense, and keep the heart
Awake to Love and Beauty! and sometimes
'Tis well to be bereft of promised good,
That we may lift the Soul, and contemplate
With lively joy the joys we cannot share.
My gentle-hearted Charles! when the last rook
Beat its straight path along the dusky air
Homewards, I blessed it! deeming its black wing
 (Now a dim speck, now vanishing in light)
Had crossed the mighty orb's dilated glory,
While thou stood'st gazing; or when all was still,
Flew creeking o'er thy head, and had a charm
For thee, my gentle-hearted Charles, to whom
No sound is dissonant which tells of Life.

[1797]

GEORGE GORDON, LORD BYRON   [1788–1824]

Prometheus°

1

Titan! to whose immortal eyes
   The sufferings of mortality,
   Seen in their sad reality,
Were not as things that gods despise;
What was thy pity's recompense?   5
A silent suffering, and intense;
The rock, the vulture, and the chain,
All that the proud can feel of pain,
The agony they do not show,
The suffocating sense of woe,   10
   Which speaks but in its loneliness,
And then is jealous lest the sky
Should have a listener, nor will sigh
   Until its voice is echoless.

2

Titan! to thee the strife was given   15
   Between the suffering and the will,
   Which torture where they cannot kill;
And the inexorable Heaven,
And the deaf tyranny of Fate,
The ruling principle of Hate,   20
Which for its pleasure doth create
The things it may annihilate,
Refused thee even the boon to die:
The wretched gift Eternity
Was thine—and thou hast borne it well.   25

Prometheus: According to various Greek poets and playwrights, Prometheus, a Titan, stole fire from the gods and gave it to all mankind. As punishment, Zeus shackled Prometheus to a rock in the mountain. Each day, vultures came to eat his entrails, and he lived in agony until he was eventually freed by Hercules.

All that the Thunderer wrung from thee
Was but the menace which flung back
On him the torments of thy rack;
The fate thou didst so well foresee,
But would not to appease him tell;   30
And in thy Silence was his Sentence,
And in his Soul a vain repentance,
And evil dread so ill dissembled,
That in his hand the lightnings trembled.

3

Thy Godlike crime was to be kind,   35
    To render with thy precepts less
    The sum of human wretchedness,
And strengthen Man with his own mind;
And baffled as thou wert from high,
Still in thy patient energy,   40
In the endurance, and repulse
    Of thine impenetrable Spirit,
Which Earth and Heaven could not convulse,
    A mighty lesson we inherit:
Thou art a symbol and a sign   45
    To Mortals of their fate and force;
Like thee, Man is in part divine,
    A troubled stream from a pure source;
And Man in portions can foresee
His own funereal destiny;   50
His wretchedness, and his resistance,
And his sad unallied existence:
To which his Spirit may oppose
Itself—and equal to all woes,
    And a firm will, and a deep sense,   55
Which even in torture can descry
    Its own concenter'd recompense,
Triumphant where it dares defy,
And making Death a Victory.

                                                                [1816]

PERCY BYSSHE SHELLEY   [1792–1822]

Ode to the West Wind°

1

O wild West Wind, thou breath of Autumn's being,
Thou, from whose unseen presence the leaves dead
Are driven, like ghosts from an enchanter fleeing,

Yellow, and black, and pale, and hectic red,°
Pestilence-stricken multitudes: O Thou,   5
Who chariotest to their dark wintry bed

The winged seeds, where they lie cold and low,
Each like a corpse within its grave, until
Thine azure sister of the Spring shall blow

Her clarion° o'er the dreaming earth, and fill   10
(Driving sweet buds like flocks to feed in air)
With living hues and odours plain and hill:

Wild Spirit, which art moving everywhere;
Destroyer and Preserver; hear, O hear!

2

Thou on whose stream, 'mid the steep sky's commotion,   15
Loose clouds like Earth's decaying leaves are shed,
Shook from the tangled boughs of Heaven and Ocean,

Angels of rain and lightning: there are spread
On the blue surface of thine aery surge,
Like the bright hair uplifted from the head   20

Ode to the West Wind: This poem was conceived and chiefly written in a wood
that skirts the Arno, near Florence, and on a day when that tempestuous wind,
whose temperature is at once mild and animating, was collecting the vapours
which pour down the autumnal rains [Shelley's note].
4. hectic red: The type of fever that comes with tuberculosis.
10. clarion: A high-pitched trumpet.

Of some fierce Mænad,° even from the dim verge
Of the horizon to the zenith's height,
The locks of the approaching storm. Thou Dirge

Of the dying year, to which this closing night
Will be the dome of a vast sepulchre,   2
Vaulted with all thy congregated might

Of vapours,° from whose solid atmosphere   *clouds*
Black rain and fire and hail will burst: O hear!

3

Thou who didst waken from his summer dreams
The blue Mediterranean, where he lay,   3
Lulled by the coil of his chrystalline streams,

Beside a pumice isle in Baiæ's bay,°
And saw in sleep old palaces and towers
Quivering within the wave's intenser day,

All overgrown with azure moss and flowers   3
So sweet, the sense faints picturing them! Thou
For whose path the Atlantic's level powers

Cleave themselves into chasms, while far below
The sea-blooms and the oozy woods which wear
The sapless foliage of the ocean, know   4

Thy voice, and suddenly grow grey with fear,
And tremble and despoil themselves:° O hear!

4

If I were a dead leaf thou mightest bear;
If I were a swift cloud to fly with thee;
A wave to pant beneath thy power, and share   4

21. **Maenad:** Female followers of Dionysus, god of wine and fruitfulness. Maenads were known for their ecstatic dances.
32. **Baiae's bay:** In ancient Italy, Baiae was a seaside town known for its mineral springs. It was eventually subsumed by volcanic eruptions; hence Shelley's description of the "pumice isle."
40–42. **The sapless foliage . . . despoil themselves:** The vegetation at the bottom of the sea . . . sympathizes with that of the land in the change of seasons [Shelley's note].

The impulse of thy strength, only less free
Than thou, O Uncontrollable! If even
I were as in my boyhood, and could be

The comrade of thy wanderings over Heaven,
As then, when to outstrip thy skiey speed   50
Scarce seemed a vision; I would ne'er have striven

As thus with thee in prayer in my sore need.
Oh! lift me as a wave, a leaf, a cloud!
I fall upon the thorns of life! I bleed!

A heavy weight of hours has chained and bowed   55
One too like thee: tameless, and swift, and proud.

5

Make me thy lyre,° even as the forest is:
What if my leaves are falling like its own!
The tumult of thy mighty harmonies

Will take from both a deep, autumnal tone,   60
Sweet though in sadness. Be thou, Spirit fierce,
My spirit! Be thou me, impetuous one!

Drive my dead thoughts over the universe
Like withered leaves to quicken a new birth!
And, by the incantation of this verse,   65

Scatter, as from an unextinguished hearth
Ashes and sparks, my words among mankind!
Be through my lips to unawakened Earth

The trumpet of a prophecy! O Wind,
If Winter comes, can Spring be far behind?   70

[1819; 1820]

57. lyre: A reference to the Eolian lyre, or harp, a stringed instrument that,
when left on a windowsill or porch, uses the wind to create sound.

JOHN KEATS [1795–1821]

When I have fears that I may cease to be

When I have fears that I may cease to be
  Before my pen has gleaned my teeming brain,
Before high piled books, in charactry,°   *writing*
  Hold like rich garners° the full ripened grain;   *granaries*
When I behold, upon the night's starred face,
  Huge cloudy symbols of a high romance,
And think that I may never live to trace
  Their shadows, with the magic hand of chance;
And when I feel, fair creature of an hour,
  That I shall never look upon thee more,
Never have relish in the fairy power
  Of unreflecting love;—then on the shore
Of the wide world I stand alone, and think
Till love and fame to nothingness do sink.

[*1818;* 1848]

460

JOHN KEATS [1795–1821]

Ode to a Nightingale°

1

My heart aches, and a drowsy numbness pains
  My sense, as though of hemlock° I had drunk,
Or emptied some dull opiate to the drains
  One minute past, and Lethe°-wards had sunk:
'Tis not through envy of thy happy lot,   5
  But being too happy in thine happiness,—
    That thou, light-winged Dryad of the trees,
      In some melodious plot
  Of beechen green, and shadows numberless,
    Singest of summer in full-throated ease.   10

2

O, for a draught of vintage! that hath been
  Cool'd a long age in the deep-delved earth,
Tasting of Flora° and the country green,
  Dance, and Provençal song, and sunburnt mirth!
O for a beaker full of the warm South,   15
  Full of the true, the blushful Hippocrene,°

Ode to a Nightingale: Charles Brown, with whom Keats lived in Hampstead, wrote: "In the spring of 1819 a nightingale had built her nest near my house. Keats felt a tranquil and continual joy in her song; and one morning he took his chair from the breakfast table to the grass plot under a plum tree, where he sat for two or three hours. When he came into the house, I perceived he had some scraps of paper in his hand, and these he was quietly thrusting behind the books. On inquiry, I found those scraps, four or five in number, contained his poetic feeling on the song of our nightingale."
2. hemlock: A highly poisonous herb native to Europe and North Africa.
4. Lethe: One of the five rivers of the underworld of Hades said to cause forgetfulness.
13. Flora: Roman goddess of flowers.
16. Hippocrene: Literally "horse's fountain": refers to the fresh water spring on Mount Helicon, sacred to the muses, whose waters supposedly provide poetic inspiration.

With beaded bubbles winking at the brim,
   And purple-stained mouth;
That I might drink, and leave the world unseen,
   And with thee fade away into the forest dim: 20

3

Fade far away, dissolve, and quite forget
   What thou among the leaves hast never known,
The weariness, the fever, and the fret
   Here, where men sit and hear each other groan;
Where palsy shakes a few, sad, last gray hairs,   25
   Where youth grows pale, and spectre-thin, and dies;°
      Where but to think is to be full of sorrow
        And leaden-eyed despairs,
   Where Beauty cannot keep her lustrous eyes,
      Or new Love pine at them beyond to-morrow.   30

4

Away! away! for I will fly to thee,
   Not charioted by Bacchus° and his pards,
But on the viewless wings of Poesy,
   Though the dull brain perplexes and retards:
Already with thee! tender is the night,   35
   And haply the Queen-Moon is on her throne,
      Cluster'd around by all her starry Fays;
        But here there is no light,
   Save what from heaven is with the breezes blown
      Through verdurous° glooms and winding mossy ways.   *green-leaved* 40

5

I cannot see what flowers are at my feet,
   Nor what soft incense hangs upon the boughs,
But, in embalmed° darkness, guess each sweet   *perfumed*
   Wherewith the seasonable month endows
The grass, the thicket, and the fruit-tree wild;   45
   White hawthorn, and the pastoral eglantine;°
      Fast fading violets cover'd up in leaves;
        And mid-May's eldest child,

26. dies: A reference to Keats's brother, who died of tuberculosis.
32. Bacchus: God of wine.
46. eglantine: Another term for sweetbriar.

The coming musk-rose, full of dewy wine,
    The murmurous haunt of flies on summer eves.   50

6

Darkling° I listen; and, for many a time   *in darkness*
    I have been half in love with easeful Death,
Call'd him soft names in many a mused° rhyme,   *mediated*
    To take into the air my quiet breath;
Now more than ever seems it rich to die,   55
    To cease upon the midnight with no pain,
        While thou art pouring forth thy soul abroad
            In such an ecstasy!
    Still wouldst thou sing, and I have ears in vain—
        To thy high requiem become a sod.   60

7

Thou wast not born for death, immortal Bird!
    No hungry generations tread thee down;
The voice I hear this passing night was heard
    In ancient days by emperor and clown:
Perhaps the self-same song that found a path   65
    Through the sad heart of Ruth,° when, sick for home,
        She stood in tears amid the alien corn;°   *wheat*
            The same that oft-times hath
    Charm'd magic casements, opening on the foam
        Of perilous seas, in faery lands forlorn.   70

8

Forlorn! the very word is like a bell
    To toll me back from thee to my sole self!
Adieu! the fancy cannot cheat so well
    As she is fam'd to do, deceiving elf.
Adieu! adieu! thy plaintive anthem° fades   *hymn* 75
    Past the near meadows, over the still stream,
        Up the hill-side; and now 'tis buried deep
            In the next valley-glades:
    Was it a vision, or a waking dream?
        Fled is that music:—Do I wake or sleep?   80

                                              [1819]

---

66. **Ruth:** The young widow in the Book of Ruth in the Hebrew Bible.

ELIZABETH BARRETT BROWNING   [1806–1861]

How do I love thee?
Let me count the ways

How do I love thee? Let me count the ways.
I love thee to the depth and breadth and height
My soul can reach, when feeling out of sight
For the ends of Being and ideal Grace.
I love thee to the level of everyday's
Most quiet need, by sun and candlelight.
I love thee freely, as men strive for Right;
I love thee purely, as they turn from Praise.
I love thee with the passion put to use
In my old griefs, and with my childhood's faith.
I love thee with a love I seemed to lose
With my lost saints—I love thee with the breath,
Smiles, tears, of all my life!—and, if God choose,
I shall but love thee better after death.

[1850]

EDGAR ALLAN POE   [1809–1849]

Annabel Lee

It was many and many a year ago,
    In a kingdom by the sea,
That a maiden there lived whom you may know
    By the name of Annabel Lee;
And this maiden she lived with no other thought
    Than to love and be loved by me.

She was a child and *I* was a child,
   In this kingdom by the sea,
But we loved with a love that was more than love —
   I and my Annabel Lee —   10
With a love that the wingèd seraphs° of Heaven   *angels of the highest order*
   Coveted her and me.

And this was the reason that, long ago,
   In this kingdom by the sea,
A wind blew out of a cloud by night   15
   Chilling my Annabel Lee;
So that her highborn kinsmen came
   And bore her away from me,
To shut her up in a sepulchre
   In this kingdom by the sea.   20

The angels, not half so happy in Heaven,
   Went envying her and me:
Yes! that was the reason (as all men know,
   In this kingdom by the sea)
That the wind came out of the cloud, chilling   25
   And killing my Annabel Lee.

But our love it was stronger by far than the love
   Of those who were older than we —
   Of many far wiser than we —
And neither the angels in Heaven above   30
   Nor the demons down under the sea,
Can ever dissever my soul from the soul
   Of the beautiful Annabel Lee:

For the moon never beams without bringing me dreams
   Of the beautiful Annabel Lee;   35
And the stars never rise but I see the bright eyes
   Of the beautiful Annabel Lee;
And so, all the night-tide, I lie down by the side
Of my darling, my darling, my life and my bride,
   In her sepulchre there by the sea —   40
   In her tomb by the side of the sea.

[1849]

ALFRED, LORD TENNYSON [1809–1892]

Ulysses°

It little profits that an idle king,
By this still hearth, among these barren crags,
Matched with an agèd wife, I mete and dole
Unequal laws unto a savage race,°
That hoard, and sleep, and feed, and know not me.

I cannot rest from travel; I will drink
Life to the lees.° All times I have enjoyed
Greatly, have suffered greatly, both with those
That loved me, and alone; on shore, and when
Through scudding drifts° the rainy Hyades°
Vexed the dim sea. I am become a name;
For always roaming with a hungry heart
Much have I seen and known—cities of men
And manners, climates, councils, governments,
Myself not least, but honored of them all —

Ulysses (the Roman form of Odysseus): The hero of Homer's epic *The Odyssey*,
which tells the story of Odysseus's adventures on his voyage back to Ithaca, the
small island of which he was king, after he and the other Greek heroes defeated
Troy. It took Odysseus ten years to reach Ithaca, where his wife (Penelope) and
son (Telemachus) were waiting for him. Upon his return, he defeated the suitors
who had been trying to marry the faithful Penelope, and he resumed the
kingship and his old ways of life. Here Homer's story ends, but in Canto 26 of
the *Inferno*, Dante extended the story: Odysseus eventually became restless and
dissatisfied with his settled life and decided to return to the sea and sail west,
into the unknown sea, and seek whatever adventures he might find there.
Tennyson's poem amplifies the speech delivered in Dante's poem as Ulysses
challenges his men to accompany him on this new voyage.
3–4. mete . . . race: Administer inadequate (unequal to what is needed) laws to a
still somewhat lawless race.
6–7. drink . . . lees: Lees refers to the dregs or sediment at the bottom of beer or
wine, so Ulysses is vowing to live his life to the fullest, to drink to the last drop.
10. scudding drifts: Wind-driven spray; **Hyades:** Five stars in the constellation
Taurus whose rising was assumed to be followed by rain.

And drunk delight of battle with my peers,
Far on the ringing plains of windy Troy.
I am a part of all that I have met;
Yet all experience is an arch wherethrough
Gleams that untraveled world whose margin fades   20
Forever and forever when I move.
How dull it is to pause, to make an end,
To rust unburnished, not to shine in use!
As though to breathe were life! Life piled on life
Were all too little, and of one to me   25
Little remains; but every hour is saved
From that eternal silence, something more,
A bringer of new things; and vile it were
For some three suns° to store and hoard myself,   *years*
And this gray spirit yearning in desire   30
To follow knowledge like a sinking star,
Beyond the utmost bound of human thought.

    This is my son, mine own Telemachus,
To whom I leave the scepter and the isle —
Well-loved of me, discerning to fulfill   35
This labor, by slow prudence to make mild
A rugged people, and through soft degrees
Subdue them to the useful and the good.
Most blameless is he, centered in the sphere
Of common duties, decent not to fail   40
In offices of tenderness, and pay
Meet° adoration to my household gods,   *proper*
When I am gone. He works his work, I mine.

    There lies the port; the vessel puffs her sail;
There gloom the dark, broad seas. My mariners,   45
Souls that have toiled, and wrought, and thought with me —
That ever with a frolic welcome took
The thunder and the sunshine, and opposed
Free hearts, free foreheads—you and I are old;
Old age hath yet his honor and his toil.   50
Death closes all; but something ere the end,
Some work of noble note, may yet be done,
Not unbecoming men that strove with Gods.
The lights begin to twinkle from the rocks;
The long day wanes; the slow moon climbs; the deep   55
Moans round with many voices. Come, my friends,
'Tis not too late to seek a newer world.

Push off, and sitting well in order smite
The sounding furrows; for my purpose holds
To sail beyond the sunset, and the baths°
Of all the western stars, until I die.
It may be that the gulfs will wash us down;
It may be we shall touch the Happy Isles,°
And see the great Achilles,° whom we knew.
Though much is taken, much abides; and though
We are not now that strength which in old days
Moved earth and heaven, that which we are, we are —
One equal temper of heroic hearts,
Made weak by time and fate, but strong in will
To strive, to seek, to find, and not to yield.

[1833]

60. **baths:** The outer river or ocean surrounding the flat earth, in Greek cosmology, into which the stars descended upon setting.
63. **Happy Isles:** The Islands of the Blessed, or Elysian Fields, in Greek myth, which lay in the western seas beyond the Strait of Gibraltar and were the abode of heroes after death.
64. **Achilles:** The hero of the Greeks, and Odysseus's comrade, in Homer's *Iliad*.

ROBERT BROWNING   [1812–1889]

My Last Duchess

Ferrara°

That's my last Duchess° painted on the wall,
Looking as if she were alive. I call
That piece a wonder, now: Frà Pandolf's° hands
Worked busily a day, and there she stands.
Will't please you sit and look at her? I said
"Frà Pandolf" by design, for never read

Ferrara: The poem is based on events that occurred in the life of Alfonso II, duke of Ferrara in Italy, in the sixteenth century.
1. **last Duchess:** Ferrara's first wife, Lucrezia, died in 1561 at age seventeen after three years of marriage.
3. **Frà Pandolf:** Brother Pandolf, a fictional painter.

Strangers like you that pictured countenance,
The depth and passion of its earnest glance,
But to myself they turned (since none puts by
The curtain I have drawn for you, but I)   10
And seemed as they would ask me, if they durst,
How such a glance came there; so, not the first
Are you to turn and ask thus. Sir, 'twas not
Her husband's presence only called that spot
Of joy into the Duchess' cheek: perhaps   15
Frà Pandolf chanced to say "Her mantle laps
Over my lady's wrist too much," or "Paint
Must never hope to reproduce the faint
Half-flush that dies along her throat": such stuff
Was courtesy, she thought, and cause enough   20
For calling up that spot of joy. She had
A heart—how shall I say?—too soon made glad,
Too easily impressed; she liked whate'er
She looked on, and her looks went everywhere.
Sir, 'twas all one! My favor at her breast,   25
The dropping of the daylight in the West,
The bough of cherries some officious fool
Broke in the orchard for her, the white mule
She rode with round the terrace—all and each
Would draw from her alike the approving speech,   30
Or blush, at least. She thanked men,—good! but thanked
Somehow—I know not how—as if she ranked
My gift of a nine-hundred-years-old name
With anybody's gift. Who'd stoop to blame
This sort of trifling? Even had you skill   35
In speech—(which I have not)—to make your will
Quite clear to such an one, and say, "Just this
Or that in you disgusts me; here you miss,
Or there exceed the mark"—and if she let
Herself be lessoned so, nor plainly set   40
Her wits to yours, forsooth, and made excuse,
— E'en then would be some stooping; and I choose
Never to stoop. Oh sir, she smiled, no doubt,
Whene'er I passed her; but who passed without
Much the same smile? This grew; I gave commands;   45
Then all smiles stopped together. There she stands
As if alive. Will't please you rise? We'll meet
The company below, then. I repeat,
The Count your master's known munificence
Is ample warrant that no just pretence   50

Of mine for dowry will be disallowed;
Though his fair daughter's self, as I avowed
At starting, is my object. Nay, we'll go
Together down, sir. Notice Neptune, though,
Taming a sea-horse, thought a rarity,
Which Claus of Innsbruck° cast in bronze for me!

[1842]

56. **Claus of Innsbruck:** A fictional sculptor.

WALT WHITMAN   [1819–1892]

From Song of Myself°

1

I celebrate myself, and sing myself,
And what I assume you shall assume,
For every atom belonging to me as good belongs to you.

I loafe and invite my soul,
I lean and loafe at my ease observing a spear of summer grass.

My tongue, every atom of my blood, form'd from this soil, this air,
Born here of parents born here from parents the same, and their
    parents the same,
I, now thirty-seven years old in perfect health begin,
Hoping to cease not till death.

Song of Myself: The poem was first published in 1855 as an untitled section of
Leaves of Grass. It was a rough, rude, and vigorous example of antebellum
American cultural politics and free verse experimentation. The version used
here, from the sixth edition (1891–1892), is much longer, more carefully crafted,
and more conventionally punctuated. Sections 1–3 introduce the persona and
the scope and method of the poem; section 6 explains grass as a symbol; sections
7–10, examples of Whitman's dynamic panoramic miniatures, are also of historical significance regarding Native and African Americans; section 14 extends the
outward sweep of 7–10; section 21 develops Whitman's theme of sex and nature;
section 24 extends the handling of the poem's persona; sections 46 and
48 recapitulate the major themes of the poem; sections 51 and 52 deal with the
absorption of the poet's persona into the converted reader.

Creeds and schools in abeyance,   10
Retiring back a while sufficed at what they are, but never forgotten,
I harbor for good or bad, I permit to speak at every hazard,
Nature without check with original energy.

2

Houses and rooms are full of perfumes, the shelves are crowded with
    perfumes,
I breathe the fragrance myself and know it and like it,   15
The distillation would intoxicate me also, but I shall not let it.
The atmosphere is not a perfume, it has no taste of the distillation,
    it is odorless,
It is for my mouth forever, I am in love with it,
I will go to the bank by the wood and become undisguised and naked,
I am mad for it to be in contact with me.   20

The smoke of my own breath,
Echoes, ripples, buzz'd whispers, love-root, silk-thread, crotch and
    vine,
My respiration and inspiration, the beating of my heart, the passing of
    blood and air through my lungs,
The sniff of green leaves and dry leaves, and of the shore and
    dark-color'd sea-rocks, and of hay in the barn,
The sound of the belch'd words of my voice loos'd to the eddies of the
    wind,   25
A few light kisses, a few embraces, a reaching around of arms,
The play of shine and shade on the trees as the supple boughs wag,
The delight alone or in the rush of the streets, or along the fields and
    hill-sides,
The feeling of health, the full-noon trill, the song of me rising from bed
    and meeting the sun.

Have you reckon'd a thousand acres much? have you reckon'd the earth
    much?   30
Have you practis'd so long to learn to read?
Have you felt so proud to get at the meaning of poems?

Stop this day and night with me and you shall possess the origin of all
    poems,
You shall possess the good of the earth and sun, (there are millions of
    suns left,)
You shall no longer take things at second or third hand, nor look
    through the eyes of the dead, nor feed on the spectres in books,   35
You shall not look through my eyes either, nor take things from me,
You shall listen to all sides and filter them from your self.

3

I have heard what the talkers were talking, the talk of the beginning
  and the end,
But I do not talk of the beginning or the end.

There was never any more inception than there is now,
Nor any more youth or age than there is now,
And will never be any more perfection than there is now,
Nor any more heaven or hell than there is now.
Urge and urge and urge,
Always the procreant urge of the world.

Out of the dimness opposite equals advance, always substance and
  increase, always sex,
Always a knit of identity, always distinction, always a breed of life.

To elaborate is no avail, learn'd and unlearn'd feel that it is so.

Sure as the most certain sure, plumb in the uprights, well entretied,°
  braced in the beams,
Stout as a horse, affectionate, haughty, electrical,
I and this mystery here we stand.

Clear and sweet is my soul, and clear and sweet is all that is not my
  soul.

Lack one lacks both, and the unseen is proved by the seen,
Till that becomes unseen and receives proof in its turn.

Showing the best and dividing it from the worst age vexes age,
Knowing the perfect fitness and equanimity of things, while they
  discuss I am silent, and go bathe and admire myself.

Welcome is every organ and attribute of me, and of any man hearty
  and clean,
Not an inch nor a particle of an inch is vile, and none shall be less
  familiar than the rest.

I am satisfied—I see, dance, laugh, sing;
As the hugging and loving bed-fellow sleeps at my side through the
  night, and withdraws at the peep of the day with stealthy tread,
Leaving me baskets cover'd with white towels swelling the house with
  their plenty,
Shall I postpone my acceptation and realization and scream at
  my eyes,

---

49. **entretied:** Cross-braced, as between two joists in carpentry.

That they turn from gazing after and down the road,
And forthwith cipher and show me to a cent,
Exactly the value of one and exactly the value of two, and which is
    ahead?   65

6

A child said *What is the grass?* fetching it to me with full hands;
How could I answer the child? I do not know what it is any more
    than he.   100

I guess it must be the flag of my disposition, out of hopeful green stuff
    woven.

Or I guess it is the handkerchief of the Lord,
A scented gift and remembrancer designedly dropt,
Bearing the owner's name someway in the corners, that we may see and
    remark, and say *Whose?*

Or I guess the grass is itself a child, the produced babe of the vegetation. 105

Or I guess it is a uniform hieroglyphic,
And it means, Sprouting alike in broad zones and narrow zones,
Growing among black folks as among white,
Kanuck,° Tuckahoe,° Congressman, Cuff,° I give them the same, I receive
    them the same.

And now it seems to me the beautiful uncut hair of graves.   110

Tenderly will I use you curling grass,
It may be you transpire from the breasts of young men,
It may be if I had known them I would have loved them,
It may be you are from old people, or from offspring taken soon out of
    their mothers' laps,
And here you are the mothers' laps.   115

This grass is very dark to be from the white heads of old mothers,
Darker than the colorless beards of old men,
Dark to come from under the faint red roofs of mouths.

O I perceive after all so many uttering tongues,
And I perceive they do not come from the roofs of mouths for nothing.   120

---

109. Kanuck: A French Canadian; **Tuckahoe:** A Virginian living in the tide-
water region and eating tuckahoe, a fungus; **Cuff:** A black person.

I wish I could translate the hints about the dead young men and
women,
And the hints about old men and mothers, and the offspring taken soon
    out of their laps.
What do you think has become of the young and old men?
And what do you think has become of the women and children?
They are alive and well somewhere,   12
The smallest sprout shows there is really no death,
And if ever there was it led forward life, and does not wait at the end to
    arrest it,
And ceas'd the moment life appear'd.

All goes onward and outward, nothing collapses,
And to die is different from what any one supposed, and luckier.   13

7

Has any one supposed it lucky to be born?
I hasten to inform him or her it is just as lucky to die, and I know it.

I pass death with the dying and birth with the new-wash'd babe, and am
    not contain'd between my hat and boots,
And peruse manifold objects, no two alike and every one good,
The earth good and the stars good, and their adjuncts all good.   13

I am not an earth nor an adjunct of an earth,
I am the mate and companion of people, all just as immortal and
    fathomless as myself,
(They do not know how immortal, but I know.)

Every kind for itself and its own, for me mine male and female,
For me those that have been boys and that love women,   14
For me the man that is proud and feels how it stings to be slighted,
For me the sweet-heart and the old maid, for me mothers and the
    mothers of mothers,
For me lips that have smiled, eyes that have shed tears,
For me children and the begetters of children.

Undrape! you are not guilty to me, nor stale nor discarded,   14
I see through the broadcloth and gingham whether or no,
And am around, tenacious, acquisitive, tireless, and cannot be shaken
    away.

8

The little one sleeps in its cradle,
I lift the gauze and look a long time, and silently brush away flies with
    my hand.

The youngster and the red-faced girl turn aside up the bushy hill,   150
I peeringly view them from the top.
The suicide sprawls on the bloody floor of the bedroom,
I witness the corpse with its dabbled hair, I note where the pistol has
  fallen.

The blab of the pave, tires of carts, sluff of boot-soles, talk of the
  promenaders,
The heavy omnibus, the driver with his interrogating thumb, the clank
  of the shod horses on the granite floor,   155
The snow-sleighs, clinking, shouted jokes, pelts of snow-balls,
The hurrahs for popular favorites, the fury of rous'd mobs,
The flap of the curtain'd litter, a sick man inside borne to the hospital,
The meeting of enemies, the sudden oath, the blows and fall,
The excited crowd, the policeman with his star quickly working his
  passage to the centre of the crowd,   160
The impassive stones that receive and return so many echoes,
What groans of over-fed or half-starv'd who fall sunstruck or in fits,
What exclamations of women taken suddenly who hurry home and give
  birth to babes,
What living and buried speech is always vibrating here, what howls
  restrain'd by decorum,
Arrests of criminals, slights, adulterous offers made, acceptances,
  rejections with convex lips,   165
I mind them or the show or resonance of them—I come and I depart.

9

The big doors of the country barn stand open and ready,
The dried grass of the harvest-time loads the slow-drawn wagon,
The clear light plays on the brown gray and green intertinged,
The armfuls are pack'd to the sagging mow.   170

I am there, I help, I came stretch'd atop of the load,
I felt its soft jolts, one leg reclined on the other,
I jump from the cross-beams and seize the clover and timothy,
And roll head over heels and tangle my hair full of wisps.

10

Alone far in the wilds and mountains I hunt,   175
Wandering amazed at my own lightness and glee,
In the late afternoon choosing a safe spot to pass the night,
Kindling a fire and broiling the fresh-kill'd game,
Falling asleep on the gather'd leaves with my dog and gun by my side.

The Yankee clipper is under her sky-sails, she cuts the sparkle and
    scud,
My eyes settle the land, I bend at her prow or shout joyously from
    the deck.

The boatmen and clam-diggers arose early and stopt for me,
I tuck'd my trowser-ends in my boots and went and had a good time;
You should have been with us that day round the chowder-kettle.

I saw the marriage of the trapper in the open air in the far west, the
    bride was a red girl,
Her father and his friends sat near cross-legged and dumbly smoking,
    they had moccasins to their feet and large thick blankets hanging
    from their shoulders,
On a bank lounged the trapper, he was drest mostly in skins, his
    luxuriant beard and curls protected his neck, he held his bride by
    the hand,
She had long eyelashes, her head was bare, her coarse straight locks
    descended upon her voluptuous limbs and reach'd to her feet.

The runaway slave came to my house and stopt outside,
I heard his motions crackling the twigs of the woodpile,
Through the swung half-door of the kitchen I saw him limpsy and
    weak,
And went where he sat on a log and led him in and assured him,
And brought water and fill'd a tub for his sweated body and bruis'd feet,
And gave him a room that enter'd from my own, and gave him some
    coarse clean clothes,
And remember perfectly well his revolving eyes and his awkwardness,
And remember putting plasters on the galls of his neck and ankles;
He staid with me a week before he was recuperated and pass'd north,
I had him sit next me at table, my fire-lock lean'd in the corner.

14

The wild gander leads his flock through the cool night,
Ya-honk he says, and sounds it down to me like an invitation,
The pert may suppose it meaningless, but I listening close,
Find its purpose and place up there toward the wintry sky.

The sharp-hoof'd moose of the north, the cat on the house-sill, the
    chickadee, the prairie-dog,
The litter of the grunting sow as they tug at her teats,
The brood of the turkey-hen and she with her half-spread wings,
I see in them and myself the same old law.

The press of my foot to the earth springs a hundred affections,
They scorn the best I can do to relate them.
I am enamour'd of growing out-doors,   255
Of men that live among cattle or taste of the ocean or woods,
Of the builders and steerers of ships and the wielders of axes and mauls,
   and the drivers of horses,
I can eat and sleep with them week in and week out.

What is commonest, cheapest, nearest, easiest, is Me,
Me going in for my chances, spending for vast returns,   260
Adorning myself to bestow myself on the first that will take me,
Not asking the sky to come down to my good will,
Scattering it freely forever.

21

I am the poet of the Body and I am the poet of the Soul,
The pleasures of heaven are with me and the pains of hell are with me,
The first I graft and increase upon myself, the latter I translate into a
   new tongue.

I am the poet of the woman the same as the man,   425
And I say it is as great to be a woman as to be a man,
And I say there is nothing greater than the mother of men.

I chant the chant of dilation or pride,
We have had ducking and deprecating about enough,
I show that size is only development.   430

Have you outstript the rest? are you the President?
It is a trifle, they will more than arrive there every one, and still
   pass on.

I am he that walks with the tender and growing night,
I call to the earth and sea half-held by the night.

Press close bare-bosom'd night — press close magnetic nourishing
   night!   435
Night of south winds — night of the large few stars!
Still nodding night — mad naked summer night.

Smile O voluptuous cool-breath'd earth!
Earth of the slumbering and liquid trees!
Earth of departed sunset — earth of the mountains misty-topt!   440
Earth of the vitreous pour of the full moon just tinged with blue!
Earth of shine and dark mottling the tide of the river!
Earth of the limpid gray of clouds brighter and clearer for my sake!

Far-swooping elbow'd earth—rich apple-blossom'd earth!
Smile, for your lover comes.   44
Prodigal, you have given me love—therefore I to you give love!
O unspeakable passionate love.

24

Walt Whitman, a kosmos, of Manhattan the son,
Turbulent, fleshy, sensual, eating, drinking and breeding,
No sentimentalist, no stander above men and women or apart from them,
No more modest than immodest.   50

Unscrew the locks from the doors!
Unscrew the doors themselves from their jambs!

Whoever degrades another degrades me,
And whatever is done or said returns at last to me.

Through me the afflatus° surging and surging, through me the current
    and index.   50

I speak the pass-word primeval, I give the sign of democracy,
By God! I will accept nothing which all cannot have their counterpart
    of on the same terms.

Through me many long dumb voices,
Voices of the interminable generations of prisoners and slaves,
Voices of the diseas'd and despairing and of thieves and dwarfs,   51
Voices of cycles of preparation and accretion,
And of the threads that connect the stars, and of wombs and of the
    father-stuff,
And of the rights of them the others are down upon,
Of the deform'd, trivial, flat, foolish, despised,
Fog in the air, beetles rolling balls of dung.   51

Through me forbidden voices,
Voices of sexes and lusts, voices veil'd and I remove the veil,
Voices indecent by me clarified and transfigur'd.

I do not press my fingers across my mouth,
I keep as delicate around the bowels as around the head and heart,   52
Copulation is no more rank to me than death is.

I believe in the flesh and the appetites,
Seeing, hearing, feeling, are miracles, and each part and tag of me is a
    miracle.

505. **afflatus:** Inspiration (from the Latin for "to blow on").

Divine am I inside and out, and I make holy whatever I touch or am
  touch'd from,
The scent of these arm-pits aroma finer than prayer,   525
This head more than churches, bibles, and all the creeds.

If I worship one thing more than another it shall be the spread of my
  own body, or any part of it,
Translucent mould of me it shall be you!
Shaded ledges and rests it shall be you!
Firm masculine colter° it shall be you!   530
Whatever goes to the tilth° of me it shall be you!
You my rich blood! your milky stream pale strippings of my life!
Breast that presses against other breasts it shall be you!
My brain it shall be your occult convolutions!
Root of wash'd sweet-flag! timorous pond-snipe! nest of guarded
  duplicate eggs! it shall be you!   535
Mix'd tussled hay of head, beard, brawn, it shall be you!
Trickling sap of maple, fibre of manly wheat, it shall be you!
Sun so generous it shall be you!
Vapors lighting and shading my face it shall be you!
You sweaty brooks and dews it shall be you!   540
Winds whose soft-tickling genitals rub against me it shall be you!
Broad muscular fields, branches of live oak, loving lounger in my
  winding paths, it shall be you!
Hands I have taken, face I have kiss'd, mortal I have ever touch'd, it
  shall be you.

46

I know I have the best of time and space, and was never measured and
  never will be measured.

I tramp a perpetual journey, (come listen all!)
My signs are a rain-proof coat, good shoes, and a staff cut from the woods,
No friend of mine takes his ease in my chair,
I have no chair, no church, no philosophy,   1205
I lead no man to a dinner-table, library, exchange,
But each man and each woman of you I lead upon a knoll,
My left hand hooking you round the waist,
My right hand pointing to landscapes of continents and the public road.

---

530. **colter:** Blade or disk on a plow for cutting the earth.
531. **tilth:** Cultivation of land.

Not I, not any one else can travel that road for you,   121
You must travel it for yourself.

It is not far, it is within reach,
Perhaps you have been on it since you were born and did not know,
Perhaps it is everywhere on water and on land.

Shoulder your duds dear son, and I will mine, and let us hasten forth,   121
Wonderful cities and free nations we shall fetch as we go.

If you tire, give me both burdens, and rest the chuff° of your hand
     on my hip,
And in due time you shall repay the same service to me,
For after we start we never lie by again.

This day before dawn I ascended a hill and look'd at the crowded
     heaven,   122
And I said to my spirit *When we become the enfolders of those orbs, and
     the pleasure and knowledge of every thing in them, shall we be fill'd and
     satisfied then?*
And my spirit said *No, we but level that lift to pass and continue beyond.*

You are also asking me questions and I hear you,
I answer that I cannot answer, you must find out for yourself.

Sit a while dear son,   122
Here are biscuits to eat and here is milk to drink,
But as soon as you sleep and renew yourself in sweet clothes, I kiss you
     with a good-by kiss and open the gate for your egress hence.

Long enough have you dream'd contemptible dreams,
Now I wash the gum from your eyes,
You must habit yourself to the dazzle of the light and of every moment
     of your life.   123

Long have you timidly waded holding a plank by the shore,
Now I will you to be a bold swimmer,
To jump off in the midst of the sea, rise again, nod to me, shout, and
     laughingly dash with your hair.

48

I have said that the soul is not more than the body,
And I have said that the body is not more than the soul,   127
And nothing, not God, is greater to one than one's self is,

1217. chuff: Weight.

And whoever walks a furlong without sympathy walks to his own
    funeral drest in his shroud,
And I or you pocketless of a dime may purchase the pick of the earth,
And to glance with an eye or show a bean in its pod confounds the
    learning of all times,
And there is no trade or employment but the young man following it
    may become a hero,   1275
And there is no object so soft but it makes a hub for the wheel'd
    universe,
And I say to any man or woman, Let your soul stand cool and composed
    before a million universes.

And I say to mankind, Be not curious about God,
For I who am curious about each am not curious about God,
(No array of terms can say how much I am at peace about God and
    about death.)   1280

I hear and behold God in every object, yet understand God not in the
    least,
Nor do I understand who there can be more wonderful than myself.

Why should I wish to see God better than this day?
I see something of God each hour of the twenty-four, and each
    moment then,
In the faces of men and women I see God, and in my own face in the
    glass,   1285
I find letters from God dropt in the street, and every one is sign'd by
    God's name,
And I leave them where they are, for I know that wheresoe'er I go,
Others will punctually come for ever and ever.

51

The past and present wilt—I have fill'd them, emptied them,
And proceed to fill my next fold of the future.   1320

Listener up there! what have you to confide to me?
Look in my face while I snuff° the sidle° of evening,
(Talk honestly, no one else hears you, and I stay only a minute longer.)

Do I contradict myself?
Very well then I contradict myself,   1325
(I am large, I contain multitudes.)
I concentrate toward them that are nigh, I wait on the door-slab.

1322. snuff: Snuff out; **sidle:** Sidewise or stealthy movement.

Who has done his day's work? who will soonest be through with his
   supper?
Who wishes to walk with me?

Will you speak before I am gone? will you prove already too late?   13:

52

The spotted hawk swoops by and accuses me, he complains of my gab
   and my loitering.

I too am not a bit tamed, I too am untranslatable,
I sound my barbaric yawp over the roofs of the world.

The last scud of day holds back for me,
It flings my likeness after the rest and true as any on the shadow'd
   wilds,   13:
It coaxes me to the vapor and the dusk.

I depart as air, I shake my white locks at the runaway sun,
I effuse my flesh in eddies, and drift it in lacy jags.

I bequeath myself to the dirt to grow from the grass I love,
If you want me again look for me under your boot-soles.   134

You will hardly know who I am or what I mean,
But I shall be good health to you nevertheless,
And filter and fibre your blood.

Failing to fetch me at first keep encouraged,
Missing me one place search another,   134
I stop somewhere waiting for you.

                                      [*1855;* 1891–1892]

WALT WHITMAN   [1819–1892]

When Lilacs Last in the Dooryard Bloom'd°

From Memories of President Lincoln

1

When lilacs° last in the dooryard bloom'd,
And the great star° early droop'd in the western sky in the night,   *Venus*
I mourn'd, and yet shall mourn with ever-returning spring.

Ever-returning spring, trinity sure to me you bring,
Lilac blooming perennial and drooping star in the west,   5
And thought of him I love.

2

O powerful western fallen star!°
O shades of night—O moody, tearful night!
O great star disappear'd—O the black murk that hides the star!
O cruel hands that hold me powerless—O helpless soul of me!   10
O harsh surrounding cloud that will not free my soul.

3

In the dooryard fronting an old farm-house near the white-wash'd
    palings,
Stands the lilac-bush tall-growing with heart-shaped leaves of rich green,
With many a pointed blossom rising delicate, with the perfume strong
    I love,
With every leaf a miracle—and from this bush in the dooryard,   15
With delicate-color'd blossoms and heart-shaped leaves of rich green,
A sprig with its flower I break.

When Lilacs Last in the Dooryard Bloom'd: This poem was written over a period
of weeks after the assassination of Abraham Lincoln on April 14, 1865. The poem
is recognized as one of the most significant elegies of American literature.
1. lilacs: Lilacs are usually a symbol of spring.
7. western fallen star: A reference to Abraham Lincoln.

4

In the swamp in secluded recesses,
A shy and hidden bird is warbling a song.

Solitary the thrush,   20
The hermit withdrawn to himself, avoiding the settlements,
Sings by himself a song.

Song of the bleeding throat,
Death's outlet song of life, (for well dear brother I know,
If thou wast not granted to sing thou would'st surely die.)   25

5

Over the breast of the spring, the land, amid cities,
Amid lanes and through old woods, where lately the violets peep'd from
    the ground, spotting the gray debris,
Amid the grass in the fields each side of the lanes, passing the endless grass,
Passing the yellow-spear'd wheat, every grain from its shroud in the
    dark-brown fields uprisen,
Passing the apple-tree blows of white and pink in the orchards,   30
Carrying a corpse to where it shall rest in the grave,
Night and day journeys a coffin.°

6

Coffin that passes through lanes and streets,
Through day and night with the great cloud darkening the land,
With the pomp of the inloop'd flags with the cities draped in black,   35
With the show of the States themselves as of crape-veil'd women
    standing,
With processions long and winding and the flambeaus° of the night,
With the countless torches lit, with the silent sea of faces and the
    unbared heads,
With the waiting depot, the arriving coffin, and the sombre faces,
With dirges through the night, with the thousand voices rising
    strong and solemn,   40
With all the mournful voices of the dirges pour'd around the coffin,

The dim-lit churches and the shuddering organs—where amid these you
    journey,
With the tolling tolling bells' perpetual clang,

32. journeys a coffin: Lincoln's body was carried by a special funeral train from
Washington, DC, to Springfield, Illinois, for burial.
37. flambeaus: Flaming torches.

Here, coffin that slowly passes,
I give you my sprig of lilac.   45

7

(Nor for you, for one alone,
Blossoms and branches green to coffins all I bring,
For fresh as the morning, thus would I chant a song for you O sane and
    sacred death.

All over bouquets of roses,
O death, I cover you over with roses and early lilies,   50
But mostly and now the lilac that blooms the first,
Copious I break, I break the sprigs from the bushes,
With loaded arms I come, pouring for you,
For you and the coffins all of you O death.)

8

O western orb sailing the heaven,   55
Now I know what you must have meant as a month since I walk'd,
As I walk'd in silence the transparent shadowy night,
As I saw you had something to tell as you bent to me night after night,
As you droop'd from the sky low down as if to my side, (while the other
    stars all look'd on,)
As we wander'd together the solemn night, (for something I know not
    what kept me from sleep,)   60
As the night advanced, and I saw on the rim of the west how full you
    were of woe,
As I stood on the rising ground in the breeze in the cool transparent
    night,
As I watch'd where you pass'd and was lost in the netherward black of
    the night,
As my soul in its trouble dissatisfied sank, as where you sad orb,
Concluded, dropt in the night, and was gone.   65

9

Sing on there in the swamp,
O singer bashful and tender, I hear your notes, I hear your call,
I hear, I come presently, I understand you,
But a moment I linger, for the lustrous star has detain'd me,
The star my departing comrade holds and detains me.   70

10

O how shall I warble myself for the dead one there I loved?
And how shall I deck my song for the large sweet soul that has gone?
And what shall my perfume be for the grave of him I love?

Sea-winds blown from east and west,
Blown from the Eastern sea and blown from the Western sea, till there
    on the prairies meeting,
These and with these and the breath of my chant,
I'll perfume the grave of him I love.

11

O what shall I hang on the chamber walls?
And what shall the pictures be that I hang on the walls,
To adorn the burial-house of him I love?

Pictures of growing spring and farms and homes,
With the Fourth-month eve at sundown, and the gray smoke lucid and
    bright,
With floods of the yellow gold of the gorgeous, indolent, sinking sun,
    burning, expanding the air,
With the fresh sweet herbage under foot, and the pale green leaves of the
    trees prolific,
In the distance the flowing glaze, the breast of the river, with a wind-
    dapple here and there,
With ranging hills on the banks, with many a line against the sky, and
    shadows,
And the city at hand with dwellings so dense, and stacks of chimneys,
And all the scenes of life and the workshops, and the workmen home-
    ward returning.

12

Lo, body and soul—this land,
My own Manhattan with spires, and the sparkling and hurrying tides,
    and the ships,
The varied and ample land, the South and the North in the light,
    Ohio's shores and flashing Missouri,
And ever the far-spreading prairies cover'd with grass and corn.

Lo, the most excellent sun so calm and haughty,
The violet and purple morn with just-felt breezes,
The gentle soft-born measureless light,
The miracle spreading bathing all, the fulfill'd noon,

The coming eve delicious, the welcome night and the stars,
Over my cities shining all, enveloping man and land.

13

Sing on, sing on you gray-brown bird,
Sing from the swamps, the recesses, pour your chant from the
    bushes,   100
Limitless out of the dusk, out of the cedars and pines.

Sing on dearest brother, warble your reedy song,
Loud human song, with voice of uttermost woe.

O liquid and free and tender!
O wild and loose to my soul—O wondrous singer!   105
You only I hear—yet the star holds me, (but will soon depart,)
Yet the lilac with mastering odor holds me.

14

Now while I sat in the day and look'd forth,
In the close of the day with its light and the fields of spring, and the
    farmers preparing their crops,
In the large unconscious scenery of my land with its lakes and forests,   110
In the heavenly aerial beauty, (after the perturb'd winds and the storms,)
Under the arching heavens of the afternoon swift passing, and the voices
    of children and women,
The many-moving sea-tides, and I saw the ships how they sail'd,
And the summer approaching with richness, and the fields all busy with
    labor,
And the infinite separate houses, how they all went on, each with its
    meals and minutia of daily usages,   115
And the streets how their throbbings throbb'd, and the cities pent—lo,
    then and there,
Falling upon them all and among them all, enveloping me with the rest,
Appear'd the cloud, appear'd the long black trail, — how deep × is
And I knew death, its thought, and the sacred knowledge of death.

Then with the knowledge of death as walking one side of me,   120
And the thought of death close-walking the other side of me,
And I in the middle as with companions, and as holding the hands of
    companions,
I fled forth to the hiding receiving night that talks not,
Down to the shores of the water, the path by the swamp in the dimness,
To the solemn shadowy cedars and ghostly pines so still.   125

And the singer so shy to the rest receiv'd me,
The gray-brown bird I know receiv'd us comrades three,
And he sang the carol of death, and a verse for him I love.

From deep secluded recesses,
From the fragrant cedars and the ghostly pines so still,   13
Came the carol of the bird.

And the charm of the carol rapt me,
As I held as if by their hands my comrades in the night,
And the voice of my spirit tallied the song of the bird.

Come lovely and soothing death,   13
Undulate round the world, serenely arriving, arriving,
In the day, in the night, to all, to each,
Sooner or later delicate death.

Prais'd be the fathomless universe,
For life and joy, and for objects and knowledge curious,   14
And for love, sweet love—but praise! praise! praise!
For the sure-enwinding arms of cool-enfolding death.

Dark mother always gliding near with soft feet,
Have none chanted for thee a chant of fullest welcome?
Then I chant it for thee, I glorify thee above all,   14
I bring thee a song that when thou must indeed come, come unfalteringly.

Approach strong deliveress,
When it is so, when thou hast taken them I joyously sing the dead,
Lost in the loving floating ocean of thee,
Laved in the flood of thy bliss O death.   15

From me to thee glad serenades,
Dances for thee I propose saluting thee, adornments and feastings for
    thee,
And the sights of the open landscape and the high-spread sky are fitting,
And life and the fields, and the huge and thoughtful night.

The night in silence under many a star,   15
The ocean shore and the husky whispering wave whose voice I know,
And the soul turning to thee O vast and well-veil'd death,
And the body gratefully nestling close to thee.

Over the tree-tops I float thee a song,
Over the rising and sinking waves, over the myriad fields and the prairies
    wide,   16
Over the dense-pack'd cities all and the teeming wharves and ways,
I float this carol with joy, with joy to thee O death.

15

To the tally of my soul,
Loud and strong kept up the gray-brown bird,
With pure deliberate notes spreading filling the night.   165

Loud in the pines and cedars dim,
Clear in the freshness moist and the swamp-perfume,
And I with my comrades there in the night.

While my sight that was bound in my eyes unclosed,
As to long panoramas of visions.   170

And I saw askant° the armies,
I saw as in noiseless dreams hundreds of battle-flags,
Borne through the smoke of the battles and pierc'd with missiles I saw
    them,
And carried hither and yon through the smoke, and torn and bloody,
And at last but a few shreds left on the staffs, (and all in silence,)   175
And the staffs all splinter'd and broken.

I saw battle-corpses, myriads of them,
And the white skeletons of young men, I saw them,
I saw the debris and debris of all the slain soldiers of the war,
But I saw they were not as was thought,   180
They themselves were fully at rest, they suffer'd not,
The living remain'd and suffer'd, the mother suffer'd,
And the wife and the child and the musing comrade suffer'd,
And the armies that remain'd suffer'd.

16

Passing the visions, passing the night,   185
Passing, unloosing the hold of my comrades' hands,
Passing the song of the hermit bird and the tallying song of my soul,
Victorious song, death's outlet song, yet varying ever-altering song,
As low and wailing, yet clear the notes, rising and falling, flooding the
    night,
Sadly sinking and fainting, as warning and warning, and yet again
    bursting with joy,   190
Covering the earth and filling the spread of the heaven,
As that powerful psalm in the night I heard from recesses,
Passing, I leave thee lilac with heart-shaped leaves,
I leave thee there in the door-yard, blooming, returning with spring.

-----

171. **askant:** Sideways or obliquely.

I cease from my song for thee,   19
From my gaze on thee in the west, fronting the west, communing with thee,
O comrade lustrous with silver face in the night.

Yet each to keep and all, retrievements out of the night,
The song, the wondrous chant of the gray-brown bird,
And the tallying chant, the echo arous'd in my soul,   20
With the lustrous and drooping star with the countenance full of woe,
With the holders holding my hand nearing the call of the bird,
Comrades mine and I in the midst, and their memory ever to keep, for
    the dead I loved so well,
For the sweetest, wisest soul of all my days and lands—and this for his
    dear sake,
Lilac and star and bird twined with the chant of my soul,   20
There in the fragrant pines and the cedars dusk and dim.

[1865–1866; 1882]

MATTHEW ARNOLD   [1822–1888]

Dover Beach

The sea is calm tonight.
The tide is full, the moon lies fair
Upon the straits; on the French coast the light
Gleams and is gone; the cliffs of England stand,
Glimmering and vast, out in the tranquil bay.
Come to the window, sweet is the night-air!
Only, from the long line of spray
Where the sea meets the moon-blanched land,
Listen! you hear the grating roar
Of pebbles which the waves draw back, and fling,
At their return, up the high strand,
Begin, and cease, and then again begin,
With tremulous cadence slow, and bring
The eternal note of sadness in.

Sophocles long ago
Heard it on the Aegean, and it brought

Into his mind the turbid ebb and flow
Of human misery; we
Find also in the sound a thought,
Hearing it by this distant northern sea.   20

The Sea of Faith
Was once, too, at the full, and round earth's shore
Lay like the folds of a bright girdle furled.
But now I only hear
Its melancholy, long, withdrawing roar,   25
Retreating, to the breath
Of the night-wind, down the vast edges drear
And naked shingles° of the world.   *pebble-covered beaches*

Ah, love, let us be true
To one another! for the world, which seems   30
To lie before us like a land of dreams,
So various, so beautiful, so new,
Hath really neither joy, nor love, nor light,
Nor certitude, nor peace, nor help for pain;
And we are here as on a darkling plain   35
Swept with confused alarms of struggle and flight,
Where ignorant armies clash by night.

[*c. 1851;* 1867]

EMILY DICKINSON   [1830–1886]

Wild Nights — Wild Nights!

Wild Nights — Wild Nights!
Were I with thee
Wild Nights should be
Our luxury!

Futile — the Winds —   5
To a Heart in port —
Done with the Compass —
Done with the Chart!

Rowing in Eden —
Ah, the Sea!
Might I but moor — Tonight —
In Thee!

[c. *1861;* 1891]

EMILY DICKINSON   [1830–1886]

Much Madness is divinest Sense

Much Madness is divinest Sense —
To a discerning Eye —
Much Sense — the starkest Madness —
'Tis the Majority
In this, as All, prevail —
Assent — and you are sane —
Demur — you're straightway dangerous —
And handled with a Chain —

[c. *1862;* 1890]

EMILY DICKINSON   [1830–1886]

I heard a Fly buzz — when I died

I heard a Fly buzz — when I died —
The Stillness in the Room
Was like the Stillness in the Air —
Between the Heaves of Storm —

The Eyes around—had wrung them dry —   5
And Breaths were gathering firm
For that last Onset—when the King
Be witnessed—in the Room —

I willed my Keepsakes—Signed away
What portion of me be   10
Assignable—and then it was
There interposed a Fly —

With Blue—uncertain stumbling Buzz —
Between the light—and me —
And then the Windows failed—and then   15
I could not see to see —

[*c. 1862;* 1890]

EMILY DICKINSON   [1830–1886]

Because I could not
stop for Death

Because I could not stop for Death —
He kindly stopped for me —
The Carriage held but just Ourselves —
And Immortality.

We slowly drove—He knew no haste   5
And I had put away
My labor and my leisure too,
For His Civility —

We passed the School, where Children strove
At Recess—in the Ring —   10
We passed the Fields of Gazing Grain —
We passed the Setting Sun —

Or rather—He passed Us —
The Dews drew quivering and chill —
For only Gossamer, my Gown —   15
My Tippet°—only Tulle° —   *scarf/silk net*

We paused before a House that seemed
A Swelling of the Ground —
The Roof was scarcely visible —
The Cornice—in the Ground —

Since then —'tis Centuries—and yet
Feels shorter than the Day
I first surmised the Horses' Heads
Were toward Eternity —

[c. *1863;* 1890]

EMILY DICKINSON   [1830–1886]

There's a certain Slant of light

There's a certain Slant of light,
Winter Afternoons—
That oppresses, like the Heft
Of Cathedral Tunes—

Heavenly Hurt, it gives us—
We can find no scar,
But internal difference—
Where the Meanings, are—

None may teach it—Any—
'Tis the Seal Despair—
An imperial affliction
Sent us of the Air—

When it comes, the Landscape listens—
Shadows—hold their breath—
When it goes, 'tis like the Distance
On the look of Death—

[c. 1890]

LEWIS CARROLL   [1832–1898]

Jabberwocky°

'Twas brillig, and the slithy toves
   Did gyre and gimble in the wabe;
All mimsy were the borogoves,
   And the mome raths outgrabe.

"Beware the Jabberwock, my son!   5
   The jaws that bite, the claws that catch!
Beware the Jubjub bird, and shun
   The frumious Bandersnatch!"

He took his vorpal sword in hand;
   Long time the manxome foe he sought—   10
So rested he by the Tumtum tree,
   And stood awhile in thought.

And, as in uffish thought he stood,
   The Jabberwock, with eyes of flame,
Came whiffling through the tulgey wood,   15
   And burbled as it came!

One, two! One, two! And through and through
   The vorpal blade went snicker-snack!
He left it dead, and with its head
   He went galumphing back.   20

"And hast thou slain the Jabberwock?
   Come to my arms, my beamish boy!
O frabjous day! Callooh! Callay!"
   He chortled in his joy.

'Twas brillig, and the slithy toves   25
   Did gyre and gimble in the wabe;
All mimsy were the borogoves,
   And the mome raths outgrabe.

[1855; 1871]

Jabberwocky: From *Through the Looking-Glass*, by Lewis Carroll.

THOMAS HARDY   [1840–1928]

The Darkling° Thrush

I leant upon a coppice° gate
  When Frost was spectre-grey,
And Winter's dregs made desolate
  The weakening eye of day.
The tangled bine-stems° scored the sky
  Like strings of broken lyres,
And all mankind that haunted nigh°   *near*
  Had sought their household fires.

The land's sharp features seemed to be
  The Century's corpse outleant,°   1
His crypt the cloudy canopy,
  The wind his death-lament.
The ancient pulse of germ and birth
  Was shrunken hard and dry,
And every spirit upon earth   1
  Seemed fervourless as I.

At once a voice arose among
  The bleak twigs overhead
In a full-hearted evensong
  Of joy illimited;   2
An aged thrush, frail, gaunt, and small,
  In blast-beruffled plume,
Had chosen thus to fling his soul
  Upon the growing gloom.

So little cause for carolings   2
  Of such ecstatic sound

Darkling: In darkness.
1. coppice: A small wood or thicket.
5. bine-stems: The flexible stem of a climbing plant.
10. Century's corpse outleant: Leaning out. The poem, written on December 31, 1900, refers to the demise of the nineteenth century.

Was written on terrestrial things
    Afar or nigh around,
That I could think there trembled through
    His happy good-night air   30
Some blessed Hope, whereof he knew
    And I was unaware.

[*1900;* 1901]

GERARD MANLEY HOPKINS [1844–1889]

God's Grandeur

The world is charged with the grándeur of God.
    It will flame out, like shining from shook foil;°   *shaken gold foil*
    It gathers to a greatness, like the ooze of oil°   *(from olives)*
Crushed. Why do men then now not reck° his rod?°   *recognize/discipline*
Génerátions have trod, have trod, have trod;   5
    And all is seared with trade; bleared, smeared, with toil;
    And wears man's smudge and shares man's smell: the soil
Is bare now, nor can foot feel, being shod.

Ánd, for° all this, náture is never spent;   *despite*
    There lives the dearest freshness deep down things;   10
And though the last lights off the black West went
    Oh, morning, at the brown brink eastward, springs —
Because the Holy Ghost óver the bent
    World broods with warm breast and with ah! bright wings.

[*1877;* 1918]

A. E. HOUSMAN   [1859–1936]

To an Athlete Dying Young

The time you won your town the race
We chaired you through the market-place;
Man and boy stood cheering by,
And home we brought you shoulder-high.

To-day, the road all runners come,
Shoulder-high we bring you home,
And set you at your threshold down,
Townsman of a stiller town.

Smart lad, to slip betimes away
From fields where glory does not stay
And early though the laurel grows
It withers quicker than the rose.

Eyes the shady night has shut
Cannot see the record cut,°   *broken*
And silence sounds no worse than cheers
After earth has stopped the ears:

Now you will not swell the rout
Of lads that wore their honours out,
Runners whom renown outran
And the name died before the man.

So set, before its echoes fade,
The fleet foot on the sill of shade,
And hold to the low lintel up
The still-defended challenge-cup.

And round that early-laurelled head
Will flock to gaze the strengthless dead,
And find unwithered on its curls
The garland briefer than a girl's.

[1896]

498

WILLIAM BUTLER YEATS [1865–1939]

The Lake Isle of Innisfree

I will arise and go now, and go to Innisfree,
And a small cabin build there, of clay and wattles made:
Nine bean-rows will I have there, a hive for the honey-bee,
And live alone in the bee-loud glade.

And I shall have some peace there, for peace comes dropping slow,   5
Dropping from the veils of the morning to where the cricket sings;
There midnight's all a glimmer, and noon a purple glow,
And evening full of the linnet's wings.

I will arise and go now, for always night and day
I hear lake water lapping with low sounds by the shore;   10
While I stand on the roadway, or on the pavements grey,
I hear it in the deep heart's core.

[1892]

WILLIAM BUTLER YEATS [1865–1939]

The Second Coming°

Turning and turning in the widening gyre
The falcon cannot hear the falconer;
Things fall apart; the centre cannot hold;
Mere anarchy is loosed upon the world,
The blood-dimmed tide is loosed, and everywhere
The ceremony of innocence is drowned;
The best lack all conviction, while the worst
Are full of passionate intensity.

Surely some revelation is at hand;
Surely the Second Coming is at hand.
The Second Coming! Hardly are those words out
When a vast image out of *Spiritus Mundi*°
Troubles my sight: somewhere in sands of the desert
A shape with lion body and the head of a man,
A gaze blank and pitiless as the sun,
Is moving its slow thighs, while all about it
Reel shadows of the indignant desert birds.
The darkness drops again; but now I know
That twenty centuries of stony sleep
Were vexed to nightmare by a rocking cradle,
And what rough beast, its hour come round at last,
Slouches towards Bethlehem to be born?

[1921]

The Second Coming: Alludes to Matthew 24:3–44, on the return of Christ at
the end of the present age. Yeats viewed history as a series of 2,000-year cycles
(imaged as gyres, cone-shaped motions). The birth of Christ in Bethlehem brought
to an end the cycle that ran from the Babylonians through the Greeks and Romans.
The approach of the year 2000, then, anticipated for Yeats the end of another era
(the Christian age). Yeats wrote this poem shortly after the Russian Revolution of
1917 (lines 4–8), which may have confirmed his sense of imminent change and of a
new beginning of an unpredictable nature (Yeats expected the new era to be violent
and despotic).
12. *Spiritus Mundi:* The spirit of the universe (Latin). Yeats believed in a Great
Memory, a universal storehouse of symbolic images from the past. Individuals,
drawing on it for images, are put in touch with the soul of the universe.

WILLIAM BUTLER YEATS   [1865–1939]

Leda and the Swan°

A sudden blow: the great wings beating still
Above the staggering girl, her thighs caressed
By the dark webs, her nape caught in his bill,
He holds her helpless breast upon his breast.

How can those terrified vague fingers push   5
The feathered glory from her loosening thighs?
And how can body, laid in that white rush,
But feel the strange heart beating where it lies?

A shudder in the loins engenders there
The broken wall, the burning roof and tower   10
And Agamemnon dead.
                Being so caught up,
So mastered by the brute blood of the air,
Did she put on his knowledge with his power
Before the indifferent beak could let her drop?

[1928]

Leda and the Swan: In Greek mythology, Leda was seduced (or raped) by Zeus,
who approached her in the form of a swan. She gave birth to Helen, whose
abduction by Paris gave rise to the Trojan War (referred to in line 10). The Greek
forces were headed by Agamemnon, who was killed (line 11) upon his return to
Greece by his wife, Clytemnestra, daughter of Leda by her husband, Tyndareus.
Yeats regarded Zeus's visit as a "violent annunciation" of the founding of Greek
civilization, with parallels to the annunciation to Mary (Luke 1:26–38), 2,000
years later, of the coming of the Christian age. See the note to "The Second
Coming" for Yeats's view of historical eras (p. 504).

EDWIN ARLINGTON ROBINSON [1869–1935]

Richard Cory

Whenever Richard Cory went down town,
We people on the pavement looked at him:
He was a gentleman from sole to crown,
Clean favored, and imperially slim.

And he was always quietly arrayed,
And he was always human when he talked;
But still he fluttered pulses when he said,
"Good-morning," and he glittered when he walked.

And he was rich — yes, richer than a king —
And admirably schooled in every grace:
In fine, we thought that he was everything
To make us wish that we were in his place.

So on we worked, and waited for the light,
And went without the meat, and cursed the bread;
And Richard Cory, one calm summer night,
Went home and put a bullet through his head.

[1897]

PAUL LAURENCE DUNBAR [1872–1906]

We Wear the Mask

We wear the mask that grins and lies,
It hides our cheeks and shades our eyes, —
This debt we pay to human guile;
With torn and bleeding hearts we smile,
And mouth with myriad subtleties.

Why should the world be over-wise,
In counting all our tears and sighs?
Nay, let them only see us, while
   We wear the mask.

We smile, but, O great Christ, our cries   10
To thee from tortured souls arise.
We sing, but oh the clay is vile
Beneath our feet, and long the mile;
But let the world dream otherwise,
   We wear the mask!   15

[1896]

ROBERT FROST   [1874–1963]

After Apple-Picking

My long two-pointed ladder's sticking through a tree
Toward heaven still,
And there's a barrel that I didn't fill
Beside it, and there may be two or three
Apples I didn't pick upon some bough.   5
But I am done with apple-picking now.
Essence of winter sleep is on the night,
The scent of apples: I am drowsing off.
I cannot rub the strangeness from my sight
I got from looking through a pane of glass   10
I skimmed this morning from the drinking trough
And held against the world of hoary grass.
It melted, and I let it fall and break.
But I was well
Upon my way to sleep before it fell,   15
And I could tell
What form my dreaming was about to take.
Magnified apples appear and disappear,
Stem end and blossom end,
And every fleck of russet showing clear.   20
My instep arch not only keeps the ache,

It keeps the pressure of a ladder-round.
I feel the ladder sway as the boughs bend.
And I keep hearing from the cellar bin
The rumbling sound
Of load on load of apples coming in.
For I have had too much
Of apple-picking: I am overtired
Of the great harvest I myself desired.
There were ten thousand thousand fruit to touch,
Cherish in hand, lift down, and not let fall.
For all
That struck the earth,
No matter if not bruised or spiked with stubble,
Went surely to the cider-apple heap
As of no worth.
One can see what will trouble
This sleep of mine, whatever sleep it is.
Were he not gone,
The woodchuck could say whether it's like his
Long sleep, as I describe its coming on,
Or just some human sleep.

[1914]

ROBERT FROST   [1874–1963]

The Road Not Taken

Two roads diverged in a yellow wood,
And sorry I could not travel both
And be one traveler, long I stood
And looked down one as far as I could
To where it bent in the undergrowth;

Then took the other, as just as fair,
And having perhaps the better claim,
Because it was grassy and wanted wear;
Though as for that, the passing there
Had worn them really about the same,

And both that morning equally lay
In leaves no step had trodden black.
Oh, I kept the first for another day!
Yet knowing how way leads on to way,
I doubted if I should ever come back.   15

I shall be telling this with a sigh
Somewhere ages and ages hence:
Two roads diverged in a wood, and I —
I took the one less traveled by,
And that has made all the difference.   20

[1916]

ROBERT FROST   [1874–1963]

Stopping by Woods on a Snowy Evening

Whose woods these are I think I know.
His house is in the village, though;
He will not see me stopping here
To watch his woods fill up with snow.

My little horse must think it queer   5
To stop without a farmhouse near
Between the woods and frozen lake
The darkest evening of the year.

He gives his harness bells a shake
To ask if there is some mistake.   10
The only other sound's the sweep
Of easy wind and downy flake.

The woods are lovely, dark, and deep,
But I have promises to keep,
And miles to go before I sleep,   15
And miles to go before I sleep.

[1923]

ROBERT FROST   [1874–1963]

Acquainted with the Night

I have been one acquainted with the night.
I have walked out in rain—and back in rain.
I have outwalked the furthest city light.

I have looked down the saddest city lane.
I have passed by the watchman on his beat
And dropped my eyes, unwilling to explain.

I have stood still and stopped the sound of feet
When far away an interrupted cry
Came over houses from another street,

But not to call me back or say good-bye;
And further still at an unearthly height,
One luminary clock against the sky

Proclaimed the time was neither wrong nor right.
I have been one acquainted with the night.

[1928]

WALLACE STEVENS   [1879–1955]

Thirteen Ways of Looking
at a Blackbird

I

Among twenty snowy mountains,
The only moving thing
Was the eye of the blackbird.

II

I was of three minds,
Like a tree   5
In which there are three blackbirds.

III

The blackbird whirled in the autumn winds.
It was a small part of the pantomime.

a dramatic entertainment

IV

A man and a woman
Are one.   10
A man and a woman and a blackbird
Are one.

V

I do not know which to prefer,
The beauty of inflections
Or the beauty of innuendoes,   15
The blackbird whistling
Or just after.

allusive remark

VI

Icicles filled the long window
With barbaric glass.
The shadow of the blackbird   20
Crossed it, to and fro.
The mood
Traced in the shadow
An indecipherable cause.

VII

O thin men of Haddam,°   25
Why do you imagine golden birds?
Do you not see how the blackbird
Walks around the feet
Of the women about you?

25. Haddam: A town in Connecticut.

VIII

I know noble accents
And lucid, inescapable rhythms;
But I know, too,
That the blackbird is involved
In what I know.

IX

When the blackbird flew out of sight,
It marked the edge
Of one of many circles.

X

At the sight of blackbirds
Flying in a green light,
Even the bawds of euphony
Would cry out sharply.

XI

He rode over Connecticut
In a glass coach.
Once, a fear pierced him,
In that he mistook
The shadow of his equipage
For blackbirds.

XII

The river is moving.
The blackbird must be flying.

XIII

It was evening all afternoon.
It was snowing
And it was going to snow.
The blackbird sat
In the cedar-limbs.

[1917]

The Emperor of Ice-Cream

Call the roller of big cigars,
The muscular one, and bid him whip
In kitchen cups concupiscent curds.
Let the wenches dawdle in such dress
As they are used to wear, and let the boys   5
Bring flowers in last month's newspapers.
Let be be finale of seem.
The only emperor is the emperor of ice-cream.

Take from the dresser of deal,°
Lacking the three glass knobs, that sheet   10
On which she embroidered fantails once
And spread it so as to cover her face.
If her horny feet protrude, they come
To show how cold she is, and dumb.
Let the lamp affix its beam.   15
The only emperor is the emperor of ice-cream.

[1923]

9. **deal:** Fir or pine wood.

GEORGIA DOUGLAS JOHNSON   [1880–1966]

Common Dust

And who shall separate the dust
Which later we shall be:
Whose keen discerning eye will scan
And solve the mystery?

509

The high, the low, the rich, the poor,
The black, the white, the red,
And all the chromatique between,
Of whom shall it be said:

Here lies the dust of Africa;
Here are the sons of Rome;
Here lies one unlabelled
The world at large his home!

Can one then separate the dust,
Will mankind lie apart,
When life has settled back again
The same as from the start?

[1920s]

MINA LOY   [1882–1966]

Moreover, the Moon—

Face of the skies
preside
over our wonder.

Fluorescent
truant of heaven
draw us under.

Silver, circular corpse
your decease
infects us with unendurable ease,

touching nerve-terminals
to thermal icicles

Coercive as coma, frail as bloom
innuendoes of your inverse dawn
suffuse the self;
our every corpuscle become an elf.

[1923]

WILLIAM CARLOS WILLIAMS   [1883–1963]

The Red Wheelbarrow

so much depends
upon

a red wheel
barrow

glazed with rain   5
water

beside the white
chickens.

[1923]

WILLIAM CARLOS WILLIAMS   [1883–1963]

This Is Just to Say

I have eaten
the plums
that were in
the icebox

and which   5
you were probably
saving
for breakfast

Forgive me
they were delicious   10
so sweet
and so cold

[1934]

The River-Merchant's Wife: A Letter

While my hair was still cut straight across my forehead
I played about the front gate, pulling flowers.
You came by on bamboo stilts, playing horse,
You walked about my seat, playing with blue plums.
And we went on living in the village of Chokan:
Two small people, without dislike or suspicion.

At fourteen I married My Lord you.
I never laughed, being bashful.
Lowering my head, I looked at the wall.
Called to, a thousand times, I never looked back.

At fifteen I stopped scowling,
I desired my dust to be mingled with yours
Forever and forever and forever.
Why should I climb the look out?

At sixteen you departed,
You went into far Ku-to-yen, by the river of swirling eddies,
And you have been gone five months.
The monkeys make sorrowful noise overhead.

You dragged your feet when you went out.
By the gate now, the moss is grown, the different mosses,
Too deep to clear them away!
The leaves fall early this autumn, in wind.
The paired butterflies are already yellow with August
Over the grass in the West garden;
They hurt me. I grow older.
If you are coming down through the narrows of the river Kiang,

Please let me know beforehand,
And I will come out to meet you
            As far as Cho-fu-Sa.

                             By Rihaku°

                               [1915]

By Rihaku: An adaptation of a Chinese poem by the famous poet Li Po
(701–762 C.E.), whose Japanese name is Rihaku.

EZRA POUND [1885–1972]

In a Station of the Metro°

The apparition of these faces in the crowd;
Petals on a wet, black bough.

                             [*1913;* 1916]

Metro: Paris subway.

H. D. (HILDA DOOLITTLE) [1886–1961]

Helen°

All Greece hates
the still eyes in the white face,
the lustre as of olives

Helen: In Greek mythology, Helen of Troy is described as the most beautiful
woman in the world. According to many narratives, including Homer's *Illiad*, she
is the daughter of Zeus and Leda and wife to the great warrior Menelaus. Helen
was abducted by Paris, the Prince of Troy, and the Trojan War was fought in
order to bring her back to Sparta.

where she stands,
and the white hands.

All Greece reviles
the wan face when she smiles,
hating it deeper still
when it grows wan and white,
remembering past enchantments
and past ills.

Greece sees, unmoved,
God's daughter, born of love,
the beauty of cool feet
and slenderest knees,
could love indeed the maid,
only if she were laid,
white ash amid funereal cypresses.

[1923]

MARIANNE MOORE   [1887–1972]

Poetry

I, too, dislike it: there are things that are important beyond all this fiddle.
 Reading it, however, with a perfect contempt for it, one discovers in
 it after all, a place for the genuine.
  Hands that can grasp, eyes
  that can dilate, hair that can rise
   if it must, these things are important not because a

high-sounding interpretation can be put upon them but because they are
 useful. When they become so derivative as to become unintelligible,
 the same thing may be said for all of us, that we
  do not admire what
  we cannot understand: the bat
   holding on upside down or in quest of something to

eat, elephants pushing, a wild horse taking a roll, a tireless wolf under
 a tree, the immovable critic twitching his skin like a horse that feels a
                    flea, the base-

ball fan, the statistician—case after case   15
    could be cited did
    one wish it; nor is it valid
        to discriminate against "business documents and

school-books"; all these phenomena are important. One must make a
        distinction
    however: when dragged into prominence by half poets, the result is not
            poetry,   20
nor till the poets among us can be
    "literalists of
    the imagination"—above
        insolence and triviality and can present

for inspection, "imaginary gardens with real toads in them," shall we have   25
    it. In the meantime, if you demand on the one hand,
    the raw material of poetry in
        all its rawness and
        that which is on the other hand
            genuine, you are interested in poetry.

                                                                        [1921]

T. S. ELIOT [1888–1965]

The Love Song of J. Alfred Prufrock

*S'io credesse che mia risposta fosse
A persona che mai tornasse al mondo,
Questa fiamma staria senza piu scosse.
Ma perciocche giammai di questo fondo
Non torno vivo alcun, s'i'odo il vero,
Senza tema d'infamia ti rispondo.*°

Let us go then, you and I,
When the evening is spread out against the sky
Like a patient etherised upon a table;
Let us go, through certain half-deserted streets,
The muttering retreats
Of restless nights in one-night cheap hotels
And sawdust restaurants with oyster-shells:
Streets that follow like a tedious argument
Of insidious intent
To lead you to an overwhelming question . . .   1
Oh, do not ask, "What is it?"
Let us go and make our visit.

In the room the women come and go
Talking of Michelangelo.

The yellow fog that rubs its back upon the window-panes,   1
The yellow smoke that rubs its muzzle on the window-panes
Licked its tongue into the corners of the evening,

Epigraph: "If I thought that my answer were being made to someone who would ever return to earth, this flame would remain without further movement; but since no one has ever returned alive from this depth, if what I hear is true, I answer you without fear of infamy" (Dante, *Inferno* 27.61–66). Dante encounters Guido de Montefeltro in the eighth circle of hell, where souls are trapped within flames (tongues of fire) as punishment for giving evil counsel. Guido tells Dante details about his evil life only because he assumes that Dante is on his way to an even deeper circle in hell and will never return to earth and be able to repeat what he has heard.

Lingered upon the pools that stand in drains,
Let fall upon its back the soot that falls from chimneys,
Slipped by the terrace, made a sudden leap,   20
And seeing that it was a soft October night,
Curled once about the house, and fell asleep.

    And indeed there will be time
For the yellow smoke that slides along the street,
Rubbing its back upon the window-panes;   25
There will be time, there will be time
To prepare a face to meet the faces that you meet;
There will be time to murder and create,
And time for all the works and days° of hands
That lift and drop a question on your plate;   30
Time for you and time for me,
And time yet for a hundred indecisions,
And for a hundred visions and revisions,
Before the taking of a toast and tea.

    In the room the women come and go   35
Talking of Michelangelo.

    And indeed there will be time
To wonder, "Do I dare?" and, "Do I dare?"
Time to turn back and descend the stair,
With a bald spot in the middle of my hair —   40
(They will say: "How his hair is growing thin!")
My morning coat, my collar mounting firmly to the chin,
My necktie rich and modest, but asserted by a simple pin —
(They will say: "But how his arms and legs are thin!")
Do I dare   45
Disturb the universe?
In a minute there is time
For decisions and revisions which a minute will reverse.

    For I have known them all already, known them all: —
Have known the evenings, mornings, afternoons,   50
I have measured out my life with coffee spoons;
I know the voices dying with a dying fall°

---

29. **works and days:** *Works and Days* is the title of a didactic poem about farming by the Greek poet Hesiod (eighth century B.C.E.) that includes instruction about doing each task at the proper time.

52. **a dying fall:** An allusion to Shakespeare's *Twelfth Night* (1.1.4): "That strain [of music] again! It had a dying fall" (a cadence that falls away).

Beneath the music from a farther room.
　So how should I presume?

And I have known the eyes already, known them all —   5
The eyes that fix you in a formulated phrase,
And when I am formulated, sprawling on a pin,
When I am pinned and wriggling on the wall,
Then how should I begin
To spit out all the butt-ends of my days and ways?   6
　And how should I presume?

And I have known the arms already, known them all —
Arms that are braceleted and white and bare
(But in the lamplight, downed with light brown hair!)
Is it perfume from a dress   6
That makes me so digress?
Arms that lie along a table, or wrap about a shawl.
　And should I then presume?
　And how should I begin?

　　　·　·　·

Shall I say, I have gone at dusk through narrow streets   7
And watched the smoke that rises from the pipes
Of lonely men in shirt-sleeves, leaning out of windows? . . .

I should have been a pair of ragged claws
Scuttling across the floors of silent seas.

　　　·　·　·

And the afternoon, the evening, sleeps so peacefully!   7
Smoothed by long fingers,
Asleep . . . tired . . . or it malingers,
Stretched on the floor, here beside you and me.
Should I, after tea and cakes and ices,
Have the strength to force the moment to its crisis?   8
But though I have wept and fasted, wept and prayed,
Though I have seen my head (grown slightly bald) brought in upon a
　　platter,°
I am no prophet — and here's no great matter;
I have seen the moment of my greatness flicker,
And I have seen the eternal Footman hold my coat, and snicker,   8
And in short, I was afraid.

82. head . . . platter: As a reward for dancing before King Herod, Salome, his
stepdaughter, asked for the head of John the Baptist to be presented to her on a
platter (Matthew 14:1–12; Mark 6:17–28).

And would it have been worth it, after all,
After the cups, the marmalade, the tea,
Among the porcelain, among some talk of you and me,
Would it have been worth while,   90
To have bitten off the matter with a smile,
To have squeezed the universe into a ball
To roll it toward some overwhelming question,
To say: "I am Lazarus,° come from the dead,
Come back to tell you all, I shall tell you all" —   95
If one, settling a pillow by her head,
    Should say: "That is not what I meant at all.
    That is not it, at all."

    And would it have been worth it, after all,
Would it have been worth while,   100
After the sunsets and the dooryards and the sprinkled streets,
After the novels, after the teacups, after the skirts that trail along the
    floor —
And this, and so much more? —
It is impossible to say just what I mean!
But as if a magic lantern threw the nerves in patterns on a screen: 105
Would it have been worth while
If one, settling a pillow or throwing off a shawl,
And turning toward the window, should say:
    "That is not it at all,
    That is not what I meant, at all."   110

          •   •   •

No! I am not Prince Hamlet, nor was meant to be;
Am an attendant lord, one that will do
To swell a progress,° start a scene or two,
Advise the prince; no doubt, an easy tool,
Deferential, glad to be of use,   115
Politic, cautious, and meticulous;
Full of high sentence,° but a bit obtuse;   *sententiousness*
At times, indeed, almost ridiculous —
Almost, at times, the Fool.

    I grow old . . . I grow old . . .   120
I shall wear the bottoms of my trousers rolled.°   *turned up, with cuffs*

---

94. Lazarus: Either the beggar Lazarus, who in Luke 16:19–31 did not return
from the dead, or Jesus' friend Lazarus, who did (John 11:1–44).
113. progress: Ceremonial journey made by a royal court.

Shall I part my hair behind? Do I dare to eat a peach?
I shall wear white flannel trousers, and walk upon the beach.
I have heard the mermaids singing, each to each.

I do not think that they will sing to me.   12

I have seen them riding seaward on the waves
Combing the white hair of the waves blown back
When the wind blows the water white and black.

We have lingered in the chambers of the sea
By sea-girls wreathed with seaweed red and brown   13
Till human voices wake us, and we drown.

[1915]

CLAUDE McKAY   [1890–1948]

America

Although she feeds me bread of bitterness,
And sinks into my throat her tiger's tooth,
Stealing my breath of life, I will confess
I love this cultured hell that tests my youth!
Her vigor flows like tides into my blood,
Giving me strength erect against her hate.
Her bigness sweeps my being like a flood.
Yet as a rebel fronts a king in state,
I stand within her walls with not a shred
Of terror, malice, not a word of jeer.
Darkly I gaze into the days ahead,
And see her might and granite wonders there,
Beneath the touch of Time's unerring hand,
Like priceless treasures sinking in the sand.

[1922]

EDNA ST. VINCENT MILLAY   [1892–1950]

What lips my lips have kissed

What lips my lips have kissed, and where, and why,
I have forgotten, and what arms have lain
Under my head till morning; but the rain
Is full of ghosts tonight, that tap and sigh
Upon the glass and listen for reply,   5
And in my heart there stirs a quiet pain
For unremembered lads that not again
Will turn to me at midnight with a cry.
Thus in the winter stands the lonely tree,
Nor knows what birds have vanished one by one,   10
Yet knows its boughs more silent than before:
I cannot say what loves have come and gone,
I only know that summer sang in me
A little while, that in me sings no more.

[1941]

WILFRED OWEN   [1893–1918]

Dulce et Decorum Est

Bent double, like old beggars under sacks,
Knock-kneed, coughing like hags, we cursed through sludge,
Till on the haunting flares we turned our backs
And towards our distant rest began to trudge.
Men marched asleep. Many had lost their boots   5
But limped on, blood-shod. All went lame; all blind;
Drunk with fatigue; deaf even to the hoots
Of tired, outstripped Five-Nines° that dropped behind.

8. Five-Nines: 5.9-inch caliber shells.

521

Gas! GAS! Quick, boys!—An ecstasy of fumbling,
Fitting the clumsy helmets just in time;   1
But someone still was yelling out and stumbling
And flound'ring like a man in fire or lime . . .
Dim, through the misty panes° and thick green light,   *of a gas mask*
As under a green sea, I saw him drowning.

In all my dreams, before my helpless sight,   1
He plunges at me, guttering, choking, drowning.

If in some smothering dreams you too could pace
Behind the wagon that we flung him in,
And watch the white eyes writhing in his face,
His hanging face, like a devil's sick of sin;   2
If you could hear, at every jolt, the blood
Come gargling from the froth-corrupted lungs,
Obscene as cancer, bitter as the cud
Of vile, incurable sores on innocent tongues,—
My friend, you would not tell with such high zest   2
To children ardent for some desperate glory,
The old Lie: Dulce et decorum est
Pro patria mori.°

                                                                      [1920]

27–28. Dulce . . . mori: It is sweet and fitting/to die for one's country (Horace,
Odes 3.12.13).

DOROTHY PARKER   [1893–1967]

Résumé

Razors pain you;
Rivers are damp;
Acids stain you;
And drugs cause cramp.
Guns aren't lawful;
Nooses give;   5
Gas smells awful;
You might as well live.

                                                                      [1926]

E. E. CUMMINGS [1894–1962]

in Just-

in Just-
spring   when the world is mud-
luscious the little
lame balloonman

whistles   far   and wee   5

and eddieandbill come
running from marbles and
piracies and it's
spring

when the world is puddle-wonderful   10

the queer
old balloonman whistles
far   and   wee
and bettyandisbel come dancing

from hop-scotch and jump-rope and   15

it's
spring
and
  the

    goat-footed   20

balloonMan   whistles
far
and
wee

[1923]

E. E. CUMMINGS [1894–1962]

"next to of course god america i

"next to of course god america i
love you land of the pilgrims' and so forth oh
say can you see by the dawn's early my
country 'tis of centuries come and go
and are no more what of it we should worry
in every language even deafanddumb
thy sons acclaim your glorious name by gorry
by jingo by gee by gosh by gum
why talk of beauty what could be more beautiful than these heroic happy dead
who rushed like lions to the roaring slaughter
they did not stop to think they died instead
then shall the voice of liberty be mute?"

He spoke.   And drank rapidly a glass of water

[1926]

LANGSTON HUGHES   [1902–1967]

Theme for English B

The instructor said,

> *Go home and write*
> *a page tonight.*
> *And let that page come out of you—*
> *Then, it will be true.*

I wonder if it's that simple?
I am twenty-two, colored, born in Winston-Salem.

524

I went to school there, then Durham, then here
to this college on the hill above Harlem.
I am the only colored student in my class.   10
The steps from the hill lead down into Harlem,
through a park, then I cross St. Nicholas,
Eighth Avenue, Seventh, and I come to the Y,
the Harlem Branch Y, where I take the elevator
up to my room, sit down, and write this page: 15

It's not easy to know what is true for you or me
at twenty-two, my age. But I guess I'm what
I feel and see and hear, Harlem, I hear you:
hear you, hear me—we two—you, me, talk on this page.
(I hear New York, too.) Me—who?   20
Well, I like to eat, sleep, drink, and be in love.
I like to work, read, learn, and understand life.
I like a pipe for a Christmas present,
or records—Bessie, bop, or Bach.
I guess being colored doesn't make me *not* like   25
the same things other folks like who are other races.
So will my page be colored that I write?
Being me, it will not be white.
But it will be
a part of you, instructor.   30
You are white—
yet a part of me, as I am a part of you.
That's American.
Sometimes perhaps you don't want to be a part of me.
Nor do I often want to be a part of you.   35
But we are, that's true!
As I learn from you,
I guess you learn from me—
although you're older—and white—
and somewhat more free.   40

This is my page for English B.

[1949]

LANGSTON HUGHES   [1902–1967]

The Negro Speaks of Rivers

I've known rivers:
I've known rivers ancient as the world and older than the
      flow of human blood in human veins.

My soul has grown deep like the rivers.

I bathed in the Euphrates when dawns were young.
I built my hut near the Congo and it lulled me to sleep.
I looked upon the Nile and raised the pyramids above it.
I heard the singing of the Mississippi when Abe Lincoln
      went down to New Orleans,° and I've seen its muddy
      bosom turn all golden in the sunset

I've known rivers:
Ancient, dusky rivers.

My soul has grown deep like the rivers.

[*1921*; 1926]

8–9. Abe Lincoln . . . New Orleans: Abraham Lincoln observed the slave trade
firsthand during boat trips on the Mississippi River in 1828 and 1831.

LANGSTON HUGHES   [1902–1967]

The Weary Blues

Droning a drowsy syncopated tune,
Rocking back and forth to a mellow croon,
    I heard a Negro play.
Down on Lenox Avenue the other night

By the pale dull pallor of an old gas light   5
   He did a lazy sway. . . .
   He did a lazy sway. . . .
To the tune o' those Weary Blues.
With his ebony hands on each ivory key.
He made that poor piano moan with melody.   10
   O Blues!
Swaying to and fro on his rickety stool
He played that sad raggy tune like a musical fool.
   Sweet Blues!
Coming from a black man's soul.   15
   O Blues!
In a deep song voice with a melancholy tone
I heard that Negro sing, that old piano moan—
   "Ain't got nobody in all this world,
   Ain't got nobody but ma self.   20
   I's gwine to quit ma frownin'
   And put ma troubles on de shelf."
Thump, thump, thump, went his foot on the floor.
He played a few chords then he sang some more—
   "I got de Weary Blues   25
   And I can't be satisfied.
   Got de Weary Blues
   And can't be satisfied—
   I ain't happy no mo'
   And I wish that I had died."   30
And far into the night he crooned that tune.
The stars went out and so did the moon.
The singer stopped playing and went to bed.
While the Weary Blues echoes through his head
He slept like a rock or a man that's dead.   35

[1932]

LANGSTON HUGHES   [1902–1967]

Harlem

What happens to a dream deferred?

> Does it dry up
> like a raisin in the sun?
> Or fester like a sore —
> And then run?
> Does it stink like rotten meat?
> Or crust and sugar over —
> like a syrupy sweet?

> Maybe it just sags
> like a heavy load.

> *Or does it explode?*

[1951]

STEVIE SMITH   [1902–1971]

Not Waving but Drowning

Nobody heard him, the dead man,
But still he lay moaning:
I was much further out than you thought
And not waving but drowning.

Poor chap, he always loved larking°
And now he's dead

5. **larking:** Playing tricks; frolicking.

It must have been too cold for him his heart gave way,
They said.

Oh, no no no, it was too cold always
(Still the dead one lay moaning)   10
I was much too far out all my life
And not waving but drowning.

[1957]

COUNTEE CULLEN   [1903–1946]

Incident

for Eric Walrond

Once riding in old Baltimore,
   Heart-filled, head-filled with glee,
I saw a Baltimorean
   Keep looking straight at me.

Now I was eight and very small,   5
   And he was no whit bigger,
And so I smiled, but he poked out
   His tongue, and called me, "Nigger."

I saw the whole of Baltimore
   From May until December;   10
Of all the things that happened there
   That's all that I remember.

[1925]

W. H. AUDEN   [1907–1973]

[Funeral Blues]

Stop all the clocks, cut off the telephone,
Prevent the dog from barking with a juicy bone,
Silence the pianos and with muffled drum
Bring out the coffin, let the mourners come.

Let aeroplanes circle moaning overhead
Scribbling on the sky the message He Is Dead,
Put crêpe bows round the white necks of the public doves,
Let the traffic policemen wear black cotton gloves.

He was my North, my South, my East and West,
My working week and my Sunday rest,
My noon, my midnight, my talk, my song;
I thought that love would last for ever: I was wrong.

The stars are not wanted now; put out every one:
Pack up the moon and dismantle the sun;
Pour away the ocean and sweep up the woods:
For nothing now can ever come to any good.

[1936]

W. H. AUDEN [1907–1973]

Musée des Beaux Arts°

About suffering they were never wrong,
The Old Masters: how well they understood
Its human position; how it takes place
While someone else is eating or opening a window or just walking dully
    along;
How, when the aged are reverently, passionately waiting   5
For the miraculous birth, there always must be
Children who did not specially want it to happen, skating
On a pond at the edge of the wood:
They never forgot
That even the dreadful martyrdom must run its course   10
Anyhow in a corner, some untidy spot
Where the dogs go on with their doggy life and the torturer's horse
Scratches its innocent behind on a tree.
In Brueghel's *Icarus*,° for instance: how everything turns away
Quite leisurely from the disaster; the ploughman may   15
Have heard the splash, the forsaken cry,
But for him it was not an important failure; the sun shone
As it had to on the white legs disappearing into the green
Water; and the expensive delicate ship that must have seen
Something amazing, a boy falling out of the sky,   20
Had somewhere to get to and sailed calmly on.

[1940]

Musée des Beaux Arts: The painting *Landscape with the Fall of Icarus* by Pieter Brueghel the Elder, on which the poem is based, is in the Musées Royaux des Beaux-Arts in Brussels.
14. Icarus: In Greek mythology, Daedalus and his son Icarus were imprisoned by King Minos of Crete. In order to escape, Daedalus created a pair of enormous wings for himself and for his son. He advised Icarus to not fly too close to the sun, as the wax that held the wings together would melt. Icarus forgot his father's advice, and when the wax melted, he fell into the ocean and drowned.

THEODORE ROETHKE   [1908–1963]

My Papa's Waltz

The whiskey on your breath
Could make a small boy dizzy;
But I hung on like death:
Such waltzing was not easy.

We romped until the pans
Slid from the kitchen shelf;
My mother's countenance
Could not unfrown itself.

The hand that held my wrist
Was battered on one knuckle;
At every step you missed
My right ear scraped a buckle.

You beat time on my head
With a palm caked hard by dirt,
Then waltzed me off to bed
Still clinging to your shirt.

[1948]

GEORGE OPPEN   [1908–1984]

Psalm

Veritas sequitur° . . .

In the small beauty of the forest
The wild deer bedding down—
That they are there!

   Their eyes
Effortless, the soft lips   5
Nuzzle and the alien small teeth
Tear at the grass

   The roots of it
Dangle from their mouths
Scattering earth in the strange woods.   10
They who are there.

   Their paths
Nibbled thru the fields, the leaves that shade them
Hang in the distances
Of sun   15

   The small nouns
Crying faith
In this in which the wild deer
Startle, and stare out.

         [1965]

Veritas sequitur: Truth follows (Latin).

533

ELIZABETH BISHOP   [1911–1979]

The Fish

I caught a tremendous fish
and held him beside the boat
half out of water, with my hook
fast in a corner of his mouth.
He didn't fight.
He hadn't fought at all.
He hung a grunting weight,
battered and venerable
and homely. Here and there
his brown skin hung in strips
like ancient wallpaper,
and its pattern of darker brown
was like wallpaper:
shapes like full-blown roses
stained and lost through age.
He was speckled with barnacles,
fine rosettes of lime,
and infested
with tiny white sea-lice,
and underneath two or three
rags of green weed hung down.
While his gills were breathing in
the terrible oxygen
— the frightening gills,
fresh and crisp with blood,
that can cut so badly —
I thought of the coarse white flesh
packed in like feathers,
the big bones and the little bones,
the dramatic reds and blacks
of his shiny entrails,
and the pink swim-bladder
like a big peony.
I looked into his eyes
which were far larger than mine

but shallower, and yellowed,
the irises backed and packed
with tarnished tinfoil
seen through the lenses
of old scratched isinglass.°   *transparent sheet of mica*   40
They shifted a little, but not
to return my stare.
— It was more like the tipping
of an object toward the light.
I admired his sullen face,   45
the mechanism of his jaw,
and then I saw
that from his lower lip
— if you could call it a lip —
grim, wet, and weaponlike,   50
hung five old pieces of fish-line,
or four and a wire leader
with the swivel still attached,
with all their five big hooks
grown firmly in his mouth.   55
A green line, frayed at the end
where he broke it, two heavier lines,
and a fine black thread
still crimped from the strain and snap
when it broke and he got away.   60
Like medals with their ribbons
frayed and wavering,
a five-haired beard of wisdom
trailing from his aching jaw.
I stared and stared   65
and victory filled up
the little rented boat,
from the pool of bilge
where oil had spread a rainbow
around the rusted engine   70
to the bailer rusted orange,
the sun-cracked thwarts,
the oarlocks on their strings,
the gunnels—until everything
was rainbow, rainbow, rainbow!   75
And I let the fish go.

[1946]

ELIZABETH BISHOP   [1911–1979]

One Art

The art of losing isn't hard to master;
so many things seem filled with the intent
to be lost that their loss is no disaster.

Lose something every day. Accept the fluster
of lost door keys, the hour badly spent.
The art of losing isn't hard to master.

Then practice losing farther, losing faster:
places, and names, and where it was you meant
to travel. None of these will bring disaster.

I lost my mother's watch. And look! my last, or
next-to-last, of three loved houses went.
The art of losing isn't hard to master.

I lost two cities, lovely ones. And, vaster,
some realms I owned, two rivers, a continent.
I miss them, but it wasn't a disaster.

— Even losing you (the joking voice, a gesture
I love) I shan't have lied. It's evident
the art of losing's not too hard to master
though it may look like (*Write it!*) like disaster.

[1976]

ROBERT HAYDEN   [1913–1980]

Those Winter Sundays

Sundays too my father got up early
and put his clothes on in the blueblack cold,
then with cracked hands that ached
from labor in the weekday weather made
banked fires blaze. No one ever thanked him.   5

I'd wake and hear the cold splintering, breaking.
When the rooms were warm, he'd call,
and slowly I would rise and dress,
fearing the chronic angers of that house,

Speaking indifferently to him,   10
who had driven out the cold
and polished my good shoes as well.
What did I know, what did I know
of love's austere and lonely offices?

[1962]

MURIEL RUKEYSER   [1913–1980]

Waiting for Icarus°

He said he would be back and we'd drink wine together
He said that everything would be better than before
He said we were on the edge of a new relation
He said he would never again cringe before his father
He said that he was going to invent full-time   5
He said he loved me that going into me

Icarus: See note to W. H. Auden's "Musée des Beaux Arts" on p. 531.

537

He said was going into the world and the sky
He said all the buckles were very firm
He said the wax was the best wax
He said Wait for me here on the beach   1
He said Just don't cry

I remember the gulls and the waves
I remember the islands going dark on the sea
I remember the girls laughing
I remember they said he only wanted to get away from me   1
I remember mother saying : Inventors are like poets,
                                       a trashy lot
I remember she told me those who try out inventions are worse
I remember she added : Women who love such are the worst of all
I have been waiting all day, or perhaps longer.   2
I would have liked to try those wings myself.
It would have been better than this.

                                                              [1973]

DUDLEY RANDALL   [1914–2000]

Ballad of Birmingham

On the bombing of a church in Birmingham, Alabama, 1963

"Mother dear, may I go downtown
Instead of out to play,
And march the streets of Birmingham
In a Freedom March today?"

"No, baby, no, you may not go,
For the dogs are fierce and wild,
And clubs and hoses, guns and jails
Aren't good for a little child."

"But, mother, I won't be alone.
Other children will go with me,   1
And march the streets of Birmingham
To make our country free."

"No, baby, no, you may not go,
For I fear those guns will fire.
But you may go to church instead   15
And sing in the children's choir."

She has combed and brushed her night-dark hair,
And bathed rose petal sweet,
And drawn white gloves on her small brown hands,
And white shoes on her feet.   20

The mother smiled to know her child
Was in the sacred place,
But that smile was the last smile
To come upon her face.

For when she heard the explosion,   25
Her eyes grew wet and wild.
She raced through the streets of Birmingham
Calling for her child.

She clawed through bits of glass and brick,
Then lifted out a shoe.   30
"Oh, here's the shoe my baby wore,
But, baby, where are you?"

[1969]

WILLIAM STAFFORD   [1914–1995]

Traveling through the Dark

Traveling through the dark I found a deer
dead on the edge of the Wilson River road.
It is usually best to roll them into the canyon:
that road is narrow; to swerve might make more dead.

By glow of the tail-light I stumbled back of the car   5
and stood by the heap, a doe, a recent killing;
she had stiffened already, almost cold.
I dragged her off; she was large in the belly.

My fingers touching her side brought me the reason —
her side was warm; her fawn lay there waiting,
alive, still, never to be born.
Beside that mountain road I hesitated.

The car aimed ahead its lowered parking lights;
under the hood purred the steady engine.
I stood in the glare of the warm exhaust turning red;
around our group I could hear the wilderness listen.

I thought hard for us all—my only swerving—,
then pushed her over the edge into the river.

[1962]

DYLAN THOMAS   [1914–1953]

Do not go gentle into that good night

Do not go gentle into that good night,
Old age should burn and rave at close of day;
Rage, rage against the dying of the light.

Though wise men at their end know dark is right,
Because their words had forked no lightning they
Do not go gentle into that good night.

Good men, the last wave by, crying how bright
Their frail deeds might have danced in a green bay,
Rage, rage against the dying of the light.

Wild men who caught and sang the sun in flight,
And learn, too late, they grieved it on its way,
Do not go gentle into that good night.

Grave men, near death, who see with blinding sight
Blind eyes could blaze like meteors and be gay,
Rage, rage against the dying of the light.

And you, my father, there on the sad height,
Curse, bless, me now with your fierce tears, I pray.
Do not go gentle into that good night.
Rage, rage against the dying of the light.

[1952]

RANDALL JARRELL   [1914–1965]

The Death of the Ball Turret Gunner°

From my mother's sleep I fell into the State,
And I hunched in its belly till my wet fur froze.
Six miles from earth, loosed from its dream of life,
I woke to black flak and the nightmare fighters.
When I died they washed me out of the turret with a hose.   5

[1945]

Ball Turret Gunner: "A ball turret was a plexiglass sphere set into the belly of a
B-17 or B-24, and inhabited by two .50 caliber machine-guns and one man, a
short small man. When this gunner tracked with his machine guns a fighter
attacking his bomber from below, he revolved with the turret; hunched upside-
down in his little sphere, he looked like the foetus in the womb. The fighters that
attacked him were armed with cannon-firing explosive shells. The hose was a
steam hose" [Jarrell's note].

GWENDOLYN BROOKS [1917–2000]

We Real Cool

The Pool Players.
Seven at the Golden Shovel.

We real cool. We
Left school. We

Lurk late. We
Strike straight. We

Sing sin. We
Thin gin. We

Jazz° June. We   *have sexual intercourse (with)*
Die soon.

[1960]

GWENDOLYN BROOKS [1917–2000]

the mother

Abortions will not let you forget.
You remember the children you got that you did not get,
The damp small pulps with a little or with no hair,
The singers and workers that never handled the air.
You will never neglect or beat
Them, or silence or buy with a sweet.
You will never wind up the sucking-thumb
Or scuttle off ghosts that come.
You will never leave them, controlling your luscious sigh,
Return for a snack of them, with gobbling mother-eye.

I have heard in the voices of the wind the voices of my dim killed children.
I have contracted. I have eased
My dim dears at the breasts they could never suck.
I have said, Sweets, if I sinned, if I seized
Your luck   15
And your lives from your unfinished reach,
If I stole your births and your names,
Your straight baby tears and your games,
Your stilted or lovely loves, your tumults, your marriages, aches,
          and your deaths,
If I poisoned the beginnings of your breaths,   20
Believe that even in my deliberateness I was not deliberate.
Though why should I whine,
Whine that the crime was other than mine?—
Since anyhow you are dead.
Or rather, or instead,   25
You were never made.
But that too, I am afraid,
Is faulty: oh, what shall I say, how is the truth to be said?
You were born, you had body, you died.
It is just that you never giggled or planned or cried.   30

Believe me, I loved you all.
Believe me, I knew you, though faintly, and I loved, I loved you
All.

                                                                                          [1945]

ROBERT LOWELL   [1917–1978]

Skunk Hour

for Elizabeth Bishop

Nautilus Island's hermit
heiress still lives through winter in her Spartan cottage;
her sheep still graze above the sea.
Her son's a bishop. Her farmer

is first selectman in our village;
she's in her dotage.

Thirsting for
the hierarchic privacy
of Queen Victoria's century,
she buys up all
the eyesores facing her shore,
and lets them fall.

The season's ill —
we've lost our summer millionaire,
who seemed to leap from an L. L. Bean
catalogue. His nine-knot yawl
was auctioned off to lobstermen.
A red fox stain covers Blue Hill.

And now our fairy
decorator brightens his shop for fall;
his fishnet's filled with orange cork,
orange, his cobbler's bench and awl;
there is no money in his work,
he'd rather marry.

One dark night,
my Tudor Ford climbed the hill's skull;
I watched for love-cars. Lights turned down,
they lay together, hull to hull,
where the graveyard shelves on the town. . . .
My mind's not right.

A car radio bleats,
"Love, O careless Love. . . ." I hear
my ill-spirit sob in each blood cell,
as if my hand were at its throat. . . .
I myself am hell;
nobody's here —

only skunks, that search
in the moonlight for a bite to eat.
They march on their soles up Main Street:
white stripes, moonstruck eyes' red fire
under the chalk-dry and spar spire
of the Trinitarian Church.

I stand on top
of our back steps and breathe the rich air —
a mother skunk with her column of kittens swills the garbage pail.   45
She jabs her wedge-head in a cup
of sour cream, drops her ostrich tail,
and will not scare.

[1963]

PHILIP LARKIN   [1922–1985]

High Windows

When I see a couple of kids
And guess he's fucking her and she's
Taking pills or wearing a diaphragm,
I know this is paradise

Everyone old has dreamed of all their lives—   5
Bonds and gestures pushed to one side
Like an outdated combine harvester,
And everyone young going down the long slide

To happiness, endlessly. I wonder if
Anyone looked at me, forty years back,   10
And thought, *That'll be the life;*
No God any more, or sweating in the dark

About hell and that, or having to hide
What you think of the priest. He
And his lot will all go down the long slide   15
Like free bloody birds. And immediately

Rather than words comes the thought of high windows:
The sun-comprehending glass,
And beyond it, the deep blue air, that shows
Nothing, and is nowhere, and is endless.   20

[1974]

DENISE LEVERTOV   [1923–1997]

The Ache of Marriage

The ache of marriage:

thigh and tongue, beloved,
are heavy with it,
it throbs in the teeth

We look for communion
and are turned away, beloved,
each and each

It is leviathan and we
in its belly
looking for joy, some joy
not to be known outside it

two by two in the ark of
the ache of it.

[1966]

MAXINE KUMIN   [1925–2014]

Morning Swim

Into my empty head there come
a cotton beach, a dock wherefrom

I set out, oily and nude
through mist, in chilly solitude.

There was no line, no roof or floor
to tell the water from the air.

Night fog thick as terry cloth
closed me in its fuzzy growth.

I hung my bathrobe on two pegs.
I took the lake between my legs.   10

Invaded and invader, I
went overhand on that flat sky.

Fish twitched beneath me, quick and tame.
In their green zone they sang my name

and in the rhythm of the swim   15
I hummed a two-four-time slow hymn.

I hummed "Abide With Me."° The beat
rose in the fine thrash of my feet,

rose in the bubbles I put out
slantwise, trailing through my mouth.   20

My bones drank water; water fell
through all my doors. I was the well

that fed the lake that met my sea
in which I sang "Abide With Me."

[1965]

17. **"Abide With Me"**: A popular Christian hymn.

KENNETH KOCH   [1925–2002]

To Stammering

Where did you come from, lamentable quality?
Before I had a life you were about to ruin my life.
The mystery of this stays with me.
"Don't brood about things," my elders said.
I hadn't any other experience of enemies from inside.   5
They were all from outside—big boys
Who cursed me and hit me; motorists; falling trees.

All these you were as bad as, yet inside. When I spoke, you were there.
I could avoid you by singing or by acting.
I acted in school plays but was no good at singing.
Immediately after the play you were there again.
You ruined the cast party.
You were not a sign of confidence.
You were not a sign of manliness.
You were stronger than good luck and bad; you survived them both.
You were slowly edged out of my throat by psychoanalysis
You who had been brought in, it seems, like a hired thug
To beat up both sides and distract them
From the main issue: oedipal love. You were horrible!
Tell them, now that you're back in your thug country,
That you don't have to be so rough next time you're called in
But can be milder and have the same effect—unhappiness and pain.

[2000]

GERALD STERN   [b. 1925]

I Remember Galileo

I remember Galileo describing the mind
as a piece of paper blown around by the wind,
and I loved the sight of it sticking to a tree
or jumping into the backseat of a car,
and for years I watched paper leap through my cities;
but yesterday I saw the mind was a squirrel caught crossing
Route 80 between the wheels of a giant truck,
dancing back and forth like a thin leaf,
or a frightened string, for only two seconds living
on the white concrete before he got away,
his life shortened by all that terror, his head
jerking, his yellow teeth ground down to dust.

It was the speed of the squirrel and his lowness to the ground,
his great purpose and the alertness of his dancing,
that showed me the difference between him and paper.
Paper will do in theory, when there is time
to sit back in a metal chair and study shadows;

but for this life I need a squirrel,
his clawed feet spread, his whole soul quivering,
the hot wind rushing through his hair,   20
the loud noise shaking him from head to tail.

   O philosophical mind, O mind of paper, I need a squirrel
finishing his wild dash across the highway,
rushing up his green ungoverned hillside.

[1979]

EMMETT WILLIAMS [1925–2007]

like attracts like°

```
like            attracts            like
 like           attracts            like
  like          attracts           like
   like         attracts           like
    like        attracts          like
     like       attracts         like
      like      attracts        like
       like     attracts       like
        likeattractslike
        likattractäike
        likätraclike
        läkäralike
        ätkäkke
```

[1958]

like attracts like: Ernst Jandl, in a note on his own work, observes: "'There must
be an infinite number of methods of writing experimental poems, but I think the
most successful methods are those which can only be used once, for then the
result is a poem identical with the method by which it is made. The method used
again would turn out exactly the same poem.' This particular poem says what it
does, and does what it says, and I can't think of three other words that would
work as well in this construction." (E.W.)

FRANK O'HARA [1926–1966]

The Day Lady° Died

It is 12:20 in New York a Friday
three days after Bastille day,° yes   *(July 14)*
it is 1959 and I go get a shoeshine
because I will get off the 4:19 in Easthampton
at 7:15 and then go straight to dinner
and I don't know the people who will feed me

I walk up the muggy street beginning to sun
and have a hamburger and a malted and buy
an ugly NEW WORLD WRITING to see what the poets
in Ghana are doing these days
                              I go on to the bank
and Miss Stillwagon (first name Linda I once heard)
doesn't even look up my balance for once in her life
and in the GOLDEN GRIFFIN I get a little Verlaine°   *French poet*
for Patsy with drawings by Bonnard° although I do
think of Hesiod,° trans. Richmond Lattimore or   *Greek poet*
Brendan Behan's° new play or *Le Balcon* or *Les Nègres*   *Irish playwright*
of Genet,° but I don't, I stick with Verlaine
after practically going to sleep with quandariness

and for Mike I just stroll into the PARK LANE
Liquor Store and ask for a bottle of Strega and
then I go back where I came from to 6th Avenue
and the tobacconist in the Ziegfeld Theatre and
casually ask for a carton of Gauloises° and a carton   *French cigarettes*
of Picayunes,° and a NEW YORK POST with her face on it *Southern cigarettes*

and I am sweating a lot by now and thinking of
leaning on the john door in the 5 SPOT
while she whispered a song along the keyboard
to Mal Waldron and everyone and I stopped breathing

[1964]

Lady: Jazz singer Billie Holiday (1915–1959).
15. Bonnard: Pierre Bonnard, French modernist painter (1867–1947).
18. Genet: Jean Genet, French playwright and novelist (1910–1986).

ALLEN GINSBERG   [1926–1997]

A Supermarket in California

What thoughts I have of you tonight, Walt Whitman, for I walked down the sidestreets under the trees with a headache self-conscious looking at the full moon.

In my hungry fatigue, and shopping for images, I went into the neon fruit supermarket, dreaming of your enumerations!

What peaches and what penumbras! Whole families shopping at night! Aisles full of husbands! Wives in the avocados, babies in the tomatoes!—and you, García Lorca,° what were you doing down by the watermelons?

I saw you, Walt Whitman, childless, lonely old grubber, poking among the meats in the refrigerator and eyeing the grocery boys.

I heard you asking questions of each: Who killed the pork chops? What price bananas? Are you my Angel?   5

I wandered in and out of the brilliant stacks of cans following you, and followed in my imagination by the store detective.

We strode down the open corridors together in our solitary fancy tasting artichokes, possessing every frozen delicacy, and never passing the cashier.

Where are we going, Walt Whitman? The doors close in an hour. Which way does your beard point tonight?

(I touch your book and dream of our odyssey in the supermarket and feel absurd.)

Will we walk all night through solitary streets? The trees add shade to shade, lights out in the houses, we'll both be lonely.   10

Will we stroll dreaming of the lost America of love past blue automobiles in driveways, home to our silent cottage?

3. García Lorca: Federico García Lorca, Spanish surrealist poet and playwright (1898–1936).

Ah, dear father, graybeard, lonely old courage-teacher, what America
did you have when Charon° quit poling his ferry and you got out on a
smoking bank and stood watching the boat disappear on the black
waters of Lethe?°

Berkeley, 1955

[1956]

12. **Charon:** The boatman in Greek mythology who carried the dead across the
river Styx to Hades. **Lethe:** River of Forgetfulness in Hades.

W. S. MERWIN   [b. 1927]

One of the Butterflies

The trouble with pleasure is the timing
it can overtake me without warning
and be gone before I know it is here
it can stand facing me unrecognized
while I am remembering somewhere else
in another age or someone not seen
for years and never to be seen again
in this world and it seems that I cherish
only now a joy I was not aware of
when it was here although it remains   1
out of reach and will not be caught or named
or called back and if I could make it stay
as I want to it would turn into pain

[2009]

GALWAY KINNELL   [1927–2014]

Prayer

Whatever happens. Whatever
what is is is what
I want. Only
that. But that.

[1993]

GALWAY KINNELL   [1927–2014]

When one has lived a long time alone

When one has lived a long time alone,
among regrets so immense the past occupies
nearly all the room there is in consciousness,
one notices in the snake's eyes, which look back
without giving any less attention to the future,   5
the first coating of the opaque, milky-blue
leucoma snakes get when about to throw their skins
and become new—meanwhile continuing,
of course, to grow old—the same *bleu passé*°
that bleaches the corneas of the blue-eyed   10
when they lie back at the end and look for heaven,
a fading one knows means they will never find it
when one has lived a long time alone.

[1995]

9. bleu passé: Faded blue (French).

JAMES WRIGHT [1927–1980]

Lying in a Hammock at William Duffy's Farm in Pine Island, Minnesota

Over my head, I see the bronze butterfly,
Asleep on the black trunk,
Blowing like a leaf in green shadow.
Down the ravine behind the empty house,
The cowbells follow one another
Into the distances of the afternoon.
To my right,
In a field of sunlight between two pines,
The droppings of last year's horses
Blaze up into golden stones.
I lean back, as the evening darkens and comes on.
A chicken hawk floats over, looking for home.
I have wasted my life.

[1972]

JOHN ASHBERY [b. 1927]

They Knew What They Wanted

They all kissed the bride.
They all laughed.
They came from beyond space.
They came by night.

They came to a city.   5
They came to blow up America.
They came to rob Las Vegas.
They dare not love.

They died with their boots on.
They shoot horses, don't they?   10
They go boom.
They got me covered.

They flew alone.
They gave him a gun.
They just had to get married.   15
They live. They loved life.

They live by night.
They drive by night.
They knew Mr. Knight.
They were expendable.   20

They met in Argentina.
They met in Bombay.
They met in the dark.
They might be giants.

They made me a fugitive.   25
They made me a criminal.
They only kill their masters.
They shall have music.

They were sisters.
They still call me Bruce.   30
They won't believe me.
They won't forget.

[2009]

PHILIP LEVINE [1928–2015]

What Work Is

We stand in the rain in a long line
waiting at Ford Highland Park. For work.
You know what work is—if you're
old enough to read this you know what
work is, although you may not do it.
Forget you. This is about waiting,
shifting from one foot to another.
Feeling the light rain falling like mist
into your hair, blurring your vision
until you think you see your own brother
ahead of you, maybe ten places.
You rub your glasses with your fingers,
and of course it's someone else's brother,
narrower across the shoulders than
yours but with the same sad slouch, the grin
that does not hide the stubbornness,
the sad refusal to give in to
rain, to the hours wasted waiting,
to the knowledge that somewhere ahead
a man is waiting who will say, "No,
we're not hiring today," for any
reason he wants. You love your brother,
now suddenly you can hardly stand
the love flooding you for your brother,
who's not beside you or behind or
ahead because he's home trying to
sleep off a miserable night shift
at Cadillac so he can get up
before noon to study his German.
Works eight hours a night so he can sing
Wagner, the opera you hate most,
the worst music ever invented.
How long has it been since you told him
you loved him, held his wide shoulders,

opened your eyes wide and said those words,   35
and maybe kissed his cheek? You've never
done something so simple, so obvious,
not because you're too young or too dumb,
not because you're jealous or even mean
or incapable of crying in   40
the presence of another man, no,
just because you don't know what work is.

[1991]

ANNE SEXTON   [1928–1974]

Cinderella

You always read about it:
the plumber with twelve children
who wins the Irish Sweepstakes.
From toilets to riches.
That story.   5

Or the nursemaid,
some luscious sweet from Denmark
who captures the oldest son's heart.
From diapers to Dior.°
That story.   10

Or a milkman who serves the wealthy,
eggs, cream, butter, yogurt, milk,
the white truck like an ambulance
who goes into real estate
and makes a pile.   15
From homogenized to martinis at lunch.

Or the charwoman
who is on the bus when it cracks up

---

9. **Dior:** Fashions designed by the French house of Dior, established by Christian
Dior (1905–1957).

and collects enough from the insurance.
　From mops to Bonwit Teller.°
　That story.

Once
the wife of a rich man was on her deathbed
and she said to her daughter Cinderella:
Be devout. Be good. Then I will smile
down from heaven in the seam of a cloud.
The man took another wife who had
two daughters, pretty enough
but with hearts like blackjacks.
Cinderella was their maid.
She slept on the sooty hearth each night
and walked around looking like Al Jolson.°
Her father brought presents home from town,
jewels and gowns for the other women
but the twig of a tree for Cinderella.
She planted that twig on her mother's grave
and it grew to a tree where a white dove sat.
Whenever she wished for anything the dove
would drop it like an egg upon the ground.
The bird is important, my dears, so heed him.

Next came the ball, as you all know.
It was a marriage market.
The prince was looking for a wife.
All but Cinderella were preparing
and gussying up for the big event.
Cinderella begged to go too.
Her stepmother threw a dish of lentils
into the cinders and said: Pick them
up in an hour and you shall go.
The white dove brought all his friends;
all the warm wings of the fatherland came,
and picked up the lentils in a jiffy.
No, Cinderella, said the stepmother,
you have no clothes and cannot dance.
That's the way with stepmothers.

---

20. Bonwit Teller: A fashionable and expensive department store.
32. Al Jolson: American entertainer (1888–1950), known particularly for singing in blackface.

Cinderella went to the tree at the grave
and cried forth like a gospel singer:
Mama! Mama! My turtledove,
send me to the prince's ball!
The bird dropped down a golden dress   60
and delicate little gold slippers.
Rather a large package for a simple bird.
So she went. Which is no surprise.
Her stepmother and sisters didn't
recognize her without her cinder face   65
and the prince took her hand on the spot
and danced with no other the whole day.

As nightfall came she thought she'd better
get home. The prince walked her home
and she disappeared into the pigeon house   70
and although the prince took an axe and broke
it open she was gone. Back to her cinders.
These events repeated themselves for three days.
However on the third day the prince
covered the palace steps with cobbler's wax   75
and Cinderella's gold shoe stuck upon it.

Now he would find whom the shoe fit
and find his strange dancing girl for keeps.
He went to their house and the two sisters
were delighted because they had lovely feet.   80
The eldest went into a room to try the slipper on
but her big toe got in the way so she simply
sliced it off and put on the slipper.
The prince rode away with her until the white dove
told him to look at the blood pouring forth.   85
That is the way with amputations.
They don't just heal up like a wish.
The other sister cut off her heel
but the blood told as blood will.
The prince was getting tired.   90
He began to feel like a shoe salesman.
But he gave it one last try.
This time Cinderella fit into the shoe
like a love letter into its envelope.

At the wedding ceremony   95
the two sisters came to curry favor

and the white dove pecked their eyes out.
Two hollow spots were left
like soup spoons.

Cinderella and the prince   10
lived, they say, happily ever after,
like two dolls in a museum case
never bothered by diapers or dust,
never arguing over the timing of an egg,
never telling the same story twice,   1(
never getting a middle-aged spread,
their darling smiles pasted on for eternity.
Regular Bobbsey Twins.°
That story.

[1971]

108. **Bobbsey Twins:** Principal characters in a popular series of children's
books, published between 1904 and 1979. In illustrations they are depicted as
carefully dressed, always smiling, and in idyllic circumstances.

ADRIENNE RICH [1929–2012]

Aunt Jennifer's Tigers

Aunt Jennifer's tigers prance across a screen,
Bright topaz denizens of a world of green.
They do not fear the men beneath the tree;
They pace in sleek chivalric certainty.

Aunt Jennifer's fingers fluttering through her wool
Find even the ivory needle hard to pull.
The massive weight of Uncle's wedding band
Sits heavily upon Aunt Jennifer's hand.

When Aunt is dead, her terrified hands will lie
Still ringed with ordeals she was mastered by.
The tigers in the panel that she made
Will go on prancing, proud and unafraid.

[1951]

ADRIENNE RICH   [1929–2012]

Diving into the Wreck

First having read the book of myths,
and loaded the camera,
and checked the edge of the knife-blade,
I put on
the body-armor of black rubber   5
the absurd flippers
the grave and awkward mask.
I am having to do this
not like Cousteau° with his
assiduous team   10
aboard the sun-flooded schooner
but here alone.

There is a ladder.
The ladder is always there
hanging innocently   15
close to the side of the schooner.
We know what it is for,
we who have used it.
Otherwise
it's a piece of maritime floss   20
some sundry equipment.

I go down.
Rung after rung and still
the oxygen immerses me
the blue light   25
the clear atoms
of our human air.
I go down.
My flippers cripple me,

---

9. **Cousteau:** Jacques-Yves Cousteau (1910–1997), French underwater explorer, photographer, and author.

I crawl like an insect down the ladder
and there is no one
to tell me when the ocean
will begin.

First the air is blue and then
it is bluer and then green and then
black I am blacking out and yet
my mask is powerful
it pumps my blood with power
the sea is another story
the sea is not a question of power
I have to learn alone
to turn my body without force
in the deep element.

And now: it is easy to forget
what I came for
among so many who have always
lived here
swaying their crenellated° fans
between the reefs
and besides
you breathe differently down here.

I came to explore the wreck.
The words are purposes.
The words are maps.
I came to see the damage that was done
and the treasures that prevail.
I stroke the beam of my lamp
slowly along the flank
of something more permanent
than fish or weed

the thing I came for:
the wreck and not the story of the wreck
the thing itself and not the myth
the drowned face° always staring
toward the sun

48. **crenellated:** Notched; *crenels* are the open spaces between the solid portions
of a battlement.
64. **drowned face:** The ornamental female figurehead on the prow of an old
sailing ship.

the evidence of damage
worn by salt and sway into this threadbare beauty
the ribs of the disaster
curving their assertion
among the tentative haunters.   70

This is the place.
And I am here, the mermaid whose dark hair
streams black, the merman in his armored body
We circle silently
about the wreck   75
we dive into the hold.
I am she: I am he

whose drowned face sleeps with open eyes
whose breasts still bear the stress
whose silver, copper, vermeil° cargo lies   80
obscurely inside barrels
half-wedged and left to rot
we are the half-destroyed instruments
that once held to a course
the water-eaten log   85
the fouled compass

We are, I am, you are
by cowardice or courage
the one who find our way
back to this scene   90
carrying a knife, a camera
a book of myths
in which
our names do not appear.

                                                          [1973]

80. vermeil: Gilded silver, bronze, or copper.

LINDA PASTAN   [b. 1932]

love poem

I want to write you
a love poem as headlong
as our creek
after thaw
when we stand
on its dangerous
banks and watch it carry
with it every twig
every dry leaf and branch
in its path
every scruple
when we see it
so swollen
with runoff
that even as we watch
we must grab
each other
and step back
we must grab each
other or
get our shoes
soaked we must
grab each other

[1988]

ETHERIDGE KNIGHT [1931–1991]

Hard Rock Returns to Prison from the Hospital for the Criminal Insane

Hard Rock / was / "known not to take no shit
From nobody," and he had the scars to prove it:
Split purple lips, lumbed ears, welts above
His yellow eyes, and one long scar that cut
Across his temple and plowed through a thick   5
Canopy of kinky hair.

The WORD / was / that Hard Rock wasn't a mean nigger
Anymore, that the doctors had bored a hole in his head,
Cut out part of his brain, and shot electricity
Through the rest. When they brought Hard Rock back,   10
Handcuffed and chained, he was turned loose,
Like a freshly gelded stallion, to try his new status.
And we all waited and watched, like a herd of sheep,
To see if the WORD was true.

As we waited we wrapped ourselves in the cloak   15
Of his exploits: "Man, the last time, it took eight
Screws° to put him in the Hole."° "Yeah, remember when he
Smacked the captain with his dinner tray?" "He set
The record for time in the Hole—67 straight days!"
"Ol Hard Rock! man, that's one crazy nigger."   20
And then the jewel of a myth that Hard Rock had once bit
A screw on the thumb and poisoned him with syphilitic spit.

The testing came, to see if Hard Rock was really tame.
A hillbilly called him a black son of a bitch
And didn't lose his teeth, a screw who knew Hard Rock   25
From before shook him down and barked in his face.

17. Screws: Guards; **Hole:** Solitary confinement.

And Hard Rock did *nothing*. Just grinned and looked silly,
His eyes empty like knot holes in a fence.

And even after we discovered that it took Hard Rock
Exactly 3 minutes to tell you his first name,
We told ourselves that he had just wised up,
Was being cool; but we could not fool ourselves for long,
And we turned away, our eyes on the ground. Crushed.
He had been our Destroyer, the doer of things
We dreamed of doing but could not bring ourselves to do,
The fears of years, like a biting whip,
Had cut deep bloody grooves
Across our backs.

[1968]

SYLVIA PLATH   [1932–1963]

Morning Song

Love set you going like a fat gold watch.
The midwife slapped your footsoles, and your bald cry
Took its place among the elements.

Our voices echo, magnifying your arrival. New statue
In a drafty museum, your nakedness
Shadows our safety. We stand round blankly as walls.

I'm no more your mother
Than the cloud that distils a mirror to reflect its own slow
Effacement at the wind's hand.

All night your moth-breath
Flickers among the flat pink roses. I wake to listen:
A far sea moves in my ear.

One cry, and I stumble from bed, cow-heavy and floral
In my Victorian nightgown.
Your mouth opens clean as a cat's. The window square

Whitens and swallows its dull stars. And now you try
Your handful of notes;
The clear vowels rise like balloons.

[*1961;* 1965]

SYLVIA PLATH   [1932–1963]

Daddy

You do not do, you do not do
Any more, black shoe
In which I have lived like a foot
For thirty years, poor and white,
Barely daring to breathe or Achoo.   5

Daddy, I have had to kill you.
You died before I had time—
Marble-heavy, a bag full of God,
Ghastly statue with one grey toe
Big as a Frisco seal   10

And a head in the freakish Atlantic
Where it pours bean green over blue
In the waters off beautiful Nauset.
I used to pray to recover you.
Ach, du.°   *Oh, you (German)*   15

In the German tongue, in the Polish town
Scraped flat by the roller
Of wars, wars, wars.
But the name of the town is common.
My Polack friend   20

Says there are a dozen or two.
So I never could tell where you
Put your foot, your root,
I never could talk to you.
The tongue stuck in my jaw.   25

It stuck in a barb wire snare.
Ich, ich, ich, ich,°   *I (German)*
I could hardly speak.
I thought every German was you.
And the language obscene   30

An engine, an engine
Chuffing me off like a Jew.

A Jew to Dachau, Auschwitz, Belsen.°
I began to talk like a Jew.
I think I may well be a Jew.

The snows of the Tyrol,° the clear beer of Vienna
Are not very pure or true.
With my gypsy ancestress and my weird luck
And my Taroc pack and my Taroc pack
I may be a bit of a Jew.

I have always been scared of *you*,
With your Luftwaffe,° your gobbledygoo.
And your neat moustache
And your Aryan eye, bright blue.
Panzer°-man, panzer-man, O You—

Not God but a swastika
So black no sky could squeak through.
Every woman adores a Fascist,
The boot in the face, the brute
Brute heart of a brute like you.

You stand at the blackboard, daddy,
In the picture I have of you,
A cleft in your chin instead of your foot
But no less a devil for that, no not
Any less the black man who

Bit my pretty red heart in two.
I was ten when they buried you.
At twenty I tried to die
And get back, back, back to you.
I thought even the bones would do.

But they pulled me out of the sack,
And they stuck me together with glue.
And then I knew what to do.
I made a model of you,
A man in black with a Meinkampf° look

---

33. **Dachau, Auschwitz, Belsen:** Nazi concentration camps.
36. **the Tyrol:** An alpine region in western Austria and northern Italy.
42. **Luftwaffe:** The Nazi air force in World War II.
45. **Panzer:** An armored unit in the German army in World War II.
65. **Meinkampf:** *Mein Kampf* (or *My Struggle*), the title of Adolf Hitler's autobiography.

And a love of the rack and the screw.
And I said I do, I do.
So daddy, I'm finally through.
The black telephone's off at the root,
The voices just can't worm through.   70

If I've killed one man, I've killed two—
The vampire who said he was you
And drank my blood for a year,
Seven years, if you want to know.
Daddy, you can lie back now.   75

There's a stake in your fat black heart
And the villagers never liked you.
They are dancing and stamping on you.
They always *knew* it was you.
Daddy, daddy, you bastard, I'm through.   80

[1962]

AUDRE LORDE   [1934–1992]

Coal

I   is the total black
being spoken
from the earth's inside.
There are many kinds of open
how a diamond comes   5
into a knot of flame
how sound comes into a word
colored
by who pays what for speaking.

Some words are open   10
diamonds on a glass window
singing out within the crash
of passing sun
other words are stapled wagers

in a perforated book
buy and sign and tear apart
and come whatever wills all chances
the stub remains
an ill-pulled tooth
with a ragged edge.

Some words live in my throat
breeding like adders
others
know sun
seeking like gypsies
over my tongue
to explode through my lips
like young sparrows
bursting from shell.

Some words
bedevil me.

Love is a word, another kind of open.
As the diamond comes
into a knot of flame
I am Black
because I come from the earth's inside
take my word for jewel
in the open light.

[*1962;* rev. 1992]

MARY OLIVER   [b. 1935]

First Snow

The snow
began here
this morning and all day
continued, its white
rhetoric everywhere
calling us back to *why, how,*

whence such beauty and *what*
the meaning; such
an oracular fever! flowing
past windows, an energy it seemed   10
would never ebb, never settle
less than lovely! and only now,
deep into night,
it has finally ended.
The silence   15
is immense,
and the heavens still hold
a million candles; nowhere
the familiar things:
stars, the moon,   20
the darkness we expect
and nightly turn from. Trees
glitter like castles
of ribbons, the broad fields
smolder with light, a passing   25
creekbed lies
heaped with shining hills;
and though the questions
that have assailed us all day
remain—not a single   30
answer has been found—
walking out now
into the silence and the light
under the trees,
and through the fields,   35
feels like one.

[1983]

LUCILLE CLIFTON   [1936–2010]

at the cemetery, walnut grove plantation, south carolina, 1989

among the rocks
at walnut grove
your silence drumming
in my bones,
tell me your names.

nobody mentioned slaves
and yet the curious tools
shine with your fingerprints.
nobody mentioned slaves
but somebody did this work
who had no guide, no stone,
who moulders under rock.

tell me your names,
tell me your bashful names
and i will testify.

the inventory lists ten slaves
but only men were recognized.

among the rocks
at walnut grove
some of these honored dead
were dark
some of these dark
were slaves
some of these slaves
were women
some of them did this
honored work.
tell me your names

foremothers, brothers,
tell me your dishonored names.   30
here lies
here lies
here lies
here lies
hear   35

[1991]

LUCILLE CLIFTON   [1936–2010]

homage to my hips

these hips are big hips.
they need space to
move around in.
they don't fit into little
petty places. these hips   5
are free hips.
they don't like to be held back.
these hips have never been enslaved,
they go where they want to go
they do what they want to do.   10
these hips are mighty hips.
these hips are magic hips.
i have known them
to put a spell on a man and
spin him like a top!   15

[1980]

C. K. WILLIAMS   [1936–2015]

On the Métro

On the métro, I have to ask a young woman to move the packages beside
  her to make room for me;
She's reading, her foot propped on the seat in front of her, and barely
  looks up as she pulls them to her.
I sit, take out my own book—Cioran, *The Temptation to Exist*—and
  notice her glancing up from hers
to take in the title of mine, and then, as Gombrowicz puts it, she "affirms
  herself physically," that is,
she's *present* in a way she hadn't been before; though she hasn't moved an
  inch, she's allowed herself
to come more sharply into focus, be more accessible to my sensual perception, so I can't help but remark
her strong figure and very tan skin—(how literally golden young women
  can look at the end of summer).
She leans back now, and as the train rocks and her arm brushes mine she
  doesn't pull it away;
she seems to be allowing our surfaces to unite: the fine hairs on both our
  forearms, sensitive, alive,
achingly alive, bring news of someone touched, someone sensed, and
  thus acknowledged, *known.*

I understand that in no way is she offering more than this, and in truth I
  have no desire for more,
but it's still enough for me to be taken by a surge, first of warmth then of
  something like its opposite:
a memory—a lovely girl I'd mooned for from afar, across the table from
  me in the library in school,
our feet I thought touching, touching even again, and then, with all I
  craved that touch to mean,
my having to realize it wasn't her flesh my flesh for that gleaming time
  had pressed, but a table leg.
The young woman today removes her arm now, stands, swaying against
  the lurch of the slowing train,
and crossing before me brushes my knee and does that thing again, asserts her bodily being again,

(Gombrowicz again), then quickly moves to the door of the car and de-
    scends, not once looking back,
(to my relief not looking back), and I allow myself the thought that
    though I must be to her again
as senseless as that table of my youth, as wooden, as unfeeling, perhaps
    there was a moment I was not.   20

[2006]

CHARLES SIMIC   [b. 1938]

Eyes Fastened with Pins

How much death works,
No one knows what a long
Day he puts in. The little
Wife always alone
Ironing death's laundry.   5
The beautiful daughters
Setting death's supper table.
The neighbors playing
Pinochle in the backyard
Or just sitting on the steps   10
Drinking beer. Death,
Meanwhile, in a strange
Part of town looking for
Someone with a bad cough,
But the address somehow wrong,   15
Even death can't figure it out
Among all the locked doors . . .
And the rain beginning to fall.
Long windy night ahead.
Death with not even a newspaper   20
To cover his head, not even
A dime to call the one pining away,
Undressing slowly, sleepily,
And stretching naked
On death's side of the bed.   25

[1977]

MICHAEL S. HARPER [b. 1938]

Nightmare Begins Responsibility

I place these numbed wrists to the pane
watching white uniforms whisk over
him in the tube-kept
prison
fear what they will do in experiment
watch my gloved stickshifting gasolined hands
breathe *boxcar-information-please* infirmary tubes
distrusting white-pink mending paperthin
silkened end hairs, distrusting tubes
shrunk in his *trunk-skincapped*
shaven head, in thighs
distrusting-white-hands-picking-baboon-light
on this son who will not make his second night
of this wardstrewn intensive airpocket
where his father's asthmatic
hymns of *night-train*, train done gone
his mother can only know that he has flown
up into essential calm unseen corridor
going boxscarred home, *mamaborn, sweetsonchild*
gonedowntown into *researchtestingwarehousebatteryacid*
mama-son-done-gone/me telling her 'nother
train tonight, no music, no breathstroked
heartbeat in my infinite distrust of them:

and of my distrusting self
white-doctor-who-breathed-for-him-all-night
say it for two sons gone,
say nightmare, say it loud
panebreaking heartmadness:
nightmare begins responsibility.

[1975]

576

SEAMUS HEANEY [1939–2013]

Mid-Term Break

I sat all morning in the college sick bay
Counting bells knelling classes to a close.
At two o'clock our neighbours drove me home.

In the porch I met my father crying—
He had always taken funerals in his stride—   5
And Big Jim Evans saying it was a hard blow.

The baby cooed and laughed and rocked the pram°   *baby carriage*
When I came in, and I was embarrassed
By old men standing up to shake my hand

And tell me they were "sorry for my trouble,"   10
Whispers informed strangers I was the eldest,
Away at school, as my mother held my hand

In hers and coughed out angry tearless sighs.
At ten o'clock the ambulance arrived
With the corpse, stanched and bandaged by the nurses.   15

Next morning I went up into the room. Snowdrops
And candles soothed the bedside; I saw him
For the first time in six weeks. Paler now,

Wearing a poppy bruise on his left temple,
He lay in the four foot box as in his cot.   20
No gaudy scars, the bumper knocked him clear.

A four foot box, a foot for every year.

[1966]

SEAMUS HEANEY [1939–2013]

Digging

Between my finger and my thumb
The squat pen rests; snug as a gun.

Under my window, a clean rasping sound
When the spade sinks into gravelly ground:
My father, digging. I look down

Till his straining rump among the flowerbeds
Bends low, comes up twenty years away
Stooping in rhythm through potato drills
Where he was digging.

The coarse boot nestled on the lug, the shaft
Against the inside knee was levered firmly.
He rooted out tall tops, buried the bright edge deep
To scatter new potatoes that we picked
Loving their cool hardness in our hands.

By God, the old man could handle a spade.
Just like his old man.

My grandfather cut more turf in a day
Than any other man on Toner's bog.
Once I carried him milk in a bottle
Corked sloppily with paper. He straightened up
To drink it, then fell to right away
Nicking and slicing neatly, heaving sods
Over his shoulder, going down and down
For the good turf. Digging.

The cold smell of potato mould, the squelch and slap
Of soggy peat, the curt cuts of an edge
Through living roots awaken in my head.
But I've no spade to follow men like them.

Between my finger and my thumb
The squat pen rests.
I'll dig with it.

[1966]

TED KOOSER   [b. 1939]

Abandoned Farmhouse

He was a big man, says the size of his shoes
on a pile of broken dishes by the house;
a tall man too, says the length of the bed
in an upstairs room; and a good, God-fearing man,
says the Bible with a broken back   5
on the floor below the window, dusty with sun;
but not a man for farming, say the fields
cluttered with boulders and the leaky barn.

A woman lived with him, says the bedroom wall
papered with lilacs and the kitchen shelves   10
covered with oilcloth, and they had a child,
says the sandbox made from a tractor tire.
Money was scarce, say the jars of plum preserves
and canned tomatoes sealed in the cellar hole.
And the winters cold, say the rags in the window frames.   15
It was lonely here, says the narrow country road.

Something went wrong, says the empty house
in the weed-choked yard. Stones in the fields
say he was not a farmer; the still-sealed jars
in the cellar say she left in a nervous haste.   20
And the child? Its toys are strewn in the yard
like branches after a storm—a rubber cow,
a rusty tractor with a broken plow,
a doll in overalls. Something went wrong, they say.

[1980]

579

QUINCY TROUPE   [b. 1939]

A Poem For "Magic"°

for Earvin "Magic" Johnson,
Donnell Reid & Richard Franklin

take it to the hoop, "magic" johnson,
take the ball dazzling down the open lane
herk & jerk & raise your six-feet, nine-inch frame
into air sweating screams of your neon name
"magic" johnson, nicknamed "windex" way back
in high school
                        cause you wiped glass backboards
so clean, where you first juked & shook
wiled your way to glory
                        a new-style fusion of shake-&-bake
energy, using everything possible, you created your own
space to fly through—any moment now
we expect your wings to spread feathers for that spooky takeoff
of yours—then, shake & glide & ride up in space
till you hammer home a clothes-lining deuce off glass
now, come back down with a reverse hoodoo gem
off the spin & stick in sweet, popping nets clean
from twenty feet, right side
put the ball on the floor again, "magic"
slide the dribble behind your back, ease it deftly
between your bony stork legs, head bobbing everwhichaway
up & down, you see everything on the court
off the high yoyo patter
                        stop & go dribble

"**Magic**": Earvin "Magic" Johnson Jr. (b. 1959), star basketball player at Lansing (Michigan) Everett High School (1973–1977) and Michigan State University (1977–1979) and for the Los Angeles Lakers (1979–1991 and 1996). He was honored in 1996 as one of the Fifty Greatest Players in National Basketball Association History.

you thread a needle-rope pass sweet home   25
to kareem cutting through the lane
                                his skyhook pops the cords
now, lead the fastbreak, hit worthy on the fly
now, blindside a pinpoint behind-the-back pass for two more
off the fake, looking the other way, you raise off-balance   30
into electric space
sweating chants of your name
turn, 180 degrees off the move, your legs scissoring space
like a swimmer's yoyoing motion in deep water
stretching out now toward free flight   35
you double-pump through human trees
                                hang in place
slip the ball into your left hand
then deal it like a las vegas card dealer off squared glass
into nets, living up to your singular nickname   40
so "bad" you cartwheel the crowd toward frenzy
wearing now your electric smile, neon as your name

in victory, we suddenly sense your glorious uplift
your urgent need to be champion
& so we cheer with you, rejoice with you   45
                        for this quicksilver, quicksilver,
quicksilver moment of fame
so put the ball on the floor again, "magic"
juke & dazzle, shake & bake down the lane
take the sucker to the hoop, "magic" johnson,   50
recreate reverse hoodoo gems off the spin
deal alley-oop dunkathon magician passes
now, double-pump, scissor, vamp through space
hang in place
                        & put it all up in the sucker's face, "magic" johnson,   55
& deal the roundball like the juju man that you am
like the sho-nuff shaman that you am, "magic,"
like the sho-nuff spaceman you am

                                                [*1991*; rev. 1996]

AL YOUNG   [b. 1939]

A Dance for Ma Rainey°

I'm going to be just like you, Ma
Rainey this monday morning
clouds puffing up out of my head
like those balloons
that float above the faces of white people
in the funnypapers

I'm going to hover in the corners
of the world, Ma
& sing from the bottom of hell
up to the tops of high heaven
& send out scratchless waves of yellow
& brown & that basic black honey
misery

I'm going to cry so sweet
& so low
& so dangerous,
Ma,
that the message is going to reach you
back in 1922
where you shimmer
snaggle-toothed
perfumed &
powdered
in your bauble beads

hair pressed & tied back
throbbing with that sick pain
I know
& hide so well

Ma Rainey: Gertrude Pridgett (1886–1939), known after her marriage as Ma Rainey, was a noted vaudeville entertainer and blues singer, credited as being the "Mother of the Blues."

582

that pain that blues
jives the world with   30
aching to be heard
that downness
that bottomlessness
first felt by some stolen delta nigger
swamped under with redblooded american agony;   35
reduced to the sheer shit
of existence
that bred
& battered us all,
Ma,   40
the beautiful people
our beautiful brave black people
who no longer need to jazz
or sing to themselves in murderous vibrations
or play the veins of their strong tender arms   45
with needles
to prove we're still here

                                                            [1969]

JAMES WELCH   [b. 1940]

Christmas Comes to
Moccasin Flat

Christmas comes like this: Wise men
unhurried, candles bought on credit (poor price
for calves), warriors face down in wine sleep.
Winds cheat to pull heat from smoke.

Friends sit in chinked cabins, stare out   5
plastic windows and wait for commodities.
Charlie Blackbird, twenty miles from church
and bar, stabs his fire with flint.

When drunks drain radiators for love
or need, chiefs eat snow and talk of change,   10

an urge to laugh pounding their ribs.
Elk play games in high country.

Medicine Woman, clay pipe and twist tobacco,
calls each blizzard by name and predicts
five o'clock by spitting at her television.
Children lean into her breath to beg a story:

Something about honor and passion,
warriors back with meat and song,
a peculiar evening star, quick vision of birth.
Blackbird feeds his fire. Outside, a quick 30 below.

[1976]

MARTHA COLLINS   [b. 1940]

14 from *White Papers*

black keys from trees white keys locked
on black shoulders locked together above
skeleton ribs keys to 45 keyboards from one
tusk *the word ivory rang through the air*
one tusk + one slave to carry it bought
together if slave survived the long march
sold for spice or sugar plantations if not
replaced by other slaves five Africans died
for each tusk 2 million for 400,000 American
pianos including the one my grandmother
played not to mention grieving villages
burned women children left to die the dead
elephants whose tusks went to Connecticut
where they were cut bleached and polished
while my grandmother played in Illinois
my mother played and I—there were many old
pianos and slaves were used till the 20th century:
an African slave could have carried a tusk
that was cut into white keys I played, starting
with middle C and going up and down

[2012]

ROBERT PINSKY [b. 1940]

Shirt

The back, the yoke, the yardage. Lapped seams,
The nearly invisible stitches along the collar
Turned in a sweatshop by Koreans or Malaysians

Gossiping over tea and noodles on their break
Or talking money or politics while one fitted   5
This armpiece with its overseam to the band

Of cuff I button at my wrist. The presser, the cutter,
The wringer, the mangle. The needle, the union,
The treadle, the bobbin. The code. The infamous blaze

At the Triangle Factory° in nineteen-eleven.   *(in New York City)* 10
One hundred and forty-six died in the flames
On the ninth floor, no hydrants, no fire escapes—

The witness in a building across the street
Who watched how a young man helped a girl to step
Up to the windowsill, then held her out   15

Away from the masonry wall and let her drop.
And then another. As if he were helping them up
To enter a streetcar, and not eternity.

A third before he dropped her put her arms
Around his neck and kissed him. Then he held   20
Her into space, and dropped her. Almost at once

He stepped to the sill himself, his jacket flared
And fluttered up from his shirt as he came down,
Air filling up the legs of his gray trousers—

Like Hart Crane's Bedlamite,° "shrill shirt ballooning."   25
Wonderful how the pattern matches perfectly
Across the placket and over the twin bar-tacked

25. Bedlamite: Reference to image in Hart Crane's famous book-length poem
The Bridge (lines 17–20 of the section titled, "The Brooklyn Bridge.")

Corners of both pockets, like a strict rhyme
Or a major chord. Prints, plaids, checks,
Houndstooth, Tattersall, Madras. The clan tartans

Invented by mill-owners inspired by the hoax of Ossian,°
To control their savage Scottish workers, tamed
By a fabricated heraldry: MacGregor,

Bailey, MacMartin. The kilt, devised for workers
To wear among the dusty clattering looms.
Weavers, carders, spinners. The loader,

The docker, the navvy.° The planter, the picker, the sorter
Sweating at her machine in a litter of cotton
As slaves in calico headrags sweated in fields:

George Herbert,° your descendant is a Black
Lady in South Carolina, her name is Irma
And she inspected my shirt. Its color and fit

And feel and its clean smell have satisfied
Both her and me. We have culled its cost and quality
Down to the buttons of simulated bone,

The buttonholes, the sizing, the facing, the characters
Printed in black on neckband and tail. The shape,
The label, the labor, the color, the shade. The shirt.

[1990]

31. Ossian: Legendary Gaelic poet, hero of a cycle of traditional tales and
poems that place him in the third century CE. The hoax involved Scottish
author James Macpherson (1736–1796), who published two epic poems that he
said were translations of works written by Ossian but were in fact mostly
composed by Macpherson himself.
37. navvy: An unskilled laborer.
40. George Herbert: English metaphysical poet (1593–1633). See Biographical
Notes (p. 1381).

BILLY COLLINS [b. 1941]

Forgetfulness

The name of the author is the first to go
followed obediently by the title, the plot,
the heartbreaking conclusion, the entire novel
which suddenly becomes one you have never read, never even heard of,

as if, one by one, the memories you used to harbor   5
decided to retire to the southern hemisphere of the brain,
to a little fishing village where there are no phones.

Long ago you kissed the names of the nine Muses good-bye
and watched the quadratic equation pack its bag,
and even now as you memorize the order of the planets,   10

something else is slipping away, a state flower perhaps,
the address of an uncle, the capital of Paraguay.

Whatever it is you are struggling to remember
it is not poised on the tip of your tongue,
not even lurking in some obscure corner of your spleen.   15

It has floated away down a dark mythological river
whose name begins with an *L* as far as you can recall,
well on your own way to oblivion where you will join those
who have even forgotten how to swim and how to ride a bicycle.

No wonder you rise in the middle of the night   20
to look up the date of a famous battle in a book on war.
No wonder the moon in the window seems to have drifted
out of a love poem that you used to know by heart.

[2002]

TOI DERRICOTTE   [b. 1941]

A Note on My Son's Face

I

Tonight, I look, thunderstruck
at the gold head of my grandchild.
Almost asleep, he buries his feet
between my thighs;
his little straw eyes
close in the near dark.
I smell the warmth of his raw
slightly foul breath, the new death
waiting to rot inside him.
Our breaths equalize our heartbeats;
every muscle of the chest uncoils,
the arm bones loosen in the nest
of nerves. I think of the peace
of walking through the house,
pointing to the name of this, the name of that,
an educator of a new man.

Mother. Grandmother. Wise
Snake-woman who will show the way;
Spider-woman whose black tentacles
hold him precious. Or will tear off his head,
her teeth over the little husband,
the small fist clotted in trust at her breast.

This morning, looking at the face of his father,
I remembered how, an infant, his face was too dark,
nose too broad, mouth too wide.
I did not look in that mirror
and see the face that could save me
from my own darkness.
Did he, looking in my eye, see
what I turned from:
my own dark grandmother
bending over gladioli in the field,

her shaking black hand defenseless
at the shining cock of flower?

I wanted that face to die,   35
to be reborn in the face of a white child.
I wanted the soul to stay the same,
for I loved to death,
to damnation and God-death,
the soul that broke out of me.   40
I crowed: My Son! My Beautiful!
But when I peeked in the basket,
I saw the face of a black man.

Did I bend over his nose
and straighten it with my fingers   45
like a vine growing the wrong way?
Did he feel my hand in malice?

Generations we prayed and fucked
for this light child,
the shining god of the second coming;   50
we bow down in shame
and carry the children of the past
in our wallets, begging forgiveness.

II

A picture in a book,
a lynching.   55
The bland faces of men who watch
a Christ go up in flames, smiling,
as if he were a hooked
fish, a felled antelope, some
wild thing tied to boards and burned.   60
His charring body
gives off light—a halo
burns out of him.
His face scorched featureless;
the hair matted to the scalp   65
like feathers.
One man stands with his hand on his hip,
another with his arm
slung over the shoulder of a friend,
as if this moment were large enough   70
to hold affection.

III

How can we wake
from a dream
we are born into,
that shines around us,
the terrible bright air?

Having awakened,
having seen our own bloody hands,
how can we ask forgiveness,
bring before our children the real
monster of their nightmares?

The worst is true.
Everything you did not want to know.

[1989]

RICHARD GARCIA   [b. 1941]

Why I Left the Church

Maybe it was
because the only time
I hit a baseball
it smashed the neon cross
on the church across
the street. Even
twenty-five years later
when I saw Father Harris
I would wonder
if he knew it was me.
Maybe it was the demon-stoked
rotisseries of purgatory
where we would roast
hundreds of years
for the smallest of sins.
Or was it the day
I wore my space helmet

to catechism? Clear plastic
with a red-and-white
inflatable rim.   20
Sister Mary Bernadette
pointed toward the door
and said, "Out! Come back
when you're ready."
I rose from my chair   25
and kept rising
toward the ceiling
while the children
screamed and Sister
kept crossing herself.   30
The last she saw of me
was my shoes disappearing
through cracked plaster.
I rose into the sky and beyond.
It is a good thing   35
I am wearing my helmet,
I thought as I floated
and turned in the blackness
and brightness of outer space,
my body cold on one side and hot   40
on the other. It would
have been very quiet
if my blood had not been
rumbling in my ears so loud.
I remember thinking,   45
Maybe I will come back
when I'm ready.
But I won't tell
the other children
what it was like.   50
I'll have to make something up.

[1993]

SHARON OLDS [b. 1942]

I Go Back to May 1937

I see them standing at the formal gates of their colleges,
I see my father strolling out
under the ochre sandstone arch, the
red tiles glinting like bent
plates of blood behind his head, I
see my mother with a few light books at her hip
standing at the pillar made of tiny bricks with the
wrought-iron gate still open behind her, its
sword-tips black in the May air,
they are about to graduate, they are about to get married,
they are kids, they are dumb, all they know is they are
innocent, they would never hurt anybody.
I want to go up to them and say Stop,
don't do it—she's the wrong woman,
he's the wrong man, you are going to do things
you cannot imagine you would ever do,
you are going to do bad things to children,
you are going to suffer in ways you never heard of,
you are going to want to die. I want to go
up to them there in the late May sunlight and say it,
her hungry pretty blank face turning to me,
her pitiful beautiful untouched body,
his arrogant handsome blind face turning to me,
his pitiful beautiful untouched body,
but I don't do it. I want to live. I
take them up like the male and female
paper dolls and bang them together
at the hips like chips of flint as if to
strike sparks from them, I say
Do what you are going to do, and I will tell about it.

[1987]

592

MARILYN HACKER   [b. 1942]

Villanelle

Every day our bodies separate,
explode torn and dazed.
Not understanding what we celebrate

we grope through languages and hesitate
and touch each other, speechless and amazed;   5
and every day our bodies separate

us further from our planned, deliberate
ironic lives. I am afraid, disphased,
not understanding what we celebrate

when our fused limbs and lips communicate   10
the unlettered power we have raised.
Every day our bodies' separate

routines are harder to perpetuate.
In wordless darkness we learn wordless praise,
not understanding what we celebrate;   15

wake to ourselves, exhausted, in the late
morning as the wind tears off the haze,
not understanding how we celebrate
our bodies. Every day we separate.

[1974]

JAMES TATE [1943–2015]

The Lost Pilot

for my father, 1922–1944

Your face did not rot
like the others—the co-pilot,
for example, I saw him

yesterday. His face is corn-
mush: his wife and daughter,
the poor ignorant people, stare

as if he will compose soon.
He was more wronged than Job.
But your face did not rot

like the others—it grew dark,
and hard like ebony;
the features progressed in their

distinction. If I could cajole
you to come back for an evening,
down from your compulsive

orbiting, I would touch you,
read your face as Dallas,
your hoodlum gunner, now,

with the blistered eyes, reads
his braille editions. I would
touch your face as a disinterested

scholar touches an original page.
However frightening, I would
discover you, and I would not

turn you in; I would not make
you face your wife, or Dallas,
or the co-pilot, Jim. You

could return to your crazy
orbiting, and I would not try
to fully understand what   30

it means to you. All I know
is this: when I see you,
as I have seen you at least

once every year of my life,
spin across the wilds of the sky   35
like a tiny, African god,

I feel dead. I feel as if I were
the residue of a stranger's life,
that I should pursue you.

My head cocked toward the sky,   40
I cannot get off the ground,
and, you, passing over again,

fast, perfect, and unwilling
to tell me that you are doing
well, or that it was mistake   45

that placed you in that world,
and me in this; or that misfortune
placed these worlds in us.

                                            [1991]

LOUISE GLÜCK   [b. 1943]

Mock Orange

It is not the moon, I tell you.
It is these flowers
lighting the yard.

I hate them.
I hate them as I hate sex,   5
the man's mouth
sealing my mouth, the man's
paralyzing body—

and the cry that always escapes,
the low, humiliating
premise of union—

In my mind tonight
I hear the question and pursuing answer
fused in one sound
that mounts and mounts and then
is split into the old selves,
the tired antagonisms. Do you see?
We were made fools of.
And the scent of mock orange
drifts through the window.

How can I rest?
How can I be content
when there is still
that odor in the world?

[1985]

EAVAN BOLAND [b. 1944]

The Pomegranate

The only legend I have ever loved is
the story of a daughter lost in hell.
And found and rescued there.
Love and blackmail are the gist of it.
Ceres° and Persephone the names.

---

5. **Ceres:** Roman name of Demeter, the goddess of crops and harvest. Her daughter Persephone was kidnapped by Pluto (or Hades) and taken to the underworld. Demeter, grieving and angry, refused to let seeds germinate or crops grow. To save the human race from extinction, Zeus finally ordered Pluto to release Persephone. Pluto told her she was free to leave but tricked her by offering a pomegranate seed; anyone who eats food in the underworld must return there. Zeus therefore arranged a compromise: Persephone would spend a third of each year in the land of the dead with Pluto (winter, when Demeter went into mourning), but she would be with her mother for the other two-thirds of each year (spring and summer).

And the best thing about the legend is
I can enter it anywhere. And have.
As a child in exile in
a city of fogs and strange consonants,
I read it first and at first I was   10
an exiled child in the crackling dusk of
the underworld, the stars blighted. Later
I walked out in a summer twilight
searching for my daughter at bed-time.
When she came running I was ready   15
to make any bargain to keep her.
I carried her back past whitebeams
and wasps and honey-scented buddleias.
But I was Ceres then and I knew
winter was in store for every leaf   20
on every tree on that road.
Was inescapable for each one we passed.
And for me.
                              It is winter
and the stars are hidden.   25
I climb the stairs and stand where I can see
my child asleep beside her teen magazines,
her can of Coke, her plate of uncut fruit.
The pomegranate! How did I forget it?
She could have come home and been safe   30
and ended the story and all
our heart-broken searching but she reached
out a hand and plucked a pomegranate.
She put out her hand and pulled down
the French sound for apple° and   *pomme* 35
the noise of stone° and the proof   *granite*
that even in the place of death,
at the heart of legend, in the midst
of rocks full of unshed tears
ready to be diamonds by the time   40
the story was told, a child can be
hungry. I could warn her. There is still a chance.
The rain is cold. The road is flint-coloured.
The suburb has cars and cable television.
The veiled stars are above ground.   45
It is another world. But what else
can a mother give her daughter but such
beautiful rifts in time?
If I defer the grief I will diminish the gift.

The legend will be hers as well as mine.
She will enter it. As I have.
She will wake up. She will hold
the papery flushed skin in her hand.
And to her lips. I will say nothing.

[*1994;* 1995]

BERNADETTE MAYER   [b. 1945]

Sonnet

(You jerk you didn't call me up)

You jerk you didn't call me up
I haven't seen you in so long
You probably have a fucking tan
& besides that instead of making love tonight
You're drinking your parents to the airport
I'm through with you bourgeois boys
All you ever do is go back to ancestral comforts
Only money can get—even Catullus was rich but

Nowadays you guys settle for a couch
By a soporific color cable t.v. set
Instead of any arc of love, no wonder
The G.I. Joe team blows it every other time

Wake up! It's the middle of the night
You can either make love or die at the hands of
              the Cobra Commander

———————

To make love, turn to page 121.
To die, turn to page 172.

[1992]

KAY RYAN   [b. 1945]

Drops in the Bucket

At first
each drop
makes its
own pock
against the tin.   5
In time
there is a
thin lacquer
which is
layered and   10
relayered
till there's
a quantity
of water
with its   15
own skin
and sense
of purpose,
shocked at
each new violation   20
of its surface.

[2011]

WENDY COPE   [b. 1945]

Reading Scheme

Here is Peter. Here is Jane. They like fun.
Jane has a big doll. Peter has a ball.
Look, Jane, look! Look at the dog! See him run!

Here is Mummy. She has baked a bun.
Here is the milkman. He has come to call.
Here is Peter. Here is Jane. They like fun.

Go Peter! Go Jane! Come, milkman, come!
The milkman likes Mummy. She likes them all.
Look, Jane, look! Look at the dog! See him run!

Here are the curtains. They shut out the sun.
Let us peep! On tiptoe Jane! You are small!
Here is Peter. Here is Jane. They like fun.

I hear a car, Jane. The milkman looks glum.
Here is Daddy in his car. Daddy is tall.
Look, Jane, look! Look at the dog! See him run!

Daddy looks very cross. Has he a gun?
Up milkman! Up milkman! Over the wall!
Here is Peter. Here is Jane. They like fun.
Look, Jane, look! Look at the dog! See him run!

[1986]

LARRY LEVIS [1946–1996]

My Story in a Late Style of Fire

Whenever I listen to Billie Holiday, I am reminded
That I, too, was once banished from New York City.
Not because of drugs or because I was interesting enough
For any wan, overworked patrolman to worry about—
His expression usually a great, gauzy spiderweb of bewilderment   5
Over his face—I was banished from New York City by a woman.
Sometimes, after we had stopped laughing, I would look
At her & see a cold note of sorrow or puzzlement go
Over her face as if someone else were there, behind it,
Not laughing at all. We were, I think, "in love." No, I'm sure.   10
If my house burned down tomorrow morning, & if I & my wife
And son stood looking on at the flames, & if, then,
Someone stepped out of the crowd of bystanders
And said to me: "Didn't you once know . . . ?" *No*. But if
One of the flames, rising up in the scherzo of fire, turned   15
All the windows blank with light, & if that flame could speak,
And if it said to me: "You loved her, didn't you?" I'd answer,
Hands in my pockets, "Yes." And then I'd let fire & misfortune
Overwhelm my life. Sometimes, remembering those days,
I watch a warm, dry wind bothering a whole line of elms   20
And maples along a street in this neighborhood until
They're all moving at once, until I feel just like them,
Trembling & in unison. None of this matters now,
But I never felt alone all that year, & if I had sorrows,
I also had laughter, the affliction of angels & children.   25
Which can set a whole house on fire if you'd let it. And even then
You might still laugh to see all of your belongings set you free
In one long choiring of flames that sang only to you—
Either because no one else could hear them, or because
No one else wanted to. And, mostly, because they know.   30
They know such music cannot last, & that it would
Tear them apart if they listened. In those days,
I was, in fact, already married, just as I am now,
Although to another woman. And that day I could have stayed

601

In New York. I had friends there. I could have strayed
Up Lexington Avenue, or down to Third, & caught a faint
Glistening of the sea between the buildings. But all I wanted
Was to hold her all morning, until her body was, again,
A bright field, or until we both reached some thicket
As if at the end of a lane, or at the end of all desire,
And where we could, therefore, be alone again, & make
Some dignity out of loneliness. As, mostly, people cannot do.
Billie Holiday, whose life was shorter & more humiliating
Than my own, would have understood all this, if only
Because even in her late addiction & her bloodstream's
Hallelujahs, she, too, sang often of some affair, or someone
Gone, & therefore permanent. And sometimes she sang for
Nothing, even then, & it isn't anyone's business, if she did.
That morning, when *she* asked me to leave, wearing only
That apricot tinted, fraying chemise, I wanted to stay.
But I also wanted to go to lose her suddenly, almost
For no reason, & certainly without any explanation.
I remember looking down at a pair of singular tracks
Made in a light snow the night before, at how they were
Gradually effacing themselves beneath the tires
Of the morning traffic, & thinking that my only other choice
Was fire, ashes, abandonment, solitude. All of which happened
Anyway, & soon after, & by divorce. I know this isn't much.
But I wanted to explain this life to you, even if
I had to become, over the years, someone else to do it.
You have to think of me what you think of me. I had
To live my life, even its late, florid style. Before
You judge this, think of her. Then think of fire,
Its laughter, the music of splintering beams & glass,
The flames reaching through the second story of a house
Almost as if to—mistakenly—rescue someone who
Left you years ago. It is so American, fire. So like us.
Its desolation. And its eventual, brief triumph.

[1985]

MARILYN NELSON   [b. 1946]

Emmett Till's name still catches in my throat,°

like syllables waylaid in a stutterer's mouth.
A fourteen-year-old stutterer, in the South
to visit relatives and to be taught
the family's ways. His mother had finally bought
that White Sox cap; she'd made him swear an oath   5
to be careful around white folks. She'd told him the truth
of many a Mississippi anecdote:
Some white folks have blind souls. In his suitcase
she'd packed dungarees, T-shirts, underwear,
and comic books. She'd given him a note   10
for the conductor, waved to his chubby face,
wondered if he'd remember to brush his hair.
Her only child. A body left to bloat.

                                            [2005]

Excerpt from *A Wreath for Emmett Till* by Marilyn Nelson.

LINDA HOGAN   [b. 1947]

Crow Law

The temple where crow worships
walks forward in tall, black grass.
Betrayal is crow's way of saying grace
to the wolf
so it can eat   5

603

what is left
when blood is on the ground,
until what remains of moose
is crow
walking out
the sacred temple of ribs
in a dance of leaving
the red tracks of scarce and private gods.
It is the oldest war
where moose becomes wolf and crow,
where the road ceases
to become the old forest
where crow is calling,
where we are still afraid.

[1993]

YUSEF KOMUNYAKAA   [b. 1947]

Facing It

My black face fades,
hiding inside the black granite.
I said I wouldn't,
dammit: No tears.
I'm stone. I'm flesh.
My clouded reflection eyes me
like a bird of prey, the profile of night
slanted against morning. I turn
this way—the stone lets me go.
I turn that way—I'm inside
the Vietnam Veterans Memorial
again, depending on the light
to make a difference.
I go down the 58,022 names,
half-expecting to find
my own in letters like smoke.
I touch the name Andrew Johnson;
I see the booby trap's white flash.

Names shimmer on a woman's blouse
but when she walks away   20
the names stay on the wall.
Brushstrokes flash, a red bird's
wings cutting across my stare.
The sky. A plane in the sky.
A white vet's image floats   25
closer to me, then his pale eyes
look through mine. I'm a window.
He's lost his right arm
inside the stone. In the black mirror
a woman's trying to erase names: 30
No, she's brushing a boy's hair.

[1988]

AI   [1947–2010]

Hoover, Edgar J.

1

I'm the man behind the man
behind the man
and I have got my hands
in everybody's pockets.
I know who's been sticking his plug   5
in Marilyn Monroe's socket.
The shock it would give,
if everybody knew what King Arthur Jack
won't do to keep his rocket fueled.
I have files on everyone who counts,   10
yet they would amount to nothing,
if I did not have the will to use them.
Citizens must know their place,
but so must the president,
who simply decided one day   15
to hock his family jewels to the Mob.
They call me a cruel sonofabitch

just to aggravate me,
but my strength is truth.
I have the proof
of every kind of infidelity
and that makes me the one free man
in a country of prisoners
of lust, greed, hatred, need
greater than the fear of reprisal,
all the recognized sins
and all those unrecognizable,
except to me and God. Maybe God.
Sometimes my whole body aches
and I lie down on the floor,
just staring at the ceiling,
until I am feeling in control again,
my old confidence surging back
through me like electricity
and I get up, Frankenstein, revived
by the weakness of others
and as unstoppable as a handful of pills
that might kill you on a night like this,
like the night when Marilyn kissed it all goodbye.
It only came up roses after her show closed.
Too bad she had to row, row her boat
in lava lake.
They said they would make her a star.
Now far out in space,
her face big as a planet,
she looks down
on the whole pathetic, human race, wasting time,
as it shivers and shakes
down the conga line
behind Jack, Bobby, and me too.
When the voice on the phone
cried *"We're through"* and hung up,
she took an overdose,
trusting someone to save her,
but now she whispers,
"Honey, don't trust anybody
and never, ever fuck the head of state."

2

I had a head bald
as a licked clean plate
and a face . . .   60
Nobody ever said grace at my table,
yet, the god of judgment hovered over my head.
He led me down
dark halls to motel rooms,
where a locked door   65
and heavy perfume
could neither conceal, nor contain
the fumes of love that proclaimed
another fallen angel by his name.
Martin Luther King, Jr. preaches freedom,   70
but it means slavery for the white man.
It hands our keys to the robbers
and says, please, don't take anything.
Look at him on his knees
before pussy's altar.   75
Tomorrow with his wife beside him
he won't falter, as he shouts
from the pulpit about equality.
His words are a disease sweeping
through the colored people.   80
I can stop it if I choose.
I can release the tapes, the photographs
and end the so-called peaceful revolution,
but my solution is to sabotage discreetly,
to let someone else take the blame,   85
the Klan, or even another smoke,
who's younger and not broken in by privilege.
Someone like that Malcolm X,
that showstopping nigger,
who respects no boundaries   90
and hates the white man,
because he understands him.
He doesn't want to vote,
he doesn't want to tote that bail
in the name of integration.   95
He wants to sail back into blackness
and I say let him.
There is no such thing as freedom
and there never will be,

even for the white man.
The X-man knows it is eat, or be eaten
and Grandpa Hoover
has the biggest teeth.

3

They all wanted me
to take the A train to anonymity,
those who would seduce their own mothers,
after an audience with the Pope.
The Holy joke I call him.
I'd like to get a tape, or two,
of that crew in Rome.
A two-way mirror
somewhere in the Vatican, the camera rolling,
while some Cardinal is jerking off
over a silver bowl,
until his Vesuvius erupts again and again.
But I digress.
Now Lyndon Johnson and a negress,
that *is* delicious,
something best served on a platter.
Save it until after the elections
when it really matters.
I'm so scattered lately.
I feel like shattering all my Waterford crystal.
Ask me anything you want, but don't touch me.
I keep my pistol loaded.
Don't say I told you. Do.
I want the lowdown sonsofbitches
who betray me to know
I'm on to them like a fly on shit.
I will not rest,
until I spit in their mouths
and piss on their faces. The fools.
J. Edgar Hoover runs this country.
J. Edgar Hoover rules.

[2000]

JANE KENYON [1947–1995]

Happiness

There's just no accounting for happiness,
or the way it turns up like a prodigal
who comes back to the dust at your feet
having squandered a fortune far away.

And how can you not forgive?   5
You make a feast in honor of what
was lost, and take from its place the finest
garment, which you saved for an occasion
you could not imagine, and you weep night and day
to know that you were not abandoned,   10
that happiness saved its most extreme form
for you alone.

No, happiness is the uncle you never
knew about, who flies a single-engine plane
onto the grassy landing strip, hitchhikes   15
into town, and inquires at every door
until he finds you asleep midafternoon
as you so often are during the unmerciful
hours of your despair.

It comes to the monk in his cell.   20
It comes to the woman sweeping the street
with a birch broom, to the child
whose mother has passed out from drink.
It comes to the lover, to the dog chewing
a sock, to the pusher, to the basketmaker,   25
and to the clerk stacking cans of carrots
in the night.
            It even comes to the boulder
in the perpetual shade of pine barrens,
to rain falling on the open sea,   30
to the wineglass, weary of holding wine.

[1995]

609

HEATHER McHUGH   [b. 1948]

What He Thought

for Fabbio Doplicher

We were supposed to do a job in Italy
and, full of our feeling for
ourselves (our sense of being
Poets from America) we went
from Rome to Fano, met
the mayor, mulled
a couple matters over (what's
cheap date, they asked us; what's
flat drink). Among Italian literati

we could recognize our counterparts:
the academic, the apologist,
the arrogant, the amorous,
the brazen and the glib—and there was one

administrator (the conservative), in suit
of regulation gray, who like a good tour guide
with measured pace and uninflected tone narrated
sights and histories the hired van hauled us past.
Of all, he was most politic and least poetic,
so it seemed. Our last few days in Rome
(when all but three of the New World Bards had flown)
I found a book of poems this
unprepossessing one had written: it was there
in the *pensione* room (a room he'd recommended)
where it must have been abandoned by
the German visitor (was there a bus of *them*?)
to whom he had inscribed and dated it a month before.
I couldn't read Italian, either, so I put the book
back into the wardrobe's dark. We last Americans

were due to leave tomorrow. For our parting evening then
our host chose something in a family restaurant, and there
we sat and chatted, sat and chewed,
till, sensible it was our last

610

big chance to be poetic, make
our mark, one of us asked
                                   "What's poetry?   35
Is it the fruits and vegetables and
marketplace of Campo dei Fiori, or
the statue there?" Because I was

the glib one, I identified the answer
instantly, I didn't have to think—"The truth   40
is both, it's both," I blurted out. But that
was easy. That was easiest to say. What followed
taught me something about difficulty,
for our underestimated host spoke out,
all of a sudden, with a rising passion, and he said: 45

The statue represents Giordano Bruno,
brought to be burned in the public square
because of his offense against
authority, which is to say
the Church. His crime was his belief   50
the universe does not revolve around
the human being: God is no
fixed point or central government, but rather is
poured in waves through all things. All things
move. "If God is not the soul itself, He is   55
the soul of the soul of the world." Such was
his heresy. The day they brought him
forth to die, they feared he might
incite the crowd (the man was famous
for his eloquence). And so his captors   60
placed upon his face
an iron mask, in which

he could not speak. That's
how they burned him. That is how
he died: without a word, in front   65
of everyone.
                And poetry—
                      (we'd all
put down our forks by now, to listen to
the man in gray; he went on   70
softly)—
                poetry is what

he thought, but did not say.

                                                    [1994]

LESLIE MARMON SILKO   [b. 1948]

Prayer to the Pacific

I traveled to the ocean
　　　　distant
　　　　　　　　from my southwest land of sandrock
　　　　　　　　to the moving blue water
　　　　　　　　Big as the myth of origin.

Pale
pale water in the yellow-white light of
　　　　　　　　sun　floating west
　　　　　　　　　　to China
　　　　　　　　where ocean herself was born.
Clouds that blow across the sand are wet.

Squat in the wet sand and speak to the Ocean:
　　　　　　　　I return to you　turquoise　the red coral you sent us,
　　　　　　　　　　sister spirit of Earth.
Four round stones in my pocket　I carry back the ocean
　　　　　　　　　　to suck and to taste.

Thirty thousand years ago
　　　　　　　　Indians came riding across the ocean
　　　　　　　　carried by giant sea turtles.

Waves were high that day
　　　　　　　　great sea turtles waded　slowly out
　　　　　　　　　　from the gray sundown sea.

Grandfather Turtle rolled in the sand　four times
　　　　　　　　and disappeared
　　　　　　　　　　swimming into the sun.

And so　from that time
　　　　　　　immemorial,
　　　　　　　　　as the old people say,
rain clouds drift from the west
　　　　　　　　gift from the ocean.

Green leaves in the wind
Wet earth on my feet
              swallowing raindrops
                        clear from China.

[1981]

SEKOU SUNDIATA   [1948–2007]

Blink Your Eyes

Remembering Sterling A. Brown

I was on my way to see my woman
but the Law said I was on my way
thru a red light red light red light
and if you saw my woman
you could understand,   5
I was just being a man
It wasn't about no light
it was about my ride
and if you saw my ride
you could dig that too, you dig?   10
Sunroof stereo radio black leather
bucket seats sit low you know,
the body's cool, but the tires are worn.
Ride when the hard time come, ride
when they're gone, in other words   15
the light was green.

I could wake up in the morning
without a warning
and my world could change:
blink your eyes.   20
All depends, all depends on the skin,
all depends on the skin you're living in.

Up to the window comes the Law
with his hand on his gun

what's up? what's happening?
I said I guess
that's when I really broke the law.
He said *a routine, step out the car*
a routine, assume the position.
Put your hands up in the air
you know the routine, like you just don't care.
License and registration.
Deep was the night and the light
from the North Star on the car door, deja vu
we've been through this before,
why did you stop me?
Somebody had to stop you.
I watch the news, you always lose.
You're unreliable, that's undeniable.
This is serious, you could be dangerous.

I could wake up in the morning
without a warning
and my world could change:
blink your eyes.
All depends, all depends on the skin,
all depends on the skin you're living in.

New York City, they got laws
can't no bruthas drive outdoors,
in certain neighborhoods, on particular streets
near and around certain types of people.
They got laws.
All depends, all depends on the skin,
all depends on the skin you're living in.

[1995]

AGHA SHAHID ALI   [1949–2001]

Even the Rain

What will suffice for a true-love knot? Even the rain?
But he has bought grief's lottery, bought even the rain.

"Our glosses / wanting in this world" — Can you remember?
Anyone! — "when we thought / the poets taught" even the rain?

After we died — *That was it!* — God left us in the dark.   5
And as we forgot the dark, we forgot even the rain.

Drought was over. Where was I? Drinks were on the house.
For mixers, my love, you'd poured — what? — even the rain.

Of this pear-shaped orange's perfumed twist, I will say:
Extract Vermouth from the bergamot, even the rain.   10

How did the Enemy love you — with earth? air? and fire?
He held just one thing back till he got even: the rain.

This is God's site for a new house of executions?
You swear by the Bible, Despot, even the rain.

After the bones — those flowers — this was found in the urn: 15
The lost river, ashes from the ghat,° even the rain.

What was I to prophesy if not the end of the world?
A salt pillar for the lonely lot, even the rain.

How the air raged, desperate, streaming the earth with flames —
To help burn down my house, Fire sought even the rain.   20

He would raze the mountains, he would level the waves;
he would, to smooth his epic plot, even the rain.

New York belongs at daybreak to only me, just me —
To make this claim Memory's brought even the rain.

They've found the knife that killed you, but whose prints are these?   25
No one has such small hands, Shahid, not even the rain.

[2003]

16. ghat: Steps that lead down to the bank of a river.

615

VICTOR HERNÁNDEZ CRUZ   [b. 1949]

Problems with Hurricanes

A campesino° looked at the air
And told me:
With hurricanes it's not the wind
or the noise or the water.
I'll tell you he said:
it's the mangoes, avocados
Green plantains and bananas
flying into town like projectiles.

How would your family
feel if they had to tell
The generations that you
got killed by a flying
Banana.

Death by drowning has honor
If the wind picked you up
and slammed you
Against a mountain boulder
This would not carry shame
But
to suffer a mango smashing
Your skull
or a plantain hitting your
Temple at 70 miles per hour
is the ultimate disgrace.

The campesino takes off his hat—
As a sign of respect
towards the fury of the wind
And says:
Don't worry about the noise

1. **campesino:** Someone (particularly a farmer or farm laborer) who lives in a
rural area in Latin America.

Don't worry about the water   30
Don't worry about the wind—
If you are going out
beware of mangoes
And all such beautiful
sweet things.   35

[1991]

CAROLYN FORCHÉ   [b. 1950]

The Colonel

What you have heard is true. I was in his house. His wife carried a tray
of coffee and sugar. His daughter filed her nails, his son went out for the
night. There were daily papers, pet dogs, a pistol on the cushion beside
him. The moon swung bare on its black cord over the house. On the television was a cop show. It was in English. Broken bottles were embedded   5
in the walls around the house to scoop the kneecaps from a man's legs or
cut his hands to lace. On the windows there were gratings like those in
liquor stores. We had dinner, rack of lamb, good wine, a gold bell was on
the table for calling the maid. The maid brought green mangoes, salt, a
type of bread. I was asked how I enjoyed the country. There was a brief   10
commercial in Spanish. His wife took everything away. There was some
talk then of how difficult it had become to govern. The parrot said hello
on the terrace. The colonel told it to shut up, and pushed himself from
the table. My friend said to me with his eyes: say nothing. The colonel
returned with a sack used to bring groceries home. He spilled many   15
human ears on the table. They were like dried peach halves. There is no
other way to say this. He took one of them in his hands, shook it in our
faces, dropped it into a water glass. It came alive there. I am tired of fooling around he said. As for the rights of anyone, tell your people they can
go fuck themselves. He swept the ears to the floor with his arm and held   20
the last of his wine in the air. Something for your poetry, no? he said.
Some of the ears on the floor caught this scrap of his voice. Some of the
ears on the floor were pressed to the ground.

[1978]

RAY A. YOUNG BEAR   [b. 1950]

From the Spotted Night

In the blizzard
while chopping wood
the mystical whistler
beckons my attention.
Once there were longhouses
here. A village.
In the abrupt spring floods
swimmers retrieved our belief.
So their spirit remains.
From the spotted night
distant jets transform
into fireflies who float
towards me like incandescent
snowflakes.
The leather shirt
which is suspended
on a wire hanger
above the bed's headboard
is humanless; yet when one
stands outside the house,
the strenuous sounds
of dressers and boxes
being moved can be heard.
We believe someone wears
the shirt and rearranges
the heavy furniture,
although nothing
is actually changed.
Unlike the Plains Indian shirts
which repelled lead bullets,
ricocheting from them
in fiery sparks,
this shirt is the means;
this shirt *is* the bullet.

[1990]

JORIE GRAHAM [b. 1950]

Prayer

Over a dock railing, I watch the minnows, thousands, swirl
themselves, each a minuscule muscle, but also, without the
way to *create* current, making of their unison (turning, reinfolding,
entering and exiting their own unison in unison) making of themselves a
visual current, one that cannot freight or sway by   5
minutest fractions the water's downdrafts and upswirls, the
dockside cycles of finally-arriving boat-wakes, there where
they hit deeper resistance, water that seems to burst into
itself (it has those layers), a real current though mostly
invisible sending into the visible (minnows) arrowing   10
                    motion that forces change—
this is freedom. This is the force of faith. Nobody gets
what they want. Never again are you the same. The longing
is to be pure. What you get is to be changed. More and more by
each glistening minute, through which infinity threads itself,   15
also oblivion, of course, the aftershocks of something
at sea. Here, hands full of sand, letting it sift through
in the wind, I look in and say take this, this is
what I have saved, take this, hurry. And if I listen
now? Listen, I was not saying anything. It was only   20
something I did. I could not choose words. I am free to go.
I cannot of course come back. Not to this. Never.
It is a ghost posed on my lips. Here: never.

[2002]

MARIE HOWE   [b. 1950]

Death, the last visit

Hearing a low growl in your throat, you'll know that it's started.
It has nothing to ask you. It has only something to say, and
it will speak in your own tongue.

Locking its arm around you, it will hold you as long as you ever wanted.
Only this time it will be long enough. It will not let go.
Burying your face in its dark shoulder, you'll smell mud and hair and
          water.

You'll taste your mother's sour nipple, your favorite salty cock
and swallow a word you thought you'd spit out once and be done with.
Through half-closed eyes you'll see that its shadow looks like yours,

a perfect fit. You could weep with gratefulness. It will take you
as you like it best, hard and fast as a slap across your face,
or so sweet and slow you'll scream give it to me give it to me until it does.

Nothing will ever reach this deep. Nothing will ever clench this hard.
At last (the little girls are clapping, shouting) someone has pulled
the drawstring of your gym bag closed enough and tight. At last

someone has knotted the lace of your shoe so it won't ever come undone.
Even as you turn into it, even as you begin to feel yourself stop,
you'll whistle with amazement between your residual teeth oh jesus

oh sweetheart, oh holy mother, nothing nothing nothing ever felt this good.

[1988]

JOY HARJO [b. 1951]

She Had Some Horses

She had some horses.

She had horses who were bodies of sand.
She had horses who were maps drawn of blood.
She had horses who were skins of ocean water.
She had horses who were the blue air of sky.   5
She had horses who were fur and teeth.
She had horses who were clay and would break.
She had horses who were splintered red cliff.

She had some horses.

She had horses with long, pointed breasts.   10
She had horses with full, brown thighs.
She had horses who laughed too much.
She had horses who threw rocks at glass houses.
She had horses who licked razor blades.

She had some horses.   15

She had horses who danced in their mothers' arms.
She had horses who thought they were the sun and their
bodies shone and burned like stars.
She had horses who waltzed nightly on the moon.
She had horses who were much too shy, and kept quiet   20
in stalls of their own making.

She had some horses.

She had horses who liked Creek Stomp Dance songs.
She had horses who cried in their beer.
She had horses who spit at male queens who made   25
them afraid of themselves.
She had horses who said they weren't afraid.
She had horses who lied.
She had horses who told the truth, who were stripped
bare of their tongues.   30

621

She had some horses.

She had horses who called themselves, "horse."
She had horses who called themselves, "spirit," and kept
their voices secret and to themselves.
She had horses who had no names.
She had horses who had books of names.

She had some horses.

She had horses who whispered in the dark, who were afraid to speak.
She had horses who screamed out of fear of the silence, who
carried knives to protect themselves from ghosts.
She had horses who waited for destruction.
She had horses who waited for resurrection.

She had some horses.

She had horses who got down on their knees for any saviour.
She had horses who thought their high price had saved them.
She had horses who tried to save her, who climbed in her
bed at night and prayed as they raped her.

She had some horses.

She had some horses she loved.
She had some horses she hated.

These were the same horses.

[1983]

CHERRIE MORAGA   [b. 1952]

Loving in the War Years

Loving you is like living
in the war years.
I *do* think of Bogart & Bergman
not clear who's who
but still singin a long smoky
mood into the piano bar
drinks straight up
the last bottle in the house
while bombs split
outside, a broken
world.

A world war going on
but you and I still insisting
in each our own heads
still thinkin how   15
if I could only make some contact
with that woman across the keyboard
we size each other up
        yes . . .

Loving you has this kind of desperation   20
to it, like do or die, I
having eyed you from the first
time you made the decision to move
from your stool
to live dangerously.   25

All on the hunch
that in our exchange of photos
of old girlfriends, names
of cities and memories
back in the states   30
the fronts we've manned
out here on the continent
all this on the hunch
that *this* time there'll be
no need for resistance.   35

Loving in the war years
calls for this kind of risking
without a home to call our own
I've got to take you as you come
to me, each time like a stranger   40
all over again. Not knowing
what deaths you saw today
I've got to take you
as you come, battle bruised
refusing our enemy, fear.   45

We're all we've got. You and I

maintaining
this war time morality
where being queer
and female is as rude   50
as we can get.

                                                        [1983]

RAY GONZÁLEZ   [b. 1952]

Praise the Tortilla, Praise Menudo, Praise Chorizo

I praise the tortilla in honor of El Panzón,
who hit me in school every day and made me see
how the bruises on my arms looked like
the brown clouds on my mother's tortillas.
I praise the tortilla because I know
they can fly into our hands like
eager flesh of the one we love,
those soft yearnings we delight in biting
as we tear the tortilla and wipe the plate clean.

I praise the menudo° as visionary food that it is,
the tripas y posole° tight flashes of color
we see as the red caldo° smears across our notebooks
like a vision we have not had in years,
our lives going down like the empty bowl
of menudo exploding in our stomachs
with the chili piquin° of our poetic dreams.

I praise the chorizo° and smear it
across my face and hands,
the dayglow brown of it painting me
with the desire to find out
what happened to la familia,
why the chorizo sizzled in the pan
and covered the house with a smell
of childhood we will never have again,

10. **menudo:** Mexican soup made with hominy and tripe; said to have special powers.
11. **tripas y posole:** Tripe and hominy.
12. **caldo:** Soup.
16. **chili piquin:** Type of pepper, added to menudo or other soups.
17. **chorizo:** Mexican sausage.

the chorizo burrito hot in our hands,   25
as we ran out to play and show the vatos°
it's time to cut the chorizo,
tell it like it is before la manteca° runs down
our chins and drips away.

[1992]

26. vatos: Guys.
28. la manteca: Lard or grease.

MARY RUEFLE   [b. 1952]

Rain Effect°

A bride and a groom sitting in an open buggy
in the rain, holding hands but not looking
at each other, waiting for the rain to stop,
waiting for the marriage to begin, embarrassed
by the rain, the effect of the rain on the bridal   5
veil, the wet horse with his mane in his eyes,
the rain cold as the sea, the sea deep as love,
big drops of rain falling on the leather seat,
the rain beaded on a rose pinned to the groom's
lapel, the rain on the bride's bouquet,   10
on the baby's breath there, the sound of the rain
hitting the driver's top hat, the rain
shining like satin on the black street,
on the tips of patent leather shoes, Hokusai's
father who polished mirrors for a living, Hokusai's   15
father watching the sky for clouds, Hokusai's father's son
drawing rain over a bridge and over the people crossing
the bridge, Hokusai's father's son drawing the rain
for hours, Hokusai's father rubbing a mirror, the rain
cold as the sea, the sea cold as love, the sea swelling   20
to a tidal wave, at the tip of the wave white.

[2001]

Rain Effect: This ekphrastic poem was inspired by the paintings of Katsushika
Hokusai (1760–1849).

ALBERTO RÍOS   [b. 1952]

Nani°

Sitting at her table, she serves
the sopa de arroz° to me   *rice soup*
instinctively, and I watch her,
the absolute *mamá*, and eat words
I might have had to say more
out of embarrassment. To speak,
now-foreign words I used to speak,
too, dribble down her mouth as she serves
me albondigas.° No more   *meatballs*
than a third are easy to me.
By the stove she does something with words
and looks at me only with her
back. I am full. I tell her
I taste the mint, and watch her speak
smiles at the stove. All my words
make her smile. Nani never serves
herself, she only watches me
with her skin, her hair. I ask for more.

I watch the *mamá* warming more
tortillas for me. I watch her
fingers in the flame for me.
Near her mouth, I see a wrinkle speak
of a man whose body serves
the ants like she serves me, then more words
from more wrinkles about children, words
about this and that, flowing more
easily from these other mouths. Each serves
as a tremendous string around her,
holding her together. They speak
nani was this and that to me

Nani: Diminutive for "grandmother."

626

and I wonder just how much of me
will die with her, what were the words
I could have been, was. Her insides speak
through a hundred wrinkles, now, more
than she can bear, steel around her,   35
shouting, then, What is this thing she serves?

She asks me if I want more.
I own no words to stop her.
Even before I speak, she serves.

[1982]

GARY SOTO [b. 1952]

Moving Away

Remember that we are moving away   brother
From those years
In the same house with a white stepfather
What troubled him has been forgotten

But what troubled us has settled   5
Like dirt
In the nests of our knuckles
And cannot be washed away

All those times you woke shivering
In the night   10
From a coldness I
Could not understand
And cupped a crucifix beneath the covers

All those summers we hoed our yard
In the afternoon sun   15
The heat waving across our faces
And we waved back wasps
While the one we hated
Watched us from under a tree and said nothing

We will remember those moments   brother

And now that we are far
From one another
What I want to speak of
Is the quiet of a room just before daybreak
And you next to me   sleeping

[1977]

JIMMY SANTIAGO BACA   [b. 1952]

Family Ties

Mountain barbecue.
They arrive, young cousins singly,
older aunts and uncles in twos and threes,
like trees. I play with a new generation
of children, my hands in streambed silt
of their lives, a scuba diver's hands, dusting
surface sand for buried treasure.
Freshly shaved and powdered faces
of uncles and aunts surround taco
and tamale tables. Mounted elk head on wall,
brass rearing horse cowboy clock
on fireplace mantle. Sons and daughters
converse round beer and whiskey table.
Tempers ignite on land grant issues.
Children scurry round my legs.
Old bow-legged men toss horseshoes on lawn,
other farmhands from Mexico sit on a bench,
broken lives repaired for this occasion.
I feel no love or family tie here. I rise
to go hiking, to find abandoned rock cabins
in the mountains. We come to a grass clearing,
my wife rolls her jeans up past ankles,
wades ice cold stream, and I barefooted,
carry a son in each arm and follow.
We cannot afford a place like this.

At the party again, I eat bean and chile
burrito, and after my third glass of rum,
we climb in the car and my wife drives
us home. My sons sleep in the back,
dream of the open clearing,   30
they are chasing each other with cattails
in the sunlit pasture, giggling,
as I stare out the window
at no trespassing signs white flashing past.

[1989]

NAOMI SHIHAB NYE   [b. 1952]

Gate A-4

Wandering around the Albuquerque Airport Terminal, after learning my   1
flight had been delayed four hours, I heard an announcement: "If anyone
in the vicinity of Gate A-4 understands any Arabic, please come to the
gate immediately."

Well—one pauses these days. Gate A-4 was my own gate. I went there.   2

An older woman in full traditional Palestinian embroidered dress, just   3
like my grandma wore, was crumpled to the floor, wailing loudly. "Help,"
said the flight service person. "Talk to her. What is her problem? We told
her the flight was going to be late and she did this."

I stooped to put my arm around the woman and spoke to her   4
haltingly. "Shu-dow-a, Shu-bid-uck Habibti? Stani schway, Min fadlick,
Shu-bit-se-wee?" The minute she heard any words she knew, however
poorly used, she stopped crying. She thought the flight had been cancelled entirely. She needed to be in El Paso for major medical treatment
the next day. I said, "No, we're fine, you'll get there, just later, who is picking you up? Let's call him."

We called her son and I spoke with him in English. I told him I would   5
stay with his mother till we got on the plane and would ride next to
her—Southwest. She talked to him. Then we called her other sons just
for the fun of it. Then we called my dad and he and she spoke for a while
in Arabic and found out of course they had ten shared friends. Then I

thought just for the heck of it why not call some Palestinian poets I know and let them chat with her? This all took up about two hours.

She was laughing a lot by then. Telling about her life, patting my knee, answering questions. She had pulled a sack of homemade *mamool* cookies—little powdered sugar crumbly mounds stuffed with dates and nuts—out of her bag—and was offering them to all the women at the gate. To my amazement, not a single woman declined one. It was like a sacrament. The traveler from Argentina, the mom from California, the lovely woman from Laredo—we were all covered with the same powdered sugar. And smiling. There is no better cookie.

And then the airline broke out free beverages from huge coolers and two little girls from our flight ran around serving us all apple juice and they were covered with powdered sugar, too. And I noticed my new best friend—by now we were holding hands—had a potted plant poking out of her bag, some medicinal thing, with green furry leaves. Such an old country traveling tradition. Always carry a plant. Always stay rooted to somewhere.

And I looked around that gate of late and weary ones and thought, This is the world I want to live in. The shared world. Not a single person in that gate—once the crying of confusion stopped—seemed apprehensive about any other person. They took the cookies. I wanted to hug all those other women, too.

This can still happen anywhere. Not everything is lost.

[2008]

RITA DOVE   [b. 1952]

Fifth Grade Autobiography

I was four in this photograph fishing
with my grandparents at a lake in Michigan.
My brother squats in poison ivy.
His Davy Crockett cap
sits squared on his head so the raccoon tail
flounces down the back of his sailor suit.

My grandfather sits to the far right
in a folding chair,

and I know his left hand is on
the tobacco in his pants pocket   10
because I used to wrap it for him
every Christmas. Grandmother's hips
bulge from the brush, she's leaning
into the ice chest, sun through the trees
printing her dress with soft   15
luminous paws.

I am staring jealously at my brother;
the day before he rode his first horse, alone.
I was strapped in a basket
behind my grandfather.   20
He smelled of lemons. He's died—

but I remember his hands.

[1989]

TONY HOAGLAND   [b. 1953]

History of Desire

When you're seventeen, and drunk
on the husky, late-night flavor
of your first girlfriend's voice
along the wires of the telephone

what else to do but steal   5
your father's El Dorado from the drive,
and cruise out to the park on Driscoll Hill?
Then climb the county water tower

and aerosol her name in spraycan orange
a hundred feet above the town?   10
Because only the letters of that word,
DORIS, next door to yours,

in yard-high, iridescent script,
are amplified enough to tell the world
who's playing lead guitar   15
in the rock band of your blood.

You don't consider for a moment
the shock in store for you in 10 A.D.,
a decade after Doris, when,
out for a drive on your visit home,

you take the Smallville Road, look up
and see RON LOVES DORIS
still scorched upon the reservoir.
This is how history catches up—

by holding still until you
bump into yourself.
What makes you blush, and shove
the pedal of the Mustang

almost through the floor
as if you wanted to spray gravel
across the features of the past,
or accelerate into oblivion?

Are you so out of love that you
can't move fast enough away?
But if desire is acceleration,
experience is circular as any

Indianapolis. We keep coming back
to what we are—each time older,
more freaked out, or less afraid.
And you are older now.

You should stop today.
In the name of Doris, stop.

[1992]

HARRYETTE MULLEN   [b. 1953]

Elliptical

They just can't seem to ... They should try harder to ... They
ought to be more ... We all wish they weren't so ... They
never ... They always ... Sometimes they ... Once in a while

they . . . However it is obvious that they . . . Their overall ten-
dency has been . . . The consequences of which have been . . .
They don't appear to understand that . . . If only they would
make an effort to . . . But we know how difficult it is for them to
. . . Many of them remain unaware of . . . Some who should
know better simply refuse to . . . Of course, their perspective
has been limited by . . . On the other hand, they obviously feel
entitled to . . . Certainly we can't forget that they . . . Nor can it
be denied that they . . . We know that this has had an enormous
impact on their . . . Nevertheless their behavior strikes us as . . .
Our interactions unfortunately have been . . .

[2002]

JANE HIRSHFIELD   [b. 1953]

My Species

even
a small purple artichoke
boiled
in its own bittered
and darkening   5
waters
grows tender,
grows tender and sweet

patience, I think,
my species   10

keep testing the spiny leaves

the spiny heart

[2015]

MARK DOTY [b. 1953]

A Display of Mackerel

They lie in parallel rows,
on ice, head to tail,
each a foot of luminosity

barred with black bands,
which divide the scales'
radiant sections

like seams of lead
in a Tiffany window.
Iridescent, watery

prismatics: think abalone,
the wildly rainbowed
mirror of a soapbubble sphere,

think sun on gasoline.
Splendor, and splendor,
and not a one in any way

distinguished from the other
—nothing about them
of individuality. Instead

they're *all* exact expressions
of the one soul,
each a perfect fulfilment

of heaven's template,
mackerel essence. As if,
after a lifetime arriving

at this enameling, the jeweler's
made uncountable examples,
each as intricate

in its oily fabulation
as the one before
Suppose we could iridesce,

like these, and lose ourselves
entirely in the universe
of shimmer—would you want

to be yourself only,
unduplicatable, doomed   35
to be lost? They'd prefer,

plainly, to be flashing participants,
multitudinous. Even now
they seem to be bolting

forward, heedless of stasis.   40
They don't care they're dead
and nearly frozen,

just as, presumably,
they didn't care that they were living:
all, all for all,   45

the rainbowed school
and its acres of brilliant classrooms,
in which no verb is singular,

or every one is. How happy they seem,
even on ice, to be together, selfless,   50
which is the price of gleaming.

[1995]

KIM ADDONIZIO   [b. 1954]

First Kiss

Afterwards you had that drunk, drugged look
my daughter used to get, when she had let go
of my nipple, her mouth gone slack and her eyes
turned vague and filmy, as though behind them
the milk was rising up to fill her   5
whole head, that would loll on the small
white stalk of her neck so I would have to hold her
closer, amazed at the sheer power
of satiety, which was nothing like the needing

to be fed, the wild flailing and crying until she fastened
herself to me and made the seal tight
between us, and sucked, drawing the liquid down and
out of my body; no, *this* was the crowning
moment, this giving of herself, knowing
she could show me how helpless
she was—that's what I saw, that night when you
pulled your mouth from mine and
leaned back against a chain-link fence,
in front of a burned-out church: a man
who was going to be that vulnerable,
that easy and impossible to hurt.

[2004]

LORNA DEE CERVANTES   [b. 1954]

Freeway 280

Las casitas° near the gray cannery,   *little houses*
nestled amid wild abrazos° of climbing roses   *bear hugs*
and man-high red geraniums
are gone now. The freeway conceals it
all beneath a raised scar.

But under the fake windsounds of the open lanes,
in the abandoned lots below, new grasses sprout,
wild mustard remembers, old gardens
come back stronger than they were,
trees have been left standing in their yards.
Albaricoqueros, cerezos, nogales° . . .   *apple, cherry, walnut trees*
Viejitas° come here with paper bags to gather greens.   *old women*
Espinaca, verdolagas, yerbabuena° . . .   *spinach, purslane, mint*

I scramble over the wire fence
that would have kept me out.
Once, I wanted out, wanted the rigid lanes
to take me to a place without sun,
without the smell of tomatoes burning
on swing shift in the greasy summer air.

Maybe it's here   20
en los campos extraños de esta ciudad°
where I'll find it, that part of me
mown under
like a corpse
or a loose seed.   25

[1981]

21. en . . . ciudad: In the strange fields of this city.

THYLIAS MOSS   [b. 1954]

The Lynching

They should have slept, would have
but had to fight the darkness, had
to build a fire and bathe a man in
flames. No

other soap's as good when   5
the dirt is the skin. Black since
birth, burnt by birth. His father
is not in heaven. No parent

of atrocity is in heaven. My father chokes
in the next room. It is night, darkness   10
has replaced air. We are white like
incandescence

yet lack light. The God in my father
does not glow. The only lamp
is the burning black man. Holy   15
burning, holy longing, remnants of

a genie after greed. My father
baptizes by fire same as Jesus will.
Becomes a holy ghost when
he dons his sheet, a clerical collar   20

out of control, Dundee Mills percale,
fifty percent cotton, dixie, confederate

and fifty percent polyester, man-made, man-
ipulated, unnatural, mulatto fiber, warp

of miscegenation.
After the bath, the man is hung as if
just his washed shirt, the parts
of him most capable of sin removed.

Charred, his flesh is bark, his body
a trunk. No sign of roots. I can't leave
him. This is limbo. This is the life after
death coming if God is an invention as were

slaves. So I spend the night, his thin moon-begot
shadow as mattress; something smoldering
keeps me warm. Patches of skin fall onto me
in places I didn't know needed mending.

[1991]

CORNELIUS EADY   [b. 1954]

I'm a Fool to Love You

Some folks will tell you the blues is a woman,
Some type of supernatural creature.
My mother would tell you, if she could,
About her life with my father,
A strange and sometimes cruel gentleman.
She would tell you about the choices
A young black woman faces.
Is falling in with some man
A deal with the devil
In blue terms, the tongue we use
When we don't want nuance
To get in the way,
When we need to talk straight.
My mother chooses my father
After choosing a man
Who was, as we sing it,

Of no account.
This man made my father look good,
That's how bad it was.
He made my father seem like an island   20
In the middle of a stormy sea,
He made my father look like a rock.
And is the blues the moment you realize
You exist in a stacked deck,
You look in a mirror at your young face,   25
The face my sister carries,
And you know it's the only leverage
You've got.
Does this create a hurt that whispers
How you going to do?   30
Is the blues the moment
You shrug your shoulders
And agree, a girl without money
Is nothing, dust
To be pushed around by any old breeze.   35
Compared to this,
My father seems, briefly,
To be a fire escape.
This is the way the blues works
Its sorry wonders,   40
Makes trouble look like
A feather bed,
Makes the wrong man's kisses
A healing.

                                                      [1997]

PATRICIA SMITH [b. 1955]

Skinhead

They call me skinhead, and I got my own beauty.
It is knife-scrawled across my back in sore, jagged letters,
it's in the way my eyes snap away from the obvious.
I sit in my dim matchbox,

on the edge of a bed tousled with my ragged smell,
slide razors across my hair,
count how many ways
I can bring blood closer to the surface of my skin.
These are the duties of the righteous,
the ways of the anointed.

The face that moves in my mirror is huge and pockmarked,
scraped pink and brilliant, apple-cheeked,
I am filled with my own spit.
Two years ago, a machine that slices leather
sucked in my hand and held it,
whacking off three fingers at the root.
I didn't feel nothing till I looked down
and saw one of them on the floor
next to my boot heel,
and I ain't worked since then.

I sit here and watch niggers take over my TV set,
walking like kings up and down the sidewalks in my head,
walking like their fat black mamas *named* them freedom.
My shoulders tell me that ain't right.
So I move out into the sun
where my beauty makes them lower their heads,
or into the night
with a lead pipe up my sleeve,
a razor tucked in my boot.
I was born to make things right.

It's easy now to move my big body into shadows,
to move from a place where there was nothing
into the stark circle of a streetlight,
the pipe raised up high over my head.
It's a kick to watch their eyes get big,
round and gleaming like cartoon jungle boys,
right in that second when they know
the pipe's gonna come down, and I got this thing
I like to say, listen to this, I like to say
"Hey, nigger, Abe Lincoln's been dead a long time."

I get hard listening to their skin burst.
I was born to make things right.

Then this newspaper guy comes around,
seems I was a little sloppy kicking some fag's ass

and he opened his hole and screamed about it.   45
This reporter finds me curled up in my bed,
those TV flashes licking my face clean.
Same ol' shit.
Ain't got no job, the coloreds and spics got 'em all.
Why ain't I working? Look at my hand, asshole.   50
No, I ain't part of no organized group,
I'm just a white boy who loves his race,
fighting for a pure country.

Sometimes it's just me. Sometimes three. Sometimes 30.
AIDS will take care of the faggots,   55
then it's gon' be white on black in the streets.
Then there'll be three million.
I tell him that.

So he writes it up
and I come off looking like some kind of freak,   60
like I'm Hitler himself. I ain't that lucky,
but I got my own beauty.
It is in my steel-toed boots,
in the hard corners of my shaved head.

I look in the mirror and hold up my mangled hand,   65
only the baby finger left, sticking straight up,
I know it's the wrong goddamned finger,
but fuck you all anyway.
I'm riding the top rung of the perfect race,
my face scraped pink and brilliant.   70
I'm your baby, America, your boy,
drunk on my own spit, I am goddamned fuckin' beautiful.

And I was born

and raised
right here.   75

[1992]

MARILYN CHIN   [b. 1955]

How I Got That Name

an essay on assimilation

I am Marilyn Mei Ling Chin.
Oh, how I love the resoluteness
of that first person singular
followed by that stalwart indicative
of "be," without the uncertain i-n-g
of "becoming." Of course,
the name had been changed
somewhere between Angel Island° and the sea,
when my father the paperson°
in the late 1950s
obsessed with a bombshell blonde°   *(Marilyn Monroe)*
transliterated "Mei Ling" to "Marilyn."
And nobody dared question
his initial impulse—for we all know
lust drove men to greatness,
not goodness, not decency.
And there I was, a wayward pink baby,
named after some tragic white woman
swollen with gin and Nembutal.°
My mother couldn't pronounce the "r."
She dubbed me "Numba one female offshoot"
for brevity: henceforth, she will live and die
in sublime ignorance, flanked
by loving children and the "kitchen deity."
While my father dithers,

8. Angel Island: An island in San Francisco Bay, site of the Angel Island Immigration Station that processed approximately one million Asian immigrants between 1910 and 1940.
9. paperson: A "paper son" is a term used for young Chinese males entering the United States who claimed to be sons of U.S. citizens but were, in fact, sons on paper only.
19. Nembutal: A short-acting barbituate (Pentobarbital) prescribed as a sedative but also used as an intoxicant.

a tomcat in Hong Kong trash—
a gambler, a petty thug,
who bought a chain of chopsuey joints
in Piss River, Oregon,
with bootlegged Gucci cash.   30
Nobody dared question his integrity given
his nice, devout daughters
and his bright, industrious sons
as if filial piety were the standard
by which all earthly men were measured.   35

*

Oh, how trustworthy our daughters,
how thrifty our sons!
How we've managed to fool the experts
in education, statistics and demography—
We're not very creative but not adverse to rote-learning.   40
Indeed, they can *use* us.
But the "Model Minority" is a tease.
We know you are watching now,
so we refuse to give you any!
Oh, bamboo shoots, bamboo shoots!   45
The further west we go, we'll hit east;
the deeper down we dig, we'll find China.
History has turned its stomach
on a black polluted beach—
where life doesn't hinge   50
on that red, red wheelbarrow,°
but whether or not our new lover
in the final episode of *Santa Barbara*°
will lean over a scented candle
and call us a "bitch."   55
Oh God, where have we gone wrong?
We have no inner resources!

*

Then, one redolent spring morning
the Great Patriarch Chin
peered down from his kiosk in heaven   60
and saw that his descendants were ugly.

51. red wheelbarrow: See the poem by William Carlos Williams on page 531.
53. *Santa Barbara:* American television soap opera, 1984–1993, that focused on
the lives of the wealthy Capwell family of Santa Barbara, California.

One had a squarish head and a nose without a bridge.
Another's profile—long and knobbed as a gourd.
A third, the sad, brutish one
may never, never marry.
And I, his least favorite—
"not quite boiled, not quite cooked,"
a plump pomfret simmering in my juices—
too listless to fight for my people's destiny.
"To kill without resistance is not slaughter"
says the proverb. So, I wait for imminent death.
The fact that this death is also metaphorical
is testament to my lethargy.

*

So here lies Marilyn Mei Ling Chin,
married once, twice to so-and-so, a Lee and a Wong,
granddaughter of Jack "the patriarch"
and the brooding Suilin Fong,
daughter of the virtuous Yuet Kuen Wong
and G. G. Chin the infamous,
sister of a dozen, cousin of a million,
survived by everybody and forgotten by all.
She was neither black nor white,
neither cherished nor vanquished,
just another squatter in her own bamboo grove
minding her poetry—
when one day heaven was unmerciful,
and a chasm opened where she stood.
Like the jowls of a mighty white whale,°
or the jaws of a metaphysical Godzilla,°
it swallowed her whole.
She did not flinch nor writhe,
nor fret about the afterlife,
but stayed! Solid as wood, happily
a little gnawed, tattered, mesmerized
by all that was lavished upon her
and all that was taken away!

[1994]

---

88. **mighty white whale:** The whale in Herman Melville's 1851 novel *Moby Dick*.
89. **Godzilla:** A monster which appeared first in Ishiro Honda's 1954 film
Godzilla and became a pop culture icon in twenty-eight additional films.

KIMIKO HAHN   [b. 1955]

Mother's Mother

> *. . . There is no mother tongue.*
> —ELAINE SHOWALTER

The mother draws the shade down halfway
so the sunlight does not blind the pages
and she reads the story, *mukashi mukashi aruhi,*°
which is the way every story begins
whether about a boy riding a tortoise beneath the sea   5
or a girl born from a bamboo stalk.
Her daughter does not speak Japanese
though she can write her name in the *kana*°
that resembles tv antennae

キ ミ コ °

and she knows not everyone speaks the same language: 10
see you, ciao, adios, sayonara. She knows
her mother knows more than one way to say things
and Japanese, which is also how she *looks*,
is the language her mother was taught,
like the island of Japan,   15
almost as far from this little house on the island of Maui.

The chickens are so loud grandma.
Ursuai ne.°
So dusty.
Kitanai°   20
So—
She wants to learn every word her grandma knows.

3. *mukashi mukashi aruhi:* Once upon a time.
8. *kana:* A general term for the syllabic Japanese scripts *hiragana* and *katakana*,
which were adapted from the logographic characters of Chinese origin known in
Japan as *Kanji* and are easier to master.
9. キ ミ コ: Ki-mi-ko.
18. *Ursuai ne:* Annoying, isn't it?
20. *Kitanai:* Dirty, filthy.

She wants to be like her grandma
who she sees her mother loves and does not want to leave.
She wants to stay with her grandma also
and knows from her mother's shoulders they will not see her again.

If there is no mother tongue for women
there is for immigrant children
who play on the black volcanic beaches,
on the sharp coral reefs, in the salty rain, the plantation houses,
the fields of burning cane, the birds-of-paradise.
Who see the shark fins in the sunlight and linger on the blanket.

There is a mother's tongue and it is conveyed
by this mother to her daughters
who will carry the words at least in song
because when mother dies there will be no one else
unless there is an aunt or cousin
to correct the tense or word choice
with such affection and cause.

そうよね。°

The same cause found in domestic arts and survival.
When the mother dies the daughter
or the daughter-in-law, or even the son,
becomes that figure in part
and the words the older woman knew
are the words this person will parent
despite lineage and its repressive roots.
Its often awful branches.
The root words and radicals the daughter memorizes.

氷　シ°

So when I toss my hair from my eyes I feel
it's mother tossing her head and when I cough
it is her cough I hear.
And when I tell my child to say *mama*
it may be that I am speaking to myself
as much as I am speaking to the small mouth
a few inches from my face.

[1999]

---

39. そうよね。: That's just the way it is, isn't it?
48. 氷　シ: It is endless (the process of learning Japanese characters).

CATHY SONG [b. 1955]

Heaven

He thinks when we die we'll go to China.
Think of it—a Chinese heaven
where, except for his blond hair,
the part that belongs to his father,
everyone will look like him.   5
China, that blue flower on the map,
bluer than the sea
his hand must span like a bridge
to reach it.
An octave away.   10

I've never seen it.
It's as if I can't sing that far.
But look—
on the map, this black dot.
Here is where we live,   15
on the pancake plains
just east of the Rockies,
on the other side of the clouds.
A mile above the sea,
the air is so thin, you can starve on it.   20
No bamboo trees
but the alpine equivalent,
reedy aspen with light, fluttering leaves.
Did a boy in Guangzhou° dream of this
as his last stop?   25

I've heard the trains at night
whistling past our yards,
what we've come to own,
the broken fences, the whiny dog, the rattletrap cars.
It's still the wild west,   30

24. **Guangzhou:** A large seaport city in southeastern China (also known as Canton).

mean and grubby,
the shootouts and fistfights in the back alley.
With my son the dreamer
and my daughter, who is too young to walk,
I've sat in this spot
and wondered why here?
Why in this short life,
this town, this creek they call a river?

He had never planned to stay,
the boy who helped to build
the railroads° for a dollar a day.
He had always meant to go back.
When did he finally know
that each mile of track led him further away,
that he would die in his sleep,
dispossessed,
having seen Gold Mountain,°
the icy wind tunneling through it,
these landlocked, makeshift ghost towns?

It must be in the blood,
this notion of returning.
It skipped two generations, lay fallow,
the garden an unmarked grave.
On a spring sweater day
it's as if we remember him.
I call to the children.
We can see the mountains
shimmering blue above the air.
If you look really hard
says my son the dreamer,
leaning out from the laundry's rigging,
the work shirts fluttering like sails,
you can see all the way to heaven.

[1988]

40–41. **build the railroads:** The Central Pacific Railroad used mostly Chinese
immigrant laborers to lay the western section of tracks for the first transcontinental
railroad.
47. **Gold Mountain:** The name the Chinese gave to California and British Columbia
during the gold rush of the nineteenth century.

LI-YOUNG LEE   [b. 1957]

Eating Alone

I've pulled the last of the year's young onions.
The garden is bare now. The ground is cold,
brown and old. What is left of the day flames
in the maples at the corner of my
eye. I turn, a cardinal vanishes.   5
By the cellar door, I wash the onions,
then drink from the icy metal spigot.

Once, years back, I walked beside my father
among the windfall pears. I can't recall
our words. We may have strolled in silence. But   10
I still see him bend that way—left hand braced
on knee, creaky—to lift and hold to my
eye a rotten pear. In it, a hornet
spun crazily, glazed in slow, glistening juice.

It was my father I saw this morning   15
waving to me from the trees. I almost
called to him, until I came close enough
to see the shovel, leaning where I had
left it, in the flickering, deep green shade.

White rice steaming, almost done. Sweet green peas   20
fried in onions. Shrimp braised in sesame
oil and garlic. And my own loneliness.
What more could I, a young man, want.

[1986]

MARTÍN ESPADA   [b. 1957]

Alabanza: In Praise of Local 100

for the 43 members of Hotel Employees and Restaurant Employees
Local 100, working at the Windows on the World restaurant,
who lost their lives in the attack on the World Trade Center

Alabanza. Praise the cook with a shaven head
and a tattoo on his shoulder that said *Oye,*
a blue-eyed Puerto Rican with people from Fajardo,
the harbor of pirates centuries ago.
Praise the lighthouse in Fajardo, candle
glimmering white to worship the dark saint of the sea.
Alabanza. Praise the cook's yellow Pirates cap
worn in the name of Roberto Clemente, his plane
that flamed into the ocean loaded with cans for Nicaragua,
for all the mouths chewing the ash of earthquakes.
Alabanza. Praise the kitchen radio, dial clicked
even before the dial on the oven, so that music and Spanish
rose before bread. Praise the bread. *Alabanza.*

Praise Manhattan from a hundred and seven flights up,
like Atlantis glimpsed through the windows of an ancient aquarium.
Praise the great windows where immigrants from the kitchen
could squint and almost see their world, hear the chant of nations:
Ecuador, México, Republica Dominicana,
Haiti, Yemen, Ghana, Bangladesh.
Alabanza. Praise the kitchen in the morning,
where the gas burned blue on every stove
and exhaust fans fired their diminutive propellers,
hands cracked eggs with quick thumbs
or sliced open cartons to build an altar of cans.
Alabanza. Praise the busboy's music, the *chime-chime*
of his dishes and silverware in the tub.
Alabanza. Praise the dish-dog, the dishwasher
who worked that morning because another dishwasher

650

could not stop coughing, or because he needed overtime
to pile the sacks of rice and beans for a family   30
floating away on some Caribbean island plagued by frogs.
Alabanza. Praise the waitress who heard the radio in the kitchen
and sang to herself about a man gone. *Alabanza.*

After the thunder wilder than thunder,
after the shudder deep in the glass of the great windows,   35
after the radio stopped singing like a tree full of terrified frogs,
after night burst the dam of day and flooded the kitchen,
for a time the stoves glowed in darkness like the lighthouse in Fajardo,
like a cook's soul. Soul I say, even if the dead cannot tell us
about the bristles of God's beard because God has no face,   40
soul I say, to name the smoke-beings flung in constellations
across the night sky of this city and cities to come.
Alabanza I say, even if God has no face.

Alabanza. When the war began, from Manhattan and Kabul
two constellations of smoke rose and drifted to each other,   45
mingling in icy air, and one said with an Afghan tongue:
Teach me to dance. We have no music here.
And the other said with a Spanish tongue:
I will teach you. Music is all we have.

                                                          [2003]

DENISE DUHAMEL   [b. 1961]

Kinky

They decide to exchange heads.
Barbie squeezes the small opening under her chin
over Ken's bulging neck socket. His wide jaw line jostles
atop his girlfriend's body, loosely,
like one of those nodding novelty dogs   5
destined to gaze from the back windows of cars.
The two dolls chase each other around the orange Country Camper
unsure what they'll do when they're within touching distance.
Ken wants to feel Barbie's toes between his lips,
take off one of her legs and force his whole arm inside her.   10

With only the vaguest suggestion of genitals,
all the alluring qualities they possess as fashion dolls,
up until now, have done neither of them much good.
But suddenly Barbie is excited looking at her own body
under the weight of Ken's face. He is part circus freak,
part thwarted hermaphrodite. And she is imagining
she is somebody else—maybe somebody middle class and ordinary,
maybe another teenage model being caught in a scandal.

The night had begun with Barbie getting angry
at finding Ken's blow-up doll, folded and stuffed
under the couch. He was defensive and ashamed, especially about
not having the breath to inflate her. But after a round
of pretend-tears, Barbie and Ken vowed to try
to make their relationship work. With their good memories
as sustaining as good food, they listened to late-night radio
talk shows, one featuring Doctor Ruth. *When all else fails,
just hold each other*, the small sex therapist crooned.
Barbie and Ken, on cue, groped in the dark,
their interchangeable skin glowing, the color of Band-Aids.
Then, they let themselves go—soon Barbie was begging Ken
to try on her spandex miniskirt. She showed him how
to pivot as though he were on a runway. Ken begged
to tie Barbie onto his yellow surfboard and spin her
on the kitchen table until she grew dizzy. *Anything,
anything*, they both said to the other's requests,
their mirrored desires bubbling from the most unlikely places.

[1997]

ELIZABETH ALEXANDER   [b. 1962]

The Venus Hottentot°

(1825)

1. CUVIER°

Science, science, science!
Everything is beautiful

blown up beneath my glass.
Colors dazzle insect wings.

A drop of water swirls   5
like marble. Ordinary

crumbs become stalactites
set in perfect angles

of geometry I'd thought
impossible. Few will   10

ever see what I see
through this microscope.

Cranial measurements
crowd my notebook pages,

and I am moving closer,   15
close to how these numbers

signify aspects of
national character.

The Venus Hottentot: This is a stage name that was ascribed to Saartjie Baartman
(c. 1790-1815), a Khoi woman from South Africa who was displayed as a curiosity
in circuses and exhibition halls throughout her adult life. "Hottentot" was a derog-
atory term used to describe the Khoi people, who had been victims of cruelty and
exploitation throughout the colonization of South Africa.
Cuvier: Georges Cuvier (1769-1832) was a prominent anatomist of the nineteenth
century. When Saartje Baartman died in 1815, Cuvier performed the autopsy on
her body. He preserved Bartmann's brains and genitals in jars, and they were on
display in the Museé de l'Homme in Paris for decades.

Her genitalia
will float inside a labeled

pickling jar in the Musée
de l'Homme on a shelf

above Broca's brain:
"The Venus Hottentot."

Elegant facts await me.
Small things in this world are mine.

2.

There is unexpected sun today
in London, and the clouds that
most days sift into this cage
where I am working have dispersed.
I am a black cutout against
a captive blue sky, pivoting
nude so the paying audience
can view my naked buttocks.

I am called "Venus Hottentot."
I left Capetown with a promise
of revenue: half the profits
and my passage home: A boon!
Master's brother proposed the trip;
the magistrate granted me leave.
I would return to my family
a duchess, with watered-silk

dresses and money to grow food,
rouge and powders in glass pots,
silver scissors, a lorgnette,
voile and tulle instead of flax,
cerulean blue instead
of indigo. My brother would
devour sugar-studded non-
pareils, pale taffy, damask plums.

That was years ago. London's
circuses are florid and filthy,
swarming with cabbage-smelling
citizens who stare and query,
"Is it muscle? bone? or fat?"

My neighbor to the left is
The Sapient Pig, "The Only
Scholar of His Race." He plays

at cards, tells time and fortunes
by scraping his hooves. Behind   60
me is Prince Kar-mi, who arches
like a rubber tree and stares back
at the crowd from under the crook
of his knee. A professional
animal trainer shouts my cues.   65
There are singing mice here.

"The Ball of Duchess DuBarry":
In the engraving I lurch
toward the *belles dames*, mad-eyed, and
they swoon. Men in capes and pince-nez   70
shield them. Tassels dance at my hips.
In this newspaper lithograph
my buttocks are shown swollen
and luminous as a planet.

Monsieur Cuvier investigates   75
between my legs, poking, prodding,
sure of his hypothesis.
I half expect him to pull silk
scarves from inside me, paper poppies,
then a rabbit! He complains   80
at my scent and does not think
I comprehend, but I speak

English. I speak Dutch. I speak
a little French as well, and
languages Monsieur Cuvier   85
will never know have names.
Now I am bitter and now
I am sick. I eat brown bread,
drink rancid broth. I miss good sun,
miss Mother's *sadza*.° My stomach   90

is frequently queasy from mutton
chops, pale potatoes, blood sausage.

---

90. *sadza*: Cooked cornmeal—a staple food in Southern Africa.

I was certain that this would be
better than farm life. I am
the family entrepreneur!
But there are hours in every day
to conjur my imaginary
daughters, in banana skirts

and ostrich-feather fans.
Since my own genitals are public
I have made other parts private.
In my silence I possess
mouth, larynx, brain, in a single
gesture. I rub my hair
with lanolin, and pose in profile
like a painted Nubian

archer, imagining gold leaf
woven through my hair, and diamonds.
Observe the wordless Odalisque.
I have not forgotten my Xhosa
clicks. My flexible tongue
and healthy mouth bewilder
this man with his rotting teeth.
If he were to let me rise up

from this table, I'd spirit
his knives and cut out his black heart,
seal it with science fluid inside
a bell jar, place it on a low
shelf in a white man's museum
so the whole world could see
it was shriveled and hard,
geometric, deformed, unnatural.

[1990]

CLAUDIA RANKINE [b. 1963]

You are in the dark, in the car . . . °

***

You are in the dark, in the car, watching the black-tarred street being swallowed by speed; he tells you his dean is making him hire a person of color when there are so many great writers out there.

You think maybe this is an experiment and you are being tested or retro-actively insulted or you have done something that communicates this is an okay conversation to be having.   5

Why do you feel okay saying this to me? You wish the light would turn red or a police siren would go off so you could slam on the brakes, slam into the car ahead of you, be propelled forward so quickly both your faces would suddenly be exposed to the wind.   10

As usual you drive straight through the moment with the expected back-ing off of what was previously said. It is not only that confrontation is headache producing; it is also that you have a destination that doesn't include acting like this moment isn't inhabitable, hasn't happened be-fore, and the before isn't part of the now as the night darkens and the   15
time shortens between where we are and where we are going.

***

When you arrive in your driveway and turn off the car, you remain be-hind the wheel another ten minutes. You fear the night is being locked in and coded on a cellular level and want time to function as a power wash. Sitting there staring at the closed garage door you are reminded that a   20
friend once told you there exists a medical term—John Henryism—for people exposed to stresses stemming from racism. They achieve them-selves to death trying to dodge the build up of erasure. Sherman James, the researcher who came up with the term, claimed the physiological costs were high. You hope by sitting in silence you are bucking the trend.   25

***

From *Citizen* (2014) by Claudia Rankine.

657

When the stranger asks, Why do you care? you just stand there staring at him. He has just referred to the boisterous teenagers in Starbucks as niggers. Hey, I am standing right here, you responded, not necessarily expecting him to turn to you.

He is holding the lidded paper cup in one hand and a small paper bag in the other. They are just being kids. Come on, no need to get all KKK on them, you say.

Now there you go, he responds.

The people around you have turned away from their screens. The teenagers are on pause. There I go? you ask, feeling irritation begin to rain down. Yes, and something about hearing yourself repeating this stranger's accusation in a voice usually reserved for your partner makes you smile.

***

A man knocked over her son in the subway. You feel your own body wince. He's okay, but the son of a bitch kept walking. She says she grabbed the stranger's arm and told him to apologize: I told him to look at the boy and apologize. And yes, you want it to stop, you want the black child pushed to the ground to be seen, to be helped to his feet and be brushed off, not brushed off by the person that did not see him, has never seen him, has perhaps never seen anyone who is not a reflection of himself.

The beautiful thing is that a group of men began to stand behind me like a fleet of bodyguards, she says, like newly found uncles and brothers.

***

The new therapist specializes in trauma counseling. You have only ever spoken on the phone. Her house has a side gate that leads to a back entrance she uses for patients. You walk down a path bordered on both sides with deer grass and rosemary to the gate, which turns out to be locked.

At the front door the bell is a small round disc that you press firmly. When the door finally opens, the woman standing there yells, at the top of her lungs, Get away from my house. What are you doing in my yard?

It's as if a wounded Doberman pinscher or a German shepherd has gained the power of speech. And though you back up a few steps, you manage to tell her you have an appointment. You have an appointment? she spits back. Then she pauses. Everything pauses. Oh, she says, followed by, oh, yes, that's right. I am sorry.

I am so sorry, so, so sorry.

***

[2014]

TAYLOR MALI   [b. 1965]

What Teachers Make

He says the problem with teachers is
What's a kid going to learn
from someone who decided his best option in life
was to become a teacher?
He reminds the other dinner guests that it's true   5
what they say about teachers:
Those who can, do; those who can't, teach.
I decide to bite my tongue instead of his
and resist the temptation to remind the dinner guests
that it's also true what they say about lawyers.   10
Because we're eating, after all, and this is polite conversation.

I mean, you're a teacher, Taylor.
Be honest. What do you make?

And I wish he hadn't done that—asked me to be honest—
because, you see, I have this policy about honesty and ass-kicking: 15
if you ask for it, then I have to let you have it.
You want to know what I make?
I make kids work harder than they ever thought they could.
I can make a C+ feel like a Congressional Medal of Honor
and an A– feel like a slap in the face.   20
How dare you waste my time
with anything less than your very best.
I make kids sit through 40 minutes of study hall
in absolute silence. *No, you may not work in groups.*
No, you may not ask a question.   25
Why won't I let you go to the bathroom?
Because you're bored.
And you don't really have to go to the bathroom, do you?
I make parents tremble in fear when I call home:
Hi. This is Mr. Mali. I hope I haven't called at a bad time,   30
I just wanted to talk to you about something your son said today.
To the biggest bully in the grade, he said,
"Leave the kid alone. I still cry sometimes, don't you?

659

It's no big deal."
And that was noblest act of courage I have ever seen.
I make parents see their children for who they are
and what they can be.

You want to know what I make? I make kids wonder,
I make them question.
I make them criticize.
I make them apologize and mean it.
I make them write.
I make them read, read, read.
I make them spell *definitely beautiful, definitely beautiful, definitely beautiful*
over and over and over again until they will never misspell
either one of those words again.
I make them show all their work in math
and hide it on their final drafts in English.
I make them understand that if you've got *this*,
then you follow *this*,
and if someone ever tries to judge you
by what you make, you give them *this*.

Here, let me break it down for you, so you know what I say is true:
Teachers make a goddamn difference! Now what about you?

[2002]

SHERMAN ALEXIE   [b. 1966]

Postcards to Columbus

Beginning at the front door of the White House, travel west
for 500 years, pass through small towns and house fires, ignore
hitchhikers and stranded motorists, until you find yourself
back at the beginning of this journey, this history and country

folded over itself like a Mobius strip. Christopher Columbus
where have you been? Lost between Laramie and San Francisco
or in the reservation HUD house, building a better mousetrap?
Seymour saw you shooting free throws behind the Tribal School

in a thunderstorm. Didn't you know lightning strikes the earth
800 times a second? But, Columbus, how could you ever imagine
how often our lives change? *Electricity is lightning pretending
to be permanent* and when the Indian child pushes the paper clip

into the electrical outlet, it's applied science, insane economics
of supply and demand, the completion of a 20th century circuit.
Christopher Columbus, you are the most successful real estate agent   15
who ever lived, sold acres and acres of myth, a house built on stilts

above the river salmon travel by genetic memory. Beneath the burden
of 15,000 years my tribe celebrated this country's 200th birthday
by refusing to speak English and we'll honor the 500th anniversary
of your invasion, Columbus, by driving blindfolded cross-country   20

naming the first tree we destroy *America*. We'll make the first guardrail
we crash through our national symbol. Our flag will be a white sheet
stained with blood and piss. Columbus, can you hear me over white
noise of your television set? Can you hear ghosts of drums approaching?

[1993]

NATASHA TRETHEWEY [b. 1966]

History Lesson

I am four in this photograph, standing
on a wide strip of Mississippi beach,
my hands on the flowered hips

of a bright bikini. My toes dig in,
curl around wet sand. The sun cuts   5
the rippling Gulf in flashes with each

tidal rush. Minnows dart at my feet
glinting like switchblades. I am alone
except for my grandmother, other side

of the camera, telling me how to pose.   10
It is 1970, two years after they opened
the rest of this beach to us,

forty years since the photograph
where she stood on a narrow plot
of sand marked *colored*, smiling,   15

her hands on the flowered hips
of a cotton meal-sack dress.

[2000]

HONORÉE FANONNE JEFFERS [b. 1967]

Unidentified Female Student, Former Slave (Talladega College, circa 1885)

You might have heard a story like this one well
but I'm telling this one to you now.
I was five when the soldiers came.

Master worked me twenty years longer.
How could I know? One day he left me alone
and an unwatched pot started to boil. By the time

he came back home I was cleaned of him and singing,
There's a man going round taking names.
Ready, set, and I was gone, walking. Could I see

beyond his yard? Did I have a thought to read or write
or count past God's creation? A barefooted
girl!—and you remember, you woman who will take

your pen to write my life. This is what the truth was like:
Master's clouds followed me to the steps of this school.
Dear reader, when you think on this years after I have died

and I am dust, think on a great and awful morning
when I learned my freedom. Think that the skin on my
back was scared when I dared step out into the world,

when my Master stood trembling and weeping
on his front porch and he cursed me beyond knowing.

[2003]

ALLISON JOSEPH   [b. 1967]

On Being Told I Don't Speak
Like a Black Person

Emphasize the "h," you hignorant ass,
was what my mother was told
when colonial-minded teachers
slapped her open palm with a ruler
in that Jamaican schoolroom.   5
Trained in England, they tried
to force their pupils to speak
like Eliza Doolittle after
her transformation, fancying themselves
British as Henry Higgins,°   10
despite dark, sun-ripened skin.
Mother never lost her accent,
though, the music of her voice
charming everyone, an infectious lilt
I can imitate, not duplicate.   15
No one in the States told her
to eliminate the accent,
my high school friends adoring
the way her voice would lift
when she called me to the phone,   20
A-ll-i-son, it's friend Cathy.
Why don't you sound like her?,
they'd ask. I didn't sound
like anyone or anything,
no grating New Yorker nasality,   25

8–10. Eliza Doolittle . . . Henry Higgins: Flower-girl with a strong Cockney
(working-class) accent in George Bernard Shaw's play *Pygmalion* and the
musical based on it, *My Fair Lady*. Henry Higgins, a linguistics professor, takes
on the challenge of teaching her how to speak (and act and dress) like a proper
British lady.

663

no fastidious British mannerisms
like the ones my father affected
when he wanted to sell someone
something. And I didn't sound
like a Black American,
college acquaintances observed,
sure they knew what a black person
was supposed to sound like.
Was I supposed to sound lazy,
dropping syllables here, there,
not finishing words but
slurring the final letter so that
each sentence joined the next,
sliding past the listener?
Were certain words off limits,
too erudite, too scholarly
for someone with a natural tan?
I asked what they meant,
and they stuttered, blushed,
said you know, Black English,
applying what they'd learned
from that semester's text.
Does everyone in your family
speak alike?, I'd question,
and they'd say don't take this the
wrong way, nothing personal.

Now I realize there's nothing
more personal than speech,
that I don't have to defend
how I speak, how any person,
black, white, chooses to speak.
Let us speak. Let us talk
with the sounds of our mothers
and fathers still reverberating
in our minds, wherever our mothers
or fathers come from:
Arkansas, Belize, Alabama,
Brazil, Aruba, Arizona.
Let us simply speak
to one another,
listen and prize the inflections,
differences, never assuming

how any person will sound
until her mouth opens,
until his mouth opens,   70
greetings familiar
in any language.

                                                                    [1999]

BRIAN TURNER   [b. 1967]

What Every Soldier Should Know

To yield to force is an act of necessity, not of will;
it is at best an act of prudence.
—JEAN-JACQUES ROUSSEAU

If you hear gunfire on a Thursday afternoon,
it could be for a wedding, or it could be for you.

Always enter a home with your right foot;
the left is for cemeteries and unclean places.

O-guf! Tera armeek is rarely useful.   5
It means *Stop! Or I'll shoot.*

Sabah el khair is effective.
It means *Good Morning.*

Inshallah means *Allah be willing.*
Listen well when it is spoken.   10

You will hear the RPG coming for you.
Not so the roadside bomb.

There are bombs under the overpasses,
in trashpiles, in bricks, in cars.

There are shopping carts with clothes soaked   15
in foogas, a sticky gel of homemade napalm.

Parachute bombs and artillery shells
sewn into the carcasses of dead farm animals.

A graffiti sprayed onto the overpasses:
I will kell you, American.

Men wearing vests rigged with explosives
walk up, raise their arms and say *Inshallah.*

There are men who earn eighty dollars
to attack you, five thousand to kill.

Small children who will play with you,
old men with their talk, women who offer chai—

and any one of them
may dance over your body tomorrow.

[2007]

TERRANCE HAYES   [b. 1971]

Talk

like a nigger now, my white friend, M, said
after my M.L.K. and Ronald Reagan impersonations,
the two of us alone and shirtless in the locker room,

and if you're thinking my knuckles knocked
a few times against his jaw or my fingers knotted
at his throat, you're wrong because I pretended

I didn't hear him, and when he didn't ask it again,
we slipped into our middle school uniforms
since it was November, the beginning

of basketball season, and jogged out
onto the court to play together
in that vision all Americans wish for

their children, and the point is we slipped
into our uniform harmony, and spit out *Go Team!*,
our hands stacked on and beneath the hands

of our teammates and that was as close
as I have come to passing for one
of the members of The Dream, my white friend

thinking I was so far from that word
that he could say it to me, which I guess   20
he could since I didn't let him taste the salt

and iron in the blood, I didn't teach him
what it's like to squint through a black eye,
and if I had I wonder if he would have grown

up to be the kind of white man who believes   25
all blacks are thugs or if he would have learned
to bite his tongue or let his belly be filled

by shame, but more importantly, would I be
the kind of black man who believes silence
is worth more than talk or that it can be   30

a kind of grace, though I'm not sure
that's the kind of black man I've become,
and in any case, M, wherever you are,

I'd just like to say I heard it, but let it go
because I was afraid to lose our friendship   35
or afraid we'd lose the game—which we did anyway.

[2006]

JEN BERVIN   [b. 1972]

64°

When **I have seen** by Time's fell hand defaced
The rich proud cost of outworn buried age,
When sometime lofty **towers** I see **down-razed**,
And brass eternal slave to mortal rage;
When I have seen the hungry ocean gain
Advantage on the kingdom of the shore,
And the firm soil win of the wat'ry main,
Increasing store with **loss** and **loss** with store;
When I have seen such interchange of state,
Or state itself confounded to decay,
Ruin hath taught me thus to ruminate—
That Time will come and take my love away.
    This thought is as a death, which cannot choose
    But weep to have that which it fears to lose.

64: Erasure of Sonnet 64 by William Shakespeare. From *Nets* (2004) by Jen
Bervin.

EDUARDO CORRAL   [b. 1973]

In Colorado My Father
Scoured and Stacked Dishes

in a Tex-Mex restaurant. His co-workers,
unable to utter his name, renamed him Jalapeño.

If I ask for a goldfish, he spits a glob of phlegm
into a jar of water. The silver letters

on his black belt spell *Sangrón*. Once, borracho,
at dinner, he said: Jesus wasn't a snowman.

Arriba Durango. Arriba Orizaba. Packed
into a car trunk, he was smuggled into the States.

Frijolero. Greaser. In Tucson he branded
cattle. He slept in a stable. The horse blankets   10

oddly fragrant: wood smoke, lilac. He's an illegal.
I'm an Illegal-American. Once, in a grove

of saguaro, at dusk, I slept next to him. I woke
with his thumb in my mouth. ¿No qué no

tronabas pistolita? He learned English   15
by listening to the radio. The first four words

he memorized: In God We Trust. The fifth:
Percolate. Again and again I borrow his clothes.

He calls me Scarecrow. In Oregon he picked apples.
Braeburn. Jonagold. Cameo. Nightly,   20

to entertain his cuates, around a campfire,
he strummed a guitarra, sang corridos. Arriba

Durango. Arriba Orizaba. Packed into
a car trunk, he was smuggled into the States.

Greaser. Beaner. Once, borracho, at breakfast,   25
he said: The heart can only be broken

once, like a window, ¡No mames! His favorite
belt buckle: an águila perched on a nopal.

If he laughs out loud, his hands tremble.
Bugs Bunny wants to deport him. César Chávez   30

wants to deport him. When I walk through
the desert, I wear his shirt. The gaze of the moon

stitches the buttons of his shirt to my skin.
The snake hisses. The snake is torn.

[2012]

ROSS GAY   [b. 1974]

A Small Needful Fact

Is that Eric Garner worked
for some time for the Parks and Rec.
Horticultural Department, which means,
perhaps, that with his very large hands,
perhaps, in all likelihood,
he put gently into the earth
some plants which, most likely,
some of them, in all likelihood,
continue to grow, continue
to do what such plants do, like house
and feed small and necessary creatures,
like being pleasant to touch and smell,
like converting sunlight
into food, like making it easier
for us to breathe.

[2015]

AIMEE NEZHUKUMATATHIL   [b. 1974]

Dear Amy
Nehzooukammyatootill,

*(a found poem, composed entirely of e-mails
from various high school students)*

If I were to ask you a question about your book
and sum it up into one word it would be, *Why?*
I think I like Walt Whitman better than you. I just don't
get literature, but for a fast hour and a half read, your book

670

takes the cake. I liked how you organized the lines   5
in that one poem to represent a growing twisting bonsai tree.
Are you going to get a rude reaction when you meet
that one guy in that one poem? I guess you never know.

You are very young to be a poet. I also like how your poems take
up an entire page (it makes our reading assignment go faster).   10
In class we spend so much time dissecting your poems
and then deeply analyzing them. I think I like Walt Whitman

better than you, but don't take offense—you are very good too!
You are young. You are young and pure and really just want
to have a good time. Thank you we have taken a debate   15
and you are a far better poet than Walt Whitman. And I loved

how your poems were easy to read and understand. Hello
my name is Alicia. We read your book and I just loved it.
We also read Walt Whitman's *Leaves of Grass*. There
was no competition there. I liked your book a whole lot better.   20

It was an easy read. But poetry is not my favorite type
of literature. Sometimes I am offered drinks and guys
try to talk to me but I too just brush it off and keep dancing.
Every once and a while the creepy mean guys try to offer you

things and then they say something. What would you do?   25
Lastly, I was wondering if you ever wrote a poem that really
didn't have a deeper meaning but everyone still tried
to give it one anyways? Walt Whitman is better than you.

[2011]

JERICHO BROWN   [b. 1976]

Host

We want pictures of everything
Below your waist, and we want
Pictures of your waist. We can't
Talk right now, but we will text you
Into coitus. All thumbs. All bi   5

Coastal and discreet and masculine
And muscular. No whites. Every
Body a top. We got a career
To think about. No face. We got
Kids to remember. No one over 29.
No one under 30. Our exes hurt us
Into hurting them. Disease free. No
Drugs. We like to get high with
The right person. You
Got a girl? Bring your boy.
We visiting. Room at the W.
Name's D. Name's J. We DeeJay.
We Trey. We Troy. We Q. We not
Sending a face. Where should we
Go tonight? You coming through? Please
Know what a gym looks like. Not much
Time. No strings. No place, no
Face. Be clean. We haven't met
Anyone here yet. Why is it so hard
To make friends? No games. You
Still coming through? Latinos only.
Blacks will do. We can take one right
Now. Text it to you. Be there next
Week. Be there in June. We not a phone
Person. We can host, but we won't meet
Without a recent pic and a real name
And the sound of your deepest voice.

[2014]

NATALIE DIAZ   [b. 1978]

When My Brother Was an Aztec

he lived in our basement and sacrificed my parents
   every morning. It was awful. Unforgivable. But they kept coming
     back for more. They loved him, was all they could say.

It started with him stumbling along *la Avenida de los Muertos*,
   my parents walking behind like effigies in a procession

he might burn to the ground at any moment. They didn't know

what else to do except be there to pick him up when he died.
    They forgot who was dying, who was already dead. My brother
        quit wearing shirts when a carnival of dirty-breasted women

made him their leader, following him up and down the stairs —   10
    They were acrobats, moving, twitching like snakes — They fed him
        crushed diamonds and fire. He gobbled the gifts. My parents

begged him to pluck their eyes out. He thought he was
    Huitzilopochtli, a god, half-man half-hummingbird. My parents
        at his feet, wrecked honeysuckles, he lowered his swordlike mouth,   15

gorged on them, draining color until their eyebrows whitened.
    My brother shattered and quartered them before his basement festivals —
        waved their shaking hearts in his fists,

while flea-ridden dogs ran up and down the steps, licking their asses,
    turning tricks. Neighbors were amazed my parents' hearts kept   20
        growing back — It said a lot about my parents, or parents' hearts.

My brother flung them into *cenotes*, dropped them from cliffs,
    punched holes into their skulls like useless jars or vases,
        broke them to pieces and fed them to gods ruling

the ratty crotches of street fair whores with pocked faces   25
    spreading their thighs in flophouses with no electricity. He slept
        in filthy clothes smelling of rotten peaches and matches, fell in love

with sparkling spoonfuls the carnival dog-women fed him. My parents
    lost their appetites for food, for sons. Like all bad kings, my brother
        wore a crown, a green baseball cap turned backwards   30

with a Mexican flag embroidered on it. When he wore it
    in the front yard, which he treated like his personal *zócalo*,
        all his realm knew he had the power that day, had all the jewels

a king could eat or smoke or shoot. The slave girls came
    to the fence and ate out of his hands. He fed them *maíz*   35
        through the chain links. My parents watched from the window,

crying over their house turned zoo, their son who was
    now a rusted cage. The Aztec held court in a salt cedar grove
        across the street where peacocks lived. My parents crossed fingers

so he'd never come back, lit *novena* candles   40
    so he would. He always came home with turquoise and jade
        feathers and stinking of peacock shit. My parents gathered

what he'd left of their bodies, trying to stand without legs,
    trying to defend his blows with missing arms, searching for their fingers
    to pray, to climb out of whatever dark belly my brother, the Aztec,
    their son, had fed them to.

[2012]

AMIT MAJMUDAR   [b. 1979]

Arms and the Man

There's no confusing docs and soldiers in
The fitness center here at Walter Reed.
Black socks and sneakers, whitecoat-pale, knob-kneed,
I watch their sets, then nod and move the pin

Six slots back up into the human range.
This one is called the military press.
It works the deltoids so these Atlases
Can shoulder worlds and raise them into change.

I rub a shoulder's twinge, my first set done.
A treadmill dials to a whine nearby.
A soldier, six feet seven, thumps his run.

I don't know why I stare. A moment's lag,
And then I see the shriveled sleeve that lies
At half-mast by him, like a grieving flag.

[2010]

TARFIA FAIZULLAH   [b. 1980]

En Route to Bangladesh, Another Crisis of Faith

*—at Dubai International Airport and ending
with a line by César Vallejo*

Because I must walk
    through the eye-shaped
shadows cast by these
    curved gold leaves thick
atop each constructed   5
    palm tree, past displays
of silk scarves, lit
    silhouettes of blue-bottled
perfume—because
    I grip, as though for the first   10
time, a paper bag
    of french fries from McDonald's,
and lick, from each fingertip,
    the fat and salt as I stand alone
to the side of this moving   15
    walkway gliding me past dark-
eyed men who do not look
    away when I stare squarely
back—because standing
    in line to the restroom I want   20
only to pluck from her
    black sweater this one shimmering
blond hair clinging fast—
    because I must rest the Coke, cold
in my hand, beside this   25
    toilet seat warmed by her thighs,
her thighs, and hers.
    Here, at the narrow mouth
of this long, humid
    corridor leading to the plane,   30

675

I take my place among
       this damp, dark horde of men
and women who look like me—
       because I look like them—
because I am ashamed
       of their bodies that reek so
unabashedly of body—
       because I can—because I am
an American, *a star*
       of blood on the surface of muscle.

[2014]

PATRICIA LOCKWOOD   [b. 1982]

Rape Joke

The rape joke is that you were 19 years old.

The rape joke is that he was your boyfriend.

The rape joke it wore a goatee. A goatee.

Imagine the rape joke looking in the mirror, perfectly reflecting back itself, and grooming itself to look more like a rape joke. "Ahhhh," it thinks. "Yes. *A goatee.*"

No offense.

The rape joke is that he was seven years older. The rape joke is that you had known him for years, since you were too young to be interesting to him. You liked that use of the word *interesting*, as if you were a piece of knowledge that someone could be desperate to acquire, to assimilate, and to spit back out in different form through his goateed mouth.

Then suddenly you were older, but not very old at all.

The rape joke is that you had been drinking wine coolers. Wine coolers! Who drinks wine coolers? People who get raped, according to the rape joke.

The rape joke is he was a bouncer, and kept people out for a living.

Not you!   10

The rape joke is that he carried a knife, and would show it to you, and   11
would turn it over and over in his hands as if it were a book.

He wasn't threatening you, you understood. He just really liked his knife.   12

The rape joke is he once almost murdered a dude by throwing him   13
through a plate-glass window. The next day he told you and he was trembling, which you took as evidence of his sensitivity.

How can a piece of knowledge be stupid? But of course you were so stupid.   14

The rape joke is that sometimes he would tell you you were going on a   15
date and then take you over to his best friend Peewee's house and make
you watch wrestling while they all got high.

The rape joke is that his best friend was named Peewee.   16

OK, the rape joke is that he worshiped The Rock.   17

Like the dude was completely in love with The Rock. He thought it was   18
so great what he could do with his eyebrow.

The rape joke is he called wrestling "a soap opera for men." Men love   19
drama too, he assured you.

The rape joke is that his bookshelf was just a row of paperbacks about   20
serial killers. You mistook this for an interest in history, and laboring
under this misapprehension you once gave him a copy of Günter Grass's
My Century, which he never even tried to read.

It gets funnier.   21

The rape joke is that he kept a diary. I wonder if he wrote about the rape   22
in it.

The rape joke is that you read it once, and he talked about another girl.   23
He called her Miss Geography, and said "he didn't have those urges when
he looked at her anymore," not since he met you. Close call, Miss
Geography!

The rape joke is that he was your father's high-school student—your fa-   24
ther taught World Religion. You helped him clean out his classroom at
the end of the year, and he let you take home the most beat-up textbooks.

The rape joke is that he knew you when you were 12 years old. He once   25
helped your family move two states over, and you drove from Cincinnati
to St. Louis with him, all by yourselves, and he was kind to you, and you
talked the whole way. He had chaw in his mouth the entire time, and you

told him he was disgusting and he laughed, and spat the juice through his goatee into a Mountain Dew bottle.

The rape joke is that *come on*, you should have seen it coming. This rape joke is practically writing itself.

The rape joke is that you were facedown. The rape joke is you were wearing a pretty green necklace that your sister had made for you. Later you cut that necklace up. The mattress felt a specific way, and your mouth felt a specific way open against it, as if you were speaking, but you know you were not. As if your mouth were open ten years into the future, reciting a poem called Rape Joke.

The rape joke is that time is different, becomes more horrible and more habitable, and accommodates your need to go deeper into it.

Just like the body, which more than a concrete form is a capacity.

You know the body of time is *elastic*, can take almost anything you give it, and heals quickly.

The rape joke is that of course there was blood, which in human beings is so close to the surface.

The rape joke is you went home like nothing happened, and laughed about it the next day and the day after that, and when you told people you laughed, and that was the rape joke.

It was a year before you told your parents, because he was like a son to them. The rape joke is that when you told your father, he made the sign of the cross over you and said, "I absolve you of your sins, in the name of the Father, and of the Son, and of the Holy Spirit," which even in its total wrongheadedness, was so completely sweet.

The rape joke is that you were crazy for the next five years, and had to move cities, and had to move states, and whole days went down into the sinkhole of thinking about why it happened. Like you went to look at your backyard and suddenly it wasn't there, and you were looking down into the center of the earth, which played the same red event perpetually.

The rape joke is that after a while you weren't crazy anymore, but close call, Miss Geography.

The rape joke is that for the next five years all you did was write, and never about yourself, about anything else, about apples on the tree, about islands, dead poets and the worms that aerated them, and there was no warm body in what you wrote, it was elsewhere.

The rape joke is that this is finally artless. The rape joke is that you do not   37
write artlessly.

The rape joke is if you write a poem called Rape Joke, you're asking for   38
it to become the only thing people remember about you.

The rape joke is that you asked why he did it. The rape joke is he said he   39
didn't know, like what else would a rape joke say? The rape joke said
YOU were the one who was drunk, and the rape joke said you remembered it wrong, which made you laugh out loud for one long split-open
second. The wine coolers weren't Bartles & Jaymes, but it would be funnier for the rape joke if they were. It was some pussy flavor, like Passionate Mango or Destroyed Strawberry, which you drank down without
question and trustingly in the heart of Cincinnati Ohio.

Can rape jokes be funny at all, is the question.   40

Can any part of the rape joke be funny. The part where it ends — haha,   41
just kidding! Though you did dream of killing the rape joke for years,
spilling all of its blood out, and telling it that way.

The rape joke cries out for the right to be told.   42

The rape joke is that this is just how it happened.   43

The rape joke is that the next day he gave you Pet Sounds. No really. Pet   44
Sounds. He said he was sorry and then he gave you Pet Sounds. Come
on, that's a little bit funny.

Admit it.   45

[2013]

SOLMAZ SHARIF [b. 1986]

from Reaching Guantánamo

Dear Salim,

Love, are you well? Do they   you?
I worry so much. Lately, my hair   ,even
my skin   . The doctors tell me it's
I believe them. It shouldn't
. Please don't worry.
                    in the yard, and moths
have gotten to your mother's
                    ,remember?
I have enclosed some   —made this
batch just for you. Please eat well. Why
did you   me to remarry? I told
        and he couldn't   it.
I would never
Love, I'm singing that   you loved,
remember, the line that went
"   "? I'm holding
the   just for you.

Yours,

[2010]

680

PART THREE

9 Plays

QUESTIONS FOR ACTIVE READING: DRAMA

- *What actually happens within the frame of the play? What transpired before the play started? What do you speculate will happen once the play is over? For example, the events of the past bear heavily upon the characters in August Wilson's* Fences *(p. 1030), well before the action of the actual play begins.*

- *Every character has unique attributes and relationships with other characters. What do you learn about each character through their interaction with others? How do the characters speak? Do they use slang? A regional dialect? Does someone hesitate or speak in fits and starts? What do characters withhold or reveal through their dialogue? For example, in Tennessee Williams's* Cat on a Hot Tin Roof *(p. 951), how does the Southern dialect of the characters inform your understanding of their character and relationship to place?*

- *Setting can determine how characters act and what obstacles may stand in their way. What does the setting of the play reveal to you? For example, how does the setting in Susan Glaspell's* Trifles *(p. 939)—an abandoned farmhouse in a farming community—affect the series of events in the play?*

- *Scenes are the building blocks of any dramatic text. Can you identify each scene? What does each one accomplish?*

- *Typically, dramatic texts establish tension right away. What is the central tension of the dramatic text? Where do you first learn of the tension or problem? Does it get resolved by the end of the play? If not, why not? For example, early on in Oscar Wilde's* The Importance of Being Earnest *(p. 889), the main characters discuss the advantages and disadvantages of marriage. What kind of commentary do the characters provide in order to give you some insight into their concerns?*

- *You can tell a lot about a play based on how the writer manipulates time. How does time move in the play? Sequentially? Are there flashbacks? Speculations about the future? How long does it take for time to transpire in the play? How do you know?*

- *Are there moments of dramatic irony—that is, moments in which you as an audience member know something that the characters onstage do not? (Sophocles's* Oedipus Rex, *p. 685, provides some excellent moments of dramatic irony.) Why does the playwright create this gap in a character's knowledge? How does it affect you as a viewer?*

- *What does this play reveal about the culture in which it was produced? For example, what does Shakespeare's* Othello *(p. 728) reveal about attitudes toward race during the Renaissance?*

- *What insights do you gather from this dramatic text? Does the play challenge your value system, as in the case of Ayad Akhtar's* Disgraced *(p. 1156)? Do the characters undergo a transformation that is surprising, troubling, or inspiring, and what does that reveal about the play itself?*

SOPHOCLES   [496?–406 B.C.]

Oedipus the King

TRANSLATED BY DAVID GRENE

Characters

OEDIPUS, *King of Thebes*
JOCASTA, *His Wife*
CREON, *His Brother-in-Law*
TEIRESIAS, *an Old Blind Prophet*
A PRIEST
FIRST MESSENGER
SECOND MESSENGER
A HERDSMAN
CHORUS OF OLD MEN OF THEBES

Scene: *In front of the palace of Oedipus at Thebes. To the right of the stage near the altar stands the Priest with a crowd of children. Oedipus emerges from the central door.*

OEDIPUS: Children, young sons and daughters of old Cadmus,°
   why do you sit here with your suppliant crowns?
   The town is heavy with a mingled burden
   of sounds and smells, of groans and hymns and incense;
   I did not think it fit that I should hear   5
   of this from messengers but came myself,—
   I Oedipus whom all men call the Great.   *(He turns to the Priest.)*
   You're old and they are young; come, speak for them.
   What do you fear or want, that you sit here
   suppliant? Indeed I'm willing to give all   10
   that you may need; I would be very hard
   should I not pity suppliants like these.
PRIEST: O ruler of my country, Oedipus,
   you see our company around the altar;
   you see our ages; some of us, like these,   15
   who cannot yet fly far, and some of us
   heavy with age; these children are the chosen

1. **Cadmus:** Founder and first king of Thebes.

685

among the young, and I the priest of Zeus.
Within the market place sit others crowned
with suppliant garlands, at the double shrine
of Pallas° and the temple where Ismenus
gives oracles by fire. King, you yourself
have seen our city reeling like a wreck
already; it can scarcely lift its prow
out of the depths, out of the bloody surf.
A blight is on the fruitful plants of the earth,
A blight is on the cattle in the fields,
a blight is on our women that no children
are born to them; a God that carries fire,
a deadly pestilence, is on our town,
strikes us and spares not, and the house of Cadmus
is emptied of its people while black Death
grows rich in groaning and in lamentation.
We have not come as suppliants to this altar
because we thought of you as of a God,
but rather judging you the first of men
in all the chances of this life and when
we mortals have to do with more than man.
You came and by your coming saved our city,
freed us from tribute which we paid of old
to the Sphinx,° cruel singer. This you did
in virtue of no knowledge we could give you,
in virtue of no teaching; it was God
that aided you, men say, and you are held
with God's assistance to have saved our lives.
Now Oedipus, Greatest in all men's eyes,
here falling at your feet we all entreat you,
find us some strength for rescue.
Perhaps you'll hear a wise word from some God,
perhaps you will learn something from a man
(for I have seen that for the skilled of practice
the outcome of their counsels live the most).
Noblest of men, go, and raise up our city,

---

21. Pallas: Pallas Athene, goddess of wisdom and daughter of Zeus.
41. Sphinx: A mythical creature with the body of a lion, wings of a bird, and the face of a woman. The Sphinx stumped Thebans with her riddle and killed those that could not answer it. Oedipus solved the riddle, the Sphinx killed herself, and Oedipus became king of Thebes.

go,—and give heed. For now this land of ours
calls you its savior since you saved it once.   55
So, let us never speak about your reign
as of a time when first our feet were set
secure on high, but later fell to ruin.
Raise up our city, save it and raise it up.
Once you have brought us luck with happy omen;   60
be no less now in fortune.
If you will rule this land, as now you rule it,
better to rule it full of men than empty.
For neither tower nor ship is anything
when empty, and none live in it together.   65
OEDIPUS: I pity you, children. You have come full of longing,
but I have known the story before you told it
only too well. I know you are all sick,
yet there is not one of you, sick though you are,
that is as sick as I myself.   70
Your several sorrows each have single scope
and touch but one of you. My spirit groans
for city and myself and you at once.
You have not roused me like a man from sleep;
know that I have given many tears to this,   75
gone many ways wandering in thought,
but as I thought I found only one remedy
and that I took. I sent Menoeceus' son
Creon, Jocasta's brother, to Apollo,°
to his Pythian temple,   80
that he might learn there by what act or word
I could save this city. As I count the days,
it vexes me what ails him; he is gone
far longer than he needed for the journey.
But when he comes, then, may I prove a villain,   85
if I shall not do all the God commands.
PRIEST: Thanks for your gracious words. Your servants here
signal that Creon is this moment coming.
OEDIPUS: His face is bright. O holy Lord Apollo,
grant that his news too may be bright for us   90
and bring us safety.
PRIEST: It is happy news,
I think, for else his head would not be crowned
with sprigs of fruitful laurel.

79. Apollo: Oracular god of the sun, light, and truth, and son of Zeus.

OEDIPUS: We will know soon,
  he's within hail. Lord Creon, my good brother,
  what is the word you bring us from the God?   (*Creon enters.*)
CREON: A good word,—for things hard to bear themselves
  if in the final issue all is well
  I count complete good fortune.
OEDIPUS: What do you mean?
  What you have said so far   10
  leaves me uncertain whether to trust or fear.
CREON: If you will hear my news before these others
  I am ready to speak, or else to go within.
OEDIPUS: Speak it to all;
  the grief I bear, I bear it more for these   10
  than for my own heart.
CREON: I will tell you, then,
  what I heard from the God.
  King Phoebus° in plain words commanded us
  to drive out a pollution from our land,
  pollution grown ingrained within the land;   11
  drive it out, said the God, not cherish it,
  till it's past cure.
OEDIPUS: What is the rite
  of purification? How shall it be done?
CREON: By banishing a man, or expiation
  of blood by blood, since it is murder guilt   11
  which holds our city in this destroying storm.
OEDIPUS: Who is this man whose fate the God pronounces?
CREON: My Lord, before you piloted the state
  we had a king called Laius.°
OEDIPUS: I know of him by hearsay. I have not seen him.   12
CREON: The God commanded clearly: let some one
  punish with force this dead man's murderers.
OEDIPUS: Where are they in the world? Where would a trace
  of this old crime be found? It would be hard
  to guess where.
CREON: The clue is in this land;   12
  that which is sought is found;
  the unheeded thing escapes:
  so said the God.

108. King Phoebus: Apollo.   **119. Laius:** Former king of Thebes.

OEDIPUS: Was it at home,
  or in the country that death came upon him,
  or in another country travelling?   130
CREON: He went, he said himself, upon an embassy,
  but never returned when he set out from home.
OEDIPUS: Was there no messenger, no fellow traveller
  who knew what happened? Such a one might tell
  something of use.   135
CREON: They were all killed save one. He fled in terror
  and he could tell us nothing in clear terms
  of what he knew, nothing, but one thing only.
OEDIPUS: What was it?
  If we could even find a slim beginning   140
  in which to hope, we might discover much.
CREON: This man said that the robbers they encountered
  were many and the hands that did the murder
  were many; it was no man's single power.
OEDIPUS: How could a robber dare a deed like this   145
  were he not helped with money from the city,
  money and treachery?
CREON: That indeed was thought.
  But Laius was dead and in our trouble
  there was none to help.
OEDIPUS: What trouble was so great to hinder you   150
  inquiring out the murder of your king?
CREON: The riddling Sphinx induced us to neglect
  mysterious crimes and rather seek solution
  of troubles at our feet.
OEDIPUS: I will bring this to light again. King Phoebus   155
  fittingly took this care about the dead,
  and you too fittingly.
  And justly you will see in me an ally,
  a champion of my country and the God.
  For when I drive pollution from the land   160
  I will not serve a distant friend's advantage,
  but act in my own interest. Whoever
  he was that killed the king may readily
  wish to dispatch me with his murderous hand;
  so helping the dead king I help myself.   165
  Come, children, take your suppliant boughs and go;
  up from the altars now. Call the assembly
  and let it meet upon the understanding
  that I'll do everything. God will decide

whether we prosper or remain in sorrow.   17

PRIEST: Rise, children—it was this we came to seek,
which of himself the king now offers us.
May Phoebus who gave us the oracle
come to our rescue and stay the plague.   (*Exeunt*° *all but the Chorus.*)

CHORUS (*Strophe*°): What is the sweet spoken word of God from the
    shrine of Pytho° rich in gold   17
that has come to glorious Thebes?
I am stretched on the rack of doubt, and terror and trembling hold
my heart, O Delian Healer,° and I worship full of fears
for what doom you will bring to pass, new or renewed in the
    revolving years.
Speak to me, immortal voice,   18
child of golden Hope.

(*Antistrophe*°) First I call on you, Athene, deathless daughter of Zeus,
and Artemis, Earth Upholder,
who sits in the midst of the market place in the throne which men
    call Fame,
and Phoebus, the Far Shooter, three averters of Fate,   18
come to us now, if ever before, when ruin rushed upon the state,
you drove destruction's flame away
out of our land.

(*Strophe*) Our sorrows defy number;
all the ship's timbers are rotten;   19
taking of thought is no spear for the driving away of the plague.
There are no growing children in this famous land;
there are no women bearing the pangs of childbirth.
You may see them one with another, like birds swift on the wing,
quicker than fire unmastered,   19
speeding away to the coast of the Western God.

(*Antistrophe*) In the unnumbered deaths
of its people the city dies;
those children that are born lie dead on the naked earth
unpitied, spreading contagion of death; and grey haired mothers
    and wives   20

Exeunt: Stage direction indicating that the characters have left the stage.
Strophe: The song sung by the Chorus, dancing from stage right to stage left.
175. shrine of Pytho: Delphi, site of the oracle and shrine dedicated to Apollo.
178. Delian Healer: Apollo.   **Antistrophe:** The song sung after the strophe by
the Chorus, dancing back from stage left to stage right.

everywhere stand at the altar's edge, suppliant, moaning;
the hymn to the healing God rings out but with it the wailing voices
   are blended.
From these our sufferings grant us, O golden Daughter of Zeus,
   glad-faced deliverance.

(*Strophe*) There is no clash of brazen shields but our fight is with
   the War God,   205
a War God ringed with the cries of men, a savage God who burns us;
grant that he turn in racing course backwards out of our country's
   bounds
to the great palace of Amphitrite° or where the waves of the Thracian
   sea
deny the stranger safe anchorage.
Whatsoever escapes the night   210
at last the light of day revisits;
so smite the War God, Father Zeus,
beneath your thunderbolt,
for you are the Lord of the lightning, the lightning that carries fire.

(*Antistrophe*) And your unconquered arrow shafts, winged by the
   golden corded bow,   215
Lycean King,° I beg to be at our side for help;
and the gleaming torches of Artemis with which she scours the Lycean
   hills,
and I call on the God with the turban of gold, who gave his name to
   this country of ours,
the Bacchic God° with the wind flushed face,
Evian One, who travel   220
with the Maenad company,°
combat the God that burns us
with your torch of pine;
for the God that is our enemy is a God unhonoured among the Gods.
                                 (*Oedipus returns.*)

OEDIPUS: For what you ask me—if you will hear my words,   225
   and hearing welcome them and fight the plague,
   you will find strength and lightening of your load.

   Hark to me; what I say to you, I say
   as one that is a stranger to the story
   as stranger to the deed. For I would not   230

---

208. Amphitrite: Sea goddess and wife of Poseidon.   **216. Lycean King:** Apollo.
219. Bacchic God: Bacchus, also known as Dionysus, god of wine and wild
celebration.   **221. Maenad company:** Female followers of Bacchus.

be far upon the track if I alone
were tracing it without a clue. But now,
since after all was finished, I became
a citizen among you, citizens—
now I proclaim to all the men of Thebes: 23
who so among you knows the murderer
by whose hand Laius, son of Labdacus,
died—I command him to tell everything
to me,—yes, though he fears himself to take the blame
on his own head; for bitter punishment   24
he shall have none, but leave this land unharmed.
Or if he knows the murderer, another,
a foreigner, still let him speak the truth.
For I will pay him and be grateful, too.
But if you shall keep silence, if perhaps   24
some one of you, to shield a guilty friend,
or for his own sake shall reject my words—
hear what I shall do then:
I forbid that man, whoever he be, my land,
my land where I hold sovereignty and throne;   25
and I forbid any to welcome him
or cry him greeting or make him a sharer
in sacrifice or offering to the Gods,
or give him water for his hands to wash.
I command all to drive him from their homes,   25
since he is our pollution, as the oracle
of Pytho's God proclaimed him now to me.
So I stand forth a champion of the God
and of the man who died.
Upon the murderer I invoke this curse—   26
whether he is one man and all unknown,
or one of many—may he wear out his life
in misery to miserable doom!
If with my knowledge he lives at my hearth
I pray that I myself may feel my curse.   26
On you I lay my charge to fulfill all this
for me, for the God, and for this land of ours
destroyed and blighted, by the God forsaken.

Even were this no matter of God's ordinance
it would not fit you so to leave it lie,   27
unpurified, since a good man is dead
and one that was a king. Search it out.

Since I am now the holder of his office,
and have his bed and wife that once was his,
and had his line not been unfortunate   275
we would have common children—(fortune leaped
upon his head)—because of all these things,
I fight in his defence as for my father,
and I shall try all means to take the murderer
of Laius the son of Labdacus   280
the son of Polydorus and before him
of Cadmus and before him of Agenor.°
Those who do not obey me, may the Gods
grant no crops springing from the ground they plough
nor children to their women! May a fate   285
like this, or one still worse than this consume them!
For you whom these words please, the other Thebans,
may Justice as your ally and all the Gods
live with you, blessing you now and for ever!

CHORUS: As you have held me to my oath, I speak: 290
   I neither killed the king nor can declare
   the killer; but since Phoebus set the quest
   it is his part to tell who the man is.

OEDIPUS: Right; but to put compulsion on the Gods
   against their will—no man can do that.   295

CHORUS: May I then say what I think second best?

OEDIPUS: If there's a third best, too, spare not to tell it.

CHORUS: I know that what the Lord Teiresias
   sees, is most often what the Lord Apollo
   sees. If you should inquire of this from him   300
   you might find out most clearly.

OEDIPUS: Even in this my actions have not been sluggard.
   On Creon's word I have sent two messengers
   and why the prophet is not here already
   I have been wondering.

CHORUS: His skill apart   305
   there is besides only an old faint story.

OEDIPUS: What is it?
   I look at every story.

CHORUS: It was said
   that he was killed by certain wayfarers.

OEDIPUS: I heard that, too, but no one saw the killer.   310

---

282. Labdacus, Polydorus, Cadmus, and Agenor: Referring to the father,
grandfather, great-grandfather, and great-great-grandfather of Laius.

CHORUS: Yet if he has a share of fear at all,
  his courage will not stand firm, hearing your curse.
OEDIPUS: The man who in the doing did not shrink
  will fear no word.
CHORUS: Here comes his prosecutor:
  led by your men the godly prophet comes   31
  in whom alone of mankind truth is native.

                    (*Enter Teiresias, led by a little boy.*)

OEDIPUS: Teiresias, you are versed in everything,
  things teachable and things not to be spoken,
  things of the heaven and earth-creeping things.
  You have no eyes but in your mind you know   32
  with what a plague our city is afflicted.
  My lord, in you alone we find a champion,
  in you alone one that can rescue us.
  Perhaps you have not heard the messengers,
  but Phoebus sent in answer to our sending   32
  an oracle declaring that our freedom
  from this disease would only come when we
  should learn the names of those who killed King Laius,
  and kill them or expel from our country.
  Do not begrudge us oracles from birds,°   33
  or any other way of prophecy
  within your skill; save yourself and the city,
  save me; redeem the debt of our pollution
  that lies on us because of this dead man.
  We are in your hands; pains are most nobly taken   33
  to help another when you have means and power.
TEIRESIAS: Alas, how terrible is wisdom when
  it brings no profit to the man that's wise!
  This I knew well, but had forgotten it,
  else I would not have come here.
OEDIPUS: What is this?   34
  How sad you are now you have come!
TEIRESIAS: Let me
  go home. It will be easiest for us both
  to bear our several destinies to the end
  if you will follow my advice.
OEDIPUS: You'd rob us
  of this your gift of prophecy? You talk   34

---

330. oracles from birds: Bird flight, a method by which prophets predicted the
future using the flight of birds.

as one who had no care for law nor love
for Thebes who reared you.
TEIRESIAS: Yes, but I see that even your own words
miss the mark; therefore I must fear for mine.
OEDIPUS: For God's sake if you know of anything,   350
do not turn from us; all of us kneel to you,
all of us here, your suppliants.
TEIRESIAS: All of you here know nothing. I will not
bring to the light of day my troubles, mine—
rather than call them yours.
OEDIPUS: What do you mean?   355
You know of something but refuse to speak.
Would you betray us and destroy the city?
TEIRESIAS: I will not bring this pain upon us both,
neither on you nor on myself. Why is it
you question me and waste your labour? I   360
will tell you nothing.
OEDIPUS: You would provoke a stone! Tell us, you villain,
tell us, and do not stand there quietly
unmoved and balking at the issue.
TEIRESIAS: You blame my temper but you do not see   365
your own that lives within you; it is me
you chide.
OEDIPUS: Who would not feel his temper rise
at words like these with which you shame our city?
TEIRESIAS: Of themselves things will come, although I hide them   370
and breathe no word of them.
OEDIPUS: Since they will come
tell them to me.
TEIRESIAS: I will say nothing further.
Against this answer let your temper rage
as wildly as you will.
OEDIPUS: Indeed I am
so angry I shall not hold back a jot   375
of what I think. For I would have you know
I think you were complotter^c of the deed
and doer of the deed save in so far
as for the actual killing. Had you had eyes
I would have said alone you murdered him.   380
TEIRESIAS: Yes? Then I warn you faithfully to keep
the letter of your proclamation and

377. **complotter:** One who is part of a plot or conspiracy.

from this day forth to speak no word of greeting
to these nor me; you are the land's pollution.

OEDIPUS: How shamelessly you started up this taunt!   38
How do you think you will escape?

TEIRESIAS: I have.
I have escaped; the truth is what I cherish
and that's my strength.

OEDIPUS: And who has taught you truth?
Not your profession surely!

TEIRESIAS: You have taught me,
for you have made me speak against my will.   39

OEDIPUS: Speak what? Tell me again that I may learn it better.

TEIRESIAS: Did you not understand before or would you
provoke me into speaking?

OEDIPUS: I did not grasp it,
not so to call it known. Say it again.

TEIRESIAS: I say you are the murderer of the king   39
whose murderer you seek.

OEDIPUS: Not twice you shall
say calumnies like this and stay unpunished.

TEIRESIAS: Shall I say more to tempt your anger more?

OEDIPUS: As much as you desire; it will be said
in vain.

TEIRESIAS: I say that with those you love best   40
you live in foulest shame unconsciously
and do not see where you are in calamity.

OEDIPUS: Do you imagine you can always talk
like this, and live to laugh at it hereafter?

TEIRESIAS: Yes, if the truth has anything of strength.   40

OEDIPUS: It has, but not for you; it has no strength
for you because you are blind in mind and ears
as well as in your eyes.

TEIRESIAS: You are a poor wretch
to taunt me with the very insults which
every one soon will heap upon yourself.   41

OEDIPUS: Your life is one long night so that you cannot
hurt me or any other who sees the light.

TEIRESIAS: It is not fate that I should be your ruin,
Apollo is enough; it is his care
to work this out.

OEDIPUS: Was this your own design   41
or Creon's?

TEIRESIAS: Creon is no hurt to you,
    but you are to yourself.
OEDIPUS: Wealth, sovereignty and skill outmatching skill
    for the contrivance of an envied life!
    Great store of jealousy fill your treasury chests,   420
    if my friend Creon, friend from the first and loyal,
    thus secretly attacks me, secretly
    desires to drive me out and secretly
    suborns this juggling, trick devising quack,
    this wily beggar who has only eyes   425
    for his own gains, but blindness in his skill.
    For, tell me, where have you seen clear, Teiresias,
    with your prophetic eyes? When the dark singer,
    the sphinx, was in your country, did you speak
    word of deliverance to its citizens?   430
    And yet the riddle's answer was not the province
    of a chance comer. It was a prophet's task
    and plainly you had no such gift of prophecy
    from birds nor otherwise from any God
    to glean a word of knowledge. But I came,   435
    Oedipus, who knew nothing and I stopped her.
    I solved the riddle by my wit alone.
    Mine was no knowledge got from birds. And now
    you would expel me,
    because you think that you will find a place   440
    by Creon's throne. I think you will be sorry,
    both you and your accomplice, for your plot
    to drive me out. And did I not regard you
    as an old man, some suffering would have taught you
    that what was in your heart was treason.   445
CHORUS: We look at this man's words and yours, my king,
    and we find both have spoken them in anger.
    We need no angry words but only thought
    how we may best hit the God's meaning for us.
TEIRESIAS: If you are king, at least I have the right   450
    no less to speak in my defence against you.
    Of that much I am master. I am no slave
    of yours, but Loxias', and so I shall not
    enroll myself with Creon for my patron.
    Since you have taunted me with being blind,   455
    here is my word for you.
    You have your eyes but see not where you are

in sin, nor where you live, nor whom you live with.
Do you know who your parents are? Unknowing
you are an enemy to kith and kin   46
in death, beneath the earth, and in this life.
A deadly footed, double striking curse,
from father and mother both, shall drive you forth
out of this land, with darkness on your eyes,
that now have such straight vision. Shall there be   46
a place will not be harbour to your cries,
a corner of Cithaeron° will not ring
in echo to your cries, soon, soon,—
when you shall learn the secret of your marriage,
which steered you to a haven in this house,—   47
haven no haven, after lucky voyage?
And of the multitude of other evils
establishing a grim equality
between you and your children, you know nothing.
So, muddy with contempt my words and Creon's!   47
Misery shall grind no man as it will you.

OEDIPUS: Is it endurable that I should hear
such words from him? Go and a curse go with you!
Quick, home with you! Out of my house at once!

TEIRESIAS: I would not have come either had you not called me.   48

OEDIPUS: I did not know then you would talk like a fool—
or it would have been long before I called you.

TEIRESIAS: I am a fool then, as it seems to you—
but to the parents who have bred you, wise.

OEDIPUS: What parents? Stop! Who are they of all the world?   48

TEIRESIAS: This day will show your birth and will destroy you.

OEDIPUS: How needlessly your riddles darken everything.

TEIRESIAS: But it's in riddle answering you are strongest.

OEDIPUS: Yes. Taunt me where you will find me great.

TEIRESIAS: It is this very luck that has destroyed you.   49

OEDIPUS: I do not care, if it has saved this city.

TEIRESIAS: Well, I will go. Come, boy, lead me away.

OEDIPUS: Yes, lead him off. So long as you are here,
you'll be a stumbling block and a vexation;
once gone, you will not trouble me again.

TEIRESIAS: I have said   49
what I came here to say not fearing your

---

467. Cithaeron: Mountain in Greece and the location where Oedipus was
abandoned as a baby.

countenance: there is no way you can hurt me.
I tell you, king, this man, this murderer
(whom you have long declared you are in search of,
indicting him in threatening proclamation   500
as murderer of Laius)—he is here.
In name he is a stranger among citizens
but soon he will be shown to be a citizen
true native Theban, and he'll have no joy
of the discovery: blindness for sight   505
and beggary for riches his exchange,
he shall go journeying to a foreign country
tapping his way before him with a stick.
He shall be proved father and brother both
to his own children in his house; to her   510
that gave him birth, a son and husband both;
a fellow sower in his father's bed
with that same father that he murdered.
Go within, reckon that out, and if you find me
mistaken, say I have no skill in prophecy.   515

(Exeunt separately Teiresias and Oedipus.)

CHORUS (*Strophe*): Who is the man proclaimed
　by Delphi's prophetic rock
　as the bloody handed murderer,
　the doer of deeds that none dare name?
Now is the time for him to run   520
　with a stronger foot
　than Pegasus
for the child of Zeus leaps in arms upon him
　with fire and the lightning bolt,
and terribly close on his heels   525
are the Fates that never miss.

(*Antistrophe*) Lately from snowy Parnassus[c]
　clearly the voice flashed forth,
　bidding each Theban track him down,
　the unknown murderer.   530
In the savage forests he lurks and in
　the caverns like
　the mountain bull.
He is sad and lonely, and lonely his feet
　that carry him far from the navel of earth;   535

---

527. Parnassus: Mountain in Greece that was sacred to Apollo.

but its prophecies, ever living,
flutter around his head.

(*Strophe*) The augur has spread confusion,
terrible confusion;
I do not approve what was said   54
nor can I deny it.
I do not know what to say;
I am in a flutter of foreboding;
I never heard in the present
nor past of a quarrel between   54
the sons of Labdacus and Polybus,
that I might bring as proof
in attacking the popular fame
of Oedipus, seeking
to take vengeance for undiscovered   55
death in the line of Labdacus.

(*Antistrophe*) Truly Zeus and Apollo are wise
and in human things all knowing;
but amongst men there is no
distinct judgment, between the prophet   55
and me—which of us is right.
One man may pass another in wisdom
but I would never agree
with those that find fault with the king
till I should see the word   56
proved right beyond doubt. For once
in visible form the Sphinx
came on him and all of us
saw his wisdom and in that test
he saved the city. So he will not be condemned by my mind.   56

(Enter Creon.)

CREON: Citizens, I have come because I heard
deadly words spread about me, that the king
accuses me. I cannot take that from him.
If he believes that in these present troubles
he has been wronged by me in word or deed   57
I do not want to live on with the burden
of such a scandal on me. The report
injures me doubly and most vitally—
for I'll be called a traitor to my city
and traitor also to my friends and you.   57

CHORUS: Perhaps it was a sudden gust of anger
   that forced that insult from him, and no judgment.
CREON: But did he say that it was in compliance
   with schemes of mine that the seer told him lies?
CHORUS: Yes, he said that, but why, I do not know.   580
CREON: Were his eyes straight in his head? Was his mind right
   when he accused me in this fashion?
CHORUS: I do not know; I have no eyes to see
   what princes do. Here comes the king himself.   (*Enter Oedipus.*)
OEDIPUS: You, sir, how is it you come here? Have you so much   585
   brazen-faced daring that you venture in
   my house although you are proved manifestly
   the murderer of that man, and though you tried,
   openly, highway robbery of my crown?
   For God's sake, tell me what you saw in me,   590
   what cowardice or what stupidity,
   that made you lay a plot like this against me?
   Did you imagine I should not observe
   the crafty scheme that stole upon me or
   seeing it, take no means to counter it?   595
   Was it not stupid of you to make the attempt,
   to try to hunt down royal power without
   the people at your back or friends? For only
   with the people at your back or money can
   the hunt end in the capture of a crown.   600
CREON: Do you know what you're doing? Will you listen
   to words to answer yours, and then pass judgment?
OEDIPUS: You're quick to speak, but I am slow to grasp you,
   for I have found you dangerous,—and my foe.
CREON: First of all hear what I shall say to that.   605
OEDIPUS: At least don't tell me that you are not guilty.
CREON: If you think obstinacy without wisdom
   a valuable possession, you are wrong.
OEDIPUS: And you are wrong if you believe that one,
   a criminal, will not be punished only   610
   because he is my kinsman.
CREON: This is but just—
   but tell me, then, of what offense I'm guilty?
OEDIPUS: Did you or did you not urge me to send
   to this prophetic mumbler?
CREON: I did indeed,
   and I shall stand by what I told you.   615

OEDIPUS: How long ago is it since Laius. . . .
CREON: What about Laius? I don't understand.
OEDIPUS: Vanished—died—was murdered?
CREON: It is long,
  a long, long time to reckon.
OEDIPUS: Was this prophet
  in the profession then?
CREON: He was, and honoured   62(
  as highly as he is today.
OEDIPUS: At that time did he say a word about me?
CREON: Never, at least when I was near him.
OEDIPUS: You never made a search for the dead man?
CREON: We searched, indeed, but never learned of anything.   62!
OEDIPUS: Why did our wise old friend not say this then?
CREON: I don't know; and when I know nothing, I
  usually hold my tongue.
OEDIPUS: You know this much,
  and can declare this much if you are loyal.
CREON: What is it? If I know, I'll not deny it.   63(
OEDIPUS: That he would not have said that I killed Laius
  had he not met you first.
CREON: You know yourself
  whether he said this, but I demand that I
  should hear as much from you as you from me.
OEDIPUS: Then hear,—I'll not be proved a murderer.   63!
CREON: Well, then. You're married to my sister.
OEDIPUS: Yes,
  that I am not disposed to deny.
CREON: You rule
  this country giving her an equal share
  in the government?
OEDIPUS: Yes, everything she wants
  she has from me.
CREON: And I, as thirdsman to you,   64(
  am rated as the equal of you two?
OEDIPUS: Yes, and it's there you've proved yourself false friend.
CREON: Not if you will reflect on it as I do.
  Consider, first, if you think any one
  would choose to rule and fear rather than rule   64!
  and sleep untroubled by a fear if power
  were equal in both cases. I, at least,
  I was not born with such a frantic yearning
  to be a king—but to do what kings do.

And so it is with every one who has learned   650
wisdom and self-control. As it stands now,
the prizes are all mine—and without fear.
But if I were the king myself, I must
do much that went against the grain.
How should despotic rule seem sweeter to me   655
than painless power and an assured authority?
I am not so besotted yet that I
want other honours than those that come with profit.
Now every man's my pleasure; every man greets me;
now those who are your suitors fawn on me,—   660
success for them depends upon my favour.
Why should I let all this go to win that?
My mind would not be traitor if it's wise;
I am no treason lover, of my nature,
nor would I ever dare to join a plot.   665
Prove what I say. Go to the oracle
at Pytho and inquire about the answers,
if they are as I told you. For the rest,
if you discover I laid any plot
together with the seer, kill me, I say,   670
not only by your vote but by my own.
But do not charge me on obscure opinion
without some proof to back it. It's not just
lightly to count your knaves as honest men,
nor honest men as knaves. To throw away   675
an honest friend is, as it were, to throw
your life away, which a man loves the best.
In time you will know all with certainty;
time is the only test of honest men,
one day is space enough to know a rogue.   680
CHORUS: His words are wise, king, if one fears to fall.
    Those who are quick of temper are not safe.
OEDIPUS: When he that plots against me secretly
    moves quickly, I must quickly counterplot.
    If I wait taking no decisive measure   685
    his business will be done, and mine be spoiled.
CREON: What do you want to do then? Banish me?
OEDIPUS: No, certainly; kill you, not banish you.
CREON: I do not think that you've your wits about you.
OEDIPUS: For my own interests, yes.
CREON: But for mine, too,   690
    you should think equally.

OEDIPUS: You are a rogue.

CREON: Suppose you do not understand?

OEDIPUS: But yet
  I must be ruler.

CREON: Not if you rule badly.

OEDIPUS: O, city, city!

CREON: I too have some share
  in the city; it is not yours alone.   69

CHORUS: Stop, my lords! Here—and in the nick of time
  I see Jocasta coming from the house;
  with her help lay the quarrel that now stirs you.   (*Enter Jocasta.*)

JOCASTA: For shame! Why have you raised this foolish squabbling
  brawl? Are you not ashamed to air your private   70
  griefs when the country's sick? Go in, you, Oedipus,
  and you, too, Creon, into the house. Don't magnify
  your nothing troubles.

CREON: Sister, Oedipus,
  your husband, thinks he has the right to do
  terrible wrongs—he has but to choose between   70
  two terrors: banishing or killing me.

OEDIPUS: He's right, Jocasta; for I find him plotting
  with knavish tricks against my person.

CREON: That God may never bless me! May I die
  accursed, if I have been guilty of   71
  one tittle of the charge you bring against me!

JOCASTA: I beg you, Oedipus, trust him in this,
  spare him for the sake of this his oath to God,
  for my sake, and the sake of those who stand here.

CHORUS: Be gracious, be merciful,   71
  we beg of you.

OEDIPUS: In what would you have me yield?

CHORUS: He has been no silly child in the past.
  He is strong in his oath now.
  Spare him.   72

OEDIPUS: Do you know what you ask?

CHORUS: Yes.

OEDIPUS: Tell me then.

CHORUS: He has been your friend before all men's eyes; do not cast him
  away dishonoured on an obscure conjecture.   72

OEDIPUS: I would have you know that this request of yours
  really requests my death or banishment.

CHORUS: May the Sun God, king of Gods, forbid! May I die without God's
  blessing, without friends' help, if I had any such thought. But my spirit

is broken by my unhappiness for my wasting country; and this would 730
    but add troubles amongst ourselves to the other troubles.
OEDIPUS: Well, let him go then—if I must die ten times for it,
    or be sent out dishonoured into exile.
    It is your lips that prayed for him I pitied,
    not his; wherever he is, I shall hate him. 735
CREON: I see you sulk in yielding and you're dangerous
    when you are out of temper; natures like yours
    are justly heaviest for themselves to bear.
OEDIPUS: Leave me alone! Take yourself off, I tell you.
CREON: I'll go, you have not known me, but they have, 740
    and they have known my innocence. (*Exit.*)
CHORUS: Won't you take him inside, lady?
JOCASTA: Yes, when I've found out what was the matter.
CHORUS: There was some misconceived suspicion of a story, and on the
    other side the sting of injustice. 745
JOCASTA: So, on both sides?
CHORUS: Yes.
JOCASTA: What was the story?
CHORUS: I think it best, in the interests of the country, to leave it where
    it ended. 750
OEDIPUS: You see where you have ended, straight of judgment
    although you are, by softening my anger.
CHORUS: Sir, I have said before and I say again—be sure that I would
    have been proved a madman, bankrupt in sane council, if I should put
    you away, you who steered the country I love safely when she 755
    was crazed with troubles. God grant that now, too, you may prove a
    fortunate guide for us.
JOCASTA: Tell me, my lord, I beg of you, what was it
    that roused your anger so?
OEDIPUS: Yes, I will tell you.
    I honour you more than I honour them. 760
    It was Creon and the plots he laid against me.
JOCASTA: Tell me—if you can clearly tell the quarrel—
OEDIPUS: Creon says
    that I'm the murderer of Laius.
JOCASTA: Of his own knowledge or on information?
OEDIPUS: He sent this rascal prophet to me, since 765
    he keeps his own mouth clean of any guilt.
JOCASTA: Do not concern yourself about this matter;
    listen to me and learn that human beings
    have no part in the craft of prophecy.
    Of that I'll show you a short proof. 770

There was an oracle once that came to Laius,—
I will not say that it was Phoebus' own,
but it was from his servants—and it told him
that it was fate that he should die a victim
at the hands of his own son, a son to be born   77
of Laius and me. But, see now, he,
the king, was killed by foreign highway robbers
at a place where three roads meet—so goes the story;
and for the son—before three days were out
after his birth King Laius pierced his ankles   78
and by the hands of others cast him forth
upon a pathless hillside. So Apollo
failed to fulfill his oracle to the son,
that he should kill his father, and to Laius
also proved false in that the thing he feared,   78
death at his son's hands, never came to pass.
So clear in this case were the oracles,
so clear and false. Give them no heed, I say;
what God discovers need of, easily
he shows to us himself.

OEDIPUS: O dear Jocasta,   79
    as I hear this from you, there comes upon me
    a wandering of the soul—I could run mad.

JOCASTA: What trouble is it, that you turn again
    and speak like this?

OEDIPUS: I thought I heard you say
    that Laius was killed at a crossroads.   79

JOCASTA: Yes, that was how the story went and still
    that word goes round.

OEDIPUS: Where is this place, Jocasta,
    where he was murdered?

JOCASTA: Phocis is the country
    and the road splits there, one of two roads from Delphi,
    another comes from Daulia.

OEDIPUS: How long ago is this?   80

JOCASTA: The news came to the city just before
    you became king and all men's eyes looked to you.
    What is it, Oedipus, that's in your mind?

OEDIPUS: What have you designed, O Zeus, to do with me?

JOCASTA: What is the thought that troubles your heart?   80

OEDIPUS: Don't ask me yet—tell me of Laius—
    How did he look? How old or young was he?

JOCASTA: He was a tall man and his hair was grizzled
   already—nearly white—and in his form
   not unlike you.
OEDIPUS: O God, I think I have   810
   called curses on myself in ignorance.
JOCASTA: What do you mean? I am terrified
   when I look at you.
OEDIPUS: I have a deadly fear
   that the old seer had eyes. You'll show me more
   if you can tell me one more thing.
JOCASTA: I will.   815
   I'm frightened,—but if I can understand,
   I'll tell you all you ask.
OEDIPUS: How was his company?
   Had he few with him when he went this journey,
   or many servants, as would suit a prince?
JOCASTA: In all there were but five, and among them   820
   a herald; and one carriage for the king.
OEDIPUS: It's plain—its plain—who was it told you this?
JOCASTA: The only servant that escaped safe home.
OEDIPUS: Is he at home now?
JOCASTA: No, when he came home again
   and saw you king and Laius was dead,   825
   he came to me and touched my hand and begged
   that I should send him to the fields to be
   my shepherd and so he might see the city
   as far off as he might. So I
   sent him away. He was an honest man,   830
   as slaves go, and was worthy of far more
   than what he asked of me.
OEDIPUS: O, how I wish that he could come back quickly!
JOCASTA: He can. Why is your heart so set on this?
OEDIPUS: O dear Jocasta, I am full of fears   835
   that I have spoken far too much; and therefore
   I wish to see this shepherd.
JOCASTA: He will come;
   but, Oedipus, I think I'm worthy too
   to know what it is that disquiets you.
OEDIPUS: It shall not be kept from you, since my mind   840
   has gone so far with its forebodings. Whom
   should I confide in rather than you, who is there
   of more importance to me who have passed

through such a fortune?
Polybus was my father, king of Corinth,   84?
and Merope,° the Dorian, my mother.
I was held greatest of the citizens
in Corinth till a curious chance befell me
as I shall tell you—curious, indeed,
but hardly worth the store I set upon it.   85?
There was a dinner and at it a man,
a drunken man, accused me in his drink
of being bastard. I was furious
but held my temper under for that day.
Next day I went and taxed my parents with it;   85?
they took the insult very ill from him,
the drunken fellow who had uttered it.
So I was comforted for their part, but
still this thing rankled always, for the story
crept about widely. And I went at last   86?
to Pytho, though my parents did not know.
But Phoebus sent me home again unhonoured
in what I came to learn, but he foretold
other and desperate horrors to befall me,
that I was fated to lie with my mother,   86?
and show to daylight an accursed breed
which men would not endure, and I was doomed
to be murderer of the father that begot me.
When I heard this I fled, and in the days
that followed I would measure from the stars   870
the whereabouts of Corinth—yes, I fled
to somewhere where I should not see fulfilled
the infamies told in that dreadful oracle.
And as I journeyed I came to the place
where, as you say, this king met with his death.   87?
Jocasta, I will tell you the whole truth.
When I was near the branching of the crossroads,
going on foot, I was encountered by
a herald and a carriage with a man in it,
just as you tell me. He that led the way   88?
and the old man himself wanted to thrust me
out of the road by force. I became angry
and struck the coachman who was pushing me.
When the old man saw this he watched his moment,

845–846. Polybus...Merope: King and queen that adopted and raised Oedipus.

and as I passed he struck me from his carriage,   885
full on the head with his two pointed goad.
But he was paid in full and presently
my stick had struck him backwards from the car
and he rolled out of it. And then I killed them
all. If it happened there was any tie   890
of kinship twixt this man and Laius,
who is then now more miserable than I,
what man on earth so hated by the Gods,
since neither citizen nor foreigner
may welcome me at home or even greet me,   895
but drive me out of doors? And it is I,
I and no other have so cursed myself.
And I pollute the bed of him I killed
by the hands that killed him. Was I not born evil?
Am I not utterly unclean? I had to fly   900
and in my banishment not even see
my kindred nor set foot in my own country,
or otherwise my fate was to be yoked
in marriage with my mother and kill my father,
Polybus who begot me and had reared me.   905
Would not one rightly judge and say that on me
these things were sent by some malignant God?
O no, no, no—O holy majesty
of God on high, may I not see that day!
May I be gone out of men's sight before   910
I see the deadly taint of this disaster
come upon me.
CHORUS: Sir, we too fear these things. But until you see this man face to
    face and hear his story, hope.
OEDIPUS: Yes, I have just this much of hope—to wait until the herdsman
    comes.   915
JOCASTA: And when he comes, what do you want with him?
OEDIPUS: I'll tell you; if I find that his story is the same as yours, I at least
    will be clear of this guilt.
JOCASTA: Why what so particularly did you learn from my story?
OEDIPUS: You said that he spoke of highway *robbers* who killed Laius. 920
    Now if he uses the same number, it was not I who killed him. One man
    cannot be the same as many. But if he speaks of a man travelling alone,
    then clearly the burden of the guilt inclines towards me.
JOCASTA: Be sure, at least, that this was how he told the story. He cannot
    unsay it now, for everyone in the city heard it—not I alone. But, Oedipus, 925
    even if he diverges from what he said then, he shall never prove that the

murder of Laius squares rightly with the prophecy— for Loxias declared
that the king should be killed by his own son. And that poor creature did
not kill him surely,—for he died himself first. So as far as prophecy goes,
henceforward I shall not look to the right hand or the left.   93

OEDIPUS: Right. But yet, send some one for the peasant to bring him
here; do not neglect it.

JOCASTA: I will send quickly. Now let me go indoors. I will do nothing
except what pleases you.   (*Exeunt.*)

CHORUS (*Strophe*): May destiny ever find me   93
pious in word and deed
prescribed by the laws that live on high:
laws begotten in the clear air of heaven,
whose only father is Olympus;
no mortal nature brought them to birth,   94
no forgetfulness shall lull them to sleep;
for God is great in them and grows not old.

(*Antistrophe*) Insolence breeds the tyrant, insolence
if it is glutted with a surfeit, unseasonable, unprofitable,
climbs to the roof-top and plunges   94
sheer down to the ruin that must be,
and there its feet are no service.
But I pray that the God may never
abolish the eager ambition that profits the state.
For I shall never cease to hold the God as our protector.   95

(*Strophe*) If a man walks with haughtiness
of hand or word and gives no heed
to Justice and the shrines of Gods
despises—may an evil doom
smite him for his ill-starred pride of heart!—   95
he reaps gains without justice
and will not hold from impiety
and his fingers itch for untouchable things.
When such things are done, what man shall contrive
to shield his soul from the shafts of the God?   96
When such deeds are held in honour,
why should I honour the Gods in the dance?

(*Antistrophe*) No longer to the holy place,
to the navel of earth I'll go
to worship, nor to Abae°   96

965. **Abae:** A town in ancient Greece that was renowned for its oracle.

nor to Olympia,
unless the oracles are proved to fit,
for all men's hands to point at.
O Zeus, if you are rightly called
the sovereign lord, all-mastering,   970
let this not escape you nor your ever-living power!
The oracles concerning Laius
are old and dim and men regard them not.
Apollo is nowhere clear in honour; God's service perishes.

                    (Enter Jocasta, carrying garlands.)

JOCASTA: Princes of the land, I have had the thought to go   975
to the Gods' temples, bringing in my hand
garlands and gifts of incense, as you see.
For Oedipus excites himself too much
at every sort of trouble, not conjecturing,
like a man of sense, what will be from what was,   980
but he is always at the speaker's mercy,
when he speaks terrors. I can do no good
by my advice, and so I came as suppliant
to you, Lycaean Apollo, who are nearest.
These are the symbols of my prayer and this   985
my prayer: grant us escape free of the curse.
Now when we look to him we are all afraid;
he's pilot of our ship and he is frightened.   *(Enter Messenger.)*

MESSENGER: Might I learn from you, sirs, where is the house of Oedipus?
Or best of all, if you know, where is the king himself?   990

CHORUS: This is his house and he is within doors. This lady is his wife
and mother of his children.

MESSENGER: God bless you, lady, and God bless your household! God
bless Oedipus' noble wife!

JOCASTA: God bless you, sir, for your kind greeting! What do you want of   995
us that you have come here? What have you to tell us?

MESSENGER: Good news, lady. Good for your house and for your
husband.

JOCASTA: What is your news? Who sent you to us?

MESSENGER: I come from Corinth and the news I bring will give you
pleasure. Perhaps a little pain too.   1000

JOCASTA: What is this news of double meaning?

MESSENGER: The people of the Isthmus will choose Oedipus to be their
king. That is the rumour there.

JOCASTA: But isn't their king still old Polybus?

MESSENGER: No. He is in his grave. Death has got him.   1005

JOCASTA: Is that the truth? Is Oedipus' father dead?

MESSENGER: May I die myself if it be otherwise!

JOCASTA (*to a servant*): Be quick and run to the King with the news! O oracles of the Gods, where are you now? It was from this man Oedipus fled, lest he should be his murderer! And now he is dead, in the course of nature, and not killed by Oedipus.   (*Enter Oedipus.*) 101

OEDIPUS: Dearest Jocasta, why have you sent for me?

JOCASTA: Listen to this man and when you hear reflect what is the outcome of the holy oracles of the Gods.

OEDIPUS: Who is he? What is his message for me? 101

JOCASTA: He is from Corinth and he tells us that your father Polybus is dead and gone.

OEDIPUS: What's this you say, sir? Tell me yourself.

MESSENGER: Since this is the first matter you want clearly told: Polybus has gone down to death. You may be sure of it. 102

OEDIPUS: By treachery or sickness?

MESSENGER: A small thing will put old bodies asleep.

OEDIPUS: So he died of sickness, it seems,—poor old man!

MESSENGER: Yes, and of age—the long years he had measured.

OEDIPUS: Ha! Ha! O dear Jocasta, why should one 102
    look to the Pythian hearth?° Why should one look
    to the birds screaming overhead? They prophesied
    that I should kill my father! But he's dead,
    and hidden deep in earth, and I stand here
    who never laid a hand on spear against him,— 103
    unless perhaps he died of longing for me,
    and thus I am his murderer. But they,
    the oracles, as they stand—he's taken them
    away with him, they're dead as he himself is,
    and worthless.

JOCASTA: That I told you before now. 103

OEDIPUS: You did, but I was misled by my fear.

JOCASTA: Then lay no more of them to heart, not one.

OEDIPUS: But surely I must fear my mother's bed?

JOCASTA: Why should man fear since chance is all in all
    for him, and he can clearly foreknow nothing? 104
    Best to live lightly, as one can, unthinkingly.
    As to your mother's marriage bed,—don't fear it.
    Before this, in dreams too, as well as oracles,

1026. **Pythian hearth:** Delphi.

many a man has lain with his own mother.
But he to whom such things are nothing bears   1045
his life most easily.
OEDIPUS: All that you say would be said perfectly
if she were dead; but since she lives I must
still fear, although you talk so well, Jocasta.
JOCASTA: Still in your father's death there's light of comfort?   1050
OEDIPUS: Great light of comfort; but I fear the living.
MESSENGER: Who is the woman that makes you afraid?
OEDIPUS: Merope, old man, Polybus' wife.
MESSENGER: What about her frightens the queen and you?
OEDIPUS: A terrible oracle, stranger, from the Gods.   1055
MESSENGER: Can it be told? Or does the sacred law
forbid another to have knowledge of it?
OEDIPUS: O no! Once on a time Loxias said
that I should lie with my own mother and
take on my hands the blood of my own father.   1060
And so for these long years I've lived away
from Corinth; it has been to my great happiness;
but yet it's sweet to see the face of parents.
MESSENGER: This was the fear which drove you out of Corinth?
OEDIPUS: Old man, I did not wish to kill my father.   1065
MESSENGER: Why should I not free you from this fear, sir,
since I have come to you in all goodwill?
OEDIPUS: You would not find me thankless if you did.
MESSENGER: Why, it was just for this I brought the news,—
to earn your thanks when you had come safe home.   1070
OEDIPUS: No, I will never come near my parents.
MESSENGER: Son,
it's very plain you don't know what you're doing.
OEDIPUS: What do you mean, old man? For God's sake, tell me.
MESSENGER: If your homecoming is checked by fears like these.
OEDIPUS: Yes, I'm afraid that Phoebus may prove right.   1075
MESSENGER: The murder and the incest?
OEDIPUS: Yes, old man;
that is my constant terror.
MESSENGER: Do you know
that all your fears are empty?
OEDIPUS: How is that,
if they are father and mother and I their son?
MESSENGER: Because Polybus was no kin to you in blood.   1080
OEDIPUS: What, was not Polybus my father?

MESSENGER: No more than I but just so much.
OEDIPUS: How can
    my father be my father as much as one
    that's nothing to me?
MESSENGER: Neither he nor I
    begat you.
OEDIPUS: Why then did he call me son?   1085
MESSENGER: A gift he took you from these hands of mine.
OEDIPUS: Did he love so much what he took from another's hand?
MESSENGER: His childlessness before persuaded him.
OEDIPUS: Was I a child you bought or found when I
    was given to him?
MESSENGER: On Cithaeron's slopes   1090
    in the twisting thickets you were found.
OEDIPUS: And why
    were you a traveller in those parts?
MESSENGER: I was
    in charge of mountain flocks.
OEDIPUS: You were a shepherd?
    A hireling vagrant?
MESSENGER: Yes, but at least at that time
    the man that saved your life, son.   1095
OEDIPUS: What ailed me when you took me in your arms?
MESSENGER: In that your ankles should be witnesses.
OEDIPUS: Why do you speak of that old pain?
MESSENGER: I loosed you;
    the tendons of your feet were pierced and fettered, —
OEDIPUS: My swaddling clothes brought me a rare disgrace.   1100
MESSENGER: So that from this you're called your present name.°
OEDIPUS: Was this my father's doing or my mother's?
    For God's sake, tell me.
MESSENGER: I don't know, but he
    who gave you to me has more knowledge than I.
OEDIPUS: You yourself did not find me then? You took me   1105
    from someone else?
MESSENGER: Yes, from another shepherd.
OEDIPUS: Who was he? Do you know him well enough
    to tell?
MESSENGER: He was called Laius' man.
OEDIPUS: You mean the king who reigned here in the old days?
MESSENGER: Yes, he was that man's shepherd.

1101. name: *Oedipus* literally translates to "swollen foot."

OEDIPUS: Is he alive   1110
  still, so that I could see him?
MESSENGER: You who live here
  would know that best.
OEDIPUS: Do any of you here
  know of this shepherd whom he speaks about
  in town or in the fields? Tell me. It's time
  that this was found out once for all.   1115
CHORUS: I think he is none other than the peasant
  whom you have sought to see already; but
  Jocasta here can tell us best of that.
OEDIPUS: Jocasta, do you know about this man
  whom we have sent for? Is he the man he mentions?   1120
JOCASTA: Why ask of whom he spoke? Don't give it heed;
  nor try to keep in mind what has been said.
  It will be wasted labour.
OEDIPUS: With such clues
  I could not fail to bring my birth to light.
JOCASTA: I beg you—do not hunt this out—I beg you,   1125
  if you have any care for your own life.
  What I am suffering is enough.
OEDIPUS: Keep up
  your heart, Jocasta. Though I'm proved a slave,
  thrice slave, and though my mother is thrice slave,
  you'll not be shown to be of lowly lineage.   1130
JOCASTA: O be persuaded by me, I entreat you;
  do not do this.
OEDIPUS: I will not be persuaded to let be
  the chance of finding out the whole thing clearly.
JOCASTA: It is because I wish you well that I   1135
  give you this counsel—and it's the best counsel.
OEDIPUS: Then the best counsel vexes me, and has
  for some while since.
JOCASTA: O Oedipus, God help you!
  God keep you from the knowledge of who you are!
OEDIPUS: Here, some one, go and fetch the shepherd for me;   1140
  and let her find her joy in her rich family!
JOCASTA: O Oedipus, unhappy Oedipus!
  that is all I can call you, and the last thing
  that I shall ever call you.   (*Exit.*)
CHORUS: Why has the queen gone, Oedipus, in wild   1145
  grief rushing from us? I am afraid that trouble
  will break out of this silence.

OEDIPUS: Break out what will! I at least shall be
  willing to see my ancestry, though humble.
  Perhaps she is ashamed of my low birth,
  for she has all a woman's high-flown pride.
  But I account myself a child of Fortune,
  beneficent Fortune, and I shall not be
  dishonoured. She's the mother from whom I spring;
  the months, my brothers, marked me, now as small,
  and now again as mighty. Such is my breeding,
  and I shall never prove so false to it,
  as not to find the secret of my birth.

CHORUS (*Strophe*): If I am a prophet and wise of heart
  you shall not fail, Cithaeron,
  by the limitless sky, you shall not! —
  to know at tomorrow's full moon
  that Oedipus honours you,
  as native to him and mother and nurse at once;
  and that you are honoured in dancing by us, as finding
    favour in sight of our king.
  Apollo, to whom we cry, find these things pleasing!

  (*Antistrophe*) Who was it bore you, child? One of
  the long-lived nymphs who lay with Pan —
  the father who treads the hills?
  Or was she a bride of Loxias, your mother? The grassy slopes
  are all of them dear to him. Or perhaps Cyllene's king°
  or the Bacchants' God that lives on the tops
  of the hills received you a gift from some
  one of the Helicon Nymphs, with whom he mostly plays?
                 (*Enter an old man, led by Oedipus' servants.*)

OEDIPUS: If some one like myself who never met him
  may make a guess, — I think this is the herdsman,
  whom we were seeking. His old age is consonant
  with the other. And besides, the men who bring him
  I recognize as my own servants. You
  perhaps may better me in knowledge since
  you've seen the man before.

CHORUS: You can be sure
  I recognize him. For if Laius
  had ever an honest shepherd, this was he.

1172. Cyllene's king: Hermes, the messenger god.

OEDIPUS: You, sir, from Corinth, I must ask you first,   1185
  is this the man you spoke of?
MESSENGER: This is he
  before your eyes.
OEDIPUS: Old man, look here at me
  and tell me what I ask you. Were you ever
  a servant of King Laius?
HERDSMAN: I was,—
  no slave he bought but reared in his own house.   1190
OEDIPUS: What did you do as work? How did you live?
HERDSMAN: Most of my life was spent among the flocks.
OEDIPUS: In what part of the country did you live?
HERDSMAN: Cithaeron and the places near to it.
OEDIPUS: And somewhere there perhaps you knew this man?   1195
HERDSMAN: What was his occupation? Who?
OEDIPUS: This man here,
  have you had any dealings with him?
HERDSMAN: No—
  not such that I can quickly call to mind.
MESSENGER: That is no wonder, master. But I'll make him remember
  what he does not know. For I know, that he well knows the country   1200
  of Cithaeron, how he with two flocks, I with one kept company for
  three years—each year half a year—from spring till autumn time
  and then when winter came I drove my flocks to our fold home
  again and he to Laius' steadings. Well—am I right or not in what I
  said we did?   1205
HERDSMAN: You're right—although it's a long time ago.
MESSENGER: Do you remember giving me a child
  to bring up as my foster child?
HERDSMAN: What's this?
  Why do you ask this question?
MESSENGER: Look old man,
  here he is—here's the man who was that child!   1210
HERDSMAN: Death take you! Won't you hold your tongue?
OEDIPUS: No, no,
  do not find fault with him, old man. Your words
  are more at fault than his.
HERDSMAN: O best of masters,
  how do I give offense?
OEDIPUS: When you refuse
  to speak about the child of whom he asks you.   1215
HERDSMAN: He speaks out of his ignorance, without meaning.

OEDIPUS: If you'll not talk to gratify me, you
　　will talk with pain to urge you.
HERDSMAN: 　　　　　　　　O please, sir,
　　don't hurt an old man, sir.
OEDIPUS (TO THE SERVANTS): Here, one of you,
　　twist his hands behind him.
HERDSMAN: 　　　　　　　Why, God help me, why? 　　122
　　What do you want to know?
OEDIPUS: 　　　　　　　You gave a child
　　to him,—the child he asked you of?
HERDSMAN: 　　　　　　　　　I did.
　　I wish I'd died the day I did.
OEDIPUS: 　　　　　　　You will
　　unless you tell me truly.
HERDSMAN: 　　　　　　And I'll die
　　far worse if I should tell you.
OEDIPUS: 　　　　　　　　This fellow 　　122
　　is bent on more delays, as it would seem.
HERDSMAN: O no, no! I have told you that I gave it.
OEDIPUS: Where did you get this child from? Was it your own or did
　　you get it from another?
HERDSMAN: 　　　　　　Not
　　my own at all; I had it from some one. 　　123
OEDIPUS: One of these citizens? or from what house?
HERDSMAN: O master, please—I beg you, master, please
　　don't ask me more.
OEDIPUS: 　　　　　You're a dead man if I
　　ask you again.
HERDSMAN: 　　It was one of the children
　　of Laius.
OEDIPUS: 　A slave? Or born in wedlock? 　　123
HERDSMAN: O God, I am on the brink of frightful speech.
OEDIPUS: And I of frightful hearing. But I must hear.
HERDSMAN: The child was called his child; but she within,
　　your wife would tell you best how all this was.
OEDIPUS: *She* gave it to you?
HERDSMAN: 　　　　　　Yes, she did, my lord. 　　124
OEDIPUS: To do what with it?
HERDSMAN: 　　　　　　Make away with it.
OEDIPUS: She was so hard—its mother?
HERDSMAN: 　　　　　　　　　Aye, through fear
　　of evil oracles.

OEDIPUS: Which?
HERDSMAN: They said that he
    should kill his parents.
OEDIPUS: How was it that you
    gave it away to this old man?
HERDSMAN: O master,   1245
    I pitied it, and thought that I could send it
    off to another country and this man
    was from another country. But he saved it
    for the most terrible troubles. If you are
    the man he says you are, you're bred to misery.   1250
OEDIPUS: O, O, O, they will all come,
    all come out clearly! Light of the sun, let me
    look upon you no more after today!
    I who first saw the light bred of a match
    accursed, and accursed in my living   1255
    with them I lived with, cursed in my killing.
                            (*Exeunt all but the Chorus.*)
CHORUS (*Strophe*): O generations of men, how I
    count you as equal with those who live
    not at all!
    What man, what man on earth wins more   1260
    of happiness than a seeming
    and after that turning away?
    Oedipus, you are my pattern of this,
    Oedipus, you and your fate!
    Luckless Oedipus, whom of all men   1265
    I envy not at all.

    (*Antistrophe*) In as much as he shot his bolt
    beyond the others and won the prize
    of happiness complete—
    O Zeus—and killed and reduced to nought   1270
    the hooked taloned maid of the riddling speech,
    standing a tower against death for my land:
    hence he was called my king and hence
    was honoured the highest of all
    honours; and hence he ruled   1275
    in the great city of Thebes.

    (*Strophe*) But now whose tale is more miserable?
    Who is there lives with a savager fate?
    Whose troubles so reverse his life as his?

O Oedipus, the famous prince   128
for whom a great haven
the same both as father and son
sufficed for generation,
how, O how, have the furrows ploughed
by your father endured to bear you, poor wretch,   128
and hold their peace so long?

(*Antistrophe*) Time who sees all has found you out
against your will; judges your marriage accursed,
begetter and begot at one in it.

O child of Laius,   129
would I had never seen you.
I weep for you and cry
a dirge of lamentation.

To speak directly, I drew my breath
from you at the first and so now I lull   129
my mouth to sleep with your name.   (*Enter a second messenger.*)

SECOND MESSENGER: O Princes always honoured by our country,
    what deeds you'll hear of and what horrors see,
    what grief you'll feel, if you as true born Thebans
    care for the house of Labdacus's sons.   130
    Phasis nor Ister cannot purge this house,
    I think, with all their streams, such things
    it hides, such evils shortly will bring forth
    into the light, whether they will or not;
    and troubles hurt the most   130
    when they prove self-inflicted.

CHORUS: What we had known before did not fall short
    of bitter groaning's worth; what's more to tell?

SECOND MESSENGER: Shortest to hear and tell—our glorious queen
    Jocasta's dead.

CHORUS: Unhappy woman! How?   131

SECOND MESSENGER: By her own hand. The worst of what was done
    you cannot know. You did not see the sight.
    Yet in so far as I remember it
    you'll hear the end of our unlucky queen.
    When she came raging into the house she went   131
    straight to her marriage bed, tearing her hair
    with both her hands, and crying upon Laius
    long dead—Do you remember, Laius,
    that night long past which bred a child for us
    to send you to your death and leave   132
    a mother making children with her son?

And then she groaned and cursed the bed in which
she brought forth husband by her husband, children
by her own child, an infamous double bond.
How after that she died I do not know,— 1325
for Oedipus distracted us from seeing.
He burst upon us shouting and we looked
to him as he paced frantically around,
begging us always: Give me a sword, I say,
to find this wife no wife, this mother's womb, 1330
this field of double sowing whence I sprang
and where I sowed my children! As he raved
some god showed him the way—none of us there.
Bellowing terribly and led by some
invisible guide he rushed on the two doors,— 1335
wrenching the hollow bolts out of their sockets,
he charged inside. There, there, we saw his wife
hanging, the twisted rope around her neck.
When he saw her, he cried out fearfully
and cut the dangling noose. Then, as she lay, 1340
poor woman, on the ground, what happened after,
was terrible to see. He tore the brooches—
the gold chased brooches fastening her robe—
away from her and lifting them up high
dashed them on his own eyeballs, shrieking out 1345
such things as: they will never see the crime
I have committed or had done upon me!
Dark eyes, now in the days to come look on
forbidden faces, do not recognize
those whom you long for—with such imprecations 1350
he struck his eyes again and yet again
with the brooches. And the bleeding eyeballs gushed
and stained his beard—no sluggish oozing drops
but a black rain and bloody hail poured down.

So it has broken—and not on one head 1355
but troubles mixed for husband and for wife.
The fortune of the days gone by was true
good fortune—but today groans and destruction
and death and shame—of all ills can be named
not one is missing. 1360
CHORUS: Is he now in any ease from pain?
SECOND MESSENGER: He shouts
for some one to unbar the doors and show him
to all the men of Thebes, his father's killer,
his mother's—no I cannot say the word,

it is unholy—for he'll cast himself,   13
out of the land, he says, and not remain
to bring a curse upon his house, the curse
he called upon it in his proclamation. But
he wants for strength, aye, and some one to guide him;
his sickness is too great to bear. You, too,   13
will be shown that. The bolts are opening.
Soon you will see a sight to waken pity
even in the horror of it.   (*Enter the blinded Oedipus.*)

CHORUS: This is a terrible sight for men to see!
I never found a worse!   13
Poor wretch, what madness came upon you!
What evil spirit leaped upon your life
to your ill-luck—a leap beyond man's strength!
Indeed I pity you, but I cannot
look at you, though there's much I want to ask   13
and much to learn and much to see.
I shudder at the sight of you.

OEDIPUS: O, O,
where am I going? Where is my voice
borne on the wind to and fro?   13
Spirit, how far have you sprung?

CHORUS: To a terrible place whereof men's ears
may not hear, nor their eyes behold it.

OEDIPUS: Darkness!
Horror of darkness enfolding, resistless, unspeakable visitant
    sped by an ill wind in haste!   13
madness and stabbing pain and memory
of evil deeds I have done!

CHORUS: In such misfortunes it's no wonder
if double weighs the burden of your grief.

OEDIPUS: My friend,   13
you are the only one steadfast, the only one that attends on me;
you still stay nursing the blind man.
Your care is not unnoticed. I can know
your voice, although this darkness is my world.

CHORUS: Doer of dreadful deeds, how did you dare   14
so far to do despite to your own eyes?
what spirit urged you to it?

OEDIPUS: It was Apollo, friends, Apollo,
that brought this bitter bitterness, my sorrows to completion.
But the hand that struck me   14
was none but my own.
Why should I see

whose vision showed me nothing sweet to see?
CHORUS: These things are as you say.
OEDIPUS: What can I see to love?   1410
   What greeting can touch my ears with joy?
   Take me away, and haste—to a place out of the way!
   Take me away, my friends, the greatly miserable,
   the most accursed, whom God too hates
   above all men on earth!   1415
CHORUS: Unhappy in your mind and your misfortune,
   would I had never known you!
OEDIPUS: Curse on the man who took
   the cruel bonds from off my legs, as I lay in the field.
   He stole me from death and saved me,   1420
   no kindly service.
   Had I died then
   I would not be so burdensome to friends.
CHORUS: I, too, could have wished it had been so.
OEDIPUS: Then I would not have come   1425
   to kill my father and marry my mother infamously.
   Now I am godless and child of impurity,
   begetter in the same seed that created my wretched self.
   If there is any ill worse than ill,
   that is the lot of Oedipus.   1430
CHORUS: I cannot say your remedy was good;
   you would be better dead than blind and living.
OEDIPUS: What I have done here was best done—don't tell me
   otherwise, do not give me further counsel.
   I do not know with what eyes I could look   1435
   upon my father when I die and go
   under the earth, nor yet my wretched mother—
   those two to whom I have done things deserving
   worse punishment than hanging. Would the sight
   of children, bred as mine are, gladden me?   1440
   No, not these eyes, never. And my city,
   its towers and sacred places of the Gods,
   of these I robbed my miserable self
   when I commanded all to drive *him* out,
   the criminal since proved by God impure   1445
   and of the race of Laius.
   To this guilt I bore witness against myself—
   with what eyes shall I look upon my people?
   No. If there were a means to choke the fountain
   of hearing I would not have stayed my hand   1450
   from locking up my miserable carcase,

seeing and hearing nothing; it is sweet
to keep our thoughts out of the range of hurt.

Cithaeron, why did you receive me? why
having received me did you not kill me straight?   145
And so I had not shown to men my birth.

O Polybus and Corinth and the house,
the old house that I used to call my father's—
what fairness you were nurse to, and what foulness
festered beneath! Now I am found to be   146
a sinner and a son of sinners. Crossroads,
and hidden glade, oak and the narrow way
at the crossroads, that drank my father's blood
offered you by my hands, do you remember
still what I did as you looked on, and what   146
I did when I came here? O marriage, marriage!
you bred me and again when you had bred
bred children of your child and showed to men
brides, wives and mothers and the foulest deeds
that can be in this world of ours.   147

Come—it's unfit to say what is unfit
to do.—I beg of you in God's name hide me
somewhere outside your country, yes, or kill me,
or throw me into the sea, to be forever
out of your sight. Approach and deign to touch me   147
for all my wretchedness, and do not fear.
No man but I can bear my evil doom.

CHORUS: Here Creon comes in fit time to perform
or give advice in what you ask of us.
Creon is left sole ruler in your stead.   148

OEDIPUS: Creon! Creon! What shall I say to him?
How can I justly hope that he will trust me?
In what is past I have been proved towards him
an utter liar.   (*Enter Creon.*)

CREON: Oedipus, I've come
not so that I might laugh at you nor taunt you   148
with evil of the past. But if you still
are without shame before the face of men
reverence at least the flame that gives all life,
our Lord the Sun, and do not show unveiled
to him pollution such that neither land   149
nor holy rain nor light of day can welcome.   (*To a servant*)

Be quick and take him in. It is most decent
that only kin should see and hear the troubles
of kin.

OEDIPUS: I beg you, since you've torn me from   1495
my dreadful expectations and have come
in a most noble spirit to a man
that has used you vilely—do a thing for me.
I shall speak for your own good, not for my own.

CREON: What do you need that you would ask of me?   1500

OEDIPUS: Drive me from here with all the speed you can
to where I may not hear a human voice.

CREON: Be sure, I would have done this had not I
wished first of all to learn from the God the course
of action I should follow.

OEDIPUS: But his word   1505
has been quite clear to let the parricide,°
the sinner, die.

CREON: Yes, that indeed was said.
But in the present need we had best discover
what we should do.

OEDIPUS: And will you ask about
a man so wretched?

CREON: Now even you will trust   1510
the God.

OEDIPUS: So. I command you—and will beseech you—
to her that lies inside that house give burial
as you would have it; she is yours and rightly
you will perform the rites for her. For me—
never let this my father's city have me   1515
living a dweller in it. Leave me live
in the mountains where Cithaeron is, that's called
my mountain, which my mother and my father
while they were living would have made my tomb.
So I may die by their decree who sought   1520
indeed to kill me. Yet I know this much:
no sickness and no other thing will kill me.
I would not have been saved from death if not
for some strange evil fate. Well, let my fate
go where it will.

                    Creon, you need not care   1525

1506. parricide: One who kills his parent or another close relative.

about my sons; they're men and so wherever
they are, they will not lack a livelihood.
But my two girls—so sad and pitiful—
whose table never stood apart from mine,
and everything I touched they always shared—   15:
O Creon, have a thought for them! And most
I wish that you might suffer me to touch them
and sorrow with them.
> (*Enter Antigone and Ismene, Oedipus' two daughters.*)

O my lord! O true noble Creon! Can I
really be touching them, as when I saw?   15
What shall I say?
Yes, I can hear them sobbing—my two darlings!
and Creon has had pity and has sent me
what I loved most?
Am I right?   15<

CREON: You're right: it was I gave you this
because I knew from old days how you loved them
as I see now.

OEDIPUS: God bless you for it, Creon,
and may God guard you better on your road
than he did me!
                   O children,   154
where are you? Come here, come to my hands,
a brother's hands which turned your father's eyes,
those bright eyes you knew once, to what you see,
a father seeing nothing, knowing nothing,
begetting you from his own source of life.   15£
I weep for you—I cannot see your faces—
I weep when I think of the bitterness
there will be in your lives, how you must live
before the world. At what assemblages
of citizens will you make one? to what   15£
gay company will you go and not come home
in tears instead of sharing in the holiday?
And when you're ripe for marriage, who will he be,
the man who'll risk to take such infamy
as shall cling to my children, to bring hurt   15€
on them and those that marry with them? What
curse is not there? "Your father killed his father
and sowed the seed where he had sprung himself
and begot you out of the womb that held him."
These insults you will hear. Then who will marry you?   156
No one, my children; clearly you are doomed

to waste away in barrenness unmarried.
Son of Menoeceus,° since you are all the father
left these two girls, and we, their parents, both
are dead to them—do not allow them wander   1570
like beggars, poor and husbandless.
They are of your own blood.
And do not make them equal with myself
in wretchedness; for you can see them now
so young, so utterly alone, save for you only.   1575
Touch my hand, noble Creon, and say yes.
If you were older, children, and were wiser
there's much advice I'd give you. But as it is,
let this be what you pray: give me a life
wherever there is opportunity   1580
to live, and better life than was my father's.

CREON: Your tears have had enough of scope; now go within the house.

OEDIPUS: I must obey, though bitter of heart.

CREON: In season, all is good.

OEDIPUS: Do you know on what conditions I obey?

CREON: You tell me them,   1585
and I shall know them when I hear.

OEDIPUS: That you shall send me out
to live away from Thebes.

CREON: That gift you must ask of the God.

OEDIPUS: But I'm now hated by the Gods.

CREON: So quickly you'll obtain your prayer.

OEDIPUS: You consent then?

CREON: What I do not mean, I do not use to say.

OEDIPUS: Now lead me away from here.

CREON: Let go the children, then, and come. 1590

OEDIPUS: Do not take them from me.

CREON: Do not seek to be master in everything,
for the things you mastered did not follow you throughout your life.

                    (*As Creon and Oedipus go out*)

CHORUS: You that live in my ancestral Thebes, behold this Oedipus,—
him who knew the famous riddles and was a man most masterful;
not a citizen who did not look with envy on his lot—   1595
see him now and see the breakers of misfortune swallow him!
Look upon that last day always. Count no mortal happy till
he has passed the final limit of his life secure from pain.

                                        [c. 430 BCE]

1568. Son of Menoeceus: Creon

WILLIAM SHAKESPEARE [1564–1616]

Othello the Moor of Venice

The Names of the Actors
OTHELLO, THE MOOR
BRABANTIO, [*a Venetian senator,*] *father to Desdemona*
CASSIO, *an honorable lieutenant* [*to Othello*]
IAGO, [*Othello's ancient,*] *a villain*
RODERIGO, *a gulled gentleman*
DUKE OF VENICE
SENATORS [*of Venice*]
MONTANO, *governor of Cyprus*
LODOVICO AND GRATIANO, [*kinsmen to Brabantio,*] *two noble Venetians*
SAILORS
CLOWNS
DESDEMONA, *wife to Othello*
EMILIA, *wife to Iago*
BIANCA, *a courtesan*
[MESSENGER, HERALD, OFFICERS, VENETIAN GENTLEMEN, MUSICIANS, ATTENDANTS]

Scene: *Venice and Cyprus*

ACT I   *Scene I*

(*A street in Venice.*)

(*Enter Roderigo and Iago.*)

RODERIGO: Tush, never tell me! I take it much unkindly

Note: *Othello* was first published in 1622, some six years after Shakespeare's death, in a slender book called a "quarto" (made up of printer's paper folded twice, creating four leaves—eight pages—approximately 9½ by 12 inches in size). The following year the play was printed a second time, in the 1623 collected edition of Shakespeare's plays called the First Folio (with paper folded once, creating pages twice as large as a quarto). The Folio text is around 160 lines longer, but the quarto text contains some things omitted from the Folio text. The play as printed here mainly follows the Folio text, but passages from the quarto text have been inserted and enclosed in square brackets.

That thou, Iago, who hast had my purse
As if the strings were thine, shouldst know of this.°
IAGO: 'Sblood,° but you'll not hear me!
    If ever I did dream of such a matter,   5
    Abhor me.
RODERIGO: Thou told'st me thou didst hold him in thy hate.
IAGO: Despise me if I do not. Three great ones of the city,
    In personal suit to make me his lieutenant,
    Off-capped to him;° and, by the faith of man,   10
    I know my price; I am worth no worse a place.
    But he, as loving his own pride and purposes,
    Evades them with a bombast circumstance.°
    Horribly stuffed with epithets of war;
    [And, in conclusion,]   15
    Nonsuits° my mediators; for, "Certes," says he,
    "I have already chose my officer."
    And what was he?
    Forsooth, a great arithmetician,°
    One Michael Cassio, a Florentine   20
    (A fellow almost damned in a fair wife°)
    That never set a squadron in the field,
    Nor the division of a battle knows
    More than a spinster; unless the bookish theoric,
    Wherein the togèd consuls can propose°   25
    As masterly as he. Mere prattle without practice
    Is all his soldiership. But he, sir, had th' election;
    And I (of whom his eyes had seen the proof
    At Rhodes, at Cyprus, and on other grounds
    Christian and heathen) must be belee'd and calmed°   30
    By debitor and creditor; this counter-caster,°
    He, in good time, must his lieutenant be,
    And I—God bless the mark!—his Moorship's ancient.°
RODERIGO: By heaven, I rather would have been his hangman.
IAGO: Why, there's no remedy; 'tis the curse of service.   35
    Preferment goes by letter and affection,°

---

3. **this:** I.e., Desdemona's elopement.   4. **'Sblood:** By God's blood.   10. **him:**
I.e., Othello.   13. **a bombast circumstance:** Pompous circumlocutions.
16. **Nonsuits:** Rejects.   19. **arithmetician:** Theoretician.   21. **almost . . . wife:**
(An obscure allusion; Cassio is unmarried, but see 4.1.125–26).   25. **Wherein . . .
propose:** In which the toga-wearing senators can debate.   30. **belee'd and
calmed:** Left in the lurch.   31. **counter-caster:** Bookkeeper.   33. **ancient:**
Ensign.   36. **affection:** Favoritism

And not by old gradation, where each second
Stood heir to th' first. Now, sir, be judge yourself,
Whether I in any just term am affined°
To love the Moor.

RODERIGO: I would not follow him then.

IAGO: O, sir, content you;
I follow him to serve my turn upon him.
We cannot all be masters, nor all masters
Cannot be truly followed. You shall mark
Many a duteous and knee-crooking knave
That, doting on his own obsequious bondage,
Wears out his time, much like his master's ass,
For naught but provender; and when he's old, cashiered.°
Whip me such honest knaves! Others there are
Who, trimmed° in forms and visages of duty,
Keep yet their hearts attending on themselves;
And, throwing but shows of service on their lords,
Do well thrive by them, and when they have lined their coats,°
Do themselves homage. These fellows have some soul;
And such a one do I profess myself. For, sir,
It is as sure as you are Roderigo,
Were I the Moor, I would not be Iago.
In following him, I follow but myself;
Heaven is my judge, not I for love and duty,
But seeming so, for my peculiar end;
For when my outward action doth demonstrate
The native act and figure of my heart°
In compliment extern,° 'tis not long after
But I will wear my heart upon my sleeve
For daws to peck at; I am not what I am.°

RODERIGO: What a full fortune does the thick-lips° owe°
If he can carry't thus!

IAGO: Call up her father,
Rouse him. Make after him, poison his delight,
Proclaim him in the streets. Incense her kinsmen,
And though he in a fertile climate dwell,
Plague him with flies; though that his joy be joy,

---

39. affined: Obliged.   **48. cashiered:** Dismissed.   **50. trimmed:** Dressed
up.   **53. lined their coats:** Filled their purses.   **62. The . . . heart:** What I really
believe and intend.   **63. compliment extern:** Outward appearance.   **65. what I
am:** What I seem.   **66. thick-lips:** An Elizabethan epithet for blacks, including
Moors; **owe:** Own.

Yet throw such changes of vexation on't
As it may lose some color.
RODERIGO: Here is her father's house. I'll call aloud.
IAGO: Do, with like timorous° accent and dire yell   75
  As when, by night and negligence, the fire
  Is spied in populous cities.
RODERIGO: What, ho, Brabantio! Signior Brabantio, ho!
IAGO: Awake! What, ho, Brabantio! Thieves! thieves! thieves!
  Look to your house, your daughter, and your bags!   80
  Thieves! thieves!

(Brabantio at a window.°)

BRABANTIO *(above)*: What is the reason of this terrible summons?
  What is the matter there?
RODERIGO: Signior, is all your family within?
IAGO: Are your doors locked?
BRABANTIO: Why, wherefore ask you this?   85
IAGO: Zounds, sir, y' are robbed! For shame, put on your gown!
  Your heart is burst; you have lost half your soul.
  Even now, now, very now, an old black ram
  Is tupping° your white ewe. Arise, arise!
  Awake the snorting° citizens with the bell.   90
  Or else the devil will make a grandsire of you.
  Arise, I say!
BRABANTIO: What, have you lost your wits?
RODERIGO: Most reverend signior, do you know my voice?
BRABANTIO: Not I. What are you?   95
RODERIGO: My name is Roderigo.
BRABANTIO: The worser welcome!
  I have charged thee not to haunt about my doors.
  In honest plainness thou hast heard me say
  My daughter is not for thee; and now, in madness,
  Being full of supper and distemp'ring° draughts,   100
  Upon malicious knavery dost thou come
  To start° my quiet.
RODERIGO: Sir, sir, sir—
BRABANTIO: But thou must needs be sure
  My spirit and my place have in them power   105
  To make this bitter to thee.

---

75. timorous: Terrifying. **[S.D.] Brabantio at a window:** (added from quarto).
89. tupping: Copulating with. **90. snorting:** Snoring. **100. distemp'ring:**
Intoxicating. **102. start:** Startle, disturb.

RODERIGO: Patience, good sir.
BRABANTIO: What tell'st thou me of robbing? This is Venice;
  My house is not a grange.°
RODERIGO: Most grave Brabantio,
  In simple° and pure soul I come to you.
IAGO: Zounds, sir, you are one of those that will not serve God if the devil
  bid you. Because we come to do you service, and you think we are ruf-
  fians, you'll have your daughter covered with a Barbary horse; you'll
  have your nephews° neigh to you; you'll have coursers for cousins, and
  gennets for germans.°
BRABANTIO: What profane wretch art thou?
IAGO: I am one, sir, that comes to tell you your daughter and the Moor
  are now making the beast with two backs.
BRABANTIO: Thou art a villain.
IAGO: You are—a senator.
BRABANTIO: This thou shalt answer. I know thee, Roderigo.
RODERIGO: Sir, I will answer anything. But I beseech you,
  If 't be your pleasure and most wise consent,
  As partly I find it is, that your fair daughter,
  At this odd-even° and dull watch o' th' night,
  Transported, with° no worse nor better guard
  But with a knave of common hire, a gondolier,
  To the gross clasps of a lascivious Moor—
  If this be known to you, and your allowance,°
  We then have done you bold and saucy wrongs;
  But if you know not this, my manners tell me
  We have your wrong rebuke. Do not believe
  That, from the sense° of all civility,
  I thus would play and trifle with your reverence.
  Your daughter, if you have not given her leave,
  I say again, hath made a gross revolt,
  Tying her duty, beauty, wit, and fortunes
  In an extravagant and wheeling° stranger
  Of here and everywhere. Straight satisfy yourself.
  If she be in her chamber, or your house,
  Let loose on me the justice of the state
  For thus deluding you.

---

108. **grange:** Isolated farmhouse. 109. **simple:** Sincere. 113. **nephews:** I.e.,
grandsons. 114. **gennets for germans:** Spanish horses for near kinsmen.
123. **odd-even:** Between night and morning. 124. **with:** By. 127. **allowance:**
Approval. 131. **from the sense:** Contrary to. 136. **extravagant and wheeling:**
Expatriate and roving.

BRABANTIO: Strike on the tinder, ho!   140
  Give me a taper!° Call up all my people!
  This accident° is not unlike my dream.
  Belief of it oppresses me already.
  Light, I say! light!   (*Exit [above].*)
IAGO: Farewell, for I must leave you.
  It seems not meet,° nor wholesome to my place,°   145
  To be produced°—as, if I stay, I shall—
  Against the Moor. For I do know the state,
  However this may gall him with some check,°
  Cannot with safety cast° him; for he's embarked
  With such loud reason to the Cyprus wars,   150
  Which even now stand in act,° that for their souls
  Another of his fathom° they have none
  To lead their business; in which regard,
  Though I do hate him as I do hell-pains,
  Yet, for necessity of present life,°   155
  I must show out a flag and sign of love,
  Which is indeed but sign. That you shall surely find him,
  Lead to the Sagittary° the raisèd search;
  And there will I be with him. So farewell.   (*Exit.*)

(*Enter [below] Brabantio in his nightgown,° and Servants with torches.*)

BRABANTIO: It is too true an evil. Gone she is;   160
  And what's to come of my despisèd time
  Is naught but bitterness. Now, Roderigo,
  Where didst thou see her?—O unhappy girl!—
  With the Moor, say'st thou?—Who would be a father?—
  How didst thou know 'twas she!—O, she deceives me   165
  Past thought!—What said she to you?—Get moe° tapers!
  Raise all my kindred!—Are they married, think you?
RODERIGO: Truly I think they are.
BRABANTIO: O heaven! How got she out? O treason of the blood!
  Fathers, from hence trust not your daughters' minds   170
  By what you see them act. Is there not charms
  By which the property° of youth and maidhood
  May be abused? Have you not read, Roderigo,
  Of some such thing?

---

141. **taper:** Candle. 142. **accident:** Occurrence. 145. **meet:** Fitting; **place:**
Position. 146. **produced:** Called as a witness. 148. **check:** Reprimand.
149. **cast:** Discharge. 151. **stand in act:** Are going on. 152. **fathom:** Capacity. 155. **life:** Livelihood. 158. **Sagittary:** An inn. [S.D.] **nightgown:** Dressing gown. 166. **moe:** More. 172. **property:** Nature.

RODERIGO: Yes, sir, I have indeed.
BRABANTIO: Call up my brother.—O, would you had had her!—
   Some one way, some another.—Do you know
   Where we may apprehend her and the Moor?
RODERIGO: I think I can discover him, if you please
   To get good guard and go along with me.
BRABANTIO: I pray you lead on. At every house I'll call;
   I may command at most.—Get weapons, ho!
   And raise some special officers of night.—
   On, good Roderigo; I'll deserve° your pains.   (*Exeunt.*)

Scene II

(*Before the lodgings of Othello.*)

(*Enter Othello, Iago, and Attendants with torches.*)

IAGO: Though in the trade of war I have slain men,
   Yet do I hold it very stuff o' th' conscience
   To do no contrived° murther. I lack iniquity
   Sometimes to do me service. Nine or ten times
   I had thought t' have yerked° him here under the ribs.
OTHELLO: 'Tis better as it is.
IAGO: Nay, but he prated,
   And spoke such scurvy and provoking terms
   Against your honor
   That with the little godliness I have
   I did full hard forbear him.° But I pray you, sir,
   Are you fast° married? Be assured of this,
   That the magnifico° is much beloved,
   And hath in his effect° a voice potential°
   As double° as the Duke's. He will divorce you,
   Or put upon you what restraint and grievance
   The law, with all his might to enforce it on,
   Will give him cable.
OTHELLO: Let him do his spite.
   My services which I have done the signiory°
   Shall out-tongue his complaints. 'Tis yet to know°—

---

183. deserve: Show gratitude for. SCENE II. 3. contrived: Premeditated
5. yerked: Stabbed. 10. I . . . him: I restrained myself with difficulty from
attacking him. 11. fast: Securely. 12. magnifico: Grandee (Brabantio).
13. in his effect: At his command; potential: Powerful. 14. double: Doubly
influential. 18. signiory: Venetian government. 19. yet to know: Still not
generally known.

Which, when I know that boasting is an honor,   20
I shall promulgate—I fetch my life and being
From men of royal siege;° and my demerits°
May speak unbonneted to as proud a fortune
As this that I have reached.° For know, Iago,
But that I love the gentle Desdemona,   25
I would not my unhousèd° free condition
Put into circumscription and confine
For the sea's worth. But look what lights come yond?
IAGO: Those are the raisèd father and his friends.
    You were best go in.
OTHELLO: Not I; I must be found.   30
    My parts, my title, and my perfect soul°
    Shall manifest me rightly. Is it they?
IAGO: By Janus, I think no.

(*Enter Cassio, with torches, Officers.*)

OTHELLO: The servants of the Duke, and my lieutenant.
    The goodness of the night upon you, friends!   35
    What is the news?
CASSIO: The Duke does greet you, general;
    And he requires your haste-post-haste appearance
    Even on the instant.
OTHELLO: What's the matter, think you?
CASSIO: Something from Cyprus, as I may divine.
    It is a business of some heat.° The galleys   40
    Have sent a dozen sequent° messengers
    This very night at one another's heels,
    And many of the consuls,° raisèd and met,
    Are at the Duke's already. You have been hotly called for;
    When, being not at your lodging to be found,   45
    The Senate hath sent about three several° quests
    To search you out.
OTHELLO: 'Tis well I am found by you.
    I will but spend a word here in the house,
    And go with you.   [*Exit.*]
CASSIO: Ancient, what makes° he here?

22. **siege:** Rank; **demerits:** Deserts.   23–24. **May speak . . . reached:** Are equal,
I modestly assert, to those of Desdemona's family.   26. **unhousèd:** Unrestrained.
31. **My parts . . . soul:** My natural gifts, my position, and my stainless conscience.
40. **heat:** Urgency.   41. **sequent:** Consecutive.   43. **consuls:** Senators.
46. **several:** Separate.   49. **makes:** Does.

IAGO: Faith, he to-night hath boarded a land carack.°
    If it prove lawful prize,° he's made for ever.
CASSIO: I do not understand.
IAGO: He's married.
CASSIO: To who?

[*Enter Othello.*]

IAGO: Marry,° to—Come, captain, will you go?
OTHELLO: Have with you.
CASSIO: Here comes another troop to seek for you.

(*Enter Brabantio, Roderigo, and others with lights and weapons.*)

IAGO: It is Brabantio. General, be advised.°
    He comes to bad intent.
OTHELLO: Holla! stand there!
RODERIGO: Signior, it is the Moor.
BRABANTIO: Down with him, thief!

[*They draw on both sides.*]

IAGO: You, Roderigo! Come, sir, I am for you.
OTHELLO: Keep up° your bright swords, for the dew will rust them.
    Good signior, you shall more command with years
    Than with your weapons.
BRABANTIO: O thou foul thief, where hast thou stowed my daughter?
    Damned as thou art, thou hast enchanted her!
    For I'll refer me to all things of sense,°
    If she in chains of magic were not bound,
    Whether a maid so tender, fair, and happy,
    So opposite to marriage that she shunned
    The wealthy curlèd darlings of our nation,
    Would ever have, t' incur a general mock,
    Run from her guardage° to the sooty bosom
    Of such a thing as thou—to fear, not to delight.
    Judge me the world if 'tis not gross in sense°
    That thou hast practiced on her with foul charms,
    Abused her delicate youth with drugs or minerals
    That weaken motion.° I'll have't disputed on;
    'Tis probable, and palpable to thinking.

---

50. carack: Treasure ship.   **51. prize:** Booty.   **53. Marry:** By Mary (a mild oath).
55. be advised: Be on your guard.   **59. Keep up:** I.e., sheath.   **64. I'll . . . sense:**
I'll submit my case to everyone.   **70. guardage:** Guardianship.   **72. gross in**
sense: Obvious.   **75. motion:** Perception.

I therefore apprehend and do attach° thee
For an abuser of the world, a practicer
Of arts inhibited° and out cf warrant.°
Lay hold upon him. If he do resist,   80
Subdue him at his peril.
OTHELLO: Hold your hands,
Both you of my inclining and the rest.
Were it my cue to fight, I should have known it
Without a prompter. Where will you that I go
To answer this your charge?
BRABANTIO: To prison, till fit time   85
Of law and course of direct session°
Call thee to answer.
OTHELLO: What if I do obey?
How may the Duke be therewith satisfied,
Whose messengers are here about my side
Upon some present business of the state   90
To bring me to him?
OFFICER: 'Tis true, most worthy signior.
The Duke's in council, and your noble self
I am sure is sent for.
BRABANTIO: How? The Duke in council?
In this time of the night? Bring him away.
Mine's not an idle° cause. The Duke himself,   95
Or any of my brothers of the state,
Cannot but feel this wrong as 'twere their own;
For if such actions may have passage free,°
Bondslaves and pagans shall our statesmen be.   (*Exeunt.*)

Scene III

(*The Venetian Senate Chamber.*)

(*Enter Duke and Senators, set at a table, with lights and Attendants.*)

DUKE: There is no composition° in these news
That gives them credit.
FIRST SENATOR: Indeed they are disproportioned.°
My letters say a hundred and seven galleys.

---

77. **attach:** Arrest.   79. **arts inhibited:** Prohibited arts, black magic;   **out of warrant:** Illegal.   86. **direct session:** Regular trial.   95. **idle:** Trifling. 98. **may . . . free:** Are allowed to go unrestrained.   SCENE III.   1. **composition:** Consistency.   2. **disproportioned:** Inconsistent.

DUKE: And mine a hundred forty.
SECOND SENATOR: And mine two hundred.
  But though they jump° not on a just° account—
  As in these cases where the aim° reports
  'Tis oft with difference—yet do they all confirm
  A Turkish fleet, and bearing up to Cyprus.
DUKE: Nay, it is possible enough to judgment.
  I do not so secure me° in the error
  But the main article° I do approve°
  In fearful sense.
SAILOR (*within*): What, ho! what, ho! what, ho!
OFFICER: A messenger from the galleys.

(*Enter Sailor.*)

DUKE: Now, what's the business?
SAILOR: The Turkish preparation makes for Rhodes.
  So was I bid report here to the state
  By Signior Angelo.
DUKE: How say you by° this change?
FIRST SENATOR: This cannot be
  By no assay° of reason. 'Tis a pageant
  To keep us in false gaze.° When we consider
  Th' importancy of Cyprus to the Turk,
  And let ourselves again but understand
  That, as it more concerns the Turk than Rhodes,
  So may he with more facile question bear° it,
  For that it stands not in such warlike brace,°
  But altogether lacks th' abilities
  That Rhodes is dressed in—if we make thought of this,
  We must not think the Turk is so unskillful
  To leave that latest which concerns him first,
  Neglecting an attempt of ease and gain
  To wake and wage° a danger profitless.
DUKE: Nay, in all confidence, he's not for Rhodes.
OFFICER: Here is more news.

(*Enter a Messenger.*)

MESSENGER: The Ottomites, reverend and gracious,

---

5. **jump:** Agree; **just:** Exact.   6. **aim:** Conjecture.   10. **so secure me:** Take such comfort.   11. **article:** Substance; **approve:** Accept.   17. **by:** About.   18. **assay:** Test.   19. **in false gaze:** Looking the wrong way.   23. **with . . . bear:** More easily capture.   24. **brace:** Posture of defense.   30. **wake and wage:** Rouse and risk.

Steering with due course toward the isle of Rhodes,
Have there injointed them° with an after fleet.   35
FIRST SENATOR: Ay, so I thought. How many, as you guess?
MESSENGER: Of thirty sail; and now they do restem°
  Their backward course, bearing with frank appearance°
  Their purposes toward Cyprus. Signior Montano,
  Your trusty and most valiant servitor,   40
  With his free duty recommends you thus,
  And prays you to believe him.
DUKE: 'Tis certain then for Cyprus.
  Marcus Luccicos,° is not he in town?
FIRST SENATOR: He's now in Florence.   45
DUKE: Write from us to him, post, post-haste. Dispatch.
FIRST SENATOR: Here comes Brabantio and the valiant Moor.

(*Enter Brabantio, Othello, Cassio, Iago, Roderigo, and Officers.*)

DUKE: Valiant Othello, we must straight employ you
  Against the general enemy Ottoman.   [*To Brabantio.*]
  I did not see you. Welcome, gentle signior.   50
  We lacked your counsel and your help to-night.
BRABANTIO: So did I yours. Good your grace, pardon me.
  Neither my place, nor aught I heard of business,
  Hath raised me from my bed; nor doth the general care
  Take hold on me; for my particular grief   55
  Is of so floodgate° and o'erbearing nature
  That it engluts° and swallows other sorrows,
  And it is still itself.
DUKE: Why, what's the matter?
BRABANTIO: My daughter! O, my daughter!
ALL: Dead?
BRABANTIO: Ay, to me.
  She is abused,° stol'n from me, and corrupted   60
  By spells and medicines bought of mountebanks;
  For nature so prepost'rously to err,
  Being not deficient,° blind, or lame of sense,
  Sans witchcraft could not.
DUKE: Whoe'er he be that in this foul proceeding   65
  Hath thus beguiled your daughter of herself,

---

35. injointed them: Joined themselves. **37. restem:** Steer again. **38. frank appearance:** Undisguised intent. **44. Marcus Luccicos:** (Presumably a Venetian envoy). **56. floodgate:** Torrential. **57. engluts:** Engulfs. **60. abused:** Deceived. **63. deficient:** Feeble-minded.

And you of her, the bloody book of law
You shall yourself read in the bitter letter
After your own sense; yea, though our proper° son
Stood in your action.°

BRABANTIO: Humbly I thank your grace.
Here is the man—this Moor, whom now, it seems,
Your special mandate for the state affairs
Hath hither brought.

ALL: We are very sorry for't.

DUKE [*to Othello*]: What, in your own part, can you say to this?

BRABANTIO: Nothing, but this is so.

OTHELLO: Most potent, grave, and reverend signiors,
My very noble, and approved° good masters,
That I have ta'en away this old man's daughter,
It is most true; true I have married her.
The very head and front of my offending
Hath this extent, no more. Rude° am I in my speech,
And little blessed with the soft phrase of peace;
For since these arms of mine had seven years' pith°
Till now some nine moons wasted,° they have used
Their dearest action in the tented field;
And little of this great world can I speak
More than pertains to feats of broil and battle;
And therefore little shall I grace my cause
In speaking for myself. Yet, by your gracious patience,
I will a round° unvarnished tale deliver
Of my whole course of love—what drugs, what charms,
What conjuration, and what mighty magic
(For such proceeding am I charged withal°)
I won his daughter.

BRABANTIO: A maiden never bold;
Of spirit so still and quiet that her motion
Blushed° at herself; and she—in spite of nature,
Of years,° of country, credit, everything—
To fall in love with what she feared to look on!
It is a judgment maimed and most imperfect
That will confess perfection so could err

69. our proper: My own.   70. Stood in your action: Were accused by you.
77. approved: Tested by experience.   81. Rude: Unpolished.   83. pith: Strength
(i.e., since I was seven years old).   84. Till . . . wasted: Until about nine months
ago.   90. round: Plain.   93. withal: With.   95–96. her motion Blushed: Her
own emotions caused her to blush.   97. years: (Difference in age).

Against all rules of nature, and must be driven
To find out practices° of cunning hell
Why this should be. I therefore vouch° again
That with some mixtures pow'rful o'er the blood,°
Or with some dram, conjured° to this effect,   105
He wrought upon her.

DUKE: To vouch this is no proof,
Without more certain and more overt test
Than these thin habits° and poor likelihoods
Of modern seeming° do prefer against him.

FIRST SENATOR: But, Othello, speak.   110
Did you by indirect and forcèd° courses
Subdue and poison this young maid's affections?
Or came it by request, and such fair question°
As soul to soul affordeth?

OTHELLO: I do beseech you,
Send for the lady to the Sagittary   115
And let her speak of me before her father.
If you do find me foul in her report,
The trust, the office, I do hold of you
Not only take away, but let your sentence
Even fall upon my life.

DUKE: Fetch Desdemona hither.   120

OTHELLO: Ancient, conduct them; you best know the place.
                    (*Exit [Iago, with] two or three [Attendants]*.)
And till she come, as truly as to heaven
I do confess the vices of my blood,
So justly to your grave ears I'll present
How I did thrive in this fair lady's love,   125
And she in mine.

DUKE: Say it, Othello.

OTHELLO: Her father loved me, oft invited me;
Still° questioned me the story of my life
From year to year—the battles, sieges, fortunes   130
That I have passed.
I ran it through, even from my boyish days
To th' very moment that he bade me tell it.
Wherein I spoke of most disastrous chances,

---

102. **practices:** Plots.   103. **vouch:** Assert.   104. **blood:** Passions.   105. **dram,
conjured:** Potion, prepared by magic.   108. **thin habits:** Slight appearances.
109. **modern seeming:** Everyday supposition.   111. **forcèd:** Violent.
113. **question:** Conversation.   129. **Still:** Continually.

Of moving accidents by flood and field;
Of hairbreadth scapes i' th' imminent deadly breach;
Of being taken by the insolent foe
And sold to slavery; of my redemption thence
And portance° in my travels' history;
Wherein of anters° vast and deserts idle,
Rough quarries, rocks, and hills whose heads touch heaven,
It was my hint° to speak—such was the process;
And of the Cannibals that each other eat,
The Anthropophagi,° and men whose heads
Do grow beneath their shoulders. This to hear
Would Desdemona seriously incline;
But still the house affairs would draw her thence;
Which ever as she could with haste dispatch,
She'ld come again, and with a greedy ear
Devour up my discourse. Which I observing,
Took once a pliant° hour, and found good means
To draw from her a prayer of earnest heart
That I would all my pilgrimage dilate,°
Whereof by parcels° she had something heard,
But not intentively.° I did consent,
And often did beguile her of her tears
When I did speak of some distressful stroke
That my youth suffered. My story being done,
She gave me for my pains a world of sighs.
She swore, i' faith, 'twas strange, 'twas passing° strange;
'Twas pitiful, 'twas wondrous pitiful.
She wished she had not heard it; yet she wished
That heaven had made her such a man. She thanked me;
And bade me, if I had a friend that loved her,
I should but teach him how to tell my story,
And that would woo her. Upon this hint° I spake.
She loved me for the dangers I had passed,
And I loved her that she did pity them.
This only is the witchcraft I have used.
Here comes the lady. Let her witness it.

(*Enter Desdemona, Iago, Attendants.*)

---

139. portance: Behavior.   **140. anters:** Propitous caves.   **142. hint:** Occasion.
144. Anthropophagi: Man-eaters.   **151. pliant:** Suitable.   **153. dilate:** Recount
in full.   **154. parcels:** Portions.   **155. intentively:** With full attention.
160. passing: Exceedingly.   **166. hint:** Opportunity.

DUKE: I think this tale would win my daughter too.
  Good Brabantio,
  Take up this mangled matter at the best.°
  Men do their broken weapons rather use
  Than their bare hands.
BRABANTIO: I pray you hear her speak.   175
  If she confess that she was half the wooer,
  Destruction on my head if my bad blame
  Light on the man! Come hither, gentle mistress.
  Do you perceive in all this noble company
  Where most you owe obedience?
DESDEMONA: My noble father,   180
  I do perceive here a divided duty.
  To you I am bound for life and education;°
  My life and education both do learn me
  How to respect you: you are the lord of duty;°
  I am hitherto your daughter. But here's my husband;   185
  And so much duty as my mother showed
  To you, preferring you before her father,
  So much I challenge° that I may profess
  Due to the Moor my lord.
BRABANTIO: God be with you! I have done.
  Please it your grace, on to the state affairs.   190
  I had rather to adopt a child than get° it.
  Come hither, Moor.
  I here do give thee that with all my heart
  Which, but thou hast already, with all my heart
  I would keep from thee. For your sake,° jewel,   195
  I am glad at soul I have no other child;
  For thy escape° would teach me tyranny,
  To hang clogs on them. I have done, my lord.
DUKE: Let me speak like yourself° and lay a sentence°
  Which, as a grise° or step, may help these lovers   200
  [Into your favor.]
  When remedies are past, the griefs are ended
  By seeing the worst, which late on hopes depended.
  To mourn a mischief that is past and gone
  Is the next way to draw new mischief on.   205
  What cannot be preserved when fortune takes,

---

173. Take . . . best: Make the best of this situation.   182. education: Upbringing.   184. of duty: To whom duty is due.   188. challenge: Claim the right.
191. get: Beget.   195. For your sake: Because of you.   197. escape: Esca-
pade.   199. like yourself: As you should; sentence: Maxim.   200. grise: Step.

Patience her injury a mock'ry makes.
The robbed that smiles steals something from the thief;
He robs himself that spends a bootless grief.

BRABANTIO: So let the Turk of Cyprus us beguile: 2
We lose it not so long as we can smile.
He bears the sentence well that nothing bears
But the free comfort which from thence he hears;
But he bears both the sentence and the sorrow
That to pay grief must of poor patience borrow.   2
These sentences, to sugar, or to gall,
Being strong on both sides, are equivocal.
But words are words. I never yet did hear
That the bruisèd heart was piercèd through the ear.
Beseech you, now to the affairs of state.   2

DUKE: The Turk with a most mighty preparation makes for Cyprus.
Othello, the fortitude° of the place is best known to you; and though
we have there a substitute of most allowed° sufficiency, yet opinion,° a
more sovereign mistress of effects, throws a more safer voice on you.
You must therefore be content to slubber° the gloss of your new for-   2.
tunes with this more stubborn and boist'rous expedition.

OTHELLO: The tyrant custom, most grave senators,
Hath made the flinty and steel couch of war
My thrice-driven bed of down. I do agnize
A natural and prompt alacrity   2.
I find in hardness;° and do undertake
These present wars against the Ottomites.
Most humbly, therefore, bending to your state,
I crave fit disposition for my wife,
Due reference of place, and exhibition,°   2:
With such accommodation and besort°
As levels° with her breeding.

DUKE: If you please,
Be't at her father's.

BRABANTIO: I will not have it so.

OTHELLO: Nor I.

DESDEMONA: Nor I. I would not there reside,   2·
To put my father in impatient thoughts
By being in his eye. Most gracious Duke,

---

222. **fortitude:** Fortification.   223. **allowed:** Acknowledged; **opinion:** Public
opinion.   225. **slubber:** Sully.   229–31. **agnize . . . hardness:** Recognize in
myself a natural and easy response to hardship.   235. **exhibition:** Allowance of
money.   236. **besort:** Suitable company.   237. **levels:** Corresponds.

To my unfolding lend your prosperous° ear,
And let me find a charter in your voice,
T' assist my simpleness.°   245
DUKE: What would you, Desdemona?
DESDEMONA: That I did love the Moor to live with him,
    My downright violence, and storm of fortunes,°
    May trumpet to the world. My heart's subdued
    Even to the very quality of my lord.   250
    I saw Othello's visage in his mind,
    And to his honors and his valiant parts
    Did I my soul and fortunes consecrate.
    So that, dear lords, if I be left behind,
    A moth of peace, and he go to the war,   255
    The rites for which I love him are bereft me,
    And I a heavy interim shall support
    By his dear° absence. Let me go with him.
OTHELLO: Let her have your voice.°
    Vouch with me, heaven, I therefore beg it not   260
    To please the palate of my appetite,
    Not to comply with heat°—the young affects°
    In me defunct—and proper satisfaction;
    But to be free and bounteous to her mind;
    And heaven defend your good souls that you think   265
    I will your serious and great business scant
    When she is with me. No, when light-winged toys
    Of feathered Cupid seel° with wanton dullness
    My speculative and officed instruments,°
    That° my disports corrupt and taint my business,   270
    Let housewives make a skillet of my helm,
    And all indign° and base adversities
    Make head against my estimation!°
DUKE: Be it as you shall privately determine,
    Either for her stay or going. Th' affair cries haste,   275
    And speed must answer it.
FIRST SENATOR: You must away to-night.
OTHELLO: With all my heart.

243. prosperous: Favorable.   245. simpleness: Lack of skill.   248. My . . .
fortunes: My clear and complete breaking of social customs.   258. dear: Griev-
ous.   259. voice: Consent.   262. heat: Passions. young affects: Tendencies of
youth.   268. seel: Blind.   269. My . . . instruments: My perceptive and responsible faculties.   270. That: So that.   272. indign: Unworthy.   273. estimation:
Reputation.

DUKE: At nine i' th' morning here we'll meet again.
  Othello, leave some officer behind,
  And he shall our commission bring to you,
  With such things else of quality and respect
  As doth import° you.
OTHELLO: So please your grace, my ancient;
  A man he is of honesty and trust.
  To his conveyance I assign my wife,
  With what else needful your good grace shall think
  To be sent after me.
DUKE: Let it be so.
  Good night to every one.
       [*To Brabantio.*]   And, noble signior,
  If virtue no delighted° beauty lack,
  Your son-in-law is far more fair than black.
FIRST SENATOR: Adieu, brave Moor. Use Desdemona well.
BRABANTIO: Look to her, Moor, if thou hast eyes to see:
  She has deceived her father, and may thee.
                    (*Exeunt [Duke, Senators, Officers, etc.*].)
OTHELLO: My life upon her faith!—Honest Iago,
  My Desdemona must I leave to thee.
  I prithee let thy wife attend on her,
  And bring them after in the best advantage.°
  Come, Desdemona. I have but an hour
  Of love, of worldly matters and direction,
  To spend with thee. We must obey the time.
                    (*Exit Moor and Desdemona.*)
RODERIGO: Iago,—
IAGO: What say'st thou, noble heart?
RODERIGO: What will I do, think'st thou?
IAGO: Why, go to bed and sleep.
RODERIGO: I will incontinently° drown myself.
IAGO: If thou dost, I shall never love thee after. Why, thou silly gentleman!
RODERIGO: It is silliness to live when to live is torment; and then have we
  a prescription to die when death is our physician.
IAGO: O villainous! I have looked upon the world for four times seven
  years; and since I could distinguish betwixt a benefit and an injury, I
  never found man that knew how to love himself. Ere I would say I
  would drown myself for the love of a guinea hen,° I would change my
  humanity with a baboon.

282. import: Concern.   **288. delighted:** Delightful.   **296. in the best advantage:** At the best opportunity.   **304. incontinently:** Forthwith.   **312. guinea
hen:** Prostitute (slang).

RODERIGO: What should I do? I confess it is my shame to be so fond,° but
it is not in my virtue° to amend it.   315
IAGO: Virtue? a fig! 'Tis in ourselves that we are thus or thus. Our bodies
are our gardens, to which our wills are gardeners; so that if we will
plant nettles or sow lettuce, set hyssop and weed up thyme, supply it
with one gender° of herbs or distract it with many—either to have it
sterile with idleness or manured with industry—why, the power and   320
corrigible authority° of this lies in our wills. If the balance of our lives
had not one scale of reason to poise° another of sensuality, the blood
and baseness° of our natures would conduct us to most preposterous
conclusions. But we have reason to cool our raging motions,° our carnal strings, our unbitted° lusts; whereof I take this that you call love to 325
be a sect or scion.°
RODERIGO: It cannot be.
IAGO: It is merely a lust of the blood and a permission of the will. Come,
be a man! Drown thyself? Drown cats and blind puppies! I have pro-
fessed me thy friend, and I confess me knit to thy deserving with cables 330
of perdurable toughness. I could never better stead thee than now.
Put money in thy purse. Follow thou the wars; defeat thy favor° with
an usurped beard. I say, put money in thy purse. It cannot be that
Desdemona should long continue her love to the Moor—put money in
thy purse—nor he his to her. It was a violent commencement in her,   335
and thou shalt see an answerable sequestration°—put but money in
thy purse. These Moors are changeable in their wills—fill thy purse
with money. The food that to him now is as luscious as locusts shall be
to him shortly as bitter as coloquintida.° She must change for youth:
when she is sated with his body, she will find the error of her choice.   340
[She must have change, she must.] Therefore put money in thy purse.
If thou wilt needs damn thyself, do it a more delicate way than drowning. Make° all the money thou canst. If sanctimony and a frail vow
betwixt an erring° barbarian and a supersubtle Venetian be not too
hard for my wits and all the tribe of hell, thou shalt enjoy her. There-   345
fore make money. A pox of drowning thyself! 'Tis clean out of the way.
Seek thou rather to be hanged in compassing thy joy than to be
drowned and go without her.

---

314. fond: Foolish.   315. virtue: Strength, ability.   319. gender: Species.
321. corrigible authority: Corrective power.   322. poise: Counterbalance.
322–23. blood and baseness: Animal instincts.   324. motions: Appetites.
325. unbitted: Uncontrolled.   326. sect or scion: Offshoot, cutting.
332. defeat thy favor: Disguise thy appearance.   336. sequestration:
Estrangement.   339. coloquintida: A medicine.   343. Make: Raise.
344. erring: Wandering.

RODERIGO: Wilt thou be fast to my hopes, if I depend on the issue?
IAGO: Thou art sure of me. Go, make money. I have told thee often, and I   3
    retell thee again and again, I hate the Moor. My cause is hearted;° thine
    hath no less reason. Let us be conjunctive° in our revenge against him.
    If thou canst cuckold him, thou dost thyself a pleasure, me a sport.
    There are many events in the womb of time, which will be delivered.
    Traverse,° go, provide thy money! We will have more of this to-morrow.   3
    Adieu.
RODERIGO: Where shall we meet i' th' morning?
IAGO: At my lodging.
RODERIGO: I'll be with thee betimes.°
IAGO: Go to, farewell—Do you hear, Roderigo?   3
[RODERIGO: What say you?
IAGO: No more of drowning, do you hear?
RODERIGO: I am changed.
IAGO: Go to, farewell. Put money enough in your purse.]
RODERIGO: I'll sell all my land.   (*Exit.*)   3
IAGO: Thus do I ever make my fool my purse;
    For I mine own gained knowledge should profane
    If I would time expend with such a snipe°
    But for my sport and profit. I hate the Moor;
    And it is thought abroad° that 'twixt my sheets   3
    H'as done my office. I know not if't be true;
    But I, for mere suspicion in that kind,
    Will do as if for surety.° He holds me well;°
    The better shall my purpose work on him.
    Cassio's a proper man. Let me see now: 3
    To get his place, and to plume up° my will
    In double knavery—How, how?—Let's see:—
    After some time, to abuse° Othello's ears
    That he° is too familiar with his° wife.
    He hath a person and a smooth dispose°   3
    To be suspected—framed to make women false.
    The Moor is of a free° and open nature
    That thinks men honest that but seem to be so;
    And will as tenderly be led by th' nose

---

351. **hearted:** Fixed in my heart.   352. **conjunctive:** United.   355. **Traverse:**
Forward march.   359. **betimes:** Early.   368. **snipe:** Fool.   370. **thought abroad:**
Rumored.   373. **do . . . surety:** Act on it as if certain; **well:** In high regard.
376. **plume up:** Gratify.   378. **abuse:** Deceive.   379. **he:** (Cassio); **his:**
(Othello's).   380. **dispose:** Manner.   382. **free:** Frank.

As asses are.   385
I have't! It is engend'red! Hell and night
Must bring this monstrous birth to the world's light.   (*Exit.*)

ACT II   *Scene I*

(*An open place in Cyprus, near the harbor.*)

(*Enter Montano and two Gentlemen.*)

MONTANO: What from the cape can you discern at sea?
FIRST GENTLEMAN: Nothing at all: it is a high-wrought flood.°
    I cannot 'twixt the heaven and the main
    Descry a sail.
MONTANO: Methinks the wind hath spoke aloud at land;   5
    A fuller blast ne'er shook our battlements.
    If it hath ruffianed° so upon the sea,
    What ribs of oak, when mountains° melt on them,
    Can hold the mortise?° What shall we hear of this?
SECOND GENTLEMAN: A segregation° of the Turkish fleet.   10
    For do but stand upon the foaming shore,
    The chidden billow seems to pelt the clouds;
    The wind-shaked surge, with high and monstrous mane,
    Seems to cast water on the burning Bear
    And quench the Guards° of th' ever-fixèd pole.°   15
    I never did like molestation° view
    On the enchafèd° flood.
MONTANO: If that° the Turkish fleet
    Be not ensheltered and embayed, they are drowned;
    It is impossible to bear it out.

(*Enter a third Gentleman.*)

THIRD GENTLEMAN: News, lads! Our wars are done.   20
    The desperate tempest hath so banged the Turks
    That their designment halts.° A noble ship of Venice
    Hath seen a grievous wrack° and sufferance°
    On most part of their fleet.

ACT II, SCENE I.   2. high-wrought flood: Very agitated sea.   7. ruffianed: Raged.
8. mountains: I.e., of water.   9. hold the mortise: Hold their joints together.
10. segregation: Scattering.   15. Guards: Stars near the North Star; pole: Pole-
star.   16. molestation: Tumult.   17. enchafèd: Angry; If that: If.   22. design-
ment halts: Plan is crippled.   23. wrack: Shipwreck; sufferance: Disaster.

MONTANO: How? Is this true?

THIRD GENTLEMAN: The ship is here put in,
  A Veronesa;° Michael Cassio,
  Lieutenant to the warlike Moor Othello,
  Is come on shore; the Moor himself at sea,
  And is in full commission here for Cyprus.

MONTANO: I am glad on't. 'Tis a worthy governor.

THIRD GENTLEMAN: But this same Cassio, though he speak of comfort
  Touching the Turkish loss, yet he looks sadly
  And prays the Moor be safe, for they were parted
  With foul and violent tempest.

MONTANO: Pray heaven he be;
  For I have served him, and the man commands
  Like a full° soldier. Let's to the seaside, ho!
  As well to see the vessel that's come in
  As to throw out our eyes for brave Othello,
  Even till we make the main and th' aerial blue
  An indistinct regard.°

THIRD GENTLEMAN: Come, let's do so;
  For every minute is expectancy
  Of more arrivance.

(*Enter Cassio.*)

CASSIO: Thanks, you the valiant of this warlike isle,
  That so approve° the Moor! O, let the heavens
  Give him defense against the elements,
  For I have lost him on a dangerous sea!

MONTANO: Is he well shipped?

CASSIO: His bark is stoutly timbered, and his pilot
  Of very expert and approved allowance;°
  Therefore my hopes, not surfeited to death,°
  Stand in bold cure.°
  (*Within.*)   A sail, a sail, a sail!   (*Enter a messenger.*)

CASSIO: What noise?

MESSENGER: The town is empty; on the brow o' th' sea
  Stand ranks of people, and they cry "A sail!"

CASSIO: My hopes do shape him for the governor.

(*A shot.*)

---

26. Veronesa: Ship furnished by Verona.   **36. full:** Perfect.   **40. An indistinct regard:** Indistinguishable.   **44. approve:** Commend, admire.   **49. approved allowance:** Tested reputation.   **50. surfeited to death:** Overindulged.   **51. in bold cure:** A good chance of fulfillment.

SECOND GENTLEMAN: They do discharge their shot of courtesy:
  Our friends at least.
CASSIO: I pray you, sir, go forth
  And give us truth who 'tis that is arrived.
SECOND GENTLEMAN: I shall.   *(Exit.)*
MONTANO: But, good lieutenant, is your general wived?   60
CASSIO: Most fortunately. He hath achieved a maid
  That paragons° description and wild fame;
  One that excels the quirks° of blazoning° pens,
  And in th' essential vesture of creation
  Does tire the ingener.°

(Enter Second Gentleman.)

               How now? Who has put in?   65
SECOND GENTLEMAN: 'Tis one Iago, ancient to the general.
CASSIO: He's had most favorable and happy speed:
  Tempests themselves, high seas, and howling winds,
  The guttered° rocks and congregated sands,
  Traitors ensteeped° to clog the guiltless keel,   70
  As having sense of beauty, do omit
  Their mortal° natures, letting go safely by
  The divine Desdemona.
MONTANO: What is she?
CASSIO: She that I spake of, our great captain's captain,
  Left in the conduct of the bold Iago,   75
  Whose footing° here anticipates our thoughts
  A se'nnight's° speed. Great Jove, Othello guard,
  And swell his sail with thine own pow'rful breath,
  That he may bless this bay with his tall ship,
  Make love's quick pants in Desdemona's arms,   80
  Give renewed fire to our extinct spirits,
  [And bring all Cyprus comfort!]

(Enter Desdemona, Iago, Roderigo, and Emilia [with Attendants].)

                 O, behold!
  The riches of the ship is come on shore!
  You men of Cyprus, let her have your knees.°
  Hail to thee, lady! and the grace of heaven,   85

---

62. **paragons:** Surpasses.   63. **quirks:** Ingenuities; **blazoning:** Describing in
heraldic language.   64–65. **And . . . ingener:** Merely to describe her as God made
her exhausts her praiser.   69. **guttered:** Jagged.   70. **ensteeped:** Submerged.
72. **mortal:** Deadly.   76. **footing:** Landing.   77. **se'nnight's:** Week's.   84. **knees:**
I.e., kneeling.

Before, behind thee, and on every hand,
Enwheel thee round!
DESDEMONA: I thank you, valiant Cassio.
What tidings can you tell me of my lord?
CASSIO: He is not yet arrived; nor know I aught
But that he's well and will be shortly here.
DESDEMONA: O but I fear! How lost you company?
CASSIO: The great contention of the sea and skies
Parted our fellowship.
        (*Within.*)   A sail, a sail! [*A shot.*]
                                         But hark. A sail!
SECOND GENTLEMAN: They give their greeting to the citadel;
This likewise is a friend.
CASSIO: See for the news.
                                         [*Exit Gentleman.*]
Good ancient, you are welcome.
        [*To Emilia.*]   Welcome, mistress. —
Let it not gall your patience, good Iago,
That I extend my manners. 'Tis my breeding
That gives me this bold show of courtesy.
        [*Kisses Emilia.*°]
IAGO: Sir, would she give you so much of her lips   1
As of her tongue she oft bestows on me,
You would have enough.
DESDEMONA: Alas, she has no speech!
IAGO: In faith, too much.
I find it still° when I have list° to sleep.
Marry, before your ladyship, I grant,   1
She puts her tongue a little in her heart
And chides with thinking.
EMILIA: You have little cause to say so.
IAGO: Come on, come on! You are pictures out of doors,°
Bells° in your parlors, wildcats in your kitchens,   1
Saints° in your injuries, devils being offended,
Players in your housewifery,° and housewives° in your beds.
DESDEMONA: O, fie upon thee, slanderer!
IAGO: Nay, it is true, or else I am a Turk:°
You rise to play, and go to bed to work.   1

[S.D.] **Kisses Emilia:** (Kissing was a common Elizabethan form of social courtesy.) **104. still:** Always; **list:** Desire. **109. pictures out of doors:** Well-
behaved in public. **110. Bells:** Noisy, jangling. **111. Saints:** Martyrs.
112. housewifery: Housekeeping; **housewives:** Hussies. **114. Turk:** Infidel,
not to be believed.

EMILIA: You shall not write my praise.
IAGO: No, let me not.
DESDEMONA: What wouldst thou write of me, if thou shouldst praise me?
IAGO: O gentle lady, do not put me to't,
　　For I am nothing if not critical.
DESDEMONA: Come on, assay.°—There's one gone to the harbor?   120
IAGO: Ay, madam.
DESDEMONA: I am not merry; but I do beguile
　　The thing I am by seeming otherwise.—
　　Come, how wouldst thou praise me?
IAGO: I am about it; but indeed my invention   125
　　Comes from my pate as birdlime° does from frieze°—
　　It plucks out brains and all. But my Muse labors,
　　And thus she is delivered:
　　If she be fair and wise, fairness and wit—
　　The one's for use, the other useth it.   130
DESDEMONA: Well praised! How if she be black° and witty?
IAGO: If she be black, and thereto have a wit,
　　She'll find a white° that shall her blackness fit.
DESDEMONA: Worse and worse!
EMILIA: How if fair and foolish?   135
IAGO: She never yet was foolish that was fair,
　　For even her folly° helped her to an heir.
DESDEMONA: These are old fond° paradoxes to make fools laugh i' th'
　　alehouse. What miserable praise hast thou for her that's foul° and
　　foolish?   140
IAGO: There's none so foul, and foolish thereunto,
　　But does foul pranks which fair and wise ones do.
DESDEMONA: O heavy ignorance! Thou praisest the worst best. But what
　　praise couldst thou bestow on a deserving woman indeed—one that in
　　the authority of her merit did justly put on the vouch° of very malice   145
　　itself?
IAGO: She that was ever fair, and never proud;
　　Had tongue at will, and yet was never loud;
　　Never lacked gold, and yet went never gay;°
　　Fled from her wish, and yet said "Now I may";°   150
　　She that, being ang'red, her revenge being nigh,

---

120. assay: Try.   126. birdlime: A sticky paste; frieze: Rough cloth.   131. black:
Brunette.   133. white: Wight (a person), and a fair person (pun).   137. folly:
Wantonness.   138. fond: Foolish.   139. foul: Ugly.   145. put on the vouch:
Compel the approval.   149. gay: Lavishly clothed.   150. Fled . . . may": Resisted
temptation even when she had a choice.

Bade her wrong stay,° and her displeasure fly;
She that in wisdom never was so frail
To change the cod's head for the salmon's tail;°
She that could think, and ne'er disclose her mind;   1
See suitors following, and not look behind:
She was a wight (if ever such wight° were)—

DESDEMONA: To do what?

IAGO: To suckle fools and chronicle small beer.°

DESDEMONA: O most lame and impotent conclusion! Do not learn of him, 1
Emilia, though he be thy husband. How say you, Cassio? Is he not a
most profane and liberal° counsellor?

CASSIO: He speaks home,° madam. You may relish him more in the soldier than in the scholar.

IAGO [aside]: He takes her by the palm. Ay, well said, whisper! With as 1
little a web as this will I ensnare as great a fly as Cassio. Ay, smile upon
her, do! I will give thee in thine own courtship.°—You say true; 'tis so,
indeed!—If such tricks as these strip you out of your lieutenantry, it
had been better you had not kissed your three fingers so oft—which
now again you are most apt to play the sir° in. Very good! well kissed! 1
an excellent courtesy! 'Tis so, indeed. Yet again your fingers to your
lips? Would they were clyster pipes° for your sake! (Trumpet within.)
The Moor! I know his trumpet.

CASSIO: 'Tis truly so.

DESDEMONA: Let's meet him and receive him.   1

CASSIO: Lo, where he comes.

(Enter Othello and Attendants.)

OTHELLO: O my fair warrior!

DESDEMONA: My dear Othello!

OTHELLO: It gives me wonder great as my content
To see you here before me. O my soul's joy!
If after every tempest come such calms,   1
May the winds blow till they have wakened death!
And let the laboring bark climb hills of seas
Olympus-high, and duck again as low
As hell's from heaven! If it were now to die,

---

152. **Bade . . . stay:** Decided to put up with her injury patiently.   154. **To . . . tail:**
I.e., to exchange the good for the poor but expensive.   157. **wight:** Person, human
being.   159. **chronicle small beer:** Keep petty household accounts.   162. **profane and liberal:** Worldly and licentious.   163. **home:** Bluntly.   167. **give . . .
courtship:** Manacle you by means of your courtly manners.   170. **sir:** Courtly
gentleman.   172. **clyster pipes:** Syringes.

'Twere now to be most happy;° for I fear   185
My soul hath her content so absolute
That not another comfort like to this
Succeeds in unknown fate.
DESDEMONA: The heavens forbid
  But that our loves and comforts should increase
  Even as our days do grow.
OTHELLO: Amen to that, sweet powers!   190
  I cannot speak enough of this content;
  It stops me here; it is too much of joy.
  And this, and this, the greatest discords be

(*They kiss.*)

  That e'er our hearts shall make!
IAGO [*aside*]:   O, you are well tuned now!
  But I'll set down° the pegs that make this music,   195
  As honest as I am.
OTHELLO: Come, let us to the castle.
  News, friends! Our wars are done; the Turks are drowned.
  How does my old acquaintance of this isle? —
  Honey, you shall be well desired° in Cyprus;
  I have found great love amongst them. O my sweet,   200
  I prattle out of fashion, and I dote
  In mine own comforts. I prithee, good Iago,
  Go to the bay and disembark my coffers.
  Bring thou the master° to the citadel;
  He is a good one, and his worthiness   205
  Does challenge° much respect. — Come, Desdemona,
  Once more well met at Cyprus.
                (*Exit Othello [with all but Iago and Roderigo].*)
IAGO [*to an Attendant, who goes out*]: Do thou meet me presently at the
  harbor. [*To Roderigo.*] Come hither. If thou be'st valiant (as they say
  base men being in love have then a nobility in their natures more than 210
  is native to them), list me. The lieutenant to-night watches on the court
  of guard.° First, I must tell thee this: Desdemona is directly in love
  with him.
RODERIGO: With him? Why, 'tis not possible.
IAGO: Lay thy finger thus,° and let thy soul be instructed. Mark me with 215
  what violence she first loved the Moor, but° for bragging and telling

---

185. **happy:** Fortunate.   195. **set down:** Loosen.   199. **well desired:** Warmly
welcomed.   204. **master:** Ship captain.   206. **challenge:** Deserve.   211–12. **court
of guard:** Headquarters.   215. **thus:** I.e., on your lips.   216. **but:** Only.

her fantastical lies; and will she love him still for prating? Let not thy
discreet heart think it. Her eye must be fed; and what delight shall she
have to look on the devil? When the blood is made dull with the act of
sport,° there should be, again to inflame it and to give satiety a fresh   2;
appetite, loveliness in favor,° sympathy° in years, manners, and beauties; all which the Moor is defective in. Now for want of these required
conveniences,° her delicate tenderness will find itself abused,° begin to
heave the gorge,° disrelish and abhor the Moor. Very nature° will in-
struct her in it and compel her to some second choice. Now, sir, this   2;
granted—as it is a most pregnant° and unforced position—who
stands so eminent in the degree of° this fortune as Cassio does? A
knave very voluble; no further conscionable° than in putting on the
mere form of civil and humane° seeming for the better compassing of
his salt° and most hidden loose affection? Why, none! why, none! A   2;
slipper° and subtle knave; a finder-out of occasions; that has an eye can
stamp° and counterfeit advantages,° though true advantage never
present itself; a devilish knave! Besides, the knave is handsome, young,
and hath all those requisites in him that folly and green° minds look
after. A pestilent complete knave! and the woman hath found him   2;
already.
RODERIGO: I cannot believe that in her; she's full of most blessed
  condition.°
IAGO: Blessed fig's-end! The wine she drinks is made of grapes. If she had
  been blessed, she would never have loved the Moor. Blessed pudding!   24
  Didst thou not see her paddle with the palm of his hand? Didst not
  mark that?
RODERIGO: Yes, that I did; but that was but courtesy.
IAGO: Lechery, by this hand! an index° and obscure° prologue to the history of lust and foul thoughts. They met so near with their lips that   24
  their breaths embraced together. Villainous thoughts, Roderigo! When
  these mutualities° so marshal the way, hard at hand comes the master
  and main exercise, th' incorporate° conclusion. Pish! But, sir, be you
  ruled by me: I have brought you from Venice. Watch you to-night;

220. the act of sport: Sex.   221. favor: Appearance; sympathy: Similarity.
223. conveniences: Compatibilities;   abused: Cheated.   224. heave the gorge:
Be nauseated;   Very nature: Her very instincts.   226. pregnant: Evident.
227. in the degree of: As next in line for.   228. conscionable: Conscientious.   229. humane: Polite.   230. salt: Lecherous.   231. slipper: Slippery.
232. stamp: Coin; advantages: Opportunities.   234. folly and green: Foolish
and inexperienced.   237–238. condition: Character.   244. index: Table of contents; obscure: Hidden.   247. mutualities: Exchanges.   248. incorporate:
Carnal.

for the command, I'll lay't upon you.° Cassio knows you not. I'll not be 250
far from you: do you find some occasion to anger Cassio, either by
speaking too loud, or tainting° his discipline, or from what other
course you please which the time shall more favorably minister.°
RODERIGO: Well.
IAGO: Sir, he's rash and very sudden in choler,° and haply with his trun- 255
cheon may strike at you. Provoke him that he may; for even out of that
will I cause these of Cyprus to mutiny; whose qualification° shall come
into no true taste° again but by the displanting of Cassio. So shall you
have a shorter journey to your desires by the means I shall then have
to prefer° them; and the impediment most profitably removed with- 260
out the which there were no expectation of our prosperity.
RODERIGO: I will do this if you can bring it to any opportunity.
IAGO: I warrant thee. Meet me by and by at the citadel; I must fetch his
necessaries ashore. Farewell.
RODERIGO: Adieu.   (*Exit.*) 265
IAGO: That Cassio loves her, I do well believe't;
    That she loves him, 'tis apt° and of great credit.
    The Moor, howbeit that I endure him not,
    Is of a constant, loving, noble nature,
    And I dare think he'll prove to Desdemona   270
    A most dear husband. Now I do love her too;
    Not out of absolute lust, though peradventure
    I stand accountant° for as great a sin,
    But partly led to diet° my revenge,
    For that I do suspect the lusty Moor   275
    Hath leaped into my seat; the thought whereof
    Doth, like a poisonous mineral, gnaw my innards;
    And nothing can or shall content my soul
    Till I am evened with him, wife for wife;
    Or failing so, yet that I put the Moor   280
    At least into a jealousy so strong
    That judgment cannot cure. Which thing to do,
    If this poor trash of Venice, whom I trash°
    For° his quick hunting, stand the putting on,°

---

250. **for . . . you:** I'll put you in charge.   252. **tainting:** Discrediting.   253. **minister:** Provide.   255. **sudden in choler:** Violent in anger.   257. **qualification:**
Appeasement.   258. **true taste:** Satisfactory state.   260. **prefer:** Advance.
267. **apt:** Probable.   273. **accountant:** Accountable.   274. **diet:** Feed.   283. **I
trash:** I weight down (in order to keep under control).   284. **For:** In order to
develop; **stand the putting on:** Responds to my inciting.

I'll have our Michael Cassio on the hip,°
Abuse him to the Moor in the rank garb°
(For I fear Cassio with my nightcap too),
Make the Moor thank me, love me, and reward me
For making him egregiously an ass
And practicing upon° his peace and quiet
Even to madness. 'Tis here, but yet confused:
Knavery's plain face is never seen till used.   (*Exit.*)

Scene II

(*A street in Cyprus.*)

(*Enter Othello's Herald, with a proclamation.*)

HERALD: It is Othello's pleasure, our noble and valiant general, that,
upon certain tidings now arrived, importing the mere perdition° of the
Turkish fleet, every man put himself into triumph; some to dance,
some to make bonfires, each man to what sport and revels his addiction leads him. For, besides these beneficial news, it is the celebration
of his nuptial. So much was his pleasure should be proclaimed. All
offices° are open, and there is full liberty of feasting from the present hour of five till the bell have told eleven. Heaven bless the isle of
Cyprus and our noble general Othello!   (*Exit.*)

Scene III

(*The Cyprian Castle.*)

(*Enter Othello, Desdemona, Cassio, and Attendants.*)

OTHELLO: Good Michael, look you to the guard to-night.
    Let's teach ourselves that honorable stop,
    Not to outsport discretion.°
CASSIO: Iago hath direction what to do;
    But not withstanding, with my personal eye
    Will I look to't.
OTHELLO: Iago is most honest.
    Michael, good night. To-morrow with your earliest

---

285. on the hip: At my mercy.   286. rank garb: Gross manner.   290. practicing
upon: Plotting against.   SCENE II.   2. mere perdition: Complete destruction.
7. offices: Kitchens and storerooms.   SCENE III.   3. outsport discretion: Let
celebrating go too far.

Let me have speech with you.
     [*To Desdemona.*]   Come, my dear love.
The purchase made, the fruits are to ensue;
That profit 's yet to come 'tween me and you.—   10
Good night.
               (*Exit [Othello with Desdemona and Attendants]*.)

(*Enter Iago.*)

CASSIO: Welcome, Iago. We must to the watch.

IAGO: Not this hour, lieutenant; 'tis not yet ten o' th' clock. Our general cast° us thus early for the love of his Desdemona; who let us not therefore blame. He hath not yet made wanton the night with her, and she 15 is sport for Jove.

CASSIO: She's a most exquisite lady.

IAGO: And, I'll warrant her, full of game.

CASSIO: Indeed, she's a most fresh and delicate creature.

IAGO: What an eye she has! Methinks it sounds a parley to provocation. 20

CASSIO: An inviting eye; and yet methinks right modest.

IAGO: And when she speaks, is it not an alarum to love?

CASSIO: She is indeed perfection.

IAGO: Well, happiness to their sheets! Come, lieutenant, I have a stoup° of wine, and here without are a brace of Cyprus gallants that would 25 fain have a measure to the health of black Othello.

CASSIO: Not to-night, good Iago. I have very poor and unhappy brains for drinking; I could well wish courtesy would invent some other custom of entertainment.

IAGO: O, they are our friends. But one cup! I'll drink for you. 30

CASSIO: I have drunk but one cup to-night, and that was craftily qualified° too; and behold what innovation° it makes here. I am unfortunate in the infirmity and dare not task my weakness with any more.

IAGO: What, man! 'Tis a night of revels: the gallants desire it.

CASSIO: Where are they? 35

IAGO: Here at the door; I pray you call them in.

CASSIO: I'll do't, but it dislikes me.   (*Exit.*)

IAGO: If I can fasten but one cup upon him
With that which he hath drunk to-night already,
He'll be as full of quarrel and offense 40
As my young mistress' dog. Now my sick fool Roderigo,
Whom love hath turned almost the wrong side out,
To Desdemona hath to-night caroused

---

14. cast: Dismissed. **24. stoup:** Two-quart tankard. **31–32. qualified:** Diluted.
32. innovation: Disturbance.

Potations pottle-deep;° and he's to watch.
Three lads of Cyprus—noble swelling spirits,
That hold their honors in a wary distance,°
The very elements° of this warlike isle—
Have I to-night flustered with flowing cups,
And they watch too. Now, 'mongst this flock of drunkards
Am I to put our Cassio in some action
That may offend the isle.

(*Enter Cassio, Montano, and Gentlemen; [Servants following with wine].*)

                        But here they come.
If consequence do but approve my dream,
My boat sails freely, both with wind and stream.
CASSIO: 'Fore God, they have given me a rouse° already.
MONTANO: Good faith, a little one; not past a pint, as I am a soldier.
IAGO: Some wine, ho!
    [*Sings.*]   And let me the canakin° clink, clink;
             And let me the canakin clink
                A soldier's a man;
                A life's but a span,
            Why then, let a soldier drink.
    Some wine, boys!
CASSIO: 'Fore God, an excellent song!
IAGO: I learned it in England, where indeed they are most potent in pot-
    ting. Your Dane, your German, and your swag-bellied Hollander—
    Drink, ho!—are nothing to your English.
CASSIO: Is your Englishman so expert in his drinking?
IAGO: Why, he drinks° you with facility your Dane dead drunk; he sweats
    not to overthrow your Almain;° he gives your Hollander a vomit ere
    the next pottle can be filled.
CASSIO: To the health of our general!
MONTANO: I am for it, lieutenant, and I'll do you justice.
IAGO: O sweet England!
    [*Sings.*]   King Stephen was a worthy peer;
             His breeches cost him but a crown;
             He held 'em sixpence all too dear,
                With that he called the tailor lown.°
             He was a wight of high renown,
                And thou art but of low degree.

---

44. pottle-deep: Bottoms up.   **46. That . . . distance:** Are very sensitive about
their honor.   **47. very elements:** True representatives.   **54. rouse:** Bumper.
57. canakin: Small drinking cup.   **69. Almain:** German.   **77. lown:** Rascal.

    'Tis pride that pulls the country down;   80
      Then take thine auld cloak about thee.
  Some wine, ho!
CASSIO: 'Fore God, this is a more exquisite song than the other.
IAGO: Will you hear't again?
CASSIO: No, for I hold him to be unworthy of his place that does those   85
  things.° Well, God's above all; and there be souls must be saved, and
  there be souls must not be saved.
IAGO: It's true, good lieutenant.
CASSIO: For mine own part—no offense to the general, nor any man of
  quality—I hope to be saved.   90
IAGO: And so do I too, lieutenant.
CASSIO: Ay, but, by your leave, not before me. The lieutenant is to be
  saved before the ancient. Let's have no more of this; let's to our af-
  fairs.—God forgive us our sins!—Gentlemen, let's look to our busi-
  ness. Do not think, gentlemen, I am drunk. This is my ancient; this is   95
  my right hand, and this is my left. I am not drunk now. I can stand well
  enough, and I speak well enough.
ALL: Excellent well!
CASSIO: Why, very well then. You must not think then that I am drunk.
                      (*Exit.*)
MONTANO: To th' platform, masters. Come, let's set the watch.   100
IAGO: You see this fellow that is gone before.
  He's a soldier fit to stand by Caesar
  And give direction; and do but see his vice.
  'Tis to his virtue a just equinox,°
  The one as long as th' other. 'Tis pity of him.   105
  I fear the trust Othello puts him in,
  On some odd time of his infirmity,
  Will shake this island.
MONTANO: But is he often thus?
IAGO: 'Tis evermore his prologue to his sleep:
  He'll watch the horologe a double set°   110
  If drink rock not his cradle.
MONTANO: It were well
  The general were put in mind of it.
  Perhaps he sees it not, or his good nature
  Prizes the virtue that appears in Cassio
  And looks not on his evils. Is not this true?   115

(*Enter Roderigo.*)

85–86. does . . . things: I.e., behaves in this fashion. **104. just equinox:** Exact
equivalent. **110. watch . . . set:** Stay awake twice around the clock (horologe).

IAGO [*aside to him*]: How now, Roderigo?
  I pray you, after the lieutenant, go!   (*Exit Roderigo.*)
MONTANO: And 'tis great pity that the noble Moor
  Should hazard such a place as his own second
  With one of an ingraft° infirmity.   1.
  It were an honest action to say
  So to the Moor.
IAGO: Not I, for this fair island!
  I do love Cassio well and would do much
  To cure him of this evil.
      (*Within.*) Help! help!
                 But hark! What noise?   1:

(*Enter Cassio, driving in Roderigo.*)

CASSIO: Zounds, you rogue! you rascal!
MONTANO: What's the matter, lieutenant?
CASSIO: A knave to teach me my duty?
  I'll beat the knave into a twiggen° bottle.
RODERIGO: Beat me?
CASSIO: Dost thou prate, rogue? [*Strikes him.*]
MONTANO: Nay, good lieutenant!
                     [*Stays him.*]
  I pray you, sir, hold your hand.
CASSIO: Let me go, sir,   1:
  Or I'll knock you o'er the mazzard.°
MONTANO: Come, come, you're drunk!
CASSIO: Drunk?

(*They fight.*)

IAGO [*aside to Roderigo*]: Away, I say! Go out and cry a mutiny!
                  (*Exit Roderigo.*)
  Nay, good lieutenant. God's will, gentlemen!
  Help, ho!—lieutenant—sir—Montano—sir—   1:
  Help, masters!—Here's a goodly watch indeed!

(*A bell rung.*)

  Who's that which rings the bell? Diablo,° ho!
  The town will rise.° God's will, lieutenant, hold!
  You'll be shamed for ever.

(*Enter Othello and Gentlemen with weapons.*)

---

120. ingraft: I.e., ingrained. **128. twiggen:** Wicker-covered. **131. mazzard:**
Head. **137. Diablo:** The devil. **138. rise:** Grow riotous.

OTHELLO: What is the matter here?
MONTANO: Zounds, I bleed still. I am hurt to th' death.   140
  He dies!
OTHELLO: Hold for your lives!
IAGO: Hold, hold! Lieutenant—sir—Montano—gentlemen!
  Have you forgot all sense of place and duty?
  Hold! The general speaks to you. Hold, for shame!   145
OTHELLO: Why, how now ho? From whence ariseth this?
  Are we turned Turks, and to ourselves do that
  Which heaven hath forbid the Ottomites?
  For Christian shame put by this barbarous brawl!
  He that stirs next to carve for° his own rage   150
  Holds his soul light;° he dies upon his motion.°
  Silence that dreadful bell! It frights the isle
  From her propriety.° What is the matter, masters?
  Honest Iago, that looks dead with grieving,
  Speak. Who began this? On thy love, I charge thee.   155
IAGO: I do not know. Friends all, but now, even now,
  In quarter,° and in terms like bride and groom
  Devesting them for bed; and then, but now—
  As if some planet had unwitted men—
  Swords out, and tilting one at other's breast   160
  In opposition bloody. I cannot speak
  Any beginning to this peevish odds,°
  And would in action glorious I had lost
  Those legs that brought me to a part of it!
OTHELLO: How comes it, Michael, you are thus forgot?°   165
CASSIO: I pray you pardon me; I cannot speak.
OTHELLO: Worthy Montano, you were wont to be civil;
  The gravity and stillness of your youth
  The world hath noted, and your name is great
  In mouths of wisest censure.° What's the matter   170
  That you unlace° your reputation thus
  And spend your rich opinion° for the name
  Of a night-brawler? Give me answer to it.
MONTANO: Worthy Othello, I am hurt to danger.
  Your officer, Iago, can inform you,   175

---

150. carve for: Indulge.   151. Holds . . . light: Values his life lightly; **upon his
motion:** If he moves.   153. propriety: Proper self.   157. quarter: Friendliness.
162. peevish odds: Childish quarrel.   165. are thus forgot: Have forgotten
yourself this way.   170. censure: Judgment.   171. unlace: Undo.   172. rich
opinion: High reputation.

While I spare speech, which something now offends° me,
Of all that I do know; nor know I aught
By me that's said or done amiss this night,
Unless self-charity be sometimes a vice,
And to defend ourselves it be a sin
When violence assails us.

OTHELLO: Now, by heaven,
My blood° begins my safer guides° to rule,
And passion, having my best judgment collied,°
Assays° to lead the way. If I once stir
Or do but lift this arm, the best of you
Shall sink in my rebuke. Give me to know
How this foul rout began, who set it on;
And he that is approved in° this offense,
Though he had twinned with me, both at a birth,
Shall lose me. What! in a town of war,
Yet wild, the people's hearts brimful of fear,
To manage° private and domestic quarrel?
In night, and on the court and guard of safety?
'Tis monstrous. Iago, who began't?

MONTANO: If partially affined, or leagued in office,°
Thou dost deliver more or less than truth,
Thou art no soldier.

IAGO: Touch me not so near.
I had rather have this tongue cut from my mouth
Than it should do offense to Michael Cassio;
Yet I persuade myself, to speak the truth
Shall nothing wrong him. This it is, general.
Montano and myself being in speech,
There comes a fellow crying out for help,
And Cassio following him with determined sword
To execute° upon him. Sir, this gentleman
Steps in to Cassio and entreats his pause.°
Myself the crying fellow did pursue,
Lest by his clamor—as it so fell out—
The town might fall in fright. He, swift of foot,
Outran my purpose; and I returned then rather°

---

176. **offends:** Pains.   182. **blood:** Passion; **safer guides:** Reason.   183. **collied:** Darkened.   184. **Assays:** Tries.   188. **approved in:** Proved guilty of.   192. **manage:** Carry on.   195. **partially . . . office:** Prejudiced by comradeship or official relations.   205. **execute:** Work his will.   206. **his pause:** Him to stop.
210. **rather:** Sooner.

For that I heard the clink and fall of swords,
And Cassio high in oath;° which till to-night
I ne'er might say before. When I came back—
For this was brief—I found them close together
At blow and thrust, even as again they were   215
When you yourself did part them.
More of this matter cannot I report;
But men are men; the best sometimes forget.°
Though Cassio did some little wrong to him,
As men in rage strike those that wish them best,   220
Yet surely Cassio I believe received
From him that fled some strange indignity,
Which patience could not pass.°
OTHELLO: I know, Iago,
Thy honesty and love doth mince this matter,
Making it light to Cassio. Cassio, I love thee;   225
But never more be officer of mine.

(*Enter Desdemona, attended.*)

Look if my gentle love be not raised up!
I'll make thee an example.
DESDEMONA: What's the matter?
OTHELLO: All's well now, sweeting; come away to bed.
[*To Montano.*]
Sir, for your hurts, myself will be your surgeon.   230
Lead him off.

[*Montano is led off.*]

Iago, look with care about the town
And silence those whom this vile brawl distracted.°
Come, Desdemona; 'tis the soldiers' life
To have their balmy slumbers waked with strife.   235
                     (*Exit [with all but Iago and Cassio].*)
IAGO: What, are you hurt, lieutenant?
CASSIO: Ay, past all surgery.
IAGO: Marry, God forbid!
CASSIO: Reputation, reputation, reputation! O, I have lost my reputation!
    I have lost the immortal part of myself, and what remains is bestial. 240
    My reputation, Iago, my reputation!
IAGO: As I am an honest man. I thought you had received some bodily
    wound. There is more sense in that than in reputation. Reputation is

---

212. high in oath: Cursing.   **218. forget:** Forget themselves.   **223. pass:** Pass
over, ignore.   **233. distracted:** Excited.

an idle and most false imposition; oft got without merit and lost without deserving. You have lost no reputation at all unless you repute yourself such a loser. What, man! there are ways to recover° the general again. You are but now cast in his mood°—a punishment more in policy than in malice, even so as one would beat his offenseless dog to affright an imperious lion. Sue to him again, and he's yours.

CASSIO: I will rather sue to be despised than to deceive so good a commander with so slight, so drunken, and so indiscreet an officer. Drunk! and speak parrot!° and squabble! swagger! swear! and discourse fustian° with one's own shadow! O thou invisible spirit of wine, if thou hast no name to be known by, let us call thee devil!

IAGO: What was he that you followed with your sword? What had he done to you?

CASSIO: I know not.

IAGO: Is't possible?

CASSIO: I remember a mass of things, but nothing distinctly; a quarrel, but nothing wherefore. O God, that men should put an enemy in their mouths to steal away their brains! that we should with joy, pleasance, revel, and applause° transform ourselves into beasts!

IAGO: Why, but you are now well enough. How came you thus recovered?

CASSIO: It hath pleased the devil drunkenness to give place to the devil wrath. One unperfectness shows me another, to make me frankly despise myself.

IAGO: Come, you are too severe a moraler.° As the time, the place, and the condition of this country stands, I could heartily wish this had not so befall'n; but since it is as it is, mend it for your own good.

CASSIO: I will ask him for my place again: he shall tell me I am a drunkard! Had I as many mouths as Hydra,° such an answer would stop them all. To be now a sensible man, by and by a fool, and presently a beast! O strange! Every inordinate° cup is unblest, and the ingredient° is a devil.

IAGO: Come, come, good wine is a good familiar creature if it be well used. Exclaim no more against it. And, good lieutenant, I think you think I love you.

CASSIO: I have well approved it,° sir. I drunk!

IAGO: You or any man living may be drunk at some time, man. I'll tell you what you shall do. Our general's wife is now the general. I may say so in this respect, for that he hath devoted and given up himself to the

---

246. **recover:** Regain favor with.   247. **in his mood:** Dismissed because of his anger.   252. **parrot:** Meaningless phrases.   252–53. **fustian:** Bombastic nonsense.   262. **applause:** Desire to please.   267. **moraler:** Moralizer.   271. **Hydra:** Monster with many heads.   273. **inordinate:** Excessive; **ingredient:** Contents.   278. **approved:** Proved.

contemplation, mark, and denotement of her parts and graces. Confess
yourself freely to her; importune her help to put you in your place
again. She is of so free,° so kind, so apt, so blessed a disposition she
holds it a vice in her goodness not to do more than she is requested.   285
This broken joint between you and her husband entreat her to splinter;° and my fortunes against any lay° worth naming, this crack of your
love shall grow stronger than it was before.

CASSIO: You advise me well.

IAGO: I protest, in the sincerity of love and honest kindness.   290

CASSIO: I think it freely; and betimes in the morning will I beseech the
virtuous Desdemona to undertake for me. I am desperate of my fortunes if they check me here.°

IAGO: You are in the right. Good night, lieutenant; I must to the watch.

CASSIO: Good night, honest Iago.   (*Exit Cassio.*) 295

IAGO: And what's he then that says I play the villain,
When this advice is free I give and honest,
Probal° to thinking, and indeed the course
To win the Moor again? For 'tis most easy
Th' inclining Desdemona to subdue°   300
In any honest suit; she's framed as fruitful
As the free elements. And then for her
To win the Moor—were't to renounce his baptism,
All seals and symbols of redeemèd sin—
His soul is so enfettered to her love   305
That she may make, unmake, do what she list,
Even as her appetite shall play the god
With his weak function.° How am I then a villain
To counsel Cassio to this parallel° course,
Directly to his good? Divinity° of hell!   310
When devils will the blackest sins put on,°
They do suggest at first with heavenly shows,
As I do now. For whiles this honest fool
Plies Desdemona to repair his fortunes,
And she for him pleads strongly to the Moor,   315
I'll pour this pestilence into his ear,
That she repeals him° for her body's lust;
And by how much she strives to do him good,

---

284. free: Bounteous.   **286–87. splinter:** Bind up with splints; **lay:** Wager.
292–93. I . . . here: I despair of my future if my career is stopped short here.
298. Probal: Probable.   **300. subdue:** Persuade.   **308. function:** Intelligence
(weakened by his fondness for her).   **309. parallel:** Corresponding.
310. Divinity: Theology.   **311. put on:** Incite.   **317. repeals him:** Seeks his recall.

She shall undo her credit with the Moor.
So will I turn her virtue into pitch,   3
And out of her own goodness make the net
That shall enmesh them all.

(*Enter Roderigo.*)

                                                How, now, Roderigo?
RODERIGO: I do follow here in the chase, not like a hound that hunts, but
   one that fills up the cry.° My money is almost spent; I have been to-
   night exceedingly well cudgelled; and I think the issue will be—I shall   3
   have so much experience for my pains; and so, with no money at all,
   and a little more wit, return again to Venice.
IAGO: How poor are they that have not patience!
   What wound did ever heal but by degrees?
   Thou know'st we work by wit, and not by witchcraft;   3
   And wit depends on dilatory time.
   Does't not go well? Cassio hath beaten thee,
   And thou by that small hurt hast cashiered Cassio.°
   Though other things grow fair against the sun,
   Yet fruits that blossom first will first be ripe.°   3
   Content thyself awhile. By the mass, 'tis morning!
   Pleasure and action make the hours seem short.
   Retire thee; go where thou art billeted.
   Away, I say! Thou shalt know more hereafter.
   Nay, get thee gone!   (*Exit Roderigo.*)
                              Two things are to be done: 3
   My wife must move for Cassio to her mistress;
   I'll set her on;
   Myself the while to draw the Moor apart
   And bring him jump° when he may Cassio find
   Soliciting his wife. Ay, that's the way!   3
   Dull no device by coldness and delay.   (*Exit.*)

ACT III   *Scene I*

(*Before the chamber of Othello and Desdemona.*)

(*Enter Cassio, with Musicians and the Clown.*)

324. cry: Pack.   **333. cashiered Cassio:** Maneuvered Cassio's discharge.   **334–
35. Though . . . ripe:** Although fruit ripens in the sun, yet the first fruit to ripen
will come from the earliest blossoms.   **344. jump:** At the exact moment.

CASSIO: Masters, play here, I will content° your pains:
   Something that's brief; and bid "Good morrow, general."

[*They play.*]

CLOWN: Why, masters, ha' your instruments been in Naples,° that they
   speak i' th' nose thus?
MUSICIAN: How, sir, how?   5
CLOWN: Are these, I pray you, called wind instruments?
MUSICIAN: Ay, marry, are they, sir.
CLOWN: O, thereby hangs a tail.
MUSICIAN: Whereby hangs a tale, sir?
CLOWN: Marry, sir, by many a wind instrument that I know. But, masters,   10
   here's money for you; and the general so likes your music that he de-
   sires you, for love's sake, to make no more noise with it.
MUSICIAN: Well, sir, we will not.
CLOWN: If you have any music that may not be heard, to't again: but, as
   they say, to hear music the general does not greatly care.   15
MUSICIAN: We have none such, sir.
CLOWN: Then put up your pipes in your bag, for I'll away. Go, vanish into
   air, away!   (*Exit Musician [with his fellows].*)
CASSIO: Dost thou hear, my honest friend?
CLOWN: No, I hear not your honest friend. I hear you.   20
CASSIO: Prithee keep up thy quillets.° There's a poor piece of gold for
   thee. If the gentlewoman that attends the general's wife be stirring, tell
   her there's one Cassio entreats her a little favor of speech. Wilt thou do
   this?
CLOWN: She is stirring sir. If she will stir hither, I shall seem to notify 25
   unto her.
CASSIO: [Do, good my friend.]   (*Exit Clown.*)

(*Enter Iago.*)

                          In happy time,° Iago.
IAGO: You have not been abed then?
CASSIO: Why, no; the day had broke
   Before we parted. I have made bold, Iago,   30
   To send in to your wife: my suit to her
   Is that she will to virtuous Desdemona
   Procure me some access.
IAGO: I'll send her to you presently;
   And I'll devise a mean to draw the Moor

ACT III, SCENE I.   **1. content:** Reward   **3. Naples:** (Notorious for its association
with venereal disease).   **21. quillets:** Quips.   **27. In happy time:** Well met.

Out of the way, that your converse and business
May be more free.
CASSIO: I humbly thank you for't.   (*Exit* [*Iago*].)
                         I never knew
A Florentine° more kind and honest.

(*Enter Emilia.*)

EMILIA: Good morrow, good lieutenant. I am sorry
For your displeasure:° but all will sure be well.
The general and his wife are talking of it,
And she speaks for you stoutly. The Moor replied
That he you hurt is of great fame in Cyprus
And great affinity,° and that in wholesome wisdom
He might not but refuse you; but he protests he loves you,
And needs no other suitor but his likings
[To take the safest occasion° by the front°]
To bring you in again.
CASSIO: Yet I beseech you,
If you think fit, or that it may be done,
Give me advantage of some brief discourse
With Desdemona alone.
EMILIA: Pray you come in.
I will bestow you where you shall have time
To speak your bosom° freely.
CASSIO: I am much bound to you.   (*Exeunt.*)

Scene II

(*The castle.*)

(*Enter Othello, Iago, and Gentlemen.*)

OTHELLO: These letters give, Iago, to the pilot
And by him do my duties° to the Senate.
That done, I will be walking on the works;°
Repair there to me.
IAGO: Well, my good lord, I'll do't.
OTHELLO: This fortification, gentlemen, shall we see't?
GENTLEMEN: We'll wait upon your lordship.   (*Exeunt.*)

---

38. Florentine: I.e., even a Florentine (like Cassio; Iago was a Venetian).
40. displeasure: Fall from favor.   **44. affinity:** Family connections.   **47. occasion:** Opportunity; **front:** Forelock.   **53. your bosom:** Your inmost thoughts.
SCENE II.   **2. do my duties:** Convey my respects.   **3. works:** Fortifications.

Scene III

(*The castle grounds.*)

(*Enter Desdemona, Cassio, and Emilia.*)

DESDEMONA: Be thou assured, good Cassio, I will do
All my abilities in thy behalf.
EMILIA: Good madam, do. I warrant it grieves my husband
As if the cause were his.
DESDEMONA: O, that's an honest fellow. Do not doubt, Cassio,   5
But I will have my lord and you again
As friendly as you were.
CASSIO: Bounteous madam,
Whatever shall become of Michael Cassio,
He's never anything but your true servant.
DESDEMONA: I know't; I thank you. You do love my lord;   10
You have known him long; and be you well assured
He shall in strangeness° stand no farther off
Than in a politic distance.°
CASSIO: Ay, but, lady,
That policy may either last so long,
Or feed upon such nice and waterish diet,°   15
Or breed itself so out of circumstance,
That, I being absent, and my place supplied,
My general will forget my love and service.
DESDEMONA: Do not doubt° that; before Emilia here
I give thee warrant of thy place. Assure thee,   20
If I do vow a friendship, I'll perform it
To the last article. My lord shall never rest;
I'll watch him tame° and talk him out of patience;
His bed shall seem a school, his board a shrift;°
I'll intermingle everything he does   25
With Cassio's suit. Therefore be merry, Cassio,
For thy solicitor shall rather die
Than give thy cause away.

(*Enter Othello and Iago [at a distance].*)

EMILIA: Madam, here comes my lord.
CASSIO: Madam, I'll take my leave.   30

SCENE III.   **12. strangeness:** Aloofness.   **13. Than . . . distance:** Than wise policy
requires.   **15. Or . . . diet:** Or be continued for such slight reasons.   **19. doubt:**
Fear.   **23. watch him tame:** Keep him awake until he gives in.   **24. board a**
shrift: Confessional.

DESDEMONA: Why, stay, and hear me speak.
CASSIO: Madam, not now: I am very ill at ease,
  Unfit for mine own purposes.
DESDEMONA: Well, do your discretion.   (*Exit Cassio.*)
IAGO: Ha! I like not that.
OTHELLO: What dost thou say?
IAGO: Nothing, my lord; or if—I know not what.
OTHELLO: Was not that Cassio parted from my wife?
IAGO: Cassio, my lord? No, sure, I cannot think it,
  That he would steal away so guilty-like,
  Seeing your coming.
OTHELLO: I do believe 'twas he.
DESDEMONA: How now, my lord?
  I have been talking with a suitor here,
  A man that languishes in your displeasure.
OTHELLO: What is't you mean?
DESDEMONA: Why, your lieutenant, Cassio. Good my lord,
  If I have any grace or power to move you,
  His present° reconciliation take;
  For if he be not one that truly loves you,
  That errs in ignorance, and not in cunning,°
  I have no judgment in an honest face,
  I prithee call him back.
OTHELLO: Went he hence now?
DESDEMONA: Yes, faith; so humbled
  That he hath left part of his grief with me
  To suffer with him. Good love, call him back.
OTHELLO: Not now, sweet Desdemon; some other time.
DESDEMONA: But shall't be shortly?
OTHELLO: The sooner, sweet, for you.
DESDEMONA: Shall't be to-night at supper?
OTHELLO: No, not to-night.
DESDEMONA: To-morrow dinner then?
OTHELLO: I shall not dine at home;
  I meet the captains at the citadel.
DESDEMONA: Why then, to-morrow night, or Tuesday morn,
  On Tuesday noon or night, or Wednesday morn.
  I prithee name the time, but let it not
  Exceed three days. I' faith, he's penitent;
  And yet his trespass, in our common reason
  (Save that, they say, the wars must make examples

_____

47. present: Immediate. **49. in cunning:** Knowingly.

Out of their best), is not almost° a fault
T' incur a private check.° When shall he come?
Tell me, Othello. I wonder in my soul
What you could ask me that I should deny
Or stand so mamm'ring on.° What? Michael Cassio,   70
That came a-wooing with you, and so many a time,
When I have spoke of you dispraisingly,
Hath ta'en your part—to have so much to do
To bring him in?° By'r Lady, I could do much—
OTHELLO: Prithee no more. Let him come when he will!   75
I will deny thee nothing.
DESDEMONA: Why, this is not a boon;
'Tis as I should entreat you wear your gloves,
Or feed on nourishing dishes, or keep you warm,
Or sue to you to do a peculiar profit
To your own person. Nay, when I have a suit   80
Wherein I mean to touch your love indeed,
It shall be full of poise and difficult weight,
And fearful° to be granted.
OTHELLO: I will deny thee nothing!
Whereon I do beseech thee grant me this,
To leave me but a little to myself.   85
DESDEMONA: Shall I deny you? No. Farewell, my lord.
OTHELLO: Farewell, my Desdemon: I'll come to thee straight.°
DESDEMONA: Emilia, come.—Be as your fancies teach you;°
    Whate'er you be, I am obedient.   (*Exit* [*with Emilia*].)
OTHELLO: Excellent wretch!° Perdition catch my soul   90
    But I do love thee! and when I love thee not,
    Chaos is come again.
IAGO: My noble lord—
OTHELLO: What dost thou say, Iago?
IAGO: Did Michael Cassio, when you wooed my lady,
    Know of your love?   95
OTHELLO: He did, from first to last. Why dost thou ask?
IAGO: But for a satisfaction of my thought;
    No further harm.
OTHELLO: Why of thy thought, Iago?
IAGO: I did not think he had been acquainted with her.

66. not almost: Hardly.   **67. a private check:** Even a private reprimand.
70. mamm'ring on: Hesitating about.   **74. To bring him in:** To restore him to
favor.   **83. fearful:** Dangerous.   **87. straight:** Straightway.   **88. Be . . . you:**
Please yourself.   **90. wretch:** (A term of endearment).

OTHELLO: O, yes, and went between us° very oft.
IAGO: Indeed?
OTHELLO: Indeed? Ay, indeed! Discern'st thou aught in that?
   Is he not honest?
IAGO: Honest, my lord?
OTHELLO: Honest. Ay, honest.
IAGO: My lord, for aught I know.
OTHELLO: What dost thou think?
IAGO: Think, my lord?
OTHELLO: Think, my lord?
   By heaven, he echoes me,
   As if there were some monster in his thought
   Too hideous to be shown. Thou dost mean something:
   I heard thee say even now, thou lik'st not that,
   When Cassio left my wife. What didst not like?
   And when I told thee he was of my counsel
   In my whole course of wooing, thou cried'st "Indeed?"
   And didst contract and purse thy brow together,
   As if thou then hadst shut up in thy brain
   Some horrible conceit.° If thou dost love me,
   Show me thy thought
IAGO: My lord, you know I love you.
OTHELLO: I think thou dost;
   And, for° I know thou'rt full of love and honesty
   And weigh'st thy words before thou giv'st them breath,
   Therefore these stops° of thine fright me the more;
   For such things in a false disloyal knave
   Are tricks of custom;° but in a man that's just
   They are close dilations, working from the heart
   That passion cannot rule.°
IAGO: For Michael Cassio,
   I dare be sworn I think that he is honest.
OTHELLO: I think so too.
IAGO: Men should be what they seem;
   Or those that be not, would they might seem none!°
OTHELLO: Certain, men should be what they seem.
IAGO: Why then, I think Cassio's an honest man.

---

100. went . . . us: (I.e., as messenger).   **115. conceit:** Fancy.   **118. for:** Because.   **120. stops:** Pauses.   **122. tricks of custom:** Customary, or usual, tricks.   **123–24. close dilations . . . rule:** Secret emotions which well up and cannot be restrained.   **127. seem none:** I.e., not pretend to be men when they are really monsters.

OTHELLO: Nay, yet there's more in this. 130
  I prithee speak to me as to thy thinkings,
  As thou dost ruminate, and give thy worst of thoughts
  The worst of words.
IAGO: Good my lord, pardon me:
  Though I am bound to every act of duty,
  I am not bound to that all slaves are free to.° 135
  Utter my thoughts? Why, say they are vile and false,
  As where's that palace whereinto foul things
  Sometimes intrude not? Who has a breast so pure
  But some uncleanly apprehensions
  Keep leets and law days,° and in Sessions sit 140
  With meditations lawful?
OTHELLO: Thou dost conspire against thy friend, Iago,
  If thou but think'st him wronged, and mak'st his ear
  A stranger to thy thoughts.
IAGO: I do beseech you—
  Though I perchance am vicious° in my guess 145
  (As I confess it is my nature's plague
  To spy into abuses, and oft my jealousy°
  Shapes faults that are not), that your wisdom yet
  From one that so imperfectly conjects°
  Would take no notice, nor build yourself a trouble 150
  Out of his scattering° and unsure observance.
  It were not for your quiet nor your good,
  Nor for my manhood, honesty, and wisdom,
  To let you know my thoughts.
OTHELLO: What dost thou mean?
IAGO: Good name in man and woman, dear my lord, 155
  Is the immediate° jewel of their souls.
  Who steals my purse steals trash; 'tis something, nothing;
  'Twas mine, 'tis his, and has been slave to thousands;
  But he that filches from me my good name
  Robs me of that which not enriches him 160
  And makes me poor indeed.
OTHELLO: By heaven, I'll know thy thoughts!
IAGO: You cannot, if° my heart were in your hand;
  Nor shall not whilst 'tis in my custody.

---

135. bound . . . free to: Bound to tell that which even slaves are allowed to keep
to themselves. 140. leets and law days: Sittings of the courts. 145. vicious:
Wrong. 147. jealousy: Suspicion. 149. conjects: Conjectures. 151. scattering: Random. 156. immediate: Nearest the heart. 163. if: Even if.

OTHELLO: Ha!
IAGO: O, beware, my lord, of jealousy!
  It is the green-eyed monster, which doth mock°
  The meat it feeds on. That cuckold lives in bliss
  Who, certain of his fate, loves not his wronger;
  But O, what damnèd minutes tells he o'er
  Who dotes, yet doubts—suspects, yet strongly loves!
OTHELLO: O misery!
IAGO: Poor and content is rich, and rich enough;
  But riches fineless° is as poor as winter
  To him that ever fears he shall be poor.
  Good God, the souls of all my tribe defend
  From jealousy!
OTHELLO: Why, why is this?
  Think'st thou I'ld make a life of jealousy,
  To follow still the changes of the moon
  With fresh suspicions? No! To be once in doubt
  Is once to be resolved. Exchange me for a goat
  When I shall turn the business of my soul
  To such exsufflicate and blown° surmises,
  Matching this inference. 'Tis not to make me jealous
  To say my wife is fair, feeds well, loves company,
  Is free of speech, sings, plays, and dances;
  Where virtue is, these are more virtuous.
  Nor from mine own weak merits will I draw
  The smallest fear or doubt of her revolt,°
  For she had eyes, and chose me. No, Iago;
  I'll see before I doubt; when I doubt, prove;
  And on the proof there is no more but this—
  Away at once with love or jealousy!
IAGO: I am glad of this; for now I shall have reason
  To show the love and duty that I bear you
  With franker spirit. Therefore, as I am bound,
  Receive it from me. I speak not yet of proof.
  Look to your wife; observe her well with Cassio;
  Wear your eyes thus, not jealous nor secure:°
  I would not have your free and noble nature,
  Out of self-bounty,° be abused. Look to't.
  I know our country disposition well:

166. **mock:** Play with, like a cat with a mouse.   173. **fineless:** Unlimited.
182. **exsufflicate and blown:** Spat out and flyblown.   188. **revolt:** Unfaithful-
ness.   198. **secure:** Overconfident.   200. **self-bounty:** Natural goodness.

    In Venice they do let God see the pranks
    They dare not show their husbands; their best conscience
    Is not to leave't undone, but keep't unknown.
OTHELLO: Dost thou say so?   205
IAGO: She did deceive her father, marrying you;
    And when she seemed to shake and fear your looks,
    She loved them most.
OTHELLO: And so she did.
IAGO: Why, go to then!
    She that, so young, could give out such a seeming
    To seel° her father's eyes up close as oak°—   210
    He thought 'twas witchcraft—but I am much to blame.
    I humbly do beseech you of your pardon
    For too much loving you.
OTHELLO: I am bound to thee for ever.
IAGO: I see this hath a little dashed your spirits.
OTHELLO: Not a jot, not a jot.
IAGO: I' faith, I fear it has.   215
    I hope you will consider what is spoke
    Comes from my love. But I do see y' are moved.
    I am to pray you not to strain my speech
    To grosser issues° nor to larger reach
    Than to suspicion.   220
OTHELLO: I will not.
IAGO: Should you do so, my lord,
    My speech should fall into such vile success°
    As my thoughts aim not at. Cassio's my worthy friend—
    My lord, I see y' are moved.
OTHELLO: No, not much moved:
    I do not think but Desdemona's honest.°   225
IAGO: Long live she so! and long live you to think so!
OTHELLO: And yet, how nature erring from itself—
IAGO: Ay, there's the point! as (to be bold with you)
    Not to affect° many proposèd matches
    Of her own clime, complexion, and degree,°   230
    Whereto we see in all things nature tends—
    Foh! one may smell in such a will most rank,°

---

210. seel: Close (a term from falconry); **close as oak:** Tight as oak grain.
219. To grosser issues: To mean something more monstrous.   **222. vile
success:** Evil outcome.   **225. honest:** Chaste.   **229. affect:** Prefer.
230. clime . . . degree: Country, color, and rank.   **232. will most rank:** Desire
most lustful.

Foul disproportions,° thought unnatural—
But pardon me—I do not in position°
Distinctly speak of her; though I may fear
Her will, recoiling° to her better judgment,
May fall to match° you with her country forms,
And happily° repent.
OTHELLO: Farewell, farewell!
  If more thou dost perceive, let me know more.
  Set on thy wife to observe. Leave me, Iago.
IAGO: My lord, I take my leave.   [*Going.*]
OTHELLO: Why did I marry? This honest creature doubtless
  Sees and knows more, much more, than he unfolds.
IAGO [returns]: My lord, I would I might entreat your honor
  To scan this thing no further: leave it to time.
  Although 'tis fit that Cassio have his place,
  For sure he fills it up with great ability,
  Yet, if you please to hold off a while,
  You shall by that perceive him and his means.
  Note if your lady strain his entertainment°
  With any strong or vehement importunity;
  Much will be seen in that. In the mean time
  Let me be thought too busy° in my fears
  (As worthy cause I have to fear I am)
  And hold her free,° I do beseech your honor.
OTHELLO: Fear not my government.°
IAGO: I once more take my leave.   (*Exit.*)
OTHELLO: This fellow 's of exceeding honesty,
  And knows all qualities,° with a learned spirit
  Of° human dealings. If I do prove her haggard,°
  Though that her jesses° were my dear heartstrings,
  I'd whistle her off and let her down the wind
  To prey at fortune.° Haply, for I am black
  And have not those soft parts of conversation°
  That chamberers° have, or for I am declined

233. **disproportions:** Abnormality.   234. **position:** Definite assertion.
236. **recoiling:** Reverting.   237. **fall to match:** Happen to compare.
238. **happily:** Haply, perhaps.   250. **strain his entertainment:** Urge his recall.
253. **busy:** Meddlesome.   255. **hold her free:** Consider her guiltless.
256. **government:** Self-control.   259. **qualities:** Natures.   259–60. **learnèd
spirit Of:** Mind informed about.   260. **haggard:** A wild hawk.   261. **jesses:**
Thongs for controlling a hawk.   262–63. **whistle . . . fortune:** Turn her out and
let her take care of herself.   264. **soft . . . conversation:** Ingratiating manners.
265. **chamberers:** Courtiers.

Into the vale of years—yet that's not much—
She's gone. I am abused, and my relief
Must be to loathe her. O curse of marriage,
That we can call these delicate creatures ours,
And not their appetites! I had rather be a toad   270
And live upon the vapor of a dungeon
Than keep a corner in the thing I love
For others' uses. Yet 'tis the plague of great ones;°
Prerogatived° are they less than the base.
'Tis destiny unshunnable, like death.   275
Even then this forkèd plague° is fated to us
When we do quicken.° Look where she comes.

(*Enter Desdemona and Emilia.*)

If she be false, O, then heaven mocks itself!
I'll not believe't.
DESDEMONA: How now, my dear Othello?
Your dinner, and the generous° islanders   280
By you invited, do attend your presence.
OTHELLO: I am to blame.
DESDEMONA: Why do you speak so faintly?
Are you not well?
OTHELLO: I have a pain upon my forehead, here.
DESDEMONA: Faith, that's with watching;° 'twill away again.   285
Let me but bind it hard, within this hour
It will be well.
OTHELLO: Your napkin° is too little;

[*He pushes the handkerchief from him, and it falls unnoticed.*]

Let it° alone. Come, I'll go in with you.
DESDEMONA: I am very sorry that you are not well.   (*Exit [with Othello].*)
EMILIA: I am glad I have found this napkin;   290
This was her first remembrance from the Moor,
My wayward husband hath a hundred times
Wooed me to steal it; but she so loves the token
(For he conjured her she should ever keep it)
That she reserves it evermore about her   295
To kiss and talk to. I'll have the work ta'en out°
And give't Iago.

---

273. great ones: Prominent men.   **274. Prerogatived:** Privileged.   **276. forkèd plague:** I.e., horns of a cuckold.   **277. do quicken:** Are born.   **280. generous:** Noble.   **285. watching:** Working late.   **287. napkin:** Handkerchief.   **288. it:** I.e., his forehead.   **296. work ta'en out:** Pattern copied.

What he will do with it heaven knows, not I;
I nothing but to please his fantasy.°

(*Enter Iago.*)

IAGO: How now? What do you here alone?
EMILIA: Do not you chide; I have a thing for you.
IAGO: A thing for me? It is a common° thing°—
EMILIA: Ha?
IAGO: To have a foolish wife.
EMILIA: O, is that all? What will you give me now
   For that same handkerchief?
IAGO: What handkerchief?
EMILIA: What handkerchief!
   Why, that the Moor first gave to Desdemona;
   That which so often you did bid me steal.
IAGO: Hast stol'n it from her?
EMILIA: No, faith; she let it drop by negligence,
   And to th' advantage,° I, being here, took't up.
   Look, here it is.
IAGO: A good wench! Give it me.
EMILIA: What will you do with't, that you have been so earnest
   To have me filch it?
IAGO: Why, what is that to you?

[*Snatches it.*]

EMILIA: If it be not for some purpose of import,°
   Give't me again. Poor lady, she'll run mad
   When she shall lack it.
IAGO: Be not acknown on't;° I have use for it.
   Go, leave me.   (*Exit Emilia.*)
   I will in Cassio's lodgings lose this napkin
   And let him find it. Trifles light as air
   Are to the jealous confirmations strong
   As proofs of holy writ. This may do something.
   The Moor already changes with my poison:
   Dangerous conceits° are in their nature poisons,
   Which at the first are scarce found to distaste,°
   But with a little act° upon the blood
   Burn like the mines of sulphur.

---

299. fantasy: Whim.   **302. common:** Available to everyone; **thing:** Slang term for vagina.   **312. to th' advantage:** Opportunely.   **316. import:** Importance.
319. Be . . . on't: Do not acknowledge it.   **326. conceits:** Ideas.   **327. distaste:** Be distasteful.   **328. act:** Action.

(Enter Othello.)

I did say so.

Look where he comes! Not poppy nor mandragora,°   330
Nor all the drowsy syrups of the world,
Shall ever med'cine thee to that sweet sleep
Which thou owedst yesterday.
OTHELLO: Ha! ha! false to me?
IAGO: Why, how now, general? No more of that!
OTHELLO: Avaunt! be gone! Thou hast set me on the rack.   335
  I swear 'tis better to be much abused
  Than but to know't a little.
IAGO: How now, my lord?
OTHELLO: What sense had I of her stol'n hours of lust?
  I saw't not, thought it not, it harmed not me;
  I slept the next night well, fed well, was free° and merry;   340
  I found not Cassio's kisses on her lips
  He that is robbed, not wanting° what is stol'n,
  Let him not know't, and he's not robbed at all.
IAGO: I am sorry to hear this.
OTHELLO: I had been happy if the general camp,   345
  Pioneers° and all, had tasted her sweet body,
  So° I had nothing known. O, now for ever
  Farewell the tranquil mind! farewell content!
  Farewell the plumèd troop, and the big° wars
  That make ambition virtue! O, farewell!   350
  Farewell the neighing steed and the shrill trump,
  The spirit-stirring drum, th' ear-piercing fife,
  The royal banner, and all quality,
  Pride, pomp, and circumstance° of glorious war!
  And O you mortal engines° whose rude throats   355
  Th' immortal Jove's dread clamors counterfeit,°
  Farewell! Othello's occupation's gone!
IAGO: Is't possible, my lord?
OTHELLO: Villain, be sure thou prove my love a whore!
  Be sure of it; give me the ocular proof;   360
  Or, by the worth of mine eternal soul,
  Thou hadst been better have been born a dog
  Than answer my waked wrath!

---

330. mandragora: A sleep-inducing drug made from mandrake roots. **340. free:** Carefree. **342. wanting:** Missing. **346. Pioneers:** Sappers, laborers. **347. So:** So long as. **349. big:** Mighty. **354. circumstance:** Pageantry. **355. mortal engines:** Deadly artillery. **356. counterfeit:** Imitate.

IAGO: Is't come to this?
OTHELLO: Make me to see't; or at the least so prove it
   That the probation° bear no hinge nor loop
   To hang a doubt on—or woe upon thy life!
IAGO: My noble lord—
OTHELLO: If thou dost slander her and torture me,
   Never pray more; abandon all remorse;°
   On horror's head horrors accumulate;
   Do deeds to make heaven weep, all earth amazed;
   For nothing canst thou to damnation add
   Greater than that.
IAGO: O grace! O heaven forgive me!
   Are you a man? Have you a soul or sense?—
   God b' wi' you! take mine office. O wretched fool,°
   That lov'st to make thine honesty a vice!°
   O monstrous world! Take note, take note, O world,
   To be direct and honest is not safe.
   I thank you for this profit;° and from hence°
   I'll love no friend, sith love breeds such offense.
OTHELLO: Nay, stay. Thou shouldst be honest.
IAGO: I should be wise; for honesty's a fool
   And loses that it works for.
OTHELLO: By the world,
   I think my wife be honest, and think she is not;
   I think that thou art just, and think thou art not.
   I'll have some proof. Her name, that was as fresh
   As Dian's° visage, is now begrimed and black
   As mine own face. If there be cords, or knives,
   Poison, or fire, or suffocating streams,
   I'll not endure it. Would I were satisfied!°
IAGO: I see, sir, you are eaten up with passion:
   I do repent me that I put it to you.
   You would be satisfied?
OTHELLO: Would? Nay, I will.
IAGO: And may; but how? how satisfied, my lord?
   Would you, the supervisor,° grossly gape on?
   Behold her topped?

---

365. probation: Proof. **369. remorse:** Penitence, hope of salvation. **375. O
wretched fool:** (Iago addressing himself). **376. make . . . vice:** Take honesty
too far. **379. profit:** Profitable lesson; **hence:** Henceforth. **387. Dian:** Diana,
goddess of the moon and of chastity. **390. satisfied:** Completely informed.
395. supervisor: Spectator.

OTHELLO: Death and damnation! O!
IAGO: It were a tedious difficulty, I think,
    To bring them to that prospect. Damn them then,
    If ever mortal eyes do see them bolster°
    More than their own! What then? How then?   400
    What shall I say? Where's satisfaction?
    It is impossible you should see this,
    Were they as prime° as goats, as hot as monkeys,
    As salt° as wolves in pride,° and fools as gross
    As ignorance made drunk. But yet, I say,   405
    If imputation and strong circumstances
    Which lead directly to the door of truth
    Will give you satisfaction, you may have't.
OTHELLO: Give me a living reason she's disloyal.
IAGO: I do not like the office.   410
    But sith I am ent'red in this cause so far,
    Pricked° to't by foolish honesty and love,
    I will go on. I lay with Cassio lately,
    And being troubled with a raging tooth,
    I could not sleep.   415
    There are a kind of men so loose of soul
    That in their sleeps will mutter their affairs.
    One of this kind is Cassio.
    In sleep I heard him say, "Sweet Desdemona,
    Let us be wary, let us hide our loves!"   420
    And then, sir, would he grip and wring my hand,
    Cry "O sweet creature!" and then kiss me hard,
    As if he plucked up kisses by the roots
    That grew upon my lips; then laid his leg
    Over my thigh, and sighed, and kissed, and then   425
    Cried "Cursèd fate that gave thee to the Moor!"
OTHELLO: O monstrous! monstrous!
IAGO: Nay, this was but his dream.
OTHELLO: But this denoted a foregone conclusion;°
    'Tis a shrewd doubt,° though it be but a dream.
IAGO: And this may help to thicken other proofs   430
    That do demonstrate thinly.
OTHELLO: I'll tear her all to pieces!
IAGO: Nay, but be wise. Yet we see nothing done;

399. bolster: Lie together.   403. prime: Lustful.   404. salt: Lecherous; pride:
Heat.   412. Pricked: Spurred.   428. foregone conclusion: Previous experience.
429. a shrewd doubt: Cursedly suspicious.

She may be honest yet. Tell me but this—
Have you not sometimes seen a handkerchief
Spotted with strawberries in your wife's hand?
OTHELLO: I gave her such a one; 'twas my first gift.
IAGO: I know not that; but such a handkerchief—
   I am sure it was your wife's—did I to-day
   See Cassio wipe his beard with.
OTHELLO: If it be that—
IAGO: If it be that, or any that was hers,
   It speaks against her with the other proofs.
OTHELLO: O, that the slave had forty thousand lives!
   One is too poor, too weak for my revenge.
   Now do I see 'tis true. Look here, Iago:
   All my fond love thus do I blow to heaven.
   'Tis gone.
   Arise, black vengeance, from the hollow hell!
   Yield up, O love, thy crown and hearted throne
   To tyrannous hate! Swell, bosom, with thy fraught,°
   For 'tis of aspics'° tongues!
IAGO: Yet be content.
OTHELLO: O, blood, blood, blood!
IAGO: Patience, I say. Your mind perhaps may change.
OTHELLO: Never, Iago. Like to the Pontic sea,°
   Whose icy current and compulsive course
   Ne'er feels retiring ebb, but keeps due on
   To the Propontic and the Hellespont,
   Even so my bloody thoughts, with violent pace,
   Shall ne'er look back, ne'er ebb to humble love,
   Till that a capable° and wide revenge
   Swallow them up.
   (*He kneels.*)   Now, by yond marble heaven,
   In the due reverence of a sacred vow
   I here engage my words.
IAGO: Do not rise yet.
(*Iago kneels.*)
   Witness, you ever-burning lights above,
   You elements that clip° us round about,
   Witness that here Iago doth give up
   The execution° of his wit,° hands, heart

---

449. fraught: Burden.   **450. aspics:** Deadly poisonous snakes.   **453. Pontic
sea:** Black Sea.   **459. capable:** All-embracing.   **464. clip:** Encompass.
466. execution: Activities; **wit:** Mind.

To wronged Othello's service! Let him command,
And to obey shall be in me remorse,°
What bloody business ever.°

[*They rise.*]

OTHELLO: I greet thy love,
   Not with vain thanks but with acceptance bounteous,   470
   And will upon the instant put thee to't.
   Within these three days let me hear thee say
   That Cassio's not alive.
IAGO: My friend is dead; 'tis done at your request.
   But let her live.   475
OTHELLO: Damn her, lewd minx!° O, damn her! damn her!
   Come, go with me apart. I will withdraw
   To furnish me with some swift means of death
   For the fair devil. Now art thou my lieutenant.
IAGO: I am your own forever.   (*Exeunt.*) 480

Scene IV

(*The environs of the castle.*)

(*Enter Desdemona, Emilia, and Clown.*)

DESDEMONA: Do you know, sirrah, where Lieutenant Cassio lies?°
CLOWN: I dare not say he lies anywhere.
DESDEMONA: Why, man?
CLOWN: He's a soldier, and for me to say a soldier lies is stabbing.
DESDEMONA: Go to. Where lodges he?   5
CLOWN: To tell you where he lodges is to tell you where I lie.
DESDEMONA: Can anything be made of this?
CLOWN: I know not where he lodges; and for me to devise a lodging, and
   say he lies here or he lies there, were to lie in mine own throat.
DESDEMONA: Can you enquire him out, and be edified by report?   10
CLOWN: I will catechize the world for him; that is, make questions, and
   by them answer.
DESDEMONA: Seek him, bid him come hither. Tell him I have moved° my
   lord on his behalf and hope all will be well.
CLOWN: To do this is within the compass of man's wit, and therefore I'll 15
   attempt the doing of it.   (*Exit.*)

468. remorse: Pity. 469. ever: Soever. 476. minx: Wanton. SCENE IV. 1. lies:
Lives, lodges. 13. moved: Made proposals to.

DESDEMONA: Where should I lose that handkerchief, Emilia?
EMILIA: I know not, madam.
DESDEMONA: Believe me, I had rather have lost my purse
  Full of crusadoes;° and but my noble Moor
  Is true of mind, and made of no such baseness
  As jealous creatures are, it were enough
  To put him to ill thinking.
EMILIA: Is he not jealous?
DESDEMONA: Who? he? I think the sun where he was born
  Drew all such humors° from him.

(*Enter Othello.*)

EMILIA: Look where he comes.
DESDEMONA: I will not leave him now till Cassio
  Be called to him—How is't with you, my lord?
OTHELLO: Well, my good lady. [*Aside.*] O, hardness to dissemble!—
  How do you, Desdemona?
DESDEMONA: Well, my good lord.
OTHELLO: Give me your hand. This hand is moist, my lady.
DESDEMONA: It yet hath felt no age nor known no sorrow.
OTHELLO: ˙This argues fruitfulness and liberal heart.
  Hot, hot, and moist. This hand of yours requires
  A sequester° from liberty, fasting and prayer,
  Much castigation, exercise devout;
  For here's a young and sweating devil here
  That commonly rebels. 'Tis a good hand,
  A frank one.
DESDEMONA: You may, indeed, say so;
  For 'twas that hand that gave away my heart.
OTHELLO: A liberal hand! The hearts of old gave hands;
  But our new heraldry° is hands, not hearts.
DESDEMONA: I cannot speak of this. Come now, your promise!
OTHELLO: What promise, chuck?
DESDEMONA: I have sent to bid Cassio come speak with you.
OTHELLO: I have a salt and sorry rheum° offends me.
  Lend me thy handkerchief.
DESDEMONA: Here, my lord.
OTHELLO: That which I gave you.
DESDEMONA: I have it not about me.
OTHELLO: Not?

---

20. crusadoes: Portuguese gold coins.   **25. humors:** Inclinations.   **34. seques-**
ter: Removal.   **42. heraldry:** Heraldic symbolism.   **46. salt . . . rheum:** Distressing head cold.

DESDEMONA: No, faith, my lord.
OTHELLO: That's a fault.
　　That handkerchief   50
　　Did an Egyptian° to my mother give.
　　She was a charmer,° and could almost read
　　The thoughts of people. She told her, while she kept it,
　　'Twould make her amiable° and subdue my father
　　Entirely to her love; but if she lost it   55
　　Or made a gift of it, my father's eye
　　Should hold her loathèd, and his spirits should hunt
　　After new fancies. She, dying, gave it me,
　　And bid me, when my fate would have me wive,
　　To give it her. I did so; and take heed on't;   60
　　Make it a darling like your precious eye.
　　To lose't or give't away were such perdition°
　　As nothing else could match.
DESDEMONA: Is't possible?
OTHELLO: 'Tis true. There's magic in the web of it.
　　A sibyl that had numb'red in the world   65
　　The sun to course two hundred compasses,°
　　In her prophetic fury sewed the work;
　　The worms were hallowed that did breed the silk;
　　And it was dyed in mummy° which the skillful
　　Conserved of maidens' hearts.
DESDEMONA: I' faith? Is't true?   70
OTHELLO: Most veritable. Therefore look to't well.
DESDEMONA: Then would to God that I had never seen't!
OTHELLO: Ha! Wherefore?
DESDEMONA: Why do you speak so startingly and rash?
OTHELLO: Is't lost? Is't gone? Speak, is it out o' th' way?   75
DESDEMONA: Heaven bless us!
OTHELLO: Say you?
DESDEMONA: It is not lost. But what an if it were?
OTHELLO: How?
DESDEMONA: I say it is not lost.
OTHELLO: Fetch't, let me see't!   80
DESDEMONA: Why, so I can, sir; but I will not now.
　　This is a trick to put° me from my suit:
　　Pray you let Cassio be received again.

---

51. Egyptian: Gypsy. **52. charmer:** Sorceress. **54. amiable:** Lovable.
62. perdition: Disaster. **66. compasses:** Annual rounds. **69. mummy:** A drug
made from mummies. **82. put:** Divert.

OTHELLO: Fetch me the handkerchief! My mind misgives.
DESDEMONA: Come, come!
  You'll never meet a more sufficient man.
OTHELLO: The handkerchief!
[DESDEMONA: I pray talk me of Cassio.
OTHELLO: The handkerchief!]
DESDEMONA: A man that all his time°
  Hath founded his good fortunes on your love,
  Shared dangers with you—
OTHELLO: The handkerchief!
DESDEMONA: I' faith, you are to blame.
OTHELLO: Zounds!   (*Exit Othello.*)
EMILIA: Is not this man jealous?
DESDEMONA: I ne'er saw this before.
  Sure there's some wonder in this handkerchief;
  I am most unhappy in the loss of it.
EMILIA: 'Tis not a year or two shows us a man.
  They are all but° stomachs, and we all but food;
  They eat us hungerly, and when they are full,   1
  They belch us.

(*Enter Iago and Cassio.*)

                 Look you—Cassio and my husband!
IAGO: There is no other way; 'tis she must do't.
  And lo the happiness!° Go and importune her.
DESDEMONA: How now, good Cassio? What's the news with you?
CASSIO: Madam, my former suit. I do beseech you   1
  That by your virtuous means I may again
  Exist, and be a member of his love
  Whom I with all the office° of my heart
  Entirely honor. I would not be delayed.
  If my offense be of such mortal° kind   1
  That neither service past, nor present sorrows,
  Nor purposed merit in futurity,
  Can ransom me into his love again,
  But to know so must be my benefit.
  So shall I clothe me in a forced content,   1
  And shut myself up in° some other course,
  To fortune's alms.
DESDEMONA: Alas, thrice-gentle Cassio!

---

88. all . . . time: During his whole career.   99. but: Nothing but.   103. happiness: Good luck.   108. office: Loyal service.   110. mortal: Fatal.   116. shut
myself up in: Confine myself to.

My advocation° is not now in tune.
My lord is not my lord; nor should I know him,
Were he in favor° as in humor altered.   120
So help me every spirit sanctified
As I have spoken for you all my best
And stood within the blank° of his displeasure
For my free speech! You must a while be patient.
What I can do I will; and more I will   125
Than for myself I dare. Let that suffice you.

IAGO: Is my lord angry?

EMILIA: He went hence but now,
And certainly in strange unquietness.

IAGO: Can he be angry? I have seen the cannon
When it hath blown his ranks into the air   130
And, like the devil, from his very arm
Puffed his own brother—and is he angry?
Something of moment then. I will go meet him.
There's matter in't indeed if he be angry.

DESDEMONA: I prithee do so.   (*Exit [Iago].*)
                          Something sure of state,°   135
Either from Venice or some unhatched practice°
Made demonstrable here in Cyprus to him,
Hath puddled° his clear spirit; and in such cases
Men's natures wrangle with inferior things,
Though great ones are their object. 'Tis even so;   140
For let our finger ache, and it endues°
Our other, healthful members even to a sense
Of pain. Nay, we must think men are not gods,
Nor of them look for such observancy°
As fits the bridal. Beshrew me much, Emilia,   145
I was, unhandsome warrior° as I am,
Arraigning his unkindness with my soul;°
But now I find I had suborned the witness,
And he's indicted falsely.

EMILIA: Pray heaven it be state matters, as you think,   150
And no conception nor no jealous toy°
Concerning you.

DESDEMONA: Alas the day! I never gave him cause.

---

118. advocation: Advocacy. 120. favor: Appearance. 123. blank: Bull's-eye of
the target. 135. state: Public affairs. 136. unhatched practice: Budding plot.
138. puddled: Muddied. 141. endues: Brings. 144. observancy: Attentive-
ness. 146. unhandsome warrior: Inadequate soldier. 147. Arraigning . . . soul:
Indicting his unkindness before the bar of my soul. 151. toy: Fancy.

EMILIA: But jealous souls will not be answered so;
    They are not ever jealous for the cause,
    But jealous for° they're jealous. 'Tis a monster
    Begot upon itself,° born on itself.
DESDEMONA: Heaven keep that monster from Othello's mind!
EMILIA: Lady, amen.
DESDEMONA: I will go seek him. Cassio, walk here about:
    If I do find him fit, I'll move your suit
    And seek to effect it to my uttermost.
CASSIO: I humbly thank your ladyship.

                                  (*Exeunt Desdemona and Emilia.*)

(*Enter Bianca.*)

BIANCA: Save° you, friend Cassio!
CASSIO: What make you from home?
    How is't with you, my most fair Bianca?
    I' faith, sweet love, I was coming to your house.
BIANCA: And I was going to your lodging, Cassio.
    What, keep a week away? seven days and nights?
    Eightscore eight hours? and lovers' absent hours,
    More tedious than the dial° eightscore times?
    O weary reck'ning!
CASSIO: Pardon me, Bianca:
    I have this while with leaden thoughts been pressed;
    But I shall in a more continuate° time
    Strike off this score° of absence. Sweet Bianca,

[*Gives her Desdemona's handkerchief.*]

    Take me this work out.°
BIANCA: O Cassio, whence came this?
    This is some token from a newer friend.
    To the felt absence now I feel a cause.
    Is't come to this? Well, well.
CASSIO: Go to, woman!
    Throw your vile guesses in the devil's teeth,
    From whence you have them. You are jealous now
    That this is from some mistress, some remembrance.
    No, by my faith, Bianca.
BIANCA: Why, whose is it?

---

156. for: Because. **157. Begot . . . itself:** Self-engendered. **164. Save:** God save. **170. dial:** Complete revolution of the clock (or sundial). **173. continuate:** Uninterrupted. **174. Strike . . . score:** Settle this account. **175. Take . . . out:** Copy this embroidery for me.

CASSIO: I know not, sweet; I found it in my chamber.
  I like the work° well; ere it be demanded,
  As like enough it will, I'd have it copied.   185
  Take it and do't, and leave me for this time.
BIANCA: Leave you? Wherefore?
CASSIO: I do attend here on the general
  And think it no addition,° nor my wish,
  To have him see me womaned.
BIANCA: Why, I pray you?   190
CASSIO: Not that I love you not.
BIANCA: But that you do not love me!
  I pray you bring me on the way a little,
  And say if I shall see you soon at night.
CASSIO: 'Tis but a little way that I can bring you,
  For I attend here; but I'll see you soon.   195
BIANCA: 'Tis very good. I must be circumstanced.°   (*Exeunt.*)

ACT IV   *Scene I*

(*The environs of the castle.*)

(*Enter Othello and Iago.*)

IAGO: Will you think so?
OTHELLO: Think so, Iago?
IAGO: What
  To kiss in private?
OTHELLO: An unauthorized kiss.
IAGO: Or to be naked with her friend in bed
  An hour or more, not meaning any harm?
OTHELLO: Naked in bed, Iago, and not mean harm?   5
  It is hypocrisy against the devil.°
  They that mean virtuously, and yet do so,
  The devil their virtue tempts, and they tempt heaven.
IAGO: So° they do nothing, 'tis a venial slip.
  But if I give my wife a handkerchief—   10
OTHELLO: What then?
IAGO: Why, then 'tis hers, my lord; and being hers,
  She may, I think, bestow't on any man.

---

184. work: Needlework. **189. addition:** (To my reputation). **196. circum-stanced:** Governed by circumstances. ACT IV, SCENE I. **6. hypocrisy . . . devil:** I.e., feigned sin instead of feigned virtue. **9. So:** So long as.

OTHELLO: She is protectress of her honor too;
  May she give that?
IAGO: Her honor is an essence that's not seen;
  They have it very oft that have it not.
  But for the handkerchief—
OTHELLO: By heaven, I would most gladly have forgot it!
  Thou said'st—O, it comes o'er my memory
  As doth the raven o'er the infected° house,
  Boding to all!—he had my handkerchief.
IAGO: Ay, what of that?
OTHELLO: That's not so good now.
IAGO: What
  If I had said I had seen him do you wrong?
  Or heard him say—as knaves be such abroad
  Who having, by their own importunate suit,
  Or voluntary dotage of some mistress,
  Convincèd or supplied° them, cannot choose
  But they must blab—
OTHELLO: Hath he said anything?
IAGO: He hath, my lord; but be you well assured,
  No more than he'll unswear.
OTHELLO: What hath he said?
IAGO: Faith, that he did—I know not what he did.
OTHELLO: What? what?
IAGO: Lie—
OTHELLO: With her?
IAGO: With her, on her; what you will.
OTHELLO: Lie with her? lie on her?—We say "lie on her" when they
  belie° her.—Lie with her! Zounds, that's fulsome.°—Handkerchief—
  confessions—handkerchief!—To confess, and be hanged for his
  labor—first to be hanged, and then to confess! I tremble at it. Nature
  would not invest herself in such shadowing passion without some instruction.° It is not words that shakes me thus.—Pish! Noses, ears,
  and lips? Is't possible?—Confess?—Handkerchief?—O devil!

(*Falls in a trance.*)

IAGO: Work on,
  My med'cine, work! Thus credulous fools are caught,
  And many worthy and chaste dames even thus,

---

21. infected: Plague-stricken.   **28. Convincèd or supplied:** Overcome or grati-
fied.   **36–37. belie:** Slander.   **37. fulsome:** Foul.   **39–41. Nature . . . instruction:**
My natural faculties would not be so overcome by passion without reason.

All guiltless, meet reproach.—What, ho! my lord!
My lord, I say! Othello!
(*Enter Cassio.*)   How now, Cassio?
CASSIO: What's the matter?
IAGO: My lord is fall'n into an epilepsy.
This is his second fit; he had one yesterday.   50
CASSIO: Rub him about the temples.
IAGO: No, forbear.
The lethargy° must have his quiet course.
If not, he foams at mouth, and by and by
Breaks out to savage madness. Look, he stirs.
Do you withdraw yourself a little while.   55
He will recover straight. When he is gone,
I would on great occasion speak with you.   [*Exit Cassio.*]
How is it, general? Have you not hurt your head?
OTHELLO: Dost thou mock me?
IAGO: I mock you? No, by heaven.
Would you would bear your fortune like a man!   60
OTHELLO: A hornèd man's° a monster and a beast.
IAGO: There's many a beast then in a populous city,
And many a civil° monster.
OTHELLO: Did he confess it?
IAGO: Good sir, be a man.
Think every bearded fellow that's but yoked   65
May draw with you. There's millions now alive
That nightly lie in those unproper° beds
Which they dare swear peculiar:° your case is better.
O, 'tis the spite of hell, the fiend's arch-mock,
To lip a wanton in a secure° couch,   70
And to suppose her chaste! No, let me know;
And knowing what I am, I know what she shall be.
OTHELLO: O, thou art wise! 'Tis certain.
IAGO: Stand you awhile apart;
Confine yourself but in a patient list.°
Whilst you were here, o'erwhelmèd with your grief—   75
A passion most unsuiting such a man—
Cassio came hither. I shifted him away
And laid good 'scuse upon your ecstasy;°

---

52. **lethargy:** Coma.   61. **hornèd man:** Cuckold.   63. **civil:** City-dwelling.
67. **unproper:** Not exclusively their own.   68. **peculiar:** Exclusively their own.
70. **secure:** Free from fear of rivalry   74. **in a patient list:** Within the limits of
self-control.   78. **ecstasy:** Trance.

Bade him anon return, and here speak with me;
The which he promised. Do but encave° yourself
And mark the fleers, the gibes, and notable scorns
That dwell in every region of his face;
For I will make him tell the tale anew—
Where, how, how oft, how long ago, and when
He hath, and is again to cope° your wife.
I say, but mark his gesture. Marry, patience!
Or I shall say y'are all in all in spleen,°
And nothing of a man.

OTHELLO: Dost thou hear, Iago?
I will be found most cunning in my patience;
But—dost thou hear?—most bloody.

IAGO: That's not amiss:
But yet keep time in all. Will you withdraw?

                                   [*Othello retires.*]

Now will I question Cassio of Bianca,
A huswife° that by selling her desires
Buys herself bread and clothes. It is a creature
That dotes on Cassio, as 'tis the strumpet's plague
To beguile many and be beguiled by one.
He, when he hears of her, cannot refrain
From the excess of laughter. Here he comes.

(*Enter Cassio.*)

As he shall smile, Othello shall go mad;
And his unbookish° jealousy must conster°
Poor Cassio's smiles, gestures, and light behavior
Quite in the wrong. How do you now, lieutenant?

CASSIO: The worser that you give me the addition°
Whose want even kills me.

IAGO: Ply Desdemona well, and you are sure on't.
Now, if this suit lay in Bianca's power,
How quickly should you speed!

CASSIO: Alas, poor caitiff!°

OTHELLO: Look how he laughs already!

IAGO: I never knew a woman love man so.

CASSIO: Alas, poor rogue! I think, i' faith, she loves me.

---

80. **encave:** Conceal. 85. **cope:** Meet. 87. **all in all in spleen:** Wholly overcome
by your passion. 93. **huswife:** Hussy. 100. **unbookish:** Uninstructed; **conster:**
Construe, interpret. 103. **addition:** Title. 107. **caitiff:** Wretch.

OTHELLO: Now he denies it faintly, and laughs it out.
IAGO: Do you hear, Cassio?
OTHELLO: Now he importunes him
  To tell it o'er. Go to! Well said, well said!
IAGO: She gives out that you shall marry her.
  Do you intend it?   115
CASSIO: Ha, ha, ha!
OTHELLO: Do you triumph, Roman? Do you triumph?
CASSIO: I marry her? What, a customer?° Prithee bear some charity to
  my wit;° do not think it so unwholesome.° Ha, ha, ha!
OTHELLO: So, so, so, so! They laugh that win!   120
IAGO: Faith, the cry goes that you shall marry her.
CASSIO: Prithee, say true.
IAGO: I am a very villain else.
OTHELLO: Have you scored me?° Well.
CASSIO: This is the monkey's own giving out. She is persuaded I will 125
  marry her out of her own love and flattery, not out of my promise.
OTHELLO: Iago beckons° me; now he begins the story.
CASSIO: She was here even now; she haunts me in every place. I was t'
  other day talking on the sea bank with certain Venetians, and thither
  comes the bauble,° and, by this hand, she falls me thus about my   130
  neck—
OTHELLO: Crying "O dear Cassio!" as it were. His gesture imports it.
CASSIO: So hangs, and lolls, and weeps upon me; so shakes and pulls me!
  Ha, ha, ha!
OTHELLO: Now he tells how she plucked him to my chamber. O, I see that 135
  nose of yours, but not that dog I shall throw it to.
CASSIO: Well, I must leave her company.

(*Enter Bianca.*)

IAGO: Before me!° Look where she comes.
CASSIO: 'Tis such another fitchew!° marry, a perfumed one. What do you
  mean by this haunting of me?   140
BIANCA: Let the devil and his dam haunt you! What did you mean by that
  same handkerchief you gave me even now? I was a fine fool to take it.
  I must take out the whole work? A likely piece of work that you should
  find it in your chamber and know not who left it there! This is some

---

118. customer: Prostitute.   118–19. bear . . . wit: Be more generous in assessing my intelligence.   119. unwholesome: Impaired, defective.   124. scored
me: Settled my account.   127. beckons: Signals.   130. bauble: Plaything.
138. Before me: By my soul.   139. fitchew: Polecat (slang for whore).

n, and I must take out the work? There! Give it your
.° Wheresoever you had it, I'll take out no work on't.
ow, my sweet Bianca? How now? how now?
.. ƆY neaven, that should be my handkerchief!

BIANCA: An° you'll come to supper to-night, you may; an you will not,
come when you are next prepared for.   (*Exit*.)

IAGO: After her, after her!

CASSIO: Faith, I must; she'll rail in the street else.

IAGO: Will you sup there?

CASSIO: Yes, I intend so.

IAGO: Well, I may chance to see you; for I would very fain speak with
you.

CASSIO: Prithee come. Will you?

IAGO: Go to! say no more.   (*Exit Cassio*.)

OTHELLO [*comes forward*]: How shall I murder him, Iago?

IAGO: Did you perceive how he laughed at his vice?°

OTHELLO: O Iago!

IAGO: And did you see the handkerchief?

OTHELLO: Was that mine?

IAGO: Yours, by this hand! And to see how he prizes° the foolish woman
your wife! She gave it him, and he hath giv'n it his whore.

OTHELLO: I would have him nine years a-killing—A fine woman! a fair
woman! a sweet woman!

IAGO: Nay, you must forget that.

OTHELLO: Ay, let her rot, and perish, and be damned to-night; for she
shall not live. No, my heart is turned to stone; I strike it, and it hurts
my hand. O, the world hath not a sweeter creature! She might lie by an
emperor's side and command him tasks.

IAGO: Nay, that's not your way.

OTHELLO: Hang her! I do but say what she is. So delicate with her needle!
an admirable musician! O, she will sing the savageness out of a bear!
Of so high and plenteous wit and invention°—

IAGO: She's the worse for all this.

OTHELLO: O, a thousand thousand times! And then, of so gentle a condition!°

IAGO: Ay, too gentle.°

OTHELLO: Nay, that's certain. But yet the pity of it, Iago! O Iago, the pity
of it, Iago!

145–46. **hobby-horse:** Harlot.   149. **An:** If.   160. **vice:** I.e., vicious conduct.
164. **prizes:** Values.   176. **invention:** Imagination.   178–79. **condition:** Disposition.   180. **gentle:** Generous.

IAGO: If you are so fond over her iniquity, give her patent° to offend; for
if it touch not you, it comes near nobody.

OTHELLO: I will chop her into messes!° Cuckold me!   185

IAGO: O, 'tis foul in her.

OTHELLO: With mine officer!

IAGO: That's fouler.

OTHELLO: Get me some poison, Iago, this night. I'll not expostulate with
her, lest her body and beauty unprovide° my mind again. This night, 190
Iago!

IAGO: Do it not with poison. Strangle her in her bed, even the bed she
hath contaminated.

OTHELLO: Good, good! The justice of it pleases. Very good!

IAGO: And for Cassio, let me be his undertaker;° you shall hear more by 195
midnight.

OTHELLO: Excellent good!

(*A trumpet.*)

What trumpet is that same?

IAGO: I warrant something from Venice.

(*Enter Lodovico, Desdemona, and Attendants.*)

                                        'Tis Lodovico.

This comes from the Duke; and see, your wife is with him.   200

LODOVICO: God save you, worthy general!

OTHELLO: With all my heart, sir.

LODOVICO: The Duke and senators of Venice greet you.

[*Gives him a letter.*]

OTHELLO: I kiss the instrument of their pleasures.

[*Opens the letter and reads.*]

DESDEMONA: And what's the news, good cousin Lodovico?

IAGO: I am very glad to see you, signior.   205
Welcome to Cyprus.

LODOVICO: I thank you. How does Lieutenant Cassio?

IAGO: Lives, sir.

DESDEMONA: Cousin, there's fall'n between him and my lord
An unkind° breach; but you shall make all well.

OTHELLO: Are you sure of that?   210

DESDEMONA: My lord?

---

183. patent: License.   185. messes: Small pieces.   190. unprovide: Disarm.
195. be his undertaker: Undertake to deal with him.   209. unkind: Unnatural.

OTHELLO [reads]: "This fail you not to do, as you will—"
LODOVICO: He did not call; he's busy in the paper.
   Is there division 'twixt thy lord and Cassio?
DESDEMONA: A most unhappy one. I would do much   21
   T' atone° them, for the love I bear to Cassio.
OTHELLO: Fire and brimstone!
DESDEMONA: My lord?
OTHELLO: Are you wise?
DESDEMONA: What, is he angry?
LODOVICO: May be the letter moved him;
   For, as I think, they do command him home,
   Deputing Cassio in his government.   22
DESDEMONA: By my troth, I am glad on't.
OTHELLO: Indeed?
DESDEMONA: My lord?
OTHELLO: I am glad to see you mad.°
DESDEMONA: Why, sweet Othello—
OTHELLO: Devil!

[*Strikes her.*]

DESDEMONA: I have not deserved this.
LODOVICO: My lord, this would not be believed in Venice,   22
   Though I should swear I saw't. 'Tis very much.
   Make her amends; she weeps.
OTHELLO: O devil, devil!
   If that the earth could teem° with woman's tears,
   Each drop she falls would prove a crocodile.°
   Out of my sight!
DESDEMONA: I will not stay to offend you.   [*Going.*] 23
LODOVICO: Truly, an obedient lady.
   I do beseech your lordship call her back.
OTHELLO: Mistress!
DESDEMONA: My lord?
OTHELLO: What would you with her, sir?
LODOVICO: Who? I, my lord?   23
OTHELLO: Ay! You did wish that I would make her turn.
   Sir, she can turn, and turn, and yet go on
   And turn again; and she can weep, sir, weep;
   And she's obedient; as you say, obedient,

---

216. atone: Reconcile. **222. mad:** I.e., waggish. **228. teem:** Breed.
229. crocodile: (Crocodiles were supposed to shed hypocritical tears to lure
men to destruction.)

Very obedient.—Proceed you in your tears.—   240
Concerning this, sir—O well-painted passion!°—
I am commanded home.—Get you away;
I'll send for you anon.—Sir, I obey the mandate
And will return to Venice.—Hence, avaunt!

                                        [*Exit Desdemona.*]

Cassio shall have my place. And, sir, to-night   245
I do entreat that we may sup together.
You are welcome, sir, to Cyprus—Goats and monkeys!

                                                        [*Exit.*]

LODOVICO: Is this the noble Moor whom our full Senate
    Call all in all sufficient? Is this the nature
    Whom passion could not shake? whose solid virtue   250
    The shot of accident nor dart of chance
    Could neither graze nor pierce?
IAGO: He is much changed.
LODOVICO: Are his wits safe? Is he not light of brain?
IAGO: He's that he is; I may not breathe my censure.
    What he might be—if what he might he is not—   255
    I would to heaven he were!
LODOVICO: What, strike his wife?
IAGO: Faith, that was not so well; yet would I knew
    That stroke would prove the worst!
LODOVICO: Is it his use?°
    Or did the letters work upon his blood°
    And new-create this fault?
IAGO: Alas, alas!   260
    It is not honesty in me to speak
    What I have seen and known. You shall observe him,
    And his own courses will denote° him so
    That I may save my speech. Do but go after
    And mark how he continues.   265
LODOVICO: I am sorry that I am deceived in him.   (*Exeunt.*)

                            Scene II

(*Within the castle.*)

(*Enter Othello and Emilia.*)

OTHELLO: You have seen nothing then?
EMILIA: Nor ever heard, nor ever did suspect.

---

241. passion: Grief. **258. use:** Custom. **259. blood:** Passions. **263. courses
will denote:** Actions will reveal.

OTHELLO: Yes, you have seen Cassio and she together.
EMILIA: But then I saw no harm, and then I heard
　Each syllable that breath made up between them.
OTHELLO: What, did they never whisper?
EMILIA: Never, my lord.
OTHELLO: Nor send you out o' th' way?
EMILIA: Never.
OTHELLO: To fetch her fan, her gloves, her mask, nor nothing?
EMILIA: Never, my lord.
OTHELLO: That's strange.
EMILIA: I durst, my lord, to wager she is honest,
　Lay down my soul at stake.° If you think other,
　Remove your thought; it doth abuse your bosom.°
　If any wretch have put this in your head,
　Let heaven requite it with the serpent's curse!°
　For if she be not honest, chaste, and true,
　There's no man happy; the purest of their wives
　Is foul as slander.
OTHELLO: Bid her come hither. Go.   (*Exit Emilia.*)
　She says enough; yet she's a simple bawd
　That cannot say as much.° This is a subtle whore,
　A closet lock and key of villainous secrets;
　And yet she'll kneel and pray; I seen her do't.

(*Enter Desdemona and Emilia.*)

DESDEMONA: My lord, what is your will?
OTHELLO: Pray, chuck, come hither.
DESDEMONA: What is your pleasure?
OTHELLO: Let me see your eyes.
　Look in my face.
DESDEMONA: What horrible fancy's this?
OTHELLO [*to Emilia*]: Some of your function, mistress.
　Leave procreants° alone and shut the door;
　Cough or cry hem if anybody come.
　Your mystery, your mystery!° Nay, dispatch!

(*Exit Emilia.*)

DESDEMONA: Upon my knees, what doth your speech import?
　I understand a fury in your words,
　[But not the words.]

SCENE II. **13. at stake:** As the wager. **14. abuse your bosom:** Deceive your heart.
16. serpent's curse: (cf. Genesis 3:14). **20–21. yet . . . much:** Yet any procuress
who couldn't make up as believable a story as this would have to be pretty stupid. **28. procreants:** Mating couples. **30. mystery:** Trade, occupation.

OTHELLO: Why, what art thou?
DESDEMONA: Your wife, my lord; your true
  And loyal wife.
OTHELLO: Come, swear it, damn thyself;   35
  Lest, being like one of heaven,° the devils themselves
  Should fear to seize thee. Therefore be double-damned—
  Swear thou art honest.°
DESDEMONA: Heaven doth truly know it.
OTHELLO: Heaven truly knows that thou art false as hell.
DESDEMONA: To whom, my lord? With whom? How am I false?   40
OTHELLO: Ah, Desdemona! away! away! away!
DESDEMONA: Alas the heavy day! Why do you weep?
  Am I the motive of these tears, my lord?
  If haply you my father do suspect
  An instrument° of this your calling back,   45
  Lay not your blame on me. If you have lost him,
  Why, I have lost him too.
OTHELLO: Had it pleased heaven
  To try me with affliction, had they rained
  All kinds of sores and shames on my bare head,
  Steeped me in poverty to the very lips,   50
  Given to captivity me and my utmost hopes,
  I should have found in some place of my soul
  A drop of patience. But, alas, to make me
  A fixèd figure for the time of scorn°
  To point his slow unmoving finger at!   55
  Yet could I bear that too; well, very well.
  But there where I have garnered up my heart,
  Where either I must live or bear no life,
  The fountain from the which my current runs
  Or else dries up—to be discarded thence,   60
  Or keep it as a cistern for foul toads
  To knot and gender in—turn thy complexion there,°
  Patience, thou young and rose-lipped cherubin!
  Ay, there look grim as hell!
DESDEMONA: I hope my noble lord esteems me honest.   65
OTHELLO: O, ay; as summer flies are in the shambles,°
  That quicken° even with blowing. O thou weed,

---

36. being . . . heaven: Looking like an angel. **38. honest:** Chaste. **45. An instrument:** To be the cause. **54. time of scorn:** Scornful world. **62. turn thy complexion there:** Change your color at that point. **66. shambles:** Slaughterhouse. **67. quicken:** Come to life.

Who art so lovely fair, and smell'st so sweet,
That the sense aches at thee, would thou hadst ne'er been born!
DESDEMONA: Alas, what ignorant sin have I committed?
OTHELLO: Was this fair paper, this most goodly book,
Made to write "whore" upon? What committed?
Committed? O thou public commoner!°
I should make very forges of my cheeks
That would to cinders burn up modesty,
Did I but speak thy deeds. What committed?
Heaven stops the nose at it, and the moon winks;°
The bawdy wind, that kisses all it meets,
Is hushed within the hollow mine of earth
And will not hear it. What committed?
Impudent strumpet!
DESDEMONA: By heaven, you do me wrong!
OTHELLO: Are not you a strumpet?
DESDEMONA: No, as I am a Christian!
If to preserve this vessel for my lord
From any other foul unlawful touch
Be not to be a strumpet, I am none.
OTHELLO: What, not a whore?
DESDEMONA: No, as I shall be saved!
OTHELLO: Is't possible?
DESDEMONA: O, heaven forgive us!
OTHELLO: I cry you mercy° then.
I took you for that cunning whore of Venice
That married with Othello.—[*Calling.*] You, mistress,
That have the office opposite to Saint Peter
And keep the gate of hell!

(*Enter Emilia.*)

                    You, you, ay, you!
We have done our course; there's money for your pains:
I pray you turn the key, and keep our counsel.
EMILIA: Alas, what does this gentleman conceive?
How do you, madam? How do you, my good lady?
DESDEMONA: Faith, half asleep.°
EMILIA: Good madam, what's the matter with my lord?
DESDEMONA: With who?
EMILIA: Why, with my lord, madam.

---

73. commoner: Harlot.   77. winks: Closes her eyes.   88. cry you mercy: Beg
your pardon.   97. half asleep: I.e., stunned.

DESDEMONA: Who is thy lord?
EMILIA: He that is yours, sweet lady.
DESDEMONA: I have none. Do not talk to me, Emilia.
 I cannot weep; nor answer have I none
 But what should go by water. Prithee to-night
 Lay on my bed my wedding sheets, remember;   105
 And call thy husband hither.
EMILIA: Here's a change indeed!   (*Exit.*)
DESDEMONA: 'Tis meet° I should be used so, very meet.
 How have I been behaved, that he might stick
 The small'st opinion° on my least misuse?°

(*Enter Iago and Emilia.*)

IAGO: What is your pleasure, madam? How is't with you?   110
DESDEMONA: I cannot tell. Those that do teach young babes
 Do it with gentle means and easy tasks:
 He might have chid me so; for, in good faith,
 I am a child to chiding.
IAGO: What is the matter, lady?
EMILIA: Alas, Iago, my lord hath so bewhored her,   115
 Thrown such despite and heavy terms upon her
 As true hearts cannot bear.
DESDEMONA: Am I that name, Iago?
IAGO: What name, fair lady?
DESDEMONA: Such as she said my lord did say I was.
EMILIA: He called her whore. A beggar in his drink   120
 Could not have laid such terms upon his callet.°
IAGO: Why did he so?
DESDEMONA: I do not know; I am sure I am none such.
IAGO: Do not weep, do not weep. Alas the day!
EMILIA: Hath she forsook so many noble matches,   125
 Her father and her country, and her friends,
 To be called whore? Would it not make one weep?
DESDEMONA: It is my wretched fortune.
IAGO: Beshrew him for't!
 How comes this trick° upon him?
DESDEMONA: Nay, heaven doth know.
EMILIA: I will be hanged if some eternal villain,   130
 Some busy and insinuating° rogue,

---

107. **meet:** Fitting.   109. **small'st opinion:** Least suspicion; **least misuse:**
Slightest misconduct.   121. **callet:** Whore.   129. **trick:** Freakish behavior.
131. **insinuating:** Ingratiating.

Some cogging, cozening° slave, to get some office,
Have not devised this slander. I'll be hanged else.
IAGO: Fie, there is no such man! It is impossible.
DESDEMONA: If any such there be, heaven pardon him!   13
EMILIA: A halter° pardon him! and hell gnaw his bones!
  Why should he call her whore? Who keeps her company?
  What place? what time? what form? what likelihood?
  The Moor 's abused by some most villainous knave,
  Some base notorious knave, some scurvy fellow.   14
  O heaven, that such companions° thou 'dst unfold,°
  And put in every honest hand a whip
  To lash the rascals naked through the world
  Even from the east to th' west!
IAGO: Speak within door.°
EMILIA: O, fie upon them! Some such squire he was   14
  That turned your wit the seamy side without
  And made you to suspect me with the Moor.
IAGO: You are a fool. Go to.
DESDEMONA: Alas, Iago,
  What shall I do to win my lord again?
  Good friend, go to him; for, by this light of heaven,   15
  I know not how I lost him. Here I kneel:
  If e'er my will did trespass 'gainst his love
  Either in discourse° of thought or actual deed,
  Or that° mine eyes, mine ears, or any sense
  Delighted them in any other form,   15
  Or that I do not yet,° and ever did,
  And ever will (though he do shake me off
  To beggarly divorcement) love him dearly,
  Comfort forswear° me! Unkindness may do much;
  And his unkindness may defeat° my life,   16
  But never taint my love. I cannot say "whore."
  It does abhor me now I speak the word;
  To do the act that might the addition° earn
  Not the world's mass of vanity° could make me.
IAGO: I pray you be content. 'Tis but his humor.   16
  The business of the state does him offense,
  [And he does chide with you.]

---

132. **cogging, cozening:** Cheating, defrauding.   136. **halter:** Hangman's noose.
141. **companions:** Rogues; **unfold:** Expose.   144. **within door:** With restraint.
153. **discourse:** Course.   154. **that:** If.   156. **yet:** Still.   159. **Comfort forswear:**
May happiness forsake.   160. **defeat:** Destroy.   163. **addition:** Title.   164. **vanity:** Showy riches.

DESDEMONA: If 'twere no other—
IAGO: 'Tis but so, I warrant.

[*Trumpets within.*]

Hark how these instruments summon you to supper.
The messengers of Venice stay the meat: 170
Go in, and weep not. All things shall be well.
                              (*Exeunt Desdemona and Emilia.*)

(*Enter Roderigo.*)

How now, Roderigo?
RODERIGO: I do not find that thou deal'st justly with me.
IAGO: What in the contrary?
RODERIGO: Every day thou daff'st me with some device,° Iago, and rather, 175
    as it seems to me now, keep'st from me all conveniency° than suppliest
    me with the least advantage° of hope. I will indeed no longer endure it;
    nor am I yet persuaded to put up° in peace what already I have fool-
    ishly suffered.
IAGO: Will you hear me, Roderigo?   180
RODERIGO: Faith, I have heard too much; for your words and perfor-
    mances are no kin together.
IAGO: You charge me most unjustly.
RODERIGO: With naught but truth. I have wasted myself out of my means.
    The jewels you have had from me to deliver to Desdemona would half 185
    have corrupted a votarist.° You have told me she hath received them,
    and returned me expectations and comforts of sudden respect° and
    acquaintance; but I find none.
IAGO: Well, go to; very well.
RODERIGO: Very well! go to! I cannot go to, man; nor 'tis not very well. By 190
    this hand, I say 'tis very scurvy, and begin to find myself fopped° in it.
IAGO: Very well.
RODERIGO: I tell you 'tis not very well. I will make myself known to Des-
    demona. If she will return me my jewels, I will give over my suit and
    repent my unlawful solicitation; if not, assure yourself I will seek sat- 195
    isfaction of you.
IAGO: You have said now.
RODERIGO: Ay, and said nothing but what I protest intendment° of doing.
IAGO: Why, now I see there's mettle in thee; and even from this instant do
    build on thee a better opinion than ever before. Give me thy hand, 200

---

175. thou . . . device: You put me off with some trick.   176. conveniency: Favorable opportunities.   177. advantage: Increase.   178. put up: Tolerate.
186. votarist: Nun.   187. sudden respect: Immediate notice.   191. fopped:
Duped.   198. protest intendment: Declare my intention.

Roderigo. Thou has taken against me a most just exception; but yet I protest I have dealt most directly° in thy affair.

RODERIGO: It hath not appeared.

IAGO: I grant indeed it hath not appeared, and your suspicion is not without wit and judgment. But, Roderigo, if thou hast that in thee indeed   20
which I have greater reason to believe now than ever, I mean purpose, courage, and valor, this night show it. If thou the next night following enjoy not Desdemona, take me from this world with treachery and devise engines for° my life.

RODERIGO: Well, what is it? Is it within reason and compass?   21

IAGO: Sir, there is especial commission come from Venice to depute Cassio in Othello's place.

RODERIGO: Is that true? Why, then Othello and Desdemona return again to Venice.

IAGO: O, no; he goes into Mauritania and takes away with him the fair   21
Desdemona, unless his abode be lingered here° by some accident; wherein none can be so determinate° as the removing of Cassio.

RODERIGO: How do you mean removing of him?

IAGO: Why, by making him uncapable of Othello's place—knocking out his brains.   22

RODERIGO: And that you would have me to do?

IAGO: Ay, if you dare do yourself a profit and a right. He sups to-night with a harlotry, and thither will I go to him. He knows not yet of his honorable fortune. If you will watch his going thence, which I will fashion to fall out° between twelve and one, you may take him at your   22
pleasure. I will be near to second your attempt, and he shall fall between us. Come, stand not amazed at it, but go along with me. I will show you such a necessity in his death that you shall think yourself bound to put it on him. It is now high supper time, and the night grows to waste. About it!   23

RODERIGO: I will hear further reason for this.

IAGO: And you shall be satisfied.   (*Exeunt.*)

Scene III

(*Within the castle.*)

(*Enter Othello, Lodovico, Desdemona, Emilia, and Attendants.*)

LODOVICO: I do beseech you, sir, trouble yourself no further.

---

202. directly: Straightforwardly.   **209. engines for:** Plots against.
216. abode . . . here: Stay here be extended.   **217. determinate:** Effective.
225. fall out: Occur.

OTHELLO: O, pardon me; 'twill do me good to walk.
LODOVICO: Madam, good night. I humbly thank your ladyship.
DESDEMONA: Your honor is most welcome.
OTHELLO: Will you walk, sir?
  O, Desdemona—   5
DESDEMONA: My lord?
OTHELLO: Get you to bed on th' instant; I will be returned forthwith.
  Dismiss your attendant there. Look't be done.
DESDEMONA: I will, my lord.

            (*Exit [Othello, with Lodovico and Attendants]*.)

EMILIA: How goes it now? He looks gentler than he did.   10
DESDEMONA: He says he will return incontinent.°
  He hath commanded me to go to bed,
  And bade me to dismiss you.
EMILIA: Dismiss me?
DESDEMONA: It was his bidding; therefore, good Emilia,
  Give me my nightly wearing, and adieu.   15
  We must not now displease him.
EMILIA: I would you had never seen him!
DESDEMONA: So would not I. My love doth so approve him
  That even his stubbornness,° his checks,° his frowns—
  Prithee unpin me—have grace and favor in them.   20
EMILIA: I have laid those sheets you bade me on the bed.
DESDEMONA: All's one.° Good faith, how foolish are our minds!
  If I do die before thee, prithee shroud me
  In one of those same sheets.
EMILIA: Come, come! You talk.°
DESDEMONA: My mother had a maid called Barbary.   25
  She was in love; and he she loved proved mad°
  And did forsake her. She had a song of "Willow";
  An old thing 'twas; but it expressed her fortune,
  And she died singing it. That song to-night
  Will not go from my mind; I have much to do   30
  But to go hang° my head all at one side
  And sing it like poor Barbary. Prithee dispatch.
EMILIA: Shall I go fetch your nightgown?°
DESDEMONA: No, unpin me here.
  This Lodovico is a proper man.

SCENE III. **11. incontinent**: At once. **19. stubbornness**: Roughness; **checks**:
Rebukes. **22. All's one**: It doesn't matter. **24. talk**: Prattle. **26. mad**: Wild,
faithless. **30–31. I . . . hang**: I can hardly keep from hanging. **33. nightgown**:
Dressing gown.

EMILIA: A very handsome man.

DESDEMONA: He speaks well.

EMILIA: I know a lady in Venice would have walked barefoot to Palestine for a touch of his nether lip.

DESDEMONA (*sings*): "The poor soul sat sighing by a sycamore tree
    Sing all a green willow;
  Her hand on her bosom, her head on her knee,
    Sing willow, willow, willow.
  The fresh streams ran by her and murmured her moans;
    Sing willow, willow, willow;
  Her salt tears fell from her, and soft'ned the stones"—
Lay by these.
    "Sing willow, willow, willow"—
Prithee hie thee;° he'll come anon.
    "Sing all a green willow must be my garland.
  Let nobody blame him; his scorn I approve"—
Nay, that's not next. Hark! who is't that knocks?

EMILIA: It's the wind.

DESDEMONA (*sings*): "I called my love false love; but what said he then?
    Sing willow, willow, willow:
  If I court moe women, you'll couch with moe men."
So get thee gone; good night. Mine eyes do itch.
Doth that bode weeping?

EMILIA: 'Tis neither here nor there.

DESDEMONA: I have heard it said so. O, these men, these men!
Dost thou in conscience think—tell me, Emilia—
That there be women do abuse their husbands
In such gross kind?

EMILIA: There be some such, no question.

DESDEMONA: Wouldst thou do such a deed for all the world?

EMILIA: Why, would not you?

DESDEMONA: No, by this heavenly light!

EMILIA: Nor I neither by this heavenly light.
I might do't as well i' th' dark.

DESDEMONA: Wouldst thou do such a deed for all the world?

EMILIA: The world's a huge thing; it is a great price for a small vice.

DESDEMONA: In troth, I think thou wouldst not.

EMILIA: In troth, I think I should; and undo't when I had done it. Marry, I would not do such a thing for a joint-ring,° nor for measures of lawn, nor for gowns, petticoats, nor caps, nor any petty exhibition;° but, for all the whole world—'Ud's pity! who would not make her

---

48. hie thee: Hurry.   70. joint-ring: Ring made in separable halves.
71. exhibition: Gift.

husband a cuckold to make him a monarch? I should venture purgatory
for't.

DESDEMONA: Beshrew me if I would do such a wrong   75
    For the whole world.

EMILIA: Why, the wrong is but a wrong i' th' world; and having the world
    for your labor, 'tis a wrong in your own world, and you might quickly
    make it right.

DESDEMONA: I do not think there is any such woman.   80

EMILIA: Yes, a dozen; and as many to th' vantage° as
    would store° the world they played for.
    But I do think it is their husbands' faults
    If wives do fall. Say that they slack their duties
    And pour our treasures into foreign laps;°   85
    Or else break out in peevish° jealousies
    Throwing restraint upon us; or say they strike us,
    Or scant our former having° in despite—
    Why, we have galls;° and though we have some grace,
    Yet have we some revenge. Let husbands know   90
    Their wives have sense like them. They see, and smell,
    And have their palates both for sweet and sour,
    As husbands have. What is it that they do
    When they change us for others? Is it sport?
    I think it is. And doth affection breed it?   95
    I think it doth. Is't frailty that thus errs?
    It is so too. And have not we affections,
    Desires for sport, and frailty, as men have?
    Then let them use us well; else let them know,
    The ills we do, their ills instruct us so.   100

DESDEMONA: Good night, good night. God me such usage° send,
    Not to pick bad from bad, but by bad mend!°   (*Exeunt.*)

ACT V   *Scene I*

(*A street in Cyprus.*)

(*Enter Iago and Roderigo.*)

81. to th' vantage: Besides.   82. store: Populate.   84–85. slack . . . laps: Are
unfaithful.   86. peevish: Senseless.   88. having: Allowance.   89. galls: Spirits
to resent.   101. usage: Habits.   102. Not . . . mend: As not to learn bad ways
from others' badness, but to mend my ways by learning what evil is.

IAGO: Here, stand behind this bulk;° straight will he come.
  Wear thy good rapier bare, and put it home.
  Quick, quick! Fear nothing; I'll be at thy elbow.
  It makes us, or it mars us—think on that,
  And fix most firm thy resolution.
RODERIGO: Be near at hand; I may miscarry in't.
IAGO: Here, at thy hand. Be bold, and take thy stand.

[*Stands aside.*]

RODERIGO: I have no great devotion to the deed,
  And yet he hath given me satisfying reasons.
  'Tis but a man gone. Forth my sword! He dies!   1
IAGO: I have rubbed this young quat° almost to the sense,°
  And he grows angry. Now whether he kill Cassio,
  Or Cassio him, or each do kill the other,
  Every way makes my gain. Live Roderigo,
  He calls me to a restitution large   1
  Of gold and jewels that I bobbed° from him
  As gifts to Desdemona.
  It must not be. If Cassio do remain,
  He hath a daily beauty in his life
  That makes me ugly; and besides, the Moor   2
  May unfold me to him; there stand I in much peril.
  No, he must die. Be't so! I hear him coming.

(*Enter Cassio.*)

RODERIGO: I know his gait. 'Tis he. Villain, thou diest!

[*Makes a pass at Cassio.*]

CASSIO: That thrust had been mine enemy indeed
  But that my coat° is better than thou know'st.   2
  I will make proof° of thine.

[*Draws, and wounds Roderigo.*]

RODERIGO: O, I am slain!

[*Iago darts from concealment behind Cassio, wounds him in the leg, and exits.*]

CASSIO: I am maimed for ever. Help, ho! Murder! murder!

[*Falls.*]

(*Enter Othello.*)

ACT V, SCENE I.   **1. bulk:** Projecting shop-front.   **11. quat:** Pimple; **sense:** Quick.
16. bobbed: Swindled.   **25. coat:** Undershirt of mail.   **26. proof:** A test.

OTHELLO: The voice of Cassio. Iago keeps his word.
RODERIGO: O, villain that I am!
OTHELLO: It is even so.
CASSIO: O, help, ho! light! a surgeon!   30
OTHELLO: 'Tis he. O brave Iago, honest and just,
 That hast such noble sense of thy friend's wrong!
 Thou teachest me. Minion,° your dear lies dead,
 And your unblest fate hies.° Strumpet, I come.
 Forth of my heart those charms, thine eyes, are blotted.   35
 Thy bed, lust-stained, shall with lust's blood be spotted.

           (*Exit Othello.*)

(*Enter Lodovico and Gratiano.*)

CASSIO: What, ho? No watch? No passage?° Murder! murder!
GRATIANO: 'Tis some mischance. The cry is very direful.
CASSIO: O, help!
LODOVICO: Hark!   40
RODERIGO: O wretched villain!
LODOVICO: Two or three groan. It is a heavy° night.
 These may be counterfeits. Let's think't unsafe
 To come in to the cry without more help.
RODERIGO: Nobody come? Then shall I bleed to death.   45
LODOVICO: Hark!

(*Enter Iago, with a light.*)

GRATIANO: Here's one comes in his shirt, with light and weapons.
IAGO: Who's there? Whose noise is this that cries on° murder?
LODOVICO: We do not know.
IAGO: Did not you hear a cry?
CASSIO: Here, here! For heaven's sake, help me!
IAGO: What's the matter?   50
GRATIANO: This is Othello's ancient, as I take it.
LODOVICO: The same indeed, a very valiant fellow.
IAGO: What are you here that cry so grievously?
CASSIO: Iago? O, I am spoiled, undone by villains!
 Give me some help.   55
IAGO: O me, lieutenant! What villains have done this?
CASSIO: I think that one of them is hereabout
 And cannot make° away.
IAGO: O treacherous villains!

---

33. Minion: Mistress (Desdemona). **34. hies:** Hurries on. **37. passage:** Passersby. **42. heavy:** Cloudy, dark. **48. cries on:** Raises the cry of. **58. make:** Get.

[*To Lodovico and Gratiano.*]

    What are you there? Come in, and give some help.
RODERIGO: O, help me here!
CASSIO: That's one of them.
IAGO: O murd'rous slave! O villain!

[*Stabs Roderigo.*]

RODERIGO: O damned Iago! O inhuman dog!
IAGO: Kill men i' th' dark?—Where be these bloody thieves?—
   How silent is this town!—Ho! murder! murder!—
   What may you be? Are you of good or evil?
LODOVICO: As you shall prove us, praise us.
IAGO: Signior Lodovico?
LODOVICO: He, sir.
IAGO: I cry you mercy.° Here's Cassio hurt by villains.
GRATIANO: Cassio?
IAGO: How is't, brother?
CASSIO: My leg is cut in two.
IAGO: Marry,° heaven forbid!
   Light, gentlemen. I'll bind it with my shirt.

(*Enter Bianca.*)

BIANCA: What is the matter, ho? Who is't that cried?
IAGO: Who is't that cried?
BIANCA: O my dear Cassio! my sweet Cassio!
   O Cassio, Cassio, Cassio!
IAGO: O notable strumpet!—Cassio, may you suspect
   Who they should be that have thus mangled you?
CASSIO: No.
GRATIANO: I am sorry to find you thus. I have been to seek you.
IAGO: Lend me a garter. So. O for a chair°
   To bear him easily hence!
BIANCA: Alas, he faints! O Cassio, Cassio, Cassio!
IAGO: Gentlemen all, I do suspect this trash
   To be a party in this injury.—
   Patience a while, good Cassio.—Come, come!
   Lend me a light. Know we this face or no?
   Alas, my friend and my dear countryman
   Roderigo? No—Yes, sure.—O heaven, Roderigo!
GRATIANO: What, of Venice?

---

69. I . . . mercy: I beg your pardon. **72. Marry:** (From "By Mary"). **82. chair:**
Litter (an enclosed seat carried on poles by two bearers).

IAGO: Even he, sir. Did you know him?
GRATIANO: Know him? Ay.
IAGO: Signior Gratiano? I cry your gentle° pardon.
  These bloody accidents° must excuse my manners
  That so neglected you.
GRATIANO: I am glad to see you.   95
IAGO: How do you, Cassio?—O, a chair, a chair!
GRATIANO: Roderigo?
IAGO: He, he, 'tis he!

[A chair brought in.]

  O, that's well said;° the chair.
  Some good man bear him carefully from hence.   100
  I'll fetch the general's surgeon. [To Bianca.] For you, mistress,
  Save you your labor.—He that lies slain here, Cassio,
  Was my dear friend. What malice was between you?
CASSIO: None in the world; nor do I know the man.
IAGO [To Bianca]: What, look you pale?—O, bear him out o' th' air.   105

                    [Cassio and Roderigo are borne off.]

  Stay you, good gentlemen.—Look you pale, mistress?—
  Do you perceive the gastness° of her eye?—
  Nay, if you stare, we shall hear more anon.
  Behold her well; I pray you look upon her.
  Do you see, gentlemen? Nay, guiltiness will speak.   110
  Though tongues were out of use.

(Enter Emilia.)

EMILIA: 'Las, what's the matter? What's the matter, husband?
IAGO: Cassio hath here been set on in the dark
  By Roderigo, and fellows that are scaped.
  He's almost slain, and Roderigo dead.   115
EMILIA: Alas, good gentlemen! alas, good Cassio!
IAGO: This is the fruits of whoring. Prithee, Emilia,
  Go know of° Cassio where he supped to-night.

[To Bianca.]

  What, do you shake at that?
BIANCA: He supped at my house; but I therefore shake not.   120
IAGO: O, did he so? I charge you go with me.
EMILIA: Fie, fie upon thee, strumpet!

93. gentle: Noble.   94. accidents: Sudden events.   99. well said: Well done.
107. gastness: Terror.   118. know of: Learn from.

BIANCA: I am no strumpet, but of life as honest°
  As you that thus abuse me.
EMILIA: As I? Foh! fie upon thee!
IAGO: Kind gentlemen, let's go see poor Cassio dressed.°   1

[*To Bianca.*]

  Come, mistress, you must tell 's another tale.
  Emilia, run you to the citadel
  And tell my lord and lady what hath happed.

                                                        [*Exit Emilia.*]
  Will you go on afore?   (*Exeunt [all but Iago].*)
            This is the night
  That either makes me or fordoes° me quite.   [*Exit.*] 1

Scene II

(*A bedchamber in the castle.*)

(*Desdemona [asleep] in her bed. Enter Othello with a light.*)

OTHELLO: It is the cause, it is the cause,° my soul.
  Let me not name it to you, you chaste stars!
  It is the cause. Yet I'll not shed her blood,
  Nor scar that whiter skin of hers than snow,
  And smooth as monumental alabaster.°
  Yet she must die, else she'll betray more men.
  Put out the light, and then put out the light.
  If I quench thee, thou flaming minister,°
  I can again thy former light restore,
  Should I repent me;° but once put out thy light,
  Thou cunning'st pattern° of excelling nature,
  I know not where is that Promethean heat°
  That can thy light relume.° When I have plucked the rose,
  I cannot give it vital growth again;
  It needs must wither. I'll smell thee on the tree.

(*He kisses her.*)

  O balmy breath, that dost almost persuade
  Justice to break her sword! One more, one more!

123. honest: Chaste.   125. Cassio dressed: Cassio's wounds dressed.   130. for-
does: Destroys.   SCENE II.   1. cause: Cause of justice.   5. monumental alabaster: Alabaster stone used for tombs and monuments.   8. minister: Servant.
10. repent me: Change my mind.   11. cunning'st pattern: Skillfully wrought
example.   12. Promethean heat: Divine fire.   13. relume: Relight.

Be thus when thou art dead, and I will kill thee,
And love thee after. One more, and that's the last!
So sweet was ne'er so fatal. I must weep,   20
But they are cruel tears. This sorrow's heavenly;
It strikes where it doth love. She wakes.
DESDEMONA: Who's there? Othello?
OTHELLO: Ay, Desdemona.
DESDEMONA: Will you come to bed, my lord?
OTHELLO: Have you prayed to-night, Desdemon?
DESDEMONA: Ay, my lord.   25
OTHELLO: If you bethink yourself of any crime°
   Unreconciled as yet to heaven and grace,
   Solicit° for it straight.
DESDEMONA: Alack, my lord, what may you mean by that?
OTHELLO: Well, do it, and be brief; I will walk by.   30
   I would not kill thy unpreparèd spirit.
   No, heaven forfend!° I would not kill thy soul.
DESDEMONA: Talk you of killing?
OTHELLO: Ay, I do.
DESDEMONA: Then heaven
   Have mercy on me!
OTHELLO: Amen, with all my heart!
DESDEMONA: If you say so, I hope you will not kill me.   35
OTHELLO: Hum!
DESDEMONA: And yet I fear you; for you're fatal then
   When your eyes roll so. Why I should fear I know not,
   Since guiltiness I know not; but yet I feel I fear.
OTHELLO: Think on thy sins.
DESDEMONA: They are loves I bear to you.   40
OTHELLO: Ay, and for that thou diest.
DESDEMONA: That death's unnatural that kills for loving.
   Alas, why gnaw you so your nether lip?
   Some bloody passion shakes your very frame.
   These are portents,° but yet I hope, I hope,   45
   They do not point on me.
OTHELLO: Peace and be still!
DESDEMONA: I will so. What's the matter?
OTHELLO: That handkerchief which I so loved and gave thee
   Thou gav'st to Cassio.
DESDEMONA: No, by my life and soul!
   Send for the man and ask him.

26. crime: Sin. **28. Solicit:** Pray. **32. forfend:** Forbid. **45. portents:** Signs
of impending violence.

OTHELLO: Sweet soul, take heed,
  Take heed of perjury; thou art on thy deathbed.
DESDEMONA: Ay, but not yet to die.
OTHELLO: Yes, presently.°
  Therefore confess thee freely of thy sin;
  For to deny each article with oath
  Cannot remove nor choke the strong conception°
  That I do groan withal. Thou art to die.
DESDEMONA: Then Lord have mercy on me!
OTHELLO: I say amen.
DESDEMONA: And have you mercy too! I never did
  Offend° you in my life; never loved Cassio
  But with such general warranty of heaven
  As I might love. I never gave him token.
OTHELLO: By heaven, I saw my handkerchief in's hand!
  O perjured woman! thou dost stone my heart,°
  And mak'st me call what I intend to do
  A murder, which I thought a sacrifice.
  I saw the handkerchief.
DESDEMONA: He found it then.
  I never gave it him. Send for him hither.
  Let him confess a truth.
OTHELLO: He hath confessed.
DESDEMONA: What, my lord?
OTHELLO: That he hath used thee.
DESDEMONA: How? Unlawfully?
OTHELLO: Ay.
DESDEMONA: He will not say so.
OTHELLO: No, his mouth is stopped.
  Honest Iago hath ta'en order° for't.
DESDEMONA: O, my fear interprets. What, is he dead?
OTHELLO: Had all his hairs been lives, my great revenge
  Had stomach for them all.
DESDEMONA: Alas, he is betrayed, and I undone!   [*She weeps.*]
OTHELLO: Out, strumpet! Weep'st thou for him to my face?
DESDEMONA: O, banish me, my lord, but kill me not!
OTHELLO: Down, strumpet!
DESDEMONA: Kill me to-morrow; let me live to-night!
OTHELLO: Nay, if you strive—
DESDEMONA: But half an hour!

---

52. presently: At once. **55. conception:** Belief. **59. Offend:** Wrong. **63. stone my heart:** Turn my heart to stone. **72. ta'en order:** Taken measures.

OTHELLO: Being done, there is no pause.
DESDEMONA: But while I say one prayer!
OTHELLO: It is too late.

(*Smothers her.*)

  [DESDEMONA: O Lord, Lord, Lord!]

(*Emilia at the door.*)

EMILIA (*calls within*): My lord, my lord! What, ho! my lord, my lord!   85
OTHELLO: What noise is this? Not dead? not yet quite dead?
   I that am cruel am yet merciful;
   I would not have thee linger in thy pain.
   So, so.
EMILIA (*within*): What, ho! my lord, my lord!
OTHELLO: Who's there?   90
EMILIA (*within*): O, good my lord, I would speak a word with you!
OTHELLO: Yes, 'tis Emilia.—By and by.°—She's dead.—
   'Tis like° she comes to speak of Cassio's death.
   The noise was here. Ha! no more moving?
   Still as the grave.—Shall she come in? Were't good!—   95
   I think she stirs again. No.—What's best to do?
   If she come in, she'll sure speak to my wife.
   My wife! my wife! what wife? I have no wife.
   O, insupportable! O heavy hour!
   Methinks it should be now a huge eclipse   100
   Of sun and moon, and that th' affrighted globe
   Should yawn° at alteration.
EMILIA (*within*):   I do beseech you
   That I may speak with you, O good my lord!
OTHELLO: I had forgot thee. O, come in, Emilia.
   Soft, by and by.—Let me the curtains draw.—   105

[*Closes the bed-curtains.*]

   Where art thou?

[*Opens the door.*]

(*Enter Emilia.*)

                 What's the matter with thee now?
EMILIA: O my good lord, yonder's foul murder done!
OTHELLO: What? Now?

---

92. By and by: Just a moment (addressed to Emilia).   **93. like:** Likely.
102. yawn: Open, as in an earthquake.

EMILIA: But now, my lord.
OTHELLO: It is the very error° of the moon.
  She comes more nearer earth than she was wont
  And makes men mad.
EMILIA: Cassio, my lord, hath killed a young Venetian
  Called Roderigo.
OTHELLO: Roderigo killed?
  And Cassio killed?
EMILIA: No, Cassio is not killed.
OTHELLO: Not Cassio killed? Then murder's out of tune,
  And sweet revenge grows harsh.
DESDEMONA: O, falsely, falsely murdered?
EMILIA: O, Lord! what cry is that?
OTHELLO: That? What?
EMILIA: Out and alas! that was my lady's voice.
  Help! help, ho! help! O lady, speak again!
  Sweet Desdemona! O sweet mistress, speak!
DESDEMONA: A guiltless death I die.
EMILIA: O, who hath done this deed?
DESDEMONA: Nobody—I myself. Farewell.
  Commend° me to my kind lord. O, farewell!

(*She dies.*)

OTHELLO: Why, how should she be murd'red?
EMILIA: Alas, who knows?
OTHELLO: You heard her say herself, it was not I.
EMILIA: She said so. I must needs report the truth.
OTHELLO: She's like a liar gone to burning hell!
  'Twas I that killed her.
EMILIA: O, the more angel she,
  And you the blacker devil!
OTHELLO: She turned to folly, and she was a whore.
EMILIA: Thou dost belie° her, and thou art a devil.
OTHELLO: She was false as water.°
EMILIA: Thou art rash as fire to say
  That she was false. O, she was heavenly true!
OTHELLO: Cassio did top her. Ask thy husband else.°
  O, I were damned beneath all depth in hell
  But that I did proceed upon just grounds
  To this extremity. Thy husband knew it all.

110. error: Straying off course.   126. Commend: Remember.   134. belie:
Slander.   135. water: (Which is yielding).   137. else: If you don't believe me.

EMILIA: My husband?
OTHELLO: Thy husband.
EMILIA: That she was false to wedlock?
OTHELLO: Ay, with Cassio. Nay, had she been true,
  If heaven would make me such another world   145
  Of one entire and perfect chrysolite,°
  I'ld not have sold her for it.
EMILIA: My husband?
OTHELLO: Ay 'twas he that told me first.
  An honest man he is, and hates the slime
  That sticks on filthy deeds.
EMILIA: My husband?   150
OTHELLO: What needs this iterance,° woman? I say thy husband.
EMILIA: O mistress, villainy hath made mocks with° love!
  My husband say that she was false?
OTHELLO: He, woman.
  I say, thy husband. Dost understand the word?
  My friend, thy husband; honest, honest Iago.   155
EMILIA: If he say so, may his pernicious soul
  Rot half a grain a day! he lies to th' heart.
  She was too fond of her most filthy bargain.
OTHELLO: Ha! [*He draws.*]
EMILIA: Do thy worst.   160
  This deed of thine is no more worthy heaven
  Than thou wast worthy her.
OTHELLO: Peace, you were best.°
EMILIA: Thou hast not half the power to do me harm
  As I have to be hurt.° O gull! O dolt!
  As ignorant as dirt! thou hast done a deed—   165
  I care not for thy sword; I'll make thee known,
  Though I lost twenty lives. Help! help! Ho! help!
  The Moor hath killed my mistress! Murder! murder!

(*Enter Montano, Gratiano, Iago, and others.*)

MONTANO: What is the matter? How now, general?
EMILIA: O, are you come, Iago? You have done well,   170
  That men must lay their murders on your neck.°
GRATIANO: What is the matter?
EMILIA: Disprove this villain, if thou be'st a man.

146. chrysolite: (Precious topaz).   151. iterance: Repetition.   152. mocks
with: A mockery of.   162. Peace . . . best: You had better keep quiet.   164. to
be hurt: To endure hurt.   171. on your neck: To your charge.

He says thou told'st him that his wife was false.
I know thou didst not; thou'rt not such a villain.
Speak, for my heart is full.
IAGO: I told him what I thought, and told no more
Than what he found himself was apt and true.
EMILIA: But did you ever tell him she was false?
IAGO: I did.
EMILIA: You told a lie, an odious damnèd lie!
Upon my soul, a lie! a wicked lie!
She false with Cassio? Did you say with Cassio?
IAGO: With Cassio, mistress. Go to, charm° your tongue.
EMILIA: I will not charm my tongue; I am bound to speak:
My mistress here lies murdered in her bed—
ALL: O heavens forfend!
EMILIA: And your reports have set the murder on.
OTHELLO: Nay, stare not, masters. It is true indeed.
GRATIANO: 'Tis a strange truth.
MONTANO: O monstrous act!
EMILIA: Villainy, villainy, villainy!
I think upon't—I think I smell't!—O villainy!
I thought so then.—I'll kill myself for grief.—
O villainy, villainy!
IAGO: What, are you mad? I charge you get you home.
EMILIA: Good gentlemen, let me have leave to speak.
'Tis proper I obey him, but not now.
Perchance, Iago, I will ne'er go home.
OTHELLO: O! O! O!   (*Falls on the bed.*)
EMILIA: Nay, lay thee down and roar!
For thou hast killed the sweetest innocent
That e'er did lift up eye.°
OTHELLO: O, she was foul!

[*Rises.*]

I scarce did know you, uncle. There lies your niece,
Whose breath, indeed, these hands have newly stopped.
I know this act shows° horrible and grim.
GRATIANO: Poor Desdemon! I am glad thy father's dead.
Thy match was mortal to him, and pure grief
Shore his old thread in twain. Did he live now,
This sight would make him do a desperate turn;°

---

184. charm: Cast a spell on, silence.   **201. lift up eye:** Lift her eyes to heaven.
204. shows: Appears.   **208. turn:** Act.

Yea, curse his better angel from his side,
And fall to reprobation.°   210
OTHELLO: 'Tis pitiful; but yet Iago knows
    That she with Cassio hath the act of shame
    A thousand times committed. Cassio confessed it;
    And she did gratify° his amorous works
    With that recognizance° and pledge of love   215
    Which I first gave her. I saw it in his hand.
    It was a handkerchief, an antique token
    My father gave my mother.
EMILIA: O God! O heavenly God!
IAGO: Zounds, hold your peace
EMILIA: 'Twill out, 'twill out! I peace?   220
    No, I will speak as liberal as the north,°
    Let heaven and men and devils, let them all,
    All, all, cry shame against me, yet I'll speak.
IAGO: Be wise, and get you home.
EMILIA: I will not.

[*Iago draws and threatens Emilia.*]

GRATIANO: Fie!
    Your sword upon a woman?   225
EMILIA: O thou dull Moor, that handkerchief thou speak'st of
    I found by fortune, and did give my husband;
    For often with a solemn earnestness—
    More than indeed belonged to such a trifle—
    He begged of me to steal't.
IAGO: Villainous whore!   230
EMILIA: She give it Cassio? No, alas, I found it,
    And I did give't my husband.
IAGO: Filth, thou liest!
EMILIA: By heaven, I do not, I do not, gentlemen.
    O murd'rous coxcomb!° what should such a fool
    Do with so good a wife?
OTHELLO: Are there no stones° in heaven   235
    But what serves for the thunder? Precious° villain!

(*The Moor runs at Iago [but is disarmed by Montano].*)

---

210. reprobation: Rejection by God, damnation.   **214. gratify:** Reward.
215. recognizance: Token.   **221. liberal as the north:** Unchecked as the north
wind blows.   **234. coxcomb:** Fool.   **235. stones:** Bolts like those used for
thunderbolts.   **236. Precious:** Absolute.

(*Iago kills his wife.*)

GRATIANO: The woman falls. Sure he hath killed his wife.
EMILIA: Ay, ay. O, lay me by my mistress' side.   (*Exit Iago.*)
GRATIANO: He's gone, but his wife's killed.
MONTANO: 'Tis a notorious° villain. Take you this weapon,
    Which I have here recovered from the Moor.
    Come, guard the door without. Let him not pass,
    But kill him rather. I'll after that same villain,
    For 'tis a damnèd slave.

                    (*Exit [Montano, with all but Othello and Emilia].*)

OTHELLO: I am not valiant neither;
    But every puny whipster° gets my sword.
    But why should honor outlive honesty?
    Let it go all.
EMILIA: What did thy song bode, lady?
    Hark, canst thou hear me? I will play the swan,
    And die in music. [*Sings.*] "Willow, willow, willow."
    Moor, she was chaste. She loved thee, cruel Moor:
    So come my soul to bliss as I speak true.
    So speaking as I think, alas, I die.

(*She dies.*)

OTHELLO: I have another weapon in this chamber;
    It is a sword of Spain, the ice brook's° temper.
    O, here it is.—Uncle, I must come forth.
GRATIANO (*within*): If thou attempt it, it will cost thee dear.
    Thou hast no weapon, and perforce must suffer.
OTHELLO: Look in upon me then and speak with me,
    Or, naked° as I am, I will assault thee.

[*Enter Gratiano.*]

GRATIANO: What is the matter?
OTHELLO: Behold, I have a weapon;
    A better never did itself sustain
    Upon a soldier's thigh. I have seen the day
    That with this little arm and this good sword
    I have made my way through more impediments
    Than twenty times your stop.° But O vain boast!

---

240. **notorious:** Reprehensible.   245. **puny whipster:** Whippersnapper.
254. **ice brook:** I.e., a Spanish blade, tempered in cold running water.
259. **naked:** Disarmed.   265. **stop:** Power to stop.

Who can control his fate? 'Tis not so now.
Be not afraid, though you do see me weaponed.
Here is my journey's end, here is my butt,°
And very seamark° of my utmost sail:
Do you go back dismayed? 'Tis a lost° fear.   270
Man but a rush° against Othello's breast,
And he retires. Where should Othello go?
Now, how dost thou look now? O ill-starred wench!
Pale as thy smock! When we shall meet at compt,°
This look of thine will hurl my soul from heaven,   275
And fiends will snatch at it. Cold, cold, my girl?
Even like thy chastity.
O cursèd, cursèd slave! Whip me, ye devils,
From the possession of this heavenly sight!
Blow me about in winds! roast me in sulphur!   280
Wash me in steep-down gulfs of liquid fire!
Oh Desdemon! dead Desdemon! dead! Oh! Oh!

(*Enter Lodovico, Montano, Iago* [*as prisoner*]*, and Officers; Cassio in a chair.*)

LODOVICO: Where is this rash and most unfortunate man?
OTHELLO: That's he that was Othello. Here I am.
LODOVICO: Where is that viper? Bring the villain forth.   285
OTHELLO: I look down towards his feet°—but that's a fable.
   If that thou be'st a devil, I cannot kill thee.

[*Wounds Iago.*]

LODOVICO: Wrench his sword from him.

[*Othello is disarmed.*]

IAGO: I bleed, sir, but not killed.
OTHELLO: I am not sorry neither. I'ld have thee live;
   For in my sense, 'tis happiness to die.   290
LODOVICO: O thou Othello that wert once so good.
   Fall'n in the practice° of a damnèd slave,
   What shall be said to thee?
OTHELLO: Why, anything;
   An honorable murderer, if you will;
   For naught did I in hate, but all in honor.   295

268. **butt:** Limit.   269. **seamark:** Beacon, destination.   270. **lost:** Wasted.
271. **Man but a rush:** Wield only a reed.   274. **compt:** Final accounting, Last
Judgment.   286. **I . . . feet:** I.e., to see if they are cloven, like the Devil's.
292. **practice:** Plot.

LODOVICO: This wretch hath part confessed his villainy.
  Did you and he consent in° Cassio's death?
OTHELLO: Ay.
CASSIO: Dear general, I never gave you cause.
OTHELLO: I do believe it, and I ask your pardon.
  Will you, I pray, demand that demi-devil
  Why he hath thus ensnared my soul and body?
IAGO: Demand me nothing. What you know, you know.
  From this time forth I never will speak word.
LODOVICO: What, not to pray?
GRATIANO: Torments° will ope your lips.
OTHELLO: Well, thou dost best.
LODOVICO: Sir, you shall understand what hath befall'n,
  Which, as I think, you know not. Here is a letter
  Found in the pocket of the slain Roderigo;
  And here another. The one of them imports
  The death of Cassio to be undertook
  By Roderigo.
OTHELLO: O villain!
CASSIO: Most heathenish and most gross!
LODOVICO: Now here's another discontented° paper
  Found in the pocket too; and this, it seems,
  Roderigo meant t' have sent this damnèd villain;
  But that, belike, Iago in the nick°
  Came in and satisfied him.
OTHELLO: O thou pernicious caitiff!—
  How came you, Cassio, by that handkerchief
  That was my wife's?
CASSIO: I found it in my chamber;
  And he himself confessed but even now
  That there he dropped it for a special purpose
  Which wrought to his desire.
OTHELLO: O fool! fool! fool!
CASSIO: There is besides in Roderigo's letter,
  How he upbraids Iago that he made him
  Brave° me upon the watch; whereon it came°
  That I was cast;° and even but now he spake,
  After long seeming dead—Iago hurt him,
  Iago set him on.

---

297. **consent in:** Agree upon.   305. **Torments:** Torture.   314. **discontented:**
Full of discontent.   317. **nick:** Nick of time.   326. **Brave:** Defy; **Whereon it
came:** whereof it came about.   327. **cast:** Dismissed.

LODOVICO [*to Othello*]: You must forsake this room and go with us.   330
    Your power and your command is taken off,°
    And Cassio rules in Cyprus. For this slave,
    If there be any cunning cruelty
    That can torment him much and hold him long,°
    It shall be his. You shall close prisoner rest°   335
    Till that the nature of your fault be known
    To the Venetian state. Come, bring away.
OTHELLO: Soft you!° a word or two before you go.
    I have done the state some service, and they know't.
    No more of that. I pray you, in your letters,   340
    When you shall these unlucky° deeds relate,
    Speak of me as I am. Nothing extenuate,
    Nor set down aught in malice. Then must you speak
    Of one that loved not wisely, but too well;
    Of one not easily jealous, but, being wrought,°   345
    Perplexed° in the extreme; of one whose hand,
    Like the base Judean,° threw a pearl away
    Richer than all his tribe; of one whose subdued° eyes,
    Albeit unusèd to the melting mood,
    Drop tears as fast as the Arabian trees   350
    Their med'cinable gum. Set you down this.
    And say besides that in Aleppo once,
    Where a malignant and a turbaned Turk
    Beat a Venetian and traduced the state,
    I took by th' throat the circumcisèd dog   355
    And smote him—thus.

(*He stabs himself.*)

LODOVICO: O bloody period!°
GRATIANO: All that's spoke is marred.
OTHELLO: I kissed thee ere I killed thee. No way but this,
    Killing myself, to die upon a kiss.

(*He [falls upon the bed and] dies.*)

CASSIO: This did I fear, but thought he had no weapon;   360
    For he was great of heart.

---

331. off: Away.   **334. hold him long:** Keep him alive a long time.   **335. rest:**
Remain.   **338. Soft you:** Wait a moment.   **341. unlucky:** Fatal.   **345. wrought:**
Worked into a frenzy.   **346. Perplexed:** Distraught.   **347. Judean:** Judas Iscariot
(?) (quarto reads "Indian").   **348. subdued:** I.e., conquered by grief.   **357. period:**
Ending.

LODOVICO [*to Iago*]:   O Spartan dog,
  More fell° than anguish, hunger, or the sea!
  Look on the tragic loading of this bed.
  This is thy work. The object poisons sight;
  Let it be hid.° Gratiano, keep° the house,
  And seize upon° the fortunes of the Moor,
  For they succeed on you. [*To Cassio*] To you, lord governor,
  Remains the censure° of this hellish villain,
  The time, the place, the torture. O, enforce it!
  Myself will straight aboard, and to the state
  This heavy act with heavy heart relate.

                                                   (*Exeunt.*)

                                                    [1604]

363. fell: Cruel.   **365. Let it be hid:** I.e., draw the bed curtains.   **366. seize
upon:** Take legal possession of.   **368. censure:** Judicial sentence.

HENRIK IBSEN   [1828–1906]

A Doll House

TRANSLATED BY B. FARQUHARSON SHARP

Dramatis personae
TORVALD HELMER
NORA, *his wife*
DOCTOR RANK
MRS. LINDE
NILS KROGSTAD
Helmer's three young children
ANNE, *their nurse*
A Housemaid
A Porter

Scene: *The action takes place in Helmer's house.*

ACT I

Scene: *A room furnished comfortably and tastefully, but not extravagantly. At the back, a door to the right leads to the entrance-hall, another to the left leads to Helmer's study. Between the doors stands a piano. In the middle of the left-hand wall is a door, and beyond it a window. Near the window are a round table, arm-chairs and a small sofa. In the right-hand wall, at the farther end, another door; and on the same side, nearer the footlights, a stove, two easy chairs and a rocking-chair; between the stove and the door, a small table. Engravings on the walls; a cabinet with china and other small objects; a small book-case with well-bound books. The floors are carpeted, and a fire burns in the stove. It is winter.*

A bell rings in the hall; shortly afterwards the door is heard to open. Enter Nora, humming a tune and in high spirits. She is in outdoor dress and carries a number of parcels; these she lays on the table to the right. She leaves the outer door open after her, and through it is seen a Porter who is carrying a Christmas Tree and a basket, which he gives to the Maid who has opened the door.

NORA: Hide the Christmas Tree carefully, Helen. Be sure the children do not see it until this evening, when it is dressed. (*To the Porter, taking out her purse.*) How much?

PORTER: Sixpence.

NORA: There is a shilling. No, keep the change. (*The Porter thanks her, and goes out. Nora shuts the door. She is laughing to herself, as she takes off her hat and coat. She takes a packet of macaroons from her pocket and eats one or two; then goes cautiously to her husband's door and listens.*) Yes, he is in. (*Still humming, she goes to the table on the right.*)

HELMER (*calls out from his room*): Is that my little lark twittering out there?

NORA (*busy opening some of the parcels*): Yes, it is!

HELMER: Is it my little squirrel bustling about?

NORA: Yes!

HELMER: When did my squirrel come home?

NORA: Just now. (*Puts the bag of macaroons into her pocket and wipes her mouth.*) Come in here, Torvald, and see what I have bought.

HELMER: Don't disturb me. (*A little later, he opens the door and looks into the room, pen in hand.*) Bought, did you say? All these things? Has my little spendthrift been wasting money again?

NORA: Yes but, Torvald, this year we really can let ourselves go a little. This is the first Christmas that we have not needed to economise.

HELMER: Still, you know, we can't spend money recklessly.

NORA: Yes, Torvald, we may be a wee bit more reckless now, mayn't we? Just a tiny wee bit! You are going to have a big salary and earn lots and lots of money.

HELMER: Yes, after the New Year; but then it will be a whole quarter before the salary is due.

NORA: Pooh! we can borrow until then.

HELMER: Nora! (*Goes up to her and takes her playfully by the ear.*) The same little featherhead! Suppose, now, that I borrowed fifty pounds to-day, and you spent it all in the Christmas week, and then on New Year's Eve a slate fell on my head and killed me, and—

NORA (*putting her hands over his mouth*): Oh! don't say such horrid things.

HELMER: Still, suppose that happened,—what then?

NORA: If that were to happen, I don't suppose I should care whether I owed money or not.

HELMER: Yes, but what about the people who had lent it?

NORA: They? Who would bother about them? I should not know who they were.

HELMER: That is like a woman! But seriously, Nora, you know what I think about that. No debt, no borrowing. There can be no freedom or beauty about a home life that depends on borrowing and debt. We two have kept bravely on the straight road so far, and we will go on the same way for the short time longer that there need be any struggle.

NORA (*moving towards the stove*): As you please, Torvald.

HELMER (*following her*): Come, come, my little skylark must not droop her wings. What is this! Is my little squirrel out of temper? (*Taking out his purse.*) Nora, what do you think I have got here?

NORA (*turning round quickly*): Money!

HELMER: There you are. (*Gives her some money.*) Do you think I don't know what a lot is wanted for housekeeping at Christmas-time?

NORA (*counting*): Ten shillings—a pound—two pounds! Thank you, thank you, Torvald; that will keep me going for a long time.

HELMER: Indeed it must.

NORA: Yes, yes, it will. But come here and let me show you what I have bought. And all so cheap! Look, here is a new suit for Ivar, and a sword; and a horse and a trumpet for Bob; and a doll and dolly's bedstead for Emmy,—they are very plain, but anyway she will soon break them in pieces. And here are dress-lengths and hand-kerchiefs for the maids; old Anne ought really to have something better.

HELMER: And what is in this parcel?

NORA (*crying out*): No, no! you mustn't see that until this evening.

HELMER: Very well. But now tell me, you extravagant little person, what would you like for yourself?

NORA: For myself? Oh, I am sure I don't want anything.

HELMER: Yes, but you must. Tell me something reasonable that you would particularly like to have.

NORA: No, I really can't think of anything—unless, Torvald—

HELMER: Well?

NORA (*playing with his coat buttons, and without raising her eyes to his*): If you really want to give me something, you might—you might—

HELMER: Well, out with it!

NORA (*speaking quickly*): You might give me money, Torvald. Only just as much as you can afford; and then one of these days I will buy something with it.

HELMER: But, Nora—

NORA: Oh, do! dear Torvald; please, please do! Then I will wrap it up in beautiful gilt paper and hang it on the Christmas Tree. Wouldn't that be fun?

HELMER: What are little people called that are always wasting money?

NORA: Spendthrifts—I know. Let us do as you suggest, Torvald, and then I shall have time to think what I am most in want of. That is a very sensible plan, isn't it?

HELMER (*smiling*): Indeed it is—that is to say, if you were really to save out of the money I give you, and then really buy something for your-self. But if you spend it all on the housekeeping and any number of unnecessary things, then I merely have to pay up again.

NORA: Oh but, Torvald—

HELMER: You can't deny it, my dear little Nora. (*Puts his arm round her waist.*) It's a sweet little spendthrift, but she uses up a deal of money. One would hardly believe how expensive such little persons are!

NORA: It's a shame to say that. I do really save all I can.

HELMER (*laughing*): That's very true,—all you can. But you can't save anything!

NORA (*smiling quietly and happily*): You haven't any idea how many expenses we skylarks and squirrels have, Torvald.

HELMER: You are an odd little soul. Very like your father. You always find some new way of wheedling money out of me, and, as soon as you have got it, it seems to melt in your hands. You never know where it has gone. Still, one must take you as you are. It is in the blood; for indeed it is true that you can inherit these things, Nora.

NORA: Ah, I wish I had inherited many of papa's qualities.

HELMER: And I would not wish you to be anything but just what you are, my sweet little skylark. But, do you know, it strikes me that you are looking rather—what shall I say—rather uneasy today?

NORA: Do I?

HELMER: You do, really. Look straight at me.

NORA (*looks at him*): Well?

HELMER (*wagging his finger at her*): Hasn't Miss Sweet Tooth been breaking rules in town today?

NORA: No; what makes you think that?

HELMER: Hasn't she paid a visit to the confectioner's?

NORA: No, I assure you, Torvald—

HELMER: Not been nibbling sweets?

NORA: No, certainly not.

HELMER: Not even taken a bite at a macaroon or two?

NORA: No, Torvald, I assure you really—

HELMER: There, there, of course I was only joking.

NORA (*going to the table on the right*): I should not think of going against your wishes.

HELMER: No, I am sure of that; besides, you gave me your word— (*Going up to her.*) Keep your little Christmas secrets to yourself, my darling. They will all be revealed to-night when the Christmas Tree is lit, no doubt.

NORA: Did you remember to invite Doctor Rank?

HELMER: No. But there is no need; as a matter of course he will come to dinner with us. However, I will ask him when he comes in this morning. I have ordered some good wine. Nora, you can't think how I am looking forward to this evening.

NORA: So am I! And how the children will enjoy themselves, Torvald!

HELMER: It is splendid to feel that one has a perfectly safe appointment, and a big enough income. It's delightful to think of, isn't it?

NORA: It's wonderful!

HELMER: Do you remember last Christmas? For a full three weeks beforehand you shut yourself up every evening until long after midnight, making ornaments for the Christmas Tree, and all the other fine things that were to be a surprise to us. It was the dullest three weeks I ever spent!

NORA: I didn't find it dull.

HELMER (*smiling*): But there was precious little result, Nora.

NORA: Oh, you shouldn't tease me about that again. How could I help the cat's going in and tearing everything to pieces?

HELMER: Of course you couldn't, poor little girl. You had the best of intentions to please us all, and that's the main thing. But it is a good thing that our hard times are over.

NORA: Yes, it is really wonderful.

HELMER: This time I needn't sit here and be dull all alone, and you needn't ruin your dear eyes and your pretty little hands —

NORA (*clapping her hands*): No, Torvald, I needn't any longer, need I! It's wonderfully lovely to hear you say so! (*Taking his arm.*) Now I will tell you how I have been thinking we ought to arrange things, Torvald. As soon as Christmas is over — (*A bell rings in the hall.*) There's the bell. (*She tidies the room a little.*) There's some one at the door. What a nuisance!

HELMER: If it is a caller, remember I am not at home.

MAID (*in the doorway*): A lady to see you, ma'am, — a stranger.

NORA: Ask her to come in.

MAID (*to Helmer*): The doctor came at the same time, sir.

HELMER: Did he go straight into my room?

MAID: Yes, sir.

(*Helmer goes into his room. The Maid ushers in Mrs. Linde, who is in travelling dress, and shuts the door.*)

MRS. LINDE (*in a dejected and timid voice*): How do you do, Nora?

NORA (*doubtfully*): How do you do —

MRS. LINDE: You don't recognise me, I suppose.

NORA: No, I don't know — yes, to be sure, I seem to — (*Suddenly.*) Yes! Christine! Is it really you?

MRS. LINDE: Yes, it is I.

NORA: Christine! To think of my not recognising you! And yet how could I — (*In a gentle voice.*) How you have altered, Christine!

MRS. LINDE: Yes, I have indeed. In nine, ten long years —

NORA: Is it so long since we met? I suppose it is. The last eight years have been a happy time for me, I can tell you. And so now you have come into the town, and have taken this long journey in winter—that was plucky of you.

MRS. LINDE: I arrived by steamer this morning.

NORA: To have some fun at Christmas-time, of course. How delightful! We will have such fun together! But take off your things. You are not cold, I hope. (*Helps her.*) Now we will sit down by the stove, and be cosy. No, take this armchair; I will sit here in the rocking-chair. (*Takes her hands.*) Now you look like your old self again; it was only the first moment—You are a little paler, Christine, and perhaps a little thinner.

MRS. LINDE: And much, much older, Nora.

NORA: Perhaps a little older; very, very little; certainly not much. (*Stops suddenly and speaks seriously.*) What a thoughtless creature I am, chattering away like this. My poor, dear Christine, do forgive me.

MRS. LINDE: What do you mean, Nora?

NORA (*gently*): Poor Christine, you are a widow.

MRS. LINDE: Yes; it is three years ago now.

NORA: Yes, I knew; I saw it in the papers. I assure you, Christine, I meant ever so often to write to you at the time, but I always put it off and something always prevented me.

MRS. LINDE: I quite understand, dear.

NORA: It was very bad of me, Christine. Poor thing, how you must have suffered. And he left you nothing?

MRS. LINDE: No.

NORA: And no children?

MRS. LINDE: No.

NORA: Nothing at all, then.

MRS. LINDE: Not even any sorrow or grief to live upon.

NORA (*looking incredulously at her*): But, Christine, is that possible?

MRS. LINDE (*smiles sadly and strokes her hair*): It sometimes happens, Nora.

NORA: So you are quite alone. How dreadfully sad that must be. I have three lovely children. You can't see them just now, for they are out with their nurse. But now you must tell me all about it.

MRS. LINDE: No, no; I want to hear about you.

NORA: No, you must begin. I mustn't be selfish today; today I must only think of your affairs. But there is one thing I must tell you. Do you know we have just had a great piece of good luck?

MRS. LINDE: No, what is it?

NORA: Just fancy, my husband has been made manager of the Bank!

MRS. LINDE: Your husband? What good luck!

NORA: Yes, tremendous! A barrister's profession is such an uncertain thing, especially if he won't undertake unsavoury cases; and naturally Torvald has never been willing to do that, and I quite agree with him.

You may imagine how pleased we are! He is to take up his work in the Bank at the New Year, and then he will have a big salary and lots of commissions. For the future we can live quite differently—we can do just as we like. I feel so relieved and so happy, Christine! It will be splendid to have heaps of money and not need to have any anxiety, won't it?

MRS. LINDE: Yes, anyhow I think it would be delightful to have what one needs.

NORA: No, not only what one needs, but heaps and heaps of money.

MRS. LINDE (*smiling*): Nora, Nora, haven't you learned sense yet? In our schooldays you were a great spendthrift.

NORA (*laughing*): Yes, that is what Torvald says now. (*Wags her finger at her.*) But "Nora, Nora" is not so silly as you think. We have not been in a position for me to waste money. We have both had to work.

MRS. LINDE: You too?

NORA: Yes; odds and ends, needlework, crotchet-work, embroidery, and that kind of thing. (*Dropping her voice.*) And other things as well. You know Torvald left his office when we were married? There was no prospect of promotion there, and he had to try and earn more than before. But during the first year he over-worked himself dreadfully. You see, he had to make money every way he could, and he worked early and late; but he couldn't stand it, and fell dreadfully ill, and the doctors said it was necessary for him to go south.

MRS. LINDE: You spent a whole year in Italy, didn't you?

NORA: Yes. It was no easy matter to get away, I can tell you. It was just after Ivar was born; but naturally we had to go. It was a wonderfully beautiful journey, and it saved Torvald's life. But it cost a tremendous lot of money, Christine.

MRS. LINDE: So I should think.

NORA: It cost about two hundred and fifty pounds. That's a lot, isn't it?

MRS. LINDE: Yes, and in emergencies like that it is lucky to have the money.

NORA: I ought to tell you that we had it from papa.

MRS. LINDE: Oh, I see. It was just about that time that he died, wasn't it?

NORA: Yes; and, just think of it, I couldn't go and nurse him. I was expecting little Ivar's birth every day and I had my poor sick Torvald to look after. My dear, kind father—I never saw him again, Christine. That was the saddest time I have known since our marriage.

MRS. LINDE: I know how fond you were of him. And then you went off to Italy?

NORA: Yes; you see we had money then, and the doctors insisted on our going, so we started a month later.

MRS. LINDE: And your husband came back quite well?

NORA: As sound as a bell!

MRS. LINDE: But—the doctor?

NORA: What doctor?

MRS. LINDE: I thought your maid said the gentleman who arrived here just as I did, was the doctor?

NORA: Yes, that was Doctor Rank, but he doesn't come here professionally. He is our greatest friend, and comes in at least once everyday. No, Torvald has not had an hour's illness since then, and our children are strong and healthy and so am I. (*Jumps up and claps her hands.*) Christine! Christine! it's good to be alive and happy!—But how horrid of me; I am talking of nothing but my own affairs. (*Sits on a stool near her, and rests her arms on her knees.*) You mustn't be angry with me. Tell me, is it really true that you did not love your husband? Why did you marry him?

MRS. LINDE: My mother was alive then, and was bedridden and helpless, and I had to provide for my two younger brothers; so I did not think I was justified in refusing his offer.

NORA: No, perhaps you were quite right. He was rich at that time, then?

MRS. LINDE: I believe he was quite well off. But his business was a precarious one; and, when he died, it all went to pieces and there was nothing left.

NORA: And then?—

MRS. LINDE: Well, I had to turn my hand to anything I could find—first a small shop, then a small school, and so on. The last three years have seemed like one long working-day, with no rest. Now it is at an end, Nora. My poor mother needs me no more, for she is gone; and the boys do not need me either; they have got situations and can shift for themselves.

NORA: What a relief you must feel it—

MRS. LINDE: No, indeed; I only feel my life unspeakably empty. No one to live for anymore. (*Gets up restlessly.*) That was why I could not stand the life in my little backwater any longer. I hope it may be easier here to find something which will busy me and occupy my thoughts. If only I could have the good luck to get some regular work—office work of some kind—

NORA: But, Christine, that is so frightfully tiring, and you look tired out now. You had far better go away to some watering-place.

MRS. LINDE (*walking to the window*): I have no father to give me money for a journey, Nora.

NORA (*rising*): Oh, don't be angry with me!

MRS. LINDE (*going up to her*): It is you that must not be angry with me, dear. The worst of a position like mine is that it makes one so bitter. No one to work for, and yet obliged to be always on the lookout for chances. One must live, and so one becomes selfish. When you told me of the happy turn your fortunes have taken—you will hardly believe it—I was delighted not so much on your account as on my own.

NORA: How do you mean?—Oh, I understand. You mean that perhaps Torvald could get you something to do.

MRS. LINDE: Yes, that was what I was thinking of.

NORA: He must, Christine. Just leave it to me; I will broach the subject very cleverly—I will think of something that will please him very much. It will make me so happy to be of some use to you.

MRS. LINDE: How kind you are, Nora, to be so anxious to help me! It is doubly kind in you, for you know so little of the burdens and troubles of life.

NORA: I—? I know so little of them?

MRS. LINDE (*smiling*): My dear! Small household cares and that sort of thing!—You are a child, Nora.

NORA (*tosses her head and crosses the stage*): You ought not to be so superior.

MRS. LINDE: No?

NORA: You are just like the others. They all think that I am incapable of anything really serious—

MRS. LINDE: Come, come—

NORA: —that I have gone through nothing in this world of cares.

MRS. LINDE: But, my dear Nora, you have just told me all your troubles.

NORA: Pooh!—those were trifles. (*Lowering her voice.*) I have not told you the important thing.

MRS. LINDE: The important thing? What do you mean?

NORA: You look down upon me altogether, Christine—but you ought not to. You are proud, aren't you, of having worked so hard and so long for your mother?

MRS. LINDE: Indeed, I don't look down on anyone. But it is true that I am both proud and glad to think that I was privileged to make the end of my mother's life almost free from care.

NORA: And you are proud to think of what you have done for your brothers?

MRS. LINDE: I think I have the right to be.

NORA: I think so, too. But now, listen to this: I too have something to be proud and glad of.

MRS. LINDE: I have no doubt you have. But what do you refer to?

NORA: Speak low. Suppose Torvald were to hear. He mustn't on any account—no one in the world must know, Christine, except you.

MRS. LINDE: But what is it?

NORA: Come here. (*Pulls her down on the sofa beside her.*) Now I will show you that I too have something to be proud and glad of. It was I who saved Torvald's life.

MRS. LINDE: "Saved"? How?

NORA: I told you about our trip to Italy. Torvald would never have recovered if he had not gone there—

MRS. LINDE: Yes, but your father gave you the necessary funds.

NORA (*smiling*): Yes, that is what Torvald and all the others think, but—

MRS. LINDE: But—

NORA: Papa didn't give us a shilling. It was I who procured the money.

MRS. LINDE: You? All that large sum?

NORA: Two hundred and fifty pounds. What do you think of that?

MRS. LINDE: But, Nora, how could you possibly do it? Did you win a prize in the Lottery?

NORA (*contemptuously*): In the Lottery? There would have been no credit in that.

MRS. LINDE: But where did you get it from, then?

NORA (*humming and smiling with an air of mystery*): Hm, hm! Aha!

MRS. LINDE: Because you couldn't have borrowed it.

NORA: Couldn't I? Why not?

MRS. LINDE: No, a wife cannot borrow without her husband's consent.

NORA (*tossing her head*): Oh, if it is a wife who has any head for business— a wife who has the wit to be a little bit clever—

MRS. LINDE: I don't understand it at all, Nora.

NORA: There is no need you should. I never said I had borrowed the money. I may have got it some other way. (*Lies back on the sofa.*) Perhaps I got it from some other admirer. When anyone is as attractive as I am—

MRS. LINDE: You are a mad creature.

NORA: Now, you know you're full of curiosity, Christine.

MRS. LINDE: Listen to me, Nora dear. Haven't you been a little bit imprudent?

NORA (*sits up straight*): Is it imprudent to save your husband's life?

MRS. LINDE: It seems to me imprudent, without his knowledge, to—

NORA: But it was absolutely necessary that he should not know! My goodness, can't you understand that? It was necessary he should have no idea what a dangerous condition he was in. It was to me that the doctors came and said that his life was in danger, and that the only thing to save him was to live in the south. Do you suppose I didn't try, first of all, to get what I wanted as if it were for myself? I told him how much I should love to travel abroad like other young wives; I tried tears and entreaties with him; I told him that he ought to remember the condition I was in, and that he ought to be kind and indulgent to me; I even hinted that he might raise a loan. That nearly made him angry, Christine. He said I was thoughtless, and that it was his duty as my husband not to indulge me in my whims and caprices — as I believe he called them. Very well, I thought, you must be saved — and that was how I came to devise a way out of the difficulty —

MRS. LINDE: And did your husband never get to know from your father that the money had not come from him?

NORA: No, never. Papa died just at that time. I had meant to let him into the secret and beg him never to reveal it. But he was so ill then — alas, there never was any need to tell him.

MRS. LINDE: And since then have you never told your secret to your husband?

NORA: Good Heavens, no! How could you think so? A man who has such strong opinions about these things! And besides, how painful and humiliating it would be for Torvald, with his manly independence, to know that he owed me anything! It would upset our mutual relations altogether; our beautiful happy home would no longer be what it is now.

MRS. LINDE: Do you mean never to tell him about it?

NORA (*meditatively, and with a half smile*): Yes — someday, perhaps, after many years, when I am no longer as nice-looking as I am now. Don't laugh at me! I mean, of course, when Torvald is no longer as devoted to me as he is now; when my dancing and dressing-up and reciting have palled on him; then it may be a good thing to have something in reserve — (*Breaking off.*) What nonsense! That time will never come. Now, what do you think of my great secret, Christine? Do you still think I am of no use? I can tell you, too, that this affair has caused me a lot of worry. It has been by no means easy for me to meet my engagements punctually. I may tell you that there is something that is called, in business, quarterly interest, and another thing called payment in installments, and it is always so dreadfully difficult to manage them. I have had to save a little here and there, where I could, you understand. I have not been able to put aside much from my housekeeping money, for Torvald must have a good table. I couldn't let my children be shabbily dressed; I have felt obliged to use up all he gave me for them, the sweet little darlings!

MRS. LINDE: So it has all had to come out of your own necessaries of life, poor Nora?

NORA: Of course. Besides, I was the one responsible for it. Whenever Torvald has given me money for new dresses and such things, I have never spent more than half of it; I have always bought the simplest and cheapest things. Thank Heaven, any clothes look well on me, and so Torvald has never noticed it. But it was often very hard on me, Christine — because it is delightful to be really well dressed, isn't it?

MRS. LINDE: Quite so.

NORA: Well, then I have found other ways of earning money. Last winter I was lucky enough to get a lot of copying to do; so I locked myself up and sat writing every evening until quite late at night. Many a time I was desperately tired; but all the same it was a tremendous pleasure to sit there working and earning money. It was like being a man.

MRS. LINDE: How much have you been able to pay off in that way?

NORA: I can't tell you exactly. You see, it is very difficult to keep an account of a business matter of that kind. I only know that I have paid every penny that I could scrape together. Many a time I was at my wits' end. (*Smiles.*) Then I used to sit here and imagine that a rich old gentleman had fallen in love with me—

MRS. LINDE: What! Who was it?

NORA: Be quiet!—that he had died; and that when his will was opened it contained, written in big letters, the instruction: "The lovely Mrs. Nora Helmer is to have all I possess paid over to her at once in cash."

MRS. LINDE: But, my dear Nora—who could the man be?

NORA: Good gracious, can't you understand? There was no old gentleman at all; it was only something that I used to sit here and imagine, when I couldn't think of any way of procuring money. But it's all the same now; the tiresome old person can stay where he is, as far as I am concerned; I don't care about him or his will either, for I am free from care now. (*Jumps up.*) My goodness, it's delightful to think of, Christine! Free from care! To be able to be free from care, quite free from care; to be able to play and romp with the children; to be able to keep the house beautifully and have everything just as Torvald likes it! And, think of it, soon the spring will come and the big blue sky! Perhaps we shall be able to take a little trip—perhaps I shall see the sea again! Oh, it's a wonderful thing to be alive and be happy. (*A bell is heard in the hall.*)

MRS. LINDE (*rising*): There is the bell; perhaps I had better go.

NORA: No, don't go; no one will come in here; it is sure to be for Torvald.

SERVANT (*at the hall door*): Excuse me, ma'am—there is a gentleman to see the master, and as the doctor is with him—

NORA: Who is it?

KROGSTAD (*at the door*): It is I, Mrs. Helmer (*Mrs. Linde starts, trembles, and turns to the window.*)

NORA (*takes a step towards him, and speaks in a strained, low voice*): You? What is it? What do you want to see my husband about?

KROGSTAD: Bank business—in a way. I have a small post in the Bank, and I hear your husband is to be our chief now—

NORA: Then it is—

KROGSTAD: Nothing but dry business matters, Mrs. Helmer; absolutely nothing else.

NORA: Be so good as to go into the study, then. (*She bows indifferently to him and shuts the door into the hall; then comes back and makes up the fire in the stove.*)

MRS. LINDE: Nora—who was that man?

NORA: A lawyer, of the name of Krogstad.

MRS. LINDE: Then it really was he.

NORA: Do you know the man?

MRS. LINDE: I used to—many years ago. At one time he was a solicitor's clerk in our town.

NORA: Yes, he was.

MRS. LINDE: He is greatly altered.

NORA: He made a very unhappy marriage.

MRS. LINDE: He is a widower now, isn't he?

NORA: With several children. There now, it is burning up. (*Shuts the door of the stove and moves the rocking-chair aside.*)

MRS. LINDE: They say he carries on various kinds of business.

NORA: Really! Perhaps he does; I don't know anything about it. But don't let us think of business; it is so tiresome.

DOCTOR RANK (*comes out of Helmer's study. Before he shuts the door he calls to him*): No, my dear fellow, I won't disturb you; I would rather go in to your wife for a little while. (*Shuts the door and sees Mrs. Linde.*) I beg your pardon; I am afraid I am disturbing you too.

NORA: No, not at all. (*Introducing him.*) Doctor Rank, Mrs. Linde.

RANK: I have often heard Mrs. Linde's name mentioned here. I think I passed you on the stairs when I arrived, Mrs. Linde?

MRS. LINDE: Yes, I go up very slowly; I can't manage stairs well.

RANK: Ah! some slight internal weakness?

MRS. LINDE: No, the fact is I have been overworking myself.

RANK: Nothing more than that? Then I suppose you have come to town to amuse yourself with our entertainments?

MRS. LINDE: I have come to look for work.

RANK: Is that a good cure for overwork?

MRS. LINDE: One must live, Doctor Rank.

RANK: Yes, the general opinion seems to be that it is necessary.

NORA: Look here, Doctor Rank—you know you want to live.

RANK: Certainly. However wretched I may feel, I want to prolong the agony as long as possible. All my patients are like that. And so are those who are morally diseased; one of them, and a bad case too, is at this very moment with Helmer—

MRS. LINDE (*sadly*): Ah!

NORA: Whom do you mean?

RANK: A lawyer of the name of Krogstad, a fellow you don't know at all. He suffers from a diseased moral character, Mrs. Helmer; but even he began talking of its being highly important that he should live.

NORA: Did he? What did he want to speak to Torvald about?

RANK: I have no idea; I only heard that it was something about the Bank.

NORA: I didn't know this—what's his name—Krogstad had anything to do with the Bank.

RANK: Yes, he has some sort of appointment there. (*To Mrs. Linde.*) I don't know whether you find also in your part of the world that there are certain people who go zealously snuffing about to smell out moral corruption, and, as soon as they have found some, put the person concerned into some lucrative position where they can keep their eye on him. Healthy natures are left out in the cold.

MRS. LINDE: Still I think the sick are those who most need taking care of.

RANK (*shrugging his shoulders*): Yes, there you are. That is the sentiment that is turning Society into a sick-house.

(*Nora, who has been absorbed in her thoughts, breaks out into smothered laughter and claps her hands.*)

RANK: Why do you laugh at that? Have you any notion what Society really is?

NORA: What do I care about tiresome Society? I am laughing at something quite different, something extremely amusing. Tell me, Doctor Rank, are all the people who are employed in the Bank dependent on Torvald now?

RANK: Is that what you find so extremely amusing?

NORA (*smiling and humming*): That's my affair! (*Walking about the room.*) It's perfectly glorious to think that we have—that Torvald has so much power over so many people. (*Takes the packet from her pocket.*) Doctor Rank, what do you say to a macaroon?

RANK: What, macaroons? I thought they were forbidden here.

NORA: Yes, but these are some Christine gave me.

MRS. LINDE: What! I?—

NORA: Oh, well, don't be alarmed! You couldn't know that Torvald had forbidden them. I must tell you that he is afraid they will spoil my teeth. But, bah!—once in a way—That's so, isn't it, Doctor Rank? By your leave! (*Puts a macaroon into his mouth.*) You must have one too, Christine. And I shall have one, just a little one—or at most two. (*Walking about.*) I am tremendously happy. There is just one thing in the world now that I should dearly love to do.

RANK: Well, what is that?

NORA: It's something I should dearly love to say, if Torvald could hear me.

RANK: Well, why can't you say it?

NORA: No, I daren't; it's so shocking.

MRS. LINDE: Shocking?

RANK: Well, I should not advise you to say it. Still, with us you might. What is it you would so much like to say if Torvald could hear you?

NORA: I should just love to say—Well, I'm damned!

RANK: Are you mad?

MRS. LINDE: Nora, dear—!

RANK: Say it, here he is!

NORA (*hiding the packet*): Hush! Hush! Hush! (*Helmer comes out of his room, with his coat over his arm and his hat in his hand.*)

NORA: Well, Torvald dear, have you got rid of him?

HELMER: Yes, he has just gone.

NORA: Let me introduce you—this is Christine, who has come to town.

HELMER: Christine—? Excuse me, but I don't know—

NORA: Mrs. Linde, dear; Christine Linde.

HELMER: Of course. A school friend of my wife's, I presume?

MRS. LINDE: Yes, we have known each other since then.

NORA: And just think, she has taken a long journey in order to see you.

HELMER: What do you mean?

MRS. LINDE: No, really, I—

NORA: Christine is tremendously clever at book-keeping, and she is frightfully anxious to work under some clever man, so as to perfect herself—

HELMER: Very sensible, Mrs. Linde.

NORA: And when she heard you had been appointed manager of the Bank—the news was telegraphed, you know—she travelled here as quick as she could. Torvald, I am sure you will be able to do something for Christine, for my sake, won't you?

HELMER: Well, it is not altogether impossible. I presume you are a widow, Mrs. Linde?

MRS. LINDE: Yes.

HELMER: And have had some experience of book-keeping?

MRS. LINDE: Yes, a fair amount.

HELMER: Ah! well, it's very likely I may be able to find something for you—

NORA (*clapping her hands*): What did I tell you? What did I tell you?

HELMER: You have just come at a fortunate moment, Mrs. Linde.

MRS. LINDE: How am I to thank you?

HELMER: There is no need. (*Puts on his coat.*) But to-day you must excuse me—

RANK: Wait a minute; I will come with you. (*Brings his fur coat from the hall and warms it at the fire.*)

NORA: Don't be long away, Torvald dear.

HELMER: About an hour, not more.

NORA: Are you going too, Christine?

MRS. LINDE (*putting on her cloak*): Yes, I must go and look for a room.

HELMER: Oh, well then, we can walk down the street together.

NORA (*helping her*): What a pity it is we are so short of space here; I am afraid it is impossible for us—

MRS. LINDE: Please don't think of it! Good-bye, Nora dear, and many thanks.

NORA: Good-bye for the present. Of course you will come back this evening. And you too, Dr. Rank. What do you say? If you are well enough? Oh, you must be! Wrap yourself up well. (*They go to the door all talking together. Children's voices are heard on the staircase.*)

NORA: There they are! There they are! (*She runs to open the door. The Nurse comes in with the children.*) Come in! Come in! (*Stoops and kisses them.*) Oh, you sweet blessings! Look at them, Christine! Aren't they darlings?

RANK: Don't let us stand here in the draught.

HELMER: Come along, Mrs. Linde; the place will only be bearable for a mother now!

(*Rank, Helmer, and Mrs. Linde go downstairs. The Nurse comes forward with the children; Nora shuts the hall door.*)

NORA: How fresh and well you look! Such red cheeks like apples and roses. (*The children all talk at once while she speaks to them.*) Have you had great fun? That's splendid! What, you pulled both Emmy and Bob along on the sledge?—both at once?—that was good. You are a clever boy, Ivar. Let me take her for a little, Anne. My sweet little baby doll! (*Takes the baby from the Maid and dances it up and down.*) Yes, yes, mother will dance with Bob too. What! Have you been snowballing? I wish I had been there too! No, no, I will take their things off, Anne; please let me do it, it is such fun. Go in now, you look half frozen. There is some hot coffee for you on the stove.

(*The Nurse goes into the room on the left. Nora takes off the children's things and throws them about, while they all talk to her at once.*)

NORA: Really! Did a big dog run after you? But it didn't bite you? No, dogs don't bite nice little dolly children. You mustn't look at the parcels, Ivar. What are they? Ah, I daresay you would like to know. No, no—it's something nasty! Come, let us have a game! What shall we play at? Hide and Seek? Yes, we'll play Hide and Seek. Bob shall hide first. Must I hide? Very well, I'll hide first. (*She and the children laugh and shout, and romp in and out of the room; at last Nora hides under the table, the children rush in and out for her, but do not see her; they hear her smothered laughter, run to the table, lift up the cloth and find her. Shouts of laughter. She crawls forward and pretends to frighten them. Fresh laughter. Meanwhile there has been a knock at the hall door, but none of them has noticed it. The door is half opened, and Krogstad appears. He waits a little; the game goes on.*)

KROGSTAD: Excuse me, Mrs. Helmer.

NORA (*with a stifled cry, turns round and gets up on to her knees*): Ah! what do you want?

KROGSTAD: Excuse me, the outer door was ajar; I suppose someone forgot to shut it.

NORA (*rising*): My husband is out, Mr Krogstad.

KROGSTAD: I know that.

NORA: What do you want here, then?

KROGSTAD: A word with you.

NORA: With me?—(*To the children, gently.*) Go in to nurse. What? No, the strange man won't do mother any harm. When he has gone we will have another game. (*She takes the children into the room on the left, and shuts the door after them.*) You want to speak to me?

KROGSTAD: Yes, I do.

NORA: To-day? It is not the first of the month yet.

KROGSTAD: No, it is Christmas Eve, and it will depend on yourself what sort of a Christmas you will spend.

NORA: What do you mean? To-day it is absolutely impossible for me—

KROGSTAD: We won't talk about that until later on. This is something different. I presume you can give me a moment?

NORA: Yes—yes, I can—although—

KROGSTAD: Good. I was in Olsen's Restaurant and saw your husband going down the street—

NORA: Yes?

KROGSTAD: With a lady.

NORA: What then?

KROGSTAD: May I make so bold as to ask if it was a Mrs. Linde?

NORA: It was.

KROGSTAD: Just arrived in town?

NORA: Yes, to-day.

KROGSTAD: She is a great friend of yours, isn't she?

NORA: She is. But I don't see—

KROGSTAD: I knew her too, once upon a time.

NORA: I am aware of that.

KROGSTAD: Are you? So you know all about it; I thought as much. Then I can ask you, without beating about the bush—is Mrs. Linde to have an appointment in the Bank?

NORA: What right have you to question me, Mr. Krogstad?—You, one of my husband's subordinates! But since you ask, you shall know. Yes, Mrs. Linde *is* to have an appointment. And it was I who pleaded her cause, Mr. Krogstad, let me tell you that.

KROGSTAD: I was right in what I thought, then.

NORA (*walking up and down the stage*): Sometimes one has a tiny little bit of influence, I should hope. Because one is a woman, it does not necessarily follow that—. When anyone is in a subordinate position, Mr. Krogstad, they should really be careful to avoid offending anyone who—who—

KROGSTAD: Who has influence?

NORA: Exactly.

KROGSTAD (*changing his tone*): Mrs. Helmer, you will be so good as to use your influence on my behalf.

NORA: What? What do you mean?

KROGSTAD: You will be so kind as to see that I am allowed to keep my subordinate position in the Bank.

NORA: What do you mean by that? Who proposes to take your post away from you?

KROGSTAD: Oh, there is no necessity to keep up the pretence of ignorance. I can quite understand that your friend is not very anxious to expose herself to the chance of rubbing shoulders with me; and I quite understand, too, whom I have to thank for being turned off.

NORA: But I assure you—

KROGSTAD: Very likely; but, to come to the point, the time has come when I should advise you to use your influence to prevent that.

NORA: But, Mr. Krogstad, I *have* no influence.

KROGSTAD: Haven't you? I thought you said yourself just now—

NORA: Naturally I did not mean you to put that construction on it. What should make you think I have any influence of that kind with my husband?

KROGSTAD: Oh, I have known your husband from our student days. I don't suppose he is any more unassailable than other husbands.

NORA: If you speak slightingly of my husband, I shall turn you out of the house.

KROGSTAD: You are bold, Mrs. Helmer.

NORA: I am not afraid of you any longer. As soon as the New Year comes, I shall in a very short time be free of the whole thing.

KROGSTAD (*controlling himself*): Listen to me, Mrs. Helmer. If necessary, I am prepared to fight for my small post in the Bank as if I were fighting for my life.

NORA: So it seems.

KROGSTAD: It is not only for the sake of the money; indeed, that weighs least with me in the matter. There is another reason—well, I may as well tell you. My position is this. I daresay you know, like everybody else, that once, many years ago, I was guilty of an indiscretion.

NORA: I think I have heard something of the kind.

KROGSTAD: The matter never came into court; but every way seemed to be closed to me after that. So I took to the business that you know of. I had to do something; and, honestly, I don't think I've been one of the worst. But now I must cut myself free from all that. My sons are growing up; for their sake I must try and win back as much respect as I can in the town. This post in the Bank was like the first step up for me—and now your husband is going to kick me downstairs again into the mud.

NORA: But you must believe me, Mr. Krogstad; it is not in my power to help you at all.

KROGSTAD: Then it is because you haven't the will; but I have means to compel you.

NORA: You don't mean that you will tell my husband that I owe you money?

KROGSTAD: Hm!—suppose I were to tell him?

NORA: It would be perfectly infamous of you. (*Sobbing.*) To think of his learning my secret, which has been my joy and pride, in such an ugly, clumsy way—that he should learn it from you! And it would put me in a horribly disagreeable position—

KROGSTAD: Only disagreeable?

NORA (*impetuously*): Well, do it, then!—and it will be the worse for you. My husband will see for himself what a blackguard you are, and you certainly won't keep your post then.

KROGSTAD: I asked you if it was only a disagreeable scene at home that you were afraid of?

NORA: If my husband does get to know of it, of course he will at once pay you what is still owing, and we shall have nothing more to do with you.

KROGSTAD (*coming a step nearer*): Listen to me, Mrs. Helmer. Either you have a very bad memory or you know very little of business. I shall be obliged to remind you of a few details.

NORA: What do you mean?

KROGSTAD: When your husband was ill, you came to me to borrow two hundred and fifty pounds.

NORA: I didn't know anyone else to go to.

KROGSTAD: I promised to get you that amount—

NORA: Yes, and you did so.

KROGSTAD: I promised to get you that amount, on certain conditions. Your mind was so taken up with your husband's illness, and you were so anxious to get the money for your journey, that you seem to have paid no attention to the conditions of our bargain. Therefore it will not be amiss if I remind you of them. Now, I promised to get the money on the security of a bond which I drew up.

NORA: Yes, and which I signed.

KROGSTAD: Good. But below your signature there were a few lines constituting your father a surety for the money; those lines your father should have signed.

NORA: Should? He did sign them.

KROGSTAD: I had left the date blank; that is to say, your father should himself have inserted the date on which he signed the paper. Do you remember that?

NORA: Yes, I think I remember—

KROGSTAD: Then I gave you the bond to send by post to your father. Is that not so?

NORA: Yes.

KROGSTAD: And you naturally did so at once, because five or six days afterwards you brought me the bond with your father's signature. And then I gave you the money.

NORA: Well, haven't I been paying it off regularly?

KROGSTAD: Fairly so, yes. But—to come back to the matter in hand— that must have been a very trying time for you, Mrs. Helmer.

NORA: It was, indeed.

KROGSTAD: Your father was very ill, wasn't he?

NORA: He was very near his end.

KROGSTAD: And he died soon afterwards?

NORA: Yes.

KROGSTAD: Tell me, Mrs. Helmer, can you by any chance remember what day your father died?—on what day of the month, I mean.

NORA: Papa died on the 29th of September.

KROGSTAD: That is correct; I have ascertained it for myself. And, as that is so, there is a discrepancy (*taking a paper from his pocket*) which I cannot account for.

NORA: What discrepancy? I don't know—

KROGSTAD: The discrepancy consists, Mrs. Helmer, in the fact that your father signed this bond three days after his death.

NORA: What do you mean? I don't understand—

KROGSTAD: Your father died on the 29th of September. But, look here; your father has dated his signature the 2nd of October. It is a discrepancy, isn't it? (*Nora is silent.*) Can you explain it to me? (*Nora is still silent.*) It is a remarkable thing, too, that the words "2nd of October," as well as the year, are not written in your father's handwriting but in one that I think I know. Well, of course it can be explained; your father may have forgotten to date his signature, and someone else may have dated it haphazard before they knew of his death. There is no harm in that. It all depends on the signature of the name; and *that* is genuine, I suppose, Mrs. Helmer? It was your father himself who signed his name here?

NORA (*after a short pause, throws her head up and looks defiantly at him*): No, it was not. It was I that wrote papa's name.

KROGSTAD: Are you aware that is a dangerous confession?

NORA: In what way? You shall have your money soon.

KROGSTAD: Let me ask you a question; why did you not send the paper to your father?

NORA: It was impossible; papa was so ill. If I had asked him for his signature, I should have had to tell him what the money was to be used for; and when he was so ill himself I couldn't tell him that my husband's life was in danger—it was impossible.

KROGSTAD: It would have been better for you if you had given up your trip abroad.

NORA: No, that was impossible. That trip was to save my husband's life; I couldn't give that up.

KROGSTAD: But did it never occur to you that you were committing a fraud on me?

NORA: I couldn't take that into account; I didn't trouble myself about you at all. I couldn't bear you, because you put so many heartless difficulties in my way, although you knew what a dangerous condition my husband was in.

KROGSTAD: Mrs. Helmer, you evidently do not realise clearly what it is that you have been guilty of. But I can assure you that my one false step, which lost me all my reputation, was nothing more or nothing worse than what you have done.

NORA: You? Do you ask me to believe that you were brave enough to run a risk to save your wife's life?

KROGSTAD: The law cares nothing about motives.

NORA: Then it must be a very foolish law.

KROGSTAD: Foolish or not, it is the law by which you will be judged, if I produce this paper in court.

NORA: I don't believe it. Is a daughter not to be allowed to spare her dying father anxiety and care? Is a wife not to be allowed to save her husband's life? I don't know much about law; but I am certain that there must be laws permitting such things as that. Have you no knowledge of such laws—you who are a lawyer? You must be a very poor lawyer, Mr. Krogstad.

KROGSTAD: Maybe. But matters of business—such business as you and I have had together—do you think I don't understand that? Very well. Do as you please. But let me tell you this—if I lose my position a second time, you shall lose yours with me. (*He bows, and goes out through the hall.*)

NORA (*appears buried in thought for a short time, then tosses her head*): Nonsense! Trying to frighten me like that!—I am not so silly as he thinks. (*Begins to busy herself putting the children's things in order.*) And yet—? No, it's impossible! I did it for love's sake.

CHILDREN (*in the doorway on the left*): Mother, the stranger man has gone out through the gate.

NORA: Yes, dears, I know. But, don't tell anyone about the stranger man. Do you hear? Not even papa.

CHILDREN: No, mother; but will you come and play again?

NORA: No, no,—not now.

CHILDREN: But, mother, you promised us.

NORA: Yes, but I can't now. Run away in; I have such a lot to do. Run away in, my sweet little darlings. (*She gets them into the room by degrees and shuts the door on them; then sits down on the sofa, takes up a piece of needlework and sews a few stitches, but soon stops.*) No! (*Throws down the work, gets up, goes to the hall door and calls out.*) Helen! bring the Tree in. (*Goes to the table on the left, opens a drawer, and stops again.*) No, no! it is quite impossible!

MAID (*coming in with the Tree*): Where shall I put it, ma'am?

NORA: Here, in the middle of the floor.

MAID: Shall I get you anything else?

NORA: No, thank you. I have all I want.   (*Exit Maid.*)

NORA (*begins dressing the tree*): A candle here—and flowers here—. The horrible man! It's all nonsense—there's nothing wrong. The Tree shall be splendid! I will do everything I can think of to please you, Torvald!— I will sing for you, dance for you—(*Helmer comes in with some papers under his arm.*) Oh! are you back already?

HELMER: Yes. Has anyone been here?

NORA: Here? No.

HELMER: That is strange. I saw Krogstad going out of the gate.

NORA: Did you? Oh yes, I forgot, Krogstad was here for a moment.

HELMER: Nora, I can see from your manner that he has been here begging you to say a good word for him.

NORA: Yes.

HELMER: And you were to appear to do it of your own accord; you were to conceal from me the fact of his having been here; didn't he beg that of you too?

NORA: Yes, Torvald, but—

HELMER: Nora, Nora, and you would be a party to that sort of thing? To have any talk with a man like that, and give him any sort of promise? And to tell me a lie into the bargain?

NORA: A lie—?

HELMER: Didn't you tell me no one had been here? (*Shakes his finger at her.*) My little song-bird must never do that again. A song-bird must have a clean beak to chirp with—no false notes! (*Puts his arm around her waist.*) That is so, isn't it? Yes, I am sure it is. (*Lets her go.*) We will say no more about it. (*Sits down by the stove.*) How warm and snug it is here! (*Turns over his papers.*)

NORA (*after a short pause, during which she busies herself with the Christmas Tree*): Torvald!

HELMER: Yes.

NORA: I am looking forward tremendously to the fancy-dress ball at the Stenborgs' the day after to-morrow.

HELMER: And I am tremendously curious to see what you are going to surprise me with.

NORA: It was very silly of me to want to do that.

HELMER: What do you mean?

NORA: I can't hit upon anything that will do; everything I think of seems so silly and insignificant.

HELMER: Does my little Nora acknowledge that at last?

NORA (*standing behind his chair with her arms on the back of it*): Are you very busy, Torvald?

HELMER: Well—

NORA: What are all those papers?

HELMER: Bank business.

NORA: Already?

HELMER: I have got authority from the retiring manager to undertake the necessary changes in the staff and in the rearrangement of the work; and I must make use of the Christmas week for that, so as to have everything in order for the new year.

NORA: Then that was why this poor Krogstad—

HELMER: Hm!

NORA (*leans against the back of his chair and strokes his hair*): If you hadn't been so busy I should have asked you a tremendously big favour, Torvald.

HELMER: What is that? Tell me.

NORA: There is no one has such good taste as you. And I do so want to look nice at the fancy-dress ball. Torvald, couldn't you take me in hand and decide what I shall go as, and what sort of a dress I shall wear?

HELMER: Aha! so my obstinate little woman is obliged to get someone to come to her rescue?

NORA: Yes, Torvald, I can't get along a bit without your help.

HELMER: Very well, I will think it over, we shall manage to hit upon something.

NORA: That is nice of you. (*Goes to the Christmas Tree. A short pause.*) How pretty the red flowers look—. But, tell me, was it really something very bad that this Krogstad was guilty of?

HELMER: He forged someone's name. Have you any idea what that means?

NORA: Isn't it possible that he was driven to do it by necessity?

HELMER: Yes; or, as in so many cases, by imprudence. I am not so heartless as to condemn a man altogether because of a single false step of that kind.

NORA: No, you wouldn't, would you, Torvald?

HELMER: Many a man has been able to retrieve his character, if he has openly confessed his fault and taken his punishment.

NORA: Punishment—?

HELMER: But Krogstad did nothing of that sort; he got himself out of it by a cunning trick, and that is why he has gone under altogether.

NORA: But do you think it would—?

HELMER: Just think how a guilty man like that has to lie and play the hypocrite with every one, how he has to wear a mask in the presence of those near and dear to him, even before his own wife and children. And about the children—that is the most terrible part of it all, Nora.

NORA: How?

HELMER: Because such an atmosphere of lies infects and poisons the whole life of a home. Each breath the children take in such a house is full of the germs of evil.

NORA (*coming nearer him*): Are you sure of that?

HELMER: My dear, I have often seen it in the course of my life as a lawyer. Almost everyone who has gone to the bad early in life has had a deceitful mother.

NORA: Why do you only say—mother?

HELMER: It seems most commonly to be the mother's influence, though naturally a bad father's would have the same result. Every lawyer is familiar with the fact. This Krogstad, now, has been persistently poisoning his own children with lies and dissimulation; that is why I say he has lost all moral character. (*Holds out his hands to her.*) That is why my sweet little Nora must promise me not to plead his cause. Give me your hand on it. Come, come, what is this? Give me your hand. There now, that's settled. I assure you it would be quite impossible for me to work with him; I literally feel physically ill when I am in the company of such people.

NORA (*takes her hand out of his and goes to the opposite side of the Christmas Tree*): How hot it is in here; and I have such a lot to do.

HELMER (*getting up and putting his papers in order*): Yes, and I must try and read through some of these before dinner; and I must think about your costume, too. And it is just possible I may have something ready in gold paper to hang up on the Tree. (*Puts his hand on her head.*) My precious little singing-bird! (*He goes into his room and shuts the door after him.*)

NORA (*after a pause, whispers*): No, no—it isn't true. It's impossible; it must be impossible.

(*The Nurse opens the door on the left.*)

NURSE: The little ones are begging so hard to be allowed to come in to mamma.

NORA: No, no, no! Don't let them come in to me! You stay with them, Anne.

NURSE: Very well, ma'am. (*Shuts the door.*)

NORA (*pale with terror*): Deprave my little children? Poison my home? (*A short pause. Then she tosses her head.*) It's not true. It can't possibly be true.

ACT II

The Same Scene: *The Christmas Tree is in the corner by the piano, stripped of its ornaments and with burnt-down candle-ends on its dishevelled branches. Nora's cloak and hat are lying on the sofa. She is alone in the room, walking about uneasily. She stops by the sofa and takes up her cloak.*

NORA (*drops her cloak*): Someone is coming now! (*Goes to the door and listens.*) No—it is no one. Of course, no one will come to-day, Christmas Day—nor to-morrow either. But, perhaps—(*opens the door and looks out*). No, nothing in the letter-box; it is quite empty. (*Comes forward.*) What rubbish! of course he can't be in earnest about it. Such a thing couldn't happen; it is impossible—I have three little children.

(*Enter the Nurse from the room on the left, carrying a big cardboard box.*)

NURSE: At last I have found the box with the fancy dress.

NORA: Thanks; put it on the table.

NURSE (*doing so*): But it is very much in want of mending.

NORA: I should like to tear it into a hundred thousand pieces.

NURSE: What an idea! It can easily be put in order—just a little patience.

NORA: Yes, I will go and get Mrs. Linde to come and help me with it.

NURSE: What, out again? In this horrible weather? You will catch cold, ma'am, and make yourself ill.

NORA: Well, worse than that might happen. How are the children?

NURSE: The poor little souls are playing with their Christmas presents, but—

NORA: Do they ask much for me?

NURSE: You see, they are so accustomed to have their mamma with them.

NORA: Yes, but, nurse, I shall not be able to be so much with them now as I was before.

NURSE: Oh well, young children easily get accustomed to anything.

NORA: Do you think so? Do you think they would forget their mother if she went away altogether?

NURSE: Good heavens!—went away altogether?

NORA: Nurse, I want you to tell me something I have often wondered about—how could you have the heart to put your own child out among strangers?

NURSE: I was obliged to, if I wanted to be little Nora's nurse.

NORA: Yes, but how could you be willing to do it?

NURSE: What, when I was going to get such a good place by it? A poor girl who has got into trouble should be glad to. Besides, that wicked man didn't do a single thing for me.

NORA: But I suppose your daughter has quite forgotten you.

NURSE: No, indeed she hasn't. She wrote to me when she was confirmed, and when she was married.

NORA (*putting her arms round her neck*): Dear old Anne, you were a good mother to me when I was little.

NURSE: Little Nora, poor dear, had no other mother but me.

NORA: And if my little ones had no other mother, I am sure you would— What nonsense I am talking! (*Opens the box.*) Go in to them. Now I must—. You will see to-morrow how charming I shall look.

NURSE: I am sure there will be no one at the ball so charming as you, ma'am. (*Goes into the room on the left.*)

NORA (*begins to unpack the box, but soon pushes it away from her*): If only I dared go out. If only no one would come. If only I could be sure nothing would happen here in the meantime. Stuff and nonsense! No one will come. Only I mustn't think about it. I will brush my muff. What lovely, lovely gloves! Out of my thoughts, out of my thoughts! One, two, three, four, five, six—(*Screams.*) Ah! there is someone coming—. (*Makes a movement towards the door, but stands irresolute.*)

(*Enter Mrs. Linde from the hall, where she has taken off her cloak and hat.*)

NORA: Oh, it's you, Christine. There is no one else out there, is there? How good of you to come!

MRS. LINDE: I heard you were up asking for me

NORA: Yes, I was passing by. As a matter of fact, it is something you could help me with. Let us sit down here on the sofa. Look here. To-morrow evening there is to be a fancy-dress ball at the Stenborgs', who live above us; and Torvald wants me to go as a Neapolitan fisher-girl, and dance the Tarantella that I learned at Capri.

MRS. LINDE: I see; you are going to keep up the character.

NORA: Yes, Torvald wants me to. Look, here is the dress; Torvald had it made for me there, but now it is all so torn, and I haven't any idea—

MRS. LINDE: We will easily put that right. It is only some of the trimming come unsewn here and there. Needle and thread? Now then, that's all we want.

NORA: It *is* nice of you.

MRS. LINDE (*sewing*): So you are going to be dressed up to-morrow, Nora. I will tell you what—I shall come in for a moment and see you in your fine feathers. But I have completely forgotten to thank you for a delightful evening yesterday.

NORA (*gets up, and crosses the stage*): Well, I don't think yesterday was as pleasant as usual. You ought to have come to town a little earlier, Christine. Certainly Torvald does understand how to make a house dainty and attractive.

MRS. LINDE: And so do you, it seems to me; you are not your father's daughter for nothing. But tell me, is Doctor Rank always as depressed as he was yesterday?

NORA: No; yesterday it was very noticeable. I must tell you that he suffers from a very dangerous disease. He has consumption of the spine, poor creature. His father was a horrible man who committed all sorts of excesses; and that is why his son was sickly from childhood, do you understand?

MRS. LINDE (*dropping her sewing*): But, my dearest Nora, how do you know anything about such things?

NORA (*walking about*): Pooh! When you have three children, you get visits now and then from—from married women, who know something of medical matters, and they talk about one thing and another.

MRS. LINDE: (*goes on sewing. A short silence*) Does Doctor Rank come here everyday?

NORA: Everyday regularly. He is Torvald's most intimate friend, and a great friend of mine too. He is just like one of the family.

MRS. LINDE: But tell me this—is he perfectly sincere? I mean, isn't he the kind of man that is very anxious to make himself agreeable?

NORA: Not in the least. What makes you think that?

MRS. LINDE: When you introduced him to me yesterday, he declared he had often heard my name mentioned in this house; but afterwards I noticed that your husband hadn't the slightest idea who I was. So how could Doctor Rank—?

NORA: That is quite right, Christine. Torvald is so absurdly fond of me that he wants me absolutely to himself, as he says. At first he used to seem almost jealous if I mentioned any of the dear folk at home, so naturally I gave up doing so. But I often talk about such things with Doctor Rank, because he likes hearing about them.

MRS. LINDE: Listen to me, Nora. You are still very like a child in many things, and I am older than you in many ways and have a little more experience. Let me tell you this—you ought to make an end of it with Doctor Rank.

NORA: What ought I to make an end of?

MRS. LINDE: Of two things, I think. Yesterday you talked some nonsense about a rich admirer who was to leave you money—

NORA: An admirer who doesn't exist, unfortunately! But what then?

MRS. LINDE: Is Doctor Rank a man of means?

NORA: Yes, he is.

MRS. LINDE: And has no one to provide for?

NORA: No, no one; but—

MRS. LINDE: And comes here everyday?

NORA: Yes, I told you so.

MRS. LINDE: But how can this well-bred man be so tactless?

NORA: I don't understand you at all.

MRS. LINDE: Don't prevaricate, Nora. Do you suppose I don't guess who lent you the two hundred and fifty pounds?

NORA: Are you out of your senses? How can you think of such a thing! A friend of ours, who comes here everyday! Do you realise what a horribly painful position that would be?

MRS. LINDE: Then it really isn't he?

NORA: No, certainly not. It would never have entered into my head for a moment. Besides, he had no money to lend then; he came into his money afterwards.

MRS. LINDE: Well, I think that was lucky for you, my dear Nora.

NORA: No, it would never have come into my head to ask Doctor Rank. Although I am quite sure that if I had asked him—

MRS. LINDE: But of course you won't.

NORA: Of course not. I have no reason to think it could possibly be necessary. But I am quite sure that if I told Doctor Rank—

MRS. LINDE: Behind your husband's back?

NORA: I must make an end of it with the other one, and that will be behind his back too. I *must* make an end of it with him.

MRS. LINDE: Yes, that is what I told you yesterday, but—

NORA (*walking up and down*): A man can put a thing like that straight much easier than a woman—

MRS. LINDE: One's husband, yes.

NORA: Nonsense! (*Standing still.*) When you pay off a debt you get your bond back, don't you?

MRS. LINDE: Yes, as a matter of course.

NORA: And can tear it into a hundred thousand pieces, and burn it up— the nasty dirty paper!

MRS. LINDE (*looks hard at her, lays down her sewing and gets up slowly*): Nora, you are concealing something from me.

NORA: Do I look as if I were?

MRS. LINDE: Something has happened to you since yesterday morning. Nora, what is it?

NORA (*going nearer to her*): Christine! (*Listens.*) Hush! there's Torvald come home. Do you mind going in to the children for the present? Torvald can't bear to see dressmaking going on. Let Anne help you.

MRS. LINDE (*gathering some of the things together*): Certainly—but I am not going away from here until we have had it out with one another. (*She goes into the room on the left, as Helmer comes in from the hall.*)

NORA (*going up to Helmer*): I have wanted you so much, Torvald dear.

HELMER: Was that the dressmaker?

NORA: No, it was Christine; she is helping me to put my dress in order. You will see I shall look quite smart.

HELMER: Wasn't that a happy thought of mine, now?

NORA: Splendid! But don't you think it is nice of me, too, to do as you wish?

HELMER: Nice?—because you do as your husband wishes? Well, well, you little rogue, I am sure you did not mean it in that way. But I am not going to disturb you; you will want to be trying on your dress, I expect.

NORA: I suppose you are going to work.

HELMER: Yes. (*Shows her a bundle of papers.*) Look at that. I have just been into the bank. (*Turns to go into his room.*)

NORA: Torvald.

HELMER: Yes.

NORA: If your little squirrel were to ask you for something very, very prettily—?

HELMER: What then?

NORA: Would you do it?

HELMER: I should like to hear what it is, first.

NORA: Your squirrel would run about and do all her tricks if you would be nice, and do what she wants.

HELMER: Speak plainly.

NORA: Your skylark would chirp about in every room, with her song rising and falling—

HELMER: Well, my skylark does that anyhow.

NORA: I would play the fairy and dance for you in the moonlight, Torvald.

HELMER: Nora—you surely don't mean that request you made to me this morning?

NORA (*going near him*): Yes, Torvald, I beg you so earnestly—

HELMER: Have you really the courage to open up that question again?

NORA: Yes, dear, you *must* do as I ask; you *must* let Krogstad keep his post in the bank.

HELMER: My dear Nora, it is his post that I have arranged Mrs. Linde shall have.

NORA: Yes, you have been awfully kind about that; but you could just as well dismiss some other clerk instead of Krogstad.

HELMER: This is simply incredible obstinacy! Because you chose to give him a thoughtless promise that you would speak for him, I am expected to—

NORA: That isn't the reason, Torvald. It is for your own sake. This fellow writes in the most scurrilous newspapers; you have told me so yourself. He can do you an unspeakable amount of harm. I am frightened to death of him—

HELMER: Ah, I understand; it is recollections of the past that scare you.

NORA: What do you mean?

HELMER: Naturally you are thinking of your father.

NORA: Yes—yes, of course. Just recall to your mind what these malicious creatures wrote in the papers about papa, and how horribly they slandered him. I believe they would have procured his dismissal if the Department had not sent you over to inquire into it, and if you had not been so kindly disposed and helpful to him.

HELMER: My little Nora, there is an important difference between your father and me. Your father's reputation as a public official was not above suspicion. Mine is, and I hope it will continue to be so, as long as I hold my office.

NORA: You never can tell what mischief these men may contrive. We ought to be so well off, so snug and happy here in our peaceful home, and have no cares—you and I and the children, Torvald! That is why I beg you so earnestly—

HELMER: And it is just by interceding for him that you make it impossible for me to keep him. It is already known at the Bank that I mean to dismiss Krogstad. Is it to get about now that the new manager has changed his mind at his wife's bidding—

NORA: And what if it did?

HELMER: Of course!—if only this obstinate little person can get her way! Do you suppose I am going to make myself ridiculous before my whole staff, to let people think that I am a man to be swayed by all sorts of outside influence? I should very soon feel the consequences of it, I can tell you! And besides, there is one thing that makes it quite impossible for me to have Krogstad in the Bank as long as I am manager.

NORA: Whatever is that?

HELMER: His moral failings I might perhaps have overlooked, if necessary—

NORA: Yes, you could—couldn't you?

HELMER: And I hear he is a good worker, too. But I knew him when we were boys. It was one of those rash friendships that so often prove an incubus in afterlife. I may as well tell you plainly, we were once on very intimate terms with one another. But this tactless fellow lays no restraint on himself when other people are present. On the contrary, he thinks it gives him the right to adopt a familiar tone with me, and every minute it is "I say, Helmer, old fellow!" and that sort of thing. I assure you it is extremely painful for me. He would make my position in the Bank intolerable.

NORA: Torvald, I don't believe you mean that.

HELMER: Don't you? Why not?

NORA: Because it is such a narrow-minded way of looking at things.

HELMER: What are you saying? Narrow-minded? Do you think I am narrow-minded?

NORA: No, just the opposite, dear—and it is exactly for that reason.

HELMER: It's the same thing. You say my point of view is narrow-minded, so I must be so too. Narrow-minded! Very well—I must put an end to this. (*Goes to the hall door and calls.*) Helen!

NORA: What are you going to do?

HELMER (*looking among his papers*): Settle it. (*Enter Maid.*) Look here; take this letter and go downstairs with it at once. Find a messenger and tell him to deliver it, and be quick. The address is on it, and here is the money.

MAID: Very well, sir. (*Exit with the letter.*)

HELMER (*putting his papers together*): Now then, little Miss Obstinate.

NORA (*breathlessly*): Torvald—what was that letter?

HELMER: Krogstad's dismissal.

NORA: Call her back, Torvald! There is still time. Oh Torvald, call her back! Do it for my sake—for your own sake—for the children's sake! Do you hear me, Torvald? Call her back! You don't know what that letter can bring upon us.

HELMER: It's too late.

NORA: Yes, it's too late.

HELMER: My dear Nora, I can forgive the anxiety you are in, although really it is an insult to me. It is, indeed. Isn't it an insult to think that I should be afraid of a starving quill-driver's vengeance? But I forgive you nevertheless, because it is such eloquent witness to your great love for me. (*Takes her in his arms.*) And that is as it should be, my own darling Nora. Come what will, you may be sure I shall have both courage and strength if they be needed. You will see I am man enough to take everything upon myself.

NORA (*in a horror-stricken voice*): What do you mean by that?

HELMER: Everything, I say—

NORA (*recovering herself*): You will never have to do that.

HELMER: That's right. Well, we will share it, Nora, as man and wife should. That is how it shall be. (*Caressing her.*) Are you content now? There! there!—not these frightened dove's eyes! The whole thing is only the wildest fancy!—Now, you must go and play through the Tarantella and practise with your tambourine. I shall go into the inner office and shut the door, and I shall hear nothing; you can make as much noise as you please. (*Turns back at the door.*) And when Rank comes, tell him where he will find me. (*Nods to her, takes his papers and goes into his room, and shuts the door after him.*)

NORA (*bewildered with anxiety, stands as if rooted to the spot, and whispers*): He was capable of doing it. He will do it. He will do it in spite of everything.—No, not that! Never, never! Anything rather than that! Oh, for some help, some way out of it! (*The door-bell rings.*) Doctor Rank! Anything rather than that—anything, whatever it is! (*She puts her hands over her face, pulls herself together, goes to the door and opens it. Rank is standing without, hanging up his coat. During the following dialogue it begins to grow dark.*)

NORA: Good-day, Doctor Rank. I knew your ring. But you mustn't go in to Torvald now; I think he is busy with something.

RANK: And you?

NORA (*brings him in and shuts the door after him*): Oh, you know very well I always have time for you.

RANK: Thank you. I shall make use of as much of it as I can.

NORA: What do you mean by that? As much of it as you can?

RANK: Well, does that alarm you?

NORA: It was such a strange way of putting it. Is anything likely to happen?

RANK: Nothing but what I have long been prepared for. But I certainly didn't expect it to happen so soon.

NORA (*gripping him by the arm*): What have you found out? Doctor Rank, you must tell me.

RANK (*sitting down by the stove*): It is all up with me. And it can't be helped.

NORA (*with a sigh of relief*): Is it about yourself?

RANK: Who else? It is no use lying to one's self. I am the most wretched of all my patients, Mrs. Helmer. Lately I have been taking stock of my internal economy. Bankrupt! Probably within a month I shall lie rotting in the churchyard.

NORA: What an ugly thing to say!

RANK: The thing itself is cursedly ugly, and the worst of it is that I shall have to face so much more that is ugly before that. I shall only make one more examination of myself; when I have done that, I shall know pretty certainly when it will be that the horrors of dissolution will begin. There is something I want to tell you. Helmer's refined nature gives him an unconquerable disgust at everything that is ugly; I won't have him in my sick-room.

NORA: Oh, but, Doctor Rank—

RANK: I won't have him there. Not on any account. I bar my door to him. As soon as I am quite certain that the worst has come, I shall send you my card with a black cross on it, and then you will know that the loathsome end has begun.

NORA: You are quite absurd to-day. And I wanted you so much to be in a really good humour.

RANK: With death stalking beside me?—To have to pay this penalty for another man's sin? Is there any justice in that? And in every single family, in one way or another, some such inexorable retribution is being exacted—

NORA (*putting her hands over her ears*): Rubbish! Do talk of something cheerful.

RANK: Oh, it's a mere laughing matter, the whole thing. My poor innocent spine has to suffer for my father's youthful amusements.

NORA (*sitting at the table on the left*): I suppose you mean that he was too partial to asparagus and pâté de foie gras, don't you?

RANK: Yes, and to truffles.

NORA: Truffles, yes. And oysters too, I suppose?

RANK: Oysters, of course, that goes without saying.

NORA: And heaps of port and champagne. It is sad that all these nice things should take their revenge on our bones.

RANK: Especially that they should revenge themselves on the unlucky bones of those who have not had the satisfaction of enjoying them.

NORA: Yes, that's the saddest part of it all.

RANK (*with a searching look at her*): Hm!—

NORA (*after a short pause*): Why did you smile?

RANK: No, it was you that laughed.

NORA: No, it was you that smiled, Doctor Rank!

RANK (*rising*): You are a greater rascal than I thought.

NORA: I am in a silly mood to-day.

RANK: So it seems.

NORA (*putting her hands on his shoulders*): Dear, dear Doctor Rank, death mustn't take you away from Torvald and me.

RANK: It is a loss you would easily recover from. Those who are gone are soon forgotten.

NORA (*looking at him anxiously*): Do you believe that?

RANK: People form new ties, and then—

NORA: Who will form new ties?

RANK: Both you and Helmer, when I am gone. You yourself are already on the high road to it, I think. What did that Mrs. Linde want here last night?

NORA: Oho!—you don't mean to say you are jealous of poor Christine?

RANK: Yes, I am. She will be my successor in this house. When I am done for, this woman will—

NORA: Hush! don't speak so loud. She is in that room.

RANK: To-day again. There, you see.

NORA: She has only come to sew my dress for me. Bless my soul, how unreasonable you are! (*Sits down on the sofa.*) Be nice now, Doctor Rank, and to-morrow you will see how beautifully I shall dance, and you can imagine I am doing it all for you—and for Torvald too, of course. (*Takes various things out of the box.*) Doctor Rank, come and sit down here, and I will show you something.

RANK (*sitting down*): What is it?

NORA: Just look at those!

RANK: Silk stockings.

NORA: Flesh-coloured. Aren't they lovely? It is so dark here now, but to-morrow—. No, no, no! you must only look at the feet. Oh well, you may have leave to look at the legs too.

RANK: Hm!—

NORA: Why are you looking so critical? Don't you think they will fit me?

RANK: I have no means of forming an opinion about that.

NORA (*looks at him for a moment*): For shame! (*Hits him lightly on the ear with the stockings.*) That's to punish you. (*Folds them up again.*)

RANK: And what other nice things am I to be allowed to see?

NORA: Not a single thing more, for being so naughty. (*She looks among the things, humming to herself.*)

RANK (*after a short silence*): When I am sitting here, talking to you as intimately as this, I cannot imagine for a moment what would have become of me if I had never come into this house.

NORA (*smiling*): I believe you do feel thoroughly at home with us.

RANK (*in a lower voice, looking straight in front of him*): And to be obliged to leave it all—

NORA: Nonsense, you are not going to leave it.

RANK (*as before*): And not be able to leave behind one the slightest token of one's gratitude, scarcely even a fleeting regret—nothing but an empty place which the first comer can fill as well as any other.

NORA: And if I asked you now for a—? No!

RANK: For what?

NORA: For a big proof of your friendship—

RANK: Yes, yes!

NORA: I mean a tremendously big favour.

RANK: Would you really make me so happy for once?

NORA: Ah, but you don't know what it is yet.

RANK: No—but tell me.

NORA: I really can't, Doctor Rank. It is something out of all reason; it means advice, and help, and a favour—

RANK: The bigger a thing it is the better. I can't conceive what it is you mean. Do tell me. Haven't I your confidence?

NORA: More than anyone else. I know you are my truest and best friend, and so I will tell you what it is. Well, Doctor Rank, it is something you must help me to prevent. You know how devotedly, how inexpressibly deeply Torvald loves me; he would never for a moment hesitate to give his life for me.

RANK (*leaning towards her*): Nora—do you think he is the only one—?

NORA (*with a slight start*): The only one—?

RANK: The only one who would gladly give his life for your sake.

NORA (*sadly*): Is that it?

RANK: I was determined you should know it before I went away, and there will never be a better opportunity than this. Now you know it, Nora. And now you know, too, that you can trust me as you would trust no one else.

NORA (*rises, deliberately and quietly*): Let me pass.

RANK (*makes room for her to pass him, but sits still*): Nora!

NORA (*at the hall door*): Helen, bring in the lamp. (*Goes over to the stove.*) Dear Doctor Rank, that was really horrid of you.

RANK: To have loved you as much as anyone else does? Was that horrid?

NORA: No, but to go and tell me so. There was really no need—

RANK: What do you mean? Did you know—? (*Maid enters with lamp, puts it down on the table, and goes out.*) Nora—Mrs. Helmer—tell me, had you any idea of this?

NORA: Oh, how do I know whether I had or whether I hadn't? I really can't tell you—To think you could be so clumsy, Doctor Rank! We were getting on so nicely.

RANK: Well, at all events you know now that you can command me, body and soul. So won't you speak out?

NORA (*looking at him*): After what happened?

RANK: I beg you to let me know what it is.

NORA: I can't tell you anything now.

RANK: Yes, yes. You mustn't punish me in that way. Let me have permission to do for you whatever a man may do.

NORA: You can do nothing for me now. Besides, I really don't need any help at all. You will find that the whole thing is merely fancy on my part. It really is so—of course it is! (*Sits down in the rocking-chair, and looks at him with a smile.*) You are a nice sort of man, Doctor Rank!— don't you feel ashamed of yourself, now the lamp has come?

RANK: Not a bit. But perhaps I had better go—for ever?

NORA: No, indeed, you shall not. Of course you must come here just as before. You know very well Torvald can't do without you.

RANK: Yes, but you?

NORA: Oh, I am always tremendously pleased when you come.

RANK: It is just that, that put me on the wrong track. You are a riddle to me. I have often thought that you would almost as soon be in my company as in Helmer's.

NORA: Yes—you see there are some people one loves best, and others whom one would almost always rather have as companions.

RANK: Yes, there is something in that.

NORA: When I was at home, of course I loved papa best. But I always thought it tremendous fun if I could steal down into the maids' room, because they never moralised at all, and talked to each other about such entertaining things.

RANK: I see—it is *their* place I have taken.

NORA (*jumping up and going to him*): Oh, dear, nice Doctor Rank, I never meant that at all. But surely you can understand that being with Torvald is a little like being with papa—

(*Enter Maid from the hall.*)

MAID: If you please, ma'am. (*Whispers and hands her a card.*)

NORA (*glancing at the card*): Oh! (*Puts it in her pocket.*)

RANK: Is there anything wrong?

NORA: No, no, not in the least. It is only something—it is my new dress—

RANK: What? Your dress is lying there.

NORA: Oh, yes, that one; but this is another. I ordered it. Torvald mustn't know about it—

RANK: Oho! Then that was the great secret.

NORA: Of course. Just go in to him; he is sitting in the inner room. Keep him as long as—

RANK: Make your mind easy; I won't let him escape. (*Goes into Helmer's room.*)

NORA (*to the Maid*): And he is standing waiting in the kitchen?

MAID: Yes; he came up the back stairs.

NORA: But didn't you tell him no one was in?

MAID: Yes, but it was no good.

NORA: He won't go away?

MAID: No; he says he won't until he has seen you, ma'am.

NORA: Well, let him come in—but quietly. Helen, you mustn't say anything about it to anyone. It is a surprise for my husband.

MAID: Yes, ma'am, I quite understand. (*Exit.*)

NORA: This dreadful thing is going to happen! It will happen in spite of me! No, no, no, it can't happen—it shan't happen! (*She bolts the door of Helmer's room. The Maid opens the hall door for Krogstad and shuts it after him. He is wearing a fur coat, high boots and a fur cap.*)

NORA (*advancing towards him*): Speak low—my husband is at home.

KROGSTAD: No matter about that.

NORA: What do you want of me?

KROGSTAD: An explanation of something.

NORA: Make haste then. What is it?

KROGSTAD: You know, I suppose, that I have got my dismissal.

NORA: I couldn't prevent it, Mr. Krogstad. I fought as hard as I could on your side, but it was no good.

KROGSTAD: Does your husband love you so little, then? He knows what I can expose you to, and yet he ventures—

NORA: How can you suppose that he has any knowledge of the sort?

KROGSTAD: I didn't suppose so at all. It would not be the least like our dear Torvald Helmer to show so much courage—

NORA: Mr. Krogstad, a little respect for my husband, please.

KROGSTAD: Certainly—all the respect he deserves. But since you have kept the matter so carefully to yourself, I make bold to suppose that you have a little clearer idea, than you had yesterday, of what it actually is that you have done?

NORA: More than you could ever teach me.

KROGSTAD: Yes, such a bad lawyer as I am.

NORA: What is it you want of me?

KROGSTAD: Only to see how you were, Mrs. Helmer. I have been thinking about you all day long. A mere cashier, a quill-driver, a— well, a man like me—even he has a little of what is called feeling, you know.

NORA: Show it, then; think of my little children.

KROGSTAD: Have you and your husband thought of mine? But never mind about that. I only wanted to tell you that you need not take this matter too seriously. In the first place there will be no accusation made on my part.

NORA: No, of course not; I was sure of that.

KROGSTAD: The whole thing can be arranged amicably; there is no reason why anyone should know anything about it. It will remain a secret between us three.

NORA: My husband must never get to know anything about it.

KROGSTAD: How will you be able to prevent it? Am I to understand that you can pay the balance that is owing?

NORA: No, not just at present.

KROGSTAD: Or perhaps that you have some expedient for raising the money soon?

NORA: No expedient that I mean to make use of.

KROGSTAD: Well, in any case, it would have been of no use to you now. If you stood there with ever so much money in your hand, I would never part with your bond.

NORA: Tell me what purpose you mean to put it to.

KROGSTAD: I shall only preserve it—keep it in my possession. No one who is not concerned in the matter shall have the slightest hint of it. So that if the thought of it has driven you to any desperate resolution—

NORA: It has.

KROGSTAD: If you had it in your mind to run away from your home—

NORA: I had.

KROGSTAD: Or even something worse—

NORA: How could you know that?

KROGSTAD: Give up the idea.

NORA: How did you know I had thought of *that*?

KROGSTAD: Most of us think of that at first. I did, too—but I hadn't the courage.

NORA (*faintly*): No more had I.

KROGSTAD (*in a tone of relief*): No, that's it, isn't it—you hadn't the courage either?

NORA: No, I haven't—I haven't.

KROGSTAD: Besides, it would have been a great piece of folly. Once the first storm at home is over—. I have a letter for your husband in my pocket.

NORA: Telling him everything?

KROGSTAD: In as lenient a manner as I possibly could.

NORA (*quickly*): He mustn't get the letter. Tear it up. I will find some means of getting money.

KROGSTAD: Excuse me, Mrs. Helmer, but I think I told you just now—

NORA: I am not speaking of what I owe you. Tell me what sum you are asking my husband for, and I will get the money.

KROGSTAD: I am not asking your husband for a penny.

NORA: What do you want, then?

KROGSTAD: I will tell you. I want to rehabilitate myself, Mrs. Helmer; I want to get on; and in that your husband must help me. For the last year and a half I have not had a hand in anything dishonourable, and all that time I have been struggling in most restricted circumstances. I was content to work my way up step by step. Now I am turned out, and I am not going to be satisfied with merely being taken into favour again. I want to get on, I tell you. I want to get into the Bank again, in a higher position. Your husband must make a place for me—

NORA: That he will never do!

KROGSTAD: He will; I know him; he dare not protest. And as soon as I am in there again with him, then you will see! Within a year I shall be the manager's right hand. It will be Nils Krogstad and not Torvald Helmer who manages the Bank.

NORA: That's a thing you will never see!

KROGSTAD: Do you mean that you will—?

NORA: I have courage enough for it now.

KROGSTAD: Oh, you can't frighten me. A fine, spoilt lady like you—

NORA: You will see, you will see.

KROGSTAD: Under the ice, perhaps? Down into the cold, coal-black water? And then, in the spring, to float up to the surface, all horrible and unrecognisable, with your hair fallen out—

NORA: You can't frighten me.

KROGSTAD: Nor you me. People don't do such things, Mrs. Helmer. Besides, what use would it be? I should have him completely in my power all the same.

NORA: Afterwards? When I am no longer—

KROGSTAD: Have you forgotten that it is I who have the keeping of your reputation? (*Nora stands speechlessly looking at him.*) Well, now, I have warned you. Do not do anything foolish. When Helmer has had my letter, I shall expect a message from him. And be sure you remember that it is your husband himself who has forced me into such ways as this again. I will never forgive him for that. Good-bye, Mrs. Helmer. (*Exit through the hall.*)

NORA (*goes to the hall door, opens it slightly and listens*): He is going. He is not putting the letter in the box. Oh no, no! that's impossible! (*Opens the door by degrees.*) What is that? He is standing outside. He is not going downstairs. Is he hesitating? Can he—? (*A letter drops into the box; then*

Krogstad's footsteps are heard, till they die away as he goes downstairs. Nora utters a stifled cry, and runs across the room to the table by the sofa. A short pause.)

NORA: In the letter-box. (*Steals across to the hall door.*) There it lies— Torvald, Torvald, there is no hope for us now!

(*Mrs. Linde comes in from the room on the left, carrying the dress.*)

MRS. LINDE: There, I can't see anything more to mend now. Would you like to try it on—?

NORA (*in a hoarse whisper*): Christine, come here.

MRS. LINDE (*throwing the dress down on the sofa*): What is the matter with you? You look so agitated!

NORA: Come here. Do you see that letter? There, look—you can see it through the glass in the letter-box.

MRS. LINDE: Yes, I see it.

NORA: That letter is from Krogstad.

MRS. LINDE: Nora—it was Krogstad who lent you the money!

NORA: Yes, and now Torvald will know all about it.

MRS. LINDE: Believe me, Nora, that's the best thing for both of you.

NORA: You don't know all. I forged a name.

MRS. LINDE: Good heavens—!

NORA: I only want to say this to you, Christine—you must be my witness.

MRS. LINDE: Your witness? What do you mean? What am I to—?

NORA: If I should go out of my mind—and it might easily happen—

MRS. LINDE: Nora!

NORA: Or if anything else should happen to me—anything, for instance, that might prevent my being here—

MRS. LINDE: Nora! Nora! you are quite out of your mind.

NORA: And if it should happen that there were some one who wanted to take all the responsibility, all the blame, you understand—

MRS. LINDE: Yes, yes—but how can you suppose—?

NORA: Then you must be my witness, that it is not true, Christine. I am not out of my mind at all! I am in my right senses now, and I tell you no one else has known anything about it; I, and I alone, did the whole thing. Remember that.

MRS. LINDE: I will, indeed. But I don't understand all this.

NORA: How should you understand it? A wonderful thing is going to happen!

MRS. LINDE: A wonderful thing?

NORA: Yes, a wonderful thing!—But it is so terrible, Christine; it *mustn't* happen, not for all the world.

MRS. LINDE: I will go at once and see Krogstad.

NORA: Don't go to him; he will do you some harm.

MRS. LINDE: There was a time when he would gladly do anything for my sake.

NORA: He?

MRS. LINDE: Where does he live?

NORA: How should I know—? Yes (*feeling in her pocket*), here is his card. But the letter, the letter—!

HELMER (*calls from his room, knocking at the door*): Nora!

NORA (*cries out anxiously*): Oh, what's that? What do you want?

HELMER: Don't be so frightened. We are not coming in; you have locked the door. Are you trying on your dress?

NORA: Yes, that's it. I look so nice, Torvald.

MRS. LINDE (*who has read the card*): I see he lives at the corner here.

NORA: Yes, but it's no use. It is hopeless. The letter is lying there in the box.

MRS. LINDE: And your husband keeps the key?

NORA: Yes, always.

MRS. LINDE: Krogstad must ask for his letter back unread, he must find some pretence—

NORA: But it is just at this time that Torvald generally—

MRS. LINDE: You must delay him. Go in to him in the meantime. I will come back as soon as I can. (*She goes out hurriedly through the hall door.*)

NORA (*goes to Helmer's door, opens it and peeps in*): Torvald!

HELMER (*from the inner room*): Well? May I venture at last to come into my own room again? Come along, Rank, now you will see—(*Halting in the doorway.*) But what is this?

NORA: What is what, dear?

HELMER: Rank led me to expect a splendid transformation.

RANK (*in the doorway*): I understood so, but evidently I was mistaken.

NORA: Yes, nobody is to have the chance of admiring me in my dress until to-morrow.

HELMER: But, my dear Nora, you look so worn out. Have you been practising too much?

NORA: No, I have not practised at all.

HELMER: But you will need to—

NORA: Yes, indeed I shall, Torvald. But I can't get on a bit without you to help me; I have absolutely forgotten the whole thing.

HELMER: Oh, we will soon work it up again.

NORA: Yes, help me, Torvald. Promise that you will! I am so nervous about it—all the people—. You must give yourself up to me entirely this evening. Not the tiniest bit of business—you mustn't even take a pen in your hand. Will you promise, Torvald dear?

HELMER: I promise. This evening I will be wholly and absolutely at your service, you helpless little mortal. Ah, by the way, first of all I will just—(*Goes towards the hall door.*)

NORA: What are you going to do there?

HELMER: Only see if any letters have come.

NORA: No, no! don't do that, Torvald!

HELMER: Why not?

NORA: Torvald, please don't. There is nothing there.

HELMER: Well, let me look. (*Turns to go to the letter-box. Nora, at the piano, plays the first bars of the Tarantella. Helmer stops in the doorway.*) Aha!

NORA: I can't dance to-morrow if I don't practise with you.

HELMER (*going up to her*): Are you really so afraid of it, dear?

NORA: Yes, so dreadfully afraid of it. Let me practise at once; there is time now, before we go to dinner. Sit down and play for me, Torvald dear; criticise me, and correct me as you play.

HELMER: With great pleasure, if you wish me to. (*Sits down at the piano.*)

NORA (*takes out of the box a tambourine and a long variegated shawl. She hastily drapes the shawl round her. Then she springs to the front of the stage and calls out*): Now play for me! I am going to dance!

(*Helmer plays and Nora dances. Rank stands by the piano behind Helmer, and looks on.*)

HELMER (*as he plays*): Slower, slower!

NORA: I can't do it any other way.

HELMER: Not so violently, Nora!

NORA: This is the way.

HELMER (*stops playing*): No, no—that is not a bit right.

NORA (*laughing and swinging the tambourine*): Didn't I tell you so?

RANK: Let me play for her.

HELMER (*getting up*): Yes, do. I can correct her better then.

(*Rank sits down at the piano and plays. Nora dances more and more wildly. Helmer has taken up a position beside the stove, and during her dance gives her frequent instructions. She does not seem to hear him; her hair comes down and falls over her shoulders; she pays no attention to it, but goes on dancing. Enter Mrs. Linde.*)

MRS. LINDE (*standing as if spell-bound in the doorway*): Oh!—

NORA (*as she dances*): Such fun, Christine!

HELMER: My dear darling Nora, you are dancing as if your life depended on it.

NORA: So it does.

HELMER: Stop, Rank; this is sheer madness. Stop, I tell you! (*Rank stops playing, and Nora suddenly stands still. Helmer goes up to her.*) I could never have believed it. You have forgotten everything I taught you.

NORA (*throwing away the tambourine*): There, you see.

HELMER: You will want a lot of coaching.

NORA: Yes, you see how much I need it. You must coach me up to the last minute. Promise me that, Torvald!

HELMER: You can depend on me.

NORA: You must not think of anything but me, either to-day or to-morrow; you mustn't open a single letter—not even open the letter-box—

HELMER: Ah, you are still afraid of that fellow—

NORA: Yes, indeed I am.

HELMER: Nora, I can tell from your looks that there is a letter from him lying there.

NORA: I don't know; I think there is; but you must not read anything of that kind now. Nothing horrid must come between us until this is all over.

RANK (*whispers to Helmer*): You mustn't contradict her.

HELMER (*taking her in his arms*): The child shall have her way. But to-morrow night, after you have danced—

NORA: Then you will be free. (*The Maid appears in the doorway to the right.*)

MAID: Dinner is served, ma'am.

NORA: We will have champagne, Helen.

MAID: Very good, ma'am. (*Exit.*)

HELMER: Hullo!—are we going to have a banquet?

NORA: Yes, a champagne banquet until the small hours. (*Calls out.*) And a few macaroons, Helen—lots, just for once.

HELMER: Come, come, don't be so wild and nervous. Be my own little skylark, as you used.

NORA: Yes, dear, I will. But go in now and you too, Doctor Rank. Christine, you must help me to do up my hair.

RANK (*whispers to Helmer as they go out*): I suppose there is nothing—she is not expecting anything?

HELMER: Far from it, my dear fellow; it is simply nothing more than this childish nervousness I was telling you of. (*They go into the right-hand room.*)

NORA: Well!

MRS. LINDE: Gone out of town.

NORA: I could tell from your face.

MRS. LINDE: He is coming home to-morrow evening. I wrote a note for him.

NORA: You should have let it alone; you must prevent nothing. After all, it is splendid to be waiting for a wonderful thing to happen.

MRS. LINDE: What is it that you are waiting for?

NORA: Oh, you wouldn't understand. Go in to them, I will come in a moment. (*Mrs. Linde goes into the dining-room. Nora stands still for a little while, as if to compose herself. Then she looks at her watch.*) Five o'clock. Seven hours until midnight; and then four-and-twenty hours until the next midnight. Then the Tarantella will be over. Twenty-four and seven? Thirty-one hours to live.

HELMER (*from the doorway on the right*): Where's my little skylark?

NORA (*going to him with her arms outstretched*): Here she is!

ACT III

The Same Scene: *The table has been placed in the middle of the stage, with chairs round it. A lamp is burning on the table. The door into the hall stands open. Dance music is heard in the room above. Mrs. Linde is sitting at the table idly turning over the leaves of a book; she tries to read, but does not seem able to collect her thoughts. Every now and then she listens intently for a sound at the outer door.*

MRS. LINDE (*looking at her watch*): Not yet—and the time is nearly up. If only he does not—. (*Listens again.*) Ah, there he is. (*Goes into the hall and opens the outer door carefully. Light footsteps are heard on the stairs. She whispers.*) Come in. There is no one here.

KROGSTAD (*in the doorway*): I found a note from you at home. What does this mean?

MRS. LINDE: It is absolutely necessary that I should have a talk with you.

KROGSTAD: Really? And is it absolutely necessary that it should be here?

MRS. LINDE: It is impossible where I live; there is no private entrance to my rooms. Come in; we are quite alone. The maid is asleep, and the Helmers are at the dance upstairs.

KROGSTAD (*coming into the room*): Are the Helmers really at a dance to-night?

MRS. LINDE: Yes, why not?

KROGSTAD: Certainly—why not?

MRS. LINDE: Now, Nils, let us have a talk.

KROGSTAD: Can we two have anything to talk about?

MRS. LINDE: We have a great deal to talk about.

KROGSTAD: I shouldn't have thought so.

MRS. LINDE: No, you have never properly understood me.

KROGSTAD: Was there anything else to understand except what was obvious to all the world—a heartless woman jilts a man when a more lucrative chance turns up?

MRS. LINDE: Do you believe I am as absolutely heartless as all that? And do you believe that I did it with a light heart?

KROGSTAD: Didn't you?

MRS. LINDE: Nils, did you really think that?

KROGSTAD: If it were as you say, why did you write to me as you did at the time?

MRS. LINDE: I could do nothing else. As I had to break with you, it was my duty also to put an end to all that you felt for me.

KROGSTAD (*wringing his hands*): So that was it. And all this—only for the sake of money!

MRS. LINDE: You must not forget that I had a helpless mother and two little brothers. We couldn't wait for you, Nils; your prospects seemed hopeless then.

KROGSTAD: That may be so, but you had no right to throw me over for anyone else's sake.

MRS. LINDE: Indeed I don't know. Many a time did I ask myself if I had the right to do it.

KROGSTAD (*more gently*): When I lost you, it was as if all the solid ground went from under my feet. Look at me now—I am a shipwrecked man clinging to a bit of wreckage.

MRS. LINDE: But help may be near.

KROGSTAD: It *was* near; but then you came and stood in my way.

MRS. LINDE: Unintentionally, Nils. It was only to-day that I learned it was your place I was going to take in the Bank.

KROGSTAD: I believe you, if you say so. But now that you know it, are you not going to give it up to me?

MRS. LINDE: No, because that would not benefit you in the least.

KROGSTAD: Oh, benefit, benefit—I would have done it whether or no.

MRS. LINDE: I have learned to act prudently. Life, and hard, bitter necessity have taught me that.

KROGSTAD: And life has taught me not to believe in fine speeches.

MRS. LINDE: Then life has taught you something very reasonable. But deeds you must believe in?

KROGSTAD: What do you mean by that?

MRS. LINDE: You said you were like a shipwrecked man clinging to some wreckage.

KROGSTAD: I had good reason to say so.

MRS. LINDE: Well, I am like a shipwrecked woman clinging to some wreckage—no one to mourn for, no one to care for.

KROGSTAD: It was your own choice.

MRS. LINDE: There was no other choice—then.

KROGSTAD: Well, what now?

MRS. LINDE: Nils, how would it be if we two shipwrecked people could join forces?

KROGSTAD: What are you saying?

MRS. LINDE: Two on the same piece of wreckage would stand a better chance than each on their own.

KROGSTAD: Christine!

MRS. LINDE: What do you suppose brought me to town?

KROGSTAD: Do you mean that you gave me a thought?

MRS. LINDE: I could not endure life without work. All my life, as long as I can remember, I have worked, and it has been my greatest and only pleasure. But now I am quite alone in the world—my life is so dreadfully empty and I feel so forsaken. There is not the least pleasure in working for one's self. Nils, give me someone and something to work for.

KROGSTAD: I don't trust that. It is nothing but a woman's overstrained sense of generosity that prompts you to make such an offer of yourself.

MRS. LINDE: Have you ever noticed anything of the sort in me?

KROGSTAD: Could you really do it? Tell me—do you know all about my past life?

MRS. LINDE: Yes.

KROGSTAD: And do you know what they think of me here?

MRS. LINDE: You seemed to me to imply that with me you might have been quite another man.

KROGSTAD: I am certain of it.

MRS. LINDE: Is it too late now?

KROGSTAD: Christine, are you saying this deliberately? Yes, I am sure you are. I see it in your face. Have you really the courage, then—?

MRS. LINDE: I want to be a mother to someone, and your children need a mother. We two need each other. Nils, I have faith in your real character—I can dare anything together with you.

KROGSTAD (*grasps her hands*): Thanks, thanks, Christine! Now I shall find a way to clear myself in the eyes of the world. Ah, but I forgot—

MRS. LINDE (*listening*): Hush! The Tarantella! Go, go!

KROGSTAD: Why? What is it?

MRS. LINDE: Do you hear them up there? When that is over, we may expect them back.

KROGSTAD: Yes, yes—I will go. But it is all no use. Of course you are not aware what steps I have taken in the matter of the Helmers.

MRS. LINDE: Yes, I know all about that.

KROGSTAD: And in spite of that have you the courage to—?

MRS. LINDE: I understand very well to what lengths a man like you might be driven by despair.

KROGSTAD: If I could only undo what I have done!

MRS. LINDE: You cannot. Your letter is lying in the letter-box now.

KROGSTAD: Are you sure of that?

MRS. LINDE: Quite sure, but—

KROGSTAD (*with a searching look at her*): Is that what it all means?—that you want to save your friend at any cost? Tell me frankly. Is that it?

MRS. LINDE: Nils, a woman who has once sold herself for another's sake, doesn't do it a second time.

KROGSTAD: I will ask for my letter back.

MRS. LINDE: No, no.

KROGSTAD: Yes, of course I will. I will wait here until Helmer comes; I
will tell him he must give me my letter back—that it only concerns my
dismissal—that he is not to read it—

MRS. LINDE: No, Nils, you must not recall your letter.

KROGSTAD: But, tell me, wasn't it for that very purpose that you asked me
to meet you here?

MRS. LINDE: In my first moment of fright, it was. But twenty-four hours
have elapsed since then, and in that time I have witnessed incredible
things in this house. Helmer must know all about it. This unhappy
secret must be disclosed; they must have a complete understanding
between them, which is impossible with all this concealment and
falsehood going on.

KROGSTAD: Very well, if you will take the responsibility. But there is one
thing I can do in any case, and I shall do it at once.

MRS. LINDE (listening): You must be quick and go! The dance is over; we
are not safe a moment longer.

KROGSTAD: I will wait for you below.

MRS. LINDE: Yes, do. You must see me back to my door.

KROGSTAD: I have never had such an amazing piece of good fortune in
my life! (Goes out through the outer door. The door between the room and
the hall remains open.)

MRS. LINDE (tidying up the room and laying her hat and cloak ready): What
a difference! what a difference! Some-one to work for and live
for—a home to bring comfort into. That I will do, indeed. I wish
they would be quick and come—(Listens.) Ah. there they are now. I
must put on my things. (Takes up her hat and cloak. Helmer's and Nora's
voices are heard outside; a key is turned, and Helmer brings Nora almost
by force into the hall. She is in an Italian costume with a large black shawl
around her; he is in evening dress, and a black domino which is flying
open.)

NORA (hanging back in the doorway, and struggling with him): No, no, no!—
don't take me in. I want to go upstairs again; I don't want to leave
so early.

HELMER: But, my dearest Nora—

NORA: Please, Torvald dear—please, please—only an hour more.

HELMER: Not a single minute, my sweet Nora. You know that was our
agreement. Come along into the room; you are catching cold standing
there. (He brings her gently into the room, in spite of her resistance.)

MRS. LINDE: Good-evening.

NORA: Christine!

HELMER: You here, so late, Mrs. Linde?

MRS. LINDE: Yes, you must excuse me; I was so anxious to see Nora in her dress.

NORA: Have you been sitting here waiting for me?

MRS. LINDE: Yes, unfortunately I came too late, you had already gone upstairs; and I thought I couldn't go away again without having seen you.

HELMER (*taking off Nora's shawl*): Yes, take a good look at her. I think she is worth looking at. Isn't she charming, Mrs. Linde?

MRS. LINDE: Yes, indeed she is.

HELMER: Doesn't she look remarkably pretty? Everyone thought so at the dance. But she is terribly self-willed, this sweet little person. What are we to do with her? You will hardly believe that I had almost to bring her away by force.

NORA: Torvald, you will repent not having let me stay, even if it were only for half an hour.

HELMER: Listen to her, Mrs. Linde! She had danced her Tarantella, and it had been a tremendous success, as it deserved—although possibly the performance was a trifle too realistic—a little more so, I mean, than was strictly compatible with the limitations of art. But never mind about that! The chief thing is, she had made a success—she had made a tremendous success. Do you think I was going to let her remain there after that, and spoil the effect? No, indeed! I took my charming little Capri maiden—my capricious little Capri maiden, I should say—on my arm; took one quick turn round the room; a curtsey on either side, and, as they say in novels, the beautiful apparition disappeared. An exit ought always to be effective, Mrs. Linde; but that is what I cannot make Nora understand. Pooh! this room is hot. (*Throws his domino on a chair, and opens the door of his room.*) Hullo! it's all dark in here. Oh, of course—excuse me—. (*He goes in, and lights some candles.*)

NORA (*in a hurried and breathless whisper*): Well?

MRS. LINDE (*in a low voice*): I have had a talk with him.

NORA: Yes, and—

MRS. LINDE: Nora, you must tell your husband all about it.

NORA (*in an expressionless voice*): I knew it.

MRS. LINDE: You have nothing to be afraid of as far as Krogstad is concerned; but you must tell him.

NORA: I won't tell him.

MRS. LINDE: Then the letter will.

NORA: Thank you, Christine. Now I know what I must do. Hush—!

HELMER (*coming in again*): Well, Mrs. Linde, have you admired her?

MRS. LINDE: Yes, and now I will say good-night.

HELMER: What, already? Is this yours, this knitting?

MRS. LINDE (*taking it*): Yes, thank you, I had very nearly forgotten it.

HELMER: So you knit?

MRS. LINDE: Of course.

HELMER: Do you know, you ought to embroider.

MRS. LINDE: Really? Why?

HELMER: Yes, it's far more becoming. Let me show you. You hold the embroidery thus in your left hand, and use the needle with the right—like this—with a long, easy sweep. Do you see?

MRS. LINDE: Yes, perhaps—

HELMER: But in the case of knitting—that can never be anything but ungraceful; look here—the arms close together, the knitting-needles going up and down—it has a sort of Chinese effect—. That was really excellent champagne they gave us.

MRS. LINDE: Well,—good-night, Nora, and don't be self-willed any more.

HELMER: That's right, Mrs. Linde.

MRS. LINDE: Good-night, Mr. Helmer.

HELMER (*accompanying her to the door*): Good-night, good-night. I hope you will get home all right. I should be very happy to—but you haven't any great distance to go. Good-night, good-night. (*She goes out; he shuts the door after her, and comes in again.*) Ah!—at last we have got rid of her. She is a frightful bore, that woman.

NORA: Aren't you very tired, Torvald?

HELMER: No, not in the least.

NORA: Nor sleepy?

HELMER: Not a bit. On the contrary, I feel extraordinarily lively. And you?—you really look both tired and sleepy.

NORA: Yes, I am very tired. I want to go to sleep at once.

HELMER: There, you see it was quite right of me not to let you stay there any longer.

NORA: Everything you do is quite right, Torvald.

HELMER (*kissing her on the forehead*): Now my little skylark is speaking reasonably. Did you notice what good spirits Rank was in this evening?

NORA: Really? Was he? I didn't speak to him at all.

HELMER: And I very little, but I have not for a long time seen him in such good form. (*Looks for a while at her and then goes nearer to her.*) It is delightful to be at home by ourselves again, to be all alone with you—you fascinating, charming little darling!

NORA: Don't look at me like that, Torvald.

HELMER: Why shouldn't I look at my dearest treasure?—at all the beauty that is mine, all my very own?

NORA (*going to the other side of the table*): You mustn't say things like that to me to-night.

HELMER (*following her*): You have still got the Tarantella in your blood, I see. And it makes you more captivating than ever. Listen—the guests are beginning to go now. (*In a lower voice.*) Nora—soon the whole house will be quiet.

NORA: Yes, I hope so.

HELMER: Yes, my own darling Nora. Do you know, when I am out at a party with you like this, why I speak so little to you, keep away from you, and only send a stolen glance in your direction now and then?— do you know why I do that? It is because I make believe to myself that we are secretly in love, and you are my secretly promised bride, and that no one suspects there is anything between us.

NORA: Yes, yes—I know very well your thoughts are with me all the time.

HELMER: And when we are leaving, and I am putting the shawl over your beautiful young shoulders—on your lovely neck—then I imagine that you are my young bride and that we have just come from the wedding, and I am bringing you for the first time into our home—to be alone with you for the first time—quite alone with my shy little darling! All this evening I have longed for nothing but you. When I watched the seductive figures of the Tarantella, my blood was on fire; I could endure it no longer, and that was why I brought you down so early—

NORA: Go away, Torvald! You must let me go. I won't—

HELMER: What's that? You're joking, my little Nora! You won't—you won't? Am I not your husband—? (*A knock is heard at the outer door.*)

NORA (*starting*): Did you hear—?

HELMER (*going into the hall*): Who is it?

RANK (*outside*): It is I. May I come in for a moment?

HELMER (*in a fretful whisper*): Oh, what does he want now? (*Aloud.*) Wait a minute! (*Unlocks the door.*) Come, that's kind of you not to pass by our door.

RANK: I thought I heard your voice, and felt as if I should like to look in. (*With a swift glance round.*) Ah, yes!—these dear familiar rooms. You are very happy and cosy in here, you two.

HELMER: It seems to me that you looked after yourself pretty well upstairs too.

RANK: Excellently. Why shouldn't I? Why shouldn't one enjoy everything in this world?—at any rate as much as one can, and as long as one can. The wine was capital—

HELMER: Especially the champagne.

RANK: So you noticed that too? It is almost incredible how much I managed to put away!

NORA: Torvald drank a great deal of champagne to-night too.

RANK: Did he?

NORA: Yes, and he is always in such good spirits afterwards.

RANK: Well, why should one not enjoy a merry evening after a well-spent day?

HELMER: Well spent? I am afraid I can't take credit for that.

RANK (*clapping him on the back*): But I can, you know!

NORA: Doctor Rank, you must have been occupied with some scientific investigation to-day.

RANK: Exactly.

HELMER: Just listen!—little Nora talking about scientific investigations!

NORA: And may I congratulate you on the result?

RANK: Indeed you may.

NORA: Was it favourable, then?

RANK: The best possible, for both doctor and patient—certainty.

NORA (*quickly and searchingly*): Certainty?

RANK: Absolute certainty. So wasn't I entitled to make a merry evening of it after that?

NORA: Yes, you certainly were, Doctor Rank.

HELMER: I think so too, so long as you don't have to pay for it in the morning.

RANK: Oh well, one can't have anything in this life without paying for it.

NORA: Doctor Rank—are you fond of fancy-dress balls?

RANK: Yes, if there is a fine lot of pretty costumes.

NORA: Tell me—what shall we two wear at the next?

HELMER: Little featherbrain!—are you thinking of the next already?

RANK: We two? Yes, I can tell you. You shall go as a good fairy—

HELMER: Yes, but what do you suggest as an appropriate costume for that?

RANK: Let your wife go dressed just as she is in everyday life.

HELMER: That was really very prettily turned. But can't you tell us what you will be?

RANK: Yes, my dear friend, I have quite made up my mind about that.

HELMER: Well?

RANK: At the next fancy-dress ball I shall be invisible.

HELMER: That's a good joke!

RANK: There is a big black hat—have you never heard of hats that make you invisible? If you put one on, no one can see you.

HELMER (*suppressing a smile*): Yes, you are quite right.

RANK: But I am clean forgetting what I came for. Helmer, give me a cigar—one of the dark Havanas.

HELMER: With the greatest pleasure. (*Offers him his case.*)

RANK (*takes a cigar and cuts off the end*): Thanks.

NORA (*striking a match*): Let me give you a light.

RANK: Thank you. (*She holds the match for him to light his cigar.*) And now good-bye!

HELMER: Good-bye, good-bye, dear old man!

NORA: Sleep well, Doctor Rank.

RANK: Thank you for that wish.

NORA: Wish me the same.

RANK: You? Well, if you want me to sleep well! And thanks for the light. (*He nods to them both and goes out.*)

HELMER (*in a subdued voice*): He has drunk more than he ought.

NORA (*absently*): Maybe. (*Helmer takes a bunch of keys out of his pocket and goes into the hall.*) Torvald! what are you going to do there?

HELMER: Empty the letter-box; it is quite full; there will be no room to put the newspaper in to-morrow morning.

NORA: Are you going to work to-night?

HELMER: You know quite well I'm not. What is this? Someone has been at the lock.

NORA: At the lock—?

HELMER: Yes, someone has. What can it mean? I should never have thought the maid—. Here is a broken hairpin. Nora, it is one of yours.

NORA (*quickly*): Then it must have been the children—

HELMER: Then you must get them out of those ways. There, at last I have got it open. (*Takes out the contents of the letter-box, and calls to the kitchen.*) Helen!—Helen, put out the light over the front door. (*Goes back into the room and shuts the door into the hall. He holds out his hand full of letters.*) Look at that—look what a heap of them there are. (*Turning them over.*) What on earth is that?

NORA (*at the window*): The letter—No! Torvald, no!

HELMER: Two cards—of Rank's.

NORA: Of Doctor Rank's?

HELMER (*looking at them*): Doctor Rank. They were on the top. He must have put them in when he went out.

NORA: Is there anything written on them?

HELMER: There is a black cross over the name. Look there—what an uncomfortable idea! It looks as if he were announcing his own death.

NORA: It is just what he is doing.

HELMER: What? Do you know anything about it? Has he said anything to you?

NORA: Yes. He told me that when the cards came it would be his leave-taking from us. He means to shut himself up and die.

HELMER: My poor old friend! Certainly I knew we should not have him very long with us. But so soon! And so he hides himself away like a wounded animal.

NORA: If it has to happen, it is best it should be without a word—don't you think so, Torvald?

HELMER (*walking up and down*): He had so grown into our lives. I can't think of him as having gone out of them. He, with his sufferings and his loneliness, was like a cloudy background to our sunlit happiness. Well, perhaps it is best so. For him, anyway. (*Standing still.*) And perhaps for us too, Nora. We two are thrown quite upon each other now. (*Puts his arms round her.*) My darling wife, I don't feel as if I could hold you tight enough. Do you know, Nora, I have often wished that you might be threatened by some great danger, so that I might risk my life's blood, and everything, for your sake.

NORA (*disengages herself, and says firmly and decidedly*): Now you must read your letters, Torvald.

HELMER: No, no; not to-night. I want to be with you, my darling wife.

NORA: With the thought of your friend's death—

HELMER: You are right, it has affected us both. Something ugly has come between us—the thought of the horrors of death. We must try and rid our minds of that. Until then—we will each go to our own room.

NORA (*hanging on his neck*): Good-night, Torvald—Good-night!

HELMER (*kissing her on the forehead*): Good-night, my little singing-bird. Sleep sound, Nora. Now I will read my letters through. (*He takes his letters and goes into his room, shutting the door after him.*)

NORA (*gropes distractedly about, seizes Helmer's domino, throws it round her, while she says in quick, hoarse, spasmodic whispers*): Never to see him again. Never! Never! (*Puts her shawl over her head.*) Never to see my children again either—never again. Never! Never!—Ah! the icy, black water—the unfathomable depths—If only it were over! He has got it now—now he is reading it. Good-bye, Torvald and my children! (*She is about to rush out through the hall, when Helmer opens his door hurriedly and stands with an open letter in his hand.*)

HELMER: Nora!

NORA: Ah!—

HELMER: What is this? Do you know what is in this letter?

NORA: Yes, I know. Let me go! Let me get out!

HELMER (*holding her back*): Where are you going?

NORA (*trying to get free*): You shan't save me, Torvald!

HELMER (*reeling*): True? Is this true, that I read here? Horrible! No, no—it is impossible that it can be true.

NORA: It is true. I have loved you above everything else in the world.

HELMER: Oh, don't let us have any silly excuses.

NORA (*taking a step towards him*): Torvald—!

HELMER: Miserable creature—what have you done?

NORA: Let me go. You shall not suffer for my sake. You shall not take it upon yourself.

HELMER: No tragedy airs, please. (*Locks the hall door.*) Here you shall stay and give me an explanation. Do you understand what you have done? Answer me! Do you understand what you have done?

NORA (*looks steadily at him and says with a growing look of coldness in her face*): Yes, now I am beginning to understand thoroughly.

HELMER (*walking about the room*): What a horrible awakening! All these eight years—she who was my joy and pride—a hypocrite, a liar— worse, worse—a criminal! The unutterable ugliness of it all!—For shame! For shame! (*Nora is silent and looks steadily at him. He stops in front of her.*) I ought to have suspected that something of the sort would happen. I ought to have foreseen it. All your father's want of principle— be silent!—all your father's want of principle has come out in you. No religion, no morality, no sense of duty—. How I am punished for having winked at what he did! I did it for your sake, and this is how you repay me.

NORA: Yes, that's just it.

HELMER: Now you have destroyed all my happiness. You have ruined all my future. It is horrible to think of! I am in the power of an unscrupulous man; he can do what he likes with me, ask anything he likes of me, give me any orders he pleases—I dare not refuse. And I must sink to such miserable depths because of a thoughtless woman!

NORA: When I am out of the way, you will be free.

HELMER: No fine speeches, please. Your father had always plenty of those ready, too. What good would it be to me if you were out of the way, as you say? Not the slightest. He can make the affair known everywhere; and if he does, I may be falsely suspected of having been a party to your criminal action. Very likely people will think I was behind it all—that it was I who prompted you! And I have to thank you for all this—you whom I have cherished during the whole of our married life. Do you understand now what it is you have done for me?

NORA (*coldly and quietly*): Yes.

HELMER: It is so incredible that I can't take it in. But we must come to some understanding. Take off that shawl. Take it off, I tell you. I must try and appease him some way or another. The matter must be hushed up at any cost. And as for you and me, it must appear as if everything between us were just as before—but naturally only in the eyes of the world. You will still remain in my house, that is a matter of course. But I shall not allow you to bring up the children; I dare not trust them to you. To think that I should be obliged to say so to one whom I have loved so dearly, and whom I still—. No, that is all over. From this moment happiness is not the question; all that concerns us is to save the remains, the fragments, the appearance—

(*A ring is heard at the front-door bell.*)

HELMER (*with a start*): What is that? So late. Can the worst—? Can he—? Hide yourself, Nora. Say you are ill.

(*Nora stands motionless. Helmer goes and unlocks the hall door.*)

MAID (*half-dressed, comes to the door*): A letter for the mistress.

HELMER: Give it to me. (*Takes the letter, and shuts the door.*) Yes, it is from him. You shall not have it; I will read it myself.

NORA: Yes, read it.

HELMER (*standing by the lamp*): I scarcely have the courage to do it. It may mean ruin for both of us. No, I must know. (*Tears open the letter, runs his eye over a few lines, looks at a paper enclosed, and gives a shout of joy.*) Nora! (*She looks at him questioningly.*) Nora!—No, I must read it once again—. Yes, it is true! I am saved! Nora, I am saved!

NORA: And I?

HELMER: You too, of course; we are both saved, both you and I. Look, he sends you your bond back. He says he regrets and repents—that a happy change in his life—never mind what he says! We are saved, Nora! No one can do anything to you. Oh, Nora, Nora!—no, first I must destroy these hateful things. Let me see—. (*Takes a look at the bond.*) No, no, I won't look at it. The whole thing shall be nothing but a bad dream to me. (*Tears up the bond and both letters, throws them all into the stove, and watches them burn.*) There—now it doesn't exist any longer. He says that since Christmas Eve you—. These must have been three dreadful days for you, Nora.

NORA: I have fought a hard fight these three days.

HELMER: And suffered agonies, and seen no way out but—. No, we won't call any of the horrors to mind. We will only shout with joy, and keep saying, "It's all over! It's all over!" Listen to me, Nora. You don't seem to realise that it is all over. What is this?—such a cold, set face! My poor little Nora, I quite understand; you don't feel as if you could believe that I have forgiven you. But it is true, Nora, I swear it; I have forgiven you everything. I know that what you did, you did out of love for me.

NORA: That is true.

HELMER: You have loved me as a wife ought to love her husband. Only you had not sufficient knowledge to judge of the means you used. But do you suppose you are any the less dear to me, because you don't understand how to act on your own responsibility? No, no; only lean on me; I will advise you and direct you. I should not be a man if this womanly helplessness did not just give you a double attractiveness in my eyes. You must not think anymore about the hard things I said in my first moment of consternation, when I thought everything was going to overwhelm me. I have forgiven you, Nora; I swear to you I have forgiven you.

NORA: Thank you for your forgiveness. (*She goes out through the door to the right.*)

HELMER: No, don't go—. (*Looks in.*) What are you doing in there?

NORA (*from within*): Taking off my fancy dress.

HELMER (*standing at the open door*): Yes, do. Try and calm yourself, and make your mind easy again, my frightened little singing-bird. Be at rest, and feel secure; I have broad wings to shelter you under. (*Walks up and down by the door.*) How warm and cosy our home is, Nora. Here is shelter for you; here I will protect you like a hunted dove that I have saved from a hawk's claws; I will bring peace to your poor beating heart. It will come, little by little, Nora, believe me. To-morrow morning you will look upon it all quite differently; soon everything will be just as it was before. Very soon you won't need me to assure you that I have forgiven you; you will yourself feel the certainty that I have done so. Can you suppose I should ever think of such a thing as repudiating you, or even reproaching you? You have no idea what a true man's heart is like, Nora. There is something so indescribably sweet and satisfying, to a man, in the knowledge that he has forgiven his wife— forgiven her freely, and with all his heart. It seems as if that had made her, as it were, doubly his own; he has given her a new life, so to speak; and she has in a way become both wife and child to him. So you shall be for me after this, my little scared, helpless darling. Have no anxiety about anything, Nora; only be frank and open with me, and I will serve as will and conscience both to you—. What is this? Not gone to bed? Have you changed your things?

NORA (*in everyday dress*): Yes, Torvald, I have changed my things now.

HELMER: But what for?—so late as this.

NORA: I shall not sleep to-night.

HELMER: But, my dear Nora—

NORA (*looking at her watch*): It is not so very late. Sit down here, Torvald. You and I have much to say to one another. (*She sits down at one side of the table.*)

HELMER: Nora—what is this?—this cold, set face?

NORA: Sit down. It will take some time; I have a lot to talk over with you.

HELMER (*sits down at the opposite side of the table*): You alarm me, Nora!— and I don't understand you.

NORA: No, that is just it. You don't understand me, and I have never understood you either—before to-night. No, you mustn't interrupt me. You must simply listen to what I say. Torvald, this is a settling of accounts.

HELMER: What do you mean by that?

NORA (*after a short silence*): Isn't there one thing that strikes you as strange in our sitting here like this?

HELMER: What is that?

NORA: We have been married now eight years. Does it not occur to you that this is the first time we two, you and I, husband and wife, have had a serious conversation?

HELMER: What do you mean by serious?

NORA: In all these eight years—longer than that—from the very beginning of our acquaintance, we have never exchanged a word on any serious subject.

HELMER: Was it likely that I would be continually and forever telling you about worries that you could not help me to bear?

NORA: I am not speaking about business matters. I say that we have never sat down in earnest together to try and get at the bottom of anything.

HELMER: But, dearest Nora, would it have been any good to you?

NORA: That is just it; you have never understood me. I have been greatly wronged, Torvald—first by papa and then by you.

HELMER: What! By us two—by us two, who have loved you better than anyone else in the world?

NORA (*shaking her head*): You have never loved me. You have only thought it pleasant to be in love with me.

HELMER: Nora, what do I hear you saying?

NORA: It is perfectly true, Torvald. When I was at home with papa, he told me his opinion about everything, and so I had the same opinions; and if I differed from him I concealed the fact, because he would not have liked it. He called me his doll-child, and he played with me just as I used to play with my dolls. And when I came to live with you—

HELMER: What sort of an expression is that to use about our marriage?

NORA (*undisturbed*): I mean that I was simply transferred from papa's hands into yours. You arranged everything according to your own taste, and so I got the same tastes as you—or else I pretended to, I am really not quite sure which—I think sometimes the one and sometimes the other. When I look back on it, it seems to me as if I had been living here like a poor woman—just from hand to mouth. I have existed merely to perform tricks for you, Torvald. But you would have it so. You and papa have committed a great sin against me. It is your fault that I have made nothing of my life.

HELMER: How unreasonable and how ungrateful you are, Nora! Have you not been happy here?

NORA: No, I have never been happy. I thought I was, but it has never really been so.

HELMER: Not—not happy!

NORA: No, only merry. And you have always been so kind to me. But our home has been nothing but a playroom. I have been your doll-wife, just as at home I was papa's doll-child; and here the children have been my dolls. I thought it great fun when you played with me, just as they thought it great fun when I played with them. That is what our marriage has been, Torvald.

HELMER: There is some truth in what you say—exaggerated and strained as your view of it is. But for the future it shall be different. Playtime shall be over, and lesson-time shall begin.

NORA: Whose lessons? Mine, or the children's?

HELMER: Both yours and the children's, my darling Nora.

NORA: Alas, Torvald, you are not the man to educate me into being a proper wife for you.

HELMER: And you can say that!

NORA: And I—how am I fitted to bring up the children?

HELMER: Nora!

NORA: Didn't you say so yourself a little while ago—that you dare not trust me to bring them up?

HELMER: In a moment of anger! Why do you pay any heed to that?

NORA: Indeed, you were perfectly right. I am not fit for the task. There is another task I must undertake first. I must try and educate myself—you are not the man to help me in that. I must do that for myself. And that is why I am going to leave you now.

HELMER (springing up): What do you say?

NORA: I must stand quite alone, if I am to understand myself and everything about me. It is for that reason that I cannot remain with you any longer.

HELMER: Nora, Nora!

NORA: I am going away from here now, at once. I am sure Christine will take me in for the night—

HELMER: You are out of your mind! I won't allow it! I forbid you!

NORA: It is no use forbidding me anything any longer. I will take with me what belongs to myself. I will take nothing from you, either now or later.

HELMER: What sort of madness is this!

NORA: To-morrow I shall go home—I mean, to my old home. It will be easiest for me to find something to do there.

HELMER: You blind, foolish woman!

NORA: I must try and get some sense, Torvald.

HELMER: To desert your home, your husband and your children! And you don't consider what people will say!

NORA: I cannot consider that at all. I only know that it is necessary for me.

HELMER: It's shocking. This is how you would neglect your most sacred
  duties.
NORA: What do you consider my most sacred duties?
HELMER: Do I need to tell you that? Are they not your duties to your
  husband and your children?
NORA: I have other duties just as sacred.
HELMER: That you have not. What duties could those be?
NORA: Duties to myself.
HELMER: Before all else, you are a wife and a mother.
NORA: I don't believe that any longer. I believe that before all else I am a
  reasonable human being, just as you are—or, at all events, that I must
  try and become one. I know quite well, Torvald, that most people
  would think you right, and that views of that kind are to be found in
  books; but I can no longer content myself with what most people say,
  or with what is found in books. I must think over things for myself and
  get to understand them.
HELMER: Can you not understand your place in your own home? Have
  you not a reliable guide in such matters as that?—have you no
  religion?
NORA: I am afraid, Torvald, I do not exactly know what religion is.
HELMER: What are you saying?
NORA: I know nothing but what the clergyman said, when I went to be
  confirmed. He told us that religion was this, and that, and the other.
  When I am away from all this, and am alone, I will look into that
  matter too. I will see if what the clergyman said is true, or at all events
  if it is true for me.
HELMER: This is unheard of in a girl of your age! But if religion cannot
  lead you aright, let me try and awaken your conscience. I suppose you
  have some moral sense? Or—answer me—am I to think you have
  none?
NORA: I assure you, Torvald, that is not an easy question to answer. I
  really don't know. The thing perplexes me altogether. I only know that
  you and I look at it in quite a different light. I am learning, too, that the
  law is quite another thing from what I supposed; but I find it impossible to convince myself that the law is right. According to it a woman
  has no right to spare her old dying father, or to save her husband's life.
  I can't believe that.
HELMER: You talk like a child. You don't understand the conditions of
  the world in which you live.
NORA: No, I don't. But now I am going to try. I am going to see if I can
  make out who is right, the world or I.
HELMER: You are ill, Nora; you are delirious; I almost think you are out
  of your mind.

NORA: I have never felt my mind so clear and certain as to-night.

HELMER: And is it with a clear and certain mind that you forsake your husband and your children?

NORA: Yes, it is.

HELMER: Then there is only one possible explanation.

NORA: What is that?

HELMER: You do not love me anymore.

NORA: No, that is just it.

HELMER: Nora!—and you can say that?

NORA: It gives me great pain, Torvald, for you have always been so kind to me, but I cannot help it. I do not love you any more.

HELMER (*regaining his composure*): Is that a clear and certain conviction too?

NORA: Yes, absolutely clear and certain. That is the reason why I will not stay here any longer.

HELMER: And can you tell me what I have done to forfeit your love?

NORA: Yes, indeed I can. It was to-night, when the wonderful thing did not happen; then I saw you were not the man I had thought you.

HELMER: Explain yourself better. I don't understand you.

NORA: I have waited so patiently for eight years; for, goodness knows, I knew very well that wonderful things don't happen every day. Then this horrible misfortune came upon me; and then I felt quite certain that the wonderful thing was going to happen at last. When Krogstad's letter was lying out there, never for a moment did I imagine that you would consent to accept this man's conditions. I was so absolutely certain that you would say to him: Publish the thing to the whole world. And when that was done—

HELMER: Yes, what then?—when I had exposed my wife to shame and disgrace?

NORA: When that was done, I was so absolutely certain, you would come forward and take everything upon yourself, and say: I am the guilty one.

HELMER: Nora—!

NORA: You mean that I would never have accepted such a sacrifice on your part? No, of course not. But what would my assurances have been worth against yours? That was the wonderful thing which I hoped for and feared; and it was to prevent that, that I wanted to kill myself.

HELMER: I would gladly work night and day for you, Nora—bear sorrow and want for your sake. But no man would sacrifice his honour for the one he loves.

NORA: It is a thing hundreds of thousands of women have done.

HELMER: Oh, you think and talk like a heedless child.

NORA: Maybe. But you neither think nor talk like the man I could bind myself to. As soon as your fear was over—and it was not fear for what threatened me, but for what might happen to you—when the whole thing was past, as far as you were concerned it was exactly as if nothing at all had happened. Exactly as before, I was your little skylark, your doll, which you would in future treat with doubly gentle care, because it was so brittle and fragile. (*Getting up.*) Torvald—it was then it dawned upon me that for eight years I had been living here with a strange man, and had borne him three children—. Oh, I can't bear to think of it! I could tear myself into little bits!

HELMER (*sadly*): I see, I see. An abyss has opened between us—there is no denying it. But, Nora, would it not be possible to fill it up?

NORA: As I am now, I am no wife for you.

HELMER: I have it in me to become a different man.

NORA: Perhaps—if your doll is taken away from you.

HELMER: But to part!—to part from you! No, no, Nora, I can't understand that idea.

NORA (*going out to the right*): That makes it all the more certain that it must be done. (*She comes back with her cloak and hat and a small bag which she puts on a chair by the table.*)

HELMER: Nora, Nora, not now! Wait until to-morrow.

NORA (*putting on her cloak*): I cannot spend the night in a strange man's room.

HELMER: But can't we live here like brother and sister—?

NORA (*putting on her hat*): You know very well that would not last long. (*Puts the shawl round her.*) Good-bye, Torvald. I won't see the little ones. I know they are in better hands than mine. As I am now, I can be of no use to them.

HELMER: But some day, Nora—some day?

NORA: How can I tell? I have no idea what is going to become of me.

HELMER: But you are my wife, whatever becomes of you.

NORA: Listen, Torvald. I have heard that when a wife deserts her husband's house, as I am doing now, he is legally freed from all obligations towards her. In any case, I set you free from all your obligations. You are not to feel yourself bound in the slightest way, any more than I shall. There must be perfect freedom on both sides. See, here is your ring back. Give me mine.

HELMER: That too?

NORA: That too.

HELMER: Here it is.

NORA: That's right. Now it is all over. I have put the keys here. The maids know all about everything in the house—better than I do. To-morrow, after I have left her, Christine will come here and pack up my own things that I brought with me from home. I will have them sent after me.

HELMER: All over! All over!—Nora, shall you never think of me again?

NORA: I know I shall often think of you, the children, and this house.

HELMER: May I write to you, Nora?

NORA: No—never. You must not do that.

HELMER: But at least let me send you—

NORA: Nothing—nothing—

HELMER: Let me help you if you are in want.

NORA: No. I can receive nothing from a stranger.

HELMER: Nora—can I never be anything more than a stranger to you?

NORA (*taking her bag*): Ah, Torvald, the most wonderful thing of all would have to happen.

HELMER: Tell me what that would be!

NORA: Both you and I would have to be so changed that—. Oh, Torvald, I don't believe any longer in wonderful things happening.

HELMER: But I will believe in it. Tell me! So changed that—?

NORA: That our life together would be a real wedlock. Good-bye. (*She goes out through the hall.*)

HELMER (*sinks down on a chair at the door and buries his face in his hands*): Nora! Nora! (*Looks round, and rises.*) Empty. She is gone. (*A hope flashes across his mind.*) The most wonderful thing of all—?

(*The sound of a door shutting is heard from below.*)

[1879]

OSCAR WILDE [1854–1900]

The Importance of Being Earnest

A TRIVIAL COMEDY FOR SERIOUS PEOPLE

The Persons of the Play
JOHN WORTHING, J.P., *of the Manor House, Woolton, Hertfordshire*
ALGERNON MONCRIEFF, *his friend*
REV. CANON CHASUBLE, D.D., *rector of Woolton*
MERRIMAN, *butler to Mr. Worthing*
LANE, *Mr. Moncrieff's manservant*
LADY BRACKNELL
HON. GWENDOLEN FAIRFAX, *her daughter*
CECILY CARDEW, *John Worthing's ward*
MISS PRISM, *her governess*

The Scenes of the Play
Act I: *Algernon Moncrieff's Flat in Half-Moon Street, W.*
Act II: *The Garden at the Manor House, Woolton*
Act III: *Morning Room at the Manor House, Woolton*

FIRST ACT

Scene: *Morning room in Algernon's flat in Half-Moon Street.*

The room is luxuriously and artistically furnished. The sound of a piano is heard in the adjoining room.

(Lane is arranging afternoon tea on the table, and after the music has ceased, Algernon enters.)

ALGERNON: Did you hear what I was playing, Lane?
LANE: I didn't think it polite to listen, sir.
ALGERNON: I'm sorry for that, for your sake. I don't play accurately— anyone can play accurately—but I play with wonderful expression. As far as the piano is concerned, sentiment is my forte. I keep science for Life.

889

LANE: Yes, sir.

ALGERNON: And, speaking of the science of Life, have you got the cucumber sandwiches cut for Lady Bracknell?

LANE: Yes, sir. (*Hands them on a salver.*)

ALGERNON (*inspects them, takes two, and sits down on the sofa*): Oh! . . . by the way, Lane, I see from your book that on Thursday night, when Lord Shoreham and Mr. Worthing were dining with me, eight bottles of champagne are entered as having been consumed.

LANE: Yes, sir; eight bottles and a pint.

ALGERNON: Why is it that at a bachelor's establishment the servants invariably drink the champagne? I ask merely for information.

LANE: I attribute it to the superior quality of the wine, sir. I have often observed that in married households the champagne is rarely of a first-rate brand.

ALGERNON: Good Heavens! Is marriage so demoralizing as that?

LANE: I believe it *is* a very pleasant state, sir. I have had very little experience of it myself up to the present. I have only been married once. That was in consequence of a misunderstanding between myself and a young person.

ALGERNON (*languidly*): I don't know that I am much interested in your family life, Lane.

LANE: No, sir; it is not a very interesting subject. I never think of it myself.

ALGERNON: Very natural, I am sure. That will do, Lane, thank you.

LANE: Thank you, sir.   (*Lane goes out.*)

ALGERNON: Lane's views on marriage seem somewhat lax. Really, if the lower orders don't set us a good example, what on earth is the use of them? They seem, as a class, to have absolutely no sense of moral responsibility.

(*Enter Lane.*)

LANE: Mr. Ernest Worthing.

(*Enter Jack.*)   (*Lane goes out.*)

ALGERNON: How are you, my dear Ernest? What brings you up to town?

JACK: Oh, pleasure, pleasure! What else should bring one anywhere? Eating as usual, I see, Algy!

ALGERNON (*stiffly*): I believe it is customary in good society to take some slight refreshment at five o'clock. Where have you been since last Thursday?

JACK (*sitting down on the sofa*): In the country.

ALGERNON: What on earth do you do there?

JACK (*pulling off his gloves*): When one is in town one amuses oneself. When one is in the country one amuses other people. It is excessively boring.

ALGERNON: And who are the people you amuse?

JACK (*airily*): Oh, neighbors, neighbors.

ALGERNON: Got nice neighbors in your part of Shropshire?

JACK: Perfectly horrid! Never speak to one of them.

ALGERNON: How immensely you must amuse them! (*Goes over and takes sandwich.*) By the way, Shropshire is your county, is it not?

JACK: Eh? Shropshire? Yes, of course. Hallo! Why all these cups? Why cucumber sandwiches? Why such reckless extravagance in one so young? Who is coming to tea?

ALGERNON: Oh! merely Aunt Augusta and Gwendolen.

JACK: How perfectly delightful!

ALGERNON: Yes, that is all very well; but I am afraid Aunt Augusta won't quite approve of your being here.

JACK: May I ask why?

ALGERNON: My dear fellow, the way you flirt with Gwendolen is perfectly disgraceful. It is almost as bad as the way Gwendolen flirts with you.

JACK: I am in love with Gwendolen. I have come up to town expressly to propose to her.

ALGERNON: I thought you had come up for pleasure? . . . I call that business.

JACK: How utterly unromantic you are!

ALGERNON: I really don't see anything romantic in proposing. It is very romantic to be in love. But there is nothing romantic about a definite proposal. Why, one may be accepted. One usually is, I believe. Then the excitement is all over. The very essence of romance is uncertainty. If ever I get married, I'll certainly try to forget the fact.

JACK: I have no doubt about that, dear Algy. The Divorce Court was specially invented for people whose memories are so curiously constituted.

ALGERNON: Oh! there is no use speculating on that subject. Divorces are made in Heaven—(*Jack puts out his hand to take a sandwich. Algernon at once interferes.*) Please don't touch the cucumber sandwiches. They are ordered specially for Aunt Augusta. (*Takes one and eats it.*)

JACK: Well, you have been eating them all the time.

ALGERNON: That is quite a different matter. She is my aunt. (*Takes plate from below.*) Have some bread and butter. The bread and butter is for Gwendolen. Gwendolen is devoted to bread and butter.

JACK (*advancing to table and helping himself*): And very good bread and butter it is too.

ALGERNON: Well, my dear fellow, you need not eat as if you were going to eat it all. You behave as if you were married to her already. You are not married to her already, and I don't think you ever will be.

JACK: Why on earth do you say that?

ALGERNON: Well, in the first place, girls never marry the men they flirt with. Girls don't think it right.

JACK: Oh, that is nonsense!

ALGERNON: It isn't. It is a great truth. It accounts for the extraordinary number of bachelors that one sees all over the place. In the second place, I don't give my consent.

JACK: Your consent!

ALGERNON: My dear fellow, Gwendolen is my first cousin. And before I allow you to marry her, you will have to clear up the whole question of Cecily. (*Rings bell.*)

JACK: Cecily! What on earth do you mean? What do you mean, Algy, by Cecily? I don't know anyone of the name of Cecily.

(*Enter Lane.*)

ALGERNON: Bring me that cigarette case Mr. Worthing left in the smoking-room the last time he dined here.

LANE: Yes, sir.   (*Lane goes out.*)

JACK: Do you mean to say you have had my cigarette case all this time? I wish to goodness you had let me know. I have been writing frantic letters to Scotland Yard about it. I was very nearly offering a large reward.

ALGERNON: Well, I wish you would offer one. I happen to be more than usually hard up.

JACK: There is no good offering a large reward now that the thing is found.

(*Enter Lane with the cigarette case on a salver. Algernon takes it at once. Lane goes out.*)

ALGERNON: I think that is rather mean of you, Ernest, I must say. (*Opens case and examines it.*) However, it makes no matter, for, now that I look at the inscription inside, I find that the thing isn't yours after all.

JACK: Of course it's mine. (*Moving to him.*) You have seen me with it a hundred times, and you have no right whatsoever to read what is written inside. It is a very ungentlemanly thing to read a private cigarette case.

ALGERNON: Oh! it is absurd to have a hard-and-fast rule about what one should read and what one shouldn't. More than half of modern culture depends on what one shouldn't read.

JACK: I am quite aware of the fact, and I don't propose to discuss modern culture. It isn't the sort of thing one should talk of in private. I simply want my cigarette case back.

ALGERNON: Yes; but this isn't your cigarette case. This cigarette case is a present from someone of the name of Cecily, and you said you didn't know anyone of that name.

JACK: Well, if you want to know, Cecily happens to be my aunt.

ALGERNON: Your aunt!

JACK: Yes. Charming old lady she is, too. Lives at Tunbridge Wells. Just give it back to me, Algy.

ALGERNON (*retreating to back of sofa*): But why does she call herself little Cecily if she is your aunt and lives at Tunbridge Wells? (*Reading.*) "From little Cecily with her fondest love."

JACK (*moving to sofa and kneeling upon it*): My dear fellow, what on earth is there in that? Some aunts are tall, some aunts are not tall. That is a matter that surely an aunt may be allowed to decide for herself. You seem to think that every aunt should be exactly like your aunt! That is absurd! For Heaven's sake give me back my cigarette case. (*Follows Algy round the room.*)

ALGERNON: Yes. But why does your aunt call you her uncle? "From little Cecily, with her fondest love to her dear Uncle Jack." There is no objection, I admit, to an aunt being a small aunt, but why an aunt, no matter what her size may be, should call her own nephew her uncle, I can't quite make out. Besides, your name isn't Jack at all; it is Ernest.

JACK: It isn't Ernest; it's Jack.

ALGERNON: You have always told me it was Ernest. I have introduced you to everyone as Ernest. You answer to the name of Ernest. You look as if your name was Ernest. You are the most earnest looking person I ever saw in my life. It is perfectly absurd your saying that your name isn't Ernest. It's on your cards. Here is one of them. (*Taking it from case.*) "Mr. Ernest Worthing, B. 4, The Albany." I'll keep this as a proof that your name is Ernest if ever you attempt to deny it to me, or to Gwendolen, or to anyone else. (*Puts the card in his pocket.*)

JACK: Well, my name is Ernest in town and Jack in the country, and the cigarette case was given to me in the country.

ALGERNON: Yes, but that does not account for the fact that your small Aunt Cecily, who lives at Tunbridge Wells, calls you her dear uncle. Come, old boy, you had much better have the thing out at once.

JACK: My dear Algy, you talk exactly as if you were a dentist. It is very vulgar to talk like a dentist when one isn't a dentist. It produces a false impression.

ALGERNON: Well, that is exactly what dentists always do. Now, go on! Tell me the whole thing. I may mention that I have always suspected you of being a confirmed and secret Bunburyist; and I am quite sure of it now.

JACK: Bunburyist? What on earth do you mean by a Bunburyist?

ALGERNON: I'll reveal to you the meaning of that incomparable expression as soon as you are kind enough to inform me why you are Ernest in town and Jack in the country.

JACK: Well, produce my cigarette case first.

ALGERNON: Here it is. (*Hands cigarette case.*) Now produce your explanation, and pray make it improbable. (*Sits on sofa.*)

JACK: My dear fellow, there is nothing improbable about my explanation at all. In fact it's perfectly ordinary. Old Mr. Thomas Cardew, who adopted me when I was a little boy, made me in his will guardian to his granddaughter, Miss Cecily Cardew. Cecily, who addresses me as her uncle from motives of respect that you could not possibly appreciate, lives at my place in the country under the charge of her admirable governess, Miss Prism.

ALGERNON: Where is that place in the country, by the way?

JACK: That is nothing to you, dear boy. You are not going to be invited. . . . I may tell you candidly that the place is not in Shropshire.

ALGERNON: I suspected that, my dear fellow! I have Bunburyed all over Shropshire on two separate occasions. Now, go on. Why are you Ernest in town and Jack in the country?

JACK: My dear Algy, I don't know whether you will be able to understand my real motives. You are hardly serious enough. When one is placed in the position of guardian, one has to adopt a very high moral tone on all subjects. It's one's duty to do so. And as a high moral tone can hardly be said to conduce very much to either one's health or one's happiness, in order to get up to town I have always pretended to have a younger brother of the name of Ernest, who lives in the Albany, and gets into the most dreadful scrapes. That, my dear Algy, is the whole truth pure and simple.

ALGERNON: The truth is rarely pure and never simple. Modern life would be very tedious if it were either, and modern literature a complete impossibility!

JACK: That wouldn't be at all a bad thing.

ALGERNON: Literary criticism is not your forte, my dear fellow. Don't try it. You should leave that to people who haven't been at a University. They do it so well in the daily papers. What you really are is a Bunburyist. I was quite right in saying you were a Bunburyist. You are one of the most advanced Bunburyists I know.

JACK: What on earth do you mean?

ALGERNON: You have invented a very useful young brother called Ernest, in order that you may be able to come up to town as often as you like. I have invented an invaluable permanent invalid called Bunbury, in order that I may be able to go down into the country whenever I choose. Bunbury is perfectly invaluable. If it wasn't for Bunbury's extraordinary bad health, for instance, I wouldn't be able to dine with you at Willis's tonight, for I have been really engaged to Aunt Augusta for more than a week.

JACK: I haven't asked you to dine with me anywhere tonight.

ALGERNON: I know. You are absurdly careless about sending out invitations. It is very foolish of you. Nothing annoys people so much as not receiving invitations.

JACK: You had much better dine with your Aunt Augusta.

ALGERNON: I haven't the smallest intention of doing anything of the kind. To begin with, I dined there on Monday, and once a week is quite enough to dine with one's own relations. In the second place, whenever I do dine there I am always treated as a member of the family, and sent down with either no woman at all, or two. In the third place, I know perfectly well whom she will place me next to, tonight. She will place me next Mary Farquhar, who always flirts with her own husband across the dinner table. That is not very pleasant. Indeed, it is not even decent . . . and that sort of thing is enormously on the increase. The amount of women in London who flirt with their own husbands is perfectly scandalous. It looks so bad. It is simply washing one's clean linen in public. Besides, now that I know you to be a confirmed Bunburyist, I naturally want to talk to you about Bunburying. I want to tell you the rules.

JACK: I'm not a Bunburyist at all. If Gwendolen accepts me, I am going to kill my brother, indeed I think I'll kill him in any case. Cecily is a little too much interested in him. It is rather a bore. So I am going to get rid of Ernest. And I strongly advise you to do the same with Mr. . . . with your invalid friend who has the absurd name.

ALGERNON: Nothing will induce me to part with Bunbury, and if you ever get married, which seems to me extremely problematic, you will be very glad to know Bunbury. A man who marries without knowing Bunbury has a very tedious time of it.

JACK: That is nonsense. If I marry a charming girl like Gwendolen, and she is the only girl I ever saw in my life that I would marry, I certainly won't want to know Bunbury.

ALGERNON: Then your wife will. You don't seem to realize, that in married life three is company and two is none.

JACK (*sententiously*): That, my dear young friend, is the theory that the corrupt French Drama has been propounding for the last fifty years.

ALGERNON: Yes; and that the happy English home has proved in half the time.

JACK: For heaven's sake, don't try to be cynical. It's perfectly easy to be cynical.

ALGERNON: My dear fellow, it isn't easy to be anything nowadays. There's such a lot of beastly competition about. (*The sound of an electric bell is heard.*) Ah! that must be Aunt Augusta. Only relatives, or creditors, ever ring in that Wagnerian manner. Now, if I get her out of the way for ten minutes, so that you can have an opportunity for proposing to Gwendolen, may I dine with you tonight at Willis's?

JACK: I suppose so, if you want to.

ALGERNON: Yes, but you must be serious about it. I hate people who are not serious about meals. It is so shallow of them.

(*Enter Lane.*)

LANE: Lady Bracknell and Miss Fairfax.

(*Algernon goes forward to meet them. Enter Lady Bracknell and Gwendolen.*)

LADY BRACKNELL: Good afternoon, dear Algernon, I hope you are behaving very well.

ALGERNON: I'm feeling very well, Aunt Augusta.

LADY BRACKNELL: That's not quite the same thing. In fact the two things rarely go together. (*Sees Jack and bows to him with icy coldness.*)

ALGERNON (*to Gwendolen*): Dear me, you are smart!

GWENDOLEN: I am always smart! Aren't I, Mr. Worthing?

JACK: You're quite perfect, Miss Fairfax.

GWENDOLEN: Oh! I hope I am not that. It would leave no room for developments, and I intend to develop in many directions. (*Gwendolen and Jack sit down together in the corner.*)

LADY BRACKNELL: I'm sorry if we are a little late, Algernon, but I was obliged to call on dear Lady Harbury. I hadn't been there since her poor husband's death. I never saw a woman so altered; she looks quite twenty years younger. And now I'll have a cup of tea, and one of those nice cucumber sandwiches you promised me.

ALGERNON: Certainly, Aunt Augusta. (*Goes over to tea table.*)

LADY BRACKNELL: Won't you come and sit here, Gwendolen?

GWENDOLEN: Thanks, mamma, I'm quite comfortable where I am.

ALGERNON (*picking up empty plate in horror*): Good heavens! Lane! Why are there no cucumber sandwiches? I ordered them specially.

LANE (*gravely*): There were no cucumbers in the market this morning, sir. I went down twice.

ALGERNON: No cucumbers!

LANE: No, sir. Not even for ready money.

ALGERNON: That will do, Lane, thank you.

LANE: Thank you, sir.

ALGERNON: I am greatly distressed, Aunt Augusta, about there being no cucumbers, not even for ready money.

LADY BRACKNELL: It really makes no matter, Algernon. I had some crumpets with Lady Harbury, who seems to me to be living entirely for pleasure now.

ALGERNON: I hear her hair has turned quite gold from grief.

LADY BRACKNELL: It certainly has changed its color. From what cause I, of course, cannot say. (*Algernon crosses and hands tea.*) Thank you. I've quite a treat for you tonight, Algernon. I am going to send you down with Mary Farquhar. She is such a nice woman, and so attentive to her husband. It's delightful to watch them.

ALGERNON: I am afraid, Aunt Augusta, I shall have to give up the pleasure of dining with you tonight after all.

LADY BRACKNELL (*frowning*): I hope not, Algernon. It would put my table completely out. Your uncle would have to dine upstairs. Fortunately he is accustomed to that.

ALGERNON: It is a great bore, and, I need hardly say, a terrible disappointment to me, but the fact is I have just had a telegram to say that my poor friend Bunbury is very ill again. (*Exchanges glances with Jack.*) They seem to think I should be with him.

LADY BRACKNELL: It is very strange. This Mr. Bunbury seems to suffer from curiously bad health.

ALGERNON: Yes; poor Bunbury is a dreadful invalid.

LADY BRACKNELL: Well, I must say, Algernon, that I think it is high time that Mr. Bunbury made up his mind whether he was going to live or to die. This shilly-shallying with the question is absurd. Nor do I in any way approve of the modern sympathy with invalids. I consider it morbid. Illness of any kind is hardly a thing to be encouraged in others. Health is the primary duty of life. I am always telling that to your poor uncle, but he never seems to take much notice . . . as far as any improvement in his ailments goes. I should be obliged if you would ask Mr. Bunbury, from me, to be kind enough not to have a relapse on Saturday, for I rely on you to arrange my music for me. It is my last reception, and one wants something that will encourage conversation, particularly at the end of the season when everyone has practically said whatever they had to say, which, in most cases, was probably not much.

ALGERNON: I'll speak to Bunbury, Aunt Augusta, if he is still conscious, and I think I can promise you he'll be all right by Saturday. Of course the music is a great difficulty. You see, if one plays good music, people don't listen, and if one plays bad music, people don't talk. But I'll run over the program I've drawn out, if you will kindly come into the next room for a moment.

LADY BRACKNELL: Thank you, Algernon. It is very thoughtful of you. (*Rising, and following Algernon.*) I'm sure the program will be delightful, after a few expurgations. French songs I cannot possibly allow. People always seem to think that they are improper, and either look shocked, which is vulgar, or laugh, which is worse. But German sounds a thoroughly respectable language, and indeed, I believe is so. Gwendolen, you will accompany me.

GWENDOLEN: Certainly, mamma.

(*Lady Bracknell and Algernon go into the music room, Gwendolen remains behind.*)

JACK: Charming day it has been, Miss Fairfax.

GWENDOLEN: Pray don't talk to me about the weather, Mr. Worthing. Whenever people talk to me about the weather, I always feel quite certain that they mean something else. And that makes me so nervous.

JACK: I do mean something else.

GWENDOLEN: I thought so. In fact, I am never wrong.

JACK: And I would like to be allowed to take advantage of Lady Bracknell's temporary absence . . .

GWENDOLEN: I would certainly advise you to do so. Mamma has a way of coming back suddenly into a room that I have often had to speak to her about.

JACK (*nervously*): Miss Fairfax, ever since I met you I have admired you more than any girl . . . I have ever met since . . . I met you.

GWENDOLEN: Yes, I am quite aware of the fact. And I often wish that in public, at any rate, you had been more demonstrative. For me you have always had an irresistible fascination. Even before I met you I was far from indifferent to you. (*Jack looks at her in amazement.*) We live, as I hope you know, Mr. Worthing, in an age of ideals. The fact is constantly mentioned in the more expensive monthly magazines, and has reached the provincial pulpits, I am told: and my ideal has always been to love someone of the name of Ernest. There is something in that name that inspires absolute confidence. The moment Algernon first mentioned to me that he had a friend called Ernest, I knew I was destined to love you.

JACK: You really love me, Gwendolen?

GWENDOLEN: Passionately!

JACK: Darling! You don't know how happy you've made me.

GWENDOLEN: My own Ernest!

JACK: But you don't really mean to say that you couldn't love me if my name wasn't Ernest?

GWENDOLEN: But your name is Ernest.

JACK: Yes, I know it is. But supposing it was something else? Do you mean to say you couldn't love me then?

GWENDOLEN (*glibly*): Ah! that is clearly a metaphysical speculation, and like most metaphysical speculations has very little reference at all to the actual facts of real life, as we know them.

JACK: Personally, darling, to speak quite candidly, I don't much care about the name of Ernest . . . I don't think the name suits me at all.

GWENDOLEN: It suits you perfectly. It is a divine name. It has a music of its own. It produces vibrations.

JACK: Well, really, Gwendolen, I must say that I think there are lots of other much nicer names. I think Jack, for instance, a charming name.

GWENDOLEN: Jack? . . . No, there is very little music in the name Jack, if any at all, indeed. It does not thrill. It produces absolutely no vibrations. . . . I have known several Jacks, and they all, without exception, were more than usually plain. Besides, Jack is a notorious domesticity for John! And I pity any woman who is married to a man called John. She would probably never be allowed to know the entrancing pleasure of a single moment's solitude. The only really safe name is Ernest.

JACK: Gwendolen, I must get christened at once—I mean we must get married at once. There is no time to be lost.

GWENDOLEN: Married, Mr. Worthing?

JACK (*astounded*): Well . . . surely. You know that I love you, and you led me to believe, Miss Fairfax, that you were not absolutely indifferent to me.

GWENDOLEN: I adore you. But you haven't proposed to me yet. Nothing has been said at all about marriage. The subject has not even been touched on.

JACK: Well . . . may I propose to you now?

GWENDOLEN: I think it would be an admirable opportunity. And to spare you any possible disappointment, Mr. Worthing, I think it only fair to tell you quite frankly beforehand that I am fully determined to accept you.

JACK: Gwendolen!

GWENDOLEN: Yes, Mr. Worthing, what have you got to say to me?

JACK: You know what I have got to say to you.

GWENDOLEN: Yes, but you don't say it.

JACK: Gwendolen, will you marry me? (*Goes on his knees.*)

GWENDOLEN: Of course I will, darling. How long you have been about it! I am afraid you have had very little experience in how to propose.

JACK: My own one, I have never loved anyone in the world but you.

GWENDOLEN: Yes, but men often propose for practice. I know my brother Gerald does. All my girlfriends tell me so. What wonderfully blue eyes you have, Ernest! They are quite, quite blue. I hope you will always look at me just like that, especially when there are other people present.

(*Enter Lady Bracknell.*)

LADY BRACKNELL: Mr. Worthing! Rise, sir, from this semi-recumbent posture. It is most indecorous.

GWENDOLEN: Mamma! (*He tries to rise; she restrains him.*) I must beg you to retire. This is no place for you. Besides, Mr. Worthing has not quite finished yet.

LADY BRACKNELL: Finished what, may I ask?

GWENDOLEN: I am engaged to Mr. Worthing, mamma.

(*They rise together.*)

LADY BRACKNELL: Pardon me, you are not engaged to anyone. When you do become engaged to someone, I, or your father, should his health permit him, will inform you of the fact. An engagement should come on a young girl as a surprise, pleasant or unpleasant, as the case may be. It is hardly a matter that she could be allowed to arrange for herself. . . . And now I have a few questions to put to you, Mr. Worthing. While I am making these inquiries, you, Gwendolen, will wait for me below in the carriage.

GWENDOLEN (*reproachfully*): Mamma!

LADY BRACKNELL: In the carriage, Gwendolen! (*Gwendolen goes to the door. She and Jack blow kisses to each other behind Lady Bracknell's back. Lady Bracknell looks vaguely about as if she could not understand what the noise was. Finally turns round.*) Gwendolen, the carriage!

GWENDOLEN: Yes, mamma. (*Goes out, looking back at Jack.*)

LADY BRACKNELL (*sitting down*): You can take a seat, Mr. Worthing.

(*Looks in her pocket for notebook and pencil.*)

JACK: Thank you, Lady Bracknell, I prefer standing.

LADY BRACKNELL (*pencil and notebook in hand*): I feel bound to tell you that you are not down on my list of eligible young men, although I have the same list as the dear Duchess of Bolton has. We work together, in fact. However, I am quite ready to enter your name, should your answers be what a really affectionate mother requires. Do you smoke?

JACK: Well, yes, I must admit I smoke.

LADY BRACKNELL: I am glad to hear it. A man should always have an occupation of some kind. There are far too many idle men in London as it is. How old are you?

JACK: Twenty-nine.

LADY BRACKNELL: A very good age to be married at. I have always been of opinion that a man who desires to get married should know either everything or nothing. Which do you know?

JACK (*after some hesitation*): I know nothing, Lady Bracknell.

LADY BRACKNELL: I am pleased to hear it. I do not approve of anything that tampers with natural ignorance. Ignorance is like a delicate exotic fruit; touch it and the bloom is gone. The whole theory of modern education is radically unsound. Fortunately in England, at any rate,

education produces no effect whatsoever. If it did, it would prove a
serious danger to the upper classes, and probably lead to acts of violence in Grosvenor Square. What is your income?

JACK: Between seven and eight thousand a year.

LADY BRACKNELL (*makes a note in her book*): In land, or in investments?

JACK: In investments, chiefly.

LADY BRACKNELL: That is satisfactory. What between the duties expected
of one during one's lifetime, and the duties exacted from one after
one's death, land has ceased to be either a profit or a pleasure. It gives
one position, and prevents one from keeping it up. That's all that can
be said about land.

JACK: I have a country house with some land, of course, attached to it,
about fifteen hundred acres, I believe; but I don't depend on that for
my real income. In fact, as far as I can make out, the poachers are the
only people who make anything out of it.

LADY BRACKNELL: A country house! How many bedrooms? Well, that
point can be cleared up afterwards. You have a town house, I hope? A
girl with a simple, unspoiled nature, like Gwendolen, could hardly be
expected to reside in the country.

JACK: Well, I own a house in Belgrave Square, but it is let by the year to
Lady Bloxham. Of course, I can get it back whenever I like, at six
months' notice.

LADY BRACKNELL: Lady Bloxham? I don't know her.

JACK: Oh, she goes about very little. She is a lady considerably advanced
in years.

LADY BRACKNELL: Ah, nowadays that is no guarantee of respectability of
character. What number in Belgrave Square?

JACK: 149.

LADY BRACKNELL (*shaking her head*): The unfashionable side. I thought
there was something. However, that could easily be altered.

JACK: Do you mean the fashion, or the side?

LADY BRACKNELL (*sternly*): Both, if necessary, I presume. What are your
politics?

JACK: Well, I am afraid I really have none. I am a Liberal Unionist.

LADY BRACKNELL: Oh, they count as Tories. They dine with us. Or come
in the evening, at any rate. Now to minor matters. Are your parents
living?

JACK: I have lost both my parents.

LADY BRACKNELL: Both? To lose one parent may be regarded as a
misfortune—to lose *both* seems like carelessness. Who was your
father? He was evidently a man of some wealth. Was he born in what
the Radical papers call the purple of commerce, or did he rise from the
ranks of aristocracy?

JACK: I am afraid I really don't know. The fact is, Lady Bracknell, I said I had lost my parents. It would be nearer the truth to say that my parents seem to have lost me. . . . I don't actually know who I am by birth. I was . . . well, I was found.

LADY BRACKNELL: Found!

JACK: The late Mr. Thomas Cardew, an old gentleman of a very charitable and kindly disposition, found me, and gave me the name of Worthing, because he happened to have a first-class ticket for Worthing in his pocket at the time. Worthing is a place in Sussex. It is a seaside resort.

LADY BRACKNELL: Where did the charitable gentleman who had a first-class ticket for this seaside resort find you?

JACK (*gravely*): In a handbag.

LADY BRACKNELL: A handbag?

JACK (*very seriously*): Yes, Lady Bracknell. I was in a handbag—a somewhat large, black leather handbag, with handles to it—an ordinary handbag, in fact.

LADY BRACKNELL: In what locality did this Mr. James, or Thomas, Cardew come across this ordinary handbag?

JACK: In the cloak room at Victoria Station. It was given to him in mistake for his own.

LADY BRACKNELL: The cloak room at Victoria Station?

JACK: Yes. The Brighton line.

LADY BRACKNELL: The line is immaterial. Mr. Worthing, I confess I feel somewhat bewildered by what you have just told me. To be born, or at any rate, bred in a handbag, whether it had handles or not, seems to me to display a contempt for the ordinary decencies of family life that reminds one of the worst excesses of the French Revolution. And I presume you know what that unfortunate movement led to? As for the particular locality in which the handbag was found, a cloak room at a railway station might serve to conceal a social indiscretion—has probably, indeed, been used for that purpose before now—but it could hardly be regarded as an assured basis for a recognized position in good society.

JACK: May I ask you then what you would advise me to do? I need hardly say I would do anything in the world to ensure Gwendolen's happiness.

LADY BRACKNELL: I would strongly advise you, Mr. Worthing, to try and acquire some relations as soon as possible, and to make a definite effort to produce at any rate one parent, of either sex, before the season is quite over.

JACK: Well, I don't see how I could possibly manage to do that. I can produce the handbag at any moment, it is in my dressing room at home. I really think that should satisfy you, Lady Bracknell.

LADY BRACKNELL: Me, sir! What has it to do with me? You can hardly imagine that I and Lord Bracknell would dream of allowing our only daughter—a girl brought up with the utmost care—to marry into a cloak room, and form an alliance with a parcel? Good morning, Mr. Worthing!

(*Lady Bracknell sweeps out in majestic indignation.*)

JACK: Good morning! (*Algernon, from the other room, strikes up the Wedding March. Jack looks perfectly furious, and goes to the door.*) For goodness' sake don't play that ghastly tune, Algy! How idiotic you are!

(*The music stops, and Algernon enters cheerily.*)

ALGERNON: Didn't it go off all right, old boy? You don't mean to say Gwendolen refused you? I know it is a way she has. She is always refusing people. I think it is most ill-natured of her.

JACK: Oh, Gwendolen is as right as a trivet. As far as she is concerned, we are engaged. Her mother is perfectly unbearable. Never met such a Gorgon . . . I don't really know what a Gorgon is like, but I am quite sure that Lady Bracknell is one. In any case, she is a monster, without being a myth, which is rather unfair . . . I beg your pardon, Algy, I suppose I shouldn't talk about your own aunt in that way before you.

ALGERNON: My dear boy, I love hearing my relations abused. It is the only thing that makes me put up with them at all. Relations are simply a tedious pack of people who haven't got the remotest knowledge of how to live, nor the smallest instinct about when to die.

JACK: Oh, that is nonsense!

ALGERNON: It isn't!

JACK: Well, I won't argue about the matter. You always want to argue about things.

ALGERNON: That is exactly what things were originally made for.

JACK: Upon my word, if I thought that, I'd shoot myself . . . (*A pause.*) You don't think there is any chance of Gwendolen becoming like her mother in about a hundred and fifty years, do you, Algy?

ALGERNON: All women become like their mothers. That is their tragedy. No man does. That's his.

JACK: Is that clever?

ALGERNON: It is perfectly phrased! and quite as true as any observation in civilized life should be.

JACK: I am sick to death of cleverness. Everybody is clever nowadays. You can't go anywhere without meeting clever people. The thing has become an absolute public nuisance. I wish to goodness we had a few fools left.

ALGERNON: We have.

JACK: I should extremely like to meet them. What do they talk about?

ALGERNON: The fools? Oh! about the clever people, of course.

JACK: What fools!

ALGERNON: By the way, did you tell Gwendolen the truth about your being Ernest in town, and Jack in the country?

JACK (*in a very patronizing manner*): My dear fellow, the truth isn't quite the sort of thing one tells to a nice sweet refined girl. What extraordinary ideas you have about the way to behave to a woman!

ALGERNON: The only way to behave to a woman is to make love to her, if she is pretty, and to someone else if she is plain.

JACK: Oh, that is nonsense.

ALGERNON: What about your brother? What about the profligate Ernest?

JACK: Oh, before the end of the week I shall have got rid of him. I'll say he died in Paris of apoplexy. Lots of people die of apoplexy, quite suddenly, don't they?

ALGERNON: Yes, but it's hereditary, my dear fellow. It's a sort of thing that runs in families. You had much better say a severe chill.

JACK: You are sure a severe chill isn't hereditary, or anything of that kind?

ALGERNON: Of course it isn't!

JACK: Very well, then. My poor brother Ernest is carried off suddenly in Paris, by a severe chill. That gets rid of him.

ALGERNON: But I thought you said that . . . Miss Cardew was a little too much interested in your poor brother Ernest? Won't she feel his loss a good deal?

JACK: Oh, that is all right. Cecily is not a silly romantic girl, I am glad to say. She has got a capital appetite, goes on long walks, and pays no attention at all to her lessons.

ALGERNON: I would rather like to see Cecily.

JACK: I will take very good care you never do. She is excessively pretty, and she is only just eighteen.

ALGERNON: Have you told Gwendolen yet that you have an excessively pretty ward who is only just eighteen?

JACK: Oh! one doesn't blurt these things out to people. Cecily and Gwendolen are perfectly certain to be extremely great friends. I'll bet you anything you like that half an hour after they have met, they will be calling each other sister.

ALGERNON: Women only do that when they have called each other a lot of other things first. Now, my dear boy, if we want to get a good table at Willis's, we really must go and dress. Do you know it is nearly seven?

JACK (*irritably*): Oh! it always is nearly seven.

ALGERNON: Well, I'm hungry.

JACK: I never knew you when you weren't. . . .

ALGERNON: What shall we do after dinner? Go to the theater?

JACK: Oh no! I loathe listening.

ALGERNON: Well, let us go to the club?

JACK: Oh, no! I hate talking.

ALGERNON: Well, we might trot around to the Empire at ten?

JACK: Oh no! I can't bear looking at things. It is so silly.

ALGERNON: Well, what shall we do?

JACK: Nothing!

ALGERNON: It is awfully hard work doing nothing. However, I don't mind hard work where there is no definite object of any kind.

(*Enter Lane.*)

LANE: Miss Fairfax.

(*Enter Gwendolen. Lane goes out.*)

ALGERNON: Gwendolen, upon my word!

GWENDOLEN: Algy, kindly turn your back. I have something very particular to say to Mr. Worthing.

ALGERNON: Really, Gwendolen, I don't think I can allow this at all.

GWENDOLEN: Algy, you always adopt a strictly immoral attitude towards life. You are not quite old enough to do that. (*Algernon retires to the fireplace.*)

JACK: My own darling!

GWENDOLEN: Ernest, we may never be married. From the expression on mamma's face I fear we never shall. Few parents nowadays pay any regard to what their children say to them. The old-fashioned respect for the young is fast dying out. Whatever influence I ever had over mamma, I lost at the age of three. But although she may prevent us from becoming man and wife, and I may marry someone else, and marry often, nothing that she can possibly do can alter my eternal devotion to you.

JACK: Dear Gwendolen!

GWENDOLEN: The story of your romantic origin, as related to me by mamma, with unpleasing comments, has naturally stirred the deeper fibers of my nature. Your Christian name has an irresistible fascination. The simplicity of your character makes you exquisitely incomprehensible to me. Your town address at the Albany I have. What is your address in the country?

JACK: The Manor House, Woolton, Hertfordshire.

(*Algernon, who has been carefully listening, smiles to himself, and writes the address on his shirt-cuff. Then picks up the Railway Guide.*)

GWENDOLEN: There is a good postal service, I suppose? It may be necessary to do something desperate. That of course will require serious consideration. I will communicate with you daily.

JACK: My own one!

GWENDOLEN: How long do you remain in town?

JACK: Till Monday.

GWENDOLEN: Good! Algy, you may turn round now.

ALGERNON: Thanks, I've turned round already.

GWENDOLEN: You may also ring the bell.

JACK: You will let me see you to your carriage, my own darling?

GWENDOLEN: Certainly.

JACK (*to Lane, who now enters*): I will see Miss Fairfax out.

LANE: Yes, sir. (*Jack and Gwendolen go off.*)

(*Lane presents several letters on a salver to Algernon. It is to be surmised that they are bills, as Algernon after looking at the envelopes, tears them up.*)

ALGERNON: A glass of sherry, Lane.

LANE: Yes, sir.

ALGERNON: Tomorrow, Lane, I'm going Bunburying.

LANE: Yes, sir.

ALGERNON: I shall probably not be back till Monday. You can put up my dress clothes, my smoking jacket, and all the Bunbury suits . . .

LANE: Yes, sir. (*Handing sherry.*)

ALGERNON: I hope tomorrow will be a fine day, Lane.

LANE: It never is, sir.

ALGERNON: Lane, you're a perfect pessimist.

LANE: I do my best to give satisfaction, sir.

(*Enter Jack. Lane goes off.*)

JACK: There's a sensible, intellectual girl! the only girl I ever cared for in my life. (*Algernon is laughing immoderately.*) What on earth are you so amused at?

ALGERNON: Oh, I'm a little anxious about poor Bunbury, that is all.

JACK: If you don't take care, your friend Bunbury will get you into a serious scrape some day.

ALGERNON: I love scrapes. They are the only things that are never serious.

JACK: Oh, that's nonsense, Algy. You never talk anything but nonsense.

ALGERNON: Nobody ever does.

(*Jack looks indignantly at him, and leaves the room. Algernon lights a cigarette, reads his shirt-cuff, and smiles.*)

ACT-DROP

SECOND ACT

Scene: *Garden at the Manor House. A flight of gray stone steps leads up to the house. The garden, an old-fashioned one, full of roses. Time of year, July. Basket chairs, and a table covered with books, are set under a large yew tree.*

(*Miss Prism discovered seated at the table. Cecily is at the back watering flowers.*)

MISS PRISM (*calling*): Cecily, Cecily! Surely such a utilitarian occupation as the watering of flowers is rather Moulton's duty than yours? Especially at a moment when intellectual pleasures await you. Your German grammar is on the table. Pray open it at page fifteen. We will repeat yesterday's lesson.

CECILY (*coming over very slowly*): But I don't like German. It isn't at all a becoming language. I know perfectly well that I look quite plain after my German lesson.

MISS PRISM: Child, you know how anxious your guardian is that you should improve yourself in every way. He laid particular stress on your German, as he was leaving for town yesterday. Indeed, he always lays stress on your German when he is leaving for town.

CECILY: Dear Uncle Jack is so very serious! Sometime he is so serious that I think he cannot be quite well.

MISS PRISM (*drawing herself up*): Your guardian enjoys the best of health, and his gravity of demeanor is especially to be commended in one so comparatively young as he is. I know no one who has a higher sense of duty and responsibility.

CECILY: I suppose that is why he often looks a little bored when we three are together.

MISS PRISM: Cecily! I am surprised at you. Mr. Worthing has many troubles in his life. Idle merriment and triviality would be out of place in his conversation. You must remember his constant anxiety about that unfortunate young man his brother.

CECILY: I wish Uncle Jack would allow that unfortunate young man, his brother, to come down here sometimes. We might have a good influence over him, Miss Prism. I am sure you certainly would. You know German, and geology, and things of that kind influence a man very much. (*Cecily begins to write in her diary.*)

MISS PRISM (*shaking her head*): I do not think that even I could produce any effect on a character that according to his own brother's admission is irretrievably weak and vacillating. Indeed I am not sure that I would desire to reclaim him. I am not in favor of this modern mania for turning bad people into good people at a moment's notice. As a man sows so let him reap. You must put away your diary, Cecily. I really don't see why you should keep a diary at all.

CECILY: I keep a diary in order to enter the wonderful secrets of my life. If I didn't write them down I should probably forget all about them.

MISS PRISM: Memory, my dear Cecily, is the diary that we all carry about with us.

CECILY: Yes, but it usually chronicles the things that have never happened, and couldn't possibly have happened. I believe that Memory is responsible for nearly all the three-volume novels that Mudie sends us.

MISS PRISM: Do not speak slightingly of the three-volume novel, Cecily. I wrote one myself in earlier days.

CECILY: Did you really, Miss Prism? How wonderfully clever you are! I hope it did not end happily? I don't like novels that end happily. They depress me so much.

MISS PRISM: The good ended happily, and the bad unhappily. That is what Fiction means.

CECILY: I suppose so. But it seems very unfair. And was your novel ever published?

MISS PRISM: Alas! no. The manuscript unfortunately was abandoned. I use the word in the sense of lost or mislaid. To your work, child, these speculations are profitless.

CECILY (*smiling*): But I see dear Dr. Chasuble coming up through the garden.

MISS PRISM (*rising and advancing*): Dr. Chasuble! This is indeed a pleasure.

(*Enter Canon Chasuble.*)

CHASUBLE: And how are we this morning? Miss Prism, you are, I trust, well?

CECILY: Miss Prism has just been complaining of a slight headache. I think it would do her so much good to have a short stroll with you in the Park, Dr. Chasuble.

MISS PRISM: Cecily, I have not mentioned anything about a headache.

CECILY: No, dear Miss Prism, I know that, but I felt instinctively that you had a headache. Indeed I was thinking about that, and not about my German lesson, when the Rector came in.

CHASUBLE: I hope, Cecily, you are not inattentive.

CECILY: Oh, I am afraid I am.

CHASUBLE: That is strange. Were I fortunate enough to be Miss Prism's pupil, I would hang upon her lips. (*Miss Prism glares.*) I spoke metaphorically.—My metaphor was drawn from bees. Ahem! Mr. Worthing, I suppose, has not returned from town yet?

MISS PRISM: We do not expect him till Monday afternoon.

CHASUBLE: Ah yes, he usually likes to spend his Sunday in London. He is not one of those whose sole aim is enjoyment, as, by all accounts, that unfortunate young man his brother seems to be. But I must not disturb Egeria and her pupil any longer.

MISS PRISM: Egeria? My name is Laetitia, Doctor.

CHASUBLE (*bowing*): A classical allusion merely, drawn from the Pagan authors. I shall see you both no doubt at Evensong?

MISS PRISM: I think, dear Doctor, I will have a stroll with you. I find I have a headache after all, and a walk might do it good.

CHASUBLE: With pleasure, Miss Prism, with pleasure. We might go as far as the schools and back.

MISS PRISM: That would be delightful. Cecily, you will read your Political Economy in my absence. The chapter on the Fall of the Rupee you may omit. It is somewhat too sensational. Even these metallic problems have their melodramatic side. (*Goes down the garden with Dr. Chasuble.*)

CECILY (*picks up books and throws them back on table*): Horrid Political Economy! Horrid Geography! Horrid, horrid German!

(*Enter Merriman with a card on a salver.*)

MERRIMAN: Mr. Ernest Worthing has just driven over from the station. He has brought his luggage with him.

CECILY (*takes the card and reads it*): "Mr. Ernest Worthing, B. 4, The Albany, W." Uncle Jack's brother! Did you tell him Mr. Worthing was in town?

MERRIMAN: Yes, Miss. He seemed very much disappointed. I mentioned that you and Miss Prism were in the garden. He said he was anxious to speak to you privately for a moment.

CECILY: Ask Mr. Ernest Worthing to come here. I suppose you had better talk to the housekeeper about a room for him.

MERRIMAN: Yes, Miss. (*Merriman goes off.*)

CECILY: I have never met any really wicked person before. I feel rather frightened. I am so afraid he will look just like everyone else. (*Enter Algernon, very gay and debonair.*) He does!

ALGERNON (*raising his hat*): You are my little cousin Cecily, I'm sure.

CECILY: You are under some strange mistake. I am not little. In fact, I believe I am more than usually tall for my age. (*Algernon is rather taken aback.*) But I am your cousin Cecily. You, I see from your card, are Uncle Jack's brother, my cousin Ernest, my wicked cousin Ernest.

ALGERNON: Oh! I am not really wicked at all, cousin Cecily. You mustn't think that I am wicked.

CECILY: If you are not, then you have certainly been deceiving us all in a very inexcusable manner. I hope you have not been leading a double life, pretending to be wicked and being really good all the time. That would be hypocrisy.

ALGERNON (*looks at her in amazement*): Oh! Of course I have been rather reckless.

CECILY: I am glad to hear it.

ALGERNON: In fact, now you mention the subject, I have been very bad in my own small way.

CECILY: I don't think you should be so proud of that, though I am sure it must have been very pleasant.

ALGERNON: It is much pleasanter being here with you.

CECILY: I can't understand how you are here at all. Uncle Jack won't be back till Monday afternoon.

ALGERNON: That is a great disappointment. I am obliged to go up by the first train on Monday morning. I have a business appointment that I am anxious . . . to miss.

CECILY: Couldn't you miss it anywhere but in London?

ALGERNON: No: the appointment is in London.

CECILY: Well, I know, of course, how important it is not to keep a business engagement, if one wants to retain any sense of the beauty of life, but still I think you had better wait till Uncle Jack arrives. I know he wants to speak to you about your emigrating.

ALGERNON: About my what?

CECILY: Your emigrating. He has gone up to buy your outfit.

ALGERNON: I certainly wouldn't let Jack buy my outfit. He has no taste in neckties at all.

CECILY: I don't think you will require neckties. Uncle Jack is sending you to Australia.

ALGERNON: Australia? I'd sooner die.

CECILY: Well, he said at dinner on Wednesday night, that you would have to choose between this world, the next world, and Australia.

ALGERNON: Oh, well! The accounts I have received of Australia and the next world are not particularly encouraging. This world is good enough for me, cousin Cecily.

CECILY: Yes, but are you good enough for it?

ALGERNON: I'm afraid I'm not that. That is why I want you to reform me. You might make that your mission, if you don't mind, cousin Cecily.

CECILY: I'm afraid I've no time, this afternoon.

ALGERNON: Well, would you mind my reforming myself this afternoon?

CECILY: It is rather Quixotic of you. But I think you should try.

ALGERNON: I will. I feel better already.

CECILY: You are looking a little worse.

ALGERNON: That is because I am hungry.

CECILY: How thoughtless of me. I should have remembered that when one is going to lead an entirely new life, one requires regular and wholesome meals. Won't you come in?

ALGERNON: Thank you. Might I have a buttonhole first? I never have any appetite unless I have a buttonhole first.

CECILY: A Maréchal Niel°? (*Picks up scissors.*)

ALGERNON: No, I'd sooner have a pink rose.

CECILY: Why? (*Cuts a flower.*)

ALGERNON: Because you are like a pink rose, cousin Cecily.

CECILY: I don't think it can be right for you to talk to me like that. Miss Prism never says such things to me.

ALGERNON: Then Miss Prism is a shortsighted old lady. (*Cecily puts the rose in his buttonhole.*) You are the prettiest girl I ever saw.

CECILY: Miss Prism says that all good looks are a snare.

ALGERNON: They are a snare that every sensible man would like to be caught in.

CECILY: Oh! I don't think I would care to catch a sensible man. I shouldn't know what to talk to him about.

(*They pass into the house. Miss Prism and Dr. Chasuble return.*)

MISS PRISM: You are too much alone, dear Dr. Chasuble. You should get married. A misanthrope I can understand—a womanthrope, never!

CHASUBLE (*with a scholar's shudder*): Believe me, I do not deserve so neologistic a phrase. The precept as well as the practice of the Primitive Church was distinctly against matrimony.

MISS PRISM (*sententiously*): That is obviously the reason why the Primitive Church has not lasted up to the present day. And you do not seem to realize, dear Doctor, that by persistently remaining single, a man converts himself into a permanent public temptation. Men should be more careful; this very celibacy leads weaker vessels astray.

CHASUBLE: But is a man not equally attractive when married?

MISS PRISM: No married man is ever attractive except to his wife.

CHASUBLE: And often, I've been told, not even to her.

MISS PRISM: That depends on the intellectual sympathies of the woman. Maturity can always be depended on. Ripeness can be trusted. Young women are green. (*Dr. Chasuble starts.*) I spoke horticulturally. My metaphor was drawn from fruits. But where is Cecily?

CHASUBLE: Perhaps she followed us to the schools.

(*Enter Jack slowly from the back of the garden. He is dressed in the deepest mourning, with crape hat-band and black gloves.*)

MISS PRISM: Mr. Worthing!

CHASUBLE: Mr. Worthing?

MISS PRISM: This is indeed a surprise. We did not look for you till Monday afternoon.

Maréchal Niel: A yellow rose.

JACK (*shakes Miss Prism's hand in a tragic manner*): I have returned sooner than I expected. Dr. Chasuble, I hope you are well?

CHASUBLE: Dear Mr. Worthing, I trust this garb of woe does not betoken some terrible calamity?

JACK: My brother.

MISS PRISM: More shameful debts and extravagance?

CHASUBLE: Still leading his life of pleasure?

JACK (*shaking his head*): Dead!

CHASUBLE: Your brother Ernest dead?

JACK: Quite dead.

MISS PRISM: What a lesson for him! I trust he will profit by it.

CHASUBLE: Mr. Worthing, I offer you my sincere condolence. You have at least the consolation of knowing that you were always the most generous and forgiving of brothers.

JACK: Poor Ernest! He had many faults, but it is a sad, sad blow.

CHASUBLE: Very sad indeed. Were you with him at the end?

JACK: No. He died abroad; in Paris, in fact. I had a telegram last night from the manager of the Grand Hotel.

CHASUBLE: Was the cause of death mentioned?

JACK: A severe chill, it seems.

MISS PRISM: As a man sows, so shall he reap.

CHASUBLE (*raising his hand*): Charity, dear Miss Prism, charity! None of us are perfect. I myself am peculiarly susceptible to drafts. Will the interment take place here?

JACK: No. He seemed to have expressed a desire to be buried in Paris.

CHASUBLE: In Paris! (*Shakes his head.*) I fear that hardly points to any very serious state of mind at the last. You would no doubt wish me to make some slight allusion to this tragic domestic affliction next Sunday. (*Jack presses his hand convulsively.*) My sermon on the meaning of the manna in the wilderness can be adapted to almost any occasion, joyful, or, as in the present case, distressing. (*All sigh.*) I have preached it at harvest celebrations, christenings, confirmations, on days of humiliation and festal days. The last time I delivered it was in the Cathedral, as a charity sermon on behalf of the Society for the Prevention of Discontent among the Upper Orders. The Bishop, who was present, was much struck by some of the analogies I drew.

JACK: Ah! That reminds me, you mentioned christenings, I think, Dr. Chasuble? I suppose you know how to christen all right? (*Dr. Chasuble looks astounded.*) I mean, of course, you are continually christening, aren't you?

MISS PRISM: It is, I regret to say, one of the Rector's most constant duties in this parish. I have often spoken to the poorer classes on the subject. But they don't seem to know what thrift is.

CHASUBLE: But is there any particular infant in whom you are interested, Mr. Worthing? Your brother was, I believe, unmarried, was he not?

JACK: Oh yes.

MISS PRISM (*bitterly*): People who live entirely for pleasure usually are.

JACK: But it is not for any child, dear Doctor. I am very fond of children. No! the fact is, I would like to be christened myself, this afternoon, if you have nothing better to do.

CHASUBLE: But surely, Mr. Worthing, you have been christened already?

JACK: I don't remember anything about it.

CHASUBLE: But have you any grave doubts on the subject?

JACK: I certainly intend to have. Of course I don't know if the thing would bother you in any way, or if you think I am a little too old now.

CHASUBLE: Not at all. The sprinkling, and, indeed, the immersion of adults is a perfectly canonical practice.

JACK: Immersion!

CHASUBLE: You need have no apprehensions. Sprinkling is all that is necessary, or indeed I think advisable. Our weather is so changeable. At what hour would you wish the ceremony performed?

JACK: Oh, I might trot round about five if that would suit you.

CHASUBLE: Perfectly, perfectly! In fact I have two similar ceremonies to perform at that time. A case of twins that occurred recently in one of the outlying cottages on your own estate. Poor Jenkins the carter, a most hard-working man.

JACK: Oh! I don't see much fun in being christened along with other babies. It would be childish. Would half-past five do?

CHASUBLE: Admirably! Admirably! (*Takes out watch.*) And now, dear Mr. Worthing, I will not intrude any longer into a house of sorrow. I would merely beg you not to be too much bowed down by grief. What seem to us bitter trials are often blessings in disguise.

MISS PRISM: This seems to me a blessing of an extremely obvious kind.

(*Enter Cecily from the house.*)

CECILY: Uncle Jack! Oh, I am pleased to see you back. But what horrid clothes you have got on! Do go and change them.

MISS PRISM: Cecily!

CHASUBLE: My child! my child! (*Cecily goes towards Jack; he kisses her brow in a melancholy manner.*)

CECILY: What is the matter, Uncle Jack? Do look happy! You look as if you had toothache, and I have got such a surprise for you. Who do you think is in the dining room? Your brother!

JACK: Who?

CECILY: Your brother Ernest. He arrived about half an hour ago.

JACK: What nonsense! I haven't got a brother!

CECILY: Oh, don't say that. However badly he may have behaved to you in the past he is still your brother. You couldn't be so heartless as to disown him. I'll tell him to come out. And you will shake hands with him, won't you, Uncle Jack? (*Runs back into the house.*)

CHASUBLE: These are very joyful tidings.

MISS PRISM: After we had all been resigned to his loss, his sudden return seems to me peculiarly distressing.

JACK: My brother is in the dining room? I don't know what it all means. I think it is perfectly absurd.

(*Enter Algernon and Cecily hand in hand. They come slowly up to Jack.*)

JACK: Good heavens! (*Motions Algernon away.*)

ALGERNON: Brother John, I have come down from town to tell you that I am very sorry for all the trouble I have given you, and that I intend to lead a better life in the future. (*Jack glares at him and does not take his hand.*)

CECILY: Uncle Jack, you are not going to refuse your own brother's hand?

JACK: Nothing will induce me to take his hand. I think his coming down here disgraceful. He knows perfectly well why.

CECILY: Uncle Jack, do be nice. There is some good in everyone. Ernest has just been telling me about his poor invalid friend Mr. Bunbury whom he goes to visit so often. And surely there must be much good in one who is kind to an invalid, and leaves the pleasures of London to sit by a bed of pain.

JACK: Oh! he has been talking about Bunbury, has he?

CECILY: Yes, he has told me all about poor Mr. Bunbury, and his terrible state of health.

JACK: Bunbury! Well, I won't have him talk to you about Bunbury or about anything else. It is enough to drive one perfectly frantic.

ALGERNON: Of course I admit that the faults were all on my side. But I must say that I think that Brother John's coldness to me is peculiarly painful. I expected a more enthusiastic welcome, especially considering it is the first time I have come here.

CECILY: Uncle Jack, if you don't shake hands with Ernest, I will never forgive you.

JACK: Never forgive me?

CECILY: Never, never, never!

JACK: Well, this is the last time I shall ever do it. (*Shakes hands with Algernon and glares.*)

CHASUBLE: It's pleasant, is it not, to see so perfect a reconciliation? I think we might leave the two brothers together.

MISS PRISM: Cecily, you will come with us.

CECILY: Certainly, Miss Prism. My little task of reconciliation is over.

CHASUBLE: You have done a beautiful action today, dear child.

MISS PRISM: We must not be premature in our judgments.

CECILY: I feel very happy. (*They all go off.*)

JACK: You young scoundrel. Algy, you must get out of this place as soon as possible. I don't allow any Bunburying here.

(*Enter Merriman.*)

MERRIMAN: I have put Mr. Ernest's things in the room next to yours, sir. I suppose that is all right?

JACK: What?

MERRIMAN: Mr. Ernest's luggage, sir. I have unpacked it and put it in the room next to your own.

JACK: His luggage?

MERRIMAN: Yes, sir. Three portmanteaus, a dressing case, two hat-boxes, and a large luncheon basket.

ALGERNON: I am afraid I can't stay more than a week this time.

JACK: Merriman, order the dogcart at once. Mr. Ernest has been suddenly called back to town.

MERRIMAN: Yes, sir.   (*Goes back into the house.*)

ALGERNON: What a fearful liar you are, Jack. I have not been called back to town at all.

JACK: Yes, you have.

ALGERNON: I haven't heard anyone call me.

JACK: Your duty as a gentleman calls you back.

ALGERNON: My duty as a gentleman has never interfered with my pleasures in the smallest degree.

JACK: I can quite understand that.

ALGERNON: Well, Cecily is a darling.

JACK: You are not to talk of Miss Cardew like that. I don't like it.

ALGERNON: Well, I don't like your clothes. You look perfectly ridiculous in them. Why on earth don't you go up and change? It is perfectly childish to be in deep mourning for a man who is actually staying for a whole week with you in your house as a guest. I call it grotesque.

JACK: You are certainly not staying with me for a whole week as a guest or anything else. You have got to leave . . . by the four-five train.

ALGERNON: I certainly won't leave you so long as you are in mourning. It would be most unfriendly. If I were in mourning you would stay with me, I suppose. I should think it very unkind if you didn't.

JACK: Well, will you go if I change my clothes?

ALGERNON: Yes, if you are not too long. I never saw anybody take so long to dress, and with such little result.

JACK: Well, at any rate, that is better than being always overdressed as you are.

ALGERNON: If I am occasionally a little overdressed, I make up for it by being always immensely overeducated.

JACK: Your vanity is ridiculous, your conduct an outrage, and your presence in my garden utterly absurd. However, you have got to catch the four-five, and I hope you will have a pleasant journey back to town. This Bunburying, as you call it, has not been a great success for you. (*Goes into the house.*)

ALGERNON: I think it has been a great success. I'm in love with Cecily, and that is everything.

(*Enter Cecily at the back of the garden. She picks up the can and begins to water the flowers.*)

But I must see her before I go, and make arrangements for another Bunbury. Ah, there she is.

CECILY: Oh, I merely came back to water the roses. I thought you were with Uncle Jack.

ALGERNON: He's gone to order the dogcart for me.

CECILY: Oh, is he going to take you for a nice drive?

ALGERNON: He's going to send me away.

CECILY: Then have we got to part?

ALGERNON: I am afraid so. It's very painful parting.

CECILY: It is always painful to part from people whom one has known for a very brief space of time. The absence of old friends one can endure with equanimity. But even a momentary separation from anyone to whom one has just been introduced is almost unbearable.

ALGERNON: Thank you.

(*Enter Merriman.*)

MERRIMAN: The dogcart is at the door, sir. (*Algernon looks appealingly at Cecily.*)

CECILY: It can wait, Merriman . . . for . . . five minutes.

MERRIMAN: Yes, Miss.   (*Exit Merriman.*)

ALGERNON: I hope, Cecily, I shall not offend you if I state quite frankly and openly that you seem to me to be in every way the visible personification of absolute perfection.

CECILY: I think your frankness does you great credit, Ernest. If you will allow me I will copy your remarks into my diary. (*Goes over to table and begins writing in diary.*)

ALGERNON: Do you really keep a diary? I'd give anything to look at it. May I?

CECILY: Oh no. (*Puts her hand over it.*) You see, it is simply a very young girl's record of her own thoughts and impressions, and consequently meant for publication. When it appears in volume form I hope you will order a copy. But pray, Ernest, don't stop. I delight in taking down from dictation. I have reached "absolute perfection." You can go on. I am quite ready for more.

ALGERNON (*somewhat taken aback*): Ahem! Ahem!

CECILY: Oh, don't cough, Ernest. When one is dictating one should speak fluently and not cough. Besides, I don't know how to spell a cough. (*Writes as Algernon speaks.*)

ALGERNON (*speaking very rapidly*): Cecily, ever since I first looked upon your wonderful and incomparable beauty, I have dared to love you wildly, passionately, devotedly, hopelessly.

CECILY: I don't think that you should tell me that you love me wildly, passionately, devotedly, hopelessly. Hopelessly doesn't seem to make much sense, does it?

ALGERNON: Cecily!

(*Enter Merriman.*)

MERRIMAN: The dogcart is waiting, sir.

ALGERNON: Tell it to come round next week, at the same hour.

MERRIMAN (*looks at Cecily, who makes no sign*): Yes, sir.

(*Merriman retires.*)

CECILY: Uncle Jack would be very much annoyed if he knew you were staying on till next week, at the same hour.

ALGERNON: Oh, I don't care about Jack. I don't care for anybody in the whole world but you. I love you, Cecily. You will marry me, won't you?

CECILY: You silly boy! Of course. Why, we have been engaged for the last three months.

ALGERNON: For the last three months?

CECILY: Yes, it will be exactly three months on Thursday.

ALGERNON: But how did we become engaged?

CECILY: Well, ever since dear Uncle Jack first confessed to us that he had a younger brother who was very wicked and bad, you of course have formed the chief topic of conversation between myself and Miss Prism. And of course a man who is much talked about is always very attractive. One feels there must be something in him after all. I daresay it was foolish of me, but I fell in love with you, Ernest.

ALGERNON: Darling! And when was the engagement actually settled?

CECILY: On the 14th of February last. Worn out by your entire ignorance of my existence, I determined to end the matter one way or the other, and after a long struggle with myself I accepted you under this dear old tree here. The next day I bought this little ring in your name, and this is the little bangle with the true lovers' knot I promised you always to wear.

ALGERNON: Did I give you this? It's very pretty, isn't it?

CECILY: Yes, you've wonderfully good taste, Ernest. It's the excuse I've always given for your leading such a bad life. And this is the box in which I keep all your dear letters. (*Kneels at table, opens box, and produces letters tied up with blue ribbon.*)

ALGERNON: My letters! But my own sweet Cecily, I have never written you any letters.

CECILY: You need hardly remind me of that, Ernest. I remember only too well that I was forced to write your letters for you. I always wrote three times a week, and sometimes oftener.

ALGERNON: Oh, do let me read them, Cecily?

CECILY: Oh, I couldn't possibly. They would make you far too conceited. (*Replaces box.*) The three you wrote me after I had broken off the engagement are so beautiful, and so badly spelled, that even now I can hardly read them without crying a little.

ALGERNON: But was our engagement ever broken off?

CECILY: Of course it was. On the 22nd of last March. You can see the entry if you like. (*Shows diary.*) "Today I broke off my engagement with Ernest. I feel it is better to do so. The weather still continues charming."

ALGERNON: But why on earth did you break if off? What had I done? I had done nothing at all. Cecily, I am very much hurt indeed to hear you broke it off. Particularly when the weather was so charming.

CECILY: It would hardly have been a really serious engagement if it hadn't been broken off at least once. But I forgave you before the week was out.

ALGERNON (*crossing to her, and kneeling*): What a perfect angel you are, Cecily.

CECILY: You dear romantic boy. (*He kisses her, she puts her fingers through his hair.*) I hope your hair curls naturally, does it?

ALGERNON: Yes, darling, with a little help from others.

CECILY: I am so glad.

ALGERNON: You'll never break off our engagement again, Cecily?

CECILY: I don't think I could break it off now that I have actually met you. Besides, of course, there is the question of your name.

ALGERNON: Yes, of course. (*Nervously.*)

CECILY: You must not laugh at me, darling, but it had always been a girl-ish dream of mine to love someone whose name was Ernest. (*Algernon rises, Cecily also.*) There is something in that name that seems to inspire absolute confidence. I pity any poor married woman whose husband is not called Ernest.

ALGERNON: But, my dear child, do you mean to say you could not love me if I had some other name?

CECILY: But what name?

ALGERNON: Oh, any name you like—Algernon—for instance . . .

CECILY: But I don't like the name of Algernon.

ALGERNON: Well, my own dear, sweet, loving little darling, I really can't see why you should object to the name of Algernon. It is not at all a bad name. In fact, it is rather an aristocratic name. Half of the chaps who get into the Bankruptcy Court are called Algernon. But seriously, Cecily . . . (*Moving to her.*) . . . if my name was Algy, couldn't you love me?

CECILY (*rising*): I might respect you, Ernest, I might admire your character, but I fear that I should not be able to give you my undivided attention.

ALGERNON: Ahem! Cecily! (*Picking up hat.*) Your Rector here is, I suppose, thoroughly experienced in the practice of all the rites and ceremonials of the Church?

CECILY: Oh, yes. Dr. Chasuble is a most learned man. He has never written a single book, so you can imagine how much he knows.

ALGERNON: I must see him at once on a most important christening—I mean on most important business.

CECILY: Oh!

ALGERNON: I shan't be away more than half an hour.

CECILY: Considering that we have been engaged since February the 14th, and that I only met you today for the first time, I think it is rather hard that you should leave me for so long a period as half an hour. Couldn't you make it twenty minutes?

ALGERNON: I'll be back in no time. (*Kisses her and rushes down the garden.*)

CECILY: What an impetuous boy he is! I like his hair so much. I must enter his proposal in my diary.

(*Enter Merriman.*)

MERRIMAN: A Miss Fairfax has just called to see Mr. Worthing. On very important business, Miss Fairfax states.

CECILY: Isn't Mr. Worthing in his library?

MERRIMAN: Mr. Worthing went over in the direction of the Rectory some time ago.

CECILY: Pray ask the lady to come out here; Mr. Worthing is sure to be back soon. And you can bring tea.

MERRIMAN: Yes, Miss.   (*Goes out.*)

CECILY: Miss Fairfax! I suppose one of the many good elderly women who are associated with Uncle Jack in some of his philanthropic work in London. I don't quite like women who are interested in philanthropic work. I think it is so forward of them.

(*Enter Merriman.*)

MERRIMAN: Miss Fairfax.

(*Enter Gwendolen.*)   (*Exit Merriman.*)

CECILY (*advancing to meet her*): Pray let me introduce myself to you. My name is Cecily Cardew.

GWENDOLEN: Cecily Cardew? (*Moving to her and shaking hands.*) What a very sweet name! Something tells me that we are going to be great friends. I like you already more than I can say. My first impressions of people are never wrong.

CECILY: How nice of you to like me so much after we have known each other such a comparatively short time. Pray sit down.

GWENDOLEN (*still standing up*): I may call you Cecily, may I not?

CECILY: With pleasure!

GWENDOLEN: And you will always call me Gwendolen, won't you?

CECILY: If you wish.

GWENDOLEN: Then that is all quite settled, is it not?

CECILY: I hope so. (*A pause. They both sit down together.*)

GWENDOLEN: Perhaps this might be a favorable opportunity for my mentioning who I am. My father is Lord Bracknell. You have never heard of papa, I suppose?

CECILY: I don't think so.

GWENDOLEN: Outside the family circle, papa, I am glad to say, is entirely unknown. I think that is quite as it should be. The home seems to me to be the proper sphere for the man. And certainly once a man begins to neglect his domestic duties he becomes painfully effeminate, does he not? And I don't like that. It makes men so very attractive. Cecily, mamma, whose views on education are remarkably strict, has brought me up to be extremely shortsighted; it is part of her system; so do you mind my looking at you through my glasses?

CECILY: Oh! not at all, Gwendolen. I am very fond of being looked at.

GWENDOLEN (*after examining Cecily carefully through a lorgnette*): You are here on a short visit, I suppose.

CECILY: Oh no! I live here.

GWENDOLEN (*severely*): Really? Your mother, no doubt, or some female relative of advanced years, resides here also?

CECILY: Oh no! I have no mother, nor, in fact, any relations.

GWENDOLEN: Indeed?

CECILY: My dear guardian, with the assistance of Miss Prism, has the arduous task of looking after me.

GWENDOLEN: Your guardian?

CECILY: Yes, I am Mr. Worthing's ward.

GWENDOLEN: Oh! It is strange he never mentioned to me that he had a ward. How secretive of him! He grows more interesting hourly. I am not sure, however, that the news inspires me with feelings of unmixed delight. (*Rising and going to her.*) I am very fond of you, Cecily; I have liked you ever since I met you! But I am bound to state that now that I know that you are Mr. Worthing's ward, I cannot help expressing a wish you were—well just a little older than you seem to be—and not quite so very alluring in appearance. In fact, if I may speak candidly——

CECILY: Pray do! I think that whenever one has anything unpleasant to say, one should always be quite candid.

GWENDOLEN: Well, to speak with perfect candor, Cecily, I wish that you were fully forty-two, and more than usually plain for your age. Ernest has a strong upright nature. He is the very soul of truth and honor. Disloyalty would be as impossible to him as deception. But even men of the noblest possible moral character are extremely susceptible to the influence of the physical charms of others. Modern, no less than Ancient History, supplies us with many most painful examples of what I refer to. If it were not so, indeed, History would be quite unreadable.

CECILY: I beg your pardon, Gwendolen, did you say Ernest?

GWENDOLEN: Yes.

CECILY: Oh, but it is not Mr. Ernest Worthing who is my guardian. It is his brother—his elder brother.

GWENDOLEN (*sitting down again*): Ernest never mentioned to me that he had a brother.

CECILY: I am sorry to say they have not been on good terms for a long time.

GWENDOLEN: Ah! that accounts for it. And now that I think of it I have never heard any man mention his brother. The subject seems distasteful to most men. Cecily, you have lifted a load from my mind. I was growing almost anxious. It would have been terrible if any cloud had come across a friendship like ours, would it not? Of course you are quite, quite sure that it is not Mr. Ernest Worthing who is your guardian?

CECILY: Quite sure. (*A pause.*) In fact, I am going to be his.

GWENDOLEN (*inquiringly*): I beg your pardon?

CECILY (*rather shy and confidingly*): Dearest Gwendolen, there is no reason why I should make a secret of it to you. Our little county newspaper is sure to chronicle the fact next week. Mr. Ernest Worthing and I are engaged to be married.

GWENDOLEN (*quite politely, rising*): My darling Cecily, I think there must be some slight error. Mr. Ernest Worthing is engaged to me. The announcement will appear in the *Morning Post* on Saturday at the latest.

CECILY (*very politely, rising*): I am afraid you must be under some misconception. Ernest proposed to me exactly ten minutes ago. (*Shows diary*.)

GWENDOLEN (*examines diary through her lorgnette carefully*): It is certainly very curious, for he asked me to be his wife yesterday afternoon at 5:30. If you would care to verify the incident, pray do so. (*Produces diary of her own*.) I never travel without my diary. One should always have something sensational to read in the train. I am so sorry, dear Cecily, if it is any disappointment to you, but I am afraid I have the prior claim.

CECILY: It would distress me more than I can tell you, dear Gwendolen, if it caused you any mental or physical anguish, but I feel bound to point out that since Ernest proposed to you he clearly has changed his mind.

GWENDOLEN (*meditatively*): If the poor fellow has been entrapped into any foolish promise I shall consider it my duty to rescue him at once, and with a firm hand.

CECILY (*thoughtfully and sadly*): Whatever unfortunate entanglement my dear boy may have got into, I will never reproach him with it after we are married.

GWENDOLEN: Do you allude to me, Miss Cardew, as an entanglement? You are presumptuous. On an occasion of this kind it becomes more than a moral duty to speak one's mind. It becomes a pleasure.

CECILY: Do you suggest, Miss Fairfax, that I entrapped Ernest into an engagement? How dare you? This is no time for wearing the shallow mask of manners. When I see a spade I call it a spade.

GWENDOLEN (*satirically*): I am glad to say that I have never seen a spade. It is obvious that our social spheres have been widely different.

(*Enter Merriman, followed by the footman. He carries a salver, tablecloth, and plate stand. Cecily is about to retort. The presence of the servants exercises a restraining influence, under which both girls chafe.*)

MERRIMAN: Shall I lay tea here as usual, Miss?

CECILY (*sternly, in a calm voice*): Yes, as usual.

(*Merriman begins to clear table and lay cloth. A long pause. Cecily and Gwendolen glare at each other.*)

GWENDOLEN: Are there many interesting walks in the vicinity, Miss Cardew?

CECILY: Oh! yes! a great many. From the top of one of the hills quite close one can see five counties.

GWENDOLEN: Five counties! I don't think I should like that. I hate crowds.

CECILY (*sweetly*): I suppose that is why you live in town?

(*Gwendolen bites her lip, and beats her foot nervously with her parasol.*)

GWENDOLEN (*looking round*): Quite a well-kept garden this is, Miss Cardew.

CECILY: So glad you like it, Miss Fairfax.

GWENDOLEN: I had no idea there were any flowers in the country.

CECILY: Oh, flowers are as common here, Miss Fairfax, as people are in London.

GWENDOLEN: Personally I cannot understand how anybody manages to exist in the country, if anybody who is anybody does. The country always bores me to death.

CECILY: Ah! This is what the newspapers call agricultural depression, is it not? I believe the aristocracy are suffering very much from it just at present. It is almost an epidemic amongst them, I have been told. May I offer you some tea, Miss Fairfax?

GWENDOLEN (*with elaborate politeness*): Thank you. (*Aside.*) Detestable girl! But I require tea!

CECILY (*sweetly*): Sugar?

GWENDOLEN (*superciliously*): No, thank you. Sugar is not fashionable any more. (*Cecily looks angrily at her, takes up the tongs and puts four lumps of sugar into the cup.*)

CECILY (*severely*): Cake or bread and butter?

GWENDOLEN (*in a bored manner*): Bread and butter, please. Cake is rarely seen at the best houses nowadays.

CECILY (*cuts a very large slice of cake, and puts it on the tray*): Hand that to Miss Fairfax.

(*Merriman does so, and goes out with footman. Gwendolen drinks the tea and makes a grimace. Puts down cup at once, reaches out her hand to the bread and butter, looks at it, and finds it is cake. Rises in indignation.*)

GWENDOLEN: You have filled my tea with lumps of sugar, and though I asked most distinctly for bread and butter, you have given me cake. I am known for the gentleness of my disposition, and the extraordinary sweetness of my nature, but I warn you, Miss Cardew, you may go too far.

CECILY (*rising*): To save my poor, innocent, trusting boy from the machinations of any other girl there are no lengths to which I would not go.

GWENDOLEN: From the moment I saw you I distrusted you. I felt that you were false and deceitful. I am never deceived in such matters. My first impressions of people are invariably right.

CECILY: It seems to me, Miss Fairfax, that I am trespassing on your valuable time. No doubt you have many other calls of a similar character to make in the neighborhood.

(*Enter Jack.*)

GWENDOLEN (*catching sight of him*): Ernest! My own Ernest!

JACK: Gwendolen! Darling! (*Offers to kiss her.*)

GWENDOLEN (*drawing back*): A moment! May I ask if you are engaged to be married to this young lady? (*Points to Cecily.*)

JACK (*laughing*): To dear little Cecily! Of course not! What could have put such an idea into your pretty little head?

GWENDOLEN: Thank you. You may! (*Offers her cheek.*)

CECILY (*very sweetly*): I knew there must be some misunderstanding, Miss Fairfax. The gentleman whose arm is at present round your waist is my dear guardian, Mr. John Worthing.

GWENDOLEN: I beg your pardon?

CECILY: This is Uncle Jack.

GWENDOLEN (*receding*): Jack! Oh!

(*Enter Algernon.*)

CECILY: Here is Ernest.

ALGERNON (*goes straight over to Cecily without noticing anyone else*): My own love! (*Offers to kiss her.*)

CECILY (*drawing back*): A moment, Ernest! May I ask you—are you engaged to be married to this young lady?

ALGERNON (*looking round*): To what young lady? Good heavens! Gwendolen!

CECILY: Yes! to good heavens, Gwendolen, I mean to Gwendolen.

ALGERNON (*laughing*): Of course not! What could have put such an idea into your pretty little head?

CECILY: Thank you. (*Presenting her cheek to be kissed.*) You may. (*Algernon kisses her.*)

GWENDOLEN: I felt there was some slight error, Miss Cardew. The gentleman who is now embracing you is my cousin, Mr. Algernon Moncrieff.

CECILY (*breaking away from Algernon*): Algernon Moncrieff! Oh! (*The two girls move towards each other and put their arms round each other's waists as if for protection.*)

CECILY: Are you called Algernon?

ALGERNON: I cannot deny it.

CECILY: Oh!

GWENDOLEN: Is your name really John?

JACK (*standing rather proudly*): I could deny it if I liked, I could deny anything if I liked. But my name certainly is John. It has been John for years.

CECILY (*to Gwendolen*): A gross deception has been practiced on both of us.

GWENDOLEN: My poor wounded Cecily!

CECILY: My sweet wronged Gwendolen!

GWENDOLEN (*slowly and seriously*): You will call me sister, will you not? (*They embrace. Jack and Algernon groan and walk up and down.*)

CECILY (*rather brightly*): There is just one question I would like to be allowed to ask my guardian.

GWENDOLEN: An admirable idea! Mr. Worthing, there is just one question I would like to be permitted to put to you. Where is your brother Ernest? We are both engaged to be married to your brother Ernest, so it is a matter of some importance to us to know where your brother Ernest is at present.

JACK (*slowly and hesitatingly*): Gwendolen—Cecily—it is very painful for me to be forced to speak the truth. It is the first time in my life that I have ever been reduced to such a painful position, and I am really quite inexperienced in doing anything of the kind. However I will tell you quite frankly that I have no brother Ernest. I have no brother at all. I never had a brother in my life, and I certainly have not the smallest intention of ever having one in the future.

CECILY (*surprised*): No brother at all?

JACK (*cheerily*): None!

GWENDOLEN (*severely*): Had you never a brother of any kind?

JACK (*pleasantly*): Never. Not even of any kind.

GWENDOLEN: I am afraid it is quite clear, Cecily, that neither of us is engaged to be married to anyone.

CECILY: It is not a very pleasant position for a young girl suddenly to find herself in. Is it?

GWENDOLEN: Let us go into the house. They will hardly venture to come after us there.

CECILY: No, men are so cowardly, aren't they?

(*They retire into the house with scornful looks.*)

JACK: This ghastly state of things is what you call Bunburying, I suppose?

ALGERNON: Yes, and a perfectly wonderful Bunbury it is. The most wonderful Bunbury I have ever had in my life.

JACK: Well, you've no right whatsoever to Bunbury here.

ALGERNON: That is absurd. One has a right to Bunbury anywhere one chooses. Every serious Bunburyist knows that.

JACK: Serious Bunburyist! Good heavens!

ALGERNON: Well, one must be serious about something, if one wants to have any amusement in life. I happen to be serious about Bunburying. What on earth you are serious about I haven't got the remotest idea. About everything, I should fancy. You have such an absolutely trivial nature.

JACK: Well, the only small satisfaction I have in the whole of this wretched business is that your friend Bunbury is quite exploded. You won't be able to run down to the country quite so often as you used to do, dear Algy. And a very good thing too.

ALGERNON: Your brother is a little off-color, isn't he, dear Jack? You won't be able to disappear to London quite so frequently as your wicked custom was. And not a bad thing either.

JACK: As for your conduct towards Miss Cardew, I must say that your taking in a sweet, simple, innocent girl like that is quite inexcusable. To say nothing of the fact that she is my ward.

ALGERNON: I can see no possible defense at all for your deceiving a brilliant, clever, thoroughly experienced young lady like Miss Fairfax. To say nothing of the fact that she is my cousin.

JACK: I wanted to be engaged to Gwendolen, that is all. I love her.

ALGERNON: Well, I simply wanted to be engaged to Cecily. I adore her.

JACK: There is certainly no chance of your marrying Miss Cardew.

ALGERNON: I don't think there is much likelihood, Jack, of you and Miss Fairfax being united.

JACK: Well, that is no business of yours.

ALGERNON: If it was my business, I wouldn't talk about it. (*Begins to eat muffins.*) It is very vulgar to talk about one's business. Only people like stockbrokers do that, and then merely at dinner parties.

JACK: How can you sit there, calmly eating muffins when we are in this horrible trouble, I can't make out. You seem to me to be perfectly heartless.

ALGERNON: Well, I can't eat muffins in an agitated manner. The butter would probably get on my cuffs. One should always eat muffins quite calmly. It is the only way to eat them.

JACK: I say it's perfectly heartless your eating muffins at all, under the circumstances.

ALGERNON: When I am in trouble, eating is the only thing that consoles me. Indeed, when I am in really great trouble, as anyone who knows me intimately will tell you, I refuse everything except food and drink. At the present moment I am eating muffins because I am unhappy. Besides, I am particularly fond of muffins. (*Rising.*)

JACK (*rising*): Well, that is no reason why you should eat them all in that greedy way. (*Takes muffins from Algernon.*)

ALGERNON (*offering tea cake*): I wish you would have tea cake instead. I don't like tea cake.

JACK: Good heavens! I suppose a man may eat his own muffins in his own garden.

ALGERNON: But you have just said it was perfectly heartless to eat muffins.

JACK: I said it was perfectly heartless of you, under the circumstances. That is a very different thing.

ALGERNON: That may be. But the muffins are the same. (*He seizes the muffin dish from Jack.*)

JACK: Algy, I wish to goodness you would go.

ALGERNON: You can't possibly ask me to go without having some dinner. It's absurd. I never go without my dinner. No one ever does, except vegetarians and people like that. Besides I have just made arrangements with Dr. Chasuble to be christened at a quarter to six under the name of Ernest.

JACK: My dear fellow, the sooner you give up that nonsense the better. I made arrangements this morning with Dr. Chasuble to be christened myself at 5:30, and I naturally will take the name of Ernest. Gwendolen would wish it. We can't both be christened Ernest. It's absurd. Besides, I have a perfect right to be christened if I like. There is no evidence at all that I ever have been christened by anybody. I should think it extremely probable I never was, and so does Dr. Chasuble. It is entirely different in your case. You have been christened already.

ALGERNON: Yes, but I have not been christened for years.

JACK: Yes, but you have been christened. That is the important thing.

ALGERNON: Quite so. So I know my constitution can stand it. If you are not quite sure about your ever having been christened, I must say I think it rather dangerous your venturing on it now. It might make you very unwell. You can hardly have forgotten that someone very closely connected with you was very nearly carried off this week in Paris by a severe chill.

JACK: Yes, but you said yourself that a severe chill was not hereditary.

ALGERNON: It usen't to be, I know — but I daresay it is now. Science is always making wonderful improvements in things.

JACK (*picking up the muffin dish*): Oh, that is nonsense; you are always talking nonsense.

ALGERNON: Jack, you are at the muffins again! I wish you wouldn't. There are only two left. (*Takes them.*) I told you I was particularly fond of muffins.

JACK: But I hate tea cake.

ALGERNON: Why on earth then do you allow tea cake to be served up for your guests? What ideas you have of hospitality!

JACK: Algernon! I have already told you to go. I don't want you here. Why don't you go!

ALGERNON: I haven't quite finished my tea yet! and there is still one muffin left. (*Jack groans, and sinks into a chair. Algernon still continues eating.*)

ACT-DROP

THIRD ACT

Scene: *Morning room at the Manor House.*

(*Gwendolen and Cecily are at the window, looking out into the garden.*)

GWENDOLEN: The fact that they did not follow us at once into the house, as anyone else would have done, seems to me to show that they have some sense of shame left.

CECILY: They have been eating muffins. That looks like repentance.

GWENDOLEN (*after a pause*): They don't seem to notice us at all. Couldn't you cough?

CECILY: But I haven't got a cough.

GWENDOLEN: They're looking at us. What effrontery!

CECILY: They're approaching. That's very forward of them.

GWENDOLEN: Let us preserve a dignified silence.

CECILY: Certainly. It's the only thing to do now.

(*Enter Jack followed by Algernon. They whistle some dreadful popular air from a British Opera.*)

GWENDOLEN: This dignified silence seems to produce an unpleasant effect.

CECILY: A most distasteful one.

GWENDOLEN: But we will not be the first to speak.

CECILY: Certainly not.

GWENDOLEN: Mr. Worthing, I have something very particular to ask you. Much depends on your reply.

CECILY: Gwendolen, your common sense is invaluable. Mr. Moncrieff, kindly answer me the following question. Why did you pretend to be my guardian's brother?

ALGERNON: In order that I might have an opportunity of meeting you.

CECILY (*to Gwendolen*): That certainly seems a satisfactory explanation, does it not?

GWENDOLEN: Yes, dear, if you can believe him.

CECILY: I don't. But that does not affect the wonderful beauty of his answer.

GWENDOLEN: True. In matters of grave importance, style, not sincerity is the vital thing. Mr. Worthing, what explanation can you offer to me for pretending to have a brother? Was it in order that you might have an opportunity of coming up to town to see me as often as possible?

JACK: Can you doubt it, Miss Fairfax?

GWENDOLEN: I have the gravest doubts upon the subject. But I intend to crush them. This is not the moment for German skepticism. (*Moving to*

Cecily.) Their explanations appear to be quite satisfactory, especially Mr. Worthing's. That seems to me to have the stamp of truth upon it.

CECILY: I am more than content with what Mr. Moncrieff said. His voice alone inspires one with absolute credulity.

GWENDOLEN: Then you think we should forgive them?

CECILY: Yes. I mean no.

GWENDOLEN: True! I had forgotten. There are principles at stake that one cannot surrender. Which of us should tell them? The task is not a pleasant one.

CECILY: Could we not both speak at the same time?

GWENDOLEN: An excellent idea! I nearly always speak at the same time as other people. Will you take the time from me?

CECILY: Certainly. (*Gwendolen beats time with uplifted finger.*)

GWENDOLEN AND CECILY (*speaking together*): Your Christian names are still an insuperable barrier. That is all!

JACK AND ALGERNON (*speaking together*): Our Christian names! Is that all? But we are going to be christened this afternoon.

GWENDOLEN (*to Jack*): For my sake you are prepared to do this terrible thing?

JACK: I am.

CECILY (*to Algernon*): To please me you are ready to face this fearful ordeal?

ALGERNON: I am!

GWENDOLEN: How absurd to talk of the equality of the sexes! Where questions of self-sacrifice are concerned, men are infinitely beyond us.

JACK: We are. (*Clasps hands with Algernon.*)

CECILY: They have moments of physical courage of which we women know absolutely nothing.

GWENDOLEN (*to Jack*): Darling!

ALGERNON (*to Cecily*): Darling. (*They fall into each other's arms.*)

(*Enter Merriman. When he enters he coughs loudly, seeing the situation.*)

MERRIMAN: Ahem! Ahem! Lady Bracknell!

JACK: Good heavens!

(*Enter Lady Bracknell. The couples separate in alarm. Exit Merriman.*)

LADY BRACKNELL: Gwendolen! What does this mean?

GWENDOLEN: Merely that I am engaged to be married to Mr. Worthing, mamma.

LADY BRACKNELL: Come here. Sit down. Sit down immediately. Hesitation of any kind is a sign of mental decay in the young, of physical weakness in the old. (*Turns to Jack.*) Apprised, sir, of my daughter's sudden flight by her trusty maid, whose confidence I purchased by means of a small coin, I followed her at once by a luggage train. Her unhappy father is, I am glad to say, under the impression that she is attending a more than usually lengthy lecture by the University Extension Scheme on the Influence of a Permanent Income on Thought. I do not propose to undeceive him. Indeed I have never undeceived him on any question. I would consider it wrong. But of course, you will clearly understand that all communication between yourself and my daughter must cease immediately from this moment. On this point, as indeed on all points, I am firm.

JACK: I am engaged to be married to Gwendolen, Lady Bracknell!

LADY BRACKNELL: You are nothing of the kind, sir. And now, as regards Algernon! . . . Algernon!

ALGERNON: Yes, Aunt Augusta.

LADY BRACKNELL: May I ask if it is in this house that your invalid friend Mr. Bunbury resides?

ALGERNON (*stammering*): Oh! No! Bunbury doesn't live here. Bunbury is somewhere else at present. In fact, Bunbury is dead.

LADY BRACKNELL: Dead! When did Mr. Bunbury die? His death must have been extremely sudden.

ALGERNON (*airily*): Oh! I killed Bunbury this afternoon. I mean poor Bunbury died this afternoon.

LADY BRACKNELL: What did he die of?

ALGERNON: Bunbury? Oh, he was quite exploded.

LADY BRACKNELL: Exploded! Was he the victim of a revolutionary outrage? I was not aware that Mr. Bunbury was interested in social legislation. If so, he is well punished for his morbidity.

ALGERNON: My dear Aunt Augusta, I mean he was found out! The doctors found out that Bunbury could not live, that is what I mean—so Bunbury died.

LADY BRACKNELL: He seems to have had great confidence in the opinion of his physicians. I am glad, however, that he made up his mind at the last to some definite course of action, and acted under proper medical advice. And now that we have finally got rid of this Mr. Bunbury, may I ask, Mr. Worthing, who is that young person whose hand my nephew Algernon is now holding in what seems to me a peculiarly unnecessary manner?

JACK: That lady is Miss Cecily Cardew, my ward.

(*Lady Bracknell bows coldly to Cecily.*)

ALGERNON: I am engaged to be married to Cecily, Aunt Augusta.

LADY BRACKNELL: I beg your pardon?

CECILY: Mr. Moncrieff and I are engaged to be married, Lady Bracknell.

LADY BRACKNELL (*with a shiver, crossing to the sofa and sitting down*): I do not know whether there is anything peculiarly exciting in the air of this particular part of Hertfordshire, but the number of engagements that go on seems to me considerably above the proper average that statistics have laid down for our guidance. I think some preliminary inquiry on my part would not be out of place. Mr. Worthing, is Miss Cardew at all connected with any of the larger railway stations in London? I merely desire information. Until yesterday I had no idea that there were any families or persons whose origin was a Terminus. (*Jack looks perfectly furious, but restrains himself.*)

JACK (*in a clear, cold voice*): Miss Cardew is the granddaughter of the late Mr. Thomas Cardew of 149, Belgrave Square, S.W.; Gervase Park, Dorking, Surrey; and the Sporran, Fifeshire, N.B.

LADY BRACKNELL: That sounds not unsatisfactory. Three addresses always inspire confidence, even in tradesmen. But what proof have I of their authenticity?

JACK: I have carefully preserved the Court Guides of the period. They are open to your inspection, Lady Bracknell.

LADY BRACKNELL (*grimly*): I have known strange errors in that publication.

JACK: Miss Cardew's family solicitors are Messrs. Markby, Markby, and Markby.

LADY BRACKNELL: Markby, Markby, and Markby? A firm of the very highest position in their profession. Indeed I am told that one of the Mr. Markbys is occasionally to be seen at dinner parties. So far I am satisfied.

JACK (*very irritably*): How extremely kind of you, Lady Bracknell! I have also in my possession, you will be pleased to hear, certificates of Miss Cardew's birth, baptism, whooping cough, registration, vaccination, confirmation, and the measles; both the German and the English variety.

LADY BRACKNELL: Ah! A life crowded with incident, I see; though perhaps somewhat too exciting for a young girl. I am not myself in favor of premature experiences. (*Rises, looks at her watch.*) Gwendolen! the time approaches for our departure. We have not a moment to lose. As a matter of form, Mr. Worthing, I had better ask you if Miss Cardew has any little fortune?

JACK: Oh! about a hundred and thirty thousand pounds in the Funds. That is all. Good-bye, Lady Bracknell. So pleased to have seen you.

LADY BRACKNELL (*sitting down again*): A moment, Mr. Worthing. A hundred and thirty thousand pounds! And in the Funds! Miss Cardew seems to me a most attractive young lady, now that I look at her. Few girls of the present day have any really solid qualities, any of the qualities that last, and improve with time. We live, I regret to say, in an age of surfaces. (*To Cecily.*) Come over here, dear. (*Cecily goes across.*) Pretty child! your dress is sadly simple, and your hair seems almost as Nature might have left it. But we can soon alter all that. A thoroughly experienced French maid produces a really marvelous result in a very brief space of time. I remember recommending one to young Lady Lancing, and after three months her own husband did not know her.

JACK (*aside*): And after six months nobody knew her.

LADY BRACKNELL (*glares at Jack for a few moments; then bends, with a practiced smile, to Cecily*): Kindly turn round, sweet child. (*Cecily turns completely round.*) No, the side view is what I want. (*Cecily presents her profile.*) Yes, quite as I expected. There are distinct social possibilities in your profile. The two weak points in our age are its want of principle and its want of profile. The chin a little higher, dear. Style largely depends on the way the chin is worn. They are worn very high, just at present. Algernon!

ALGERNON: Yes, Aunt Augusta!

LADY BRACKNELL: There are distinct social possibilities in Miss Cardew's profile.

ALGERNON: Cecily is the sweetest, dearest, prettiest girl in the whole world. And I don't care twopence about social possibilities.

LADY BRACKNELL: Never speak disrespectfully of Society, Algernon. Only people who can't get into it do that. (*To Cecily.*) Dear child, of course you know that Algernon has nothing but his debts to depend upon. But I do not approve of mercenary marriages. When I married Lord Bracknell I had no fortune of any kind. But I never dreamed for a moment of allowing that to stand in my way. Well, I suppose I must give my consent.

ALGERNON: Thank you, Aunt Augusta.

LADY BRACKNELL: Cecily, you may kiss me!

CECILY (*kisses her*): Thank you, Lady Bracknell.

LADY BRACKNELL: You may also address me as Aunt Augusta for the future.

CECILY: Thank you, Aunt Augusta.

LADY BRACKNELL: The marriage, I think, had better take place quite soon.

ALGERNON: Thank you, Aunt Augusta.

CECILY: Thank you, Aunt Augusta.

LADY BRACKNELL: To speak frankly, I am not in favor of long engagements. They give people the opportunity of finding out each other's character before marriage, which I think is never advisable.

JACK: I beg your pardon for interrupting you, Lady Bracknell, but this engagement is quite out of the question. I am Miss Cardew's guardian, and she cannot marry without my consent until she comes of age. That consent I absolutely decline to give.

LADY BRACKNELL: Upon what grounds may I ask? Algernon is an extremely, I may almost say an ostentatiously, eligible young man. He has nothing, but he looks everything. What more can one desire?

JACK: It pains me very much to have to speak frankly to you, Lady Brack-nell, about your nephew, but the fact is that I do not approve at all of his moral character. I suspect him of being untruthful. (*Algernon and Cecily look at him in indignant amazement.*)

LADY BRACKNELL: Untruthful! My nephew Algernon? Impossible! He is an Oxonian.

JACK: I fear there can be no possible doubt about the matter. This after-noon, during my temporary absence in London on an important question of romance, he obtained admission to my house by means of the false pretense of being my brother. Under an assumed name he drank, I've just been informed by my butler, an entire pint bottle of my Perrier-Jouet, Brut, '89; a wine I was specially reserving for myself. Continuing his disgraceful deception, he succeeded in the course of the afternoon in alienating the affections of my only ward. He subsequently stayed to tea, and devoured every single muffin. And what makes his conduct all the more heartless is, that he was per-fectly well aware from the first that I have no brother, that I never had a brother, and that I don't intend to have a brother, not even of any kind. I distinctly told him so myself yesterday afternoon.

LADY BRACKNELL: Ahem! Mr. Worthing, after careful consideration I have decided entirely to overlook my nephew's conduct to you.

JACK: That is very generous of you, Lady Bracknell. My own decision, however, is unalterable. I decline to give my consent.

LADY BRACKNELL (*to Cecily*): Come here, sweet child. (*Cecily goes over.*) How old are you, dear?

CECILY: Well, I am really only eighteen, but I always admit to twenty when I go to evening parties.

LADY BRACKNELL: You are perfectly right in making some slight altera-tion. Indeed, no woman should ever be quite accurate about her age. It looks so calculating. . . . (*In a meditative manner.*) Eighteen, but admit-ting to twenty at evening parties. Well, it will not be very long before you are of age and free from the restraints of tutelage. So I don't think your guardian's consent is, after all, a matter of any importance.

JACK: Pray excuse me, Lady Bracknell, for interrupting you again, but it is only fair to tell you that according to the terms of her grandfather's will Miss Cardew does not come legally of age till she is thirty-five.

LADY BRACKNELL: That does not seem to me to be a grave objection. Thirty-five is a very attractive age. London society is full of women of the very highest birth who have, of their own free choice, remained thirty-five for years. Lady Dumbleton is an instance in point. To my own knowledge she has been thirty-five ever since she arrived at the age of forty, which was many years ago now. I see no reason why our dear Cecily should not be even still more attractive at the age you mention than she is at present. There will be a large accumulation of property.

CECILY: Algy, could you wait for me till I was thirty-five?

ALGERNON: Of course I could, Cecily. You know I could.

CECILY: Yes, I felt it instinctively, but I couldn't wait all that time. I hate waiting even five minutes for anybody. It always makes me rather cross. I am not punctual myself, I know, but I do like punctuality in others, and waiting, even to be married, is quite out of the question.

ALGERNON: Then what is to be done, Cecily?

CECILY: I don't know, Mr. Moncrieff.

LADY BRACKNELL: My dear Mr. Worthing, as Miss Cardew states positively that she cannot wait till she is thirty-five—a remark which I am bound to say seems to me to show a somewhat impatient nature—I would beg of you to reconsider your decision.

JACK: But my dear Lady Bracknell, the matter is entirely in your own hands. The moment you consent to my marriage with Gwendolen, I will most gladly allow your nephew to form an alliance with my ward.

LADY BRACKNELL (*rising and drawing herself up*): You must be quite aware that what you propose is out of the question.

JACK: Then a passionate celibacy is all that any of us can look forward to.

LADY BRACKNELL: This is not the destiny I propose for Gwendolen. Algernon, of course, can choose for himself. (*Pulls out her watch.*) Come, dear; (*Gwendolen rises.*) we have already missed five, if not six, trains. To miss any more might expose us to comment on the platform.

(*Enter Dr. Chasuble.*)

CHASUBLE: Everything is quite ready for the christenings.

LADY BRACKNELL: The christenings, sir! Is not that somewhat premature?

CHASUBLE (*looking rather puzzled, and pointing to Jack and Algernon*): Both these gentlemen have expressed a desire for immediate baptism.

LADY BRACKNELL: At their age? The idea is grotesque and irreligious! Algernon, I forbid you to be baptized. I will not hear of such excesses. Lord Bracknell would be highly displeased if he learned that that was the way in which you wasted your time and money.

CHASUBLE: Am I to understand then that there are to be no christenings at all this afternoon?

JACK: I don't think that, as things are now, it would be of much practical value to either of us, Dr. Chasuble.

CHASUBLE: I am grieved to hear such sentiments from you, Mr. Worthing. They savor of the heretical views of the Anabaptists, views that I have completely refuted in four of my unpublished sermons. However, as your present mood seems to be one peculiarly secular, I will return to the church at once. Indeed, I have just been informed by the pew-opener that for the last hour and a half Miss Prism has been waiting for me in the vestry.

LADY BRACKNELL (*starting*): Miss Prism! Did I hear you mention a Miss Prism?

CHASUBLE: Yes, Lady Bracknell. I am on my way to join her.

LADY BRACKNELL: Pray allow me to detain you for a moment. This matter may prove to be one of vital importance to Lord Bracknell and myself. Is this Miss Prism a female of repellent aspect, remotely connected with education?

CHASUBLE (*somewhat indignantly*): She is the most cultivated of ladies, and the very picture of respectability.

LADY BRACKNELL: It is obviously the same person. May I ask what position she holds in your household?

CHASUBLE (*severely*): I am a celibate, madam.

JACK (*interposing*): Miss Prism, Lady Bracknell, has been for the last three years Miss Cardew's esteemed governess and valued companion.

LADY BRACKNELL: In spite of what I hear of her, I must see her at once. Let her be sent for.

CHASUBLE (*looking off*): She approaches; she is nigh.

(*Enter Miss Prism hurriedly.*)

MISS PRISM: I was told you expected me in the vestry, dear Canon. I have been waiting for you there for an hour and three quarters. (*Catches sight of Lady Bracknell who has fixed her with a stony glare. Miss Prism grows pale and quails. She looks anxiously round as if desirous to escape.*)

LADY BRACKNELL (*in a severe, judicial voice*): Prism! (*Miss Prism bows her head in shame.*) Come here, Prism! (*Miss Prism approaches in a humble manner.*) Prism! Where is that baby? (*General consternation. The Canon starts back in horror. Algernon and Jack pretend to be anxious to shield Cecily and Gwendolen from hearing the details of a terrible public scandal.*) Twenty-eight years ago, Prism, you left Lord Bracknell's house, Number 104, Upper Grosvenor Street, in charge of a perambulator that contained a baby, of the male sex. You never returned. A few weeks later, through the elaborate investigations of the Metropolitan police, the perambulator was discovered at midnight, standing by itself in a remote corner of Bayswater. It contained the manuscript of a three-volume novel of more than usually revolting sentimentality. (*Miss Prism starts in involuntary indignation.*) But the baby was not there! (*Everyone looks at Miss Prism.*) Prism! Where is that baby? (*A pause.*)

MISS PRISM: Lady Bracknell, I admit with shame that I do not know. I only wish I did. The plain facts of the case are these. On the morning of the day you mention, a day that is forever branded on my memory, I prepared as usual to take the baby out in its perambulator. I had also with me a somewhat old, but capacious handbag, in which I had intended to place the manuscript of a work of fiction that I had written during my few unoccupied hours. In a moment of mental abstraction, for which I never can forgive myself, I deposited the manuscript in the bassinette, and placed the baby in the handbag.

JACK (*who has been listening attentively*): But where did you deposit the handbag?

MISS PRISM: Do not ask me, Mr. Worthing.

JACK: Miss Prism, this is a matter of no small importance to me. I insist on knowing where you deposited the handbag that contained that infant.

MISS PRISM: I left it in the cloak room of one of the larger railway stations in London.

JACK: What railway station?

MISS PRISM (*quite crushed*): Victoria. The Brighton line. (*Sinks into a chair.*)

JACK: I must retire to my room for a moment. Gwendolen, wait here for me.

GWENDOLEN: If you are not too long, I will wait here for you all my life.

(*Exit Jack in great excitement.*)

CHASUBLE: What do you think this means, Lady Bracknell?

LADY BRACKNELL: I dare not even suspect, Dr. Chasuble. I need hardly tell you that in families of high position strange coincidences are not supposed to occur. They are hardly considered the thing.

(*Noises heard overhead as if someone was throwing trunks about. Everyone looks up.*)

CECILY: Uncle Jack seems strangely agitated.

CHASUBLE: Your guardian has a very emotional nature.

LADY BRACKNELL: This noise is extremely unpleasant. It sounds as if he was having an argument. I dislike arguments of any kind. They are always vulgar, and often convincing.

CHASUBLE (*looking up*): It has stopped now. (*The noise is redoubled.*)

LADY BRACKNELL: I wish he would arrive at some conclusion.

GWENDOLEN: This suspense is terrible. I hope it will last.

(*Enter Jack with a handbag of black leather in his hand.*)

JACK (*rushing over to Miss Prism*): Is this the handbag, Miss Prism? Examine it carefully before you speak. The happiness of more than one life depends on your answer.

MISS PRISM (*calmly*): It seems to be mine. Yes, here is the injury it received through the upsetting of a Gower Street omnibus in younger and happier days. Here is the stain on the lining caused by the explosion of a temperance beverage, an incident that occurred at Leamington. And here, on the lock, are my initials. I had forgotten that in an extravagant mood I had had them placed there. The bag is undoubtedly mine. I am delighted to have it so unexpectedly restored to me. It has been a great inconvenience being without it all these years.

JACK (*in a pathetic voice*): Miss Prism, more is restored to you than this handbag. I was the baby you placed in it.

MISS PRISM (*amazed*): You?

JACK (*embracing her*): Yes . . . mother!

MISS PRISM (*recoiling in indignant astonishment*): Mr. Worthing! I am unmarried!

JACK: Unmarried! I do not deny that is a serious blow. But after all, who has the right to cast a stone against one who has suffered? Cannot repentance wipe out an act of folly? Why should there be one law for men, and another for women? Mother, I forgive you. (*Tries to embrace her again.*)

MISS PRISM (*still more indignant*): Mr. Worthing, there is some error. (*Pointing to Lady Bracknell.*) There is the lady who can tell you who you really are.

JACK (*after a pause*): Lady Bracknell, I hate to seem inquisitive, but would you kindly inform me who I am?

LADY BRACKNELL: I am afraid that the news I have to give you will not altogether please you. You are the son of my poor sister, Mrs. Moncrieff, and consequently Algernon's elder brother.

JACK: Algy's elder brother! Then I have a brother after all. I knew I had a brother! I always said I had a brother! Cecily—how could you have ever doubted that I had a brother? (*Seizes hold of Algernon.*) Dr. Chasuble, my unfortunate brother. Miss Prism, my unfortunate brother. Gwendolen, my unfortunate brother. Algy, you young scoundrel, you will have to treat me with more respect in the future. You have never behaved to me like a brother in all your life.

ALGERNON: Well, not till today, old boy, I admit. I did my best, however, though I was out of practice. (*Shakes hands.*)

GWENDOLEN (*to Jack*): My own! But what own are you? What is your Christian name, now that you have become someone else?

JACK: Good heavens! . . . I had quite forgotten that point. Your decision on the subject of my name is irrevocable, I suppose?

GWENDOLEN: I never change, except in my affections.

CECILY: What a noble nature you have, Gwendolen!

JACK: Then the question had better be cleared up at once. Aunt Augusta, a moment. At the time when Miss Prism left me in the handbag, had I been christened already?

LADY BRACKNELL: Every luxury that money could buy, including christening, had been lavished on you by your fond and doting parents.

JACK: Then I was christened! That is settled. Now, what name was I given? Let me know the worst.

LADY BRACKNELL: Being the eldest son you were naturally christened after your father.

JACK (*irritably*): Yes, but what was my father's Christian name?

LADY BRACKNELL (*meditatively*): I cannot at the present moment recall what the General's Christian name was. But I have no doubt he had one. He was eccentric, I admit. But only in later years. And that was the result of the Indian climate, and marriage, and indigestion, and other things of that kind.

JACK: Algy! Can't you recollect what our father's Christian name was?

ALGERNON: My dear boy, we were never even on speaking terms. He died before I was a year old.

JACK: His name would appear in the Army Lists of the period, I suppose, Aunt Augusta?

LADY BRACKNELL: The General was essentially a man of peace, except in his domestic life. But I have no doubt his name would appear in any military directory.

JACK: The Army Lists of the last forty years are here. These delightful records should have been my constant study. (*Rushes to bookcase and tears the books out.*) M. Generals . . . Mallam, Maxbohm, Magley, what ghastly names they have—Markby, Migsby, Mobbs, Moncrieff! Lieutenant 1840, Captain, Lieutenant Colonel, Colonel, General 1869, Christian names, Ernest John. (*Puts book very quietly down and speaks quite calmly.*) I always told you, Gwendolen, my name was Ernest, didn't I? Well it is Ernest after all. I mean it naturally is Ernest.

LADY BRACKNELL: Yes, I remember now that the General was called Ernest. I knew I had some particular reason for disliking the name.

GWENDOLEN: Ernest! My own Ernest! I felt from the first that you could have no other name!

JACK: Gwendolen, it is a terrible thing for a man to find out suddenly that all his life he has been speaking nothing but the truth. Can you forgive me?

GWENDOLEN: I can. For I feel that you are sure to change.

JACK: My own one!

CHASUBLE (*to Miss Prism*): Laetitia! (*Embraces her.*)

MISS PRISM (*enthusiastically*): Frederick! At last!

ALGERNON: Cecily! (*Embraces her.*) At last!

JACK: Gwendolen! (*Embraces her.*) At last!

LADY BRACKNELL: My nephew, you seem to be displaying signs of triviality.

JACK: On the contrary, Aunt Augusta, I've now realized for the first time in my life the vital Importance of Being Earnest.

CURTAIN

[1899]

SUSAN GLASPELL [1882–1948]

Trifles

Characters
GEORGE HENDERSON, *county attorney*
HENRY PETERS, *sheriff*
LEWIS HALE, *a neighboring farmer*
MRS. PETERS
MRS. HALE

Scene: *The kitchen in the now abandoned farmhouse of John Wright, a gloomy kitchen, and left without having been put in order—the walls covered with a faded wall paper. Down right is a door leading to the parlor. On the right wall above this door is a built-in kitchen cupboard with shelves in the upper portion and drawers below. In the rear wall at right, up two steps is a door opening onto stairs leading to the second floor. In the rear wall at left is a door to the shed and from there to the outside. Between these two doors is an old-fashioned black iron stove. Running along the left wall from the shed door is an old iron sink and sink shelf, in which is set a hand pump. Downstage of the sink is an uncurtained window. Near the window is an old wooden rocker. Center stage is an unpainted wooden kitchen table with straight chairs on either side. There is a small chair down right. Unwashed pans under the sink, a loaf of bread outside the breadbox, a dish towel on the table—other signs of incompleted work. At the rear the shed door opens and the Sheriff comes in followed by the County Attorney and Hale. The Sheriff and Hale are men in middle life, the County Attorney is a young man; all are much bundled up and go at once to the stove. They are followed by the two women—the Sheriff's wife, Mrs. Peters, first: she is a slight wiry woman, a thin nervous face. Mrs. Hale is larger and would ordinarily be called more comfortable looking, but she is disturbed now and looks fearfully about as she enters. The women have come in slowly, and stand close together near the door.*

COUNTY ATTORNEY (*at stove rubbing his hands*): This feels good. Come up to the fire, ladies.
MRS. PETERS (*after taking a step forward*): I'm not—cold.
SHERIFF (*unbuttoning his overcoat and stepping away from the stove to right of table as if to mark the beginning of official business*): Now, Mr. Hale, before we move things about, you explain to Mr. Henderson just what you saw when you came here yesterday morning.
COUNTY ATTORNEY (*crossing down to left of the table*): By the way, has anything been moved? Are things just as you left them yesterday?

SHERIFF (*looking about*): It's just about the same. When it dropped below zero last night I thought I'd better send Frank out this morning to make a fire for us—(*sits right of center table*) no use getting pneumonia with a big case on, but I told him not to touch anything except the stove—and you know Frank.

COUNTY ATTORNEY: Somebody should have been left here yesterday.

SHERIFF: Oh—yesterday. When I had to send Frank to Morris Center for that man who went crazy—I want you to know I had my hands full yesterday. I knew you could get back from Omaha by today and as long as I went over everything here myself——

COUNTY ATTORNEY: Well, Mr. Hale, tell just what happened when you came here yesterday morning.

HALE (*crossing down to above table*): Harry and I had started to town with a load of potatoes. We came along the road from my place and as I got here I said, "I'm going to see if I can't get John Wright to go in with me on a party telephone." I spoke to Wright about it once before and he put me off, saying folks talked too much anyway, and all he asked was peace and quiet—I guess you know about how much he talked himself; but I thought maybe if I went to the house and talked about it before his wife, though I said to Harry that I didn't know as what his wife wanted made much difference to John——

COUNTY ATTORNEY: Let's talk about that later, Mr. Hale. I do want to talk about that, but tell now just what happened when you got to the house.

HALE: I didn't hear or see anything; I knocked at the door, and still it was all quiet inside. I knew they must be up, it was past eight o'clock. So I knocked again, and I thought I heard someone say, "Come in." I wasn't sure, I'm not sure yet, but I opened the door—this door (*indicating the door by which the two women are still standing*) and there in that rocker—(*pointing to it*) sat Mrs. Wright. (*They all look at the rocker down left*.)

COUNTY ATTORNEY: What—was she doing?

HALE: She was rockin' back and forth. She had her apron in her hand and was kind of—pleating it.

COUNTY ATTORNEY: And how did she—look?

HALE: Well, she looked queer.

COUNTY ATTORNEY: How do you mean—queer?

HALE: Well, as if she didn't know what she was going to do next. And kind of done up.

COUNTY ATTORNEY (*takes out notebook and pencil and sits left of center table*): How did she seem to feel about your coming?

HALE: Why, I don't think she minded—one way or other. She didn't pay much attention. I said, "How do, Mrs. Wright, it's cold, ain't it?" And she said, "Is it?"—and went on kind of pleating at her apron. Well, I was surprised: she didn't ask me to come up to the stove, or to set down, but just sat there, not even looking at me, so I said, "I want to see John." And then she—laughed. I guess you would call it a laugh. I thought of Harry and the team outside, so I said a little sharp: "Can't I see John?" "No," she says, kind o' dull like. "Ain't he home?" says I. "Yes," says she, "he's home." "Then why can't I see him?" I asked her, out of patience. "'Cause he's dead," says she. "*Dead?*" says I. She just nodded her head, not getting a bit excited, but rockin' back and forth. "Why—where is he?" says I, not knowing what to say. She just pointed upstairs—like that. (*Himself pointing to the room above.*) I started for the stairs, with the idea of going up there. I walked from there to here—then I says, "Why, what did he die of?" "He died of a rope round his neck," says she, and just went on pleatin' at her apron. Well, I went out and called Harry. I thought I might—need help. We went upstairs and there he was lyin'——

COUNTY ATTORNEY: I think I'd rather have you go into that upstairs, where you can point it all out. Just go on now with the rest of the story.

HALE: Well, my first thought was to get that rope off. It looked . . . (*stops: his face twitches*) . . . but Harry, he went up to him, and he said, "No, he's dead all right, and we'd better not touch anything." So we went right back downstairs. She was still sitting that same way. "Has anybody been notified?" I asked. "No," says she, unconcerned. "Who did this, Mrs. Wright?" said Harry. He said it businesslike—and she stopped pleatin' of her apron. "I don't know," she says. "You don't *know?*" says Harry. "No," says she. "Weren't you sleepin' in the bed with him?" says Harry. "Yes," says she, "but I was on the inside." "Somebody slipped a rope round his head and strangled him and you didn't wake up?" says Harry. "I didn't wake up," she said after him. We must 'a' looked as if we didn't see how that could be, for after a minute she said, "I sleep sound." Harry was going to ask her more questions but I said maybe we ought to let her tell her story first to the coroner, or the sheriff, so Harry went fast as he could to Rivers' place, where there's a telephone.

COUNTY ATTORNEY: And what did Mrs. Wright do when she knew that you had gone for the coroner?

HALE: She moved from the rocker to that chair over there (*pointing to a small chair in the down right corner*) and just sat there with her hands held together and looking down. I got a feeling that I ought to make some conversation, so I said I had come in to see if John wanted to put in a telephone, and at that she started to laugh, and then she stopped and looked at me—scared. (*The County Attorney, who has had his notebook out, makes a note.*) I dunno, maybe it wasn't scared. I wouldn't like to say it was. Soon Harry got back, and then Dr. Lloyd came and you, Mr. Peters, and so I guess that's all I know that you don't.

COUNTY ATTORNEY (*rising and looking around*): I guess we'll go upstairs first—and then out to the barn and around there. (*To the Sheriff.*) You're convinced that there was nothing important here—nothing that would point to any motive?

SHERIFF: Nothing here but kitchen things. (*The County Attorney, after again looking around the kitchen, opens the door of a cupboard closet in right wall. He brings a small chair from right—gets on it and looks on a shelf. Pulls his hand away, sticky.*)

COUNTY ATTORNEY: Here's a nice mess. (*The women draw nearer up to center.*)

MRS. PETERS (*to the other woman*): Oh, her fruit; it did freeze. (*To the Lawyer.*) She worried about that when it turned so cold. She said the fire'd go out and her jars would break.

SHERIFF (*rises*): Well, can you beat the woman! Held for murder and worryin' about her preserves.

COUNTY ATTORNEY (*getting down from chair*): I guess before we're through she may have something more serious than preserves to worry about. (*Crosses down right center.*)

HALE: Well, women are used to worrying over trifles. (*The two women move a little closer together.*)

COUNTY ATTORNEY (*with the gallantry of a young politician*): And yet, for all their worries, what would we do without the ladies? (*The women do not unbend. He goes below the center table to the sink, takes a dipperful of water from the pail, and pouring it into a basin, washes his hands. While he is doing this the Sheriff and Hale cross to cupboard, which they inspect. The County Attorney starts to wipe his hands on the roller towel, turns it for a cleaner place.*) Dirty towels! (*Kicks his foot against the pans under the sink.*) Not much of a housekeeper, would you say, ladies?

MRS. HALE (*stiffly*): There's a great deal of work to be done on a farm.

COUNTY ATTORNEY: To be sure. And yet (*with a little bow to her*) I know there are some Dickson County farmhouses which do not have such roller towels. (*He gives it a pull to expose its full-length again.*)

MRS. HALE: Those towels get dirty awful quick. Men's hands aren't always clean as they might be.

COUNTY ATTORNEY: Ah, loyal to your sex, I see. But you and Mrs. Wright were neighbors. I suppose you were friends, too.

MRS. HALE (*shaking her head*): I've not seen much of her of late years. I've not been in this house—it's more than a year.

COUNTY ATTORNEY (*crossing to women up center*): And why was that? You didn't like her?

MRS. HALE: I liked her all well enough. Farmer's wives have their hands full, Mr. Henderson. And then——

COUNTY ATTORNEY: Yes——?

MRS. HALE (*looking about*): It never seemed a very cheerful place.

COUNTY ATTORNEY: No—it's not cheerful. I shouldn't say she had the homemaking instinct.

MRS. HALE: Well, I don't know as Wright had, either.

COUNTY ATTORNEY: You mean that they didn't get on very well?

MRS. HALE: No, I don't mean anything. But I don't think a place'd be any cheerfuller for John Wright's being in it.

COUNTY ATTORNEY: I'd like to talk more of that a little later. I want to get the lay of things upstairs now. (*He goes past the women to up right where the steps lead to a stair door.*)

SHERIFF: I suppose anything Mrs. Peters does'll be all right. She was to take in some clothes for her, you know, and a few little things. We left in such a hurry yesterday.

COUNTY ATTORNEY: Yes, but I would like to see what you take, Mrs. Peters, and keep an eye out for anything that might be of use to us.

MRS. PETERS: Yes, Mr. Henderson. (*The men leave by up right door to stairs. The women listen to the men's steps on the stairs, then look about the kitchen.*)

MRS. HALE (*crossing left to sink*): I'd hate to have men coming into my kitchen, snooping around and criticizing. (*She arranges the pans under sink which the lawyer had shoved out of place.*)

MRS. PETERS: Of course it's no more than their duty. (*Crosses to cupboard up right.*)

MRS. HALE: Duty's all right, but I guess that deputy sheriff that came out to make the fire might have got a little of this on. (*Gives the roller towel a pull.*) Wish I'd thought of that sooner. Seems mean to talk about her for not having things slicked up when she had to come away in such a hurry. (*Crosses right to Mrs. Peters at cupboard.*)

MRS. PETERS (*who has been looking through cupboard, lifts one end of towel that covers a pan*): She had bread set. (*Stands still.*)

MRS. HALE (*eyes fixed on a loaf of bread beside the breadbox, which is on a low shelf of the cupboard*): She was going to put this in there. (*Picks up loaf, abruptly drops it. In a manner of returning to familiar things.*) It's a shame about her fruit. I wonder if it's all gone. (*Gets up on chair and looks.*) I think there's some here that's all right, Mrs. Peters. Yes—here; (*holding it toward the window*) this is cherries, too. (*Looking again.*) I declare I believe that's the only one. (*Gets down, jar in hand. Goes to the sink and wipes it off on the outside.*) She'll feel awful bad after all her hard work in the hot weather. I remember the afternoon I put up my cherries last summer. (*She puts the jar on the big kitchen table, center of the room. With a sigh, is about to sit down in the rocking chair. Before she is seated realizes what chair it is; with a slow look at it, steps back. The chair which she has touched rocks back and forth. Mrs. Peters moves to center table and they both watch the chair rock for a moment or two.*)

MRS. PETERS (*shaking off the mood which the empty rocking chair has evoked. Now in a businesslike manner she speaks*): Well I must get those things from the front room closet. (*She goes to the door at the right but, after looking into the other room, steps back.*) You coming with me, Mrs. Hale? You could help me carry them. (*They go in the other room; reappear, Mrs. Peters carrying a dress, petticoat, and skirt, Mrs. Hale following with a pair of shoes.*) My, it's cold in there. (*She puts the clothes on the big table and hurries to the stove.*)

MRS. HALE (*right of center table examining the skirt*): Wright was close. I think maybe that's why she kept so much to herself. She didn't even belong to the Ladies' Aid. I suppose she felt she couldn't do her part, and then you don't enjoy things when you feel shabby. I heard she used to wear pretty clothes and be lively, when she was Minnie Foster, one of the town girls singing in the choir. But that—oh, that was thirty years ago. This all you want to take in?

MRS. PETERS: She said she wanted an apron. Funny thing to want, for there isn't much to get you dirty in jail, goodness knows. But I suppose just to make her feel more natural. (*Crosses to cupboard.*) She said they was in the top drawer in this cupboard. Yes, here. And then her little shawl that always hung behind the door. (*Opens stair door and looks.*) Yes, here it is. (*Quickly shuts door leading upstairs.*)

MRS. HALE (*abruptly moving toward her*): Mrs. Peters?

MRS. PETERS: Yes, Mrs. Hale? (*At up right door.*)

MRS. HALE: Do you think she did it?

MRS. PETERS (*in a frightened voice*): Oh, I don't know.

MRS. HALE: Well, I don't think she did. Asking for an apron and her little shawl. Worrying about her fruit.

MRS. PETERS (*starts to speak, glances up, where footsteps are heard in the room above. In a low voice*): Mr. Peters says it looks bad for her. Mr. Henderson is awful sarcastic in a speech and he'll make fun of her sayin' she didn't wake up.

MRS. HALE: Well, I guess John Wright didn't wake when they was slipping that rope under his neck.

MRS. PETERS (*crossing slowly to table and placing shawl and apron on table with other clothing*): No, it's strange. It must have been done awful crafty and still. They say it was such a—funny way to kill a man, rigging it all up like that.

MRS. HALE (*crossing to left of Mrs. Peters at table*): That's just what Mr. Hale said. There was a gun in the house. He says that's what he can't understand.

MRS. PETERS: Mr. Henderson said coming out that what was needed for the case was a motive: something to show anger, or—sudden feeling.

MRS. HALE (*who is standing by the table*): Well, I don't see any signs of anger around here. (*She puts her hand on the dish towel, which lies on the table, stands looking down at table, one-half of which is clean, the other half messy.*) It's wiped to here. (*Makes a move as if to finish work, then turns and looks at loaf of bread outside the breadbox. Drops towel. In that voice of coming back to familiar things.*) Wonder how they are finding things upstairs. (*Crossing below table to down right.*) I hope she had it a little more red-up up there. You know, it seems kind of *sneaking*. Locking her up in town and then coming out here and trying to get her own house to turn against her!

MRS. PETERS: But, Mrs. Hale, the law is the law.

MRS. HALE: I s'pose 'tis. (*Unbuttoning her coat.*) Better loosen up your things, Mrs. Peters. You won't feel them when you go out. (*Mrs. Peters takes off her fur tippet, goes to hang it on chair back left of table, stands looking at the work basket on floor near down left window.*)

MRS. PETERS: She was piecing a quilt. (*She brings the large sewing basket to the center table and they look at the bright pieces, Mrs. Hale above the table and Mrs. Peters left of it.*)

MRS. HALE: It's a log cabin pattern. Pretty, isn't it? I wonder if she was goin' to quilt it or just knot it? (*Footsteps have been heard coming down the stairs. The Sheriff enters followed by Hale and the County Attorney.*)

SHERIFF: They wonder if she was going to quilt it or just knot it! (*The men laugh, the women look abashed.*)

COUNTY ATTORNEY (*rubbing his hands over the stove*): Frank's fire didn't do much up there, did it? Well, let's go out to the barn and get that cleared up. (*The men go outside by up left door.*)

MRS. HALE (*resentfully*): I don't know as there's anything so strange, our takin' up our time with little things while we're waiting for them to get the evidence. (*She sits in chair right of table smoothing out a block with decision.*) I don't see as it's anything to laugh about.

MRS. PETERS (*apologetically*): Of course they've got awful important things on their minds. (*Pulls up a chair and joins Mrs. Hale at the left of the table.*)

MRS. HALE (*examining another block*): Mrs. Peters, look at this one. Here, this is the one she was working on, and look at the sewing! All the rest of it has been so nice and even. And look at this! It's all over the place! Why, it looks as if she didn't know what she was about! (*After she has said this they look at each other, then start to glance back at the door. After an instant Mrs. Hale has pulled at a knot and ripped the sewing.*)

MRS. PETERS: Oh, what are you doing, Mrs. Hale?

MRS. HALE (*mildly*): Just pulling out a stitch or two that's not sewed very good. (*Threading a needle.*) Bad sewing always made me fidgety.

MRS. PETERS (*with a glance at the door, nervously*): I don't think we ought to touch things.

MRS. HALE: I'll just finish up this end. (*Suddenly stopping and leaning forward.*) Mrs. Peters?

MRS. PETERS: Yes, Mrs. Hale?

MRS. HALE: What do you suppose she was so nervous about?

MRS. PETERS: Oh—I don't know. I don't know as she was nervous. I sometimes sew awful queer when I'm just tired. (*Mrs. Hale starts to say something, looks at Mrs. Peters, then goes on sewing.*) Well, I must get these things wrapped up. They may be through sooner than we think. (*Putting apron and other things together.*) I wonder where I can find a piece of paper, and string. (*Rises.*)

MRS. HALE: In that cupboard, maybe.

MRS. PETERS (*crosses right looking in cupboard*): Why, here's a bird-cage. (*Holds it up.*) Did she have a bird, Mrs. Hale?

MRS. HALE: Why, I don't know whether she did or not—I've not been here for so long. There was a man around last year selling canaries cheap, but I don't know as she took one; maybe she did. She used to sing real pretty herself.

MRS. PETERS (*glancing around*): Seems funny to think of a bird here. But she must have had one, or why would she have a cage? I wonder what happened to it?

MRS. HALE: I s'pose maybe the cat got it.

MRS. PETERS: No, she didn't have a cat. She's got that feeling some people have about cats—being afraid of them. My cat got in her room and she was real upset and asked me to take it out.

MRS. HALE: My sister Bessie was like that. Queer, ain't it?

MRS. PETERS (*examining the cage*): Why, look at this door. It's broke. One hinge is pulled apart. (*Takes a step down to Mrs. Hale's right.*)

MRS. HALE (*looking too*): Looks as if someone must have been rough with it.

MRS. PETERS: Why, yes. (*She brings the cage forward and puts it on the table.*)

MRS. HALE (*glancing toward up left door*): I wish if they're going to find any evidence they'd be about it. I don't like this place.

MRS. PETERS: But I'm awful glad you came with me, Mrs. Hale. It would be lonesome for me sitting here alone.

MRS. HALE: It would, wouldn't it? (*Dropping her sewing.*) But I tell you what I do wish, Mrs. Peters. I wish I had come over sometimes when she was here. I—(*looking around the room*)—wish I had.

MRS. PETERS: But of course you were awful busy, Mrs. Hale—your house and your children.

MRS. HALE (*rises and crosses left*): I could've come. I stayed away because it weren't cheerful—and that's why I ought to have come. I—(*looking *out left window*)—I've never liked this place. Maybe it's because it's down in a hollow and you don't see the road. I dunno what it is, but it's a lonesome place and always was. I wish I had come over to see Minnie Foster sometimes. I can see now—(*Shakes her head.*)

MRS. PETERS (*left of table and above it*): Well, you mustn't reproach yourself, Mrs. Hale. Somehow we just don't see how it is with other folks until—something turns up.

MRS. HALE: Not having children makes less work—but it makes a quiet house, and Wright out to work all day, and no company when he did come in. (*Turning from window.*) Did you know John Wright, Mrs. Peters?

MRS. PETERS: Not to know him; I've seen him in town. They say he was a good man.

MRS. HALE: Yes—good; he didn't drink, and kept his word as well as most, I guess, and paid his debts. But he was a hard man, Mrs. Peters. Just to pass the time of day with him—(*Shivers.*) Like a raw wind that gets to the bone. (*Pauses, her eye falling on the cage.*) I should think she would 'a' wanted a bird. But what do you suppose went with it?

MRS. PETERS: I don't know, unless it got sick and died. (*She reaches over and swings the broken door, swings it again, both women watch it.*)

MRS. HALE: You weren't raised round here, were you? (*Mrs. Peters shakes her head.*) You didn't know—her?

MRS. PETERS: Not till they brought her yesterday.

MRS. HALE: She—come to think of it, she was kind of like a bird herself—real sweet and pretty, but kind of timid and—fluttery. How— she—did—change. (*Silence: then as if struck by a happy thought and relieved to get back to everyday things. Crosses right above Mrs. Peters to cupboard, replaces small chair used to stand on to its original place down right.*) Tell you what, Mrs. Peters, why don't you take the quilt in with you? It might take up her mind.

MRS. PETERS: Why, I think that's a real nice idea, Mrs. Hale. There couldn't possibly be any objection to it could there? Now, just what would I take? I wonder if her patches are in here—and her things. (*They look in the sewing basket.*)

MRS. HALE (*crosses to right of table*): Here's some red. I expect this has got sewing things in it. (*Brings out a fancy box.*) What a pretty box. Looks like something somebody would give you. Maybe her scissors are in here. (*Opens box. Suddenly puts her hand to her nose.*) Why———(*Mrs. Peters bends nearer, then turns her face away.*) There's something wrapped up in this piece of silk.

MRS. PETERS: Why, this isn't her scissors.

MRS. HALE (*lifting the silk*): Oh, Mrs. Peters—it's———(*Mrs. Peters bends closer.*)

MRS. PETERS: It's the bird.

MRS. HALE: But, Mrs. Peters—look at it! Its neck! Look at its neck! It's all—other side *to.*

MRS. PETERS: Somebody—wrung—its—neck. (*Their eyes meet. A look of growing comprehension, of horror. Steps are heard outside. Mrs. Hale slips box under quilt pieces, and sinks into her chair. Enter Sheriff and County Attorney. Mrs. Peters steps down left and stands looking out of window.*)

COUNTY ATTORNEY (*as one turning from serious things to little pleasantries*): Well, ladies, have you decided whether she was going to quilt it or knot it? (*Crosses to center above table.*)

MRS. PETERS: We think she was going to—knot it. (*Sheriff crosses to right of stove, lifts stove lid, and glances at fire, then stands warming hands at stove.*)

COUNTY ATTORNEY: Well, that's interesting, I'm sure. (*Seeing the bird-cage.*) Has the bird flown?

MRS. HALE (*putting more quilt pieces over the box*): We think the—cat got it.

COUNTY ATTORNEY (*preoccupied*): Is there a cat? (*Mrs. Hale glances in a quick covert way at Mrs. Peters.*)

MRS. PETERS (*turning from window takes a step in*): Well, not *now.* They're superstitious, you know. They leave.

COUNTY ATTORNEY (*to Sheriff Peters, continuing an interrupted conversation*): No sign at all of anyone having come from the outside. Their own rope. Now let's go up again and go over it piece by piece. (*They start upstairs.*) It would have to have been someone who knew just the———(*Mrs. Peters sits down left of table. The two women sit there not looking at one another, but as if peering into something and at the same time holding back. When they talk now it is in the manner of feeling their way over strange ground, as if afraid of what they are saying, but as if they cannot help saying it.*)

MRS. HALE (*hesitatively and in hushed voice*): She liked the bird. She was going to bury it in that pretty box.

MRS. PETERS (*in a whisper*): When I was a girl—my kitten—there was a boy took a hatchet, and before my eyes—and before I could get there———(*Covers her face an instant.*) If they hadn't held me back I would have—(*catches herself, looks upstairs where steps are heard, falters weakly*)—hurt him.

MRS. HALE (*with a slow look around her*): I wonder how it would seem never to have had any children around. (*Pause.*) No, Wright wouldn't like the bird—a thing that sang. She used to sing. He killed that, too.

MRS. PETERS (*moving uneasily*): We don't know who killed the bird.

MRS. HALE: I knew John Wright.

MRS. PETERS: It was an awful thing was done in this house that night, Mrs. Hale. Killing a man while he slept, slipping a rope around his neck that choked the life out of him.

MRS. HALE: His neck. Choked the life out of him. (*Her hand goes out and rests on the bird-cage.*)

MRS. PETERS (*with rising voice*): We don't know who killed him. We don't know.

MRS. HALE (*her own feelings not interrupted*): If there'd been years and years of nothing, then a bird to sing to you, it would be awful—still, after the bird was still.

MRS. PETERS (*something within her speaking*): I know what stillness is. When we homesteaded in Dakota, and my first baby died—after he was two years old, and me with no other then——

MRS. HALE (*moving*): How soon do you suppose they'll be through looking for the evidence?

MRS. PETERS: I know what stillness is. (*Pulling herself back.*) The law has got to punish crimes, Mrs. Hale.

MRS. HALE (*not as if answering that*): I wish you'd seen Minnie Foster when she wore a white dress with blue ribbons and stood up there in the choir and sang. (*A look around the room.*) Oh, I wish I'd come over here once in a while! That was a crime! That was a crime! Who's going to punish that?

MRS. PETERS (*looking upstairs*): We mustn't—take on.

MRS. HALE: I might have known she needed help! I know how things can be—for women. I tell you, it's queer, Mrs. Peters. We live close together and we live far apart. We all go through the same things—it's all just a different kind of the same thing. (*Brushes her eyes, noticing the jar of fruit, reaches out for it.*) If I was you I wouldn't tell her her fruit was gone. Tell her it ain't. Tell her it's all right. Take this in to prove it to her. She—she may never know whether it was broke or not.

MRS. PETERS (*takes the jar, looks about for something to wrap it in; takes petticoat from the clothes brought from the other room, very nervously begins winding this around the jar. In a false voice*): My, it's a good thing the men couldn't hear us. Wouldn't they just laugh! Getting all stirred up over a little thing like a—dead canary. As if that could have anything to do with—with—wouldn't they *laugh*! (*The men are heard coming downstairs.*)

MRS. HALE (*under her breath*): Maybe they would—maybe they wouldn't.

COUNTY ATTORNEY: No, Peters, it's all perfectly clear except a reason for doing it. But you know juries when it comes to women. If there was some definite thing. (*Crosses slowly to above table. Sheriff crosses down right. Mrs. Hale and Mrs. Peters remain seated at either side of table.*) Something to show—something to make a story about—a thing that would connect up with this strange way of doing it———(*The women's eyes meet for an instant. Enter Hale from outer door.*)

HALE (*remaining by door*): Well, I've got the team around. Pretty cold out there.

COUNTY ATTORNEY: I'm going to stay awhile by myself. (*To the Sheriff.*) You can send Frank out for me, can't you? I want to go over everything. I'm not satisfied that we can't do better.

SHERIFF: Do you want to see what Mrs. Peters is going to take in? (*The Lawyer picks up the apron, laughs.*)

COUNTY ATTORNEY: Oh, I guess they're not very dangerous things the ladies have picked out. (*Moves a few things about, disturbing the quilt pieces which cover the box. Steps back.*) No, Mrs. Peters doesn't need supervising. For that matter a sheriff's wife is married to the law. Ever think of it that way, Mrs. Peters?

MRS. PETERS: Not—just that way.

SHERIFF (*chuckling*): Married to the law. (*Moves to down right door to the other room.*) I just want you to come in here a minute, George. We ought to take a look at these windows.

COUNTY ATTORNEY (*scoffingly*): Oh, windows!

SHERIFF: We'll be right out, Mr. Hale. (*Hale goes outside. The Sheriff follows the County Attorney into the room. Then Mrs. Hale rises, hands tight together, looking intensely at Mrs. Peters, whose eyes make a slow turn, finally meeting Mrs. Hale's. A moment Mrs. Hale holds her, then her own eyes point the way to where the box is concealed. Suddenly Mrs. Peters throws back quilt pieces and tries to put the box in the bag she is carrying. It is too big. She opens box, starts to take bird out, cannot touch it, goes to pieces, stands there helpless. Sound of a knob turning in the other room. Mrs. Hale snatches the box and puts it in the pocket of her big coat. Enter County Attorney and Sheriff, who remains down right.*)

COUNTY ATTORNEY (*crosses to up left door facetiously*): Well, Henry, at least we found out that she was not going to quilt it. She was going to—what is it you call it, ladies?

MRS. HALE (*standing center below table facing front, her hand against her pocket*): We call it—knot it, Mr. Henderson.

[1916]

TENNESSEE WILLIAMS [1911–1983]

Cat on a Hot Tin Roof

And you, my father, there on the sad height,
Curse, bless, me now with your fierce tears, I pray.
Do not go gentle into that good night,
Rage, rage against the dying of the light!
— DYLAN THOMAS

Production Notes by Tennessee Williams

The set is the bed-sitting-room of a plantation home in the Mississippi Delta. It is along an upstairs gallery which probably runs around the entire house; it has two pairs of very wide doors opening onto the gallery, showing white balustrades against a fair summer sky that fades into dusk and night during the course of the play, which occupies precisely the time of its performance, excepting, of course, the fifteen minutes of intermission.

Perhaps the style of the room is not what you would expect in the home of the Delta's biggest cotton-planter. It is Victorian with a touch of the Far East. It hasn't changed much since it was occupied by the original owners of the place, Jack Straw and Peter Ochello, a pair of old bachelors who shared this room all their lives together. In other words, the room must evoke some ghosts; it is gently and poetically haunted by a relationship that must have involved a tenderness which was uncommon. This may be irrelevant or unnecessary, but I once saw a reproduction of a faded photograph of the verandah of Robert Louis Stevenson's home on that Samoan Island where he spent his last years, and there was a quality of tender light on weathered wood, such as porch furniture made of bamboo and wicker, exposed to tropical suns and tropical rains, which came to mind when I thought about the set for this play, bringing also to mind the grace and comfort of light, the reassurance it gives, on a late and fair afternoon in summer, the way that no matter what, even dread of death, is gently touched and soothed by it. For the set is the background for a play that deals with human extremities of emotion, and it needs that softness behind it.

The bathroom door, showing only pale-blue tile and silver towel racks, is in one side wall; the hall door in the opposite wall. Two articles of furniture need mention: a big double bed which staging should make a functional part of the set as often as suitable, the surface of which should be slightly raked to

951

make figures on it seen more easily; and against the wall space between the two huge double doors upstage: a monumental monstrosity peculiar to our times, a *huge* console combination of radio-phonograph (hi-fi with three speakers) TV set *and* liquor cabinet, bearing and containing many glasses and bottles, all in one piece, which is a composition of muted silver tones, and the opalescent tones of reflecting glass, a chromatic link, this thing, between the sepia (tawny gold) tones of the interior and the cool (white and blue) tones of the gallery and sky. This piece of furniture (?!), this monument, is a very complete and compact little shrine to virtually all the comforts and illusions behind which we hide from such things as the characters in the play are faced with. . . .

The set should be far less realistic than I have so far implied in this description of it. I think the walls below the ceiling should dissolve mysteriously into air; the set should be roofed by the sky; stars and moon suggested by traces of milky pallor, as if they were observed through a telescope lens out of focus.

Anything else I can think of? Oh, yes, fanlights (transoms shaped like an open glass fan) above all the doors in the set, with panes of blue and amber, and above all, the designer should take as many pains to give the actors room to move about freely (to show their restlessness, their passion for breaking out) as if it were a set for a ballet.

An evening in summer. The action is continuous, with two intermissions.

Characters of the Play

MARGARET
BRICK
MAE, *sometimes called Sister Woman*
BIG MAMA
DIXIE, *a little girl*
BIG DADDY
REVEREND TOOKER
GOOPER, *sometimes called Brother Man*
DOCTOR BAUGH, *pronounced "Baw"*
LACEY, *a Negro servant*
SOOKEY, *another*
Another little girl and two small boys

(The playing script of Act III also includes TRIXIE, another little girl, also DAISY, BRIGHTIE and SMALL, servants.)

ACT I

At the rise of the curtain someone is taking a shower in the bathroom, the door of which is half open. A pretty young woman, with anxious lines in her face, enters the bedroom and crosses to the bathroom door.

MARGARET (*shouting above roar of water*): One of those no-neck monsters hit me with a hot buttered biscuit so I have t' change!

(*Margaret's voice is both rapid and drawling. In her long speeches she has the vocal tricks of a priest delivering a liturgical chant, the lines are almost sung, always continuing a little beyond her breath so she has to gasp for another. Sometimes she intersperses the lines with a little wordless singing, such as "Da-da-daaaa!"*)

  (*Water turns off and Brick calls out to her, but is still unseen. A tone of politely feigned interest, masking indifference, or worse, is characteristic of his speech with Margaret.*)

BRICK: Wha'd you say, Maggie? Water was on s' loud I couldn't hearya. . . .
MARGARET: Well, I!—just remarked that!—one of th' no-neck monsters messed up m' lovely lace dress so I got t'—cha-a-ange. . . .

(*She opens and kicks shut drawers of the dresser.*)

BRICK: Why d'ya call Gooper's kiddies no-neck monsters?
MARGARET: Because they've got no necks! Isn't that a good enough reason?
BRICK: Don't they have any necks?
MARGARET: None visible. Their fat little heads are set on their fat little bodies without a bit of connection.
BRICK: That's too bad.
MARGARET: Yes, it's too bad because you can't wring their necks if they've got no necks to wring! Isn't that right, honey?

(*She steps out of her dress, stands in a slip of ivory satin and lace.*)

  Yep, they're no-neck monsters, all no-neck people are monsters . . .

(*Children shriek downstairs.*)

  Hear them? Hear them screaming? I don't know where their voice boxes are located since they don't have necks. I tell you I got so nervous at that table tonight I thought I would throw back my head and utter a scream you could hear across the Arkansas border an' parts of Louisiana an' Tennessee. I said to your charming sister-in-law, Mae, honey, couldn't you feed those precious little things at a separate table with an oilcloth cover? They make such a mess an' the lace cloth looks so

pretty! She made enormous eyes at me and said, "Ohhh, noooooo! On
Big Daddy's birthday? Why, he would never forgive me!" Well, I want
you to know, Big Daddy hadn't been at the table two minutes with
those five no-neck monsters slobbering and drooling over their food
before he threw down his fork an' shouted, "Fo' God's sake, Gooper,
why don't you put them pigs at a trough in th' kitchen?"—Well, I
swear, I simply could have di-ieed!

Think of it, Brick, they've got five of them and number six is coming.
They've brought the whole bunch down here like animals to display at
a county fair. Why, they have those children doin' tricks all the time!
"Junior, show Big Daddy how you do this, show Big Daddy how you do
that, say your little piece fo' Big Daddy, Sister. Show your dimples,
Sugar. Brother, show Big Daddy how you stand on your head!"—It
goes on all the time, along with constant little remarks and innuendos
about the fact that you and I have not produced any children, are
totally childless and therefore totally useless!—Of course it's comical
but it's also disgusting since it's so obvious what they're up to!

BRICK (*without interest*): What are they up to, Maggie?
MARGARET: Why, you know what they're up to!
BRICK (*appearing*): No, I don't know what they're up to.

(*He stands there in the bathroom doorway drying his hair with a towel and
hanging onto the towel rack because one ankle is broken, plastered and bound.
He is still slim and firm as a boy. His liquor hasn't started tearing him down
outside. He has the additional charm of that cool air of detachment that people
have who have given up the struggle. But now and then, when disturbed, something flashes behind it, like lightning in a fair sky, which shows that at some
deeper level he is far from peaceful. Perhaps in a stronger light he would show
some signs of deliquescence, but the fading, still warm light from the gallery
treats him gently.*)

MARGARET: I'll tell you what they're up to, boy of mine!—They're up to
    cutting you out of your father's estate, and—

(*She freezes momentarily before her next remark. Her voice drops as if it were
somehow a personally embarrassing admission.*)

    —Now we know that Big Daddy's dyin' of—*cancer*. . . .

(*There are voices on the lawn below: long-drawn calls across distance. Margaret
raises her lovely bare arms and powders her armpits with a light sigh.*)

    (*She adjusts the angle of a magnifying mirror to straighten an eyelash, then
rises fretfully saying:*)

There's so much light in the room it—

BRICK (*softly but sharply*): Do we?
MARGARET: Do we what?
BRICK: Know Big Daddy's dyin' of cancer?
MARGARET: Got the report today.
BRICK: Oh . . .
MARGARET (*letting down bamboo blinds which cast long, goldfretted shadows over the room*): Yep, got th' report just now . . . it didn't surprise me, Baby. . . .

(*Her voice has range, and music; sometimes it drops low as a boy's and you have a sudden image of her playing boy's games as a child.*)

I recognized the symptoms soon's we got here last spring and I'm wil-
lin' to bet you that Brother Man and his wife were pretty sure of it, too.
That more than likely explains why their usual summer migration to
the coolness of the Great Smokies was passed up this summer in favor
of—hustlin' down here ev'ry whipstitch with their whole screamin'
tribe! And why so many allusions have been made to Rainbow Hill
lately. You know what Rainbow Hill is? Place that's famous for treatin'
alcoholics an' dope fiends in the movies!
BRICK: I'm not in the movies.
MARGARET: No, and you don't take dope. Otherwise you're a perfect candidate for Rainbow Hill, Baby, and that's where they aim to ship
you—over my dead body! Yep, over my dead body they'll ship you
there, but nothing would please them better. Then Brother Man could
get a-hold of the purse strings and dole out remittances to us, maybe
get power of attorney and sign checks for us and cut off our credit
wherever, whenever he wanted! Son-of-a-bitch!—How'd you like that,
Baby?—Well, you've been doin' just about ev'rything in your power to
bring it about, you've just been doin' ev'rything you can think of to aid
and abet them in this scheme of theirs! Quittin' work, devoting yourself to the occupation of drinkin'!—Breakin' your ankle last night on
the high school athletic field: doin' what? Jumpin' hurdles? At two or
three in the morning? Just fantastic! Got in the paper. *Clarksdale Register* carried a nice little item about it, human interest story about a
well-known former athlete stagin' a one-man track meet on the Glorious Hill High School athletic field last night, but was slightly out of
condition and didn't clear the first hurdle! Brother Man Gooper claims
he exercised his influence t' keep it from goin' out over AP or UP or
every goddam "P."
  But, Brick? You still have one big advantage!

(*During the above swift flood of words, Brick has reclined with contrapuntal leisure on the snowy surface of the bed and has rolled over carefully on his side or belly.*)

BRICK (*wryly*): Did you *say* something, Maggie?

MARGARET: Big Daddy dotes on you, honey. And he can't stand Brother Man and Brother Man's wife, that monster of fertility, Mae; she's downright odious to him! Know how I know? By little expressions that flicker over his face when that woman is holding fo'th on one of her choice topics such as—how she refused twilight sleep!—when the twins were delivered! Because she feels motherhood's an experience that a woman ought to experience fully!—in order to fully appreciate the wonder and beauty of it! HAH!

(*This loud "HAH!" is accompanied by a violent action such as slamming a drawer shut.*)

—and how she made Brother Man come in an' stand beside her in the delivery room so he would not miss out on the "wonder and beauty" of it either!—producin' those no-neck monsters. . . .

(*A speech of this kind would be antipathetic from almost anybody but Margaret; she makes it oddly funny, because her eyes constantly twinkle and her voice shakes with laughter which is basically indulgent.*)

—Big Daddy shares my attitude toward those two! As for me, well—I give him a laugh now and then and he tolerates me. In fact!—I sometimes suspect that Big Daddy harbors a little unconscious "lech" fo' me. . . .

BRICK: What makes you think that Big Daddy has a lech for you, Maggie?

MARGARET: Way he always drops his eyes down my body when I'm talkin' to him, drops his eyes to my boobs an' licks his old chops! Ha ha!

BRICK: That kind of talk is disgusting.

MARGARET: Did anyone ever tell you that you're an ass-aching Puritan, Brick?

I think it's mighty fine that that ole fellow, on the doorstep of death, still takes in my shape with what I think is deserved appreciation!

And you wanta know something else? Big Daddy didn't know how many little Maes and Goopers had been produced! "How many kids have you got?" he asked at the table, just like Brother Man and his wife were new acquaintances to him! Big Mama said he was jokin', but that ole boy wasn't jokin', Lord, no!

And when they infawmed him that they had five already and were turning out number six!—the news seemed to come as a sort of unpleasant surprise . . .

(*Children yell below.*)

Scream, monsters!

(*Turns to Brick with a sudden, gay, charming smile which fades as she notices that he is not looking at her but into fading gold space with a troubled expression.*)

(*It is constant rejection that makes her humor "bitchy."*)

Yes, you should of been at that supper-table, Baby.

(*Whenever she calls him "baby" the word is a soft caress.*)

Y'know, Big Daddy, bless his ole sweet soul, he's the dearest ole thing in the world, but he does hunch over his food as if he preferred not to notice anything else. Well, Mae an' Gooper were side by side at the table, direckly across from Big Daddy, watchin' his face like hawks while they jawed an' jabbered about the cuteness an' brillance of th' no-neck monsters!

(*She giggles with a hand fluttering at her throat and her breast and her long throat arched.*

(*She comes downstage and recreates the scene with voice and gesture.*)

And the no-neck monsters were ranged around the table, some in high chairs and some on th' *Books of Knowledge*, all in fancy little paper caps in honor of Big Daddy's birthday, and all through dinner, well, I want you to know that Brother Man an' his partner never once, for one moment, stopped exchanging pokes an' pinches an' kicks an' signs an' signals!—Why, they were like a couple of cardsharps fleecing a sucker.—Even Big Mama, bless her ole sweet soul, she isn't th' quickest an' brightest thing in the world, she finally noticed, at last, an' said to Gooper, "Gooper, what are you an' Mae makin' all these signs at each other about?"—I swear t' goodness, I nearly choked on my chicken!

(*Margaret, back at the dressing table, still doesn't see Brick. He is watching her with a look that is not quite definable—Amused? shocked? contemptuous?—part of those and part of something else.*)

Y'know—your brother Gooper still cherishes the illusion he took a giant step up on the social ladder when he married Miss Mae Flynn of the Memphis Flynns.

(*Margaret moves about the room as she talks, stops before the mirror, moves on.*)

But I have a piece of Spanish news for Gooper. The Flynns never had a thing in this world but money and they lost that, they were nothing at all but fairly successful climbers. Of course, Mae Flynn came out in

Memphis eight years before I made my debut in Nashville, but I had friends at Ward-Belmont who came from Memphis and they used to come to see me and I used to go to see them for Christmas and spring vacations, and so I know who rates an' who doesn't rate in Memphis society. Why, y'know ole Papa Flynn, he barely escaped doing time in the Federal pen for shady manipulations on th' stock market when his chain stores crashed, and as for Mae having been a cotton carnival queen, as they remind us so often, lest we forget, well, that's one honor that I don't envy her for!—Sit on a brass throne on a tacky float an' ride down Main Street, smilin', bowin', and blowin' kisses to all the trash on the street—

(*She picks out a pair of jeweled sandals and rushes to the dressing table.*)

Why, year before last, when Susan McPheeters was singled out fo' that honor, y'know what happened to her? Y'know what happened to poor little Susie McPheeters?

BRICK (*absently*): No. What happened to little Susie McPheeters?

MARGARET: Somebody spit tobacco juice in her face.

BRICK (*dreamily*): Somebody spit tobacco juice in her face?

MARGARET: That's right, some old drunk leaned out of a window in the Hotel Gayoso and yelled, "Hey, Queen, hey, hey, there, Queenie!" Poor Susie looked up and flashed him a radiant smile and he shot out a squirt of tobacco juice right in poor Susie's face.

BRICK: Well, what d'you know about that.

MARGARET (*gaily*): What do I know about it? I was there, I saw it!

BRICK (*absently*): Must have been kind of funny.

MARGARET: Susie didn't think so. Had hysterics. Screamed like a banshee. They had to stop th' parade an' remove her from her throne an' go on with—

(*She catches sight of him in the mirror, gasps slightly, wheels about to face him. Count ten.*)

—Why are you looking at me like that?

BRICK (*whistling softly, now*): Like what, Maggie?

MARGARET (*intensely, fearfully*): The way y' were lookin' at me just now, befo' I caught your eye in the mirror and you started t' whistle! I don't know how t' describe it but it froze my blood!—I've caught you lookin' at me like that so often lately. What are you thinkin' of when you look at me like that?

BRICK: I wasn't conscious of lookin' at you, Maggie.

MARGARET: Well, I was conscious of it! What were you thinkin'?

BRICK: I don't remember thinking of anything, Maggie.

MARGARET: Don't you think I know that—? Don't you—?—Think I know that—?

BRICK (*coolly*): Know *what*, Maggie?

MARGARET (*struggling for expression*): That I've gone through this— *hideous!—transformation*, become—*hard! Frantic!*

(*Then she adds, almost tenderly:*)

—*cruel!!*
   That's what you've been observing in me lately. How could y' help but observe it? That's all right. I'm not—thin-skinned any more, can't afford t' be thin-skinned any more.

(*She is now recovering her power.*)

   —But Brick? Brick?

BRICK: Did you say something?

MARGARET: I was *goin'* t' say something: that I get—lonely. Very!

BRICK: Ev'rybody gets that . . .

MARGARET: Living with someone you love can be lonelier—than living entirely *alone!*—if the one that y' love doesn't love you. . . .

(*There is a pause. Brick hobbles downstage and asks, without looking at her:*)

BRICK: Would you like to live alone, Maggie?

(*Another pause: then—after she has caught a quick, hurt breath:*)

MARGARET: *No!—God!—I wouldn't!*

(*Another gasping breath. She forcibly controls what must have been an impulse to cry out. We see her deliberately, very forcibly, going all the way back to the world in which you can talk about ordinary matters.*)

   Did you have a nice shower?

BRICK: Uh-huh.

MARGARET: Was the water cool?

BRICK: No.

MARGARET: But it made y' feel fresh, huh?

BRICK: Fresher. . . .

MARGARET: I know something would make y' feel *much* fresher!

BRICK: What?

MARGARET: An alcohol rub. Or cologne, a rub with cologne!

BRICK: That's good after a workout but I haven't been workin' out, Maggie.

MARGARET: You've kept in good shape, though.

BRICK (*indifferently*): You think so, Maggie?

MARGARET: I always thought drinkin' men lost their looks, but I was
  plainly mistaken.
BRICK (*wryly*): Why, thanks, Maggie.
MARGARET: You're the only drinkin' man I know that it never seems t' put
  fat on.
BRICK: I'm gettin' softer, Maggie.
MARGARET: Well, sooner or later it's bound to soften you up. It was just
  beginning to soften up Skipper when—

(*She stops short.*)

I'm sorry. I never could keep my fingers off a sore—I wish you *would*
lose your looks. If you did it would make the martyrdom of Saint Maggie a little more bearable. But no such goddam luck. I actually believe
you've gotten better looking since you've gone on the bottle. Yeah, a
person who didn't know you would think you'd never had a tense nerve
in your body or a strained muscle.

(*There are sounds of croquet on the lawn below: the click of mallets, light voices,
near and distant.*)

Of course, you always had that detached quality as if you were playing
a game without much concern over whether you won or lost, and now
that you've lost the game, not lost but just quit playing, you have that
rare sort of charm that usually only happens in very old or hopelessly
sick people, the charm of the defeated.—You look so cool, so cool, so
enviably cool.

(*Music is heard.*)

They're playing croquet. The moon has appeared and it's white, just
beginning to turn a little bit yellow. . . .
  You were a wonderful lover. . . .
  Such a wonderful person to go to bed with, and I think mostly
because you were really indifferent to it. Isn't that right? Never had any
anxiety about it, did it naturally, easily, slowly, with absolute confidence and perfect calm, more like opening a door for a lady or seating
her at a table than giving expression to any longing for her. Your indifference made you wonderful at lovemaking—*strange?*—but true. . . .
  You know, if I thought you would never, never, *never* make love to me
again—I would go downstairs to the kitchen and pick out the longest
and sharpest knife I could find and stick it straight into my heart, I
swear that I would!
  But one thing I don't have is the charm of the defeated, my hat is still
in the ring, and I am determined to win!

(*There is the sound of croquet mallets hitting croquet balls.*)

—What is the victory of a cat on a hot tin roof?—I wish I knew. . . .
Just staying on it, I guess, as long as she can. . . .

(*More croquet sounds.*)

Later tonight I'm going to tell you I love you an' maybe by that time
you'll be drunk enough to believe me. Yes, they're playing croquet. . . .
  Big Daddy is dying of cancer. . . .
  What were you thinking of when I caught you looking at me like
that? Were you thinking of Skipper?

(*Brick takes up his crutch, rises.*)

Oh, excuse me, forgive me, but laws of silence don't work! No, laws of
silence don't work. . . .

(*Brick crosses to the bar, takes a quick drink, and rubs his head with a towel.*)

Laws of silence don't work. . . .
  When something is festering in your memory or your imagination,
laws of silence don't work, it's just like shutting a door and locking it
on a house on fire in hope of forgetting that the house is burning. But
not facing a fire doesn't put it out. Silence about a thing just magnifies
it. It grows and festers in silence, becomes malignant. . . .
  Get dressed, Brick.

(*He drops his crutch.*)

BRICK: I've dropped my crutch.

(*He has stopped rubbing his hair dry but still stands hanging onto the towel
rack in a white towel-cloth robe.*)

MARGARET: Lean on me.
BRICK: No, just give me my crutch.
MARGARET: Lean on my shoulder.
BRICK: *I don't want to lean on your shoulder, I want my crutch!*

(*This is spoken like sudden lightning.*)

Are you going to give me my crutch or do I have to get down on my
knees on the floor and—
MARGARET: *Here, here, take it, take it!*

(*She has thrust the crutch at him.*)

BRICK (*hobbling out*): Thanks . . .

MARGARET: We mustn't scream at each other, the walls in this house have ears. . . .

(*He hobbles directly to liquor cabinet to get a new drink.*)

—but that's the first time I've heard you raise your voice in a long time, Brick. A crack in the wall?—Of composure?
   —I think that's a good sign. . . .
A sign of nerves in a player on the defensive!

(*Brick turns and smiles at her coolly over his fresh drink.*)

BRICK: It just hasn't happened yet, Maggie.
MARGARET: What?
BRICK: The click I get in my head when I've had enough of this stuff to make me peaceful. . . .
   Will you do me a favor?
MARGARET: Maybe I will. What favor?
BRICK: Just, just keep your voice down!
MARGARET (*in a hoarse whisper*): I'll do you that favor, I'll speak in a whisper, if not shut up completely, if *you* will do *me* a favor and make that drink your last one till after the party.
BRICK: What party?
MARGARET: Big Daddy's birthday party.
BRICK: Is this Big Daddy's birthday?
MARGARET: You know this is Big Daddy's birthday!
BRICK: No, I don't, I forgot it.
MARGARET: Well, I remembered it for you. . . .

(*They are both speaking as breathlessly as a pair of kids after a fight, drawing deep exhausted breaths and looking at each other with faraway eyes, shaking and panting together as if they had broken apart from a violent struggle.*)

BRICK: Good for you, Maggie.
MARGARET: You just have to scribble a few lines on this card.
BRICK: You scribble something, Maggie.
MARGARET: It's got to be your handwriting; it's your present, I've given him my present; it's got to be your handwriting!

(*The tension between them is building again, the voices becoming shrill once more.*)

BRICK: I didn't get him a present.
MARGARET: I got one for you.
BRICK: All right. You write the card, then.
MARGARET: And have him know you didn't remember his birthday?

BRICK: I didn't remember his birthday.

MARGARET: You don't have to prove you didn't!

BRICK: I don't want to fool him about it.

MARGARET: Just write "Love, Brick!" for God's—

BRICK: No.

MARGARET: You've *got* to!

BRICK: I don't have to do anything I don't want to do. You keep forgetting the conditions on which I agreed to stay on living with you.

MARGARET (*out before she knows it*): I'm not living with you. We occupy the same cage.

BRICK: You've got to remember the conditions agreed on.

MARGARET: They're impossible conditions!

BRICK: Then why don't you—?

MARGARET: HUSH! Who is out there? Is somebody at the door?

(*There are footsteps in hall.*)

MAE (*outside*): May I enter a moment?

MARGARET: Oh, *you!* Sure. Come in, Mae.

(*Mae enters bearing aloft the bow of a young lady's archery set.*)

MAE: Brick, is this thing yours?

MARGARET: Why, Sister Woman—that's my Diana Trophy. Won it at the intercollegiate archery contest on the Ole Miss campus.

MAE: It's a mighty dangerous thing to leave exposed round a house full of nawmal rid-blooded children attracted t'weapons.

MARGARET: "Nawmal rid-blooded children attracted t'weapons" ought t'be taught to keep their hands off things that don't belong to them.

MAE: Maggie, honey, if you had children of your own you'd know how funny that is. Will you please lock this up and put the key out of reach?

MARGARET: Sister Woman, nobody is plotting the destruction of your kiddies.—Brick and I still have our special archers' license. We're goin' deer-huntin' on Moon Lake as soon as the season starts. I love to run with dogs through chilly woods, run, run leap over obstructions—

(*She goes into the closet carrying the bow.*)

MAE: How's the injured ankle, Brick?

BRICK: Doesn't hurt. Just itches.

MAE: Oh, my! Brick—Brick, you should've been downstairs after supper! Kiddies put on a show. Polly played the piano, Buster an' Sonny drums, an' then they turned out the lights an' Dixie an' Trixie puhfawmed a toe dance in fairy costume with *spahkluhs!* Big Daddy just beamed! He just beamed!

MARGARET (*from the closet with a sharp laugh*): Oh, I bet. It breaks my heart that we missed it!

(*She reenters.*)

But Mae? Why did y'give dawgs' names to all your kiddies?
MAE: *Dogs'* names?

(*Margaret has made this observation as she goes to raise the bamboo blinds, since the sunset glare has diminished. In crossing she winks at Brick.*)

MARGARET (*sweetly*): Dixie, Trixie, Buster, Sonny, Polly!—Sounds like four dogs and a parrot . . . animal act in a circus!
MAE: Maggie?

(*Margaret turns with a smile.*)

Why are you so catty?
MARGARET: Cause I'm a cat! But why can't *you* take a joke, Sister Woman?
MAE: Nothin' pleases me more than a joke that's funny. You know the real names of our kiddies. Buster's real name is Robert. Sonny's real name is Saunders. Trixie's real name is Marlene and Dixie's—

(*Someone downstairs calls for her. "Hey, Mae!"—She rushes to door, saying:*)

Intermission is over!
MARGARET (*as Mae closes door*): I wonder what Dixie's real name is?
BRICK: Maggie, being catty doesn't help things any . . .
MARGARET: I know! *WHY!*—Am I so catty?—Cause I'm consumed with envy an' eaten up with longing?—Brick, I've laid out your beautiful Shantung silk suit from Rome and one of your monogrammed silk shirts. I'll put your cuff links in it, those lovely star sapphires I get you to wear so rarely. . . .
BRICK: I can't get trousers on over this plaster cast.
MARGARET: Yes, you can, I'll help you.
BRICK: I'm not going to get dressed, Maggie.
MARGARET: Will you just put on a pair of white silk pajamas?
BRICK: Yes, I'll do that, Maggie.
MARGARET: *Thank* you, thank you so *much!*
BRICK: Don't mention it.
MARGARET: *Oh, Brick!* How long does it have t' go on? This punishment? Haven't I done time enough, haven't I served my term, can't I apply for a—pardon?

BRICK: Maggie, you're spoiling my liquor. Lately your voice always sounds like you'd been running upstairs to warn somebody that the house was on fire!

MARGARET: Well, no wonder, no wonder. Y'know what I feel like, Brick?

(*Children's and grownups' voices are blended, below, in a loud but uncertain rendition of "My Wild Irish Rose."*)

I feel all the time like a cat on a hot tin roof!

BRICK: Then jump off the roof, jump off it, cats can jump off roofs and land on their four feet uninjured!

MARGARET: Oh, yes!

BRICK: Do it! —fo' God's sake, do it . . .

MARGARET: Do what?

BRICK: Take a lover!

MARGARET: I can't see a man but you! Even with my eyes closed, I just see you! Why don't you get ugly, Brick, why don't you please get fat or ugly or something so I could stand it?

(*She rushes to hall door, opens it, listens.*)

The concert is still going on! Bravo, no-necks, bravo!

(*She slams and locks door fiercely.*)

BRICK: What did you lock the door for?

MARGARET: To give us a little privacy for a while.

BRICK: You know better, Maggie.

MARGARET: No, I don't know better. . . .

(*She rushes to gallery doors, draws the rose-silk drapes across them.*)

BRICK: Don't make a fool of yourself.

MARGARET: I don't mind makin' a fool of myself over you!

BRICK: I mind, Maggie. I feel embarrassed for you.

MARGARET: Feel embarrassed! But don't continue my torture. I can't live on and on under these circumstances.

BRICK: You agreed to—

MARGARET: I know but—

BRICK: —Accept that condition!

MARGARET: *I CAN'T! CAN'T! CAN'T!*

(*She seizes his shoulder.*)

BRICK: Let go!

(*He breaks away from her and seizes the small boudoir chair and raises it like a lion-tamer facing a big circus cat.*)

(*Count five. She stares at him with her fist pressed to her mouth, then bursts into shrill, almost hysterical laughter. He remains grave for a moment, then grins and puts the chair down.*
(*Big Mama calls through closed door.*)

BIG MAMA: Son? Son? Son?

BRICK: What is it, Big Mama?

BIG MAMA (*outside*): Oh, son! We got the most wonderful news about Big Daddy. I just had t' run up an' tell you right this—

(*She rattles the knob.*)

—What's this door doin', locked, faw? You all think there's robbers in the house?

MARGARET: Big Mama, Brick is dressin', he's not dressed yet.

BIG MAMA: That's all right, it won't be the first time I've seen Brick not dressed. Come on, open this door!

(*Margaret, with a grimace, goes to unlock and open the hall door, as Brick hobbles rapidly to the bathroom and kicks the door shut. Big Mama has disappeared from the hall.*)

MARGARET: Big Mama?

(*Big Mama appears through the opposite gallery doors behind Margaret, huffing and puffing like an old bulldog. She is a short, stout woman; her sixty years and 170 pounds have left her somewhat breathless most of the time; she's always tensed like a boxer, or rather, a Japanese wrestler. Her "family" was maybe a little superior to Big Daddy's, but not much. She wears a black or silver lace dress and at least half a million in flashy gems. She is very sincere.*)

BIG MAMA (*loudly, startling Margaret*): Here—I come through Gooper's and Mae's gall'ry door. Where's Brick? *Brick*—Hurry on out of there, son, I just have a second and want to give you the news about Big Daddy.—I hate locked doors in a house. . . .

MARGARET (*with affected lightness*): I've noticed you do, Big Mama, but people have got to have *some* moments of privacy, don't they?

BIG MAMA: No, ma'am, not in *my* house. (*without pause*) Whacha took off you' dress faw? I thought that little lace dress was so sweet on yuh, honey.

MARGARET: I thought it looked sweet on me, too, but one of m' cute little table-partners used it for a napkin so—!

BIG MAMA (*picking up stockings on floor*): What?

MARGARET: You know, Big Mama, Mae and Gooper's so touchy about those children—thanks, Big Mama . . .

(*Big Mama has thrust the picked-up stockings in Margaret's hand with a grunt.*)

—that you just don't dare to suggest there's any room for improvement in their—

BIG MAMA: Brick, hurry out!—Shoot, Maggie, you just don't like children.

MARGARET: I do SO like children! Adore them!—well brought up!

BIG MAMA (*gentle—loving*): Well, why don't you have some and bring them up well, then, instead of all the time pickin' on Gooper's an' Mae's?

GOOPER (*shouting up the stairs*): Hey, hey, Big Mama, Betsy an' Hugh got to go, waitin' t' tell yuh g'by!

BIG MAMA: Tell 'em to hold their hawses, I'll be right down in a jiffy!

(*She turns to the bathroom door and calls out.*)

Son? Can you hear me in there?

(*There is a muffled answer.*)

We just got the full report from the laboratory at the Ochsner Clinic, completely negative, son, ev'rything negative, right on down the line! Nothin' a-tall's wrong with him but some little functional thing called a spastic colon. Can you hear me, son?

MARGARET: He can hear you, Big Mama.

BIG MAMA: Then why don't he say something? God Almighty, a piece of news like that should make him shout. It made *me* shout, I can tell you. I shouted and sobbed and fell right down on my knees!— Look!

(*She pulls up her skirt.*)

See the bruises where I hit my kneecaps? Took both doctors to haul me back on my feet!

(*She laughs—she always laughs like hell at herself.*)

Big Daddy was furious with me! But ain't that wonderful news?

(*Facing bathroom again, she continues:*)

After all the anxiety we been through to git a report like that on Big Daddy's birthday? Big Daddy tried to hide how much of a load that news took off his mind, but didn't fool *me*. He was mighty close to crying about it *himself*!

(*Goodbyes are shouted downstairs, and she rushes to door.*)

Hold those people down there, don't let them go!—Now, git dressed, we're all comin' up to this room fo' Big Daddy's birthday party because of your ankle.—How's his ankle, Maggie?

MARGARET: Well, he broke it, Big Mama.

BIG MAMA: I know he broke it.

(*A phone is ringing in hall. A Negro voice answers: "Mistuh Polly's res'dence."*)

I mean does it hurt him much still.

MARGARET: I'm afraid I can't give you that information, Big Mama. You'll have to ask Brick if it hurts much still or not.

SOOKEY (*in the hall*): It's Memphis, Mizz Polly, it's Miss Sally in Memphis.

BIG MAMA: Awright, Sookey.

(*Big Mama rushes into the hall and is heard shouting on the phone:*)

Hello, Miss Sally. How are you, Miss Sally?—Yes, well, I was just gonna call you about it. *Shoot!*—

(*She raises her voice to a bellow.*)

Miss Sally? Don't ever call me from the Gayoso Lobby, too much talk goes on in that hotel lobby, no wonder you can't hear me! Now listen, Miss Sally. They's nothin' serious wrong with Big Daddy. We got the report just now, they's nothin' wrong but a thing called a—spastic! *SPASTIC!*—colon . . .

(*She appears at the hall door and calls to Margaret.*)

—Maggie, come out here and talk to that fool on the phone. I'm shouted breathless!

MARGARET (*goes out and is heard sweetly at phone*): Miss Sally? This is Brick's wife, Maggie. So nice to hear your voice. Can you hear *mine?* Well, *good!*—Big Mama just wanted you to know that they've got the report from the Ochsner Clinic and what Big Daddy has is a spastic colon. Yes. Spastic colon, Miss Sally. That's right, spastic colon. *G'bye, Miss Sally, hope I'll see you real soon!*

(*Hangs up a little before Miss Sally was probably ready to terminate the talk. She returns through the hall door.*)

She heard me perfectly. I've discovered with deaf people the thing to do is not shout at them but just enunciate clearly. My rich old Aunt Cornelia was deaf as the dead but I could make her hear me just by sayin' each word slowly, distinctly, close to her ear. I read her the

Commercial Appeal ev'ry night, read her the classified ads in it, even, she never missed a word of it. But was she a mean ole thing! Know what I got when she died? Her unexpired subscriptions to five magazines and the Book-of-the-Month Club and a LIBRARY full of ev'ry dull book ever written! All else went to her hellcat of a sister . . . meaner than she was, even!

(*Big Mama has been straightening things up in the room during this speech.*)

BIG MAMA (*closing closet door on discarded clothes*): Miss Sally sure is a case! Big Daddy says she's always got her hand out fo' something. He's not mistaken. That poor ole thing always has her hand out fo' somethin'. I don't think Big Daddy gives her as much as he should.

(*Somebody shouts for her downstairs and she shouts:*)

I'm comin'!

(*She starts out. At the hall door, turns and jerks a forefinger, first toward the bathroom door, then toward the liquor cabinet, meaning: "Has Brick been drinking?" Margaret pretends not to understand, cocks her head and raises her brows as if the pantomimic performance was completely mystifying to her.*)

(*Big Mama rushes back to Margaret:*)

Shoot! *Stop playin' so dumb!*—I mean has he been drinkin' that stuff much yet?
MARGARET (*with a little laugh*): Oh! I think he had a highball after supper.
BIG MAMA: Don't laugh about it!—Some single men stop drinkin' when they git married and others start! Brick never touched liquor before he—!
MARGARET (*crying out*): *THAT'S NOT FAIR!*
BIG MAMA: Fair or not fair I want to ask you a question, one question: D'you make Brick happy in bed?
MARGARET: Why don't you ask if he makes *me* happy in bed?
BIG MAMA: Because I know that—
MARGARET: *It works both ways!*
BIG MAMA: Something's not right! You're childless and my son drinks!

(*Someone has called her downstairs and she has rushed to the door on the line above. She turns at the door and points at the bed.*)

—When a marriage goes on the rocks, the rocks are *there*, right *there*!
MARGARET: *That's*—

(*Big Mama has swept out of the room and slammed the door.*)

—not—*fair* . . .

(*Margaret is alone, completely alone, and she feels it. She draws in, hunches her shoulders, raises her arms with fists clenched, shuts her eyes tight as a child about to be stabbed with a vaccination needle. When she opens her eyes again, what she sees is the long oval mirror and she rushes straight to it, stares into it with a grimace and says: "Who are you?"—Then she crouches a little and answers herself in a different voice which is high, thin, mocking: "I am Maggie the Cat!"—Straightens quickly as bathroom door opens a little and Brick calls out to her.*)

BRICK: Has Big Mama gone?
MARGARET: She's gone.

(*He opens the bathroom door and hobbles out, with his liquor glass now empty, straight to the liquor cabinet. He is whistling softly. Margaret's head pivots on her long, slender throat to watch him.*

(*She raises a hand uncertainly to the base of her throat, as if it was difficult for her to swallow, before she speaks:*)

You know, our sex life didn't just peter out in the usual way, it was cut off short, long before the natural time for it to, and it's going to revive again, just as sudden as that. I'm confident of it. That's what I'm keeping myself attractive for. For the time when you'll see me again like other men see me. Yes, like other men see me. They still see me, Brick, and they like what they see. Uh-huh. Some of them would give their—
  Look, Brick!

(*She stands before the long oval mirror, touches her breast and then her hips with her two hands.*)

How high my body stays on me!—Nothing has fallen on me—not a fraction. . . .

(*Her voice is soft and trembling: a pleading child's. At this moment as he turns to glance at her—a look which is like a player passing a ball to another player, third down and goal to go—she has to capture the audience in a grip so tight that she can hold it till the first intermission without any lapse of attention.*)

Other men still want me. My face looks strained, sometimes, but I've kept my figure as well as you've kept yours, and men admire it. I still turn heads on the street. Why, last week in Memphis everywhere that I went men's eyes burned holes in my clothes, at the country club and in restaurants and department stores, there wasn't a man I met or walked by that didn't just eat me up with his eyes and turn around when I passed him and look back at me. Why, at Alice's party for her New York cousins, the best-lookin' man in the crowd—followed me upstairs and tried to force his way in the powder room with me, followed me to the door and tried to force his way in!

BRICK: Why didn't you let him, Maggie?

MARGARET: Because I'm not that common, for one thing. Not that I wasn't almost tempted to. You like to know who it was? It was Sonny Boy Maxwell, that's who!

BRICK: Oh, yeah, Sonny Boy Maxwell, he was a good end-runner but had a little injury to his back and had to quit.

MARGARET: He has no injury now and has no wife and still has a lech for me!

BRICK: I see no reason to lock him out of a powder room in that case.

MARGARET: And have someone catch me at it? I'm not that stupid. Oh, I might sometime cheat on you with someone, since you're so insultingly eager to have me do it!—But if I do, you can be damned sure it will be in a place and a time where no one but me and the man could possibly know. Because I'm not going to give you any excuse to divorce me for being unfaithful or anything else. . . .

BRICK: Maggie, I wouldn't divorce you for being unfaithful or anything else. Don't you know that? Hell. I'd be relieved to know that you'd found yourself a lover.

MARGARET: Well, I'm taking no chances. No. I'd rather stay on this hot tin roof.

BRICK: A hot tin roof's 'n uncomfo'table place t' stay on. . . .

(He starts to whistle softly.)

MARGARET *(through his whistle):* Yeah, but I can stay on it just as long as I have to.

BRICK: You could leave me, Maggie.

(He resumes whistle. She wheels about to glare at him.)

MARGARET: *Don't want to and will not!* Besides if I did, you don't have a cent to pay for it but what you get from Big Daddy and he's dying of cancer!

(For the first time a realization of Big Daddy's doom seems to penetrate to Brick's consciousness, visibly, and he looks at Margaret.)

BRICK: Big Mama just said he *wasn't*, that the report was okay.

MARGARET: That's what she thinks because she got the same story that they gave Big Daddy. And was just as taken in by it as he was, poor ole things. . . .

But tonight they're going to tell her the truth about it. When Big Daddy goes to bed, they're going to tell her that he is dying of cancer.

(*She slams the dresser drawer.*)

—It's malignant and it's terminal.
BRICK: Does Big Daddy know it?
MARGARET: Hell, do they *ever* know it? Nobody says, "You're dying." You have to fool them. They have to fool *themselves*.
BRICK: Why?
MARGARET: *Why?* Because human beings dream of life everlasting, that's the reason! But most of them want it on earth and not in heaven.

(*He gives a short, hard laugh at her touch of humor.*)

Well. . . . (*She touches up her mascara.*) That's how it is, anyhow. . . . (*She looks about.*) Where did I put down my cigarette? Don't want to burn up the home-place, at least not with Mae and Gooper and their five monsters in it!

(*She has found it and sucks at it greedily. Blows out smoke and continues:*)

So this is Big Daddy's last birthday. And Mae and Gooper, they know it, oh, *they* know it, all right. They got the first information from the Ochsner Clinic. That's why they rushed down here with their no-neck monsters. Because. Do you know something? Big Daddy's made no will? Big Daddy's never made out any will in his life, and so this campaign's afoot to impress him, forcibly as possible, with the fact that you drink and I've borne no children!

(*He continues to stare at her a moment, then mutters something sharp but not audible and hobbles rather rapidly out onto the long gallery in the fading, much faded, gold light.*)

MARGARET (*continuing her liturgical chant*): Y'know, I'm *fond* of Big Daddy, I am genuinely fond of that old man, I really *am*, you know. . . .
BRICK (*faintly, vaguely*): Yes, I know you are. . . .
MARGARET: I've always sort of admired him in spite of his coarseness, his four-letter words and so forth. Because Big Daddy *is* what he *is*, and he makes no bones about it. He hasn't turned gentleman farmer, he's still a Mississippi redneck, as much of a redneck as he must have been when he was just overseer here on the old Jack Straw and Peter Ochello place. But he got hold of it an' built it into th' biggest an' finest plantation in the Delta. — I've always *liked* Big Daddy. . . .

(*She crosses to the proscenium.*)

Well, this is Big Daddy's last birthday. I'm sorry about it. But I'm facing the facts. It takes money to take care of a drinker and that's the office that I've been elected to lately.

BRICK: You don't have to take care of me.

MARGARET: Yes, I do. Two people in the same boat have got to take care of each other. At least you want money to buy more Echo Spring when this supply is exhausted, or will you be satisfied with a ten-cent beer?

Mae an' Gooper are plannin' to freeze us out of Big Daddy's estate because you drink and I'm childless. But we can defeat that plan. We're *going* to defeat that plan! *Brick, y'know, I've been so God damn disgustingly poor all my life!* — That's the *truth*, Brick!

BRICK: I'm not sayin' it isn't.

MARGARET: Always had to suck up to people I couldn't stand because they had money and I was poor as Job's turkey. You don't know what that's like. Well, I'll tell you, it's like you would feel a thousand miles away from Echo Spring! — And had to get back to it on that broken ankle . . . without a crutch!

That's how it feels to be as poor as Job's turkey and have to suck up to relatives that you hated because they had money and all you had was a bunch of hand-me-down clothes and a few old moldy three-percent government bonds. My daddy loved his liquor, he fell in love with his liquor the way you've fallen in love with Echo Spring! — And my poor Mama, having to maintain some semblance of social position, to keep appearances up, on an income of one hundred and fifty dollars a month on those old government bonds!

When I came out, the year that I made my debut, I had just two evening dresses! One Mother made me from a pattern in *Vogue*, the other a hand-me-down from a snotty rich cousin I hated!

—The dress that I married you in was my grandmother's weddin' gown. . . .

So that's why I'm like a cat on a hot tin roof!

(*Brick is still on the gallery. Someone below calls up to him in a warm Negro voice, "Hiya, Mistuh Brick, how yuh feelin'?" Brick raises his liquor glass as if that answered the question.*)

MARGARET: You can be young without money, but you can't be old without it. You've got to be old *with* money because to be old without it is just too awful, you've got to be one or the other, either *young* or *with money*, you can't be old and *without* it. — That's the *truth*, Brick. . . .

(*Brick whistles softly, vaguely.*)

Well, now I'm dressed, I'm all dressed, there's nothing else for me to do.

(*Forlornly, almost fearfully.*)

I'm dressed, all dressed, nothing else for me to do. . . .

(*She moves about restlessly, aimlessly, and speaks, as if to herself.*)

I know when I made my mistake.—What am I—? Oh!—my bracelets. . . .

(*She starts working a collection of bracelets over her hands onto her wrists, about six on each, as she talks.*)

I've thought a whole lot about it and now I know when I made my mistake. Yes, I made my mistake when I told you the truth about that thing with Skipper. Never should have confessed it, a fatal error, tellin' you about that thing with Skipper.

BRICK: Maggie, shut up about Skipper. I mean it, Maggie; you got to shut up about Skipper.

MARGARET: You ought to understand that Skipper and I—

BRICK: You don't think I'm serious, Maggie? You're fooled by the fact that I am saying this quiet? Look, Maggie. What you're doing is a dangerous thing to do. You're—you're—you're—foolin' with something that—nobody ought to fool with.

MARGARET: This time I'm going to finish what I have to say to you. Skipper and I made love, if love you could call it, because it made both of us feel a little bit closer to you. You see, you son of a bitch, you asked too much of people, of me, of him, of all the unlucky poor damned sons of bitches that happen to love you, and there was a whole pack of them, yes, there was a pack of them besides me and Skipper, you asked too goddam much of people that loved you, you—superior creature!—you godlike being!—And so we made love to each other to dream it was you, both of us! Yes, yes, yes! Truth, truth! What's so awful about it? I like it, I think the truth is—yeah! I shouldn't have told you. . . .

BRICK (*holding his head unnaturally still and uptilted a bit*): It was Skipper that told me about it. Not you, Maggie.

MARGARET: I told you!

BRICK: After he told me!

MARGARET: What does it matter who—?

(*Brick turns suddenly out upon the gallery and calls:*)

BRICK: Little girl! Hey, little girl!

LITTLE GIRL (*at a distance*): What, Uncle Brick?

BRICK: Tell the folks to come up!—Bring everybody upstairs!
MARGARET: I can't stop myself! I'd go on telling you this in front of them all, if I had to!
BRICK: Little girl! Go on, go on, will you? Do what I told you, call them!
MARGARET: Because it's got to be told and you, you!—you never let me!

(*She sobs, then controls herself, and continues almost calmly.*)

It was one of those beautiful, ideal things they tell about in the Greek legends, it couldn't be anything else, you being you, and that's what made it so sad, that's what made it so awful, because it was love that never could be carried through to anything satisfying or even talked about plainly. Brick, I tell you, you got to believe me, Brick, I *do* understand all about it! I—I think it was—*noble!* Can't you tell I'm sincere when I say I respect it? My only point, the only point that I'm making, is life has got to be allowed to continue even after the *dream* of life is—all—over. . . .

(*Brick is without his crutch. Leaning on furniture, he crosses to pick it up as she continues as if possessed by a will outside herself:*)

Why I remember when we double-dated at college, Gladys Fitzgerald and I and you and Skipper, it was more like a date between you and Skipper. Gladys and I were just sort of tagging along as if it was necessary to chaperone you!—to make a good public impression—
BRICK (*turns to face her, half lifting his crutch*): Maggie, you want me to hit you with this crutch? Don't you know I could kill you with this crutch?
MARGARET: Good Lord, man, d' you think I'd care if you did?
BRICK: One man has one great good true thing in his life. One great good thing which is true!—I had friendship with Skipper.—You are naming it dirty!
MARGARET: I'm not naming it dirty! I am naming it clean.
BRICK: Not love with you, Maggie, but friendship with Skipper was that one great true thing, and you are naming it dirty!
MARGARET: Then you haven't been listenin', not understood what I'm saying! I'm naming it so damn clean that it killed poor Skipper!—You two had something that had to be kept on ice, yes, incorruptible, yes!—and death was the only icebox where you could keep it. . . .
BRICK: I married you, Maggie. Why would I marry you, Maggie, if I was—?
MARGARET: Brick, don't brain me yet, let me finish!—I know, believe me I know, that it was only Skipper that harbored even any *unconscious* desire for anything not perfectly pure between you two!—Now let me skip a little. You married me early that summer we graduated out of

Ole Miss, and we were happy, weren't we, we were blissful, yes, hit heaven together ev'ry time that we loved! But that fall you an' Skipper turned down wonderful offers of jobs in order to keep on bein' football heroes — pro-football heroes. You organized the Dixie Stars that fall, so you could keep on bein' teammates forever! But somethin' was not right with it! — *Me included!* — between you. Skipper began hittin' the bottle . . . you got a spinal injury — couldn't play the Thanksgivin' game in Chicago, watched it on TV from a traction bed in Toledo. I joined Skipper. The Dixie Stars lost because poor Skipper was drunk. We drank together that night all night in the bar of the Blackstone and when cold day was comin' up over the Lake an' we were comin' out drunk to take a dizzy look at it, I said, "SKIPPER! STOP LOVIN' MY HUSBAND OR TELL HIM HE'S GOT TO LET YOU ADMIT IT TO HIM!" — one way or another!

HE SLAPPED ME HARD ON THE MOUTH! — then turned and ran without stopping once, I'm sure, all the way back into his room at the Blackstone. . . .

— When I came to his room that night, with a little scratch like a shy little mouse at his door, he made that pitiful, ineffectual little attempt to prove that what I had said wasn't true. . . .

(*Brick strikes at her with crutch, a blow that shatters the gemlike lamp on the table.*)

— In this way, I destroyed him, by telling him truth that he and his world which he was born and raised in, yours and his world, had told him could not be told?

— From then on Skipper was nothing at all but a receptacle for liquor and drugs. . . .

— *Who shot cock robin? I with my —*

(*She throws back her head with tight shut eyes.*)

— *merciful arrow!*

(*Brick strikes at her; misses.*)

Missed me! — Sorry, — I'm not tryin' to whitewash my behavior, Christ, no! Brick, I'm not good. I don't know why people have to pretend to be good, nobody's good. The rich or the well-to-do can afford to respect moral patterns, conventional moral patterns, but I could never afford to, yeah, but — I'm honest! Give me credit for just that, will you *please?* — Born poor, raised poor, expect to die poor unless I manage to get us something out of what Big Daddy leaves when he dies of cancer! But Brick?! — *Skipper is dead! I'm alive!* Maggie the cat is —

(*Brick hops awkwardly forward and strikes at her again with his crutch.*)

—*alive! I am alive, alive! I am . . .*

(*He hurls the crutch at her, across the bed she took refuge behind, and pitches forward on the floor as she completes her speech.*)

—*alive!*

(*A little girl, Dixie, bursts into the room, wearing an Indian war bonnet and firing a cap pistol at Margaret and shouting: "Bang, bang, bang!"*

(*Laughter downstairs floats through the open hall door. Margaret had crouched gasping to bed at child's entrance. She now rises and says with cool fury:*)

Little girl, your mother or someone should teach you—(*gasping*)—to knock at a door before you come into a room. Otherwise people might think that you—lack—good breeding. . . .

DIXIE: Yanh, yanh, yanh, what is Uncle Brick doin' on th' floor?

BRICK: I tried to kill your Aunt Maggie, but I failed—and I fell. Little girl, give me my crutch so I can get up off th' floor.

MARGARET: Yes, give your uncle his crutch, he's a cripple, honey, he broke his ankle last night jumping hurdles on the high school athletic field!

DIXIE: What were you jumping hurdles for, Uncle Brick?

BRICK: Because I used to jump them, and people like to do what they used to do, even after they've stopped being able to do it. . . .

MARGARET: That's right, that's your answer, now go away, little girl.

(*Dixie fires cap pistol at Margaret three times.*)

Stop, you stop that, monster! You little no-neck monster!

(*She seizes the cap pistol and hurls it through gallery doors.*)

DIXIE (*with a precocious instinct for the cruelest thing*): You're jealous!—You're just jealous because you can't have babies!

(*She sticks out her tongue at Margaret as she sashays past her with her stomach stuck out, to the gallery. Margaret slams the gallery doors and leans panting against them. There is a pause. Brick has replaced his spilt drink and sits, faraway, on the great four-poster bed.*)

MARGARET: You see?—they gloat over us being childless, even in front of their five little no-neck monsters!

(*Pause. Voices approach on the stairs.*)

Brick?—I've been to a doctor in Memphis, a—a gynecologist. . . .
I've been completely examined, and there is no reason why we can't
have a child whenever we want one. And this is my time by the calendar to conceive. Are you listening to me? Are you? Are you LISTEN-
ING TO ME!

BRICK: Yes. I hear you, Maggie.

(*His attention returns to her inflamed face.*)

—But how in hell on earth do you imagine—that you're going to have
a child by a man that can't stand you?

MARGARET: That's a problem that I will have to work out.

(*She wheels about to face the hall door.*)

Here they come!

(*The lights dim.*)

CURTAIN

ACT II

*There is no lapse of time. Margaret and Brick are in the same positions they held at
the end of Act I.*

MARGARET (*at door*): *Here they come!*

(*Big Daddy appears first, a tall man with a fierce, anxious look, moving carefully not to betray his weakness even, or especially, to himself.*)

BIG DADDY: Well, Brick.

BRICK: Hello, Big Daddy.—Congratulations!

BIG DADDY:—Crap. . . .

(*Some of the people are approaching through the hall, others along the gallery:
voices from both directions. Gooper and Reverend Tooker become visible outside gallery doors, and their voices come in clearly.*
  (*They pause outside as Gooper lights a cigar.*)

REVEREND TOOKER (*vivaciously*): Oh, but St. Paul's in Grenada has three
memorial windows, and the latest one is a Tiffany stained-glass window that cost twenty-five hundred dollars, a picture of Christ the Good
Shepherd with a Lamb in His arms.

GOOPER: Who give that window, Preach?

REVEREND TOOKER: Clyde Fletcher's widow. Also presented St. Paul's with a baptismal font.

GOOPER: Y'know what somebody ought t' give your church is a *coolin'* system, Preach.

REVEREND TOOKER: Yes, siree, Bob! And y'know what Gus Hamma's family gave in his memory to the church at Two Rivers? A complete new stone parish-house with a basketball court in the basement and a—

BIG DADDY (*uttering a loud barking laugh which is far from truly mirthful*): Hey, Preach! What's all this talk about memorials, Preach? Y' think somebody's about t' kick off around here? 'S that it?

(*Startled by this interjection, Reverend Tooker decides to laugh at the question almost as loud as he can.*

(*How he would answer the question we'll never know, as he's spared that embarrassment by the voice of Gooper's wife, Mae, rising high and clear as she appears with "Doc" Baugh, the family doctor, through the hall door.*)

MAE (*almost religiously*):—Let's see now, they've had their *tyyy*phoid shots, and their tetanus shots, their diphtheria shots and their hepatitis shots and their polio shots, they got *those* shots every month from May through September, and—Gooper? Hey! Gooper!—What all have the kiddies been shot faw?

MARGARET (*overlapping a bit*): Turn on the hi-fi, Brick! Let's have some music t' start off th' party with!

(*The talk becomes so general that the room sounds like a great aviary of chattering birds. Only Brick remains unengaged, leaning upon the liquor cabinet with his faraway smile, an ice cube in a paper napkin with which he now and then rubs his forehead. He doesn't respond to Margaret's command. She bounds forward and stoops over the instrument panel of the console.*)

GOOPER: We gave 'em that thing for a third anniversary present, got three speakers in it.

(*The room is suddenly blasted by the climax of a Wagnerian opera or a Beethoven symphony.*)

BIG DADDY: *Turn that dam thing off!*

(*Almost instant silence, almost instantly broken by the shouting charge of Big Mama, entering through hall door like a charging rhino.*)

BIG MAMA: *Wha's my Brick, wha's mah precious baby!!*

BIG DADDY: *Sorry! Turn it back on!*

(*Everyone laughs very loud. Big Daddy is famous for his jokes at Big Mama's expense, and nobody laughs louder at these jokes than Big Mama herself,*

*though sometimes they're pretty cruel and Big Mama has to pick up or fuss with
something to cover the hurt that the loud laugh doesn't quite cover.)*

*(On this occasion, a happy occasion because the dread in her heart has also
been lifted by the false report on Big Daddy's condition, she giggles, grotesquely,
coyly, in Big Daddy's direction and bears down upon Brick, all very quick and
alive.)*

BIG MAMA: Here he is, here's my precious baby! What's that you've got in
your hand? You put that liquor down, son, your hand was made fo'
holdin' somethin' better than that!

GOOPER: Look at Brick put it down!

*(Brick has obeyed Big Mama by draining the glass and handing it to her. Again
everyone laughs, some high, some low.)*

BIG MAMA: Oh, you bad boy, you, you're my bad little boy. Give Big
Mama a kiss, you bad boy, you!—Look at him shy away, will you?
Brick never liked bein' kissed or made a fuss over, I guess because he's
always had too much of it!

Son, you turn that thing off!

(Brick has switched on the TV set.)

I can't stand TV, radio was bad enough but TV has gone it one better, I
mean—*(plops wheezing in chair)*—one worse, ha ha! Now what'm I sittin' down here faw? I want t' sit next to my sweetheart on the sofa, hold
hands with him and love him up a little!

*(Big Mama has on a black and white figured chiffon. The large irregular pat-
terns, like the markings of some massive animal, the luster of her great diamonds and many pearls, the brilliants set in the silver frames of her glasses, her
riotous voice, booming laugh, have dominated the room since she entered. Big
Daddy has been regarding her with a steady grimace of chronic annoyance.)*

BIG MAMA *(still louder)*: Preacher, Preacher, hey, Preach! Give me you'
hand an' help me up from this chair!

REVEREND TOOKER: None of your tricks, Big Mama!

BIG MAMA: What tricks? You give me you' hand so I can get up an'—

*(Reverend Tooker extends her his hand. She grabs it and pulls him into her lap
with a shrill laugh that spans an octave in two notes.)*

Ever seen a preacher in a fat lady's lap? Hey, hey, folks! Ever seen a
preacher in a fat lady's lap?

*(Big Mama is notorious throughout the Delta for this sort of inelegant horse-
play. Margaret looks on with indulgent humor, sipping Dubonnet "on the rocks"*

and watching Brick, but Mae and Gooper exchange signs of humorless anxiety over these antics, the sort of behavior which Mae thinks may account for their failure to quite get in with the smartest young married set in Memphis, despite all. One of the Negroes, Lacy or Sookey, peeks in, cackling. They are waiting for a sign to bring in the cake and champagne. But Big Daddy's not amused. He doesn't understand why, in spite of the infinite mental relief he's received from the doctor's report, he still has these same old fox teeth in his guts. "This spastic thing sure is something," he says to himself, but aloud he roars at Big Mama:)

BIG DADDY: *BIG MAMA, WILL YOU QUIT HORSIN'?*—You're too old an' too fat fo' that sort of crazy kid stuff an' besides a woman with your blood pressure—she had two hundred last spring!—is riskin' a stroke when you mess around like that. . . .

BIG MAMA: *Here comes Big Daddy's birthday!*

(Negroes in white jackets enter with an enormous birthday cake ablaze with candles and carrying buckets of champagne with satin ribbons about the bottle necks.)

(Mae and Gooper strike up song, and everybody, including the Negroes and Children, joins in. Only Brick remains aloof.)

EVERYONE: Happy birthday to you.
Happy birthday to you.
Happy birthday, Big Daddy—

(Some sing: "Dear, Big Daddy!")

Happy birthday to you.

(Some sing: "How old are you?")

(Mae has come down center and is organizing her children like a chorus. She gives them a barely audible: "One, two, three!" and they are off in the new tune.)

CHILDREN: Skinamarinka—dinka—dink
Skinamarinka—do
We love you.
Skinamarinka—dinka—dink
Skinamarinka—do.

(All together, they turn to Big Daddy.)

Big Daddy, you!

(They turn back front, like a musical comedy chorus.)

We love you in the morning;
We love you in the night.

We love you when we're with you,
And we love you out of sight.
Skinamarinka—dinka—dink
Skinamarinka—do.

(*Mae turns to Big Mama.*)

Big Mama, too!

(*Big Mama bursts into tears. The Negroes leave.*)

BIG DADDY: Now Ida, what the hell is the matter with you?
MAE: She's just so happy.
BIG MAMA: I'm just so happy, Big Daddy, I have to cry or something.

(*Sudden and loud in the hush:*)

Brick, do you know the wonderful news that Doc Baugh got from the clinic about Big Daddy? Big Daddy's one hundred per cent!
MARGARET: Isn't that wonderful?
BIG MAMA: He's just one hundred per cent. Passed the examination with flying colors. Now that we know there's nothing wrong with Big Daddy but a spastic colon, I can tell you something. I was worried sick, half out of my mind, for fear that Big Daddy might have a thing like—

(*Margaret cuts through this speech, jumping up and exclaiming shrilly:*)

MARGARET: Brick, honey, aren't you going to give Big Daddy his birthday present?

(*Passing by him, she snatches his liquor glass from him.*)

(*She picks up a fancily wrapped package.*)

Here it is, Big Daddy, this is from Brick!
BIG MAMA: This is the biggest birthday Big Daddy's ever had, a hundred presents and bushels of telegrams from—
MAE (*at same time*): What is it, Brick?
GOOPER: I bet 500 to 50 that Brick don't *know* what it is.
BIG MAMA: The fun of presents is not knowing what they are till you open the package. Open your present, Big Daddy.
BIG DADDY: Open it you'self. I want to ask Brick somethin'! Come here, Brick.
MARGARET: Big Daddy's callin' you, Brick.

(*She is opening the package.*)

BRICK: Tell Big Daddy I'm crippled.
BIG DADDY: I see you're crippled. I want to know how you got crippled.

MARGARET (*making diversionary tactics*): *Oh, look, oh, look, why, it's a cash-mere robe!*

(*She holds the robe up for all to see.*)

MAE: You sound surprised, Maggie.

MARGARET: I never saw one before.

MAE: That's funny.—*Hah!*

MARGARET (*turning on her fiercely, with a brilliant smile*): Why is it funny? All my family ever had was family—and luxuries such as cashmere robes still surprise me!

BIG DADDY (*ominously*): Quiet!

MAE (*heedless in her fury*): I don't see how you could be so surprised when you bought it yourself at Loewenstein's in Memphis last Saturday. You know how I know?

BIG DADDY: I said, Quiet!

MAE:—I know because the salesgirl that sold it to you waited on me and said, Oh, Mrs. Pollitt, your sister-in-law just bought a cashmere robe for your husband's father!

MARGARET: Sister Woman! Your talents are wasted as a housewife and mother, you really ought to be with the FBI or—

BIG DADDY: QUIET!

(*Reverend Tooker's reflexes are slower than the others'. He finishes a sentence after the bellow.*)

REVEREND TOOKER (*to Doc Baugh*):—the Stork and the Reaper are running neck and neck!

(*He starts to laugh gaily when he notices the silence and Big Daddy's glare. His laugh dies falsely.*)

BIG DADDY: Preacher, I hope I'm not butting in on more talk about memorial stained-glass windows, am I, Preacher?

(*Reverend Tooker laughs feebly, then coughs dryly in the embarrassed silence.*)

Preacher?

BIG MAMA: Now, Big Daddy, don't you pick on Preacher!

BIG DADDY (*raising his voice*): You ever hear that expression all hawk and no spit? You bring that expression to mind with that little dry cough of yours, all hawk an' no spit. . . .

(*The pause is broken only by a short startled laugh from Margaret, the only one there who is conscious of and amused by the grotesque.*)

MAE (*raising her arms and jangling her bracelets*): I wonder if the mosquitoes are active tonight?

BIG DADDY: What's that, Little Mama? Did you make some remark?

MAE: Yes, I said I wondered if the mosquitoes would eat us alive if we went out on the gallery for a while.

BIG DADDY: Well, if they do, I'll have your bones pulverized for fertilizer!

BIG MAMA (*quickly*): Last week we had an airplane spraying the place and I think it done some good, at least I haven't had a—

BIG DADDY (*cutting her speech*): Brick, they tell me, if what they tell me is true, that you done some jumping last night on the high school athletic field?

BIG MAMA: Brick, Big Daddy is talking to you, son.

BRICK (*smiling vaguely over his drink*): What was that, Big Daddy?

BIG DADDY: They said you done some jumping on the high school track field last night.

BRICK: That's what they told me, too.

BIG DADDY: Was it jumping or humping that you were doing out there? What were you doing out there at three a.m., layin' a woman on that cinder track?

BIG MAMA: Big Daddy, you are off the sick-list, now, and I'm not going to excuse you for talkin' so—

BIG DADDY: Quiet!

BIG MAMA:—*nasty* in front of Preacher and—

BIG DADDY: *QUIET!*—I ast you, Brick, if you was cuttin' you'self a piece o' poon-tang last night on that cinder track? I thought maybe you were chasin' poon-tang on that track an' tripped over something in the heat of the chase—'sthat it?

(*Gooper laughs, loud and false, others nervously following suit. Big Mama stamps her foot, and purses her lips, crossing to Mae and whispering something to her as Brick meets his father's hard, intent, grinning stare with a slow, vague smile that he offers all situations from behind the screen of his liquor.*)

BRICK: No, sir, I don't think so. . . .

MAE (*at the same time, sweetly*): Reverend Tooker, let's you and I take a stroll on the widow's walk.

(*She and the preacher go out on the gallery as Big Daddy says:*)

BIG DADDY: Then what the hell were you doing out there at three o'clock in the morning?

BRICK: Jumping the hurdles, Big Daddy, runnin' and jumpin' the hurdles, but those high hurdles have gotten too high for me, now.

BIG DADDY: Cause you was drunk?

BRICK (*his vague smile fading a little*): Sober I wouldn't have tried to jump the *low* ones. . . .

BIG MAMA (*quickly*): Big Daddy, blow out the candles on your birthday cake!

MARGARET (*at the same time*): I want to propose a toast to Big Daddy Pollitt on his sixty-fifth birthday, the biggest cotton planter in—

BIG DADDY (*bellowing with fury and disgust*): *I told you to stop it, now stop it, quit this—!*

BIG MAMA (*coming in front of Big Daddy with the cake*): Big Daddy, I will not allow you to talk that way, not even on your birthday, I—

BIG DADDY: I'll talk like I want to on my birthday, Ida, or any other goddam day of the year and anybody here that don't like it knows what they can do!

BIG MAMA: You don't mean that!

BIG DADDY: What makes you think I don't mean it?

(*Meanwhile various discreet signals have been exchanged and Gooper has also gone out on the gallery.*)

BIG MAMA: I just know you don't mean it.

BIG DADDY: You don't know a goddam thing and you never did!

BIG MAMA: Big Daddy, you don't mean that.

BIG DADDY: Oh, yes, I do, oh, yes, I do, I mean it! I put up with a whole lot of crap around here because I thought I was dying. And you thought I was dying and you started taking over, well, you can stop taking over now, Ida, because I'm not gonna die, you can just stop now this business of taking over because you're not taking over because I'm not dying, I went through the laboratory and the goddam exploratory operation and there's nothing wrong with me but a spastic colon. And I'm not dying of cancer which you thought I was dying of. Ain't that so? Didn't you think that I was dying of cancer, Ida?

(*Almost everybody is out on the gallery but the two old people glaring at each other across the blazing cake.*)

(*Big Mama's chest heaves and she presses a fat fist to her mouth.*)

(*Big Daddy continues, hoarsely:*)

Ain't that so, Ida? Didn't you have an idea I was dying of cancer and now you could take control of this place and everything on it? I got that impression, I seemed to get that impression. Your loud voice everywhere, your fat old body butting in here and there!

BIG MAMA: Hush! The Preacher!

BIG DADDY: Rut the goddam preacher!

(*Big Mama gasps loudly and sits down on the sofa which is almost too small for her.*)

Did you hear what I said? I said rut the goddam preacher!

(*Somebody closes the gallery doors from outside just as there is a burst of fireworks and excited cries from the children.*)

BIG MAMA: I never seen you act like this before and I can't think what's got in you!

BIG DADDY: I went through all that laboratory and operation and all just so I would know if you or me was boss here! Well, now it turns out that I am and you ain't—and that's my birthday present—and my cake and champagne!—because for three years now you been gradually taking over. Bossing. Talking. Sashaying your fat old body around the place I made! I made this place! I was overseer on it! I was the overseer on the old Straw and Ochello plantation. I quit school at ten! I quit school at ten years old and went to work like a nigger in the fields. And I rose to be overseer of the Straw and Ochello plantation. And old Straw died and I was Ochello's partner and the place got bigger and bigger and bigger and bigger and bigger! I did all that myself with no goddam help from you, and now you think you're just about to take over. Well, I am just about to tell you that you are not just about to take over, you are not just about to take over a God damn thing. Is that clear to you, Ida? Is that very plain to you, now? Is that understood completely? I been through the laboratory from A to Z. I've had the goddam exploratory operation, and nothing is wrong with me but a spastic colon—made spastic, I guess, by *disgust!* By all the goddam lies and liars that I have had to put up with, and all the goddam hypocrisy that I lived with all these forty years that we been livin' together!

Hey! Ida!! Blow out the candles on the birthday cake! Purse up your lips and draw a deep breath and blow out the goddam candles on the cake!

BIG MAMA: Oh, Big Daddy, oh, oh, oh, Big Daddy!

BIG DADDY: What's the matter with you?

BIG MAMA: *In all these years you never believed that I loved you??*

BIG DADDY: Huh?

BIG MAMA: *And I did, I did so much, I did love you!*—I even loved your hate and your hardness, Big Daddy!

(*She sobs and rushes awkwardly out onto the gallery.*)

BIG DADDY (*to himself*): *Wouldn't it be funny if that was true.* . . .

(*A pause is followed by a burst of light in the sky from the fireworks.*)

BRICK! HEY, BRICK!

(*He stands over his blazing birthday cake.*)
   (*After some moments, Brick hobbles in on his crutch, holding his glass.*
   Margaret follows him with a bright, anxious smile.)

   I didn't call you, Maggie. I called Brick.
MARGARET: I'm just delivering him to you.

(*She kisses Brick on the mouth which he immediately wipes with the back of his hand. She flies girlishly back out. Brick and his father are alone.*)

BIG DADDY: Why did you do that?
BRICK: Do what, Big Daddy?
BIG DADDY: Wipe her kiss off your mouth like she'd spit on you.
BRICK: I don't know. I wasn't conscious of it.
BIG DADDY: That woman of yours has a better shape on her than Gooper's but somehow or other they got the same look about them.
BRICK: What sort of look is that, Big Daddy?
BIG DADDY: I don't know how to describe it but it's the same look.
BRICK: They don't look peaceful, do they?
BIG DADDY: No, they sure in hell don't.
BRICK: They look nervous as cats?
BIG DADDY: That's right, they look nervous as cats.
BRICK: Nervous as a couple of cats on a hot tin roof?
BIG DADDY: That's right, boy, they look like a couple of cats on a hot tin roof. It's funny that you and Gooper being so different would pick out the same type of woman.
BRICK: Both of us married into society, Big Daddy.
BIG DADDY: Crap . . . I wonder what gives them both that look?
BRICK: Well. They're sittin' in the middle of a big piece of land, Big Daddy, twenty-eight thousand acres is a pretty big piece of land and so they're squaring off on it, each determined to knock off a bigger piece of it than the other whenever you let it go.
BIG DADDY: I got a surprise for those women. I'm not gonna let it go for a long time yet if that's what they're waiting for.
BRICK: That's right, Big Daddy. You just sit tight and let them scratch each other's eyes out. . . .
BIG DADDY: You bet your life I'm going to sit tight on it and let those sons of bitches scratch their eyes out, ha ha ha. . . .
   But Gooper's wife's a good breeder, you got to admit she's fertile. Hell, at supper tonight she had them all at the table and they had to put a couple of extra leafs in the table to make room for them, she's got five head of them, now, and another one's comin'.
BRICK: Yep, number six is comin'. . . .

BIG DADDY: Brick, you know, I swear to God, I don't know the way it happens?

BRICK: The way what happens, Big Daddy?

BIG DADDY: You git you a piece of land, by hook or crook, an' things start growin' on it, things accumulate on it, and the first thing you know it's completely out of hand, completely out of hand!

BRICK: Well, they say nature hates a vacuum, Big Daddy.

BIG DADDY: That's what they say, but sometimes I think that a vacuum is a hell of a lot better than some of the stuff that nature replaces it with. Is someone out there by that door?

BRICK: Yep.

BIG DADDY: Who?

(*He has lowered his voice.*)

BRICK: Someone int'rested in what we say to each other.

BIG DADDY: Gooper?—*GOOPER!*

(*After a discreet pause, Mae appears in the gallery door.*)

MAE: Did you call Gooper, Big Daddy?

BIG DADDY: Aw, it was you.

MAE: Do you want Gooper, Big Daddy?

BIG DADDY: No, and I don't want you. I want some privacy here, while I'm having a confidential talk with my son Brick. Now it's too hot in here to close them doors, but if I have to close those rutten doors in order to have a private talk with my son Brick, just let me know and I'll close 'em. Because I hate eavesdroppers, I don't like any kind of sneakin' an' spyin'.

MAE: Why, Big Daddy—

BIG DADDY: You stood on the wrong side of the moon, it threw your shadow!

MAE: I was just—

BIG DADDY: You was just nothing but *spyin'* an' you *know* it!

MAE (*begins to sniff and sob*): Oh, Big Daddy, you're so unkind for some reason to those that really love you!

BIG DADDY: Shut up, shut up, shut up! I'm going to move you and Gooper out of that room next to this! It's none of your goddam business what goes on in here at night between Brick an' Maggie. You listen at night like a couple of rutten peekhole spies and go and give a report on what you hear to Big Mama an' she comes to me and says they say such and such and so and so about what they heard goin' on between Brick an' Maggie, and Jesus, it makes me sick. I'm goin' to move you an' Gooper out of that room, I can't stand sneakin' an' spyin', it makes me sick. . . .

(*Mae throws back her head and rolls her eyes heavenward and extends her arms as if invoking God's pity for this unjust martyrdom; then she presses a handkerchief to her nose and flies from the room with a loud swish of skirts.*)

BRICK (*now at the liquor cabinet*): They listen, do they?
BIG DADDY: Yeah. They listen and give reports to Big Mama on what goes on in here between you and Maggie. They say that—

(*He stops as if embarrassed.*)

—You won't sleep with her, that you sleep on the sofa. Is that true or not true? If you don't like Maggie, get rid of Maggie!—What are you doin' there now?
BRICK: Fresh'nin' up my drink.
BIG DADDY: Son, you know you got a real liquor problem?
BRICK: Yes, sir, yes, I know.
BIG DADDY: Is that why you quit sports-announcing, because of this liquor problem?
BRICK: Yes, sir, yes, sir, I guess so.

(*He smiles vaguely and amiably at his father across his replenished drink.*)

BIG DADDY: Son, don't guess about it, it's too important.
BRICK (*vaguely*): Yes, sir.
BIG DADDY: And listen to me, don't look at the damn chandelier. . . .

(*Pause. Big Daddy's voice is husky.*)

—Somethin' else we picked up at th' big fire sale in Europe.

(*Another pause.*)

Life is important. There's nothing else to hold onto. A man that drinks is throwing his life away. Don't do it, hold onto your life. There's nothing else to hold onto. . . .
    Sit down over here so we don't have to raise our voices, the walls have ears in this place.
BRICK (*hobbling over to sit on the sofa beside him*): All right, Big Daddy.
BIG DADDY: Quit!—how'd that come about? Some disappointment?
BRICK: I don't know. Do you?
BIG DADDY: I'm askin' you, God damn it! How in hell would I know if you don't?
BRICK: I just got out there and found that I had a mouth full of cotton. I was always two or three beats behind what was goin' on on the field and so I—
BIG DADDY: Quit!
BRICK (*amiably*): Yes, quit.

BIG DADDY: Son?

BRICK: Huh?

BIG DADDY (*inhales loudly and deeply from his cigar; then bends suddenly a little forward, exhaling loudly and raising a hand to his forehead*): — Whew! — ha ha! — I took in too much smoke, it made me a little lightheaded. . . .

(*The mantel clock chimes.*)

Why is it so damn hard for people to talk?

BRICK: Yeah. . . .

(*The clock goes on sweetly chiming till it has completed the stroke of ten.*)

— Nice peaceful-soundin' clock, I like to hear it all night. . . .

(*He slides low and comfortable on the sofa; Big Daddy sits up straight and rigid with some unspoken anxiety. All his gestures are tense and jerky as he talks. He wheezes and pants and sniffs through his nervous speech, glancing quickly, shyly, from time to time, at his son.*)

BIG DADDY: We got that clock the summer we wint to Europe, me an' Big Mama on that damn Cook's Tour, never had such an awful time in my life, I'm tellin' you, son, those gooks over there, they gouge your eyeballs out in their grand hotels. And Big Mama bought more stuff than you could haul in a couple of boxcars, that's no crap. Everywhere she wint on this whirlwind tour, she bought, bought, bought. Why, half that stuff she bought is still crated up in the cellar, under water last spring!

(*He laughs.*)

That Europe is nothin' on earth but a great big auction, that's all it is, that bunch of old worn-out places, it's just a big fire-sale, the whole rutten thing, an' Big Mama wint wild in it, why, you couldn't hold that woman with a mule's harness! Bought, bought, bought! — lucky I'm a rich man, yes siree, Bob, an' half that stuff is mildewin' in th' basement. It's lucky I'm a rich man, it sure is lucky, well, I'm a rich man, Brick, yep, I'm a mighty rich man.

(*His eyes light up for a moment.*)

Y'know how much I'm worth? Guess, Brick! Guess how much I'm worth!

(*Brick smiles vaguely over his drink.*)

Close on ten million in cash an' blue-chip stocks, outside, mind you, of twenty-eight thousand acres of the richest land this side of the valley Nile!

(A puff and crackle and the night sky blooms with an eerie greenish glow. Children shriek on the gallery.)

But a man can't buy his life with it, he can't buy back his life with it when his life has been spent, that's one thing not offered in the Europe fire-sale or in the American markets or any markets on earth, a man can't buy his life with it, he can't buy back his life when his life is finished. . . .

That's a sobering thought, a very sobering thought, and that's a thought that I was turning over in my head, over and over and over—until today. . . .

I'm wiser and sadder, Brick, for this experience which I just gone through. They's one thing else that I remember in Europe.

BRICK: What is that, Big Daddy?

BIG DADDY: The hills around Barcelona in the country of Spain and the children running over those bare hills in their bare skins beggin' like starvin' dogs with howls and screeches, and how fat the priests are on the streets of Barcelona, so many of them and so fat and so pleasant, ha ha!—Y'know I could feed that country? I got money enough to feed that goddam country, but the human animal is a selfish beast and I don't reckon the money I passed out there to those howling children in the hills around Barcelona would more than upholster one of the chairs in this room, I mean pay to put a new cover on this chair!

Hell, I threw them money like you'd scatter feed corn for chickens, I threw money at them just to get rid of them long enough to climb back into th' car and—drive away. . . .

And then in Morocco, them Arabs, why, prostitution begins at four or five, that's no exaggeration, why, I remember one day in Marrakech, that old walled Arab city, I set on a broken-down wall to have a cigar, it was fearful hot there and this Arab woman stood in the road and looked at me till I was embarrassed, she stood stock still in the dusty hot road and looked at me till I was embarrassed. But listen to this. She had a naked child with her, a little naked girl with her, barely able to toddle, and after a while she set this child on the ground and give her a push and whispered something to her.

This child come toward me, barely able t' walk, come toddling up to me and—

Jesus, it makes you sick t' remember a thing like this!

It stuck out its hand and tried to unbutton my trousers!

That child was not yet five! Can you believe me? Or do you think that I am making this up? I went back to the hotel and said to Big Mama, Git packed! We're clearing out of this country. . . .

BRICK: Big Daddy, you're on a talkin' jag tonight.

BIG DADDY (*ignoring this remark*): Yes, sir, that's how it is, the human ani-
    mal is a beast that dies but the fact that he's dying don't give him pity
    for others, no, sir, it—
    —Did you say something?

BRICK: Yes.

BIG DADDY: What?

BRICK: Hand me over that crutch so I can get up.

BIG DADDY: Where you goin'?

BRICK: I'm takin' a little short trip to Echo Spring.

BIG DADDY: To where?

BRICK: Liquor cabinet. . . .

BIG DADDY: Yes, sir, boy—

(*He hands Brick the crutch.*)

—the human animal is a beast that dies and if he's got money he buys
    and buys and buys and I think the reason he buys everything he can
    buy is that in the back of his mind he has the crazy hope that one of his
    purchases will be life everlasting!—Which it never can be. . . . The
    human animal is a beast that—

BRICK (*at the liquor cabinet*): Big Daddy, you sure are shootin' th' breeze
    here tonight.

(*There is a pause and voices are heard outside.*)

BIG DADDY: I been quiet here lately, spoke not a word, just sat and stared
    into space. I had something heavy weighing on my mind but tonight
    that load was took off me. That's why I'm talking.—The sky looks
    diff'rent to me. . . .

BRICK: You know what I like to hear most?

BIG DADDY: What?

BRICK: Solid quiet. Perfect unbroken quiet.

BIG DADDY: Why?

BRICK: Because it's more peaceful.

BIG DADDY: Man, you'll hear a lot of that in the grave.

(*He chuckles agreeably.*)

BRICK: Are you through talkin' to me?

BIG DADDY: Why are you so anxious to shut me up?

BRICK: Well, sir, ever so often you say to me, Brick, I want to have a talk
    with you, but when we talk, it never materializes. Nothing is said. You
    sit in a chair and gas about this and that and I look like I listen. I try to
    look like I listen, but I don't listen, not much. Communication

is—awful hard between people an'—somehow between you and me, it just don't—

BIG DADDY: Have you ever been scared? I mean have you ever felt downright terror of something?

(*He gets up.*)

Just one moment. I'm going to close these doors. . . .

(*He closes doors on gallery as if he were going to tell an important secret.*)

BRICK: What?

BIG DADDY: Brick?

BRICK: Huh?

BIG DADDY: Son, I thought I had it!

BRICK: Had what? Had what, Big Daddy?

BIG DADDY: Cancer!

BRICK: Oh . . .

BIG DADDY: I thought the old man made out of bones had laid his cold and heavy hand on my shoulder!

BRICK: Well, Big Daddy, you kept a tight mouth about it.

BIG DADDY: A pig squeals. A man keeps a tight mouth about it, in spite of a man not having a pig's advantage.

BRICK: What advantage is that?

BIG DADDY: Ignorance—of mortality—is a comfort. A man don't have that comfort, he's the only living thing that conceives of death, that knows what it is. The others go without knowing which is the way that anything living should go, go without knowing, without any knowledge of it, and yet a pig squeals, but a man sometimes, he can keep a tight mouth about it. Sometimes he—

(*There is a deep, smoldering ferocity in the old man.*)

—can keep a tight mouth about it. I wonder if—

BRICK: What, Big Daddy?

BIG DADDY: A whiskey highball would injure this spastic condition?

BRICK: No, sir, it might do it good.

BIG DADDY (*grins suddenly, wolfishly*): *Jesus, I can't tell you! The sky is open! Christ, it's open again! It's open, boy, it's open!*

(*Brick looks down at his drink.*)

BRICK: You feel better, Big Daddy?

BIG DADDY: Better? Hell! I can breathe!—All of my life I been like a doubled-up fist. . . .

(*He pours a drink.*)

—Poundin', smashin', drivin'!—now I'm going to loosen these doubled-up hands and touch things *easy* with them. . . .

(*He spreads his hands as if caressing the air.*)

You know what I'm contemplating?

BRICK (*vaguely*): No, sir. What are you contemplating?

BIG DADDY: Ha ha!—*Pleasure!*—pleasure with *women!*

(*Brick's smile fades a little but lingers.*)

Brick, this stuff burns me!—

—Yes, boy. I'll tell you something that you might not guess. I still have desire for women and this is my sixty-fifth birthday.

BRICK: I think that's mighty remarkable, Big Daddy.

BIG DADDY: Remarkable?

BRICK: *Admirable*, Big Daddy.

BIG DADDY: You're damn right it is, remarkable and admirable both. I realize now that I never had me enough. I let many chances slip by because of scruples about it, scruples, convention—crap. . . . All that stuff is bull, bull, bull!—It took the shadow of death to make me see it. Now that shadow's lifted, I'm going to cut loose and have, what is it they call it, have me a—ball!

BRICK: A ball, huh?

BIG DADDY: That's right, a ball, a ball! Hell!—I slept with Big Mama till, let's see, five years ago, till I was sixty and she was fifty-eight, and never even liked her, never did!

(*The phone has been ringing down the hall. Big Mama enters, exclaiming:*)

BIG MAMA: Don't you men hear that phone ring? I heard it way out on the gall'ry.

BIG DADDY: There's five rooms off this front gall'ry that you could go through. Why do you go through this one?

(*Big Mama makes a playful face as she bustles out the hall door.*)

Hunh!—Why, when Big Mama goes out of a room, I can't remember what that woman looks like, but when Big Mama comes back into the room, boy, then I see what she looks like, and I wish I didn't!

(*Bends over laughing at this joke till it hurts his guts and he straightens with a grimace. The laugh subsides to a chuckle as he puts the liquor glass a little distrustfully down on the table.*)

(*Brick has risen and hobbled to the gallery doors.*)

Hey! Where you goin'?

BRICK: Out for a breather.

BIG DADDY: Not yet you ain't. Stay here till this talk is finished, young fellow.

BRICK: I thought it was finished, Big Daddy.

BIG DADDY: It ain't even begun.

BRICK: My mistake. Excuse me. I just wanted to feel that river breeze.

BIG DADDY: Turn on the ceiling fan and set back down in that chair.

(*Big Mama's voice rises, carrying down the hall.*)

BIG MAMA: Miss Sally, you're a case! You're a caution, Miss Sally. Why didn't you give me a chance to explain it to you?

BIG DADDY: Jesus, she's talking to my old maid sister again.

BIG MAMA: Well, goodbye, now, Miss Sally. You come down real soon, Big Daddy's dying to see you! Yaisss, goodbye, Miss Sally. . . .

(*She hangs up and bellows with mirth. Big Daddy groans and covers his ears as she approaches.*)

(*Bursting in:*)

Big Daddy, that was Miss Sally callin' from Memphis again! You know what she done, Big Daddy? She called her doctor in Memphis to git him to tell her what that spastic thing is! Ha-*HAAAA!*—And called back to tell me how relieved she was that—Hey! Let me in!

(*Big Daddy has been holding the door half closed against her.*)

BIG DADDY: Naw I ain't. I told you not to come and go through this room. You just back out and go through those five other rooms.

BIG MAMA: Big Daddy? Big Daddy? Oh, Big Daddy!—You didn't mean those things you said to me, did you?

(*He shuts door firmly against her but she still calls.*)

Sweetheart? Sweetheart? Big Daddy? You didn't mean those awful things you said to me?—I know you didn't. I know you didn't mean those things in your heart. . . .

(*The childlike voice fades with a sob and her heavy footsteps retreat down the hall. Brick has risen once more on his crutches and starts for the gallery again.*)

BIG DADDY: All I ask of that woman is that she leave me alone. But she can't admit to herself that she makes me sick. That comes of having slept with her too many years. Should of quit much sooner but that old woman she never got enough of it—and I was good in bed . . . I never should of wasted so much of it on her. . . . They say you got just so many and each one is numbered. Well, I got a few left in me, a few, and

I'm going to pick me a good one to spend 'em on! I'm going to pick me a choice one, I don't care how much she costs, I'll smother her in—minks! Ha ha! I'll strip her naked and smother her in minks and choke her with diamonds! Ha ha! I'll strip her naked and choke her with diamonds and smother her with minks and hump her from hell to breakfast. *Ha aha ha ha ha!*

MAE (*gaily at door*): Who's that laughin' in there?

GOOPER: Is Big Daddy laughin' in there?

BIG DADDY: Crap!—them two—*drips.* . . .

(*He goes over and touches Brick's shoulder.*)

Yes, son. Brick, boy.—I'm—*happy!* I'm happy, son, I'm happy!

(*He chokes a little and bites his under lip, pressing his head quickly, shyly against his son's head and then, coughing with embarrassment, goes uncertainly back to the table where he set down the glass. He drinks and makes a grimace as it burns his guts. Brick sighs and rises with effort.*)

What makes you so restless? Have you got ants in your britches?

BRICK: Yes, sir . . .

BIG DADDY: Why?

BRICK:—Something—hasn't—happened. . . .

BIG DADDY: Yeah? What is that!

BRICK (*sadly*):—the click. . . .

BIG DADDY: Did you say click?

BRICK: Yes, click.

BIG DADDY: What click?

BRICK: A click that I get in my head that makes me peaceful.

BIG DADDY: I sure in hell don't know what you're talking about, but it disturbs me.

BRICK: It's just a mechanical thing.

BIG DADDY: What is a mechanical thing?

BRICK: This click that I get in my head that makes me peaceful. I got to drink till I get it. It's just a mechanical thing, something like a—like a—like a—

BIG DADDY: Like a—

BRICK: Switch clicking off in my head, turning the hot light off and the cool night on and—

(*He looks up, smiling sadly.*)

—all of a sudden there's—peace!

BIG DADDY (*whistles long and soft with astonishment; he goes back to Brick and clasps his son's two shoulders*): Jesus! I didn't know it had gotten that bad with you. Why, boy, you're—*alcoholic!*

BRICK: That's the truth, Big Daddy. I'm alcoholic.

BIG DADDY: This shows how I—let things go!

BRICK: I have to hear that little click in my head that makes me peaceful. Usually I hear it sooner than this, sometimes as early as—noon, but— —Today it's—dilatory. . . .
—I just haven't got the right level of alcohol in my bloodstream yet!

(*This last statement is made with energy as he freshens his drink.*)

BIG DADDY: Uh—huh. Expecting death made me blind. I didn't have no idea that a son of mine was turning into a drunkard under my nose.

BRICK (*gently*): Well, now you do, Big Daddy, the news has penetrated.

BIG DADDY: UH-huh, yes, now I do, the news has—penetrated. . . .

BRICK: And so if you'll excuse me—

BIG DADDY: No, I won't excuse you.

BRICK: —I'd better sit by myself till I hear that click in my head, it's just a mechanical thing but it don't happen except when I'm alone or talking to no one. . . .

BIG DADDY: You got a long, long time to sit still, boy, and talk to no one, but now you're talkin' to me. At least I'm talking to you. And you set there and listen until I tell you the conversation is over!

BRICK: But this talk is like all the others we've ever had together in our lives! It's nowhere, nowhere!—it's—it's *painful*, Big Daddy. . . .

BIG DADDY: All right, then let it be painful, but don't you move from that chair!—I'm going to remove that crutch. . . .

(*He seizes the crutch and tosses it across room.*)

BRICK: I can hop on one foot, and if I fall, I can crawl!

BIG DADDY: If you ain't careful you're gonna crawl off this plantation and then, by Jesus, you'll have to hustle your drinks along Skid Row!

BRICK: That'll come, Big Daddy.

BIG DADDY: Naw, it won't. You're my son and I'm going to straighten you out; now that *I'm* straightened out, I'm going to straighten out you!

BRICK: Yeah?

BIG DADDY: Today the report come in from Ochsner Clinic. Y'know what they told me?

(*His face glows with triumph.*)

The only thing that they could detect with all the instruments of science in that great hospital is a little spastic condition of the colon! And nerves torn to pieces by all that worry about it.

(*A little girl bursts into room with a sparkler clutched in each fist, hops and shrieks like a monkey gone mad and rushes back out again as Big Daddy strikes at her.* (*Silence. The two men stare at each other. A woman laughs gaily outside.*)

I want you to know I breathed a sigh of relief almost as powerful as the Vicksburg tornado!

BRICK: You weren't ready to go?

BIG DADDY: GO WHERE?—crap. . . .
   —When you are gone from here, boy, you are long gone and no where! The human machine is not no different from the animal machine or the fish machine or the bird machine or the reptile machine or the insect machine! It's just a whole God damn lot more complicated and consequently more trouble to keep together. Yep. I thought I had it. The earth shook under my foot, the sky come down like the black lid of a kettle and I couldn't breathe!—Today!!—that lid was lifted, I drew my first free breath in—how many years?—God!— three. . . .

(*There is laughter outside, running footsteps, the soft, plushy sound and light of exploding rockets.*)
   (*Brick stares at him soberly for a long moment; then makes a sort of startled sound in his nostrils and springs up on one foot and hops across the room to grab his crutch, swinging on the furniture for support. He gets the crutch and flees as if in horror for the gallery. His father seizes him by the sleeve of his white silk pajamas.*)

Stay here, you son of a bitch!—till I say go!

BRICK: I can't

BIG DADDY: You sure in hell will, God damn it.

BRICK: No, I can't. We talk, you talk, in—circles! We get no where, no where! It's always the same, you say you want to talk to me and don't have a ruttin' thing to say to me!

BIG DADDY: Nothin' to say when I'm tellin' you I'm going to live when I thought I was dying?!

BRICK: Oh—*that!*—Is that what you have to say to me?

BIG DADDY: Why, you son of a bitch! Ain't that, ain't that—*important?!*

BRICK: Well, you said that, that's said, and now I—

BIG DADDY: Now you set back down.

BRICK: You're all balled up, you—

BIG DADDY: I ain't balled up!

BRICK: You are, you're all balled up!

BIG DADDY: Don't tell me what I am, you drunken whelp! I'm going to tear this coat sleeve off if you don't set down!

BRICK: Big Daddy—

BIG DADDY: Do what I tell you! I'm the boss here, now! I want you to know I'm back in the driver's seat now!

(*Big Mama rushes in, clutching her great heaving bosom.*)

What in hell do you want in here, Big Mama?

BIG MAMA: Oh, Big Daddy! Why are you shouting like that? I just cain't stainnnnnnnnd—it. . . .

BIG DADDY (*raising the back of his hand above his head*): GIT!—outa here.

(*She rushes back out, sobbing.*)

BRICK (*softly, sadly*): Christ. . . .

BIG DADDY (*fiercely*): Yeah! Christ!—is right . . .

(*Brick breaks loose and hobbles toward the gallery.*)

(*Big Daddy jerks his crutch from under Brick so he steps with the injured ankle. He utters a hissing cry of anguish, clutches a chair and pulls it over on top of him on the floor.*)

Son of a—tub of—hog fat. . . .

BRICK: Big Daddy! Give me my crutch.

(*Big Daddy throws the crutch out of reach.*)

Give me that crutch, Big Daddy.

BIG DADDY: Why do you drink?

BRICK: Don't know, give me my crutch!

BIG DADDY: You better think why you drink or give up drinking!

BRICK: Will you please give me my crutch so I can get up off this floor?

BIG DADDY: First you answer my question. Why do you drink? Why are you throwing your life away, boy, like somethin' disgusting you picked up on the street?

BRICK (*getting onto his knees*): Big Daddy, I'm in pain, I stepped on that foot.

BIG DADDY: Good! I'm glad you're not too numb with the liquor in you to feel some pain!

BRICK: You—spilled my—drink . . .

BIG DADDY: I'll make a bargain with you. You tell me why you drink and I'll hand you one. I'll pour you the liquor myself and hand it to you.

BRICK: Why do I drink?

BIG DADDY: Yea! Why?

BRICK: Give me a drink and I'll tell you.
BIG DADDY: Tell me first!
BRICK: I'll tell you in one word.
BIG DADDY: What word?
BRICK: DISGUST!

(*The clock chimes softly, sweetly. Big Daddy gives it a short, outraged glance.*)

Now how about that drink?
BIG DADDY: What are you disgusted with? You got to tell me that, first.
  Otherwise being disgusted don't make no sense!
BRICK: Give me my crutch.
BIG DADDY: You heard me, you got to tell me what I asked you first.
BRICK: I told you, I said to kill my disgust!
BIG DADDY: DISGUST WITH WHAT!
BRICK: You strike a hard bargain.
BIG DADDY: What are you disgusted with?—an' I'll pass you the liquor.
BRICK: I can hop on one foot, and if I fall, I can crawl.
BIG DADDY: You want liquor that bad?
BRICK (*dragging himself up, clinging to bedstead*): Yeah, I want it that bad.
BIG DADDY: If I give you a drink, will you tell me what it is you're dis-
  gusted with, Brick?
BRICK: Yes, sir, I will try to.

(*The old man pours him a drink and solemnly passes it to him.*
  (*There is silence as Brick drinks.*)

Have you ever heard the word "mendacity"?
BIG DADDY: Sure. Mendacity is one of them five dollar words that cheap
  politicians throw back and forth at each other.
BRICK: You know what it means?
BIG DADDY: Don't it mean lying and liars?
BRICK: Yes, sir, lying and liars.
BIG DADDY: Has someone been lying to you?
CHILDREN: (*chanting in chorus offstage*): We want Big Dad-dee! We want
  Big Dad-dee!

(*Gooper appears in the gallery door.*)

GOOPER: Big Daddy, the kiddies are shouting for you out there.
BIG DADDY (*fiercely*): Keep out, Gooper!
GOOPER: 'Scuse *me!*

(*Big Daddy slams the doors after Gooper.*)

BIG DADDY: Who's been lying to you, has Margaret been lying to you,
  has your wife been lying to you about something, Brick?

BRICK: Not her. That wouldn't matter.
BIG DADDY: Then who's been lying to you, and what about?
BRICK: No one single person and no one lie. . . .
BIG DADDY: Then what, what then, for Christ's sake?
BRICK: —The whole, the whole—thing. . . .
BIG DADDY: Why are you rubbing your head? You got a headache?
BRICK: No, I'm tryin' to—
BIG DADDY: —Concentrate, but you can't because your brain's all soaked with liquor, is that the trouble? Wet brain!

(*He snatches the glass from Brick's hand.*)

What do you know about this mendacity thing? Hell! I could write a book on it! Don't you know that? I could write a book on it and still not cover the subject? Well, I could, I could write a goddam book on it and still not cover the subject anywhere near enough!!—Think of all the lies I got to put up with!—Pretenses! Ain't that mendacity? Having to pretend stuff you don't think or feel or have any idea of? Having for instance to act like I care for Big Mama!—I haven't been able to stand the sight, sound, or smell of that woman for forty years now!—even when I *laid* her!—regular as a piston. . . .

Pretend to love that son of a bitch of a Gooper and his wife Mae and those five same screechers out there like parrots in a jungle? Jesus! Can't stand to look at 'em!

Church!—it bores the bejesus out of me but I go!—I go an' sit there and listen to the fool preacher!

Clubs!—Elks! Masons! Rotary!—*crap!*

(*A spasm of pain makes him clutch his belly. He sinks into a chair and his voice is softer and hoarser.*)

You I *do* like for some reason, did always have some kind of real feeling for—affection—respect—yes, always. . . .

You and being a success as a planter is all I ever had any devotion to in my whole life!—and that's the truth. . . .

I don't know why, but it is!

I've lived with mendacity!—Why can't *you* live with it? Hell, you *got* to live with it, there's nothing *else* to *live* with except mendacity, is there?
BRICK: Yes, sir. Yes, sir there is something else that you can live with!
BIG DADDY: What?
BRICK (*lifting his glass*): This!—Liquor. . . .
BIG DADDY: That's not living, that's dodging away from life.
BRICK: I want to dodge away from it.
BIG DADDY: Then why don't you kill yourself, man?

BRICK: I like to drink. . . .

BIG DADDY: Oh, God, I can't talk to you. . . .

BRICK: I'm sorry, Big Daddy.

BIG DADDY: Not as sorry as I am. I'll tell you something. A little while back when I thought my number was up—

(*This speech should have torrential pace and fury.*)

— before I found out it was just this—spastic—colon. I thought about you. Should I or should I not, if the jig was up, give you this place when I go—since I hate Gooper an' Mae an' know that they hate me, and since all five same monkeys are little Maes an' Goopers.—And I thought, No!—Then I thought, Yes!—I couldn't make up my mind. I hate Gooper and his five same monkeys and that bitch Mae! Why should I turn over twenty-eight thousand acres of the richest land this side of the valley Nile to not my kind?—But why in hell, on the other hand, Brick—should I subsidize a goddam fool on the bottle?—Liked or not liked, well, maybe even—*loved!*—Why should I do that?—Subsidize worthless behavior? Rot? Corruption?

BRICK (*smiling*): I understand.

BIG DADDY: Well, if you do, you're smarter than I am, God damn it, because I don't understand. And this I will tell you frankly. I didn't make up my mind at all on that question and still to this day I ain't made out no will!—Well, now I don't *have* to. The pressure is gone. I can just wait and see if you pull yourself together or if you don't.

BRICK: That's right, Big Daddy.

BIG DADDY: You sound like you thought I was kidding.

BRICK (*rising*): No, sir, I know you're not kidding.

BIG DADDY: But you don't care—?

BRICK (*hobbling toward the gallery door*): No, sir, I don't care. . . .
    Now how about taking a look at your birthday fireworks and getting some of that cool breeze off the river?

(*He stands in the gallery doorway as the night sky turns pink and green and gold with successive flashes of light.*)

BIG DADDY: *WAIT!*—Brick. . . .

(*His voice drops. Suddenly there is something shy, almost tender, in his restraining gesture.*)

Don't let's—leave it like this, like them other talks we've had, we've always—talked around things, we've—just talked around things for some rutten reason, I don't know what, it's always like something was

left not spoken, something avoided because neither of us was honest
enough with the—other. . . .

BRICK: I never lied to you, Big Daddy.

BIG DADDY: Did I ever to *you?*

BRICK: No, sir. . . .

BIG DADDY: Then there is at least two people that never lied to each other.

BRICK: But we've never *talked* to each other.

BIG DADDY: We can *now.*

BRICK: Big Daddy, there don't seem to be anything much to say.

BIG DADDY: You say that you drink to kill your disgust with lying.

BRICK: You said to give you a reason.

BIG DADDY: Is liquor the only thing that'll kill this disgust?

BRICK: Now. Yes.

BIG DADDY: But not once, huh?

BRICK: Not when I was still young an' believing. A drinking man's someone who wants to forget he isn't still young an' believing.

BIG DADDY: Believing what?

BRICK: Believing. . . .

BIG DADDY: Believing *what?*

BRICK (*stubbornly evasive*): Believing. . . .

BIG DADDY: I don't know what the hell you mean by believing and I don't
think you know what you mean by believing, but if you still got sports
in your blood, go back to sports announcing and—

BRICK: Sit in a glass box watching games I can't play? Describing what I
can't do while players do it? Sweating out their disgust and confusion
in contests I'm not fit for? Drinkin' a coke, half bourbon, so I can stand
it? That's no goddam good any more, no help—time just outran me,
Big Daddy—got there first . . .

BIG DADDY: I think you're passing the buck.

BRICK: You know many drinkin' men?

BIG DADDY (*with a slight, charming smile*): I have known a fair number of
that species.

BRICK: Could any of them tell you why he drank?

BIG DADDY: Yep, you're passin' the buck to things like time and disgust with "mendacity" and—crap!—if you got to use that kind of
language about a thing, it's ninety-proof bull, and I'm not buying
any.

BRICK: I had to give you a reason to get a drink!

BIG DADDY: You started drinkin' when your friend Skipper died.

(*Silence for five beats. Then Brick makes a startled movement, reaching for his
crutch.*)

BRICK: What are you suggesting?
BIG DADDY: I'm suggesting nothing.

(*The shuffle and clop of Brick's rapid hobble away from his father's steady, grave attention.*)

—But Gooper an' Mae suggested that there was something not right exactly in your—
BRICK (*stopping short downstage as if backed to a wall*): "Not right"?
BIG DADDY: Not, well, exactly *normal* in your friendship with—
BRICK: They suggested that, too? I thought that was Maggie's suggestion.

(*Brick's detachment is at last broken through. His heart is accelerated; his forehead sweat-beaded; his breath becomes more rapid and his voice hoarse. The thing they're discussing, timidly and painfully on the side of Big Daddy, fiercely, violently on Brick's side, is the inadmissible thing that Skipper died to disavow between them. The fact that if it existed it had to be disavowed to "keep face" in the world they lived in, may be at the heart of the "mendacity" that Brick drinks to kill his disgust with. It may be the root of his collapse. Or maybe it is only a single manifestation of it, not even the most important. The bird that I hope to catch in the net of this play is not the solution of one man's psychological problem. I'm trying to catch the true quality of experience in a group of people, that cloudy, flickering, evanescent—fiercely charged!—interplay of live human beings in the thundercloud of a common crisis. Some mystery should be left in the revelation of character in a play, just as a great deal of mystery is always left in the revelation of character in life, even in one's own character to himself. This does not absolve the playwright of his duty to observe and probe as clearly and deeply as he* legitimately *can: but it should steer him away from "pat" conclusions, facile definitions which make a play just a play, not a snare for the truth of human experience.*)

(*The following scene should be played with great concentration, with most of the power leashed but palpable in what is left unspoken.*)

Who else's suggestion is it, is it *yours?* How many others thought that Skipper and I were—
BIG DADDY (*gently*): Now, hold on, hold on a minute, son.—I knocked around in my time.
BRICK: What's that got to do with—
BIG DADDY: I said "Hold on!"—I bummed, I bummed this country till I was—
BRICK: Whose suggestion, who else's suggestion is it?
BIG DADDY: Slept in hobo jungles and railroad Y's and flophouses in all cities before I—

BRICK: Oh, *you* think so, too, you call me your son and a queer. Oh! Maybe that's why you put Maggie and me in this room that was Jack Straw's and Peter Ochello's, in which that pair of old sisters slept in a double bed where both of 'em died!

BIG DADDY: *Now just don't go throwing rocks at —*

(*Suddenly Reverend Tooker appears in the gallery doors, his head slightly, playfully, fatuously cocked, with a practised clergyman's smile, sincere as a bird call blown on a hunter's whistle, the living embodiment of the pious, conventional lie.*)

(*Big Daddy gasps a little at this perfectly timed, but incongruous, apparition.*)

—What're you lookin' for, Preacher?

REVEREND TOOKER: The gentleman's lavatory, ha ha!—heh, heh . . .

BIG DADDY (*with strained courtesy*):—Go back out and walk down to the other end of the gallery, Reverend Tooker, and use the bathroom connected with my bedroom, and if you can't find it, ask them where it is!

REVEREND TOOKER: Ah, thanks.

(*He goes out with a deprecatory chuckle.*)

BIG DADDY: It's hard to talk in this place . . .

BRICK: Son of a—!

BIG DADDY (*leaving a lot unspoken*):—I seen all things and understood a lot of them, till 1910. Christ, the year that—I had worn my shoes through, hocked my—I hopped off a yellow dog freight car half a mile down the road, slept in a wagon of cotton outside the gin—Jack Straw an' Peter Ochello took me in. Hired me to manage this place which grew into this one.—When Jack Straw died—why, old Peter Ochello quit eatin' like a dog does when its master's dead, and died, too!

BRICK: Christ!

BIG DADDY: I'm just saying I understand such—

BRICK (*violently*): Skipper is dead. I have not quit eating!

BIG DADDY: No, but you started drinking.

(*Brick wheels on his crutch and hurls his glass across the room shouting.*)

BRICK: YOU THINK SO, TOO?

BIG DADDY: *Shhh!*

(*Footsteps run on the gallery. There are women's calls.*)
(*Big Daddy goes toward the door.*)

Go way!—Just broke a glass. . . .

(*Brick is transformed, as if a quiet mountain blew suddenly up in volcanic flame.*)

BRICK: You think so, too? You think so, too? You think me an' Skipper did, did, did!—*sodomy!*—together?

BIG DADDY: Hold—!

BRICK: That what you—

BIG DADDY: —*ON*—a minute!

BRICK: You think we did dirty things between us, Skipper an'—

BIG DADDY: Why are you shouting like that? Why are you—

BRICK: —Me, is that what you think of Skipper, is that—

BIG DADDY: —so excited? I don't think nothing. I don't know nothing. I'm simply telling you what—

BRICK: You think that Skipper and me were a pair of dirty old men?

BIG DADDY: Now that's—

BRICK: Straw? Ochello? A couple of—

BIG DADDY: Now just—

BRICK: —ducking sissies? Queers? Is that what you—

BIG DADDY: Shhh.

BRICK: —think?

(*He loses his balance and pitches to his knees without noticing the pain. He grabs the bed and drags himself up.*)

BIG DADDY: Jesus!—Whew. . . . Grab my hand!

BRICK: Naw, I don't want your hand. . . .

BIG DADDY: Well, I want yours. Git up!

(*He draws him up, keeps an arm about him with concern and affection.*)

You broken out in a sweat! You're panting like you'd run a race with—

BRICK (*freeing himself from his father's hold*): Big Daddy, you shock me, Big Daddy, you, you—*shock* me! Talkin' so—

(*He turns away from his father.*)

—casually!—about a—thing like that . . .

　—Don't you know how people *feel* about things like that? How, how *disgusted* they are by things like that? Why, at Ole Miss when it was discovered a pledge to our fraternity, Skipper's and mine, did a, *attempted* to do a, unnatural thing with—

　We not only dropped him like a hot rock!—We told him to git off the campus, and he did, he got!—All the way to—

(*He halts, breathless.*)

BIG DADDY: —Where?

BRICK: —North Africa, last I heard!

BIG DADDY: Well, I have come back from further away than that, I have just now returned from the other side of the moon, death's country, son, and I'm not easy to shock by anything here.

(*He comes downstage and faces out.*)

Always, anyhow, lived with too much space around me to be infected by ideas of other people. One thing you can grow on a big place more important than cotton!—is *tolerance!*—I grown it.

(*He returns toward Brick.*)

BRICK: Why can't exceptional friendship, *real, real, deep, deep friendship!* between two men be respected as something clean and decent without being thought of as—

BIG DADDY: It can, it is, for God's sake.

BRICK: —*Fairies*. . . .

(*In his utterance of this word, we gauge the wide and profound reach of the conventional mores he got from the world that crowned him with early laurel.*)

BIG DADDY: I told Mae an' Gooper—

BRICK: Frig Mae and Gooper, frig all dirty lies and liars!—Skipper and me had a clean, true thing between us!—had a clean friendship, practically all our lives, till Maggie got the idea you're talking about. Normal? No!—It was too rare to be normal, any true thing between two people is too rare to be normal. Oh, once in a while he put his hand on my shoulder or I'd put mine on his, oh, maybe even, when we were touring the country in pro-football an' shared hotel-rooms we'd reach across the space between the two beds and shake hands to say goodnight, yeah, one or two times we—

BIG DADDY: Brick, nobody thinks that that's not normal!

BRICK: Well, they're mistaken, it was! It was a pure an' true thing an' that's not normal.

(*They both stare straight at each other for a long moment. The tension breaks and both turn away as if tired.*)

BIG DADDY: Yeah, it's—hard t'—talk. . . .

BRICK: All right, then, let's—let it go. . . .

BIG DADDY: Why did Skipper crack up? Why have you?

(*Brick looks back at his father again. He has already decided, without knowing that he has made this decision, that he is going to tell his father that he is dying of cancer. Only this could even the score between them: one inadmissible thing in return for another.*)

BRICK (*ominously*): All right. You're asking for it, Big Daddy. We're finally going to have that real true talk you wanted. It's too late to stop it, now, we got to carry it through and cover every subject.

(*He hobbles back to the liquor cabinet.*)

Uh-huh.

(*He opens the ice bucket and picks up the silver tongs with slow admiration of their frosty brightness.*)

Maggie declares that Skipper and I went into pro-football after we left "Ole Miss" because we were scared to grow up . . .

(*He moves downstage with the shuffle and clop of a cripple on a crutch. As Margaret did when her speech became "recitative," he looks out into the house, commanding its attention by his direct, concentrated gaze—a broken, "tragically elegant" figure telling simply as much as he knows of "the Truth":*)

—Wanted to—keep on tossing—those long, long!—high, high!—passes that—couldn't be intercepted except by time, the aerial attack that made us famous! And so we did, we did, we kept it up for one season, that aerial attack, we held it high!—Yeah, but—
—that summer, Maggie, she laid the law down to me, said, Now or never, and so I married Maggie. . . .
BIG DADDY: How was Maggie in bed?
BRICK (*wryly*): Great! the greatest!

(*Big Daddy nods as if he thought so.*)

She went on the road that fall with the Dixie Stars. Oh, she made a great show of being the world's best sport. She wore a—wore a—tall bearskin cap! A shako, they call it, a dyed moleskin coat, a moleskin coat dyed red!—Cut up crazy! Rented hotel ballrooms for victory celebrations, wouldn't cancel them when it—turned out—defeat. . . .
MAGGIE THE CAT! Ha ha!

(*Big Daddy nods.*)

—But Skipper, he had some fever which came back on him which doctors couldn't explain and I got that injury—turned out to be just a shadow on the X-ray plate—and a touch of bursitis. . . .
I lay in a hospital bed, watched our games on TV, saw Maggie on the bench next to Skipper when he was hauled out of a game for stumbles, fumbles!—Burned me up the way she hung on his arm!—Y'know, I think that Maggie had always felt sort of left out because she and me

never got any closer together than two people just get in bed, which is not much closer than two cats on a—fence humping. . . .

So! She took this time to work on poor dumb Skipper. He was a less than average student at Ole Miss, you know that, don't you?!—Poured in his mind the dirty, false idea that what we were, him and me, was a frustrated case of that ole pair of sisters that lived in this room, Jack Straw and Peter Ochello!—He, poor Skipper, went to bed with Maggie to prove it wasn't true, and when it didn't work out, he thought it *was* true!—Skipper broke in two like a rotten stick—nobody ever turned so fast to a lush—or died of it so quick. . . .

—Now are you satisfied?

(*Big Daddy has listened to this story, dividing the grain from the chaff. Now he looks at his son.*)

BIG DADDY: Are *you* satisfied?

BRICK: With what?

BIG DADDY: That half-ass story!

BRICK: What's half-ass about it?

BIG DADDY: Something's left out of that story. What did you leave out?

(*The phone has started ringing in the hall. As if it reminded him of something, Brick glances suddenly toward the sound and says:*)

BRICK: Yes!—I left out a long-distance call which I had from Skipper, in which he made a drunken confession to me and on which I hung up!—last time we spoke to each other in our lives. . . .

(*Muted ring stops as someone answers phone in a soft, indistinct voice in hall.*)

BIG DADDY: You hung up?

BRICK: Hung up. Jesus! Well—

BIG DADDY: Anyhow now!—we have tracked down the lie with which you're disgusted and which you are drinking to kill your disgust with, Brick. You been passing the buck. This disgust with mendacity is disgust with yourself.

You!—dug the grave of your friend and kicked him in it!—before you'd face truth with him!

BRICK: *His* truth, not *mine!*

BIG DADDY: His truth, okay! But you wouldn't face it with him!

BRICK: Who *can* face truth? Can *you?*

BIG DADDY: Now don't start passin' the rotten buck again, boy!

BRICK: *How about these birthday congratulations, these many, many happy returns of the day, when ev'rybody but you knows there won't be any!*

(*Whoever has answered the hall phone lets out a high, shrill laugh; the voice becomes audible saying:* "No, no, you got it all wrong! Upside down! Are you crazy?"

(*Brick suddenly catches his breath as he realized that he has made a shocking disclosure. He hobbles a few paces, then freezes, and without looking at his father's shocked face, says:*)

Let's, let's—go out, now, and—

(*Big Daddy moves suddenly forward and grabs hold of the boy's crutch like it was a weapon for which they were fighting for possession.*)

BIG DADDY: Oh, no, no! No one's going out! What did you start to say?

BRICK: I don't remember.

BIG DADDY: "Many happy returns when they know there won't be any"?

BRICK: Aw, hell, Big Daddy, forget it. Come on out on the gallery and look at the fireworks they're shooting off for your birthday. . . .

BIG DADDY: First you finish that remark you were makin' before you cut off. "Many happy returns when they know there won't be any"?—Ain't that what you just said?

BRICK: Look, now. I can get around without that crutch if I have to but it would be a lot easier on the furniture an' glassware if I didn' have to go swinging along like Tarzan of th'—

BIG DADDY: FINISH! WHAT YOU WAS SAYIN'!

(*An eerie green glow shows in sky behind him.*)

BRICK (*sucking the ice in his glass, speech becoming thick*): Leave th' place to Gooper and Mae an' their five little same little monkeys. All I want is—

BIG DADDY: "LEAVE TH' PLACE," did you say?

BRICK (*vaguely*): All twenty-eight thousand acres of the richest land this side of the valley Nile.

BIG DADDY: Who said I was "leaving the place" to Gooper or anybody? This is my sixty-fifth birthday! I got fifteen years or twenty years left in me! I'll outlive *you!* I'll bury you an' have to pay for your coffin!

BRICK: Sure. Many happy returns. Now let's go watch the fireworks, come on, let's—

BIG DADDY: Lying, have they been lying? About the report from th'—clinic? Did they, did they—find something?—*Cancer.* Maybe?

BRICK: Mendacity is a system that we live in. Liquor is one way out an' death's the other. . . .

(*He takes the crutch from Big Daddy's loose grip and swings out on the gallery leaving the doors open.*)

(*A song, "Pick a Bale of Cotton," is heard.*)

MAE (*appearing in door*): *Oh, Big Daddy, the field hands are singin' fo' you!*
BIG DADDY (*shouting hoarsely*): BRICK! BRICK!
MAE: He's outside drinkin', Big Daddy.
BIG DADDY: *BRICK!*

(*Mae retreats, awed by the passion of his voice. Children call Brick in tones mocking Big Daddy. His face crumbles like broken yellow plaster about to fall into dust.*)
(*There is a glow in the sky. Brick swings back through the doors, slowly, gravely, quite soberly.*)

BRICK: I'm sorry, Big Daddy. My head don't work any more and it's hard for me to understand how anybody could care if he lived or died or was dying or cared about anything but whether or not there was liquor left in the bottle and so I said what I said without thinking. In some ways I'm no better than the others, in some ways worse because I'm less alive. Maybe it's being alive that makes them lie, and being almost *not* alive makes me sort of accidentally truthful—I don't know but—anyway—we've been friends . . .
    —And being friends is telling each other the truth. . . .

(*There is a pause.*)

You told *me!* I told *you!*

(*A child rushes into the room and grabs a fistful of firecrackers and runs out again.*)

CHILD (*screaming*): Bang, bang, bang, bang, bang, bang, bang, bang, bang!
BIG DADDY (*slowly and passionately*): CHRIST—DAMN—ALL—LYING SONS OF—LYING BITCHES!

(*He straightens at last and crosses to the inside door. At the door he turns and looks back as if he had some desperate question he couldn't put into words. Then he nods reflectively and says in a hoarse voice:*)

Yes, all liars, all liars, all lying dying liars!

(*This is said slowly, slowly, with a fierce revulsion. He goes on out.*)

—Lying! Dying! Liars!

(*His voice dies out. There is the sound of a child being slapped. It rushes, hideously bawling, through room and out the hall door.*
    (*Brick remains motionless as the lights dim out and the curtain falls.*)

CURTAIN

ACT III

There is no lapse of time. Mae enters with Reverend Tooker.

MAE: Where is Big Daddy! Big Daddy?

BIG MAMA (*entering*): Too much smell of burnt fireworks makes me feel a little bit sick at my stomach.—Where is Big Daddy?

MAE: That's what I want to know, where has Big Daddy gone?

BIG MAMA: He must have turned in, I reckon he went to baid. . . .

(*Gooper enters.*)

GOOPER: Where is Big Daddy?

MAE: We don't know where he is!

BIG MAMA: I reckon he's gone to baid.

GOOPER: Well, then, now we can talk.

BIG MAMA: What *is* this talk, *what* talk?

(*Margaret appears on gallery, talking to Dr. Baugh.*)

MARGARET (*musically*): My family freed their slaves ten years before abolition, my great-great-grandfather gave his slaves their freedom five years before the war between the States started!

MAE: Oh, for God's sake! Maggie's climbed back up in her family tree!

MARGARET (*sweetly*): What, Mae?—Oh, where's Big Daddy?!

(*The pace must be very quick. Great Southern animation.*)

BIG MAMA (*addressing them all*): I think Big Daddy was just worn out. He loves his family, he loves to have them around him, but it's a strain on his nerves. He wasn't himself tonight, Big Daddy wasn't himself, I could tell he was all worked up.

REVEREND TOOKER: I think he's remarkable.

BIG MAMA: Yaisss! Just remarkable. Did you all notice the food he ate at that table? Did you all notice the supper he put away? Why, he ate like a hawss!

GOOPER: I hope he doesn't regret it.

BIG MAMA: Why, that man—ate a huge piece of cawn-bread with molasses on it! Helped himself twice to hoppin' john.

MARGARET: Big Daddy loves hoppin' john.—We had a real country dinner.

BIG MAMA (*overlapping Margaret*): Yais, he simply adores it! An' candied yams? That man put away enough food at that table to stuff a nigger *field* hand!

GOOPER (*with grim relish*): I hope he don't have to pay for it later on. . . .

BIG MAMA (*fiercely*): What's *that*, Gooper?

MAE: Gooper says he hopes Big Daddy doesn't suffer tonight.

BIG MAMA: Oh, shoot, Gooper says, Gooper says! Why should Big Daddy suffer for satisfying a normal appetite? There's nothin' wrong with that man but nerves, he's sound as a dollar! And now he knows he is an' that's why he ate such a supper. He had a big load off his mind, knowin' he wasn't doomed t'—what he thought he was doomed to. . . .

MARGARET (*sadly and sweetly*): Bless his old sweet soul. . . .

BIG MAMA (*vaguely*): Yais, bless his heart, where's Brick?

MAE: Outside.

GOOPER:—Drinkin' . . .

BIG MAMA: I know he's drinkin'. You all don't have to keep tellin' *me* Brick is drinkin'. Cain't I see he's drinkin' without you continually tellin' me that boy's drinkin'?

MARGARET: Good for you, Big Mama!

(*She applauds.*)

BIG MAMA: Other people *drink* and *have* drunk an' will *drink*, as long as they make that stuff an' put it in bottles.

MARGARET: That's the truth. I never trusted a man that didn't drink.

MAE: Gooper never drinks. Don't you trust Gooper?

MARGARET: Why, Gooper don't you drink? If I'd known you didn't drink, I wouldn't of made that remark—

BIG MAMA: *Brick?*

MARGARET:—at least not in your presence.

(*She laughs sweetly.*)

BIG MAMA: *Brick!*

MARGARET: He's still on the gall'ry. I'll go bring him in so we can talk.

BIG MAMA (*worriedly*): I don't know what this mysterious family conference is about.

(*Awkward silence. Big Mama looks from face to face, then belches slightly and mutters, "Excuse me. . . ." She opens an ornamental fan suspended about her throat, a black lace fan to go with her black lace gown and fans her wilting corsage, sniffing nervously and looking from face to face in the uncomfortable silence as Margaret calls "Brick?" and Brick sings to the moon on the gallery.*)

I don't know what's wrong here, you all have such long faces! Open that door on the hall and let some air circulate through here, will you please, Gooper?

MAE: I think we'd better leave that door closed, Big Mama, till after the talk.

BIG MAMA: Reveren' Tooker, will *you* please open that door?!

REVEREND TOOKER: I sure will, Big Mama.

MAE: I just didn't think we ought t' take any chance of Big Daddy hearin' a word of this discussion.

BIG MAMA: *I swan!* Nothing's going to be said in Big Daddy's house that he cain't hear if he wants to!

GOOPER: Well, Big Mama, it's—

(*Mae gives him a quick, hard poke to shut him up. He glares at her fiercely as she circles before him like a burlesque ballerina, raising her skinny bare arms over her head, jangling her bracelets, exclaiming:*)

MAE: *A breeze! A breeze!*

REVEREND TOOKER: I think this house is the coolest house in the Delta.— Did you all know that Halsey Banks' widow put air-conditioning units in the church and rectory at Friar's Point in memory of Halsey?

(*General conversation has resumed; everybody is chatting so that the stage sounds like a big bird-cage.*)

GOOPER: Too bad nobody cools your church off for you. I bet you sweat in that pulpit these hot Sundays, Reverend Tooker.

REVEREND TOOKER: Yes, my vestments are drenched.

MAE (*at the same time to Dr. Baugh*): You think those vitamin B12 injections are what they're cracked up t' be, Doc Baugh?

DOCTOR BAUGH: Well, if you want to be stuck with something I guess they're as good to be stuck with as anything else.

BIG MAMA (*at gallery door*): *Maggie, Maggie, aren't you comin' with Brick?*

MAE (*suddenly and loudly, creating a silence*): *I have a strange feeling, I have a peculiar feeling!*

BIG MAMA (*turning from gallery*): What feeling?

MAE: That Brick said somethin' he shouldn't of said t' Big Daddy.

BIG MAMA: Now what on earth could Brick of said t' Big Daddy that he shouldn't say?

GOOPER: Big Mama, there's somethin'—

MAE: NOW, WAIT!

(*She rushes up to Big Mama and gives her a quick hug and kiss. Big Mama pushes her impatiently off as the Reverend Tooker's voice rises serenely in a little pocket of silence:*)

REVEREND TOOKER: Yes, last Sunday the gold in my chasuble faded into th' purple. . . .

GOOPER: Reveren' you must of been preachin' hell's fire last Sunday!

(*He guffaws at this witticism but the Reverend is not sincerely amused. At the same time Big Mama has crossed over to Dr. Baugh and is saying to him:*)

BIG MAMA (*her breathless voice rising high-pitched above the others*): In my day they had what they call the Keeley cure for heavy drinkers. But now I understand they just take some kind of tablets, they call them "Annie Bust" tablets. But Brick don't need to take *nothin'*.

(*Brick appears in gallery doors with Margaret behind him.*)

BIG MAMA (*unaware of his presence behind her*): That boy is just broken up over Skipper's death. You know how poor Skipper died. They gave him a big, big dose of that sodium amytal stuff at his home and then they called the ambulance and give him another big, big dose of it at the hospital and that and all of the alcohol in his system fo' months an' months an' months just proved too much for his heart. . . . I'm scared of needles! I'm more scared of a needle than the knife. . . . I think more people have been needled out of this world than—

(*She stops short and wheels about.*)

OH!—here's Brick! My precious baby—

(*She turns upon Brick with short, fat arms extended, at the same time uttering a loud, short sob, which is both comic and touching.*

(*Brick smiles and bows slightly, making a burlesque gesture of gallantry for Maggie to pass before him into the room. Then he hobbles on his crutch directly to the liquor cabinet and there is absolute silence, with everybody looking at Brick as everybody has always looked at Brick when he spoke or moved or appeared. One by one he drops ice cubes in his glass, then suddenly, but not quickly, looks back over his shoulder with a wry, charming smile, and says:*)

BRICK: I'm sorry! Anyone else?
BIG MAMA (*sadly*): No, son. I wish you wouldn't!
BRICK: I wish I didn't have to, Big Mama, but I'm still waiting for that click in my head which makes it all smooth out!
BIG MAMA: Aw, Brick, you—BREAK MY HEART!
MARGARET (*at the same time*): Brick, go sit with Big Mama!
BIG MAMA: I just cain't *staiiiiiiiii-nnnnnd*—it. . . .

(*She sobs.*)

MAE: Now that we're all assembled—
GOOPER: We kin talk. . . .

BIG MAMA: Breaks my heart. . . .

MARGARET: Sit with Big Mama, Brick, and hold her hand.

(*Big Mama sniffs very loudly three times, almost like three drum beats in the pocket of silence.*)

BRICK: You do that, Maggie. I'm a restless cripple. I got to stay on my crutch.

(*Brick hobbles to the gallery door; leans there as if waiting.*)
  (*Mae sits beside Big Mama, while Gooper moves in front and sits on the end of the couch, facing her. Reverend Tooker moves nervously into the space between them; on the other side, Dr. Baugh stands looking at nothing in particular and lights a cigar. Margaret turns away.*)

BIG MAMA: Why're you all *surroundin'* me—like this? Why're you all starin' at me like this an' makin' signs at each other?

(*Reverend Tooker steps back startled.*)

MAE: Calm yourself, Big Mama.

BIG MAMA: Calm you'self, *you'self*, Sister Woman. How could I calm myself with everyone starin' at me as if big drops of blood had broken out on m'face? What's this all about, annh! What?

(*Gooper coughs and takes a center position.*)

GOOPER: Now, Doc Baugh.

MAE: Doc Baugh?

BRICK (*suddenly*): SHHH!—

(*Then he grins and chuckles and shakes his head regretfully.*)

  —Naw!—that wasn't th' click.

GOOPER: Brick, shut up or stay out there on the gallery with your liquor! We got to talk about a serious matter. Big Mama wants to know the complete truth about the report we got today from the Ochsner Clinic.

MAE (*eagerly*):—on Big Daddy's condition!

GOOPER: Yais, on Big Daddy's condition, we got to face it.

DOCTOR BAUGH: Well. . . .

BIG MAMA (*terrified, rising*): Is there? Something? Something that I? Don't—Know?

(*In these few words, this startled, very soft, question, Big Mama reviews the history of her forty-five years with Big Daddy, her great, almost embarrassingly true-hearted and simple-minded devotion to Big Daddy, who must have had something Brick has, who made himself loved so much by the "simple expedient" of not loving enough to disturb his charming detachment, also once coupled, like Brick's, with virile beauty.)*

(Big Mama has a dignity at this moment: she almost stops being fat.)

DOCTOR BAUGH (*after a pause, uncomfortably*): Yes?—Well—
BIG MAMA: *I*!!!—want to—*knowwwwww. . . .*

(Immediately she thrusts her fist to her mouth as if to deny that statement.)

(Then, for some curious reason, she snatches the withered corsage from her breast and hurls it on the floor and steps on it with her short, fat feet.)

—*Somebody must be lyin'!—I want to know!*

MAE: Sit down, Big Mama, sit down on this sofa.
MARGARET (*quickly*): Brick, go sit with Big Mama.
BIG MAMA: *What is it, what is it?*
DOCTOR BAUGH: I never have seen a more thorough examination than Big Daddy Pollitt was given in all my experience with the Ochsner Clinic.
GOOPER: It's one of the best in the country.
MAE: It's *THE* best in the country—bar none!

(For some reason she gives Gooper a violent poke as she goes past him. He slaps at her hand without removing his eyes from his mother's face.)

DOCTOR BAUGH: Of course they were ninety-nine and nine-tenths percent sure before they even started.
BIG MAMA: Sure of what, sure of what, sure of—*what?—what!*

(She catches her breath in a startled sob. Mae kisses her quickly. She thrusts Mae fiercely away from her, staring at the doctor.)

MAE: Mommy, be a brave girl!
BRICK (*in the doorway, softly*): "By the light, by the light,
    Of the sil-ve-ry mo-ooo-n . . ."
GOOPER: Shut up!—Brick.
BRICK: —Sorry. . . .

(He wanders out on the gallery.)

DOCTOR BAUGH: But now, you see, Big Mama, they cut a piece off this growth, a specimen of the tissue and—
BIG MAMA: Growth? You told Big Daddy—
DOCTOR BAUGH: Now wait.
BIG MAMA (*fiercely*): You told me and Big Daddy there wasn't a thing wrong with him but—
MAE: Big Mama, they always—

GOOPER: Let Doc Baugh talk, will yuh?

BIG MAMA:—little spastic condition of—

(*Her breath gives out in a sob.*)

DOCTOR BAUGH: Yes, that's what we told Big Daddy. But we had this bit of tissue run through the laboratory and I'm sorry to say the test was positive on it. It's—well—malignant. . . .

(*Pause.*)

BIG MAMA:—Cancer?! Cancer?!

(*Dr. Baugh nods gravely.*
Big Mama gives a long gasping cry.)

MAE and GOOPER: Now, now, now, Big Mama, you had to know. . . .

BIG MAMA: *WHY DIDN'T THEY CUT IT OUT OF HIM? HANH? HANH?*

DOCTOR BAUGH: Involved too much, Big Mama, too many organs affected.

MAE: Big Mama, the liver's affected and so's the kidneys, both! It's gone way past what they call a—

GOOPER: A surgical risk.

MAE:—Uh-huh. . . .

(*Big Mama draws a breath like a dying gasp.*)

REVEREND TOOKER: Tch, tch, tch, tch, tch!

DOCTOR BAUGH: Yes, it's gone past the knife.

MAE: *That's why he's turned yellow, Mommy!*

BIG MAMA: *Git away from me, git away from me, Mae!*

(*She rises abruptly.*)

    I want Brick! Where's Brick? Where is my only son?

MAE: Mama! Did she say *"only* son"?

GOOPER: What does that make *me*?

MAE: A sober responsible man with five precious children!—*Six!*

BIG MAMA: I want Brick to tell me! Brick! Brick!

MARGARET (*rising from her reflections in a corner*): Brick was so upset he went back out.

BIG MAMA: *Brick!*

MARGARET: Mama, let *me* tell you!

BIG MAMA: No, no, leave me alone, you're not my blood!

GOOPER: *Mama, I'm your son! Listen to me!*

MAE: Gooper's your son, Mama, he's your first-born!

BIG MAMA: Gooper never liked Daddy.

MAE (*as if terribly shocked*): *That's not TRUE!*

(*There is a pause. The minister coughs and rises.*)

REVEREND TOOKER (*to Mae*): I think I'd better slip away at this point.

MAE (*sweetly and sadly*): Yes, Doctor Tooker, you go.

REVEREND TOOKER (*discreetly*): Goodnight, goodnight, everybody, and God bless you all . . . on this place. . . .

(*He slips out.*)

DOCTOR BAUGH: That man is a good man but lacking in tact. Talking about people giving memorial windows—if he mentioned one memorial window, he must have spoke of a dozen, and saying how awful it was when somebody died intestate, the legal wrangles, and so forth.

(*Mae coughs, and points at Big Mama.*)

DOCTOR BAUGH: Well, Big Mama. . . .

(*He sighs.*)

BIG MAMA: It's all a mistake, I know it's just a bad dream.

DOCTOR BAUGH: We're gonna keep Big Daddy as comfortable as we can.

BIG MAMA: Yes, it's just a bad dream, that's all it is, it's just an awful dream.

GOOPER: In my opinion Big Daddy is having some pain but won't admit that he has it.

BIG MAMA: Just a dream, a bad dream.

DOCTOR BAUGH: That's what lots of them do, they think if they don't admit they're having the pain they can sort of escape the fact of it.

GOOPER (*with relish*): Yes, they get sly about it, they get real sly about it.

MAE: Gooper and I think—

GOOPER: Shut up, Mae!—Big Daddy ought to be started on morphine.

BIG MAMA: Nobody's going to give Big Daddy morphine.

DOCTOR BAUGH: Now, Big Mama, when that pain strikes it's going to strike mighty hard and Big Daddy's going to need the needle to bear it.

BIG MAMA: I tell you, nobody's going to give him morphine.

MAE: Big Mama, you don't want to see Big Daddy suffer, you know you—

(*Gooper standing beside her gives her a savage poke.*)

DOCTOR BAUGH (*placing a package on the table*): I'm leaving this stuff here, so if there's a sudden attack you all won't have to send out for it.

MAE: I know how to give a hypo.

GOOPER: Mae took a course in nursing during the war.

MARGARET: Somehow I don't think Big Daddy would want Mae to give him a hypo.

MAE: You think he'd want *you* to do it?

(*Dr. Baugh rises.*)

GOOPER: Doctor Baugh is goin'.
DOCTOR BAUGH: Yes, I got to be goin'. Well, keep your chin up, Big Mama.
GOOPER (*with jocularity*): She's gonna keep *both* chins up, aren't you Big
    Mama?

(*Big Mama sobs.*)

    Now stop that, Big Mama.
MAE: Sit down with me, Big Mama.
GOOPER (*at door with Dr. Baugh*): Well, Doc, we sure do appreciate all you
    done. I'm telling you, we're surely obligated to you for—

(*Dr. Baugh has gone out without a glance at him.*)

GOOPER:—I guess that doctor has got a lot on his mind but it wouldn't
    hurt him to act a little more human. . . .

(*Big Mama sobs.*)

    Now be a brave girl, Mommy.

BIG MAMA: It's not true, I know that it's just not true!
GOOPER: Mama, those tests are infallible!
BIG MAMA: Why are you so determined to see your father daid?
MAE: Big Mama!
MARGARET (*gently*): I know what Big Mama means.
MAE (*fiercely*): Oh, do you?
MARGARET (*quietly and very sadly*): Yes, I think I do.
MAE: For a newcomer in the family you sure do show a lot of
    understanding.
MARGARET: Understanding is needed on this place.
MAE: I guess you must have needed a lot of it in your family, Maggie,
    with your father's liquor problem and now you've got Brick with his!
MARGARET: Brick does not have a liquor problem at all. Brick is devoted
    to Big Daddy. This thing is a terrible strain on him.
BIG MAMA: Brick is Big Daddy's boy, but he drinks too much and it wor-
    ries me and Big Daddy, and, Margaret, you've got to cooperate with us,
    you've got to cooperate with Big Daddy and me in getting Brick
    straightened out. Because it will break Big Daddy's heart if Brick don't
    pull himself together and take hold of things.
MAE: Take hold of *what* things, Big Mama?
BIG MAMA: The place.

(*There is a quick violent look between Mae and Gooper.*)

GOOPER: Big Mama, you've had a shock.

MAE: Yais, we've all had a shock, but . . .

GOOPER: Let's be realistic—

MAE: —Big Daddy would never, would *never*, be foolish enough to—

GOOPER: —put this place in irresponsible hands!

BIG MAMA: Big Daddy ain't going to leave the place in anybody's hands; Big Daddy is *not* going to die. I want you to get that in your heads, all of you!

MAE: Mommy, Mommy, Big Mama, we're just as hopeful an' optimistic as you are about Big Daddy's prospects, we have faith in *prayer*—but nevertheless there are certain matters that have to be discussed an' dealt with, because otherwise—

GOOPER: Eventualities have to be considered and now's the time. . . . Mae, will you please get my briefcase out of our room?

MAE: Yes, honey.

(*She rises and goes out through the hall door.*)

GOOPER (*standing over Big Mama*): Now Big Mom. What you said just now was not at all true and you know it. I've always loved Big Daddy in my own quiet way. I never made a show of it, and I know that Big Daddy has always been fond of me in a quiet way, too, and he never made a show of it neither.

(*Mae returns with Gooper's briefcase.*)

MAE: Here's your briefcase, Gooper, honey.

GOOPER (*handing the briefcase back to her*): Thank you. . . . Of ca'use, my relationship with Big Daddy is different from Brick's.

MAE: You're eight years older'n Brick an' always had t'carry a bigger load of th' responsibilities than Brick ever had t'carry. He never carried a thing in his life but a football or a highball.

GOOPER: Mae, will y' let me talk, please?

MAE: Yes, honey.

GOOPER: Now, a twenty-eight thousand acre plantation's a mighty big thing t'run.

MAE: Almost singlehanded.

(*Margaret has gone out onto the gallery, and can be heard calling softly to Brick.*)

BIG MAMA: You never had to run this place! What are you talking about? As if Big Daddy was dead and in his grave, you had to run it? Why, you just helped him out with a few business details and had your law practice at the same time in Memphis!

MAE: Oh, Mommy, Mommy, Big Mommy! Let's be fair! Why, Gooper has given himself body and soul to keeping this place up for the past five years since Big Daddy's health started failing. Gooper won't say it, Gooper never thought of it as a duty, he just did it. And what did Brick do? Brick kept living in his past glory at college! Still a football player at twenty-seven!

MARGARET (*returning alone*): Who are you talking about, now? Brick? A football player? He isn't a football player and you know it. Brick is a sport's announcer on TV and one of the best-known ones in the country!

MAE: I'm talking about what he was.

MARGARET: Well, I wish you would just stop talking about my husband.

GOOPER: I've got a right to discuss my brother with other members of MY OWN family which don't include *you*. Why don't you go out there and drink with Brick?

MARGARET: I've never seen such malice toward a brother.

GOOPER: How about his for me? Why, he can't stand to be in the same room with me!

MARGARET: This is a deliberate campaign of vilification for the most disgusting and sordid reason on earth, and I know what it is! It's *avarice, avarice, greed, greed!*

BIG MAMA: *Oh, I'll scream! I will scream in a moment unless this stops!*

(*Gooper has stalked up to Margaret with clenched fists at his sides as if he would strike her. Mae distorts her face again into a hideous grimace behind Margaret's back.*)

MARGARET: We only remain on the place because of Big Mom and Big Daddy. If it is true what they say about Big Daddy we are going to leave here just as soon as it's over. Not a moment later.

BIG MAMA (*sobs*): Margaret. Child. Come here. Sit next to Big Mama.

MARGARET: Precious Mommy. I'm sorry, I'm so sorry, I—!

(*She bends her long graceful neck to press her forehead to Big Mama's bulging shoulder under its black chiffon.*)

GOOPER: How beautiful, how touching, this display of devotion!

MAE: Do you know why she's childless? She's childless because that big beautiful athlete husband of hers won't go to bed with her!

GOOPER: You jest won't let me do this in a nice way, will yah? Awright— Mae and I have five kids with another one coming! I don't give a goddam if Big Daddy likes me or don't like me or did or never did or will or will never! I'm just appealing to a sense of common decency and fair play. I'll tell you the truth. I've resented Big Daddy's partiality to Brick ever since Brick was born, and the way I've been treated like I was just barely good enough to spit on and sometimes not even good enough for that. Big Daddy is dying of cancer, and it's spread all through him and it's attacked all his vital organs including the kidneys and right now he is sinking into uremia, and you all know what uremia is, it's poisoning of the whole system due to the failure of the body to eliminate its poisons.

MARGARET (*to herself, downstage, hissingly*): *Poisons, poisons! Venomous thoughts and words! In hearts and minds!—That's poisons!*

GOOPER (*overlapping her*): I am asking for a square deal, and I expect to get one. But if I don't get one, if there's any peculiar shenanigans going on around here behind my back, or before me, well, I'm not a corporation lawyer for nothing, I know how to protect my own interests.—*OH! A late arrival!*

(*Brick enters from the gallery with a tranquil, blurred smile, carrying an empty glass with him.*)

MAE: Behold the conquering hero comes!

GOOPER: The fabulous Brick Pollitt! Remember him?—Who could forget him!

MAE: He looks like he's been injured in a game!

GOOPER: Yep, I'm afraid you'll have to warm the bench at the Sugar Bowl this year, Brick!

(*Mae laughs shrilly.*)

Or was it the Rose Bowl that he made that famous run in?

MAE: The punch bowl, honey. It was in the punch bowl, the cut-glass punch bowl!

GOOPER: Oh, that's right, I'm getting the bowls mixed up!

MARGARET: Why don't you stop venting your malice and envy on a sick boy?

BIG MAMA: *Now you two hush, I mean it, hush, all of you, hush!*

GOOPER: All right, Big Mama. A family crisis brings out the best and the worst in every member of it.

MAE: *That's* the truth.

MARGARET: *Amen!*

BIG MAMA: *I said, hush!* I won't tolerate any more catty talk in my house.

(*Mae gives Gooper a sign indicating briefcase.*)

(*Brick's smile has grown both brighter and vaguer. As he prepares a drink, he sings softly:*)

BRICK: *Show me the way to go home,*
 I'm tired and I wanta go to bed,
 I had a little drink about an hour ago—

GOOPER (*at the same time*): Big Mama, you know it's necessary for me t'go back to Memphis in th' mornin' t'represent the Parker estate in a lawsuit.

(*Mae sits on the bed and arranges papers she has taken from the briefcase.*)

BRICK (*continuing the song*): *Wherever I may roam,*
   On land or sea or foam.
BIG MAMA: Is it, GOOPER?
MAE: Yaiss.
GOOPER: That's why I'm forced to—to bring up a problem that—
MAE: Somethin' that's too important t' be put off!
GOOPER: If Brick was sober, he ought to be in on this.
MARGARET: Brick is present; we're here.
GOOPER: Well, good. I will now give you this outline my partner, Tom Bullitt, an' me have drawn up—a sort of dummy—trusteeship.
MARGARET: Oh, that's it! You'll be in charge an' dole out remittances, will you?
GOOPER: This we did as soon as we got the report on Big Daddy from th' Ochsner Laboratories. We did this thing, I mean we drew up this dummy outline with the advice and assistance of the Chairman of the Boa'd of Directors of th' Southern Plantahs Bank and Trust Company in Memphis, C. C. Bellowes, a man who handles estates for all th' prominent fam'lies in West Tennessee and th' Delta.
BIG MAMA: Gooper?
GOOPER (*crouching in front of Big Mama*): Now this is not—not final, or anything like it. This is just a preliminary outline. But it does provide a basis—a design—a—possible, feasible—*plan!*
MARGARET: Yes, I'll bet.
MAE: It's a plan to protect the biggest estate in the Delta from irresponsibility an'—
BIG MAMA: Now you listen to me, all of you, you listen here! They's not goin' to be any more catty talk in my house! And Gooper, you put that away before I grab it out of your hand and tear it right up! I don't know what the hell's in it, and I don't want to know what the hell's in it. I'm talkin' in Big Daddy's language now; I'm his *wife*, not his *widow*, I'm still his *wife!* And I'm talkin' to you in his language an'—
GOOPER: Big Mama, what I have here is—
MAE: Gooper explained that it's just a plan. . . .
BIG MAMA: I don't care what you got there. Just put it back where it came from, an' don't let me see it again, not even the outside of the envelope of it! Is that understood? Basis! Plan! Preliminary! Design! I say—what is it Big Daddy always says when he's disgusted?

BRICK (*from the bar*): Big Daddy says "crap" when he's disgusted.

BIG MAMA (*rising*): That's right—*CRAP!* I say *CRAP* too, like Big Daddy!

MAE: Coarse language doesn't seem called for in this—

GOOPER: Somethin' in me is *deeply outraged* by hearin' you talk like this.

BIG MAMA: *Nobody's goin' to take nothin'!*—till Big Daddy lets go of it, and maybe, just possibly, not—not even then! No, not even then!

BRICK: *You can always hear me singin' this song,*
Show me the way to go home.

BIG MAMA: Tonight Brick looks like he used to look when he was a little boy, just like he did when he played wild games and used to come home all sweaty and pink-cheeked and sleepy, with his—red curls shining. . . .

(*She comes over to him and runs her fat shaky hand through his hair. He draws aside as he does from all physical contact and continues the song in a whisper, opening the ice bucket and dropping in the ice cubes one by one as if he were mixing some important chemical formula.*)

BIG MAMA (*continuing*): Time goes by so fast. Nothin' can outrun it. Death commences too early—almost before you're half acquainted with life—you meet with the other. . . .

Oh, you know we just got to love each other an' stay together, all of us, just as close as we can, especially now that such a *black* thing has come and moved into this place without invitation.

(*Awkwardly embracing Brick, she presses her head to his shoulder.*)
(*Gooper has been returning papers to Mae who has restored them to briefcase with an air of severely tried patience.*)

GOOPER: Big Mama? Big Mama?

(*He stands behind her, tense with sibling envy.*)

BIG MAMA (*oblivious of Gooper*): Brick, you hear me, don't you?

MARGARET: Brick hears you, Big Mama, he understands what you're saying.

BIG MAMA: Oh, Brick, son of Big Daddy! Big Daddy does so love you! Y'know what would be his fondest dream come true? If before he passed on, if Big Daddy has to pass on, you gave him a child of yours, a grandson as much like his son as his son is like Big Daddy!

MAE (*zipping briefcase shut: an incongruous sound*): *Such a pity that Maggie an' Brick can't oblige!*

MARGARET (*suddenly and quietly but forcefully*): Everybody listen.

(*She crosses to the center of the room, holding her hands rigidly together.*)

MAE: Listen to what, Maggie?

MARGARET: I have an announcement to make.

GOOPER: A sports announcement, Maggie?

MARGARET: Brick and I are going to—*have a child!*

(*Big Mama catches her breath in a loud gasp.*)
  (*Pause. Big Mama rises.*)

BIG MAMA: Maggie! Brick! This is too good to believe!

MAE: That's right, too good to believe.

BIG MAMA: Oh, my, my! This is Big Daddy's dream, his dream come true!
  I'm going to tell him right now before he—

MARGARET: We'll tell him in the morning. Don't disturb him now.

BIG MAMA: I want to tell him before he goes to sleep, I'm going to tell him
  his dream's come true this minute! And Brick! A child will make you
  pull yourself together and quit this drinking!

(*She seizes the glass from his hand.*)

  The responsibilities of a father will—

(*Her face contorts and she makes an excited gesture; bursting into sobs, she
rushes out, crying.*)

  I'm going to tell Big Daddy right this minute!

(*Her voice fades out down the hall.*)
  (*Brick shrugs slightly and drops an ice cube into another glass. Margaret
crosses quickly to his side, saying something under her breath, and she pours
the liquor for him, staring up almost fiercely into his face.*)

BRICK (*coolly*): Thank you, Maggie, that's a nice big shot.

(*Mae has joined Gooper and she gives him a fierce poke, making a low hissing
sound and a grimace of fury.*)

GOOPER (*pushing her aside*): Brick, could you possibly spare me one small
  shot of that liquor?

BRICK: Why, help yourself, Gooper boy.

GOOPER: I will.

MAE (*shrilly*): Of course we know that this is—

GOOPER: *Be still, Mae!*

MAE: I won't be still! I know she's made this up!

GOOPER: God damn it, I said to shut up!

MARGARET: Gracious! I didn't know that my little announcement was
  going to provoke such a storm!

MAE: *That* woman isn't *pregnant!*

GOOPER: Who said she was?

MAE: *She* did.

GOOPER: The doctor didn't. Doc Baugh didn't.

MARGARET: I haven't gone to Doc Baugh.

GOOPER: Then who'd you go to, Maggie?

MARGARET: One of the best gynecologists in the South.

GOOPER: Uh huh, uh huh!—I see. . . .

(*He takes out pencil and notebook.*)

    —May we have his name, please?

MARGARET: No, you may not, Mister Prosecuting Attorney!

MAE: He doesn't have any name, he doesn't exist!

MARGARET: Oh, he exists all right, and so does my child, Brick's baby!

MAE: You can't conceive a child by a man that won't sleep with you
    unless you think you're—

(*Brick has turned on the phonograph. A scat song cuts Mae's speech.*)

GOOPER: *Turn that off!*

MAE: We know it's a lie because we hear you in here; he won't sleep with
    you, we hear you! So don't imagine you're going to put a trick over on
    us, to fool a dying man with a—

(*A long drawn cry of agony and rage fills the house. Margaret turns phonograph
down to a whisper.*)

    (*The cry is repeated.*)

MAE (*awed*): Did you hear that, Gooper, did you hear that?

GOOPER: Sounds like the pain has struck.

MAE: Go see, Gooper!

GOOPER: Come along and leave these lovebirds together in their nest!

(*He goes out first. Mae follows but turns at the door, contorting her face and
hissing at Margaret.*)

MAE: *Liar!*

(*She slams the door.*)

    (*Margaret exhales with relief and moves a little unsteadily to catch hold of
Brick's arm.*)

MARGARET: Thank you for—keeping still . . .

BRICK: OK, Maggie.

MARGARET: It was gallant of you to save my face!

BRICK:—It hasn't happened yet.

MARGARET: What?

BRICK: The click. . . .

MARGARET: —the click in your head that makes you peaceful, honey?

BRICK: Uh-huh. It hasn't happened. . . . I've got to make it happen before I can sleep. . . .

MARGARET: —I—know what you—mean. . . .

BRICK: Give me that pillow in the big chair, Maggie.

MARGARET: I'll put it on the bed for you.

BRICK: No, put it on the sofa, where I sleep.

MARGARET: Not tonight, Brick.

BRICK: I want it on the sofa. That's where I sleep.

(*He has hobbled to the liquor cabinet. He now pours down three shots in quick succession and stands waiting, silent. All at once he turns with a smile and says:*)

> There!

MARGARET: What?

BRICK: The *click*. . . .

(*His gratitude seems almost infinite as he hobbles out on the gallery with a drink. We hear his crutch as he swings out of sight. Then, at some distance, he begins singing to himself a peaceful song.*)
  (*Margaret holds the big pillow forlornly as if it were her only companion, for a few moments, then throws it on the bed. She rushes to the liquor cabinet, gathers all the bottles in her arms, turns about undecidedly, then runs out of the room with them, leaving the door ajar on the dim yellow hall. Brick is heard hobbling back along the gallery, singing his peaceful song. He comes back in, sees the pillow on the bed, laughs lightly, sadly, picks it up. He has it under his arm as Margaret returns to the room. Margaret softly shuts the door and leans against it, smiling softly at Brick.*)

MARGARET: Brick, I used to think that you were stronger than me and I didn't want to be overpowered by you. But now, since you've taken to liquor—you know what?—I guess it's bad, but now I'm stronger than you and I can love you more truly!
  Don't move that pillow. I'll move it right back if you do!
  —Brick?

(*She turns out all the lamps but a single rose-silk-shaded one by the bed.*)

> I really have been to a doctor and I know what to do and—Brick?—this is my time by the calendar to conceive!

BRICK: Yes, I understand, Maggie. But how are you going to conceive a child by a man in love with his liquor?

MARGARET: By locking his liquor up and making him satisfy my desire before I unlock it!

BRICK: Is that what you've done, Maggie?

MARGARET: Look and see. That cabinet's mighty empty compared to before!

BRICK: Well, I'll be a son of a—

(*He reaches for his crutch but she beats him to it and rushes out on the gallery, hurls the crutch over the rail and comes back in, panting.*

There are running footsteps. Big Mama bursts into the room, her face all awry, gasping, stammering.)

BIG MAMA: Oh, my God, oh, my God, oh, my God, where is it?

MARGARET: Is this what you want, Big Mama?

(*Margaret hands her the package left by the doctor.*)

BIG MAMA: I can't bear it, oh, God! Oh, Brick! Brick, baby!

(*She rushes at him. He averts his face from her sobbing kisses. Margaret watches with a tight smile.*)

My son, Big Daddy's boy! Little Father!

(*The groaning cry is heard again. She runs out, sobbing.*)

MARGARET: And so tonight we're going to make the lie true, and when that's done, I'll bring the liquor back here and we'll get drunk together, here, tonight, in this place that death has come into. . . .
—What do you say?

BRICK: I don't say anything. I guess there's nothing to say.

MARGARET: Oh, you weak people, you weak, beautiful people!—who give up.—What you want is someone to—

(*She turns out the rose-silk lamp.*)

—take hold of you.—Gently, gently, with love! And—

(*The curtain begins to fall slowly.*)

I *do* love you, Brick, I *do*!

BRICK (*smiling with charming sadness*): Wouldn't it be funny if that was true?

THE CURTAIN COMES DOWN

THE END

[1955]

AUGUST WILSON [1945–2005]

Fences

Characters

TROY MAXSON
JIM BONO, *Troy's friend*
ROSE, *Troy's wife*
LYONS, *Troy's oldest son by previous marriage*
GABRIEL, *Troy's brother*
CORY, *Troy and Rose's son*
RAYNELL, *Troy's daughter*

Setting: *The setting is the yard which fronts the only entrance to the Maxson house-hold, an ancient two-story brick house set back off a small alley in a big-city neigh-borhood. The entrance to the house is gained by two or three steps leading to a wooden porch badly in need of paint.*

A relatively recent addition to the house and running its full width, the porch lacks congruence. It is a sturdy porch with a flat roof. One or two chairs of dubious value sit at one end where the kitchen window opens onto the porch. An old-fashioned icebox stands silent guard at the opposite end.

The yard is a small dirt yard, partially fenced, except for the last scene, with a wooden sawhorse, a pile of lumber, and other fence-building equipment set off to the side. Opposite is a tree from which hangs a ball made of rags. A baseball bat leans against the tree. Two oil drums serve as garbage receptacles and sit near the house at right to complete the setting.

The Play: Near the turn of the century, the destitute of Europe sprang on the city with tenacious claws and an honest and solid dream. The city devoured them. They swelled its belly until it burst into a thousand furnaces and sewing machines, a thousand butcher shops and bakers' ovens, a thousand churches and hospitals and funeral parlors and money-lenders. The city grew. It nourished itself and offered each man a partnership limited only by his talent, his guile, and his willingness and capacity for hard work. For the immigrants of Europe, a dream dared and won true.

The descendants of African slaves were offered no such welcome or participation. They came from places called the Carolinas and the Virginias, Georgia, Alabama, Mississippi, and Tennessee. They came strong, eager, searching. The city rejected them and they fled and settled along the river-banks and under bridges in shallow, ramshackle houses made of sticks and tarpaper. They collected rags and wood. They sold the use of their muscles and their bodies. They cleaned houses and washed clothes, they shined shoes, and in quiet desperation and vengeful pride, they stole, and lived in pursuit of their own dream. That they could breathe free, finally, and stand to meet life with the force of dignity and whatever eloquence the heart could call upon.

By 1957, the hard-won victories of the European immigrants had solidified the industrial might of America. War had been confronted and won with new energies that used loyalty and patriotism as its fuel. Life was rich, full, and flourishing. The Milwaukee Braves won the World Series, and the hot winds of change that would make the sixties a turbulent, racing, dangerous, and provocative decade had not yet begun to blow full.

ACT I

Scene I

(*It is 1957. Troy and Bono enter the yard, engaged in conversation. Troy is fifty-three years old, a large man with thick, heavy hands; it is this largeness that he strives to fill out and make an accommodation with. Together with his blackness, his largeness informs his sensibilities and the choices he has made in his life.*)

(*Of the two men, Bono is obviously the follower. His commitment to their friend-ship of thirty-odd years is rooted in his admiration of Troy's honesty, capacity for hard work, and his strength, which Bono seeks to emulate.*)

(*It is Friday night, payday, and the one night of the week the two men engage in a ritual of talk and drink. Troy is usually the most talkative and at times he can be crude and almost vulgar, though he is capable of rising to profound heights of expres-sion. The men carry lunch buckets and wear or carry burlap aprons and are dressed in clothes suitable to their jobs as garbage collectors.*)

BONO: Troy, you ought to stop that lying!
TROY: I ain't lying! The nigger had a watermelon this big.

(*He indicates with his hands.*)

Talking about . . . "What watermelon, Mr. Rand?" I liked to fell out! "What watermelon, Mr. Rand?" . . . And it sitting there big as life.
BONO: What did Mr. Rand say?
TROY: Ain't said nothing. Figure if the nigger too dumb to know he car-rying a watermelon, he wasn't gonna get much sense out of him. Try-ing to hide that great big old watermelon under his coat. Afraid to let the white man see him carry it home.
BONO: I'm like you . . . I ain't got no time for them kind of people.
TROY: Now what he look like getting mad cause he see the man from the union talking to Mr. Rand?

BONO: He come to me talking about . . . "Maxson gonna get us fired." I told him to get away from me with that. He walked away from me calling you a troublemaker. What Mr. Rand say?

TROY: Ain't said nothing. He told me to go down the Commissioner's office next Friday. They called me down there to see them.

BONO: Well, as long as you got your complaint filed, they can't fire you. That's what one of them white fellows tell me.

TROY: I ain't worried about them firing me. They gonna fire me cause I asked a question? That's all I did. I went to Mr. Rand and asked him, "Why? Why you got the white mens driving and the colored lifting?" Told him, "what's the matter, don't I count? You think only white fellows got sense enough to drive a truck. That ain't no paper job! Hell, anybody can drive a truck. How come you got all whites driving and the colored lifting?" He told me "take it to the union." Well, hell, that's what I done! Now they wanna come up with this pack of lies.

BONO: I told Brownie if the man come and ask him any questions . . . just tell the truth! It ain't nothing but something they done trumped up on you cause you filed a complaint on them.

TROY: Brownie don't understand nothing. All I want them to do is change the job description. Give everybody a chance to drive the truck. Brownie can't see that. He ain't got that much sense.

BONO: How you figure he be making out with that gal be up at Taylors' all the time . . . that Alberta gal?

TROY: Same as you and me. Getting just as much as we is. Which is to say nothing.

BONO: It is, huh? I figure you doing a little better than me . . . and I ain't saying what I'm doing.

TROY: Aw, nigger, look here . . . I know you. If you had got anywhere near that gal, twenty minutes later you be looking to tell somebody. And the first one you gonna tell . . . that you gonna want to brag to . . . is gonna be me.

BONO: I ain't saying that. I see where you be eyeing her.

TROY: I eye all the women. I don't miss nothing. Don't never let nobody tell you Troy Maxson don't eye the women.

BONO: You been doing more than eyeing her. You done bought her a drink or two.

TROY: Hell yeah, I bought her a drink! What that mean? I bought you one, too. What that mean cause I buy her a drink? I'm just being polite.

BONO: It's all right to buy her one drink. That's what you call being polite. But when you wanna be buying two or three . . . that's what you call eyeing her.

TROY: Look here, as long as you known me . . . you ever known me to chase after women?

BONO: Hell yeah! Long as I done known you. You forgetting I knew you when.

TROY: Naw, I'm talking about since I been married to Rose?

BONO: Oh, not since you been married to Rose. Now, that's the truth, there. I can say that.

TROY: All right then! Case closed.

BONO: I see you be walking up around Alberta's house. You supposed to be at Taylors' and you be walking up around there.

TROY: What you watching where I'm walking for? I ain't watching after you.

BONO: I seen you walking around there more than once.

TROY: Hell, you liable to see me walking anywhere! That don't mean nothing cause you see me walking around there.

BONO: Where she come from anyway? She just kinda showed up one day.

TROY: Tallahassee. You can look at her and tell she one of them Florida gals. They got some big healthy women down there. Grow them right up out the ground. Got a little bit of Indian in her. Most of them niggers down in Florida got some Indian in them.

BONO: I don't know about that Indian part. But she damn sure big and healthy. Woman wear some big stockings. Got them great big old legs and hips as wide as the Mississippi River.

TROY: Legs don't mean nothing. You don't do nothing but push them out of the way. But them hips cushion the ride!

BONO: Troy, you ain't got no sense.

TROY: It's the truth! Like you riding on Goodyears!

(*Rose enters from the house. She is ten years younger than Troy, her devotion to him stems from her recognition of the possibilities of her life without him: a succession of abusive men and their babies, a life of partying and running the streets, the Church, or aloneness with its attendant pain and frustration. She recognizes Troy's spirit as a fine and illuminating one and she either ignores or forgives his faults, only some of which she recognizes. Though she doesn't drink, her presence is an integral part of the Friday night rituals. She alternates between the porch and the kitchen, where supper preparations are under way.*)

ROSE: What you all out here getting into?

TROY: What you worried about what we getting into for? This is men talk, woman.

ROSE: What I care what you all talking about? Bono, you gonna stay for supper?

BONO: No, I thank you, Rose. But Lucille say she cooking up a pot of pigfeet.

TROY: Pigfeet! Hell, I'm going home with you. Might even stay the night if you got some pigfeet. You got something in there to top them pigfeet, Rose?

ROSE: I'm cooking up some chicken. I got some chicken and collard greens.

TROY: Well, go on back in the house and let me and Bono finish what we was talking about. This is men talk. I got some talk for you later. You know what kind of talk I mean. You go on and powder it up.

ROSE: Troy Maxson, don't you start that now!

TROY (*puts his arm around her*): Aw, woman . . . come here. Look here, Bono . . . when I met this woman . . . I got out that place, say, "Hitch up my pony, saddle up my mare . . . there's a woman out there for me somewhere. I looked here. Looked there. Saw Rose and latched on to her." I latched on to her and told her—I'm gonna tell you the truth—I told her, "Baby, I don't wanna marry, I just wanna be your man." Rose told me . . . tell him what you told me, Rose.

ROSE: I told him if he wasn't the marrying kind, then move out the way so the marrying kind could find me.

TROY: That's what she told me. "Nigger, you in my way. You blocking the view! Move out the way so I can find me a husband." I thought it over two or three days. Come back—

ROSE: Ain't no two or three days nothing. You was back the same night.

TROY: Come back, told her . . . "Okay, baby . . . but I'm gonna buy me a banty rooster and put him out there in the backyard . . . and when he see a stranger come, he'll flap his wings and crow . . ." Look here, Bono, I could watch the front door by myself . . . it was that back door I was worried about.

ROSE: Troy, you ought not talk like that. Troy ain't doing nothing but telling a lie.

TROY: Only thing is . . . when we first got married . . . forget the rooster . . . we ain't had no yard!

BONO: I hear you tell it. Me and Lucille was staying down there on Logan Street. Had two rooms with the outhouse in the back. I ain't mind the outhouse none. But when that goddamn wind blow through there in the winter . . . that's what I'm talking about! To this day I wonder why in the hell I ever stayed down there for six long years. But see, I didn't know I could do no better. I thought only white folks had inside toilets and things.

ROSE: There's a lot of people don't know they can do no better than they doing now. That's just something you got to learn. A lot of folks still shop at Bella's.

TROY: Ain't nothing wrong with shopping at Bella's. She got fresh food.

ROSE: I ain't said nothing about if she got fresh food. I'm talking about what she charge. She charge ten cents more than the A&P.

TROY: The A&P ain't never done nothing for me. I spends my money where I'm treated right. I go down to Bella, say, "I need a loaf of bread,

I'll pay you Friday." She give it to me. What sense that make when I got money to go and spend it somewhere else and ignore the person who done right by me? That ain't in the Bible.

ROSE: We ain't talking about what's in the Bible. What sense it make to shop there when she overcharge?

TROY: You shop where you want to. I'll do my shopping where the people been good to me.

ROSE: Well, I don't think it's right for her to overcharge. That's all I was saying.

BONO: Look here . . . I got to get on. Lucille going be raising all kind of hell.

TROY: Where you going, nigger? We ain't finished this pint. Come here, finish this pint.

BONO: Well, hell, I am . . . if you ever turn the bottle loose.

TROY (*hands him the bottle*): The only thing I say about the A&P is I'm glad Cory got that job down there. Help him take care of his school clothes and things. Gabe done moved out and things getting tight around here. He got that job. . . . He can start to look out for himself.

ROSE: Cory done went and got recruited by a college football team.

TROY: I told that boy about that football stuff. The white man ain't gonna let him get nowhere with that football. I told him when he first come to me with it. Now you come telling me he done went and got more tied up in it. He ought to go and get recruited in how to fix cars or something where he can make a living.

ROSE: He ain't talking about making no living playing football. It's just something the boys in school do. They gonna send a recruiter by to talk to you. He'll tell you he ain't talking about making no living play-ing football. It's a honor to be recruited.

TROY: It ain't gonna get him nowhere. Bono'll tell you that.

BONO: If he be like you in the sports . . . he's gonna be all right. Ain't but two men ever played baseball as good as you. That's Babe Ruth and Josh Gibson.° Them's the only two men ever hit more home runs than you.

TROY: What it ever get me? Ain't got a pot to piss in or a window to throw it out of.

ROSE: Times have changed since you was playing baseball, Troy. That was before the war. Times have changed a lot since then.

TROY: How in hell they done changed?

ROSE: They got lots of colored boys playing ball now. Baseball and football.

BONO: You right about that, Rose. Times have changed, Troy. You just come along too early.

Josh Gibson: (1911–1947), notable 1930s baseball player, considered the Babe Ruth of the Negro leagues.

TROY: There ought not never have been no time called too early! Now you take that fellow . . . what's that fellow they had playing right field for the Yankees back then? You know who I'm talking about, Bono. Used to play right field for the Yankees.

ROSE: Selkirk?

TROY: Selkirk! That's it! Man batting .269, understand? .269. What kind of sense that make? I was hitting .432 with thirty-seven home runs! Man batting .269 and playing right field for the Yankees! I saw Josh Gibson's daughter yesterday. She walking around with raggedy shoes on her feet. Now I bet you Selkirk's daughter ain't walking around with raggedy shoes on her feet! I bet you that!

ROSE: They got a lot of colored baseball players now. Jackie Robinson was the first. Folks had to wait for Jackie Robinson.

TROY: I done seen a hundred niggers play baseball better than Jackie Robinson. Hell, I know some teams Jackie Robinson couldn't even make! What you talking about Jackie Robinson. Jackie Robinson wasn't nobody. I'm talking about if you could play ball then they ought to have let you play. Don't care what color you were. Come telling me I come along too early. If you could play . . . then they ought to have let you play.

(*Troy takes a long drink from the bottle.*)

ROSE: You gonna drink yourself to death. You don't need to be drinking like that.

TROY: Death ain't nothing. I done seen him. Done wrassled with him. You can't tell me nothing about death. Death ain't nothing but a fastball on the outside corner. And you know what I'll do to that! Lookee here, Bono . . . am I lying? You get one of them fastballs, about waist high, over the outside corner of the plate where you can get the meat of the bat on it . . . and good god! You can kiss it goodbye. Now, am I lying?

BONO: Naw, you telling the truth there. I seen you do it.

TROY: If I'm lying . . . that 450 feet worth of lying!

(*Pause.*)

That's all death is to me. A fastball on the outside corner.

ROSE: I don't know why you want to get on talking about death.

TROY: Ain't nothing wrong with talking about death. That's part of life. Everybody gonna die. You gonna die, I'm gonna die. Bono's gonna die. Hell, we all gonna die.

ROSE: But you ain't got to talk about it. I don't like to talk about it.

TROY: You the one brought it up. Me and Bono was talking about baseball . . . you tell me I'm gonna drink myself to death. Ain't that right, Bono? You know I don't drink this but one night out of the week. That's

Friday night. I'm gonna drink just enough to where I can handle it.
Then I cuts it loose. I leave it alone. So don't you worry about me
drinking myself to death. 'Cause I ain't worried about Death. I done
seen him. I done wrestled with him.

Look here, Bono . . . I looked up one day and Death was marching
straight at me. Like Soldiers on Parade! The Army of Death was marching straight at me. The middle of July, 1941. It got real cold just like it
be winter. It seem like Death himself reached out and touched me on
the shoulder. He touch me just like I touch you. I got cold as ice and
Death standing there grinning at me.

ROSE: Troy, why don't you hush that talk.

TROY: I say . . . What you want, Mr. Death? You be wanting me? You
done brought your army to be getting me? I looked him dead in the
eye. I wasn't fearing nothing. I was ready to tangle. Just like I'm ready
to tangle now. The Bible say be ever vigilant. That's why I don't get but
so drunk. I got to keep watch.

ROSE: Troy was right down there in Mercy Hospital. You remember he had
pneumonia? Laying there with a fever talking plumb out of his head.

TROY: Death standing there staring at me . . . carrying that sickle in his
hand. Finally he say, "You want bound over for another year?" See, just
like that . . . "You want bound over for another year?" I told him,
"Bound over hell! Let's settle this now!"

It seem like he kinda fell back when I said that, and all the cold went
out of me. I reached down and grabbed that sickle and threw it just as
far as I could throw it . . . and me and him commenced to wrestling.

We wrestled for three days and three nights. I can't say where I found
the strength from. Every time it seemed like he was gonna get the best
of me, I'd reach way down deep inside myself and find the strength to
do him one better.

ROSE: Every time Troy tell that story he find different ways to tell it. Different things to make up about it.

TROY: I ain't making up nothing. I'm telling you the facts of what happened. I wrestled with Death for three days and three nights and I'm
standing here to tell you about it.

(*Pause.*)

All right. At the end of the third night we done weakened each other
to where we can't hardly move. Death stood up, throwed on his
robe . . . had him a white robe with a hood on it. He throwed on that
robe and went off to look for his sickle. Say, "I'll be back." Just like
that. "I'll be back." I told him, say, "Yeah, but . . . you gonna have to
find me!" I wasn't no fool. I wasn't going looking for him. Death ain't
nothing to play with. And I know he's gonna get me. I know I got to

join his army . . . his camp followers. But as long as I keep my strength and see him coming . . . as long as I keep up my vigilance . . . he's gonna have to fight to get me. I ain't going easy.

BONO: Well, look here, since you got to keep up your vigilance . . . let me have the bottle.

TROY: Aw hell, I shouldn't have told you that part. I should have left out that part.

ROSE: Troy be talking that stuff and half the time don't even know what he be talking about.

TROY: Bono know me better than that.

BONO: That's right. I know you. I know you got some Uncle Remus° in your blood. You got more stories than the devil got sinners.

TROY: Aw hell, I done seen him too! Done talked with the devil.

ROSE: Troy, don't nobody wanna be hearing all that stuff.

(*Lyons enters the yard from the street. Thirty-four years old, Troy's son by a previous marriage, he sports a neatly trimmed goatee, sport coat, white shirt, tieless and buttoned at the collar. Though he fancies himself a musician, he is more caught up in the rituals and "idea" of being a musician than in the actual practice of the music. He has come to borrow money from Troy, and while he knows he will be successful, he is uncertain as to what extent his lifestyle will be held up to scrutiny and ridicule.*)

LYONS: Hey, Pop.

TROY: What you come "Hey, Popping" me for?

LYONS: How you doing, Rose?

(*He kisses her.*)

Mr. Bono. How you doing?

BONO: Hey, Lyons . . . how you been?

TROY: He must have been doing all right. I ain't seen him around here last week.

ROSE: Troy, leave your boy alone. He come by to see you and you wanna start all that nonsense.

TROY: I ain't bothering Lyons.

(*Offers him the bottle.*)

Here . . . get you a drink. We got an understanding. I know why he come by to see me and he know I know.

LYONS: Come on, Pop . . . I just stopped by to say hi . . . see how you was doing.

TROY: You ain't stopped by yesterday.

Uncle Remus: Fictional black narrator in the collection of black folktales adapted by Joel Chandler Harris.

ROSE: You gonna stay for supper, Lyons? I got some chicken cooking in
the oven.

LYONS: No, Rose . . . thanks. I was just in the neighborhood and thought
I'd stop by for a minute.

TROY: You was in the neighborhood all right, nigger. You telling the truth
there. You was in the neighborhood cause it's my payday.

LYONS: Well, hell, since you mentioned it . . . let me have ten dollars.

TROY: I'll be damned! I'll die and go to hell and play blackjack with the
devil before I give you ten dollars.

BONO: That's what I wanna know about . . . that devil you done seen.

LYONS: What . . . Pop done seen the devil? You too much, Pops.

TROY: Yeah, I done seen him. Talked to him too!

ROSE: You ain't seen no devil. I done told you that man ain't had nothing
to do with the devil. Anything you can't understand, you want to call it
the devil.

TROY: Look here, Bono . . . I went down to see Hertzberger about some
furniture. Got three rooms for two-ninety-eight. That what it say on the
radio. "Three rooms . . . two-ninety-eight." Even made up a little song
about it. Go down there . . . man tell me I can't get no credit. I'm working every day and can't get no credit. What to do? I got an empty house
with some raggedy furniture in it. Cory ain't got no bed. He's sleeping
on a pile of rags on the floor. Working every day and can't get no credit.
Come back here—Rose'll tell you—madder than hell. Sit down . . . try
to figure what I'm gonna do. Come a knock on the door. Ain't been living here but three days. Who know I'm here? Open the door . . . devil
standing there bigger than life. White fellow . . . got on good clothes
and everything. Standing there with a clipboard in his hand. I ain't had
to say nothing. First words come out of his mouth was . . . "I understand you need some furniture and can't get no credit." I liked to fell
over. He say, "I'll give you all the credit you want, but you got to pay the
interest on it." I told him, "Give me three rooms worth and charge
whatever you want." Next day a truck pulled up here and two men
unloaded them three rooms. Man what drove the truck give me a book.
Say send ten dollars, first of every month to the address in the book
and everything will be all right. Say if I miss a payment the devil was
coming back and it'll be hell to pay. That was fifteen years ago. To this
day . . . the first of the month I send my ten dollars, Rose'll tell you.

ROSE: Troy lying.

TROY: I ain't never seen that man since. Now you tell me who else that
could have been but the devil? I ain't sold my soul or nothing like that,
you understand. Naw, I wouldn't have truck with the devil about nothing like that. I got my furniture and pays my ten dollars the first of the
month just like clockwork.

BONO: How long you say you been paying this ten dollars a month?

TROY: Fifteen years!

BONO: Hell, ain't you finished paying for it yet? How much the man done charged you?

TROY: Ah hell, I done paid for it. I done paid for it ten times over! The fact is I'm scared to stop paying it.

ROSE: Troy lying. We got that furniture from Mr. Glickman. He ain't paying no ten dollars a month to nobody.

TROY: Aw hell, woman. Bono know I ain't that big a fool.

LYONS: I was just getting ready to say . . . I know where there's a bridge for sale.

TROY: Look here, I'll tell you this . . . it don't matter to me if he was the devil. It don't matter if the devil give credit. Somebody has got to give it.

ROSE: It ought to matter. You going around talking about having truck with the devil . . . God's the one you gonna have to answer to. He's the one gonna be at the Judgment.

LYONS: Yeah, well, look here, Pop . . . let me have that ten dollars. I'll give it back to you. Bonnie got a job working at the hospital.

TROY: What I tell you, Bono? The only time I see this nigger is when he wants something. That's the only time I see him.

LYONS: Come on, Pop, Mr. Bono don't want to hear all that. Let me have the ten dollars. I told you Bonnie working.

TROY: What that mean to me? "Bonnie working." I don't care if she working. Go ask her for the ten dollars if she working. Talking about "Bonnie working." Why ain't you working?

LYONS: Aw, Pop, you know I can't find no decent job. Where am I gonna get a job at? You know I can't get no job.

TROY: I told you I know some people down there. I can get you on the rubbish if you want to work. I told you that the last time you came by here asking me for something.

LYONS: Naw, Pop . . . thanks. That ain't for me. I don't wanna be carrying nobody's rubbish. I don't wanna be punching nobody's time clock.

TROY: What's the matter, you too good to carry people's rubbish? Where you think that ten dollars you talking about come from? I'm just supposed to haul people's rubbish and give my money to you cause you too lazy to work. You too lazy to work and wanna know why you ain't got what I got.

ROSE: What hospital Bonnie working at? Mercy?

LYONS: She's down at Passavant working in the laundry.

TROY: I ain't got nothing as it is. I give you that ten dollars and I got to eat beans the rest of the week. Naw . . . you ain't getting no ten dollars here.

LYONS: You ain't got to be eating no beans. I don't know why you wanna say that.

TROY: I ain't got no extra money. Gabe done moved over to Miss Pearl's paying her the rent and things done got tight around here. I can't afford to be giving you every payday.

LYONS: I ain't asked you to give me nothing. I asked you to loan me ten dollars. I know you got ten dollars.

TROY: Yeah, I got it. You know why I got it? Cause I don't throw my money away out there in the streets. You living the fast life . . . wanna be a musician . . . running around in them clubs and things . . . then, you learn to take care of yourself. You ain't gonna find me going and asking nobody for nothing. I done spent too many years without.

LYONS: You and me is two different people, Pop.

TROY: I done learned my mistake and learned to do what's right by it. You still trying to get something for nothing. Life don't owe you nothing. You owe it to yourself. Ask Bono. He'll tell you I'm right.

LYONS: You got your way of dealing with the world . . . I got mine. The only thing that matters to me is the music.

TROY: Yeah, I can see that! It don't matter how you gonna eat . . . where your next dollar is coming from. You telling the truth there.

LYONS: I know I got to eat. But I got to live too. I need something that gonna help me to get out of the bed in the morning. Make me feel like I belong in the world. I don't bother nobody. I just stay with my music cause that's the only way I can find to live in the world. Otherwise there ain't no telling what I might do. Now I don't come criticizing you and how you live. I just come by to ask you for ten dollars. I don't wanna hear all that about how I live.

TROY: Boy, your mamma did a hell of a job raising you.

LYONS: You can't change me, Pop. I'm thirty-four years old. If you wanted to change me, you should have been there when I was growing up. I come by to see you . . . ask for ten dollars and you want to talk about how I was raised. You don't know nothing about how I was raised.

ROSE: Let the boy have ten dollars, Troy.

TROY (*to Lyons*): What the hell you looking at me for? I ain't got no ten dollars. You know what I do with my money.

(*To Rose.*)

Give him ten dollars if you want him to have it.

ROSE: I will. Just as soon as you turn it loose.

TROY (*handing Rose the money*): There it is. Seventy-six dollars and forty-two cents. You see this, Bono? Now, I ain't gonna get but six of that back.

ROSE: You ought to stop telling that lie. Here, Lyons. (*She hands him the money.*)

LYONS: Thanks, Rose. Look . . . I got to run . . . I'll see you later.

TROY: Wait a minute. You gonna say, "thanks, Rose" and ain't gonna look to see where she got that ten dollars from? See how they do me, Bono?

LYONS: I know she got it from you, Pop. Thanks. I'll give it back to you.

TROY: There he go telling another lie. Time I see that ten dollars . . . he'll be owing me thirty more.

LYONS: See you, Mr. Bono.

BONO: Take care, Lyons!

LYONS: Thanks, Pop. I'll see you again.

(*Lyons exits the yard.*)

TROY: I don't know why he don't go and get him a decent job and take care of that woman he got.

BONO: He'll be all right, Troy. The boy is still young.

TROY: The *boy* is thirty-four years old.

ROSE: Let's not get off into all that.

BONO: Look here . . . I got to be going. I got to be getting on. Lucille gonna be waiting.

TROY (*puts his arm around Rose*): See this woman, Bono? I love this woman. I love this woman so much it hurts. I love her so much . . . I done run out of ways of loving her. So I got to go back to basics. Don't you come by my house Monday morning talking about time to go to work . . . 'cause I'm still gonna be stroking!

ROSE: Troy! Stop it now!

BONO: I ain't paying him no mind, Rose. That ain't nothing but gin-talk. Go on, Troy. I'll see you Monday.

TROY: Don't you come by my house, nigger! I done told you what I'm gonna be doing.

(*The lights go down to black.*)

Scene II

(*The lights come up on Rose hanging up clothes. She hums and sings softly to herself. It is the following morning.*)

ROSE (*sings*): Jesus, be a fence all around me every day
   Jesus, I want you to protect me as I travel on my way.
   Jesus, be a fence all around me every day.

(*Troy enters from the house.*)

Jesus, I want you to protect me
As I travel on my way.
(*To Troy.*) 'Morning. You ready for breakfast? I can fix it soon as I finish
hanging up these clothes.

TROY: I got the coffee on. That'll be all right. I'll just drink some of that
this morning.

ROSE: That 651 hit yesterday. That's the second time this month. Miss
Pearl hit for a dollar . . . seem like those that need the least always get
lucky. Poor folks can't get nothing.

TROY: Them numbers don't know nobody. I don't know why you fool
with them. You and Lyons both.

ROSE: It's something to do.

TROY: You ain't doing nothing but throwing your money away.

ROSE: Troy, you know I don't play foolishly. I just play a nickel here and
a nickel there.

TROY: That's two nickels you done thrown away.

ROSE: Now I hit sometimes . . . that makes up for it. It always comes in
handy when I do hit. I don't hear you complaining then.

TROY: I ain't complaining now. I just say it's foolish. Trying to guess out
of six hundred ways which way the number gonna come. If I had all
the money niggers, these Negroes, throw away on numbers for one
week—just one week—I'd be a rich man.

ROSE: Well, you wishing and calling it foolish ain't gonna stop folks from
playing numbers. That's one thing for sure. Besides . . . some good
things come from playing numbers. Look where Pope done bought
him that restaurant off of numbers.

TROY: I can't stand niggers like that. Man ain't had two dimes to rub
together. He walking around with his shoes all run over bumming
money for cigarettes. All right. Got lucky there and hit the numbers . . .

ROSE: Troy, I know all about it.

TROY: Had good sense, I'll say that for him. He ain't throwed his money
away. I seen niggers hit the numbers and go through two thousand
dollars in four days. Man bought him that restaurant down there . . .
fixed it up real nice . . . and then didn't want nobody to come in it!
A Negro go in there and can't get no kind of service. I seen a white fellow come in there and order a bowl of stew. Pope picked all the meat
out the pot for him. Man ain't had nothing but a bowl of meat! Negro
come behind him and ain't got nothing but the potatoes and carrots.
Talking about what numbers do for people, you picked a wrong
example. Ain't done nothing but make a worser fool out of him than he
was before.

ROSE: Troy, you ought to stop worrying about what happened at work
yesterday.

TROY: I ain't worried. Just told me to be down there at the Commissioner's office on Friday. Everybody think they gonna fire me. I ain't worried about them firing me. You ain't got to worry about that.

(*Pause.*)

Where's Cory? Cory in the house? (*Calls.*) Cory?

ROSE: He gone out.

TROY: Out, huh? He gone out 'cause he know I want him to help me with this fence. I know how he is. That boy scared of work.

(*Gabriel enters. He comes halfway down the alley and, hearing Troy's voice, stops.*)

TROY (*continues*): He ain't done a lick of work in his life.

ROSE: He had to go to football practice. Coach wanted them to get in a little extra practice before the season start.

TROY: I got his practice . . . running out of here before he get his chores done.

ROSE: Troy, what is wrong with you this morning? Don't nothing set right with you. Go on back in there and go to bed . . . get up on the other side.

TROY: Why something got to be wrong with me? I ain't said nothing wrong with me.

ROSE: You got something to say about everything. First it's the numbers . . . then it's the way the man runs his restaurant . . . then you done got on Cory. What's it gonna be next? Take a look up there and see if the weather suits you . . . or is it gonna be how you gonna put up the fence with the clothes hanging in the yard.

TROY: You hit the nail on the head then.

ROSE: I know you like I know the back of my hand. Go on in there and get you some coffee . . . see if that straighten you up. 'Cause you ain't right this morning.

(*Troy starts into the house and sees Gabriel. Gabriel starts singing. Troy's brother, he is seven years younger than Troy. Injured in World War II, he has a metal plate in his head. He carries an old trumpet tied around his waist and believes with every fiber of his being that he is the Archangel Gabriel. He carries a chipped basket with an assortment of discarded fruits and vegetables he has picked up in the strip district and which he attempts to sell.*)

GABRIEL (*singing*): Yes, ma'am, I got plums
    You ask me how I sell them
    Oh ten cents apiece
    Three for a quarter
    Come and buy now
    'Cause I'm here today
    And tomorrow I'll be gone

(*Gabriel enters.*)

   Hey, Rose!
ROSE: How you doing, Gabe?
GABRIEL: There's Troy . . . Hey, Troy!
TROY: Hey, Gabe.

(*Exit into kitchen.*)

ROSE (*to Gabriel*): What you got there?
GABRIEL: You know what I got, Rose. I got fruits and vegetables.
ROSE (*looking in basket*): Where's all these plums you talking about?
GABRIEL: I ain't got no plums today, Rose. I was just singing that. Have
   some tomorrow. Put me in a big order for plums. Have enough plums
   tomorrow for St. Peter and everybody.

(*Troy reenters from kitchen, crosses to steps.*)
(*To Rose.*)

   Troy's mad at me.
TROY: I ain't mad at you. What I got to be mad at you about? You ain't
   done nothing to me.
GABRIEL: I just moved over to Miss Pearl's to keep out from in your way.
   I ain't mean no harm by it.
TROY: Who said anything about that? I ain't said anything about that.
GABRIEL: You ain't mad at me, is you?
TROY: Naw . . . I ain't mad at you, Gabe. If I was mad at you I'd tell you
   about it.
GABRIEL: Got me two rooms. In the basement. Got my own door too.
   Wanna see my key?

(*He holds up a key.*)

   That's my own key! Ain't nobody else got a key like that. That's my key!
   My two rooms!
TROY: Well, that's good, Gabe. You got your own key . . . that's good.
ROSE: You hungry, Gabe? I was just fixing to cook Troy his breakfast.
GABRIEL: I'll take some biscuits. You got some biscuits? Did you know
   when I was in heaven . . . every morning me and St. Peter would sit
   down by the gate and eat some big fat biscuits? Oh, yeah! We had us a
   good time. We'd sit there and eat us them biscuits and then St. Peter
   would go off to sleep and tell me to wake him up when it's time to open
   the gates for the judgment.
ROSE: Well, come on . . . I'll make up a batch of biscuits.

(*Rose exits into the house.*)

GABRIEL: Troy . . . St. Peter got your name in the book. I seen it. It say . . . Troy Maxson. I say . . . I know him! He got the same name like what I got. That's my brother!

TROY: How many times you gonna tell me that, Gabe?

GABRIEL: Ain't got my name in the book. Don't have to have my name. I done died and went to heaven. He got your name though. One morning St. Peter was looking at his book . . . marking it up for the judgment . . . and he let me see your name. Got it in there under M. Got Rose's name . . . I ain't seen it like I seen yours . . . but I know it's in there. He got a great big book. Got everybody's name what was ever been born. That's what he told me. But I seen your name. Seen it with my own eyes.

TROY: Go on in the house there. Rose going to fix you something to eat.

GABRIEL: Oh, I ain't hungry. I done had breakfast with Aunt Jemimah. She come by and cooked me up a whole mess of flapjacks. Remember how we used to eat them flapjacks?

TROY: Go on in the house and get you something to eat now.

GABRIEL: I got to go sell my plums. I done sold some tomatoes. Got me two quarters. Wanna see?

(*He shows Troy his quarters.*)

I'm gonna save them and buy me a new horn so St. Peter can hear me when it's time to open the gates.

(*Gabriel stops suddenly. Listens.*)

Hear that? That's the hellhounds. I got to chase them out of here. Go on get out of here! Get out!

(*Gabriel exits singing.*)

Better get ready for the judgment
Better get ready for the judgment
My Lord is coming down

(*Rose enters from the house.*)

TROY: He gone off somewhere.

GABRIEL (*offstage*): Better get ready for the judgment
Better get ready for the judgment morning
Better get ready for the judgment
My God is coming down

ROSE: He ain't eating right. Miss Pearl say she can't get him to eat nothing.

TROY: What you want me to do about it, Rose? I done did everything I can for the man. I can't make him get well. Man got half his head blown away . . . what you expect?

Rose: Seem like something ought to be done to help him.

Troy: Man don't bother nobody. He just mixed up from that metal plate he got in his head. Ain't no sense for him to go back into the hospital.

Rose: Least he be eating right. They can help him take care of himself.

Troy: Don't nobody wanna be locked up, Rose. What you wanna lock him up for? Man go over there and fight the war ... messin' around with them Japs, get half his head blown off ... and they give him a lousy three thousand dollars. And I had to swoop down on that.

Rose: Is you fixing to go into that again?

Troy: That's the only way I got a roof over my head ... cause of that metal plate.

Rose: Ain't no sense you blaming yourself for nothing. Gabe wasn't in no condition to manage that money. You done what was right by him. Can't nobody say you ain't done what was right by him. Look how long you took care of him ... till he wanted to have his own place and moved over there with Miss Pearl.

Troy: That ain't what I'm saying, woman! I'm just stating the facts. If my brother didn't have that metal plate in his head ... I wouldn't have a pot to piss in or a window to throw it out of. And I'm fifty-three years old. Now see if you can understand that!

(*Troy gets up from the porch and starts to exit the yard.*)

Rose: Where you going off to? You been running out of here every Saturday for weeks. I thought you was gonna work on this fence?

Troy: I'm gonna walk down to Taylors'. Listen to the ball game. I'll be back in a bit. I'll work on it when I get back.

(*He exits the yard. The lights go to black.*)

Scene III

(*The lights come up on the yard. It is four hours later. Rose is taking down the clothes from the line. Cory enters carrying his football equipment.*)

Rose: Your daddy like to had a fit with you running out of here this morning without doing your chores.

Cory: I told you I had to go to practice.

Rose: He say you were supposed to help him with this fence.

Cory: He been saying that the last four or five Saturdays, and then he don't never do nothing but go down to Taylors'. Did you tell him about the recruiter?

Rose: Yeah, I told him.

Cory: What he say?

ROSE: He ain't said nothing too much. You get in there and get started on your chores before he gets back. Go on and scrub down them steps before he gets back here hollering and carrying on.

CORY: I'm hungry. What you got to eat, Mama?

ROSE: Go on and get started on your chores. I got some meat loaf in there. Go on and make you a sandwich . . . and don't leave no mess in there.

(*Cory exits into the house. Rose continues to take down the clothes. Troy enters the yard and sneaks up and grabs her from behind.*)

Troy! Go on, now. You liked to scared me to death. What was the score of the game? Lucille had me on the phone and I couldn't keep up with it.

TROY: What I care about the game? Come here, woman. (*He tries to kiss her.*)

ROSE: I thought you went down Taylors' to listen to the game. Go on, Troy! You supposed to be putting up this fence.

TROY (*attempting to kiss her again*): I'll put it up when I finish with what is at hand.

ROSE: Go on, Troy. I ain't studying you.

TROY (*chasing after her*): I'm studying you . . . fixing to do my homework!

ROSE: Troy, you better leave me alone.

TROY: Where's Cory? That boy brought his butt home yet?

ROSE: He's in the house doing his chores.

TROY (*calling*): Cory! Get your butt out here, boy!

(*Rose exits into the house with the laundry. Troy goes over to the pile of wood, picks up a board, and starts sawing. Cory enters from the house.*)

TROY: You just now coming in here from leaving this morning?

CORY: Yeah, I had to go to football practice.

TROY: Yeah, what?

CORY: Yessir.

TROY: I ain't but two seconds off you noway. The garbage sitting in there overflowing . . . you ain't done none of your chores . . . and you come in here talking about "Yeah."

CORY: I was just getting ready to do my chores now, Pop . . .

TROY: Your first chore is to help me with this fence on Saturday. Everything else come after that. Now get that saw and cut them boards.

(*Cory takes the saw and begins cutting the boards. Troy continues working. There is a long pause.*)

CORY: Hey, Pop . . . why don't you buy a TV?

TROY: What I want with a TV? What I want one of them for?

CORY: Everybody got one. Earl, Ba Bra . . . Jesse!

TROY: I ain't asked you who had one. I say what I want with one?

CORY: So you can watch it. They got lots of things on TV. Baseball games and everything. We could watch the World Series.

TROY: Yeah . . . and how much this TV cost?

CORY: I don't know. They got them on sale for around two hundred dollars.

TROY: Two hundred dollars, huh?

CORY: That ain't that much, Pop.

TROY: Naw, it's just two hundred dollars. See that roof you got over your head at night? Let me tell you something about that roof. It's been over ten years since that roof was last tarred. See now . . . the snow come this winter and sit up there on that roof like it is . . . and it's gonna seep inside. It's just gonna be a little bit . . . ain't gonna hardly notice it. Then the next thing you know, it's gonna be leaking all over the house. Then the wood rot from all that water and you gonna need a whole new roof. Now, how much you think it cost to get that roof tarred?

CORY: I don't know.

TROY: Two hundred and sixty-four dollars . . . cash money. While you thinking about a TV, I got to be thinking about the roof . . . and whatever else go wrong around here. Now if you had two hundred dollars, what would you do . . . fix the roof or buy a TV?

CORY: I'd buy a TV. Then when the roof started to leak . . . when it needed fixing . . . I'd fix it.

TROY: Where you gonna get the money from? You done spent it for a TV. You gonna sit up and watch the water run all over your brand new TV.

CORY: Aw, Pop. You got money. I know you do.

TROY: Where I got it at, huh?

CORY: You got it in the bank.

TROY: You wanna see my bankbook? You wanna see that seventy-three dollars and twenty-two cents I got sitting up in there.

CORY: You ain't got to pay for it all at one time. You can put a down payment on it and carry it on home with you.

TROY: Not me. I ain't gonna owe nobody nothing if I can help it. Miss a payment and they come and snatch it right out your house. Then what you got? Now, soon as I get two hundred dollars clear, then I'll buy a TV. Right now, as soon as I get two hundred and sixty-four dollars, I'm gonna have this roof tarred.

CORY: Aw . . . Pop!

TROY: You go on and get you two hundred dollars and buy one if ya want it. I got better things to do with my money.

CORY: I can't get no two hundred dollars. I ain't never seen two hundred dollars.

TROY: I'll tell you what . . . you get you a hundred dollars and I'll put the other hundred with it.

CORY: All right, I'm gonna show you.

TROY: You gonna show me how you can cut them boards right now.

(*Cory begins to cut the boards. There is a long pause.*)

CORY: The Pirates won today. That makes five in a row.

TROY: I ain't thinking about the Pirates. Got an all-white team. Got that boy . . . that Puerto Rican boy . . . Clemente. Don't even half-play him. That boy could be something if they give him a chance. Play him one day and sit him on the bench the next.

CORY: He gets a lot of chances to play.

TROY: I'm talking about playing regular. Playing every day so you can get your timing. That's what I'm talking about.

CORY: They got some white guys on the team that don't play every day. You can't play everybody at the same time.

TROY: If they got a white fellow sitting on the bench . . . you can bet your last dollar he can't play! The colored guy got to be twice as good before he get on the team. That's why I don't want you to get all tied up in them sports. Man on the team and what it get him? They got colored on the team and don't use them. Same as not having them. All them teams the same.

CORY: The Braves got Hank Aaron and Wes Covington. Hank Aaron hit two home runs today. That makes forty-three.

TROY: Hank Aaron ain't nobody. That's what you supposed to do. That's how you supposed to play the game. Ain't nothing to it. It's just a matter of timing . . . getting the right follow-through. Hell, I can hit forty-three home runs right now!

CORY: Not off no major-league pitching, you couldn't.

TROY: We had better pitching in the Negro leagues. I hit seven home runs off of Satchel Paige.° You can't get no better than that!

CORY: Sandy Koufax. He's leading the league in strikeouts.

TROY: I ain't thinking of no Sandy Koufax.

CORY: You got Warren Spahn and Lew Burdette. I bet you couldn't hit no home runs off of Warren Spahn.

TROY: I'm through with it now. You go on and cut them boards.

(*Pause.*)

Your mama tell me you done got recruited by a college football team? Is that right?

CORY: Yeah. Coach Zellman say the recruiter gonna be coming by to talk to you. Get you to sign the permission papers.

Satchel Paige: (1906?–1982), renowned black pitcher in the Negro leagues and Major League Baseball.

TROY: I thought you supposed to be working down there at the A&P. Ain't you suppose to be working down there after school?

CORY: Mr. Stawicki say he gonna hold my job for me until after the football season. Say starting next week I can work weekends.

TROY: I thought we had an understanding about this football stuff? You suppose to keep up with your chores and hold that job down at the A&P. Ain't been around here all day on a Saturday. Ain't none of your chores done . . . and now you telling me you done quit your job.

CORY: I'm gonna be working weekends.

TROY: You damn right you are! And ain't no need for nobody coming around here to talk to me about signing nothing.

CORY: Hey, Pop . . . you can't do that. He's coming all the way from North Carolina.

TROY: I don't care where he coming from. The white man ain't gonna let you get nowhere with that football noway. You go on and get your book-learning so you can work yourself up in that A&P or learn how to fix cars or build houses or something, get you a trade. That way you have something can't nobody take away from you. You go on and learn how to put your hands to some good use. Besides hauling people's garbage.

CORY: I get good grades, Pop. That's why the recruiter wants to talk with you. You got to keep up your grades to get recruited. This way I'll be going to college. I'll get a chance . . .

TROY: First you gonna get your butt down there to the A&P and get your job back.

CORY: Mr. Stawicki done already hired somebody else 'cause I told him I was playing football.

TROY: You a bigger fool than I thought . . . to let somebody take away your job so you can play some football. Where you gonna get your money to take out your girlfriend and whatnot? What kind of foolishness is that to let somebody take away your job?

CORY: I'm still gonna be working weekends.

TROY: Naw . . . naw. You getting your butt out of here and finding you another job.

CORY: Come on, Pop! I got to practice. I can't work after school and play football too. The team needs me. That's what Coach Zellman say . . .

TROY: I don't care what nobody else say. I'm the boss . . . you understand? I'm the boss around here. I do the only saying what counts.

CORY: Come on, Pop!

TROY: I asked you . . . did you understand?

CORY: Yeah . . .

TROY: What?!

CORY: Yessir.

TROY: You go on down there to that A&P and see if you can get your job back. If you can't do both . . . then you quit the football team. You've got to take the crookeds with the straights.

CORY: Yessir.

(*Pause.*)

Can I ask you a question?

TROY: What the hell you wanna ask me? Mr. Stawicki the one you got the questions for.

CORY: How come you ain't never liked me?

TROY: Liked you? Who the hell say I got to like you? What law is there say I got to like you? Wanna stand up in my face and ask a damn fool-ass question like that. Talking about liking somebody. Come here, boy, when I talk to you.

(*Cory comes over to where Troy is working. He stands slouched over and Troy shoves him on his shoulder.*)

Straighten up, goddammit! I asked you a question . . . what law is there say I got to like you?

CORY: None.

TROY: Well, all right then! Don't you eat every day?

(*Pause.*)

Answer me when I talk to you! Don't you eat every day?

CORY: Yeah.

TROY: Nigger, as long as you in my house, you put that sir on the end of it when you talk to me!

CORY: Yes . . . sir.

TROY: You eat every day.

CORY: Yessir!

TROY: Got a roof over your head.

CORY: Yessir!

TROY: Got clothes on your back.

CORY: Yessir.

TROY: Why you think that is?

CORY: Cause of you.

TROY: Ah, hell I know it's 'cause of me . . . but why do you think that is?

CORY (*hesitant*): Cause you like me.

TROY: Like you? I go out of here every morning . . . bust my butt . . . putting up with them crackers° every day . . . cause I like you? You about the biggest fool I ever saw.

crackers: Reference to white people, often used to belittle underprivileged whites.

(*Pause.*)

It's my job. It's my responsibility! You understand that? A man got to
take care of his family. You live in my house . . . sleep you behind on my
bedclothes . . . fill you belly up with my food . . . cause you my son. You
my flesh and blood. Not cause I like you! Cause it's my duty to take care
of you. I owe a responsibility to you! Let's get this straight right here . . .
before it go along any further . . . I ain't got to like you. Mr. Rand don't
give me my money come payday cause he likes me. He gives me cause
he owe me. I done give you everything I had to give you. I gave you
your life! Me and your mama worked that out between us. And liking
your black ass wasn't part of the bargain. Don't you try and go through
life worrying about if somebody like you or not. You best be making
sure they doing right by you. You understand what I'm saying, boy?

CORY: Yessir.

TROY: Then get the hell out of my face, and get on down to that A&P.

(*Rose has been standing behind the screen door for much of the scene. She enters as Cory exits.*)

ROSE: Why don't you let the boy go ahead and play football, Troy? Ain't
no harm in that. He's just trying to be like you with the sports.

TROY: I don't want him to be like me! I want him to move as far away
from my life as he can get. You the only decent thing that ever happened to me. I wish him that. But I don't wish him a thing else from
my life. I decided seventeen years ago that boy wasn't getting involved
in no sports. Not after what they did to me in the sports.

ROSE: Troy, why don't you admit you was too old to play in the major
leagues? For once . . . why don't you admit that?

TROY: What do you mean too old? Don't come telling me I was too old. I
just wasn't the right color. Hell, I'm fifty-three years old and can do
better than Selkirk's .269 right now!

ROSE: How's was you gonna play ball when you were over forty? Sometimes I can't get no sense out of you.

TROY: I got good sense, woman. I got sense enough not to let my boy get
hurt over playing no sports. You been mothering that boy too much.
Worried about if people like him.

ROSE: Everything that boy do . . . he do for you. He wants you to say
"Good job, son." That's all.

TROY: Rose, I ain't got time for that. He's alive. He's healthy. He's got to
make his own way. I made mine. Ain't nobody gonna hold his hand
when he get out there in that world.

ROSE: Times have changed from when you was young, Troy. People
change. The world's changing around you and you can't even see it.

TROY (*slow, methodical*): Woman . . . I do the best I can do. I come in here every Friday. I carry a sack of potatoes and a bucket of lard. You all line up at the door with your hands out. I give you the lint from my pockets. I give you my sweat and my blood. I ain't got no tears. I done spent them. We go upstairs in that room at night . . . and I fall down on you and try to blast a hole into forever. I get up Monday morning . . . find my lunch on the table. I go out. Make my way. Find my strength to carry me through to the next Friday.

(*Pause.*)

That's all I got, Rose. That's all I got to give. I can't give nothing else.

(*Troy exits into the house. The lights go down to black.*)

Scene IV

(*It is Friday. Two weeks later. Cory starts out of the house with his football equipment. The phone rings.*)

CORY (*calling*): I got it!

(*He answers the phone and stands in the screen door talking.*)

Hello? Hey, Jesse. Naw . . . I was just getting ready to leave now.
ROSE (*calling*): Cory!
CORY: I told you, man, them spikes is all tore up. You can use them if you want, but they ain't no good. Earl got some spikes.
ROSE (*calling*): Cory!
CORY (*calling to Rose*): Mam? I'm talking to Jesse.

(*Into phone.*)

When she say that? (*Pause.*) Aw, you lying, man. I'm gonna tell her you said that.
ROSE (*calling*): Cory, don't you go nowhere!
CORY: I got to go to the game, Ma!

(*Into the phone.*)

Yeah, hey, look, I'll talk to you later. Yeah, I'll meet you over Earl's house. Later. Bye, Ma.

(*Cory exits the house and starts out the yard.*)

ROSE: Cory, where you going off to? You got that stuff all pulled out and thrown all over your room.
CORY (*in the yard*): I was looking for my spikes. Jesse wanted to borrow my spikes.

ROSE: Get up there and get that cleaned up before your daddy get back in here.

CORY: I got to go to the game! I'll clean it up *when I get back*.

(*Cory exits.*)

ROSE: That's all he need to do is see that room all messed up.

(*Rose exits into the house. Troy and Bono enter the yard. Troy is dressed in clothes other than his work clothes.*)

BONO: He told him the same thing he told you. Take it to the union.

TROY: Brownie ain't got that much sense. Man wasn't thinking about nothing. He wait until I confront them on it . . . then he wanna come crying seniority.

(*Calls.*)

Hey, Rose!

BONO: I wish I could have seen Mr. Rand's face when he told you.

TROY: He couldn't get it out of his mouth! Liked to bit his tongue! When they called me down there to the Commissioner's office . . . he thought they was gonna fire me. Like everybody else.

BONO: I didn't think they was gonna fire you. I thought they was gonna put you on the warning paper.

TROY: Hey, Rose!

(*To Bono.*)

Yeah, Mr. Rand like to bit his tongue.

(*Troy breaks the seal on the bottle, takes a drink, and hands it to Bono.*)

BONO: I see you run right down to Taylors' and told that Alberta gal.

TROY (*calling*): Hey, Rose! (*To Bono.*) I told everybody. Hey, Rose! I went down there to cash my check.

ROSE (*entering from the house*): Hush all that hollering, man! I know you out here. What they say down there at the Commissioner's office?

TROY: You supposed to come when I call you, woman. Bono'll tell you that.

(*To Bono.*)

Don't Lucille come when you call her?

ROSE: Man, hush your mouth. I ain't no dog . . . talk about "come when you call me."

TROY (*puts his arm around Rose*): You hear this Bono? I had me an old dog used to get uppity like that. You say, "C'mere, Blue!" . . . and he just lay there and look at you. End up getting a stick and chasing him away trying to make him come.

ROSE: I ain't studying you and your dog. I remember you used to sing that old song.

TROY (*he sings*): Hear it ring! Hear it ring! I had a dog his name was Blue.

ROSE: Don't nobody wanna hear you sing that old song.

TROY (*sings*): You know Blue was mighty true.

ROSE: Used to have Cory running around here singing that song.

BONO: Hell, I remember that song myself.

TROY (*sings*): You know Blue was a good old dog.
    Blue treed a possum in a hollow log.
    That was my daddy's song. My daddy made up that song.

ROSE: I don't care who made it up. Don't nobody wanna hear you sing it.

TROY (*makes a song like calling a dog*): Come here, woman.

ROSE: You come in here carrying on, I reckon they ain't fired you. What they say down there at the Commissioner's office?

TROY: Look here, Rose . . . Mr. Rand called me into his office today when I got back from talking to them people down there . . . it come from up top . . . he called me in and told me they was making me a driver.

ROSE: Troy, you kidding!

TROY: No I ain't. Ask Bono.

ROSE: Well, that's great, Troy. Now you don't have to hassle them people no more.

(*Lyons enters from the street.*)

TROY: Aw hell, I wasn't looking to see you today. I thought you was in jail. Got it all over the front page of the *Courier* about them raiding Sefus' place . . . where you be hanging out with all them thugs.

LYONS: Hey, Pop . . . that ain't got nothing to do with me. I don't go down there gambling. I go down there to sit in with the band. I ain't got nothing to do with the gambling part. They got some good music down there.

TROY: They got some rogues . . . is what they got.

LYONS: How you been, Mr. Bono? Hi, Rose.

BONO: I see where you playing down at the Crawford Grill tonight.

ROSE: How come you ain't brought Bonnie like I told you. You should have brought Bonnie with you, she ain't been over in a month of Sundays.

LYONS: I was just in the neighborhood . . . thought I'd stop by.

TROY: Here he come . . .

BONO: Your daddy got a promotion on the rubbish. He's gonna be the first colored driver. Ain't got to do nothing but sit up there and read the paper like them white fellows.

LYONS: Hey, Pop . . . if you knew how to read you'd be all right.

BONO: Naw . . . naw . . . you mean if the nigger knew how to drive he'd be all right. Been fighting with them people about driving and ain't even got a license. Mr. Rand know you ain't got no driver's license?

TROY: Driving ain't nothing. All you do is point the truck where you want it to go. Driving ain't nothing.

BONO: Do Mr. Rand know you ain't got no driver's license? That's what I'm talking about. I ain't asked if driving was easy. I asked if Mr. Rand know you ain't got no driver's license.

TROY: He ain't got to know. The man ain't got to know my business. Time he find out, I have two or three driver's licenses.

LYONS (*going into his pocket*): Say, look here, Pop . . .

TROY: I knew it was coming. Didn't I tell you, Bono? I know what kind of "Look here, Pop" that was. The nigger fixing to ask me for some money. It's Friday night. It's my payday. All them rogues down there on the avenue . . . the ones that ain't in jail . . . and Lyons is hopping in his shoes to get down there with them.

LYONS: See, Pop . . . if you give somebody else a chance to talk some-time, you'd see that I was fixing to pay you back your ten dollars like I told you. Here . . . I told you I'd pay you when Bonnie got paid.

TROY: Naw . . . you go ahead and keep that ten dollars. Put it in the bank. The next time you feel like you wanna come by here and ask me for something . . . you go on down there and get that.

LYONS: Here's your ten dollars, Pop. I told you I don't want you to give me nothing. I just wanted to borrow ten dollars.

TROY: Naw . . . you go on and keep that for the next time you want to ask me.

LYONS: Come on, Pop . . . here go your ten dollars.

ROSE: Why don't you go on and let the boy pay you back, Troy?

LYONS: Here you go, Rose. If you don't take it I'm gonna have to hear about it for the next six months.

(*He hands her the money.*)

ROSE: You can hand yours over here too, Troy.

TROY: You see this, Bono. You see how they do me.

BONO: Yeah, Lucille do me the same way.

(*Gabriel is heard singing offstage. He enters.*)

GABRIEL: Better get ready for the Judgment! Better get ready for . . . Hey! . . . Hey! . . . There's Troy's boy!

LYONS: How are you doing, Uncle Gabe?

GABRIEL: Lyons . . . The King of the Jungle! Rose . . . hey, Rose. Got a flower for you.

(*He takes a rose from his pocket.*)

Picked it myself. That's the same rose like you is!

ROSE: That's right nice of you, Gabe.

LYONS: What you been doing, Uncle Gabe?

GABRIEL: Oh, I been chasing hellhounds and waiting on the time to tell St. Peter to open the gates.

LYONS: You been chasing hellhounds, huh? Well . . . you doing the right thing, Uncle Gabe. Somebody got to chase them.

GABRIEL: Oh, yeah . . . I know it. The devil's strong. The devil ain't no pushover. Hellhounds snipping at everybody's heels. But I got my trumpet waiting on the judgment time.

LYONS: Waiting on the Battle of Armageddon, huh?

GABRIEL: Ain't gonna be too much of a battle when God get to waving that Judgment sword. But the people's gonna have a hell of a time trying to get into heaven if them gates ain't open.

LYONS (*putting his arm around Gabriel*): You hear this, Pop. Uncle Gabe, you all right!

GABRIEL (*laughing with Lyons*): Lyons! King of the Jungle.

ROSE: You gonna stay for supper, Gabe. Want me to fix you a plate?

GABRIEL: I'll take a sandwich, Rose. Don't want no plate. Just wanna eat with my hands. I'll take a sandwich.

ROSE: How about you, Lyons? You staying? Got some short ribs cooking.

LYONS: Naw, I won't eat nothing till after we finished playing.

(*Pause.*)

You ought to come down and listen to me play, Pop.

TROY: I don't like that Chinese music. All that noise.

ROSE: Go on in the house and wash up, Gabe . . . I'll fix you a sandwich.

GABRIEL (*to Lyons, as he exits*): Troy's mad at me.

LYONS: What you mad at Uncle Gabe for, Pop.

ROSE: He thinks Troy's mad at him cause he moved over to Miss Pearl's.

TROY: I ain't mad at the man. He can live where he want to live at.

LYONS: What he move over there for? Miss Pearl don't like nobody.

ROSE: She don't mind him none. She treats him real nice. She just don't allow all that singing.

TROY: She don't mind that rent he be paying . . . that's what she don't mind.

ROSE: Troy, I ain't going through that with you no more. He's over there cause he want to have his own place. He can come and go as he please.

TROY: Hell, he could come and go as he please here. I wasn't stopping him. I ain't put no rules on him.

ROSE: It ain't the same thing, Troy. And you know it.

(*Gabriel comes to the door.*)

Now, that's the last I wanna hear about that. I don't wanna hear nothing else about Gabe and Miss Pearl. And next week . . .

GABRIEL: I'm ready for my sandwich, Rose.

ROSE: And next week . . . when that recruiter come from that school . . . I want you to sign that paper and go on and let Cory play football. Then that'll be the last I have to hear about that.

TROY (*to Rose as she exits into the house*): I ain't thinking about Cory nothing.

LYONS: What . . . Cory got recruited? What school he going to?

TROY: That boy walking around here smelling his piss . . . thinking he's grown. Thinking he's gonna do what he want, irrespective of what I say. Look here, Bono . . . I left the Commissioner's office and went down to the A&P . . . that boy ain't working down there. He lying to me. Telling me he got his job back . . . telling me he working weekends . . . telling me he working after school . . . Mr. Stawicki tell me he ain't working down there at all!

LYONS: Cory just growing up. He's just busting at the seams trying to fill out your shoes.

TROY: I don't care what he's doing. When he get to the point where he wanna disobey me . . . then it's time for him to move on. Bono'll tell you that. I bet he ain't never disobeyed his daddy without paying the consequences.

BONO: I ain't never had a chance. My daddy came on through . . . but I ain't never knew him to see him . . . or what he had on his mind or where he went. Just moving on through. Searching out the New Land. That's what the old folks used to call it. See a fellow moving around from place to place . . . woman to woman . . . called it searching out the New Land. I can't say if he ever found it. I come along, didn't want no kids. Didn't know if I was gonna be in one place long enough to fix on them right as their daddy. I figured I was going searching too. As it turned out I been hooked up with Lucille near about as long as your daddy been with Rose. Going on sixteen years.

TROY: Sometimes I wish I hadn't known my daddy. He ain't cared nothing about no kids. A kid to him wasn't nothing. All he wanted was for you to learn how to walk so he could start you to working. When it come time for eating . . . he ate first. If there was anything left over, that's what you got. Man would sit down and eat two chickens and give you the wing.

LYONS: You ought to stop that, Pop. Everybody feed their kids. No matter how hard times is . . . everybody care about their kids. Make sure they have something to eat.

TROY: The only thing my daddy cared about was getting them bales of cotton in to Mr. Lubin. That's the only thing that mattered to him.

Sometimes I used to wonder why he was living. Wonder why the devil hadn't come and got him. "Get them bales of cotton in to Mr. Lubin" and find out he owe him money . . .

LYONS: He should have just went on and left when he saw he couldn't get nowhere. That's what I would have done.

TROY: How he gonna leave with eleven kids? And where he gonna go? He ain't knew how to do nothing but farm. No, he was trapped and I think he knew it. But I'll say this for him . . . he felt a responsibility toward us. Maybe he ain't treated us the way I felt he should have . . . but without that responsibility he could have walked off and left us . . . made his own way.

BONO: A lot of them did. Back in those days what you talking about . . . they walk out their front door and just take on down one road or another and keep on walking.

LYONS: There you go! That's what I'm talking about.

BONO: Just keep on walking till you come to something else. Ain't you never heard of nobody having the walking blues? Well, that's what you call it when you just take off like that.

TROY: My daddy ain't had them walking blues! What you talking about? He stayed right there with his family. But he was just as evil as he could be. My mama couldn't stand him. Couldn't stand that evilness. She run off when I was about eight. She sneaked off one night after he had gone to sleep. Told me she was coming back for me. I ain't never seen her no more. All his women run off and left him. He wasn't good for nobody.

When my turn come to head out, I was fourteen and got to sniffing around Joe Canewell's daughter. Had us an old mule we called Greyboy. My daddy sent me out to do some plowing and I tied up Greyboy and went to fooling around with Joe Canewell's daughter. We done found us a nice little spot, got real cozy with each other. She about thirteen and we done figured we was grown anyway . . . so we down there enjoying ourselves . . . ain't thinking about nothing. We didn't know Greyboy had got loose and wandered back to the house and my daddy was looking for me. We down there by the creek enjoying ourselves when my daddy come up on us. Surprised us. He had them leather straps off the mule and commenced to whupping me like there was no tomorrow. I jumped up, mad and embarrassed. I was scared of my daddy. When he commenced to whupping on me . . . quite naturally I run to get out of the way.

(*Pause.*)

Now I thought he was mad cause I ain't done my work. But I see where he was chasing me off so he could have the gal for himself. When I see

what the matter of it was, I lost all fear of my daddy. Right there is
where I become a man . . . at fourteen years of age.

(*Pause.*)

Now it was my turn to run him off. I picked up them same reins that
he had used on me. I picked up them reins and commenced to whupping on him. The gal jumped up and run off . . . and when my daddy
turned to face me, I could see why the devil had never come to get
him . . . cause he was the devil himself. I don't know what happened.
When I woke up, I was laying right there by the creek, and Blue . . . this
old dog we had . . . was licking my face. I thought I was blind. I couldn't
see nothing. Both my eyes were swollen shut. I layed there and cried. I
didn't know what I was gonna do. The only thing I knew was the time
had come for me to leave my daddy's house. And right there the world
suddenly got big. And it was a long time before I could cut it down to
where I could handle it.

   Part of that cutting down was when I got to the place where I could
feel him kicking in my blood and knew that the only thing that separated us was the matter of a few years.

(*Gabriel enters from the house with a sandwich.*)

LYONS: What you got there, Uncle Gabe?
GABRIEL: Got me a ham sandwich. Rose gave me a ham sandwich.
TROY: I don't know what happened to him. I done lost touch with
   everybody except Gabriel. But I hope he's dead. I hope he found some
   peace.
LYONS: That's a heavy story, Pop. I didn't know you left home when you
   was fourteen.
TROY: And didn't know nothing. The only part of the world I knew was
   the forty-two acres of Mr. Lubin's land. That's all I knew about life.
LYONS: Fourteen's kinda young to be out on your own. (*Phone rings.*) I
   don't even think I was ready to be out on my own at fourteen. I don't
   know what I would have done.
TROY: I got up from the creek and walked on down to Mobile. I was
   through with farming. Figured I could do better in the city. So I walked
   the two hundred miles to Mobile.
LYONS: Wait a minute . . . you ain't walked no two hundred miles, Pop.
   Ain't nobody gonna walk no two hundred miles. You talking about
   some walking there.
BONO: That's the only way you got anywhere back in them days.
LYONS: Shhh. Damn if I wouldn't have hitched a ride with somebody!
TROY: Who you gonna hitch it with? They ain't had no cars and things
   like they got now. We talking about 1918.

ROSE (*entering*): What you all out here getting into?

TROY (*to Rose*): I'm telling Lyons how good he got it. He don't know nothing about this I'm talking.

ROSE: Lyons, that was Bonnie on the phone. She say you supposed to pick her up.

LYONS: Yeah, okay, Rose.

TROY: I walked on down to Mobile and hitched up with some of them fellows that was heading this way. Got up here and found out . . . not only couldn't you get a job . . . you couldn't find no place to live. I thought I was in freedom. Shhh. Colored folks living down there on the riverbanks in whatever kind of shelter they could find for themselves. Right down there under the Brady Street Bridge. Living in shacks made of sticks and tarpaper. Messed around there and went from bad to worse. Started stealing. First it was food. Then I figured, hell, if I steal money I can buy me some food. Buy me some shoes too! One thing led to another. Met your mama. I was young and anxious to be a man. Met your mama and had you. What I do that for? Now I got to worry about feeding you and her. Got to steal three times as much. Went out one day looking for somebody to rob . . . that's what I was, a robber. I'll tell you the truth. I'm ashamed of it today. But it's the truth. Went to rob this fellow . . . pulled out my knife . . . and he pulled out a gun. Shot me in the chest. It felt just like somebody had taken a hot branding iron and laid it on me. When he shot me I jumped at him with my knife. They told me I killed him and they put me in the penitentiary and locked me up for fifteen years. That's where I met Bono. That's where I learned how to play baseball. Got out that place and your mama had taken you and went on to make life without me. Fifteen years was a long time for her to wait. But that fifteen years cured me of that robbing stuff. Rose'll tell you. She asked me when I met her if I had gotten all that foolishness out of my system. And I told her, "Baby, it's you and baseball all what count with me." You hear me, Bono? I meant it too. She say, "Which one comes first?" I told her, "Baby, ain't no doubt it's baseball . . . but you stick and get old with me and we'll both outlive this baseball." Am I right, Rose? And it's true.

ROSE: Man, hush your mouth. You ain't said no such thing. Talking about, "Baby, you know you'll always be number one with me." That's what you was talking.

TROY: You hear that, Bono. That's why I love her.

BONO: Rose'll keep you straight. You get off the track, she'll straighten you up.

ROSE: Lyons, you better get on up and get Bonnie. She waiting on you.

LYONS (*gets up to go*): Hey, Pop, why don't you come on down to the Grill and hear me play?

TROY: I ain't going down there. I'm too old to be sitting around in them clubs.

BONO: You got to be good to play down at the Grill.

LYONS: Come on, Pop . . .

TROY: I got to get up in the morning.

LYONS: You ain't got to stay long.

TROY: Naw, I'm gonna get my supper and go on to bed.

LYONS: Well, I got to go. I'll see you again.

TROY: Don't you come around my house on my payday.

ROSE: Pick up the phone and let somebody know you coming. And bring Bonnie with you. You know I'm always glad to see her.

LYONS: Yeah, I'll do that, Rose. You take care now. See you, Pop. See you, Mr. Bono. See you, Uncle Gabe.

GABRIEL: Lyons! King of the Jungle!

(*Lyons exits.*)

TROY: Is supper ready, woman? Me and you got some business to take care of. I'm gonna tear it up too.

ROSE: Troy, I done told you now!

TROY (*puts his arm around Bono*): Aw hell, woman . . . this is Bono. Bono like family. I done known this nigger since . . . how long I done know you?

BONO: It's been a long time.

TROY: I done known this nigger since Skippy was a pup. Me and him done been through some times.

BONO: You sure right about that.

TROY: Hell, I done know him longer than I known you. And we still standing shoulder to shoulder. Hey, look here, Bono . . . a man can't ask for no more than that.

(*Drinks to him.*)

I love you, nigger.

BONO: Hell, I love you too . . . but I got to get home see my woman. You got yours in hand. I got to go get mine.

(*Bono starts to exit as Cory enters the yard, dressed in his football uniform. He gives Troy a hard, uncompromising look.*)

CORY: What you do that for, Pop?

(*He throws his helmet down in the direction of Troy.*)

ROSE: What's the matter? Cory . . . what's the matter?

CORY: Papa done went up to the school and told Coach Zellman I can't play football no more. Wouldn't even let me play the game. Told him to tell the recruiter not to come.

ROSE: Troy . . .

TROY: What you Troying me for. Yeah, I did it. And the boy know why I did it.

CORY: Why you wanna do that to me? That was the one chance I had.

ROSE: Ain't nothing wrong with Cory playing football, Troy.

TROY: The boy lied to me. I told the nigger if he wanna play football . . . to keep up his chores and hold down that job at the A&P. That was the conditions. Stopped down there to see Mr. Stawicki . . .

CORY: I can't work after school during the football season, Pop! I tried to tell you that Mr. Stawicki's holding my job for me. You don't never want to listen to nobody. And then you wanna go and do this to me!

TROY: I ain't done nothing to you. You done it to yourself.

CORY: Just cause you didn't have a chance! You just scared I'm gonna be better than you, that's all.

TROY: Come here.

ROSE: Troy . . .

(*Cory reluctantly crosses over to Troy.*)

TROY: All right! See. You done made a mistake.

CORY: I didn't even do nothing!

TROY: I'm gonna tell you what your mistake was. See . . . you swung at the ball and didn't hit it. That's strike one. See, you in the batter's box now. You swung and you missed. That's strike one. Don't you strike out!

(*Lights fade to black.*)

ACT II

Scene I

(*The following morning. Cory is at the tree hitting the ball with the bat. He tries to mimic Troy, but his swing is awkward, less sure. Rose enters from the house.*)

ROSE: Cory, I want you to help me with this cupboard.

CORY: I ain't quitting the team. I don't care what Poppa say.

ROSE: I'll talk to him when he gets back. He had to go see about your Uncle Gabe. The police done arrested him. Say he was disturbing the peace. He'll be back directly. Come on in here and help me clean out the top of this cupboard.

(*Cory exits into the house. Rose sees Troy and Bono coming down the alley.*)

Troy . . . what they say down there?

TROY: Ain't said nothing. I give them fifty dollars and they let him go. I'll talk to you about it. Where's Cory?

ROSE: He's in there helping me clean out these cupboards.

TROY: Tell him to get his butt out here.

(*Troy and Bono go over to the pile of wood. Bono picks up the saw and begins sawing.*)

TROY (*to Bono*): All they want is the money. That makes six or seven times I done went down there and got him. See me coming they stick out their hands.

BONO: Yeah. I know what you mean. That's all they care about . . . that money. They don't care about what's right.

(*Pause.*)

Nigger, why you got to go and get some hard wood? You ain't doing nothing but building a little old fence. Get you some soft pine wood. That's all you need.

TROY: I know what I'm doing. This is outside wood. You put pine wood inside the house. Pine wood is inside wood. This here is outside wood. Now you tell me where the fence is gonna be?

BONO: You don't need this wood. You can put it up with pine wood and it'll stand as long as you gonna be here looking at it.

TROY: How you know how long I'm gonna be here, nigger? Hell, I might just live forever. Live longer than old man Horsely.

BONO: That's what Magee used to say.

TROY: Magee's a damn fool. Now you tell me who you ever heard of gonna pull their own teeth with a pair of rusty pliers.

BONO: The old folks . . . my granddaddy used to pull his teeth with pliers. They ain't had no dentists for the colored folks back then.

TROY: Get clean pliers! You understand? Clean pliers! Sterilize them! Besides we ain't living back then. All Magee had to do was walk over to Doc Goldblum's.

BONO: I see where you and that Tallahassee gal . . . that Alberta . . . I see where you all done got tight.

TROY: What you mean "got tight"?

BONO: I see where you be laughing and joking with her all the time.

TROY: I laughs and jokes with all of them, Bono. You know me.

BONO: That ain't the kind of laughing and joking I'm talking about.

(*Cory enters from the house.*)

CORY: How you doing, Mr. Bono?

TROY: Cory? Get that saw from Bono and cut some wood. He talking about the wood's too hard to cut. Stand back there, Jim, and let that young boy show you how it's done.

BONO: He's sure welcome to it.

(*Cory takes the saw and begins to cut the wood.*)

Whew-e-e! Look at that. Big old strong boy. Look like Joe Louis. Hell, must be getting old the way I'm watching that boy whip through that wood.

CORY: I don't see why Mama want a fence around the yard noways.

TROY: Damn if I know either. What the hell she keeping out with it? She ain't got nothing nobody want.

BONO: Some people build fences to keep people out . . . and other people build fences to keep people in. Rose wants to hold on to you all. She loves you.

TROY: Hell, nigger, I don't need nobody to tell me my wife loves me. Cory . . . go on in the house and see if you can find that other saw.

CORY: Where's it at?

TROY: I said find it! Look for it till you find it!

(*Cory exits into the house.*)

What's that supposed to mean? Wanna keep us in?

BONO: Troy . . . I done known you seem like damn near my whole life. You and Rose both. I done know both of you all for a long time. I remember when you met Rose. When you was hitting them baseball out the park. A lot of them old gals was after you then. You had the pick of the litter. When you picked Rose, I was happy for you. That was the first time I knew you had any sense. I said . . . My man Troy knows what he's doing . . . I'm gonna follow this nigger . . . he might take me somewhere. I been following you too. I done learned a whole heap of things about life watching you. I done learned how to tell where the shit lies. How to tell it from the alfalfa. You done learned me a lot of things. You showed me how to not make the same mistakes . . . to take life as it comes along and keep putting one foot in front of the other.

(*Pause.*)

Rose a good woman, Troy.

TROY: Hell, nigger, I know she a good woman. I been married to her for eighteen years. What you got on your mind, Bono?

BONO: I just say she a good woman. Just like I say anything. I ain't got to have nothing on my mind.

TROY: You just gonna say she a good woman and leave it hanging out there like that? Why you telling me she a good woman?

BONO: She loves you, Troy. Rose loves you.

TROY: You saying I don't measure up. That's what you trying to say. I don't measure up cause I'm seeing this other gal. I know what you trying to say.

BONO: I know what Rose means to you, Troy. I'm just trying to say I don't
   want to see you mess up.
TROY: Yeah, I appreciate that, Bono. If you was messing around on
   Lucille I'd be telling you the same thing.
BONO: Well, that's all I got to say. I just say that because I love you both.
TROY: Hell, you know me . . . I wasn't out there looking for nothing. You
   can't find a better woman than Rose. I know that. But seems like this
   woman just stuck onto me where I can't shake her loose. I done wrestled with it, tried to throw her off me . . . but she just stuck on tighter.
   Now she's stuck on for good.
BONO: You's in control . . . that's what you tell me all the time. You responsible for what you do.
TROY: I ain't ducking the responsibility of it. As long as it sets right in my
   heart . . . then I'm okay. Cause that's all I listen to. It'll tell me right
   from wrong every time. And I ain't talking about doing Rose no bad
   turn. I love Rose. She done carried me a long ways and I love and respect her for that.
BONO: I know you do. That's why I don't want to see you hurt her. But
   what you gonna do when she find out? What you got then? If you try
   and juggle both of them . . . sooner or later you gonna drop one of
   them. That's common sense.
TROY: Yeah, I hear what you saying, Bono. I been trying to figure a way
   to work it out.
BONO: Work it out right, Troy. I don't want to be getting all up between
   you and Rose's business . . . but work it so it come out right.
TROY: Ah hell, I get all up between you and Lucille's business. When you
   gonna get that woman that refrigerator she been wanting? Don't tell
   me you ain't got no money now. I know who your banker is. Mellon
   don't need that money bad as Lucille want that refrigerator. I'll tell you
   that.
BONO: Tell you what I'll do . . . when you finish building this fence for
   Rose . . . I'll buy Lucille that refrigerator.
TROY: You done stuck your foot in your mouth now!

(*Troy grabs up a board and begins to saw. Bono starts to walk out the yard.*)

   Hey, nigger . . . where you going?
BONO: I'm going home. I know you don't expect me to help you now.
   I'm protecting my money. I wanna see you put that fence up by your-
   self. That's what I want to see. You'll be here another six months with-
   out me.
TROY: Nigger, you ain't right.
BONO: When it comes to my money . . . I'm right as fireworks on the
   Fourth of July.

TROY: All right, we gonna see now. You better get out your bankbook.

(*Bono exits, and Troy continues to work. Rose enters from the house.*)

ROSE: What they say down there? What's happening with Gabe?

TROY: I went down there and got him out. Cost me fifty dollars. Say he was disturbing the peace. Judge set up a hearing for him in three weeks. Say to show cause why he shouldn't be recommitted.

ROSE: What was he doing that cause them to arrest him?

TROY: Some kids was teasing him and he run them off home. Say he was howling and carrying on. Some folks seen him and called the police. That's all it was.

ROSE: Well, what's you say? What'd you tell the judge?

TROY: Told him I'd look after him. It didn't make no sense to recommit the man. He stuck out his big greasy palm and told me to give him fifty dollars and take him on home.

ROSE: Where's he at now? Where'd he go off to?

TROY: He's gone on about his business. He don't need nobody to hold his hand.

ROSE: Well, I don't know. Seem like that would be the best place for him if they did put him into the hospital. I know what you're gonna say. But that's what I think would be best.

TROY: The man done had his life ruined fighting for what? And they wanna take and lock him up. Let him be free. He don't bother nobody.

ROSE: Well, everybody got their own way of looking at it I guess. Come on and get your lunch. I got a bowl of lima beans and some cornbread in the oven. Come on get something to eat. Ain't no sense you fretting over Gabe.

(*Rose turns to go into the house.*)

TROY: Rose . . . got something to tell you.

ROSE: Well, come on . . . wait till I get this food on the table.

TROY: Rose!

(*She stops and turns around.*)

I don't know how to say this.

(*Pause.*)

I can't explain it none. It just sort of grows on you till it gets out of hand. It starts out like a little bush . . . and the next thing you know it's a whole forest.

ROSE: Troy . . . what is you talking about?

TROY: I'm talking, woman, let me talk. I'm trying to find a way to tell you . . . I'm gonna be a daddy. I'm gonna be somebody's daddy.

ROSE: Troy . . . you're not telling me this? You're gonna be . . . what?
TROY: Rose . . . now . . . see . . .
ROSE: You telling me you gonna be somebody's daddy? You telling your wife this?

(*Gabriel enters from the street. He carries a rose in his hand.*)

GABRIEL: Hey, Troy! Hey, Rose!
ROSE: I have to wait eighteen years to hear something like this.
GABRIEL: Hey, Rose . . . I got a flower for you.

(*He hands it to her.*)

That's a rose. Same rose like you is.
ROSE: Thanks, Gabe.
GABRIEL: Troy, you ain't mad at me is you? Them bad mens come and put me away. You ain't mad at me is you?
TROY: Naw, Gabe, I ain't mad at you.
ROSE: Eighteen years and you wanna come with this.
GABRIEL (*takes a quarter out of his pocket*): See what I got? Got a brand new quarter.
TROY: Rose . . . it's just . . .
ROSE: Ain't nothing you can say, Troy. Ain't no way of explaining that.
GABRIEL: Fellow that give me this quarter had a whole mess of them. I'm gonna keep this quarter till it stop shining.
ROSE: Gabe, go on in the house there. I got some watermelon in the frigidaire. Go on and get you a piece.
GABRIEL: Say, Rose . . . you know I was chasing hellhounds and them bad mens come and get me and take me away. Troy helped me. He come down there and told them they better let me go before he beat them up. Yeah, he did!
ROSE: You go on and get you a piece of watermelon, Gabe. Them bad mens is gone now.
GABRIEL: Okay, Rose . . . gonna get me some watermelon. The kind with the stripes on it.

(*Gabriel exits into the house.*)

ROSE: Why, Troy? Why? After all these years to come dragging this in to me now. It don't make no sense at your age. I could have expected this ten or fifteen years ago, but not now.
TROY: Age ain't got nothing to do with it, Rose.
ROSE: I done tried to be everything a wife should be. Everything a wife could be. Been married eighteen years and I got to live to see the day you tell me you been seeing another woman and done fathered a child by her. And you know I ain't never wanted no half nothing in my

family. My whole family is half. Everybody got different fathers and mothers . . . my two sisters and my brother. Can't hardly tell who's who. Can't never sit down and talk about Papa and Mama. It's your papa and your mama and my papa and my mama . . .

TROY: Rose . . . stop it now.

ROSE: I ain't never wanted that for none of my children. And now you wanna drag your behind in here and tell me something like this.

TROY: You ought to know. It's time for you to know.

ROSE: Well, I don't want to know, goddamn it!

TROY: I can't just make it go away. It's done now. I can't wish the circumstance of the thing away.

ROSE: And you don't want to either. Maybe you want to wish me and my boy away. Maybe that's what you want? Well, you can't wish us away. I've got eighteen years of my life invested in you. You ought to have stayed upstairs in my bed where you belong.

TROY: Rose . . . now listen to me . . . we can get a handle on this thing. We can talk this out . . . come to an understanding.

ROSE: All of a sudden it's "we." Where was "we" at when you was down there rolling around with some godforsaken woman? "We" should have come to an understanding before you started making a damn fool of yourself. You're a day late and a dollar short when it comes to an understanding with me.

TROY: It's just . . . She gives me a different idea . . . a different understanding about myself. I can step out of this house and get away from the pressures and problems . . . be a different man. I ain't got to wonder how I'm gonna pay the bills or get the roof fixed. I can just be a part of myself that I ain't never been.

ROSE: What I want to know . . . is do you plan to continue seeing her. That's all you can say to me.

TROY: I can sit up in her house and laugh. Do you understand what I'm saying. I can laugh out loud . . . and it feels good. It reaches all the way down to the bottom of my shoes.

(*Pause.*)

Rose, I can't give that up.

ROSE: Maybe you ought to go on and stay down there with her . . . if she's a better woman than me.

TROY: It ain't about nobody being a better woman or nothing. Rose, you ain't the blame. A man couldn't ask for no woman to be a better wife than you've been. I'm responsible for it. I done locked myself into a pattern trying to take care of you all that I forgot about myself.

ROSE: What the hell was I there for? That was my job, not somebody else's.

TROY: Rose, I done tried all my life to live decent . . . to live a clean . . .
hard . . . useful life. I tried to be a good husband to you. In every way I
knew how. Maybe I come into the world backwards, I don't know.
But . . . you born with two strikes on you before you come to the plate.
You got to guard it closely . . . always looking for the curve ball on the
inside corner. You can't afford to let none get past you. You can't afford
a call strike. If you going down . . . you going down swinging. Everything lined up against you. What you gonna do. I fooled them, Rose. I
bunted. When I found you and Cory and a halfway decent job . . . I was
safe. Couldn't nothing touch me. I wasn't gonna strike out no more. I
wasn't going back to the penitentiary. I wasn't gonna lay in the streets
with a bottle of wine. I was safe. I had me a family. A job. I wasn't
gonna get that last strike. I was on first looking for one of them boys to
knock me in. To get me home.

ROSE: You should have stayed in my bed, Troy.

TROY: Then when I saw that gal . . . she firmed up my backbone. And I
got to thinking that if I tried . . . I just might be able to steal second. Do
you understand after eighteen years I wanted to steal second.

ROSE: You should have held me tight. You should have grabbed me and
held on.

TROY: I stood on first base for eighteen years and I thought . . . well, goddamn it . . . go on for it!

ROSE: We're not talking about baseball! We're talking about you going
off to lay in bed with another woman . . . and then bring it home to me.
That's what we're talking about. We ain't talking about no baseball.

TROY: Rose, you're not listening to me. I'm trying the best I can to explain it to you. It's not easy for me to admit that I been standing in the
same place for eighteen years.

ROSE: I been standing with you! I been right here with you, Troy. I got a
life too. I gave eighteen years of my life to stand in the same spot with
you. Don't you think I ever wanted other things? Don't you think I had
dreams and hopes? What about my life? What about me. Don't you
think it ever crossed my mind to want to know other men? That I wanted
to lay up somewhere and forget about my responsibilities? That I wanted
someone to make me laugh so I could feel good? You not the only one
who's got wants and needs. But I held on to you, Troy. I took all my feelings, my wants and needs, my dreams . . . and I buried them inside you.
I planted a seed and watched and prayed over it. I planted myself inside you and waited to bloom. And it didn't take me no eighteen years to
find out the soil was hard and rocky and it wasn't never gonna bloom.

But I held on to you, Troy. I held you tighter. You was my husband. I
owed you everything I had. Every part of me I could find to give you.
And upstairs in that room . . . with the darkness falling in on me . . . I

gave everything I had to try and erase the doubt that you wasn't the finest man in the world. And wherever you was going . . . I wanted to be there with you. Cause you was my husband. Cause that's the only way I was gonna survive as your wife. You always talking about what you give . . . and what you don't have to give. But you take too. You take . . . and don't even know nobody's giving!

(*Rose turns to exit into the house; Troy grabs her arm.*)

TROY: You say I take and don't give!
ROSE: Troy! You're hurting me!
TROY: You say I take and don't give.
ROSE: Troy . . . you're hurting my arm! Let go!
TROY: I done give you everything I got. Don't you tell that lie on me.
ROSE: Troy!
TROY: Don't you tell that lie on me!

(*Cory enters from the house.*)

CORY: Mama!
ROSE: Troy. You're hurting me.
TROY: Don't you tell me about no taking and giving.

(*Cory comes up behind Troy and grabs him. Troy, surprised, is thrown off balance just as Cory throws a glancing blow that catches him on the chest and knocks him down. Troy is stunned, as is Cory.*)

ROSE: Troy. Troy. No!

(*Troy gets to his feet and starts at Cory.*)

Troy . . . no. Please! Troy!

(*Rose pulls on Troy to hold him back. Troy stops himself.*)

TROY (*to Cory*): All right. That's strike two. You stay away from around me, boy. Don't you strike out. You living with a full count. Don't you strike out.

(*Troy exits out the yard as the lights go down.*)

Scene II

(*It is six months later, early afternoon. Troy enters from the house and starts to exit the yard. Rose enters from the house.*)

ROSE: Troy, I want to talk to you.
TROY: All of a sudden, after all this time, you want to talk to me, huh? You ain't wanted to talk to me for months. You ain't wanted to talk to

me last night. You ain't wanted no part of me then. What you wanna talk to me about now?

ROSE: Tomorrow's Friday.

TROY: I know what day tomorrow is. You think I don't know tomorrow's Friday? My whole life I ain't done nothing but look to see Friday coming and you got to tell me it's Friday.

ROSE: I want to know if you're coming home.

TROY: I always come home, Rose. You know that. There ain't never been a night I ain't come home.

ROSE: That ain't what I mean . . . and you know it. I want to know if you're coming straight home after work.

TROY: I figure I'd cash my check . . . hang out at Taylors' with the boys . . . maybe play a game of checkers . . .

ROSE: Troy, I can't live like this. I won't live like this. You livin' on borrowed time with me. It's been going on six months now you ain't been coming home.

TROY: I be here every night. Every night of the year. That's 365 days.

ROSE: I want you to come home tomorrow after work.

TROY: Rose . . . I don't mess up my pay. You know that now. I take my pay and I give it to you. I don't have no money but what you give me back. I just want to have a little time to myself . . . a little time to enjoy life.

ROSE: What about me? When's my time to enjoy life?

TROY: I don't know what to tell you, Rose. I'm doing the best I can.

ROSE: You ain't been home from work but time enough to change your clothes and run out . . . and you wanna call that the best you can do?

TROY: I'm going over to the hospital to see Alberta. She went into the hospital this afternoon. Look like she might have the baby early. I won't be gone long.

ROSE: Well, you ought to know. They went over to Miss Pearl's and got Gabe today. She said you told them to go ahead and lock him up.

TROY: I ain't said no such thing. Whoever told you that is telling a lie. Pearl ain't doing nothing but telling a big fat lie.

ROSE: She ain't had to tell me. I read it on the papers.

TROY: I ain't told them nothing of the kind.

ROSE: I saw it right there on the papers.

TROY: What it say, huh?

ROSE: It said you told them to take him.

TROY: Then they screwed that up, just the way they screw up everything. I ain't worried about what they got on the paper.

ROSE: Say the government send part of his check to the hospital and the other part to you.

TROY: I ain't got nothing to do with that if that's the way it works. I ain't made up the rules about how it work.

ROSE: You did Gabe just like you did Cory. You wouldn't sign the paper for Cory . . . but you signed for Gabe. You signed that paper.

(*The telephone is heard ringing inside the house.*)

TROY: I told you I ain't signed nothing, woman! The only thing I signed was the release form. Hell, I can't read, I don't know what they had on that paper! I ain't signed nothing about sending Gabe away.

ROSE: I said send him to the hospital . . . you said let him be free . . . now you done went down there and signed him to the hospital for half his money. You went back on yourself, Troy. You gonna have to answer for that.

TROY: See now . . . you been over there talking to Miss Pearl. She done got mad cause she ain't getting Gabe's rent money. That's all it is. She's liable to say anything.

ROSE: Troy, I seen where you signed the paper.

TROY: You ain't seen nothing I signed. What she doing got papers on my brother anyway? Miss Pearl telling a big fat lie. And I'm gonna tell her about it too! You ain't seen nothing I signed. Say . . . you ain't seen nothing I signed.

(*Rose exits into the house to answer the telephone. Presently she returns.*)

ROSE: Troy . . . that was the hospital. Alberta had the baby.

TROY: What she have? What is it?

ROSE: It's a girl.

TROY: I better get on down to the hospital to see her.

ROSE: Troy . . .

TROY: Rose . . . I got to go see her now. That's only right . . . what's the matter . . . the baby's all right, ain't it?

ROSE: Alberta died having the baby.

TROY: Died . . . you say she's dead? Alberta's dead?

ROSE: They said they done all they could. They couldn't do nothing for her.

TROY: The baby? How's the baby?

ROSE: They say it's healthy. I wonder who's gonna bury her.

TROY: She had family, Rose. She wasn't living in the world by herself.

ROSE: I know she wasn't living in the world by herself.

TROY: Next thing you gonna want to know if she had any insurance.

ROSE: Troy, you ain't got to talk like that.

TROY: That's the first thing that jumped out your mouth. "Who's gonna bury her?" Like I'm fixing to take on that task for myself.

ROSE: I am your wife. Don't push me away.

TROY: I ain't pushing nobody away. Just give me some space. That's all. Just give me some room to breathe.

(*Rose exits into the house. Troy walks about the yard.*)

TROY (*with a quiet rage that threatens to consume him*): All right . . . Mr.
Death. See now . . . I'm gonna tell you what I'm gonna do. I'm gonna
take and build me a fence around this yard. See? I'm gonna build me a
fence around what belongs to me. And then I want you to stay on the
other side. See? You stay over there until you're ready for me. Then
you come on. Bring your army. Bring your sickle. Bring your wrestling
clothes. I ain't gonna fall down on my vigilance this time. You ain't
gonna sneak up on me no more. When you ready for me . . . when
the top of your list say Troy Maxson . . . that's when you come around
here. You come up and knock on the front door. Ain't nobody else got
nothing to do with this. This is between you and me. Man to man. You
stay on the other side of that fence until you ready for me. Then you
come up and knock on the front door. Anytime you want. I'll be ready
for you.

(*The lights go down to black.*)

Scene III

(*The lights come up on the porch. It is late evening three days later. Rose sits
listening to the ball game waiting for Troy. The final out of the game is made and
Rose switches off the radio. Troy enters the yard carrying an infant wrapped in
blankets. He stands back from the house and calls.*)
   (*Rose enters and stands on the porch. There is a long, awkward silence, the
weight of which grows heavier with each passing second.*)

TROY: Rose . . . I'm standing here with my daughter in my arms. She
ain't but a wee bittie little old thing. She don't know nothing about
grownups' business. She innocent . . . and she ain't got no mama.
ROSE: What you telling me for, Troy?

(*She turns and exits into the house.*)

TROY: Well . . . I guess we'll just sit out here on the porch.

(*He sits down on the porch. There is an awkward indelicateness about the way
he handles the baby. His largeness engulfs and seems to swallow it. He speaks
loud enough for Rose to hear.*)

A man's got to do what's right for him. I ain't sorry for nothing I done.
It felt right in my heart.

(*To the baby.*)

What you smiling at? Your daddy's a big man. Got these great big old
hands. But sometimes he's scared. And right now your daddy's scared

cause we sitting out here and ain't got no home. Oh, I been homeless before. I ain't had no little baby with me. But I been homeless. You just be out on the road by your lonesome and you see one of them trains coming and you just kinda go like this . . .

(*He sings as a lullaby.*)

Please, Mr. Engineer let a man ride the line
Please, Mr. Engineer let a man ride the line
I ain't got no ticket please let me ride the blinds

(*Rose enters from the house. Troy hearing her steps behind him, stands and faces her.*)

She's my daughter, Rose. My own flesh and blood. I can't deny her no more than I can deny them boys.

(*Pause.*)

You and them boys is my family. You and them and this child is all I got in the world. So I guess what I'm saying is . . . I'd appreciate it if you'd help me take care of her.

ROSE: Okay, Troy . . . you're right. I'll take care of your baby for you . . . cause . . . like you say . . . she's innocent . . . and you can't visit the sins of the father upon the child. A motherless child has got a hard time.

(*She takes the baby from him.*)

From right now . . . this child got a mother. But you a womanless man.

(*Rose turns and exits into the house with the baby. Lights go down to black.*)

Scene IV

(*It is two months later. Lyons enters from the street. He knocks on the door and calls.*)

LYONS: Hey, Rose! (*Pause.*) Rose!

ROSE (*from inside the house*): Stop that yelling. You gonna wake up Raynell. I just got her to sleep.

LYONS: I just stopped by to pay Papa this twenty dollars I owe him. Where's Papa at?

ROSE: He should be here in a minute. I'm getting ready to go down to the church. Sit down and wait on him.

LYONS: I got to go pick up Bonnie over her mother's house.

ROSE: Well, sit it down there on the table. He'll get it.

LYONS (*enters the house and sets the money on the table*): Tell Papa I said thanks. I'll see you again.

ROSE: All right, Lyons. We'll see you.

(*Lyons starts to exit as Cory enters.*)

CORY: Hey, Lyons.

LYONS: What's happening, Cory. Say man, I'm sorry I missed your graduation. You know I had a gig and couldn't get away. Otherwise, I would
have been there, man. So what you doing?

CORY: I'm trying to find a job.

LYONS: Yeah I know how that go, man. It's rough out here. Jobs are
scarce.

CORY: Yeah, I know.

LYONS: Look here, I got to run. Talk to Papa . . . he know some people.
He'll be able to help get you a job. Talk to him . . . see what he say.

CORY: Yeah . . . all right, Lyons.

LYONS: You take care. I'll talk to you soon. We'll find some time to talk.

(*Lyons exits the yard. Cory wanders over to the tree, picks up the bat, and assumes a batting stance. He studies an imaginary pitcher and swings. Dissatisfied with the result, he tries again. Troy enters. They eye each other for a beat.
Cory puts the bat down and exits the yard. Troy starts into the house as Rose
exits with Raynell. She is carrying a cake.*)

TROY: I'm coming in and everybody's going out.

ROSE: I'm taking this cake down to the church for the bake sale. Lyons
was by to see you. He stopped by to pay you your twenty dollars. It's
laying in there on the table.

TROY (*going into his pocket*): Well . . . here go this money.

ROSE: Put it in there on the table, Troy. I'll get it.

TROY: What time you coming back?

ROSE: Ain't no use in you studying me. It don't matter what time I come
back.

TROY: I just asked you a question, woman. What's the matter . . . can't I
ask you a question?

ROSE: Troy, I don't want to go into it. Your dinner's in there on the stove.
All you got to do is heat it up. And don't you be eating the rest of them
cakes in there. I'm coming back for them. We having a bake sale at the
church tomorrow.

(*Rose exits the yard. Troy sits down on the steps, takes a pint bottle from his
pocket, opens it, and drinks. He begins to sing.*)

TROY: Hear it ring! Hear it ring!
  Had an old dog his name was Blue
  You know Blue was mighty true
  You know Blue was a good old dog

Blue trees a possum in a hollow log
You know from that he was a good old dog

(*Bono enters the yard.*)

BONO: Hey, Troy.

TROY: Hey, what's happening, Bono?

BONO: I just thought I'd stop by to see you.

TROY: What you stop by and see me for? You ain't stopped by in a month of Sundays. Hell, I must owe you money or something.

BONO: Since you got your promotion I can't keep up with you. Used to see you every day. Now I don't even know what route you working.

TROY: They keep switching me around. Got me out in Greentree now . . . hauling white folks' garbage.

BONO: Greentree, huh? You lucky, at least you ain't got to be lifting them barrels. Damn if they ain't getting heavier. I'm gonna put in my two years and call it quits.

TROY: I'm thinking about retiring myself.

BONO: You got it easy. You can *drive* for another five years.

TROY: It ain't the same, Bono. It ain't like working the back of the truck. Ain't got nobody to talk to . . . feel like you working by yourself. Naw, I'm thinking about retiring. How's Lucille?

BONO: She all right. Her arthritis get to acting up on her sometime. Saw Rose on my way in. She going down to the church, huh?

TROY: Yeah, she took up going down there. All them preachers looking for somebody to fatten their pockets.

(*Pause.*)

Got some gin here.

BONO: Naw, thanks. I just stopped by to say hello.

TROY: Hell, nigger . . . you can take a drink. I ain't never known you to say no to a drink. You ain't got to work tomorrow.

BONO: I just stopped by. I'm fixing to go over to Skinner's. We got us a domino game going over his house every Friday.

TROY: Nigger, you can't play no dominoes. I used to whup you four games out of five.

BONO: Well, that learned me. I'm getting better.

TROY: Yeah? Well, that's all right.

BONO: Look here . . . I got to be getting on. Stop by sometime, huh?

TROY: Yeah, I'll do that, Bono. Lucille told Rose you bought her a new refrigerator.

BONO: Yeah, Rose told Lucille you had finally built your fence . . . so I figured we'd call it even.

TROY: I knew you would.

BONO: Yeah . . . okay. I'll be talking to you.
TROY: Yeah, take care, Bono. Good to see you. I'm gonna stop over.
BONO: Yeah. Okay, Troy.

(*Bono exits. Troy drinks from the bottle.*)

TROY: Old Blue died and I dig his grave
   Let him down with a golden chain
   Every night when I hear old Blue bark
   I know Blue treed a possum in Noah's Ark.
   Hear it ring! Hear it ring!

(*Cory enters the yard. They eye each other for a beat. Troy is sitting in the middle of the steps. Cory walks over.*)

CORY: I got to get by.
TROY: Say what? What's you say?
CORY: You in my way. I got to get by.
TROY: You got to get by where? This is my house. Bought and paid for. In full. Took me fifteen years. And if you wanna go in my house and I'm sitting on the steps . . . you say excuse me. Like your mama taught you.
CORY: Come on, Pop . . . I got to get by.

(*Cory starts to maneuver his way past Troy. Troy grabs his leg and shoves him back.*)

TROY: You just gonna walk over top of me?
CORY: I live here too!
TROY (*advancing toward him*): You just gonna walk over top of me in my own house?
CORY: I ain't scared of you.
TROY: I ain't asked if you was scared of me. I asked you if you was fixing to walk over top of me in my own house? That's the question. You ain't gonna say excuse me? You just gonna walk over top of me?
CORY: If you wanna put it like that.
TROY: How else am I gonna put it?
CORY: I was walking by you to go into the house cause you sitting on the steps drunk, singing to yourself. You can put it like that.
TROY: Without saying excuse me???

(*Cory doesn't respond.*)

   I asked you a question. Without saying excuse me???
CORY: I ain't got to say excuse me to you. You don't count around here no more.
TROY: Oh, I see . . . I don't count around here no more. You ain't got to say excuse me to your daddy. All of a sudden you done got so grown

that your daddy don't count around here no more . . . Around here in his own house and yard that he done paid for with the sweat of his brow. You done got so grown to where you gonna take over. You gonna take over my house. Is that right? You gonna wear my pants. You gonna go in there and stretch out on my bed. You ain't got to say excuse me cause I don't count around here no more. Is that right?

CORY: That's right. You always talking this dumb stuff. Now, why don't you just get out my way.

TROY: I guess you got someplace to sleep and something to put in your belly. You got that, huh? You got that? That's what you need. You got that, huh?

CORY: You don't know what I got. You ain't got to worry about what I got.

TROY: You right! You one hundred percent right! I done spent the last seventeen years worrying about what you got. Now it's your turn, see? I'll tell you what to do. You grown . . . we done established that. You a man. Now, let's see you act like one. Turn your behind around and walk out this yard. And when you get out there in the alley . . . you can forget about this house. See? 'Cause this is my house. You go on and be a man and get your own house. You can forget about this. Cause this is mine. You go on and get yours 'cause I'm through with doing for you.

CORY: You talking about what you did for me . . . what'd you ever give me?

TROY: Them feet and bones! That pumping heart, nigger! I give you more than anybody else is ever gonna give you.

CORY: You ain't never gave me nothing! You ain't never done nothing but hold me back. Afraid I was gonna be better than you. All you ever did was try and make me scared of you. I used to tremble every time you called my name. Every time I heard your footsteps in the house. Wondering all the time . . . what's Papa gonna say if I do this? . . . What's he gonna say if I do that? . . . What's Papa gonna say if I turn on the radio? And Mama, too . . . she tries . . . but she's scared of you.

TROY: You leave your mama out of this. She ain't got nothing to do with this.

CORY: I don't know how she stand you . . . after what you did to her.

TROY: I told you to leave your mama out of this!

(*He advances toward Cory.*)

CORY: What you gonna do . . . give me a whupping? You can't whup me no more. You're too old. You just an old man.

TROY (*shoves him on his shoulder*): Nigger! That's what you are. You just another nigger on the street to me!

CORY: You crazy! You know that?

TROY: Go on now! You got the devil in you. Get on away from me!

CORY: You just a crazy old man . . . talking about I got the devil in me.
TROY: Yeah, I'm crazy! If you don't get on the other side of that yard . . . I'm
    gonna show you how crazy I am! Go on . . . get the hell out of my yard.
CORY: It ain't your yard. You took Uncle Gabe's money he got from the
    army to buy this house and then you put him out.
TROY (*Troy advances on Cory*): Get your black ass out of my yard!

(*Troy's advance backs Cory up against the tree. Cory grabs up the bat.*)

CORY: I ain't going nowhere! Come on . . . put me out! I ain't scared of you.
TROY: That's my bat!
CORY: Come on!
TROY: Put my bat down!
CORY: Come on, put me out.

(*Cory swings at Troy, who backs across the yard.*)

    What's the matter? You so bad . . . put me out!

(*Troy advances toward Cory.*)

CORY (*backing up*): Come on! Come on!
TROY: You're gonna have to use it! You wanna draw that bat back on
    me . . . you're gonna have to use it.
CORY: Come on! . . . Come on!

(*Cory swings the bat at Troy a second time. He misses. Troy continues to advance toward him.*)

TROY: You're gonna have to kill me! You wanna draw that bat back on
    me. You're gonna have to kill me.

(*Cory, backed up against the tree, can go no farther. Troy taunts him. He sticks
out his head and offers him a target.*)

    Come on! Come on!

(*Cory is unable to swing the bat. Troy grabs it.*)

TROY: Then I'll show you.

(*Cory and Troy struggle over the bat. The struggle is fierce and fully engaged.
Troy ultimately is the stronger and takes the bat from Cory and stands over him
ready to swing. He stops himself.*)

    Go on and get away from around my house.

(*Cory, stung by his defeat, picks himself up, walks slowly out of the yard and up
the alley.*)

CORY: Tell Mama I'll be back for my things.

TROY: They'll be on the other side of that fence.

(*Cory exits.*)

TROY: I can't taste nothing. Helluljah! I can't taste nothing no more. (*Troy assumes a batting posture and begins to taunt Death, the fastball on the outside corner.*) Come on! It's between you and me now! Come on! Anytime you want! Come on! I be ready for you . . . but I ain't gonna be easy.

(*The lights go down on the scene.*)

Scene V

(*The time is 1965. The lights come up in the yard. It is the morning of Troy's funeral. A funeral plaque with a light hangs beside the door. There is a small garden plot off to the side. There is noise and activity in the house as Rose, Gabriel, and Bono have gathered. The door opens and Raynell, seven years old, enters dressed in a flannel nightgown. She crosses to the garden and pokes around with a stick. Rose calls from the house.*)

ROSE: Raynell!
RAYNELL: Mam?
ROSE: What you doing out there?
RAYNELL: Nothing.

(*Rose comes to the door.*)

ROSE: Girl, get in here and get dressed. What you doing?
RAYNELL: Seeing if my garden growed.
ROSE: I told you it ain't gonna grow overnight. You got to wait.
RAYNELL: It don't look like it never gonna grow. Dag!
ROSE: I told you a watched pot never boils. Get in here and get dressed.
RAYNELL: This ain't even no pot, Mama.
ROSE: You just have to give it a chance. It'll grow. Now you come on and do what I told you. We got to be getting ready. This ain't no morning to be playing around. You hear me?
RAYNELL: Yes, mam.

(*Rose exits into the house. Raynell continues to poke at her garden with a stick. Cory enters. He is dressed in a Marine corporal's uniform, and carries a duffel bag. His posture is that of a military man, and his speech has a clipped sternness.*)

CORY (*to Raynell*): Hi.

(*Pause.*)

I bet your name is Raynell.
RAYNELL: Uh huh.

CORY: Is your mama home?

(*Raynell runs up on the porch and calls through the screen door.*)

RAYNELL: Mama . . . there's some man out here. Mama?

(*Rose comes to the door.*)

ROSE: Cory? Lord have mercy! Look here, you all!

(*Rose and Cory embrace in a tearful reunion as Bono and Lyons enter from the house dressed in funeral clothes.*)

BONO: Aw, looka here . . .
ROSE: Done got all grown up!
CORY: Don't cry, Mama. What you crying about?
ROSE: I'm just so glad you made it.
CORY: Hey Lyons. How you doing, Mr. Bono.

(*Lyons goes to embrace Cory.*)

LYONS: Look at you, man. Look at you. Don't he look good, Rose. Got
   them Corporal stripes.
ROSE: What took you so long?
CORY: You know how the Marines are, Mama. They got to get all their
   paperwork straight before they let you do anything.
ROSE: Well, I'm sure glad you made it. They let Lyons come. Your Uncle
   Gabe's still in the hospital. They don't know if they gonna let him out
   or not. I just talked to them a little while ago.
LYONS: A Corporal in the United States Marines.
BONO: Your daddy knew you had it in you. He used to tell me all the time.
LYONS: Don't he look good, Mr. Bono?
BONO: Yeah, he remind me of Troy when I first met him.

(*Pause.*)

   Say, Rose, Lucille's down at the church with the choir. I'm gonna go
   down and get the pallbearers lined up. I'll be back to get you all.
ROSE: Thanks, Jim.
CORY: See you, Mr. Bono.
LYONS (*with his arm around Raynell*): Cory . . . look at Raynell. Ain't she
   precious? She gonna break a whole lot of hearts.
ROSE: Raynell, come and say hello to your brother. This is your brother
   Cory. You remember Cory.
RAYNELL: No, Mam.
CORY: She don't remember me, Mama.
ROSE: Well, we talk about you. She heard us talk about you. (*To Raynell.*)
   This is your brother Cory. Come on and say hello.
RAYNELL: Hi.

CORY: Hi. So you're Raynell. Mama told me a lot about you.

ROSE: You all come on into the house and let me fix you some breakfast. Keep up your strength.

CORY: I ain't hungry, Mama.

LYONS: You can fix me something, Rose. I'll be in there in a minute.

ROSE: Cory, you sure you don't want nothing. I know they ain't feeding you right.

CORY: No, Mama . . . thanks. I don't feel like eating. I'll get something later.

ROSE: Raynell . . . get on upstairs and get that dress on like I told you.

(*Rose and Raynell exit into the house.*)

LYONS: So . . . I hear you thinking about getting married.

CORY: Yeah, I done found the right one, Lyons. It's about time.

LYONS: Me and Bonnie been split up about four years now. About the time Papa retired. I guess she just got tired of all them changes I was putting her through.

(*Pause.*)

I always knew you was gonna make something out yourself. Your head was always in the right direction. So . . . you gonna stay in . . . make it a career . . . put in your twenty years?

CORY: I don't know. I got six already, I think that's enough.

LYONS: Stick with Uncle Sam and retire early. Ain't nothing out here. I guess Rose told you what happened with me. They got me down the workhouse. I thought I was being slick cashing other people's checks.

CORY: How much time you doing?

LYONS: They give me three years. I got that beat now. I ain't got but nine more months. It ain't so bad. You learn to deal with it like anything else. You got to take the crookeds with the straights. That's what Papa used to say. He used to say that when he struck out. I seen him strike out three times in a row . . . and the next time up he hit the ball over the grandstand. Right out there in Homestead Field. He wasn't satisfied hitting in the seats . . . he want to hit it over everything! After the game he had two hundred people standing around waiting to shake his hand. You got to take the crookeds with the straights. Yeah, Papa was something else.

CORY: You still playing?

LYONS: Cory . . . you know I'm gonna do that. There's some fellows down there we got us a band . . . we gonna try and stay together when we get out . . . but yeah, I'm still playing. It still helps me to get out of bed in the morning. As long as it do that I'm gonna be right there playing and trying to make some sense out of it.

ROSE (*calling*): Lyons, I got these eggs in the pan.

LYONS: Let me go on and get these eggs, man. Get ready to go bury Papa.

(*Pause.*)

How you doing? You doing all right?

(*Cory nods. Lyons touches him on the shoulder and they share a moment of silent grief. Lyons exits into the house. Cory wanders about the yard. Raynell enters.*)

RAYNELL: Hi.
CORY: Hi.
RAYNELL: Did you used to sleep in my room?
CORY: Yeah . . . that used to be my room.
RAYNELL: That's what Papa call it. "Cory's room." It got your football in the closet.

(*Rose comes to the door.*)

ROSE: Raynell, get in there and get them good shoes on.
RAYNELL: Mama, can't I wear these. Them other one hurt my feet.
ROSE: Well, they just gonna have to hurt your feet for a while. You ain't said they hurt your feet when you went down to the store and got them.
RAYNELL: They didn't hurt then. My feet done got bigger.
ROSE: Don't you give me no backtalk now. You get in there and get them shoes on.

(*Raynell exits into the house.*)

Ain't too much changed. He still got that piece of rag tied to that tree. He was out here swinging that bat. I was just ready to go back in the house. He swung that bat and then he just fell over. Seem like he swung it and stood there with this grin on his face . . . and then he just fell over. They carried him on down to the hospital, but I knew there wasn't no need . . . why don't you come on in the house?
CORY: Mama . . . I got something to tell you. I don't know how to tell you this . . . but I've got to tell you . . . I'm not going to Papa's funeral.
ROSE: Boy, hush your mouth. That's your daddy you talking about. I don't want hear that kind of talk this morning. I done raised you to come to this? You standing there all healthy and grown talking about you ain't going to your daddy's funeral?
CORY: Mama . . . listen . . .
ROSE: I don't want to hear it, Cory. You just get that thought out of your head.
CORY: I can't drag Papa with me everywhere I go. I've got to say no to him. One time in my life I've got to say no.
ROSE: Don't nobody have to listen to nothing like that. I know you and your daddy ain't seen eye to eye, but I ain't got to listen to that kind of talk this morning. Whatever was between you and your daddy . . . the time has come to put it aside. Just take it and set it over there on the

shelf and forget about it. Disrespecting your daddy ain't gonna make you a man, Cory. You got to find a way to come to that on your own. Not going to your daddy's funeral ain't gonna make you a man.

CORY: The whole time I was growing up . . . living in his house . . . Papa was like a shadow that followed you everywhere. It weighed on you and sunk into your flesh. It would wrap around you and lay there until you couldn't tell which one was you anymore. That shadow digging in your flesh. Trying to crawl in. Trying to live through you. Everywhere I looked, Troy Maxson was staring back at me . . . hiding under the bed . . . in the closet. I'm just saying I've got to find a way to get rid of that shadow, Mama.

ROSE: You just like him. You got him in you good.

CORY: Don't tell me that, Mama.

ROSE: You Troy Maxson all over again.

CORY: I don't want to be Troy Maxson. I want to be me.

ROSE: You can't be nobody but who you are, Cory. That shadow wasn't nothing but you growing into yourself. You either got to grow into it or cut it down to fit you. But that's all you got to make life with. That's all you got to measure yourself against that world out there. Your daddy wanted you to be everything he wasn't . . . and at the same time he tried to make you into everything he was. I don't know if he was right or wrong . . . but I do know he meant to do more good than he meant to do harm. He wasn't always right. Sometimes when he touched he bruised. And sometimes when he took me in his arms he cut.

When I first met your daddy I thought . . . Here is a man I can lay down with and make a baby. That's the first thing I thought when I seen him. I was thirty years old and had done seen my share of men. But when he walked up to me and said, "I can dance a waltz that'll make you dizzy," I thought, Rose Lee, here is a man that you can open yourself up to and be filled to bursting. Here is a man that can fill all them empty spaces you been tipping around the edges of. One of them empty spaces was being somebody's mother.

I married your daddy and settled down to cooking his supper and keeping clean sheets on the bed. When your daddy walked through the house he was so big he filled it up. That was my first mistake. Not to make him leave some room for me. For my part in the matter. But at that time I wanted that. I wanted a house that I could sing in. And that's what your daddy gave me. I didn't know to keep up his strength I had to give up little pieces of mine. I did that. I took on his life as mine and mixed up the pieces so that you couldn't hardly tell which was which anymore. It was my choice. It was my life and I didn't have to live it like that. But that's what life offered me in the way of being a woman and I took it. I grabbed hold of it with both hands.

By the time Raynell came into the house, me and your daddy had done lost touch with one another. I didn't want to make my blessing off of nobody's misfortune . . . but I took on to Raynell like she was all them babies I had wanted and never had.

(*The phone rings.*)

Like I'd been blessed to relive a part of my life. And if the Lord see fit to keep up my strength . . . I'm gonna do her just like your daddy did you . . . I'm gonna give her the best of what's in me.

RAYNELL (*entering, still with her old shoes*): Mama . . . Reverend Tollivier on the phone.

(*Rose exits into the house.*)

RAYNELL: Hi.
CORY: Hi.
RAYNELL: You in the Army or the Marines?
CORY: Marines.
RAYNELL: Papa said it was the Army. Did you know Blue?
CORY: Blue? Who's Blue?
RAYNELL: Papa's dog what he sing about all the time.
CORY (*singing*): Hear it ring! Hear it ring!
  I had a dog his name was Blue
  You know Blue was mighty true
  You know Blue was a good old dog
  Blue treed a possum in a hollow log
  You know from that he was a good old dog.
  Hear it ring! Hear it ring!

(*Raynell joins in singing.*)

CORY AND RAYNELL: Blue treed a possum out on a limb
  Blue looked at me and I looked at him
  Grabbed that possum and put him in a sack
  Blue stayed there till I came back
  Old Blue's feets was big and round
  Never allowed a possum to touch the ground.

  Old Blue died and I dug his grave
  I dug his grave with a silver spade
  Let him down with a golden chain
  And every night I call his name
  Go on Blue, you good dog you
  Go on Blue, you good dog you
RAYNELL: Blue laid down and died like a man
  Blue laid down and died . . .

BOTH: Blue laid down and died like a man
   Now he's treeing possums in the Promised Land
   I'm gonna tell you this to let you know
   Blue's gone where the good dogs go
   When I hear old Blue bark
   When I hear old Blue bark
   Blue treed a possum in Noah's Ark
   Blue treed a possum in Noah's Ark.

(*Rose comes to the screen door.*)

ROSE: Cory, we gonna be ready to go in a minute.

CORY (*to Raynell*): You go on in the house and change them shoes like Mama told you so we can go to Papa's funeral.

RAYNELL: Okay, I'll be back.

(*Raynell exits into the house. Cory gets up and crosses over to the tree. Rose stands in the screen door watching him. Gabriel enters from the alley.*)

GABRIEL (*calling*): Hey, Rose!

ROSE: Gabe?

GABRIEL: I'm here, Rose. Hey Rose, I'm here!

(*Rose enters from the house.*)

ROSE: Lord . . . Look here, Lyons!

LYONS: See, I told you, Rose . . . I told you they'd let him come.

CORY: How you doing, Uncle Gabe?

LYONS: How you doing, Uncle Gabe?

GABRIEL: Hey, Rose. It's time. It's time to tell St. Peter to open the gates. Troy, you ready? You ready, Troy. I'm gonna tell St. Peter to open the gates. You get ready now.

(*Gabriel, with great fanfare, braces himself to blow. The trumpet is without a mouthpiece. He puts the end of it into his mouth and blows with great force, like a man who has been waiting some twenty-odd years for this single moment. No sound comes out of the trumpet. He braces himself and blows again with the same result. A third time he blows. There is a weight of impossible description that falls away and leaves him bare and exposed to a frightful realization. It is a trauma that a sane and normal mind would be unable to withstand. He begins to dance. A slow, strange dance, eerie and life-giving. A dance of atavistic signature and ritual. Lyons attempts to embrace him. Gabriel pushes Lyons away. He begins to howl in what is an attempt at song, or perhaps a song turning back into itself in an attempt at speech. He finishes his dance and the gates of heaven stand open as wide as God's closet.*)

That's the way that go!

[1987]

LYNN NOTTAGE   [b. 1964]

Ruined

Characters

MAMA NADI, *A madam, a businesswoman, attractive, early forties*
JOSEPHINE, *One of Mama's girls, early twenties*
SOPHIE, *One of Mama's girls, eighteen*
SALIMA, *One of Mama's girls, nineteen*
CHRISTIAN, *A traveling salesman, early forties*
MR. HARARI, *A Lebanese diamond merchant, early forties*
JEROME KISEMBE, *A rebel leader*
COMMANDER OSEMBENGA, *A military leader for the current government*
FORTUNE, *A Government Soldier, Salima's husband*
SIMON, *A Government Soldier, Fortune's cousin*
LAURENT, *A Government Soldier, Osembenga's assistant*
REBEL SOLDIERS
GOVERNMENT SOLDIERS
AID WORKER

Setting: *A small mining town. The Democratic Republic of Congo.*

ACT ONE

Scene 1

A small mining town. The sounds of the tropical Ituri rain forest. The Democratic Republic of Congo.
   A bar, makeshift furniture and a rundown pool table. A lot of effort has gone into making the worn bar cheerful. A stack of plastic washtubs rests in the corner. An old car battery powers the audio system, a covered birdcage sits conspicuously in the corner of the room.
   Mama Nadi, early forties, an attractive woman with an arrogant stride and majestic air, watches Christian, early forties, a perpetually cheerful traveling salesman, knock back a Fanta. His good looks have been worn down by hard living on the road. He wears a suit that might have been considered stylish when new, but it's now nearly ten years old, and overly loved.

CHRISTIAN: Ah. Cold. The only cold Fanta in twenty-five kilometers. You
   don't know how good this tastes.

(*Mama flashes a warm flirtatious smile, then pours herself a Primus beer.*)

1089

MAMA: And where the hell have you been?

CHRISTIAN: It was no easy task getting here.

MAMA: I've been expecting you for the last three weeks. How am I supposed do business? No soap, no cigarettes, no condoms. Not even a half liter of petrol for the generator.

CHRISTIAN: Why are you picking a fight with me already? I didn't create this damn chaos. Nobody, and I'm telling you, nobody could get through on the main road. Every two kilometers a boy with a Kalashnikov and pockets that need filling. Toll, tax, tariff. They invent reasons to lighten your load.

MAMA: Then why does Mr. Harari always manage to get through?

CHRISTIAN: Mr. Harari doesn't bring you things you need, does he? Mr. Harari has interests that supercede his safety. Me, I still hope to have a family one day. (*Laughs heartily.*)

MAMA: And my lipstick?

CHRISTIAN: Your lipstick? Aye! Did you ask me for lipstick?

MAMA: Of course, I did, you idiot!

CHRISTIAN: Look at the way you speak to me, chérie. *Comment est-ce possible?* You should be happy I made it here in one piece.

(*Christian produces a tube of lipstick from his pocket.*)

Play nice, or I'll give this to Josephine. She knows just how to show her appreciation.

MAMA: Yes, but you always take home a little more than you ask for with Josephine. I hope you know how to use a condom.

(*Christian laughs.*)

CHRISTIAN: Are you jealous?

MAMA: Leave me alone, you're too predictable. (*Turns away, dismissive.*)

CHRISTIAN: Where are you going? Hey, hey what are you doing? (*Teasingly.*) Chérie, I know you wanted me to forget, so you could yell at me, but you won't get the pleasure this time.

(*Christian taunts her with the lipstick. Mama resists the urge to smile.*)

MAMA: Oh shut up and give it to me.

(*He passes her the lipstick.*)

Thank you, Christian.

CHRISTIAN: I didn't hear you—

MAMA: Don't press your luck. And it better be red.

(*Mama grabs a sliver of a broken mirror from behind the rough-hewn bar, and gracefully applies the lipstick.*)

CHRISTIAN: You don't have to say it. I know you want a husband.

MAMA: Like a hole in my head.

CHRISTIAN (*reciting*): What, is this love?
An unexpected wind,
A fluctuation,
Fronting the coming of a storm.
Resolve, a thorny bush
Blown asunder and swept away.

There, chérie. I give you a poem in lieu of the kiss you won't allow me.

(*Christian laughs, warmly. Mama puts out a bowl of peanuts, a peace offering.*)

MAMA: Here. I saved you some groundnuts, professor.

CHRISTIAN: That's all you saved for me?

MAMA: Be smart, and I'll show you the door in one second.

(*Mama scolds him with her eyes.*)

CHRISTIAN: Ach, ach . . . why are you wearing my grandmama's face?

(*Christian mocks her expression. Mama laughs and downs her beer.*)

MAMA: You sure you don't want a beer?

CHRISTIAN: You know me better than that, chérie, I haven't had a drop of liquor in four years.

MAMA (*teasing*): It's cold.

CHRISTIAN: Tst!

(*Christian cracks open a few peanuts, and playfully pops them into his mouth. The parrot squawks.*)

What's there? In the cage?

MAMA: Oh, that, a gray parrot. Old Papa Batunga passed.

CHRISTIAN: When?

MAMA: Last Thursday. No one wanted the damn bird. It complains too much.

CHRISTIAN (*Amused*): Yeah, what does it say?

(*Christian walks to the birdcage, and peers under the covering.*)

MAMA: Who the hell knows. It speaks pygmy. Old Papa was the last of his tribe. That stupid bird was the only thing he had left to talk to.

CHRISTIAN (*to the bird*): Hello?

MAMA: He believed as long as the words of the forest people were spoken, the spirits would stay alive.

CHRISTIAN: For true?

MAMA: Yeah, well, when that bird dies this place is gonna lose part of its story.

CHRISTIAN (*poking his finger into the cage*): What are you going to do with him?

MAMA: Sell it. I don't want it. It stinks.

CHRISTIAN (*still poking; to the parrot*): Hello.

MAMA: Hey, hey don't put your fingers in there.

CHRISTIAN: Look. He likes me. So, Mama, you haven't asked me what else I've brought for you? Go see. (*Quickly withdraws his finger.*) Ow. Shit. He bit me.

MAMA: Well, you shouldn't be messing with it. (*Laughs.*)

CHRISTIAN: Ow, damn it.

MAMA (*impatiently*): Don't be a cry baby, what did you bring me? Well? . . . Are you going to keep me guessing?

CHRISTIAN (*sitting back down*): Go on. Take a peek in the truck. And don't say I don't think about you.

MAMA (*smiling*): How many?

CHRISTIAN: Three.

MAMA: Three? But, I can't use three right now. You know that.

CHRISTIAN: Of course you can. And I'll give you a good price if you take all of them.

(*Mama goes to the doorway, and peers out at the offerings, unimpressed.*)

MAMA: I don't know. They look used. Worn.

CHRISTIAN: C'mon, Mama. Take another look. A full look. You've said it yourself business is good.

(*Mama considers, then finally:*)

MAMA: Okay, one. That one in front. (*Points into the distance.*)

CHRISTIAN: Three. C'mon, don't make me travel back with them.

MAMA: Just one. How much?

CHRISTIAN: Do you know how difficult it was getting here? The road was completely washed out—

MAMA: All right, all right. I don't need the whole damn saga. Just tell me, how much for the one?

CHRISTIAN: The same as usual plus twenty-five, because . . . because . . . You understand it wasn't easy to get here with the—

MAMA: I'll give you fifteen.

CHRISTIAN: Ahh! Fifteen? No. That's nothing. Twenty-two. C'mon.

MAMA: Twenty. My best offer.

(*Christian mulls it over. He's reluctant.*)

CHRISTIAN: Aye. Okay. Okay. Damn it. Yes. Yes. But I expect another cold Fanta. One from the bottom this time.

(*Christian, defeated, exits. Mama smiles victoriously, and retrieves another soda from the cooler. She reapplies her lipstick for good measure, then counts out her money.*
  Christian reenters proudly bearing two cartons of Ugandan cigarettes. A moment later two women in ragged clothing step tentatively into the bar: Sophie, a luminous beauty with an air of defiance, and Salima, a sturdy peasant woman whose face betrays a world-weariness. They hold hands. Mama studies the women, then:)

MAMA: I said one. That one.

(*Mama points to Sophie.*)

CHRISTIAN: It's been a good week, and I'll tell you what, I'll give you two for the price of one. Why not?
MAMA: Are you deaf? No. Tst! I don't need two more mouths to feed and pester me.

(*Mama continues to examine each woman.*)

CHRISTIAN: Take both. Feed them as one. Please, Mama, I'll throw in the cigarettes for cost.
MAMA: But, I'll only pay for one.
CHRISTIAN: Of course. We agree, why are we arguing?
MAMA (*yelling*): Josephine! Josephine! Where is that stupid woman?

(*Josephine, a sexy woman in a short western-style miniskirt and high heels appears in the beaded doorway. She surveys the new women with obvious contempt.*)
  Take them out back. Get them washed and some proper clothing.

JOSEPHINE: *Kuya apa* (*Beat.*) *sasa.*° (*Beckons to the women. They reluctantly follow.*)
MAMA: Wait.

(*Mama gestures to Salima, who clings to Sophie.*)

  You. Come here.

(*Salima doesn't move.*)

  Come.

(*Salima clings to Sophie, then slowly walks toward Mama.*)

---

kuya apa: Come here. *sasa*: Now.

What's your name?

SALIMA (*whispers*): Salima.

MAMA: What?

SALIMA: Salima.

(*Mama examines Salima's rough hands.*)

MAMA: Rough. (*With disdain.*) A digger. We'll have to do something about that.

(*Salima yanks her hand away. Mama registers the bold gesture.*)

And you, come. (*Sophie walks to Mama.*) You're a pretty thing, what's your name?

SOPHIE (*gently*): Sophie.

MAMA: Do you have a smile?

SOPHIE: Yes.

MAMA: Then let me see it.

(*Sophie struggles to find a halfhearted smile.*)

Good. Go get washed up.

(*A moment.*)

JOSEPHINE (*snaps*): C'mon, now!

(*Salima looks to Sophie. The women follow behind Josephine. Sophie walks with some pain and effort.*)

MAMA: Did you at least tell them this time?

CHRISTIAN: Yes. They know and they came willingly.

MAMA: And . . . ?

CHRISTIAN: Salima is from a tiny village. No place really. She was, captured by rebel soldiers, *Mayi-mayi,* the poor thing spent nearly five months in the bush as their concubine.

MAMA: And what of her people?

CHRISTIAN: She says her husband is a farmer. And from what I understand, her village won't have her back. Because . . . But she's a simple girl, she doesn't have much learning, I wouldn't worry about her.

MAMA: And the other?

CHRISTIAN: Sophie. Sophie is . . .

MAMA: Is what?

CHRISTIAN: . . . is . . . ruined.

(*A moment.*)

MAMA (*enraged*): You brought me a girl that's ruined?

CHRISTIAN: She cost you nothing.

MAMA: I paid money for her, not the other one. The other one is plain. I have half a dozen girls like her, I don't need to feed another plain girl.

CHRISTIAN: I know this, okay, don't get worked-up. Sophie is a good girl, she won't trouble you.

MAMA: How do I know that?

CHRISTIAN (*defensively*): Because I am telling you. She's seen some very bad times.

MAMA: Yeah? And why is that my concern?

CHRISTIAN: Take her on, just for a month. You'll see she's a good girl. Hard worker.

(*Mama gestures toward her own genitals.*)

MAMA: But damaged, am I right?

CHRISTIAN: Yes . . . Look, militia did ungodly things to the child, took her with . . . a bayonet and then left her for dead. And she was—

MAMA (*Snaps*): I don't need to hear it. Are you done?

CHRISTIAN (*passionately*): Things are gonna get busy, Mama. All along the road people are talking about how this red dirt is rich with coltan.° Suddenly everyone has a shovel, and wants to stake a claim since that boastful pygmy dug up his fortune in the reserve. I guarantee there'll be twice as many miners here by September. And you know all those bastards will be thirsty. So, take her, put her to work for you.

MAMA: And what makes you think I have any use for her?

CHRISTIAN (*pleads*): The girl cooks, cleans and she sings like an angel. And you . . . you haven't had nice music here since that one, that beauty Camille got the AIDS.

MAMA: No. A girl like this is bad luck. I can't have it. Josephine! Josephine!

CHRISTIAN: And, Mama, she's pretty pretty. She'll keep the miners eyes happy. I promise.

MAMA: Stop it already, no. You're like a hyena. Won't you shut up, now.

(*Josephine enters, put upon.*)

JOSEPHINE: Yes, Mama.

MAMA: Bring the girl, Sophie, back.

CHRISTIAN: Wait. Give us a minute, Josephine.

(*Josephine doesn't move.*)

---

coltan: A metallic ore used to create electronic products.

Mama, please. Look, okay, I'm asking you to do me this favor. I've done many things for you over the years. And I don't ask you for a lot in return. Please. The child has no place else to go.

MAMA: I'm sorry, but I'm running a business not a mission. Take her to the sisters in Bunia, let her weave baskets for them. Josephine, why are you standing there like a fool . . . go get the girl.

CHRISTIAN: Wait.

JOSEPHINE (*annoyed*): Do you want me to stay or to go?

MAMA (*snaps*): Get her!

(*Josephine sucks her teeth and exits.*)

CHRISTIAN (*with a tinge of resentment*): Tst! I remembered your lipstick and everything.

MAMA: Don't look at me that way. I open my doors, and tomorrow I'm refugee camp overrun with suffering. Everyone has their hand open since this damned war began. I can't do it. I keep food in the mouths of eight women when half the country's starving, so don't give me shit about taking on one more girl.

CHRISTIAN: Look. Have anything you want off of my truck. Anything! I even have some . . . some Belgian chocolate.

MAMA: You won't let up. Why are you so damn concerned with this girl? Huh?

CHRISTIAN: C'mon, Mama, please.

MAMA: Chocolate. I always ask you for chocolate, and you always tell me it turns in this heat. How many times have you refused me this year. Huh? But, she must be very very important to you. I see that. Do you want to fuck her or something?

(*A moment.*)

CHRISTIAN: She's my sister's only daughter. Okay? I told my family I'd find a place for her . . . And here at least I know she'll be safe. Fed.

(*He stops himself and gulps down his soda.*)

And as you know the village isn't a place for a girl who has been . . . ruined. It brings shame, dishonor to the family.

MAMA (*ironically*): But it's okay for her to be here, huh? I'm sorry, but, I can't. I don't have room for another broken girl.

CHRISTIAN: She eats like a bird. Nothing.

(*Sophie enters.*)

SOPHIE: Madame.

MAMA (*defensively*): It's "Mademoiselle."

(*Mama stares at Sophie, thinking, her resolve slowly softening.*)

Come here.

(*Sophie walks over to Mama.*)

How old are you?

(*Sophie meets Mama's eyes.*)

SOPHIE: Eighteen.
MAMA: Yeah? Do you have a beau?
SOPHIE: No.

(*Mama's surprised by her haughtiness.*)

MAMA: Are you a student?
SOPHIE: Yes, I was to sit for the university exam.
MAMA: I bet you were good at your studies. Am I right?
SOPHIE: Yes.
MAMA: A *petit bureaucrat* in the making.

(*Sophie shifts with discomfort. Her body aches, tears escape her eyes. Mama uses her skirt to wipe Sophie's eyes.*)

Did they hurt you badly?
SOPHIE (*whispered*): . . . Yes.
MAMA: I bet they did.

(*Mama studies Sophie. She considers, then decides:*)

Christian, go get me the chocolate.
CHRISTIAN: Does that mean . . . ?
MAMA: I'm doing this for you, cuz you've been good to me. (*Whispers to Christian.*) But this is the last time you bring me damaged goods. Understood? It's no good for business.
CHRISTIAN: Thank you. It's the last time. I promise. Thank you.
MAMA (*to Sophie*): You sing?
SOPHIE (*softly*): Yes.
MAMA: Do you know any popular songs?
SOPHIE: Yes. A few.
CHRISTIAN: Speak up!

(*Christian exits.*)

SOPHIE: Yes, Mad . . . (*Catching herself.*) . . . emoiselle.
MAMA: Mama. You do math? Stuff like that?
SOPHIE: Yes, Mama.
MAMA: Good.

(*Mama lifts Sophie's chin with her fingers, enviously examining her face.*)

Yes, you're very pretty. I can see how that caused you problems. Do you know what kind of place this is?

SOPHIE: Yes, Mama. I think so.

MAMA: Good.

(*Mama carefully applies red lipstick to Sophie's mouth.*)

Then we have no problems. I expect my girls to be well behaved and clean. That's all. I provide a bed, food and clothing. If things are good, everyone gets a little. If things are bad, then Mama eats first. Am I making myself clear?

(*Sophie nods.*)

Good. Red is your color.

(*Sophie doesn't respond.*)

Thank you, Mama.

SOPHIE: Thank you, Mama.

(*Mama pours a glass of local home-brewed liquor. She holds it out.*)

MAMA: Here. It'll help the pain down below. I know it hurts, because it smells like the rot of meat. So wash good.

(*Sophie takes the glass, and slowly drinks the liquor down.*)

Don't get too dependent on drink. It'll make you sloppy, and I have no tolerance for sloppiness. Understood?

(*Christian, put upon, reenters with a faded, but pretty, box of chocolates.*)

CHRISTIAN: Handmade. Imported. *Très bon*. I hope you're impressed. A Belgian shopkeeper in Bunia ordered them. Real particular. I had a hell of a time trying to find these Goddamn chocolates. And then, poof, she's gone. And now I'm stuck with twenty boxes, I tried to pawn them off on Pastor Robbins, but apparently he's on a diet.

(*Mama opens the box, surveying the chocolates. She's in seventh heaven. She offers a piece to Sophie, who timidly selects a piece.*)

SOPHIE: Merci.

(*Mama bites into the chocolate.*)

MAMA: Mmm.

CHRISTIAN: Happy? That's what the good life in Belgium tastes like.

MAMA: Caramel. (*Savoring.*) Good God, I haven't had caramel in ages. You bastard, you've been holding out on me! Mmm. Smell 'em, the smell reminds me of my mother. She'd take me and my brothers to

Kisangani. And she'd buy us each an enormous bag of caramels wrapped in that impossible plastic. You know why? So we wouldn't tell my grandfather about all of the uncles she visited in the big town. She'd sit us on the bank of the river, watching the boats and eating sweaty caramels, while she "visited with uncles." And as long as there were sweets, we didn't breathe a word, not a murmur, to old Papa.

(*Sophie eats her chocolate, smiling for the first time. Christian reaches for a chocolate, but Mama quickly slaps his hand away.*)

CHRISTIAN: What about me?
MAMA: What about you?
CHRISTIAN: Don't I get one?
MAMA: No!

(*This amuses Sophie. She smiles.*)

CHRISTIAN: Why are you smiling? You're a lucky girl. You're lucky you have such a good uncle. A lot of men would've left you for dead.

(*Sophie's smile disappears.*)

MAMA: Never mind him. (*To Christian.*) Go already and bring the other stuff in before the vultures steal it!
CHRISTIAN: Sophie. I'm . . . you . . . you be a good girl. Don't make Mama angry.
SOPHIE: I won't Uncle.

(*Christian exits, an apology in his posture. Sophie licks her chocolate-covered fingers as the lights fade.*)

Scene 2

A month later. The bar. Josephine cranks the generator. Colorful Christmas lights flicker. The generator hums on. Music and lights provide a festive atmosphere. The birdcage rests in the back of the bar. Periodically the bird makes a raucous.

At the bar, drunk and disheveled Rebel Soldiers drain their beers and laugh too loudly. Salima, wearing a shiny gold midriff, a colorful traditional wrap and mismatched yellow heels, shoots pool, doing her best to ignore the occasional lustful leers of the Soldiers.

Jerome Kisembe, the rebel leader dressed in military uniform, holds court. Mama, toting bowls of peanuts, wears a bright red kerchief around her neck, in recognition of the rebel leader's colors. Josephine dirty-dances for Mr. Harari, a tipsy Lebanese diamond merchant, who sports surprisingly pristine clothing. He is barefoot.

Sophie plows through an upbeat dance song, accompanied by a guitar and drums.

SOPHIE (*sings*): The liquid night slowly pours in
    Languor peels away like a curtain
    Spirits rise and tongues loosen
    And the weary ask to be forgiven.
    You come here to forget,
    You say drive away all regret
    And dance like it's the ending
    The ending of the war.
    The day's heavy door closes quick
    Leaving the scold of the sun behind
    Dusk ushers in the forest's music
    And your body's free to unwind.

(*Josephine dances for the men. They give her tips.*)

    You come here to forget,
    You say drive away all regret
    And dance like it's the ending
    The ending of the war.
    But can the music be all forgiving
    Purge the wear and tear of the living?
    Will the sound drown out your sorrow,
    So you'll remember nothing tomorrow?

(*A drunk Rebel Soldier stands, and demands attention.*)

REBEL SOLDIER #1: Another! Hey!
MAMA: I hear you! I hear you!
REBEL SOLDIER #1: C'mon! Another!

(*He clumsily slams the bottle on the counter. He gestures to Sophie.*)

    Psst! You! Psst! Psst!

(*Another Rebel Soldier gives Sophie a catcall. Sophie ignores him. Rebel Soldier #1 turns his attention back to Mama.*)

    Her! Why won't she come talk to me?
MAMA: You want to talk to her. Behave, and let me see your money.

(*Kisembe, haughty, lets out a roar of a laugh.*)

REBEL SOLDIER #1: The damn beer drained my pocket. It cost too much!
    You're a fucking thief!
MAMA: Then go somewhere else. And mind your tongue. (*Turns away.*)
REBEL SOLDIER #1: Hey. Wait. Wait. I want her to talk to me. Mama, lookie!
    I have this. (*Proudly displays a cloth filled with little chunks of ore.*)

MAMA: What is it? Huh? Coltan? Where'd you get it?

REBEL SOLDIER #1 (*boasting*): From a miner on the reserve.

MAMA: He just gave it to you?

REBEL SOLDIER #1 (*snickering*): Yeah, he give it to me. Dirty poacher been diggin' up our forest, we run 'em off. Run them good, gangsta style: "Muthafucka run!" Left 'em for the fucking scavengers.

(*The Rebel Soldier strikes a hip-hop "gangsta-style" pose. The other Soldiers laugh. Mr. Harari, unamused, ever so slightly registers the conversation. Mama laughs.*)

MAMA: Coltan? Let me see. Ah, that's nothing, it's worthless my friend. A month ago, yes, but now you can't get a handful of meal for it. Too many prospectors. Every miner that walks in here has a bucket of it. Bring me a gram of gold, then we talk.

REBEL SOLDIER #1: What do you mean? Liar! In the city, this would fetch me plenty.

MAMA: This ain't the city, is it, Soldier?

(*He aggressively grabs Mama's wrist.*)

This is a nice place for a drink. Yeah? I don't abide by bush laws. If you want to drink like a man, you drink like a man. You want to behave like gorilla, then go back into the bush.

(*The Soldiers laugh. The Rebel Soldier unhands Mama.*)

REBEL SOLDIER #1: C'mon, Mama, this is worth plenty! Yeah?

(*Again, he gestures to Sophie. He's growing increasingly belligerent.*)

Bitch. Why won't she talk to me?

(*Frustrated, he puts the cloth back in his pocket. He broods, silently watching Sophie sway to the music. Then all of a sudden he collects himself, and drunkenly makes his way toward her.*)

I'll teach her manners! Respect me!

(*He pounds his chest, another Soldier goads him on. Sophie stiffens. The music stops. Mama quickly steps between them.*)

MAMA: But . . . as the coltan is all you have. I'll take it this time. Now go sit down. Sit down. Please.

REBEL SOLDIER #1 (*excited*): Yeah? Now, I want her to talk to me! Will she talk to me?

MAMA: Okay. Okay. Sit.

(*He pulls out the cloth again. He gently removes several pieces of the ore.*)

Don't be stingy. Tst! Let me see all of it.

(*He reluctantly relinquishes the weathered cloth to Mama.*)

(*smiling*) Salima! Salima, come!

(*Salima bristles at the sound of her name. She reluctantly approaches the Soldier. Mama shows her off to him.*)

REBEL SOLDIER #1: What about her? (*Gestures to Sophie.*)
MAMA: Salima is better dancer. (*Salima dances, seductively.*) I promise. Okay. Everyone is happy.
KISEMBE: Solider, everyone is happy!

(*Salima sizes up the drunken Soldier.*)

SALIMA: So, "Gangsta," you wanna dance with me?

(*She places his arms around her waist. He longingly looks over at Sophie, then pulls Salima close. He leads aggressively.*)

Easy.
MAMA: Sophie.

(*Sophie, relieved, resumes singing. Salima and the Rebel Soldier dance.*)

SOPHIE (*sings*): Have another beer, my friend,
  Douse the fire of your fears, my friend,
  Get drunk and foolish on the moment,
  Brush aside the day's heavy judgment.
  Yes, have another beer, my friend,
  Wipe away the angry tears, my friend,
  Get drunk and foolish on the moment,
  Brush aside the day's heavy judgment.
  Cuz you come here to forget,
  You say drive away all regret,
  And dance like it's the ending
  The ending of the war.
  The ending of the war.
  The ending of the war.

(*Applause. Mr. Harari tips Sophie. Mama having quenched the fire, fetches her lockbox from a hiding place beneath the counter, and puts the ore inside.*)

MR. HARARI: That one, she's pretty. (*Gestures to Sophie.*)
JOSEPHINE (*with disdain*): Sophie?! She's broken. All of the girls think she's bad luck.

(*Josephine leads Mr. Harari to the table. He sits.*)

MR. HARARI: What are you wearing? Where's the dress I bought you?
JOSEPHINE: If I had known you were coming, I'd have put it on.
MR. HARARI: Then what are you waiting for, my darling?

(*Josephine exits quickly. Mama, toting her lockbox, joins Mr. Harari at his table.*)

MAMA: What happened to your shoes, Mr. Harari?
MR. HARARI: Your fucking country, some drunk child doing his best impersonation of a rebel soldier liberated my shoes. Every time I come here I have to buy a new fucking pair of shoes.

(*Laughter from the pool table.*)

MAMA: You're lucky he only wanted your shoes. *Sante.*

(*The Soldier gets too friendly with Salima. She lurches away, and falls against the pool table.*)

REBEL SOLDIER #1: Hey!
KISEMBE: Ach, ach, behave, I'm trying to play here.

(*The Solider grabs Salima onto his lap. Mr. Harari weighs the situation.*)

MR. HARARI (*to Mama*): You took that poor man's coltan. Shame on you. He probably doesn't know what he gave away for the taste of that woman. (*To Soldier.*) Savor it! The toll to enter that tunnel was very expensive, my friend. (*To Mama.*) We both know how much it would fetch on the market.
MAMA: Yeah, so? Six months ago it was just more black dirt. I don't get why everyone's crawling over each other for it.
MR. HARARI: Well, my darling, in this damnable age of the mobile phone it's become quite the precious ore, no? And for what ever reason, God has seen fit to bless your backward country with an abundance of it. Now, if that young man had come to me, I would've given him enough money to buy pussy for a month. Even yours. So who's the bigger thief, you or him?
MAMA: He give it to me, you saw. So, does that make me a thief or merely more clever than you.

(*Mr. Harari laughs.*)

MR. HARARI: My darling, you'd do well in Kisangani.
MAMA: I do well here, and I'd get homesick in Kisangani. It's a filthy city full of bureaucrats and thieves.
MR. HARARI: Very funny, but I imagine you'd enjoy it, terribly. And I mean that as a compliment.

MAMA: Do you have a minute?

MR. HARARI: Of course.

KISEMBE: Soldier! Soldier!

REBEL SOLDIER #2: Chief.

KISEMBE: Bring me my mobile! What're you, an old man? Hurry!

(*Mama empties a bag containing stones onto a cloth on the table.*)

MAMA: What do you think? Huh?

MR. HARARI (*referring to the diamonds*): Just looking, I can tell you, most of these are worthless. I'm sorry.

(*Mama takes out another stone, and places it on the table.*)

MAMA: What about that one?

(*Mama points to the rough stone. Mr. Harari examines the diamond on the table, then meticulously places a loup to his eye and examines it. He looks over his shoulder.*)

MR. HARARI (*whispers*): Hm. It's a raw diamond. Where'd you get this?

MAMA: Don't you worry. I'm holding it for someone.

MR. HARARI (*continues to examine the diamond*): Nice. Yes, you see, there. It carries the light well.

MAMA: Yeah, yeah, but is it worth anything?

MR. HARARI: Well . . .

MAMA: Well . . .

MR. HARARI: Depends.

(*Mama smiles.*)

It's raw, and the market—

MAMA: Yeah, yeah, but, what are we talking? Huh? A new generator or a plot of land?

MR. HARARI (*chuckling*): Slow down, I can offer you a fairly good price. But, be reasonable, darling, I'm an independent with a family that doesn't appreciate how hard I work.

(*Mama takes back the diamond.*)

MAMA: You sound like old Papa. He was like you, Mr. Harari, work too much, always want more, no rest. When there was famine his bananas were rotting. He used to say as long as the forest grows a man will never starve.

MR. HARARI: Does he still have his farm?

MAMA (*smiling to herself*): You know better, Mr. Harari, you're in the Congo. Things slip from our fingers like butter. No. When I was eleven, this white man with skin the color of wild berries turned up with a piece of paper. It say he have rights to my family land. (*With acid.*) Just like that. Taken! And you want to hear a joke? Poor old Papa bought magic from a friend, he thought a handful of powder would give him back his land. (*Examining the diamond.*) Everyone talk talk diamonds, but I . . . I want a powerful slip of paper that says I can cut down forests and dig holes and build to the moon if I choose. I don't want someone to turn up at my door, and take my life from me. Not ever again. But tell, how does a woman like me get a piece of land, without having to pick up a fucking gun?

(*Mr. Harari cautiously watches the Rebel Soldiers.*)

MR. HARARI: These, these idiots keep changing the damn rules on us. You file papers, and the next day the office is burned down. You buy land, and the next day the chief's son has built a fucking house on it. I don't know why anybody bothers. Madness. And look at them. (*Gestures to the Rebel Soldiers.*) A hungry pygmy digs a hole in the forest, and suddenly every two-bit militia is battling for the keys to hell.

MAMA: True, chérie, but someone must provide them with beer and distractions.

(*Mr. Harari laughs. Mama scoops up the stones and places them back into her lockbox.*)

MR. HARARI: Just, be careful, where will I drink if anything happens to you?

(*Mr. Harari gives Mama a friendly kiss.*)

MAMA: Don't worry about me. Everything is beautiful.

(*Josephine enters proudly sporting an elegant traditional dress.*)

JOSEPHINE: What do you think?

(*Mr. Harari shifts his gaze to Josephine.*)

MR. HARARI: Such loveliness. Doesn't she look beautiful?
MAMA: Yes, very. *Karibu.*°
MR. HARARI: I just might have to take you home with me.
JOSEPHINE (*excited*): Promise.
MR. HARARI: Of course.

(*Josephine hitches up her dress and straddles Mr. Harari. She kisses him.*)

KISEMBE (*shouts*): Mama! Mama!

Karibu: Welcome.

MAMA: Okay, okay, chief, *sawa sawa*.°

KISEMBE: Two more Primus. And, Mama, why can't I get mobile service in this pit?

MAMA: You tell me, you're important, go make it happen!

MR. HARARI: Who's that?

JOSEPHINE: Him? Jerome Kisembe, leader of the rebel militia. He's very powerful. He have sorcerer that give him a charm so he can't be touched by bullet. He's fearless. He is the boss man, the government and the church and anything else he wants to be.

(*Mr. Harari studies Kisembe.*)

Don't look so hard at a man like that.

(*Josephine grabs Mr. Harari's face and kisses him. Mama clears the beer bottles from Kisembe's table. The Soldier gropes at Salima, he nips her on the neck.*)

SALIMA: Ow! You jackass.

(*Salima pulls away from the Soldier and heads for the door. Mama races after her, catching her arm forcefully.*)

MAMA: What's your problem?

SALIMA: Did you see what he did?

MAMA: You selfish girl. Now get back to him.

(*Mama shoves Salima back toward the Soldier. Sophie, watching, runs over to Salima.*)

SOPHIE: Are you all right, Salima?

SALIMA: The dog bit me. (*Whispered.*) I'm not going back over there.

SOPHIE: You have to.

SALIMA: He's filth! It's a man like him that—

SOPHIE: Don't. Mama's looking.

SALIMA (*tears welling up in her eyes*): Do you know what he said to me—

SOPHIE: They'll say anything to impress a lady. Half of them are lies. Dirty fucking lies! Go back, don't listen. I'll sing the song you like.

(*Sophie gives Salima a kiss on the cheek. Salima's eyes shoot daggers at Mama, but she reluctantly returns to the drunken Soldier. Sophie launches into another song. Josephine dirty-dances for Mr. Harari.*)

> Have another beer, my friend,
> Wipe away the angry tears, my friend,
> Get drunk and foolish on the moment,

sawa sawa: Okay okay.

Brush aside the day's heavy judgment.
Cuz you come here to forget,
You say drive away all regret
And dance like it's the ending
And dance like it's the ending

(*The music crescendos.*)

The ending
The ending
The ending
And dance like it's the ending . . .

(*Mama watches Salima like a hawk. The lights fade.*)

Scene 3

Morning. Living quarters behind the bar. Ragged wood-and-straw beds. A poster of a popular African American pop star hangs over Josephine's bed. Sophie paints Salima's fingernails, as she peruses a worn fashion magazine. Salima shifts in place, agitated.

SALIMA (*impatiently*): C'mon, c'mon, c'mon, Sophie. Finish before she comes back.

SOPHIE: Keep still, will ya. Stop moving. She's with Mr. Harari.

SALIMA: She's gonna kill me if she find out I use her nail polish.

SOPHIE: Well, keep it up, and she's gonna find out one of these days.

SALIMA: But, not today. So hurry!

(*Sophie makes a mistake with Salima's nails. Salima violently yanks her hand away.*)

Aye girl, look what you did! *Pumbafu!*°

SOPHIE: What's your problem?!

SALIMA: Nothing. Nothing. I'm fine.

(*Salima, frustrated, stands up and walks away.*)

SOPHIE: Yeah? You've been short with me all morning? Don't turn away. I'm talking to you.

SALIMA: "Smile, Salima. Talk pretty." Them soldiers don't respect nothing. Them miners, they easy, they want drink, company, and it's over. But the soldiers, they want more of you, and—

SOPHIE: Did that man do something to hurt you?

Pumbafu: Stupid.

SALIMA: You know what he say? He say fifteen Hema men were shot dead
and buried in their own mining pit, in mud so thick it swallow them
right into the ground without mercy. He say, one man stuff the coltan
into his mouth to keep the soldiers from stealing his hard work, and
they split his belly open with a machete. "It'll show him for stealing,"
he say, bragging like I should be congratulating him. And then he
fucked me, and when he was finished he sat on the floor and wept. He
wanted me to hold him. Comfort him.

SOPHIE: And, did you?

SALIMA: No. I'm Hema. One of those men could be my brother.

SOPHIE: Don't even say that.

(*Salima is overcome by the possibility.*)

SALIMA: I . . . I . . . miss my family. My husband. My baby—

SOPHIE: Stop it! We said we wouldn't talk about it.

SALIMA: This morning I was thinking about Beatrice and how much she
liked banana. I feed her like this. I squeeze banana between my fingers
and let her suck them, and she'd make a funny little face. Such delight.
Delight. (*emotionally.*) Delight! Delight!

SOPHIE: Shhh! Lower your voice.

SALIMA: Please, let me say my baby's name, Beatrice.

SOPHIE: Shhh!

SALIMA: I wanna go home!

SOPHIE: Now, look at me. Look here, if you leave, where will you go?
Huh? Sleep in the bush? Scrounge for food in a stinking refugee camp.

SALIMA: But I wanna—!

SOPHIE: What? Be thrown back out there? Where will you go? Huh? Your
husband? Your village? How much goodness did they show you?

SALIMA (*wounded*): Why did you say that?

SOPHIE: I'm sorry, but you know it's true. There is a war going on, and it
isn't safe for a woman alone. You know that! It's better this way. Here.

SALIMA: You, you don't have to be with them. Sometimes their hands are
so full of rage that it hurts to be touched. This night, I look over at you
singing, and you seem almost happy like a sunbird that can fly away if
you reach out to touch it.

SOPHIE: Is that what you think? While I'm singing, I'm praying the pain
will be gone, but what those men did to me lives inside of my body.
Every step I take I feel them in me. Punishing me. And it will be that
way for the rest of my life.

(*Salima touches Sophie's face.*)

SALIMA: I'm pregnant.

SOPHIE: What?
SALIMA: I'm pregnant. I can't tell Mama. (*Tears fill her eyes.*)

(*Sophie hugs Salima.*)

SOPHIE: No. Shh. Shh. Okay. Okay.
SALIMA: She'll turn me out.

(*Sophie breaks away from Salima and digs in a basket for a book.*)

What are you doing?
SOPHIE: Shh. Look, look.

(*Sophie pulls money from between the pages of the book and empties the bills onto the bed.*)

SALIMA: Sophie?!
SOPHIE: Shhh. This is for us. We won't be here forever. Okay.
SALIMA: Where'd you get . . . the money?
SOPHIE: Don't worry. Mama may be many things, but she don't count so good. And when there's enough we'll get a bus to Bunia. I promise. But you can't say anything, not even to Josephine. Okay?
SALIMA: But if Mama finds out that you're—
SOPHIE: Shhhh. She won't.

(*Josephine, bedraggled, enters and throws herself on the bed.*)

JOSEPHINE: What you two whispering about?
SOPHIE: Nothing.

(*Sophie hides the nail polish and book beneath the mattress.*)

JOSEPHINE: God, I'm starving. And there's never anything to eat. I thought you were going to save me some fufu.°
SOPHIE: I did, I put it on the shelf under the cloth.
SALIMA: I bet that stupid monkey took it again. Pesky creature.
JOSEPHINE: It ain't the monkey, it's Emeline's nasty child. He's a menace. That boy's buttocks would be raw if he were mine.

(*Josephine takes off her shirt, revealing an enormous disfiguring black scar circumventing her stomach. She tries to hide it. Sophie's eyes are drawn to the scar.*)

(*To Salima.*) But, if it's you who's been pinching my supper, don't think I won't find out. I ain't the only one who's noticed that you getting fat fat off the same food we eating. (*To Sophie.*) What are you looking at? (*Tosses her shirt to Sophie.*) Hang up my shirt! *Sasa!*

fufu: A staple food in West African cuisine made of ground root vegetables.

(*Sophie hangs Josephine's shirt on a nail.*)

SALIMA: Tst. (*Whispers under her breath.*)
JOSEPHINE: And what's wrong with her?
SALIMA: Nothing.

(*Josephine suspiciously sniffs the air. Then puts on a traditional colorful wrap. A moment. Salima sits back on the bed. Josephine notices her magazine on the bed.*)

JOSEPHINE: Hey, girl, why is my fashion magazine here? Huh?
SALIMA: I . . . I had a quick look.
JOSEPHINE: What do you want with it? Can you even read?
SALIMA: Oh, shut your mouth, I like looking at the photographs.
JOSEPHINE: Oh, c'mon, girl, you've seen them a dozen times. It's the same photographs that were there yesterday.
SALIMA: So why do you care if I look at them?
SOPHIE: *Atsha, makelle.*° Let her see it, Josephine. Let's not have the same argument.
JOSEPHINE: There.
SALIMA (*whispered*): Bitch.
JOSEPHINE: What?
SALIMA: Thank you.
JOSEPHINE: Yeah, that's what I thought.

(*Josephine tosses the magazine at Salima.*)

Girl, I really should charge you for all the times your dirty fingers fuss with it. (*Sucks her teeth.*)
SOPHIE: Oh, give us peace, she doesn't feel well.
JOSEPHINE: No?

(*Salima, moping, thumbs through the magazine, doing her best to ignore Josephine.*)

SALIMA: The only reason I don't read is cuz my younger sister get school, and I get good husband.
JOSEPHINE: So where is he?!

(*Salima ignores her. Josephine turns on the portable radio hanging over her bed.*)

Atsha, makelle: Stop the noise.

ANNOUNCER (*voice-over*): *Nous avons reçu des rapports que les bandits armés de Lendu et des groupes rivaux de Hema combattent pour la commande de la ville—*
SALIMA: What's he say?
SOPHIE: Lendu and Hema, fighting near Bunia.

(*Josephine quickly turns the radio dial. Congolese hip-hop music plays. She does a few quick suggestive steps, then lights a cigarette.*)

JOSEPHINE: Hey. Hey. Guess what? Guess what? I'm going to Kisangani next month.
SOPHIE: What?
JOSEPHINE: Mr. Harari is going to take me. Watch out, chérie, he's promised to set me up in a high-rise apartment. Don't hate, all of this fineness belongs in the city.
SOPHIE: For true?
JOSEPHINE: What, you think I'm lying?
SOPHIE: No, no, that's real cool. Josephine. The big town. You been?
JOSEPHINE: Me? . . . No. No. (*To Salima.*) And I know you haven't.
SALIMA: How do you know? Huh? I was planning to go some time next year. My husband—
JOSEPHINE (*sarcastically*): What, he was going to sell his yams in the market?
SALIMA: I'll ask you not to mention my family.
JOSEPHINE: And if I do?
SALIMA: I'm asking you kindly this time.

(*Josephine recognizes the weight of her words but forges on.*)

JOSEPHINE: I'm tired of hearing about your family. (*Blows smoke at Salima.*)
SALIMA: Mention them again, and I swear to God I'll beat your ass.
JOSEPHINE: Yeah?
SALIMA: Yeah. You don't know what the hell you're talking about.
JOSEPHINE: I don't? All right. I'm stupid! I don't! You are smarter than all of us. Yeah? That's what you think, huh? *Kiwele wele.*° You wait, girl. I'll forgive you, I will, when you say, "Josephine you were so so right."
SOPHIE: Just shut up!
JOSEPHINE: Hey, I'm done.

(*Josephine blows a kiss. Salima, enraged, starts for the door.*)

SOPHIE: Salima, Salima.

(*Salima is gone.*)

Kiwele wele: Dummy.

JOSEPHINE (*Taunting*): Salima!

(*Josephine falls on the bed laughing.*)

SOPHIE: What's wrong with you? What did Salima do to you? You make me sick. (*Flicks off the radio.*)

JOSEPHINE: Hey, *jolie fille*. (*Makes kissing sounds.*)

SOPHIE: Don't talk to me.

JOSEPHINE: I can't talk to you? Who put you on the top shelf? You flutter about here as if God touched only you. What you seem to forget is that this is a whorehouse, chérie.

SOPHIE: Yeah, but, I'm not a whore.

JOSEPHINE: A mere trick of fate. I'm sorry, but let me say what we all know, you are something worse than a whore. So many men have had you that you're worthless.

(*A moment. Sophie, wounded, turns and limps away silently.*)

   Am I wrong?

SOPHIE: . . . Yes.

JOSEPHINE: Am I wrong?

SOPHIE: Yes.

JOSEPHINE: My father was chief!

(*Sophie is at the door. Josephine confronts her.*)

   My father was chief! The most important man in my village, and when the soldiers raided us, who was kind to me? Huh? Not his second wife: "There! She is the chief's daughter!" Or the cowards who pretended not to know me. And did any of them bring a blanket to cover me, did anyone move to help me? NO! So you see, you ain't special!

(*The lights fade.*)

Scene 4

Dusk. The generator hums. Sophie sings. The bar bustles with activity: Miners, Prostitutes, Musicians and Government Soldiers. Laughter. A Miner chats up Salima. Josephine sits at a table with a Soldier.

SOPHIE (*sings*): A rare bird on a limb
   Sings a song heard by a few,
   A few patient and distant listeners
   Hear, its sweet sweet call,
   A sound that haunts the forest,

A cry that tells a story, harmonious,
But time forgotten.
To be seen, is to be doomed
It must evade, evade capture,
And yet the bird
Still cries out to be heard.
And yet the bird
Still cries out to be heard.
And yet the bird
Still cries out to be heard.

(*Mama enters. She feeds the parrot.*)

MAMA: Hello. Talk to me. You hungry? Yes?
CHRISTIAN (*Entering*): Mama!

(*Mama is surprised by Christian. Her face lights up.*)

MAMA: Ah, professor!

(*Mama cracks open a couple of sodas. Christian places a box of chocolates and several cartons of cigarettes on the counter then launches into a poem:*)

CHRISTIAN: The tidal dance,
    A nasty tug of war,
    Two equally implacable partners
    Day fighting night . . .

And so forth and so on. Forgive me, I bring you an early poem, but I'm afraid it's running away from my memory. I still hope one day you will hear the music and dance with me.
MAMA (*dismissive*): You're a ridiculous man.

(*Mama passes a cold soda to Christian. He blows a kiss to Sophie.*)

CHRISTIAN: Lovely, chérie. It's what I've been waiting for.
MAMA: You're the only man I know who doesn't crave a cold beer at the end of a long drive.
CHRISTIAN: Last time I had a drink, I lost several years of my life.

(*Mama hands him a list.*)

    What's this?
MAMA: A list of everything I know you forgot to bring me.

(*Christian examines the list.*)

CHRISTIAN: What? When'd you learn to spell so good?

MAMA: Oh, close your mouth. Sophie wrote it down. She's a smart girl, been helping me.

CHRISTIAN (*teasing*): You see how things work out. And you, you wanted to turn her away—

MAMA: Are you finished?

(*Salima and the Miner laugh and play pool.*)

I looked out for you on Friday. What the hell happened?

CHRISTIAN: I had to deliver supplies to the mission. Have you heard? Pastor Robbins been missing for a couple days.

(*The Soldier whispers something in Josephine's ear. She laughs loudly, flirtatiously.*)

I told them I'd ask about.

MAMA: The white preacher? I'm not surprised. He's gotta big fucking mouth. The mission's better off without him. The only thing that old bastard ever did was pass out flaky aspirin and maybe a round of penicillin if you were dying.

CHRISTIAN: Well, the rumor is the pastor's been treating wounded rebel soldiers.

MAMA (*concerned*): Really?

CHRISTIAN: That's what I'm hearing. Things are getting ugly over that way.

MAMA: Since when?

CHRISTIAN: Last week or so. The militias, they're battling for control of the area. It is impossible.

MAMA: What about Yaka-yaka mine? Has the fighting scared off the miners?

CHRISTIAN: I don't know about the miners, but it's scaring me.

(*Salima and the Miner laugh.*)

I was just by Yaka-yaka. When I was there six months ago, it was a forest filled with noisy birds, now it looks like God spooned out heaping mouthfuls of earth, and every stupid bastard is trying to get a taste of it. It's been ugly, chérie, but never like this. Not here.

MAMA: No more talk.

(*She's spooked, but doesn't want to show it. She signals for the Musicians to play an upbeat song. The song plays softly.*)

There will always be squabbles, ancient and otherwise.

(*Josephine takes the Soldier to the back.*)

Me, I thank God for deep dirty holes like Yaka-yaka. In my house I try to keep everyone happy.

people? That is what I want to know? What has he given you Mama?
Hm? A new roof? Food? Peace?

MAMA: I don't need a man to give me anything.

OSEMBENGA: Make a joke, but Kisembe has one goal and that is to make
himself rich on your back, Mama.

(*Osembenga grows loud and more forthright as he speaks. The music stops. The
bar grows quiet. Tension.*)

He will burn your crops, steal your women, and make slaves of your
men all in the name of peace and reconciliation. Don't believe him. He,
and men like him, these careless militias wage a diabolical campaign.
They leave stains everywhere they go. And remember the land he
claims as his own, it is a national reserve, it is the people's land, our
land. And yet he will tell you the government has taken everything,
though we're actually paving the way for democracy.

MAMA: I know that, but the government needs to let him know that. But
you, I'm only seeing you for the first time. Kisembe, I hear his name
every day.

OSEMBENGA: Then hear my name, Commander Osembenga, *banga liwa.*°

(*A moment. Mama absorbs the news, she seems genuinely humbled. Christian
backs away as if to disappear.*)

You will hear my name quite a bit from now on.

MAMA: Commander Osembenga, forgive me for not knowing your name.
Karibu.° It's a pleasure to have such an important man in our com-
pany. Allow me to pour you a glass of our very best whiskey. From the
U.S. of A.

OSEMBENGA: Thank you. A clean glass.

MAMA: Of course. *Karibu.*

(*Mama fetches Osembenga a glass of whiskey. She makes a show of wiping out
the cloudy glass. She pours him a generous glass of whiskey and places the
bottle in front of him.*)

(*Seductively.*) We take good care of our visitors. And we offer very good
company. Clean company, not like other places. You are safe here. If
you need something, anything while—

OSEMBENGA: You are a practical woman. I know that you have the sense
to keep your doors closed to rebel dogs. Am I right?

(*Osembenga gently takes Mama's hand. She allows the intimacy. Christian
looks on. Contempt.*)

banga liwa: Fear death.   *Karibu*: Welcome.

MAMA: Of course.

(*A Miner, covered in mud, sneaks in.*)

Hey, hey, my friend. Wash your hands and feet in the bucket outside!

(*The Miner, annoyed, scrambles out of the bar.*)

These fucking miners have no respect for nothing. I have to tell that one every time.

(*Christian retreats to the bar, fuming. Osembenga takes note of him. Christian quickly averts his gaze.*)

(*Obsequiously.*) Anything you need.

OSEMBENGA: I will keep that in mind.

MAMA: Ladies.

(*She beckons to Josephine and Salima, who join Osembenga at the table. The Government Soldiers groan.*)

JOSEPHINE: Commander.

(*Josephine places her hand on Osembenga's thigh.*)

MAMA: Excuse me a moment.

(*Christian grabs Mama's arm as she passes.*)

CHRISTIAN: Watch that one.

MAMA: What? It's always good to have friends in the government, no?

(*Mama clears bottles. The Miner reenters. He sits at the bar.*)

GOVERNMENT SOLDIER #1 (*abandoned by Josephine, belligerently*): Another.

MAMA: Show me your money.

(*The Soldier holds up his money.*)

Sophie! Sophie! What are you standing around for? I'm losing money as you speak. Quick. Quick. Two beers.

(*Sophie carries two beers over to the Soldier. He places his money on the table. Sophie picks it up and quickly slips it under her shirt. She doesn't realize Mama is watching her. The drunken Soldier grabs her onto his lap. Christian protectively rises. Sophie skillfully extracts herself from the Soldier's lap.*)

CHRISTIAN: Are you okay?

SOPHIE: Yes.

(*Sophie, shaken, exits. Christian smiles to himself, and lights a cigarette. The drunken Soldier, annoyed, plops down next to Christian.*)

GOVERNMENT SOLDIER #1: *Ça va, Papa?*
CHRISTIAN: *Bien merci.*

(*The Soldier stares down Christian.*)

GOVERNMENT SOLDIER #1: You give me a cigarette, my friend?
CHRISTIAN (*nervously*): Sorry, this is my last one.
GOVERNMENT SOLDIER #1: Yeah? You, buy me cigarette?
CHRISTIAN: What?
GOVERNMENT SOLDIER #1 (*showing off*): Buy me cigarette!
CHRISTIAN: Sure.

(*Christian reluctantly digs into his pocket, and places money on the counter. Mama drops a cigarette on the counter. The Soldier scoops it up triumphantly, and walks away.*)

And? Merci?

(*The Soldier stops short, and menacingly stares down Christian.*)

OSEMBENGA: Soldier, show this good man the bush hasn't robbed you of your manners.

(*A moment.*)

GOVERNMENT SOLDIER #1: Merci.

(*Christian acknowledges Osembenga with a polite nod.*)

OSEMBENGA: Of course.

(*Osembenga smiles, and gestures to Mama.*)

MAMA: Yes, Commander?
OSEMBENGA (*referring to Christian, whispers*): Who is he?
MAMA: Passing through.

(*The Soldier, embarrassed, angrily drives the Miner out of his bar seat. The Miner retreats.*)

OSEMBENGA: What's his business?
MAMA: Salesman. He's nobody.
OSEMBENGA: I don't trust him.
MAMA: Does he look dangerous to you?
OSEMBENGA: Everyone looks dangerous to me, until I've shared a drink with them.

(*Osembenga sizes up Christian, deciding.*)

Give him a glass of whiskey, and tell him I hope he finds success here.

(*Mama pours a glass of whiskey. She walks over to Christian.*)

MAMA: Good news, the commander has bought you a drink of whiskey and hopes that you'll find prosperity.

CHRISTIAN: That's very generous, but you know I don't drink. Please, tell him thanks, but no thanks.

(*A moment.*)

MAMA: The commander is buying you a drink.

(*Mama places the glass in Christian's hand. She signals to the musicians to play.*)

Raise your glass to him, and smile.

CHRISTIAN: Thank you, but I don't drink.

MAMA (*whispered*): Oh, you most certainly do, today. You will drink every last drop of what he offers, and when he buys you another round you'll drink that as well. You will drink until he decides you've had enough.

(*Christian looks over at the smiling Osembenga. He raises his glass to Osembenga across the room, contemplating the drink for a long hard moment.*)

OSEMBENGA: Drink up!

CHRISTIAN: I—

MAMA: Please. (*Whispered.*) He's a very important man.

CHRISTIAN: Please, Mama.

MAMA: He can help us, or he can cause us many problems. It's your decision. Remember, if you don't step on the dog's tail, he won't bite you.

OSEMBENGA: Drink up!

(*The Government Soldiers egg Christian on. Unnerved, Christian, slowly and with difficulty, drinks the liquor, wincing. Osembenga laughs. He signals for Mama to pour Christian another. She does. Again, the Soldiers cheer Christian on.*)

Good. (*Shouts.*) To health and prosperity!

(*Christian contemplates the second drink. Osembenga raises his glass. Christian nervously knocks back the second shot of whiskey, and, again, winces. Osembenga smiles. He signals for Mama to pour another. The Soldiers cheer. Mama pours him another.*)

CHRISTIAN: Don't make—

MAMA: Trust me.

(*She places the glass in his hand. Christian walks over to Osembenga's table. We aren't sure whether he is going to throw the drink in his face or toast him. He forcefully thrusts his drink in the air. Blackout.*)

Scene 5

Morning. The bar. Sophie reads from the pages of a romance novel. Josephine and Salima sit listening, rapt. It is a refuge.

SOPHIE (*reading*): "The others had left the party, they were alone. She was now painfully aware that there was only the kiss left between them. She felt herself stiffen as he leaned into her. The hairs on her forearms stood on end, and the room suddenly grew several degrees warmer—"

JOSEPHINE: Oh, kiss her!

SALIMA: Shh!

SOPHIE: "His lips met hers. She could taste him, smell him, and all at once her body was infused with—"

(*Mama enters with the lockbox. Sophie protectively slips the book behind her back. Mama grabs it.*)

MAMA: What's this?

SOPHIE: . . . A romance, Uncle Christian bought it.

MAMA: A romance?

SOPHIE: Yes.

(*Mama examines the book. The women's eyes plead with her not to take it.*)

MAMA: Josephine, we need water in the back, and Salima, the broom is waiting for you in the yard.

SALIMA: Ah, Mama, let her finish the chapter.

MAMA: Are you giving me lip? I didn't think so. Come here. Hurry.

(*Salima reluctantly walks over to Mama. Mama grabs her wrist and runs her hand over Salima's stomach.*)

You must be happy here. You're getting fat fat!

SALIMA: I didn't notice.

MAMA: Well, I have.

(*Salima, petrified, isn't sure where Mama's going. Then:*)

You did good last night.

SALIMA (*surprised*): Thank you.

(*Mama tosses the book back to Sophie.*)

JOSEPHINE: You don't care for romance, Mama?

MAMA: Me? No, the problem is I already know how it's going to end. There'll be kissing, fucking, a betrayal, and then the woman will foolishly surrender her heart to an undeserving man. Okay. Move. Move. Ach. Ach. Sophie wait.

(*Salima grabs the broom and exits.*)

JOSEPHINE (*gesturing to Sophie*): What about her?
MAMA: I need her help.
JOSEPHINE: Tst!
MAMA: You have a problem with that? You count good?

(*Josephine stares down Sophie. Sophie isn't having it. Mama laughs. Salima pokes her head in the door.*)

SALIMA: Mama. Someone's coming around the bend.
MAMA (*surprised*): So early?
JOSEPHINE: Tst! Another stupid miner looking to get his cock wet.
SALIMA: No, I think it's Mr. Harari.
JOSEPHINE: What?
SALIMA: "Come with me to the city, my darling."
JOSEPHINE: Don't hate!
SOPHIE: "I'm going to buy you a palace in Lebanon, my darling."

(*This strikes a nerve.*)

JOSEPHINE: Hey, hey. At least I have somebody, I take care of him good.
    And he comes back.

(*Josephine seductively approaches Sophie. She grabs her close.*)

    Joke, laugh, *jolie fille*, but we all know a man wants a woman who's
    complete.
SOPHIE: Okay, stop—
JOSEPHINE: He wants her to open up and allow him to release himself, he
    wants to pour the whole world into her.
SOPHIE: I said stop!
JOSEPHINE: Can you be that woman?
MAMA: Let her alone. Go get the water!
JOSEPHINE: I was firstborn child! My father was chief!
MAMA: Yeah, and my father was whoever put money in my mama's
    pocket! Chief, farmer who the hell cares? Go!

(*Josephine storms off. Salima follows.*)

    Give Josephine a good smack in the mouth, and she won't bother you
    no more.

(*She plops the lockbox on the table.*)

    Here. Count last night's money. Let me know how we did.

(*Sophie opens the lockbox. Mama skillfully funnels water into a whiskey bottle.*)

    I don't know where all these men are coming from, but I'm happy for it.

(*Sophie pulls out the money, a worn ribbon, and then a small stone.*)

SOPHIE: Why do you keep this pebble?

MAMA: That? It doesn't look like anything. Stupid man, give it to me to hold for one night of company and four beers not even cold enough to quench his thirst. He said he'd be back for it and he'd pay me. It's a raw diamond. It probably took him a half year of sifting through mud to dig it up, and he promised his simple wife a Chinese motor scooter and fabric from Senegal. And there it is, some unfortunate woman's dream.

SOPHIE: What will you do with it?

MAMA (*chuckling to herself*): Do? Ha!

(*Mama knocks back a shot of watered-down whiskey.*)

It still tastes like whiskey. I don't know, but as long as they are foolish enough to give it to me, I'll keep accepting it. My mother taught me that you can follow behind everyone and walk in the dust, or you can walk ahead through the unbroken thorny brush. You may get blood on your ankles, but you arrive first and not covered in the residue of others. This land is fertile and blessed in many regards, and the men ain't the only one's entitled to its bounty.

SOPHIE: What if the man comes back for his stone?

MAMA: A lot of people would sell it, run away. But it is my insurance policy, it is what keeps me from becoming like them. There must always be a part of you that this war can't touch. It's a damn shame, but I keep it for that stupid woman. Enough talk, how'd we do?

SOPHIE: Good. If we—

MAMA: We?

SOPHIE: Charged a little more for the beer, just a few more francs. By the end of the year we'll have enough to buy a new generator.

MAMA: Yeah? A new generator? Good. You're quick with numbers. Yes. You counted everything from last night. Your tips?

SOPHIE: Yes.

MAMA: Yes?

(*A moment. Mama reaches into Sophie's chest and produces a fold of money.*)

MAMA: Is this yours?

SOPHIE: Yes. I was—

MAMA: Yes? So tell me what you're planning to do with my money. (*With edge.*) Cuz it's my money.

SOPHIE: I—

MAMA: I, I, I . . . what?

SOPHIE: It's not what you think, Mama.

MAMA: No, you're not trying to run off with my money? "Take her in, give her food." Your uncle begged me. What am I supposed to do? I trust you. Everyone say, she bad luck, but I think this is a smart girl, maybe

Mama won't have to do everything by herself. You read books, you speak good, like white man—but is this who you want to be?

SOPHIE: I'm sorry, Mama.

MAMA: No. No. I will put you out on your ass. I will let you walk naked down that road, is that what you want? What did you think you were going to do with my money?!

(*Mama grabs Sophie, pulls her to the door.*)

SOPHIE: Mama! Please! . . .

MAMA: You want to be out there? Huh? Huh? Then go! Go!

(*Sophie struggles, terrified.*)

Huh? What were you going to do?

SOPHIE: A man that come in here said he can help me. He said there is an operation for girls.

MAMA: Don't you lie to me.

SOPHIE: Listen, listen, please listen, they can repair the damage.

(*A moment. Mama releases Sophie.*)

MAMA: An operation?

SOPHIE: Yes, he give me this paper. Look, look.

MAMA: And it can make it better?

SOPHIE: Yes.

(*Mama makes a show of putting the money into her lockbox.*)

MAMA: Hm. Congratulations! You're the first girl bold enough to steal from me. (*Laughs.*) Where are your books?

SOPHIE: Under my bed.

MAMA: Go bring them to me. I know you better than you think, girl.

(*The lights fade.*)

Scene 6

The bar. Morning light pours in. Josephine struggles with a drunk Miner. She finally manages to push him out of the bar, then exits into the back. Salima quickly sneaks food from under the counter. She stuffs fufu into her mouth. The bird squawks as if to tell on her.

SALIMA: Shh! Shh!

(*Christian, winded and on edge, comes rushing into the bar. He is covered in dirt.*)

Professor!

CHRISTIAN: Get Mama!

(*Salima quickly exits. Christian paces. Mama enters.*)

MAMA: Professor! (*Beat.*) What, what is it?
CHRISTIAN: The white pastor's dead.
MAMA: What?

(*Christian sits, then immediately stands.*)

CHRISTIAN: He was dead for over a week before anyone found his body. He was only a hundred meters from the chapel. The cook said it was Osembenga's soldiers. They accused the pastor of aiding rebels. Do you hear what I am saying?

(*Mama takes in his words, they bite her.*)

They cut him up beyond recognition. Cut out his eyes and tongue. (*Nauseated by the notion.*)
MAMA: The pastor? I'm sorry to hear that.

(*Mama pours herself a whiskey.*)

CHRISTIAN: Can I have one of those, please?
MAMA: Are you sure?
CHRISTIAN: Just give it to me damn it!

(*Mama hesitantly pours Christian a drink. She stares at him.*)

What?

(*He gulps it down.*)

The policeman said there were no witnesses. No one saw anything, and so there is nothing he can do. Bury him, he said. Me? I barely know the man, and people who worked with him for years were mute, no one knew anything. He was butchered, and no one knows anything.
MAMA: Take it easy.
CHRISTIAN: These ignorant country boys, who wouldn't be able to tell left from right, they put on a uniform and suddenly they're making decisions for us. Give me another.
MAMA: The Fantas are cold.
CHRISTIAN: I don't want a Fanta.

(*Mama reluctantly pours Christian another drink. His hand slightly quivers as he knocks back the liquor.*)

They've killed a white man. Do you know what that means? A missionary. They're pushing this way. They won't think twice about killing us.
MAMA: A dead pastor, is just another dead man, and people here see that every day. I can't think about it right now. I have ten girls to feed, and a business to run.

(*Mama buries her face in her palms, overwhelmed.*)

CHRISTIAN: Come with me, Mama. We'll go to Kinshasa where there's no trouble. Between the two of us . . . The two of us. We'll open a small place. Serve food, drink, dancing.

(*Mama isn't convinced. Christian reaches for the bottle of whiskey, she snatches it away. Christian slams the bar.*
Two ragged Soldiers, Fortune and Simon, enter like a whirlwind. They carry beat-up rifles and wear dirty ill-fitting uniforms. Fortune also carries an iron pot. They are on edge, which makes Mama very uneasy.)

MAMA: Yes?
FORTUNE: Is this the place of Mama Nadi?
MAMA: Yes, that is me. What can I do for you?
FORTUNE: We'll have a meal and a beer.
MAMA: Okay, no problem. I have fish and fufu from last night.
FORTUNE: Yeah. Good. Good.
MAMA: It ain't hot.
SIMON: We'll have it.

(*Mama eyes the men suspiciously. Christian, petrified, does his best to mask it.*)

MAMA: Please don't be offended, but I'll need to see your money.

(*Fortune removes a pile of worn bills from his pocket. The men move to sit.*)

Hey. Hey. Hey. Empty your weapons.

(*The men hesitate.*)

SIMON: No, our wea—
MAMA: It's the rule. If you want to be fed.

(*The men reluctantly remove their clips from their guns and hand them to Mama.*)

FORTUNE (*to Christian*): Good morning.
CHRISTIAN: Good morning.
SIMON: Do you have a place for us to wash up?
FORTUNE: In the back maybe.

(*Fortune gestures toward the backdoor.*)

MAMA (*suspicious*): I can bring you a basin of water.

(*They sit. Sophie enters, she's surprised to find Christian and the Soldiers.*)

SOPHIE: Uncle.
CHRISTIAN: *Bonjour, mon amour.*

SOPHIE: What happened to—
CHRISTIAN: Shh. I'm okay.

(*Sophie notes the caution in his tone.*)

FORTUNE AND SIMON: Good morning. How are you?

(*The men politely rise.*)

SOPHIE (*timidly*): Good morning.

(*The men sit.*)

MAMA: Bring some water for the basin.
FORTUNE: Please.

(*Sophie exits with the basin. Mama serves beer.*)

   Thank you.
MAMA: You come from the east?
FORTUNE: No.
MAMA: Farmers?
FORTUNE: NO! We're soldiers! We follow Commander Osembenga!

(*Sophie returns with the full basin, but Christian signals for her to leave. Christian grows increasingly nervous. He watches the men like a hawk.*)

MAMA: Easy. I don't mean to insult you, Soldier. But you look like good
   men. Men who don't follow trouble.

(*Fortune seems reluctant to speak.*)

SIMON: We are—
FORTUNE: I'm told there is a woman here named Salima. Is that true?
CHRISTIAN: There—
MAMA: Why? Who is looking for her?
FORTUNE: Is she here!? I asked you, is she here!?
MAMA: I'd adjust your tone, mister.
FORTUNE: Please, I'm looking for a woman named Salima.
MAMA: I have to ask inside.

(*Christian and Mama exchange a look.*)

FORTUNE: She's from Kaligili. She has a small scar on her right cheek.
   Just so.
MAMA: A lot of women come and go. I'll ask around. And may I say who's
   looking for her?
FORTUNE: Fortune, her husband.

(*Christian registers this discovery.*)

MAMA: Excuse me. I'll go ask inside.

(*Mama exits. Christian disappears into his drink.*)

SIMON: We'll find her, Fortune. C'mon, drink up. When was your last cold beer?

FORTUNE: I'm not thirsty.

(*Simon drinks.*)

SIMON: Ah, that's nice. It's nice, man.

(*Fortune paces.*)

FORTUNE: Come on, come on, where is she?

SIMON: Be patient. Man, if she's here we'll find her.

FORTUNE: Why is it taking so long?

SIMON: Take it easy.

FORTUNE: You heard it, the man on the road described Salima. It is her.

(*Simon laughs.*)

What?

(*Fortune paces.*)

SIMON: You say that every time. Maybe it is, maybe it isn't We've been walking for months, and in every village there is a Salima. You are certain. So please, don't—

MAMA (*reemerging*): There is no Salima here.

FORTUNE (*shocked*): What? No! She is here!

MAMA: I'm sorry, you are mistaken. You got bad information.

FORTUNE: Salima! Salima Mukengeshayi!!

MAMA: I said she is not here.

FORTUNE: You lying witch! Salima!

MAMA: Call me names, but there's still no Salima here. I think maybe the woman you're looking for is dead.

FORTUNE: She is here! Goddamn you, she is here.

(*Fortune flips over the table. Mama grabs a machete. Christian brandishes the whiskey bottle like a weapon.*)

MAMA: Please, I said she is not here. And if you insist I will show you how serious I am.

SIMON: We don't want trouble.

MAMA: Now go. Get out! Get the hell out of here.

FORTUNE (*Shouts*): Tell Salima, I will be back for her!

(*The parrot raises hell. Christian scolds Mama with his eyes. Blackout.*)

ACT TWO

Scene 1

Fortune, in his ill-fitting uniform, stands outside the bar, like a centurion guarding the gates.
  Josephine teases two drunk Government Soldiers and a Miner. Guitar. Drums. Mama and Sophie sing a dance song. Mr. Harari and Christian watch. Festive.

MAMA (*sings*): Hey, monsieur, come play, monsieur,
  Hey, monsieur, come play, monsieur,
  The Congo sky rages electric
  As bullets fly like hell's rain,
  Wild flowers wilt and the forest decays.
  But here we're pouring Champagne.

MAMA AND SOPHIE (*sing*): Cuz a warrior knows no peace,
  When a hungry lion's awake
  But when that lion's asleep,
  The warrior is free to play.

SOPHIE (*sings*): Drape your weariness on my shoulder,
  Sweep travel dust from your heart.
  Villages die as soldiers grow bolder,
  We party as the world falls apart.

MAMA AND SOPHIE (*sing*): Cuz a warrior knows no peace,
  When a hungry lion's awake.
  But when that lion's asleep,
  The warrior is free to play.

(*The drum beats out a furious rhythm. Josephine answers with a dance, which begins playfully, seductively, then slowly becomes increasingly frenzied. She releases her anger, her pain . . . everything. She desperately grabs at the air as if trying to hold on to something. She abruptly stops, overwhelmed. Sophie goes to her aid.*)

MAMA AND SOPHIE (*sing*): Hey, monsieur, come play, monsieur,
  Hey, monsieur, come play, monsieur,

(*Sophie leads a spent Josephine to the back.*)

MAMA: The door never closes at Mama's place.
  The door never closes at Mama's place.

(*Mr. Harari nurses a beer as he watches Sophie and Mama sing. Christian, drunk and disheveled, struggles to remain erect.*)

MAMA (*sings*): The door never closes at Mama's place.

(*Soldier laughter. Distant gunfire.*)

Scene 2

Lights fade. The back room.
  Josephine sleeps. Salima quickly pulls down her shirt hiding her pregnant stomach as Mama enters eating a mango.

MAMA (*to Salima*): Are you going to hang here in the shadows until for-ever? I have thirsty miners with a good day in their pockets.

SALIMA: Sorry, Mama, but—

MAMA: I need one of you to go make them happy, show them their hard work isn't for naught. (*Clicks her tongue.*) C'mon. C'mon.

SALIMA (*whispered*): But . . .

MAMA: Josephine!

JOSEPHINE: Ah! Why is it always me?

(*Josephine rises. She exits in a huff, brushing past Sophie, who is just entering after bathing. Salima nervously looks to the door.*)

SALIMA: Is Fortune still outside?

MAMA: Your husband? Yes. He's still standing there, he couldn't be more quiet than if he were a stake driven into the ground. I don't like quiet men.

SALIMA: He's always been so.

MAMA: Well, I wish he wouldn't be "so" outside of my door.

(*Salima involuntarily smiles.*)

SALIMA: Why won't he go already? I don't want him to see me.

SOPHIE: He's not leaving until he sees you, Salima.

(*Sophie dresses.*)

MAMA: Ha. What for? So he can turn his lip up at her again.

SOPHIE: No. C'mon, he's been out there for two nights. If he doesn't love you, why would he still be there.

SALIMA: Yeah?

MAMA: Tst! Both of you are so stupid. He'll see you, love will flood into his eyes, he'll tell you everything you want to hear, and then one morn-ing, I know how it happens, he will begin to ask ugly questions, but he won't be able to hear the answers. And no matter what you say, he won't be satisfied. I know. And, chérie, don't look away from me, will you be able to tell him the truth? Huh? We know, don't we? The woman he loved is dead.

SOPHIE: That's not true. He—
MAMA (*to Salima*): He left her for dead. See. This is your home now. Mama takes care of you.

(*Mama takes Salima in her arms.*)

But if you want to go back out there, go. But they, your village, your people, they won't understand. Oh, they'll say they will, but they won't. Because, you know, underneath everything, they will be thinking she's damaged. She's been had by too many men. She let them, those dirty men, touch her. She's a whore. And Salima, are you strong enough to stomach their hate? It will be worse than anything you've felt yet.

SOPHIE: But he—
MAMA: I'm not being cruel, but your simple life, the one you remember, that . . . Yeah the one you're so fond of . . . it's vapor, chérie. It's gone.

(*Tears flood Salima's eyes.*)

Now, uh-uh, don't cry. We keep our faces pretty. I will send him away. Okay? Okay?

SALIMA: Okay.
MAMA: We'll make him go away. Yeah?
SALIMA: Okay. Good.
SOPHIE: No, Mama, please, let her at least talk to him. He wants to take her home.
MAMA: You read too many of those romance novels where everything is forgiven with a kiss. Enough, my miners are waiting.

(*Mama suspiciously eyes Salima's belly and exits.*)

SOPHIE: If you don't want to see him, then at least go out there and tell him. He's been sitting outside in the rain for two days, and he's not going to leave.
SALIMA: Let him sit.
SOPHIE: Go, talk to him. Maybe you'll feel differently.
SALIMA: He doesn't know that I'm pregnant. When he sees me, he'll hate me all over again.
SOPHIE: You don't know that. He came all this way.

(*A moment.*)

SALIMA: Stupid man. Why did he have to come?
SOPHIE: All you ever talk about is wanting to get away from here. Go with him, Salima. Get the hell out of here! Go!

SALIMA: He called me a filthy dog, and said I tempted them. Why else would it happen? Five months in the bush, passed between the soldiers like a wash rag. Used. I was made poison by their fingers, that is what he said. He had no choice but to turn away from me, because I dishonored him.

SOPHIE: He was hurting. It was sour pride.

SALIMA: Why are you defending him!? Then you go with him!

SOPHIE: I'm not def—

SALIMA: Do you know what I was doing on that morning? (*A calm washes over her*) I was working in our garden, picking the last of the sweet tomatoes. I put Beatrice down in the shade of a frangipani tree,° because my back was giving me some trouble. Forgiven? Where was Fortune? He was in town fetching a new iron pot. "Go," I said. "Go, today, man, or you won't have dinner tonight!" I had been after him for a new pot for a month. And finally on that day the damn man had to go and get it. A new pot. The sun was about to crest, but I had to put in another hour before it got too hot. It was such a clear and open sky. This splendid bird, a peacock, had come into the garden to taunt me, and was showing off its feathers. I stooped down and called to the bird: "Wssht, Wssht." And I felt a shadow cut across my back, and when I stood four men were there over me, smiling, wicked schoolboy smiles. "Yes?" I said. And the tall soldier slammed the butt of his gun into my cheek. Just like that. It was so quick, I didn't even know I'd fallen to the ground. Where did they come from? How could I not have heard them?

SOPHIE: You don't have to—

SALIMA: One of the soldiers held me down with his foot. He was so heavy, thick like an ox and his boot was cracked and weathered like it had been left out in the rain for weeks. His boot was pressing my chest and the cracks in the leather had the look of drying sorghum. His foot was so heavy, and it was all I could see as the others . . . "took" me. My baby was crying. She was a good baby. Beatrice never cried, but she was crying, screaming. "Shhh," I said. "Shhh." And right then . . . (*Closes her eyes.*) A soldier stomped on her head with his boot. And she was quiet.

(*A moment. Salima releases:*)

Where was everybody? WHERE WAS EVERYBODY?!

(*Sophie hugs Salima.*)

---

frangipani tree: Another name for the plumeria tree.

SOPHIE: It's okay. Take a breath.

SALIMA: I fought them!

SOPHIE: I know.

SALIMA: I did!

SOPHIE: I know.

SALIMA: But they still took me from my home. They took me through the bush—raiding thieves. Fucking demons! "She is for everyone, soup to be had before dinner," that is what someone said. They tied me to a tree by my foot, and the men came whenever they wanted soup. I make fires, I cook food, I listen to their stupid songs, I carry bullets, I clean wounds, I wash blood from their clothing, and, and, and . . . I lay there as they tore me to pieces, until I was raw . . . five months. Five months. Chained like a goat. These men fighting . . . fighting for our liberation. Still I close my eyes and I see such terrible things. Things I cannot stand to have in my head. How can men be this way?

(*A moment.*)

It was such a clear and open sky. So, so beautiful. How could I not hear them coming?

SOPHIE: Those men were on a path and we were there. It happened.

SALIMA: A peacock wandered into my garden, and the tomatoes were ripe beyond belief. Our fields of red sorghum were so perfect, it was going to be a fine season. Fortune thought so, too, and we could finally think about planning a trip on the ferry to visit his brother. Oh God please give me back that morning. "Forget the pot, Fortune. Stay . . ." "Stay," that's what I would tell him. What did I do, Sophie? I must have done something. How did I get in the middle of their fight?

SOPHIE: You were picking sweet tomatoes. That's all. You didn't do anything wrong.

(*Sophie kisses Salima on the cheek.*)

SALIMA: It isn't his baby. It's the child of a monster, and there's no telling what it will be. Now, he's willing to forgive me, and is it that simple, Sophie? But what happens when the baby is born, will he be able to forgive the child, will I? And, and . . . and even if I do, I don't think I'll be able to forgive him.

SOPHIE: You can't know that until you speak to him.

SALIMA: I walked into the family compound expecting wide open arms. An embrace. Five months, suffering. I suffered every single second of it. And my family gave me the back of their heads. And he, the man I loved since I was fourteen, chased me away with a green switch. He beat my ankles raw. And I dishonored him? I dishonored him?! Where was he? Buying a pot? He was too proud to bear my shame . . . but not proud enough to protect me from it. Let him sit in the rain.

SOPHIE: Is that really what you want?
SALIMA: Yes.
SOPHIE: He isn't going to leave.
SALIMA: Then I'm sorry for him.

(*The lights shift to moonlight.*)

Scene 3

Rain, moonlight. Outside the bar, Fortune stands in the rain. His posture is erect. Music and laughter pour out of the bar. Mama seductively stands in the doorway. She watches Fortune for a moment.

MAMA: The sky doesn't look like it's gonna let up for a long time. My mama used to say, "Careful of the cold rain, it carries more men to their death than a storm of arrows."
FORTUNE: Why won't you let me see her?
MAMA: Young man, the woman you're looking for isn't here. But if you want company, I have plenty of that. What do you like? (*Seductively.*) I know the challenges of a soldier's life, I hear stories from men every day. And there's nothing better than a gentle hand to pluck out the thorns, and heal the heart.

(*Mama runs her hand up her thigh. She laughs. Fortune turns away, disgusted. Mama smiles.*)

FORTUNE: Please . . . tell my wife, I love her.
MAMA: Yeah. Yeah. I've heard it before. You're not the first man to come here for his wife. But, Soldier, are you sure this is the place you want to be looking for her?
FORTUNE: Here. Give this to her.

(*Fortune lifts an iron pot.*)

MAMA: A pot?

(*Mama laughs.*)

FORTUNE: Yes, please. Just give it to her.
MAMA: Very charming. A pot. Is this how you intend to woo a woman?

(*Fortune shoves it into her hands.*)

You're a nice-looking young man. You seem decent. Go from here. Take care of your land and your mother.

(*Two tipsy Government Soldiers tumble out of the bar.*)

GOVERNMENT SOLDIER #2: Just one more time. One. More. Time.

GOVERNMENT SOLDIER #3: Shut up! That girl doesn't want you.
GOVERNMENT SOLDIER #2: Oh yes, she do. She don't know it, but she do.

(*Drunk, Government Soldier #2 crumples to the ground. Government Soldier #3 finds this hysterically funny.*)

MAMA (*to Fortune*): Go home. Have I made myself clear?

(*Mama goes into the bar. Fortune fumes.*)

FORTUNE (*to Soldier #3*): Idiot! Pick him up! God is watching you.

(*Soldier #3 lifts up his friend, as Simon, out of breath, comes running up to Fortune. Josephine seductively fills the doorway.*)

JOSEPHINE: Ay! Ay! Don't leave me so soon. Where are you going?
SIMON: Fortune! Fortune!

(*The two Soldiers disappear into the night.*)

JOSEPHINE: Come back! Let me show you something sweet and pretty. Come.

(*Josephine laughs.*)

SIMON: Fortune! (*He doubles-over out of breath.*) The commander is gathering everyone. We march out tomorrow morning. The militia is moving on the next village.
FORTUNE: What about Salima? I can't leave her.
SIMON: But we have our orders. We have to go.
JOSEPHINE (*seductively*): Hello, baby. Come say hello to me.
SIMON (*His face lights up*): God help me, look at that sweetness.

(*Simon licks his lips. Josephine does several down-and-dirty pelvic thrusts. Fortune tries not to smile.*)

   Quick. Let me hold some money, so I can go inside and talk to this good-time girl. C'mon, c'mon . . . c'mon, Fortune. (*To Josephine.*) What's your name?
JOSEPHINE: Josephine. Come inside, baby.
FORTUNE: Don't let the witch tempt you.

(*Josephine laughs and disappears inside.*)

SIMON: Let's enjoy ourselves, man, tonight . . . At least let me have one more taste of pleasure. A little taste. Just the tip of my tongue. C'mon, man, let me hold some money. (*Laughs.*)

(*Fortune does not respond. He silently prays.*)

   How long are you gonna do this? Huh? We've been up and down the road. It's time to consider that maybe she's dead.

FORTUNE: Then leave!

(*Simon, frustrated, starts to go.*)

SIMON: This makes no sense. You can't stay here, the rebel militia are moving this way. And if they find you, they'll kill you. We have to go by morning, with or without her.

FORTUNE: Go!

SIMON: Are you sure? You're becoming like Emmanuel Bwiza whose wife drowned in the river when we were children. Remember, the old fool got drunk on bitterness and lost heself. Look here, Fortune, the men are making a joke of you. They're saying, "Why won't the man just take another woman." "Why is he chasing a damaged girl?"

(*Fortune, enraged, grabs Simon around the neck. The friends struggle.*)

FORTUNE (*challenges*): Say it again!

SIMON: It is not me saying it. It is the other men in the brigade.

FORTUNE: Who?

SIMON: If I tell you, are you going to fight all of them?

FORTUNE: Tell me who!

SIMON: Everyone. Every damn one of them. Okay.

(*Fortune releases Simon.*)

Man, *mavi yako!*° It's time to forget her. I'm your cousin, and for three months I've been walking with you, right? Got dirty, got bloody with you. But now, I'm begging you, stop looking. It's time.

FORTUNE: No, I've prayed on this.

SIMON: Come out of the rain. We'll go inside and spend the last of our money, and forget her. C'mon, Fortune. Let's get stupid drunk. Huh? Huh? C'mon.

(*Simon tries to drag Fortune into the bar. Fortune resists. Fuming, he raises his fist to Simon.*)

If you are angry, then be angry at the men who took her. Think about how they did you, they reached right into your pocket and stole from you. I know Salima since we were children. I love her the same as you. She'd want you to avenge her honor. That is the only way to heal your soul.

(*Fortune contemplates his words.*)

FORTUNE: Kill?

SIMON: Yes.

---

mavi yako: Shit.

(*Fortune laughs ironically.*)

FORTUNE: We are farmers. What are we doing? They tell us shoot and we shoot. But for what are we getting? Salima? A better crop? No, man, we're moving further and further away from home. I want my wife! That's all. I want my family.

SIMON: The commander gave us orders to kill all deserters.

FORTUNE: Are you going to kill me?

(*A moment.*)

SIMON: I wouldn't have said it a month ago, but I'll say it now. She's gone.

(*Simon walks off into the darkness. Fortune stands outside the bar in the pouring rain.*
    Gunfire. A firefight. The sounds of the forest.)

Scene 4

The bar. Christian, drunk and haggard, is in the middle of an energetic story. He stands at the bar nursing a beer. Mr. Harari, Sophie and Mama stand around listening.

CHRISTIAN (*with urgency*): No, no, no . . . listen, listen to me, I've just come from there, and it's true. I saw a boy, take a machete to a man, sever his neck, a clean blow, and lift the head in the air like a trophy. May God be my witness. Men were hollering: "We strong warriors, we taste victory. We will kill!"

MAMA: Shh, keep it down?!

CHRISTIAN: Oh shit, my hand, my hand is still shaking. This . . . this man Osembenga is evil. He plays at democracy. This word we bandy about, "democracy," and the first opportunity we get, we spit on our neighbors and why? Because he has cattle and I don't. Because he is and I am not. But nobody has and nobody will have, except for men like you, Mr. Harari, who have the good sense to come and go, and not give a damn.

MAMA: Oh, hush up.

CHRISTIAN: But we have to pretend that all this ugliness means nothing. We wash the blood off with buckets of frigid water, and whitewash our walls. Our leaders tell us: "Follow my rules, your life will be better," their doctors say, "Take this pill, your life will be better," "Plant these seeds, your life will be better," "Read this book, your life will be better," "Kill your neighbor, your life will be better—"

MAMA: Stop. Take it outside. You know I don't allow this talk in here. My doors are open to everybody. And that way trouble doesn't settle here.

CHRISTIAN: Well, someone has to say it, otherwise what? We let it go on. Huh?

MAMA: Professor, enough! Stop it now. Leave the philosophizing and preaching to the wretched politicians. I mean it! I won't have it here!

CHRISTIAN: One day it will be at your door, Mama.

MAMA: And then I'll shut it. People come here to leave behind what ever mess they've made out there. That includes you, professor.

(*Two Rebel Soldiers, fresh from battle, appear from the back of the bar in various stages of undress. Josephine and Kisembe, doped-up and on edge, also enter from the back. Kisembe has scary unpredictable energy. Josephine buttons his shirt. He pushes her away.*)

Sophie, turn on the music.

(*Sophie turns on the radio. Congolese hip-hop music plays. Christian attempts to disappear behind his drink. Sophie stands behind the bar, drying glasses, trying not to be noticed. Mama walks over to greet the men. The Parrot squawks.*)

Colonel Kisembe, I hope my girls gave you good company.

KISEMBE: Very. It is good to be back, Mama. Where's everyone?

MAMA: You tell me. It's been this way for a week. I haven't seen but a handful of miners. I bake bread and it goes stale.

KISEMBE: It is Commander Osembenga. He is giving us some trouble.

CHRISTIAN: He's a crazy bastard!

KISEMBE: His men set fire to several of our villages, now everyone has fled deeper into the bush.

MAMA: I saw smoke over the trees.

REBEL SOLDIER #3: The mission. They burn everything to save bullets.

(*Sophie gasps and covers her mouth.*)

KISEMBE: They took machetes to anything that moves. This is their justice.

(*Josephine spots Mr. Harari. She is torn about where to place her affection.*)

Believe me, when we find Osembenga and his collaborators, he will be shown the same mercy he showed our people. It's what they deserve. (*To Christian*) Am I right? You? Am I right?

CHRISTIAN (*reluctantly*): You are right. But—

KISEMBE: I'm sorry. It's how it has to be. They have done this to us. I see you agree, Mama.

MAMA: Of course.

(*Everyone in the bar grows uneasy, afraid of Kisembe's intense erratic energy. They're barely listening to his rhetoric, instead focused on trying not to set him off.*)

KISEMBE: They say we are the renegades. We don't respect the rule of law . . . but how else do we protect ourselves against their aggression? Huh? How do we feed our families? Ay? They bring soldiers from Uganda, drive us from our land and make us refugees . . . and then turn us into criminals when we protest or try to protect ourselves. How can we let the government carve up our most valuable land to serve to companies in China. It's our land. Ask the Mbuti, they can describe every inch of the forest as if were their own flesh. Am I telling the truth?

MAMA: Here's to the truth!

(*Kisembe, pleased with his own words, places a cigarette in his mouth. A young Rebel Soldier quickly lights it for him. Kisembe challenges Christian with his eyes. Christian averts his gaze. He nervously raises his glass.*)

CHRISTIAN: The truth!

(*A moment. Mr. Harari uses the awkward silence to interject.*)

MR. HARARI: Has, um, Osembenga shut down production at Yaka-yaka mine?

KISEMBE: And you are?

MR. HARARI: I'm sorry, Colonel, may I offer you my card?

(*Mr. Harari passes Kisembe his card. Kisembe examines it.*)

KISEMBE: Ha-ra-i?

MR. HARARI: Aziz Harari. Yes. Please. I handle mostly minerals, some precious stones, but I have contacts for everything. My mobile is always on. Let me buy you a drink.

(*Mr. Harari signals Sophie to bring a bottle of whiskey over to Kisembe. She pours two glasses.*)

KISEMBE: Thank you.

(*Kisembe takes the bottle of whiskey and slips the card into his pocket, by way of dismissing Mr. Harari, who backs away. Mama wraps her arms around Kisembe's shoulders.*)

MAMA: Come, gentlemen. You will be treated like warriors here.

KISEMBE: I wish we could stay all night, but duty calls.

(*Kisembe signals to his men. They follow him toward the door.*)

MAMA: No! So soon? Josephine!

(*Mama signals to Josephine, who refuses to budge. Instead she sits on Mr. Harari's lap. Mr. Harari tenses.*)

MR. HARARI (*whispers*): Go!
JOSEPHINE: No.

(*Kisembe and his men collect their guns and leave. A moment. A huge sigh of relief. Exhale. Christian slaps his thigh and stands. He does a spot-on impersonation of the haughty swagger of the rebel leader.*)

CHRISTIAN: "Girl. Quick. Quick. Bring me a beer, so I can wash it down with Osembenga's blood."

(*Sophie and Josephine laugh. Mr. Harari is too nervous to enjoy the show.*)

SOPHIE: Yes, Colonel.
CHRISTIAN (*continuing to imitate Kisembe*): "Woman, are you addressing me as 'Colonel'?"
SOPHIE: Yes, Colonel.
CHRISTIAN: "Don't you know who I am? I am from here on in to be known as the Great Commander of All Things Wise and Wonderful, with the Heart of a Hundred Lions in Battle."
SOPHIE: I'm so sorry, Great Commander of All Things Wise and . . .
CHRISTIAN: "Wonderful with the Heart of a Hundred Lions in Battle. Don't you forget that!"

(*Christian does a playful mocking warrior dance. Josephine taps out a rhythm on the counter. A Drummer joins in. Mama laughs.*)

MAMA: You are a fool!

(*Mama retreats to the back with empty bottles. Unseen, the formidable Commander Osembenga and a sullen Government Soldier, Laurent, enter. They wear black berets and muddy uniforms. A moment. Christian stops his dance abruptly.*)

OSEMBENGA: Don't stop you. Go on.
CHRISTIAN: Commander Osembenga.
OSEMBENGA: Continue.

(*Osembenga smiles and claps his hands. Christian continues his dance, now drained of its verve and humor. Osembenga laughs. Then he stops clapping, releasing Christian from the dance. Christian, humiliated, retreats to the bar. Osembenga acknowledges Mr. Harari with a polite nod.*)

Where is Mama?
SOPHIE: She's in the back. (*Yells.*) Mama! Mama!
OSEMBENGA (*suspiciously*): I saw a truck leaving? Whose was it?
CHRISTIAN (*lying*): Uh . . . aid worker.
OSEMBENGA: Oh? Good-looking vehicle. Expensive. Eight cylinders.
CHRISTIAN: Yes.
OSEMBENGA: Sturdy. It looked like it could take the road during rainy season.
CHRISTIAN: Probably.

(*Osembenga approves.*)

SOPHIE: Mama!

MAMA (*entering from off, annoyed*): Why are you calling me?! You know I'm busy.

(*Mama stops short when she sees Osembenga. She conjures a warm smile.*)

(*Surprised.*) Commander Osembenga. *Karibu.* (*Nervously.*) We . . . how are you?

(*Mama glances at the door.*)

OSEMBENGA: Run ragged, if the truth be told. Two Primus, cold, and a pack of cigarettes.

(*Mama directs Sophie to get the beer. Osembenga strokes Mama's backside. She playfully swats away his hand.*)

You look good, today.

MAMA: You should have seen me yesterday.

OSEMBENGA: I wish I had, but I was otherwise engaged.

MAMA: Yeah? We heard you had some trouble. Kisembe.

OSEMBENGA: Is that what is being said? Not trouble! Slight irritation. But you'd be pleased to know, we're close to shutting down Kisembe and his militia. We finally have him on the run. He won't be troubling the people here very much longer.

MAMA: Is that so?

OSEMBENGA: My guess, he's heading east. He'll need to come through here. He can't hide from me. It's the only passable road.

MAMA: I saw smoke over the trees.

OSEMBENGA: That bastard and his cronies attacked the hospital.

MR. HARARI: The hospital? Why?

OSEMBENGA: Because they are imbeciles. I don't know. Looking for medicine. Speed. Morphine. Who the hell knows? They rounded-up and killed mostly Hema patients. (*To Sophie.*) Tsst. Tsst. You, bring me some groundnuts. (*To Mama.*) It was chaos. When we arrived we found the hospital staff tied by their hands and cut up like meat.

LAURENT: One man's heart was missing.

(*Sophie covers her mouth with disgust.*)

MAMA (*disgusted*): What?

OSEMBENGA: And he accuses us of being the barbarians? Don't worry, I've given my soldiers the liberty to control the situation. I am afraid this is what must be done. They force our hand.

(*Osembenga takes sadistic delight in this notion. Sophie cringes as she places beer and peanuts on the table for the Soldiers. Osembenga grabs Sophie's wrist, and pulls her toward him.*)

(*Laughing.*) Come here, you pretty pretty thing. What? You don't like what I'm wearing?

(*Sophie tries to gently pry herself loose. Christian, sensing tension, moves toward them. Laurent rises.*)

You don't like men in uniforms? You don't like men, maybe. Is that it?

(*A moment. Sophie now struggles to free herself.*)

MAMA (*sensing the tension*): Sophie, come here. Let—
OSEMBENGA (*smiling*): Hey. We are talking. We are talking, yeah?

(*Osembenga pulls Sophie onto his lap. He shoves his hand up her skirt. She gasps and struggles harder.*)

Am I ugly? Is that what you're trying to tell me.
SOPHIE (*hisses*): Let go of me!

(*Sophie violently pushes away from Osembenga. Christian rushes in to protect her, as Osembenga lunges for her. Mama blocks Osembenga's path. Laurent rises to aid Osembenga.*)

MAMA: Sophie, shush! Enough. Commander, ignore her, there are other girls for you. Come. Come.
OSEMBENGA: Bring this girl around back, my men will teach her a lesson. She needs proper schooling.

(*Laurent shoves Christian out of the way, and grabs Sophie. This is the first time we've seen Mama scared. Sophie spits on Osembenga's feet.*)

MAMA: Sophie.

(*Mama, horrified, bends down and wipes the spit from Osembenga's shoes. Osembenga glares at Sophie.*)

SOPHIE (*shouting as if possessed*): I am dead.
MAMA: No!
SOPHIE (*possessed*): I am dead! Fuck a corpse! What would that make you?

(*Osembenga is thrown.*)

OSEMBENGA: I'm trying to bring order here, and this girl spits on my feet. Do you see what I have to deal with? Do you? This is the problem.

(*Christian quickly pulls Sophie away.*)

MAMA: Gentlemen, Commander, this is not our way . . . we want you to be comfortable and happy here, let me show you the pleasures of Mama Nadi's.

(*A moment. A standoff.*)

OSEMBENGA: Then, Mama, you show me.

(*Osembenga checks his anger. He smiles. Mama understands. She follows Osembenga into the back. Sophie desperately scrubs her hands in the basin. Mr. Harari pours himself a healthy drink.*)

MR. HARARI: Okay. Let's not overreact. Everything's going to be fine.
CHRISTIAN (*whispers*): Sophie, are you crazy? What are you doing?

(*Josephine compassionately stops Sophie, who is scrubbing her hands raw.*)

JOSEPHINE: Stop it. Stop it. (*Hugs Sophie tightly.*) Shh. Shh.

(*Mama furiously reenters. She slaps Sophie across the face.*)

MAMA: Next time I will put you out for the vultures. I don't care if that was the man who slit your mother's throat. Do you understand me? You could have gotten all of us killed. What do you have to say to me?
SOPHIE: Sorry, Mama.
MAMA: You're lucky the commander is generous. I had to plead with him to give you another chance. Now you go in there, and you make sure that his cock is clean. Am I making myself clear?
SOPHIE: Please—
MAMA: Now get outta my sight.

(*Mama grabs Sophie and thrusts her into the back. Mr. Harari, Christian and Josephine stare at Mama. A moment. Mama goes behind the bar and pours herself a drink.*)

What?
CHRISTIAN: Don't make her do that! This girl is—
MAMA: What if Osembenga had been more than offended. What then? Who would protect my business if he turned on me? It is but for the grace of God, that he didn't beat her to the ground. And now I have to give away business to keep him and his filthy soldiers happy.
CHRISTIAN: But if—
MAMA: Not a word from you. You have a problem, then leave.
CHRISTIAN: "Business." When you say it, it sounds vulgar, polluted.
MAMA: Are you going to lecture me, professor? Turn your dirty finger away from me.

(*Christian is stung by her words.*)

CHRISTIAN: Mama?

MAMA: What, chérie? (*Laughs.*)

CHRISTIAN (*wounded*): Forget it! Bring me another beer. There's my money. (*Slams the money down on the counter.*) You understand *that*, don't you? You like that? There's your fucking money.

(*Mama slowly picks up the money and puts it in her apron. She ceremoniously cracks open a beer and places it in front of Christian.*)

MAMA: Drink up, you fucking drunk.

CHRISTIAN: What's wrong with you?

(*Christian snatches up his beer. He drinks it down quickly and deliberately.*)

MAMA: You men kill me. You come in here, drink your beer, take your pleasure, and then wanna judge the way I run my "business." The front door swings both ways. I don't force anyone's hand. My girls, Emilene, Mazima, Josephine, ask them, they'd rather be here, than back out there in their villages where they are taken without regard. They're safer with me than in their own homes, because this country is picked clean, while men, poets like you, drink beer, eat nuts and look for some place to disappear. And I am without mercy, is that what you're saying? Because I give them something other than a beggar's cup. (*With ferocity.*) I didn't come here as Mama Nadi, I found her the same way miners find their wealth in the muck. I stumbled off of that road without two twigs to start a fire. I turned a basket of sweets and soggy biscuits into a business. I don't give a damn what any of you think. This is my place, Mama Nadi's.

(*Christian crosses to leave.*)

Of course.

(*Mama's words stop him.*)

CHRISTIAN: The black rope of water towing
A rusted ferry fighting the current of time,
An insatiable flow,
Drifting
Without enough kerosene to get through the dark nights,
The destination always a port away.

MAMA (*spits*): It's wind. If you can't place it on a scale, it's nothing.

(*Christian heads for the door.*)

You'll be back when you need another beer.

CHRISTIAN: I don't think so.

(*Christian absorbs the blow, then storms outside in a huff. Josephine and Mr. Harari exit to the back. Mama is left alone to contemplate her actions.*)

Scene 5

Outside the bar. Osembenga and Laurent stumble out of Mama Nadi's place, laughing.

OSEMBENGA: I always like the taste of something new.

FORTUNE (*approaching them*): Commander! Commander!

OSEMBENGA: Yes?

FORTUNE: I'm sorry to disturb you, but I . . .

OSEMBENGA: Yes?

FORTUNE: I saw Jerome Kisembe.

OSEMBENGA: Who are you?

FORTUNE: I am Fortune Mukengeshayi, I'm with your brigade.

OSEMBENGA: Jerome Kisembe?

FORTUNE: Yes . . . He was inside Mama Nadi's.

OSEMBENGA: Inside here?

FORTUNE: Yes, I saw him. She was hiding him. I heard him say the rebels are heading south along this road. He will join them tomorrow.

OSEMBENGA: Mama Nadi's?! Here?!

FORTUNE: He drove south in a white truck! Please, she is holding my wife. I just want to get her back.

OSEMBENGA (*to Laurent*): Quick, quick. We'll go after him. Call ahead, prepare the brigade to move out.

(*They quickly exit.*)

Scene 6

Dawn. Morning light pours into the bar. Mr. Harari paces. His traveling bag is perched near the door. Mama wipes down the bar.

MAMA: Would you like a drink while you wait?

(*Artillery fire, closer than expected.*)

MR. HARARI: Yes. Thank you. A little palm wine.

(*Mama, settles her nerves, and pours them both a palm wine.*)

MAMA: It looks like it's going to rain, you might wanna wait until—

MR. HARARI: I can't. Thank goodness, I found a lift with one of the aid workers. My driver, fucking idiot, took off last night. (*Jokes.*) Apparently he doesn't care for the sound of gunfire.

MAMA: I told you, you didn't pay him enough.

MR. HARARI: This fucking war, ay mother, no one owns it! It's everybody's and nobody's.

MAMA: Tst!

MR. HARARI: It keeps fracturing and redefining itself. Militias form over-night, and suddenly a drunken foot solider with a tribal vendetta is a rebel leader, and in possession of half of the enriched land, but you can't reason with him, because he's only thinking as far as his next drink.

MAMA: Yes, and what is new?

MR. HARARI: The man I shake hands with in the morning is my enemy by sundown. And why? His whims. Because?! His witch doctor says I'm the enemy. I don't know whose hand to grease other than the one di-rectly in front of me. At least I understood Mobutu's brand of chaos. Now, I'm a relative beginner, I must relearn the terms every few months, and make new friends, but who? It's difficult to say, so I must befriend everybody and nobody. And it's utterly exhausting.

MAMA: Let all the mother-hating soldiers fight it out. Cuz, in the end, do you think that will change anything here?

MR. HARARI: God only knows. The main road is crowded with folks heading east. There is no shame in leaving, Mama. Part of being in business is knowing when to cut your losses and get out.

MAMA: I have the only pool table in fifty kilometers. Where will people drink if anything happens to me?

MR. HARARI: The commander knows Kisembe was here. Eventually you must fly your colors. Take a side.

MAMA: He pays me in gold, he pays me in coltan. What is worth more? You tell me. What is their argument? I don't know. Who will win? Who cares? There's an old proverb, "Two hungry birds fight over a kernel, just then a third one swoops down and carries it off. Whoops!"

MR. HARARI: You are the most devilish of optimists. You—I don't worry so much about you. But what about a lovely girl like Sophie?

(*His words hit her. Mr. Harari knocks back his drink, then heads for the door, looking out for his ride.*)

Until next time!

(*Distant gunfire. Mr. Harari anxiously stands in the doorway. Mama goes to the bar, she appears conflicted. An internal battle.*)

MAMA: Ah . . . One thing, Mr. Harari. Before you leave, can I ask you a favor?

MR. HARARI: Of course.

(*Mama opens the lockbox, and carefully lays out the diamond.*)

MAMA: This.

(*Mr. Harari's eyes light up.*)

MR. HARARI: Your insurance policy.

MAMA (*with irony*): Yes. My restaurant, my garden to dig in, and a chief's fortune of cows. (*Laughs.*)

MR. HARARI: You are ready to sell?

MAMA: Yes. Take this. (*Hands him Sophie's piece of paper.*) It has the name of a man in Bunia, a doctor. (*With urgency.*) He won't trouble you with questions. Use my name.

MR. HARARI: Slow, slow, what do you want me—

MAMA: Just listen. I want you to take her to—

MR. HARARI (*confused*): Josephine? (*Genuinely surprised.*) Be realistic, how would a girl like Josephine survive in the city.

MAMA: No, listen—

MR. HARARI: I can't. She is a country thing, not refined at all.

MAMA: No, listen . . . I'm talking about Sophie. This will raise enough money for an operation, and whatever she needs to get settled.

MR. HARARI: Sophie?

MAMA: Yes.

MR. HARARI: Why? Operation? What?

MAMA: It's a long conversation, and there isn't time.

MR. HARARI: This is more than—

MAMA: Enough for a life. I know.

MR. HARARI: Are you sure? This diamond will fetch a fairly decent price, you can settle over the border in Uganda. Start fresh.

MAMA: I have ten girls here. What will I do with them? Is there enough room for all of us in the car? No. I can't go. Since I was young, people have found reasons to push me out of my home, men have laid claim to my possessions, but I am not running now. This is my place. Mama Nadi's.

MR. HARARI: But I'm not—

MAMA: You do this for me. I don't want the other women to know. So let's do this quickly.

MR. HARARI: And the doctor's name is on the paper. I'm to call when I get there.

MAMA: Yes. And you give Sophie the money. The money for the stone. Understand? Promise me. It's important. All of it.

MR. HARARI: . . . Yes. Are you sure?

MAMA: Yes.

(*Mama reluctantly passes the diamond to Mr. Harari.*)

Thank you. I'll get her.

(*Mama quickly exits. Mr. Harari examines the diamond. An Aid Worker comes rushing in.*)

AID WORKER: I'm loaded. We have to go now! Now! Three vehicles are coming in fast. We can't be here.
MR. HARARI: But . . . What about—
AID WORKER (*panicked*): Now! I can't wait. C'mon. C'mon.

(*Distant gunfire.*)

MR. HARARI: I have to—
AID WORKER: They'll be okay. Us, men, they'll come after us—
MR. HARARI: One minute. (*Calling to Mama, off.*) Mama! Mama! Come! Mama! I—
AID WORKER: I have to go! I can't wait.

(*The Aid Worker doesn't have time to listen. He races out. The engine revs.*)

MR. HARARI: Mama! Mama!

(*Mr. Harari seems torn, a moment, then he decides. He places the diamond in his pocket and leaves. Silence. Then distant gunfire. Mama enters, frantically pulling Sophie.*)

MAMA: When you get there, he has the money to take care of everything. Settle. Make a good life, hear.
SOPHIE: Why are you doing this for me?
MAMA: Stop, don't ask me stupid questions, just go. Go!

(*She tucks a piece of paper into Sophie's hand.*)

   This is my cousin's wife, all I have is her address. But a motorbike will take you. You say that I am your friend.
SOPHIE: Thank you, Mama. I—
MAMA: No time. You send word through Mr. Harari. Let me know that everything goes well. Okay.

(*Sophie hugs Mama. She exits. Mama, elated, goes to pour herself a celebratory drink. She doesn't see Sophie reenter until:*)

SOPHIE: He's gone.

(*The stage is flooded with intense light. The sound of chaos, shouting, gunfire, grows with intensity. Government Soldiers pour in. A siege. A white hot flash. The generator blows! Streams of natural light pour into the bar. Fortune, Commander Osembenga, Simon and Soldiers stand over Sophie and Mama.*)

FORTUNE: He was here! I saw him here!

(*Osembenga stands over Mama.*)

OSEMBENGA: This soldier said he saw Jerome Kisembe here.
MAMA: This soldier is a liar.

FORTUNE: I swear to you! He was here with two men. The same night you were here, Commander!

MAMA: We are friends. Why would I lie to you? This soldier has been menacing us for days. He's crazy. A liar!

FORTUNE: This woman is the devil! She's a witch! She enchanted my wife.

OSEMBENGA: Again. Where is Kisembe?

MAMA: I don't know. Why would I play these games? Don't you think I know better. He is a simple digger. And me, I wouldn't give him what he wants, so he tells tales. Commander, we are friends. You know me. I am with you. Of course. Come, let me get you some whiskey—

OSEMBENGA: *Funga kinua yaké!* °

(*Osembenga signals to his Soldiers. Chaos. They find Mama's lockbox, break it open and take her money. A Soldier drags Josephine from the back. They throw Mama, Sophie and Josephine onto the floor.*)

MAMA: NO!

OSEMBENGA: This can stop. Tell me where I can find Kisembe.

MAMA: I don't know where he is.

OSEMBENGA (*points to Josephine*): Take that one.

(*A Soldier grabs Josephine. He is ready to sexually violate her. Josephine desperately struggles to get away. The Soldier tears away at her clothing. The women scream, fight.*)

JOSEPHINE: No! No! Tell him, Mama. He was here.

(*Osembenga turns his rage on Mama.*)

MAMA: Please!

(*Salima slowly enters as if in a trance. A pool of blood forms in the middle of her dress, blood drips down her legs.*)

SALIMA (*screams*): STOP! Stop it!

FORTUNE: Salima!

SALIMA (*screams*): For the love of God, stop this! Haven't you done enough to us. Enough! Enough!

(*The Soldiers stop abruptly, shocked by Salima's defiant voice.*)

MAMA: What did you do?!

(*Fortune violently pushes the Soldiers out of the way and races to Salima.*)

funga kinua yaké: Shut her mouth.

FORTUNE: Salima! Salima!
SALIMA: Fortune.

(*Fortune scoops Salima into his arms. Mama breaks away from the Soldiers.*)

MAMA: Quick go get some hot water and cloth. Salima look at me. You
    have to look at me; keep your eyes on me. Don't think of anything else.
    C'mon look at me.

(*Salima smiles triumphantly. She takes Fortune's hand.*)

SALIMA (*to Osembenga, the Soldiers and Fortune*): You will not fight your
    battles on my body anymore.

(*Salima collapses to the floor. Fortune cradles her in his arms. She dies.
Blackout.*)

Scene 7

*The sounds of the tropical Ituri rain forest. The bar. The bird quietly chatters. Sophie
methodically sweeps the dirt floor with a thatched broom. Josephine washes the
countertop. Mama stands in the doorway.*

SOPHIE (*sings*): Have another beer, my friend,
    Douse the fire of your fears, my friend,
    Get drunk and foolish on the moment,
    Brush aside the day's heavy judgment.

(*Mama anxiously watches the road. Excited, she spots a passing truck.*)

SOPHIE (*sings*): Cuz you come here to forget,
    You say drive away all regret,
    And dance like it's the ending . . .
MAMA: Dust rising.
JOSEPHINE (*eagerly*): Who is it?
MAMA (*Excited*): I don't know. Blue helmets heading north. Hello? Hello?

(*Mama seductively waves. Nothing. Disappointed, she retreats to the table.*)

Damn them. How the hell are we supposed to do business? They're
draining our blood.
JOSEPHINE: Hey, Sophie, give me a hand.

(*Josephine and Sophie pick up the basin of water and exit. Mama buries her
face in her hands. Christian enters. He whistles. Mama looks up, doing her best
to contain her excitement. Christian brushes the travel dust from his brand-new
brown suit.*)

MAMA: Look who it is. The wind could have brought me a paying customer, but instead I get you.

CHRISTIAN: Lovely. I'm glad to see after all these months you haven't lost any of your wonderful charm. You're looking fine as ever.

MAMA: Yeah? I'm making do with nothing.

(*Christian smiles.*)

Who'd you bribe to get past the roadblock?

CHRISTIAN: I have my ways, and as it turns out the officer on duty has a fondness for Nigerian soap operas and Belgian chocolates.

(*Mama finally lets herself smile.*)

I'm surprised to find you're still here.

MAMA: Were you expecting me to disappear into the forest and live off roots with the Mbuti? I'm staying put. The war's on the back of the gold diggers, you follow them you follow trouble. What are you wearing?

CHRISTIAN: You like?

MAMA: They didn't have your size?

CHRISTIAN: Very funny. Chérie, your eyes tell me everything I need to know.

MAMA: Tst!

CHRISTIAN: What, you have something in your teeth?

MAMA: Business must be good. Yeah?

CHRISTIAN: No, but a man's got to have at least one smart change of clothing, even in times like these . . . I heard what happened.

(*A moment.*)

MAMA: *C'est la vie.* Salima was a good girl.

(*Sophie enters.*)

SOPHIE: Uncle!

(*They exchange a long hug.*)

CHRISTIAN: Sophie, *mon amour.* I have something for you.

SOPHIE: *Un livre?*

CHRISTIAN: . . . Yes.

SOPHIE: Merci.

(*He hands her a package. She rips open the brown paper. She pulls out a handful of magazines and a book.*)

CHRISTIAN: And this. A letter from your mother. Don't expect too much.

(*Sophie, shocked, grabs the letter.*)

SOPHIE (*overwhelmed*): Excuse me.
CHRISTIAN: Go!

(*Sophie exits.*)

MAMA: I'm surprised to see you. I thought you were through with me.
CHRISTIAN: I was. I didn't come here to see you.
MAMA (*wounded*): Oh?
CHRISTIAN: And—
MAMA: Yes?

(*A moment.*)

. . . Hello, yes?
CHRISTIAN (*hesitantly, but genuinely*): I . . . I debated whether even to come, but damn it, I missed you.

(*Mama laughs.*)

You have nothing to say to me?
MAMA: Do you really want me to respond to your foolishness?
CHRISTIAN (*wounded*): You are a mean-spirited woman. I don't know why I expect the sun to shine where only mold thrives.

(*His frankness catches Mama off guard.*)

MAMA: I don't like your tone.
CHRISTIAN: We have unfinished "business"!
MAMA: Look around, there's no business here. There's nothing left.

(*Christian looks around. He looks at Mama. He shakes his head and smiles.*)

CHRISTIAN (*blurts*): Then, Mama, settle down with me.
MAMA: Go home!
CHRISTIAN: What?!
MAMA: You heard me, go the hell home. I don't wanna hear it. I have too much on my mind for this shit.
CHRISTIAN: That's all you have to say. I looked death in the eye on the river road. A boy nearly took out my liver with a bayonet. I'm serious. I drop and kiss the ground that he was a romantic, and spared me when I told him I was a man on a mission.

(*Mama cracks open a cold beer.*)

MAMA: It's cold, why can't you be happy with that?
CHRISTIAN: Because, it isn't what I want? Bring me a Fanta, please.

(*Mama smiles and gets him a Fanta.*)

MAMA: I'll put on some music.
CHRISTIAN: What's the point, you never dance with me.

(*Mama laughs.*)

MAMA: Oh shut up, relax. I'll roast some groundnuts. Huh?

(*A moment.*)

CHRISTIAN: Why not us?
MAMA: What would we do, professor? How would it work? The two of
    us? Imagine. You'd wander. I'd get impatient. I see how men do. We'd
    argue, fight and I'd grow resentful. You'd grow jealous. We know this
    story. It's tiresome.
CHRISTIAN: You know everything, don't you? And if I said, I'd stay, help
    you run things. Make a legitimate business. A shop. Fix the door. Hang
    the mirror. Protect you. Make love to you.
MAMA: Do I look like I need protection?
CHRISTIAN: No, but you look like you need someone to make love to you.
MAMA: Do I now?
CHRISTIAN: Yes. How long has it been, Mama, since you allowed a man to
    touch you? Huh? A man like me, who isn't looking through you for a
    way home.

(*Mama laughs at him.*)

MAMA: Enough. God. You're getting pathetic.
CHRISTIAN: Maybe. But damn it against my better judgment . . . I love
    you.
MAMA (*with contempt*): Love. What's the point in all this shit? Love is too
    fragile a sentiment for out here. Think about what happens to the
    things we "love." It isn't worth it. "Love." It is a poisonous word. It will
    change us. It will cost us more than it returns. Don't you think? It'll
    be an unnecessary burden for people like us. And it'll eventually
    strangle us!
CHRISTIAN: Do you hear what you're saying?
MAMA: It's the truth. Deal with it!
CHRISTIAN: Hm . . . Why do I bother. If you can't put it on a scale it is
    nothing, right?! Pardon me.

(*Christian, flustered by her response, walks to the door.*)

MAMA: Where are you going?!

(*Mama watches suddenly panicked.*)

Hey! You heard me. Don't be a baby.

(*Christian stops before exiting.*)

CHRISTIAN: We joke. It's fun. But honestly I'm worn bare. I've been driving this route a long time and I'm getting to the age where I'd like to sleep in the same bed every night. I need familiar company, food that is predictable, conversation that's too easy. If you don't know what I'm talking about, then I'll go. But, please, I'd like to have the truth . . . why not us?

(*A moment. Mama says nothing. Christian starts to leave, but her words catch him.*)

MAMA (*with surprising vulnerability*): I'm ruined. (*Louder.*) I'm ruined.

(*He absorbs her words.*)

CHRISTIAN: God, I don't know what those men did to you, but I'm sorry for it. I may be an idiot for saying so, but I think we, and I speak as a man, can do better.

(*He goes to comfort her. She pulls away until he's forced to hold her in a tight embrace.*)

MAMA: No! Don't touch me! No!

(*She struggles to free herself, but eventually succumbs to his heartfelt embrace. She breaks down in tears. He kisses her.*)

SOPHIE (*entering*): Oh, I'm sorry. (*Smiles to herself.*)
MAMA (*pulling away*): Why are you standing there looking like a lost elephant.
SOPHIE: Sorry, Mama.

(*Sophie slips out.*)

MAMA: Don't think this changes anything.
CHRISTIAN: Wait there.
MAMA: Where are you going?

(*Christian straightens his suit.*)

CHRISTIAN: I swear to you, this is the last time I'll ask.
    A branch lists to and fro,
    An answer to the insurgent wind,
    A circle dance,
    Grace nearly broken,
    But it ends peacefully,
    Stillness welcome.

(*Christian holds his hand out to Mama. A moment. Finally, she takes his hand. He pulls her into his arms. They begin to dance. At first she's a bit stiff and resistant, but slowly she gives in. Possibility. Guitar music: "A Rare Bird" guitar solo. Sophie drags Josephine into the room. They watch the pair dance.*)

JOSEPHINE (*joyfully*): Go, Mama.
PARROT: Mama! Primus! Mama! Primus!

(*Mama and Christian continue their measured dance. The lights slowly fade.*)

[2009]

AYAD AKHTAR   [b. 1970]

Disgraced

Setting: *A spacious apartment on New York's Upper East Side.*

Time: *2011–2012. The first two scenes take place in late summer of 2011. The third scene takes place three months later during fall. The fourth scene takes place six months later during spring.*

The play should be performed without intermission.

Scene 1

Lights come up.

High ceilings, parquet floors, crown molding. The works.

Upstage—a dining table. Behind it, a swinging door leads to a kitchen.

Upstage right—an open doorway leads to a hall that disappears from view.

Upstage left—a terrace and windows looking out over further buildings in the distance. Through which the season will show in each scene.

Downstage—a living room. A couch and chairs gathered together around a coffee table.

The stage left wall is covered with a large painting: A vibrant, two-paneled image in luscious whites and blues, with patterns reminiscent of an Islamic garden. The effect is lustrous and magnetic.

Below, a marble fireplace. And on the mantel, a statue of Siva. Along one or more of the walls, bookshelves.

To one side, a small table on which a half-dozen bottles of alcohol sit.

Downstage right—a vestibule and the front door.

(The furnishings are spare and tasteful. Perhaps with subtle flourishes of the Orient.)

On stage: Emily—early 30s, white, lithe and lovely—sits at the end of the dining table. A large pad before her and a book open to a large reproduction of Velázquez's Portrait of Juan de Pareja.

Emily assesses her model...

Amir—40, of South Asian origin, in an Italian suit jacket and a crisp, collared shirt, but only boxers underneath. He speaks with a perfect American accent.

Posing for his wife.

She sketches him. Until...

AMIR: You sure you don't want me to put pants on?
EMILY (*showing the Velázquez painting*): I only need you from the waist up.
AMIR: I still don't get it.
EMILY: You said it was fine.
AMIR: It is fine. It's just ...
EMILY: What?
AMIR: The more I think about it ...
EMILY: Mmm-hmm.
AMIR: I think it's a little weird. That you want to paint me after seeing a painting of a slave.
EMILY: He was Velázquez's assistant, honey.
AMIR: His slave.
EMILY: Until Velázquez freed him.
AMIR: Okay.
EMILY: I mean how many times have we stopped in front of that painting?
AMIR: It's a good painting. No idea what it has to do with what happened last night. I mean, the guy was a dick.
EMILY: He wasn't just a dick. He was a dick to you. And I could tell why.
AMIR: Honey, it's not the first time—
EMILY: A man, a waiter, looking at you.
AMIR: Looking at us.
EMILY: Not seeing you. Not seeing who you really are. Not until you started to deal with him. And the deftness with which you did that. You made him see that gap. Between what he was assuming about you and what you really are.
AMIR: The guy's a racist. So what?
EMILY: Sure. But I started to think about the Velázquez painting. And how people must have reacted when they first saw it. They think they're looking at a picture of a Moor. An assistant.
AMIR: A slave.
EMILY: Fine. A slave.
But whose portrait—it turns out—has more nuance and complexity than his renditions of kings and queens. And God knows how many of those he painted.

AMIR: You know what I think? I think you should just call your black
    Spanish boyfriend and get him up here to sit for you. He's still in New
    York, isn't he?
EMILY: Honey, I have no idea.
AMIR: You don't have to rub it in, babe.
    I know all men are not created equal—
EMILY (*gesturing for him to take the pose*): Could you do the thing?
AMIR (*adjusting his arm*): Way to make a guy feel wanted—
    If anything, I guess I should be grateful to José, right? Broke your dad
    in. I mean at least I spoke English.
EMILY: Dad's still traumatized. He brought up that Thanksgiving on the
    phone the other day.

(*Assessing her sketch.*)

    Anyway—I don't know what you're so worried about. It's not like any-
    body's gonna see this.
AMIR: Baby. Jerry Saltz loved your last show.
EMILY: He liked it. He didn't love it. It didn't sell.
AMIR: Selling's not everything.

Amir's cell phone RINGS.

EMILY: Selling's not everything? You really believe that?

Emily grabs the phone and tosses it to him.

AMIR: It's a client . . .
EMILY: Fine. Just . . . stay where you are?
AMIR (*into the phone*): What?

(*Listening.*)

    Paolo, I'm not your therapist. You don't pay me to listen to you. You
    pay me to listen to me.
        Yeah, but you're not listening.
        You're going. To kill. This deal.

(*Emily approaches, to adjust him.*)

    Honey . . .

(*Continuing into the phone.*)

    The point is, they buy it? They own it.
    They do what they want. That's how it works.

(*Checking . . . .*)

    Paolo. I'm getting another call. It's about the contract. I gotta go.

(*Switching over.*)

You enjoying your Cheerios?

Well, what the fuck else was keeping you from calling me back?

I don't care that it's Saturday morning. You're paid six figures to return my calls.

(*Breaking away and going to a contract on the table.*)

Paragraph four, subsection three. Last sentence.

Why are those three words still in there?

You missed that? No. What actually happened is I told you to fix it and you didn't.

Then behave like it.

(*Hanging up.*)

Fucking career paralegal.

EMILY: Wow.

AMIR: I don't catch his little fuck-up? It costs the client eight hundred fifty grand.

EMILY (*sketching*): It's actually kinda hot.

AMIR (*coming over to see the sketch over her shoulder*): You're so good.

(*Pointing at the picture of the Velázquez painting.*)

What's his name again?

EMILY: Juan de Pareja.

AMIR: It's a little fucked up. Give me that at least.

EMILY (*sexy*): I happen to know you like it a little fucked up.

They kiss.

AMIR: I should call Mort.

EMILY (*as Amir punches numbers*): You want more coffee?

Amir nods. Emily exits.

AMIR: (*into the phone*): Hey, Mort . . .

Good, good. So listen, I talked to Paolo again.

Seller's remorse.

It's a moot point. His board's gonna vote against him.

What do you want me to do?

Okay. I'll feed him the line on litigation. He doesn't have the stomach for that. By the time I'm through with him, he'll go into PTSD every time he sees my name on his caller ID.

Emily returns with coffee.

AMIR (CONT'D): She's right here . . .

(*To Emily.*)

Mort says hi.

EMILY: Tell him hi.

AMIR: She says hi . . .

We have plans for Labor Day, Mort.

Don't worry about it. Enjoy the weekend . . .

Sounds good. See you then.

EMILY: Hamptons?

AMIR: Honey, Jory and Isaac.

Bucks County.

It's taken forever to make that happen . . .

EMILY: I know, I know.

It's got me a little freaked out. Isaac's a big deal.

AMIR: And he is going to love your work.

EMILY: How is Mort?

AMIR: Obsessed with the idea that meditation is going to bring down his cholesterol.

EMILY: Haven't seen him in ages.

AMIR: I barely see him. He hardly comes in. A couple of hours a day at most when he does show up.

EMILY: Pays to be the boss.

AMIR: I mean, basically, I'm doing his job. I don't mind.

EMILY: He loves you.

AMIR: He depends on me.

EMILY: Okay.

He spent I don't know how much on that birthday present for you?

AMIR: Couple grand at least.

EMILY: Excuse me.

AMIR: Honey, I really am pretty much doing his job.

EMILY: So he gets you a book. Or a bottle of scotch. Or takes you to dinner. Why'd he get you a statue of Siva?°

(*Beat.*)

He doesn't think you're Hindu, does he?

AMIR: He may have mentioned something once . . .

You realize I'm going to end up with my name on that firm?

EMILY: Leibowitz, Bernstein, Harris, and Kapoor.

AMIR: My mother will roll over in her grave . . .

EMILY: Your mother would be proud.

AMIR: It's not the family name, so she might not care, seeing it alongside all those Jewish ones . . .

From the kitchen: the intercom BUZZES.

Amir looks over, surprised. Emily puts down her pencil. Heads for the kitchen.

Siva: Shiva, the Hindu god of destruction.

EMILY: That'll be Abe.

AMIR (*surprised*): Abe?

EMILY (*disappearing into the kitchen*): Your nephew?

AMIR: Oh, right. Wait . . .

EMILY (*at the intercom, off stage*): Yes?
    Send him up.

As Emily now returns . . .

AMIR: You're not gonna let this thing go, are you?

EMILY: I don't like what's happening. Somebody's gotta do something about it.

AMIR: I went to see that guy in prison. What more do you two want?

There's a KNOCKING on the door.

Amir puts on his pants on his way to the door.

He opens it. To find . . .

ABE—22, of South Asian origin. But as American as American gets. Vibrant and endearing. He's wearing a Kidrobot T-shirt under a hoodie, skinny jeans, and high-tops.

As Amir is buckling his belt.

ABE (*looking over at Emily, back to Amir*): Should I come back?

AMIR: No, no.

ABE: You sure?

AMIR: Yeah. I'm sure. Come in, Hussein.

ABE: Uncle.

AMIR: What?

ABE: Could you just call me—

AMIR (*finishing his thought*): I've known you your whole life as Hussein. I'm not gonna start calling you Abe now.

Abe shakes his head. Turning to Emily.

EMILY: Hi, Abe.

ABE: Hi, Aunt Emily.

Abe turns to Amir, lighthearted.

ABE (CONT'D) (*pointing*): See? How hard can it be?

AMIR: Abe Jensen?
    Really?

ABE: You know how much easier things are for me since I changed my name? It's in the Quran. It says you can hide your religion if you have to.

AMIR: I'm not talking about the Quran. I'm talking about you being called Abe Jensen.

Just lay off it with me and your folks at least.

ABE: It's gotta be one thing or the other. I can't be all mixed up.

EMILY (*off Amir's reaction*): Amir. You changed your name, too.

ABE: You got lucky.

    You didn't have to change your first name.

    Could be Christian. Jewish.

    Plus, you were born here. It's different.

EMILY: You want something, sweetie? Coffee, juice?

ABE: Nah. I'm good.

AMIR: So what's up?

EMILY: I'll let you gentlemen talk.

AMIR: No need. Everybody knows you're in on this.

(*To Abe.*)

So you've been calling her, too?

ABE: You weren't calling me back.

AMIR: Why are we still talking about this?

    I'm a corporate lawyer. In mergers and acquisitions—

EMILY: Who started in the public defender's—

AMIR: That was years ago.

(*Beat.*)

Your man should have been more careful . . .

ABE: Imam Fareed didn't do anything.

    Every church in the country collects money. It's how they keep their doors open. We're entitled, too.

    He's running a mosque—

EMILY: He's got the right.

    Just because they're collecting money doesn't mean it's for Hamas.

AMIR: What does any of this have to do with me?

EMILY: It doesn't matter to you that an innocent man is in prison?

AMIR: I don't know Patriot Act law. The guy's already got a legal team.

    Those guys Ken and Alex are amazing.

ABE: They're not Muslim.

AMIR: There we go.

ABE: What?

AMIR: What I thought.

    I'm not gonna be part of a legal team just because your imam is a bigot.

ABE: He's not a bigot. He'd just be more comfortable if there was a Muslim on the case, too . . .

AMIR: More comfortable if he wasn't being represented by a couple of Jews?

ABE: No.

AMIR: Really?

ABE (*beat*): He liked you. He said you were a good man.

AMIR: Well, he might not feel the same if he knew how I really felt about his religion.

ABE (*offhand*): That's just a phase.

AMIR (*taken aback*): Excuse me?

ABE: That's what Mom says Grandma used to say about you.
      That you were working something out. That you were such a good Muslim when you were a kid. And that you had to go the *other way* for a while.

AMIR (*dumbfounded*): The *other way*?

(*Considering.*)

    Sit down, Hussein. I want to tell you something.

ABE: So just tell me.

AMIR: No. I want you to sit down.

Abe sits.

AMIR (CONT'D): When was the first time you had a crush?

ABE: I thought you wanted to tell me something.

AMIR: I'm getting to it.
      Your first crush . . .

ABE (*glancing at Emily*): Umm . . .
      Fifth grade. A girl named Nasleema . . .

AMIR: I was in sixth.
      Her name was Rivkah.

EMILY: I thought your first crush was Susan.

AMIR: That was the first girl I ever kissed. Rivkah was the first girl I ever got up in the morning thinking about. One time she went away to Disney World for a week, and I was *a mess*. Didn't even want to go to school if I couldn't see her.

(*Remembering.*)

    She was a looker. Dark hair, dark eyes. Dimples. Perfect white skin.

EMILY: Why didn't you ever tell me about her?

AMIR: I didn't want you to hate my mother . . .

(*Off Emily's perplexed look.*)

    Just wait . . .

(*Back to Abe.*)

    So Rivkah and I'd gotten to the point where we were trading notes. And one day, my mother found one of the notes.

Of course it was signed, Rivkah.
Rivkah? my mom says. *That's a Jewish name.*

(*Beat.*)

I wasn't clear on what exactly a Jew was at the time, other than they'd
stolen land from the Palestinians, and something about how God
hated them more than other people . . .
I couldn't imagine God could have hated this little girl.
So I tell my mom, *No, she's not Jewish.*
But she knew the name was Jewish.
If I ever hear that name in this house again, Amir, she said, *I'll break
your bones. You will end up with a Jew over my dead body.*
Then she spat in my face.

EMILY: My God.

AMIR: *That's so you don't ever forget,* she says.
Next day?
Rivkah comes up to me in the hall with a note. *Hi, Amir,* she says. Eyes
sparkling.
I look at her and say, *You've got the name of a Jew.*
She smiles. *Yes, I'm Jewish,* she says.

(*Beat.*)

Then *I* spit in *her* face.

EMILY: That's horrible.

ABE: Man. That's effed up.

AMIR: So, when my older sister goes on to you about *this way* and the
other way, now you'll have a better idea of the *phase* I'm really going
through . . .
It's called *intelligence.*

Pause.

EMILY: I'm surprised.

AMIR: By what?

EMILY: I don't know. Your mother was very open with me . . .

AMIR: Let's just say I made it abundantly clear not to mess with you.

EMILY: I thought she liked me.

ABE: Seemed like it to me.

EMILY: She kissed me on her deathbed.

AMIR: You won her over. You were openhearted, gracious.

EMILY: You make it sound like there was some whole battle going on.

AMIR: Well . . .

EMILY: About what?

AMIR: White women have no self-respect.

How can someone respect themselves when they think they have to take off their clothes to make people like them?
They're whores.

EMILY: What are you saying?

AMIR: What Muslims around the world say about white women—

ABE (*coming in*): Not everyone says that.

AMIR: Have you heard it or not?

ABE: Yeah.

AMIR: And more than once?

ABE: Yes.

AMIR: And from your mother?

Abe nods.

AMIR (CONT'D): I rest my case.

Pause.

ABE: Imam Fareed is not like that. If you got to know him better, you'd realize. He's actually your kind of guy. Once a month, we're doing a Friday prayer that's mixed.

EMILY: And—he let me sit in his mosque and sketch every day for weeks.

AMIR: He was probably hoping you'd convert. Who knows, you probably will.

EMILY: Don't be dismissive.

AMIR: I don't understand what you see in it.

EMILY: In what?

AMIR: In Islam?

EMILY: When we were in the mosque in Cordoba . . . Remember that? The pillars and arches?

AMIR: Those were great.

EMILY: Remember what you said?

AMIR: I'm sure you're going to remind me.

EMILY: That it actually made you feel like praying.

AMIR: That's kind of the point of a mosque, honey.

EMILY: And that Matisse show° you loved so much? He got all that from Mogul miniatures. Carpets. Moroccan tiles.

AMIR: Fine. I got it.

EMILY: There's so much beauty and wisdom in the Islamic tradition. Look at Ibn Arabi, Mulla Sadra°—

AMIR (*coming in abruptly*): But the thing is? It's not just beauty and wisdom.

Matisse show: Henri Matisse (1869–1954), a French artist who was at the forefront of modern art.

Ibn Arabi, Mulla Sadra: Ibn Arabi (1165–1240), a Sufi Muslim poet and scholar who lived in Southern Spain; Mulla Sadra (1571–1640), a Muslim philosopher whose theories contributed to a golden age of Islam.

Pause.

ABE: Uncle. Don't think of him as a Muslim if you don't want to. Just think of him as a wise man. Who so many people depend on.

AMIR: I hear you, Huss. I really do.

ABE: So come to the hearing next Thursday.

AMIR: Next Thursday's a busy day at work.

ABE: An old man who didn't do anything wrong is in prison.

AMIR (*rough*): And there's nothing I can do about it.

EMILY: Honey . . .

Silence.

ABE: I should probably head out.

AMIR: I didn't mean to snap at you . . .

ABE: Just think about it?

AMIR: Okay. Fine.

Abe hugs his uncle . . .

EMILY: You okay, sweetie?

ABE: Yeah. Fine.

   I really should go.

(*With a kiss.*)

   Bye.

EMILY: Bye.

He leaves.

Once he's gone . . .

AMIR: It will never cease to amaze me. My parents move to this country with my sister, never make her a citizen. When she's old enough? They send her back, marry her off in Pakistan. She has kids with the guy, and lo and behold—he wants to come here. And what do they do? Spend all their spare time at an Islamic center.

EMILY: His heart's in the right place, Amir.

AMIR: Okay. I know.

EMILY: Is yours?

AMIR: What is that supposed to mean?

EMILY (*coming right in*): I mean, why would you have worked in the public defender's if you didn't care about justice?

AMIR: Public defenders have the hottest girlfriends.

EMILY: I'd like to think there was some part of you that *believed* in what you were doing. I mean, I don't know . . .

AMIR: No . . . Of course.

EMILY: But when it comes to the imam, it's like you don't care. Like you don't think he's human.

AMIR: You and Hussein wanted me to see him? So I went.

I went to talk to him in prison. And the man spent an hour trying to get me to pray again. He's been in prison four months and all he can do—

EMILY (*cutting him off*): You told me. So what? So a man who has nothing left but his dignity and his faith is still trying to be useful in the only way he knows how?

I mean, if he feels he needs one of his own people around him—

AMIR: I'm not one of his own people.

EMILY: You are. And in a way that's unique. And that can be helpful to him. Why can't you see that?

AMIR: Can we stop talking about this?

EMILY: We never talk about this. Not really.

Silence.

Amir stares at his wife for a long moment. Something stirring.

EMILY (CONT'D): Amir. I love you.

Lights Out.

Scene 2

Two weeks later.

Emily sits at the dining table. With a cup of morning coffee, the day's paper open before her.

Amir stands opposite her.

EMILY (*reading*): "The defendant, surrounded by a gauntlet of attorneys, struck a defiant tone. He spoke eloquently of the injustices he'd experienced, and what he called an 'unconscionable lack of due process.' Amir Kapoor of Leibowitz, Bernstein, Harris supported the imam, stating, 'As far as anybody knows, there isn't a case. And if the Justice Department has one, it's time they started making it.'"

(*Beat.*)

I don't think you look like counsel for the defense.

AMIR: That's because you know I'm not.

EMILY: It's because it doesn't say you are.

AMIR (*taking the paper*): "The defendant, surrounded by a gauntlet of attorneys, struck a defiant tone." And then she quotes an attorney. Me. Implying that I'm one of the gauntlet of attorneys. She doesn't quote another attorney.

EMILY: But she says you're just supporting him.

AMIR: I don't see a *just*. There's no *just supporting him*.

EMILY: It's implied.

AMIR: I think it reads very clearly that I was supporting his defiant tone. That I was supporting him being defiant.

EMILY: Isn't he justified?

AMIR: That's not my point, Em.

EMILY: Maybe it should be.

AMIR: The man's basically an alleged terrorist.

(*Off another look at the paper.*)

Amir Kapoor supported the imam . . .

EMILY: Even if it does make you look—

AMIR (*leaping in*): So it does?

EMILY: I don't think it does. But even *if* it does, why is that a bad thing? What you did is right. You're standing up for due process.

AMIR: It's just . . .

EMILY: What?

AMIR: Don't you think people are going to think . . .

(*Beat.*)

I guess they'll look at the name; if they know anything at all—

EMILY (*over*): Amir.

AMIR: —they'll know the name isn't Muslim.

(*Beat.*)

EMILY: Amir. What's going on?

(*Beat.*)

If this bothers you so much, call the *Times*. Have them retract.

AMIR: But the thing is, I did say this.

EMILY (*proudly*): I remember.

AMIR: But after clearly saying I was *not* counsel for the defendant.

(*Beat*)

Why did they have to mention the firm?

Pause.

EMILY: Baby.
    You did the right thing. I am so proud of you. So was Abe. And you'll see. Mort's gonna be proud of you, too.

AMIR: Mort's not the one I'm worried about.

EMILY: This is going to be good for you at work.

AMIR: Good for me?

EMILY: Look at Goldman.
AMIR: Goldman?
EMILY: Sachs.
    Jamie? He took all that philanthropy so seriously . . .
AMIR: What does your douche-bag banker ex-boyfriend have to do with this?
EMILY: Isn't that how it works?
    Isn't that how all you guys cover up the fact that all anybody cares about in your world is making money?
AMIR: I have to get going.

(*Still caught up by the paper.*)

    " . . . supported the imam . . ."
EMILY: Honey, honey. Look at me. Stop it.

The intercom BUZZES.

Sudden silence.

EMILY (CONT'D): That's Isaac.
AMIR (*off Emily's shift*): Yeah?
EMILY: Well, I mean he's here.
AMIR: Okay.
EMILY: What?
AMIR (*disgusted*): Nothing.
EMILY: Do you want to keep talking about this?
AMIR: I need to go.
EMILY: Are you annoyed with me?

(*Beat.*)

    Honey, this is a big deal. I have a studio visit with a curator from the Whitney.
AMIR: And who do you think made it happen?
EMILY: Really? Now? Can we talk about this tonight?
AMIR (*curt*): There's nothing to talk about.

Amir exits to the bedroom.

Emily goes to the intercom.

EMILY: Hi. Yes. Send him up.

(*To Amir, off stage.*)

    I mean, I'm sure no one'll see it. It's buried in the back . . .
AMIR (*returning*): Don't.
EMILY: Don't what?
AMIR: I know your mind is elsewhere.
EMILY: I just . . . I think you're overthinking this.

AMIR: Let me get this straight: Some waiter is a dick to me in a restaurant and you want to make a painting. But if it's something that actually might affect my livelihood, you don't even want to believe there could be a problem.

EMILY: What does one thing have to do with the other?

KNOCKING at the door.

Beat. Tense standoff.

Amir checks his pockets.

AMIR: I left my phone in the bedroom.

He exits again.

Emily gathers herself as she heads to the door . . .

And opens it to show . . .

ISAAC—40, white, smart, attractive. A curator at the Whitney.

ISAAC: Hi.

EMILY: Hi. How are you?

ISAAC: Great.

EMILY: Find it okay?

ISAAC: Quick ride up Madison. Couldn't be easier.

We hear SOUNDS offstage of Amir slamming around in the bedroom. Looking for his phone.

EMILY: Amir's on his way out . . .

Amir reenters.

The tension between him and Emily still palpable.

AMIR: Isaac.

ISAAC: Hello, sir.

AMIR: Good to see you.

(*Beat.*)

Thanks again for a wonderful weekend in the country.

ISAAC: Was our pleasure.

AMIR: I—uh—gotta run. I'm late for work.

ISAAC: You'll probably still get there before my wife.

AMIR: Always do.

(*To Emily, coldly.*)

See you later.

EMILY: Bye, honey.

(*To Amir, intimately.*)

It's gonna be fine. You'll see.

Amir exits.

Beat.

ISAAC: Is this a bad time?
EMILY: No. No.
ISAAC: You sure?
EMILY: Yeah.
ISAAC: I mean—okay.
EMILY: Can I get you some coffee, tea?
ISAAC: Sure. Coffee'd be great.
EMILY: Milk? Sugar?
ISAAC: Black is fine.

Emily heads for the kitchen.

Leaving Isaac onstage. He takes a look around. Perhaps just a hint intrusively.

He picks up a book off the shelf.

Emily returns with a mug.

ISAAC (CONT'D): Constable's great, isn't he?
EMILY: Love him.
ISAAC: It's one of the things I love about going to Frieze° every year. My little pilgrimage to see the Constables at the Tate.°

(*Putting the book back.*)

You ever been?
EMILY: Tate, yes.
Frieze, no. Though my dealer suggested I go this year.

Isaac takes the mug.

ISAAC: Thanks.
So I've spent a lot of time thinking about our discussions since last weekend.
EMILY: About me being a white woman with no right to be using Islamic forms?

Frieze: Frieze London, an annual art fair for collectors, curators, and gallerists.

Constables at the Tate: John Constable (1776–1837) was an English landscape painter. Several of his paintings are in the collection at the Tate Gallery in London.

I think you're wrong about that.

ISAAC: I think I might be wrong, too.

Beat.

EMILY: What happened?

ISAAC: Well, I found a few images of your work online . . .

EMILY: You read Jerry's review.

ISAAC: Yes, I did.

I don't always agree with Jerry. But he did have some compelling things to say . . .

(*Turning to the painting above the mantel.*)

This is the one you wanted me to see?

EMILY: This is the one in the apartment.

There are more at the studio.

Isaac inspects the paintings for a long beat.

ISAAC: Mm-hmm . . .

I have to admit . . .

It has presence . . .

(*Stepping back, assessing.*)

The surface tending toward the convex . . .

It's a bending of the picture plane, isn't it?

EMILY: Exactly.

ISAAC: Which is why Jerry was talking about late Bonnard.°

EMILY: The mosaics in Andalusia are bending the picture plane four hundred years before Bonnard. That's what I mean. That's what I was saying. The Muslims gave us Aristotle. Without them, we probably wouldn't even have visual perspective.

ISAAC: That's quite a statement.

EMILY: And I can back it up.

(*Beat, then off Isaac's reaction.*)

What?

ISAAC: I don't know . . .

It's the earnestness. The lack of irony. It's unusual . . .

EMILY: Irony's overrated.

ISAAC: Can't say I disagree with that.

EMILY: But?

ISAAC: You know what you're going to be accused of . . .

Bonnard: Pierre Bonnard (1867–1947), a late Impressionist painter from France.

(*Off Emily's silence.*)

Orientalism . . .
    I mean, hell. You've even got the brown husband.
EMILY: Fuck you, I think.

Beat.

ISAAC: Good.
    Because that's what they're going to say.

Beat.

EMILY: Yeah. Well, we've all gotten way too wrapped up in the optics. The way we talk about things. We've forgotten to look at things for what they really are.

(*Beat.*)

When you're at Frieze this fall, after the Constables, you need to go to the Victoria and Albert. The Islamic galleries. Room forty-two. Remember that. It will change the way you see art.
ISAAC (*warmly*): Them's fightin' words.

Beat.

EMILY: The Islamic tiling tradition, Isaac? Is a doorway to the most extraordinary freedom. And which only comes through a kind of profound submission. In my case, of course it's not submission to Islam but to the formal language. The pattern. The repetition. And the quiet that this work requires of me? It's extraordinary.
ISAAC: You sound like a midcentury American minimalist, trying to obliterate the ego.
EMILY: The Islamic tradition's been doing it for a thousand years. Pardon me for thinking they may have a better handle on it.

(*Beat.*)

It's time we woke up. Time we stop paying lip service to Islam and Islamic art. We draw on the Greeks, the Romans . . . but Islam is part of who we are, too. God forbid anybody remind us of it.
ISAAC: Huh.
EMILY: What?
ISAAC: No, this is good.
EMILY: Yeah.

Lights Out.

Scene 3

Three months later.

Lights come up. On the terrace, Amir. A drink in hand.

He drinks. Drinks again. Stares down into the bottom of his glass. Burning.

Beat.

Then all at once, he SMASHES the glass on the terrace floor. Shards fly.

Beat.

The burst of violence doesn't seem to have soothed him. He comes into the apartment. Going to the bar for a glass, and another drink.

Finally, we hear—KEYS . . .

The door opens and Emily enters with grocery bags.

EMILY: Hey, honey.
AMIR: Hey.
    Where were you?
EMILY: At Gourmet Garage. Getting a few things. For tonight.
AMIR: Tonight?
EMILY: Isaac and Jory. You didn't forget, did you?
AMIR: That's why it smells so good in here.
EMILY: I made pork tenderloin. And guess what . . .

(Pulling something from the bag.)

    . . . they had La Tur! And that liver mousse you love so much.
AMIR: Great.
EMILY: Can't be bad news, right? "I'm coming to your house to eat your food and tell you you're not in the show." Nobody does that, right?
AMIR: So you're in.
EMILY: God, I hope.

Emily approaching him. Sexual.

AMIR: Honey.
EMILY: What?
AMIR: We've talked about this.

(Beat.)

    It doesn't help.
EMILY: I miss you, Amir.
AMIR: I know.

Beat.

EMILY: So I'm assuming you forgot the wine.
AMIR: I did. I'm sorry.
EMILY: Amir.
AMIR: I said I'm sorry.

Beat.

EMILY: What's wrong?
AMIR: Nothing.
EMILY: Something's wrong.

Pause.

AMIR: I had a meeting with a couple of the partners today. I mean, if you
    could call it that. I'm in my office, red-lining a contract due at six. Steven
    comes in. With Jack. Sits down. Asks me where my parents were born.
EMILY: Pakistan.
AMIR: I said India.
    That's what I put on the form when I got hired.
EMILY: Why?
AMIR: It technically *was* India when my dad was born.
EMILY: Okay.
AMIR: *But the names of the cities you've listed are not in India,* Steven
    says. *They're in Pakistan.*
    My father was born in 1946. When it was all one country, before the
    British chopped it up into two countries in 1947.
    And your mother was born when?
    1948.
    So it wasn't India anymore, was it? It was Pakistan?
    My clock is running, and I'm wasting time on a fucking history lesson.
    Turns out, Steven's trying to ascertain if I misrepresented myself.
EMILY: It sounds like you did.
AMIR: It was all India. So there's a different name on it now. So what?

(*Beat.*)

He knew about my name change. *Your birth name is not Kapoor,* Steven
    says. *It's Abdullah. Why did you change it?*
EMILY: Didn't he already know?
AMIR: I never told them.
EMILY: They must have run a background check.
AMIR: I—uh—had my Social Security number changed. When I changed
    my name.
EMILY: You did?

AMIR: Yeah. It was before I met you.

EMILY: Is that legal?

AMIR: They do it all the time. When people go through identity theft. Steven must have been digging around. He has it in for me. I knew I never should have gone to that hearing.

EMILY: That was months ago. What does that have to do with anything?

AMIR: A lot, honey. A lot.

Beat.

EMILY: Have you talked to Mort about it?

AMIR: I can't get ahold of him.

The intercom BUZZES.

EMILY: Wait a second. What time is it?

AMIR (*checking his watch*): Ten past.

EMILY: What're they doing here? I still have to get ready.

AMIR: Go get ready. I'll get it.

Amir heads for the kitchen.

AMIR (CONT'D) (*at the intercom, off stage*): Yes? Send them up.

EMILY (*as Amir reemerges*): You gonna be okay?

AMIR: I'll be fine.

EMILY: You sure?

AMIR: Yes. Go.

EMILY: Can you get the appetizers? They're on the counter in the kitchen.

AMIR: I got it.

Emily exits.

Amir goes to the door. Turning the bolt to prop the door. Then takes the bags into the kitchen.

We hear NOISES outside the door. Then the door creeps open.

WOMAN'S VOICE: Amir?

Just as Amir emerges—

AMIR: Come on in, Jor.

Enter:

Jory—mid- to late 30s, African American—is commanding, forthright, intelligent. Almost masculine.

We've seen Isaac before.

Both shed their coats as Amir gets to them.

ISAAC (*shaking hands*): Good to see you again.
AMIR: Good to see you, too.
JORY: Hey, Amir.
AMIR: Hi, Jory.
   Did we say seven thirty?
ISAAC: I was sure she said seven.
JORY (*to Isaac*): I told you.
AMIR: She's still getting ready.
JORY: No worries.
AMIR: More time to drink, right?
JORY (*showing a box*): We brought dessert.
AMIR: Magnolia Bakery? Thank you.
JORY (*heading off*): This should go in the fridge.
ISAAC (*to Amir*): I was at the Knicks game last night.
AMIR: You were?
ISAAC: Aren't you a Knicks fan?
AMIR: I'm sorry to say.
ISAAC: No dishonor in it.
AMIR: No dishonor. But lots of pain.
ISAAC: I'm a Cubs fan. Don't get me started on pain.

Jory returns to hear:

AMIR: Oh, the Bartman.
ISAAC: I mean, I didn't think he should be killed.
   But I had friends . . .
AMIR: Killed?
JORY: Who's Bartman?
ISAAC: Honey.
AMIR: The fan who stole the ball out of a Cubs outfielder's hand . . .
ISAAC: Moisés Alou. Eighth inning.
AMIR: And denied the Cubs a trip to the World Series.
ISAAC (*to Jory*): You don't remember this?
JORY: It's ringing a bell.

(*Beat.*)

   Smells great in here.
AMIR: Em's making pork tenderloin.

(*To Isaac.*)

   You eat pork, don't you?

JORY: Every chance he gets . . .
ISAAC: Gotta make up for all the lost years . . .
    Could I use your restroom?
AMIR: Down the hall on the right.
ISAAC: I remember.

Isaac crosses to the hall. Exits.

AMIR: What are you drinking?
JORY: You have scotch?
AMIR: Still have that bottle of Macallan that you gave me.
JORY: I expect more from you, Amir.
AMIR: We'll finish it tonight.
    On the rocks?
JORY: Neat.
AMIR: You're not kidding around.

Amir begins to prepare the drink . . .

JORY: You hear about Sarah?
AMIR: What about her?
JORY: She got her terrier back.
AMIR: How?
JORY: She hired a dog investigator who kidnapped it back from Frank.
AMIR: Lord.
JORY: Frank's gonna sue her.
AMIR: On what grounds?
JORY: Just to make her life miserable.
AMIR: The two of them.
JORY: Tell me about it.

(Taking a drink from Amir.)

    She and I ran into Frank at the courthouse.
AMIR: Oh, you were in court today?
JORY: Proctor insurance arbitration.
AMIR: How'd it go?
JORY: Fine. We're just dancing around the number now. They have to
    pay and they know it. They just need a little time to get used to the
    idea.
AMIR: Mort there?
JORY: Steven took it over. He has me on it now.
AMIR: But Proctor's Mort's.
JORY: Was.
AMIR: Why is that not a surprise?
JORY: Mort couldn't be bothered. Rather be meditating.

AMIR: Yeah, instead of taking his Lipitor.

JORY: You know he took me to lunch and tried to teach me to meditate? I actually tried it a couple of times. Ended up gaining five pounds. I just kept thinking about food. I'd get frustrated, give up, and pig out.

AMIR: What's up with the offer from Credit Suisse?

JORY: I'm not gonna do it.

AMIR: Didn't they come back with two hundred more?

JORY: They did.

AMIR: I told you that move would work.

JORY: You were right.

AMIR: But I don't think you can get more . . .

Beat.

JORY: The partners are countering.

AMIR: I doubt it's two hundred more.

JORY: I've put down roots.

Beat.

AMIR: Kapoor, Brathwaite.

JORY: What?

AMIR: You and me. On our own. In business.
Steven and Mort got ahead underpricing the competition. Back in the day, when they got started.

JORY: Well, downtown WASPs didn't want to be doing mergers and acquisitions.

AMIR: Yeah, fine. That's why Jews were doing it. And then mergers and acquisitions became all the rage. And guys like Steven and Mort became the establishment.
We are the new Jews.

JORY: Okay . . .

AMIR: We go about it the right way? We'll get to where LBH is now in a quarter of the time it took them.

JORY: You coming up with this on the fly?

AMIR: This afternoon.
That firm will never be ours. It's theirs. And they're always going to remind us that we were just invited to the party.

JORY: I don't think it's a bad idea.

(Beat)

Amir—

Just as . . .

. . . Isaac returns from the bathroom, holding a book.

ISAAC: Who's reading this?
    . . . Sorry, am I interrupting?
JORY: Well . . .
AMIR: Just talking shop.

Just as Emily enters, looking lovely.

EMILY: I'm so sorry.

(*To Jory.*)

    Nice to see you.
JORY: Nice to see you, too.
ISAAC: Hey, Em.
EMILY: Hi, Isaac.
ISAAC: I'm sorry, I thought I heard seven.
EMILY: Look. As long as you don't mind waiting for dinner . . .
AMIR: Honey, they got cupcakes from Magnolia.
JORY: Banana pudding, actually.
EMILY: Oh, my God. I love that stuff.
JORY: It's like crack.
AMIR: You want something to drink, Isaac?
ISAAC: Scotch'd be great. On the rocks . . .
AMIR: Honey?
EMILY: Port.
JORY: Port? Before dinner?
EMILY: I know I'm strange. I just love it so much . . .

Amir gets started on the drinks.

ISAAC (*to Emily*): So who's reading *Denial of Death?*
EMILY: I am. Since you suggested it.
AMIR (*to Isaac*): She's been raving about it.
ISAAC: The only reason people remember this anymore is because it's the
    book Woody Allen gives to Diane Keaton on their first date in *Annie
    Hall*. And tells her: "This is everything you need to know about me."
AMIR: Denial of death.
JORY (*to Isaac*): You should've given me a heads-up, too.
ISAAC: You think?
    It's an amazing book. I actually got the title for my new show from
    here . . .
AMIR: What's the title?

Amir hands out drinks.

ISAAC: The title . . . Well, first let me say—
    It's been generations and generations of consumerism and cynicism.

JORY (*over*): Get comfortable.

ISAAC (*continuing*): . . . And an art market that just feeds the frenzy. But something's shifting. There's a movement of young artists who are not buying into it anymore.

    They're asking the question—how to make art sacred again. It's an impossibly heroic task they've set for themselves. Which is why I'm calling it . . .

(*Gesturing to Jory to hold her criticism.*)

    Impossible Heroes.

(*Off Jory's reaction.*)

    She doesn't like it.

JORY: It sounds like a segment on Anderson Cooper's *360*.

AMIR: About Paralympic athletes.

JORY: The impossible heroes.

ISAAC: Very funny.

    How about you, Em? What do you think of the title? After all, it's your show now, too . . .

Beat.

EMILY: You're kidding?

ISAAC: The work you're doing with the Islamic tradition is important and new. It needs to be seen. Widely.

EMILY: Isaac, that's amazing. Thank you. Thank you so much.

Ensuing congratulations overlap . . .

JORY: Congratulations, Emily.

EMILY: Thank you.

AMIR: That's incredible. I'm so proud of you, honey.

ISAAC (*lifting his glass*): A toast is in order. To—

AMIR (*over*): To your show. And to Emily in your show.

ALL: Cheers . . .

All drink.

AMIR: So . . . how many?

ISAAC: What?

AMIR: Of her paintings?

EMILY: That's my husband. Always talking numbers.

ISAAC: I've got room for four or five.

AMIR: Five. That sounds great.

Laughter.

ISAAC *(Pointing to the canvas above the fireplace)*: I definitely want *that* one.
The couple I saw in the studio. And I've been thinking about the *Study After Velázquez's Moor*. But I'm not sure . . .

JORY: Moor?
Haven't heard that word in a minute.

EMILY: I did a portrait of Amir a few months ago . . .
After an episode we had at a . . .

Noticing Amir's reaction to her bringing up the story, Emily shifts gears . . .

EMILY (CONT'D): I'd just been to the Met and seen the Velázquez painting.

Emily goes to the bookshelf in the corner.

JORY: Which one?

EMILY: *Portrait of Juan de Pareja*—who happened to be of Moorish descent.

(Returning with the book.)

This is the original portrait.

JORY *(recognizing)*: Oh. Of course.

EMILY: It's a study after the Velázquez. I'm using the same palette, same composition. But it's a portrait of Amir.

AMIR: Your very own personal Moor.

EMILY: *Muse* is more like it . . .

ISAAC: I think I'd rather stick with the abstract pieces. Keep the impression of your work consolidated. But I'm tempted. I mean, it's a stunning portrait. Quite a tribute to you, Amir, if you ask me . . .

AMIR: You think?

ISAAC: Standing there in your black suit. Silver cuff links. Perfectly pressed lily-white dress shirt . . .

(To Emily.)

. . . which is so magnificently rendered. You can almost smell the starch on that shirt.

AMIR: Not starch, Isaac. Just ridiculous thread count.

JORY: People do not stop talking about your shirts at the office.

AMIR: Really?

JORY: Sarah was joking you must spend half what you make on shirts.

EMILY: Wouldn't be far from the truth. Charvet, always.

JORY: How much do those run?

Amir seems reluctant to reply.

EMILY: Six hundred.

JORY: Dollars?

ISAAC: So there you are, in your six-hundred-dollar Charvet shirt, like Velázquez's brilliant apprentice-slave in his lace collar, adorned in the splendors of the world you're now so clearly a part of . . .

And yet . . .

AMIR: Yeah?

ISAAC: The question remains.

AMIR: The question?

ISAAC: Of your place.

For the viewer, of course. Not you.

It's a painting, after all . . .

Pause.

AMIR: I like the stuff she was doing before.

ISAAC: The landscapes? Not a huge fan.

JORY: Isaac.

ISAAC: What? She knows that. I think it's smart she moved on. It's not as fertile a direction for her.

AMIR: I think the landscapes are very *fertile*.

EMILY: Amir . . .

AMIR: What?

EMILY: We both know why you like the landscapes.

JORY: Why?

EMILY: Because they have nothing to do with Islam.

ISAAC (*before Amir can speak*): What she's doing with the Islamic tradition has taken her to another level.

A young Western painter drawing on Islamic representation? Not *ironically?* But in *service?*

It's an unusual and remarkable statement.

AMIR: What's the statement?

ISAAC: Islam is rich and universal. Part of a spiritual and artistic heritage we can all draw from.

(*To Emily.*)

I loved that thing you said in London. At the Frieze Art Fair. About humility and the Renaissance . . .

EMILY: Right. The Renaissance is when we turned away from something bigger than ourselves. It put the individual at the center of the universe and made a cult out of the personal ego.

ISAAC: Right.

EMILY: That never happened in the Islamic tradition. It's still more connected to a wider, less personal perspective.

ISAAC: I'm using that in the catalogue.

EMILY: Stop it.

ISAAC: I'm serious. You've got a major career ahead of you.
　　　I'm just one of the first to get to the party.
　　　Emily Hughes-Kapoor. A name to be contended with.
AMIR: Hear, hear.

Toasting . . .

JORY: Kapoor.
　　　Where in India is that name from?

Pause.

AMIR: Why are you asking?
JORY: Did I say something wrong?
AMIR: No, no . . .
　　　Steven came into my office today and asked me the same thing.
JORY: He did?

Awkward pause.

EMILY: You know—it's a pretty common Punjabi name.
ISAAC: I'm headed to Delhi day after tomorrow. That's in Punjab, isn't
　　　it?
AMIR: Not really, but . . . Same country . . . So . . . Why not?

Laughs.

EMILY: What are you doing in Delhi, Isaac?
ISAAC: Sothi Sikander has designed to offer me a studio visit.
EMILY: How exciting. I love his work.

(To Jory.)

　　　You going, too?
JORY: Ezra has school.
ISAAC: Jory's being polite. It's not because Ezra has school. I have a . . .
　　　little bit of an issue when it comes to flying.
JORY: That's one way of putting it.
ISAAC: I hate flying.
　　　It's a primal thing.
　　　The thought of not being on the ground . . . opens up this door to
　　　like every fear I have—and the hysteria around security only makes it
　　　worse.
AMIR: It's a nightmare at the airports.
JORY: And now there's a whole new attraction. You get to decide between
　　　being ogled over or felt up.
ISAAC: Felt up. Definitely.
JORY: Why is that not a surprise?

ISAAC: It actually calms me down.

(*To Amir.*)

What's that like for you?

AMIR: What?

ISAAC: Security at airports.

(*Awkward beat.*)

I mean, you hear stories . . .

AMIR: Wouldn't know. I cut right to the chase.

EMILY: He volunteers himself. Goes right to the agents and offers himself up.

JORY: What? To be searched?

AMIR: I know they're looking at me. And it's not because I look like Giselle. I figure why not make it easier for everyone involved . . .

JORY: Never heard of anyone doing *that* before . . .

AMIR: On top of people being more and more *afraid* of folks who look like me, we end up being *resented*, too.

EMILY: Those agents are working hard *not* to discriminate . . .
Then here's this guy who comes up to them and calls them out . . .

AMIR: Pure, unmitigated passive aggression. That's what my wife thinks.

ISAAC: Maybe she's got a point.

JORY: I think it's kind of admirable, Amir. If everyone was so forthcoming, the world would be a very different place.

ISAAC: It's racial profiling.

JORY: Honey. I know what it is.

ISAAC: I can't imagine you'd like that if it was you?

AMIR: It's not her. That's the point.

JORY: . . . And it's probably not some Kansas grandmother in a wheelchair.

AMIR: The next terrorist attack is probably gonna come from some guy who more or less looks like me.

EMILY: I totally disagree. The next attack is coming from some white guy who's got a gun he shouldn't have . . .

AMIR: And pointing it at a guy who looks like me.

EMILY: Not necessarily.

ISAAC (*to Amir*): If every person of Middle Eastern descent started doing what you're doing . . .

AMIR: Yeah?

ISAAC: I mean, if we all got used to that kind of . . . *compliance?*
We might actually start getting a little too comfortable about our suspicions . . .

AMIR: So you do have suspicions?
ISAAC: I mean, not *me*, I'm just saying—
AMIR: Look. Hell. I don't blame you.
ISAAC: Wait. What?
EMILY (*to Amir, abruptly*): Could you get me a glass of port?

Emily hands Amir her glass. As . . .

Her cell phone RINGS—on the coffee table.

Emily checks it. Without answering.

EMILY (*to Amir*): It's Abe.
AMIR: Abe?
EMILY: Your nephew?
AMIR: What's he calling you about?
EMILY: Did he call you and you not call him back?
AMIR: Yeah.
EMILY: So he's calling me.
      You gotta work on that, honey.

(*To Jory and Isaac.*)

      You guys hungry?
JORY: Getting there.
EMILY (*getting up*): I'm starting us with a fennel salad.

(*To Jory.*)

      You eat anchovies?
JORY: Love them. And I *love* fennel.
AMIR (*pouring a drink*): Her fennel-anchovy salad is a classic. A fucking
      classic.
JORY (*to Isaac, but indicating Amir*): See, honey.
      An exemplary instance of spousal support. He never compliments me
      on my cooking.
ISAAC: I do most of the cooking.
JORY: Because you don't show me any love when I do.
ISAAC: Look. You make a good omelet.
JORY: I haven't made an omelet in ages.
ISAAC: Might be the best thing about them.
EMILY (*getting up, for the kitchen*): I can't believe you just said that.
JORY (*to Emily*): Would you like some help?
EMILY: Thank you, Jory. I would love some.
ISAAC: Just keep her away from the ingredients.

Emily and Jory exit.

ISAAC (CONT'D) (*to Amir*): So . . .

    I'm sorry if I brought up something sensitive . . .

    Between you and Emily, I mean . . .

AMIR: You didn't.

ISAAC: Oh.

AMIR: It's not a secret. Em and I don't see eye to eye on Islam. I think it's . . . a backward way of thinking. And being.

ISAAC: You don't think that's maybe a little broad?

    I mean, it happens to be one of the world's great spiritual traditions.

AMIR: Let me guess. You're reading Rumi.°

ISAAC: Amir . . .

    Actually. Yes, I've been reading Rumi. And he's great. But that's not what I'm talking about.

    Do you know Hanif Saeed?

AMIR: I don't.

ISAAC: He's sculptor, he's Muslim, he's devout. His work is an amazing testimony to the power of faith. He carves these monolithic pillar-like forms—

AMIR (*interrupting*): Have you read the Quran, Isaac?

ISAAC: I haven't.

AMIR: When it comes to Islam? Monolithic pillar-like forms don't matter . . .

Just as Emily and Jory return with the salad and bowls . . .

AMIR (CONT'D): And paintings don't matter. Only the Quran matters.

EMILY: Paintings don't matter?

AMIR: I didn't mean it like that.

EMILY: How did you mean it?

AMIR: Honey. You're aware of what the Prophet said about them?

EMILY: I am, Amir.

JORY: What did he say?

AMIR: He used to say angels don't enter a house where there are pictures and/or dogs.

JORY: What's wrong with dogs?

AMIR: Your guess is as good as mine.

ISAAC: Every religion's got idiosyncrasies. My ancestors didn't like lobster. Who doesn't like lobster? What's your point?

AMIR: My point is that what a few artists are doing, however wonderful, does not reflect the Muslim psyche.

ISAAC: *Muslim psyche?*

AMIR: Islam comes from the desert.

Rumi: Persian Sufi poet (1207–1273).

From a group of tough-minded, tough-living people.
Who saw life as something hard and relentless.
Something to be suffered . . .

JORY: Huh . . .

ISAAC: Not the only people to have suffered in a desert for centuries,
Amir. Don't know what it says about the *Jewish* psyche, if that's the
word we're going to use.

AMIR: Desert pain. I can work with that.
   Jews reacted to the situation differently.
   They turned it over, and over, and over . . .
   I mean, look at the Talmud.° They're looking at things from a
hundred different angles, trying to negotiate with it, make it easier,
more livable . . .

JORY: Find new ways to complain about it . . .

Jory chuckles.

Isaac shoots her a look.

AMIR: Whatever they do, it's not what Muslims do.
   Muslims *don't* think about it. They submit.
   That's what Islam means, by the way. Submission.

ISAAC: I know what it means.
   Look, the problem isn't Islam. It's *Islamo-fascism.*

EMILY: Guys? Salad?

AMIR: Martin Amis, right?

ISAAC: Hitchens,° too. They're not wrong about that . . .

JORY (*Under*): I'm starving.

AMIR: You haven't read the Quran, but you've read a couple of sancti-
monious British bullies and you think you know something about
Islam?

Everyone is moving to the table . . .

EMILY: Amir . . .

AMIR: What? That's not fair game? If he's going to offer it as a counter, it's
fair game.

ISAAC: He has a point. I need to read the Koran.

EMILY (*to Isaac*): Did you want fresh pepper?

JORY: I had to read some of it in college. All I remember is the anger.

AMIR: Thank you. It's like one very long hate-mail letter to humanity.

Talmud: A set of books that offer interpretations of Jewish religious tradition.

Amis, Hitchens: Martin Amis (b. 1949) is a prolific British novelist, and
Christopher Hitchens (1949–2011), a prominent social critic and atheist.

EMILY: That's not true!

(*With the pepper.*)

Jory?

AMIR: It is *kind of*. Grant me *that* at least . . .

EMILY: I'll grant you that the Quran sees humanity as stubborn and self-interested—and it takes us to task for that. And I can't say it's wrong to do so—

ISAAC: All I was trying to say with Islamo-fascism is that there's a difference between the religion and the political use of it.

AMIR: Isaac. In Islam there's no difference. There's no distinction between church and state.

JORY: Don't you mean mosque and state?

AMIR: I do. Thank you.

I'm assuming we're all opposed to people who think the Bible is the Constitution?

Last person has been served. All begin to eat.

EMILY: *Bon appétit.*

ISAAC: *Bon appétit.*

JORY: Mmm. This is so good.

AMIR: Did I tell you, or did I tell you?

EMILY: It's so easy. You slice everything up . . .

ISAAC (*looking at his plate*): Fennel, peppers, celery . . .

EMILY: . . . carrots, radishes . . .

ISAAC: What are these?

EMILY: Baby artichokes . . .

JORY (*coming in*): What gets me just as much as people who treat the Bible like the Constitution are the people who treat the Constitution like it's the Bible. I mean, trying to figure out what a text written more than two hundred years ago really meant? Like it's going to solve our problems today?

EMILY: Like all that bullshit about the right to bear arms. It was 1791, people.

AMIR: That's my point. That's exactly what I'm saying. Honey.

ISAAC: Mmm. This is delicious, Em. Really.

EMILY: I picked up the recipe when I was on a Fulbright in Seville.

ISAAC: I love Spain. I ran with the bulls in Pamplona.

JORY: You did not run with the bulls.

ISAAC: I watched people run with the bulls. It was thrilling.

AMIR: We went to Barcelona for our honeymoon.

The chorizo. The paella. The wine.

Spanish wines are so underrated.

ISAAC: See, this is the problem I'm having . . .
    You're saying Muslims are so different. *You're* not that different.
    You have the same idea of *the good life* as I do. I wouldn't have even
known you were a Muslim if it wasn't for the article in the *Times*.

Pause.

AMIR: I'm not Muslim. I'm an *apostate*. Which means I've renounced my
    faith.
ISAAC (*overlapping*): I know what the word *apostate* means.
JORY: Isaac?
AMIR: Do you also know that—according to the Quran—it makes me
    punishable by death?
EMILY: That's not true, Amir.
AMIR: Yes, it is.
EMILY: Have you even read that part?
    Have you?
    It condemns renouncing the faith, but it doesn't specify punishment.
    The tradition has *interpreted* it as punishable by death.
JORY: Impressive . . .
EMILY: He's repeated it enough, I checked. I have a vested interest, after
    all.

Women laugh.

AMIR: Fine.
    So let's talk about something that *is* in the text.
    Wife beating.
ISAAC: Wife beating?
JORY: Great. Could you pass the bread?
EMILY: Amir, really?
AMIR (*passing the bread*): So the angel Gabriel comes to Muhammad . . .
ISAAC: Angel Gabriel?
AMIR (*mocking*): Yeah. That's how Muslims believe the Quran came to
    humanity. The angel Gabriel supposedly dictated it to Muhammad
    word for word.
ISAAC: Like Joseph Smith. Mormonism.
    An angel named Marami came down in upstate New York and talked
    to Joseph Smith—
JORY: Moroni, honey. Not Marami.
ISAAC: You sure?
JORY: It was on *South Park*.

Beat.

AMIR: So like I was saying . . .

The angel Gabriel shows up and teaches Muhammad this verse. You
know the one, honey.
   I'm paraphrasing . . .
   Men are in charge of women . . .
EMILY: Amir?
AMIR (*continuing*):
   If they don't obey . . .
   Talk to them.
   If that doesn't work . . .
   Don't sleep with them.
   And if that doesn't work . . .

(*Turning to Emily.*)

   Em?
EMILY: I'm not doing this.
AMIR: *Beat them.*
JORY: I don't remember that being in the Koran.
AMIR: Oh, it's there all right.
EMILY: The usual translation is debatable.
AMIR: Only for people who are trying to make Islam look all warm and
   fuzzy.
EMILY: The root verb can mean beat. But it can also mean leave.
   So it could be saying, if your wife doesn't listen, leave her.
   Not beat her.
ISAAC: Sounds like a pretty big difference.
AMIR: That's not how it's been interpreted for hundreds of years.
JORY (*suddenly impassioned*): No. See. Sometimes you just have to say no.
   I don't blame the French.
ISAAC: The French?
JORY: For their problem with Islam.
ISAAC: You're okay with them banning the veil?
JORY: You do have to draw the line *somewhere.*
ISAAC: Okay, Mrs. Kissinger.
EMILY: Endearing.
ISAAC: I'm married to a woman who has a Kissinger quote above her
   desk in the den . . .
JORY: *"If faced with choosing justice or order, I'll always choose order."*
EMILY: Why do you have that above your desk?
JORY: To remind me. Not to get lost in the feeling that I need to get
   justice.
   You pull yourself out of the ghetto, you realize *real soon* order is
   where it's at . . .
EMILY: Me. Justice. Always.

JORY: You know what they say? If you're young and not a liberal, you've got no heart. And if you're old and not a conservative . . .

AMIR AND JORY (*together*): . . . you've got no brain.

ISAAC: I happen to know a few very brilliant Muslim women who *choose* to wear the veil.

AMIR: You really enjoy playing the contrarian, don't you?

ISAAC: I'm not playing the contrarian.

JORY (*to Isaac, over*): Who do you know that wears the veil?

ISAAC: You wouldn't know them.

JORY: I think you're making it up.

ISAAC: I'm not.

JORY: So who?

ISAAC: Khalid's sister.

JORY: Khalid?

ISAAC: She's a professor of philosophy at Cornell.
     She wears the veil.

JORY: Khalid? Your trainer?

AMIR: You train at Equinox?

ISAAC: Yeah.

AMIR: I know Khalid. Balding? With the guns?

ISAAC: That's him. I didn't know you trained at Equinox.

JORY: What's your point?

ISAAC: Khalid may be a trainer, but he comes from a ridiculously educated Jordanian background. All the women in his family wear the veil. By choice.

EMILY: It's not always what people think. It's a source of pride for a lot of Muslim women.

AMIR: First of all, they're probably wearing headscarves. Not the veil. It's not the same thing—

JORY (*cutting in*): The veil is evil.
     You erase a face, you erase individuality.
     Nobody's making men erase their individuality.
     Why's it always come down to making the woman pay?
     Uh-uh. There is a point at which you just have to say no.

AMIR: Just say no.
     That is exactly what Muhammad *didn't* do.
     Here's the irony:
     Before becoming a prophet? He was adamant about his followers *not* abusing women.
     And then he starts talking to an angel.
     I mean, *really?*

ISAAC: I still can't believe I've never seen the parallel with Mormonism before.

AMIR: You keep saying *that* like it means something.
ISAAC: Both religions where you can have multiple wives, too.
   Though I think Mormons are okay with dogs.
AMIR: You still don't get it.
ISAAC: Get what? That you're full of self-loathing?

Jory shoots Isaac a look to kill.

AMIR: The Quran is about tribal life in a seventh-century desert, Isaac.
   The point isn't just academic.
   There's a result to believing that a book written about life in a spe-
cific society fifteen hundred years ago is the word of God:
   You start wanting to *re-create* that society.
   After all, it's the only one in which the Quran makes any literal sense.
   That's why you have people like the Taliban. They're trying to re-
create the world in the image of the one that's in the Quran.

*Amir has since gotten up from the table and is now pouring himself another
drink.*

EMILY: Honey, I think we get it.
AMIR *(to Emily)*: Actually. I'm pretty sure you don't.

(Continuing, to the others.)

   Here's the kicker. And this is the real problem:
   It goes way deeper than the Taliban.
   To be Muslim—*truly*—means not only that you *believe* all this. It
means you *fight* for it, too.
   Politics follows faith?
   No distinction between mosque and state?
   Remember all that?
   So if the point is that the world in the Quran was a better place than
this world, well, then let's go back.
   Let's stone adulterers.
   Let's cut off the hands of thieves.
   Let's kill the unbelievers.
   And so, even if you're one of those lapsed Muslims sipping your
after-dinner scotch alongside your beautiful white American wife—
and watching the news and seeing folks in the Middle East dying for
values you were taught were purer—and stricter—and truer . . . you
can't help but feel just a little a bit of pride.
ISAAC: Pride?
AMIR: Yes. Pride.

Beat.

ISAAC: Did you feel pride on September Eleventh?

AMIR (*with hesitation*): If I'm honest, yes.

EMILY: You don't really mean that, Amir.

AMIR: I was horrified by it, okay? Absolutely horrified.

JORY: Pride about what?
    About the towers coming down?
    About people getting killed?

AMIR: That we were finally winning.

JORY: *We?*

AMIR: Yeah . . . I guess I forgot . . . which *we* I was.

JORY: You're an American . . .

AMIR: It's tribal, Jor. It is in the bones.
    You have no idea how I was brought up.
    You have to work *real* hard to root that shit out.

JORY: Well, you need to keep working.

AMIR: I am.

Emily has gotten up to go to Amir.

AMIR (CONT'D): What?

EMILY: That's enough.

(*Taking his glass.*)

    I'm gonna make you some coffee.

Emily exits to the kitchen.

Long awkward pause.

AMIR: What?

(*To Isaac, conciliatory.*)

    Look . . .
    I'm sure it's not all that different than how you feel about Israel
    sometimes . . .

ISAAC: Excuse me?

AMIR: You're going to tell me you've never felt anything like that—an
    unexpected *blush* of pride, say . . .

ISAAC: Blush? I don't feel anything like a blush.

AMIR: When you hear about Israel throwing its military weight around?

ISAAC: I'm critical of Israel. A lot of Jews are.

AMIR: And when you hear Ahmadinejad° talk about wiping Israel into
    the Mediterranean, how do you feel then?

Ahmadinejad: Mahmoud Ahmadinejad (b. 1956) was president of Iran from 2005–2013.

ISAAC: Outraged. Like anybody else.
AMIR: Not everybody's outraged. A lot of folks *like* hearing that.
ISAAC: *You* like hearing that?
AMIR: I said a lot of folks . . .

Emily appears in the kitchen doorway.

ISAAC: I asked you if *you* like hearing it. Do you like hearing about Israel getting wiped into the ocean?
JORY: Isaac . . .
ISAAC: No. I want to know . . .
AMIR: Sometimes? Yes . . .
EMILY (*with hints of despair*): Amir. We're supposed to be celebrating.
AMIR (*ignoring, over*): And I'm saying it's wrong.
   And it comes from somewhere.
   And that somewhere is Islam.
ISAAC: No shit it's wrong.
   But it doesn't come from Islam.
   It comes from *you*.
   Islam has no monopoly on fundamentalism. It doesn't come from a text.
AMIR: You don't need to patronize me —
ISAAC: You've been patronizing me this whole conversation.
   You don't like organized religion? Fine.
   You have a particular antipathy for the one you were born into? Fine.
   Maybe you feel a little more strongly about it than most of us because . . . whatever? Fine.
JORY: Isaac.
ISAAC: But I'm not interested in your *absurd* — and frankly, more than a little terrifying — generalizations . . .
JORY (*firm*): Isaac.
ISAAC: What?
JORY: Stop it.
ISAAC: Okay.

Another tense pause.

AMIR: You're naive.
EMILY: Amir. Could you join me in the kitchen?

Emily exits.

AMIR (*following her out*): Naive and well-meaning. And you're on a collision course with history.

Amir crosses to the kitchen and exits.

ISAAC: I'm naive? What a fucking asshole.
JORY: He's the asshole?
ISAAC: Did you hear him?
JORY: What's gotten into you?
ISAAC: Fucking closet jihadist.
JORY: Will you shut up?
ISAAC: I will never understand what you see in this guy.
JORY: Something's off tonight.
    I think maybe he knows.

(*Off Isaac's look.*)

    About me.
ISAAC: How would he?
JORY: He's mentioned Steven a few times . . .
    I don't know? Maybe Mort told him?
ISAAC: Well. He's going to find out sooner or later.
JORY: I wanted to be the one to tell him.
    I owe him that much.
ISAAC: Then you should have told him when it happened.
JORY: I'm under confidentiality.
ISAAC: Well . . .
JORY: I think I need to tell him.

The kitchen door flies open, and Amir comes bounding back, heading for the coats.

    Emily appears behind him.

AMIR (*clearly intoxicated*): You came over here with good news. We should
    be celebrating. It's Emily's night. I'm gonna go get us some champagne.

(*Off Emily's reaction.*)

    And then we're gonna have a wonderful dinner.

Jory and Isaac share a look.

JORY: I'm gonna come with you. Is that okay?
AMIR: Of course.

Amir puts on his coat.

Jory throws on her coat.

Amir looks at Emily.

AMIR (CONT'D): What?
EMILY: Nothing.

Amir pulls open the door.

Both exit.

Emily turns to Isaac.

EMILY (CONT'D): You think I don't know what you're doing?
ISAAC: What am I doing?
EMILY: Isaac, please.
ISAAC: He's a big boy. He can't handle a little push-back?

Emily heads for the side table to pour herself another drink.

ISAAC (CONT'D): You guys get into an argument before we showed up?
EMILY: Why would we get into an argument?
ISAAC: You're married.
EMILY: I don't have the marriage you do.

(*Beat.*)

   You could have told me about the show over the phone.
ISAAC: I wanted to tell you face-to-face.
EMILY: This is my home.
      Isaac . . .
      London . . .
      Was a mistake . . .
ISAAC: I don't think you really believe that.

Isaac touches her. She pulls away.

ISAAC (CONT'D): You're in the show now, so that's it?
EMILY: If that's why you're putting me in the show . . .
ISAAC: Of course not. God.
   The whole idea for the show came from you.

Isaac makes another move toward Emily.

Which she doesn't resist at first. Until she pulls away again.

ISAAC (CONT'D): I had no idea your husband was such a mess.
   And a fucking alcoholic to boot.
EMILY: He's not an alcoholic. He had a bad day at the office.
ISAAC: Oh. So he knows.
EMILY: Knows?
ISAAC: About Jory?
EMILY: What about Jory?
ISAAC: They're making her partner.
EMILY: Wait, what?

ISAAC: They offered her a partnership. Name on the firm.
  Their counter to the offer she got from Credit Suisse.
EMILY: When did this happen?
ISAAC: Last week.
EMILY: Nobody told Amir.
ISAAC: Well, Jory's telling him right now.
EMILY: I don't understand.
ISAAC: There is not a lot to understand. They like her. They don't like him.
EMILY: Mort's like his father.
ISAAC: Mort doesn't wear the pants. Steven does.
EMILY: Amir's been there twice as long as she has.
ISAAC: Well . . .
EMILY: What?
ISAAC: The whole thing with the imam?
  That Amir represented?
EMILY: He didn't *represent* him.
ISAAC: That's not what the *Times* said.
EMILY: He went to a hearing.
ISAAC: The paper mentioned the firm and they mentioned Amir and it
  looked like he was representing a man who was raising money for
  terrorists.
EMILY: That's absurd.
ISAAC: That's not what Steven thought. He went ballistic.
EMILY: He did?
ISAAC: Don't you know this?
  Jory said your husband broke down. Was crying at a staff meeting.
  And apparently shouted something about how if the imam had been a
  rabbi, Steven wouldn't have cared.
  Steven thought the comment was anti-Semitic.
EMILY: I'm sorry, but sometimes you people have a problem.
ISAAC: We people?
EMILY: Jews. You see anti-Semitism everywhere.
ISAAC: You're married to a man who feels a blush when Ahmadinejad
  talks about wiping Jews into the ocean. Steven is a huge fund-raiser
  for Netanyahu.° I have no idea why Amir would go anywhere near a guy
  like that imam.
EMILY (*crushed*): For me. He did it for me.
  Oh, God.

Netanyahu: Benjamin Netanyahu, prime minister of Israel.

Pause.

ISAAC: He doesn't understand you. He can't understand you.
    He puts you on a pedestal.
    It's in your painting.
    Study After Velázquez.
    He's looking out at the viewer—that viewer is you. You painted it. He's looking at you.
    The expression on that face?
    Shame. Anger. Pride.
    Yeah. The pride he was talking about.
    The slave finally has the master's wife.
EMILY: You're disgusting—
ISAAC: It's the truth, Em. And you know it. You painted it.

Silence.

ISAAC (CONT'D): If what happened that night in London was a mistake, Em, it's not the last time you're going to make it.
    A man like that . . .
    You *will* cheat on him again. Maybe not with me, but you will.
EMILY: Isaac.
ISAAC: And then one day you'll leave him.
    Em. I'm in love with you.

Isaac leans in to kiss her.

Emily doesn't move. In or out.

Just as the front door opens—

Jory enters. In a huff. Returning for Isaac and her things. Ready to leave for the evening—

JORY: Isaac, we need to get out of here—

—but stopped in place by the moment of intimacy between her husband and Emily.

ISAAC: Honey?
JORY: What the fuck is going on here?

Amir enters, inflamed.

AMIR: You wait a week to tell me this? And the second I say something you don't like hearing, you walk away from me in mid-fucking sentence?
    Who *are* you?!

Jory just stares at her husband . .

AMIR (CONT'D): What?

(*Looking around.*)

What?

JORY (*to Emily*): Are you having an affair with my husband?

AMIR: Excuse me?

ISAAC (*to Jory*): Nobody's having an affair.

JORY: I walked in here and they were kissing.

EMILY: That is not true! Amir, it's not true.

JORY: They were kissing.

(*Pointing.*)

There.

EMILY: That's not what was happening.

JORY: I know what I saw.

EMILY: Isaac told me about them making you partner. I know how much longer Amir has been there than you. I was upset. I was crying.

ISAAC: I was consoling her.

JORY: By kissing her?

EMILY (*incredulous*): We weren't kissing! Why do you keep saying that?!

JORY (*to Isaac*): Are you having an affair with her? Tell me the truth.

ISAAC: Honey. I already said. We're not having an affair.

JORY: So *what the fuck* were you doing when I walked in here?

ISAAC (*going to his wife*): I was hugging her because she was crying.

JORY: Get off me!

EMILY: I was upset they made you partner.

I know how much longer Amir has been there.

I was crying.

Amir turns to Jory. Vicious.

AMIR: First you steal my job and now you try to destroy my marriage? You're fucking evil. After everything I've done for you?

Jory goes over to get her purse. As if to leave.

JORY: I know what I saw.

AMIR (*exploding*): You have any idea how much of myself I've poured into that place? That closet at the end of the hall? Where they keep the cleaning supplies? That was my first office!

Yours had a view of the fucking park!

Your first three years? Were you ever at work before anyone else in the morning?

Were you ever the last one to leave?

Cause if you were, I didn't see it.

I *still* leave the office after you do!
You think you're the nigger here?
I'm the nigger!! Me!!

ISAAC (*going to his wife*): You don't need to listen to any more out of this asshole.

JORY (*to Isaac*): Don't touch me.

AMIR (*to Isaac*): You're the asshole.

ISAAC: You better shut your mouth, buddy!

AMIR (*to Isaac*): Or what?!

ISAAC: Or I'll knock you on your *fucking* ass!

AMIR: Try me!

JORY (*to Isaac*): GET OFF ME!!

Inflamed, Isaac finally releases his wife, facing off with Amir.

When suddenly—

Amir spits in Isaac's face.

Beat.

Isaac wipes the spit from his face.

ISAAC: There's a reason they call you people animals.

Isaac turns to his wife.

Then turns to Emily.

Then walks out.

AMIR (*to Jory*): Get out.

JORY (*Collecting her things*): There's something you should know.
Your dear friend Mort is retiring.
And guess who's taking over his caseload? Not you. Me.
I asked him, *Why not Amir?*
He said something about you being duplicitous.
That it's why you're such a good litigator. But that it's impossible to trust you.

(*At the door.*)

Don't believe me?
Call Mort. Ask him yourself.
Let me guess.
He hasn't been taking your calls?

Jory walks out.

Pause.

EMILY: Have you lost your fucking mind?!

Amir turns away, withdrawing into himself. Pacing. The inward spiral deepening.

EMILY (CONT'D): Amir!

AMIR: She's right. He hasn't been taking my calls.

EMILY: I'm gonna get you that coffee.

Emily heads for the kitchen . . .

Leaving Amir onstage by himself for a moment. As he watches the swinging door sway. Back and forth.

Emily returns. A mug in hand.

AMIR: Em.

Something in Amir's tone—vulnerable, intense—stops her in place.

AMIR (CONT'D): Are you sleeping with him?

Pause.

Emily puts the mug down on the table.

Beat. Finally shakes her head.

EMILY: It was in London. When I was at Frieze.
    We were drinking. It's not an excuse . . .
    It's just . . .
    We'd just been to the Victoria and Albert. He was talking about my work.
    And . . .

Emily—seeing how her words are landing on her husband—makes her way to him.

EMILY (CONT'D): *(approaching)*: Amir, I'm so disgusted with myself. If I could take it back.

All at once, Amir hits Emily in the face. A vicious blow.

The first blow unleashes a torrent of rage, overtaking him. He hits her twice more. Maybe a third. In rapid succession. Uncontrolled violence as brutal as it needs to be in order to convey the discharge of a lifetime of discreetly building resentment.

(In order for the stage violence to seem as real as possible, obscuring it from direct view of the audience might be necessary. For it to unfold with Emily hidden by a couch, for example.)

After the last blow, Amir suddenly comes to his senses, realizing what he's done.

AMIR: Oh, my God . . .

Just as . . .

There's a KNOCKING at the door.

Beat.

And then more KNOCKING.

Finally, the door gently opens. To show:

Abe.

Abe looks over and sees—as we do—Emily emerge into full view, on the ground, her face bloodied.

Abe looks up at Amir.

Lights Out.

Scene 4

Six months later.

The dining table, a couple of chairs.

Much of the furniture gone. The rest of the room covered with the detritus of moving. Boxes, etc.

The painting above the mantel is gone.

Along one wall leans a smaller, partially wrapped canvas. It is turned away from the audience.

As the lights come up, Amir is on stage. Quietly going about the process of packing. There should be something muted about his movement/presence. As if a man chastened by life, perhaps even crippled inwardly.

He has a thought and heads for the kitchen. Just as he exits, there is a KNOCKING at the front door . . .

He reemerges. Crossing and going to the door. He opens to find:

Emily. And, to one side, Abe. Abe is wearing a Muslim skullcap. And his wardrobe is muted. Unlike the vibrant colors of the first scene.

AMIR: Em?
EMILY: Can we come in?
AMIR: Of course.

They enter.

Abe appears reluctant. Not meeting Amir's gaze.

AMIR (CONT'D): What's going on here? Everything all right?

EMILY: Not really.
AMIR: What?

Emily looks at Abe, but Abe doesn't respond.

AMIR (CONT'D): Huss?

No response.

Amir turns to Emily, making a gesture toward her, not even realizing it . . .

AMIR (CONT'D): Em?
EMILY: (*recoiling*): No, please.

(*Beat.*)

He's been coming to me. You need to hear this.

(*To Abe.*)

Tell him.
ABE: He's not going to understand.
EMILY: He got stopped by the FBI.
AMIR: What?
ABE: I didn't get stopped.
AMIR: What happened?
EMILY: Just sit down and tell him.
AMIR: What happened?
ABE: I didn't get stopped. All I was doing was sitting in Starbucks . . .
EMILY: With your friend . . .
AMIR: Don't tell me . . . Tariq?
ABE: Yeah.
AMIR: Hasn't everybody been telling you—
EMILY (*coming in*): Let him speak.
ABE: My parents are wrong about him.
AMIR: Okay.
ABE: We were at Starbucks. Just drinking coffee. Tariq starts talking to this barista who's on break. I can tell she's not into him. He's not getting the message . . . She starts asking about our kufi hats and are we Muslims. And then she asks us how we feel about Al-Qaeda. So Tariq tells her. Americans are the ones who created Al-Qaeda.

(*Off Amir's look.*)

You don't believe me?
AMIR: That's not really the—
ABE: The CIA trained the mujahideen in Afghanistan. Those are the guys that became Al-Qaeda.

AMIR: I mean, it's a little more complicated than that—
ABE: Actually, it's not, Uncle. Not really.
AMIR: Okay. What happened?
ABE: So she got snippy. And Tariq got pissed. He told her this country deserved what it got and what it was going to get.

(*Pause.*)

She goes back to work, and before we know it, the police are there. She called them. They cuff us. Take us in. Two guys from the FBI are at the station, waiting.

(*Beat.*)

We sit through this ridiculous interrogation.
AMIR: What did they ask you?
ABE: Do we believe in jihad? Do we want to blow stuff up? How often did I read the *Koran?*
AMIR: Okay . . .
ABE: Do we have girlfriends? Had I ever had sex? Do I watch porn? Do I hate America?

(*Beat.*)

They knew a lot about me. Where I'd gone to school. About Mom and Dad, where they were born. Like they already had a file.
They brought up my immigration status.
AMIR: What about it?
EMILY: It's up for renewal.
ABE: When they said that . . .

(*Hesitating.*)

. . . I laughed.
AMIR: You laughed?
ABE: I didn't mean to. It just happened.
AMIR: Were you trying to antagonize them?
ABE: No.
I mean . . .

(*Pause.*)

Look. I know what they're doing.
AMIR: What are they doing?
ABE: They're going into our community and looking for people whose immigration status is vulnerable. Then they push us to start doing stuff for them.

AMIR: Okay . . .
ABE: So what? You don't believe that either?
AMIR: I didn't say that.

Pause.

EMILY (*suddenly moving off*): I'm gonna go. He needed to talk to you . . .
AMIR: Where are you going?
ABE (*standing*): Aunt Emily. Stay. Please.

She stops.

Beat.

Finally nods, still reluctant.

EMILY: I'm gonna get some . . . water.

Emily crosses to the kitchen. Exits.

Beat.

AMIR: Is she okay?
ABE: I don't want to talk about that.

Amir starts dialing on his phone.

ABE (CONT'D): Who are you calling? You can't call Mom. She's gonna freak
    out.
AMIR: I'm calling Ken.
ABE: Ken?
AMIR: The lawyer on Imam Fareed's case . . .

(*Into the phone.*)

Hi, Ken, it's Amir. Please call me back when you get this. It's urgent.
Thanks.

(*Pause, then to Abe.*)

When you step out of your parents' house, you need to understand that
it's not a neutral world out there. Not right now. Not for you. You have
to be mindful about sending a different message.
ABE: Than what?
AMIR: Than the one that landed you in an interrogation with the FBI.

Pause.

ABE: So now what?
AMIR: Let's hear what Ken has to say. I mean, it's not good. But at least
    they let you go.

ABE: If he tells me that I have to go into our mosque and pretend I'm
planning some bullshit attack just to stay in this country—
AMIR: You don't know that's what's going to happen.
ABE: If you spent any time with your own people . . .
AMIR: Excuse me?

Beat.

ABE: What would you do? If the FBI asked you to work for them?
Hmm?
AMIR: We're not there yet . . .
ABE: (*cutting him off*): What would you do?
AMIR (*considering*): There are ways . . . to let the authorities know that . . .
you're on their side . . .
ABE: But I'm not on their side.
AMIR: You might want to rethink that. Because they make the rules.
ABE: I knew this was a mistake.
AMIR: It's not a mistake. If you're not smarter about this, you are going
to get deported.

Beat.

ABE: Yeah, well, maybe that wouldn't be the worst thing.
AMIR: To a country you haven't known since you were eight years old.
ABE: Maybe that's the problem. Maybe we never should've left.
Maybe we never should have come to this one.
AMIR: There's a reason your father came here. Same reason my father did.
They wanted to make a better life for themselves and their families—
ABE (*over*): A better life?!?
AMIR (*continuing*):—and to do it honestly. Which isn't an option in
Pakistan.
ABE (*exploding*): You don't have a better life!
AMIR: What are you talking about?
ABE: I know you were fired!
AMIR: I don't know what you think you know—
ABE (*quiet, intense*): I know what you did to her. How could you?

Beat.

AMIR: I don't know.

Beat.

ABE: You want something from these people you will never get.
AMIR: I'm still your elder. You need to show me a little respect.
ABE: Just because I'm telling you the truth doesn't mean I'm not showing
you respect.

(*Beat.*)

You forgot who you are.

AMIR (*triggered*): Really? *Abe Jensen?!*

ABE: I changed it back!

AMIR: So now you think running around with a kufi on your head, shoot-ing your mouth off in Starbucks, or sitting in a mosque and bemoan-ing the plight of Muslims around the world is going to—

ABE (*interrupting*): It's disgusting. The one thing I can be sure about with you? You'll always turn on your own people. You think it makes these people like you more when you do that? They don't. They just think you hate yourself. And they're right! You do!

I looked up to you. You have no idea—

AMIR: No. I know.

ABE: No! You have no idea what it did to me!

(*Beat.*)

I mean, if you can't make it with them . . . ?

(*Having a dawning thought.*)

The Prophet wouldn't be trying to be like one of them. He didn't conquer the world by copying other people. He made the world copy him.

AMIR: Conquer the world?

ABE: That's what *they've* done.

They've conquered the world.

We're gonna get it back.

That's our destiny. It's in the Quran.

We see Emily appear at the swinging door, listening.

Abe doesn't notice her.

ABE (CONT'D): For three hundred years they've been taking our land, drawing new borders, replacing our laws, making us want be like them. Look like them. Marry their women.

They disgraced us.

They disgraced us.

And then they pretend they don't understand the rage we've got?

Emily emerges.

Abe realizing she has heard him.

Abe moves to the door. Stops. Looks back at Emily.

ABE (CONT'D): I'm sorry.

AMIR: Hussein . . .
ABE: I'll handle it myself, Uncle.

Abe exits.

Leaving Amir and Emily.

Silence.

AMIR: My sister's been telling me about him . . . I didn't realize . . .

(*More silence.*)

   Are you reading my letters?
EMILY: Amir . . .
AMIR: I got the painting.
EMILY: I didn't want to throw it out.
AMIR: There was no note . . .

(*Beat.*)

   Look, I told your lawyer I wanted you to have the apartment. I mean,
   I wrote you that, but I have no idea if—
EMILY: The apartment's not mine.

Beat.

AMIR: If you hate me so much, why did you drop charges?
EMILY: I don't hate you, Amir.

Pause.

AMIR: I saw the write-up in *The New Yorker*. I was so proud of you.
EMILY: Oh.

Pause.

AMIR: I don't know if you've read any of my letters . . . There's a lot you
   were right about me.
      I'm finally seeing what you were seeing.
      I'm finally understanding your work.
EMILY: My work was naive.
AMIR: No, it wasn't. Why are you saying that?
EMILY: Because it's true.
AMIR: God. If you had any idea how sorry I am.
EMILY: I know.

Emily crosses. Stopping when she gets to the door.

EMILY (CONT'D): I had a part in what happened.
AMIR: Em. No.

EMILY: It's true.

(*Beat.*)

> I was selfish.
> My work . . .
> It made me blind.

AMIR: I just . . .

(*Long pause, Amir emotional.*)

> I just want you to be proud of me.
> I want you to be proud you were with me.

Beat.

EMILY: Good-bye, Amir.
> Please. Don't write me anymore.

She exits.

Long beat.

As Amir walks over to return to packing, he notices . . .

The partially wrapped canvas against the wall.

He walks over to it, picks it up. Then tears the rest of the wrapping off. From his position on stage, we will only see enough of the painting to realize:

It is Emily's portrait of him. Study After Velázquez's Moor.

He takes a searching long look.

Lights Out.

[2012]

PART FOUR

Reading and Writing about Literature

CHAPTER 1

Introduction to Reading and Writing about Literature

"Nobody reads anymore."

"People don't know how to write."

"We're becoming a nation of illiterates."

Maybe you've heard laments like these. They have sounded through our culture for several years now, indeed for at least several decades. Proclamations on the sad lack of literacy in modern life have been widely reported, as in January 2008, when Apple Computer cofounder Steve Jobs predicted that Amazon's Kindle e-book reader was doomed to failure because "people don't read anymore." (Perhaps ironically, he said this in a room full of reporters and must have known that these writers were going to quote these words in print and that millions of people would read them.) If we take these warnings seriously, it would seem that modern culture and modern education are in big trouble.

But news of the death of literacy is premature. In fact, we can make a good case that reading and writing occupy a more central place in our day-to-day life than they have at any other point in history. We are bombarded all day long with written messages. Billboards, product packaging, Web sites, blogs, flyers, wikis, advertisements, restaurant menus, e-mails, text messages, social media updates—the list goes on and on. Even while watching TV, arguably the least literary of media, we are often given a reading task: think of the "crawl" of updates that appears at the bottom of the screen during newscasts, the captions that identify interview subjects, even the station logos in the corner of the screen. The average North American in the early twenty-first century encounters literally hundreds of written messages every day, and most of us have no particular problem reading these messages. Often we don't even notice that we are doing so.

In a similar vein, most of us spend more time writing than people have at any earlier point in history. The vast majority of jobs these days require some amount of writing. Sometimes this requirement is extensive, as when engineers write sophisticated reports on their projects, while some work-related writing is as simple as a daily e-mail to communicate with others on the job. Students, of course, take notes, complete homework assignments, and write papers. Even in our leisure time, we are likely to update our social media, comment on a friend's blog post, send a text message, or write a note to a family member or friend.

If you were to keep a list of every single thing you read and wrote in a day (a list that would, of course, have to include an entry for the list you were writing), you might be surprised at how extensive that list was by the end of the day.

So, if literacy is alive and well in the modern world, why is a book like this one necessary? Why do colleges and universities offer, or even require, literature classes? Don't we already know enough about reading and writing? Do we really need to learn how to read and write about literature? The answer as to why people *do* need to learn these skills is that imaginative literature is different from most of the other writing we read every day, and reading and writing about literature requires, and builds, a very different set of skills than those we bring to a Wikipedia article or a Facebook posting.

WHY READ LITERATURE?

Let's take a moment to reflect on why we read literature. Of course, there is no single or simple answer. People read to be informed, to be entertained, to be exposed to new ideas, or to have familiar concepts reinforced. Often, people read just to enjoy a good story or to get a glimpse of how other people think and feel. But literature does much more than give us a compelling plot or a look into an author's thoughts and emotions—although at its best it does these things as well. Literature explores the larger world and the ways in which people interact with that world and with one another. So even when what we read is entirely fictional, we nevertheless learn about real life. And, indeed, by affecting our thoughts and feelings, literature can indirectly affect our actions as well. Thus literature not only reflects but even helps to shape our world.

Literature, then, is not merely informational, like so much of the reading we do in our everyday lives. It does not stand up well to haste, distractions, or multitasking. It is not meant to be browsed, skimmed, or linked away from as we search for particular facts or knowledge as efficiently as possible. Instead, it is designed for sustained reading, meaning that to do it justice we need to read it from beginning to end and pay it our full attention for all that time. What is most important in literature is rarely highlighted for us. Rather, we must use our intelligence to figure out the significance the literature holds for us, and we must realize that this significance may be different for a different reader. Because of this, reading literature helps us develop the skills of introspection, sustained attention, and deep analysis, skills that can help us in other areas of our lives as well.

WHY WRITE ABOUT LITERATURE?

Even students who enjoy reading poems, stories, or plays do not always enjoy writing about them. Some claim that having to analyze literature kills the fun they find in a good story. For others, the task of writing about literature can seem intimidating, frustrating, or just plain dull. If you share any of these prejudices, try to put them aside while we consider the value of writing about literature.

Writing about literature requires a special set of knowledge and skills. When you write about a story, a poem, or a play, you need to be particularly attentive to language, the medium of literature. This hones both analytical ability and creativity. In this sort of writing, you also need to pay close attention to your own use of language—just as you must pay attention to the language of the story, poem, or play—and doing so may have ripple effects that improve all your writing. Writing about literature, then, can help make you more thoughtful and articulate, better able to make yourself heard and understood, and obviously those are qualities that can improve your life well beyond the bounds of your literature classroom. And, far from killing the enjoyment of reading, writing about literature can increase that enjoyment and provide a sense of accomplishment as you look at the well-crafted paper you've written.

Writing about literature also has real-world usefulness. By forcing us to organize our thoughts and state clearly what we think, writing an essay helps us clarify what we know and believe. It gives us a chance to affect the thinking of our readers. Even more important, we actually learn as we write. In the process of writing, we often make new discoveries and forge new connections between ideas. We find and work through contradictions in our thinking, and we create whole new lines of thought as we work to make linear sense out of an often chaotic jumble of impressions. So, while *reading* literature can teach us much about the world, *writing* about literature often teaches us about ourselves.

WHAT TO EXPECT IN A LITERATURE CLASS

Every classroom, like every group of people in any setting, is its own unique world, with its own set of expectations and social interactions. However, there are certain features common to most literature classes, what might be considered the culture of a college or university literature class.

Unlike some other classes on campus, a literature class is not the sort of class where attendance is optional as long as you master the material and are able to pass the tests. Though your class may have a lecture component, it will almost certainly have a large discussion component as well, a give-and-take between students and instructor regarding the stories, poems, and plays you have read. In some ways, these discussions are the most important part of a literature class, and no amount of extra study on your own or sharing notes with a classmate can make up for having missed class. To follow these discussions, let alone to participate, you obviously will have to complete the reading. Whether or not your class has a stated attendance policy, to do well you need to be there and to be caught up with all reading and writing assignments. Participation is important.

Discussions in literature classes are usually interesting, because no two people come away from a particular literary text with exactly the same impressions. You may dislike a particular story and be surprised to discover that most of your fellow students loved it. A poem may leave you smiling while it makes one of your classmates cry. A character's motivation might seem obvious to you but baffle someone else. These differences arise because each reader is distinctive. Because you have lived a unique life, you have a knowledge of the world that is slightly different from any other reader's. You bring this personal history and knowledge to your reading, along with your own mind and temperament, your own likes and dislikes, and even all the knowledge gained from your past reading. Differing opinions are valid in literature classes, and each reader is in a position to enrich the conversation by speaking up in class.

Just as speaking up is part of participating, so too is attentive listening. While it is fair to regard your take on a piece of literature as valid, that doesn't mean you need only consider your own opinions. Listening to what your instructor and classmates have to say is equally important, especially when they disagree with you. If your position has value, so do theirs. Perhaps they have seen something you missed, or perhaps they consider crucial something that you had dismissed as unimportant. You may find your first impressions shifting during these discussions, or you may find them solidifying. Either of these outcomes is a good sign that you're learning. The most important thing you bring to a literary discussion is a willingness to share your own perspectives while remaining open to the possibility of learning from others.

Attentive listeners tend to make the best note takers, and having good class notes will prove incredibly helpful when you sit down to write your papers. This important skill will be covered in the next chapter.

LITERATURE AND ENJOYMENT

You may have noticed that little has been said so far about the idea that reading and writing about literature can also be fun. Some students really enjoy reading imaginative literature and writing papers about it. If you're in that group, you're lucky; your literature class will be fun and interesting for you, and—not incidentally—you'll probably do good work in the course. If you've never been fond of reading and writing about literature, though, you might spend a little time thinking about why some of your classmates enjoy this sort of work as well as what you might do to increase your own enjoyment of literature and investment in the writing process. You'll be happier and write better papers if you can put aside any previous negative experiences with literature and writing you may have had and approach your task with a positive mind-set. As you are introduced to new authors, new characters and settings, and new ideas, your literature class may surprise you. It could even end up being a favorite.

CHAPTER 2

The Role of Good Reading

Writing about literature begins, of course, with reading, so it stands to reason that good reading is the first step toward successful writing. But what exactly is "good reading"? Good reading is, generally speaking, not fast reading. In fact, often the best advice a student can receive about reading is to *slow down*. Reading well is all about paying attention, and you can't pay attention if you're texting a friend as you read or racing to get through an assignment and move on to "more important" things. If you make a point of giving yourself plenty of time and minimizing your distractions, you'll get more out of your reading and probably enjoy it more as well.

THE VALUE OF REREADING

The best reading is often rereading, and the best readers are those who are willing to go back and reread a piece of literature again and again. It is not uncommon for professional literary critics—who are, after all, some of the most skilled readers—to read a particular poem, story, or play literally dozens of times before they feel equipped to write about it. And well-written literature rewards this willingness to reread, allowing readers to continue seeing new things with each reading. If you have a favorite book you return to over and over, or a favorite song you like to listen to again and again, you intuitively understand this truth. Realistically, of course, you will not have the time to read every assigned piece many times before discussing it in class or preparing to write about it, but you should not give up or feel frustrated if you fail to "get" a piece of literature on the first reading. Be prepared to go back and reread key sections, or even a whole work, if doing so could help with your understanding.

rereading helps w understanding

CRITICAL READING

The sort of reading that works best with imaginative literature—or any other complex writing—is sometimes called "active reading" or "critical reading," though *critical* here implies not fault-finding but rather thoughtful consideration. Much of the reading we do in everyday life is passive and noncritical. We glance at street signs to see where we are; we check a sports Web site to find out how our favorite team is doing; we read packages for information about the products we use. And in general, we take in all this information passively, without questioning it or looking for deeper meaning. For many kinds of reading, this is perfectly appropriate. It would hardly make sense to ask, "*Why* is this Pine Street?" or "What do they *mean* when they say there are twelve ounces of soda in this can?" There is, however, another type of reading, one that involves asking critical questions and probing more deeply into the meaning of what we read, and this is the kind of reading most appropriate to imaginative literature (especially if we intend to discuss or write about that literature later).

THE MYTH OF "HIDDEN MEANING"

There is a persistent myth in literature classes that the purpose of reading is to scour a text for "hidden meaning." Do not be taken in by this myth. In fact, many instructors dislike the phrase *hidden meaning*, which has unpleasant and inaccurate connotations. First, it suggests a sort of willful subterfuge on the part of the author, a deliberate attempt to make his or her work difficult to understand or to exclude the reader. Second, it makes the process of reading sound like digging for buried treasure rather than a systematic intellectual process. Finally, the phrase implies that a text has a single, true meaning and that communication and understanding move in one direction only: from the crafty author to the searching reader.

In truth, the meanings in literary texts are not hidden, and your job as a reader is not to root around for them. Rather, if a text is not immediately accessible to you, it is because you need to read more actively, and meaning will then emerge in a collaborative effort as you work *with* the text to create a consistent interpretation. (This is the basis of reader-response criticism, which is explained on pages 1355–56.) Obviously, active reading requires effort. If you find this sort of reading hard, take that as a good sign. It means you're paying the sort of attention that a well-crafted poem, story, or play requires of a reader. You also should not assume that English teachers have a key that allows them to unlock the one secret truth of a text. If, as is often the case, your instructor sees more or different meanings in a piece of literature than you do, this is because he or she is trained to read actively and has probably spent much more time than you have with literature in general and more time with the particular text assigned to you.

ACTIVE READING

Annotating

If the first suggestions for active reading are to slow down and to know that a second (or even a third) reading is in order, the next suggestion is to read with a pen or pencil in hand in order to annotate your text and take notes. If you look inside a literature textbook belonging to your instructor or to an advanced literature student, chances are you'll see something of a mess—words and passages circled or underlined, comments and questions scrawled in the margins (technically called *marginalia*), and unexplained punctuation marks or other symbols decorating the pages. You should not interpret this as disrespect for the text or author or as a sign of a disordered mind. It is simply textual annotation, and it means that someone has been engaged in active reading. Perhaps an extreme example is the poet and critic Samuel Taylor Coleridge, who was famous for annotating not only his own books but also those he borrowed from friends—a habit unlikely to secure a friendship—and his marginalia actually make up one entire volume of his collected works.

If you are not accustomed to textual annotation, it may be hard to know where to begin. There is no single, widely used system of annotation, and you will almost certainly begin to develop your own techniques as you practice active reading. Here, however, are a few tips to get you started:

- **Underline, circle, or otherwise highlight passages that strike you as particularly important.** These may be anything from single words to whole paragraphs—but stick to those points in the text that really stand out, the briefer and more specific, the better. Don't worry that you need to find *the* most crucial parts of a poem, play, or story. Everyone sees things a little differently, so just note what makes an impression on *you*.

- **Make notes in the margins as to *why* certain points strike you.** Don't just underline; jot down at least a word or two in the margin to remind yourself what you were thinking when you chose to highlight a particular point. It may seem obvious to you at the moment, but when you return to the text in two weeks to write your paper, you may not remember.

- **Ask questions of the text.** Perhaps the most important aspect of active reading is the practice of asking critical questions of a text. Nobody—not even the most experienced literary critic—understands everything about a literary text immediately, and noting where you are confused or doubtful is an important first step toward resolving any confusion. Types of questions are discussed a little later in this chapter, but for now just remember that any point of confusion is fair game, from character motivation (*"Why would she do that?"*), to cultural or historical references (*"Where is Xanadu?"*), to the definitions of individual words (*"Meaning?"*). Most likely, you will eventually want to propose some possible answers, but on a first reading of the text it's enough to note that you have questions.

- **Talk back to the text.** Occasionally, something in a literary text may strike you as suspicious, offensive, or just plain wrong. Just because a story, poem, or play appears in a textbook does not mean that its author is above criticism. Try to keep an open mind and realize that there may be an explanation that would satisfy your criticism, but if you think an author has made a misstep, don't be afraid to make note of your opinion.

- **Look for unusual features of language.** In creating a mood and making a point, literary works rely much more heavily than do purely informational texts on features of language such as **style** and imagery. As a reader of literature, then, you need to heighten your awareness of style. Look for patterns of images, repeated words or phrases, and any other unusual stylistic features—right down to idiosyncratic grammar or punctuation—and make note of them in your marginalia.

- **Develop your own system of shorthand.** Annotating a text, while it obviously takes time, shouldn't become a burden or slow your reading too much, so keep your notes and questions short and to the point. Sometimes all you need is an exclamation point to indicate an important passage. An underlined term combined with a question mark in the margin can remind you that you didn't immediately understand what a word meant. Be creative, but try also to be consistent, so you'll know later what you meant by a particular symbol or comment.

Student Jarrad Nunes was assigned to read Emily Dickinson's poem "Because I could not stop for Death." Here are some of the annotations he made as he read the poem:

EMILY DICKINSON   [1830–1886]

Because I could not stop for Death

Because I could not stop for Death—
He kindly stopped for me—
The Carriage held but just Ourselves—
And Immortality.

Death personifie
kind; not the grim reap

a driver that drives t
speaker and Immortali

We slowly drove—He knew no haste
And I had put away
My labor and my leisure too,
For His Civility—

Strange punctuatio
esp. all the dashes.

We passed the School, where Children strove
At Recess—in the Ring—
We passed the Fields of Gazing Grain—
We passed the Setting Sun—

Most nouns capitalized. Wh

How does grain "gaze

Or rather—He passed Us—
The Dews drew quivering and chill—
For only Gossamer, my Gown—
My Tippet—only Tulle—

Who is "he"? The Su

Repeated sounds — dew
drew, etc.

We paused before a House that seemed
A Swelling of the Ground—
The Roof was scarcely visible—
The Cornice—in the Ground—

This "house" seems like a gra

cornice = horizontal projectic
from a wall (Dictionary.com)

Since then—'tis Centuries—and yet
Feels shorter than the Day
I first surmised the Horses' Heads
Were toward Eternity—

Eternity and Immortality, bu
no reference to God or religic
Ends with a dash, not a period. Not a final ending

[*c. 1863;* 1890]

Jarrad's annotations cover everything from major points of content, like the personification of the character Death and the absence of overt religiosity, to small notations on style. He asks lots of questions and sometimes provides tentative answers. Having annotated the poem in this way, he was ready to participate in discussions both in the classroom and online, and later he had some good starting notes when he decided to write a paper on the poem.

Note Taking

It's a good idea, especially if you are reading a difficult text or one about which you expect to be writing, to keep a notebook handy as you read, a place to make notes that would be too long or complex to fit in the margins. What should these notes contain? Essentially, they should be more extensive versions of your marginalia. Note any unusual repetitions or juxtapositions, as well as anything that surprises you or frustrates your expectations as you read. Note passages that seem particularly crucial, or particularly confusing (using page numbers, and perhaps placing an asterisk or other symbol in the margins), and write a few sentences explaining why these stood out for you. Ask plenty of questions, as explained later in this chapter.

You might want to use the same notebook that you keep with you in class so that you can make reference to your class notes while reading at home and bring the insights from your reading to your class discussions. In class, write down any information your instructor writes on the board or projects using PowerPoint or other presentation software. If he or she thought it was important enough to write down, you probably should too. Your class notes should include new terminology or vocabulary, as well as any point the instructor repeats more than once or twice. Also take note of comments by your classmates that seem especially salient to your evolving understanding of the literature, particularly points you disagree with or would not have thought of on your own. Just be sure to distinguish which ideas in your notes are yours and which you read or heard from someone else. It may be obvious to you now, but can you guarantee that a month from now, when you're writing a paper, you'll remember who produced that gem of insight?

Remember that the best note takers are not necessarily those who have amassed the most pages of notes at the end of the term. Good notes need not be well-reasoned paragraphs or even complete sentences. In fact, they seldom are. The key to taking good notes is to take them quickly, with minimal interruption to your reading or participation in a discussion. As with annotating texts, try to develop your own shorthand for note taking. Just be sure that you write enough to jog your memory when you return to the notes days, weeks, or even months later. Try to be consistent in what and how you abbreviate. One specific piece of advice, though, it's a good idea to jot down page numbers in your notes, referring to the specific lines or passages under discussion. That way, you'll have no problem matching up the notes with the texts to which they refer.

Journal Keeping

You may be assigned to keep a reading journal for your class. Of course, you should follow your instructor's guidelines, but if you aren't sure what to write in a reading journal, think of it as a place to go a step further than you do in your annotations and notes. Try out possible answers, preferably several different ones, to the questions you have raised. Expand your ideas from single phrases and sentences into entire paragraphs, and see how they hold up under this deeper probing. Although a reading journal is substantially different from a personal journal or diary, it can at times contain reflections on any connections you make between a piece of literature and your own life and ideas. Some instructors ask students to respond to their readings with Web resources, including discussion boards, e-mail messages, or blog entries. These platforms allow you to build an archive of your responses so that you can easily return to them when you begin writing a draft of your paper; in addition, you can respond to other students as they develop their ideas. Here is an example of a Blackboard discussion board response to "Because I could not stop for Death":

Forum: Because I could not stop for Death
Date: 10 Feb 2015 22:15
Author: Nunes, Jarrad
Subject: Hymn Meter

We read some Emily Dickinson poems in high school, and I remember my teacher saying that Emily Dickinson wrote all her poems in "hymnal stanzas," which are the typical meter used in hymns. My teacher used "Amazing Grace" as an example of a hymn in this style. "Because I could not stop for Death" follows this meter exactly, except in the first two lines of stanza 4, which reverses the scheme. According to Britannica Online, Dickinson was raised in a religious family, but she herself had a lot of questions and doubts about Christianity. It's notable that in this poem she never mentions God or associates death with heaven the way you might expect from a Christian.

Is this maybe a sign of her religious doubts? She must have grown up singing hymns and associating that particular rhythm with church. I wonder why
someone who was skeptical about religion would write her poems in a form
that is so strongly associated with the church.

In this brief response, the student explores questions about both form
and content. He connects his reading of the poem with insights
gleaned from both previous experience in high school and some online
research.

This kind of response will serve Jarrad well when it's time to generate
a thesis for his paper on the subject. Even if your instructor doesn't
require online forum participation or a journal for your class, many
students find keeping a journal a useful tool for getting more out of their
reading, not to mention a wealth of material to draw from when they sit
down to write a paper.

Using Reference Materials

Many students are reluctant to use the dictionary or encyclopedia while
reading, thinking they should be able to figure out the meanings of words
from their context and not wanting to interrupt their reading. But the
simple truth is that not all words are definable from context alone, and
you'll get much more out of your reading if you are willing to make the
small effort involved in looking up unfamiliar words. If you are reading
John Donne's "A Valediction: Forbidding Mourning" (page 431) and you
don't know what the word *valediction* means, you obviously start at a big
disadvantage. A quick look in a dictionary would tell you that a valediction is a speech given at a time of parting (like the one a *valedictorian*
gives at a graduation ceremony). Armed with that simple piece of information, you begin your reading of Donne's poem already knowing that it
is about leaving someone or something, and understanding the poem
becomes much simpler. Notice that the annotations for the Dickinson
poem earlier in the chapter include a definition of *cornice*.

An encyclopedia like *Britannica Online* (an online subscription service
available at most university libraries) can also be a useful tool. If, as
you're reading Dickinson's poem, you want to read her biography, *Britannica Online* can provide biographical and cultural context for her life and
work. Or, if you want to learn more about the meter of the poem, you
could look up "hymnal stanza" to develop an understanding of its use, or
"personification" to understand how the poet makes characters out of
Death and Immortality. *Britannica Online* often provides a bibliography
for further reading, so it can be a good place to start your research.

ASKING CRITICAL QUESTIONS OF LITERATURE

As mentioned, one important part of active, critical reading is asking questions. If you are reading well, your textual annotations and notes will probably be full of questions. Some of these might be simple inquiries of fact, the sort of thing that can be answered by asking your instructor or by doing some quick research. But ideally, many of your questions will be more complex and meaty than that, the sort of probing queries that may have multiple, complex, or even contradictory answers. These are the questions that will provoke you and your classmates to think still more critically about the literature you read. You need not worry—at least not at first—about finding answers to all of your questions. As you work more with the text, discussing it with your instructor and classmates, writing about it, and reading other related stories, poems, and plays, you will begin to respond to the most important of the issues you've raised. And even if you never form a satisfactory answer to some questions, they will have served their purpose if they have made you think.

Questions about literature fall into one of four categories—questions about the text, about the author, about the cultural context of the work, and about the reader. We'll discuss each of these in the next few pages.

Questions about the Text

Questions about a text focus on issues such as **genre**, **structure**, language, and style. Queries regarding the text can sometimes, though not always, be answered with a deeper examination of the story, poem, or play at hand. You might ask about the presence of certain images—or about their absence, if you have reason to expect them and find that they are not there. Sometimes authors juxtapose images or language in startling or unexpected ways, and you might ask about the purpose and effect of such **juxtaposition**. You might wonder about the meanings of specific words in the context of the work. (This is especially true with older works of literature, as meanings evolve and change over time, and a word you know today might have had a very different definition in the past.) When looking at a poem, you might inquire about the purpose and effect of sound, rhythm, rhyme, and so forth.

Your previous experiences are a big help here, including both your experiences of reading literature and your experiences in everyday life. You know from personal experience how you expect people to think and act in certain situations, and you can compare these expectations to the literature. What might motivate the characters or persons to think and act as they do? Your previous reading has likewise set up expectations for you. How does the text fulfill or frustrate these expectations? What other literature does this remind you of? What images seem arresting or unexpected? Where do the words seem particularly powerful, strange, or otherwise noteworthy?

Notice some of the questions one reader asked in his annotations upon first reading Ben Jonson's "On My First Son."

BEN JONSON   [1572–1637]

On My First Son

Farewell, thou child of my right hand, and joy;
My sin was too much hope of thee, loved boy:
Seven years thou' wert lent to me, and I thee pay,
Exacted by thy fate, on the just day.
O could I lose all father now! for why
Will man lament the state he should envy,
To have so soon 'scaped world's and flesh's rage,
And, if no other misery, yet age?
Rest in soft peace, and asked, say, "Here doth lie
Ben Jonson his best piece of poetry."
For whose sake henceforth all his vows be such
As what he loves may never like too much.

Why is hope for his child a "sin"?

The rhyme in ll. 1–2 aligns "joy" with "boy."

Why does the speaker treat the son like a bank transaction?

The word just has two meanings: exact and fair. Which does the poet mean?

What does he mean by this line? (confusing)

Here the poem works as a kind of epitaph on a tombstone. Is it actually the boy's epitaph?

The questions the student asks of the poem are, for the most part, substantial and difficult, and they will require a good deal of thinking and interpretation to get to an answer. These are the sorts of questions that prompt good discussions and good writing.

Questions about the Author

When thinking about the connection between authors and the works they produce, two contradictory impulses come into play. One is the desire to ignore the biography of the author entirely and focus solely on the work at hand, and the other is to look closely at an author's life to see what might have led him or her to write a particular poem, story, or play. It is easy to understand the first impulse. After all, we are not likely to be able to ask an author what is meant by a certain line in a play or whether an image in a story is supposed to be read symbolically. The work of literature is what we have before us, and it should stand or fall on its own merits. This was, in fact, one of the principal tenets of **New Criticism**, a method of interpretation that dominated literary criticism for much of the twentieth century and is discussed on pages 1348–49.

We cannot deny, however, that a writer's life does affect that writer's expression. An author's age, gender, religious beliefs, family structure, and many other factors have an impact on everything from topic choice to word choice. Therefore, it is sometimes appropriate to ask questions about an author as we try to come to a better understanding of a piece of literature. It is crucial, however, that we remember that not everything an author writes is to be taken at surface value. For instance, if the narrator or principal character of a story is beaten or neglected by his parents, we should not jump to the conclusion that the author was an abused child. And if this character then goes on to justify his own actions by pointing to the abuse, we should also not assume that the author endorses this justification. In other words, we must distinguish between narrative voice and the actual author as well as between what is written and what is meant.

This separation of biography and narrative is relatively easy with stories and plays that we know to be fiction; just because a character says something doesn't necessarily mean the author believes it. Poetry is a little trickier, though, because it has the reputation of being straight from the heart. Not all poetry, however, is an accurate representation of the author's thoughts or beliefs. To give just two examples, T. S. Eliot's "The Love Song of J. Alfred Prufrock" (pages 516–20) voices the thoughts of the fictional Prufrock, not of Eliot himself, and many of the poems of Robert Browning are **dramatic monologues**, delivered by speakers very different from Browning himself, including murderous noblemen and corrupt clergy. (An example of such a monologue is "My Last Duchess" on pages 468–70.)

Questions about the Cultural Context

We are all creatures of a particular time and place, and nobody, no matter how unique and iconoclastic, is immune to the subtle and pervasive force of social history. Many appropriate questions about literature, then, involve the **cultural context** of the work. What was going on in history at the time a piece of literature was written? Were there wars or other forms of social disruption? What was the standard of living for most people in the author's society? What was day-to-day life like? What were the typical religious beliefs and traditions? How was society organized in terms of power relations, work expectations, and educational possibilities? How about typical family structure? Did extended families live together? What were the expected gender roles inside (and outside) the family? All of these issues, and many more besides, have an impact on how authors see the world and how they respond to it in their writing.

As you read and ask questions of literature, you have another cultural context to be concerned with: your own. How does being a resident of twenty-first-century America affect your reading and understanding? We are every bit as influenced by issues of history, culture, and lifestyle as were authors and readers of the past, but it is harder for us to see this, since the dominant way of living tends to seem "natural" or even "universal." Indeed, one of the great benefits of reading literature is that it teaches us about history and helps us understand and appreciate diverse cultures, not the least of which is our own.

In asking and answering the following questions about Ben Jonson's culture (seventeenth-century England), an attentive reader of "On My First Son" will also note features of our own present-day society, in which childhood death is relatively rare, family roles may be different, and religious attitudes and beliefs are considerably more diverse.

- How common was childhood death in the seventeenth century? What was the life expectancy?
- Typically, how involved were fathers in young children's lives at the time?
- Is the quotation in the poem (lines 9–10) the boy's epitaph?
- How difficult was life then? What exactly does Jonson mean by the "world's and flesh's rage"?
- How common was poetry on this topic? How "original" was Jonson's poem?
- What attitudes about God and heaven were common then? What was the conception of sin?

Questions about the Reader

Except in the case of private diaries, all writing is intended to be read by somebody, and an intended audience can have a big influence on the composition of the writing in question. Think about the differences in tone and structure between a text message you send to a friend and a paper you write for a course, and you'll get some idea of the impact of intended audience on a piece of writing. It is therefore worth considering a work's originally intended readers as you seek to understand a piece more fully. Who were these intended readers? Were they actually the people who read the literature when it was first published? How are readers' expectations fulfilled or disappointed by the structure and content of the literature? How did the original readers react? Was the work widely popular, or did only certain readers enjoy it? Did it have detractors as well? Was there any controversy over the work?

Of course, in addition to the original readers of any work of literature, there are also contemporary readers, including yourself. It is often said that great literature stands the test of time and can cross cultures to speak to many different sorts of people, but your reaction to a work may be very different from that of its original audience, especially if you are far removed from the work by time or culture. In earlier centuries in Europe and America, nearly all educated people were very familiar with the Bible and with stories and myths from Greek and Roman antiquity. Writers, therefore, could assume such knowledge on the part of their readers and make liberal reference in their work to stories and characters from these sources. Today many readers are less familiar with these sources, and we often need the help of footnotes or other study aids to understand such references. So what might have been enjoyable and enlightening for the original readers of a work might sometimes be tedious or frustrating for later readers. If we are to read a work critically, we must keep both past and present audiences in mind.

The first three of the following questions deal with the original audience of "On My First Son," while the final two compare this audience and a contemporary one.

- If childhood death was common in the seventeenth century, how would Jonson's readers have related to the subject of his poem?
- Did Jonson write this for wide circulation, or was it meant just for family and friends?
- Where was the poem first published, and who was likely to read it?
- Do readers with children of their own read the poem differently? Would I?
- Now that childhood death is fairly uncommon, do we take this poem more seriously than past readers? Or less seriously?

Looking over these questions about Jonson's poem—about the text, the author, the cultural context, and the reader—you will note that there are many differences among them. Some can be answered with a simple yes or no (*Is the quotation the boy's epitaph?*), while others require much more complex responses (*What was the conception of sin in Jonson's time?*). Others are matters of conjecture, opinion, or interpretation (*Do contemporary readers take this poem more seriously?*). Some can be answered simply by rereading and considering (*How can a child's death ever be considered fair?*), while others require discussion (*Do readers with children respond to the poem differently?*) or research (*Where was the poem first published?*).

For some inquiries, you may have tentative answers, as did the reader who asked these questions when she proposed both God and fate as potential candidates for who "lent" the child to the father. Others you won't be able to answer at first. If you are genuinely curious about any of them, do a little informal research to begin formulating answers. Some basic information can be found in the brief biographies or notes about authors that appear in most textbooks. There you could learn, for instance, the dates of Jonson's birth and death and some basic facts about his life and family. A quick look at a reputable reference work or Web site could provide still more valuable background information, like the fact that Jonson also lost his first daughter and that he wrote a poem about her death as well.

CHECKLIST FOR GOOD READING

Questions to ask as you read and think about literary texts:

- ☐ Have you *slowed down* and *reread* complex passages several times?
- ☐ Are you *looking up difficult words* in the dictionary to see if they have secondary meanings?
- ☐ Are you *annotating* the text by *underlining* key phrases? Writing questions or concerns in the *margins*?
- ☐ Are you taking your reading to the next level by asking *how* or *why* these passages are compelling to you?
- ☐ Are you marking those places in the text that make you feel uncomfortable, or present a worldview that feels strange to you?
- ☐ After you read, are you *taking notes* so that you can keep track of your ideas?
- ☐ Have you identified the genre of the text? Have you described its style and **tone**?
- ☐ Have you checked *Britannica Online* or other reference sources to learn more about the author and his or her cultural context?
- ☐ Have you reflected on your perspective as a twenty-first-century *reader*, and how that might affect your interpretation of literature from another time period?

Having simply formulated some questions, you've already gone a long way toward understanding and interpreting a poem or other work of literature. If you bring such a list of questions with you to class, you will be more than ready to contribute to the discussion, and when the time comes to write an essay, you will have a rich mine of source material from which to draw.

CHAPTER 3

The Writing Process

Experts often divide the writing process into three major components: prewriting, drafting, and revision (which includes editing). Bear in mind, though, that the process for most people is not as linear as this suggests, and the three components don't always happen in a straightforward fashion. For instance, you might begin revising a partial draft before completing the drafting process. Or you may find yourself stuck at a fairly late point in the draft and decide to revisit your prewriting. Don't think that these three steps need to be completed one at a time. Different projects will likely call for different strategies, and you'll enjoy the process more if you allow yourself to go back and forth between the steps according to the needs of the particular assignment you're trying to complete.

PREWRITING

Prewriting is everything that you do before beginning an actual draft of your paper. It includes annotating and questioning texts, taking notes and participating in class, and discussing the assignment with your instructor and/or classmates. It also includes specific topics covered in this chapter: choosing a topic, developing an argument and a thesis, gathering support, and proposing an organizational strategy for the paper.

Choosing a Topic

Obviously, your choice of a topic for your paper is of key importance, since everything else follows from that first decision. Your instructor may assign a specific topic, or the choice may be left to you. The most important piece of advice for choosing a topic is to write about something that genuinely interests you. If your instructor gives your class a choice, chances are that he or she really wants to see a variety of topics and approaches and expects you to find a topic that works for *you*.

You'll write a better paper if your topic is something of genuine interest to you. A bored or uncertain writer usually writes a boring or unconvincing paper. On the other hand, if you care about your topic, your enthusiasm will show in the writing, and the paper will be far more successful.

Even if your instructor assigns a fairly specific topic, you still need to spend a little time thinking about and working with it. You want your paper to stand out from the rest, and you should do whatever you can to make the assignment your own. When you receive an assignment, give some thought as to how it might relate to your own interests and how you might call upon your background and knowledge to approach the topic in fresh and interesting ways.

Finally, if you've put in some thought and effort but still don't know what to write about, remember that you do not need to go it alone. Seek out guidance and help. Talk with other students in your class and see what they have decided to write about; although of course you don't want simply to copy someone else's topic, hearing what others think can often spark a fresh idea. And don't forget your instructor. Most teachers are more than happy to spend a little time helping you come up with a topic and an approach that will help you write a good paper.

Developing an Argument

With the possible exception of a *summary* (a brief recap of a text's most important points), all writing about literature is to some degree a form of argument. Before proceeding, though, let's dispel some of the negative connotations of the word *argument*. In everyday usage, this term can connote a heated verbal fight, and it suggests two (or more) people growing angry and, often, becoming less articulate and more abusive as time passes. It suggests combat and implies that the other party in the process is an opponent. In this sort of argument, there are winners and losers.

Clearly this is not what we have in mind when we say you will be writing argumentatively about literature. Used in a different, more traditional sense, argument refers to a writer's or speaker's attempt to establish the validity of a given position. In other words, when you write a paper, you work to convince your reader that what you are saying is valid and persuasive. The reader is not the enemy, not someone whose ideas are to be crushed and refuted, but rather a person whose thoughts and feelings you have a chance to affect. You are not arguing *against* your reader; rather, you are using your argumentative abilities to *help* your reader see the logic and value of your position.

THE THESIS

To begin writing a literary argument, then, you must take a position and have a point to make. This principal point will be the *thesis* of your paper. It is important to distinguish between a topic and a thesis: your topic is the issue or area upon which you will focus your attention, and your thesis is a statement *about* this topic.

Here is an example of a topic for Emily Dickinson's "Because I could not stop for Death" from a student journal:

> Topic: I am interested in how Dickinson portrays the character of Death.

Here is an example of a thesis statement for a paper on this topic:

> Thesis: "Because I could not stop for Death" challenges preconceptions that Dickinson's contemporaries had about death, and in doing so it makes us challenge ours as well.

It might help to phrase your thesis as a complete sentence in which the topic is the subject, followed by a predicate that makes a firm statement or claim regarding your topic. This is your **thesis statement**, and it will probably appear toward the beginning of your paper. The foremost purpose of a paper, then, is to explain, defend, and ultimately prove the truth of its thesis.

Keep the following guidelines in mind as you think about a tentative thesis for your paper:

- **Your thesis should be both clear and specific.** The purpose of a thesis is to serve as a guide to both the reader and the writer, so it needs to be understandable and to point clearly to the specific aspects of the literature that you will discuss. This does not mean it will stand alone or need no further development or explanation — after all, that's what the rest of the paper is for. But a reader who is familiar with the story, poem, or play you are writing about (and it is fair to assume a basic familiarity) should have a good sense of what your thesis means and how it relates to the literature.

- **Your thesis should be relevant.** The claim you make should not only interest you as a writer but also give your reader a reason to keep reading by sparking his or her interest and desire to know more. Not every paper is going to change lives or minds, of course, but you should at least state your thesis in such a way that your reader won't have the most dreaded of responses: "Who cares?"

- **Your thesis should be debatable.** Since the purpose of an argumentative paper is to convince a reader that your thesis is correct (or at least that it has merit), it cannot simply be an irrefutable fact. A good thesis will be something that a reasonable person, having read the literature, might disagree with or might not have considered at all. It should give you something to prove.

- **Your thesis should be original.** Again, originality does not imply that every thesis you write must be a brilliant gem that nobody but you could have discovered. But it should be something you have thought about independently, and it should avoid clichés, contain something of you, and do more than parrot back something said in your class or written in your textbook.

- **You should be able to state your thesis as a complete sentence.** This sentence, generally referred to as the *thesis statement*, should first identify your topic and then make a claim about it. (Occasionally, especially for longer papers with more complex ideas behind them, you will need more than one sentence to state your thesis clearly. Even in these cases, though, the complete thesis must both identify the topic and make a claim about it.)

- **Your thesis should be stated in strong, unambiguous language.** Avoid thesis statements that begin, "In this paper, I will prove. . . ." If you have a point to prove, just prove it. Keep the reader's attention on the topic, not on your paper. For similar reasons, avoid phrases like "in my opinion . . ." or "I think. . . ." It is assumed that the paper is made up of your thoughts and opinions, and language like this turns the reader's focus to your thought process rather than the topic at hand.

- **Your thesis should be appropriate to the assignment.** This may seem obvious, but as we work with literature, taking notes, asking questions, and beginning to think about topics and theses, it is possible to lose sight of the assignment as it was presented. After you have come up with a tentative thesis, it's a good idea to go back and review the assignment as your instructor gave it, making sure your paper will fulfill its requirements.

Let us take a look at how two students arrived at strong, workable theses for their papers. Jarrad Nunes knew that he wanted to write about how Emily Dickinson dealt with the theme of death in her poetry. His first attempt at a thesis, however, was far too weak and general:

> Emily Dickinson's poems about death are some of the most interesting ever written.

This is not so much a thesis statement as an assertion of personal preference and opinion. All we know from reading it is that Jarrad likes

Dickinson's death poems. He needs a thesis that is both more specific and more controversial:

> Dickinson's poems look at death in unconventional ways.

This version is better because it makes an assertion that can be defended, but it is still far too general. Here is the final version of Jarrad's thesis:

> "Because I could not stop for Death" challenges preconceptions that Dickinson's contemporaries had about death, and in doing so it makes us challenge ours as well.

Here we have a much stronger thesis. It limits the paper's scope by focusing on a single poem, it makes an assertion to defend (that Dickinson challenged nineteenth-century preconceptions about death), and it shows why this point is significant to a reader (because we too might have our preconceptions challenged).

Here is one more example of the process of refining and developing a thesis. When she first decided to write about the male characters in two nineteenth-century stories, Melanie Smith came up with the following:

> The husbands in the stories "The Yellow Wallpaper" by Charlotte Perkins Gilman and "The Story of an Hour" by Kate Chopin are very controlling of their wives.

This is not an adequate thesis because it is simply a statement of fact, something that will be immediately obvious to anyone who has read the stories. It left Melanie with nothing to defend, no point to prove, so she gave it a little more thought and refined her tentative thesis:

> Though the husbands in "The Yellow Wallpaper" and "The Story of an Hour" are controlling, they are not really as bad as they first appear.

At this point, the writer is definitely moving in the right direction. This version shows that she has a particular interpretation and a point to make, one that is not necessarily shared by everyone who reads the stories. However, it still doesn't give a reader much guidance about what to expect in the paper. In the end, Melanie needed two sentences to get her thesis right:

> By modern standards, the husbands of the two protagonists, particularly John in "The Yellow Wallpaper," seem almost unbearably controlling of their wives. From the vantage point of the late nineteenth century, however, their behavior looks quite different.

This version is much clearer and more precise. After reading this thesis, we are much more focused and have a good sense of what to expect in the paper as a whole.

You will note that in this discussion the phrase *tentative thesis* has come up several times. The word *tentative* is important. As you start to gather support and to write your paper, your thesis will help you focus clearly on your task and sort out which of your ideas, observations, and questions are relevant to the project at hand. But you should keep an open mind as well, realizing that your thesis is likely to evolve as you write. You are likely to change the focus in subtle or not so subtle ways, and you might even change your mind completely as you write and therefore need to create a new thesis from scratch. If this happens, don't regard it as a failure. On the contrary, it means you have succeeded in learning something genuine from the experience of writing, and that is what a literature class is all about.

Gathering Support for Your Thesis

Once you have crafted a tentative thesis, it is time to think about the evidence or support you will need to convince your reader of the claim's validity. But what exactly counts as support? What can you include in your paper as evidence that your thesis is true? Essentially, all support comes from one of three sources:

- **The text itself is the most obvious source of support.** It is not enough to *say* that a certain piece of literature says or means a certain thing. You will need to *show* this by summarizing, paraphrasing, or quoting the literature itself.

- **Other people's ideas are a good source of support.** Chances are you will find a lot of useful material for your paper if you pay attention to easily available sources of ideas from other readers. These include the notes and biographical information in your textbooks, research conducted online or in the library, lectures and discussions in class, and even informal conversations about the literature with your friends and classmates.

- **Your own thoughts are your most important source of support.** Remember that although you may want to integrate ideas and information from a variety of sources, your paper is yours and as such should reflect *your* thinking. The most indispensable source of material for your paper is your own mind; your own thoughts and words should always carry the heaviest weight in any paper you write.

One of the best ways to gather supporting ideas for your paper is **brainstorming.** You can brainstorm—alone or with classmates—even before settling on your topic and thesis, to explore the many possible threads that you could follow in your writing. When brainstorming to gather evidence, the idea is to write down, very quickly, every idea that comes to you, every possible idea that might be included in the draft of your paper. Don't censor yourself during this process. Allow yourself to write down everything that interests, puzzles, or delights you. Later you will have ample opportunity to prune your list of repetitions, tangents, or weaker ideas. For the time being, just let the ideas flow, and get as many as you can down on a piece of paper or as you can down in your notes.

At this stage, use every resource available to you to find support for your thesis. What lines in the poem, short story, or play reinforce your claims? Have you looked up words in the dictionary? Have you checked difficult concepts in a respectable encyclopedia or other reference? Have you asked your teacher for further reading suggestions? Have you read articles or book chapters that are appropriate to your topic, and are you formulating your responses to them? Treat ideas from outside sources much as you would your own brainstorming: don't censor too soon. When the time comes to organize and draft your paper, it's far better to have too many ideas and have to eliminate some than to have too few and have to root around for more.

ORGANIZING YOUR PAPER

Once you've determined what evidence to use, it is time to begin sorting and organizing it. The organizing principle for any paper is the sequence of paragraphs, so at this stage you should be thinking at the level of paragraph content. Remember that each paragraph should contain one main idea and sufficient evidence and explanation to support that idea. When added together, these paragraph-level ideas lead a reader to your paper's ultimate point—your thesis. So the first stage of organizing the content of your essay is to cluster together similar ideas in order to begin shaping the substance of individual paragraphs. The second stage is to determine the order in which these paragraphs will appear.

As you write and revise your paper, you may have different ideas about how to structure it. You may want to put the topic sentence somewhere other than at the beginning of a paragraph, or perhaps the topic is so clear that no specific topic sentence is even needed. You may devise a more interesting way to structure your introduction or conclusion. (Some additional, more specific thoughts for those tricky introductory and concluding paragraphs follow.) Unless your instructor has specified

1276 READING AND WRITING ABOUT LITERATURE

the form in which your paper is to be organized, you should feel free to experiment a bit.

For most writers, creating some version of an outline is the best way to approach the task of organizing evidence into a logical sequence for a paper. In the past, you may have been asked to write a formal outline, complete with roman numerals and capital letters. If this technique has been helpful in organizing your thoughts, by all means continue to use it. For many writers, however, an informal outline works just as well and is less cumbersome. To construct an informal outline, simply jot down a heading that summarizes the topic of each paragraph you intend to write. Then cluster your gathered evidence—quotations or paraphrases from the literature, ideas for analysis, and so on—into groups under the headings.

The following is an example of an informal outline for a paper on Shakespeare's Sonnet 116. (The full paper appears on page 427.) In this outline, the student focuses on the positive and negative language in the poem and how it results in a more interesting definition of love than he had seen in other love poems.

Introduction
    Two kinds of typical love poems: happy and sad
    Sonnet 116 is more complex and interesting
    Tentative thesis: By including both negative and positive images and
        language, this sonnet gives a complex and realistic definition of love.

Vivid images in poem
    Positive/expected: "star," "ever-fixèd mark," "rosy lips and cheeks"
    Negative/unexpected: "sickle" (deathlike), "wandering bark" (lost
        boat), "tempests"

Negative language
    Words/phrases: "Let me not," "Love is not," "never," "nor," "no," etc.
    Abstractions: "alteration," "impediments," "error"

Conclusion
    Love never changes
    Shakespeare's definition still works some 400 years later

Obviously, this is not a formal outline. It does, however, group similar items and ideas together, and it gives the writer a basic structure to follow as he moves on to drafting, the next stage of the composing process.

DRAFTING THE PAPER

You have a topic. You have a tentative thesis. You have gathered evidence. You have an outline or tentative structure in mind for this evidence. It is time to begin writing your first draft. Every writer has his or her own slightly different process for getting the words down on paper. Some begin at the beginning of the paper and work straight through to the end in a clear, organized fashion. Others begin with the first body paragraph and save the introduction for later. Still others write bits and pieces of the paper out of order and allow the overall structure to emerge at a later time.

Some writers claim that they work better at the last minute and focus better under the pressure of a looming deadline. This, however, is almost always a justification for sloppy work habits, and procrastination rarely if ever results in a superior paper. When habitual procrastinators change their working methods and give themselves more time on a project, they are frequently surprised to discover that the process is more enjoyable and the final product of their efforts better than what they have produced in the past. Start early and work steadily—it will prove more than worth it.

Try to write your first draft fairly quickly. You don't need to get every sentence just right—that's what the revision phase of writing is for. What you want now is just to get as much good raw material as possible into the mix and see what works. Don't worry too much yet about style, transitions, grammar, and so forth. In fact, you don't even need to start at the beginning or work right through to the end. If you get stuck on one part, move on. You can always come back and fill in the gaps later. Introductions can be especially tricky, particularly since you haven't yet finished the essay and don't really know what it is you're introducing. Some writers find it easier to start with the body of the essay, or to write a short, sloppy introduction as a placeholder. You can go back and work on the real introduction when the draft is complete.

Introductions, Conclusions, and Transitions

Ideally, of course, all of the parts of your paper will be equally compelling and polished, but there are certain points in a paper that most often cause trouble for writers and readers, and these points may require a little additional attention on your part. The most typical trouble spots are introductory and concluding paragraphs and the transitional sentences that connect paragraphs. Although there is no one formula to help you navigate these waters, as each writing situation and each paper are different, we offer some general guidelines that can help you think through the problems that might arise in these areas.

Introductions

Essentially, an introduction accomplishes two things. First, it gives a sense of both your topic and your approach to that topic, which is why it is common to make your thesis statement a part of the introduction. Second, an introduction compels your readers' interest and makes them want to read on and find out what your paper has to say. Some common strategies used in effective introductions are to begin with a probing rhetorical question, a vivid description, or an intriguing quotation. Weak introductions tend to speak in generalities or in philosophical ideas that are only tangentially related to the real topic of your paper. Don't spin your wheels: get specific and get to the point right away.

Consider this introduction from a student essay on Susan Glaspell's *Trifles*:

> What is the relationship between legality and morality? Susan Glaspell's short play *Trifles* asks us to ponder this question, but it provides no clear answers. Part murder mystery, part battle of the sexes, the play makes its readers confront and question many issues about laws, morals, and human relationships. In the person of Mrs. Peters, a sheriff's wife, the play chronicles one woman's moral journey from a certain, unambiguous belief in the law to a more situational view of ethics. Before it is over, this once legally minded woman is even willing to cover up the truth and let someone get away with murder.

The student poses a philosophical question at the very beginning of the paper and then offers a tentative answer. (This paper appears in its entirety on pages 1309–11.)

Conclusions

Your conclusion should give your reader something new to think about, a reason not to forget your essay as soon as the reading is done. Some writers like to use the conclusion to return to an idea, a quotation, or an image first raised in the introduction, creating a satisfying feeling of completeness and self-containment.

In this example from the same student paper, note how the student offers a tentative answer in her conclusion to the question that began the essay:

> In the end, Mrs. Peters gives in to what she believes to be emotionally right rather than what is legally permissible. She collaborates with Mrs. Hale to cover up evidence of the motive and hide the dead canary. Though very little time has gone by, she has undergone a major transformation. She may be, as the county attorney says, "married to the law," but she is also divorced from her old ideals. When she tries to cover up the evidence, a stage direction says she "goes to pieces," and Mrs. Hale has to help her. By the time she pulls herself together, the new woman she is will be a very different person from the old one. She, along with the reader, is now in a world where the relationship between legality and morality is far more complex than she had ever suspected.

Some writers use the conclusion to show the implications of their claims or the connections between the literature and real life. This is your chance to make a good final impression, so don't waste it with simple summary and restatement.

Transitions

Each paragraph is built around a different idea, and the job of the transitions is to show how these separate ideas are related to one another, to make the juxtaposition of two paragraphs seem as logical to a reader as it is to the writer. When you think a transition isn't working effectively, the first question you should ask yourself is, *why* does one paragraph follow another in this particular order? Would it make more sense to change the placement of some paragraphs, or is this really the best organizational strategy for this portion of the paper? Once you know why your paper is structured as it is, transitions become much easier to write, simply making apparent to your audience the connections you already know to be there. As you begin each new paragraph, give some consideration to the links between it and the previous paragraph, and try to make those links explicit in the opening sentence.

As with any other aspect of your writing, if you've had trouble in the past with introductions, conclusions, or transitions, one of your best sources of help is to be an attentive reader of others' writing. Pay special attention to these potential trouble spots in the writing you admire, whether by a classmate or a professional author, and see how he or she navigates them. Don't stick with the writing methods that have caused you headaches in the past. Be willing to try out different strategies, seeing which ones work best for you. In time you'll find you have a whole array of ways to approach these trouble spots, and you'll be able to find a successful response to each particular writing situation.

REVISING AND EDITING

Once you have a complete, or near-complete, draft, it's time to begin thinking about revision. Try to avoid the common pitfall of thinking of revision as locating and fixing mistakes. Revision is far more than this. Looking at the parts of the word, you can see that *re-vision* means "seeing again," and indeed the revision stage of the writing process is your chance to see your draft anew and make real and substantial improvements to every facet of it, from its organization to its tone to your word choices. Most successful writers will tell you that it is in the revision stage that the real work gets done, where the writing takes shape and begins to emerge in its final form. Most professional writers spend much more time revising than they do writing the first draft. Don't skimp on this part of the process or try to race through it.

It is a good idea not to start a major revision the minute a draft is complete. Take a break. Exercise, have a meal, do something completely different to clear your mind. If possible, put the draft aside for at least a day, so that when you return to it you'll have a fresh perspective and can begin truly re-seeing it. Print out your draft. Attempting serious revision on-screen is generally a bad idea—we see differently, and we usually see more, when we read off a printed page. Read with a pen in your hand and annotate your text just the way you would a piece of literature, looking for the strengths and weaknesses of your argument. The process laid out here consists of three phases: *global revisions*, or large-scale revisions; *local revisions*, or small-scale revisions; and a final *editing and proofreading*. If you haven't done so before, revising your paper three times may seem like a lot of work, but bear in mind that most professional writers revise their work many more times than that. Revision is the real key to writing the best paper you can.

Global Revision

On a first pass at revision—the large-scale, global part of the process—don't worry too much about details like word choice, punctuation, and so forth. Too many students focus so much on these issues that they miss the big picture. The details are important, but you will deal with them in depth later. You wouldn't want to spend your time getting the wording of a sentence just right only to decide later that the paragraph it is in weakens your argument and needs to be deleted. So at first, look at the overall picture—the argument, organization, and tone of the paper as a whole. While there's nothing wrong with making a few small improvements as you read, nothing smaller than a paragraph should concern you at this point. Here are some possibilities for how you might revise your paper globally.

GLOBAL REVISION CHECKLIST

Further develop your focus and thesis.

☐ Can your reader immediately identify what the topic of the essay will be—that is, which text(s), and which aspect of the text (for example, character development or the use of particular language features), you will analyze?

☐ Have you narrowed the scope of the thesis for your reader? How could it be further narrowed? Remember, it's not enough to say "Women are portrayed differently in X and Y." What do you mean by "differently"? Get as specific as possible.

☐ Does your thesis clearly identify a claim that is debatable but valid?

☐ Has your thinking about the issues evolved as you have written? If so, how will you change the thesis statement?

☐ Have you answered the larger "So what?" question? Do you get your reader thinking beyond your paper to the question of why this argument is important?

Reorganize your paper, if necessary.

☐ Does the order of the ideas and paragraphs make immediate sense to you, or does some alternate structure suggest itself?

☐ Experiment with different organizing principles, using the cut-and-paste feature of your word processor (or even old-fashioned paper and scissors). You can always put things back if your original organization worked better.

Expand your paper with new paragraphs or with new evidence within existing paragraphs.

☐ What textual evidence have you used? Is it sufficiently provocative and persuasive? Or does it veer off into another direction?

☐ Have you successfully integrated quotations, summaries, or paraphrases into your own writing, while at the same time acknowledging your source?

GLOBAL REVISION CHECKLIST (*continued*)

Eliminate any unnecessary, contradictory, or distracting passages.

☐ Does every piece of evidence, every sentence, and every paragraph contribute to the validity of your argument? If not, eliminate extraneous discussions and save them for another project.

Clarify difficult passages with more specific explanations or evidence.

☐ Have you worked to convey why you are citing a particular passage? What *particular* details in it provide evidence that supports your interpretation? Make sure the reasons for the presence of particular evidence are explicit in your writing. Don't assume a summary or a quotation speaks for itself.

Once you have completed your first, large-scale revision, chances are you will feel more confident about the content and structure of your paper. The thesis and focus are strong, the evidence is lined up, and the major points are clear. Print out the new version, take another break if you can, and prepare to move on to the second phase of revision, the one that takes place at the local level of words, phrases, and sentences.

Local Revision

The focus here is on style and clarity. The types of changes you will make in this stage are, essentially, small-scale versions of the changes you made in the first round of revision: adding, cutting, reorganizing, and clarifying. Are you sure about the meanings of any difficult or unusual words you have used? Is there enough variety in sentence style to keep your writing interesting? Do the same words or phrases appear again and again? Are the images vivid? Are the verbs strong? One way to assess the effectiveness of a paper's style is to read it aloud and hear how it sounds. You may feel a little foolish doing this, but many people find it very helpful.

LOCAL REVISION CHECKLIST

Consider your sentences.

☐ Do you keep the writing interesting by using a variety of sentence types and sentences of different lengths?

☐ Have you perhaps used an occasional rhetorical question to get your readers thinking? (This strategy should be used in moderation. Too many questions in a paper become distracting.)

☐ Does each sentence clearly follow from the last one? Or do you need to reorganize the sentences within a particular paragraph to provide clearer transitions between sentences?

☐ Look at the first and last sentences in each paragraph. Do they provide sufficient transitions from one paragraph to the next?

Consider your word choice.

☐ Do you use the same words and phrases again and again? If so, could you vary your word choice a bit?

☐ If you use any special literary terms, are you absolutely certain that you are using these terms correctly?

☐ Take a look at the verbs. Are many of them strong and active, or do most sentences rely on dull linking verbs like *is* or *seems*?

Final Editing and Proofreading

Once you have revised your essay a second time and achieved both content and a style that please you, it's time for final editing. This is where you make it "correct."

FINAL EDITING CHECKLIST

Check your spelling.

☐ Have you spelled everything correctly? (Should it be *their* or *there*? *It's* or *its*?)

☐ Do not rely on your computer's spell-check function. This only tells you if the word you typed is a word, not if it's the correct word. When in doubt, look it up.

Check your punctuation.

☐ Look for things that have caused you trouble in the past. Should you use a comma or a semicolon? Again, when in doubt, look it up.

☐ Pay special attention to quotations. Does the question mark go inside or outside of the quotation marks? Have you used both opening and closing quotation marks for each quotation?

Check your formatting.

☐ Is your manuscript format correct? Unless your instructor has provided other instructions, follow the format described on pages 1325–40.

☐ Have you italicized or underlined titles of plays and novels (*Othello* or *The Woman Warrior*) and put the titles of short stories and poems in quotation marks ("Love in L.A.," "The Fish")?

☐ Does your works-cited list follow MLA format, and do you properly cite your quotations in the body of the text? Nobody expects you to know all the rules on your own, but you should know where to look for them.

☐ If you have questions about citation and formatting, look them up in this book or in a good dictionary, grammar handbook, or other reference.

Here is a paragraph ready for final editing from a student essay on *Hamlet*. Notice the kinds of corrections that the student will have to make before the paragraph is done.

The supernatural relm affects the revenge tragedy in other ays than the appearance and presence of ghosts. In Hamlet, the religious concern with final absolution both inflames Hamlet's esire for revenge and causes him to hesitate in carrying out venge. Not only has Hamlet's father been murdered, but he as also Cut off even in the blossoms of [his] sin, / Unhousled, sappointed, unanel'd, / No reck'ning made, but sent to [his] ccount / With all [his] imperfections on [his] head (1.5.77-80). or Hamlet's father, being murdered is doubly disastrous; not only his life cut short. But he must burn away "the foul crimes done [his] days of nature" in purgatory before he can be granted ccess to heaven (1.5.13). A normal death would have afforded m final absolution, and thus a direct route to heaven. The same ncern that makes Hamlet's father's death even more terrible also uses Hamlet to pass on a perfect opportunity to exact revenge his father's murderer. Hamlet finds Claudius praying, alone. To ll a man in prayer means to kill a man who has had all his sins solved. Hamlet observes Claudius and reasons: "A villain kills my ther, and for that, / I, his sole son, do this same villain send / heaven." (3.3.76-78) Hamlet's concern for the supernatural terlife affects his carrying out revenge.

Spelling: "realm"

Italicize "Hamlet."

Remember to add quotation marks around the direct quotation.

This should be a comma joining two sentence fragments.

This period belongs outside the parentheses, after the act, scene, and line number.

One final word of advice as you revise your paper: ask for help. Doing so is neither cheating nor an admission of defeat. In fact, professional writers do it all the time. Despite the persistent image of writers toiling in isolation, most successful writers seek advice at various stages. More important, they are willing to listen to that advice and to rethink what they have written if it seems not to be communicating what they had intended.

PEER EDITING AND WORKSHOPS

Some instructors give class time for draft workshops, sometimes called peer editing, in which you work with your fellow students, trying to help one another improve your work-in-progress. Such workshops can benefit you in two ways. First, your classmates can offer you critiques and advice on what you might have missed in your own rereading. Second, reading and discussing papers other than your own will help you grow as a writer, showing you a variety of ways in which a topic can be approached. If you really like something about a peer's paper—say, a vivid introduction or the effective use of humor—make note of how it works within the paper and consider integrating something similar into a future paper of your own. We are not, of course, advocating copying your classmates; rather, we are pointing out that you can learn a lot from other people's writing.

Some students are uncomfortable with such workshops. They may feel they don't know enough about writing to give valid advice to others, or they may doubt whether advice from their peers is particularly valuable. But you don't need to be a great literary critic, much less an expert on style or grammar, to give genuinely useful advice to a fellow writer. Whatever your skills or limitations as a writer, you have something invaluable to give: the thoughts and impressions of a real reader working through a paper. It is only when we see how a reader responds to what we've written that we know if a paper is communicating its intended message. If you are given an opportunity to engage in peer workshops, make the most of them.

Your instructor may give you guidelines regarding what to look for in others' drafts, or you may be left more or less on your own. In either case, keep these general guidelines in mind:

- **Be respectful of one another's work.** You should, of course, treat your peers' work with the same respect and seriousness that you would want for your own. Keep your criticism constructive and avoid personal attacks, even if you disagree strongly with an opinion. You can help your fellow writers by expressing a contrary opinion in a civilized and thoughtful manner.

- **Be honest.** This means giving real, constructive criticism when it is due. Don't try to spare your workshop partner's feelings by saying "That's great" or "It's fine," when it really isn't. When asked what went badly in a peer workshop, students most commonly respond *not* that their peers were too harsh on their work but that they were not harsh enough. Wouldn't you rather hear about a problem with your work from a peer in a draft workshop than from your professor after you have already handed in the final draft? So would your classmates.

- **Look for the good as well as the bad in a draft.** No paper, no matter how rough or problematic, is completely without merit. And no paper, no matter how clever or well written, couldn't be improved. By pointing out both what works and what doesn't, you will help your classmates grow as writers.

- **Keep an eye on the time.** It's easy to get wrapped up in a discussion of an interesting paper and not allow adequate time for another paper. Say you're given half an hour to work with your draft and that of one classmate. When you reach the fifteen-minute mark, move on, no matter how interesting your discussion is. Fair is fair. On the other hand, don't stop short of the allotted time. If you are reading carefully and thinking hard about one another's drafts, it should be impossible to finish early.

- **Take notes on your draft itself or on a separate sheet.** You may be certain that you will remember what was said in a workshop, but you would be amazed how often people forget the good advice they heard and intended to follow. Better safe than sorry—take careful notes.

- **Ask questions.** Asking questions about portions of a draft you don't understand or find problematic can help its writer see what needs to be clarified, expanded, or reworked. Useful questions can range from the large scale (*What is the purpose of this paragraph?*) to the small (*Is this a quote? Who said it?*).

- **Don't assume that explaining yourself to your workshop partner can replace revision.** Sometimes your workshop partners will ask a question, and when you answer it for them, they will say, "Oh, right, that makes sense," leaving you with the impression that everything is clear now. But remember, your classmates didn't understand it from the writing alone, and you won't be there to explain it to your instructor.

- **Be specific in your comments.** Vague comments like "The introduction is good" or "It's sort of confusing here" are not much help. Aim for something more like "The introduction was funny and really made me want to read on" or "This paragraph confused me because it seems to contradict what you said in the previous one." With comments like these, a writer will have a much better sense of where to focus his or her revision energies.

- **Try to focus on the big picture.** When you are reading a draft, it's tempting to zero in on distracting little mistakes in spelling, punctuation, or word choice. While it's generally fine to point out or circle such surface matters as you go along, a draft workshop is not about correcting mistakes. It's about helping one another to re-see and rethink your papers on a global scale.

- **Push your partners to help you more.** If your workshop partners seem shy or reluctant to criticize, prompt them to say more by letting them know that you really want advice and that you are able to take criticism. Point out to them what you perceive as the trouble spots in the essay, and ask if they have any ideas to help you out. It feels good, of course, to hear that someone likes your paper and cannot imagine how to improve it. But in the long run it is even better to get real, useful advice that will lead to a better paper. If your classmates are not helping you enough, it's your responsibility to ask for more criticism.

Even if your class does not include workshop time, you can still use the many resources available to you on campus. Find one or two other members of your class and conduct your own peer workshop, reading and critiquing one another's drafts. Be sure to arrange such a meeting far enough in advance of the due date so that you will have ample time to implement any good revision advice you receive. Many campuses also have writing or tutoring centers, and the tutors in these centers, often advanced students who are skilled writers, can offer a good deal of help. Remember, again, that you should make an appointment to see a tutor well in advance of the paper's due date, and you should *not* expect a tutor or mentor to revise or "fix" your paper for you. That is, ultimately, your job. And, of course, you can also approach your instructor at any phase of the writing process and ask for advice and help.

But remember, no matter where you turn for advice, the final responsibility for your paper is yours. Any advice and help you receive from classmates, tutors, friends—or even your instructor—is just that: advice and help. It is *your* paper, and *you* must be the one to make the decisions about which advice to follow and which to ignore, and how to implement changes to improve your paper. The key is to keep an open mind, seek help from all available sources, and give yourself plenty of time to turn your first draft into a final paper that makes you truly proud.

TIPS FOR WRITING ABOUT LITERATURE

Each genre of literature—fiction, poetry, and drama—poses its own, slightly different set of assumptions, opportunities, and problems for writers, which are covered in more detail in the sections that follow. However, the following general principles can help you as you write about any form of literature:

- **Don't assume that your readers will remember (or consider important) the same ideas or incidents in the literature that you do.** You should assume that your readers have *read* the literature but not necessarily that they have reacted to it the same way you have. Therefore, whenever possible, use specific examples and evidence in the form of quotations and summaries to back up your claims.

- **Do not retell the plot or text at length.** Some writers are tempted to begin with a plot summary or even to include the text of a short poem at the beginning of a paper. However, this strategy can backfire by delaying the real substance of your paper. Be discriminating when you summarize—keep quotations short and get to the point you want to make as quickly as possible.

- **Do not assume that quotations or summaries are self-sufficient and prove your point automatically.** Summaries and quotations are a starting point; you need to analyze them thoroughly in your own words, explaining why they are important. As a general rule, each quotation or summary should be followed by at least several sentences of analysis.

- **It is customary to use the present tense when writing about literature,** even if the events discussed take place in the distant past.

  When she sees that Romeo is dead, Juliet kills herself with his knife.

- **The first time you mention an author, use his or her full name.** For subsequent references, the last name is sufficient. (Do not use first names only; it sounds as if you know an author personally.)

- **Titles of poems, short stories, and essays should be put in quotation marks. Titles of books, plays, and periodicals (magazines, newspapers, etc.) should be italicized or underlined.** In titles and in all quotations, follow spelling, capitalization, and punctuation exactly as it occurs in the work itself.

- **Give your paper a title.** A title doesn't need to be elaborate or super clever, but it should give some clue as to what the paper is about and begin setting up expectations for your reader. Simply restating the assignment, such as "Essay #2" or "Comparison and Contrast Paper," is of little help to a reader and might even suggest intellectual laziness on your part. For the same reason, avoid giving your paper the same title as the work of literature you are writing about; unless you're Shakespeare or Hemingway, don't title your paper *Hamlet* or "A Clean, Well-Lighted Place."

- **Above all, use common sense and *be consistent*.**

USING QUOTATIONS EFFECTIVELY

At some point, you will want to quote the literature you are citing, and you might also want to quote some secondary research sources as well. Quotations ground your paper in the literature you are discussing and prevent your argument from being overly abstract. They also allow the author of the literature a chance to shine through in his or her own words, showing that you respect and appreciate the author's work. Quotations bring emphasis, variety, and specificity to your writing. Be selective, though, in your use of quotations so that the dominant voice of the paper is your own, not a patchwork of the words of others. Here is general advice to help you integrate quotations effectively into your essays.

Avoiding Floating Quotations

Try to avoid floating quotations. Sometimes writers simply lift a sentence out of the original, put quotation marks around it, and identify the source (if at all) in a subsequent sentence.

> "I met a traveler from an antique land." This is how Shelley's poem "Ozymandias" begins.

Doing so can create confusion for a reader, who is momentarily left to ponder where the quotation comes from and why have you quoted it. In addition to potentially causing confusion, such quoting can read as awkward and choppy, as there is no transition between another writer's words and yours.

Use at least an attributed quotation—that is, one that names the source *within* the sentence containing the quotation, usually in a lead-in phrase.

> Shelley begins his poem "Ozymandias" with the words "I met a traveler from an antique land."

This way the reader knows right away who originally wrote or said the quoted material and knows (or at least expects) that your commentary will follow. It also provides a smoother transition between your words and the quotation.

Integrating Quotations

Whenever possible, use an integrated quotation. To do this, you make the quotation a part of your own sentence.

> When the narrator of "Ozymandias" begins by saying that he "met a traveler from an antique land," we are immediately thrust into a mysterious world.

This is the hardest sort of quoting to do since it requires that you make the quoted material fit in grammatically with your own sentence, but the payoff in clarity and sharp prose is usually well worth the extra time spent on sentence revision.

Adding to or Altering a Quotation

Sometimes, especially when you are using integrated quotations effectively, you will find that you need to slightly alter the words you are quoting. You should, of course, keep quotations exact whenever possible, but occasionally the disparity between the tense, point of view, or grammar of your sentence and that of the quoted material will necessitate some alterations. Other difficulties can arise when you quote a passage that already contains a quotation or when you need to combine quotation marks with other punctuation marks. When any of these situations arise, the following guidelines should prove useful. The examples of quoted text that follow are all drawn from this original passage from *Hamlet*, in which Hamlet and his friend Horatio are watching a gravedigger unearth old skulls in a cemetery:

> HAMLET: That skull had a tongue in it, and could sing once. How the knave jowls it to the ground, as if 'twere Cain's jaw-bone, that did the first murder! This might be the pate of a politician, which this ass now o'erreaches, one that would circumvent God, might it not?
> HORATIO: It might, my lord.
> HAMLET: Or of a courtier, which could say "Good morrow, sweet lord! How dost thou, sweet lord?" This might be my Lord Such-a-one, that prais'd my Lord Such-a-one's horse when 'a meant to beg it, might it not? (5.1.70–80)

If you ever alter anything in a quotation or add words to it in order to make it clear and grammatically consistent with your own writing, you need to signal to your readers what you have added or changed. This is done by enclosing your words within square brackets in order to distinguish them from those in the source. If, for instance, you feel Hamlet's reference to the gravedigger as "this ass" is unclear, you could clarify it either by substituting your own words, as in the first example below, or by adding the identifying phrase to the original quote, as in the second example:

> Hamlet wonders if it is "the pate of a politician, which [the gravedigger] now o'erreaches" (5.1.73–74).

> Hamlet wonders if it is "the pate of a politician, which this ass [the gravedigger] now o'erreaches" (5.1.73–74).

Omitting Words from a Quotation

To keep a quotation focused and to the point, you will sometimes want to omit words, phrases, or even whole sentences that do not contribute to your point. Any omission is signaled by ellipses, or three spaced periods, with square brackets around them. (The brackets are required to distinguish your own ellipses from any that might occur in the original source.)

> Hamlet wonders if the skull "might be the pate of a politician [. . .] that would circumvent God" (5.1.73–74).

It is usually not necessary to use ellipses at the beginning of a quotation, since a reader assumes you are quoting only a relevant portion of text, but MLA style recommends using ellipses at the end of a quotation if words are dropped at the end of the final quoted sentence.

Quotations within Quotations

If you are quoting material that itself contains a quotation, the internal quotation is set off with single quotation marks rather than the standard double quotation marks that will enclose the entire quotation.

> Hamlet wonders if he might be looking at the skull "of a courtier, which could say 'Good morrow, sweet lord! How dost thou, sweet lord?'" (5.1.76–77).

When the text you're quoting contains *only* material already in quotation marks in the original, the standard double quotation marks are all you need.

> Hamlet wonders if the courtier once said "Good morrow, sweet lord! How dost thou, sweet lord?" (5.1.76–77).

Quotation Marks with Other Punctuation

When a period or a comma comes at the end of a quotation, it should always be placed inside the closing quotation marks except when the quotation is followed by a parenthetical in-text citation, as shown below. In this case the period should follow the parenthesis.

> Hamlet muses that the skull might have belonged to "my Lord Such-a-one, that prais'd my Lord Such-a-one's horse" (5.1.78–79).

In this next example, the comma following "once" is also within the quotation marks, even though in Shakespeare's original "once" is followed by a period.

> "That skull had a tongue in it, and could sing once," muses Hamlet.

Question marks and exclamation points are placed inside quotation marks if they are part of the original quotation and outside of the marks if they are part of your own sentence but not part of the passage you are quoting. In this first example, the question is Hamlet's, and so the question mark must be placed within the quotation marks.

> Hamlet asks Horatio if the skull "might be my Lord Such-a-one, that prais'd my Lord Such-a-one's horse when 'a meant to beg it, might it not?" (5.1.78–79).

In this second example, the question is the essay writer's, and so the question mark is placed outside of the quotation marks.

> Why is Hamlet so disturbed that this skull "might be the pate of a politician"? (5.1.73)

These sorts of punctuation details are notoriously hard to remember, so you should not feel discouraged if you begin forgetting such highly specialized rules moments after reading them. At least know where you can look them up, and do so when you proofread your paper. A willingness to attend to detail is what distinguishes serious students and gives writing a polished, professional appearance. Also, the more you work with quotations, the easier it will be to remember the rules.

QUOTING FROM STORIES

The guidelines that follow should be used not only when you quote from stories but also when you quote from any prose work, be it fiction or nonfiction.

Short Quotations

For short quotations of four lines or fewer, run the quotation in with your own text, using quotation marks to signal the beginning and end of the quotation.

> Young Goodman Brown notices that the branches touched by his companion "became strangely withered and dried up, as with a week's sunshine."

Long Quotations

When a quotation is longer than four lines in your text, set it off from your essay by beginning a new line and indenting it one inch from the left margin only, as shown here. This is called a block quotation.

> Young Goodman Brown then notices something strange about his companion:
>
> > As they went, he plucked a branch of maple to serve for a walking stick, and began to strip it of the twigs and little boughs, which were wet with evening dew. The moment his fingers touched them they became strangely withered and dried up, as with a week's sunshine. Thus the pair proceeded, . . . , until suddenly, . . . Goodman Brown sat himself down on the stump of a tree and refused to go any farther. (9)

Note that no quotation marks are used with block quotations. The indentation is sufficient to signal to your readers that this is a quotation.

QUOTING FROM POEMS

Short Quotations

For quotations of up to three lines, run the text right into your own, using quotation marks just as you would with a prose quotation. However, since the placement of line endings can be significant in a poem, you need to indicate where they occur. This is done by including a slash mark, with a single space on each side, where the line breaks occur. (Some students find this awkward-looking at first, but you will quickly get used to it. Your instructor will expect you to honor the poet's choices regarding line breaks.)

> In "Sailing to Byzantium," Yeats describes an old man as "a paltry thing, / A tattered coat upon a stick" (lines 9–10).

Long Quotations

For quotations of four lines or more, "block" the material, setting it off one-half inch from the left margin, duplicating all line breaks of the original. Do not use quotation marks with block quotations.

> In the very first stanza of "The Lake Isle of Innisfree," Yeats expresses a desire to return to a simple country life:

I will arise and go now, and go to Innisfree,
And a small cabin build there, of clay and wattles made:
Nine bean-rows will I have there, a hive for the honey bee,
And live alone in the bee-loud glade.

QUOTING FROM PLAYS

Short Single-Speaker Passages

When you quote a short passage of drama with a single speaker, treat the quoted text just as you would prose fiction:

Nora's first words in *A Doll House* are "Hide the tree well, Helene. The children mustn't get a glimpse of it till this evening, after it's trimmed."

Longer or More Complex Passages

For a longer quotation, or a quotation of any length involving more than one character, you will need to block off the quotation. Begin each separate piece of dialogue indented one-half inch from the left margin with the character's name, typed in all capital letters, followed by a period. Subsequent lines of the character's speech should be indented an additional one-quarter inch. (Your word processor's "hanging indent" function is useful for achieving this effect without having to indent each separate line.) As with fiction or poetry, do not use quotation marks for block quotations.

We see the tension between Nora and her husband in their very first confrontation:

NORA. Oh, but Torvald, this year we really should let ourselves go a bit.
It's the first Christmas we haven't had to economize.
HELMER. But you know we can't go squandering.
NORA. Oh yes, Torvald, we can squander a little now. Can't we?
(1.20–23)

Verse Drama

Many older plays, including classical Greek drama and much of the work of Shakespeare and his contemporaries, are written at least partly in poetic verse. When you quote a verse drama, you must respect the line endings, just as you do in quoting poetry. The first example here shows a short quotation with slash marks that indicate line endings.

> Hamlet's most famous soliloquy begins, "To be, or not to be, that is the question: / Whether 'tis nobler in the mind to suffer / The slings and arrows of outrageous fortune" (3.1.56–58).

This second example shows a longer, block quotation in verse form.

> Hamlet then begins his most famous soliloquy:
>
> To be, or not to be, that is the question:
> Whether 'tis nobler in the mind to suffer
> The slings and arrows of outrageous fortune,
> Or to take arms against a sea of troubles,
> And by opposing end them. (3.1.56–60)

Tips for Quoting

- **Double-check the wording, spelling, and punctuation of every quotation you use.** Even if something seems "wrong" in the original source—a nonstandard spelling, a strange mark of punctuation, or even a factual error—resist the urge to correct it. When you put quotation marks around something, you indicate that you are reproducing it exactly as it first appeared. If you feel the need to clarify that an error or inconsistency is not yours, you may follow it by the word *sic* (Latin for *thus*), not italicized, in square brackets.

    > The mother in the anonymous poem "Lord Randal" asks her son "wha [sic] met ye there?"

- **Use the shortest quotation you can while still making your point.** Remember, the focus should always be on your own ideas, and the dominant voice should be yours. Don't quote a paragraph from a source when a single sentence contains the heart of what you need. Don't quote a whole sentence when you can simply integrate a few words into one of your own sentences.

- **Never assume a quotation is self-explanatory.** Each time you include a quotation, analyze it and explain why you have quoted it. Remember that your reader may have a different reaction to the quotation than you did.

- **If you are quoting a *character* in a story, play, or poem, be sure to distinguish that character from the *author*.** Hamlet says "To be or not to be," not Shakespeare, and you should make that distinction clear.
- **Take care not to distort the meaning of a quotation.** It is intellectually dishonest to quote an author or a speaker out of context or to use ellipses or additions in such a way as to change the meaning or integrity of source material. Treat your sources with the same respect you would want if you were to be quoted in a newspaper or magazine.

MANUSCRIPT FORM

If your instructor gives you directions about what your paper should look like, follow them exactly. If not, the following basic guidelines on manuscript form, recommended by the Modern Language Association of America (MLA), will work well in most instances. The most comprehensive guide to MLA style is *MLA Handbook*, 8th Edition (2016). The guiding principle here is readability—you want the look of your paper to distract as little as possible from the content.

- **Use plain white paper, black ink, and a standard, easy-to-read font.** To make your paper stand out from the masses, it might seem like a nice touch to use visual design elements like colored or decorated paper, fancy fonts, and so forth. However, your instructor has a lot of reading to do, and anything that distracts or slows down that reading is a minus, not a plus, for your paper. For the same reason, avoid illustrations, pictures of authors, and so forth, unless they are needed to clarify a point. Distinguish your paper through content and style, not flashy design.
- **Do not include a separate cover page.** Also, don't waste your time and money on report covers or folders unless asked to do so by your instructor. Many instructors, in fact, find covers cumbersome and distracting.
- **Include vital information in the upper-left corner of your first page.** This information usually consists of your name, the name of your instructor, the course number of the class, and the date you submit the paper.
- **Center your paper's title.** The title should appear in upper- and lowercase letters, and in the same font as the rest of your paper—not italicized, boldface, or set within quotation marks.

- **Page numbers should appear in the upper-right corner of each page.** Do not include the word *page* or the abbreviation *p.* with the page numbers. Use your word processing program's "header" or "running head" feature to include your last name before the page numbers.

See the sample student papers in this book for examples of correct MLA-style formatting. These basic guidelines should carry you through most situations, but if you have any questions regarding format, ask your instructor for his or her preferences.

CHAPTER 4

Common Writing Assignments

Chances are you will encounter a variety of writing assignments in your literature class, possibly ranging from a brief personal response to an extended literary research paper. Each assignment offers you two opportunities. First, writing about a particular piece (or multiple pieces) of literature forces you to think more closely than a simple reading does, so you will end up learning more about the story, poem, or play. Second, writing is your best opportunity to share your thoughts with your instructor, and possibly your classmates, so you can have an impact on someone else's thinking as well. Generally, the assignments in such a class build cumulatively on one another, so that explication and analysis, for instance, are useful techniques in a research paper, and writing a comparison and contrast paper might give you tools to help you answer a question on an essay exam. Each time you get a new assignment, ask yourself, "What did I learn from the last assignment that I might apply to this one?" This chapter outlines some of the assignments you might be given (summary, response, explication, analysis, comparison and contrast, and essay exams), provides examples of each, and demonstrates how each skill might build on the previous skill.

SUMMARY

A **summary** is a brief recap of the most important points—plot, character, and so on—in a work of literature. To demonstrate that you have understood a story or play, for instance, you may be asked to summarize its plot as homework before class discussions. A summary of Nathaniel Hawthorne's "Young Goodman Brown" (page 3) follows:

> Set in seventeenth-century Salem, Massachusetts, Nathaniel Hawthorne's "Young Goodman Brown" follows the fortunes of the title character when he leaves his young wife, Faith, for a mysterious rendezvous in a forest at night. The character he meets in the forbidding woods is unnamed, but Hawthorne hints that he may be the Devil himself. As they proceed deeper into the forest

on their unspecified but presumably unholy errand, Goodman Brown's misgivings increase, especially when they encounter his fellow townsfolk—people Goodman Brown thought were good Christians—en route to the same meeting. But when they are joined by Faith, Brown recklessly resolves to participate. At the ceremony, the new converts are called forth, but as he and Faith step forward to be anointed in blood, he rebels and urges Faith to resist. Instantly he finds himself alone in the forest, and when he returns to town the next morning, uncertain whether it was all a dream, he finds himself suspicious and wary of his neighbors and his wife. His "Faith" has been corrupted, and to the end of his days he remains a bitter and untrusting man: "his dying hour was gloom" (13).

A summary can be longer or shorter than this example, depending on your purpose. Notice that interpretation is kept to a minimum ("His 'Faith' has been corrupted") and the summary is recounted in the present tense ("he returns to town," "he remains a bitter and untrusting man").

It is rare for a full essay assignment to be based on summary alone. Keep in mind that for most of the papers you write, your readers—your teacher and possibly your classmates—are probably familiar with the literary work you are writing about, and do not need a recap of the entire work. Generally, they need only to be reminded of key points about the text that are most relevant to the argument you are making about it.

While a *summary* is not a kind of writing assignment that you will likely have to produce often in a literature course, *summarizing* is a skill you will need to develop. It is useful to be able to focus on the most important parts of a text, knowing what is most vital. Short summaries, either of a work (or part of a work) of literature or of critical essays about literature, are commonly used as part of the supporting evidence in more complex papers. When you are using secondary sources in a paper about a literary work—as when you write a literary research paper—chances are that your audience has not read the critical essays you have read. Therefore, you may need to summarize for your readers the arguments of those critical essays.

Often such summaries are only a few sentences in length and restate the author's thesis, possibly with a few examples of the kind of evidence the author uses to support the thesis. Just as often, you may want to summarize only part of a critical essay, a part that is pertinent to your paper. For example, if you have read an essay about Hawthorne's use of imagery in "Young Goodman Brown," for the purposes of your paper you may need to summarize only the section that deals with the imagery of light and darkness in the story. Ask yourself, "What do my readers need to know to follow my argument, and what evidence do I need to provide to convince them of my point of view?" Summarize accordingly.

RESPONSE

Though you may state or imply whether or not you liked the literary selection in question when you write a response paper, the main purpose is not to provide a review or a rating. Rather, the goal of such a paper is twofold: to describe your personal response to a particular reading assignment and to explain why you had this reaction. Of course, our reactions to literature are often multiple and complex, so you need to be selective in what you write. Don't try to explain every response and every thought you had while reading. Rather, choose one significant thought you had while reading and explore that in depth.

Response papers in general are somewhat informal and do not necessarily follow the thesis-and-support model common in other types of literature papers. Response papers are often fairly brief, and since you are writing about your personal responses, it's generally okay to use the first-person pronoun *I*. Remember, though, that this is not simply a personal essay in which you explore your own life and thoughts. Keep the literature as the main focus, and if you call on your own experiences, do so in order to explain and analyze some facet of the story, poem, or play. Since there are no hard-and-fast rules about response papers, be sure to read your instructor's directions carefully and follow them closely. If you have any questions, ask.

After reading Jamaica Kincaid's very short story "Girl" (page 355), take a moment to consider your own response to it and where that response comes from. Then read and consider the student response paper that follows.

Tom Lyons
Professor Tritle
English 112
17 October 2016

A Boy's View of "Girl"

It may sound peculiar for a young man to say this, but I could really relate to the character in Jamaica Kincaid's story "Girl." My father is a very old-fashioned, conservative man, and all through my childhood he constantly instructed my brother and me about proper behavior for a boy. His instructions and corrections were meant to be for our own good, but they put a lot of pressure on us from a very young age. This is similar to the experience of the young girl in Kincaid's story.

I assume the speaker in the story is the girl's mother, or at least some older female relative. She keeps saying "this is how" you do things, as though there is only one right way for every-thing. It's as if the girl can't figure out anything for herself, not even how to smile at someone she likes. I notice that the girl doesn't even have a name, and she has almost no chance to speak for herself. It seems that the mother doesn't particularly care who the girl is as an individual; what matters is just the fact that she is a girl. The mother also makes huge assumptions about what the girl is like. She thinks that the girl sings inappropriate songs in Sunday school and that she is trying to become a "slut." The poor girl never gets a chance to defend herself against these accusations.

Of course, my father was not worried about me becoming a slut, but he was very concerned that my brother and I should grow up to be strong, masculine men. The mother in the story empha-sizes the girl's domestic duties like cooking, cleaning, and sewing. My father always said that men should be good providers and that a man's work was very important. Men should also be responsible for protecting the family. I remember he went on a business trip when I was about twelve years old, and he said, "You need to take care of your mother while I'm gone." That's a big responsibility for a kid. My father thinks that our culture is too permissive and that

Tom's introduction makes clear his focus: the similarities between his own experience and that of the girl in Kincaid's story.

Tom points out particular fea-tures of the story that struck him, all related to the way the girl's mother forces her will on the girl.

Tom uses specifics from the story to demonstrate his point.

When Tom turns to his own childhood experience, he makes direct comparison to "Girl," so the focus is always on the story.

Lyons 2

any boys are not raised to be responsible men. This is similar to
ıe mother in the story, who seems to think the daughter needs to
ɛ told constantly how to be a proper woman.

This story hit home for me. It really shows how parents and
ders can pass on expectations about gender roles to future
ɛnerations. Young boys and girls do need advice and strong role
ɔdels, but parents can sometimes go too far in imposing their
vn values on the next generation. I hope that as time goes by,
ɔth boys and girls are subjected to less of this sort of pressure so
ıat they are free to develop their own unique personalities as
ɛople, not just as gender stereotypes.

Tom ends his response paper by explaining the thoughts and feelings the story provoked in him.

Works Cited

ncaid, Jamaica. "Girl." *Literature: A Portable Anthology*, edited by
Janet E. Gardner et al., 4th edition, Bedford/St. Martin's,
2017, pp. 355–56.

EXPLICATION

One common assignment is to perform an **explication** or a close-reading
of a poem or short prose passage. As the word implies, an *explication*
takes what is implicit or subtle in a work of literature and makes it explicit and clear. Literary language tends to be densely packed with meaning, and your job as you explicate it is to unfold that meaning and lay
it out for your reader. The principal technique of explication is close-
reading; indeed, explication and close-reading are so closely related that
many writers use the words virtually interchangeably. When you write
this sort of paper, you will examine a piece of literature very closely, paying special attention to such elements of the language as sentence structure, **style**, **imagery**, **figurative language** (such as **similes** and **metaphors**), word choice, and perhaps even grammar and punctuation. The
job of an explication is twofold: to point out particular, salient elements
of style and to explain the purpose and effect of these elements within
the text.

When assigned an explication or a close-reading, you might be tempted
to simply walk through a text line by line, pointing out interesting features of style as they occur. A paper written in this way, though, can de-
volve into little more than summary or restatement of the literature in

more prosaic language. A better idea is to isolate the various features of
the literature on which you will focus and then deal separately with the
specifics and implications of each.

The paper that follows is an example of a student essay that provides
an explication of a literary text. First, take a look at Robert Herrick's
"Upon Julia's Clothes," and then read the student's paper.

ROBERT HERRICK   [1591–1674]

Upon Julia's Clothes

Whenas in silks my Julia goes,
Then, then (methinks) how sweetly flows
That liquefaction of her clothes.

Next, when I cast mine eyes, and see
That brave vibration each way free,
O how that glittering taketh me!

[1648]

Barnes 1

ssica Barnes

ofessor White

glish 108

March 2016

Poetry in Motion: Herrick's "Upon Julia's Clothes"

In its brief six lines, Robert Herrick's "Upon Julia's Clothes" is celebration of the physical sensuousness of the speaker's object desire. The poem is structured like a seashell with two parts. In e first stanza, the speaker makes a seemingly simple observation: hen Julia walks past, her silken clothes seem to flow as if they're quid. In the second stanza, though, he provides a second servation: when Julia's body is "each way free" of the clothing, e speaker is completely overtaken by the beauty of Julia's "brave bration."

Jessica's intro-duction lays out clearly the focus and structure of her paper.

Herrick provides several inversions of syntax to place phasis on certain images. For example, in line 1, Herrick inverts ny Julia goes" with "in silks" to emphasize the importance of ilks" to Julia's sensuality. He creates another inversion in lines 3. The sense of the lines is as follows: "Then, then (methinks) at liquefaction of her clothes flows sweetly." Herrick rearranges e sentence to emphasize the sweetness of the flowing and to ace the emphasis on "flows" and "clothes" at the ends of the es.

In this para-graph, Jessica focuses on a specific language feature, syntax, and provides several examples from Herrick's poem.

Herrick also provides several changes in the iambic tetrameter eter to create varied lines within the poem's strict form. In line he repeats "then" two times. In doing so, he forces the reader pause deeply between each "then" and encourages the reader to editate on the poet's decision to repeat the word in the first ace. In line 6, too, Herrick alternately accelerates and deceler-es the tempo of the line. The exclamatory "O" at the beginning the line suggests that the speaker has been utterly charmed by lia's beauty. It is a long sound that slows the reader down at the ginning of the line; in addition, it provides a stress on the first lable of the line, instead of an unstressed syllable followed by a

This paragraph examines a different lan-guage feature, poetic meter.

stressed one (see, for example, "That **brave vi**bration" in line 5).
"Glittering" also disrupts the strict tetrameter of the line. Its three
syllables are compressed into two brief syllables ("**glitt**ring") so
that the next accent can fall on "**tak**eth me," which emphasizes
the fact that the speaker is totally overwhelmed by Julia's naked
body.

*Jessica begins
to tie up her
observations
about specific
language fea-
tures with some
preliminary
analysis.*

Ultimately, the poem reveals that Julia's beauty is beyond
words. We cannot know whether Julia has actually taken her
clothes off, or whether she has done so in the imagination of the
speaker. Either way, the poem provides many sounds that mirror
the "O" of line 6. The end rhyme for all of the lines in the first
stanza rhyme with the "O": *goes, flows, clothes*. Each of these
words reinforces the importance of Julia's shimmering beauty, and
the power of her movements. The "ee" rhymes at the ends of the
lines in stanza 2 — *see, free, me* — reinforce the idea that Julia's
freedom in her nakedness also frees the poet's pleasure in
imagining, or seeing, the "brave vibration" of her body.

*The final lan-
guage feature th
paper examines
is the repetition
of vowel sound*

Works Cited

Herrick, Robert. "Upon Julia's Clothes." *Literature: A Portable
Anthology*, edited by Janet E. Gardner et al., 4th edition,
Bedford/St. Martin's, 2017, p. 1268.

ANALYSIS

To analyze, by definition, is to take something apart and examine how
the individual parts relate to one another and function within the whole.
Engineers frequently analyze complex machinery, looking for ways to
improve efficiency or performance. In a similar way, you can take apart
a piece of literature to study how a particular part of it functions and
what that part contributes to the whole. Typical candidates for literary
analysis include **plot development, characterization, tone, irony, and
symbols.**

Here is an example of a student essay that provides an analysis. First,
take a look at Robert Browning's "My Last Duchess" (page 468); then
read the student's paper.

dam Walker
ofessor Blitefield
glish 203
February 2016

Possessed by the Need for Possession:
Browning's "My Last Duchess"

In "My Last Duchess," Robert Browning's duke reveals his
elings of jealousy and betrayal as he discusses the duchess's
rtrait. In his dramatic monologue, the duke's public persona as
aristocratic gentleman is shattered by the revelations of his
tual feelings about his dead duchess. The duke reveals what
sets him most: his late wife's liberal smiles and attentions to
hers besides himself. With this focus on the duchess's attentions,
owning creates a compelling portrait of a gentleman who could
t exert complete control over his former wife, and may fail to
ntrol his future wife as well.

The duke repeatedly calls attention to what he sees as the
chess's misinterpretations. The duke imagines the duchess as she
t for Fra Pandolf: "such stuff / Was courtesy, she thought, and
use enough / For calling up that spot of joy" (lines 19–21).
cording to the duke, the duchess mistook the painter's atten-
ns as courtesies. Her blush, or "spot of joy" (21) on her cheeks,
s too indiscriminate for the duke. The duke admits that the
chess blushed at his own advances, but she also blushed at the
inter, the "dropping of the daylight in the West" (26), a bough
cherries, and a white mule. The duchess's gaze is an indiscrimi-
te one: she appreciates whatever pleases her, whether it be
man, animal, or organic. This infuriates the duke, who thinks
at his "nine-hundred-years-old name" (33) ought to make him
re valuable in the eyes of the duchess.

Eventually, the duke restricts the duchess's blushes with
mmands: "This grew; I gave commands / Then all smiles
pped together. There she stands / As if alive" (45–47). These
es are concise and quick compared with the rhetoric of the other

*The introduction
names the poem
to be analyzed
and clearly ex-
plains that the
focus of the
paper will be the
duke's jealous
nature.*

*Adam quotes
specific lines
from the poem
in order to dem-
onstrate his
point. In each
case, he inte-
grates the quota-
tion cleanly into
his own prose.*

*The quotation
is immediately
followed by an
explanation of
its purpose in
the paper.*

lines in the poem. Even so, they are in some ways the most important. What made the smiles stop? Was the duchess silenced in life? Or was it her death that stopped the smiling? And why does the duke need this portrait that resembles the duchess when she was alive?

Adam uses rhetorical question to provide stylistic variety and to get the reader thinking.

Ultimately, the showing of the portrait is a way for the duke to show his possessions — and his command of his possessions — to the envoy of the Count. As the duke invites the envoy to come downstairs, he already characterizes his future bride as a kind of possession:

> I repeat,
> The Count your master's known munificence
> Is ample warrant that no just pretence
> Of mine for dowry will be disallowed;
> Though his fair daughter's self, as I avowed
> At starting, is my object. (48-53)

Note that the long quotation is blocked (indented from the left margin) and does not use quotation marks.

After alluding to the generous dowry that he will receive, the duke checks himself by saying that it is "his [the Count's] fair daughter's self" that he has found so compelling. Even so, the duke has started to limit and control the status of his future bride, suggesting that he will exert the same controls on her that he exerted on his late wife. In the end, she runs the same risk of becoming a sea horse that requires Neptune's taming.

Adam's concluding sentence alludes to the final lines of the poem.

Works Cited

Browning, Robert. "My Last Duchess." *Literature: A Portable Anthology*, edited by Janet E. Gardner et al., 4th edition, Bedford/St. Martin's, 2017, pp. 468–70.

COMPARISON AND CONTRAST

Another common paper assignment is the **comparison and contrast** essay. You might be asked to draw comparisons and contrasts within a single work of literature — say, between two characters in a story or play. Even more common is an assignment that asks you to compare and contrast a particular element—characters, setting, style, tone, and so on—in two or more stories, poems, or plays. A *comparison* emphasizes the similarities between two or more items, while a *contrast* highlights their differences. Though some papers do both, it is typical for an essay to emphasize one or the other.

If you are allowed to choose the works of literature for a comparison and contrast paper, take care to select works that have enough in common to make such a comparison interesting and valid. Even if Henrik Ibsen's *A Doll House* and Shirley Jackson's "The Lottery" are your favorites, it is difficult to imagine a well-focused paper comparing these two, as they share virtually nothing in terms of authorship, history, theme, or style, having been written in different genres, in different centuries, and on different continents. It would make far more sense to select two seventeenth-century poems or two love stories.

The paper that follows compares Robert Browning's "My Last Duchess" (page 468) and Christina Rossetti's "After Death." First, read Rossetti's poem; then read the student paper.

CHRISTINA ROSSETTI   [1830–1894]

After Death

The curtains were half drawn, the floor was swept
    And strewn with rushes, rosemary and may°
Lay thick upon the bed on which I lay,
Where through the lattice ivy-shadows crept.
He leaned above me, thinking that I slept   5
    And could not hear him; but I heard him say,
    "Poor child, poor child": and as he turned away
Came a deep silence, and I knew he wept.
He did not touch the shroud, or raise the fold
    That hid my face, or take my hand in his,   10
        Or ruffle the smooth pillows for my head:
        He did not love me living; but once dead
    He pitied me; and very sweet it is
To know he still is warm though I am cold.

[1849]

may: Green or flowering branches used for May Day celebrations.

Todd Bowen
Professor Harrison
English 215
13 May 2016

Speakers for the Dead:
Narrators in "My Last Duchess" and "After Death"

In "My Last Duchess," Robert Browning creates a duke whose tight control over his wife — and his preoccupation with his own noble rank — reveal a misogynistic character. Browning's dramatic monologue stands in stark contrast to Christina Rossetti's "After Death," a sonnet in which the speaker comes back from the dead to reveal what she observes about her lover. When paired together, these poems speak to each other in a time period that seemed to have a gothic obsession with the death of young women.

In the poems' style and structure, Browning and Rossetti create completely different portraits of women after death. In "My Last Duchess," the duke uses the actual portrait of his dead wife to create a portrait in words of a woman who smiled too liberally at men who fawned over her. The duke says, "She had / A heart — how shall I say? — too soon made glad, / Too easily impressed; she liked whate'er / She looked on, and her looks went everywhere" (lines 21-24). Throughout his long dramatic monologue, the duke meditates on several moments when the duchess betrays him by smiling at others; however, we as readers never get to hear the duchess's side of the story.

In Rossetti's "After Death," however, the tables are turned: the dead woman gets to speak back to the man who performs his grief over her death. In doing so, she carefully observes the behavior of her lover, who thinks that she is merely a lifeless corpse. In each line of the small sonnet, the speaker observes the man as he leans above her, says "Poor child, poor child" (7), and then turns away without actually touching her body. Even so, the woman suggests that this is an improvement from when she was alive: "He did not love me living; but once dead / He pitied me" (ll. 12-13). The speaker's final couplet is especially chilling: "and

Todd's concise introduction names the authors and poems that will be the subject of his comparison, as well as the paper's focus on certain shared features of the poems.

The first two body paragraphs each focus on one of the poems, providing a combination of specific evidence — mostly in the form of quotations — and analysis of this evidence.

Bowen 2

ery sweet it is / To know he still is warm though I am cold" [3-14). The speaker says that it is "sweet" to know that the man as outlived her. She doesn't explain this sweetness, but perhaps it because she can observe his emotion in a way that she never ould have while she was alive.

Note that Todd distinguishes between the poet Rossetti and the speaker of the poem.

When read together, Rossetti's "After Death" and Browning's "My Last Duchess" function as companion pieces, each speaking to he other in a kind of call-and-response. Browning's duke shuts own any speech beyond his own, talking at length in the silence f the portrait and the visitor who looks at it. His story is the only :ory that he wants to present, even if his speech reveals his own nortcomings. Rossetti's woman provides an alternative perspective f death and mourning as the woman speaks from the dead to •veal the shortcomings of the man who mourns her. Both poems rovide chilling perspectives on death, mourning, and marriage in ie Victorian period.

The concluding paragraph contains the heart of the actual comparison of the poems.

Works Cited

rowning, Robert. "My Last Duchess." *Literature: A Portable Anthology,* edited by Janet E. Gardner et al., 4th edition, Bedford/St. Martin's, 2017, pp. 468–70.

ossetti, Christina. "After Death." Gardner et al., p. 1273.

ESSAY EXAMS

The key to getting through the potentially stressful situation of an essay exam is to be prepared and to know what will be expected of you.

Preparation takes two forms: knowing the material and anticipating the questions. Knowing the material starts with keeping up with all reading and homework assignments throughout the term. You can't possibly read several weeks' or months' worth of material the night before the test and hope to remember it all. The days before the test should be used not for catching up but for review—revisiting the readings, skimming or rereading key passages, and studying your class notes. It's best to break up study sessions into manageable blocks if possible. Reviewing for two hours a night for three nights before the exam will be far more effective than a single six-hour cram session on the eve of the test.

Anticipating the questions that might be on the exam is a bit trickier, but it can be done. What themes and issues have come up again and again in class lectures or discussions? What patterns do you see in your class notes? What points did your instructor stress? These are the topics most likely to appear on the exam. Despite what you might think, it is very rare that an instructor poses intentionally obscure exam questions in an attempt to trip up students or expose their ignorance. Most often, the instructor is providing you with an opportunity to demonstrate what you know, and you should be ready to take that opportunity. You can't, of course, second-guess your instructor perfectly and know for sure what will be on the test, but you can spend some time in advance thinking about what sorts of questions you are likely to encounter and how you would answer them.

Open-Book versus Closed-Book Exams

Your exam may be open-book or closed-book; find out in advance which it will be, so that you can plan and study accordingly. In an *open-book* exam, you are allowed to use your textbook during the exam. This is a big advantage, obviously, as it allows you access to specific evidence, including quotations, to support your points. If you know the exam is going to be open-book, you might also jot down any important notes in the book itself, where you can find them readily if you need them. Use your textbook sparingly, though—just enough to find the evidence you know to be there. Don't waste time browsing the literature hoping to find inspiration or ideas. For a *closed-book* exam, you have to rely on your memory alone. But you should still try to be as specific as possible in your references to the literature, using character names, recalling plot elements, and so forth.

Develop a Plan

When you sit down to take the exam, you may have the urge to start writing right away, since your time is limited. Suppress that urge and read through the entire exam first, paying special attention to the instruction portion. Often the exam will offer you choices, such as "Answer two of the following three questions" or "Select a single poem as the basis of your answer." If you miss such cues, you may find yourself racing to write three essays and running out of time or discussing several poems shallowly instead of one in depth. Once you are certain what is expected of you, take a few more minutes to plan your answers before you start writing. A few jotted notes or an informal outline may take a moment, but it will likely save you time as you write. If you will be writing more than one essay, take care not to repeat yourself or to write more than one essay about any one piece of literature. The idea is to show your instructor your mastery of the course material, and to do so effectively you should demonstrate breadth of knowledge.

Aim for Clarity

When you do begin writing, bear in mind that instructors have different expectations for exam answers than they do for essays written outside of class. They know that in timed exams you have no time for research or extensive revisions. Clarity and concision are the keys; elegant prose style is not expected (though, of course, it will come as a pleasant surprise if you can manage it). Effective essay answers are often more formulaic than other sorts of effective writing, relying on the schematic of a straightforward introduction, simple body paragraphs, and a brief conclusion.

Your introduction should be simple and to the point. A couple of sentences is generally all that is needed, and these should avoid rhetorical flourishes or digressions. Often the best strategy is to parrot back the instructions as an opening statement. Body paragraphs for essay answers should also be simple and will often, though not always, be briefer than they would be in an essay you worked on at home. They should still be as specific as possible, making reference to and perhaps even quoting the literature to illustrate your points. Just as in a more fully developed essay, try to avoid dwelling in generalities; use specific examples and evidence. Conclusions for essay exams are usually brief, often just a sentence or two of summary.

Watch the Time

Finally, take a watch with you on exam day and keep a close eye on the time. Use all the time you are given and budget it carefully. If you have an hour to write two answers, don't spend forty-five minutes on the first. Even though you will likely be pressed for time, save a few minutes at the end to proofread your answers. Make any corrections as neatly and legibly as possible. Watch the time, but try not to watch your classmates' progress. Keep focused on your own process. Just because someone else is using his or her book a lot, you shouldn't feel you need to do the same. If someone finishes early and leaves, don't take this as a sign that you are running behind or that you are less efficient or less smart than that person. Students who don't make full use of the exam time are often underprepared; they tend to write vague and underdeveloped answers and should not be your role models.

An open-book essay exam on poetry gave students several options, including "Select two poems by different poets, each of which deals with the theme of time, and compare how the authors present this theme." A student chose William Shakespeare's Sonnet 73 (page 426) and Robert Herrick's "To the Virgins, to Make Much of Time" (page 434). Read the two poems and then the student's essay exam answer.

Midterm Essay: Option #2

Shakespeare's Sonnet 73 ("That time of year thou mayst in me behold") and Herrick's "To the Virgins, to Make Much of Time" both deal with the theme of time, and particularly the effect that time has on love. Though there are important differences in their focus and style, both poems urge their readers to love well and make the most of the time they have left.

Both poems make their points about time through a series of metaphors, and in fact they use some of the same metaphors. Herrick begins with the image of rosebuds, which bloom and then die quickly. Shakespeare's first metaphor is also drawn from the natural world of plants, in this case a tree losing its leaves in the autumn. In the sonnet, the natural world is even connected to the spiritual world of church when the poet refers to the branches of the tree as "choirs." Both poems also compare life to a single day, with the setting sun symbolizing death. Toward the end of his sonnet, Shakespeare writes of life as a fire that burns brightly in youth and then cools as a person nears death. While Herrick does not refer to fire specifically, he follows a similar line of reasoning when he mentions a time "When youth and blood are warmer" (line 10).

The most significant difference between the two poems lies in the characters of the speaker and the implied listener. Herrick offers his advice about the nature of time and its effect on love to "the Virgins" generally. He tells them to "go marry," but he offers no specifics about whom they should be marrying or how they might choose these mates. Shakespeare's poem, on the other hand, seems to be addressed to a single "you" who is in some sort of relationship with the speaker, the "me" who narrates the poem. When he urges the listener "To love that well which thou must leave ere long" (line 14), he is referring to himself as the object of love.

In the end, the differences end up overshadowing the superficial similarities of theme and purpose. Herrick's poem, with its relative lack of specificity, comes across as the sort of kindly advice an older person, perhaps an uncle, might give to any young man or woman. Shakespeare's is a more intimate, and ultimately somewhat darker, poem.

The introductory paragraph is brief and restates the assignment, adding in specifics to begin focusing the essay.

The two body paragraphs are also fairly brief, but they give lots of specific examples from the poems rather than relying on generalizations.

Because this was an open-book exam, the student was even able to incorporate brief quotations in her answer.

The organization is clear and straightforward, with one body paragraph comparing similarities between the poems and one contrasting a key difference.

The conclusion is also simple in form and purpose; it restates the main points of the body paragraphs in new language and makes the contrast more explicit.

CHAPTER 5

Writing about Stories

Fiction has long been broken down and discussed in terms of specific elements common to all stories, and chances are you will be focusing on one or more of these when you write an essay about a story.

ELEMENTS OF FICTION

The **elements of fiction** most commonly identified are **plot**, **character**, **point of view**, **setting**, **theme**, **symbolism**, and **style**. If you find yourself wondering what to write about a story, a good place to begin is isolating these elements and seeing how they work on a reader and how they combine to create the unique artifact that is a particular story.

Plot

While on some level we all read stories to find out what happens next, in truth plot is usually the least interesting of the elements of fiction. Students who have little experience writing about fiction tend to spend too much time retelling the plot. You can avoid this by bearing in mind that your readers will also have read the literature in question and don't need a thorough replay of what happened. In general, readers just need small reminders of the key points of plot about which you will write, and these should not be self-standing but rather should serve as springboards into analysis and discussion. Still, writing about the plot sometimes makes sense, especially when the plot surprises your expectations by, for instance, rearranging the chronology of events or otherwise presenting things in nonrealistic ways. When this happens in a story, the plot may indeed prove fertile ground for analysis and may be the basis of an interesting paper.

Character

Many interesting essays analyze the actions, motivations, and development of individual characters. How does the author reveal a character to the reader? How does a character grow and develop over the course of a story? Readers have to carefully examine what insights the text provides about a character, but sometimes readers have to consider what's left out. What does the reader have to infer about the character that isn't explicitly written? What does the character refrain from saying? What secrets do characters keep from others, or from themselves? These questions can be fertile ground for analysis. Although the most obvious character to write about is usually the **protagonist**, don't let your imagination stop there. Often the **antagonist** or even a minor character can be an interesting object of study. Keep in mind, too, that characters can start out as antagonistic figures and experience a transformation in the eyes of the narrator or other characters, or in the eyes of the reader. Your job in writing a paper is to consider these transformations and try to understand why a text explores these complex character developments. Usually not a lot has been said and written about less prominent characters, so you will be more free to create your own interpretations. (Playwright Tom Stoppard wrote a very successful full-length play entitled *Rosencrantz and Guildenstern Are Dead* about two of the least developed characters in *Hamlet*.)

Point of View

Related to character is the issue of point of view. The perspective from which a story is told can make a big difference in how we perceive it. Sometimes a story is told in the *first person*, from the point of view of one of the characters. Whether this is a major or a minor character, we must always remember that **first-person narrators** can be unreliable, as they do not have access to all vital information, and their own agendas can often skew the way they see events. The **narrator** of Edgar Allan Poe's "The Cask of Amontillado" (page 14) seeks to gain sympathy for a hideous act of revenge, giving us a glimpse into a deeply disturbed mind. A **third-person narrator** may be **omniscient**, knowing everything pertinent to a story; or limited, knowing, for instance, the thoughts and motives of the protagonist but not of any of the other characters. As you read a story, ask yourself what the point of view contributes and why the author may have chosen to present the story from a particular perspective.

Setting

Sometimes a setting is merely the backdrop for a story, but often place plays an important role in our understanding of a work. John Updike chooses a small, conservative New England town as the setting of his story "A & P" (page 268). It is the perfect milieu for an exploration of values and class interaction, and the story would have a very different feel and meaning if it had been set, say, in New York City. As you read, ask yourself how significant a setting is and what it adds to the meaning of a story. Remember that setting refers to time as well as place. "A & P" is about three young women walking into a small-town grocery store wearing only bathing suits, an action more shocking when the story was written in 1961 than it would be now (although it would doubtless still raise eyebrows in many places).

Theme

All **short stories** have at least one theme—an abstract concept such as *love*, *war*, *friendship*, *revenge*, or *art*—brought to life and made real through the plot, characters, and so on. Identifying a theme or themes is one of the first keys to understanding a story, but it is not the end point. Pay some attention to how the theme is developed. Is it blatant or subtle? What actions, events, or symbols make the theme apparent to you? Generally, the driving force of a story is the author's desire to convey something *about* a particular theme, to make readers think and feel in a certain way. First ask yourself what the author seems to be saying about love or war or whatever themes you have noted; second, whether you agree with the author's perceptions; and finally, why or why not.

Symbolism

Some students get frustrated when their instructors or their classmates begin to talk about **symbolism**. How do we know that an author intended a symbolic reading? Maybe that flower is just a real flower, not a stand-in for youth or for life and regeneration as some readers insist. And even if it is a symbol, how do we know we are reading it correctly? While it's true that plenty of flowers *are* simply flowers, and while students should identify symbols with caution, the more prominent an image in a story, the more likely it is meant to be read symbolically. Careful writers choose their words and images for maximum impact, filling them with as much meaning as possible and inviting their readers to interpret them. When John Steinbeck entitles his story "The Chrysanthemums," we would do well to ask if the flowers are really just plants or if we are being asked to look for a greater significance.

Style

The final element of fiction isolated here is style, sometimes spoken of under the heading of tone or language. A text may strike you as sad or lighthearted, formal or casual. It may make you feel nostalgic, or it may make your heart race with excitement. Somewhat more difficult, though, is isolating the elements of language that contribute to a particular tone or effect. Look for characteristic stylistic elements that create these effects. Is the diction elevated and difficult, or ordinary and simple? Are the sentences long and complex, or short and to the point? Is there dialogue? If so, how do the characters who speak this dialogue come across? Does the style stay consistent throughout the story, or does it change? What does the author leave out? Paying close attention to linguistic matters like these will take you far in your understanding of how a particular story achieves its effect.

STORIES FOR ANALYSIS

Read Charlotte Perkins Gilman's story "The Yellow Wallpaper" (page 64) and Kate Chopin's "The Story of an Hour" (page 48) which we have annotated below. Both stories explore issues of women's identity and freedom. The questions following the annotated story ask you to analyze how the elements of fiction work in these two stories.

KATE CHOPIN   [1851–1904]

The Story of an Hour

Knowing that Mrs. Mallard was afflicted with a heart trouble, great care was taken to break to her as gently as possible the news of her husband's death.

It was her sister Josephine who told her, in broken sentences; veiled hints that revealed in half concealing. Her husband's friend Richards was there, too, near her. It was he who had been in the newspaper office when intelligence of the railroad disaster was received, with Brently Mallard's name leading the list of "killed." He had only taken the time to assure himself of its truth by a second telegram, and had hastened to forestall any less careful, less tender friend in bearing the sad message.

Her family and friends seem t think she's deli

She did not hear the story as many women have heard the same, with a paralyzed inability to accept its significance.

She wept at once, with sudden wild abandonment, in her sister's arms. When the storm of grief had spent itself she went away to her room alone. She would have no one follow her.

There stood, facing the open window, a comfortable, roomy armchair. Into this she sank, pressed down by a physical exhaustion that haunted her body and seemed to reach into her soul.

She could see in the open square before her house the tops of trees that were all aquiver with the new spring life. The delicious breath of rain was in the air. In the street below a peddler was crying his wares. The notes of a distant song which some one was singing reached her faintly, and countless sparrows were twittering in the eaves.

A beautiful day. Why does Chopin take the time to describe it in such a short story, especially one about a death?

There were patches of blue sky showing here and there through the clouds that had met and piled one above the other in the west facing her window.

She sat with her head thrown back upon the cushion of the chair, quite motionless, except when a sob came up into her throat and shook her, as a child who had cried itself to sleep continues to sob in its dreams.

She was young, with a fair, calm face, whose lines bespoke repression and even a certain strength. But now there was a dull stare in her eyes, whose gaze was fixed away off yonder on one of those patches of blue sky. It was not a glance of reflection, but rather indicated a suspension of intelligent thought.

There was something coming to her and she was waiting for it, fearfully. What was it? She did not know; it was too subtle and elusive to name. But she felt it, creeping out of the sky, reaching toward her through the sounds, the scents, the color that filled the air.

Ominous. What could be coming? Something physical or emotional?

Now her bosom rose and fell tumultuously. She was beginning to recognize this thing that was approaching to possess her, and she was striving to beat it back with her will—as powerless as her two white slender hands would have been.

When she abandoned herself a little whispered word escaped her slightly parted lips. She said it over and over under her breath: "free, free, free!" The vacant stare and the look of terror that had followed it went from her eyes. They stayed keen and bright. Her pulses beat fast, and the coursing blood warmed and relaxed every inch of her body.

She did not stop to ask if it were or were not a monstrous joy that held her. A clear and exalted perception enabled her to dismiss the suggestion as trivial.

She knew that she would weep again when she saw the kind, tender hands folded in death; the face that had never looked save with love upon her, fixed and gray and dead. But she saw beyond that bitter moment a long procession of years to come that would belong to her absolutely. And she opened and spread her arms out to them in welcome.

There would be no one to live for her during those coming years: she would live for herself. There would be no powerful will bending hers in that blind persistence with which men and women believe they have a right to impose a private will upon a fellow-creature. A kind intention or a cruel intention made the act seem no less a crime as she looked upon it in that brief moment of illumination.

And yet she had loved him—sometimes. Often she had not. What did it matter! What could love, the unsolved mystery, count for in face of this possession of self-assertion which she suddenly recognized as the strongest impulse of her being!

"Free! Body and soul free!" she kept whispering.

Josephine was kneeling before the closed door with her lips to the keyhole, imploring for admission. "Louise, open the door! I beg; open the door—you will make yourself ill. What are you doing, Louise? For heaven's sake open the door."

"Go away. I am not making myself ill." No; she was drinking in a very elixir of life through that open window.

Her fancy was running riot along those days ahead of her. Spring days, and summer days, and all sorts of days that would be her own. She breathed a quick prayer that life might be long. It was only yesterday she had thought with a shudder that life might be long.

She arose at length and opened the door to her sister's importunities. There was a feverish triumph in her eyes, and she carried herself unwittingly like a goddess of Victory. She clasped her sister's waist, and together they descended the stairs. Richards stood waiting for them at the bottom.

Some one was opening the front door with a latchkey. It was Brently Mallard who entered, a little travel-stained, composedly carrying his gripsack and umbrella. He had been far from the scene of accident, and did not even know there had been one. He stood amazed at Josephine's piercing cry; at Richards' quick motion to screen him from the view of his wife.

How could it be? Her emotions se quick to change hard to keep up even for her.

Was their marria unhappy? Would friends and fam think so? Would husband have thought so?

Has she become more assertive? Stronger?

But Richards was too late.

When the doctors came they said she had died of heart disease—of joy that kills.

Surprising, ironic ending.

[1894]

QUESTIONS ON THE STORIES

☐ How would you summarize the plot of each story? What, if anything, makes it difficult to do so?

☐ Who, in your opinion, are the most sympathetic characters? Who are the most antagonistic? What kinds of information do we learn about the emotional lives of these characters?

☐ What is the point of view of each story? How would you compare the effects of these choices? What are the advantages and disadvantages of each choice?

☐ How would you describe the setting of each story? What details of setting contribute to the tone or atmosphere of the story?

☐ How would you describe the style of writing in each story? Is the prose formal? Archaic? Conversational? Melodramatic? Be as specific as possible, and note examples that bolster your claims.

☐ What kinds of symbols recur in each story? Are they fanciful? Ordinary? Conventional? Surprising? How do they move the narrative forward?

STUDENT ESSAY: AN ESSAY THAT COMPARES AND CONTRASTS

Melanie Smith was given the assignment to compare and contrast an element of her choosing in Kate Chopin's "The Story of an Hour" and Charlotte Perkins Gilman's "The Yellow Wallpaper" and to draw some conclusions about life in the nineteenth century. Rather than examining the female protagonists, Melanie chose to focus on the minor male characters in the stories. She wrote a point-by-point comparison designed to demonstrate that these men, despite the opinions of them that she heard expressed in class, were not bad people. Rather, they were led by their social training to behave in ways that were perfectly acceptable in their day, even if they now strike readers as oppressive.

Melanie Smith
Professor Hallet
English 109
17 May 2016

Good Husbands in Bad Marriages

When twenty-first-century readers first encounter literature of earlier times, it is easy for us to apply our own standards of conduct to the characters and situations. Kate Chopin's "The Story of an Hour" and Charlotte Perkins Gilman's "The Yellow Wallpaper" offer two good examples of this. Both written by American women in the last decade of the nineteenth century, the stories give us a look into the lives, and especially the marriages, of middle-class women of the time. By modern standards, the husbands of the two protagonists, particularly John in "The Yellow Wallpaper," seem almost unbearably controlling of their wives. From the vantage point of the late nineteenth century, however, their behavior looks quite different. Both men are essentially well-meaning and try to be good husbands. Their only real crime is that they adhere too closely to the conventional Victorian wisdom about women and marriage.

To begin with, both men are well respected in their communities. John in "The Yellow Wallpaper" is described as "a physician of high standing" who has "an intense horror of superstition, and he scoffs openly at any talk of things not to be felt and seen and put down in figures." These are just the qualities that we might expect to find in a respectable doctor, even today. It is less clear what Brently Mallard in "The Story of an Hour" does for a living. (In fact, Chopin's story is so short that we learn fairly little about any of the characters.) But he and his wife seem to live in a comfortable house, and they are surrounded by family and friends, suggesting a secure, well-connected lifestyle. In the nineteenth century, a man's most important job was to take care of his wife and family, and both men in these stories seem to be performing this job very well.

Melanie signals that she will focus on these two stories and makes a claim about them that she will go on to support.

Melanie's first observation about what the male characters have in common

Smith 2

In addition to providing a comfortable life for them, it also seems that both men love their wives. When she believes her husband has died, Mrs. Mallard thinks of his "kind, tender hands folded in death; the face that had never looked save with love upon her." Her own love for him is less certain, which may be why she feels "free" when he dies, but his love for her seems genuine. The case of John in "The Yellow Wallpaper" is a bit more complicated. To a modern reader, it seems that he treats his wife more like a child than a grown woman. He puts serious restraints on her actions, and at one point he even calls her "little girl." But he also calls her "my darling" and "dear," and she does admit, "He loves me very dearly." When he has to leave her alone, he even has his sister come to look after her, which is a kind gesture, even if it seems a bit like he doesn't trust his wife. If the narrator, who is in a position to know, doesn't doubt her husband's love, what gives us the right to judge it?

A smooth transition into the next point.

To a certain extent, we must admit that both husbands do oppress their wives by being overprotective. Part of the point of both stories is to show how even acceptable, supposedly good marriages of the day could be overly confining to women. This is especially obvious when we see how much John restricts his wife — forbidding her even to visit her cousins or to write letters — and how everyone expects her to submit to his demands. Though Mrs. Mallard isn't literally confined to a house or a room the way the narrator of "The Yellow Wallpaper" is, she stays inside the house and is looking out the window longingly when she realizes she wants to be free. But it is important for a reader not to blame the husbands, because they really don't intend to be oppressive.

Melanie establishes a similarity between the husbands.

In fact, it is true that both of the wives are in somewhat frail health. Mrs. Mallard is "afflicted with a heart trouble," and the narrator of "The Yellow Wallpaper" seems to have many physical and mental problems, so it is not surprising that their husbands worry about them. It is not evil intent that leads the men to act as they do; it is simply ignorance. John seems less innocent than

A point of similarity between the wives.

Brently because he is so patronizing and he puts such restrictions on his wife's behavior and movement, but that kind of attitude was normal for the day, and as a doctor, John seems to be doing what he really thinks is best.

All the other characters in the stories see both men as good and loving husbands, which suggests that society would have approved of their behavior. Even the wives themselves, who are the victims of these oppressive marriages, don't blame the men at all. The narrator of "The Yellow Wallpaper" even thinks she is "ungrateful" for not appreciating John's loving care more. Once we understand this, readers should not be too quick to blame the men either. The real blame falls to the society that gave these men the idea that women are frail and need protection from the world. The men may be the immediate cause of the women's suffering, but the real cause is much deeper and has to do with cultural attitudes and how the men were brought up to protect and provide for women.

Melanie returns to her original claim.

Most people who live in a society don't see the flaws in that society's conventional ways of thinking and living. We now know that women are capable and independent and that protecting them as if they were children ultimately does more harm than good. But in the late Victorian era, such an idea would have seemed either silly or dangerously radical to most people, men and women alike. Stories like these, however, could have helped their original readers begin to think about how confining these supposedly good marriages were. Fortunately, authors such as Chopin and Gilman come along from time to time and show us the problems in our conventional thinking, so society can move forward and we can begin to see how even the most well-meaning actions should sometimes be questioned.

Melanie's conclusion argues for the idea that literature is capable of challenging the status quo.

Works Cited

Chopin, Kate. "The Story of an Hour." *Literature: A Portable Anthology*, edited by Janet E. Gardner et al., 4th edition, Bedford/St. Martin's, 2017, pp. 48–50.

Gilman, Charlotte Perkins. "The Yellow Wallpaper." Gardner et al., pp. 64–77.

CHAPTER 6

Writing about Poems

Poetry may be divided into several major subgenres and types. A **narrative poem**, for instance, tells a story. An **epic**, a subgenre of narrative, is a long poem that narrates heroic events. A **lyric poem** expresses the personal thoughts and feelings of a particular poet or speaker. And many other types of poems have venerable histories.

As with stories, you should be aware of certain elements as you prepare to write about poetry. Sometimes these elements are the same as for fiction. A narrative poem, for instance, will have a **plot**, **setting**, and **characters**, and all poems speak from a particular **point of view**. To the extent that any of the elements of fiction help you understand a poem, by all means use them in your analysis. Poetry, however, does present a special set of concerns for a reader and elements of poetry frequently provide rich ground for analysis.

ELEMENTS OF POETRY

The Speaker

First, consider the speaker of the poem. Imagine that someone is saying the words of this poem aloud. Who is speaking, where is this **speaker**, and what is his or her state of mind? Sometimes the voice is that of the poet, but frequently a poem speaks from a different perspective, just as a short story might be from a point of view very different from the author's. It's not always apparent when this is the case, but some poets will signal who the speaker is in a title, such as "The Passionate Shepherd to His Love" (page 424) and "The Love Song of J. Alfred Prufrock" (page 516). Be alert to signals that will help you recognize the speaker, and remember that some poems have more than one speaker.

The Listener

Be attentive also to any other persons in the poem, particularly an implied listener. Is there a "you" to whom the poem is addressed? If the poem is being spoken aloud, who is supposed to hear it? When, early in his poem "Dover Beach" (page 490), Matthew Arnold writes, "Come to the window, sweet is the night-air!" he gives us an important clue as to how to read the poem. We should imagine both the speaker and the implied listener together in a room, with a window open to the night. As we read on, we can look for further clues as to who these two people are and why they are together on this night. Many poems create a relationship between the "I" of the speaker and the "you" of the listener; however, that is not always the case. Sometimes the speaker does not address a "you" and instead provides a more philosophical meditation that isn't explicitly addressed to a listener. Consider the effect: Do they feel more abstract? More detached from the material conditions of time and place? Do they provide certainty, or resolution? The questions about the speaker and the listener are crucial to your analysis of poetry.

Imagery

Just as you should be open to the idea that there are frequently symbols in stories, you should pay special attention to the **images** in poems. Although poems are often about such grand themes as love or death, they rarely dwell long in these abstractions. Rather, the best poetry seeks to make the abstraction concrete by creating vivid images appealing directly to the senses. A well-written poem will provide the mind of an attentive reader with sights, sounds, tastes, scents, and sensations. Since poems tend to be short and densely packed with meaning, every word and image is there for a reason. Isolate these images and give some thought to what they make you think and how they make you feel. Are they typical or unexpected?

Consider these lines from John Donne's "The Good Morrow":

> My face in thine eye, thine in mine appears,
> And true plain hearts do in the faces rest;
> Where can we find two better hemispheres,
> Without sharp north, without declining west? (lines 15–18)

Here, Donne celebrates the love between the speaker and his object of desire, comparing the faces of the lovers to two "hemispheres" on globes. Elsewhere in the poem, Donne uses imagery that is borrowed from the world of navigation and mapping; here, he suggests that the lovers' faces are an improvement upon whatever instruments explorers and learned men use to understand the world. By examining the images in a poem, their placement, juxtaposition, and effect, you will have gone a long way toward understanding the poem as a whole.

Sound and Sense

Of all the genres, poetry is the one that most self-consciously highlights language, so it is necessary to pay special attention to the sounds of a poem. In fact, it is always a good idea to read a poem aloud several times, giving yourself the opportunity to experience the role that sound plays in the poem's meaning.

Rhyme

Much of the poetry written in English before the twentieth century was written in some form of **rhyme**, and contemporary poets continue to experiment with its effects. Rhymes may seem stilted or old-fashioned to our twenty-first-century ears, but keep in mind that rhymes have powerful social meanings in the cultural context in which they're written. And even today rhyme remains a viable and significant convention in popular songs, which are, after all, a form of poetry. As you read poems, ask yourself how rhymes work. Do they create **juxtapositions**? Alignments of meaning? And what is the effect of that relationship as the poem progresses?

Assonance and Consonance

While it is important to look at the end of a line to see how the poet uses sounds, it is also important to look inside the line. Poets use **assonance**, or repeated vowel sounds, to create an aural effect. Consider these closing lines from Gerard Manley Hopkins's "God's Grandeur":

> And though the last lights off the black West went
>> Oh, morning, at the brown brink eastward, springs —
> Because the Holy Ghost óver the bent
>> World broods with warm breast and with ah! bright wings. (lines 11-14)

Throughout these lines, Hopkins pays special attention to "ee" and "oh" sounds. Notice "brink," "eastward," and "springs" in line 12, and then the continuation of the "ee" sound in "wings" in line 14. Notice "Oh" in line 12, and then "Holy," "Ghost," and "over" in line 13. As you read through each line, ask yourself: Why does the poet align these sounds? Do these sounds speed up the tempo of the line, or slow it down? What do these sounds—and words—reveal about the poet's praise of "God's Grandeur"?

Poets also use **consonance**, repeated consonant sounds, to create alignments and juxtapositions among consonants. Consider these first lines from Christopher Marlowe's "The Passionate Shepherd to His Love" (page 424):

> Come live with me and be my love,
> And we will all the pleasures prove (lines 1–2)

In line 1, Marlowe aligns "live" with "love" to suggest that there is an equation between cohabitation and romance. In line 2, he aligns the "p" sound in "pleasures prove"; in addition, though, the **slant rhyme** of "love" and "prove" also creates meaning between the lines. What "proof" is there in love? Is love what will make the speaker feel most alive?

Meter

Poetry written in English is both **accentual** and **syllabic**. That is, poets count the number of accents as well as the number of syllables as they create each line of poetry. Patterns of syllable and accent have names like "iambic pentameter" and "dactylic tetrameter," and each meter has its own unique properties and effects. Your literature instructor may help you learn about the specifics of meter, or you can find several sites online that explain the art—called **scansion**—of determining the meter of a poem. Whether or not you have a clear understanding of the many meters of poetry in English, when you read a poem, listen to each line to find out how many accents and syllables it contains. If you can determine what that meter is, consider how the poet uses—and subverts—that formula as part of a strategy for the poem.

Form

Poets writing in English use dozens of traditional forms from a variety of traditions. Some of the most common of these forms are the **sonnet**, the **villanelle**, and the **ballad**, but there are too many to name here. As you read a poem in a traditional form, think of the form as a kind of template in which poets arrange and explore challenging emotional and intellectual material. A sonnet, for example, has a concise fourteen-line structure that allows the poet to address a religious, romantic, or philosophical argument in a very compressed space. As you read a sonnet, you might ask yourself: What does its form accomplish that is different from a longer, more narrative-driven form like a ballad? The two sample poems later in this chapter provide a good opportunity to compare a short, highly conventional form with a longer one.

Note, too, that many contemporary poets write in **free verse**, which means that they don't necessarily use a strict traditional form or meter for their poems. That doesn't mean that the free verse poet is writing without rules; it just means that the poet is creating his or her own system for the unique needs of each poem.

Stanzas

A **stanza** is any grouping of lines of poetry into a unit. The term *stanza* comes from the Italian word for "room." As you read poetry, imagine each stanza as a room with its own correspondences and relationships, and consider how that stanza creates a singular effect. Sometimes a stanza can be one line long; sometimes the poet creates a block of lines with no stanza breaks. All of these choices create distinct effects for readers of poetry.

Lineation

Lineation — or how a poet uses the line breaks in the poem — is a crucial component of poetry. Sometimes poets use punctuation at the end of every line, but more often they mix end-stopped lines with enjambed lines. **Enjambment** occurs when the line is not end-stopped with a comma, dash, or period. Its meaning spills over onto the next line, creating the effect of acceleration and intensity. Poets also use **caesuras** in the middle of lines to create variety in the pattern of the line. A caesura is a deep pause created by a comma, colon, semicolon, dash, period, or white space.

TWO POEMS FOR ANALYSIS

Take a few minutes to read William Shakespeare's Sonnet 116 and T. S. Eliot's "The Love Song of J. Alfred Prufrock" and consider the student annotations and the questions that follow the poems. Both of these poems are complex, though in very different ways. What elements of poetry do you notice in these poems? What insights do you have in addition to those suggested by the annotations and questions?

WILLIAM SHAKESPEARE   [1564–1616]

Sonnet 116

Let me not to the marriage of true minds   *Consonance: marriage/mind*
Admit impediments. Love is not love
Which alters when it alteration finds,   *Repetition: love/love, alters/alteratio*
Or bends with the remover to remove.   *remover/remove.*
O, no, it is an ever-fixèd mark
That looks on tempests and is never shaken;   *Abstract ideas become specif*
It is the star to every wandering bark,°   *images: tempests, ships.*
Whose worth's unknown, although his height be taken.°
Love's not time's fool, though rosy lips and cheeks   *Rosy lips and cheeks: clas*
Within his bending sickle's compass come;   *sic love poem images.*   1
Love alters not with his brief hours and weeks,
But bears it out even to the edge of doom.°   *Sickle is a death image, unusu*
    If this be error and upon me proved,   *for a love poem.*
    I never writ, nor no man ever loved.
                                                     Final rhyme is slant rhym

[1609]

7. bark: Ship   **8. taken:** Is measured   **12. doom:** Judgment Day

The student who annotated noticed both structural features of the poem (such as the move from abstract to concrete language) and small-scale language features, such as consonance and repetitions of individual words. This provides a good beginning to understanding the poem; answering the questions that follow will deepen that understanding, making it easier to write a paper about the poem.

QUESTIONS ON THE POEM

☐ What images are most striking in this poem? Do they seem conventional? Surprising? Experimental? Why?

☐ A sonnet often reveals its own logic in order to argue for a point of view. What is the argument of this poem? Do you find it persuasive? If so, why? If not, why not?

☐ What is the rhyme structure of this sonnet? What words are aligned as a result of this scheme?

☐ How does Shakespeare use enjambment and caesura to manage the tempo of the poem? What effects does this create?

T. S. ELIOT   [1888–1965]

The Love Song of J. Alfred Prufrock

S'io credesse che mia risposta fosse
A persona che mai tornasse al mondo,
Questa fiamma staria senza piu scosse.
Ma perciocche giammai di questo fondo
Non torno vivo alcun, s'i'odo il vero,
Senza tema d'infamia ti rispondo.

Footnote says this is from Dante's Inferno. The speaker is in hell. Why start a "love song" with hell?

Let us go then, you and I,   *Who is this "you"? Where are they going?*
When the evening is spread out against the sky
Like a patient etherised upon a table;
Let us go, through certain half-deserted streets,
The muttering retreats   5
Of restless nights in one-night cheap hotels
And sawdust restaurants with oyster-shells: *Setting grubby and seedy. Depressing.*
Streets that follow like a tedious argument
Of insidious intent
To lead you to an overwhelming question . . .   10
Oh, do not ask, "What is it?"

Let us go and make our visit.   *Who are they visiting? Why*

In the room the women come and go   *New setting, in a room. Visiting "the women"*
Talking of Michelangelo.

The yellow fog that rubs its back upon the window-panes,   1
The yellow smoke that rubs its muzzle on the window-panes
Licked its tongue into the corners of the evening,   *Fog like an animal, almost*
Lingered upon the pools that stand in drains,   *a character.*
Let fall upon its back the soot that falls from chimneys,
Slipped by the terrace, made a sudden leap,   2
And seeing that it was a soft October night,
Curled once about the house, and fell asleep.   *Uses rhyme in irregular pattern*

And indeed there will be time
For the yellow smoke that slides along the street,
Rubbing its back upon the window-panes;   2
There will be time, there will be time   *Lots of repetition here, as*
To prepare a face to meet the faces that you meet;   *if he's fixated on these ideas*
There will be time to murder and create,   *and can't let go.*
And time for all the works and days° of hands
That lift and drop a question on your plate;   3
Time for you and time for me,   *He seems obsessed with time*
And time yet for a hundred indecisions,   *and how much of it there is.*
And for a hundred visions and revisions,
Before the taking of a toast and tea.

In the room the women come and go   *Another repetition. Same women?*   3
Talking of Michelangelo.   *Same room?*

And indeed there will be time
To wonder, "Do I dare?" and, "Do I dare?"
Time to turn back and descend the stair,
With a bald spot in the middle of my hair—   4
(They will say: "How his hair is growing thin!")   *Physical description: aging,*
My morning coat, my collar mounting firmly to the chin,   *thin, well dressed*
My necktie rich and modest, but asserted by a simple pin—   *Insecure*
    Indecisive
(They will say: "But how his arms and legs are thin!")
Do I dare   4
Disturb the universe?   *How could he "disturb the*
    universe"?

---

29. works and days: *Works and Days* is the title of a didactic poem about farming by the Greek poet Hesiod (eighth century B.C.E.) that includes instruction about doing each task at the proper time.

In a minute there is time
For decisions and revisions which a minute will reverse.

For I have known them all already, known them all: —   *He seems bored*
Have known the evenings, mornings, afternoons,   *with his life.* 50
I have measured out my life with coffee spoons;   *Maybe*
I know the voices dying with a dying fall°   *depressed?*
Beneath the music from a farther room.
    So how should I presume?

And I have known the eyes already, known them all—   55
The eyes that fix you in a formulated phrase,
And when I am formulated, sprawling on a pin,
When I am pinned and wriggling on the wall,   *Like a bug. More insecurity?*
Then how should I begin
To spit out all the butt-ends of my days and ways?   60
    And how should I presume?

And I have known the arms already, known them all—
Arms that are braceleted and white and bare
(But in the lamplight, downed with light brown hair!)
Is it perfume from a dress   65
That makes me so digress?
Arms that lie along a table, or wrap about a shawl.
    And should I then presume?   *He asks many questions in this section. Maybe*
    And how should I begin?   *unsure of self. Women seem to make him insecure.*

                        •   •   •

Shall I say, I have gone at dusk through narrow streets   70
And watched the smoke that rises from the pipes
Of lonely men in shirt-sleeves, leaning out of windows? . . .

    I should have been a pair of ragged claws   *Earlier he was like a bug, now like a*
Scuttling across the floors of silent seas.   *crab.*

                        •   •   •

And the afternoon, the evening, sleeps so peacefully!   75
Smoothed by long fingers,
Asleep . . . tired . . . or it malingers,
Stretched on the floor, here beside you and me.
Should I, after tea and cakes and ices,

---

52. a dying fall: An allusion to Shakespeare's *Twelfth Night* (1.1.4): "That strain
[of music] again! It had a dying fall" (a cadence that falls away).

Have the strength to force the moment to its crisis?   8

But though I have wept and fasted, wept and prayed,

Though I have seen my head (grown slightly bald) brought in upon a

      platter,°   *Lots of disconnected body parts*

I am no prophet—and here's no great matter;   *eyes, arms, claws, head*

I have seen the moment of my greatness flicker,

And I have seen the eternal Footman hold my coat, and snicker,   8

And in short, I was afraid.

                                          Eternal Footman = Death

   And would it have been worth it, after all,   *Again, he thinks someone is laughing*

After the cups, the marmalade, the tea,   *at him.*

Among the porcelain, among some talk of you and me,

Would it have been worth while,   9

To have bitten off the matter with a smile,

To have squeezed the universe into a ball

To roll it toward some overwhelming question,

To say: "I am Lazarus,° come from the dead,——— *More about death. Who is dead*

Come back to tell you all, I shall tell you all"—   *here? Prufrock himself?*

If one, settling a pillow by her head,   9

    Should say: "That is not what I meant at all.   *Sunsets and teacups seem so*

    That is not it, at all."   *much nicer, sweeter than the grim*

                                      cityscape earlier. Another new

   And would it have been worth it, after all,   *setting? How do they connect?*

Would it have been worth while,   10

After the sunsets and the dooryards and the sprinkled streets,

After the novels, after the teacups, after the skirts that trail along the

      floor—

And this, and so much more?—

It is impossible to say just what I mean!

But as if a magic lantern threw the nerves in patterns on a screen: 10

Would it have been worth while

If one, settling a pillow or throwing off a shawl,

And turning toward the window, should say: *Who is repeating this? "That is not*

    "That is not it at all,   *what I meant" = misunderstanding*

    That is not what I meant, at all."   11

•   •   •

No! I am not Prince Hamlet, nor was meant to be;   *Why compare self to*

Am an attendant lord, one that will do   *Hamlet? He's not a prince.*

                                        Not famous?

82. head . . . platter: As a reward for dancing before King Herod, Salome, his stepdaughter, asked for the head of John the Baptist to be presented to her on a platter (Matthew 14:1–12; Mark 6:17–28).

94. Lazarus: Either the beggar Lazarus, who in Luke 16:19–31 did not return from the dead, or Jesus' friend Lazarus, who did (John 11:1–44).

To swell a progress,° start a scene or two,
Advise the prince; no doubt, an easy tool,
Deferential, glad to be of use,   115
Politic, cautious, and meticulous;

Full of high sentence, but a bit obtuse;
At times, indeed, almost ridiculous—
Almost, at times, the Fool.

Worry about aging. How old is he?

    I grow old . . . I grow old . . .   120
I shall wear the bottoms of my trousers rolled.

    Shall I part my hair behind? Do I dare to eat a peach?   *A peach? How is*
I shall wear white flannel trousers, and walk upon the beach. *that daring?*
I have heard the mermaids singing, each to each.

    I do not think that they will sing to me.   125

    I have seen them riding seaward on the waves   *Setting changes again:*
Combing the white hair of the waves blown back   *now a beach.*
When the wind blows the water white and black.

    We have lingered in the chambers of the sea   *Underwater (like the crab*
By sea-girls wreathed with seaweed red and brown   *earlier).*   130
Till human voices wake us, and we drown.   *Wake us? Is this all a dream? A*
                                                                           nightmare?

[1915]

113. **progress:** Ceremonial journey made by a royal court.

    On a first reading, the student was baffled by the complexities of this poem and felt certain that it was over her head. After annotating it on a second read-through, however, she realized that she had gotten far more out of it than she originally believed and that she had begun to develop some interesting ideas about the speaker and the setting. When her class discussed the poem, she had insightful comments to add to the discussion. The following questions build on and deepen these insights.

QUESTIONS ON THE POEM

☐ What images are most striking in this poem? What makes them striking or memorable?

☐ How do the stanza breaks work in this poem? Why do you suppose Eliot chose these particular places for breaks?

☐ The rhyme and meter of the poem are highly irregular, but it's not quite free verse. Why use rhyme and meter at all? Why not make the rhyme and meter more regular?

☐ What are the various settings of the poem? How does each contribute to your understanding of the poem?

☐ What specific words would you use to sum up the character of Prufrock?

STUDENT ESSAY: AN EXPLICATION

Patrick McCorkle, the author of the paper that follows, was given the assignment to perform a close reading of one of the poems his class had studied. He needed first to pick a poem and then to choose specific features of its language to isolate and analyze. He chose Shakespeare's Sonnet 116 (page 427) because it seemed to him to offer an interesting and balanced definition of love. After rereading the poem, he became interested in several unexpectedly negative, even unsettling images that seemed out of place in a poem about the positive emotion of love. This was a good start, and it allowed him to write a draft of the paper. When he was finished, however, the essay was a little shorter and less complex than he had hoped it would be. During a peer workshop in class, he discussed the sonnet and his draft with two classmates, and together they noticed how many positive words and images appeared in the poem as well. That was the insight Patrick needed to fill out his essay and feel satisfied with the results.

McCorkle 1

atrick McCorkle

rofessor Bobrick

nglish 102

) January 2016

Shakespeare Defines Love

From the earliest written rhymes to the latest radio hit, love
among the eternal themes for poetry. Most love poetry seems to
ll into one of two categories. Either the poet sings the praises of
he beloved and the unending joys of love in overly exaggerated
erms, or the poet laments the loss of love with such bitterness
nd distress that it seems like the end of life. Anyone who has
een in love, though, can tell you that both of these views are
mited and incomplete and that real love is neither entirely joyous
or entirely sad. In Sonnet 116, "Let me not to the marriage of
ue minds," Shakespeare creates a more realistic image of love. By
alancing negative with positive images and language, this sonnet
oes a far better job than thousands of songs and poems before
nd since, defining love in all its complexities and contradictions.

Patrick identifies his topic and states his thesis.

Like many poems, Sonnet 116 relies on a series of visual
mages to paint vivid pictures for the reader, but not all of these
mages are what we might expect in a poem celebrating the
easures of lasting love. A reader can easily picture "an ever-fixèd
ark," a "tempest," a "star," a "wandering bark" (a boat lost at
ea), "rosy lips and cheeks," and a "bending sickle." Some of
hese, like stars and rosy lips, are just the sort of sunny, positive
mages we typically find in love poems of the joyous variety.
thers, though, are more unexpected. Flowers and images of
oringtime, for instance, are standard issue in happy love poetry,
ut a sickle is associated with autumn and the death of the year,
nd metaphorically with death itself in the form of the grim reaper.
ikewise, a boat tossed in a raging tempest is not exactly the
ypical poetic depiction of happy love.

Patrick introduces the poem's contradictory imagery.

Such pictures would hardly seem to provide an upbeat image
f what love is all about, and in fact they might be more at home

Patrick explains the effect of this imagery.

in one of the sad poems about the loss of love. But these tempests and sickles are more realistic than the hearts and flowers of so many lesser love poems. In fact, they show that the poet recognizes the bad times that occur in all relationships, even those strong enough to inspire love sonnets. And the negative images are tempered because of the contexts in which they occur. The "wandering bark," for instance, might represent trouble and loss, but love itself is seen as the star that will lead the boat safely back to calm waters. Meanwhile, the beloved's "rosy lips and cheeks" may fade, but real love outlives even the stroke of death's sickle, lasting "to the edge of doom."

Just as positive and negative images are juxtaposed, so are positive and negative language. The first four lines of Sonnet 116 are made up of two sentences, both negatives, beginning with the words "Let me not" and "Love is not." The negatives of the first few lines continue in phrases like "Whose worth's unknown" and "Love's not time's fool." From here, the poem goes on to dwell in abstract ideas such as "alteration," "impediments," and "error." None of this is what readers of love poems have been led to expect in their previous reading, and we might even wonder if the poet finds this love thing worth the trouble. This strange and unexpected language continues on through the last line of the poem, which contains no fewer than three negative words: "never," "nor," and "no."

Patrick integrates direct quotations from the poem into his close-reading.

Where, a reader might ask, are the expected positive descriptions of love? Where are the summer skies, the smiles and laughter? Clearly, Shakespeare doesn't mean to sweep his readers up in rosy images of a lover's bliss. Ultimately, though, even with the preponderance of negative images and words, the poem strikes a hopeful tone. The hedging about what love isn't and what it can't do are balanced with positive words and phrases, saying clearly what love is: "it is an ever-fixèd mark" and "it is the star." Love, it would seem, does not make our lives perfect, but it gives us the strength, stability, and direction to survive the bad times.

McCorkle 3

Though more than four hundred years have passed since Shakespeare wrote his sonnets, some things never change, and among these is the nature of complex human emotions. In a mere fourteen lines, Shakespeare succeeds where many others have failed through the years, providing a much more satisfying definition of love than one normally sees in one-dimensional, strictly happy or sad poetry. The love he describes is the sort that not everyone is lucky enough to find — a "marriage of true minds" — complicated, unsettling, and very real.

In his conclusion, Patrick suggests that the poem is successful because of the juxtapositions he has discussed.

Work Cited

Shakespeare, William. "Sonnet 116." *Literature: A Portable Anthology*, edited by Janet E. Gardner et al., 4th edition, Bedford/St. Martin's, 2017, p. 427.

CHAPTER 7

Writing about Plays

Perhaps the earliest literary critic in the Western tradition was Aristotle, who, in the fifth century B.C.E., set about explaining the power of the genre of **tragedy** by identifying the six **elements of drama** and analyzing the contribution each of these elements makes to the functioning of a play as a whole. The elements Aristotle identified as common to all dramas were plot, characterization, theme, diction, melody, and spectacle. Some of these are the same as or very similar to the basic components of prose fiction and poetry, but others are either unique to drama or expressed differently in dramatic texts.

ELEMENTS OF DRAMA

Plot, Character, and Theme

The words *plot*, *character*, and *theme* mean basically the same thing in drama as they do in fiction, though there is a difference in how they are presented. A story *tells* you about a series of events, whereas a play *shows* you these events happening in real time. The information that might be conveyed in descriptive passages in prose fiction must be conveyed in a play through **dialogue** (and to a lesser extent through **stage directions** and the **set** and character descriptions that sometimes occur at the start of a play). The "How to Read a Play" section later in this chapter gives suggestions and advice for understanding these special features of drama.

Diction

When Aristotle speaks of **diction**, he means the specific words that a playwright chooses to put into the mouth of a character. In a well-written play, different characters will have different ways of speaking, and these will tell us a good deal about their character and personality. Does one character sound very formal and well educated? Does another speak in slang or dialect? Does someone hesitate or speak in fits and starts, perhaps indicating distraction or nervousness? Practice paying attention to these nuances. And keep in mind that just because a character says something, that doesn't make it true. As in real life, some characters might be mistaken in what they say, or they may be hiding the truth or even telling outright lies.

Melody

When Aristotle writes of **melody**, he is referring to the fact that Greek drama was written in verse and was chanted or sung onstage. The role of melody varies substantially with the work created in different cultures and time periods. In the English Renaissance, Shakespeare and his contemporaries used iambic pentameter and occasional end-rhymes to create dramas in verse, and staged productions have often used some kind of music, whether it be instrumental, vocal, or a mix of both. Melody is much less significant in drama today, though some plays do contain songs, of course. In musical theater, and even more in opera, songs carry much of the meaning of the play. Even in a play with no overt musical component, though, the rhythm of spoken words is important, just as it is in a poem. Even an actor's tone of voice can be considered a part of melody in the Aristotelian sense

Spectacle

Spectacle refers to what we actually see onstage when we go to a play—the costumes, the actors' movements, the sets, the lights, and so forth. All of these details make a difference in how we understand and interpret a play's message. Hamlet's famous "To be or not to be" soliloquy will resonate differently with an audience if the actor playing Hamlet is wearing ripped jeans and a T-shirt, or a modern military uniform, rather than the conventional Renaissance doublet and hose. In reading a play, it is important to remember that it was not written to be read only, but rather so that it would be seen onstage in the communal setting of a theater. Reading with this in mind and trying to imagine the spectacle of a real production will increase your enjoyment of plays immensely. Specific suggestions for this sort of reading can be found in the "How to Read a Play" section of this chapter.

Setting

Setting, which Aristotle ignores completely, is just as important in drama as it is in fiction. But again, in drama it must be either displayed onstage or alluded to through the characters' words rather than being described as it might be in a story or a poem. The texts of modern plays often (though not always) begin with elaborate descriptions of the stage, furniture, major props, and so forth, which can be very useful in helping you picture a production. These tend to be absent in older plays, so in some cases you will have to use your imagination to fill in these gaps. In Act 4 of *Hamlet*, the characters are in a castle one moment and on a windswept plain the next. The only way a reader can be aware of this shift, though, is by paying close attention to the words and actions that characters use to signal a change of locale.

HOW TO READ A PLAY

Very few of us read plays for pleasure in the same way that we might take a novel with us to the beach. This isn't surprising: most playwrights, in fact, never intend for their plays to be read in this way. Drama is a living art, and if you read the play text on the page, you are getting only one part of what has made drama so important to all cultures across many time periods. Plays are written for the stage and are meant to be experienced primarily in live performance. This means that as a reader you must be especially attentive to nuances of language in a play, which often means imagining what might be happening onstage during a particular passage of speech. Using your imagination in this way—in effect, staging the play in your mind—will help you with some of the difficulties inherent in reading plays.

Watching the Play

If you have access to film versions of the play that you are examining, be sure to watch them. Do bear in mind, though, that play scripts usually undergo substantial rewriting to adapt them for film, so you will still need to read the play in its original form, perhaps making comparisons between the stage and film versions. If you are reading a Shakespeare play, you can usually choose from several film versions, many of which might be in your library's collection. Live drama, of course, is different from film. Check the listings of local theaters to see what they are staging; you might find that a theater company is performing the play that you have to read for your class.

The Director's Vision

Some of the most skilled readers of plays are theater directors. These professionals have developed the ability to read a play and instantly see and hear in their minds the many possibilities for how the play might look and sound onstage. Directors understand that a play script is just one piece of a large, collaborative process involving playwright, director, designers, actors, backstage crew, and audience. Every new production of a play is different—sometimes vastly different—from the productions that have gone before, and every play script yields nearly endless possibilities for creative staging. By altering the look and feel of a play, a director puts his or her individual stamp on it, connecting with the audience in a unique way and helping that audience understand the playwright's and the director's messages. The questions that follow are the sort that a director would consider when reading a play. As you read plays for your literature class, these questions can help you formulate a consistent and strong interpretation.

DIRECTOR'S QUESTIONS FOR PLAY ANALYSIS

- [ ] What is the main message or theme of the play? What thoughts and/or feelings could be stirred up in an audience during a performance?
- [ ] In what kind of theater would you like to stage this play? A large, high-tech space with room to accommodate a huge audience? Or something more intimate?
- [ ] What type of audience would you hope to attract to a production of this play? Older people? Young adults? Kids? Urban or rural? A mix? Who would get the most from the play's messages and themes?
- [ ] Which actors would you cast in the lead roles? Think about the sort of people you want for the various roles in terms of age, physical description, and so on. What should their voices sound like? Loud and commanding? Soft and timid?
- [ ] What kind of physical movement, blocking, or choreography would you want to see onstage? What are the most dramatic moments in the script? The most quiet or subtle?
- [ ] What would the set design look like? Would it change between acts and scenes or remain the same for the duration of the play?
- [ ] How would the characters be costumed? Period clothes? Modern dress? Something totally different? How could costuming contribute to character development?
- [ ] How much spectacle do you want? Would there be vivid sound and lighting effects? Or are you looking for a more naturalistic feel? How would this help portray the play's message?

STUDENT ESSAY: AN ANALYSIS

Sarah Johnson was free to choose the topic and focus of her paper. In the same semester as her literature class, she was enrolled in a philosophy course on ethics where she was introduced to the idea of situational ethics, the notion that exterior pressures often cause people to act in ways they might normally deem unethical, often to prevent or allay a worse evil. This philosophical concept was on Sarah's mind when she read Susan Glaspell's play *Trifles* (page 939). She noticed that the character of Mrs. Peters does indeed end up behaving in a way she would probably never have imagined for herself. This seemed an interesting concept to pursue, so Sarah decided to trace the development of Mrs. Peters' journey away from her original moral certainty.

arah Johnson

rofessor Riley

nglish 253

4 October 2016

Moral Ambiguity and Character Development

in *Trifles*

What is the relationship between legality and morality? Susan

laspell's short play *Trifles* asks us to ponder this question, but it

rovides no clear answers. Part murder mystery, part battle of the

exes, the play makes its readers confront and question many

sues about laws, morals, and human relationships. In the person

f Mrs. Peters, a sheriff's wife, the play chronicles one woman's   *Sarah focuses on*
                                                                        Mrs. Peters right
oral journey from a certain, unambiguous belief in the law to a   *away.*

ore situational view of ethics. Before it is over, this once legally

inded woman is even willing to cover up the truth and let some-

ne get away with murder.

At the beginning of the play, Mrs. Peters believes that law.

uth, and morality are one and the same. Though never unkind

pout the accused, Mrs. Wright, Mrs. Peters is at first firm in her

elief that the men will find the truth and that the crime will be

unished as it should be. Mrs. Hale feels the men are "kind of   *Sarah uses direct*
                                                                       quotations from
neaking" as they look about Mrs. Wright's abandoned house for   *the play text as*
                                                                       backup for her
vidence against her, but Mrs. Peters assures her that "the law is   *claims.*

ne law." It is not that Mrs. Peters is less sympathetic toward

omen than her companion, but she is even more sympathetic

oward the lawmen, because her version of morality is so absolute.

'hen the men deride the women's interest in so-called trifles, like

ewing and housework, Mrs. Hale takes offense. But Mrs. Peters,

onvinced that the law must prevail, defends them, saying, "It's

o more than their duty," and later, "They've got awful important

nings on their minds."

As she attempts to comply with the requirements of the law,

rs. Peters is described in a stage direction as "businesslike," and

ne tries to maintain a skeptical attitude as she waits for the truth to emerge. Asked if she thinks Mrs. Wright killed her husband, she says, "Oh, I don't know." She seems to be trying to convince herself that the accused is innocent until proven guilty, though she admits that her husband thinks it "looks bad for her." She seems to have absorbed her husband's attitudes and values and to be keeping a sort of legalistic distance from her feelings about the case.

Mrs. Hale is less convinced of the rightness of the men or the law. Even before the two women discover a possible motive for the murder, Mrs. Hale is already tampering with evidence, tearing out the erratic sewing stitches that suggest Mrs. Wright was agitated. Mrs. Peters says, "I don't think we ought to touch things," but she doesn't make any stronger move to stop Mrs. Hale, who continues to fix the sewing. At this point, we see her first beginning to waver from her previously firm stance on right and wrong.

It is not that Mrs. Peters is unsympathetic to the hard life that Mrs. Wright has led. She worries with Mrs. Hale about the accused woman's frozen jars of preserves, her half-done bread, and her unfinished quilt. But she tries to think, like the men, that these things are "trifles" and that what matters is the legal truth. But when she sees a bird with a wrung neck, things begin to change in a major way. She remembers the boy who killed her kitten when she was a child, and the sympathy she has felt for Mrs. Wright begins to turn to empathy. The empathy is enough to prompt her first lie to the men. When the county attorney spies the empty birdcage, she corroborates Mrs. Hale's story about a cat getting the bird, even though she knows there was no cat in the house.

In this paragraph, Sarah analyzes a turning point in the play text: a moment in which Mrs. Peters experiences a transformation.

Even after she has reached that point of empathy, Mrs. Peters tries hard to maintain her old way of thinking and of being. Alone again with Mrs. Hale, she says firmly, "We don't know who killed the bird," even though convincing evidence points to John Wright. More important, she says of Wright himself, "We don't know who killed him. We don't *know*." But her repetition and her "rising voice," described in a stage direction, show how agitated she has become. As a believer in the law, she should feel certain that

Johnson 3

veryone is innocent until proven guilty, but she thinks she knows
the truth, and, perhaps for the first time in her life, legal truth
does not square with moral truth. Her empathy deepens further
till when she thinks about the stillness of the house in which Mrs.
Wright was forced to live after the death of her beloved pet, which
brought song to an otherwise grim life. She knows Mrs. Wright is
childless, and she now remembers not just the death of her
childhood kitten but also the terrible quiet in her own house after
her first child died. She reaches a moment of crisis between her
two ways of thinking when she says, "I know what stillness is.
Pulling herself back.) The law has got to punish crimes, Mrs. Hale."
This is perhaps the most important line in the chronicle of her
growth as a character. First she expresses her newfound empathy
with the woman she believes to be a murderer; then, as the stage
directions say, she tries to pull herself back and return to the
comfortable moral certainty that she felt just a short time before.
It is too late for that, though.

Here and else-where, Sarah relies on stage directions as evidence for her claims about Mrs. Peters.

    In the end, Mrs. Peters gives in to what she believes to be
emotionally right rather than what is legally permissible. She collab-
orates with Mrs. Hale to cover up evidence of the motive and hide
the dead canary. Though very little time has gone by, she has under-
gone a major transformation. She may be, as the county attorney
says, "married to the law," but she is also divorced from her old
ideals. When she tries to cover up the evidence, a stage direction
says she "goes to pieces," and Mrs. Hale has to help her. By the
time she pulls herself together, the new woman she is will be a very
different person from the old one. She, along with the reader, is
now in a world where the relationship between legality and morality is far more complex than she had ever suspected.

Sarah isolates this passage to emphasize the complexity of Mrs. Peters.

Work Cited

Glaspell, Susan. *Trifles*. *Literature: A Portable Anthology*, edited by
    Janet E. Gardner et al., 4th edition, Bedford/St. Martin's,
    2017, pp. 939–50.

CHAPTER 8

Writing a Literary Research Paper

Writing a literary research paper draws on the same set of skills as writing any other paper—choosing a topic, developing a thesis, gathering and organizing support, and so on. The main difference between research writing and other sorts of writing lies in the number and types of sources from which one's support comes. All writing about literature begins with a **primary source**—the poem, story, or play on which the writing is based. Research papers also incorporate **secondary sources**, such as biographical, historical, and critical essays.

As you begin the process of research writing, the most important thing to remember is that you are writing a critical argument. Your paper should not end up reading like a book report or a catalog of what others have said about the literature. Rather, it should begin and end by making an original point based on your own ideas, and like any other paper, it needs a clear, sharply focused thesis. The sources, both primary and secondary, are there to support your thesis, not to take over the paper.

The method laid out below seems very linear and straightforward: find and evaluate sources for your paper, read them and take notes, and then write a paper integrating material from these sources. In reality, the process is rarely, if ever, this neat. As you read and write, you will discover gaps in your knowledge, or you will ask yourself new questions that will demand more research. Be flexible. Keep in mind that the process of research is recursive, requiring a writer to move back and forth between various stages. Naturally, this means that for research writing, even more than for other kinds of writing, you should start early and give yourself plenty of time to complete the project.

FINDING SOURCES

For many students, research is more or less synonymous with the Internet. It may be easy to think that all the information anybody could ever want is available online, readily and easily accessible to the public. But when it comes to literary research, this is not the case at all. True, there are plenty of Web sites and newsgroups devoted to literary figures, but the type of information available on these sites tends to be limited to a narrow range—basic biographies of authors, plot summaries, and so forth—and the quality of information is highly variable. Though serious literary scholarship does exist on the Web, proprietary online databases (available through a library portal) and print books and journals are still the better sources for you in most cases.

Online Indexes

You can begin to locate sources for your research paper by using the online indexes and databases available through your college or university library. These services sort and index journal and magazine articles to help researchers find what they are looking for. Although using these indexes is somewhat similar to using an Internet search engine, the two should not be confused. The Internet links to an array of documents— some of very high quality, some worse than useless—that are available for free to the public. By contrast, college, university, and many public libraries pay a fee to allow their users access to the more specialized and highly vetted sources found in various indexes and databases. When you use these services, you are assured that any articles you locate have been published by reliable, respected sources.

Your library probably subscribes to dozens of databases covering many fields of knowledge. These are some of the most useful ones for literary research:

- *Academic OneFile* and *Expanded Academic ASAP* (both from InfoTrac) index a combination of scholarly journals and popular magazines and provide a good starting point for articles of general interest.
- *Literary Reference Center* (EBSCO) provides full-text articles from specialized encyclopedias and reference works, including author biographies, synopses of major literary works, and articles on literary history and criticism.
- *MLA International Bibliography* (EBSCO) indexes scholarly books and articles on modern languages, literature, folklore, and linguistics; many have full-text links.
- *Humanities Index* (H. W. Wilson) indexes periodicals in the humanities, including scholarly journals and lesser-known specialized magazines; many have full-text links.
- *JSTOR* provides searchable, full-text articles digitized from more than a thousand academic journals, some dating back to the nineteenth century.

These indexes are just a sampling of those most generally applicable to literary research. Depending on your particular topic or interests, you may find yourself drawn to one of the many more specialized indexes, such as *GenderWatch* (for topics related to feminism and other gender issues), *GreenFile* (for environmental topics), and *Hispanic American Periodicals Index*, to name just a few.

If you do not know how to access or use these sources, ask the reference librarian on duty at your college library. Helping students find what they need is this person's principal job, and you will likely learn a lot from him or her. Both your librarian and your instructor can also suggest additional indexes to point you toward good secondary sources. One of the great advantages of databases and indexes is that results can be filtered and sorted according to a wide array of criteria. You can find articles written in a particular year or in a particular language; you can choose to look only at articles that have been peer-reviewed (the process that assures scholarly legitimacy); or you can select any of a number of other filters to help you find exactly what you need.

Using the Best Search Terms

When you begin searching, use fairly specific search terms to help the database focus on what you really need and to filter out irrelevant material. Let's say you are researching the nature of love in Shakespeare's sonnets. If you perform a search on the keyword or topic *Shakespeare*, you will get many thousands of hits, many of them about topics unrelated to yours. Searching on both *Shakespeare* and *sonnet*, however, will get you closer to what you want, while searching on *Shakespeare*, *sonnet*, and *love* will yield far fewer and far better, more targeted results. If your search nets you fewer results than you expected, try again with different terms (substitute *romance* for *love*, for example). Be patient, and don't be afraid to ask your instructor or librarian for help if you are experiencing difficulty.

Evaluating the Results

Once you have a screen full of results, you will be able to access a **text**, an abstract, or a citation. Some results will give you a link to the complete text of an article; just click on the link, and you can read the article on-screen, print it out, or e-mail it to yourself. Frequently, a link is provided to an abstract, a brief summary (generally just a few sentences) of the content of the full article. Reading an abstract is a good way of finding out whether it is worth tracking down the whole article for your paper.

A citation gives only the most basic information about an article—its title, its author, the date of publication, and its page numbers—and it is up to you to then find and read the whole article.

It may be tempting to settle on only those articles available immediately in full-text versions. Don't fall into this trap. Even in this electronic age, scholars and specialists still write books, as well as articles for academic journals that are not always available in electronic versions. Many of the best sources of literary research are available only in print, and the only way to obtain these is to follow the citation's lead and locate the book or journal in the library stacks. If a title or an abstract looks promising, go and retrieve the article. If you think getting up and tracking down a journal is frustrating or time-consuming, imagine how frustrating and time-consuming it will be to attempt to write a research paper without great sources.

Periodicals

At this point, you should be aware of the distinction between two types of periodicals that your search may lead to: magazines, which are directed at a general readership, and scholarly journals, which are written by and for specialists in various academic fields. *Scientific American*, for instance, is a well-respected magazine available on newsstands, whereas *The Journal of Physical Chemistry* is a scholarly journal, generally available only by subscription and read mainly by chemists and chemistry students. In the field of literary studies, there are hundreds of journals, ranging from publications covering a general period or topic (*American Literary Realism, Modern Drama*) to those devoted to specific authors (*Walt Whitman Review, Melville Society Extracts*).

While magazines like *Time* and *Newsweek* are sometimes appropriate research sources, and you certainly should not rule them out, the highest-quality and most sophisticated literary criticism tends to appear in journals. If you are uncertain whether you are looking at a scholarly journal, look for the following typical characteristics:

- Scholarly journal articles tend to be *longer* than magazine articles, ranging anywhere from five to more than fifty pages.

- Journal articles are *written by specialists* for researchers, professors, and college students. The author's professional credentials and institutional affiliation are often listed.

- Journal articles tend to be written in a given profession's *special language* and can be difficult for nonspecialists to understand. Articles in literary journals use the specialized language of literary theory and criticism.

- Journal articles are usually *peer-reviewed* or refereed, meaning that other specialists have read them and determined that they make a significant contribution to the field. Peer referees are often listed as an editorial board on the journal's masthead page.
- Journal articles usually include *footnotes or endnotes* and an often substantial references, *bibliography*, or works cited section.

Books

As mentioned earlier, many scholars still publish their most important work in print books, and the place to look for these is in your college or university library's catalog. (Public libraries, no matter how well run, seldom carry the sorts of specialized sources needed for college-level research.) Start by looking for one or two good books on your topic. Books tend to be more general in their scope than journal articles, and they can be useful at the early stages of your research to help you focus and refine your thinking. If you have given yourself sufficient time for the process, take a book or two home and skim them to determine which parts would be most useful for you. When you return to the library to perform more research, you will have a clearer sense of what you are looking for and therefore will be more efficient at completing the rest of your search.

Interlibrary Loan

If you find a promising lead but discover that your library doesn't have a particular book or has no subscription to the needed periodical, you still may be in luck. Nearly all libraries offer interlibrary loan services, which can track down books and articles from a large network of other libraries and send them to your home institution, generally free of charge. Of course, this process takes time—usually, a couple of days to a couple of weeks—and this is yet another reason to get started as early as possible on your research.

The Internet

Lastly, if your quest for books and periodicals has not yielded all the results you want, search the Internet. As with a search of a specialized index, you will do better and filter out a lot of low-quality sources if you come up with some well-focused search terms in advance. Be sure to ask your instructor or reference librarian about authoritative Web sites. Your librarian may have already created a special page on the library's Web site that provides links to the best Web sites for students of English.

If you use the Web for your research, look especially for scholarly sites, written by professors or researchers and maintained by colleges and universities. For example, if you want to research the poetry and artwork of William Blake, you might check The Blake Archive, an online project sponsored by the Library of Congress and the University of North Carolina, Chapel Hill: www.blakearchive.org/blake/. If you are interested in learning more about Walt Whitman's life and work, check The Walt Whitman Archive, a project developed and edited by Ed Folsom and Kenneth M. Price, both of whom are eminent Whitman scholars: www.whitmanarchive.org/. If you want to read the 1603 printing of *Hamlet*, check the British Library's Web site: www.bl.uk/treasures/shakespeare /homepage.html. Also potentially useful are the online equivalents of scholarly journals, as well as discussion groups or newsgroups dedicated to particular authors, literary schools, or periods.

How do you know when you have enough sources? Many instructors specify a minimum number of sources for research papers, and many students find exactly that number of sources and then look no further. Your best bet is to stop looking for sources when you think you have enough material to write a top-quality paper. Indeed, it is far better to gather up too many sources and end up not using them all than to get too few and find yourself wanting more information as you write. And remember that any "extra" research beyond what you actually cite in your paper isn't really wasted effort—every piece of information you read contributes to your background knowledge and overall understanding of your topic, making your final paper sound smarter and better informed.

EVALUATING SOURCES

As you locate research sources, you should engage in a continual process of evaluation to determine both the reliability of the potential source and its appropriateness to your particular topic and needs. Keep the following questions in mind to help you evaluate both print and electronic sources:

- **Who is the author, and what are his or her credentials?** If this information is not readily available, you might ask yourself why not. Is the author or publisher trying to hide something?

- **What is the medium of publication?** Books, journals, magazines, newspapers, and electronic publications all have something to offer a researcher, but they do not all offer the same thing. A good researcher will usually seek out a variety of sources.

- **How respectable is the publisher?** Not all publishers are created equal, and some have a much better reputation than others for reliability. Just because something is published, that doesn't make it accurate—think of all those supermarket tabloids publishing articles about alien autopsies. In general, your best sources are books from university presses and major, well-established publishers; scholarly journal articles; and articles from well-regarded magazines and newspapers such as the *Atlantic Monthly* or the *New York Times*. If you are not sure how respectable or reliable a particular publisher or source might be, ask your instructor or librarian.
- **If it's an online publication, who is hosting the site?** Though commercial sites (whose Web addresses end in *.com*) should not be ruled out, keep in mind that these sites are often driven by profit as much as a desire to educate the public. Sites hosted by educational institutions, nonprofit organizations, or the government (*.edu*, *.org*, and *.gov*, respectively) tend to be more purely educational, though they likely won't be free of an agenda either.
- **How recent is the publication?** While older publications can often be appropriate—you may be doing historical research, or you may want to refer to a classic in a certain field—newer ones are preferable, all other things being equal. Newer publications take advantage of more recent ideas and theories, and they often summarize or incorporate older sources.
- **How appropriate is the source to your specific project?** Even the highest-quality scholarly journal or a book by the top expert in a given field will be appropriate for only a very limited number of research projects. Let your topic, your tentative thesis, and your common sense be your guides.

WORKING WITH SOURCES

You now have a stack of articles and printouts of electronic sources, and perhaps a book or two as well. How do you work through these to get the support you need for your paper?

- *First*, sort the various sources by expected relevance, with those you think will be most informative and useful to you on the top of the list.
- *Next*, skim or read through everything quickly, highlighting or making note of the parts that seem most directly applicable to your paper. (Obviously, you should not mark up or otherwise deface library materials—take notes on a separate piece of paper.)

- *Then*, slow down and reread the important passages again, this time taking careful notes.
- *When taking notes*, keep yourself scrupulously well organized, making sure that you always know which of your notes refers to which source.

If you are taking notes by hand, it's a good idea to start a separate page for each source. If you are using a computer to take notes, start a separate file or section for each new source you read.

Notes will generally fall into one of four categories: quotations, paraphrases, summaries, and commentaries.

Quotations

While quotations are useful, and you will almost certainly incorporate several into your paper, resist the urge to transcribe large portions of text from your sources. Papers that rely too heavily on quotations can be unpleasant reading, with a cluttered or choppy style that results from moving back and forth between your prose and that of the various authors you quote. Reserve direct quoting for those passages that are especially relevant and that you simply can't imagine phrasing as clearly or elegantly yourself. When you do make note of a quotation, be sure also to note the pages on which it appears in the source material so that later you will be able to cite it accurately.

Paraphrases and Summaries

Most often, you should take notes in the form of **paraphrase** or summary. To paraphrase, simply put an idea or opinion drawn from a source into your own words. Generally, a paraphrase will be about equal in length to the passage being paraphrased, while a summary will be much shorter, capturing the overall point of a passage while leaving out supporting details. Here is a brief passage from *Britannica Online*'s biography of Emily Dickinson, followed by a paraphrase and a summary:

> She began writing in the 1850s; by 1860 she was boldly experimenting with language and prosody, striving for vivid, exact words and epigrammatic concision while adhering to the basic quatrains and metres of the Protestant hymn. The subjects of her deceptively simple lyrics, whose depth and intensity contrast with the apparent quiet of her life, include love, death, and nature. Her numerous letters are sometimes equal in artistry to her poems.

Paraphrase

Dickinson began writing poetry in the 1850s, and within ten years she had begun experimenting with poetic styles and forms. She used meters that were familiar to her from church hymns, but her words were chosen to be especially concise and vivid. She wrote about love, death, and nature in ways that seem simple but contain a great deal of emotional depth and intensity. She was also an avid letter-writer, and her letters show the same care and artistry as her poems.

Summary

In both her poems and her many letters, Dickinson used formal experimentation and precision to get to the heart of the themes of love, death, and nature.

Paraphrasing and summarizing are usually superior to quoting for two reasons. First, if you can summarize or paraphrase with confidence, then you know you have really understood what you have read. Second, a summary or paraphrase will be more easily transferred from your notes to your paper and will fit in well with your individual prose style. (For more on the use of summary, see pages 1263–64.) Just as with quotations, make a note of the page numbers in the source material from which your summaries and paraphrases are drawn.

Commentaries

Finally, some of your notes can be written as commentaries. When something you read strikes you as interesting, you can record your reaction to it. Do you agree or disagree strongly? Why? What exactly is the connection between the source material and your topic or tentative thesis? Making copious commentaries will help you keep your own ideas in the forefront and will keep your paper from devolving into a shopping list of other writers' priorities. Be sure to note carefully when you are commenting rather than summarizing or paraphrasing. When you are drafting your paper, you will want to distinguish carefully between which ideas are your own and which are borrowed from others.

Keeping Track of Your Sources

As you take notes on the substance of your reading, it is also essential that you record the source's author, title, and publication information for later use in compiling your works cited list, or bibliography. Nothing is more frustrating than having to retrace your research steps on a computer, or even to return to the library, just to get a page reference or the full title of a source. Most accomplished researchers actually put together their works cited list as they go along rather than waiting until the essay is drafted. Such a strategy will ensure that you have all the information you need, and it will save you from the painstaking (and potentially tedious) task of having to create the list all at once at the end of your process.

WRITING THE PAPER

After what may seem like a long time spent gathering and working with your sources, you are now ready to begin the actual writing of your paper.

Refine Your Thesis

Start by looking again at your tentative thesis. Now that you have read a lot and know much more about your topic, does your proposed thesis still seem compelling and appropriate? Is it a little too obvious, something that other writers have already said or have taken for granted? Do you perhaps need to refine or modify it in order to take into account the information you have learned and opinions you have encountered? If necessary—and it usually is—refine or revise your tentative thesis so that it can help you stay focused as you write. (For advice on what makes a good thesis, see pages 1235–38.)

Organize Your Evidence

Just as with any other essay, you will need to organize the evidence in support of your thesis. Follow whatever process for organization you have used successfully in writing other papers, while bearing in mind that this time you will probably have more, and more complex, evidence to deal with. You will likely need an outline—formal or informal—to help you put your materials in a coherent and sensible order. But, once again, flexibility is the key here. If, as you begin to work your way through the outline, some different organizational strategy begins to make sense to you, revise your outline rather than forcing your ideas into a preconceived format.

Start Your Draft

The actual drafting of the research paper is probably the part you will find most similar to writing other papers. Try to write fairly quickly and fluently, knowing you can and will add examples, fill in explanations, eliminate redundancies, and work on style during the revision phase. As with your other papers, you may want to write straight through from beginning to end, or you may want to save difficult passages like the introduction for last. Interestingly, many writers find that the process of drafting a research paper actually goes a bit more quickly than does drafting other papers, largely because their considerable research work has left them so well versed in the topic that they have a wealth of ideas for writing.

What might slow you down as you draft your research papers are the citations, which you provide so that a reader knows which ideas are your own and which come from outside sources. Before you begin drafting, familiarize yourself with the conventions for MLA in-text citations (see pages 1325–41). Each time you incorporate a quotation, paraphrase, or summary into your essay, you will need to cite the author's name and the relevant page numbers (if available) from the source material. Do not, however, get hung up at this stage trying to remember how to format and punctuate citations. There will be time to hammer out these details later, and it is important as you write to keep your focus on the big picture.

Revise

As you go through the revision process, you should do so with an eye toward full integration of your source material. Are all connections between quotations, paraphrases, or summaries and your thesis clear? Do you include sufficient commentary explaining the inclusion of all source material? Is it absolutely clear which ideas come from which research source? Most important, is the paper still a well-focused argument, meant to convince an audience of the validity of your original thesis? Bearing these questions in mind, you will be ready to make the same sorts of global revision decisions that you would for any other paper— what to add, what to cut, how to reorganize, and so forth. (See pages 1244–49 for a reminder of what to look for.)

Edit and Proofread

During the final editing and proofreading stage, include one editorial pass just for checking quotations and documentation format. Make sure each quotation is accurate and exact. Ensure that each reference to a source has an appropriate in-text citation and that your list of works cited (bibliography) is complete and correct. Double-check manuscript format and punctuation issues with the guidelines included in this book or with another appropriate resource. After putting so much time and effort into researching and writing your paper, it would be a shame to have its effectiveness diminished by small inaccuracies or errors.

UNDERSTANDING AND AVOIDING PLAGIARISM

Everyone knows that **plagiarism** is wrong. Buying or borrowing some-one else's work, downloading all or part of a paper from the Web, and sim-ilar practices are beyond reprehensible. Most colleges and universities have codes of academic honesty forbidding such practices and impos-ing severe penalties—including expulsion from the institution in some cases—on students who are caught breaking them. Many educators feel these penalties are, if anything, not severe enough. Instructors tend to be not only angered but also baffled by students who plagiarize. In addition to the obvious wrongs of cheating and lying (nobody likes being lied to), students who plagiarize are losing out on a learning opportunity, a waste of the student's time as well as the instructor's.

Not everyone, though, is altogether clear on what plagiarism entails, and a good deal of plagiarism can actually be unintentional on the part of the student. A working definition of plagiarism will help to clarify what plagiarism is:

- presenting someone else's ideas as your own
- using information from any print or electronic source without fully citing the source
- buying or "borrowing" a paper from any source
- submitting work that someone else has written, in whole or in part
- having your work edited to the point that it is no longer your work
- submitting the same paper for more than one class without the express permission of the instructors involved

Some of this is obvious. You know it is cheating to have a friend do your homework or to download a paper from the Web and submit it as your own. But the first and last items on the list are not as clear-cut or self-explanatory. What exactly does it mean to present someone else's ideas as your own? Many students believe that as long as they rephrase an idea into their own words, they have done their part to avoid plagia-rism; however, they are mistaken. Readers assume, and reasonably so, that everything in your paper is a product of your own thinking, not just your own phrasing, unless you share credit with another by document-ing your source. No matter how it is phrased, an original idea belongs to the person who first thought of it and wrote it down; in fact, the notion of possession in this context is so strong that the term applied to such ownership is *intellectual property*.

As an analogy, imagine you invented a revolutionary product, patented it, and put it up for sale. The next week, you find that your neighbor has produced the same product, painted it a different color, changed the name, and is doing a booming business selling the product. Is your neighbor any less guilty of stealing your idea just because he or she is using a new name and color for the product? Of course not. Your intellectual property, the idea behind the product, has been stolen. And you are no less guilty of plagiarism if you glean a piece of information, an opinion, or even an abstract concept from another person, put it into your own words, and "sell" it in your paper without giving proper credit.

Let us say, for example, that you find this passage about William Butler Yeats:

> Religious by temperament but unable to accept orthodox Christianity, Yeats throughout his life explored esoteric philosophies in search of a tradition that would substitute for a lost religion. He became a member of the Theosophical Society and the Order of the Golden Dawn, two groups interested in Eastern occultism, and later developed a private system of symbols and mystical ideas.

Drawing from this passage, you write:

> Yeats rejected the Christianity of his native Ireland, but he became interested in occultism and Eastern philosophy. From these sources, he developed his own system of mystical symbols that he used in his poetry.

Clearly the words of this new passage are your own, and some elements of the original have been streamlined while other information has been added. However, the essential line of reasoning and the central point of both passages are largely the same. If this second passage appears in your paper without an acknowledgment of the original source, *this is plagiarism*.

Finally, let's look at the last item on the list: submitting the same paper for more than one class without the express permission of the instructors involved. Sometimes, you will find substantial overlap in the subject matter of two or more of your classes. A literature class, for instance, has elements of history, psychology, sociology, and other disciplines, and once in a while you might find yourself working on writing projects in courses that share common features. You might be tempted to let your research and writing in such a case do double duty, and there is not necessarily anything wrong with that. However, if you wish to write a paper on a single topic for more than one class, clear these plans with both instructors first. And, of course, even if you use the same research sources for both assignments, you will almost certainly need to write two separate essays, tailoring each to meet the specifications of individual classes and disciplines.

WHAT TO DOCUMENT AND WHAT *NOT* TO DOCUMENT

Everything borrowed from another source needs to be documented. Obviously, you should document every direct quotation of any length from primary or secondary sources. Equally important is the documentation of all your paraphrases and summaries of ideas, information, and opinions, citing authors and page numbers. The rule of thumb is that if you didn't make it up yourself, you should probably document it.

The word *probably* in the previous sentence suggests that there are exceptions, and indeed there are. You do not need to document proverbial sayings ("Live and let live") or very familiar quotations ("I have a dream"), though in the case of the latter you may want to allude to the speaker in your text. You also do not need to document any information that can be considered common knowledge. Common knowledge here refers not only to information that you would expect nearly every adult to know immediately (that Shakespeare wrote *Hamlet*, for instance, or that George Washington was the first president of the United States). Common knowledge also encompasses undisputed information that you could look up in a general or specialized reference work. The average person on the street probably couldn't tell you that T. S. Eliot was born in 1888, but you don't need to say where that piece of information comes from, as it is widely available to anyone who wishes to find it.

Use both your common sense and your sense of fairness to make any necessary decisions about whether or not to document something. When in doubt, ask your instructor, and remember, it's better to document something unnecessarily than to be guilty of plagiarism.

DOCUMENTING SOURCES: MLA FORMAT

This section includes information on how to document the following:

Some students seem to believe that English teachers find footnotes and bibliographies and textual citations fun and interesting. In truth, few people know better than those who have to teach it how tedious format and documentation can be for a writer. Chances are your instructor will insist that you document your sources. There are at least three reasons for requiring documentation. First, a sense of fair play demands that we give proper credit to those whose ideas benefit us. Second, by documenting your sources, you make it possible for your readers to find the sources themselves and follow up if they become interested in something in your paper. Third, documenting your sources, and doing it accurately, enhances your credibility as a writer by highlighting your professionalism and thoroughness.

As you read the following pages, and as you work on documenting sources in your own papers, don't say that you don't understand it or that you can't learn this. If you learned the difficult and abstract skills of reading and writing, you can certainly learn something as concrete as documentation. Actually, documentation is the easy part of research writing, since there is only one right way to do it. The hard part is the creative work of discovering and presenting your original ideas and integrating them fluently with the work of others. And, of course, you don't need to actually memorize the specifics of format. Nobody does. When you need to know how to cite an anonymous newspaper article or what to include in a bibliographic entry for a radio broadcast, for instance, you can look it up. That's what professional writers do all the time.

There are many different forms and formulas for documenting sources—the APA (American Psychological Association) format commonly used in the social sciences, the CBE (Council of Biology Editors) format used in the life sciences, the *Chicago* (*Chicago Manual of Style*) format used in history, and so on. Each system highlights the type of information most relevant to experts in a particular field. If you have received contradictory instructions about documentation format for research projects in the past—include dates in your in-text references or don't; use footnotes or use endnotes—chances are you were working in different documentation systems. The format most often used in the humanities is MLA, the system developed by the Modern Language Association.

MLA format breaks down into two main elements: in-text citations and a works cited list (bibliography). In-text citations are parenthetical references that follow each quotation, paraphrase, or summary and give the briefest possible information about the source, usually the author's last name and a page number. The works cited list, which comes at the end of the paper, gives more detailed information about all sources used. The idea is that a reader coming across a parenthetical reference in your text can easily turn to the works cited list and get full details about the type of publication from which the material comes, the date of publication, and so on. (Some writers use a third element of MLA style, content endnotes, which come between the end of the paper and the works cited list and contain extra information not readily integrated into the paper. Although you may use endnotes if you wish, they are not necessary.)

The following pages describe the major types of sources you are likely to encounter and how to reference those sources both in the text of your research paper and in your works cited list. The information here, however, is not exhaustive. If you want to cite a source not covered here, or if you would like more information about MLA style and citation format, turn to the following book:

MLA Handbook, 8th edition. Modern Language Association, 2016.

In-Text Citations

The purpose of an in-text citation is to give a very brief acknowledgment of a source within the body of your essay. In MLA format, in-text citations take the form of brief parenthetical interruptions directly following each quotation, paraphrase, or summary. Some students find these interruptions a bit distracting at first, but you will quickly find that you grow accustomed to them and that soon they will not slow your reading or comprehension. The following explanations and examples of in-text citations should cover most instances you will encounter.

Citing Author and Page Number in Parentheses

Typically, a citation will contain the last name of the author being cited and a page number. The first example here shows a direct quotation, the second a paraphrase.

> One reviewer referred to *Top Girls* as, "among other things, a critique of bourgeois feminism" (Munk 33).

> When English wool was in demand, the fens were rich, but for many years now they have been among the poorest regions in England (Chamberlain 13).

Coming across these references in your text, your readers will know that they can turn to your works cited list and find out the full names of Munk and Chamberlain; the titles of what they have written; and where, when, and in what medium the works were published.

Please note:

- **In-text references contain no extraneous words or punctuation.** There is no comma between the name and the page number. Neither the word *page* nor the abbreviation *p.* precede the number. There are no extra spaces, just the name and the number.

- **Quotation marks close *before* the citation.** The in-text citation is not part of a direct quotation, so it does not belong inside the quotation marks.

- **The period that ends the sentence is placed *after* the citation.** Probably the most common error students make in MLA in-text citation is to put the period (or other closing punctuation mark) at the end of the quotation or paraphrase and then give the reference in parentheses. Doing so, however, makes the citation the beginning of the next sentence rather than the end of the one being cited.

Citing the Author in Body Text and Only the Page Number in Parentheses

If you have already named the author in your own text, for instance in a lead-in phrase, you do not need to repeat the name in parentheses, as your reader will already know which author to look for in your works cited. In this case, the parenthetical reference need only contain the page number. The two examples already given could be rewritten as follows:

> Reviewer Erika Munk referred to *Top Girls* as, "among other things, a critique of bourgeois feminism" (33).

> Martha Chamberlain writes that when English wool was in demand, the fens were rich, but for many years now they have been among the poorest regions in England (13).

Citing Multiple Pages in a Source

You may find yourself wanting to make a brief summary of an extended passage, in which case you might need to cite the inclusive pages of the summarized material.

John McGrath's Scottish theater company was destroyed by the end of government subsidies, as Elizabeth MacLennan chronicles in *The Moon Belongs to Everyone* (137-99).

Citing a Source without Page Numbers

Many electronic publications do not have page numbers. If you are citing one of these sources, simply give the author's last name either in parentheses or in a signal phrase before the quotation or summary.

Critics have noted that "Dickinson declined to make the public confession of faith that would admit her to the church" (Yezzi).

or

David Yezzi writes that "Dickinson declined to make the public confession of faith that would admit her to the church."

Citing Multiple Sources at Once

Sometimes several different sources say roughly the same thing, or at least there is substantial overlap in the parts you want to cite. Following are two ways of handling this situation; use whichever one best suits your needs.

This particular passage in the play has been the source of much critical speculation, especially by Freudian critics (Anders 19; Olsen 116; Smith 83-84; Watson 412).

A number of Freudian critics have commented on this passage, including Anders (19), Olsen (116), Smith (83-84), and Watson (412).

Citing Two or More Sources by the Same Author

It is common for one author to write multiple books or articles on the same general topic, and you might want to use more than one of them in your paper. In this case, a shortened version of the title must appear in the parenthetical reference, to show which work by the author is being quoted or cited. In citations for an article and a book about playwright Caryl Churchill, both by the author Geraldine Cousin, one would give the first word of the work's title (other than *the* or *a*, etc.). As seen here, *Common* and *Churchill* are the first words in the title of the article and the book, respectively.

> Churchill claims that this sentiment was expressed to her by one of the gangmasters she encountered in the fens (Cousin, "Common" 6).

> Churchill's notebooks from her visit to the fens record her seeing baby prams parked around the fields in which the women worked (Cousin, *Churchill* 47).

Note the comma between the author's name and the title. Note that these shortened titles are formatted (with italics or quotation marks) just as they would be in the works cited list or elsewhere in your writing, in quotation marks for an article and in italics (or underscored) for a book.

If the author is named in a signal phrase, only the shortened title and page number are needed in the parenthetical reference.

> "Violence," says Ruby Cohn, "is the only recourse in these brutalized lives on the Fen" (*Retreats* 139).

Citing a Quotation or Source within a Source

On page 58 of his book about Margaret Thatcher, Charles Moser writes:

> In a speech to Parliament in June of 1983, Thatcher said, "A return to Victorian values will encourage personal responsibility, personal initiative, self-respect, and respect for others and their property."

Let us say you do not have the text of Thatcher's original speech and that Moser doesn't make reference to a primary source that you can track down. But Moser is a reliable author, so you believe the Thatcher quotation is accurate and want to use a portion of it in your paper. This is done by giving the original speaker's name (in this case Margaret Thatcher) in your text and using the abbreviation *qtd. in* and the author from whom you got the quote (in this case Charles Moser) in the parenthetical citation.

> These "Victorian values," Thatcher claimed, would "encourage personal responsibility, personal initiative, self-respect, and respect for others" (qtd. in Moser 58).

Preparing Your Works Cited List

It is a good idea to begin preparing your list of works cited during the research process, adding new entries each time you find a source that might be useful to you. That way, when the time comes to finalize your paper, you can just edit the list you already have, making sure it contains all the necessary entries and no extraneous ones, and checking each for accuracy and format. If you wait until the end to create your works cited list, you will have to compile the whole list from scratch at a time when you are most tired and therefore least able to focus your attention on this necessary, detailed work.

A number of online resources exist to help you compose and format your works cited. Two of the best respected are *easybib.com* and *citationmachine.net*. These sites allow you to select the type of source from a menu and then enter information about author names, titles, and so on in a form. Once all the information is entered, the software formats and punctuates it appropriately, and you can then save it to your document. You can choose from MLA, APA, or other popular formats. Most instructors do not mind you using these services (ask if you are unsure how your instructor feels about this), but a word of caution is needed. These services can format and punctuate, but they cannot proofread. They will use the information exactly as you enter it, so you must double-check for accuracy before submitting the information for formatting. Many word-processing programs also have bibliography generators, but these are usually not adequate for specialized, scholarly sources and are therefore not recommended.

General Guidelines

- **Begin your list of works cited on a new page.** Continue paginating as you have throughout the paper, with your last name and the page number appearing in the upper right corner.
- **Center the heading Works Cited at the top of the page** in capital and lowercase letters; do not use italics, boldface print, or quotation marks.
- **Arrange the sources alphabetically, by the last name of the source's author** (or by title, in the case of anonymous works), regardless of the order in which the sources are cited in your paper.
- **Begin each entry flush with the left margin.** When an entry takes up more than one line, all lines after the first are indented one-half inch. (For an example, see the works cited list in the research paper by Jarrad Nunes, on page 1346.) This is called a hanging indent, and all major word processing programs can be set to format your entries this way.
- **Double-space the entire list.**
- **Do not put extra line spaces between entries.**
- **As always, carefully follow any additional or contrary instructions provided by your instructor.**

Citing Books

To list books in your works cited, include as much of the following information as is available and appropriate, in the following order and format. Each works cited entry has three basic parts, or containers:

Author's Name. *Title of Work.* Publication Information.

- **Name of the author or editor**, followed by a period, last name first for the first author or editor listed. Names of additional authors or others listed, anywhere in the entry, should appear in the regular order (first name first). (Multiple authors or editors should be listed in the order in which they appear on the book's title page. Use initials or middle names, just as they appear. You need not include titles, affiliations, and any academic degrees that precede or follow names.)
- **Title of a part of the book**, in quotation marks and followed by a period. Needed only if you cite a chapter, an introduction, or other part of a book written by someone other than the principal author or editor listed on the title page. See "A work in an anthology or compilation," "An article in a reference work," or "An introduction, preface, foreword, or afterword" on the following pages.
- **Title of the book**, italicized and followed by a period if it is the primary work being cited. If there is a subtitle, put a colon after the main title, and follow this with the full subtitle. This is the standard format for a works cited entry, even if no colon appears on the book's title page. (If the main title ends in a question mark, an exclamation point, or a dash, however, do not add a colon between the main title and the subtitle.)
- **Name of the editor** (for books with both an author and an editor), **translator**, or **compiler**, if different from the primary author(s). Place it after the title, preceded by the specific role ("Edited by" or "Translated by" or "Compiled by"), followed by a comma.
- **Edition used**, if other than the first, followed by a comma.
- **Volume used**, if a multivolume work, followed by a comma.
- **For pre-1900 sources only**, provide the city or place of publication, followed by a comma (if more than one city is listed on the title page, use only the first one); **name of the publisher**, followed by a comma; **year of publication** (if multiple copyright dates are listed, use the most recent one).
- **Page numbers.** Needed only if you cite a chapter, an introduction, or other part of a book written by someone other than the principal author or editor listed on the title page. See "A work in an anthology

or compilation," "An article in a reference work," or "An introduction, preface, foreword, or afterword" on the following pages. If you include page numbers, separate them from the year of publication by a comma and follow them with a period.

- **Series name**, if the book is part of a series.

Copy your entries directly from the book's title page, which provides more complete and accurate information than does a cover or another bibliography. The following examples cover most of the sorts of books you are likely to encounter.

A book by a single author. The simplest entry is a single-volume book by a single author, not part of a series, and without additional editors, translators, or compilers.

> Alexie, Sherman. *The Absolutely True Diary of a Part-Time Indian*. Little,
> Brown, 2007.

If a book has an editor, a translator, or a compiler in addition to an author, identify this person by role and by name, between the book's title and publisher.

> Sebald, W. G. *The Rings of Saturn*. Translated by Michael Hulse, New
> Directions, 1998.

The following example cites a third-edition book by a single author.

> Richter, David H. *The Critical Tradition: Classic Texts and Contemporary Trends*.
> 3rd ed., Bedford/St. Martin's, 2007.

A book by two or three authors. Note that in the following example only the first author's name appears in reverse order. UP (with no periods) is the abbreviation for University Press. Note also the series title, Oxford Shakespeare Topics, is included when citing a book in a series.

> Gurr, Andrew, and Mariko Ichikawa. *Staging in Shakespeare's Theaters*. Oxford
> UP, 2000. Oxford Shakespeare Topics.

A book by four or more authors. If four or more authors or editors are listed on a book's title page, you can list all names or give only the name of the first, followed by *et al.* (Latin for "and others").

> Gardner, Janet E., et al., editors. *Literature: A Portable Anthology*. 4th ed.,
> Bedford/St. Martin's, 2017.

A book by an unknown or anonymous author. Simply include all the other information, beginning with the title.

> *Gilgamesh: A New English Version.* Translated by Stephen Mitchell, Free, 2006.

A book by a corporate author. Corporate authorship refers to a book that lists an organization rather than an individual as its author. This is especially common with publications from government and nonprofit organizations.

> Bureau of the Census. *Historical Statistics of the United States, 1789-1945: A Supplement to the Statistical Abstract of the United States.* Government Printing Office, 1945.

Two or more books by the same author. If you cite more than one work by a single author, alphabetize the entries by title. For the second and all subsequent entries by the same author, replace the author's name with three hyphens.

> Bloom, Harold. *Hamlet: Poem Unlimited.* Riverhead-Penguin, 2003.

> ---. *Shakespeare's Poems and Sonnets.* Chelsea, 1999. Bloom's Major Poets.

A work in an anthology or compilation. The first example that follows is a citation from a literature anthology; the second is from a scholarly work in which each chapter is written by a different author. The title of the work or chapter being cited is usually enclosed in quotation marks. However, if the piece is a play or novel, you should italicize its title instead.

> Baldwin, James. "Sonny's Blues." *Literature: A Portable Anthology,* edited by Janet E. Gardner et al., 4th ed., Bedford/St. Martin's, 2017, pp. 223-249.

> Keyishian, Harry. "Shakespeare and the Movie Genre: The Case of *Hamlet.*" *The Cambridge Companion to Shakespeare on Film,* edited by Russell Jackson, Cambridge UP, 2000, pp. 72-81.

Two or more works in a single anthology or compilation. If you cite two or more works from a single anthology or collection, you can create a cross-reference, citing the full publication information for the collection as a whole and cross-referencing the individual pieces using only the name of the editor and page numbers of the particular work within the anthology or compilation.

READING AND WRITING ABOUT LITERATURE

Chopin, Kate. "The Story of an Hour." Gardner et al., pp. 48-50.

Gardner, Janet E., et al., editors. *Literature: A Portable Anthology*. 4th ed., Bedford/St. Martin's, 2017.

Gilman, Charlotte Perkins. "The Yellow Wallpaper." Gardner et al., pp. 64-77.

An article in a reference work. The format for citing material from dictionaries, encyclopedias, or other specialized reference works is similar to that for a work in an anthology, but the name of the reference work's editor is omitted. Often, such reference articles are anonymous anyway. The first example is for a signed article in a print book, the second for an anonymous entry in an electronic encyclopedia.

Brown, Andrew. "Sophocles." *The Cambridge Guide to Theatre*. Cambridge UP, 1988, pp. 899-900.

Durante, Amy M. "Finn Mac Cumhail." *Encyclopedia Mythica*, 17 Apr. 2011, www.pantheon.org/articles/f/finn_mac_cumhail.html.

An introduction, preface, foreword, or afterword. After the author's name, give the name of the part of the book being cited, capitalized but neither italicized nor in quotation marks, followed by the title of the book and all relevant publication information.

Dunham, Lena. Foreword. *The Liars' Club*, by Mary Karr, Penguin Classics, 2015, pp. xi-xiii.

Citing Periodicals

An article in a scholarly journal. Most scholarly journals publish several issues in each annual volume and paginate continuously throughout the entire volume. (In other words, if one issue ends on page 230, the next will begin with page 231.) Your works cited entry should list the author, article title, journal title, volume number, issue number, the season or month and year and page numbers. Follow the punctuation shown here exactly.

Fuqua, Amy. "'The Furrow of His Brow': Providence and Pragmatism in Toni Morrison's *Paradise*." *Midwest Quarterly*, vol. 54, no. 1, Autumn 2012, pp. 38-52.

An article in a magazine. For an article in a magazine, omit the volume and issue numbers (if given) and include the date of publication. The first example here shows the format for a monthly, bimonthly, or quarterly magazine; the second, which includes the date as well as the month, is appropriate for weekly and biweekly magazines.

Bryan, Christy. "Ivory Worship." *National Geographic*, Oct. 2012, pp. 28-61.

Grossman, Lev. "A Star Is Born." *Time*, 2 Nov. 2015, pp. 30-39.

An article in a newspaper. When a newspaper is separated into sections, note the letter or number designating the section as a part of the page reference. Newspapers and some magazines frequently place articles on nonconsecutive pages. When this happens, give the number of the first page only, followed by the plus sign (+).

Sherry, Allison. "Volunteers' Personal Touch Turns High-Tech Data into Votes." *The Denver Post*, 30 Oct. 2012, pp. 1A+.

A review. To cite a review, you must include the title and author of the work being reviewed between the review title and the periodical title. The first entry that follows is for a book review in a newspaper. The second is a review of a film in a magazine that includes the director's name.

Walton, James. "Noble, Embattled Souls." Review of *The Bone Clocks* and *Slade House*, by David Mitchell, *The New York Review of Books*, 3 Dec. 2015, pp. 55-58.

Lane, Anthony. "Film within a Film." Review of *Argo*, directed by Ben Affleck, and *Sinister*, directed by Scott Derrickson, *The New Yorker*, 15 Oct. 2012, pp. 98-99.

Citing Electronic Sources

Sometimes online sources do not list all the information required for a complete citation. They are, for instance, frequently anonymous, and they do not always record the dates when they were written or updated. Give as much of the information as you can find, using the formats that follow. Whenever possible, include DOIs (Digital Object Identifier) or permalinks in place of URLs. Note that the date the researcher accessed the document is optional. Include it for Web sources that do not have a publication date.

An article from an online subscription database or index. When you access an article through an online index or database (*MLA International Bibliog-*

raphy, JSTOR, etc.), treat it as you would a print source, with the addition of the title of the database (italicized), and the DOI, permalink, or URL.

> Bottomore, Stephen. "The Romance of the Cinematograph." *Film History*, vol. 24, no. 3, July 2012, pp. 341-44. *JSTOR*, doi:10.2979/filmhistory.24.3.341.

An online scholarly project or database. A full entry for an online scholarly project or database includes the editor's name; the title of the project, italicized; the name of the sponsoring organization or institution; the date of the project's most recent update; and the DOI, permalink, or URL.

> Folsom, Ed, and Kenneth M. Price, editors. *The Walt Whitman Archive*. Walt Whitman Archive, April 2016, whitmanarchive.org.

An online journal or magazine. The first entry that follows is from an online scholarly journal; the second is from an online popular magazine.

> Bryson, Devin. "The Rise of a New Senegalese Cultural Philosophy?" *African Studies Quarterly*, vol. 14, no. 3, Mar. 2014, pp. 33-56, asq.africa.ufl .edu/files/Volume-14-Issue-3-Bryson.pdf.

> Leonard, Andrew. "The Surveillance State High School." *Salon*, 27 Nov. 2012, www.salon.com/2012/11/27/the_surveillance_state_high_school/.

A professional or personal Web page. Include as much of the following information as appropriate and available: the author of the document or site; the document title, in quotation marks (if the site is divided into separate documents); the name of the site, italicized; the sponsoring organization or institution; the date of creation or most recent update; and the DOI, permalink, or URL. If the site has no official title, provide a brief identifying phrase, neither italicized nor in quotation marks, as in the second example below.

> Railton, Stephen. *Mark Twain in His Times*. Stephen Railton / U of Virginia Library, 2012, twain.lib.virginia.edu/.

> Bae, Rebecca. Home page. Iowa State U, 2015, www.engl.iastate.edu /rebecca-bae-directory-page/.

Short work from a Web site. For an individual page on a Web site, list the author (if given), followed by the rest of the information for the entire Web site, as above.

Enzinna, Wes. "Syria's Unknown Revolution." *Pulitzer Center on Crisis Reporting*,
24 Nov. 2015, pulitzercenter.org/projects/middle-east-syria-enzinna
-war-rojava.

A blog post. An entry for a blog citation includes the blogger's name (or
online handle), the title of the posting, blog title, date of posting, and the
DOI, permalink, or URL.

Cimons, Marlene. "Why Cities Could Be the Key to Solving the Climate Crisis."
Thinkprogress.org, Center for American Progress Action Fund, 10 Dec.
2015, thinkprogress.org/climate/2015/12/10/3730938/cities-key-to
-climate-crisis/.

A Facebook post or comment.

Bedford English. "Stacey Cochran explores Reflective Writing in the classroom
and as a writer: ow.ly/YkjVB." *Facebook*, 15 Feb. 2016, www.facebook
.com/BedfordEnglish/posts/10153415001259607.

A Twitter post (tweet).

Curiosity Rover. "Can you see me waving? How to spot #Mars in the night
sky: youtu.be/hv8hVvJlcJQ." *Twitter*, 5 Nov. 2015, 11:00 a.m., twitter
.com/marscuriosity/status/672859022911889408.

A posting to a discussion list or newsgroup. Give the author's name, the
title of the posting (in quotation marks) taken from the subject line, the
title of the site on which the forum is found (italicized), the sponsor of
the site, the date of posting, and the DOI, permalink, or URL. If the posting has no title, use the identifying phrase *Online posting*.

Robin, Griffith. "Write for the Reading Teacher." *Developing Digital Litera-
cies*, NCTE, 23 Oct. 2015, ncte.connectedcommunity.org/communities
/community-home/digestviewer/viewthread?GroupId=1693&MID
=24520&tab=digestviewer&CommunityKey=628d2ad6-8277-4042-a376
-2b370ddceabf.

Citing Other Miscellaneous Sources

A television or radio program. Begin with the name of the author or
another individual (director, narrator, etc.), only if you refer primarily to
the work of a particular individual. Otherwise, begin with the title of a
segment or episode (if appropriate), in quotation marks; the title of the
program, italicized; the title of the series (if applicable), italicized; the
name of the network; and the date of broadcast.

"Free Speech on College Campuses." *Washington Journal*, narrated by Peter Slen, C-SPAN, 27 Nov. 2015.

The Daily Show with Trevor Noah. Comedy Central, 18 Nov. 2015.

A film. Film citations begin with the film title (italicized), followed by the name of the director, names of featured key performers, the name of the movie studio, and the year of release.

Birdman or (The Unexpected Virtue of Ignorance). Directed by Alejandro González Iñárritu, performances by Michael Keaton, Emma Stone, Zach Galifianakis, Edward Norton, and Naomi Watts, Fox Searchlight, 2014.

An interview. Begin with the name of the person interviewed. For a published interview, give the title, if any, in quotation marks (if there is no title, simply use the designation *Interview*, neither in quotation marks nor italicized), followed by the name of the interviewer, and publication information. The first example that follows is for an interview published in a magazine. The second example is for an interview conducted personally by the author of the research paper and gives the name of the person interviewed.

Weddington, Sarah. "Sarah Weddington: Still Arguing for *Roe*." Interview by Michele Kort, *Ms.*, Winter 2013, pp. 32-35.

Akufo, Dautey. Personal interview, 11 Apr. 2016.

A lecture or speech. To cite a speech or lecture that you've attended, use the following format, listing the speaker's name; the title of the presentation, in quotation marks (if announced or published); the sponsoring organization; the location; the date; and a descriptive label such as *Address* or *Lecture*.

Smith, Anna Deavere. "On the Road: A Search for American Character." National Endowment for the Humanities, John F. Kennedy Center for the Performing Arts, Washington, 6 Apr. 2015. Address.

Generally speaking, you do not need to cite a class lecture; to quote or otherwise refer to something an instructor says in class, you may do so simply by crediting the instructor in the text of your essay.

A letter or e-mail. There are three kinds of letters: published, unpublished (in archives), and personal. A published letter includes the writer's name, the recipient's name (in quotation marks), the date of the letter, the number of the letter (if assigned by the editor), and publication information for the book or periodical in which it appears.

Wharton, Edith. Letter to Henry James, 28 Feb. 1915. *Henry James and Edith Wharton: Letters, 1900-1915*, edited by Lyall H. Powers, Scribner, 1990, pp. 323-26.

In citing an unpublished letter, give the writer's name, the title or a description of the material (for example, *Letter to Havelock Ellis*), the date, and any identifying number assigned to it. Include the name of the library or institution housing the material.

Sanger, Margaret. Letter to Havelock Ellis. 14 July 1924. Margaret Sanger Papers, Sophia Smith Collection, Smith College.

To cite a letter you received personally, include the author, the designation *Letter to the author*, and the date posted. To cite an e-mail you received personally, include the author, the subject line as the title, who the message was received by, and the date it was sent.

Green, Barclay. Letter to the author. 1 Sept. 2015.

Thornbrugh, Caitlin. "Coates Lecture." Received by Rita Anderson, 20 Oct. 2015.

A work of visual art. Give the artist's name, the title of the artwork (in italics), the date of composition, the medium of composition, and, if you saw the original artwork in person, the name and location of the institution that houses the artwork. If you saw the artwork online, be sure to provide the DOI, permalink, or URL.

Goya, Francisco. *The Family of Charles IV*. 1800. Oil on canvas. Museo del Prado, Madrid.

Clough, Charles. *January Twenty-First*. 1988-89, Joslyn Art Museum, Omaha, www.joslyn.org/ccllections-and-exhibitions/permanent-collections/modern-and-contemporary/charles-clough-january-twenty-first/.

SAMPLE RESEARCH PAPER

When choosing a research paper topic, Jarrad Nunes recalled how interesting he had found Emily Dickinson's poem "Because I could not stop for Death" (page 493), which seemed to defy his expectations of literature about death and dying. Jarrad decided to see what professional literary critics had to say on the subject and how closely their ideas matched

Jarrad S. Nunes

Professor Gardner

English 204

2 April 2016

Emily Dickinson's "Because I

could not stop for Death":

Challenging Readers' Expectations

   With a keen eye for detail and a well-known conciseness and
compression, Emily Dickinson's poetry records the abstractions
of human life so matter-of-factly that her readers often take her
technical skill for granted. Take, for example, the six-stanza poem
"Because I could not stop for Death" — a detached, but never
completely dispassionate, recollection of a human's journey to its
final conclusion. The verse is crafted so succinctly and with such
precision that its complex and vivid images are made even more
extraordinary and meaningful. At least one critic has pointed out
how Dickinson employs "rhetorical strategies that resist and
contest dominant cultural conceptions of death and immortality"
(Farland 370). We might expect literature on the theme of death
to invoke religious imagery, stillness, and a sense of dread or
foreboding, but none of this is the case. Instead, the poem
challenges the preconceptions Dickinson's contemporaries had
about death, and in doing so it makes us challenge ours as well.

   From the start, Dickinson infuses this often-grim topic with a
palpable humanity, beginning with her personification of death as
the courteous, careful carriage driver bearing the speaker's body
to rest. Literary critic Harold Bloom asserts, "The image here
of a woman and her escort, Death, meditating on the prospect
of eternity, is neither one of despair nor loss nor outrage, but of
resignation" (37). This "resignation," though, does not come
across as the predictable acceptance of God's will. In fact, any
mention of God or the soul is remarkably absent from this poem
about death and eternity. This suggests the uneasy relationship
Dickinson had with the strict religious beliefs of her society and

Jarrad focuses in on one Dickinson poem.

Because he mentions Bloom at the beginning of the sentence, Jarrad does not have to include Bloom's name in the in-text citation.

Nunes 2

er family. "Raised during the period of New England Revivalism,"
writes David Yezzi, "Dickinson declined to make the public con-
ession of faith that would admit her to the church (her father
made his twice) and by the age of thirty she left off attending
services altogether." Clearly at odds with familial and social
expectations, Dickinson nonetheless fearlessly expresses her
religious "doubt, which her poems later absorbed as ambiguity and
contradiction" (Yezzi).

Jarrad integrates Yezzi's quotation with his own writing in order to provide some cultural context.

Dickinson's narrator does not fear death, perhaps because
death is associated here not so much with endings or divine
judgment but instead with a very human journey. The driver seems
affable, "kindly stopp[ing]" and driving slowly. In stanza 2, the
narrator puts her work away to observe the driver calmly. It may
seem unlikely that she would be trusting of so ominous a character, but as critic Betsy Erkkila explains it, "Death himself comes
courting as an aristocratic gentleman with horses and a carriage"
9). David Baker carries this one step further, noting "[h]ow
homely and comfortable is this ride" and comparing it to "a mild
19th-century date." Indeed, the fact that the carriage driver has
stopped for the narrator on a day when she was too busy to do the
same emphasizes his courtesy and thoughtfulness as a character.
This is an original and deeply humanistic perception of death, in
which the personified entity is neither a black-cloaked grim reaper
nor a stern servant of God.

Along with its deep humanity, Dickinson's image of Death has
a fluidity and graceful movement that is, at first, juxtaposed
against our more frightening preconceptions of the idea. This
tangible sense of motion is perhaps best illustrated in the poem's
perfectly constructed third stanza. Here, a series of images
metaphorically re-creates a natural progression — childish play
gives way to growing grain and, eventually, to the setting of the
sun (lines 9-12). One critic has demonstrated how these three
images might represent childhood, maturity, and old age (Shaw
0). The very fact that the narrator views these scenes from a

Jarrad para-phrases Shaw's point in his own words and then provides an appropriate in-text citation.

slowly rolling carriage lends the passage a clear sense of movement and an unexpected vitality. The absurdity of this meandering vessel passing "the Setting Sun" perhaps suggests a sense of quickening as death draws near, or it may even signal the dissolution of temporal reality altogether. Regardless, the steady progression of this section is undeniable.

The strong sense of motion is continued in the fourth stanza, though with some differences. Here, the movement is less concrete, as the narrator herself moves from a life marked by careful self-control into a position in which she all but succumbs to outside forces. As "[t]he Dews drew quivering and chill" (14), the narrator has lost the ability to keep herself warm. Her earthly garments do not provide adequate protection. From her philosophical viewpoint, however, these difficulties, like death itself, are to be calmly accepted rather than feared. Indeed, before this point, there is not a single truly fearful image in this remarkable poem about death, and even here any sense of foreboding is muted.

Jarrad's smooth transition provides a link between his analyses of two stanzas.

As the poem moves into its fifth stanza, the momentum is halted temporarily, and a more traditional death image is finally introduced with the lines "We paused before a House that seemed / A Swelling of the Ground" (17-18). At this point, the character of Death seems to bid his passenger a rather unceremonial good-bye at the foot of her earthen grave. As the resting place is described, he retreats, returning to the world of the living to repeat his duty with another passenger. While the sparse but vivid description of the grave should invoke a paralyzing loneliness, Dickinson again thwarts our expectations, tempering the reader's fear by having her narrator merely pause at the sight, as if staying for a short while at a hotel or a friend's house. Once again, a usual symbol of finality is given a transitive purpose.

Jarrad consistently chooses important quotations from the poem as evidence for his claims.

The final stanza brings the narrator to a new place, Eternity. However, as one critic explains it, "Eternity, for Dickinson, is not a place at which one arrives. It is rather a journey-towards, a continual evolving" (Baker). Once again Dickinson has thwarted

eaders' expectations. While this should certainly be the logical
nd of her journey, Dickinson's exquisite use of language suggests
hat the entire account may simply be a daydream — a mental
dress rehearsal for the real death to come. Consider this account of
he poem's final stanza:

> All of this poetically elapsed time "Feels shorter than the
> Day," the day of death brought to an end by the setting sun
> of the third stanza. . . . "Surmised," carefully placed near the
> conclusion, is all the warranty one needs for reading this jour-
> ney as one that has taken place entirely in her mind . . . the
> poem returns to the very day, even the same instant, when it
> started. (Anderson 245)

*Jarrad indents
this long quo-
tation to set it
apart from his
own prose.*

hus even the most basic facts about death — its finality and
permanence — are brought into question.

Finally, "Because I could not stop for Death" indicates both
Dickinson's precise and vivid style and her unwillingness to settle
or the ordinary interpretation. Death no longer conforms to the
eaders' preconceptions, as religion, stillness, and finality give
way to humanist philosophy, motion, and continuity. The poet
bserves, experiences, and recounts her perceptions in metaphor.
he opens up many questions about the nature of death, yet she
provides no easy answers to her readers. Instead, we are provided
with an account of death that weaves in and out of time, finally
looping back on its own structure to provide a stunningly dramatic
onclusion. In six short stanzas, Dickinson cleverly exposes what
he saw as fundamental flaws in the traditional conception of
death, burial, and the eternal afterlife, and in doing so, she opens
p new pathways of thought for us all.

*In his conclu-
sion, Jarrad
reinforces his
claim: that the
poem challenges
nineteenth-
century notions
of death.*

Works Cited

Anderson, Charles R. *Emily Dickinson's Poetry: Stairway of Surprise.*   *A print book.*
Holt, 1960.

Baker, David. "Elegy and Eros." *Virginia Quarterly Review*, vol. 81,
no. 2, Spring 2005, pp. 207-20, www.vqronline.org/essay
/elegy-and-eros-configuring-grief.

Bloom, Harold. *Emily Dickinson*. Chelsea, 1999. Bloom's Major   *Book in a series.*
Poets.

Dickinson, Emily. "Because I could not stop for Death." *Literature:
A Portable Anthology*, edited by Janet E. Gardner et al., 4th
ed., Bedford/St. Martin's, 2017, pp. 493-94.

Erkkila, Betsy. "Emily Dickinson and Class." *American Literary*   *Journal article*
History, vol. 4, no. 1, Spring 1992, pp. 1-27, doi:10.1093   *online.*
/alh/4.1.1.

Farland, Maria Magdalena. "'That Tritest/Brightest Truth': Emily   *Article accessed*
Dickinson's Anti-Sentimentality." *Nineteenth-Century Litera-*   *through online*
ture, vol. 53, no. 3, December 1998, pp. 364-89. JSTOR,   *database.*
doi:10.2307/2903044.

Shaw, Mary Neff. "Dickinson's 'Because I could not stop for Death.'"
Explicator, vol. 50, no. 1, Autumn 1991, pp. 20-21. doi:10
.1080/00144940.1991.9938696.

Yezzi, David. "Straying Close to Home." Review of *Emily Dickinson*   *A book review.*
and the Art of Belief, by Roger Lundin, *Commonweal*,
9 October 1998, pp. 20-21.

CHAPTER 9

Literary Criticism and Literary Theory

Anytime you sit down to write about literature, or even to discuss a story, play, or poem with classmates, you are acting as a literary critic. The word *criticism* is often interpreted as negative and faultfinding. But literary criticism is a discipline and includes everything from a glowing review to a scathing attack to a thoughtful and balanced interpretation. Criticism can be broken down into two broad categories: evaluative and interpretive. Evaluative criticism seeks to determine how accomplished a work is and what place it should hold in the evolving story of literary history. Book reviews are the most common form of evaluative criticism. Interpretive criticism comprises all writing that seeks to explain, analyze, clarify, or question the meaning and significance of literature. Although you may engage in a certain amount of evaluative criticism in your literature class, and while your attitude about the value of literature will likely be apparent in your writing, the criticism you write for class will consist largely of interpretation.

All literary critics, including you, begin with some form of literary theory. Just as you may not have thought of yourself as a literary critic, you probably haven't thought of yourself as using literary theory. But you are doing so every time you write about literature, and it is a good idea to become familiar with some of the most prevalent types of theory. This familiarity will help you understand why so many respected literary critics seem to disagree with one another and why they write such different analyses of the same work of literature. It may also help to explain why you might disagree with your classmates, or even your instructor, in your interpretation of a particular story, poem, or play. Perhaps you are simply starting from a different theoretical base. You will be able to explain your thinking more eloquently if you understand that base.

Literary theory has the reputation of being incredibly dense and difficult. Indeed, the theories—sometimes called *schools* of criticism— discussed in the following pages are all complex, but here they are presented in their most basic, stripped-down forms. As such, these explanations are necessarily incomplete and selective. You should not feel you need to master the complexities of literary theory right now. You need only be aware of the existence of these various schools and watch for them as you read and write. Doing so will give you a better sense of what you're reading and hearing about the literature you explore, and it will make your writing more informed and articulate. There are many other schools and subschools in addition to those described here, but these are the most significant—the ones you are most likely to encounter as you continue to explore literature.

Focusing on Jamaica Kincaid's "Girl" (page 355) and T. S. Eliot's "The Love Song of J. Alfred Prufrock" (page 516), the last paragraph of each entry offers a few directions one might take in a critical reading, with the specific critical theory applied to the analysis. While these notes are by no means exhaustive, they might help spark ideas for a paper, or at least grant greater insight into the literature and theory discussed.

FORMALISM AND NEW CRITICISM

For a large part of the twentieth century, literary criticism was dominated by various types of theory that can broadly be defined as **Formalism** and **New Criticism**. (New Criticism is no longer new, having begun to fall out of prominence in the 1970s, but its name lives on.) Formalist critics focus their attention on the formal elements of a literary text—things like **structure**, **tone**, **characters**, **setting**, **symbols**, and linguistic features. Explication and close-reading (explained on pages 1267–68) are techniques of Formalist criticism. While poetry, which is quite self-consciously formal in its structure, lends itself most obviously to Formalist types of criticism, prose fiction and drama are also frequently viewed through this lens.

Perhaps the most distinguishing feature of Formalism and New Criticism is that they focus on the text itself and not on extratextual factors. Formalist critics are interested in how parts of a text relate to one another and to the whole, and they seek to create meaning by unfolding and examining these relationships. Excluded from consideration are questions about the author, the reader, history or culture, and the relationship of the literary text to other texts or artwork. Chances are you have written some Formalist criticism yourself, either in high school or in college. If you have ever written a paper on **symbolism**, character development, or the relationship between sound patterns and sense in a poem, you have been a Formalist critic.

A Formalist critic of Jamaica Kincaid's story "Girl" might choose to focus on how the language used by the speaker of this monologue illuminates her character, while a Formalist critic of T. S. Eliot's "The Love Song of J. Alfred Prufrock" might focus on Eliot's irregular use of rhyme and meter in the poem.

FEMINIST AND GENDER CRITICISM

Have you ever had a classroom discussion of a piece of literature in which the focus was on the roles of women in the literature or the culture, or on the relationships between men and women? If so, you have engaged in **feminist criticism**. Some version of feminist criticism has been around for as long as readers have been interested in gender roles, but the school rose to prominence in the 1970s at the same time the modern feminist movement was gaining steam. Most feminist criticism from this time was clearly tied to raising consciousness about the patriarchy in which many women felt trapped. Some feminist critics sought to reveal how literary texts demonstrated the repression and powerlessness of women in different periods and cultures. Others had a nearly opposite agenda, showing how female literary characters could overcome the sexist power structures that surround them and exercise power in their worlds. Still others looked to literary history and sought to rediscover and promote writing by women whose works had been far less likely than men's to be regarded as "great" literature.

Before long, however, some critics began to point out that women were not alone in feeling social pressure to conform to gender roles. Over the years, men have usually been expected to be good providers, to be strong (both physically and emotionally), and to keep their problems and feelings more or less to themselves. Though the expectations are different, men are socialized no less than women to think and behave in certain ways, and these social expectations are also displayed in works of literature. Feminist criticism has expanded in recent years to become **gender criticism**. Any literary criticism that highlights gender roles or relationships between the sexes can be a type of gender criticism, whether or not it is driven by an overt feminist agenda.

The story "Girl" would be an obvious choice for a feminist critic, since it focuses on how a young girl is socialized into the domestic roles expected of women in her society. A gender critic might also be interested in "Prufrock" and in the ways that the poem's aging speaker feels his masculinity called into question.

QUEER THEORY

Queer theory is one of the more recent critical schools to emerge out of critical interest in gender. It came into prominence in the 1990s, when some gay and lesbian literary critics perceived a need for a critical school that reflected their own particular circumstances and viewpoints. Some queer theorists insist that sexuality—or even the binary male/female division of gender itself—is culturally constructed rather than determined by physical characteristics present at birth. Many of these critics and theorists seek to destabilize the cultural norm that suggests that certain sexual preferences, marriage and family customs, and so forth are "normal" or "natural" while others are "deviant."

Queer theorists, like all literary critics, differ substantially in their focus. Some are interested in studying literary texts written by authors known or suspected to be gays, lesbians, bisexual, or transgender, particularly if these authors have been devalued in the past because of their sexual identity. Other queer theorists are interested in portrayals of gay or lesbian characters in literature by either gay or straight authors. Still others seek a "queer subtext" in canonical works of literature that have long been considered hetero-normative. (Included in this latter category are the many critics who have asked whether Shakespeare's Hamlet had something more than a traditional heterosexual friendship with his close confidant Horatio.)

At first glance, Jamaica Kincaid's "Girl" might not look like a promising candidate for examination by queer theory. But a queer theorist might, in fact, be interested in how the very possibility of homosexuality is erased by the narrator, the way the young girl is assumed to have an interest in "wharf-rat boys" and a need to know "how to love a man," though she never expresses these heterosexual urges.

MARXIST CRITICISM

Just as feminist criticism and queer theory came into their own because of the political agenda of certain critics, so too did **Marxist criticism**, which originally sought to use literature and criticism to forward a socialist political program. Early Marxist critics began with Karl Marx's (1818–1883) insistence that human interactions are economically driven and that the basic model of human progress is based on a struggle for power between different social classes. For Marxist critics, then, literature was just another battleground, another venue for the ongoing quest for individual material gain. Literary characters could be divided into powerful oppressors and their powerless victims, and literary plots and themes could be examined to uncover the economic forces that drove them. According to this model, the very acts of writing and reading literature can be characterized as production and consumption, and some Marxist critics have studied the external forces that drive education, publication, and literary tastes.

The sort of Marxist criticism that ignores all forces but socioeconomic ones is sometimes referred to as *vulgar* Marxism because, in its single-mindedness, it ignores certain complexities of individual thought and action. Its sole purpose is to expose the inequalities that underlie all societies and to thus raise the consciousness of readers and move society closer to a socialist state. Such Marxist criticism tends to be full of the language of Marxist political analysis—references to *class struggle*, to the economic *base* and *superstructure*, to the *means of production*, to worker *alienation* and *reification* (the process whereby oppressed workers lose their sense of individual humanity), and so forth.

But just as feminist criticism soon opened up into the broader and more complex school of gender criticism, so too did most Marxist criticism break free of a single-minded political agenda. You no longer have to be a committed Marxist to engage in Marxist criticism; all you need to do is acknowledge that socioeconomic forces do, in fact, affect people's lives. If you notice inequalities in power between characters in a work of literature, if you question how the class or educational background of an author affects his or her work, or if you believe that a certain type of literature—a Shakespearean sonnet, say, or a pulp western novel—appeals more to readers of a particular social background, then you are, at least in part, engaging in Marxist criticism.

Social class roles, one of the primary interests of Marxist critics, are visible in the apparently modest circumstances of the characters in "Girl" (where class and gender have a clear overlap) as well as in the more bourgeois world of porcelain teacups and perfumed dresses on display in "Prufrock."

CULTURAL STUDIES

Cultural studies is the general name given to a wide variety of critical practices, some of which might seem on the surface to have little in common with one another. Perhaps the best way to understand cultural studies is to begin with the notion that certain texts are privileged in our society while others are dismissed or derided. Privileged texts are the so-called great works of literature commonly found in anthologies and on course syllabi. Indeed, when we hear the word *literature*, these are probably the works we imagine. All other writing—from pulp romance novels to the slogans on bumper stickers—belongs to a second category of texts, those generally overlooked by traditional literary critics.

One major trend in cultural studies is the attempt to broaden the **canon**—those texts read and taught again and again and held up as examples of the finest expressions of the human experience. Critics have pointed out that canonical authors—Shakespeare, Milton, Keats, Steinbeck—tend (with obvious exceptions) to be from a fairly narrow segment of society: they are usually middle to upper-middle class, well educated, heterosexual white males. Some cultural critics, therefore, have sought out and celebrated the writing of historically disadvantaged groups such as African Americans or gay and lesbian authors. Other proponents of cultural studies turn their attention to the works of various social "outsiders," like prisoners, schoolchildren, or mental patients. This attempt at broadening the canon is designed to provide students and scholars alike with a more inclusive definition of what art and literature are all about.

Cultural critics seek to blur or erase the line separating "high" art from "low" art in the minds of the literary establishment. Some cultural critics believe that all texts are to some extent artistic expressions of a culture and that any text can therefore give us vital insights into the human experience. Rather than traditional literary objects, then, a cultural critic might choose to study such things as movies and television shows, advertisements, religious tracts, graffiti, and comic books. These texts—and virtually any other visual or verbal works you can imagine—are submitted to the same rigorous scrutiny as a sonnet or a classic novel. Some cultural critics suggest that English departments should become departments of cultural studies, in which a course on hip-hop culture would be valued as much as a course on Victorian poetry.

The poems of T. S. Eliot, including "The Love Song of J. Alfred Prufrock," occupy an important place in the early-twentieth-century literary canon. A cultural critic might seek to explain how and why Eliot came to be so firmly associated with high culture.

POSTCOLONIAL CRITICISM

One very active branch of cultural studies is **postcolonial criticism**, which focuses on writing from former British (and other, mostly European) colonies around the world. Postcolonial criticism is most strongly associated with the Indian subcontinent (India, Pakistan, and Bangladesh), large portions of Africa and the Middle East, parts of Asia (such as Singapore and Vietnam), the Caribbean, and Latin America. In such places, indigenous authors often possess attitudes, tastes, and literary traditions very different from those of their former colonial masters. Postcolonial criticism seeks to discover these attitudes and tastes, to recover literary history that was ignored or suppressed during the colonial period, and to celebrate indigenous cultures of storytelling, drama, and poetry. At the same time, it attempts to understand how occupation by a more powerful colonizing nation disrupted and changed the course of history in a particular place.

In a colonial setting, members of the ruling group tend to see as natural and ordinary attitudes that might be better understood as racist, classist, and/or religiously intolerant, such as assuming that indigenous traditions are "superstitious" or "primitive" compared to the more "civilized" culture of the imperialists. Postcolonial theorists demand that indigenous attitudes and customs be treated with full respect and understanding. Postcolonial literary theory is situated within a larger move to comprehend the effect of colonial culture on history, art, architecture, politics, law, philosophy, sociology, sex and race relations, and daily life.

A postcolonial critic reading "Girl" would likely focus his or her attention on the details of language and culture—*benna* music, for instance, or the belief that blackbirds might really be spirits—that locate the story in a particular postcolonial Caribbean setting.

HISTORICAL CRITICISM AND NEW HISTORICISM

If you have ever written a research paper that involved some background reading about the life and times of an author, you have already engaged in a form of **historical criticism**. Literary scholars have long read history books and various sorts of historical documents—from newspaper articles to personal letters—to gain insights into the composition and significance of a given work. The explanatory footnotes that often appear in literary reprints and anthologies are one obvious manifestation of this type of sleuthing. Indeed, some works of literature would be virtually inexplicable if we did not understand something of the times in which they were written and first read. If you did not know that Walt Whitman's "When Lilacs Last in the Dooryard Bloom'd" was an elegy written upon the assassination of Abraham Lincoln, it would be difficult to make any sense at all of the poem, since neither the president's name nor the cause of his death actually appear in the poem.

Likewise, historians have long turned to literary works and the visual arts in order to gain insights into the periods they study. While archives and contemporary documents can teach us a lot about the broad sweep of history—wars, leaders, the controversies of the day—it is often difficult to see from these documents what life was like for ordinary people, whose interior lives were not often documented. We may be able to learn from parish burial records, for example, how common child-hood mortality was at a particular time in English history, but only when we read Ben Jonson's poem "On My First Son" (page 433) do we begin to understand how this mortality may have affected the parents who lost their children. Likewise, the few pages of James Joyce's story "Araby" (page 85) may tell us more about how adolescent boys lived and thought in early-twentieth-century Dublin than would several volumes of social history.

One school of historical criticism, known as **New Historicism**, takes account of both what history has to teach us about literature *and* what literature has to teach us about history. (New Historicism has been around since the 1960s, and as with New Criticism, the name of the school is no longer as accurate as it once was.) New Historicists are sometimes said to read literary and nonliterary texts *in parallel*, attempt-ing to see how each illuminates the other. Typically, New Historicists examine many different types of documents—government records, peri-odicals, private diaries, bills of sale—in order to re-create, as much as possible, the rich cultural context that surrounded both an author and that author's original audience. In doing so, they seek to give modern audiences a reading experience as rich and informed as the original readers of a literary work.

A historical critic of "Prufrock" might be able to untangle the mean-ing of certain lines or images that have little meaning for contempo-rary readers. These would include, for instance, what Prufrock means when he describes his "necktie rich and modest, but asserted by a sim-ple pin" (line 43) or says, "I shall wear the bottoms of my trousers rolled" (121).

PSYCHOLOGICAL THEORIES

Early in the twenty-first century, it is easy to underestimate the enor-mous influence that the theories of the psychoanalyst Sigmund Freud (1856–1939) have had on our understanding of human behavior and motivation. For many modern readers, Freud seems to have little to say; his work is too focused on sex and too thoroughly bound by the norms of the bourgeois Viennese society in which he lived. But if you have ever wondered what the buried significance of a dream was or whether some-one had a subconscious motivation for an action, you have been affected by Freudian thinking. Freud popularized the notions that the mind can be divided into conscious and unconscious components and that we are often motivated most strongly by the unconscious. He taught us to think in terms of overt and covert desires (often referred to in Freudian language as *manifest* and *latent*) as the basis of human actions.

Like many intellectual movements of the twentieth century, psychology, and specifically Freudian psychology, has had a major influence on literary criticism. The most typical **psychological literary criticism** examines the internal mental states, the desires, and the motivations of literary characters. (In fact, Freud himself used Shakespeare's Hamlet as an example of a man whose life was ruled by what the psychoanalyst called an Oedipal complex—man's unhealthy, but not uncommon, interest in his mother's sexuality.) Another subject of psychological criticism can be the author. A critic may examine the possible unconscious urges that drove an author to write a particular story or poem. Finally, a critic might examine the psychology of readers, trying to determine what draws us to or repels us from certain literary themes or forms. If any of these aspects of literature have ever interested you, you have engaged in psychological literary criticism.

Psychological critics often interpret literature as a psychologist might interpret a dream or a wish. Special attention is often paid to symbols as the manifest representation of a deeper, less obvious meaning. Attention is also focused on the unstated motives and unconscious states of mind of characters, authors, or readers. Freud is not the only psychological theorist whose ideas are frequently used in literary analysis. Other important figures include Carl Jung (1875–1961), who gave us the notion of the collective unconscious and the influence of **archetypes** on our thinking, and Jacques Lacan (1901–1981), who had a special interest in the unconscious and the nature of language. However, you don't need to be well versed in the intricacies of psychoanalytic theory in order to be interested in the inner workings of the human mind or the ways in which they manifest themselves in literature.

The narrator of "Prufrock" is an excellent candidate for psychological study, displaying many signs of social anxiety, depression, and other recognizable psychological conditions. Or a Jungian critic of this poem might focus on archetypal symbols such as the animalistic fog early in the poem or the mermaids that appear near the end.

READER-RESPONSE THEORIES

You no doubt have heard the old question: If a tree falls in the forest and nobody hears it, did the tree make a sound? Let us rephrase that question: If a book sits on a shelf and nobody reads it, is it still a book? If you use

reader-response criticism, your answer to that question will be a resounding *no*. Of course, the book exists as a physical object, a sheaf of paper bound in a cover and printed with symbols. But, say reader-response critics, as a work of art or a conduit for meaning, no text exists without a reader.

A text, according to the various theories of reader-response criticism, is not a container filled with meaning by its author but rather an interaction between an author and a reader, and it can never be complete unless readers bring to it their own unique insights. These insights come from a number of sources, including the reader's life experience, as well as his or her beliefs, values, state of mind at the time of the reading, and, of course, previous reading experience. Reading is not a passive attempt to understand what lies within a text but an act of creation, no less so than the writing itself. Reader-response critics try to understand the process by which we make meaning out of words on a page. If you have ever wondered why a classmate or friend saw something entirely different than you did in a story or poem, then you have been a reader-response critic.

Two key terms associated with reader-response criticism are *gaps* and *process*. Gaps are those things that a text doesn't tell us, that we need to fill in and work out for ourselves. Let us say, for instance, that you read a story told from the perspective of a child, but the author never explicitly mentions the child's age. How, then, do you imagine the narrator as you read? You pay attention to his or her actions and thoughts, and you compare this to your experience of real children you have known and others whose stories you have read. In doing so, you fill in a *gap* in the text and help solidify the text's meaning. Imagine, though, that as the story continues, new clues emerge and you need to adjust your assumptions about the child's age. This highlights the idea that reading is a *process*, that the meaning of the text is not fixed and complete but rather evolving as the text unfolds in the time it takes to read.

Some reader-response critics focus on the ways that meanings of a text change over time. To illustrate this idea, let us look at a specific example. Contemporary readers of Kate Chopin's short novel *The Awakening*, first published in 1899, tend to find the book's treatment of the heroine's sexuality subtle or even invisible. Such readers are often shocked or amused to learn that the book was widely condemned at the time of its publication as tasteless and overly explicit. Expectations and tastes change over time and place, and we can tell a lot about a society by examining how it responds to works of art. Reader-response critics, therefore, sometimes ask us to look at our own reactions to literature and to ask how, if at all, they match up with those of earlier readers. When we look at reactions to *The Awakening* at the end of the nineteenth century and then at the beginning of the twenty-first, we learn not only about Chopin's culture but also about our own.

The response paper written by Tom Lyons (pages 1266–67) shows how a student with no formal background in literary theory might still approach "Girl" in a way that gives credence to the core reader-response tenet that readers bring their own meanings to literary texts.

STRUCTURALISM

Structuralism, as the name implies, is concerned with the structures that help us understand and interpret literary texts. This may sound like a return to Formalism, which, as we saw earlier, examines the formal and linguistic elements of a text. But the elements scrutinized by structuralist critics are of a different order entirely — namely, the structures that order our thinking rather than the interior architecture of poems, stories, and plays. Structuralist criticism actually derives from the work of anthropologists, linguists, and philosophers of the mid-twentieth century who sought to understand how humans think and communicate. The basic insight at the heart of the movement is the realization that we understand nothing in isolation but rather that every piece of our knowledge is part of a network of associations. Take, for instance, the question "Is Jim a good father?" In order to form a simple yes or no answer to this question, we must consider, among other things, the spectrum of "good" and "bad," the expectations our culture holds for fathers, and all we know of Jim's relationship with his children.

For a structuralist literary critic, questions about literature are answered with the same sort of attention to context. Two different types of context are especially salient—the cultural and the literary. Cultural context refers to an understanding of all aspects of an author's (and a reader's) culture, such as the organizing structures of history, politics, religion, education, work, and family. Literary context refers to all related texts, literary and nonliterary, that affect our ability to interpret a text. What had the author read that might have affected the creation of the text? What have we read that might affect our interpretation? What are the norms of the textual genre, and how does this piece of literature conform to or break from those norms?

According to structuralist critics, then, we can understand a text only by placing it within the broader contexts of culture (that of both the reader and the author) and other texts (literary and nonliterary). To fully understand one of Shakespeare's love sonnets to the mysterious "dark lady," for example, we would need to understand the conventions of romantic love, the conceptions of dark versus fair women in culturally accepted standards of beauty, and the acceptable interactions between men and women in Shakespeare's England. We would also need to relate the sonnet to the history of love poems generally, to the development of the sonnet form specifically, and to the other works in Shakespeare's cycle of 154 sonnets.

A structuralist reading of "Prufrock," then, would be likely to consider, among other things, the types of poetry that were in vogue in 1915, when the poem was first published, as well as the specific poems and poets that Eliot, who wrote literary criticism as well as poetry, most admired.

POSTSTRUCTURALISM AND DECONSTRUCTION

Poststructuralism, it will come as no surprise, begins with the insights of structuralism but carries them one step further. If, as the structuralists insist, we can understand things only in terms of other things, then perhaps there is no center point of understanding but only an endlessly interconnected web of ideas leading to other ideas leading to still other ideas. This is the starting point of poststructuralist criticism, which posits that no text has a fixed or real meaning because no meaning exists outside of the network of other meanings to which it is connected. Meaning, then, including literary meaning, is forever shifting and altering as our understanding of the world changes. The best-known version of poststructuralism is **deconstruction**, a school of philosophy and literary criticism that first gained prominence in France and that seeks to overturn the very basis of Western philosophy by undermining the notion that reality has any stable existence.

At its worst, of course, this school of thought leads to the most slippery sort of relativism. What does it matter what I think of this poem or this play? I think what I want, you think what you want. Perhaps next week I will think something different. Who cares? Every interpretation is of equal value, and none has any real value at all. At its best, though, poststructuralist criticism can lead toward truly valuable insights into literature. It reminds us that meaning within a text is contingent on all sorts of exterior understandings; it allows for several interpretations, even contradictory interpretations, to exist simultaneously; and, by insisting that no text and no meaning are absolute, it allows for a playful approach to even the most "serious" of literary objects. Indeed, one of the recurrent themes of deconstructionist criticism is the French term *jouissance*, often translated as *bliss*, which refers to a free-spirited, almost sexual enjoyment of literary language.

Having thus briefly described deconstruction, we would do well to dispel a common misconception about the word. In recent years, many people, both within and outside of academia, have begun to use *deconstruct* as a synonym for *analyze*. You might hear, for instance, "We completely deconstructed that poem in class—I understand it much better now," or "The defense attorney deconstructed the prosecutor's argument." In both these cases, what the speaker likely means has little if anything to do with the literary critical practice of deconstruction. When we take apart a text or an argument and closely examine the parts, we are engaging not in deconstruction but in analysis.

A deconstructionist reading of "Girl" might call into question the very basis for our belief in gender divisions, class structure, or the need for the socialization of young people by their elders.

These are only some of the many varieties of literary theory and criticism. In addition, you might encounter eco-criticism, which focuses on the environment and human beings' relationship with the rest of nature; religious (for example, Christian, Muslim, or Buddhist) criticism; comparative literature, which compares related works from different languages and/or cultures; various schools of critical inquiry based on race and ethnicity; and many, many more. There are even literary critics who perform textual analysis using sophisticated computer programs.

By now you may be wondering what sort of literary critic you are. You may feel that you have been a Formalist one day and a psychological critic the next. This is not surprising, and it should cause you no worry, as virtually none of these schools are mutually exclusive. Indeed, most professional critics mix and match the various schools in whatever way best suits their immediate needs. The close-reading techniques of the New Critics, for instance, are frequently adopted by those who would fervently reject the New Critical stance that social and political context be excluded from consideration. If you wished to write about the social decline of Mme. Loisel in Guy de Maupassant's story "The Necklace," you might well find yourself in the position of a Marxist–feminist–New Historicist critic. That's fine. Writing with the knowledge that you are drawing from Marxism, feminism, and New Historicism, you will almost certainly write a better-organized, better-informed, and more thorough paper than you would have had you begun with no conscious basis in literary theory.

Take a look at the annotations and notes you have made on literary works, the notes you have taken in class, and any exams or papers you have written. Are there particular themes and issues to which you keep returning, particular genres or literary features that continue to attract or interest you? If so, you may have the beginning of an answer to the question: *What sort of literary critic am I?*

Biographical Notes on the Authors
[Arranged Alphabetically]

Born in 1964 in Cairo, Egypt, **Leila Aboulela** is the author of three novels and several short stories. *Coloured Lights*, published in 2001, is the compilation of her short stories. Her novels — *The Translator* (1999), *Minaret* (2005), and *Lyrics Alley* (2010) — have earned her significant attention in the literary world, and BBC Radio turned *The Translator* into a five-part adaptation. She now lives in Aberdeen.

The daughter of a former tennis champion and a sports writer, **Kim Addonizio** was born in 1954 in Washington, DC, She has spent most of her adult life living in the San Francisco Bay area, where she teaches poetry workshops. Known for her provocative style, Addonizio has earned acclaim for both her fiction writing and her poetry. Recent works include *The Palace of Illusions* (2014), a collection of short stories, and *My Black Angel* (2014), a collection of blues poems and portraits.

Self-described as one-half Japanese, one-eighth Choctaw, one-fourth black, and one-sixteenth Irish, **Ai** (1947–2010) was born Florence Anthony in Albany, Texas, and grew up in Tucson, Arizona. She legally changed her name to "Ai," which means "love" in Japanese. She received a BA in Japanese from the University of Arizona and an MFA from the University of California at Irvine. She is the author of nine volumes of poetry, among them the award-winning *Vice* (1999) and, more recently, *No Surrender* (2010). She has taught at Wayne State University, George Mason University, the University of Kentucky, and Oklahoma State University.

A Pakistani-American actor and writer, **Ayad Akhtar** was born in 1970 in New York City and raised in Milwaukee, Wisconsin. He is a graduate of Brown and Columbia universities with degrees in theater and film directing. In 2013, he received the Pulitzer Prize for Drama for *Disgraced*. He is also the author of *American Dervish* (2012), a book published in over twenty languages worldwide. His recent play, *The Invisible Hand*, premiered at the Marin Theatre Company in Mill Valley, California, in June 2016.

Elizabeth Alexander was born in 1962 in Harlem, New York, but raised in Washington, DC. She is a poet, essayist, and playwright, and she is recognized as an important figure in African-American poetry. She is the author of several books, including *American Sublime* (2005), *The Black Interior* (2004), and *Venus Hottentot* (1990). In 2009, she recited her original poem "Praise Song for the Day" for the inauguration of Barack Obama, joining poets such as Robert Frost, Maya

Angelou, and Miller Williams who have been invited to recite their poems at previous presidential inaugurations.

Of Spokane/Coeur d'Alene Native American descent, **Sherman Alexie** was born in 1966 on the Spokane Indian Reservation in Wellpinit, Washington. He earned his BA from Washington State University in Pullman. He has published eleven books of poetry, most recently *Face* (2009); three novels, of which *Flight* (2007) is the latest; and five collections of short fiction, including *The Lone Ranger and Tonto Fistfight in Heaven* (1993), *Ten Little Indians* (2003), and *Blasphemy* (2012). His first novel for young adults, *The Absolutely True Diary of a Part-Time Indian*, received the 2007 National Book Award for Young People's Literature.

Agha Shahid Ali (1949–2001) was born in New Delhi, India, and grew up Muslim in Kashmir. He was educated at the University of Kashmir, Srinagar, and at the University of Delhi. He earned a PhD from Pennsylvania State University in 1984 and an MFA from the University of Arizona in 1985. He was a poet, critic, translator, and editor, holding teaching positions at the University of Delhi and at several colleges and universities in the United States. "Even the Rain" (page 615) showcases Ali's mastery of the *ghazal*, a traditional Persian poetic form.

Born in Camden, Ohio, **Sherwood Anderson** (1876–1941) left work as a factory manager after a nervous breakdown to pursue writing. His 1919 book *Winesburg, Ohio*, an in-depth psychological exploration featuring characters who became "grotesques," launched his career and remains one of his most enduring works. At the time, it was not as successful as one might think, and his 1925 book *Dark Laughter* was his only bestseller. Throughout the 1920s, Anderson published a variety of works, including short story collections, novels, memoirs, books of essays, and a book of poetry. His influence on later writers, such as William Faulkner, Ernest Hemingway, John Steinbeck, and Thomas Wolfe, is undeniable, and his contributions to the world of literature are impressive.

Matthew Arnold (1822–1888) was born in the small English village of Laleham and raised at Rugby School, where his father was headmaster. He attended Oxford University and, in 1857, was elected professor of poetry at Oxford, a position he held for ten years, writing mostly literary criticism. He also worked for thirty-five years as an inspector of schools and made two lecture tours of the United States.

John Ashbery (b. 1927) is an American poet who has published more than twenty-seven volumes of poetry and won nearly every major American award for poetry. Critics have praised his extensive vocabulary and reach. Langdon Hammer, the chairman of the English Department at Yale, said no poet matched the impact Ashbery has had on the last 50 years of poetry. His writing encourages readers to leave all their presumptions about verse at the door, instead asking them to consider the limits of what language can do.

Margaret Atwood was born in Ottawa in 1939 and grew up in northern Ontario, Quebec, and Toronto. She began writing while attending high school in Toronto. She received her undergraduate degree from Victoria College at the University of Toronto and her master's degree from Radcliffe College. She won the E. J. Pratt Medal for her privately printed book of poems, *Double Persephone* (1961), and has published sixteen more collections of poetry. She is perhaps best known for her thirteen novels, which include *The Handmaid's Tale* (1983), *The Robber Bride* (1994), and *The Blind Assassin* (2000; winner of the Booker Prize). She has also published ten collections of short stories, six children's books, and six books of nonfiction, and she has edited several anthologies. Her work has been translated into more than thirty languages, including Farsi, Japanese, Turkish, Finnish, Korean, Icelandic, and Estonian.

W. H. Auden (1907–1973) was born in York, England. He attended private school and later Oxford University, where he began to write poetry. He supported himself by teaching and publishing, writing books based on his travels to Iceland, Spain, and China. He also wrote (with Chester Kallman) several librettos, including the one in Igor Stravinsky's *The Rake's Progress* (1951). He lived in the United States from 1939 until his death, having become a U.S. citizen in 1946. His work combines lively intelligence, quick wit, careful craftsmanship, and social concern.

Jimmy Santiago Baca was born in 1952 in Sante Fe, New Mexico, of Chicano and Apache heritage. Abandoned by his parents at the age of two, he lived with one of his grandparents for several years before being placed in an orphanage. He lived on the streets as a youth and was imprisoned for six years for drug possession. In prison, he taught himself to read and write and began to compose poetry. A fellow inmate convinced him to submit some of his poems for publication. He has since published a dozen books of poetry, a memoir, a collection of stories and essays, a play, a screenplay, and a novel. He lives outside Albuquerque in a hundred-year-old adobe house.

Born in New York City, the son of a revivalist minister, **James Baldwin** (1924–1987) was raised in poverty in Harlem, where, at the age of fourteen, he became a preacher in the Fireside Pentecostal Church. After completing high school, he decided to become a writer and, with the help of the black American expatriate writer Richard Wright, won a grant that enabled him to move to Paris, where he lived for most of his remaining years. There he wrote the critically acclaimed *Go Tell It on the Mountain* (1953), a novel about the religious awakening of a fourteen-year-old black youth. Subsequent works, focusing on the intellectual and spiritual trials of black men in a white, racist society, included the novels *Giovanni's Room* (1956), *Another Country* (1962)—both famous at the time for their homosexual themes—*Tell Me How Long the Train's Been Gone* (1968), *If Beale Street Could Talk* (1974), *Just Above My Head* (1979), and *Harlem Quartet* (1987); the play *Blues for Mister Charlie* (1964); and the powerful nonfiction commentaries *Notes of a Native Son* (1955), *Nobody Knows My Name* (1961), and *The Fire Next Time* (1963). Baldwin's short stories are collected in *Going to Meet the Man* (1965).

Born in New York City and raised in Harlem, **Toni Cade Bambara** (1939–1995) attended Queens College, where she wrote stories, poems, scripts, and other works and was part of the staff of the literary magazine. She continued writing stories as she studied for an MA at City College. After her story collection *Gorilla, My Love* (1972) was published, her sense of herself as a black writer gradually clarified and deepened. Her other story collections include *The Black Woman* (1970), *Tales and Stories for Black Folks* (1971), and *The Sea Birds Are Still Alive* (1977). Her two novels are *The Salt Eaters* (1980) and *If Blessing Comes* (1987). *Deep Sightings and Rescue Missions*, a collection of fiction and nonfiction, appeared posthumously, in 1996.

Jen Bervin (b. 1972) is a poet and visual artist who coedited the *The Gorgeous Nothings: Emily Dickinson's Envelope Poems* (2012), a finalist for the Poetry Foundation's 2014 Pegasus Award for Criticism. She specializes in poetry, archival research, and large-scale artworks. The research for her current project, *Silk Poems*, includes contacting labs and libraries to acquire more information. Bervin is on the faculty of the graduate program at Vermont College of Fine Arts; she lives in Brooklyn, New York.

Born in Worcester, Massachusetts, **Elizabeth Bishop** (1911–1979) was raised in Nova Scotia by her grandparents after her father died and her mother was committed to an asylum. She attended Vassar College intending to study medicine but was encouraged by MARIANNE MOORE to be a poet. From 1935 to 1937, she traveled in France, Spain, northern Africa, Ireland, and Italy. She settled in Key West, Florida, for four years and then in Rio de Janeiro for almost twenty years. She wrote slowly and carefully, producing a small body of technically sophisticated, formally varied, witty, and thoughtful poetry, revealing in precise, true-to-life

images her impressions of the physical world. She served as Consultant in Poetry at the Library of Congress from 1949 to 1950.[1]

William Blake (1757–1827) was born and raised in London. His only formal schooling was in art — he studied for a year at the Royal Academy and was apprenticed to an engraver. He later worked as a professional engraver, doing commissions and illustrations, assisted by his wife, Catherine Boucher. Blake, who had started writing poetry at the age of eleven, later engraved and handprinted his own poems, in very small batches, with his own illustrations. His early work was possessed of a strong social conscience, and his mature work turned increasingly mythic and prophetic.

Eavan Boland was born in Dublin in 1944, and she was educated there as well as in London and New York. She has taught at Trinity College and University College, Dublin; Bowdoin College; and the University of Iowa. She is currently the Bella Mabury and Eloise Mabury Knapp Professor in Humanities and the Melvin and Bill Lane Professor and Director of the Creative Writing Program at Stanford University. An influential figure in Irish poetry, Boland has published a dozen volumes of poetry, including *The Journey and Other Poems* (1987), *Night Feed* (1994), *The Lost Land* (1998), *Code* (2001), *New Collected Poems* (2005),

---

[1]The first appointment of a Consultant in Poetry at the Library of Congress was made in 1937. The title was changed to Poet Laureate Consultant in Poetry in 1986. Appointments are made for one year, beginning in September, and sometimes have been renewed for a second year.

and *Domestic Violence* (2007), and she has edited several other books, including *Three Irish Poets: An Anthology* (2003) and *Irish Writers on Writing* (2007). Her poems and essays have appeared in magazines such as *The New Yorker*, *The Atlantic*, *Kenyon Review*, and *American Poetry Review*. A collection of essays, *A Journey with Two Maps: Becoming a Woman Poet*, was published in 2011. She is a regular reviewer for the *Irish Times*.

Born in 1948 into a working-class family in New York state, **T. Coraghessan Boyle** earned a bachelor's degree from the State University of New York at Potsdam before completing his MFA at the University of Iowa Writers' Workshop. His writing is often satirical and employs irony and surrealist imagery contrasted against the more mundane aspects of the baby boomer generation he usually chronicles. He has published thirteen novels and eight short-story collections. His work regularly appears in *Harper's*, *The New Yorker*, and *The Atlantic*, among other magazines, and has received numerous awards. He joined the faculty at the University of Southern California in 1978 and is now Distinguished Professor Emeritus of English there.

Born in Northampton, England, **Anne Bradstreet** (1612–1672) was educated by tutors, reading chiefly religious writings and the Bible. In 1628 she married Simon Bradstreet, a brilliant young Puritan educated at Cambridge. They were among the earliest settlers of the Massachusetts Bay Colony, in 1630, and her father and husband were leading figures in its governance. She wrote regularly in both prose and verse throughout her busy and difficult years in Massachusetts.

Born in Topeka, Kansas, **Gwendolyn Brooks** (1917–2000) was raised in Chicago and wrote her first poems at age seven. She began studying poetry at the Southside Community Art Center. Her second collection of poems, *Annie Allen* (1949), earned the first Pulitzer Prize given to an African American poet. She served as Consultant in Poetry at the Library of Congress from 1985 to 1986 and worked in community programs and poetry workshops in Chicago to encourage young African American writers.

An assistant professor in the creative writing program at Emory University in Atlanta, **Jericho Brown** (b. 1976) received the Whiting Writers Award and fellowships from the Radcliffe Institute for Advanced Study at Harvard University in recognition for his contribution to poetry. Publications such as *The Nation*, *The New Republic*, *The New Yorker*, and *The Best American Poetry* have all featured his work. He is the author of two collections: *Please* and *The New Testament*.

Born in Durham, England, **Elizabeth Barrett Browning** (1806–1861) studied with her brother's tutor. Her first book of poetry was published when she was thirteen, and she soon became the most famous female poet up until that time in English history. A riding accident at the age of sixteen left her a semi-invalid in the home of her possessive father, who forbade any of his eleven children to marry. At age thirty-nine, Elizabeth eloped with ROBERT BROWNING; the couple lived in Florence, Italy, where Elizabeth died fifteen years later. Her best-known book of poems is *Sonnets from the Portuguese*, a sequence of forty-four sonnets recording the growth of her love for her husband.

Robert Browning (1812–1889) was the son of a bank clerk in Camberwell, then a suburb of London. As an aspiring poet in 1844, Browning admired ELIZABETH BARRETT's poetry and began a correspondence with her that led to one of the world's most famous romances. His and Elizabeth's courtship lasted until 1846, when they secretly wed and ran off to Italy, where they lived until Elizabeth's death in 1861. The years in Florence were among the happiest for both of them. To her he dedicated *Men and Women* (1855), which contains his best poetry. Although she was the more popular poet during their time together, his reputation grew upon his return to London, after her death, assisted somewhat by public sympathy for him. The late 1860s were the peak of his career: he and TENNYSON were mentioned together as the foremost poets of the age.

Byron—see George Gordon, Lord Byron.

Lewis Carroll (1832–1898), born Charles Dodgson on January 27, 1832, in Daresbury, England, showed a love for writing and creating even as a child. He designed games and started writing books, even though he was shy, and he went on to publish the universally known books *Alice's Adventures in Wonderland* (1865) and its sequel, *Through the Looking-Glass and What Alice Found There* (1871). By the time of his death, *Alice's Adventures in Wonderland* was one of the most popular books in the world.

Born in Clatskanie, Oregon, **Raymond Carver** (1938–1988) lived in Port Angeles, Washington, until his death. Among the honors accorded this short-story writer and poet during his lifetime were a 1979 Guggenheim fellowship, two grants from the National Endowment for the Arts, and election to the American Academy of Arts and Letters. Carver's writing, known for its spare, stark depiction of contemporary existence, has been translated into more than twenty languages. His story collections are *Will You Please Be Quiet, Please?* (1976), nominated for a National Book Award; *Furious Seasons* (1977); *What We Talk About When We Talk About Love* (1981); *Cathedral* (1983), nominated for the Pulitzer Prize; and *Where I'm Calling From* (1988).

Born near Winchester, Virginia, **Willa Cather** (1873–1947), as a child, moved with her family to a ranch outside Red Cloud, Nebraska, a prairie frontier town. After attending high school there, she studied classics at the University of Nebraska. She then moved east; worked on a Pittsburgh newspaper; taught school in Allegheny, Pennsylvania; worked at the magazine *McClure's*, first on the staff, then as managing editor; and wrote poetry and fiction. After a volume of poetry, she wrote *The Troll Garden* (1905), a collection of stories, and *Alexander's Bridge* (1912), her first novel. Thereafter, Cather wrote full-time, often returning to western communities and landscapes for her subject; with them she felt she could plumb her own experience and examine the frontier spirit. Among the many works that followed are stories, story collections, and novels including *O Pioneers!* (1913), *Song of the Lark* (1915), *My Antonía* (1918), *One of Ours* (Pulitzer Prize, 1923), and *Death Comes for the Archbishop* (1927). Among her many honors is a gold medal from the National Institute of Arts and Letters (1944).

Lorna Dee Cervantes was born in 1954 in San Francisco and grew up in San Jose, where she studied at San Jose City College and San Jose State University. She is the author of five books of poetry: *Emplumada* (1981), which won an American Book Award, *From the Cables of Genocide: Poems of Love and Hunger* (1991), *Drive: The First Quartet* (2006), *Ciento: 100 100-Word Love Poems* (2011), and *Sueño* (2013). She is also coeditor of *Red Dirt*, a cross-cultural poetry journal, and her work has been included in many anthologies. Cervantes, who considers herself "a Chicana writer, a feminist writer, a political writer," lives in Colorado and was a professor at the University of Colorado at Boulder.

John Cheever (1912–1982) was born in Quincy, Massachusetts. Many of his pieces on life in suburban America appeared in *The New Yorker*. Sometimes called the "Chekhov of the suburbs," many of Cheever's works are rooted in a yearning for a vanishing way of life, such as the vanishing sense of community in modern suburban communities. He was known best for his short stories—*The Stories of John Cheever* earned him a Pulitzer Prize in 1978—but he was also an accomplished novelist, penning *The Wapshot Chronicle* (1957), *The Wapshot Scandal* (1964), and *Falconer* (1977).

Born the son of a grocer and the grandson of a serf in Taganrog, a seacoast town in southern Russia, Anton Chekhov (1860–1904) began writing humorous tales to support himself while studying medicine at Moscow University. In 1884 he received his medical degree and published his first collection of short stories, *Tales of Melpomene*. Other early collections are *Motley Tales* (1886), *At Twilight* (1887), and *Stones* (1888). Besides being a masterful writer of short stories, Chekhov is probably Russia's most esteemed playwright. In 1898 the Moscow Art Theatre produced his play *The Seagull*, followed by *Uncle Vanya* in 1899, *The Three Sisters* in 1901, and *The Cherry Orchard* in 1904. Chekhov, known for his sad and subtle exploration of people's inability to communicate as well as for his humanitarian activities, died at age forty-four of tuberculosis, which he contracted in his student days.

A first-generation Chinese American, Marilyn Chin was born in 1955 in Hong Kong and raised in Portland, Oregon. She is the author of three volumes of poetry, *Dwarf Bamboo* (1987), *The Phoenix Gone, The Terrace Empty* (1994), and *Rhapsody in Plain Yellow* (2002); and a novel, *Revenge of the Mooncake Vixen* (2009). She also is a coeditor of *Dissident Song: A Contemporary Asian American Anthology* (1991) and has translated poems by the modern Chinese poet Ai Qing and cotranslated poems by the Japanese poet Gozo Yoshimasu. She has received numerous awards for her poetry, including a Stegner Fellowship, the PEN/Josephine Miles Award, and four Pushcart Prizes. She is codirector of the MFA program at University of San Diego.

Born Katherine O'Flaherty, the daughter of a French Creole mother and a prosperous St. Louis businessman who died when she was four, Kate Chopin (1851–1904) was raised by her mother and a great-grandmother who sent her to Catholic school and trained her for a place in St. Louis society. At the age of eighteen, she married Oscar Chopin and accompanied him to New Orleans, where he became a cotton broker.

When her husband's business failed, the family moved to a plantation in northern Louisiana and opened a general store, which Kate managed for a year after her husband's death in 1883. She then returned to St. Louis with her six children and began a career as a writer of realistic fiction. Among her works are the story collections *Bayou Folk* (1894) and *A Night in Acadie* (1897) as well as the novel *The Awakening* (1899), shocking in its time for its frank portrayal of adultery but widely praised today for its sensitive portrayal of a woman's need for independence and sensual fulfillment.

Lucille Clifton (1936–2010) was born in Depew, New York, and studied at Howard University. She published many books of poetry, including *Blessing the Boats: New and Selected Poems, 1988–2000* (2000), which won the National Book Award. She also published a memoir and more than twenty books for children. She taught at several colleges, worked in the Office of Education in Washington, DC, served as poet laureate for the state of Maryland, and was Distinguished Professor of Humanities at St. Mary's College of Maryland. Her poems typically reflect her ethnic pride, feminist principles, and race and gender consciousness.

Samuel Taylor Coleridge (1772–1834) was born in Devonshire and sent to school in London after his father's death. He went to Jesus College, Cambridge, in 1791 and dropped out twice without a degree. In 1798 Coleridge and WILLIAM WORDSWORTH published *Lyrical Ballads*, which initiated the Romantic Movement in English poetry and established the reputations of both poets. After 1802 Coleridge became addicted to opium, which he used to treat physical discomfort and seizures. He and his wife separated, his friendship with Wordsworth ended, and he stopped producing poetry. From 1816 until his death, Coleridge lived under constant medical supervision and yet still published a journal and wrote several plays, pieces of criticism, and philosophical and religious treatises.

Born in 1941 in New York City, **Billy Collins** is the author of several collections of poems. Perhaps no poet since ROBERT FROST has managed to combine high critical acclaim with such broad popular appeal. The typical Collins poem opens on a clear and hospitable note but soon takes an unexpected turn; poems that begin in irony may end in a moment of lyric surprise. Collins sees his poetry as "a form of travel writing" and considers humor "a door into the serious." Collins is the author of numerous books of poetry, most recently *Ballistics* (2008) and *Horoscopes for the Dead* (2011). In 2009 he edited, with illustrator David Sibley, *Bright Wings: An Illustrated Anthology of Poems about Birds*. He served as Poet Laureate Consultant in Poetry at the Library of Congress from 2001 to 2003 and as New York State Poet Laureate from 2004 to 2006. He has taught at Columbia University, Sarah Lawrence College, and Lehman College/City University of New York.

Martha Collins is an American poet born in 1940 in Omaha, Nebraska. She graduated from Stanford University with a BA and earned her PhD at the University of Iowa. In her poems, Collins employs fragmentation and interruption. In her recent work, she has examined the history of racial violence and racism in America. She is the author of numerous poetry collections, including *Day Unto Day* (2014), *White Papers* (2012), *Blue Front* (2006), and *The Arrangement of Space* (1991). Collins is a professor emerita at Oberlin College, editor for Oberlin College Press, and editor-at-large for *Field* magazine.

Raised in Kent, England, **Wendy Cope** (b. 1945) is a contemporary poet known for use of parody and humor in addressing grave topics. She has published several volumes of poetry, including *Making Cocoa for Kingsley Amis* (1985) and *Serious Concerns* (1992). Critics acknowledge her sharp wit, observant eye, and accomplishments as a formal poet. Some have compared her to Philip Larkin. Cope lives in England with fellow poet Lachlan MacKinnon.

Eduardo Corral (b. 1970), a poet and teacher, earned degrees from Arizona State University and the University of Iowa Writers' Workshop. After his debut poetry collection, *Slow Lightning* (2012), he won the Yale Younger Poets Prize. His seamless blending of English and Spanish has earned him a number of awards and a legion of eager readers. He lives in New York City.

Stephen Crane (1871–1900) wrote poetry, short stories, and novels. He worked as a journalist in New York City for a number of years, and his exploration of the slums of New York City inspired his first book, *Maggie: A Girl of the Streets* (1893). The gritty realism of his second novel, *The Red Badge of Courage* (1895), brought him instant fame. Later, he worked as a war correspondent in Greece and Cuba, and his near-death experience on the *Commodore* inspired his most famous short story, "The Open Boat." He is recognized as a master of **realism** (see the glossary) and an innovator of the American short story.

Countee Cullen (1903–1946) was born either in Louisville, Kentucky; Baltimore, Maryland; or, as he himself claimed, New York City. He was adopted by the Reverend Frederick A. Cullen and his wife and grew up, as he put it, "in the conservative atmosphere of a Methodist parsonage." He studied at New York University and Harvard University. A forerunner of the Harlem Renaissance movement, he was, in the 1920s, the most popular black literary figure in America. From the 1930s until his death, he wrote less while working as a junior high school French teacher. For many years, Cullen's reputation was eclipsed by that of other Harlem Renaissance writers, particularly LANGSTON HUGHES and ZORA NEALE HURSTON; recently, however, there has been a resurgence of interest in Cullen's life and work.

E. E. Cummings (1894–1962) was born in Cambridge, Massachusetts, where his father was a Unitarian minister and a sociology lecturer at Harvard University. He graduated from Harvard and then served as an ambulance driver during World War I. *The Enormous Room* (1922) is an account of his confinement in a French prison camp during the war. After the war, he lived in rural Connecticut and Greenwich Village, with frequent visits to Paris. In his work, Cummings experimented radically with form, punctuation, spelling, and syntax, abandoning traditional techniques and structures to create a new, highly idiosyncratic means of poetic expression. At the time of his death in 1962, he was the second most widely read poet in the United States after ROBERT FROST.

Born and raised in Detroit, **Toi Derricotte** (b. 1941) earned a BA in special education from Wayne State University and an MA in English literature from New York University. She is the author of several collections of poetry as well as a memoir, *The Black Notebooks* (1997). With poet CORNELIUS EADY, she cofounded Cave Canem, which offers workshops, retreats, and publication opportunities for African American poets. Among the many honors she has received is the Distinguished Pioneering of the Arts Award from United Black Artists. Derricotte teaches creative writing at the University of Pittsburgh.

Junot Díaz (b. 1968) immigrated to the United States from the Dominican Republic at the age of six. He worked his way through Rutgers University by pumping gas, washing dishes, and performing a variety of other odd jobs. He later received an MFA from Cornell University. He published his first story collection, *Drown*, in 1996, and several years later *The New Yorker* named him one of the top twenty writers of the twenty-first century. His debut novel, *The Brief Wondrous Life of Oscar Wao*, was published in 1997 to critical acclaim and won the Pulitzer Prize. Díaz's writing often deals with the tensions of the immigrant experience and the two cultures he has had to negotiate. He currently teaches creative writing at MIT and is the fiction editor for *The Boston Review*.

Born in 1978 in the Fort Mojave Indian Village in Needles, California, **Natalie Diaz** is the author of the poetry collection *When My Brother Was an Aztec* (2012). Diaz played professional basketball in Europe and Asia before returning to school to earn her MFA. Diaz resides in Mohave Valley, Arizona, working with the last speakers of Mojave and directing a language revitalization program.

Emily Dickinson (1830–1886) was born in Amherst, Massachusetts, and lived there her entire life, leaving only rarely. She briefly attended a woman's seminary but became homesick and left before a year was out. Dickinson never married and became reclusive later in life, forgoing even the village routines and revelries she once had enjoyed. She published very few of the more than 1,700 poems she wrote; most were written for herself or for inclusion in her many letters. It was not until 1955 that a complete edition of the verses, attempting to present them as they were originally written, appeared.

Born in London to a prosperous Catholic family (through his mother he was related to statesman and author Sir Thomas More and the playwright John Heywood), **John Donne** (1572–1631) studied at Oxford University for several years but did not take a degree. He fought with WALTER RALEGH in two naval strikes against Spain. In 1601 Donne's promising political career was permanently derailed by his precipitate marriage to Anne More without her father's consent. He was briefly imprisoned, lost a very promising position with Sir Thomas Egerton, and spent years seeking political employment before finally being persuaded by King James I in 1615 to become a priest of the Church of England. His life was described by Isaac Walton later in the century as having been divided into two parts. In phase one, he was "Jack Donne" of Lincoln's Inn: when young, Donne employed a sophisticated urban wit that lent a sort of jaded tone to his earlier poetry. "A Valediction: Forbidding Mourning" presumably appeared during this stage of his life and is a typical metaphysical poem. In phase two, he was John Donne, dean of St. Paul's:

after Donne took holy orders in 1615, his poetry became markedly less amorous and more religious in tone. His Holy Sonnets, of which "Death, be not proud" is one, are as dense and complex as his earlier work but directed toward an exploration of his relationship with God.

H.D. (Hilda Doolittle) (1886–1961) published poetry under the pen name "H.D." Embodying the themes of literary modernism, Doolittle's work was constantly innovative, and she closely associated with avant-garde Imagist poets including Ezra Pound and Richard Aldington. Many of her works focus on love and war, birth and death, and sexuality. In her final year, she published *Helen in Egypt*, a famous poetic reinterpretation of the Trojan War.

Mark Doty (b. 1953) is the author of twelve collections of poetry and three memoirs—*Heaven's Coast* (1996), about the loss of his partner, Wally Roberts; *Firebird* (1999), a gay coming-of-age story that chronicles the gradual process of finding in art a place of personal belonging; and *Dog Years* (2007), about the relationships between humans and the dogs they love. He received the National Book Award for *Fire to Fire: New and Selected Poems* (2008). He has taught at Brandeis University, Sarah Lawrence College, Vermont College, and the University of Iowa Writers' Workshop. He now divides his time between New York City and Fire Island, New York, and he teaches at Rutgers University.

Rita Dove was born in 1952 in Akron, Ohio; her father was the first research chemist to break the race barrier in the tire industry. She graduated from Miami University in Oxford, Ohio, with a degree in English; after a year at Tübingen University in Germany on a Fulbright fellowship, she enrolled in the University of Iowa Writers' Workshop, where she earned her MFA in 1977. She has taught at Tuskegee Institute and Arizona State University and is now on the faculty of the University of Virginia. In 1993 she was appointed Poet Laureate Consultant in Poetry to the Library of Congress, making her the youngest person—and the first African American woman—to receive this highest official honor in American letters. She is the author of numerous collections of poetry, including *Thomas and Beulah* (1986), a book-length sequence loosely based on the lives of her grandparents, which was awarded the Pulitzer Prize in 1987.

Born in 1961 in Woonsocket, Rhode Island, **Denise Duhamel** is an American poet whose poems are known for their feminist foundation, often exploring American culture through the lens of satire. Most famously, she used the Barbie doll in her book *Kinky* (1997) to combine her knack for humor, satire, and a feminist lens. As a nod to her dedication to her craft, Duhamel received a fellowship from the National Endowment for the Arts, and her work has been included in several volumes of *Best American Poetry*. She now lives in Hollywood, Florida, and teaches creative writing and literature at Florida International University.

Paul Laurence Dunbar (1872–1906) was the first African American to gain national eminence as a poet. Born and raised in Dayton, Ohio, the son of former slaves, he was an outstanding student. The only African American in his class, he was both class president and class poet. Although he lived to be only thirty-three years old, Dunbar was prolific, writing short stories, novels, librettos, plays, songs, and essays as well as the poetry for which he became well known. Popular with both black and white readers of his day, Dunbar's style encompasses two distinct voices—the standard English of the classical poet and the evocative dialect of the turn-of-the-twentieth-century black community in America.

Born and raised in Rochester, New York, **Cornelius Eady** (b. 1954) attended Monroe Community College and Empire State College. He began writing as a teenager. His poems are his biography, their subjects ranging from blues musicians to Eady's witnessing his father's death. He has published six volumes of poetry. With poet TOI DERRICOTTE, he cofounded Cave Canem, which offers workshops, retreats, and publication opportunities for African American poets, and with composer Diedre Murray he has collaborated on two highly acclaimed music-dramas. Formerly the director of the Poetry Center at the State University of New York, Stony Brook, he is the Miller Chair in Poetry at the University of Missouri.

Edith Maud Eaton (pen name **Sui Sin Far**) (1865–1914) was the daughter of an English father and a Chinese mother. She adopted her pen name and wrote newspaper articles and short stories that addressed the plight of Chinese Americans during a time of extreme hostility toward immigrants. She is the author of *Mrs. Spring Fragrance* (1912), a collection of short stories.

Born and raised in St. Louis, **T. S. Eliot** (1888–1965) went to prep school in Massachusetts and then to Harvard University, where he earned an MA in philosophy in 1910 and started his doctoral dissertation. He studied at the Sorbonne, in Paris, and then in Marburg, Germany, in 1914, when the war forced him to leave. Relocating to Oxford, he abandoned philosophy for poetry, and he married. After teaching and working in a bank, he became an editor at Faber and Faber, and he was an editor of the journal *Criterion*. He became a British citizen and a member of the Church of England in 1927. A dominant force in English poetry for several decades, he won the Nobel Prize in Literature in 1948. He also wrote plays and essays as well as a series of poems on cats that became the basis of a musical by Andrew Lloyd Weber. The Eliot poem included in this anthology shows the poet's use of collage techniques to relate the fragmentation he saw in the culture and individual psyches of his day.

Elizabeth I (1533–1603) was one of the longest-reigning monarchs England has ever known. Fluent in four languages, a skilled diplomat, and an exceptional poet, Elizabeth ascended the throne at one of the most tumultuous points in English history and managed to resolve religious disputes, unify her nation, keep enemies at bay, and support the flourishing visual, literary, and performing arts in her realm. When she died in 1603, she had been queen for nearly forty-five years.

Ralph Ellison (1914–1994) was born in Oklahoma City. His father, an ice and coal vendor, died when Ralph was three; his mother supported herself and her son with domestic work. After studying music at the Tuskegee Institute, Ellison went to New York City in

1936, where, encouraged by the novelist Richard Wright, he became associated with the Federal Writers' Project. His first novel, *Invisible Man* (1952), received a 1953 National Book Award and became a classic in American fiction. Ellison taught literature and writing at Bard College, the University of Chicago, Rutgers University, and New York University. His other works include the collections of essays *Shadow and Act* (1964) and *Going to the Territory* (1986), and three posthumous works prepared by John F. Callahan: *The Collected Essays of Ralph Ellison* (1995); *Flying Home and Other Stories* (1996), a short-story collection; and *Juneteenth* (1999), a novel shaped and edited by Callahan from manuscripts left unfinished when Ellison died.

Louise Erdrich, born in 1954 to a Chippewa Indian mother and a German-American father, is well-known for her exploration of Native American themes in her works. Erdrich often visits the North Dakota lands, the meeting place of her ancestors, and she's published three critically acclaimed collections of poetry, *Jacklight* (1984), *Baptism of Desire* (1989), and *Original Fire: New and Selected Poems* (2003). Although Erdrich has had success in writing poetry, she is best known as a novelist, having published seven novels that tell the story of three families living in and around a reservation in the fictional town of Argus, North Dakota. Her multivoiced and nonchronological storytelling have earned her comparisons to WILLIAM FAULKNER, and her exploration of Native American experiences is like no author's before her.

Born in 1957 in Brooklyn, New York, **Martín Espada** has an eclectic résumé:

radio journalist in Nicaragua, welfare-rights paralegal, advocate for the mentally ill, night desk clerk in a transient hotel, attendant in a primate nursery, groundskeeper at a minor league ballpark, bindery worker in a printing plant, bouncer in a bar, and practicing lawyer in Chelsea, Massachusetts. He is the author of eight books of poetry, most recently *The Trouble Ball* (2011). His earlier book, *Alabanza: New and Selected Poems, 1982–2002* (2003), received the Paterson Award for Sustained Literary Achievement and was named an American Library Association Notable Book of the Year. He is an essayist, editor, and translator as well as a poet. He currently teaches at the University of Massachusetts, Amherst.

Tarfia Faizullah (b. 1980) is an American poet who won the 2009 Cohen Award. Shortly after earning her MFA from the Virginia Commonwealth University program in creative writing, she had her first book, *Seam* (2014), published. It won the Crab Orchard Series in Poetry First Book Award. Currently, Faizullah lives in Detroit, where she works as an editor for the *Asian American Literary Review* and is the codirector of Organic Weapon Arts.

Born in New Albany, Mississippi, **William Faulkner** (1897–1962) moved as a young boy to Oxford, Mississippi, the place he was to call home for the rest of his life. He completed two years of high school and a little more than one year at the University of Mississippi. After a brief stint in the Royal Air Force in Canada during World War I, he worked at various jobs before becoming a writer. His first book, *The Marble Faun* (1924), was a collection of poems. Encouraged by the writer

Sherwood Anderson, whom he met in New Orleans in 1925, Faulkner wrote his first novel, *Soldier's Pay* (1926), a work that was favorably reviewed. His third novel, *Sartoris* (1929), was the first set in Yoknapatawpha County, a fictional re-creation of the area around Oxford whose setting appeared throughout his later fiction. Over three decades Faulkner published nineteen novels, more than eighty short stories, and collections of poems and essays; he also wrote several film scripts to supplement his income. Collections of his short fiction include *Go Down, Moses* (1942); *Collected Stories* (1950), which won a National Book Award; and *Big Woods* (1955). Among his best-known novels are *The Sound and the Fury* (1929), *As I Lay Dying* (1930), *Sanctuary* (1931), *Light in August* (1932), and *Absalom, Absalom!* (1936). Faulkner was awarded the Nobel Prize in Literature in 1949; *A Fable* (1954) and *The Reivers* (1962) each won the Pulitzer Prize for fiction.

Born in St. Paul, Minnesota, **F. Scott Fitzgerald** (1896–1940) was a spoiled, undisciplined child and a failure at school. He began writing at an early age, and while attending the Newman School he had one of his plays produced in an amateur performance. At Princeton University, he worked on musical productions for the Triangle Club and wrote stories and poems, some of which were published by his friend and collaborator Edmund Wilson in the *Nassau Literary Magazine*, which Wilson edited. At the beginning of his senior year, he left Princeton to report for officer's training at Fort Leavenworth, Kansas. After basic training, he was stationed at Camp Sheridan, Alabama, and there met and fell in love with the southern belle Zelda Sayre. In 1920 his first novel, *This Side of Paradise*, was

published; it brought Fitzgerald fame and financial success. As a result of his newfound wealth, he and Zelda were able to marry and lead a glamorous, extravagant life, traveling back and forth between New York and Europe. *The Great Gatsby*, published in 1925 to critical acclaim, was probably his greatest novel, but it was a financial disappointment. His life at this time was in disorder: he was plagued by increasing alcoholism and Zelda's deterioration into madness, as well as by severe financial difficulties. After 1930 Zelda was intermittently institutionalized. In 1932 she published *Save Me the Waltz*, a novel describing the Fitzgeralds' life together as seen through her eyes. Fitzgerald's final years were spent in Hollywood trying to support himself by writing film scripts. There he met and had a love affair with the English journalist and columnist Sheilah Graham. He died in her apartment of a heart attack on December 21, 1940. His other novels include *Tender Is the Night* (1934) and *The Last Tycoon*, unfinished at the time of his death but edited by his friend Edmund Wilson and published posthumously in 1941. In addition, several collections of his short stories have been published.

Born in 1950 in Detroit, **Carolyn Forché** attended Michigan State University and earned an MFA from Bowling Green State University. She achieved immediate success as a writer, winning the Yale Younger Poets prize in 1976. Her work underwent a remarkable change following a year spent in El Salvador on a Guggenheim fellowship, when she worked with human rights activist Archbishop Oscar Humberto Romero and with Amnesty International. After seeing countless atrocities committed in

Central America, Forché began writing what she calls "poetry of witness." The volume *The Country between Us* (1981) stirred immediate controversy because of its overtly political topics and themes. "The Colonel," a prose poem in which the speaker conveys a horrific story with chilling flatness, is probably the most disturbing and memorable poem in the collection. She is the author of four books of poetry, most recently *Blue Hour* (2004), and the editor of *Against Forgetting: Twentieth-Century Poetry of Witness* (1993). She has also translated several books of poetry. She is a faculty member at George Mason University in Virginia.

Robert Frost (1874–1963) was born in San Francisco and lived there until he was eleven. When his father died, the family moved to Massachusetts, where Robert did well in school, especially in the classics, but later dropped out of both Dartmouth College and Harvard University. He went unrecognized as a poet until 1913, when he was first published in England, where he had moved with his wife and four children. Upon returning to the States, Frost quickly achieved success with more publications and became the most celebrated poet in mid-twentieth-century America. He held a teaching position at Amherst College and received many honorary degrees as well as an invitation to recite a poem at John F. Kennedy's inauguration. Although his work is principally associated with the life and landscape of New England, and although he was a poet of traditional verse forms and meters, he is also considered a quintessentially modern poet for his adherence to language as it is actually spoken, the psychological complexity of his portraits, and the degree to which his work is infused with layers of ambiguity and irony.

Richard Garcia was born in 1941 in San Francisco, a first-generation American (his mother was from Mexico, his father from Puerto Rico). While still in high school, Garcia had a poem published by City Lights in a Beat anthology. After publishing his first collection in 1972, however, he did not write poetry again for twelve years, until an unsolicited letter from Octavio Paz inspired him to resume. Since then Garcia's work has appeared widely in such literary magazines as the *Kenyon Review*, *Parnassus*, and the *Gettysburg Review*, as well as in three later collections: *Rancho Notorious* (2001), *The Persistence of Objects* (2006), and *Chickenhead* (2009). He is also the author of the bilingual children's book *My Aunt Otilia's Spirits* (1987). For twelve years he was the poet-in-residence at Children's Hospital Los Angeles, where he conducted poetry and art workshops for hospitalized children. He teaches creative writing in the Antioch University Los Angeles MFA program and at the College of Charleston.

Gabriel García Márquez (1927–2014) was born one of twelve children into a poor family in Aracataca, a small village in Colombia. He attended the University of Bogotá and gave up studying law to pursue a career as a writer, working as a journalist and film critic for *El Espectador*, a Colombian newspaper. His first short novel, *La Hojarasca* (1955; translated as *Leaf Storm* in 1972) was followed by *One Hundred Years of Solitude* (1967), his most famous work. *The Autumn of the Patriarch* (1975) and *Love in the Time of Cholera* (1988) are other novels. A political activist, García Márquez moved to Mexico in 1954, to Barcelona, Spain, in 1973, and back to Mexico in the late 1970s. He was awarded the Nobel Prize in Literature in 1982. The award cited him for novels and short stories "in which the fantastic and the realistic are combined in a richly composed world of imagination, reflecting a continent's life and conflicts." His last book was *Memories of My Melancholy Whores* (2005).

Ross Gay was born in 1974 to a black father and white mother in Youngstown, Ohio. He is the author of *Catalog of Unabashed Gratitude* (2015), *Bringing the Shovel Down* (2011), and *Against Which* (2006). His poems have been featured in numerous literary journals and magazines including *American Poetry Review; Harvard Review; Columbia: A Journal of Poetry and Art; Margie: The American Journal of Poetry;* and *Atlanta Review*. He currently teaches at Indiana University.

Born in Los Angeles in 1950, **Dagoberto Gilb** is an American writer whose work primarily focuses on life in the American Southwest. He currently lives in Texas. He has won numerous awards for his fiction including the PEN/Hemingway Award for *The Magic of Blood* (1993) and the Texas Institute of Letters Award for Fiction. He was a finalist for the PEN Faulkner Award. His collections of short works include *Woodcuts of Women* (2001) and *Gritos* (2004).

Shortly after **Charlotte Perkins Gilman** (1860–1935) was born in Hartford, Connecticut, her father left his family and provided only a small amount of support thereafter. Gilman studied at the Rhode Island School of Design and worked briefly as a commercial artist and teacher. This great-niece of Harriet Beecher Stowe became concerned at quite a young age with issues of social inequality and the circumscribed role of women. In 1884 she married Charles Stetson but left him and moved to California four years later after the birth of a child and a severe depression. Divorced, she married George Gilman, with whom she lived for thirty-five years. In 1935, afflicted by cancer, she took her own life. Charlotte Gilman wrote many influential books and articles about social problems, including *Women and Economics* (1898). From 1909 to 1917, she published her own journal. "The Yellow Wallpaper," written about 1890, draws on her experience with mental illness and has been praised for its insight and boldness.

Born in Newark, New Jersey, **Allen Ginsberg** (1926–1997) graduated from Columbia University, after a number of suspensions, in 1948. Several years later, he left for San Francisco to join other poets of the Beat Movement. His poem *Howl*, the most famous poem of the movement, was published in 1956 by Lawrence Ferlinghetti's City Lights Books; the publicity of the ensuing censorship trial brought the Beats to national attention. Ginsberg was co-founder with Anne Waldman of the Jack Kerouac School of Disembodied Poetics at the Naropa Institute in Boulder, Colorado. In his later years, he became a distinguished professor at Brooklyn College.

Born, raised, and educated in Iowa, **Susan Glaspell** (1882–1948) came to be associated with Massachusetts, where she and her husband, George Cram Cook, founded the Provincetown Players on Cape Cod. This small theater company was influential in giving a start to several serious playwrights, most notably Eugene O'Neill, and promoting realist dramas at a time when sentimental comedy and melodrama still dominated the stage. Glaspell began her writing career publishing short stories and novels, including the critically acclaimed *Fidelity* (1915). Glaspell's first several plays, including *Trifles* (1916), were one acts, and with them she began her lifelong interest in writing about the lives and special circumstances of women. She went on to write and produce a number of full-length plays as well, among the best known being *The Inheritors* (1921) and *Alison's House* (1930), which was based loosely on the life of Emily Dickinson and won a Pulitzer Prize. Though some of Glaspell's work was lighthearted, much of it dealt with serious issues of the day. Respected in its own time, Glaspell's writing fell out of fashion until it was "rediscovered" by feminist scholars and critics in the 1960s.

Louise Glück, born in 1943 in New York City, is an American poet. Known for precision, sensitivity, and insight in her poems, Glück is considered by many to be one of America's most talented contemporary poets. In 2003, she was appointed Poet Laureate Consultant in Poetry to the Library of Congress. She has won the Golden Plate Award, the Los Angeles Times Book Prize for Poetry, and the National Book Award for Poetry. She is the author of twelve books of poetry, and in all of them, she pulls readers in and asks them to imagine the world she's creating.

Ray González (b. 1952) received his MFA in creative writing from Southwest Texas State University. He has published ten books of poetry, including *The Heat of Arrivals* (winner of the 1997 Josephine Miles Book Award) and *The Hawk Temple at Tierra Grande*, winner of a 2003 Minnesota Book Award in Poetry. The editor of twelve antholo-gies, González is also the author of three books of nonfiction—*Memory Fever* (1999); *The Underground Heart* (2002), which received the 2003 Carr P. Collins/Texas Institute of Letters Award for Best Book of Nonfiction; and *Renaming the Earth* (2008)—and two collections of short stories—*The Ghost of John Wayne* (2001) and *Circling the Tortilla Dragon* (2002). He has served as poetry editor for *The Bloomsbury Review* since 1980. He teaches creative writing at the University of Minnesota.

One of the great Romantic poets, **George Gordon, Lord Byron** (1788–1824) is best known for his lighthearted and humorous verse, such as *Don Juan*. Born in London and raised in Scotland, he studied at Harrow and at Trinity College, Cambridge. He inherited the title of sixth baron Byron (with estate) at age ten. The last few years of his life were spent in Italy, but he died in Greece after joining the Greek forces in their war for independence.

Jorie Graham (b. 1950) is an American-born poet and author of numerous collections of poetry, including the Pulitzer Prize–winning *The Dream of the Unified Field: Selected Poems 1974–1992* (1995), *Overlord* (2005), *Sea Change* (2008), and *Place* (2012). With a sculptor as a mother and a journalist as a father, Graham has been influenced by visual art, mythology, history, and philosophy in her work. The influences of Modernism are apparent in her poems, especially in regard to their shape and flow.

Thomas Gray (1716–1771) was born in London and educated at Eton and at Cambridge University, where he studied literature and history. When in November 1741 his father died, Gray moved with his mother and aunt to the village of Stoke Poges, in Buckingham-shire, where he wrote his first impor-tant English poems, "Ode on the Spring," "Ode on a Distant Prospect of Eton College," and "Hymn to Adver-sity," and began his masterpiece, "Elegy Written in a Country Churchyard," called the most famous and diversified of all graveyard poems. These poems solidified his reputation as one of the most important poets of the eighteenth century. In 1757 he was named poet laureate but refused the position. In 1762 he was rejected for the Regius Professorship of Modern History at Cambridge but was given the position in 1768 when the successful candidate was killed. A painfully shy and private person, he never delivered any lectures as a professor.

Born in 1942 in New York City, **Marilyn Hacker** is the author of nine books of poetry, including *Presentation Piece* (1974), the Lamont Poetry Selection of the Academy of American Poets and a National Book Award winner, and *Selected Poems, 1965–1990* (1994), which received the Poets' Prize. Her most recent collection is *Essays on De-parture: New and Selected Poems* (2006). She was editor of the *Kenyon Review* from 1990 to 1994 and has received nu-merous honors and awards, including the PEN/Voelcker Award for Poetry in 2010. She lives in New York City and Paris. Often labeled a neoformalist, Hacker often handles traditional forms in fresh ways, as "Villanelle" illustrates.

Kimiko Hahn was born in 1955 in Mt. Kisco, New York, to two artists, a Japa-nese American mother from Hawaii and a German American father from Wisconsin. She majored in English and East Asian studies at the University of Iowa and received an MA in Japanese

literature from Columbia University. She is the author of nine volumes of po-etry, including *The Unbearable Heart* (1996), which received an American Book Award; *Toxic Flora: Poems* (2010), and *Brain Fever* (2014). In 1995 she wrote ten portraits of women for a two-hour HBO special titled *Ain't Nuthin' but a She-Thing*. She has taught at the Parsons School of Design, the Poetry Project at St. Mark's Church, and Yale University. She lives in New York and is a Distinguished Professor in the English Department at Queens College/CUNY.

Thomas Hardy (1840–1928) was born in a cottage in Higher Bockhampton, Dorset, near the regional market town of Dorchester in southwestern Eng-land. Apprenticed at age sixteen to an architect, he spent most of the next twenty years restoring old churches. Having always had an interest in litera-ture, he started writing novels in his thirties, publishing more than a dozen, including *Tess of the D'Urbervilles* (1891) and *Jude the Obscure* (1895). In 1896 Hardy gave up prose and turned to poetry, writing verse until his death at age eighty-eight. He had a consist-ently bleak, even pessimistic, outlook on life. Many of his works stress the dark effects of "hap" (happenstance, coincidence) in the world.

Born in 1951 in Tulsa, Oklahoma, to a mother of Cherokee-French descent and a Creek father, **Joy Harjo** moved to the Southwest and began writing poetry in her early twenties. She earned her BA from the University of New Mexico and her MFA from the Univer-sity of Iowa Writers' Workshop. Harjo has published numerous volumes of poetry, including *In Mad Love and War* (1990), which received an American Book Award and the Delmore Schwartz

Memorial Award. She performs her poetry and plays saxophone with her band, Poetic Justice. She is professor of English at the University of New Mexico, Albuquerque. Of "She Had Some Horses" Harjo has said, "This is the poem I'm asked most about and the one I have the least to say about. I don't know where it came from."

Michael S. Harper was born in 1938 in Brooklyn and grew up surrounded by jazz. When his family moved to Los Angeles, he worked in a variety of jobs. He attended the City College of Los Angeles; California State University, Los Angeles; and the University of Iowa Writers' Workshop. He has written more than ten books of poetry, most recently *Selected Poems* (2002) and *Use Trouble* (2009), and edited or coedited several collections of African American poetry. He is University Professor and professor of English at Brown University, where he has taught since 1970. He lives in Barrington, Rhode Island.

Born in Salem, Massachusetts, into a family descended from the New England Puritans, **Nathaniel Hawthorne** (1804–1864) graduated from Bowdoin College in Maine in 1825. For the next twelve years, he lived in Salem in relative seclusion, reading, observing the New England landscape and people, and writing his first novel, *Fanshawe* (published anonymously in 1828), and the first series of *Twice-Told Tales* (1837). (The second series, published in 1842, was reviewed by EDGAR ALLAN POE and won some notice.) To support himself, Hawthorne took a job in the Boston Custom House, resigning in 1841 to live at Brook Farm, a utopian community in West Roxbury, Massachusetts. The following year he left Brook Farm, married Sophia Peabody,

and moved to Concord, Massachusetts, where his neighbors included Ralph Waldo Emerson and Henry David Thoreau. There he wrote the stories collected in *Mosses from an Old Manse* (1846). Returning to Salem, he took a position as a customs inspector and began full-time work on what was to become his most celebrated novel, *The Scarlet Letter* (1850). The novels *The House of the Seven Gables* (1851) and *The Blithedale Romance* (1852), based on his Brook Farm experience, quickly followed. Also in 1852, he wrote a campaign biography of Franklin Pierce, a former college friend who, on becoming president, appointed Hawthorne U.S. Consul at Liverpool. Hawthorne's subsequent travels in Europe contributed to the novel *The Marble Faun* (1860), his last major work.

Raised in a poor neighborhood in Detroit, **Robert Hayden** (1913–1980) had an emotionally tumultuous childhood. Because of impaired vision, he was unable to participate in sports and spent his time reading instead. He graduated from high school in 1932 and attended Detroit City College (later Wayne State University). His first book of poems, *Heart-Shape in the Dust*, was published in 1940. After working for newspapers and on other projects, he studied under W. H. AUDEN in the graduate creative writing program at the University of Michigan, later teaching at Fisk University and the University of Michigan. His poetry gained international recognition in the 1960s; he was awarded the grand prize for poetry at the First World Festival of Negro Arts in Dakar, Senegal, in 1966 for his book *Ballad of Remembrance*. In 1976 he became the first black American to be appointed as Consultant in Poetry to the Library of Congress.

Terrance Hayes was born in 1971 in Columbia, South Carolina. In addition to being a writer, he is an accomplished artist and athlete. After receiving a BA from Coker College, where he was named an Academic All-American for his athletic and academic accomplishments, he earned an MFA from the University of Pittsburgh. His first book of poetry, *Muscular Music* (1999), won both the Whiting Writers Award and the Kate Tufts Discovery Award. His next collection, *Hip Logic* (2002), won the National Poetry Series award. *Lighthead* won the National Book Award in Poetry for 2010. His most recent collection is *How to Be Drawn* (2015). After teaching at Xavier University, he returned to Pittsburgh, where he is professor of creative writing at University of Pittsburgh.

H.D. – See Hilda Doolittle

Raised on a small farm near Castledawson, County Derry, Northern Ireland, **Seamus Heaney** (1939–2013) was educated at St. Columb's College, a Catholic boarding school situated in the city of Derry, and then at Queen's University, Belfast. As a young English teacher in Belfast in the early 1960s, he joined a poetry workshop and began writing verse, subsequently becoming a major force in contemporary Irish literature. He is the author of many volumes of poetry, translations, and essays as well as two plays. He held the chair of professor of poetry at Oxford University from 1989 to 1994. He was awarded the Nobel Prize in Literature in 1995.

Born in Oak Park, Illinois, **Ernest Hemingway** (1899–1961) led an active, vigorous life from childhood, summering in the wilds of northern Michigan with his physician father and boxing and playing football at school. His first job as a writer was as a reporter for the Kansas City *Star*. During World War I, he served as an ambulance driver in Italy; severely wounded before he had turned nineteen, he was decorated by the Italian government. Later, while working in Paris as a correspondent for the Toronto *Star*, he met Gertrude Stein, Ezra Pound, F. Scott Fitzgerald, and other artists and writers who had a significant influence on his work. Hemingway's first book, *Three Stories and Ten Poems* (1923), was followed by the well-known story collection *In Our Time* (1924; rev. and enl. ed., 1925). His novel *The Sun Also Rises* (1926) brought acclaim as well as recognition of Hemingway as the spokesman for the "lost generation." *A Farewell to Arms* (1929), based on his wartime experiences in Italy, and *For Whom the Bell Tolls* (1940), drawn from his time as a correspondent during the civil war in Spain, established his enduring reputation. During World War II, he served as a correspondent and received a Bronze Star. His frequent travels took him to Spain for the bullfights, on fishing trips to the Caribbean, and on big-game expeditions to the American West and to Africa. In his later years, he suffered from declining physical health and severe depression, which led to his suicide at his home in Ketchum, Idaho. The fullest collection of his short stories, the Finca-Vigia edition, came out in 1991. Hemingway was awarded the Nobel Prize in Literature in 1954.

The fifth son of an ancient and wealthy Welsh family, **George Herbert** (1593–1633) studied at Cambridge, graduating with honors, and was elected public orator of the university. He served in Parliament for two years, but after falling out of political favor he became rector of Bemerton, near Salisbury. Herbert was a model Anglican priest and an inspiring preacher. All his poetry, religious in nature, was published posthumously in 1633. "Easter-wings" is among the earliest of his **concrete poems** (see the Glossary).

Born in1949 in Aguas Buenas, Puerto Rico, **Victor Hernández Cruz** moved to New York City with his family at the age of five. His first book of poetry was published when he was seventeen. A year later, he moved to California's Bay Area and published his second book. In 1971, Hernández Cruz visited Puerto Rico and reconnected with his ancestral heritage; eighteen years later, he returned to Puerto Rico to live. He now divides his time between Puerto Rico and New York. He is the author of five collections of poetry, including *Maraca: New and Selected Poems, 1965–2000* (2001) and *In the Shadow of El-Andalus* (2011). He is a cofounder of the East Harlem Gut Theatre in New York and the Before Columbus Foundation, and he has taught at the University of California at Berkeley and San Diego, San Francisco State College, and the University of Michigan. Much of his work explores the relation between the English language and his native Spanish, playing with grammatical and syntactical conventions within both languages to create his own bilingual idiom.

The son of a well-to-do London goldsmith, **Robert Herrick** (1591–1674) was apprenticed to his uncle (also a goldsmith), studied at Cambridge University, then lived for nine years in London, where he hobnobbed with a group of poets that included BEN JONSON. Under familial pressure to do something more "worthwhile," Herrick became an Anglican priest. He was given the parish of

Dean Prior, Devonshire—a rural area that he hated at first—and there he quietly wrote poems about imagined mistresses and pagan rites (as in his well-known "Corinna's Going A-Maying") and deft but devout religious verse. When he returned to London in 1648, having been ejected from his pulpit by the Puritan revolution, he published his poetry in a volume with two titles, *Hesperides* for the secular poems and *Noble Numbers* for those with sacred subjects. Probably his most famous poem is "To the Virgins, to Make Much of Time," a short lyric on the traditional *carpe diem* theme (see the Glossary).

Jane Hirshfield (b. 1953) is the author of nine books of poetry, editor and cotranslator of three anthologies of poetry by women, and author of two collections of essays: *Nine Gates: Entering the Mind of Poetry* (1997) and *Ten Windows: How Great Poems Transform the World* (2015). A graduate of Princeton University, she studied Soto Zen from 1974 to 1982, including three years of monastic practice, the influence of which is apparent in her work. "For me, poetry, like Zen practice, is a path toward deeper and more life. There are ways to wake up into the actual texture of one's own existence, to widen it, to deepen and broaden it, and poetry is one of the things that does that." Hirshfield lives in the San Francisco Bay area.

Tony Hoagland was born in 1953 in Fort Bragg, North Carolina, the son of an army doctor. He grew up on military bases throughout the South. He was educated at Williams College, the University of Iowa, and the University of Arizona. He currently teaches at the University of Houston and Warren Wilson College. His collection *What Narcissism Means to Me* (2003) was a finalist for the National Book Critics Circle Award. His most recent book of poems is *Unincorporated Persons in the Late Honda Dynasty* (2010). In 2002 he received the Academy Award in Literature from the American Academy of Arts and Letters, and in 2005 he was the recipient of the Poetry Foundation's Mark Twain Award in recognition of his contribution to humor in American poetry.

Born in 1947 in Denver, **Linda Hogan** is a poet, novelist, essayist, playwright, and activist widely considered to be one of the most influential and provocative Native American figures in the contemporary American literary landscape. Because her father, who was from the Chickasaw Nation, was in the army and was transferred frequently during Hogan's childhood, she lived in various locations while she was growing up, but she considers Oklahoma to be her true home. In her late twenties, while working with children with orthopedic disabilities, she began writing during her lunch hours, though she had no previous experience as a writer and little experience reading literature. She pursued her writing by commuting to the University of Colorado, Colorado Springs, for her undergraduate degree and earning an MA in English and creative writing at the University of Colorado, Boulder, in 1978. She has published more than a dozen books—poetry, novels, and nonfiction—and received numerous awards for her work. She is a professor emeritus in the English Department at the University of Colorado.

Born in London, **Gerard Manley Hopkins** (1844–1889) was the eldest of eight children. His father was a ship insurer who also wrote a book of poetry. Hopkins studied at Balliol College, Oxford, and, after converting to Catholicism, taught in a school in Birmingham. In 1868 he became a Jesuit and burned all of his early poetry, considering it "secular" and worthless. He worked as a priest and teacher in working-class London, Glasgow, and Merseyside and later as a professor of classics at University College, Dublin. Hopkins went on to write many poems on spiritual themes but published little during his lifetime. His poems, which convey a spiritual sensuality, celebrating the wonder of nature both in their language and in their rhythms, which Hopkins called "sprung rhythm" (see **accentual meter** in the Glossary), were not widely known until they were published by his friend Robert Bridges in 1918.

A. E. Housman (1859–1936) was born in Fockbury, Worcestershire. A promising student at Oxford University, he failed his final exams (because of emotional turmoil, possibly caused by his suppressed homosexual love for a fellow student) and spent the next ten years feverishly studying and writing scholarly articles while working as a clerk at the patent office. Housman was rewarded with the chair of Latin at University College, London, and later at Cambridge University. His poetry, like his scholarship, was meticulous, impersonal in tone, and limited in output, consisting of two slender volumes—*A Shropshire Lad* (1896) and *Last Poems* (1922)—published during his lifetime and a small book titled *More Poems* (1936) that appeared after his death. His poems often take up the theme of doomed youths acting out their brief lives in the context of agricultural communities and activities, especially the English countryside and traditions that the poet loved.

Henry Howard, Earl of Surrey (1517–1547) was one of the most influential poets of the English Renaissance. As a member of King Henry VIII's court, he was involved in a number of military campaigns in Scotland, France, and Flanders. Howard had the ill fortune of being alive during a time of great court intrigue. He was accused of treason and executed when he was thirty years old. With SIR THOMAS WYATT, he introduced the **sonnet** (see the glossary) to his fellow courtier poets. He was also the first English poet to use **blank verse** (see the glossary) in his English translation of Virgil's *Aeneid*. His shorter poems, which circulated in manuscripts, were not published in print until ten years after his death.

Marie Howe (b. 1950) grew up in Rochester, New York, and was the New York State Poet from 2012 to 2014. Her first collection, *The Good Thief* (1988), focuses on speakers who communicate through biblical and mythical allusions. While some of her poems are expressed through metaphor, Howe distanced herself from figurative writing after the death of her brother, John, and detailed her losses in a transparent, grieving voice. Her other books are *What the Living Do* (1999) and *The Kingdom of Ordinary Time* (2008). Her honors include National Endowment for the Arts and Guggenheim fellowships.

Born in Joplin, Missouri, **Langston Hughes** (1902–1967) grew up in Lincoln, Illinois, and Cleveland, Ohio. He began writing poetry during his high school years. After attending Columbia University for one year, he held odd jobs as an assistant cook, a launderer, and a busboy and traveled to Africa and Europe working as a seaman. In 1924 he moved to Harlem. Hughes's first book

of poetry, *The Weary Blues*, was published in 1926. He finished his college education at Lincoln University in Pennsylvania three years later. He wrote novels, short stories, plays, songs, children's books, essays, memoirs, and poetry, and he is also known for his engagement with the world of jazz and the influence it had on his writing. His life and work were enormously important in shaping the artistic contributions of the Harlem Renaissance of the 1920s.

Zora Neale Hurston (1891–1960) was born to a family of sharecroppers in Notasula, Alabama, but grew up in Eatonville, Florida, a town founded by African Americans. After her mother's death in 1904, Hurston lived with various relatives. She never finished grade school. At sixteen she joined a traveling theater group and later did domestic work for a white household. The woman for whom she worked arranged for her to attend high school at Morgan Academy (now known as Morgan State University) in Baltimore. In her twenties, she attended Howard University, where she published her first stories in student publications and later in newspapers and magazines. In 1925 she moved to New York City and became active in the Harlem Renaissance. She collaborated with LANGSTON HUGHES in a folk comedy, *Mule Bone* (1931). Her first book, *The Eatonville Anthology* (1927), gained her national attention. At Barnard College, she took courses in anthropology and studied traditional folklore in Alabama and native culture in the Caribbean. During the 1930s and early 1940s, she completed graduate work at Columbia University and published four novels and an autobiography. Hurston published more books than any other African American woman writer of her time—novels, collections of stories, nonfiction, an autobiography—but she earned very little from her writing and spent her final years in near poverty. In the mid-1970s, her work was rediscovered, and she is now recognized as an important American author.

Henrik Ibsen (1828–1906) was born and raised in Skien, Norway, and he is still principally associated with that country, though he also lived for an extended period in Italy, where he did much of his writing. His earliest literary successes were the poetic plays *Brand* (1865) and *Peer Gynt* (1867), which were intended as closet dramas, though both eventually were performed onstage. His real breakthrough, though, came in the late 1870s, when he began to write realistic dramas that are sometimes called *problem plays* because they explore social issues and problems. Some of the problems Ibsen chose to depict, however, were too controversial for the theater of his day—the subjugation of women in marriage in *A Doll House* (1879), venereal disease and incest in *Ghosts* (1881), and the will of an individual against social and political pressure in *An Enemy of the People* (1882). Their subject matter led some critics in Norway and elsewhere to protest against public performances of these works. But despite their controversial nature, or perhaps because of it, these plays secured Ibsen's reputation as one of the most influential playwrights of the late nineteenth century. Important later works by Ibsen include *The Wild Duck* (1884), *Hedda Gabler* (1890), and *The Master Builder* (1892). Although many of his dramas resemble the tightly structured, plot-driven theatrical entity known as the **well-made play**, Ibsen's work contains subtleties of characterization and theme that raise it above commonplace theatrical experience.

Born in San Francisco and raised in Rochester, New York, **Shirley Jackson** (1919–1965) was educated at the University of Rochester and Syracuse University, where she founded and edited the campus literary magazine. After graduation she married the author and literary critic Stanley Edgar Hyman and settled in North Bennington, Vermont. She is best known for her stories and novels of gothic horror and the occult. Among her novels are *Hangsaman* (1949), *The Bird's Nest* (1954), *The Haunting of Hill House* (1959), and *We Have Always Lived in the Castle* (1962). Her short stories are collected in *The Lottery* (1949), *The Magic of Shirley Jackson* (1966), and *Come Along with Me* (1968). In 1997 *Just an Ordinary Day: The Uncollected Stories of Shirley Jackson* was published.

Born in Nashville, Tennessee, **Randall Jarrell** (1914–1965) earned his BA and MA at Vanderbilt University. From 1937 to 1939, he taught at Kenyon College, where he met John Crowe Ransom and ROBERT LOWELL, and afterward taught at the University of Texas. He served in the air force during World War II. Jarrell's reputation as a poet was established in 1945 with the publication of his second book, *Little Friend, Little Friend*, which documents the intense fears and moral struggles of young soldiers. Other volumes followed, all characterized by great technical skill, empathy, and deep sensitivity. Following the war, Jarrell began teaching at the University of North Carolina, Greensboro, and remained there, except for occasional leaves of absence to teach elsewhere, until his death. Besides poetry, he wrote a satirical novel, several children's books, numerous poetry reviews—collected in *Poetry and the Age* (1953)—and a translation of Goethe's *Faust*.

Honorée Fanonne Jeffers (b. 1967) has published fiction in addition to three books of poetry, *The Gospel of Barbecue* (2000), which won the 1999 Stan and Tom Wick Prize for Poetry and was the finalist for the 2001 Paterson Poetry Prize, *Outlandish Blues* (2003), and *Red Clay Suite* (2007). She has won the 2002 Julia Peterkin Award for Poetry and awards from the Barbara Deming Memorial Fund and the Rona Jaffe Foundation. Her poetry has been published in the anthologies *At Our Core: Women Writing about Power*, *Dark Eros*, and *Identity Lessons* and in many journals, including *Callaloo*, *Kenyon Review*, and *Prairie Schooner*. She teaches at the University of Oklahoma.

Born in Atlanta, Harlem Renaissance poet **Georgia Douglas Johnson** (1880–1966) graduated from Atlanta University Normal College and studied music at the Oberlin Conservatory and the Cleveland College of Music. She garnered literary attention for her poetry, of which she published four volumes. Her poems—given titles such as "Faith," "Youth," and "Joy"—reflected a surprising positivity. Her husband often criticized her career as a writer, but even so, she published two poems in his name, including the widely read "The Heart of a Woman." Johnson was also a powerful voice in the antilynching movement. In 2009, she was inducted into the Georgia Writers Hall of Fame.

Born in London, **Ben Jonson** (1572–1637) was the stepson of a bricklayer (his father died before he was born).

He attended Westminster School and then joined the army. Jonson later worked as an actor and was the author of such comedies as *Everyman in His Humor* (in which SHAKESPEARE acted the lead), *Volpone*, and *The Alchemist*. He wrote clear, elegant, "classical" poetry that contrasted with the intricate, subtle, **metaphysical poetry** (see the Glossary) of his contemporaries JOHN DONNE and GEORGE HERBERT. He was named poet laureate and was the idol of a generation of English writers who dubbed themselves the Sons of Ben.

Born in 1967 in London to Caribbean parents, **Allison Joseph** grew up in Toronto and the Bronx. She earned her BA from Kenyon College and her MFA from Indiana University. She is the author of seven collections of poetry. Her most recent volume is *My Father's Kites: Poems* (2010). Her poems are often attuned to the experiences of women and minorities. She holds the Judge William Holmes Cook Endowed Professorship and directs the MFA Program in Creative Writing at Southern Illinois University, Carbondale, and is editor of the *Crab Orchard Review*.

Born in Dublin, Ireland, **James Joyce** (1882–1941) was educated at Jesuit schools in preparation for the priesthood. But at an early age he abandoned Catholicism and in 1904 left Dublin for what he felt would be the broader horizons of continental Europe. Living in Paris, Zurich, and Trieste over the next twenty-five years, he tried to support himself and his family by teaching languages and singing. In 1912 he returned to Dublin briefly to arrange for the publication of his short stories. Because of the printers' fear of censorship or libel suits, the edition was burned, and *Dubliners* did not appear until

1914 in England. During World War I, Joyce lived in Zurich, where he wrote *Portrait of the Artist as a Young Man* (1916), a partly autobiographical account of his adolescent years that introduced some of the experimental techniques found in his later novels. About this time Joyce fell victim to glaucoma; for the rest of his life he suffered periods of intense pain and near blindness. His masterpiece, the novel *Ulysses* (1922), known for its "stream of consciousness" style, was written and published in periodicals between 1914 and 1921. Book publication was delayed because of obscenity charges. *Ulysses* finally was issued by Shakespeare & Company, a Paris bookstore owned and operated by Sylvia Beach, an American expatriate; U.S. publication was banned until 1933. *Finnegans Wake* (1939), an equally experimental novel, took seventeen years to write. Because of the controversy surrounding his work, Joyce earned little in royalties and often had to rely on friends for support. He died after surgery for a perforated ulcer in Zurich.

Born in Prague and raised in Bohemia, **Franz Kafka** (1883–1924), the son of middle-class German Jewish parents, studied law at the German University of Prague. After winning his degree in 1906, he was employed in the workmen's compensation division of the Austrian government. Because he wrote very slowly, he could not earn a living as a writer. At the time of his death, he had published little and asked his friend Max Brod to burn his incomplete manuscripts. Brod ignored this request and arranged posthumous publication of Kafka's major long works, *The Trial* (1925), *The Castle* (1926), and *Amerika* (1927), as well as a large number of his stories. Important stories published during his lifetime include "The Judgment" (1913), "The Metamorphosis" (1915), and "A Hunger Artist" (1924). Kafka's fiction is known for its gripping portrayals of individual helplessness before political, judicial, and paternal authority and power.

John Keats (1795–1821) was born in London. His father, a worker at a livery stable who married his employer's daughter and inherited the business, was killed by a fall from a horse when Keats was eight. When his mother died of tuberculosis six years later, Keats and his siblings were entrusted to the care of a guardian, a practical-minded man who took Keats out of school at fifteen and apprenticed him to a doctor. But as soon as he qualified for medical practice, in 1815, Keats abandoned medicine for poetry, which he had begun writing two years earlier. In 1818, the year he himself contracted tuberculosis, he also fell madly in love with a pretty, vivacious young woman named Fanny Brawne whom he could not marry because of his poverty, illness, and devotion to poetry. In the midst of such stress and emotional turmoil, his masterpieces poured out, between January and September 1819: the great odes, a number of sonnets, and several longer lyric poems. In February 1820, his health failed rapidly; he went to Italy in the autumn, in the hope that the warmer climate would improve his health, and died there on February 23, 1821. His poems are rich with sensuous, lyrical beauty and emotional resonance, reflecting both his delight in life as well as his awareness of life's brevity and difficulty.

Jane Kenyon (1947–1995) was born in Ann Arbor, Michigan, and grew up in the Midwest. She earned her BA and

MA from the University of Michigan. She was married to poet Donald Hall from 1972 until her death from leukemia in 1995. During her lifetime, she published four books of poetry— *Constance* (1993), *Let Evening Come* (1990), *The Boat of Quiet Hours* (1986), and *From Room to Room* (1978)—and a book of translation, *Twenty Poems of Anna Akhmatova* (1985). Two additional volumes were published after her death: *Otherwise: New and Selected Poems* (1996) and *A Hundred White Daffodils: Essays, Interviews, the Akhmatova Translations, Newspaper Columns, and One Poem* (1999). At the time of her death, she was New Hampshire's poet laureate.

Born in 1949 in St. John's, Antigua, and raised by devoted parents, **Jamaica Kincaid** entered college in the United States but withdrew to write. After her stories appeared in notable publications, she took a staff position on *The New Yorker*. Her first book, a story collection titled *At the Bottom of the River* (1984), won a major award from the American Academy and Institute of Arts and Letters. *Annie John* (1985), an interrelated collection, further explored life in the British West Indies as experienced by a young girl. Kincaid now lives in the United States and continues to write about her homeland in works including *A Small Place* (1988), *Lucy* (1990), *Autobiography of My Mother* (1996), *My Brother* (1997), *Talk Stories* (2002), *Mr. Potter* (2003), and *Jupiter* (2004).

Born in Providence, Rhode Island, **Galway Kinnell** (1927–2014) attended Princeton University and the University of Rochester. He served in the U.S. Navy and then visited Paris on a Fulbright fellowship. Returning to the United States, he worked for the Congress on Racial Equality and then traveled widely in the Middle East and Europe. He taught in France, Australia, and Iran as well as at numerous colleges and universities in the United States. He published many books of poetry, including *Selected Poems* (1980), for which he received both the Pulitzer Prize and the National Book Award. He also published translations of works by Yves Bonnefoy, Yvanne Goll, François Villon, and Rainer Maria Rilke. He was the Erich Maria Remarque Professor of Creative Writing at New York University.

Etheridge Knight (1931–1991) was born in Corinth, Mississippi. He dropped out of school at age sixteen and served in the U.S. Army in Korea from 1947 to 1951, returning with a shrapnel wound that caused him to fall deeper into a drug addiction that had begun during his service. In 1960 he was arrested for robbery and sentenced to eight years in an Indiana state prison. During this time, he began writing poetry. His first book, *Poems from Prison* (1968), was published one year before his release. The book was a success, and Knight joined other poets in what came to be called the Black Arts Movement, the aesthetic and spiritual sister of the Black Power concept. He went on to write several more books of poetry and receive many prestigious honors and awards, including fellowships from the National Endowment for the Arts and the Guggenheim Foundation. In 1990 he earned a BA in American poetry and in criminal justice from Martin Center University in Indianapolis.

Known for an exuberant and cosmopolitan writing style inspired by the New York School of poetry, **Kenneth**

Koch (1925–2002) expressed frustration with some of the poetry of his time, asking in his work *Fresh Air* (1956) why poems featured uninteresting subjects and forms. He disagreed with the notion that one had to be depressed or have a negative world view in order to craft exceptional poetry, and instead propped up the potential of young writers, saying they were full of natural talent. Koch was inducted into the American Academy of Arts and Letters in 1996. He passed away after a battle with leukemia in 2002.

Born in 1947 and raised in Bogalusa, Louisiana, **Yusef Komunyakaa** earned degrees at the University of Colorado, Colorado State University, and the University of California, Irvine. His numerous books of poems include *Neon Vernacular: New and Selected Poems, 1977–1989* (1994), for which he received the Pulitzer Prize and the Kingsley Tufts Poetry Award, and *Thieves of Paradise* (1998), which was a finalist for the National Book Critics Circle Award. His most recent collection is *The Emperor of Water Clocks* (2015). Other publications include *Blues Notes: Essays, Interviews and Commentaries* (2000), *The Jazz Poetry Anthology* (coedited with J. A. Sascha Feinstein, 1991), and *The Insomnia of Fire* by Nguyen Quang Thieu (cotranslated with Martha Collins, 1995). He has taught at the University of New Orleans, Indiana University, and Princeton University.

Ted Kooser was born in 1939 in Ames, Iowa. He received his BA from Iowa State University and his MA in English from the University of Nebraska, Lincoln. He is the author of eleven collections of poetry, including *Sure Signs* (1980), *One World at a Time* (1985),

Weather Central (1994), *Winter Morning Walks: One Hundred Postcards to Jim Harrison* (2000, winner of the 2001 Nebraska Book Award for poetry), and *Splitting an Order* (2014). His fiction and nonfiction books include *Local Wonders: Seasons in the Bohemian Alps* (2002, winner of the 2003 Nebraska Book Award for nonfiction) and *Braided Creek: A Conversation in Poetry* (2003), written with fellow poet and longtime friend Jim Harrison. His honors include two fellowships from the National Endowment for the Arts, a Pushcart Prize, the Stanley Kunitz Prize, and a Merit Award from the Nebraska Arts Council. He served as the Poet Laureate Consultant in Poetry to the Library of Congress from 2004 to 2006. He lives on acreage near the village of Garland, Nebraska, and is a visiting professor in the English Department of the University of Nebraska, Lincoln.

Born in Philadelphia, **Maxine Kumin** (1925–2014) received her BA and MA from Radcliffe College. She published eleven books of poetry, including *Up Country: Poems of New England* (1972), for which she received the Pulitzer Prize. She is also the author of a memoir, *Inside the Halo and Beyond: The Anatomy of a Recovery* (2000); five novels; a collection of short stories; more than twenty children's books; and four books of essays. Her most recent collection is *Short the Season: Poems* (2014). She taught at the University of Massachusetts, Columbia University, Brandeis University, and Princeton University, and she served as Consultant in Poetry to the Library of Congress.

Jhumpa Lahiri was born in 1967 in London but grew up in Rhode Island.

As a child, she wrote stories in her school notebooks. She received her BA from Barnard College, and, rejected by creative writing programs, she continued to write stories while working at an office job. She was then accepted to the graduate program at Boston University and earned an MA in English and in creative writing, and a PhD in Renaissance studies. The daughter of parents born in India who frequently took her there as a child, she has been influenced by the culture of India and the United States. Her first collection of short fiction, *Interpreter of Maladies* (1999), won the Pulitzer Prize for fiction in 2000, in addition to a number of other prestigious awards. Her first novel, *The Namesake*, was published in 2003 and made into a motion picture (2007). She published her second short-story collection, *Unaccustomed Earth*, in 2008, and her second novel, *The Lowland*, in 2013. She taught creative writing at Boston University and the Rhode Island School of Design and has been a vice president of the PEN American Center since 2005. She recently left the United States to relocate to Italy and has begun writing in Italian.

Aemilia Lanyer (1569–1645) was the first Englishwoman to establish herself as a professional poet, doing so through *Salve Deus Rex Judaeorum*, a collection of poems published in 1611. Not only was she the first female professional poet in England, she was also one of the earliest published feminists. All of her books' dedications are to women, and Lanyer argues the virtues of women with a voice that is unwavering and unapologetic.

A prominent writer in postwar England, **Philip Larkin** (1922–1985), born in Coventry, England, rose to prominence after publishing *The Less Deceived* (1955), a collection of poems, but he preferred to remain out of the limelight. As much as the public wished to pull him in, Larkin rarely took interviews or public readings; he worked as a librarian for forty years, writing when he could in his spare time. His tone as a writer often is that of a detached observer, and his poems served as a voice for thoughts that otherwise would have gone unsaid. In 2003, two decades after his death, the people of Britain voted Larkin the "nation's best-loved poet," showing the lasting impression he created.

Li-Young Lee was born in 1957 in Jakarta, Indonesia, to Chinese parents. His father, who had been personal physician to Mao Zedong, relocated his family to Indonesia, where he helped found Gamaliel University. But in 1959 the Lee family fled that country to escape anti-Chinese sentiment, settling in the United States in 1964. Lee studied at the University of Pittsburgh, the University of Arizona, and the Brockport campus of the State University of New York. He has taught at several universities, including Northwestern University and the University of Iowa. He is the author of four collections of poetry— *Rose* (1986), which won the Delmore Schwartz Memorial Poetry Award; *The City in Which I Love You* (1991), the 1990 Lamont Poetry selection; *Book of My Nights* (2001); and *Behind My Eyes* (2008)—and a memoir, *The Winged Seed: A Remembrance* (1995), which received an American Book Award from the Before Columbus Foundation. In his poems one often senses a profound sense of exile, the influence of his father's presence, and a rich, spiritual sensuality.

Denise Levertov (1923–1997) was born in Ilford, England. Her mother was Welsh, and her father was a Russian Jew who had become an Anglican priest. Educated at home, Levertov said she decided to become a writer at the age of five. Her first book, *The Double Image* (1946), brought her recognition as one of a group of poets dubbed the "New Romantics"—her poems often blend objective observation with the sensibility of a spiritual searcher. Having moved to the United States after marrying the American writer Mitchell Goodman, she turned to free-verse poetry and with her first American book, *Here and Now* (1956), became an important voice in the American avant-garde. In the 1960s, she became involved in the movement protesting the Vietnam War. Levertov went on to publish more than twenty collections of poetry, four books of prose, and three volumes of poetry in translation. From 1982 to 1993, she taught at Stanford University. She spent the last decade of her life in Seattle.

Born in Detroit, **Philip Levine** (1928–2015) received his degrees from Wayne State University and the University of Iowa. He authored sixteen books of poetry, including *The Simple Truth* (1994), which won the Pulitzer Prize, and *What Work Is*, winner of the National Book Award. He also published a collection of essays, *The Bread of Time: Toward an Autobiography* (1994), edited *The Essential Keats* (1987), and coedited and translated two books of poetry by the Spanish poet Gloria Fuertes and the Mexican poet Jaime Sabines. He divided his time between Fresno, California, and New York City, where he taught at New York University for many years.

Larry Levis (1946–1996) grew up on a farm near Fresno, California. He earned his BA from Fresno State College (now California State University), an MA from Syracuse University, and a PhD from the University of Iowa. He published six collections of poetry—several of them receiving major awards—and a collection of short fiction. He taught at the University of Missouri, the University of Utah, and Virginia Commonwealth University. He died of a heart attack at the age of forty-nine. PHILIP LEVINE wrote that he had years earlier recognized Levis as "the most gifted and determined young poet I have ever had the good fortune to have in one of my classes. . . . His early death is a staggering loss for our poetry, but what he left is a major achievement that will enrich our lives."

Born in 1972 in Beijing, **Yiyun Li** originally planned to pursue a PhD in immunology but decided to pursue a career as a writer. Many of her stories have been featured in *The New Yorker*, which named her one of the Best Young American Novelists. Her debut collection of short stories, *A Thousand Years of Good Prayers* (2006), won the PEN/Hemingway Award and many others, and her debut novel, *The Vagrants* (2010), earned her critical acclaim. She is currently an editor for a Brooklyn-based literary magazine, *A Public Space*, as well as a professor of English at University of California at Davis.

Patricia Lockwood (b. 1982) has published two poetry collections, and her poems have appeared in *The New Yorker*, the *London Review of Books*, *Tin House*, and *Poetry*. She is best known for "Rape Joke," a prose poem originally published in *The Awl*. Her first poetry collection, *Balloon Pop Outlaw Black*, was published in 2012, and quickly became one of the best-selling indie poetry titles of all time. She is also the author of *Motherland Fatherland Homelandsexuals* (2014).

Born in New York City to West Indian parents, **Audre Lorde** (1934–1992) grew up in Manhattan and attended Roman Catholic schools. While she was still in high school, her first poem appeared in *Seventeen* magazine. She earned her BA from Hunter College in New York City and her MA in library science from Columbia University. In 1968 she left her job as head librarian at Town School Library in New York City to become a lecturer and creative writer. She accepted a poet-in-residence position at Tougaloo College in Mississippi, where she discovered a love of teaching; published her first volume of poetry, *The First Cities* (1968); and met her long-term partner, Frances Clayton. Many volumes of poetry followed, several winning major awards. She also published four volumes of prose, among them *The Cancer Journals* (1980), which chronicled her struggles with cancer, and *A Burst of Light* (1988), which won a National Book Award. In the 1980s, Lorde and writer Barbara Smith founded Kitchen Table: Women of Color Press. She was also a founding member of Sisters in Support of Sisters in South Africa, an organization that worked to raise awareness about women under apartheid. She was the poet laureate of New York from 1991 to 1992.

Born in Boston into a prominent New England family, **Robert Lowell** (1917–1977) attended Harvard University and then Kenyon College, where he studied under John Crowe Ransom. At Louisiana State University, he studied with Robert Penn Warren and Cleanth Brooks as well as Allen Tate. He was always politically active—a conscientious objector during World War II and a Vietnam War protestor—and suffered from manic depression. Lowell's reputation was established early: his second book, *Lord Weary's Castle*, was awarded the Pulitzer Prize for poetry in 1947. In the mid-1950s, he began to write more directly from personal experience and loosened his adherence to traditional meter and form. The result was *Life Studies* (1959), a watershed collection of the "confessional" school that changed the landscape of modern poetry, much as T. S. Eliot's *The Waste Land* had done three decades earlier. He died suddenly from a heart attack at age sixty.

Born in England, **Mina Loy** (1882–1966) spent most of her career as a poet in Paris and New York City. Her poems, admired by the likes of EZRA POUND, T. S. ELIOT, AND WILLIAM CARLOS WILLIAMS, were known for their eccentric structure and vocabulary. After divorcing her first husband, Loy moved to New York, where she met Arthur Cravan, the man who would become her second husband. They spent a lot of time in Mexico, living in poverty, which became the subject of many of her poems. She often wrote about her marriage with Cravan, relying on boxing metaphors to describe their relationship, which was fitting, as Cravan was called the "poet-boxer" because of his personal, striking style. Loy continued to write until she died at the age of eighty-three.

The son of Indian immigrants, **Amit Majmudar** (b. 1979) grew up in the Cleveland area. Many of his poems address themes such as identity, history, spiritual faith, and mortality. He is the author of two poetry collections, *0°0°* (2009) and *Heaven and Earth* (2011), and two novels, *Partitions* (2011) and *The Abundance* (2013). Majmudar lives in Dublin, Ohio, where he works as a diagnostic nuclear radiologist, writing poetry in his spare time.

An American slam poet, humorist, and teacher, **Taylor Mali** (b. 1965) has published three books: *What Learning Leaves* (2002), *The Last Time As We Are*, (2009), and *What Teachers Make: In Praise of the Greatest Job in the World* (2012). He's been on seven National Poetry Slam teams; six of those teams won the championship. Mali spent nine years teaching English, history, and math at the K–12 level. He now lectures and conducts workshops for teachers and students all over the world.

Christopher Marlowe (1564–1593) was born in Canterbury the same year as WILLIAM SHAKESPEARE. The son of a shoemaker, he needed the help of scholarships to attend King's School, Canterbury, and Corpus Christi College, Cambridge. He was one of the most brilliant writers of his generation in narrative poetry, lyric poetry, and drama (his best-known play is *Doctor Faustus*). He died after being stabbed in a bar fight, reportedly over his bill, at the age of twenty-nine. "The Passionate Shepherd to His Love" is among the most famous of Elizabethan songs.

Born in Hull, Yorkshire, **Andrew Marvell** (1621–1678) was educated at Trinity College, Cambridge. After traveling in Europe, he worked as a tutor and in a government office (as assistant to JOHN MILTON) and later became a member of Parliament for Hull. Mar-

vell was known in his lifetime as a writer of rough satires in verse and prose. His "serious" poetry, like "To His Coy Mistress," a famous exploration of the *carpe diem* theme (see the Glossary), was not published until after his death.

Bernadette Mayer (b. 1945) is an American poet known for her experimentation with language. She has been compared to Gertrude Stein, James Joyce, and many Dadaist writers. She first won acclaim in her exhibit, *Memory* (1972), which combined photography and narration. *The Desire of Mothers to Please Others in Letters* (1994) is composed of prose poems Mayer wrote during her third pregnancy, and it features a combination of prose and poetry. Her most recent collection is *Poetry State Forest* (2008).

Heather McHugh was born in 1948 to Canadian parents in San Diego and grew up in Virginia. She is a graduate of Radcliffe College and the University of Denver. McHugh has published numerous books of poetry, including *Hinge and Sign: Poems, 1968–1993* (1994), which won both the *Boston Book Review*'s Bingham Poetry Prize and the Pollack-*Harvard Review* Prize, was a finalist for the National Book Award, and was named a "Notable Book of the Year" by the *New York Times Book Review*, and *Upgraded to Serious* (2009). She has also published a book of prose, *Broken English: Poetry and Partiality* (1993), and two books of translations. She was awarded a MacArthur Foundation grant in 2009. She teaches as a core faculty member in the MFA Program for Writers at Warren Wilson College and as Milliman Writer-in-Residence at the University of Washington, Seattle.

The son of poor farmworkers, **Claude McKay** (1890–1948) was born in Sunny Ville, Jamaica. He was educated by his older brother, who possessed a library of English novels, poetry, and scientific texts. At age twenty, McKay published a book of verse called *Songs of Jamaica*, recording his impressions of black life in Jamaica in dialect. In 1912 he traveled to the United States to attend Tuskegee Institute. He soon left to study agriculture at Kansas State University. In 1914 he moved to Harlem and became an influential member of the Harlem Renaissance. After committing himself to communism and traveling to Moscow in 1922, he lived for some time in Europe and Morocco, writing fiction. McKay later repudiated communism, converted to Roman Catholicism, and returned to the United States. He published several books of poetry as well as an autobiography, *A Long Way from Home* (1937). He wrote a number of sonnets protesting the injustices of black life in the United States, "America" among them, which are of interest for the way they use the most Anglo of forms to contain and intensify what the poem's language is saying.

W. S. Merwin (b. 1927) has published over fifty books of poetry, translation, and prose. His most recent book is *The Moon Before Morning* (2014). Merwin has garnered a number of awards, including the Pulitzer Prize, the National Book Award, and the Tanning Prize, one of the highest honors bestowed by the Academy of American Poets. He's mostly known for his indirect, impersonal style that disregards punctuation. He still writes to this day, and is currently dedicated to preserving the rain forests in Hawaii, where he lives.

Declared "some of the best sonnets of the century" by Richard Wilbur, the poems of **Edna St. Vincent Millay** (1892–1950) have proved to be long-lasting and resilient. Millay was awarded the Pulitzer Prize for poetry in 1923, when she was only the third woman to win the award. Coupled with her riveting readings and performances of the poems, Millay's active political voice helped define her legacy as a writer. She was known for her feminist activism, and she employed a unique combination of modernist attitudes and traditional forms to express herself. According to THOMAS HARDY, America had two great attractions: skyscrapers and Millay's poetry.

The son of a well-off London businessman, **John Milton** (1608–1674) was educated at St. Paul's School and at home with private tutors. After graduating with an MA from Christ's College, Cambridge, he spent the next six years reading at home. Having written verse since his university days, Milton began to write prose tracts in favor of Oliver Cromwell, in whose government he was later employed as head of a department. The strain of long hours of reading and writing for the revolutionary cause aggravated a genetic weakness and resulted in his total blindness around 1651. He wrote his most famous works—*Paradise Lost* (1667), *Paradise Regained* (1671), and *Samson Agonistes* (1671)—by dictating them to his daughter and other amanuenses.

Marianne Moore (1887–1972) was born near St. Louis and grew up in Carlisle, Pennsylvania. After studying at Bryn Mawr College and Carlisle Commercial College, she taught at a government Native American school in Carlisle. She moved to Brooklyn, where she became an assistant at the New York Public Library. She loved baseball and spent a good deal of time watching her beloved Brooklyn Dodgers. She began to write Imagist poetry and to contribute to *The Dial*, a prestigious literary magazine. From 1925 to 1929, she served as acting editor of *The Dial* and then as editor for four years. Moore was widely recognized for her work, receiving among other honors the Bollingen Prize, the National Book Award, and the Pulitzer Prize.

Cherríe Moraga (b. 1952) is a writer, playwright, and essayist of Chicana descent. Her works primarily focus on the effects of gender, sexuality, and race on the lives of women of color. She coedited *This Bridge Called My Back: Writings by Radical Women of Color* (1981) with Gloria E. Anzaldúa. The text helped facilitate the emergence of third wave feminism and won the Before Columbus Foundation American Book Award in 1986. Currently, she teaches creative writing, playwriting, Xicana-Indigenous Performance, and Indigenous Identity in Diaspora in the Arts at Stanford University.

Born in 1954 in Cleveland, Ohio, **Thylias Moss** attended Syracuse University and received her BA from Oberlin College and MFA from the University of New Hampshire. She is the author of numerous books of poetry, most recently *Tokyo Butter* (2006); a memoir, *Tale of a Sky-Blue Dress* (1998); two children's books; and two plays, *Talking to Myself* (1984) and *The Dolls in the Basement* (1984). Among her awards are a Guggenheim fellowship and a MacArthur Foundation fellowship. She lives in Ann Arbor, where she is a professor of English at the University of Michigan.

Harryette Mullen (b. 1953) is an American poet and short story writer and a professor of English at the University of California in Los Angeles. Some of her work, such as *Sleeping with the Dictionary* (2002), ventures into avant-garde territory. Shaped by the social, political, and cultural movements of African Americans, Mexican Americans, and women in the 1960s–1970s, Mullen's writing is both a compelling, challenging product of environment and an important voice in the literary community.

Marilyn Nelson was born in 1946 in Cleveland, Ohio, and grew up on numerous military bases. Her father served in the U.S. Air Force as one of the Tuskegee Airmen, and her mother was a teacher. While still in elementary school, she started writing. She earned her BA from the University of California, Davis, her MA from the University of Pennsylvania, and her PhD from the University of Minnesota. *The Homeplace* (1990), *The Fields of Praise: New and Selected Poems* (1997), and *Carver: A Life in Poems* (2001) were all finalists for the National Book Award. In addition to many collections of her own poetry for adults and for children, she has translated from Danish Halfdan Rasmussen's *Hundreds of Hens and Other Poems*. She is founder and director of Soul Mountain Retreat, a writer's colony that encourages and supports poets who belong to underrepresented racial or cultural groups. She is professor emerita of English at the University of Connecticut and was poet laureate of Connecticut from 2001 to 2006.

Aimee Nezhukumatathil (b. 1974) is the author of *Miracle Fruit* (2003), winner of the *ForeWord Magazine* Poetry Book of the Year and the Global Filipino Literary Award; *At the Drive-In*

Volcano (2007), winner of the Balcones Prize; and *Lucky Fish* (2011). Her Filipina and Malayali background lends a unique perspective to her work, and her poems often speak of love and loss. Nezhukumatathil is professor of English at SUNY-Fredonia and lives in berry country in western New York with her husband and sons.

Lynn Nottage was born in 1964 to a schoolteacher and a child psychologist in Brooklyn. She wrote her first play while attending New York's High School of Music and Art and went on to attend Brown University and the Yale School of Drama. Her plays often deal with African Americans and women and have been performed off-Broadway and regionally. Her play *Intimate Apparel* won the majority of major theater awards for the 2003–2004 theater season, and *Ruined*, first performed in 2007, won the Pulitzer Prize. She has been awarded fellowships from the MacArthur and Guggenheim foundations.

Born in 1952 in St. Louis to a Palestinian father and an American mother, **Naomi Shihab Nye** grew up in both the United States and Jerusalem. She received her BA from Trinity University in San Antonio, Texas, where she still resides with her family. She is the author of many books of poems, most recently *You and Yours* (2005), which received the Isabella Gardner Poetry Award. She has also written short stories and books for children and has edited anthologies, several of which focus on the lives of children and represent work from around the world. She is a singer-songwriter and on several occasions has traveled to the Middle East and Asia for the U.S. Information Agency, promoting international goodwill through the arts. Nye's work often attests to a universal sense of exile—from place, home, love, and oneself—and looks at the ways the human spirit confronts it.

Joyce Carol Oates was born in 1938 in Lockport, New York. She began storytelling in early childhood, composing picture stories even before she could write. Only after earning a BA from Syracuse University and an MA from the University of Wisconsin did she focus on writing as a career. Her first book was a collection of stories, *By the North Gate* (1963). Since then she has gone on to become one of the most versatile, prolific, and important American writers of her time, publishing more than one hundred books—novels, story collections, poetry, plays, children's books, and literary criticism. She has been nominated for the Nobel Prize in Literature three times. She is the Roger S. Berlind Distinguished Professor of Humanities at Princeton University.

Born in 1946 in Austin, Minnesota, **Tim O'Brien** studied at Macalester College and Harvard University. During the Vietnam War, he was drafted into the army, promoted to the rank of sergeant, and decorated with a Purple Heart. Many of his novels and stories draw on his experiences during the war. His novels are *If I Die in a Combat Zone, Box Me Up and Ship Me Home* (1973); *Northern Lights* (1975); *Going after Cacciato* (1978), winner of the National Book Award; *The Nuclear Age* (1985); *In the Lake of the Woods* (1994); and *July, July* (2002). His short-story collection is entitled *The Things They Carried* (1990). He lives in Texas and teaches alternate years in the creative writing program at Texas State University, San Marcos.

Born in Savannah, Georgia, and raised on a farm in Milledgeville, Georgia, **Flannery O'Connor** (1925–1964) graduated from Georgia State College for Women in 1945 and attended the Writers' Workshop at the University of Iowa, from which she received a master's degree in 1947. From Iowa she moved to New York City to begin her writing career but, after little more than two years, was forced by illness to return to her mother's Georgia farm. Confined as an invalid by the degenerative disease lupus, O'Connor spent her remaining fourteen years raising peacocks and writing fiction set in rural Georgia. Her works are distinguished by irreverent humor, often grotesque characters, and intense, almost mystical affirmation of the challenges of religious belief. Her work includes two novels, *Wise Blood* (1952) and *The Violent Bear It Away* (1960), and two short-story collections, *A Good Man Is Hard to Find* (1955) and *Everything That Rises Must Converge* (1965). After her death at the age of thirty-nine, a selection of occasional prose, *Mystery and Manners* (1969), was edited by her friends Sally and Robert Fitzgerald, and a collection of letters, *The Habit of Being* (1979), was edited by Sally Fitzgerald. *The Complete Stories* (1971) received the National Book Award.

Born in Baltimore and raised in Massachusetts, **Frank O'Hara** (1926–1966) studied piano at the New England Conservatory in Boston from 1941 to 1944 and served in the South Pacific and Japan during World War II. He majored in English at Harvard and received his MA in English at the University of Michigan in 1951. He moved to New York, where he worked at the Museum of Modern Art and began writing poetry seriously as well as composing essays and reviews on painting and sculpture. His first volume of poems, *A City in Winter*, thirteen poems with two drawings by the artist Larry Rivers, was published in 1952. Other collaborations with artists followed. His first major collection of poetry was *Meditations in an Emergency* (1957). His poetry is often casual, relaxed in diction, and full of specific detail, seeking to convey the immediacy of life. He described his work as "I do this I do that" poetry because his poems often read like entries in a diary, as in the opening lines of "The Day Lady Died." He was killed at forty when he was struck by a sand buggy while vacationing on Fire Island, New York.

Sharon Olds was born in 1942 in San Francisco and educated at Stanford and Columbia universities. She has written nine books of poetry—most recently *One Secret Thing* (2008)—and is the recipient of the Pulitzer Prize, the National Book Critics Circle Award, and the T. S. Eliot Prize, and fellowships from the National Endowment for the Arts and the Guggenheim Foundation. In the words of Elizabeth Frank, "[Olds] and her work are about nothing less than the joy of making—of making love, making babies, making poems, making sense of love, memory, death, the feel—the actual bodily texture, of life." She held the position of New York State Poet from 1998 until 2000. She teaches poetry workshops in New York University's graduate creative writing program along with workshops at Goldwater Hospital in New York, a public facility for physically disabled persons.

Mary Oliver was born in 1935 in Cleveland and educated at Ohio State University and Vassar College. She is the author of some twenty volumes of poetry, including *American Primitive* (1983), for which she won the Pulitzer Prize, and four books of prose. Her most recent book is *Swan: Poems and Prose Poems* (2010). She held the Catharine Osgood Foster Chair for Distinguished Teaching at Bennington College until 2001 and now lives in Provincetown, Massachusetts. Oliver is one of the most respected of poets concerned with the natural world.

George Oppen (1908–1984) was an American poet and proponent of the school of Objectivism, which emphasized simplicity and clarity in place of a more formal structure and rhyme. For an extended amount of time, Oppen abandoned poetry for political activism. During the Great Depression, he worked as a tool-and-die maker and mechanic, though he eventually forfeited his work exemption and was drafted into World War II. He was awarded the Purple Heart after being seriously wounded in battle. Oppen later returned to poetry in 1958 and won a Pulitzer Prize for poetry in 1969. Oppen's poetry is known to be sparse, and Oppen himself was known for his distrust of language. He strove to be as concise as possible. He published *Primitive* in 1978, just before the onset of Alzheimer's disease, which took his life in 1984.

Born in Oswestry, Shropshire, **Wilfred Owen** (1893–1918) attended Birkenhead Institute and Shrewsbury Technical School. When forced to withdraw from London University for financial reasons, Owen became a vicar's assistant in Dunsden, Oxfordshire. There he grew disaffected with the church and left to teach in France. In 1915, he enlisted as a soldier in World War I and was eventually made a second lieuten-

ant in the Manchester Regiment. Six months later he was hospitalized in Edinburgh, where he met Siegfried Sassoon, whose war poems had just been published. Sent back to the front, Owen was killed one week before the armistice. He is the most widely recognized of the "War Poets," a group of World War I writers who brought the realism of war to poetry.

Dorothy Parker (1893–1967) rose to fame with the Algonquin Round Table group of writers, who were celebrated New York City writers, satirists, and actors who met regularly over lunch at the Algonquin Hotel in the 1920s. Parker's work regularly appeared in numerous magazines, including *Vanity Fair* and *The New Yorker*. The Round Table group eventually separated, and Parker journeyed to Hollywood to pursue screenwriting, where she earned two Academy Award nominations. After she donated her estate to Martin Luther King Jr. in her will, the NAACP claimed her remains and created a memorial garden outside of their Baltimore headquarters. In 2014, Parker was elected to the New Jersey Hall of Fame.

Linda Pastan was born in 1932 in New York City, graduated from Radcliffe College, and earned an MA from Brandeis University. She has published many books of poetry, including *Traveling Light* (2011), and received numerous awards for them, including a Dylan Thomas Award. Her deeply emotional poetry often has grief at its center. She is known for writing short poems that address topics such as family life, domesticity, motherhood, the female experience, aging, death, loss and the fear of loss, and the fragility of life and relationships. She served as poet laureate of Maryland from 1991 to 1994 and was a staff member at the Breadloaf Writers Conference for twenty years. She lives in Potomac, Maryland.

Katherine Philips (1632–1664) was an Anglo-Welsh poet. She also achieved renown with her translations. The authorized edition of her poetry, *Poems by the Most Deservedly Admired Mrs. Katherine Philips, the Matchless Orinda,* was published in 1667 after her death. Many of her works question political authority in addition to hinting at her royalist beliefs.

Robert Pinsky was born in 1940 in Long Branch, New Jersey. He is the author of many books of poetry, including *The Figured Wheel: New and Collected Poems, 1966–1996* (1996), which won the 1997 Lenore Marshall Poetry Prize and was a Pulitzer Prize nominee. He has also published several books of criticism, two books of translation, a biography—*The Life of David* (2005)—several books on reading poetry, and *Mindwheel* (1984), an electronic novel that functions as an interactive computer game. In 1999 he coedited with Maggie Dietz *Americans' Favorite Poems: The Favorite Poem Project Anthology.* He teaches in the graduate writing program at Boston University, and in 1997 he was named Poet Laureate Consultant in Poetry to the Library of Congress.

Raised in a middle-class family in Boston, **Sylvia Plath** (1932–1963) showed early promise as a writer, having stories and poems published in magazines such as *Seventeen* while she was in high school. As a student at Smith College, she was selected for an internship at *Mademoiselle* magazine and spent a month working in New York in the summer of 1953. Upon her return home, she suffered a serious breakdown, attempted suicide, and was institutionalized. She returned to Smith College for her senior year in 1954 and received a Fulbright fellowship to study at Cambridge University in England, where she met the poet Ted Hughes. They were married in 1956. They lived in the United States as well as in England, and Plath studied under ROBERT LOWELL at Boston University. Her marriage broke up in 1962, and from her letters and poems it appears that she was approaching another breakdown at that time. On February 11, 1963, she committed suicide. Four books of poetry appeared during her lifetime, and her *Selected Poems* was published in 1985. The powerful, psychologically intense poetry for which she is best known (including "Daddy") was written after 1960, influenced by the "confessional" style of Lowell (see **confessional poetry** in the Glossary).

Born in Boston, Massachusetts, **Edgar Allan Poe** (1809–1849), the son of itinerant actors, was abandoned at one year of age by his father; his mother died soon after. The baby became the ward of John Allan of Richmond, Virginia, whose surname became Poe's middle name. When the family fortunes declined, the Allans moved to England. Poe was educated there and at the University of Virginia upon his return to Richmond. Although an excellent student, Poe drank and gambled heavily, causing Allan to withdraw him from the university after one year. Poe made his way to Boston, enlisted in the army, and eventually, with Allan's help, took an appointment at West Point. After further dissipation ended his military career, Poe set out to support himself by writing. Three volumes of poetry brought in little money, and in 1835 Poe took a position as an assistant editor of the *Southern Literary Messenger*, the first of many positions he lost because of drinking. He began to publish short stories. In 1836 he married his thirteen-year-old cousin, Virginia Clemm, and took on the support of her mother as well, increasing his financial difficulties. They went to New York City, where Poe published *The Narrative of Arthur Gordon Pym* (1838) and assembled the best stories he had published in magazines in *Tales of the Grotesque and Arabesque* (1840), his first story collection. At that time he also began to write detective stories, virtually inventing the genre. Already respected as a critic, Poe won fame as a poet with *The Raven and Other Poems* (1845). In 1847, after the death of his wife, Poe became engaged to the poet Sarah Helen Whitman, a wealthy widow six years his senior, who ultimately resisted marriage because of Poe's drinking problem. In 1849 Poe met a childhood sweetheart, Elmira Royster Shelton, now a widow, who agreed to marry him. After celebrating his apparent reversal of fortune with friends in Baltimore, he was found unconscious in the street and died shortly thereafter. Always admired in Europe, Poe's major stories of horror and detection, his major poems, and his major critical pieces on the craft of writing are considered American classics.

Ezra Pound (1885–1972) was born in Idaho but grew up outside Philadelphia; he attended the University of Pennsylvania for two years and graduated from Hamilton College. He taught for two years at Wabash College, then left for Europe, living for the next few years in London, where he edited *The Little Review* and founded several literary movements—including the Imagists and the Vorticists. After moving to Italy, he began his major work, the *Cantos*, and became involved in fascist politics. During World War II, he did radio broadcasts from Italy in support of Mussolini, for which he was indicted for treason in the United States. Judged mentally unfit for trial, he remained in an asylum in Washington, DC, until 1958, when the charges were dropped. Pound spent his last years in Italy. He is generally considered the poet most responsible for defining and promoting a Modernist aesthetic in poetry.

Walter Ralegh (1554–1618) was born to wealthy English landowners and took part in the suppression of several Irish rebellions, eventually earning himself knighthood from Queen Elizabeth I in 1585. On behalf of the queen, Ralegh set out to explore and colonize the "New World," exploring parts of South America and sending some of his followers to establish a colony near Roanoke Island, North Carolina, which was a failed endeavor. He wrote many poems, though they were not published in a compilation of any sort. At times, his voice reflected a *contemptus mundi*, or contempt for worldly concerns; in other writings, it carried a sense of melancholy toward history. Elizabeth's successor, King James I, accused Ralegh of treason and had him imprisoned and eventually put to death in October 1618.

Dudley Randall (1914–2002) was born in Washington, DC, and lived most of his life in Detroit. His first published poem appeared in the *Detroit Free Press* when he was thirteen. He worked for Ford Motor Company and then for the U.S. Postal Service and served in the South Pacific during World War II.

He graduated from Wayne State University in 1949 and then from the library school at the University of Michigan. In 1965 Randall established the Broadside Press, one of the most important publishers of modern black poetry. "Ballad of Birmingham," written in response to the 1963 bombing of a church in which four African American girls were killed, has been set to music and recorded. It became an anthem for many in the Civil Rights movement.

Of Jamaican descent, **Claudia Rankine** (b. 1963) is a poet and playwright educated at Williams College and Columbia University. She has received fellowships from the Academy of American Poets, the National Endowment for the Arts, and the Lannan Foundation. Her writing transcends genres, with *Don't Let Me Be Lonely* (2004) as a prime example. In it, she blends poetry, essay, lyrics, and television imagery. Her most recent book, *Citizen: An American Lyric* (2014), won the National Book Critics Circle Award and was widely acclaimed. Currently, Rankine lives in California and is the Aerol Arnold Chair in the University of Southern California English Department.

Adrienne Rich (1929–2012) was born in Baltimore, Maryland. She published over sixteen volumes of poetry and five volumes of critical prose, including *Tonight No Poetry Will Serve: Poems 2007–2010* (2010), *Telephone Ringing in the Labyrinth: Poems 2004–2006* (2007), and *A Human Eye: Essays on Art in Society* (2009). She also edited Muriel Rukeyser's *Selected Poems* for the Library of America. Among numerous other recognitions, she was the 2006 recipient of the National Book Foundation's Medal for Distinguished Contribution to American Letters. Her poetry

and essays have been widely translated and published internationally.

Alberto Ríos was born in 1952 in Nogales, Arizona, on the Mexican border. He earned a BA in English and in psychology, and an MFA at the University of Arizona. In addition to twelve books of poetry, he has published three collections of short stories and a memoir, *Capirotada: A Nogales Memoir* (1999). His work often fuses realism, surrealism, and magic realism. Since 1994 he has been Regents Professor of English at Arizona State University, where he has taught since 1982.

Born in Head Tide, Maine, **Edwin Arlington Robinson** (1869–1935) grew up in the equally provincial Maine town of Gardiner, the setting for much of his poetry. He was forced to leave Harvard University after two years because of his family's financial difficulties. He published his first two books of poetry in 1896 and 1897 ("Richard Cory" appeared in the latter). For the next quarter century, Robinson chose to live in poverty and write his poetry, relying on temporary jobs and charity from friends. President Theodore Roosevelt, at the urging of his son Kermit, used his influence to get Robinson a sinecure job in the New York Custom House in 1905, giving him time to write. He published numerous books of mediocre poetry in the next decade. The tide turned for him with *The Man against the Sky* (1916); the numerous volumes that followed received high praise and sold well. He was awarded three Pulitzer Prizes: for *Collected Poems* in 1921, *The Man Who Died Twice* in 1924, and *Tristram* in 1927. Robinson was the first major American poet of the twentieth century, unique in that he devoted his life to poetry and willingly paid the price in poverty and obscurity.

Theodore Roethke (1908–1963) was the son of a commercial greenhouse operator in Saginaw, Michigan. As a child, he spent much time in greenhouses, and the impressions of nature he formed there later influenced the subjects and imagery of his verse. Roethke graduated from the University of Michigan and studied at Harvard University. His eight books of poetry were held in high regard by critics, some of whom considered Roethke among the best poets of his generation. *The Waking* was awarded the Pulitzer Prize in 1954; *Words for the Wind* (1958) received the Bollingen Prize and the National Book Award. He taught at many colleges and universities, his career interrupted several times by serious mental breakdowns, and gained a reputation as an exceptional teacher of poetry writing.

Christina Rossetti (1830–1894) was an important contributor to what was known as the Pre-Raphaelite movement in English arts and literature of the late nineteenth century. She was the sister of artist and poet Dante Gabriel Rossetti, who provided the artwork for her most famous publication, *Goblin Market and Other Poems* (1862).

Mary Ruefle was born in 1952 near Pittsburgh but spent her early life moving around the United States and Europe as the daughter of a military officer. She graduated from Bennington College with a literature major. She has published ten books of poetry, including *Memling's Veil* (1982), *The Adamant* (1989; winner of the 1988 Iowa Poetry Prize), *A Little White Shadow* (2006), and *Selected Poems* (2010). She published her first collection of short stories, *The Most of It*, in 2008. Among awards she has received are a Guggenheim Fellowship, an American Academy of Arts and Letters Award in Literature, and a Whiting Foundation Writer's Award. She lives in Vermont, where she is a professor in the Vermont College MFA program.

Muriel Rukeyser (1913–1980) was an American poet and political activist. Her poems focus almost exclusively, on subjects such as equality, feminism, social justice, and Judaism. While critics had varying opinions of her work, nearly all of them cited Rukeyser's social activism. Rukeyser's poems in *The Life of Poetry* (1949) contended that poetry is essential to democracy, life, and even understanding. Rukeyser draws comparisons to Walt Whitman, and her strong voice inspired and compelled many readers and writers.

Kay Ryan (b. 1945) is the author of several books of poetry, including *Flamingo Watching* (2006), *The Niagara River* (2005), and *Say Uncle* (2000). In 2011, she won the Pulitzer Prize for Poetry, in recognition of her body of work and compilation, *The Best of It: New and Selected Poems* (2010). Her poems are often quite short, but she manages to work with internal rhyme and quirks in language, much like Emily Dickinson before her. Ryan is the recipient of several major awards, including fellowships from the John D. and Catherine T. MacArthur Foundation, the National Endowment for the Arts, the Ingram Merrill Foundation, and the Guggenheim Foundation. From 2008 to 2010, Ryan was the Poet Laureate of the United States.

Born in Newton, Massachusetts, **Anne Sexton** (1928–1974) dropped out of

Garland Junior College to get married. After suffering nervous breakdowns following the births of her two children, she was encouraged to enroll in a writing program. Studying under ROBERT LOWELL at Boston University, she was a fellow student with SYLVIA PLATH. Like the work of other "confessional" poets, Sexton's poetry is an intimate view of her life and emotions. She made the experience of being a woman a central issue in her poetry, bringing to it such subjects as menstruation and abortion as well as drug addiction. She published at least a dozen books of poetry—*Live or Die* was awarded the Pulitzer Prize for poetry in 1966—as well as four children's books coauthored with MAXINE KUMIN. Sexton's emotional problems continued, along with a growing addiction to alcohol and sedatives, and she committed suicide in 1974.

William Shakespeare (1564–1616) was born in Stratford-upon-Avon, England, where his father was a glovemaker and bailiff, and he presumably went to grammar school there. He married Anne Hathaway in 1582 and sometime before 1592 left for London to work as a playwright and actor. Shakespeare joined the Lord Chamberlain's Men (later the King's Men), an acting company for which he wrote thirty-seven plays—comedies, tragedies, histories, and romances—upon which his reputation as the finest dramatist in the English language is based. He was also arguably the finest lyric poet of his day, as exemplified by songs scattered throughout his plays, two early nondramatic poems (*Venus and Adonis* and *The Rape of Lucrece*), and the sonnet sequence expected of all noteworthy writers in the Elizabethan age. Shakespeare's sonnets were probably written in the 1590s, although they were not published

until 1609. Shakespeare retired to Stratford around 1612, and by the time he died at the age of fifty-two, he was acknowledged as a leading light of the Elizabethan stage and had become successful enough to have purchased a coat of arms for his family home.

Born in 1986 to Iranian parents in Istanbul, Turkey, **Solmaz Sharif** published her first poem, included in *A World Between: Poems, Short Stories, and Essays by Iranian-Americans* (1999), at the age of 13. Since then she has published numerous poems in many notable magazines and literary journals. In 2014, Sharif received a Ruth Lilly and Dorothy Sargent Rosenberg Poetry fellowship from the Poetry Foundation. Currently, she works as a Jones Lecturer at Stanford University.

Born into a wealthy aristocratic family in Sussex County, England, **Percy Bysshe Shelley** (1792–1822) was educated at Eton and then went on to Oxford University, where he was expelled after six months for writing a defense of atheism, the first price he would pay for his nonconformity and radical (for his time) commitment to social justice. The following year he eloped with Harriet Westbrook, daughter of a tavern keeper, despite his belief that marriage was a tyrannical and degrading social institution (she was sixteen, he eighteen). He became a disciple of the radical social philosopher William Godwin; fell in love with Godwin's daughter, Mary Wollstonecraft Godwin (the author, later, of *Frankenstein*); and went to live with her in France. Two years later, after Harriet had committed suicide, the two married and moved to Italy, where they shifted about restlessly and Shelley was generally short on money and in poor health. In such trying circumstances, he wrote his greatest works. He died at age thirty, when the boat he was in was overturned by a sudden storm.

Philip Sidney (1554–1586) was born in 1554 in Kent, England. He is known for works *Astrophil and Stella*, the first sonnet sequence ever written in English; *The Defense of Poetry*, an aesthetic treatise that has influenced generations of poets; and *The Countess of Pembroke's Arcadia*, one of the first novels written in English. With his sister Mary, he translated a number of the Psalms into English as well. He died from gangrene after he was shot in the thigh fighting for the Protestant side against the Roman Catholic Spanish in the Battle of Zutphen in the Netherlands.

Born in 1948 in Albuquerque of mixed Pueblo, Mexican, and white ancestry, **Leslie Marmon Silko** grew up on the Laguna Pueblo reservation in New Mexico. She earned her BA (with honors) from the University of New Mexico. In a long and productive writing career (she was already writing stories in elementary school), Silko has published poetry, novels, short stories, essays, letters, and film scripts. She taught creative writing first at the University of New Mexico and later at the University of Arizona. She has been named a Living Cultural Treasure by the New Mexico Humanities Council and has received the Native Writers' Circle of the Americas Lifetime Achievement Award. Her work is a graphic telling of the life of native peoples, maintaining its rich spiritual heritage while exposing the terrible consequences of European domination.

Charles Simic was born in 1938 in Belgrade, Yugoslavia. In 1953 he, his mother, and his brother joined his father in Chicago, where Charles continued to live until 1958. His first poems were published when he was twenty-one. In 1961 he was drafted into the U.S. Army, and in 1966 he earned his BA from New York University. His first book of poems, *What the Grass Says*, was published in 1967. Since then he has published more than sixty books of poetry, translations, and essays, including *The World Doesn't End: Prose Poems* (1990), for which he received the Pulitzer Prize for poetry. Since 1973 he has lived in New Hampshire, where he is a professor of English at the University of New Hampshire. In 2007 he was named Poet Laureate Consultant in Poetry to the Library of Congress.

Born in 1955 in Chicago, **Patricia Smith** is a poet, playwright, teacher, former journalist, and spoken-word performer. She is the author of *Shoulda Been Jimmy Savannah* (2013), which won the Lenore Marshall Poetry Prize, and *Teahouse of the Almighty* (2006), a National Poetry Series Prize winner. Many have noted that Smith is a testament to the power of words, as is evident throughout her body of work. Smith is also a four-time National Poetry Slam champion. She is a professor of English at CUNY/College of Staten Island in New York.

Born Florence Margaret Smith, **Stevie Smith** (1902–1971) was an English poet and novelist known for both her fiction and poetry. Her three novels, lightly fictionalized and based on events of her own life, focus on common subjects: loneliness, myth, and anecdotes drawn from middle-class British life. Her poetic style is notably dark, with many characters receptive to death. She published nine volumes of poetry, and three more were published posthumously.

Cathy Song was born in 1955 in Hawaii of Korean and Chinese ancestry and grew up in the small town of Wahiawa on Oahu. She was encouraged to write during her childhood. She left Hawaii for the East Coast, earning a BA in English from Wellesley College and an MA in creative writing from Boston University. In 1987 she returned to Honolulu, where she continues to write and teach. Her first book, *Picture Bride*, was chosen by Richard Hugo for the Yale Series of Younger Poets in 1982. Since then she has published four other books of poetry. With island poet Juliet S. Kono, she coedited and contributed poetry and prose to *Sister Stew* (1991). Her writing has earned the Hawaii Award for Literature and a Shelley Memorial Award.

Sophocles (c. 496–c. 406 BCE) was not the first important voice to emerge in drama, but as a representative of classical Greek tragedy, it is hard to imagine a more important figure. Indeed, his works were considered such models of the craft that Aristotle based much of his *Poetics* on an analysis of *Oedipus Rex*. Sophocles was born to a wealthy Athenian family and became active in many aspects of civic life as a soldier, a priest, and a statesman. Today, however, he is remembered principally for his achievements as a playwright. During a long and distinguished career, he won first prize in Greek drama competitions more often than any other writer. Though there is evidence that he wrote more than 120 plays, only seven have survived in their entirety, along with fragments of many others. In his plays, Sophocles wrestled with some of the most important issues of his time and indeed of all time—the conflict between fate and free will; between public and private morality; and

between duty to one's family, the state, and the gods—giving his work enduring appeal. *Oedipus Rex* (*Oedipus the King*, first performed in 430 BCE) is one of Sophocles's three Theban plays, the other two being *Antigone* (441 BCE) and *Oedipus at Colonus* (401 BCE, first performed posthumously).

Raised in Fresno, California, **Gary Soto** (b. 1952) earned his BA from California State University, Fresno, and an MFA from the University of California, Irvine. He worked his way through college doing such jobs as picking grapes and chopping beets. Much of his poetry comes out of and reflects his working background, that of migrant workers and tenant farmers in the fields of southern California, and provides glimpses into the lives of families in the barrio. Soto's language comes from gritty, raw, everyday American speech. His first book, *The Elements of San Joaquin*, won the 1976 United States Award from the International Poetry Forum. He has published eleven collections of poetry, eight novels, four essay collections, and numerous young adult and children's books and has edited four anthologies. He lives in Berkeley and in Fresno, California.

A contemporary of WILLIAM SHAKESPEARE, **Edmund Spenser** (1552–1599) was the greatest English nondramatic poet of his time. Best known for his romantic and national epic *The Faerie Queene*, Spenser wrote poems of a number of other types as well and was important as an innovator in meter and form (as in his development of the special form of sonnet that bears his name—the Spenserian sonnet).

Born in Hutchinson, Kansas, **William Stafford** (1914–1995) studied at the

University of Kansas and then at the University of Iowa Writers' Workshop. In between, he was a conscientious objector during World War II and worked in labor camps. In 1948 Stafford moved to Oregon, where he taught at Lewis and Clark College until he retired in 1980. His first major collection of poems, *Traveling through the Dark*, was published when Stafford was forty-eight. It won the National Book Award in 1963. He went on to publish more than sixty-five volumes of poetry and prose and came to be known as a very influential teacher of poetry. From 1970 to 1971, he was Poet Laureate Consultant in Poetry to the Library of Congress.

Gerald Stern was born in 1925 in Pittsburgh and studied at the University of Pittsburgh and Columbia University. Stern came late to poetry: he was forty-six when he published his first book. Since then he has published more than fifteen collections of poems, most recently *Divine Nothingness: Poems* (2014) and *In Beauty Bright* (2012), and received many prestigious awards, including the 1998 National Book Award for Poetry for his book *This Time: New and Selected Poems*. Stern has often been compared to WALT WHITMAN and JOHN KEATS for his exploration of the self and the sometimes ecstatic exuberance of his verse. Until his retirement in 1995, he taught at many universities, including Columbia University, New York University, Sarah Lawrence College, and the University of Pittsburgh, and for many years at the University of Iowa Writers' Workshop.

Born in Reading, Pennsylvania, **Wallace Stevens** (1879–1955) attended Harvard University for three years. He tried journalism and then attended New York University Law School, after which he worked as a legal consultant. He spent most of his life working as an executive for the Hartford Accident and Indemnity Company, spending his evenings writing some of the most imaginative and influential poetry of his time. Although now considered one of the major American poets of the twentieth century, he did not receive widespread recognition until the publication of his *Collected Poems* just a year before his death.

Sekou Sundiata (1948–2007) was born and raised in Harlem. His work was deeply influenced by the music, poetry, and oral traditions of African American culture. A self-proclaimed radical in the 1970s, for the next several decades he used poetry to comment on the life and times of our culture. His work, which encompasses print, performance, music, and theater, is praised for its fusion of soul, jazz, and hip-hop grooves with political insight, humor, and rhythmic speech. He regularly recorded and performed on tour with artists such as Craig Harris and Vernon Reid.

A native of Kansas City, Missouri, **James Tate** (1943–2015) studied at the University of Missouri and Kansas State College during his undergraduate years. He then earned his MFA at the University of Iowa Writers' Workshop in 1967, the same year his first poetry collection, *The Lost Pilot*, was published (selected by Dudley Fitts for the Yale Series of Younger Poets). Tate was the author of numerous books of poetry, including *Selected Poems* (1991), which won the Pulitzer Prize and the William Carlos Williams Award. Tate's poems often include highly unusual juxtapositions of imagery, tone, and context, as is evident in "The Wheelchair Butterfly." Tate taught at the University of Iowa, the University of California, Berkeley, Columbia University, and the University of Massachusetts, Amherst.

Born in Somersby, Lincolnshire, **Alfred, Lord Tennyson** (1809–1892), grew up in the tense atmosphere of his unhappy father's rectory. He went to Trinity College, Cambridge, but when he was forced to leave because of family and financial problems, he returned home to study and practice the craft of poetry. His early volumes, published in 1830 and 1832, received bad reviews, but his *In Memoriam* (1850), an elegy on his close friend Arthur Hallam, who died of a brain seizure, won acclaim. Tennyson was unquestionably the most popular poet of his time (the "poet of the people") and arguably the greatest of the Victorian poets. He succeeded WILLIAM WORDSWORTH as poet laureate, a position he held from 1850 until his death.

Dylan Thomas (1914–1953) was born in Swansea, Wales, and after grammar school became a journalist , working as a writer for the rest of his life. His first book of poetry, *Eighteen Poems*, appeared in 1934 and was followed by *Twenty-Five Poems* (1936), *Deaths and Entrances* (1946), and *Collected Poems* (1952). His poems are often rich in textured rhythms and images. He also wrote prose, chiefly short stories collectively appearing as *Portrait of the Artist as a Young Dog* (1940), and a number of film scripts and radio plays. His most famous work, *Under Milk Wood*, written as a play for voices, was first performed in New York on May 14, 1953. Thomas's radio broadcasts and his lecture tours and poetry readings in the United States brought him fame and popularity. Alcoholism contributed to his early death in 1953.

Natasha Trethewey was born in 1966 in Gulfport, Mississippi. She has degrees from the University of Georgia, Hollins University, and the University of Massachusetts. She has won many awards for her poetry, including the inaugural Cave Canem Poetry Prize for her first collection, *Domestic Work* (2000). Her second collection, *Bellocq's Ophelia* (2002), received the 2003 Mississippi Institute of Arts and Letters Book Prize and was a finalist for both the Academy of American Poets' James Laughlin and Lenore Marshall prizes. In 2007 her collection *Native Guard* received the Pulitzer Prize. She has taught at Auburn University, the University of North Carolina, and Duke University. From 2009 to 2010 she was the James Weldon Johnson Fellow in African American Studies at Yale University's Beinecke Rare Books and Manuscript Library. She presently teaches at Emory University, as holder of the Phillis Wheatley Distinguished Chair in Poetry.

Quincy Troupe was born in 1943 in New York City and grew up in St. Louis, Missouri. He is the author of sixteen books, including eight volumes of poetry, most recently *The Architecture of Language* (2006). He is the recipient of two American Book Awards, for his collection of poetry *Snake-Back Solos* (1980) and his nonfiction book *Miles: The Autobiography* (1989). In 1991 he received the prestigious Peabody Award for writing and coproducing the seven-part "Miles Davis Radio Project" aired on National Public Radio in 1990. *Transcircularities: New and Selected Poems* (2002) received the Milt

Kessler Award for 2003 and was a finalist for the Paterson Poetry Prize. Troupe has taught at UCLA, Ohio University, the College of Staten Island (CUNY), Columbia University (in the graduate writing program), and the University of California, San Diego. He is now professor emeritus of creative writing and American and Caribbean literature at the University of California—San Diego. He is the founding editorial director for *Code* magazine and former artistic director of "Arts on the Cutting Edge," a reading and performance series at the Museum of Contemporary Art, San Diego. He was the first official poet laureate of the state of California, appointed to the post in 2002 by Governor Gray Davis.

After a seven-year enlistment with the U.S. Army, **Brian Turner** (b. 1967) composed his first book of poetry, *Here, Bullet* (2005), which chronicled his time in Iraq. Before his tour, Turner earned an MFA from the University of Oregon and lived abroad in South Korea. He has also received a fellowship from the National Endowment for the Arts, the Amy Lowell Traveling Fellowship, and a fellowship from the Lannan Foundation. His collection, *Phantom Noise*, was published in 2010.

Born an only child in Shillington, Pennsylvania, to a mother who was a writer and a father who taught high school, **John Updike** (1932–2009) studied at Harvard University and the Ruskin School of Drawing and Fine Art at Oxford, England. On his return to the United States, he joined the staff of *The New Yorker*, where he worked from 1955 to 1957. From 1957 until his death, he lived and worked near Ipswich, Massachusetts. In addition to numerous volumes of poetry, books of

essays and speeches, and a play, Updike published some twenty novels and some ten collections of short fiction noteworthy for their incisive presentation of the quandaries of contemporary personal and social life. Among his novels are *Rabbit, Run* (1960), *The Centaur* (1963; National Book Award), *Couples* (1968), *Rabbit Redux* (1971), *Rabbit Is Rich* (1981; Pulitzer Prize), *The Witches of Eastwick* (1984), *Rabbit at Rest* (1990; Pulitzer Prize), *In the Beauty of the Lilies* (1996), *Toward the End of Time* (1997), *Bech at Bay* (1998), *Villages* (2004), and *Terrorist* (2006). His story collections include *The Same Door* (1959), *Pigeon Feathers* (1962), *Olinger Stories* (1964), *The Music School* (1966), *Museums and Women* (1972), *Too Far to Go: The Maples Stories* (1979), *Bech Is Back* (1982), *Trust Me* (1987), and *The Afterlife and Other Stories* (1994).

Alice Walker was born in 1944 in Eatonton, Georgia. Her parents were sharecropper farmers. When she was eight, she lost sight in one eye when one of her older brothers accidentally shot her with a BB gun. She was valedictorian of her high school class. Encouraged by her teachers and her mother to go to college, she attended Spelman College in Atlanta, a school for black women, for two years, and she graduated from Sarah Lawrence College. From the mid-1960s to the mid-1970s, she lived in Tougaloo, Mississippi. She was active in the civil rights movement of the 1960s and remains an involved activist today. Her first book was a collection of poetry, *Once* (1968). She is a prolific writer, having gone on to publish more than thirty books of poetry, novels, short stories, and nonfiction. Her best-known novel, *The Color Purple* (1982), won the American Book Award and the Pulitzer Prize for fiction and was made into a motion picture directed by Steven Spielberg.

James Welch (1940–2003) was born in Browning, Montana. His father was a member of the Blackfoot tribe, his mother of the Gros Ventre tribe. He attended schools on the Blackfoot and Fort Belknap reservations and took a degree from the University of Montana, where he studied under Richard Hugo. Welch published many books of poetry, fiction, and nonfiction. His hard, spare poems often evoke the bleakest side of contemporary Native American life. He received a Lifetime Achievement Award for literature from the Native Writers' Circle in 1997.

Eudora Welty (1909–2001) was born in Jackson, Mississippi, and graduated from the University of Wisconsin. She is admired for her fine photographic studies of people—*One Time, One Place* (1972) collects her photos of Mississippi in the 1930s—as well as for her fiction, which also depicts the inhabitants of rural Mississippi. Among her seven volumes of short stories, which explore the mysteries of individuals' "separateness," are *A Curtain of Green* (1941), *The Wide Net* (1943), *The Golden Apples* (1949), *The Bride of Innisfallen* (1955), and *The Collected Stories* (1980). Her novels include *Delta Wedding* (1946), *The Ponder Heart* (1954), and *The Optimist's Daughter* (1972), which won the Pulitzer Prize. Welty also wrote many reviews, articles, and books of literary criticism.

Phillis Wheatley (1753–1784), was born in West Africa and at a young age was sold into slavery and transported to North America. She was purchased by the Wheatley family of Boston, who taught her how to read, write, and to become a Christian. With the encouragement of the Wheatley family, she rose to become the first published African American female poet with her *Poems on Various Subjects, Religious and Moral* (1773). She was emancipated from slavery after the death of her master, John Wheatley. In her poems, she expressed many Christian themes, and penned several tributes to famous figures. A close reading of Wheatley's poems will reveal her conflicting views on slavery, as she both recognized its cruelty but also its role in bringing her to Christianity. Many of the famous figures in the world at the time, including George Washington and many other founding fathers, gave her high praise.

Born in rural Long Island, **Walt Whitman** (1819–1892) was the son of a farmer and carpenter. He attended grammar school in Brooklyn and took his first job as a printer's devil for the *Long Island Patriot*. Attending the opera, dabbling in politics, participating in street life, and gaining experience as a student, printer, reporter, writer, carpenter, farmer, seashore observer, and a teacher provided the bedrock for his future poetic vision of an ideal society based on the realization of self. Although Whitman liked to portray himself as uncultured, he read widely in the King James Bible as well as SHAKESPEARE, Homer, Dante, Aeschylus, and SOPHOCLES. He worked for many years in the newspaper business and began writing poetry only in 1847. In 1855, at his own expense, he published the first edition of *Leaves of Grass*, a thin volume of twelve long untitled poems. Written in a highly original and innovative **free verse** (see the

Glossary), influenced significantly by music, and with a wide-ranging subject matter, the work seemed strange to most of the poet's contemporaries — although some did recognize its value: Ralph Waldo Emerson wrote to the poet shortly after Whitman sent him a copy, saying, "I greet you at the beginning of a great career." He spent much of the remainder of his life revising and expanding this book. Today *Leaves of Grass* is considered a masterpiece of world literature, marking the beginning of modern American poetry, and Whitman is widely regarded as America's national poet.

Oscar Wilde (1854–1900) perhaps best known for his novel *The Picture of Dorian Gray* (1890) and for his play *The Importance of Being Earnest* (1895), was born in Dublin, Ireland. His mother was a poet, and Wilde showed himself to be bright and talented at a young age, earning multiple prizes at the Portora Royal School and receiving the Foundation Scholarship, the highest honor Trinity College in Dublin had to offer. While critics at the time did not always appreciate his work, Wilde proved himself a skilled writer and is one of the most revered literary names. In 1895, Wilde was tried and convicted of "gross indecency" with men, and he spent two years enduring hard labor in English prison. He continued to write while imprisoned, and left England for France upon his release. His writing career was cut short by meningitis, and he passed away at the age of forty-six.

The early poems of American poet **C. K. Williams** (1936–2015) covered political topics, such as the Vietnam War, while his later work saw a shift to more introspective topics, such as alienation and deception. In the *Nation*

and *Tar* (1983), Williams crafted unconventionally long lines of text in his poems, which became his signature style. In his lifetime, he earned just about every major poetry award, including the Pulitzer Prize, the National Book Critics Circle Award, and a Pushcart Prize, and fellowships from the Guggenheim Foundation. Williams taught at Princeton University from 1996 to 2015, just before his passing.

Emmett Williams (1925–2007) was an American poet and visual artist. He studied poetry at Kenyon College in Ohio. He lived in Europe for many years and was the founding member of the Domaine Poetique in Paris. He collaborated with Daniel Spoerri and German poet Claus Bremer in what was called the Darmstadt circle of poetry. The most memorable piece from this collaboration is the "Four-directional Song of Doubt for Five Voices." He published his autobiography in 1991.

Born Thomas Lanier Williams in Columbia, Mississippi, as a child **Tennessee Williams** (1911–1983) moved with his family to St. Louis. His childhood was not easy: his parents were ill-matched, the family had little money, and both he and his beloved sister, Rose, suffered from depression and medical problems. It took Williams three attempts at college before he finished, finally earning a degree in playwriting from the University of Iowa at the age of twenty-four. His earliest efforts at writing were unsuccessful, but in 1944 *The Glass Menagerie* opened in Chicago and later began a very successful run in New York, winning the prestigious Drama Critics Circle Award. Other successes followed, including *A Streetcar Named Desire* (1947), which won the Pulitzer Prize and helped launch the career of its young star, Marlon Brando; *Cat on a Hot Tin Roof* (1955); and *Suddenly Last Summer* (1958). The American stage in the 1940s and 1950s was not yet ready to accept overt homosexuality, so Williams transformed his own tortured searching for sexual and emotional fulfillment into plays with remarkably frank heterosexual themes. This frankness and dreamy, poetic language are key elements of his style. In his later years, Williams suffered from drug and alcohol problems and was occasionally institutionalized for these and the crippling depressions that continued to plague him. Though his later work never achieved the popular success of his early plays, Williams's reputation in the American theater is secure.

William Carlos Williams (1883–1963) was born in Rutherford, New Jersey; his father was an English emigrant and his mother was of mixed Basque descent from Puerto Rico. He decided to be both a writer and a doctor while in high school in New York City. He graduated from the medical school at the University of Pennsylvania, where he was a friend of EZRA POUND and H.D. (HILDA DOOLITTLE). After completing an internship in New York, writing poems between seeing patients, Williams practiced general medicine in Rutherford (he was ALLEN GINSBERG's pediatrician). His first book of poems was published in 1909, and he subsequently published poems, novels, short stories, plays, criticism, and essays. Initially one of the principal poets of the Imagist movement, Williams later sought to invent an entirely fresh—and distinctly American—poetic whose subject matter was centered on the everyday circumstances of life and the lives of common people. Williams, like

WALLACE STEVENS, became one of the major poets of the twentieth century and exerted great influence upon poets of his own and later generations.

Born and raised in the Hill District, an African American section of Pittsburgh that provides the backdrop to many of his plays, **August Wilson** (1945–2005) has come to be seen as one of the most important voices on the contemporary American stage. The son of a mixed-race marriage, his white father was not in the household when he was growing up. Wilson dropped out of high school but continued to read widely, beginning his serious writing with poetry, the rhythms of which can be heard in his plays. In the 1960s, he became involved in the Black Power movement and also began to turn his writing talents to the stage. His best-known work is his cycle of historical plays, known as "The Pittsburgh Cycle," which examines important elements of African American experience and consists of one play for each decade of the twentieth century. Among these are *Ma Rainey's Black Bottom* (1985), *Fences* (1987), *Joe Turner's Come and Gone* (1988), *The Piano Lesson* (1990), and *Seven Guitars* (1996). Each of these plays won the New York Drama Critics Circle Award, and the final play in the cycle, *Radio Golf* (2005), received a Tony Award nomination. *Fences* and *The Piano Lesson* each also earned Wilson the Pulitzer Prize.

Born in 1945 in Birmingham, Alabama, **Tobias Wolff** is a writer known for his memoirs, in addition to his two novels and plethora of short stories. Wolff's works embody a fascinating fusion of the biographical and existential. Whether it is the gap between what is true and what is felt to be true or between nonfiction biography and fiction, this fusion has come to define Wolff's writing. He has accumulated a number of awards, including the Rea Award for the Short Story and, on three separate occasions, the O. Henry Award, given for short stories of exceptional merit. His most recent book is *That Room* (2008).

William Wordsworth (1770–1850) was born and raised in the Lake District of England. Both his parents died by the time he was thirteen. He studied at Cambridge, toured Europe on foot, and lived in France for a year during the first part of the French Revolution. He returned to England, leaving behind a lover, Annette Vallon, and their daughter, Caroline, from whom he was soon cut off by war between England and France. He met SAMUEL TAYLOR COLERIDGE, and in 1798 they published *Lyrical Ballads*, the first great work of the English Romantic movement. He changed poetry forever by his decision to use common language in his poetry instead of heightened **poetic diction** (see the Glossary). In 1799 he and his sister Dorothy moved to Grasmere, in the Lake District, where he married Mary Hutchinson, a childhood friend. His greatest works were produced between 1797 and 1808. He continued to write for the next forty years, but his work never regained the heights of his earlier verse. In 1843 he was named poet laureate, a position he held until his death in 1850.

Raised in Martin's Ferry, Ohio, **James Wright** (1927–1980) attended Kenyon College, where the influence of John Crowe Ransom sent his early poetry in a formalist direction. After spending a year in Austria on a Fulbright fellowship, he returned to the United States and earned an MA and a PhD at the University of Washington, studying under THEODORE ROETHKE and Stanley Kunitz. He went on to teach at the University of Minnesota, Macalester College, and Hunter College. His working-class background and the poverty that he witnessed during the Depression stirred in him a sympathy for the poor and for "outsiders" of various sorts that shaped the tone and content of his poetry. He published numerous books of poetry; his *Collected Poems* received the Pulitzer Prize in 1972.

Richard Wright (1908–1960) was born in Roxie, Mississippi. He published his first short story while attending school as a teenager. He is the author of *Black Boy* (1945), a memoir of his youth, *Native Son* (1940), and *Uncle Tom's Children* (1938). Much of his work focuses on the struggles and injustices facing African Americans in the early part of the twentieth century. During the 1930s he participated in the WPA Writers' Project. For a number of years after World War II he lived as an expatriate in France and traveled widely.

The niece of Sir Philip Sidney and Mary Sidney Herbert, **Lady Mary Wroth** (1587–1653) was one of the best and most prolific women writers of the English Renaissance and an important literary patron. She wrote *Pamphilia to Amphilanthus*, the first English sonnet sequence on love themes by a woman; seventy-four poems that appeared in *Urania* (the first full-length work of prose fiction by a woman); and several other pieces. BEN JONSON said that reading her sonnets had made him "a better lover and a much better poet."

Born in Kent, **Sir Thomas Wyatt** (1503–1542) was educated at St. John's College, Cambridge. He spent most of his life as a courtier and diplomat, serving King Henry VIII as ambassador to Spain and as a member of several missions to Italy and France. In his travels, Wyatt discovered the Italian writers of the High Renaissance, whose work he translated, thus introducing the sonnet form into English. He was arrested twice and charged with treason, sent to the Tower of London, and acquitted in 1541. Aristocratic poets at the time rarely published their poems themselves: works circulated in manuscript and in published collections ("miscellanies") gathered by printers. The most important of these is a volume published by Richard Tottel in 1557 titled *Songs and Sonnets*, but more commonly known as *Tottel's Miscellany*, which includes ninety-seven of Wyatt's sonnets and delightful lyrics.

William Butler Yeats (1865–1939) was born in Sandymount, Dublin, to an Anglo-Irish family. On leaving high school in 1883, he decided to be an artist, like his father, and attended art school, but he soon gave it up to concentrate on poetry. His first poems were published in 1885 in the *Dublin University Review*. Religious by temperament but unable to accept orthodox Christianity, Yeats throughout his life explored esoteric philosophies in search of a tradition that would substitute for a lost religion. He became a member of the Theosophical Society and the Order of the Golden Dawn, two groups interested in Eastern occultism, and later developed a private system of symbols and mystical ideas. Through the influence of Lady Gregory, a writer and promoter of literature, he became interested in Irish nationalist art, helping to found the Irish National Theatre and the famous Abbey Theatre. He was actively involved in Irish politics, especially after the Easter Rising of 1916. He continued to write and to revise earlier poems, leaving behind a body of verse that, in its variety and power, placed him among the greatest twentieth-century poets of the English language. He was awarded the Nobel Prize in Literature in 1923.

Born in 1939 in Ocean Springs, Mississippi, **Al Young** lived for a decade in the South and then moved to Detroit. He attended the University of Michigan and the University of California, Berkeley. Young has been a professional guitarist and singer, a disk jockey, a medical photographer, and a warehouseman; he has written eight books of poetry, most recently *Something about the Blues: An Unlikely Collection of Poetry* (2008); five novels; memoirs; essays; and film scripts. He also has edited a number of books, including *Yardbird Lives!* (1978) and *African American Literature: A Brief Introduction and Anthology* (1995). He has taught literature and creative writing at numerous colleges and universities. In the 1970s and 1980s, Young cofounded the journals *Yardbird Reader* and *Quilt* with poet-novelist Ishmael Reed. From 2005 to 2007, he served as California's poet laureate.

Ray A. Young Bear was born in 1950 and raised in the Mesquakie Tribal Settlement near Tama, Iowa. His poetry has been influenced by his maternal grandmother, Ada Kapayou Old Bear, and his wife, Stella L. Young Bear. He attended Pomona College in California as well as Grinnell College, the University of Iowa, Iowa State University, and Northern Iowa University. He has taught creative writing and Native American literature at the Institute of American Indian Art, Eastern Washington University, the

University of Iowa, and Iowa State University. Young Bear and his wife cofounded the Woodland Song and Dance Troupe of Arts Midwest in 1983. Young Bear's group has performed traditional Mesquakie music in the United States and the Netherlands. Author of four books of poetry, a collection of short stories, and a novel, he has contributed to contemporary Native American poetry and the study of it for three decades.

Glossary of Critical and Literary Terms

This glossary provides definitions for important literary terms used in this anthology. Words and phrases highlighted in **boldface** in individual entries are defined elsewhere in the glossary.

Abstract language Any language that employs intangible, nonspecific concepts. *Love, truth,* and *beauty* are abstractions. Abstract language is the opposite of **concrete language**. Both types have different effects and are important features of an author's style.

Accent The stress, or greater emphasis, given to some syllables of words relative to that received by adjacent syllables.

Accentual meter A metrical system in which the number of accented, or stressed, syllables per line is regular—all lines have the same number, or the corresponding lines of different stanzas have the same number—while the number of unstressed syllables in lines varies randomly. Accentual meter consisting of two accented syllables in each half line linked by a system of alliteration was the hallmark of Old English poetry (up to the eleventh century), and some modern poets, such as W. H. Auden, have sought to revive it. Gerard Manley Hopkins developed a unique variety of accentual verse he called *sprung rhythm.*

Accentual-syllabic verse Verse whose meter takes into account both the number of syllables per line and the pattern of accented and unaccented syllables. The great majority of metrical poems in English are accentual-syllabic.

Act One of the principal divisions of a full-length play. Plays of the Renaissance are commonly divided into five acts. Although four acts enjoyed a brief period of popularity in the nineteenth century, two or three acts are more typical of modern and contemporary dramas.

Agon The central conflict in a play. In Greek drama, the agon is a formal structural component, often a debate between two characters or parts of the **chorus**.

Alexandrine A poetic line with six iambic feet (iambic hexameter).

Allegory (1) An extended **metaphor** in which characters, events, objects, settings, and actions stand not only for themselves but also for abstract concepts, such as death or knowledge. Allegorical plays, often religious, were popular in medieval times; a famous example is *Everyman*. (2) A form or manner, usually narrative, in which objects, persons, and actions make coherent sense on a literal level but also are equated in a

sustained and obvious way with (usually) abstract meanings that lie outside
the story. A classic example in prose is
John Bunyan's *The Pilgrim's Progress*;
in narrative poetry, Edmund Spenser's
The Faerie Queene.

Alliteration The repetition of
identical consonant sounds in the
stressed syllables of words relatively
near to each other (in the same line or
adjacent lines, usually). Alliteration is
most common at the beginnings of
words ("The soote season, that bud and
bloom forth brings") but can involve
consonants within words and at the
ends of words as well ("The adder all
her slough away she slings"). (The examples are from Surrey's "The Soote
Season" p. 421).

Allusion A figure of speech that
echoes or makes brief reference to a literary or artistic work or a historical
figure, event, or object, as, for example,
the references to Lazarus and Hamlet
in "The Love Song of J. Alfred Prufrock"
(p. 516). It is usually a way of placing
one's poem within or alongside a context that is evoked in a very economical
fashion. See also **intertextuality**.

Alternative theater Any theater—
most often political or experimental—
that sets itself up in opposition to the
conventions of the mainstream theater
of its time.

Ambiguity In expository prose, an
undesirable doubtfulness or uncertainty
of meaning or intention resulting from
imprecision in the use of one's words or
the construction of one's sentences. In
poetry, the desirable condition of admitting more than one possible meaning
resulting from the capacity of language
to function on levels other than the
literal. Related terms sometimes employed are *ambivalence* and *polysemy*.

Anagnorisis A significant recognition or discovery by a character, usually the **protagonist,** that moves the
plot forward by changing the circumstances of a play.

Anapest A metrical **foot** consisting
of three syllables, with two unaccented
syllables followed by an accented one
(˘˘´). In *anapestic meter*, anapests are
the predominant foot in a line or
poem. The following line from William
Cowper's "The Poplar Field" is in ana-
pestic meter: "Ănd thĕ whĭs | pĕrĭng
soúnd | ŏf thĕ cóol | cŏlŏnnáde."

Anaphora Repetition of the same
word or words at the beginning of two
or more lines, clauses, or sentences.
Walt Whitman employs anaphora ex-
tensively in "Song of Myself" (p. 470).

Antagonist The character (or, less
often, the force) that opposes the
protagonist.

Anticlimax In drama, a disappoint-
ingly trivial occurrence where a **climax**
would usually happen. An anticlimax
can achieve comic effect or disrupt
audience expectations of dramatic
structure. In poetry, an anticlimax is an
arrangement of details such that one of
lesser importance follows one or ones of
greater importance, where something
of greater significance is expected. A
well-known example is "Not louder
shrieks to pitying heaven are cast, /
When husbands die, or when lapdogs
breathe their last" (Alexander Pope, *The
Rape of the Lock*).

Antihero, antiheroine A character
playing a hero's part but lacking the

grandeur typically associated with a hero. Such a character may be comic or may exist to force the audience to reconsider its notions of heroism.

Antistrophe The second part of a choral ode in Greek drama. The antistrophe was traditionally sung as the chorus moved from stage left to stage right.

Antithesis A figure of speech in which contrasting words, sentences, or ideas are expressed in balanced, parallel grammatical structures. "She had some horses she loved. / She had some horses she hated," from Joy Harjo's "She Had Some Horses" (p. 621), illustrates antithesis.

Apostrophe A figure of speech in which an absent person, an abstract quality, or a nonhuman entity is addressed as though present. It is a particular type of personification. See, for example, Ben Jonson's "On My First Son" (p. 433) and Allen Ginsberg's "A Supermarket in California" (p. 551).

Approximate rhyme See **slant rhyme**.

Archetype An image, symbol, character type, or plot line that occurs frequently enough in literature, religion, myths, folktales, and fairy tales to be recognizable as an element of universal experience and that evokes a deep emotional response.

Aside A brief bit of dialogue spoken by a character to the audience or to him- or herself and assumed to be unheard by other characters onstage.

Assonance The repetition of identical or similar vowel sounds in words relatively near to one another (usually within a line or in adjacent lines) whose consonant sounds differ.

Aubade A dawn song, ordinarily expressing two lovers' regret that day has come and they must separate.

Ballad A poem that tells a story and was meant to be recited or sung; originally, a folk art transmitted orally, from person to person and from generation to generation. Many of the popular ballads were not written down and published until the eighteenth century, though their origins may have been centuries earlier. "Barbara Allen" (p. 419) is a popular Scottish ballad.

Ballad stanza A quatrain in iambic meter rhyming *abcb* with (usually) four feet in the first and third lines, three in the second and fourth. Ballad stanzas are nearly identical to common meter, though ballad stanzas usually have a more conversational, narrative-driven feel. See **common meter**.

Black comedy A type of comedy in which the traditional material of tragedy (that is, suffering, or even death) is staged to provoke laughter.

Blank verse Lines of unrhymed iambic pentameter. Blank verse is the most widely used verse form of poetry in English because it is closest to the natural rhythms of English speech. Shakespeare's plays, as well as Milton's *Paradise Lost* and *Paradise Regained*, and countless other long poems were composed in blank verse because it is well suited to narrative, dialogue, and reflection. Wordsworth's "Tintern Abbey" (p. 448) starts out as regular blank verse and then moves to a modified, less regular adaptation of blank verse.

Blocking The process of determining the stage positions, movement, and groupings of actors. Blocking generally is proposed in rehearsal by the director and may be negotiated and reworked by the actors themselves.

Brainstorming An information-gathering process in which a group or an individual writes down any and all ideas that come to mind regarding the topic of a given paper or project. The list is later fine-tuned during the organizing stage of the project.

Caesura A pause or break within a line of verse, usually signaled by a mark of punctuation.

Canon The group of literary works that form the backbone of a cultural tradition.

Carpe diem A Latin phrase from an ode by Horace meaning "seize the day." It became the label for a theme common in literature, especially in sixteenth- and seventeenth-century English love poetry, that life is short and fleeting and that therefore one must make the most of present pleasures. See Robert Herrick's "To the Virgins, to Make Much of Time" (p. 434) and Andrew Marvell's "To His Coy Mistress" (p. 439).

Catastrophe The final event of a **tragedy**, which brings about the fall or death of the **protagonist**. In plays other than classical tragedy, a **denouement** takes the place of a catastrophe.

Catharsis A purging of the emotions of pity and fear. Aristotle argued in *Poetics* that catharsis is the natural, and beneficial, outcome of viewing a **tragedy**.

Cento A poetic collage in which each line of the poem has been borrowed from another source. For example, in John Ashbery's "They Knew What They Wanted" (p. 554), each line of the poem is comprised of a movie title that begins with the word "they."

Characters, characterization Broadly speaking, characters are usually the people of a work of literature—although characters may be animals or some other beings. In fiction, characterization means the development of a character or characters throughout a story. Characterization includes the narrator's description of what characters look like and what they think, say, and do (these are sometimes very dissimilar). Their own actions and views of themselves, and other characters' views of and behavior toward them, are also means of characterization. Characters may be minor, like Goody Cloyse, or major, like Goodman Brown, both of Hawthorne's "Young Goodman Brown" (p. 3). Depending on the depth of characterization, a character may be simple or complex, flat or round. Character is one of the six **elements of drama** identified by Aristotle, and characterization is the process by which writers and actors make a character distinct and believable to an audience.

Chaucerian stanza A seven-line iambic stanza rhyming *ababbcc*, sometimes having an **alexandrine** (hexameter) closing line.

Chorus In classical Greek theater, a group of actors who perform in the **orchestra** and whose functions might include providing **exposition**, confronting or questioning the **protagonist**, and commenting on the action of the play. Much of the **spectacle** of Greek drama lay in the chorus's singing and dancing. In theater of other times and places, particularly that of the Renaissance, the functions of the Greek chorus are sometimes given to a single character identified as "Chorus."

Cliché A word that comes from the French verb *clicher*, "to stamp." A cliché is any phrase that feels pat, overused, or too familiar. Occasionally, writers will challenge an inherited cliché to create surprise; for example, see Kay Ryan's "Drops in the Bucket" (p. 599).

Climax In drama, the turning point at which a play switches from **rising action** to **falling action**. In fiction, the moment of greatest intensity and conflict in the action of a story. In Nathaniel Hawthorne's "Young Goodman Brown" (p. 3), events reach their climax when Brown and his wife stand together in the forest, at the point of conversion.

Closed form Any structural pattern or repetition of meter, rhyme, or stanza. Cf. **open form**.

Comedy Originally, any play that ended with the characters in a better condition than when the play began, though the term is now used more frequently to describe a play intended to be funny. Traditional comedy is generally distinguished by low or ordinary characters (as opposed to the great men and women of tragedy), a humble style, a series of events or role reversals that create chaos and upheaval, and a conclusion or

denouement that marks a return to normalcy and often a reintegration into society (such as with a wedding or other formal celebration).

Comic relief A funny scene or character appearing in an otherwise serious play, intended to provide the audience with a momentary break from the heavier themes of tragedy.

Common meter A poetic meter that features four lines that alternate between iambic tetrameter and iambic trimeter. It's a form that Emily Dickinson used in her poems featured in this anthology.

Complication One of the traditional elements of **plot**. Complication occurs when someone or something opposes the **protagonist**.

Compression The dropping of a syllable to make a line fit the meter, sometimes marked with an apostrophe (e.g., William Shakespeare, Sonnet 73 [p. 426], line 13: "This thou perceiv'st"). Another common device is *elision*, the dropping of a vowel at the beginning or end of a word (e.g., in lines 7 and 28 of John Donne's "A Valediction: Forbidding Mourning" [p. 431]: "'Twere profanation of our joys" and "To move, but doth, if th' other do").

Conceit A figure of speech that establishes a striking or far-fetched analogy between seemingly very dissimilar things, either the exaggerated, unrealistic comparisons found in love poems (such as in Shakespeare's Sonnet 18 [p. 426] or the complex analogies of metaphysical wit (as in John Donne's "A Valediction: Forbidding Mourning" [p. 431]).

Concrete language Any specific, physical language that appeals to one or more of the senses—sight, hearing, taste, smell, or touch. *Stones, chairs,* and *hands* are concrete words. Concrete language is the opposite of **abstract language**. Both types are important features of an author's style.

Concrete poem A poem shaped in the form of the object the poem describes or discusses. See, for example, George Herbert's "Easter-wings" (p. 435).

Confessional poetry Poetry about personal, private issues in which a poet usually speaks directly, without the use of a **persona**. See, for example, Robert Lowell's "Skunk Hour" (p. 543) and Sylvia Plath's "Daddy" (p. 567).

Conflict Antagonism between characters, ideas, or lines of action; between a character and the outside world; or between different aspects of a character's nature. Conflict is essential in a traditional plot, as in the conflict between Montresor and Fortunato in Edgar Allan Poe's "The Cask of Amontillado" (p. 14).

Connotation The range of emotional implications and associations a word may carry outside of its dictionary definitions. Cf. **denotation**.

Consonance The repetition of consonant sounds in words whose vowels are different. In perfect consonance, all consonants are the same—*live, love; chitter, chatter; reader, rider;* words in which all consonants following the main vowels are identical also are considered consonant—*dive, love; swatter, chitter; sound, bond; gate, mat; set, pit.*

Convention An unstated rule, code, practice, or characteristic established by usage. In drama, tacit acceptance of theatrical conventions prevents the audience from being distracted by unrealistic features that are necessarily part of any theater experience. Greek audiences, for instance, accepted the convention of the **chorus**, while today's audiences readily accept the convention of the **fourth wall** in realistic drama and of songs in musical comedy.

Couplet Two consecutive lines of poetry with the same **end-rhyme**. English (Shakespearean) **sonnets** end with a couplet; for an entire poem in tetrameter couplets, see Andrew Marvell's "To His Coy Mistress" (p. 439). See also **heroic couplets**.

Cultural context The milieu that gives rise to a work of literature.

Cultural studies A general name given to a wide variety of critical practices that examine and challenge why certain texts are privileged in our society while others are dismissed or derided. Rather than focusing on traditional literary objects, cultural studies critics might choose to study movies, television shows, advertisements, graffiti, or comic books, often in conjunction with **canonical** works of literature.

Dactyl A metrical foot consisting of three syllables, an accented one followed by two unaccented ones ($-\smile\smile$). In dactylic meter, dactyls are the predominant foot of a line or poem. The following lines from Thomas Hardy's "The Voice" are in dactylic meter: "Wómăn mŭch | mĭssed, hŏw yŏu | cáll tŏ mĕ, | cáll tŏ mĕ, / Sáyĭng th̆at | nów yŏu ăre | nót ăs yŏu | wére."

Deconstruction A variety of post-structuralism, deconstruction derives from the efforts of Jacques Derrida to undermine the foundations of Western philosophy, but as a literary critical practice it often emerges as a kind of close-reading that reveals irreconcilable linguistic contradictions in a text that prevents it from having a single stable meaning or message.

Denotation The basic meaning of a word; its dictionary definition(s).

Denouement Literally, "unknotting." The end of a play or other literary work, in which all elements of the plot are brought to their conclusion.

Description Language that presents specific features of a character, object, or setting; or the details of an action or event. The first paragraph of Franz Kafka's "The Metamorphosis" (p. 90) describes Gregor's startling new appearance.

Deus ex machina Literally, "god out of the machine," referring to the mechanized system used to lower an actor playing a god onto the stage in classical Greek drama. Today the term is generally used disparagingly to indicate careless plotting and an unbelievable resolution in a play.

Dialogue Words spoken by characters, often in the form of a conversation between two or more characters. In stories and other forms of prose, dialogue is commonly enclosed between quotation marks. Dialogue is an important element in characterization and plot: much of the characterization and action in Ernest Hemingway's "Hills Like White Elephants" (p. 176) is presented through its characters' dialogue.

Diction A writer's selection of words; the kind of words, phrases, and figurative language used to make up a work of literature. In fiction, particular patterns or arrangements of words in sentences and paragraphs constitute prose style. Hemingway's diction is said to be precise, concrete, and economical. Aristotle identified diction as one of the six elements of drama. See also poetic diction.

Dimeter A line of verse consisting of two metrical feet.

Double rhyme A rhyme in which an accented, rhyming syllable is followed by one or more identical, unstressed syllables: *thrilling* and *killing*, *marry* and *tarry*. Formerly known as "feminine rhyme."

Downstage The part of the stage closest to the audience.

Dramatic irony A situation in which a reader or an audience knows more than the speakers or characters, about either the outcome of events or a discrepancy between a meaning intended by a speaker or character and that recognized by the reader or audience.

Dramatic monologue A poem with only one speaker, overheard in a dramatic moment (usually addressing another character or characters who do not speak), whose words reveal what is going on in the scene and expose significant depths of the speaker's temperament, attitudes, and values. See Robert Browning's "My Last Duchess" (p. 468) and T. S. Eliot's "The Love Song of J. Alfred Prufrock" (p. 516).

Ekphrasis A description of a work of art. Sometimes the description can provide a depiction of an art object; sometimes it engages or argues with the object; sometimes it ventriloquizes the voice of the object, or perhaps sets a narrative in motion. For example, see W. H. Auden's "Musée des Beaux Arts" (p. 531).

Elegy In Greek and Roman literature, a serious, meditative poem written in "elegiac meter" (alternating hexameter and pentameter lines); since the 1600s, a sustained and formal poem lamenting the death of a particular person, usually ending with a consolation, or one setting forth meditations on death or another solemn theme. See Thomas Gray's "Elegy Written in a Country Churchyard" (p. 442). The adjective *elegiac* is also used to describe a general tone of sadness or a worldview that emphasizes suffering and loss.

Elements of drama The six features identified by Aristotle in *Poetics* as descriptive of and necessary to drama. They are, in order of the importance assigned to them by Aristotle, **plot, characterization, theme, diction, melody**, and **spectacle**.

Elements of fiction Major elements of fiction are **plot, characters, setting, point of view, style**, and **theme**. Skillful employment of these entities is essential in effective novels and stories. From beginning to end, each element is active and relates to the others dynamically.

Elements of poetry Verbal, aural, and structural features of poetry, including **diction, tone, images, figures of speech, symbols, rhythm, rhyme**, and poetic **form**, which are combined to create poems.

Elision See **compression**.

Empathy The ability of the audience to relate to, even experience, the emotions of characters onstage or in a text.

End-rhyme Rhyme occurring at the ends of lines in a poem.

End-stopped line A line of poetry whose grammatical structure and thought reach completion by its end. Cf. **run-on line**.

English sonnet A sonnet consisting of three quatrains (three four-line units, typically rhyming *abab cdcd efef*) and a couplet (two rhyming lines). Usually, the subject is introduced in the first quatrain, expanded in the second, and expanded still further in the third; the couplet adds a logical, pithy conclusion or introduces a surprising twist. Also called the *Shakespearean sonnet*.

Enjambment See **run-on line**.

Epic A long narrative poem that celebrates the achievements of great heroes and heroines, often determining the fate of a tribe or nation, written in formal language and an elevated style. Examples include Homer's *Iliad* and *Odyssey*, Virgil's *Aeneid*, and John Milton's *Paradise Lost*.

Epigram Originally, an inscription, especially an epitaph; in modern usage, a short poem, usually polished and witty with a surprising twist at the end. (Its other dictionary definition, "any terse, witty, pointed statement," generally does not apply in poetry.)

Epigraph In literature, a quotation at the beginning of a poem or on the title page or the beginning of a chapter in a book. See the epigraph from Dante's *Inferno* at the beginning of T. S. Eliot's "The Love Song of J. Alfred Prufrock" (p. 516).

Epiphany An appearance or manifestation, especially of a divine being; in literature, since James Joyce adapted the term to secular use in 1944, a sudden sense of radiance and revelation one may feel while perceiving a commonplace object; a moment or event in which the essential nature of a person, a situation, or an object is suddenly perceived, as at the end of Joyce's "Araby" (p. 85).

Episode In Greek drama, the scenes of dialogue that occur between the choral **odes**. Now the term is used to mean any small unit of drama that has its own completeness and internal unity.

Epistolary Any poem that takes the form of a written letter. For example, see William Carlos Williams's "This Is Just to Say" (p. 511).

Erasure The process by which a poet selects a nonpoetic text and "erases" words and phrases until a poem emerges. For example, see Jen Bervin's erasure of Shakespeare's "Sonnet 64" (p. 668) and Solmaz Sharif's "Reaching Guantánamo" (p. 680).

Exact rhyme Rhyme in which all sounds following the vowel sound are the same: *spite* and *night*, *art* and *heart*, *ache* and *fake*, *card* and *barred*.

Exaggeration See **hyperbole**.

Explication The process of making clear that which is implicit or subtle in a work of literature. This is achieved by performing a close-reading—reading a piece of literature with an eye toward such sentence-level elements as sentence structure, style, imagery, word choice, and figurative language—and then explaining the larger purpose and effect of those elements.

Exposition A means of filling in the audience on events that occurred offstage or before the play's beginning. Clumsily handled exposition, in which characters talk at length about things they normally would not, is characteristic of much bad drama.

Falling action The action after the **climax** in a traditionally structured play whereby the tension lessens and the play moves toward the **catastrophe** or **denouement**.

Falling meter Meter using a **foot** (usually a trochee or a dactyl) in which the first syllable is accented and those that follow are unaccented, giving a sense of stepping down. Cf. **rising meter**.

Feminine rhyme See **double rhyme**.

Feminist criticism A school of literary criticism that examines the roles of women in literature and culture as well as the relationships between men and women. Contemporary feminist criticism rose to prominence in the 1970s, when the modern feminist movement began to explore the patriarchal structures in which many women felt trapped. Some feminist critics seek to show the ways in which literary texts demonstrate the repression and powerlessness of women—or, alternately, to show how female literary characters could overcome sexist power structures. Still others seek to rediscover and promote writing by women whose works have been excluded from the mostly male **canon** of "great" literature.

Feminist theater   Any play or theater whose primary object is to shine light on the issues of women's rights and sexism.

Fiction   Generally speaking, any imaginative, usually prose, work of literature. More narrowly, narratives — **short stories**, **novellas**, or **novels** — whose plots, characters, and settings are constructions of its writer's imagination, which draws on the writer's experiences and reflections.

Figurative language   Uses of language — employing **metaphor** or **simile** or other figures of speech — that depart from standard or literal usage in order to achieve a special effect or meaning. Figurative language is often employed in poetry; although less often seen in plays and stories, it can be used powerfully in those forms. Alice Walker's "Everyday Use" (p. 310) opens with a figurative description of the family's yard.

First-person narrator   In a story told by one person, the "I" who tells the story. Sometimes the first-person narrator is purely an observer; more often he or she is directly or indirectly involved in the action of the story. Montresor is the first-person narrator of, and one of two characters in, Edgar Allan Poe's "The Cask of Amontillado" (p. 14). As a first-person narrator, he reveals much about his own emotions and motivations.

Fixed form   Poetry written in definite, repeating patterns of line, rhyme scheme, or stanza.

Flashback   A writer's way of introducing important earlier material. As a narrator tells a story, he or she may stop the flow of events and direct the reader to an earlier time. Sometimes the narrator may return to the present, sometimes remain in the past. The narrator in William Faulkner's "A Rose for Emily" (p. 168) uses flashbacks to depict the events leading up to Emily Grierson's death.

Foil   A character who exists chiefly to set off or display, usually by opposition, the important character traits of the **protagonist** or another important person.

Foot   The basic unit in metrical verse, comprising (usually) one stressed syllable and one or more unstressed syllables. See also **anapest**, **dactyl**, **iamb**, **spondee**, and **trochee**.

Foreshadowing   Words, gestures, or other actions that suggest future events or outcomes. The opening of Nathaniel Hawthorne's "Young Goodman Brown" (p. 3) foreshadows serious trouble ahead when Faith, Brown's wife, begs him to stay home with her "this night, dear husband, of all nights in the year."

Form   (1) Genre or literary type (e.g., the lyric form); (2) patterns of meter, lines, and rhymes (stanzaic form); (3) the organization of the parts of a literary work in relation to its total effect (e.g., "The form [structure] of this poem is very effective").

Formalism   A broad term for the various types of literary theory that advocate focusing attention on the text itself and not on extratextual factors.

Formalist critics are interested in the formal elements of a literary text—structure, tone, characters, setting, symbols, linguistic features—and seek to create meaning by examining the relationships between these different parts of a text.

Found poem Any poem that is "found" in nonliterary material. For example, see Aimee Nezhukumatathil's "Dear Amy Nehzooukammyatootill," (p. 670).

Fourth wall The theatrical convention, dating from the nineteenth century, whereby an audience seems to be looking and listening through an invisible fourth wall, usually into a room in a private residence. The fourth wall is primarily associated with **realism** and domestic dramas.

Free indirect discourse In fiction, the technique by which an omniscient narrator can slip into the voice and/or thoughts of a character without explicitly announcing that slip. For example, notice those moments when, in Richard Wright's "The Man Who Was Almost a Man" (p. 180), the narrator slips into the thoughts and feelings of Dave, the main character.

Free verse See **open form**.

Gender criticism A broad term for literary criticism that highlights gender roles or relationships between the sexes. In this expansive sense, **feminist criticism** is a kind of gender criticism, although the latter term is most often applied to gay and lesbian approaches to literature that explore the construction of sexual identity.

Genre A type or form of literature. While the major literary genres are **fiction, drama, poetry,** and exposition, many other subcategories of genres are recognized, including **comedy, tragedy, tragicomedy, romance, melodrama, epic, lyric, pastoral, novel, short story,** and so on.

Ghazal A centuries-old poetic form that evolved in Persia and has become enormously popular across the world. It consists of a series of self-enclosed couplets that resist narrative, all of which end with the same word (called the *radif*). The final couplet includes a proper name—usually the poet's. For an example, see Agha Shahid Ali's "Even the Rain" (p. 615).

Half rhyme See **slant rhyme**.

Hero, heroine Sometimes used to refer to any **protagonist**, the term more properly applies only to a great figure from legend or history or to a character who performs in a remarkably honorable and selfless manner.

Heroic couplets Couplets in **iambic pentameter** that usually end in a period. See Maxine Kumin's "Morning Swim" (p. 546). Also called *closed couplets*.

Hexameter A poetic line with six metrical feet. See also **alexandrine**.

Historical criticism A kind of literary criticism based on the notion that history and literature are often interrelated. For example, literary critics might read history books and various sorts of historical documents in order to gain insights into the composition and significance of a literary work.

Hubris An arrogance or inflated sense of self that can lead to a character's downfall. The **protagonists** of **tragedy** often suffer from hubris.

Hyperbole Exaggeration; a figure of speech in which something is stated more strongly than is logically warranted. Hyperbole is often used to make a point emphatically.

Iamb A metrical **foot** consisting of two syllables, an unaccented one followed by an accented one (⌣´). In iambic meter (the most widely used of English metrical forms), iambs are the predominant foot in a line or poem. The following line from Thomas Gray's "Elegy Written in a Country Churchyard" (p. 442) is in **iambic pentameter**: "The cúr | fĕw tólls | thĕ kńell | ŏf párt | ĭng dáy." See **pentameter**.

Image (1) Sometimes called a "word-picture," an image is a word or group of words that refers to a sensory experience or to an object that can be known by one or more of the senses. **Imagery** signifies all such language in a poem or other literary work collectively and can involve any of the senses; see, for example, the narrator's description of the girl he loves in James Joyce's "Araby" (p. 85): "The light from the lamp opposite our door caught the white curve of her neck, lit up her hair that rested there and, falling, lit up the hand upon the railing." See also **synesthesia**. (2) A metaphor or other comparison. **Imagery** in this sense refers to the characteristic that several images in a poem may have in common, as for example, the Christian imagery in William Blake's "The Lamb" (p. 446).

Imitation Since Aristotle, drama has been differentiated from fiction because it is said to rely on an imitation (in Greek, *mimesis*) of human actions rather than on a narration of them.

Interlude A brief, usually comic, performance inserted between the acts of a play or between courses at a formal banquet. Interludes were most popular during the Renaissance.

Internal rhyme Rhyme that occurs with words within a line, words within lines near each other, or a word within a line and one at the end of the same or a nearby line. Edgar Allan Poe's "Annabel Lee" (p. 464) offers many examples: "chilling / And killing," "Can ever dissever," "And the stars never rise but I see the bright eyes."

Intertextuality The implied presence of previous texts within a literary work or as context, usually conveyed through allusion or choice of genre. An intertextual approach assumes that interpretation of a text is incomplete until the relation of the work to its predecessors—response, opposition, and development—has been considered.

Irony A feeling, tone, mood, or attitude arising from the awareness that what *is* (reality) is opposite from, and usually worse than, what *seems* to be (appearance). What a person says may be ironic (see **verbal irony**), and a discrepancy between what a character knows or means and what a reader or an audience knows can be ironic (see **dramatic irony**). A general situation also can be seen as ironic (see **situational irony**). Irony should not be confused with mere coincidence. See also **Socratic irony**.

Italian sonnet Generally speaking, a sonnet composed of an octave (an eight-line unit), rhyming *abbaabba*, and a sestet (a six-line unit), often rhyming *cdecde* or *cdcdcd*. The octave usually develops an idea, question, or problem; then the poem pauses, or "turns," and the sestet completes the idea, answers the question, or resolves the difficulty. Sometimes called a Petrarchan sonnet. See Gerard Manley Hopkins's "God's Grandeur" (p. 497).

Juxtaposition Placement of things side by side or close together for comparison or contrast, or to create something new from the union.

Line A sequence of words printed as a separate entity on a page; the basic structural unit in a poem (except in **prose poems**).

Lineation The arrangement of lines in a poem.

Literal In accordance with the primary or strict meaning of a word or words; not figurative or metaphorical.

Litotes See **understatement**.

Lyric Originally, a poem sung to the accompaniment of a lyre; now a short poem expressing the personal emotion and ideas of a single speaker.

Marxist criticism Deriving from Karl Marx's theories of economics and class struggle, Marxist criticism sees literature as a material product of work, one that reflects or contests the ideologies that generated its production and consumption.

Masculine rhyme See **single rhyme**.

Melody One of the six elements of drama identified by Aristotle. Since the Greek chorus communicated through song and dance, melody was an important part of even the most serious play, though it is now largely confined to musical comedy.

Metaphor A figure of speech in which two things usually thought to be dissimilar are treated as if they were alike and have characteristics in common: "[Love] is the star to every wandering bark,/Whose worth's unknown, although his height be taken [...]" (William Shakespeare's "Sonnet 116," p. 427).

Metaphysical poetry The work of a number of seventeenth-century poets that was characterized by philosophical subtlety and intellectual rigor; subtle, often outrageous logic; an imitation of actual speech sometimes resulting in a "rough" meter and style; and far-fetched analogies. John Donne's "A Valediction: Forbidding Mourning" (p. 431) exemplifies the type. See also **conceit**.

Meter A steady beat, or measured pulse, created by a repeating pattern of accents or syllables, or both.

Metonymy A figure of speech in which the name of one thing is substituted for something closely associated with it, as in "The *White House* announced today . . . ," a phrase in which the name of a building is substituted for the president or the staff members who issued the announcement; "He's got *a Constable* on his wall"; "The *trains* are on strike"; or "*Wall Street* is in a panic."

Monometer   A poetic line with one metrical **foot**.

Motivation   What drives a character to act in a particular way. To be convincing to an audience, an actor must understand and make clear to the audience the character's motivation.

Narrative   A story in prose or verse; an account of events involving characters and a sequence of events told by a storyteller (narrator). A poem such as Naomi Shihab Nye's "Gate A–4" (p. 629) tells a story and is thus a **narrative poem**. Usually, the characters can be analyzed and generally understood; the events unfold in a cause-and-effect sequence; and some unity can be found among the characters, plot, point of view, style, and theme. Novels as well as stories are most often narratives, and journalism commonly employs narrative form.

Narrative poem   See **narrative**.

Narrator   The storyteller, usually an observer who is narrating from a third-person point of view or a participant in the story's action speaking in the first person. Style and tone are important clues to the nature of a narrator and the validity and objectivity of the story he or she is telling. Montresor, the narrator of Edgar Allan Poe's "The Cask of Amontillado" (p. 14), creates his own self-portrait as he relates what has happened.

Naturalism, naturalistic   A style of writing or acting meant to mimic closely the patterns of ordinary life.

Near rhyme   See **slant rhyme**.

New comedy   An ancient form of comedy that told of initially forbidden but ultimately successful love and that employed **stock characters**. New comedy is particularly associated with the Greek playwright Menander (342–292 BCE).

New Criticism   A kind of **formalism** that dominated Anglo-American literary criticism in the middle decades of the twentieth century. It emphasized close-reading, particularly of poetry, to discover how a work of literature functioned as a self-contained, self-referential aesthetic object.

New Historicism   A school of **historical criticism** that takes account of both what history has to teach us about literature *and* what literature has to teach us about history. New Historicists examine many different types of texts—government records, periodicals, private diaries, bills of sale—in order to re-create, as much as possible, the rich cultural context that surrounded both an author and that author's original audience.

Novel   An extended prose narrative or work of prose fiction, usually published alone. Nathaniel Hawthorne's *The Scarlet Letter* is a fairly short novel, Herman Melville's *Moby-Dick, or, The Whale* a very long one. The length of a novel enables its author to develop characters, plot, and settings in greater detail than a short-story writer can. Ralph Ellison's story "Battle Royal" (p. 203) is taken from his novel *Invisible Man* (1948).

Novella   A work of prose fiction that falls between the short story and the novel in size and complexity. Sometimes it is called a long short story. Franz Kafka's "The Metamorphosis" (p. 90) is a novella.

Octameter   A poetic line with eight metrical feet.

Octave The first eight lines of an Italian sonnet.

Ode (1) A multipart song sung by the chorus of Greek drama. A classical ode consists of a strophe followed by an antistrophe and sometimes by a final section called the *epode*. (2) A long lyric poem, serious (often intellectual) in tone, elevated and dignified in style, dealing with a single theme. The ode is generally more complicated in form than other lyric poems. Some odes retain a formal division into strophe, antistrophe, and epode, which reflects the form's origins in Greek tragedy.

Omniscient narrator A narrator who seems to know everything about a story's events and characters, even their inner feelings. Usually, an omniscient narrator maintains emotional distance from the characters. See Jhumpa Lahiri's "A Temporary Matter" (p. 388).

One act A short play that is complete in one act.

Onomatopoeia The use of words whose sounds supposedly resemble the sounds they denote (such as *thump*, *rattle*, *growl*, *hiss*), or a group of words whose sounds help to convey what is being described; for example, Emily Dickinson's "I heard a Fly buzz — when I died" (p. 492).

Open form A form free of any predetermined metrical and stanzaic patterns. Cf. **closed form**.

Orchestra In Greek theater, the area in front of the stage proper where the chorus performed its songs and dances. Later, a pit for musicians in front of the stage.

Organic form The idea, grounded in Plato and strong since the nineteenth century, that subject, **theme**, and **form** are essentially one, that a work "grows" from a central concept. A contrary idea, that literary works are unstable and irregular because of changes in linguistic meanings and literary conventions, has led to a critical approach called **deconstruction**.

Paradox A figure of speech in which a statement initially seeming self-contradictory or absurd turns out, seen in another light, to make good sense. The closing line of John Donne's sonnet "Death, be not proud" (p. 432) contains a paradox: "Death, thou shalt die."

Parallelism (1) A verbal arrangement in which elements of equal weight within phrases, sentences, or paragraphs are expressed in a similar grammatical order and structure. It can appear within a line or pair of lines ("And he was always quietly arrayed, / And he was always human when he talked"—Edwin Arlington Robinson, "Richard Cory" [p. 502]) or, more noticeably, as a series of parallel items, as found in Langston Hughes's "Harlem" (p. 528). (2) A principle of poetic structure in which consecutive lines in **open form** are related by a line's repeating, expanding on, or contrasting with the idea of the line or lines before it, as in the poems of Walt Whitman (pp. 470–90).

Paraphrase To restate a passage of literature or criticism in your own words, particularly useful as a method for taking research notes, or for interpreting a text. Generally, a paraphrase will be about equal in length to the passage being paraphrased, while a **summary** will be much shorter.

Pastoral A poem (also called an *eclogue*, a *bucolic*, or an *idyll*) that expresses a city poet's nostalgic image of the simple, peaceful life of shepherds and other country folk in an idealized natural setting. Christopher Marlowe's "The Passionate Shepherd to His Love" (p. 424) uses some pastoral conventions, as do certain elegies.

Pause See caesura.

Pentameter A poetic line with five metrical feet.

Peripeteia A reversal or change of fortune for a character, for better or worse.

Persona Literally, the mask through which actors spoke in Greek plays. In some critical approaches of recent decades, *persona* refers to the "character" projected by an author, the "I" of a narrative poem or novel, or the speaker whose voice is heard in a lyric poem. In this view, a poem is an artificial construct distanced from a poet's autobiographical self. Cf. voice.

Personification A figure of speech in which something nonhuman is treated as if it had human characteristics or performed human actions. Sometimes it involves abstractions, as in Thomas Gray's phrase "Fair Science frowned" ("Elegy Written in a Country Churchyard," p. 442); science cannot literally frown.

Petrarchan sonnet See Italian sonnet.

Plagiarism The act of closely imitating or outright adopting the language or ideas of another author and presenting them as one's own work without giving credit to the original author. This includes copying and pasting from any Web source. Most colleges and universities have codes of academic honesty forbidding such practices and imposing severe penalties—including expulsion from the institution in some cases—on students who are caught breaking them.

Plot (1) The sequence of major events in a story, usually related by cause and effect. **Plot development** refers to how the sequence evolves or is shaped. Plot and character are intimately related, since characters carry out the plot's action. Plots may be described as simple or complex, depending on their degree of complication. "Traditional" writers, such as Edgar Allan Poe, usually plot their stories tightly; modernist writers such as James Joyce employ looser, often ambiguous plots. (2) The action that takes place within the play. Of the six **elements of drama**, Aristotle considered plot to be the most important. Typical elements of plot include a **prologue** or **exposition, rising action, complication, climax, falling action,** and **catastrophe** or **denouement.**

Plot development See plot.

Poem A term whose meaning exceeds all attempts at definition. Here is a slightly modified version of the definition of William Harmon and C. Hugh Holman in *A Handbook to Literature* (1996): A poem is a literary composition, written or oral, typically characterized by imagination, emotion, sense impressions, and concrete language that invites attention to its own physical features, such as sound or appearance on the page.

Poetic diction   In general, specialized language used in or considered appropriate to poetry. In the late seventeenth and the eighteenth centuries, a refined use of language that excluded "common" speech from poetry as indecorous and substituted elevated circumlocutions, archaic synonyms, or such forms as *ope* and *e'er*.

Point of view   One of the elements of fiction, point of view is the perspective, or angle of vision, from which a narrator presents a story. Point of view tells us about the **narrator** as well as about the characters, setting, and theme of a story. Two common points of view are *first-person narration* and *third-person narration*. If a narrator speaks of himself or herself as "I," the narration is in the first person; if the narrator's self is not apparent and the story is told about others from some distance, using "he," "she," "it," and "they," then third-person narration is likely in force. The point of view may be omniscient (all-knowing) or limited, objective or subjective. When determining a story's point of view, it is helpful to decide whether the narrator is reporting events as they are happening or as they happened in the past; is observing or participating in the action; and is or is not emotionally involved. Shirley Jackson's "The Lottery" (p. 216) is told from the third-person objective point of view, since its narrator observes what the character is doing, thinking, and feeling, yet seems emotionally distant. Edgar Allan Poe's "The Cask of Amontillado" (p. 14) and James Joyce's "Araby" (p. 85) are told in the first-person subjective and limited point of view, since their narrators are very much involved in the action. In Kate Chopin's "The Story of an Hour" (p. 48), shifting points of view enable us to see Mrs. Mallard from the outside, as her family does (third-person objective); learn about her most private emotional responses and secrets (third-person subjective); and hear her thoughts directly as if we were inside her mind (first-person subjective)

Postcolonial criticism   A branch of cultural studies that focuses on writing from former British (and other, mostly European) colonies around the world. Postcolonial criticism seeks to recover literary history that was ignored or suppressed during the colonial period, and to celebrate indigenous cultures of storytelling, drama, and poetry. At the same time, it attempts to understand how occupation by a more powerful colonizing nation disrupted and changed the course of history in a particular place.

Poststructuralism   A theory positing that no text can have a fixed or real meaning because no meaning can exist outside the network of other meanings to which it is connected. It carries the insights of **structuralism** one step further. If, as structuralists claim, we can understand things only in terms of other things, then perhaps there is no center point of understanding, but only an endlessly interconnected web of ideas leading to other ideas leading to still other ideas. Meaning, then, is forever shifting and altering as our understanding of the world changes.

Primary source   Term used in writing about literature to refer to the literature itself—the poem, story, or play on which the writing is based. Cf. **secondary source.**

Properties, props Any movable objects, beyond scenery and costumes, used in the performance of a play. Early drama was performed with few props, but as theater moved toward **realism**, props took on greater importance.

Proscenium arch An arch across the front of a stage, sometimes with a curtain. The proscenium frames the action and provides a degree of separation between the actors and the audience.

Prose poem A poem printed as prose, with lines wrapping at the right margin rather than being divided through predetermined line breaks. See Carolyn Forché's "The Colonel" (p. 617).

Prosody The principles of versification, especially of meter, rhythm, rhyme, and stanza forms.

Protagonist The lead character of a play, though not necessarily a **hero** in the classic sense.

Psychological literary criticism A broad term for the various types of literary theory that focus on the inner workings of the human psyche and the ways in which they manifest themselves in literature. Psychological critics often interpret literature as a psychologist might interpret a dream or a wish, often paying special attention to unstated motives and to the unconscious states of mind in characters, authors, or readers.

Pun A play on words based on the similarity in sound between two words having very different meanings. Also called *paronomasia*. See Othello's use of puns on "lie" in *Othello* 4.1.35-36: "Lie with her! lie on her! We say lie on her, when / they belie her. Lie with her! that's fulsome."

Quatrain A **stanza** of four lines or other four-line unit within a larger form, such as a **sonnet**.

Queer theory One of the more recent and more challenging critical schools to emerge out of critical interest in gender. Queer theorists, like all literary critics, differ substantially in their focus: Some queer theorists are interested in studying literary texts written by authors known or suspected to be gay, lesbian, bisexual, or transgender. Other queer theorists are interested in portrayals of gay or lesbian characters in literature. Still others seek a "queer subtext" in canonical works of literature that have long been considered heteronormative.

Reader-response criticism The various theories of reader-response criticism hold that a text is an interaction between author and reader, and a text can never be complete unless readers bring to it their own unique insights. Reading, then, is not a passive attempt to understand a text but is itself an act of creation, no less than writing.

Realism Any drama (or other art) that seeks to closely mimic real life. Realism more specifically refers to a sort of drama that rose in opposition to **melodrama** in the late-nineteenth and early-twentieth centuries and that attempted to avoid some of the more artificial **conventions** of theater and present the problems of ordinary people living their everyday lives.

Recognition See **anagnorisis**.

Refrain   One or more identical or deliberately similar lines repeated throughout a poem, such as the final line of a stanza or a block of lines between stanzas or sections.

Resolution   A satisfying outcome that effectively ends the conflict of a play.

Rhyme   The repetition of the accented vowel sound of a word and all succeeding consonant sounds. See also **exact rhyme; slant rhyme.**

Rhyme scheme   The pattern of end-rhymes in a poem or stanza usually represented by a letter assigned to each word-sound, the same word-sounds having the same letter (e.g., a **quatrain's** rhyme scheme might be described as *abcb*).

Rhythm   The patterned "movement" of language created by the choice of words and their arrangement, usually described through such metaphors as fast or slow, smooth or halting, graceful or rough, deliberate or frenzied, syncopated or disjointed. Rhythm in poetry is affected by, in addition to meter, such factors as line length; line endings; pauses (or lack of them) within lines; spaces within, at the beginning or end of, or between lines; word choice; and combinations of sounds.

Rising action   The increasingly tense and complicated action leading up to the **climax** in a traditionally structured play.

Rising meter   A **foot** (usually an iamb or an anapest) in which the final, accented syllable is preceded by one or two unaccented syllables, thus giving a sense of stepping up. Cf. **falling meter.**

Romance   A play neither wholly comic nor wholly tragic, often containing elements of the supernatural. The best-known examples are Shakespeare's late plays, such as *The Winter's Tale* and *The Tempest*, which have a generally comic structure but are more ruminative in theme and spirit than traditional **comedy.**

Run-on line   A line whose sense and grammatical structure continue into the next line. In the following lines by William Stafford ("Traveling through the Dark," p. 539), the first line is run-on, the second end-stopped: "Traveling through the dark I found a deer / dead on the edge of the Wilson River road." Also called *enjambment.* Cf. **end-stopped line.**

Sarcasm   A harsh and cutting form of **verbal irony,** often involving apparent praise that is obviously not meant: "Oh, no, these are fine. I *prefer* my eggs thoroughly charred."

Satire   A work, or manner within a work, employing **comedy** and **irony** to mock a particular human characteristic or social institution. Generally, a satirist wants the audience not only to laugh but also to change its opinions or actions. See, for example, Margaret Atwood's "Happy Endings" (p. 300).

Scansion   The division of metrical verse into feet in order to determine and label its meter. Scanning a poem involves marking its stressed syllables with an accent mark (´) and its unstressed syllables with a curved line (˘), and using a vertical line to indicate the way a line divides into feet, then describing (or labeling) the type of foot used most often and the line length—that is, the number of feet in each line. See also **foot** and **line.**

Scene   One of the secondary divisions within an **act** of a play.

Secondary source   Outside source used in writing about literature: biographical, historical, or critical writing that discusses the literature but is not the literature itself. (The literature itself is considered a **primary source**.)

Sestet   The last six lines of an **Italian sonnet**.

Set   The stage dressing for a play, consisting of backdrops, furniture, and similar large items.

Setting   One of the elements of fiction, setting is the context for the action: the time, place, culture, and atmosphere in which it occurs. A work may have several settings; the relation among them may be significant to the meaning of the work. In Nathaniel Hawthorne's "Young Goodman Brown" (p. 3), for example, the larger setting is seventeenth-century Puritan Salem, Massachusetts, but Brown's mysterious journey is set in a forest, and its prelude and melancholy aftermath are set in the village.

Shakespearean sonnet   See **English sonnet**.

Shaped poem   See **concrete poem**.

Short story   A short work of narrative fiction whose plot, characters, settings, point of view, style, and theme reinforce one another, often in subtle ways, creating an overall unity.

Simile   Expression of a direct similarity, using such words as *like*, *as*, or *than*, between two things usually regarded as dissimilar. For example, see Mark Doty's comparison between mackerel and Tiffany lamps in "A Display of Mackerel" (p. 634). It is important to distinguish *simile* from *comparison*, in which the two things joined by "like" or "as" are *not* dissimilar.

Single rhyme   A rhyme in which the stressed, rhyming syllable is the final syllable: *west* and *vest*, *away* and *today*. Formerly called "masculine rhyme."

Slant rhyme   Consonance at the ends of lines; for example, *Room* and *Storm*, *firm* and *Room*, and *be* and *Fly* in Emily Dickinson's "I heard a Fly buzz—when I died" (p. 492). It can also be internal, if repeated enough to form a discernible pattern.

Socratic irony   A pose of self-deprecation, or of belittling oneself, in order to tease the reader into deeper insight.

Soliloquy   A speech delivered by a character who is alone onstage or otherwise out of hearing of the other characters. Since the character is effectively speaking to himself or herself, a soliloquy often serves as a window into the character's mind and heart.

Sonnet   A fourteen-line poem usually written in **iambic pentameter**; originally lyrical love poems, sonnets came to be used also for meditations on religious themes, death, and nature and are now open to all subjects. Some variations in form have been tried: Philip Sidney's "Loving in truth, and fain in verse my love to show" (423) is written in hexameters; George Meredith wrote sixteen-line sonnets; and American poet Robert Hayden abandons fixed rhyme altogether in "Those Winter Sundays" (p. 537).

Sonnet sequence A group of sonnets arranged so as to imply a narrative progression in the speaker's experience or attitudes; used especially in the sixteenth century. Also called a sonnet cycle. Marilyn Nelson's sonnet "Emmett Till's name still catches in my throat" (p. 603) is an excerpt from a sonnet sequence called *A Wreath for Emmett Till*.

Speaker The persona(e) voicing the poem. The speaker is sometimes the poet, though other times a poem may speak from a different perspective.

Spectacle The purely visual elements of a play, including the sets, costumes, props, lighting, and special effects. Of the six elements of drama he identified, Aristotle considered spectacle to be the least important.

Spondee A metrical foot made up of two stressed syllables (ˊˊ), with no unstressed syllables. Spondees could not, of course, be the predominant foot in a poem; they are usually substituted for iambic or trochaic feet as a way of increasing emphasis.

Sprung rhythm See accentual meter.

Stage directions Written instructions in the script telling actors how to move on the stage or how to deliver a particular line. To facilitate the reading of scripts and to distinguish them from simple dialogue, stage directions are interspersed throughout the text, typically placed in parentheses and set in italics.

Stage left, stage right Areas of the stage seen from the point of view of an actor facing an audience. Stage left,

therefore, is on the audience's right-hand side, and vice versa.

Stanza A grouping of poetic lines into a section, either according to form—each section having the same number of lines and the same prosody—or according to thought, creating irregular units comparable to paragraphs in prose.

Stress See accent.

Strophe The first part of a choral ode in Greek drama. The strophe was traditionally sung as the chorus moved from stage right to stage left.

Structuralism Based on the work of anthropologists, linguists, and philosophers of the mid-twentieth century who sought to understand how humans think and communicate, structuralism is concerned with the cognitive and cultural structures that help us understand and interpret literary texts. The basic insight at the heart of the movement is the realization that we understand nothing in isolation, but rather that every piece of knowledge is part of a network of associations.

Structure (1) The framework—the general plan, outline, or organizational pattern—of a literary work; (2) narrower patterns within the overall framework. Cf. form.

Style One of the elements of fiction, style refers to the diction (choice of words), syntax (arrangement of words), and other linguistic features of a literary work. Just as no two people have identical fingerprints or voices, so no two writers use words in exactly the same way. Style distinguishes one writer's language from another's. William Faulkner and

Ernest Hemingway, two major modern writers, had very different styles.

Subplot   A secondary **plot** that exists in addition to the main plot and involves the minor characters. In **tragedy**, particularly, a subplot might provide **comic relief**.

Substitution   The use of a different kind of foot in place of the one normally demanded by the predominant meter of a poem, as a way of adding variety, emphasizing the dominant foot by deviating from it, speeding up or slowing down the pace, or signaling a switch in meaning.

Subtext   The unspoken meaning, sense, or **motivation** of a scene or character.

Summary   A brief recap of the most important points in a work of literature, such as plot, character, or setting.

Surrealism   An artistic movement that attempted to portray or interpret the workings of the unconscious mind, especially as realized in dreams, by an irrational, noncontextual choice and arrangement of images or objects. Now more often used to refer to anything defying the normal sense of reality.

Syllabic verse   A metrical pattern in which all lines in a poem have the same number of **syllables** or all the first lines of its stanzas have the same number, all second lines the same, and so on—while the stressed syllables are random in number and placement.

Syllable   A unit of language consisting of one uninterrupted sound. "Ferry" (feh/ree) has two syllables, for example.

Symbol   Something that is itself and also stands for something else; a literary symbol is a prominent or repeated image or action that is present in a story, poem, or play and can be seen, touched, smelled, heard, tasted, or experienced imaginatively, but also conveys a cluster of abstract meanings beyond itself. Most critics agree that the wallpaper in Charlotte Perkins Gilman's "The Yellow Wallpaper" (p. 64) and the tiger in William Blake's "The Tyger" (p. 447), for example, carry symbolic meaning. See also **archetype**.

Symbolism   The use of objects or events to suggest meaning beyond their immediate, physical presence. Symbolism exists in all genres of literature, but in drama it might include visual or sound elements as well as language.

Synecdoche   A special kind of **metonymy** in which a part of a thing is substituted for the whole, as in the commonly used phrases "give me a hand," "lend me your ears," or "many mouths to feed."

Synesthesia   Description of one kind of sense experience in relation to another, such as attribution of color to sounds ("blue notes") and vice versa ("a loud tie") or of taste to sounds ("sweet music"). See, for example, "With Blue—uncertain stumbling Buzz—" (Emily Dickinson's "I heard a Fly buzz—when I died," p. 492).

Tercet   A **stanza** of three lines, each usually ending with the same rhyme; but see **terza rima**. Cf. **triplet**.

Terza rima   A poetic form consisting of three-line **stanzas** (**tercets**) with interlinked rhymes, *aba bcb cdc ded efe*, and so on, made famous by Dante's use of it in *The Divine Comedy*.

Tetrameter A poetic line with four metrical feet. Robert Frost's line "The woods are lovely, dark, and deep" ("Stopping by Woods on a Snowy Evening," p. 505) is an example of iambic tetrameter.

Text Traditionally, a piece of writing. In recent **reader-response criticism**, "text" has come to mean the words with which the reader interacts; in this view, a story, poem, or play is not an object, not a shape on the page or a spoken performance, but what is apprehended and completed in the reader's mind.

Theater in the round A circular stage completely surrounded by seating for the audience.

Theme The central idea embodied by or explored in a literary work; the general concept, explicit or implied, that the work incorporates and makes persuasive to the reader. Other literary elements, including characters, plot, settings, point of view, figurative language, symbols, and style, contribute to a theme's development.

Thesis statement A few sentences, usually located toward the beginning of a paper, declaring the position the author plans to take on the proposed topic.

Third-person narrator The type of narration being used if a storyteller is not identified, does not speak of himself or herself with the pronoun *I*, asserts no connection between the narrator and the characters in the story, and tells the story with some objectivity and distance, using the pronouns *he*, *she*, *it*, and *they* — but not *I*.

Title The name attached to a work of literature. For poetry, a title in some cases is an integral part of a poem and needs to be considered in interpreting it; see, for example, William Carlos Williams's "This is just to say" (p. 511). In other cases, a title has been added as a means of identifying a poem and is not integral to its interpretation. Sometimes a poem is untitled and the first line is used as a convenient way of referring to it, but should not be thought of as a title and does not follow the capitalization rules for titles.

Tone The implied attitude, or "stance," toward the subject and toward the reader or audience in a literary work; the "tone of voice" it seems to project (serious or playful; exaggerated or understated; formal or informal; ironic or straightforward; or a complex mixture of more than one of these). For example, the tone of Toni Cade Bambara's "The Lesson" (p. 304) is streetwise and tough, the voice of its first-person narrator.

Tragedy A play in which the **plot** moves from relative stability to death or other serious sorrow for the **protagonist**. A traditional tragedy is written in a grand style and shows a **hero** of high social stature brought down by **peripeteia** or by events beyond his or her control.

Tragicomedy A play in which **tragedy** and **comedy** are mingled in roughly equal proportion.

Trimeter A poetic line with three metrical feet.

Triplet A group of three consecutive lines with the same rhyme, often used for variation in a long sequence of couplets. Cf. **tercet**.

Trochee A metrical **foot** consisting of two syllables, an accented one followed by an unaccented one (ˊˇ). In trochaic meter, trochees are the predominant foot in a line or poem. The following lines from William Blake's introduction to *Songs of Innocence* (1789) are in trochaic meter (each line lacking the final unaccented syllable): "Pípǐng | dówn tȟe | vállěys | wíld, / Pípǐng | Sóngs ǒf | pléasǎnt | glée, / Ón ǎ | clóud Ǐ | sáw ǎ | chíld, / Aňd ȟe | laúghǐng | sáid tǒ | ḿe."

Understatement A figure of speech expressing something in an unexpectedly restrained way. Paradoxically, understatement can be a way of emphasizing something, of making people think "there must be more to it than that." When Mercutio in Shakespeare's *Romeo and Juliet*, after being stabbed by Tybalt, calls his wound "a scratch, a scratch" (3.1.92), he is understating, for the wound is serious—he calls for a doctor in the next line, and he dies a few minutes later.

Unities The elements of a play that help an audience understand the play as a unified whole. Aristotle commented on the unities of time (the action of a play usually takes place within approximately one day) and action (the play should have a single, principal plot line). Renaissance critics added a third unity—unity of place (the play has only one main setting). Though Aristotle intended these merely as observations about the most successful dramas he had seen, some later playwrights took them as inflexible laws of drama.

Unity The oneness of a short story. Generally, each of a story's elements has a unity of its own, and all reinforce one another to create an overall unity. Although a story's unity may be evident on first reading, more often discovering the unity requires rereading, reflection, and analysis. Readers who engage in these actions experience the pleasure of seeing a story come to life.

Upstage As a noun or an adjective, the part of the stage farthest from the audience, at the back of the playing area. As a verb, to draw the audience's attention away from another actor onstage.

Verbal irony A figure of speech in which what is said is nearly the opposite of what is meant (such as saying "Lovely day out" when the weather actually is miserable). The name *Arnold Friend*, in Joyce Carol Oates's "Where Are You Going, Where Have You Been?" (p. 286), is an example, for Arnold is anything but a friend to Connie.

Villanelle A nineteen-line lyric poem divided into five **tercets** and a final four-line stanza, rhyming *aba aba aba aba aba abaa*. Line 1 is repeated to form lines 6, 12, and 18; line 3 is repeated to form lines 9, 15, and 19. See Elizabeth Bishop's "One Art" (p. 536) and Dylan Thomas's "Do not go gentle into that good night" (p. 544).

Voice The supposed authorial presence in poems that do not obviously employ **persona** as a distancing device.

Volta The moment in which a poem, and especially a sonnet, shifts or takes a surprising turn. In a Petrarchan sonnet, the volta usually occurs between lines 8 and 9; in a Shakespearean sonnet, it usually occurs between lines 12 and 13. For example, see the shift in the final couplet in Shakespeare's "Sonnet 116" (p. 427).

Acknowledgments (Continued from page iv.)

Aboulela, Leila. "The Museum" from *Coloured Lights* by Leila Aboulela. (Polygon, 2001). Reprinted by permission of The Genert Co.

Addonizio, Kim. "First Kiss" Copyright © 2004 by Kim Addonizio. Reprinted from *What Is This Thing Called Love?*" by Kim Addonizio by permission of the author and W.W. Norton & Company, Inc.

Ai. "Hoover, Edgar, J.," Copyright © 1993 by Ai, from *Vice: New and Selected Poems* by Ai. Reprinted by permission of the author and W. W. Norton & Company, Inc.

Akhtar, Ayad. *Disgraced: A Play* by Ayad Akhtar. Copyright © 2013 by Ayad Akhtar. Reprinted by permission of Little, Brown and Company. All rights reserved.

Alexander, Elizabeth. "The Venus Hottentot" from *The Venus Hottentot*. Copyright © 1990 by the Rector and Visitors of the University of Virginia. Reprinted with the permission of The Permissions Company, Inc. on behalf of Graywolf Press, Minneapolis, MN. www .graywolfpress.org

Alexie, Sherman. "Postcards to Columbus" from *Old Shirts and New Skins*. Copyright © 1993 by Sherman Alexie. Reprinted by permission of the author. "The Lone Ranger and Tonto Fistfight in Heaven," from *The Lone Ranger and Tonto Fistfight in Heaven* by Sherman Alexie. Copyright © 1993, 2000 by Sherman Alexie. Used by permission of Grove/Atlantic, Inc.

Ali, Agha Shahid. "Even the Rain" from *Call Me Ishmael Tonight: A Book of Ghazals* by Agha Shahid Ali. Copyright © 2003 by Agha Shahid Ali Literary Trust. Used by permission of the author and W. W. Norton & Company, Inc.

Anderson, Sherwood. "Death in the Woods" reprinted by permission of Harold Ober Associates Incorporated. First published in the *American Mercury*. Copyright 1926 by Sherwood Anderson. Copyright renewed 1953 by Eleanor Copenhaver Anderson.

Ashbery, John. "They Knew What They Wanted" from *Planisphere* by John Ashbery. Copyright © 2009 by John Ashbery. Reprinted by permission of HarperCollins Publishers.

Atwood, Margaret. "Happy Endings," excerpted from *Good Bones and Simple Murders* by Margaret Atwood, copyright © 1983, 1992, 1994 by O.W. Toad Ltd. Used by permission of Nan A. Talese, an imprint of the Knopf Doubleday Publishing Group, a division of Penguin Random House LLC, and McClelland & Stewart, a division of Penguin Random House Canada Limited. All rights reserved.

Auden, W. H. "Stop All the Clocks" and "Musée des Beaux Arts," copyright © 1940 & renewed 1968 by W.H. Auden, from *W. H. Auden Collected Poems* by W.H. Auden. Used by permission of Random House, an imprint and division of Penguin Random House LLC.

Baca, Jimmy Santiago. "Family Ties" from *Black Mesa Poems*, copyright © 1989 by Jimmy Santiago Baca. Reprinted by permission of New Directions Publishing Corp.

Baldwin, James. "Sonny's Blues." Copyright © 1957 by James Baldwin was originally published in *Partisan Review*. Copyright renewed. Collected in *Going to Meet the Man*, published by Vintage Books. Reprinted by arrangement with the James Baldwin Estate.

Bambara, Toni Cade. "The Lesson" from *Gorilla, My Love* by Toni Cade Bambara. Copyright © 1972 by Toni Cade Bambara. Used by permision of Random House, an imprint and division of Penguin Random House LLC. All rights reserved.

Bervin, Jen. Excerpt from *Nets* (erasure of Shakespear's Sonnet 64) from *Nets* by Jen Bervin 2003. Reprinted by permission of the author and Ugly Duckling Presse.

Bishop, Elizabeth. "The Fish," and "One Art" from *The Complete Poems 1927-1979*. Copyright © 1979, 1983 by Alice Helen Methfessel. Reprinted by permission of Farrar, Straus and Giroux, LLC.

Boland, Eavan. "The Pomegranate" from *In a Time of Violence*. Copyright © 1994 by Eavan Boland. Used by permission of the author and W.W. Norton & Company, Inc.

Boyle, T. Coraghessan. "After the Plague" from *After the Plague: Stories* by T. Coraghessan Boyle, copyright © 2001 by T. Coraghessan Boyle. Used by permission of Viking Books, an imprint of Penguin Publishing Group, a division of Penguin Random House LLC.

Gilb, Dagoberto, "Shout" excerpt from *Woodcuts of Women* copyright © 2001 by Dagoberto Gilb. Used by permisison of Grove/Atlantic, Inc. Any third party use of this material, outside of this publication, is prohibited.

Ginsberg, Allen. All lines from "A Supermarket in California" from *Collected Poems 1947-1980* by Allen Ginsberg. Copyright © 1955 by Allen Ginsberg. Reprinted by permission of HarperCollins Publishers.

Glück, Louise. "Mock Orange" from *The First Four Books of Poems* by Louise Glück. Copyright © 1968, 1971, 1972, 1973, 1974, 1975, 1976, 1977, 1978, 1979, 1980, 1985, 1995 by Louise Glück. Reprinted by permission of HarperCollins Publishers.

Gonzalez, Ray. "Praise the Tortilla, Praise Menudo, Praise Chorizo" from *The Heat of Arrivals*. Copyright © 1996 by Ray Gonzalez. Reprinted with the permission of The Permissions Company, Inc., on behalf of BOA Editions, Ltd., www.boaeditions.org.

Graham, Jorie. "Prayer" from *Never* by Jorie Graham. Copyright © 2002 by Jorie Graham. Reprinted by permission of HarperCollins Publishers.

Hacker, Marilyn. "Villanelle." From *Selected Poems: 1965-1990*. Copyright © 1974 by Marilyn Hacker. Used by permission of W. W. Norton & Company, Inc.

Hahn, Kimiko. "Mother, Mother." From *Volatile*. Copyright © 1999 by Kimiko Hahn. Reprinted by permission of Hanging Loose Press.

Harjo, Joy. "She Had Some Horses" from *She Had Some Horses*. Copyright © 1983 by Joy Harjo. Used by permission of the author and W.W. Norton & Company, Inc.

Harper, Michael S. "Nightmare Begins Responsibility" from *Songlines in Michaeltree: New and Collected Poems* Copyright © 2000 by Michael S. Harper. Used with permission of the poet and the University of Illinois Press.

Hayden, Robert. "Those Winter Sundays." Copyright © 1966 by Robert Hayden, from *Collected Poems of Robert Hayden* by Robert Hayden, ed. by Frederick Glaysher. Used by permission of Liveright Publishing Corporation.

Hayes, Terrance. "Talk" from *Wind in a Box* by Terrance Hayes, copyright © 2006 by Terrance Hayes. Used by permission of Penguin Books, an imprint of Penguin Publishing Company, a division of Penguin Random House LLC.

Heaney, Seamus. "Mid-Term Break" and "Digging" from *Opened Ground: Selected Poems 1966-1996* by Seamus Heaney. Copyright © 1998 by Seamus Heaney. Reprinted by permission of Farrar, Straus and Giroux, LLC and Faber & Faber Ltd.

Hemingway, Ernest. "Hills Like White Elephants" reprinted with the permission of Scribner, a division of Simon & Schuster, Inc. from *Men Without Women* by Ernest Hemingway. Copyright © 1927 by Charles Scribner's Sons. Copyright renewed © 1955 by Ernest Hemingway. All rights reserved.

Hirshfield, Jane. "My Species" from *The Beauty: Poems* by Jane Hirshfield, compilation copyright © 2015 by Jane Hirshfield. Used by permission of Alfred A. Knopf, an imprint of the Knopf Doubleday Publishing Group, a division of Penguin Random House LLC. All rights reserved.

Hoagland, Tony. "History of Desire" from *Sweet Ruin*, copyright © 1992 by the Board of Regents of the University of Wisconsin System. Reprinted by permission of The University of Wisconsin Press.

Hogan, Linda. "Crow Law" from *The Book of Medicines*. Copyright © 1993 by Linda Hogan. Reprinted with the permission of The Permissions Company, Inc. on behalf of Coffee House Press, Minneapolis, Minnesota www.coffeehousepress.com

Howe, Marie. "Death, the last visit" from *The Good Thief*. Copyright © 1988 by Marie Howe. Reprinted with the permission of Persea Books, Inc. (New York), www.perseabooks.com

Hughes, Langston, "Theme for English B." and "The Weary Blues" copyright © 1994 by the Estate of Langston Hughes. "Harlem (2)," copyright © 1994 by The Estate of Langston Hughes. Both from *The Collected Poems of Langston Hughes by Langston Hughes*, edited by Arnold Rampersad with David Roessel, Associate Editor. Used by permission of

Tate, James. "The Lost Pilot" from *Selected Poems* © 1991 by James Tate. Reprinted by permisison of Wesleyan University Press.

Thomas, Dylan. "Do Not Go Gentle Into That Good Night" by Dylan Thomas, from *The Poems of Dylan Thomas*, copyright © 1952 by Dylan Thomas. Reprinted by permisison of New Directions Publishing Corp.

Trethewey, Natasha. "History Lesson" from *Domestic Work*. Copyright © 1998, 2000 by Natasha Trethewey. Reprinted with the permission of Graywolf Press, Minneapolis, Minnesota, www.graywolfpress.org

Troupe, Quincy. "A Poem for Magic" from *Avalanche*. Copyright © 1996 by Quincy Troupe. Reprinted with the permission of The Permissions Company, Inc. on behalf of Coffee House Press, Minneapolis, MN. www.coffeehousepress.org

Turner, Brian. "What Every Soldier Should Know" from *Here, Bullet*. Copyright © 2005 by Brian Turner. Reprinted with the permission of The Permissions Company, Inc., on behalf of Alice James Books, www.alicejamesbooks.org

Updike, John. "A&P." From *Pigeon Feathers and Other Stories* by John Updike. Copyright © 1962, copyright renewed 1990 by John Updike. Used by permission of Alfred A. Knopf, an imprint of the Knopf Doubleday Publishing Group, a division of Penguin Random House LLC. All rights reserved.

Walker, Alice. "Everyday Use" from *In Love and Trouble: Stories of Black Women* by Alice Walker. Copyright © 1973, renewed 2001 by Alice Walker. Reprinted by permission of Houghton Mifflin Harcourt Publishing Company. All rights reserved.

Welch, James. "Christmas Comes to Moccasin Flat" From *Riding the Earthboy 40* by James Welch. Copyright © 1971, 1976, 1990 by James Welch. Used by permission of Penguin Books, an imprint of Penguin Publishing Group, a division of Penguin Random House LLC.

Welty, Eudora: "Why I Live at the P.O." from *A Curtain of Green and Other Stories* by Eudora Welty. Copyright © 1941, renewed 1969 by Eudora Welty. Reprinted by permisison of Houghton Mifflin Harcourt Publishing Company. All rights reserved.

Williams, C.K. "On the Métro" from *Collected Poems* by C. K. Williams. Copyright © 2006 by C. K. Williams. Reprinted by permission of Farrar, Straus and Giroux, LLC.

Williams, Emmett. "like attracts like" from *Selected Shorter Poems (1950-1970)* New Directions Publishing Corp. Reprinted by permission of the Estate of Emmett Williams.

Williams, Tennessee. *Cat on a Hot Tin Roof* by Tennessee Williams. Copyright © 1954, 1955, 1971, 1975 by The University of the South. Reprinted by permission of New Directions Publishing Corp.

Williams, William Carlos. "The Red Wheelbarrow" and "This is Just to Say" by William Carlos Williams, from *Collected Poems: 1909-1939*, Volume I, copyright © 1938 by New Directions Publishing Corp. Reprinted by permission of New Directions Publishing Corp.

Wilson, August. "Fences" from *Fences* by August Wilson, copyright © 1986 by August Wilson. Used by permission of New American Library, an imprint of Penguin Publishing Group, a division of Random House LLC.

Wolff, Tobias. "Bullet in the Brain" from *The Night in Question: Stories* by Tobias Wolff, copyright © 1996 by Tobias Wolff. Used by permission of Alfred A. Knopf, an imprint of the Knopf Doubleday Publishing Group, a division of Penguin Random House LLC. All rights reserved.

Wright, James. "Lying in a Hammock at William Duffy's Farm in Pine Island, Minnesota" from *Collected Poems* © 1971 by James Wright. Reprinted by permission of Wesleyan University Press.

Wright, Richard. "The Man Who Was Almost a Man" from *Eight Men* by Richard Wright. Copyright © 1940, 1961 by Richard Wright; renewed © 1989 by Ellen Wright. Introduction © 1996 by Paul Gilroy. Reprinted by permission of HarperCollins Publishers.

Index of Authors, Titles, and First Lines